Cases and Materials on International Law

Cases and Materials on
International Law

Fourth Edition

Robert McCorquodale

*Professor of International Law and Human Rights, School of Law,
University of Nottingham*

Martin Dixon

University Senior Lecturer and Fellow in Law, Queens' College, Cambridge

OXFORD
UNIVERSITY PRESS

OXFORD
UNIVERSITY PRESS

Great Clarendon Street, Oxford OX2 6DP

Oxford University Press is a department of the University of Oxford.
It furthers the University's objective of excellence in research, scholarship,
and education by publishing worldwide in

Oxford New York

Auckland Bangkok Buenos Aires Cape Town Chennai
Dar es Salaam Delhi Hong Kong Istanbul Karachi Kolkata
Kuala Lumpur Madrid Melbourne Mexico City Mumbai Nairobi
São Paulo Shanghai Taipei Tokyo Toronto

Oxford is a registered trade mark of Oxford University Press
in the UK and in certain other countries

Published in the United States
by Oxford University Press Inc., New York

A Blackstone Press book

British Library Cataloguing in Publication Data

Data available

Library of Congress Cataloging in Publication Data

Data available

ISBN 0–19–925999–2

5 7 9 10 8 6 4

Typeset in ITC Stone Serif, ITC Stone Sans and Congress Sans
by RefineCatch Limited, Bungay, Suffolk
Printed in Great Britain by
Antony Rowe Ltd, Chippenham, Wiltshire

OUTLINE CONTENTS

DETAILED CONTENTS

6	**International Human Rights Law**	175

7	**Sovereignty over Territory**	234

8   Jurisdictional Sovereignty · 268

9   Immunities from National Jurisdiction · 301

PREFACE TO THE FIRST EDITION

[A]n international organisation . . . is not a native, but nor is it a visitor from abroad. It comes from the invisible depths of outer space.

Lord Donaldson MR in *Arab Monetary Fund* v
Hashim (no.3) [1990] 2 All ER 769.

Statements like this make us weep. International law is not an alien law despite the fear of it shown by judges in the national courts of many countries. Instead, international law constantly affects us and the way we live. Each day the media reports the rapid changes occurring around the world which have a significance for international law. The struggle for self-determination in the USSR and elsewhere; the attempts to control terrorism; the work of the United Nations and its relief agencies; and the urgent need to protect the environment are all matters addressed by international law. But it is also a system of law that affects the life of every individual in more mundane ways: air mail, international travel, health programmes and the transfer of money and foodstuffs are all regulated in some way by international law.

Too often the treaties, the resolutions, the statements, the cases and all the other materials dealing with these issues and those at the core of a course in International Law are not readily available. Our aim in writing this book was to include the material generally required by students, both by covering the well-trodden paths and, we hope, by introducing some material relevant to the international law of tomorrow. We have also included some material about the theories of international law—new and old—for we believe that the nature of international law is profoundly different from that of national law and so the same assumptions cannot be made about it. We hope too, to convey some of our hope for the future through potential changes in international law.

There are many people who have shared in the pleasure and stress of writing this book. In particular, our warmest gratitude to our friends and colleagues Susan Marks and Vaughan Lowe for their suggestions and insight. We were also fortunate to have students who were prepared to assist us in the dullest aspects of publishing and even to forgive the paper-filled rooms, unmarked essays, tired supervisions and occasional over-enthusiastic teaching. To Mike, Jo, Sue, Cathy, Christian and especially Alec, Marius and Redmond—thanks . . . and sorry. To Triquet and Bath, wherever you are now, good luck.

Finally, each of us has our own personal tributes. From Robert to Judy, Lex and above all Kate, thanks for the constant support, encouragement, patience and humour. From Martin, to my friends.

Martin Dixon
Robert McCorquodale
Cambridge

PREFACE TO FOURTH EDITION

One of the objectives of the United Nations, as set out in the Preamble to its Charter, was 'to establish conditions under which justice and respect for the obligations arising from treaties and other sources of international law can be maintained'. It is our intention to provide in this book the key cases and materials on current international law in an accessible manner because the more people worldwide who are aware of international law the more likely it is that this objective of the United Nations will be fulfilled.

In this book, the relevant cases and materials are presented within the context of the development of international law over time and the changing understanding of the nature of international law. This edition is fully revised and updated. We have also responded to readers' comments and welcome constructive criticism (mjd1001@cam.ac.uk or robert.mccorquodale@nottingham.ac.uk).

As our lives, both personal and professional, become increasingly busy and as Robert has moved back to the United Kingdom, we have been fortunate to have valuable assistance in preparing this edition. Rachel Lord did a marvelous job in assisting in the revision of the majority of the chapters and Paolo Galizzi's incisive comments on Chapter 12 were invaluable and much appreciated. There has also been a change in our publishers, with Oxford University Press acquiring Blackstone Press. Claire Brewer and Helen Adams at Oxford University Press have been diligent, encouraging and professional, as we have all adjusted to the new edition. Above all, we have been blessed with understanding wives and children. Our love and thanks go to Judith, William, Oliver and Emily, and Kate, Rory, Ella and Flora.

The materials in this book are as at October 2002, although some later materials have been added where time permitted.

Cambridge and Nottingham
January 2003

ACKNOWLEDGEMENTS

Grateful acknowledgement is made to all the authors and publishers of copyright material which appears in this book, and in particular to the following for permission to reprint material from the sources indicated:

P. Allott: extracts from *Eunomia: New Order for a New World* (OUP, 1990).

American Law Institute: section 404 of the *Restatement (Third) Foreign Relations Law of the United States*, copyright © 1987 by the American Law Institute. All rights reserved.

American Society of International Law, c/o the Copyright Clearance Center: extracts from *American Journal of International Law* (AJIL) and *International Legal Materials* (ILM).

R. Anand: extract from 'Attitude of Asian-African States towards certain problems of International Law' in F. E Snyder and S. Sathirathai (eds): *Third World Attitudes Toward International Law* (Nijhoff, 1987).

Australian National University, Faculty of Law, and the authors: extracts from *Australian Year Book of International Law* (AYBIL).

The Butterworths Division of Reed Elsevier (UK Ltd): extracts from *All England Law Reports* (ALR).

Cambridge Law Journal and the authors: extracts from *Cambridge Law Journal* (CLJ).

Cambridge University Press: extracts from Anthony Aust: *Modern Treaty Law and Practice* (CUP, 2000), H. Hinsley: *Sovereignty* (2e, CUP, 1986), William A. Schabas: *An Introduction to the International Criminal Court* (CUP, 2001), Gillian D. Triggs: *The Antarctic Regime, Law, Enviroment and Resources* (CUP, 1982); and *Iran-US Claim Tribunal Reports* (Grotius Publications).

Columbia Law Review: extract from F. Téson: 'The Kantian Theory of International Law' which originally appeared in 92 *Colum. L. Rev.* (1992).

Columbia University Press: extract from L. Henkin: *How Nations Behave* (2e, 1979).

Commission to Study the Organization of Peace: extract from *Regional Promotion and the Protection of Human Rights* (1980).

David Davies Memorial Institute of International Studies: extract from M. Akehurst: 'The use of force to protect nationals abroad', 5 *International Relations* (1977).

European University Institute: extracts from *European Journal of International Law*; Badinter Committee Opinion, 3 EJIL (1992); M. Craven: 'Legal differentiation and the concept of the Human Rights Treaty in International Law', 11 EJIL (2000); S. Scott: 5 EJIL (1994); and EC declarations published in 4 EJIL (1993).

David Feldman: extract from 'Monism, Dualism and Constitutional Legitimacy', 20 AYBIL (1999).

Y. Ghai: extract from 'Human Rights and Governance: The Asia Debate', 15 AYBIL (1994).

C. Greenwood: notes in 54 *Cambridge Law Journal* (1995).

Greenwood Publishing Group, Inc, Westport, CT: extract from A. Springer: *The International Law of Pollution—Protecting the Global Environment in a World of Sovereign States* (Greenwood Press, 1983).

Hague Academy of International Law: extracts from *Recueil de Cours*: J. de Arechega: 'General Course in Public International Law', 159 RC (1978); D. Bowett: 'Contemporary developments in legal techniques in the Settlement of Disputes', 180 RC (1983);

G. Fitzmaurice: 'The general principles of International Law considered from the standpoint of the Rule of Law' 92 RC (1957); L. Henkin: 'International Law; Politics, values, and functions', 13 (IV) RC (1989); O. Schachter: 'General Course in International Law', 179 RC (1982); and I. Sinclair: 'The Law of Sovereign Immunity: Recent Developments', 167 RC (1980).

Harvard College: extracts from *Harvard International Law Journal*: A. Angie: 'Finding the Peripheries: Sovereignty and Colonialism in Nineteenth-Century International Law', 40 HILJ (1999); A. Orford: 'Locating the International: Military and Monetary Interventions after the Cold War', 38 HILJ (1997); P. Sands: 'The Environment, Community and International Law', 30 HILJ (1989); and J. Trachtman: 'The Domain of WTO Dispute Resolution', 40 HILJ (1999); all copyright © by the President and Fellows of Harvard College and the Harvard International Law Journal.

Harvard Law Review Association: extract from 'Developing Countries and Multilateral Trade Agreements', 108 *Harvard Law Review* (1994), copyright © 1994 by the Harvard Law Review Association; and P. Allott: 'State Responsibility and the unmaking of International Law', 29 *Harvard International Law Journal* (1988), copyright © 1988 by the Harvard Law Review Association.

Harvard University Press: extract from Patricia Williams: *The Alchemy of Race and Rights: Diary of a Law Professor* (Harvard University Press, 1991), copyright © 1991 by the President and Fellows of Harvard College.

Human Rights Law Centre, Nottingham University: extracts from *International Human Rights Reports* (IHRR).

Incorporated Council of Law Reporting: extracts from the *Official Law Reports* (OLR) and the *Weekly Law Reports* (WLR).

Iowa Law Review: extract from Richard B. Lillich: 'Forcible Self-Help by States to Protect Human Rights', 53 *Iowa L. Rev.* (1967).

John H. Jackson: extract from 'International Law: reflections on the "Boilerroom" of International Relations' in Charlotte Ku and Paul F. Diehl (eds.): *International Law: Classic and Contemporary Readings* (Lynne Reinner Publishers, 1998).

The Johns Hopkins University Press: extract from R McCorquodale with R. Fairbrother: 'Globalization and Human rights', 21 *Human Rights Quarterly* (1999); and extract from I. Brownlie 'Humanitarian Intervention', copyright © I. Brownlie 1974, in John Norton Moore (ed): *Law and Civil War in the Modern World* (Johns Hopkins, 1974).

Juta & Co Ltd: extract from *South African Law Reports*.

Michael Kirby: extract from 'Domestic Implementation of International Human Rights Norms', 5 *Australian Journal of Human Rights* (1999).

Kluwer Law International: extracts from G. Fitzmaurice: 'Some Problems Regarding the Formal Sources of International Law' from *Symbolae Verzijl* 153 (M Nijhoff, 1958); O. Schachter: 'New Custom: Power, *Opinio Juris* and Contrary Practice' in Jerzy Makarczyk (ed): *Theory of International Law at the Threshold of the 21st Century* (Kluwer, 1996); P. Galizzi 'Economic Instruments as Tools for the protection of the International Environment', *European Environmental Law Review* 155 (1997); and M. Sornarajah: 'Power and Justice in Foreign Arbitration', 14 *Journal of International Arbitration* (1994).

Martti Koskenniemi: extracts from *From Apology to Utopia* (Finnish Lawyers Publishing Company, 1989).

Sir Hersch Lauterpacht: extract from *International Law and Human Rights* (Stevens & Sons, 1950)

LexisNexis Butterworths Australia: extracts from *Australian Law Reports* and from Michael Kirby: 5 *Australian Journal of Human Rights* (1999).

LexisNexis Butterworths New Zealand: extracts from *New Zealand Law Reports*.

A. V. Lowe: notes in 54 *Cambridge Law Journal* (1995) and extract from *Extra Territorial Jurisdiction: An Annotated Collection of Legal Materials* (Grotius, 1983).

Susan Marks: extracts from 'Torture and the Jurisdictional Immunity of Foreign States' *Cambridge Law Journal* 8 (1997), and 'Civil Liberties at the Margin: The UK Derogation and the European Court of Human Rights' 15 *Oxford Journal of Legal Studies* (1995).

Manchester University Press: extracts from Hilary Charlesworth and Christine Chinkin: *The Boundaries of International Law: A Feminist Perspective* (Manchester University Press, 2000).

John G. Merrills: extract from 'Interim Measures of Protection and the Substantive Jurisdiction of the International Court', 36 *Cambridge Law Journal* (1977).

Natural Resources Journal: extract from B. Dickson: 'The Precautionary Principle in CITES: A critical assessment', 39 NRJ (1999).

New York Law School: extracts from J. Shestack: 'Sisyphus Endures: The International Human Rights NGO', 24 *New York Law School Law Review* (1978).

New York University: extract from P. Sands: 'Turtles and Torturers: the Transformation of International Law' in 33 *New York University Journal of International Law and Politics* (2001).

Oxford University Press: extracts from P. Alston in Philip Alston (ed.): *The United Nations and Human Rights: A Critical Appraisal* (1992); M. Anderson: 'Human Rights approaches to environmental protection' in Alan E. Boyle and Michael R. Anderson (eds.): *Human Rights Approaches to Environmental Protection*; Patricia Birnie and Alan Boyle: *International Law and the Enviroment* (2e, 2002); J. L. Brierly: *The Law of Nations* (1e, 1928, and 6e, 1963); Antonio Cassese: *International Law* (2001); H. L. A. Hart: *The Concept of Law* (1961); Adam Roberts and Benedict Kingsbury: *United Nations, Divided World: The UN's Role in International Relations* (2e, 1993); J. Shestack: 'The Jurisprudence of Human Rights' in Theodor Meron (ed.): *Human Rights in International Law* (1984); Heather A. Wilson: *International Law and the Use of Force by National Liberation Movements* (OUP, 1989); and from *Our Common Future*, World Commission on Environment and Development (1987); also extracts from *British Yearbook of International Law* (BYBIL) on behalf of the Royal Insitute of International Affairs (RIIA): M. Akehurst: 'Custom as a source of International Law', 47 BYBIL (1974–5); D. Bowett: 'Reservations to non-restricted multilateral treaties', 48 BYBIL (1976); 'Jurisdiction: Changing patterns of authority over activities and resources', 53 BYBIL (1953); I. Brownlie: 'Recognition in Theory and Practice', 53 BYBIL (1982); J. Charney: 'The Persistent Objector Rule and the Development of Customary International Law', 56 BYBIL (1985); J. Crawford: 'The Criteria for Statehood in International Law', 48 BYBIL (1976–7); M. Evans: 'Delimitation and the Common Maritime Boundary', 64 BYBIL (1994); B. Sloan: 'General Assembly Resolutions Revisited', 58 BYBIL (1987); and United Kingdom Rules regarding the taking Up of International Claims by Her Majesty's Government, July 1983, 54 BYBIL (1983); also extracts from *International and Comparative Law Quarterly* (ICLQ) on behalf of the British Institute of International and Comparative Law: R. McCorquodale 'Self-Determination: A Human Rights Approach' 43 ICLQ (1994); and M. Shaw: 42 ICLQ (1993).

Oxford University Press (China Ltd): extract from Peter Wesley-Smith: *Unequal Treaty* (1980).

Palgrave Macmillan: extract from M. C. Davis: *Constitutional Confrontation in Hong Kong* (1989).

Pearson Education Ltd: extracts from *Oppenheim's International Law* 8e, edited by H. Lauterpacht (Longman, 1955); *Oppenheim's International Law* 9e, edited by R. Jennings and A. Watts (Longman, 1992); and R. Wasserstrom: 'Rights, Human Rights and Racial Discrimination' in J. Rachels: *Moral Problems: a collection of philosophical essays* (3e, Harper & Row, 1979).

Penguin Books Ltd: extract from Harold Wilson: *The Labour Government 1964–1970: A Personal Record* (Michael Joseph, 1971), copyright © Harold Wilson 1971.

Princeton University Press: extract from R McCorquodale: 'International Law, Boundaries and Imagination' in D. Miller and S. Hashmi (eds.): *Boundaries and Justice* (2001), copyright © 2001 by Princeton University Press.

Roosevelt Study Centre: extract from A. Farrag 'Human Rights and Liberties in Islam' in Jan Berting et al (eds.): *Human Rights in a Pluralist World: Individuals and Collectivities* (1990).

The Royal Insitute of International Affairs (RIIA): extracts from J. Bhagwati: 'The Agenda of the WTO' in P. Van Dijck and G. Faber (eds): *Challenges to the New World Trade Organization* (RIIA, 1996); and extracts from *British Yearbook of International Law* (BYBIL): M. Akehurst: Enforcement Action by Regional Agencies with special reference to the Organization of American States', 42 BYBIL (1967); R. Baxter: 'Multilateral Treaties as Evidence of Customary International Law', 41 BYBIL (1965); and G. Fitzmaurice: 'The Law and Procedure of the International Court of Justice: Treaty Interpretation and certain other Treaty Points', 28 BYBIL (1951).

Issa G. Shivji: extract from *The Concept of Human Rights in Africa* (CODESRIA, 1989)

Sir Ian Sinclair: extract from *The Vienna Convention on the Law of Treaties* (2e, Manchester University Press, 1984)

Singapore Journal of International and Comparative Law: extract from N. White: 'The United Nations System: Conference, Contract or Constitutional Order?', 4 *Singapore JICL* (2000).

Southern California Law Review: extract from Christopher D. Stone: 'Should Trees have Standing? Towards Legal Rights for Natural Objects', 45 *Southern California Law Review* (1972).

Springer Verlag: extracts from P-T Stoll: 'The International Environmental Law of Cooperation' in R. Wolfrum (ed): *Enforcing Environmental Standards: Economic Mechanisms as Viable Means?* (Springer Verlag, 1996).

Stanford Law School: extract from P. Gabel and D. Kennedy: 'Roll Over Beethoven', 36 *Stanford Law Review* (1984).

Sweet & Maxwell Ltd: extracts from *European Human Rights Reports* (EHRR) 20 (1994) and 34 EHRR (2002); from H. Lauterpacht: *International Law and Human Rights* (1950); and from A. Redfern and J. Hunter: *Law and Practice of International Commercial Arbitration* (3e, 1999).

Taylor & Francis, Inc, http://www.routledge-ny.com: extracts from J. Charney: 'The EEZ and Public International Law, 15 *Ocean Development and International Law* 233 (1985).

Thomson Legal & Regulatory Ltd: extracts from *Commonwealth Law Reports* (CLR) and from M. Pryles, J. Waincymer and M. Davies: *International Trade Law: Cases and Materials* (Lawbook Co, 1996), copyright © Lawbook Co, part of Thomson Legal and Regulatory Ltd, www.thomson.com.au.

United Nations Organization: extracts from reports by K. Annan: *We the Peoples: The Role of the United Nations in the Twenty-First Century* (2000), *Prevention of Armed Conflict* (2001), and *Nobel Peace Prize Lecture* (2001); also Letters and other UN materials.

United States Government Printing Office: extract from G. H. Hackworth (ed): *Digest of International law*, Vol. 5 (1943).

University of Pennsylvania Press: extracts from Hilary Charlesworth: 'What are Women's International Rights?' in R. Cook (ed.): *Human Rights of Women* (1994), copyright © 1994 by the University of Pennsylvania Press.

University of Virginia School of Law: extracts from *Virginia Journal of International Law*: Makau wa Mutua: 'The Banjul Charter and the African Cultural Fingerprint: An Evaluation of the Language of Duties', 35 VaJIL (1995); and F. Téson: ''International Human Rights and Cultural Relativism, 25 VaJIL (1985).

World Trade Organization: extracts from Reports and Declarations.

Zed Books Ltd: extract from V. Shiva 'Biotechnological Development and the Conservation of Diodiversity' in V. Shiva and I. Moser (eds.): *Biopolitics : A Feminist and Ecological Reader on Biotechnology* (1995).

TABLE OF CASES

TABLE OF STATUTES

TABLE OF TREATIES

TABLE OF OTHER DOCUMENTS

1

The Nature of the International Legal System

Introductory note

Open a newspaper, listen to the radio or watch television, and you will be confronted with events that have significance in international law. United Nations' resolutions and peacekeeping forces; the claims for independence by groups around the world; conferences on the environment and on trade; the changing political and social situation in Africa, Asia and Europe; allegations of human rights abuses in many States; attempts to control terrorism and drugs; debates concerning the future of the United Nations; and the increasing impact of European laws on the member States of the European Union, are but a few examples. Overall, as the twenty-first century begins, there is an increased interdependence in the international community.

It is these events and this interdependence that international law addresses by analysing the legal principles arising from interactions between States, actions by States and certain actions by individuals, corporations, international organisations and other actors on the international plane. International law has effects on, and is affected by, international relations, political thought and communications, as well as by the awareness of women and men in every State that they are among those addressed by the United Nations Charter as being 'We, the Peoples of the United Nations'.

International law is really a description of an entire legal system: the international legal system. It is an international legal system by which legal rules are created in order to structure and organise societies and relationships. It acknowledges the influence of political, economic, social and cultural processes upon the development of legal rules. Within this international legal system are, for example, constitutional laws, property laws, criminal laws and laws about obligations, although these terms are not normally used. It is this extensive array of laws within the international legal system that is included under the name 'international law'.

SECTION 1: **The relevance of international law**

International law is law and has relevance to our daily lives. For example, international law enables international telephone calls to be made, overseas mail to be delivered, and travel by air, sea and land to occur relatively easily. Fear of enforcement of law is rarely the sole reason why law is obeyed, but the behaviour of States and people often is modified depending on the substance of the law and its aspirational and inspirational aspects. International law does place parameters on the actions of States and others in the international community. However, there are times when the role of international law may be limited when issues of power are involved, as seen in the comments of Dean Acheson below. But international law clearly does exist and does affect the actions of all members of the international community.

D. Acheson, former United States Secretary of State
57 *American Society of International Law Proceedings* 14 (1963), pp. 14–15

[T]he law through its long history has been respectful of power, especially that power which is close to the sanctions of law. . . .

I must conclude that the propriety of the Cuban quarantine [Cuban missile crisis, 1962] is not a legal issue. The power, position and prestige of the United States had been challenged by another state; and law simply does not deal with such questions of ultimate power – power that comes close to the sources of sovereignty. I cannot believe that there are principles of law that say we must accept destruction of our way of life. One would be surprised if practical men, trained in legal history and thought, had devised and brought to a state of general acceptance a principle condemnatory of an action so essential to the continuation of pre-eminent power as that taken by the United States last October. Such a principle would be as harmful to the development of restraining procedures as it would be futile. No law can destroy the state creating the law. The survival of states is not a matter of law.

However, in the action taken in the Cuban quarantine, one can see the influence of accepted legal principles. These principles are procedural devices designed to reduce the severity of a possible clash. . . .

Wisdom for the decision was not to be found in law, but in judgment. Principles, certainly legal principles, do not decide concrete cases.

H. Waldock, *J. Brierly's The Law of Nations*
(6th edn, 1963), pp. 71–73, 77–78

Violations of the law are rare in all customary systems, and they are so in international law. . . . [That] the law is normally observed . . . receives little notice because the interest of most people in international law is not in the ordinary routine of international legal business, but in the occasions, rare but generally sensational, on which it is flagrantly broken. Such breaches generally occur either when some great political issue has arisen between states, or in that part of the system which professes to regulate the conduct of war. But our diagnosis of what is wrong with the system will be mistaken if we fail to realize that the laws of peace and the great majority of treaties are on the whole regularly observed in the daily intercourse of states. . . . If we fail to understand this, we are likely to assume, as many people do, that all would be well with international law if we could devise a better system for enforcing it. . . . It is not the existence of a police force that makes a system of law strong and respected, but the strength of the law that makes it possible for a police force to be effectively organized. The imperative character of law is felt so strongly and obedience to it has become so much a matter of habit within a . . . state that national law has developed a machinery of enforcement which generally works smoothly, though never so smoothly as to make breaches impossible. If the imperative character of international law were equally strongly felt, the institutions of definite international sanctions would easily follow.

Whether from a review of all these shortcomings we ought to conclude that international law is a failure depends upon what we assume to be its aim. It has not failed to serve the purposes for which states have chosen to use it; in fact it serves these purposes reasonably well. The layman hears little of international law as a working system, for most of its practice goes on within the walls of foreign offices, which on principle are secretive; and even if the foreign offices were inclined to be more communicative the layman would not find what they could tell him very interesting, any more than he would normally be interested in the working of a solicitor's office. For in fact the practice of international law proceeds on much the same lines as that of any other kind of law, with the foreign offices taking the place of the private legal adviser and exchanging arguments about the facts and the law, and later, more often than is sometimes supposed, with a hearing before some form of international tribunal. The volume of this work is considerable, but most of it is not sensational, and it only occasionally relates to matters of high political interest. That does not mean that the matters to which it does relate are unimportant in themselves; often they are very important to particular interests or individuals. But it means that international law is performing a useful and indeed a necessary function in international life in enabling states to carry on their day-to-day intercourse along orderly and predictable lines. That is the role for which states have chosen to use it and for that it has proved a serviceable instrument. If we are dissatisfied with this role, if we believe that it can and should be used, as national law has begun to be used, as an instrument for promoting the general welfare in positive ways, and even more if we believe that it ought to be a powerful means of maintaining international peace, then we shall have to admit that it has so far failed. But it is only fair to remember that these have not been the purposes for which states have so far chosen to use it.

L. Henkin, *How Nations Behave*

(2nd edn, 1979), pp. 320–321

[International] law works. Although there is no one to determine and adjudge the law with authoritative infallibility, there is wide agreement on the content and meaning of law and agreements, even in a world variously divided. Although there is little that is comparable to executive law enforcement in a domestic society, there are effective forces, internal and external, to induce general compliance. Nations recognize that the observance of law is in their interest, and that every violation may also bring particular undesirable consequences. It is the unusual case in which policymakers believe that the advantages of violation outweigh those of law observance, or where domestic pressures compel a government to violation even against the perceived national interest. The important violations are of political law and agreements, where basic interests of national security or independence are involved, engaging passions, prides, and prejudices, and where rational calculation of cost and advantage is less likely to occur and difficult to make. Yet, as we have seen, the most important principle of law today is commonly observed: nations have not been going to war, unilateral uses of force have been only occasional, brief, limited. Even the uncertain law against intervention, seriously breached in several instances, has undoubtedly deterred intervention in many other instances. Where political law has not deterred action it has often postponed or limited action or determined a choice among alternative actions.

None of this argument is intended to suggest that attention to law is the paramount or determinant motivation in national behavior, or even that it is always a dominant factor. A norm or obligation brings no guarantee of performance; it does add an important increment of interest in performing the obligation. Because of the requirements of law or of some prior agreement, nations modify their conduct in significant respects and in substantial degrees. It takes an extraordinary and substantially more important interest to persuade a nation to violate its obligations. Foreign policy, we know, is far from free; even the most powerful nations have learned that there are forces within their society and, even more, in the society of nations that limit their freedom of choice. When a contemplated action would violate international law or a treaty, there is additional, substantial limitation on the freedom to act.

R. Jennings and A. Watts, *Oppenheim's International Law*
(9th edn, vol. 1, 1992), pp. 4–7, 12–13

International law is the body of rules which are legally binding on states in their intercourse with each other. These rules are primarily those which govern the relations of states, but states are not the only subjects of international law. International organisations and, to some extent, also individuals may be subjects of rights conferred and duties imposed by international law. International law in the meaning of the term as used in modern times began gradually to grow from the second half of the Middle Ages. As a systematised body of rules it owes much to the Dutch jurist Hugo Grotius, whose work, *De Jure Belli ac Pacis, Libri iii*, appeared in 1625, and became a foundation of later development. . . .

International law is sometimes referred to as 'public international law' to distinguish it from private international law. Whereas the former governs the relations of states and other subjects of international law amongst themselves, the latter consists of the rules developed by states as part of their domestic law to resolve the problems which, in cases between private persons which involve a foreign element, arise over whether the court has jurisdiction and over the choice of the applicable law: in other terms, public international law arises from the juxtaposition of states, private international law from the juxtaposition of legal systems. Although the rules of private international law are part of the internal law of the state concerned, they may also have the character of public international law where they are embodied in treaties. Where this happens the failure of a state party to the treaty to observe the rule of private international law prescribed in it will lay it open to proceedings for breach of an international obligation owed to another party. Even where the rules of private international law cannot themselves be considered as rules of public international law, their application by a state as part of its internal law may directly involve the rights and obligations of the state as a matter of public international law, for example where the matter concerns the property of aliens or the extent of the state's jurisdiction. . . .

There is . . . increasing acceptance that the rules of international law are the foundation upon which the rights of states rest, and no longer merely limitations upon states' rights which, in the absence of a rule of law to the contrary, are unlimited. Although there are extensive areas in which international law accords to states a large degree of freedom of action (for example, in matters of domestic jurisdiction), it is important that freedom is derived from a legal right and not from an assertion of unlimited will, and is subject ultimately to regulation within the legal framework of the international community. In the *Military and Paramilitary Activities* (*Nicaragua* v *United States*) case the International Court of Justice upheld the essential justiciability of even those disputes raising issues of the use of force and collective self-defence.

Furthermore international law may now properly be regarded as a complete system. By this is meant not that there is always a clear and specific legal rule readily applicable to every international situation, but that every international situation is capable of being determined *as a matter of law*, either by the application of specific legal rules where they already exist, or by the application of legal rules derived, by the use of known legal techniques, from other legal rules or principles.

S. Scott, 'International Law as Ideology: Theorizing the Relationship between International Law and International Politics'
5 *European Journal of International Law* (1994) 313, pp. 324–325

The realist paradigm in international relations is unable to explain the nature and degree of the significance of international law to the system of international politics. Although international law appears to play a political role, that role cannot be conceptualized within a paradigm that posits power as the prime determinant of political outcomes and yet does not theorize the relationship between international law and power. . . .

It has been suggested that the idea of international law is integral to the international distribution of power and that it actually sustains the structure of the international political order. In political terms it does not matter whether or not the ideology is true; it is not the verity of an ideology that matters but its acceptance by international actors as a basis for interaction. Legal debate is the process of ostensibly establishing a concrete law-non-law boundary and a set of objective, applicable rules to deal with all political issues. In order for the ideology to operate successfully, lawyers must continue to find ways of demonstrating the practicality of the image of international law portrayed by the ideology. Legal discourse is founded on an assumption of legal objectivity.

This conceptualization of the relationship of international law to international politics means that many previously asked questions regarding international law have been superseded. For example, the questions as to whether and why States 'obey' international law are no longer meaningful. It can now be seen that States neither obey nor disobey international law; they simply act so as to demonstrate acceptance of the ideology of international law. While States might be concerned that international law develops in their favour, this interest is indirect; favourable terms means that the State can more readily uphold the notion of the binding quality of international law.

NOTES:
1. Jennings and Watts refer to Hugo Grotius as one of the founders of modern international law, because it was Grotius' view that States and rulers of States are bound by rules which form an international society or community with one another, even if of a rudimentary kind. However, there are other jurists who have been very influential in the development of international law as it is currently perceived, for example, Francisco Vitoria (1480–1546), Francisco Suárez (1584–1617), Alberico Gentili (1552–1608) and Emmerich de Vattel (1714–1767).
2. While international law is of a different nature to national law in its sources, institutions and development, international law is 'law' in that it seeks to ensure that there is order and structure in the international community. This order enables the members of the international community to interact together with a reasonable degree of confidence and ensures that changes in rules generally occur by a coherent and consistent process. As Henkin suggests, international law can – and does – modify behaviour, particularly of States. Just as in national law, political considerations can also determine much of the content of international law.

SECTION 2: The international community and international law

The United Nations system is central to the international community and to international law. While international law lacks a consistently effective centralised system for the determination and enforcement of international law, the United

Nations offers the possibility of some centralised action. It has some of the institutional structures – a body comprising some nominal representative of nearly all States (the General Assembly); a body with executive powers (the Security Council), and a court (the International Court of Justice) – but the limitations on the powers of these institutions means that they cannot be considered as an effective equivalent to national governmental institutions.

A. Roberts and B. Kingsbury, 'The UN's Roles in International Society since 1945' in A. Roberts and B. Kingsbury (eds), *United Nations, Divided World* (2nd edn, 1993), pp. 6–13, 16–17, 61–62

The first blueprints for the UN were drafted by the USA, the UK, the USSR, and their allies during World War II, reflecting their conceptions of the post-war international order. The Charter was finally adopted by fifty states meeting at San Francisco in June 1945. Although the nature and work of the UN has evolved considerably, the Charter has remained virtually unchanged. The UN was formally established on 24 October 1945, when its basic constitutive instrument, the UN Charter, entered into force.

In the years since 1945 the number of member states of the UN has steadily increased, due mainly to the effects of successive waves of decolonization and disintegration of states. In 1945 the UN had fifty-one original members; by the end of 1960, one hundred; by the end of 1984, one hundred and fifty-nine; and by July 1993, one hundred and eighty-four. Throughout its history, the UN has had as members the great majority of states. Despite trends towards regional integration, there have only exceptionally been enduring cases of UN member states unifying to form a single larger state: Tanzania (1964), Yemen (1990), and Germany (1990).

The most conspicuous case of non-membership was the People's Republic of China from the revolution in 1949 until 1971, during which period China was represented by the regime in Taiwan. Since 1971 the UN's claims to near-universalism have had real substance. Its members include virtually all the states of the contemporary world. No member state has ever left the UN. However, during 1950 the USSR refused to participate in the Security Council in protest against the UN's refusal to accept the government of the People's Republic of China as representative of China; and in 1965–6 Indonesia temporarily withdrew from the UN. In some cases the credentials of particular authorities to represent their state have not been accepted; and the Federal Republic of Yugoslavia (Serbia and Montenegro) was advised in 1992 by the Security Council and by the General Assembly that it could not continue the membership of the former Socialist Federal Republic of Yugoslavia, although it was able to continue participation in some UN bodies.

Six 'principal organs' of the UN were established by the Charter: the General Assembly, the Security Council, the Secretariat, the International Court of Justice (ICJ), the Trusteeship Council, and the Economic and Social Council (ECOSOC).

The *General Assembly* as the plenary body controls much of the work of the UN. It meets in regular session for approximately the last quarter of every year (with sessions spilling over well into the new year), and occasionally holds special or emergency sessions to consider specific issues. The General Assembly approves the budget, adopts priorities, calls international conferences, super-intends the operations of the Secretariat and of numerous committees and subsidiary organs, and debates and adopts resolutions on diverse issues. It played a major role in supervising European decolonization, and has also become involved in human rights supervision and election-monitoring in independent countries. The many subsidiary bodies created by the General Assembly include the United Nations Children's Fund (UNICEF), the Office of the United Nations High Commissioner for Refugees (UNHCR), the United Nations Conference on Trade and Development (UNCTAD), the United Nations Development Programme (UNDP), and the United Nations Environment Programme (UNEP). Much of the work of the General Assembly is done in permanent or *ad hoc* committees responsible for particular fields of UN activity or deliberation. The General Assembly's agenda also includes many areas of activity in which states prefer rhetoric to real action.

The fifteen-member *Security Council* is dominated by its five Permanent Members (China, France, Russia, the UK, and the USA), each of which has power to veto any draft resolution on substantive matters. The ten non-permanent members (six until a Charter amendment came into force in 1965) are elected for two-year periods by the General Assembly. The Security Council has primary responsibility for the maintenance of international peace and security, and unlike the General Assembly is able to take decisions which are supposed to be binding on all members of the UN. It meets almost continuously throughout the year, mainly to consider armed conflicts and other situations or disputes where international peace and security are threatened. It is empowered to order mandatory sanctions, call for cease-fires, and even to authorize military action on behalf of the UN.

The Security Council has also had a central role in the development of the institution of UN peacekeeping forces, which were not envisaged at all in the Charter. The blue berets or helmets worn by members of national military units working in the service of the UN have become a well-known symbol. UN peacekeeping forces, ranging from small observer units to larger forces for purposes of interposition, policing, and humanitarian assistance, have been established by the Security Council in numerous countries. . . .

The Charter provision that the Council must operate on the basis of unanimity of its Permanent Members was not the product of impractical idealism: the memoirs of some of those who helped frame the Charter confirm that they knew what they were doing in this as in many other respects. The provision, which has been interpreted in practice to mean that any one of the Permanent Members has to vote against a resolution in order to veto it, reflects a highly realistic belief that UN action will not be possible if one of the great powers seriously dissents from it.

The UN system extends beyond the six UN organs created by the Charter, and the various subsidiary bodies established subsequently by the UN, to include also a host of specialized agencies with their own separate constitutions, memberships, and budgets. These agencies constitute a distinct part of the UN system. In the words of Article 57 of the UN Charter they are 'established by intergovernmental agreement' and have 'wide international responsibilities, as defined in their basic instruments, in economic, social, cultural, educational, health, and related fields'. There are sixteen such specialized agencies associated with the UN: apart from the financial agencies – the main ones being the International Monetary Fund (IMF) and the World Bank (IBRD) – the 'big four' are the International Labour Organization (ILO); the Food and Agriculture Organization (FAO); the United Nations Educational, Scientific and Cultural Organization (UNESCO); and the World Health Organization (WHO). Other intergovernmental organizations closely associated with the UN include the International Atomic Energy Agency (IAEA) and the General Agreement on Tariffs and Trade (GATT). . . .

It is not easy to evaluate the performance of the UN separately from that of the member states. The UN is, as former US Secretary of State Dean Rusk observed, a political institution whose members 'are pursuing their national interests as they see them'. It was created by governments, and it can do little without the assent of at least the majority of them. This view is a necessary antidote to the widespread misapprehension that the UN is in the course of superseding the states system, and that the UN can and ought to take strong action on its own initiative irrespective of the views of states. But the UN cannot be adequately understood as simply the sum of its parts. Like all institutions, whatever their origins and power base, it has developed a life and an ethos of its own. The UN framework influences states' perceptions of their interests, the ordering of their priorities and preferences, and the possibilities they see of best advancing their interests. The UN has also come to embody a limited sense of a collective interest, distinct in specific cases from the particular interests of individual states. In these respects the UN has specific functions or roles against which its performance may be evaluated, even while responsibility for the quality of this performance may lie in great part with member states as well as with individual functionaries or with features of institutional design. . . .

The UN has become, over the course of its first half century, an established part of the firmament of international relations. It is involved in a huge range of activities, many of them central to the functioning of international society. The UN is best seen, not as a vehicle for completely restructuring or replacing the system of sovereign states, so much as ameliorating the problems spawned by its imperfections, and managing processes of rapid change in many distinct fields. The UN finds roles for itself in those areas of activity which are more appropriately tackled either on a truly multilateral basis, or by individuals representing, not a particular state, but the collectivity of states. To the extent that the UN is involved in the transformation of international society, it is not by creating a new and conceptually simple supranational structure, but by participating in a more general process whereby a management of different problems is allocated to different, albeit overlapping and fluctuating, levels.

'The tents have been struck, and the great caravan of humanity is once more on the march.' So said Jan Christian Smuts in 1918, at the time of the planning of the League of Nations. It is tempting to dismiss such views as merely part of the inflated rhetoric which international organizations seem so often to attract. But in our still divided world, there remains a need for an institution which can in some way, however imperfectly, articulate the twin ideas of a universal society of states and the cosmopolitan universality of humankind.

K. Annan, *We the Peoples: The Role of the United Nations in the Twenty-First Century*

Report of the Secretary-General of the United Nations to the Millennium Assembly, 2000

312. The United Nations alone can meet none of the challenges [before it]. They affect the entire international community, and they require all of us to do our part. But without a strong and effective Organization, the peoples of the world will find meeting these challenges immeasurably more difficult.

313. Whether the world's peoples have such an organization at their disposal depends ultimately, now as in the past, on the commitment of their governments to it. Now, as then, the Member States are the very foundation of the United Nation. . . .

315. Today, global affairs are no longer the exclusive province of foreign ministries, nor are states the sole source of solutions for our small planet's many problems. Many diverse and increasingly influential non-state actors have joined with national decision makers to improvise new forms of global governance. The more complex the problem at hand – whether negotiating a ban on landmines, setting limits to emissions that contribute to global warming, or creating an International Criminal Court – the more likely we are to find non-governmental organizations, private sector institutions and multilateral agencies working with sovereign states to find consensus solutions.

316. I believe two strategies will be essential to realize the potential of our Organization in the years ahead.

317. First, while our own resources as an organization are tightly constrained, those of the communities we serve are much greater. We must strive, not to usurp the role of other actors on the world stage, but to become a more effective catalyst for change and coordination among them. Our most vital role will be to stimulate collective action at the global level.

318. Second, the United Nations – like all other institutions in the world today – must fully exploit the great promise of the Information Age. The digital revolution has unleashed an unprecedented wave of technological change. Used responsibly, it can greatly improve our chances of defeating poverty and better meeting our other priority objectives. If this is to happen, we in the United Nations need to embrace the new technologies more wholeheartedly than we have in the past.

319. When it was created more than half a century ago, in the convulsive aftermath of world war, the United Nations reflected humanity's greatest hopes for a just and peaceful global community. It still embodies that dream. We remain the only global institution with the legitimacy and scope that derive from universal membership, and a mandate that encompasses development, security and human rights as well as the environment. In this sense, the United Nations is unique in world affairs.

320. We are an organization without independent military capability, and we dispose of relatively modest resources in the economic realm. Yet our influence and impact on the world is far greater than many believe to be the case – and often more than we ourselves realize. This influence derives not from any exercise of power, but from the force of the values we represent; our role in helping to establish and sustain global norms; our ability to stimulate global concern and action; and the trust we enjoy for the practical work we do on the ground to improve people's lives.

321. The importance of principles and norms is easily underestimated; but in the decades since the United Nations was created, the spreading acceptance of new norms has profoundly affected the lives of many millions of people. War was once a normal instrument of statecraft; it is now universally proscribed, except in very specific circumstances. Democracy, once challenged by authoritarianism in various guises, has not only prevailed in much of the world, but is now generally seen as the most legitimate and desirable form of government. The protection of fundamental. human rights, once considered the province of sovereign states alone, is now a universal concern transcending both governments and borders. . . .

324. The United Nations plays an equally important, but largely unsung, role in creating and sustaining the global rules without which modern societies simply could not function. The World Health Organization, for example, sets quality criteria for the pharmaceutical industry worldwide. The World Meteorological Office collates weather data from individual states and redistributes it, which in turn improves global weather forecasting. The World Intellectual Property Organization protects trademarks and patents outside their country of origin. The rights for commercial airlines to fly over borders derive from agreements negotiated by the International Civil Aviation Organization. The United Nations Statistical Commission helps secure uniformity in accounting standards.

325. Indeed, it is impossible to imagine our globalized world without the principles and practice of multilateralism to underpin it. An open world economy, in the place of mercantilism; a gradual decrease in the importance of competitive military alliances coupled with a Security Council more often able to reach decisions; the General Assembly or great gatherings of states and civil society organizations addressing humanity's common concerns – these are some of the signs, partial and halting though they may be, of an indispensable multilateral system in action. . . .

353. When the scope of our responsibilities and the hopes invested in us are measured against our resources, we confront a sobering truth. The budget for our core functions – the Secretariat operations in New York, Geneva, Nairobi, Vienna and five regional commissions – is just $1.25 billion a year. That is about 4 per cent of New York City's annual budget – and nearly a billion dollars less than the annual cost of running Tokyo's Fire Department. Our resources simply are not commensurate with our global tasks. . . .

355. The constraints are not only financial. In many areas we cannot do our job because disagreements among Member States preclude the consensus needed for effective action. This is perhaps most obvious with respect to peace operations, but it affects other areas as well. Moreover, the highly intrusive and excessively detailed mode of oversight that Member States exercise over our programme activities makes it very difficult for us to maximize efficiency or effectiveness. . . .

359. To sum up, the United Nations of the twenty-first century must continue to be guided by its founding principles. It must remain an Organization dedicated to the interests of its Member States and of their peoples. Our objectives will not change: peace, prosperity, social justice and a sustainable future. But the means we use to achieve those ends must be adapted to the challenges of the new era.

360. In future, the United Nations must increasingly serve as a catalyst for collective action, both among its Member States and between them and the vibrant constellation of new non-State actors. We must continue to be the place where new standards of international conduct are hammered out, and broad consensus on them is established. We must harness the power of technology to improve the fortunes of developing countries. Finally, we ourselves, as an organization, must become more effective, efficient, and accessible to the world's peoples. When we fail, we must be our own most demanding critics.

361. Only by these means can we become a global public trust for all the world's peoples.

NOTES:
1. As at 1 October 2002, there are 191 members of the United Nations. Both Switzerland and East Timor (under the name Timor-Leste) became members in September 2002. The member States of the United Nations are set out in the Appendix.
2. The United Nations is an institution comprised of States and governed by the United Nations Charter. While it does have some functions in addition to those given to it by States under the United Nations Charter (see Chapter 5 and the *Reparations for Injuries* Opinion, ICJ Rep 1949 174), it is limited in its activities to those that are allowed by its member States.
3. There is some involvement of entities other than States in the United Nations. For example, representative groups, such as the PLO, and non-governmental organisations, such as the International Committee of the Red Cross, have 'observer' status at the United Nations. A number of the United Nations agencies (for example, the International Labour Organization) have members who are individuals or non-governmental organisations.
4. Since the end of the Cold War, there has been a considerable change in the international community. One consequence has been pressure to change the membership and powers of the Security Council in order to reflect the present reality of international society. In particular, the permanent membership of the United Kingdom and France is questioned (perhaps both could be replaced by the European Union) and proposals have been put for permanent, semi-permanent or non-veto power permanent membership of the Security Council for Germany and Japan (which are major financial contributors to the United Nations) and for some regional powers, such as Brazil and India. These proposals face the difficult task of needing to be approved by the present permanent members of the Security Council. So far, all these proposals have not prospered and so the Security Council remains largely as it was established in 1945, though the Peoples' Republic of China and Russia have replaced the Republic of China and the Union of Society Socialist Republics as Permanent Members of the Security Council. These replacements were made without any amendment to the relevant provision (Article 23) of the United Nations Charter. In addition, the role of the International Court of Justice in reviewing the powers of the Security Council has been raised. This is discussed in Chapter 15.
5. The international community is comprised primarily of States of widely varying political, economic, cultural, social and legal backgrounds. It is also comprised of many non-State actors (see Chapter 5). While there are some common attitudes to international law, significant differences do exist, particularly between developed and developing States. Yet, despite the unequal distribution of power, international law is generally complied with.

SECTION 3: **Theories of international law**

In order for the principles of international law (or the rest of this book!) to be understood fully, it is important for its underlying assumptions to be made clear. This is particularly necessary with international law, as many of the assumptions about who is subject to international law and the rights and obligations arising from international law must be analysed before the substance of international law itself can be determined. As Susan Marks notes: 'What you hold to be true about the world depends on what you take into account, and what you take into account depends on what you think matters' (Susan Marks, *The Riddle of All Constitutions* (2000), p.121). Consequently, in many of the chapters of this book some aspects of the theories underlying the substantive law will be given. A number of the major theories are briefly described here.

J. Brierly, *The Law of Nations*
(1st edn, 1928), pp. 34–37, 51–52

The two views which may be regarded as in the orthodox tradition of international legal theory are . . . (1) a naturalist view, holding that the principles of the law or at least the most fundamental of them can be deduced from the essential nature of state-persons; and (2) a positivist view which regards the law merely as the sum of the rules by which these state-persons have consented to be bound. . . . The former of these two doctrines holds that every state, by the very fact that it is a state, is endowed with certain fundamental, or inherent, or natural, rights. Writers differ in enumerating what these rights are, but generally five rights are claimed, namely, self-preservation, independence, equality, respect, and intercourse. It is obvious that the doctrine of fundamental rights is merely the old doctrine of the natural rights of man transferred to states. . . . The positivist doctrine . . . attempts to explain the binding force of these rules [of international law] as arising from the supposed fact that states have consented to be bound by them.

H.L.A. Hart, *The Concept of Law*
(1961), p. 209

[The] absence of an international legislature, courts with compulsory jurisdiction, and centrally organized sanctions have inspired misgivings, at any rate in the breasts of legal theorists. The absence of these institutions means that the rules for states resemble that simple form of social structure, consisting only of primary rules of obligation, which, when we find it among societies of individuals, we are accustomed to contrast with a developed legal system. It is indeed arguable, as we shall show, that international law not only lacks the secondary rules of change and adjudication which provide for legislature and courts, but also a unifying rule of recognition specifying 'sources' of law and providing general criteria for the identification of its rules. These differences are indeed striking and the question 'Is international law really law?' can hardly be put aside.

M. McDougal and H. Lasswell, 'The Identification and Appraisal of Diverse Systems of Public Order'
53 AJIL 6 (1959), pp. 10–11

Fortunately, advantage may be taken of the fact that the major systems of public order are in many fundamental respects rhetorically unified. All systems proclaim the dignity of the human individual and the ideal of a worldwide public order in which this ideal is authoritatively pursued and effectively approximated. They differ in many details of the institutionalized patterns of practice by which they seek to achieve such goals in specific areas and in the world as a whole. . . .

Within the distinctions thus developed, we are able to clarify what is meant by a system of public order. The reference is to the basic features of the social process in a community – including both the identity and preferred distribution pattern of basic goal values, and implementing institutions – that are accorded protection by the legal process. Since the legal process is among the basic patterns of a community, the public order includes the protection of the legal order itself, with authority being used as a base of power to protect authority. . . .

The essential meaning of human dignity as we understand it can be succinctly stated: it refers to a social process in which values are widely and not narrowly shared, and in which private choice, rather than coercion, is emphasized as the predominant modality of power.

R. Anand, 'Attitude of Asian-African States Towards Certain Problems of International Law' in F. Snyder and S. Sathirathai (eds), *Third World Attitudes to International Law*

(1987), pp. 10–12, 15–16, 19

International law is 'no longer the almost exclusive preserve of the peoples of European blood' by whose consent, it used to be said, 'exists and for the settlement of whose differences it is applied or at least invoked' [R. Pal, [1957] 1 Ybk of ILC 158]. As it must now be assumed to embrace other peoples, it clearly requires their consent no less. Secondly, at least part of this law, created by, and for, a few prosperous, industrial nations, with a common cultural background and strong liberal, individualistic features, is hardly suitable for the present heterogeneous world society. The majority in this expanded world community consists of small, weak, poor, vulnerable, technologically and industrially underdeveloped former colonies filled with resentment against their colonial rulers, and needing and demanding the protection of the international society. This new majority has new needs and new demands and they want to mould the law according to their needs. More important, while the earlier international society was extremely nationalistic and individualistic, and put the greatest stress on sovereignty and national independence, the present society, in spite of its vast horizontal expansion, has become extremely interdependent. The fantastic scientific and technological development has already made the world too small. Not only peace but prosperity has become indivisible. The mutual interdependence of States has become the most important and all-embracing concept of the present society of nations.

The alteration in the sociological structure of the international society must, of course, be accompanied by an alteration in law. Law, it has been well said, is not a constant in a society, but is a function. In order that it may be effective, it ought to change with changes in views, powers and interests in the community. The conditions under which the classical, traditional law of nations developed the views which it contained and the interests which it protected, have all greatly changed. It is also no reproach to law to say that by its very nature it tends to be conservative and is 'a bulwark of the existing order'. The present crisis in international law . . . is merely a reflection of the struggle between the conservative forces which are trying to maintain the *status quo* and the strong demands and actions of a vast majority of States to reshape and renovate some of the old concepts of international law according to changed circumstances. . . .

Motivated by a strong desire to improve their lot, these 'underdeveloped' countries want at least fourfold development in the present system of international law. In the first instance they want to annul the former law of domination as expressed in the colonial system and the 'unequal' treaties. . . . Apart from thus trying to remove the old colonial rights or their lingering remnants, the 'new' States demand the general application of those sections of international law that formerly obtained only between the 'civilised nations'. It is on this basis that they claim the recognition of the right of self-determination, the acceptance of the quality of races without any regard to colour or creed, and want equal representation on the international bodies, such as the International Law Commission, the International Court of Justice, the Security Council and other organs of the United Nations.

Furthermore, these weak and underdeveloped States desire the development of international law so as to become a law of protection, a law which may protect the weaker States, especially economically, against the overwhelming might of the stronger ones. This is particularly apparent in their strong apprehensions in regard to the law relating to the responsibility of States, which has often been abused in the past, and their insistent demands for its modification. This latter desire is also sometimes depicted in their great stress on the otherwise dwindling concept of national sovereignty, and their particular reliance on the domestic jurisdiction clause of the United Nations Charter. Thus, it has been rightly pointed out that the great upsurge of nationalism and the idolisation of sovereignty among these countries are not merely reactions to the period of dependence, but 'means of clearing away the last traces of bondage and of preventing any further bondage, as well as 'means of firmly anchoring national consciousness in the younger States themselves.

Finally, not satisfied merely with a negative law of peace, the new majority of States demands an international law of welfare which may promote their economies and help them in raising their standards of living.

All these protests against certain aspects of international law . . . do not indicate any wholesale rejection of the present system of international law. Far from it. None of these States has ever denied the binding force of international law and they in fact accept a large part of it without question. It has been very well suggested that in order to have an effective international legal order 'we must inquire not so much what potential conflicts divide [States] but what principles and what purposes they can develop in common' [Carr, *Nationalism and After*, p. 62]. An international legal order built on common interest, and which seeks to promote the well-being and fulfil the aspirations of the world-wide community of peoples, will naturally become the focus of wider loyalties.

R. Mullerson, 'Sources of International Law: New Tendencies in Soviet Thinking'
83 AJIL 494 (1989), pp. 498–499

In a world of states adhering to different ideological and political values, one of the valuable qualities of international law is its formal definitiveness. For example, the unilateral use of armed force (except in self-defense) and interference in the internal affairs of other states are prohibited for establishing the values of both a free market economy and a socialist system. And no state or group of states has the right to decide what is in the interest of the world community as a whole, especially when the implementation of such a decision entails the infringement of formal rules of international law.

That is why it is very important to treat international law as a system of principles and rules that one can find in the formal sources of international law as recognized by the world community of states. Professor G. I. Tunkin [see extract in Chapter 2] is quite right in saying that 'McDougal's theory' [see above] leads to complete uncertainty in international law.

In this connection, it is necessary to distinguish between the normative approach to the study of international law and its normative definition. The normative approach (Kelsen was one of its most prominent representatives) presupposes that specialists in international law confine themselves to studies of the principles and norms of international law, ignoring extralegal problems as being beyond their domain of interest. Such an approach is a very restrictive one. Confining oneself in this way prevents one from seeing trends in the development of the law and from evaluating the operative effectiveness of its norms with a view to increasing it. That is why the normative approach to studies of international law is limited, one-sided and insufficient. Problems of international law must be studied in the context of economic, political, sociological, ideological and other factors. The law should be studied as a normative subsystem of the international system. In other words, the normative approach to international law should be combined with such other approaches as are made possible by sociology, political science and systems analysis.

On the other hand, the Soviet scholar does define international law as a system of principles and norms. Of course, to be effective, this normative system must be supplemented with adequate international and national mechanisms. Moreover, it is understood that the effective functioning of the norms depends on the political climate in the world, the international legal consciousness of statesmen and the political will of the world's population, as well as other factors.

T. Franck, 'Legitimacy in the International System'
82 AJIL 705 (1988), pp. 711–712

In both the state and the voluntarist international system, obedience to commands is evidence of the existence of an organized community. The international community, however, does not closely resemble the modern state, precisely because the activist state exists to issue and enforce sovereign commands, while the more passive international community exists to legitimize, or withhold legitimacy from, institutions, rules and its members and their conduct. The legitimacy of a rule, or of a rule-making or rule-applying institution, is a function of the perception of those in the community concerned that the rule, or the institution, has come into being endowed with legitimacy: that is, in accordance with right process. . . .

Four elements – the indicators of rule legitimacy in the community of states – are identified and studied in this essay. They are *determinacy*, *symbolic validation*, *coherence* and *adherence* (to a normative hierarchy). To the extent rules exhibit these properties, they appear to exert a strong pull on states to comply with their commands. To the extent these elements are not present, rules seem to be easier to avoid by a state tempted to pursue its short-term self-interest. This is not to say that the legitimacy of a rule can be deduced solely by counting how often it is obeyed or disobeyed. While its legitimacy may exert a powerful pull on state conduct, yet other pulls may be stronger in a particular circumstance. The chance to take a quick, decisive advantage may overcome the counter-pull of even a highly legitimate rule. In such circumstances, legitimacy is indicated not by obedience, but by the discomfort disobedience induces in the violator. (Student demonstrations sometimes are a sensitive indicator of such discomfort). The variable to watch is not compliance but the strength of the compliance pull, whether or not the rule achieves actual compliance in any one case.

Each rule has an inherent pull power that is independent of the circumstances in which it is exerted, and that varies from rule to rule. This pull power is its index of legitimacy. For example, the rule that makes it improper for one state to infiltrate spies into another state in the guise of diplomats is formally acknowledged by almost every state, yet it enjoys so low a degree of legitimacy as to exert virtually no pull towards compliance.

The study of legitimacy thus focuses on the inherent capacity of a rule to exert pressure on states to comply.

M. Koskenniemi, *From Apology to Utopia: The Structure of International Legal Argument*
(1989), pp. 48–49

[M]y argument is that international law is singularly useless as a means for justifying or criticizing international behaviour. Because it is based on contradictory premises it remains both over-and underlegitimizing: it is overlegitimizing as it can be ultimately invoked to justify any behaviour (apologism), it is underlegitimizing because incapable of providing a convincing argument on the legitimacy of any practices (utopianism). . . .

No coherent normative practice arises from the assumptions on which we identify international law. However, neither the demand for concreteness nor the requirement of normativity can be rejected without at the same time rejecting the idea that law is different from politics by being more "objective" than this. My suggestion will not be to develop a "more determinate" system of legal argument. Quite the contrary, I believe that lawyers should admit that if they wish to achieve justifications, they have to take a stand on political issues without assuming that there exists a privileged rationality which solves such issues for them. Before any meaningful attempt at reform may be attempted, however, the idea of legal objectivity – and with it the conventional distinction between law, politics and morality (justice) needs to be rethought.

P. Allott, *Eunomia: New Order for a New World*
(1990), pp. 417–419

20.20. International society had to find its own theory. It chose to see itself as a collection of state-societies turned inside-out, like a glove. It chose to be an unsocial society creating itself separately from the development of its subordinate societies, ignoring the idea and the ideal of democracy, depriving itself of the possibility of using social power, especially legal relations, to bring about the survival and prospering of the whole human race. . . . International society is the self-ordering of the whole human race and of all subordinate societies . . .

20.24. International law has been the primitive law of an unsocial international society. Itself a by-product of that unsocialization, it has contributed to holding back the development of international society as society. Failing to recognize itself as a society, international society has not known that it has a constitution. Not knowing its own constitution, it has ignored the generic principles of a constitution. . . .

20.26. State-societies, like all other members of international society, have social power, including legal power, to serve the purposes of international society, to will and act for its survival and prospering, that is to say, for the survival and prospering of the whole human race. They are socially and legally accountable for the exercise of their powers and the carrying out of their obligations. Non-statal societies, including industrial and commercial and financial enterprises of all kinds, exercise social power and carry out obligations on the same conditions.

20.27. The new international law will be as dynamic and as rich as the law of any subordinate society, organizing human willing and acting in every field which concerns the survival and prospering of the society of which it is the law.

H. Charlesworth, C. Chinkin and S. Wright, 'Feminist Approaches to International Law'
85 AJIL 613 (1991), pp. 615, 644

By challenging the nature and operation of international law and its context, feminist legal theory can contribute to the progressive development of international law. A feminist account of international law suggests that we inhabit a world in which men of all nations have used the statist system to establish economic and nationalist priorities to serve male elites, while basic human, social and economic needs are not met. International institutions currently echo these same priorities. By taking women seriously and describing the silences and fundamentally skewed nature of international law, feminist theory can identify possibilities for change. . . .

Modern international law is not only androcentric, but also Euro-centered in its origins, and has assimilated many assumptions about law and the place of law in society from western legal thinking. These include essentially patriarchal legal institutions, the assumption that law is objective, gender neutral and universally applicable, and the societal division into public and private spheres, which relegates many matters of concern to women to the private area regarded as inappropriate for legal regulation. . . . A feminist perspective, with its concern for gender as a category of analysis and its commitment to genuine equality between the sexes, could illuminate many areas of international law: for example, state responsibility, refugee law, the use of force and the humanitarian law of war, human rights, population control and international environmental law. Feminist research holds the promise of a fundamental restructuring of traditional international law discourse and methodology to accommodate alternative world views. As Elizabeth Gross points out ['What is Feminist Theory?' in C. Pateman and E. Gross (eds), *Feminist Challenges: Social and Political Theory* (1986), p. 197], this restructuring will not amount to the replacement of one set of 'truths' with another: '[feminist theory] aims to render patriarchal systems, methods and presumptions unable to function, unable to retain their dominance and power. It aims to make clear how such a dominance has been possible; and to make it no longer viable.'

F. Tesón, 'The Kantian Theory of International Law'
92 *Columbia Law Rev 53* (1992), pp. 53–54

This Article defends the view, first developed by Immanuel Kant, that international law and domestic justice are fundamentally connected. Despite the recent prominence of the international law of human rights, the dominant discourse in international law fails to recognize the important normative status of the individual. Traditional international legal theory focuses upon the rights and duties of states and rejects the contention that the rights of states are merely derivative of the rights and interests of the individuals who reside in them. Accordingly, international legitimacy and sovereignty are a function of whether the government politically controls the population, rather than whether it justly represents its people. This statist conceptualization of international law argues for a dual paradigm for the ordering of individuals: one domestic, the other international. Justice and legitimacy are conceptually separate. It may well be that domestic systems strive to promote justice; but international systems only seek order and compliance.

International law thus conceived, however, is incapable of serving as the normative framework for present or future political realities. While it is understandably hard for lawyers to forsake the statist assumptions of classic international legal discourse, new times call for fresh conceptual and ethical language. A liberal theory [i.e. a theory of politics founded upon individual freedom, respect for individual preferences and individual autonomy] of international law can hardly be reconciled with the statist approach. Liberal theory commits itself instead to *normative individualism*, to the premise that the primary normative unit is the individual, not the state. The end of states and governments is to benefit, serve, and protect their components, human beings; and the end of international law must also be to benefit, serve, and protect human beings, and not its components, states and governments. Respect for states is merely derivative of respect for persons. In this way, the notion of state sovereignty is redefined: the sovereignty of the state is dependent upon the state's domestic legitimacy; and therefore the principles of international justice must be congruent with the principles of internal justice.

J. Charney, 'Universal International Law'
87 AJIL 529 (1993), p. 530

Unfortunately, the traditions of the international legal system appear to work against the ability to legislate universal norms. States are said to be sovereign, thus able to determine for themselves what they must or may do. State autonomy continues to serve the international system well in traditional spheres of international relations. The freedom of states to control their own destinies and policies has substantial value: it permits diversity and the choice by each state of its own social priorities. Few if any, states favour a world government that would dictate uniform behavior for all. Consequently, many writers use the language of autonomy when they declare that international law requires the consent of the states that are governed by it. Many take the position that a state that does not wish to be bound by a new rule of international law may object to it and be exempted from its application.

If sovereignty and autonomy prevailed in all areas of international law, however, one could hardly hope to develop rules to bind all states. In a community of nearly two hundred diverse states, it is virtually impossible to obtain the acceptance of all to any norm, particularly one that requires significant expenses or changes in behavior. Complete autonomy may have been acceptable in the past when no state could take actions that would threaten the international community as a whole. Today, the enormous destructive potential of some activities and the precarious condition of some objects of international concern make full autonomy undesirable, if not potentially catastrophic.

A. Angie, 'Finding the Peripheries: Sovereignty and Colonialism in Nineteenth-Century International Law'
40 *Harvard International Law Journal* 1 (1999), pp. 78–80

I have argued that the colonial encounter, far from being peripheral to the making of international law, has been central to the formation of the discipline. By this I mean not merely the specific doctrines of the discipline, but its informing philosophy: positivism. . . . By adopting the model of cultural difference, it becomes possible to examine the complex relationship between culture and sovereignty and, specifically, the manner in which sovereignty became identified with the cultural practices of Europe. I have argued that a failure to appreciate this relationship results in a rather limited understanding of sovereignty and its operations, as well as a deficient grasp of the processes and mechanisms that resulted in the universalization of international law. . . . This . . . may assist in the important and as yet unaddressed task of writing alternative histories of the discipline. . . . An appreciation of the way in which the very vocabulary of international law was racialized from its inception raises important questions about the ways in which sovereignty operates. . . .

More generally, the nineteeenth century offers us an example of a much broader theme: the importance of the existence of the 'other' for the progress and development of the discipline itself. . . . [and] the nineteenth century is . . . an example of the nexus between international law and the civilizing mission. . . . The more alarming and likely possibility is that the civilizing mission is inherent in one form or another in the principal concepts and categories that govern our existence: ideas of modernity, progress, development, emancipation, and rights. The enormous task of identifying these biases and ridding the discipline of them continues, as does the related task of constructing an international law that fulfils its promise of advancing the cause of justice.

K. Annan, *Nobel Peace Prize Lecture*
10 December 2001, www.unhchr.ch

We have entered the third millennium through a gate of Fire. If today, after the horror of 11 September, we see better, and we see further – we will realize that humanity is indivisible. New threats make no distinction between races, nations or regions. A new insecurity has entered every mind, regardless of wealth or status. A deeper awareness of the bonds that bind us all – in pain as in prosperity – has gripped young and old. . . .

In the twenty-first century I believe the mission of the United Nations will be defined by a new, more profound, awareness of the sanctity and dignity of every human life, regardless of race or religion. This will require us to look beyond the framework of States, and beneath the surface of nations or communities. We must focus, as never before, on improving the conditions of the individual men and women who give the State or nation its richness and character. . . .

Over the past five years, I have often recalled that the United Nations' Charter begins with the words: "We the peoples." What is not always recognized is that "We the peoples" are made up of individuals whose claims to the most fundamental rights have too often been sacrificed in the supposed interests of the State or the nation. . . .

In this new century, we must start from the understanding that peace belongs not only to States or peoples, but to each and every member of those communities. The sovereignty of States must no longer be used as a shield for gross violations of human rights. Peace must be made real and tangible in the daily existence of every individual in need. Peace must be sought, above all, because it is the condition for every member of the human family to live a life of dignity and security. . . .

From this vision of the role of the United Nations in the next century flow three key priorities for the future: eradicating poverty, preventing conflict, and promoting democracy. Only in a world that is rid of poverty can all men and women make the most of their abilities. Only where individual rights are respected can differences be channelled politically and resolved peacefully. Only in a democratic environment, based on respect for diversity and dialogue, can individual self-expression and self-government be secured, and freedom of association be upheld.

NOTES:

1. Theories on the nature of the international legal system have often been placed in categories. For example, 'natural law' theories, in which law embodied principles which were in accordance with nature and morals (and often religious experience); 'positivist' theories, such as the one presented by Hart, where the legal system is made up solely of clear rules enacted by governments and is relatively divorced from moral concepts; and 'newstream' or 'postmodern' theories, such as the ones presented by Charlesworth, Chinkin and Wright, Angie and Koskenniemi, in which law is shown to be neither neutral nor objective. Positivist theories, particularly liberal positivism, in which international law is a body of rules, remain the dominant theories in international law today, though they are under challenge by the new stream theories as the latter reflect a more nuanced, diverse and dynamic approach to the international legal system. A broader explanation of the theories on the nature of international law is found in Gerry Simpson (ed) *The Nature of International Law* (2001).

2. The events of 11 September 2001, and the response of the international community to them, has highlighted the changing nature of the international legal system. No longer can it be seen as a system in which only States are actors (see Chapter 5) or in which States can only take action against other States (see Chapter 14). The continuing development of international law, particularly in regard to the extension of its application beyond States alone, means that its nature has changed over time, and will continue to change. This is reflected in the decisions of both national and international judicial bodies, and in State and non-State practice.

3. Part of the role of an international lawyer is to clarify, declare and uphold international law. Yet there is also the need (as Allott implies) for international lawyers to change the consciousness of members of the international community, so that international order and concern for the condition of all of humanity is placed above the member's narrow self-interests.

2

The Sources of International Law

Introductory note

Like the rules of other legal systems, the rules of international law come from many different 'sources'. However, given that international law currently lacks both a universal legislative body – such as a Parliament – and a universal mechanism for the interpretation of laws – such as a compulsory court structure – the 'doctrine of the sources' of international law assumes an importance that is not openly expressed in national legal systems. The *relative* absence of international legal institutions having universal competence among the members of the international community requires an articulated and stable concept of the sources of international law. In general terms, an examination of these sources may focus on the role that a particular source plays in the international legal system – for example, does the source actually *create* the law or does it *identify* the content of the law – as well as an analysis of the often quite detailed rules about how legal rules come into existence. The usual starting place is to analyse the list of matters that the International Court of Justice must consider when deciding a case before it and these are to be found in Article 38 of its Statute (below, section 2). This lists custom, conventions (i.e. treaties), general principles, judicial decisions and the writings of 'highly qualified publicists' (e.g. academics). Although it is now recognised that this is not a complete list of the 'sources', it does provide the foundation stone for any credible discussion of the relevant principles.

It is also important to appreciate that the particular 'source' of a rule of international law may have an impact on the way it is applied or interpreted by an international tribunal or international organisation. For example, rules of international law derived from 'general principles of law' tend to be interpreted more flexibly than rules derived from a bilateral treaty. This is a reflection both of the content of the rule and of the manner in which it was created. Again, on one level, the 'sources' of international law explain why the rules of the international legal system are properly regarded as 'rules of law', and this is the issue discussed in Chapter 1. On another level, as noted above, 'sources' means the methods by which those rules of law are created and, on another, the way in which those rules and the specific rights or obligations they stipulate can be identified.

SECTION 1: **General theories**

O. Schachter, 'General Course in International Law'
179 *Receuil des Cours* 9 (1982)

The principal intellectual instrument in the last century for providing objective standards of legal validation has been the doctrine of sources. That doctrine which became dominant in the nineteenth century and continues to prevail today lays down verifiable conditions for ascertaining and validating legal prescriptions. The conditions are the observable manifestations of the 'wills' of States as revealed in the *processes* by which norms are formed – namely, treaty and State practice accepted as law. (These are the principal processes; Article 38 of the Statute of the Court expands them to include general principles of law.) The emphasis in this doctrine on criteria of law applied solely on the basis of observable 'positive' facts can be linked to those intellectual currents of the nineteenth century that extolled inductive science. . . .

The doctrine of sources was more than a grand theoretical conception. It also provided the stimulus for a methodology of international law that called for detailed 'inductive' methods for ascertaining and validating law. If sources were to be used objectively and scientifically, it was necessary to examine in full detail the practice and related legal convictions (*opinio juris*) of States. Most of the major treatises in international law purported to follow this methodology though they varied considerably in their fidelity to the ideal of positivist doctrine. The favoured instruments of the positivist methodology were the national digests of State practice prepared by, or in close association with, the government of the State concerned. These digests were widely lauded and strongly encouraged by the profession. . . .

Thus, the doctrine of sources together with the digests of practice and similar material met, in principle at least, the requirement of a 'positive science of international law' based on the verifiable manifestation of the wills of the States concerned. The theory appeared realistic and practical. By and large, it seemed to be the dominant theory accepted by governments in their legal arguments, by tribunals and, to a large degree, by international lawyers. However, a closer look at the argumentation and the supporting materials indicates that there were significant deviations from the doctrine and its methodology. These deviations suggest that the idea of an inductive, factual positive science of international law may be characterized more as myth than as reality.

J. Charney, 'Universal International Law'
87 AJIL 529 (1993), pp. 530–532

The international community of the late twentieth century faces an expanding need to develop universal norms to address global concerns. Perhaps one of the most salient of these concerns is to protect the earth's environment. While many environmentally harmful activities result only in local damage, others have an impact far beyond the boundaries of the states in which they take place and may cause damage to the earth's environment as a whole. For example, the discharge of some substances into the atmosphere may adversely affect the global climate or the ozone layer. Discharges that pollute the common spaces of the oceans may also have a global impact and thus raise similar concerns. Current threats to the environment highlight the importance of establishing norms to control activities that endanger all nations and peoples, regardless of where the activities take place. Acts of international terrorism, the commission of international crimes (such as genocide and war crimes), and the use of nuclear weapons pose similar global problems and have been on the international agenda for some time.

To resolve such problems, it may be necessary to establish new rules that are binding on all subjects of international law regardless of the attitude of any particular state. For unless all states are bound, an exempted recalcitrant state could act as a spoiler for the entire international community.

Thus, states that are not bound by international laws designed to combat universal environmental threats could become havens for the harmful activities concerned. Such states might have an economic advantage over states that are bound because they would not have to bear the costs of the requisite environmental protection. They would be free riders on the system and would benefit from the environmentally protective measures introduced by others at some cost. Furthermore, the example of such free riders might undermine the system by encouraging other states not to participate, and could thus derail the entire effort. Similarly, in the case of international terrorism, one state that serves as a safe haven for terrorists can threaten all. War crimes, apartheid or genocide committed in one state might threaten international peace and security worldwide. Consequently, for certain circumstances it may be incumbent on the international community to establish international law that is binding on all states regardless of any one state's disposition.

Unfortunately, the traditions of the international legal system appear to work against the ability to legislate universal norms. States are said to be sovereign, thus able to determine for themselves what they must or may do. State autonomy continues to serve the international system well in traditional spheres of international relations. The freedom of states to control their own destinies and policies has substantial value: it permits diversity and the choice by each state of its own social priorities. Few, if any, states favour a world government that would dictate uniform behavior for all. Consequently, many writers use the language of autonomy when they declare that international law requires the consent of the states that are governed by it. Many take the position that a state that does not wish to be bound by a new rule of international law may object to it and be exempted from its application.

If sovereignty and autonomy prevailed in all areas of international law, however, one could hardly hope to develop rules to bind all states. In a community of nearly two hundred diverse states, it is virtually impossible to obtain the acceptance of all to any norm, particularly one that requires significant expenses or changes in behavior. Complete autonomy may have been acceptable in the past when no state could take actions that would threaten the international community as a whole. Today, the enormous destructive potential of some activities and the precarious condition of some objects of international concern make full autonomy undesirable, if not potentially catastrophic.

H. Charlesworth and C. Chinkin, *The Boundaries of International Law: A Feminist Perspective*
(2000), pp. 62–66

Statute of the ICJ, article 38(1)

The sources of law define how new rules are made and existing rules are repealed or abrogated. Analysis of them traditionally commences with article 38(1) of the Statute of the ICJ which lists as sources: international conventions, whether general or particular; international custom; general principles of law; judicial decisions and the teachings of the most highly qualified publicists.

International conventions are binding upon parties to them. Although the expression 'law-making treaties' is often used to describe multilateral agreements, a treaty creates rights and duties for third parties only in specified circumstances, for example when it declares or generates customary international law. Customary international law, binding upon all states, has two components: uniform and consistent state practice and *opinio juris sive necessitatis* (states' belief that the behaviour is required by law). Both requirements operate at a high level of generality. Decision-makers identifying the operative rules of customary international law must choose from among the many daily activities and statements made in the name of states, those that they regard as evidence of state practice. Emphasis is given to the official acts of government: statements and claims made by political leaders in local, regional and global public fora; diplomatic communications; judicial and administrative decisions. The chain of claim and counter-claim that typically constitutes evidence of state practice may be affected by acquiescence or silence or by 'persistent objection' to an activity. *Opinio juris* is also derived from the behaviour of a state's ruling elite.

Despite their separate categorisation in article 38(1), treaties and customary international law do not operate in isolation from each other. Customary international law is not codified in the same manner as a negotiated treaty text. However, the articulation of states' positions in negotiations can contribute to the generation of customary international law. Drafts, position papers and preliminary studies can clarify stances that may be incorporated within the text, or become part of future state practice. Customary international law that is created in this way shares some characteristics with treaty law. . . .

The content of the category of 'general principles of law recognised by all civilised nations' is controversial. When drafted as part of the Statute of the PCIJ, article 38(1)(c) was a compromise between those who regarded general principles as derived from natural law and those who saw them as drawn from national law. It is now widely accepted that article 38(1)(c) applies to principles of both international and domestic law. The concept incorporates maxims normally found within state domestic law, including procedural principles, good faith and *res judicata*. It does not, however, contemplate the incorporation of municipal law principles 'lock, stock and barrel' into international law. The drafters of the Statute of the PCIJ suggested that general principles would form a safety net to avert the danger of a *non liquet* if neither custom nor treaty law provided an answer to the question before the Court. General principles can also be used in interpreting treaties and articulating customary law.

Judicial decisions and the writings of well-known publicists are subsidiary sources of international law. Although there is no formal doctrine of precedent in international law, the articulation of principles by the ICJ, or other international adjudicators, can clarify customary international law and treaty provisions. Decisions of regional and domestic tribunals, notably state supreme courts, may also be used by decision-makers when determining the requirements of customary international law.

Other sources
The traditional schema of sources in article 38(1) preserves state control over what is deemed law, but is an incomplete reflection of the realities of contemporary international law-making. Other important modalities of law-making have been identified, for example through the resolutions of international organisations, such as the General Assembly of the UN, the practice of international organisations and international codes of conduct. An important feature of the international legal scene in the 1990s was global summits on broad, interlocking issues of international concern that have culminated in declarations and strategies for state and intergovernmental and non-governmental institutional action. Despite the high level of preparations, the often intense negotiations and the large number of participating states, traditional international legal doctrine denies the status of formally binding law to the conclusions of these conferences.

Debates on the sources of international law
Although article 38(1) was drafted over seventy years ago to guide the PCIJ, it remains widely cited as the authoritative list of the sources of international law. However, it has also generated considerable debate. Certain questions have been consistently addressed. These include the requirements for establishing a rule of customary international law; the weight to be accorded to what a state says rather than what it does; the possibility of 'instant' custom; the effect of treaties on third parties; and the content of general principles of law.

Since the decolonisation era of the 1960s, other aspects of the sources of international law have become more controversial, for example the ways in which sources are manipulated to preserve the control over substantive principle by those states that had previously dominated the international legal system. Such issues include how and why a newly emergent state is bound by the customary international law in existence at the time of its acquiring statehood; how 'law-breaking' by dissentient states transforms into new customary international law; how the requirement of uniformity applies in the generation of customary international law when the numerical majority of states dissents from the practice of the minority of economically and politically powerful states; the law-making effect of a multilateral treaty; which treaties bind a successor state, and whether it is critical that the new state came into being through decolonisation rather than secession from, or union with, an existing state. The hierarchy of sources of international law has also prompted debate, in particular the relationship between treaty and customary international law. Perhaps the most significant aspect of the debate on hierarchy is over the concept of *jus cogens* which limits state sovereignty by asserting the fundamental values of the international legal system, including those based on the integrity of the human person.

Underlying this discussion are questions about the nature of international law and the impact of power relations on the making of international law. Does individual state consent (voluntarism) remain the basis of legal obligation, as was forcefully asserted in *The Lotus Case*, or has there been a shift towards a type of international 'democracy' in which a broader notion of the international community creates law? Could this type of system embrace the views of non-state actors? The notion of consent itself has been challenged as a basis for legal, as distinct from political, obligation. . . .

The deficiencies of international law-making have been particularly highlighted in fields of international law where exclusive state interests may conflict more directly with those of non-state actors. Examples include human rights, international economic law and environmental law. Traditional international law-making assumes a monolithic state voice that silences individuals and other non-elite groups in the international arena, except insofar as their interests are championed by states. International law nevertheless has an impact upon individuals. It may be directly applicable within domestic legal systems, and domestic law in turn may influence the development of international law.

NOTES:

1. The above extracts explain in general terms what is meant by a 'doctrine of sources' and identify how such a doctrine can be developed. As they illustrate, the way in which the 'sources' of international law are viewed as an abstract legal phenomenon may have consequences for the substance of the rules of international law that are generated by those sources. The views of Charney can be regarded as an expression of the late twentieth-century doctrine of sources that seeks to divorce the law-creating process from any theory which has at its root the pure self-interest of States. Note, however, that as Schachter points out in a later work, 'customary law, new and old, are products of political aims and conditions' ('New Custom: Power, *Opinio Juris* and Contrary Practice' in *Theory of International Law at the Threshold of the 21st Century*, and see below). This at least is a reminder that a theory of the sources of international law ultimately is helpful only if it reflects the reality of how rules of law come into existence.

2. The quoted extract from Charlesworth and Chinkin is a succinct statement of how Article 38 of the Statute of the ICJ is perceived to be the foundation for a discussion of the sources of international law at the concrete level. The extract is in fact part of a general critique of an allegedly masculine conception of international law. However, as they also point out, Article 38 has generated much debate, especially as it appears to exclude the role of non-State actors from the law creation process (see Chapter 5 on Personality). Whether such actors – e.g. individuals, multinational corporations, pressure groups, terrorists/freedom fighters, Non-Governmental Organisations – *should* have such a role would be disputed by many academics and certainly by many States. Much of the international community and those who comment on it are still State-centred. For example, only States may be members of the United Nations, although many other groups do have Observer status. Indeed, even accepting that non-State actors do have a role (and this seems unarguable if one actually examines the reality of international life) *how* can such a role be effective to counter the largely

self-interested motivation of States that pervades the law creation process? Of course, the international community is no longer the cosy preserve of 50 or so like-minded States that together could effectively run the international system. That may have been the case (if ever) back in 1945. Not only has the number of States increased (on which see Chapter 5), but also non-State actors now fulfil roles that once were the preserve of States – for example, in the field of the development and enforcement of human rights standards. Yet, the doctrine of the sources of international law has yet to come to grips with this phenomenon, as indeed has so many other areas of the international legal system.

SECTION 2: Statute of the International Court of Justice 1945

Article 38

1. The Court, whose function is to decide in accordance with international law such disputes as are submitted to it, shall apply:
    (a) international conventions, whether general or particular, establishing rules expressly recognized by the contesting states;
    (b) international custom, as evidence of a general practice accepted as law;
    (c) the general principles of law recognized by civilised nations;
    (d) subject to the provisions of Article 59, judicial decisions and the teachings of the most highly qualified publicists of the various nations, as subsidiary means for the determination of rules of law.

2. This provision shall not prejudice the power of the Court to decide a case *ex aequo et bono*, if the parties agree thereto.

NOTES:
1. Although Article 38 is actually a direction to the International Court of Justice (and the Permanent Court of International Justice before it) in respect of what matters it must consider when deciding a case before it, we have noted already that it is treated as a statement of the most important of the sources of international law. This should be no surprise: after all, the ICJ is the principal judicial organ of the United Nations and we might expect that it would decide cases according to binding rules of international law! However, Article 38 is not meant to exclude other matters that may be said to give rise to international rights and obligations, such as binding resolutions of international bodies (e.g., the Security Council of the United Nations) or the unilateral acts of States. Indeed, whether the Article represents a complete list of the sources of international law rather depends on one's definitional perspective. For example, unilateral acts of States undoubtedly can create legal consequences: are they thereby 'sources' of law or 'sources' of legal obligation (if different!)?
2. It will be noted that Article 38(2) of the Statute gives the Court the power, at the request of the parties to a dispute before it, to decide a case *ex aequo et bono*. This rarely invoked provision allows the parties to request the Court to reach a decision based not only on strict rules of law, but on general conceptions of fairness, good judgement and equality. Of course, these ideals should be found liberally sprinkled among the rules of law properly so called, but Art. 38(2) could be useful if the parties were bound by a rule of international law (of a non-fundamental nature) that on the particular unusual facts of a case would produce an undesirable solution for both parties. It might then be disapplied by mutual consent.

SECTION 3: **Treaties**

Treaties are now the most important source of international law. They offer States a deliberate method by which to create binding international law. The efforts of the International Law Commission and the United Nations have produced a number of significant multilateral treaties, such as the Vienna Convention on Diplomatic Relations 1961 and the Law of the Sea Convention 1982, and such multi-national treaties are designed to set global standards within particular areas of activity. Indeed, such treaties are ideal if the aim is to establish universal standards that would not be achieved if States were left to their own devices. The recently inaugurated International Criminal Court – whose existence and legal authority stems from a multilateral treaty – is a prime example of how multilateral treaties can significantly affect the international rights and duties of States, individuals and the very working of the international legal system. However, it must not be forgotten that much of the law binding a State will take the form of a bilateral treaty between it and one other State or treaties open only to a limited group of States, such as the European Convention on State Immunity. Such bilateral or limited participation treaties, although often technical, are absolutely vital to the operation of the international legal system. Few people will get excited about an international air transit treaty between the UK and Spain, yet without the legal regulation it would provide, the planes would not fly. In order to understand fully the role of treaties as a source of law it is necessary to be aware of the rules concerning the creation and operation of treaties. These are examined in Chapter 3.

Vienna Convention on the Law of Treaties 1969
1155 UNTS 331

Article 6
Every State possesses capacity to conclude treaties.

Article 26
Every treaty in force is binding upon the parties to it and must be performed by them in good faith.

Article 34
A treaty does not create either obligations or rights for a third state without its consent.

G. Fitzmaurice, 'Some Problems Regarding the Formal Sources of International Law'
Symbolae Verzijl 153 (1958)

The sources of law are commonly classified as 'formal' and 'material'. Side by side with these there are the 'evidences' or records of law. Thus, if State practice, for instance, is a source of law, it would be incorrect to regard such things as documents embodying diplomatic representations, notes of protest, etc., as constituting sources of law. They are evidences of it because they demonstrate certain attitudes on the part of States, but it is the State practice so evidenced which is the source of law.

Accepting this classification, it is of course possible to use other terms to describe the formal and material sources. Thus they may be described as, respectively, the legal sources and the historical sources, as direct and indirect, as proximate or immediate, and remote or ultimate, and so on. Or, as has been suggested, the material sources might better be described as the 'origins' of law. But whatever the terminology used, the essence of the distinction remains the same. Material, historical, indirect sources represent, so to speak, the stuff out of which the law is made. It is they which go to form the *content* of the law. These are the sources to which the lawgiver goes, so to speak, in order to obtain ideas, or to decide what the law is to consist of, and this is broadly true whether the lawgiver be conceived of as a national legislature, or as the international community evolving customary rules through State practice. The formal, legal, and direct sources consist of the acts or facts whereby this content, whatever it may be and from whatever material source it may be drawn, is clothed with legal validity and obligatory force. The essence of the distinction therefore is between the thing which inspires the content of the law, and the thing which gives that content its obligatory character as law.

Considered in themselves, and particularly in their inception, treaties are, formally, a source of obligation rather than a source of law. In their contractual aspect they are no more a source of law than an ordinary private law contract; which simply creates rights and obligations. Such instruments (as also, on the international plane, a commercial treaty, for example) create obligations and rights, not law. In this connexion, the attempts which have been made to ascribe a law-making character to *all* treaties irrespective of the character of their content or the number of the parties to them, by postulating that some treaties create 'particular' international law and others 'general', is of extremely dubious validity. There is really no such thing as 'particular' international treaty law, though there are particular international treaty rights and obligations. The only 'law' that enters into these is derived, not from the treaty creating them – or from any treaty – but from the principle *pacta sunt servanda* – an antecedent general principle of law. The law is that the obligation must be carried out, but the obligation is not, in itself, law. A genuine law may of course be applicable only to certain particular subjects of the legal system, but if so it is usually as members of a class, not as individuals. For instance, a law relating to married women obviously applies only to women who are married. But it applies automatically and *ipso facto* to *all* such women, not merely to those individual women who have set their hands to some particular instrument. In the latter event there would be rights or obligations for the women concerned, but not law – or if law, it would be something extraneous to the right or obligation, and general, not particular – i.e. that all rights and obligations thus arising must be honoured. A statute is always, *from its inception*, law: a treaty may reflect, or lead to, law, but, *particularly* in its inception, is not, as such, 'law'. So called treaty law is really pseudo-law – *a droit fainéant*. In itself, the treaty and the 'law' it contains only applies to the parties to it. True, where it reflects (e.g. codifies) existing law, non-parties may conform to the same rules, but they do so by virtue of the rules of general law thus reflected in the treaty, not by virtue of the treaty itself. In that sense, the treaty may be an instrument in which the law is conveniently stated, and evidence of what it is, but it is still not itself the law – it is still formally not a source of law but only evidence of it. Where a treaty is, or rather becomes, a *material* source of law, because the rules it contains come to be generally regarded as representing rules of universal applicability, it will nevertheless be the case that when non-parties apply or conform to these rules, this will be because the rules are or have become rules of general law: it is in the application of this general law, not of the treaty, that non-parties will act. For them, the rules are law; but the treaty is not the law, though it may be both the material source of it, and correctly state it.

NOTES:

1. The running order of Article 38 of the Statute of the International Court of Justice suggests that treaties take precedence over the other 'sources' which follow. However, if 'international law' is to have credibility as a system of law, there is much to be said for the view that the sources of international law are not hierarchical in this way but are necessarily complimentary and interrelated. This seems to have been the view of the majority of the International Court of Justice in *Nicaragua* v *USA* ICJ Rep 1986 14 (see below), although it is true that rules of *jus cogens*, being customary rules of a fundamental nature, always take priority over treaty obligations. In the *Danube Dam Case* (see Chapter 3) the Court confirmed that *in general*, the law applicable to a treaty is the law in force when the treaty itself comes into operation, even if customary law has developed further since then. However, the Court did recognise that the treaty itself might permit evolving customary rules to be relevant to its operation. Once again this seems to be an attempt to introduce a coherency to the law irrespective of the source of any particular obligation.

2. As explained in Chapter 3, a fundamental rule in the law of treaties (with only limited exceptions) is that only States which are parties to a treaty are bound by it. With this in mind, the alleged distinction between 'law creating' and 'obligation creating' treaties may have reduced significance when trying to decide the precise obligations of a State in a real life situation. This is because, absent one of the special 'territorial status treaties', the only meaningful questions are whether the treaty has entered into force for the State concerned and, if not, whether the treaty mirrors existing rules of customary law by which the State is otherwise bound. Consequently, to describe a treaty as 'multilateral' or 'lawmaking', as opposed to 'bi-lateral' or 'obligation making', may not describe their legal effect, but their purpose. Multilateral treaties may well be intended to lay down general rules for the community at large (i.e. *intended* to be 'lawmaking') but only the parties to them are bound. Bi-lateral treaties may be *intended* to create 'obligations' for only two States, but in reality for those two States the treaty *is* 'the law' on the particular issue.

3. Many texts, and the occasional case, refer to the alleged distinction between 'formal' and 'material' sources of international law, as discussed by Fitzmaurice. This distinction is best understood as an attempt to clarify the purpose that any given source plays in the evolution of rules of international law. To describe a source as 'formal' indicates that the source is law-creating, in that it is the method by which legally binding rules come into existence. Custom, and sometimes treaties and general principles of law, are said to be formal sources. A 'material' source is a source which identifies the substance of a legal obligation rather than expressing its role as a creator of law. Material sources may include judicial decisions and, for some commentators, treaties. There is considerable debate as to whether it is possible, necessary or even desirable to classify sources in this way.

4. Questions concerning the interpretation of treaties are more fully considered in Chapter 3. However, materials that aid the implementation or understanding of a treaty might also be regarded as a 'source' of international law. In *R* v *Secretary of State for the Home Department, ex parte Robinson* [1997] 3 WLR 1162 Lord Woolf MR noted, in connection with the Convention relating to the Statutes of Refugees 1951, that 'there is no international court charged with the interpretation and implementation of the Convention, and for this reason the UNHCR *Handbook on Procedures and Criteria for Determining Refugee Status* (1979) is particularly helpful as a guide to what is the international understanding of the Convention obligations, as worked out in practice'.

SECTION 4: **Custom**

A: General considerations

Customary international law derives from the practice of States. There has been considerable discussion of the elements of customary law and these are considered in the extracts below. In particular, State practice may give rise to customary international law when that practice is uniform, consistent and general, and if it is coupled with a belief that the practice is obligatory rather than habitual (the *opinio juris*). There is, in addition, some debate as to why State practice can give rise to binding international law at all and as to whether a State's continued objection to an emerging rule can absolve it from the scope of the rule (the problem of the persistent objector).

M. Akehurst, 'Custom as a Source of International Law'
(1974–75) 47 BYBIL 53

1. Customary international law is created by State practice. State practice means any act or statement by a State from which views about customary law can be inferred; it includes physical acts, claims, declarations *in abstracto* (such as General Assembly resolutions), national laws, national judgments and omissions. Customary international law can also be created by the practice of international organizations and (in theory, at least) by the practice of individuals.

2. As regards the quantity of practice needed to create a customary rule, the number of States participating is more important than the frequency or duration of the practice. Even a practice followed by a few States, on a few occasions and for a short period of time, can create a customary rule, provided that there is no practice which conflicts with the rule, and provided that other things are equal; but other things are seldom completely equal, because there are various presumptions (e.g. the presumption in favour of the liberty of State action) which need to be taken into account.

3(a) Major inconsistencies in State practice prevent the creation of a customary rule; such inconsistencies cannot be explained away by saying that one type of practice is more important than another or that the practice of some States is more important than the practice of others.

3(b) A State is not bound by a customary rule if it has consistently opposed that rule from its inception. However, a new State is bound by rules which were well established before it became independent.

3(c) Special (e.g. regional) customs can co-exist with general customs. Apart from the number of States bound by the customs, there is little difference between special and general customs; where the number of States following one practice is roughly the same as the number of States following another practice, it may be difficult to say which is the special custom and which is the general custom.

4. *Opinio juris* is necessary for the creation of customary rules; State practice, in order to create a customary rule, must be accompanied by (or consist of) statements that certain conduct is permitted, required or forbidden by international law (a claim that conduct is permitted can be inferred from the mere existence of such conduct, but claims that conduct is required or forbidden need to be stated expressly). It is not necessary that the State making such statements believes them to be true; what is necessary is that the statements are not challenged by other States.

5. Treaties are part of State practice and can create customary rules if the requirements of *opinio juris* are met, e.g. if the treaty or its *travaux préparatoires* contain a claim that the treaty is declara-

tory of pre-existing customary law. Sometimes a treaty which is not accompanied by *opinio juris* may nevertheless be imitated in subsequent practice; but in such cases it is the subsequent practice (accompanied by *opinio juris*), and not the treaty, which creates customary rules.

North Sea Continental Shelf Cases (Federal Republic of Germany v Denmark; FRG v The Netherlands)

ICJ Rep 1969 3, International Court of Justice

By two Special Agreements, the FRG and Denmark, and the FRG and The Netherlands, submitted a dispute over the delimitation of their shared Continental Shelf to the International Court of Justice. One of the Court's tasks was to identify the rules which bound these States, and in so doing the judgments shed considerable light on the circumstances in which international custom can be created. In the result, the ICJ found that the delimitation of the continental shelf between these States (and hence giving access to the valuable oil deposits beneath them) had to be decided according to customary law because the relevant treaty (the Continental Shelf Convention 1958) had not entered into force for all parties to the dispute.

75. The Court must now consider whether State practice in the matter of continental shelf delimitation has, subsequent to the Geneva Convention [on the Continental Shelf 1958], been of such a kind as to satisfy this requirement. . . .

77. The essential point in this connection – and it seems necessary to stress it – is that even if these instances of action by non-parties to the Convention were much more numerous than they in fact are, they would not, even in the aggregate, suffice in themselves to constitute the *opinio juris*; for, in order to achieve this result, two conditions must be fulfilled. Not only must the acts concerned amount to a settled practice, but they must also be such, or be carried out in such a way, as to be evidence of a belief that this practice is rendered obligatory by the existence of a rule of law requiring it. The need for such a belief, i.e., the existence of a subjective element, is implicit in the very notion of the *opinio juris sive necessitatis*. The States concerned must therefore feel that they are conforming to what amounts to a legal obligation. The frequency, or even habitual character of the acts is not in itself enough. There are many international acts, e.g., in the field of ceremonial and protocol, which are performed almost invariably, but which are motivated only by considerations of courtesy, convenience or tradition, and not by any sense of legal duty. . . .

79. Finally, it appears that in almost all of the cases cited, the delimitations concerned were median-line delimitations between opposite States, not lateral delimitations between adjacent States. . . . [The Court] simply considers that they are inconclusive, and insufficient to bear the weight sought to be put upon them as evidence of such a settled practice, manifested in such circumstances, as would justify the inference that delimitation according to the principle of equidistance amounts to a mandatory rule of customary international law, – more particularly where lateral delimitations are concerned. . . .

81. The Court accordingly concludes that if the Geneva Convention was not in its origins or inception declaratory of a mandatory rule of customary international law enjoining the use of the equidistance principle for the delimitation of continental shelf areas between adjacent States, neither has its subsequent effect been constitutive of such a rule; and that State practice up-to-date has equally been insufficient for the purpose. . . .

83. The legal situation therefore is that the Parties are under no obligation to apply either the 1958 Convention, which is not opposable to the Federal Republic, or the equidistance method as a mandatory rule of customary law, which it is not. . . .

In sum, the general practice of States should be recognized as *prima facie* evidence that it is accepted as law. Such evidence may, of course, be controverted – even on the test of practice itself, if it shows 'much uncertainty and contradiction' (*Asylum, Judgment* . . .). It may also be controverted on the test of *opinio juris* with regard to 'the States in question' or the parties to the case.

Military and Paramilitary Activities in and against Nicaragua (Nicaragua v United States) (Merits)

ICJ Rep 1986 14, International Court of Justice

In 1984, Nicaragua brought a claim against the United States alleging certain unlawful military and paramilitary activities against Nicaraguan territory, including the mining of Nicaraguan ports and support for Nicaraguan rebels, the Contras. The United States claimed that the Court had no jurisdiction because, *inter alia*, they had entered a reservation to the jurisdiction of the ICJ excluding a matter from the Court if the dispute concerned the application of a multilateral treaty. The relevant treaty here was the UN Charter itself, particularly Article 2(4) on the non-use of force. Nicaragua argued, however, that the Court had jurisdiction because its claim against the US was also based on rules of customary law, which although similar in content to the law of the UN Charter, had not been suspended by it.

183. [T]he Court has next to consider what are the rules of customary international law applicable to the present dispute. For this purpose, it has to direct its attention to the practice and *opinio juris* of States . . . In this respect the Court must not lose sight of the Charter of the United Nations and that of the Organization of American States, notwithstanding the operation of the multilateral treaty reservation. Although the Court has no jurisdiction to determine whether the conduct of the United States constitutes a breach of those conventions, it can and must take them into account in ascertaining the content of the customary international law which the United States is also alleged to have infringed.

184. The Court notes that there is in fact evidence, to be examined below, of a considerable degree of agreement between the Parties as to the content of the customary international law relating to the non-use of force and non-intervention. This concurrence of their views does not however dispense the Court from having itself to ascertain what rules of customary international law are applicable. The mere fact that States declare their recognition of certain rules is not sufficient for the Court to consider these as being part of customary international law, and as applicable as such to those States. Bound as it is by Article 38 of its Statute to apply, *inter alia*, international custom 'as evidence of a general practice accepted as law', the Court may not disregard the essential role played by general practice. Where two States agree to incorporate a particular rule in a treaty, their agreement suffices to make that rule a legal one, binding upon them; but in the field of customary international law, the shared view of the Parties as to the content of what they regard as the rule is not enough. The Court must satisfy itself that the existence of the rule in the *opinio juris* of States is confirmed by practice.

185. In the present dispute, the Court, while exercising its jurisdiction only in respect of the application of the customary rules of non-use of force and non-intervention, cannot disregard the fact that the Parties are bound by these rules as a matter of treaty law and of customary international law. Furthermore, in the present case, apart from the treaty commitments binding the Parties to the rules in question, there are various instances of their having expressed recognition of the validity thereof as customary international law in other ways. It is therefore in the light of this

'subjective element' – the expression used by the Court in its 1969 Judgment in the *North Sea Continental Shelf* cases (*ICJ Rep 1969*, p. 44) – that the Court has to appraise the relevant practice.

186. It is not to be expected that in the practice of States the application of the rules in question should have been perfect, in the sense that States should have refrained, with complete consistency, from the use of force or from intervention in each other's internal affairs. The Court does not consider that, for a rule to be established as customary, the corresponding practice must be in absolutely rigorous conformity with the rule. In order to deduce the existence of customary rules, the Court deems it sufficient that the conduct of States should, in general, be consistent with such rules, and that instances of State conduct inconsistent with a given rule should generally have been treated as breaches of that rule, not as indications of the recognition of a new rule. If a State acts in a way prima facie incompatible with a recognized rule, but defends its conduct by appealing to exceptions or justifications contained within the rule itself, then whether or not the State's conduct is in fact justifiable on that basis, the significance of that attitude is to confirm rather than to weaken the rule.

J. Charney, 'Universal International Law'
87 AJIL 529 (1993), pp. 543–545

Traditional textbook accounts of customary international lawmaking describe an amorphous process in which a pattern of behavior developed by states acting in their self-interest over a long period of time is coupled with opinions that the practice reflects a legal obligation (*opinio juris*). Treaties may codify the practice in normative terms. Eventually, it becomes well established that new international law on the subject has emerged. The judgments in the *Paquete Habana*, *Lotus* and *North Sea* cases epitomize this process. Traditional customary law formation may have sufficed when both the scope of international law and the number of states were limited. Today, however, the subject matter has expanded substantially into areas that were traditionally the preserve of states' domestic jurisdiction. In addition, the number of states has dramatically increased, together with their diversity. The relatively exclusive ways of the past are not suitable for contemporary circumstances. While customary law is still created in the traditional way, that process has increasingly given way in recent years to a more structured method, especially in the case of important normative developments.

Rather than state practice and *opinio juris*, multilateral forums often play a central role in the creation and shaping of contemporary international law. Those forums include the United Nations General Assembly and Security Council, regional organizations, and standing and ad hoc multilateral diplomatic conferences, as well as international organizations devoted to specialized subjects. Today, major developments in international law often get their start or substantial support from proposals, reports, resolutions, treaties or protocols debated in such forums. There, representatives of states and other interested groups come together to address important international problems of mutual concern. Sometimes these efforts result in a consensus on solving the problem and express it in normative terms of general application. At other times, the potential new law is developed through the medium of international relations or the practices of specialized international institutions and at later stages is addressed in international forums. That process draws attention to the rule and helps to shape and crystallize it.

The authoritativeness of the debates at these multilateral forums varies, depending upon many factors. Among the first is how clearly it is communicated to the participating states that the rule under consideration reflects a refinement, codification, crystallization or progressive development of international law. Of crucial importance is the amount of support given to the rule under consideration. Adoption of the rule by the forum in accordance with its procedures for decision making may not be necessary or even sufficient. On the other hand, unanimous support is not required. Consensus, defined as the lack of expressed objections to the rule by any participant, may often be sufficient. The absence of objections, of course, amounts to tacit consent by participants that do not explicitly support the norm. Even opposition by a small number of participating states may not stop the movement of the proposed rule toward law. The effect of the discussion depends upon the number of objecting states, the nature of their objections, the importance of the interests they seek to protect and their geopolitical standing relative to the states that support the proposed rule. Moreover, when objections are expressed, it must be determined whether they go to the heart of the norm under consideration or to subsidiary issues. Also relevant is whether the support for the norm is widespread and encompasses all interest groups. Do the objections demonstrate that an important group of states is not supportive, precluding the widespread support of the international community, or are relatively isolated states alone raising objections?

The discussions to such forums are necessarily communicated to all states and other interested parties. According to some customary law analysts, the work and products of those forums may be characterized as state practice or *opinio juris*. Certainly, the forums may move the solutions substantially toward acquiring the status of international law. Those solutions that are also positively received by the international community through state practice or other indications of support will rapidly be absorbed into international law, notwithstanding the technical legal status of the form in which they emerged from the multilateral forum. While this process may not conform to traditional customary lawmaking, nothing in the foundations of the international legal system bars such an evolution in the international lawmaking process. The international community itself holds the authority to make changes in this process and did so through the United Nations Charter and the system that evolved from it.

O. Schachter, 'New Custom: Power, *Opinio Juris* and Contrary Practice' in J. Makarczyk (ed), *Theory of International Law at the Threshold of the 21st Century*
(1996), pp. 531–532

The fact that governments do not always practice what they preach comes as no surprise; indeed, we would be surprised if they did, at least in some areas. Still, under the canons of positivist international law, we lawyers are called upon to determine whether a putative rule of customary law meets the requirements of general and consistent practice followed by States from a sense of legal obligation. The latter requirement – the *opinio juris sive necessitatis* – calls for a 'belief' by States that the practice in question is obligatory by virtue of a rule of law requiring it. In the words of an International Court of Justice judgment, 'Not only must the acts concerned amount to a settled practice, they must also be such, or be carried out in such a way, as to be evidence of a belief that this practice is rendered obligatory by the existence of a rule of law requiring it.' As this passage indicates, custom begins with 'acts' that become a 'settled practice;' that practice may then give rise to the belief that it had become obligatory.

This generally accepted view of the relation of practice and *opinio juris* was indirectly challenged by the International Court in its 1986 Judgment in the *Nicaragua* Case. In that judgment, the Court first found the *opinio juris communis* on the non-use of force in the unanimous acceptance of relevant UN General Assembly resolutions that defined aggression. It then declared that the Court 'must satisfy itself that the existence of the rule in the *opinio juris* of States is confirmed by practice.' This sentence was seen by some critics as standing custom on its head. In place of a practice that began with the gradual accretion of acts and subsequently received the imprimatur of *opinio juris*, the Court reversed the process: an *opinio juris* expressed first as a declaration would become law if confirmed by general practice. While this passage seemed to some commentators to show a profound misunderstanding of custom, it is fair to say that it reflected a widespread professional opinion that law-declaring resolutions particularly when adopted by unanimous decisions of the General Assembly could have a creative role in the formation of custom.

NOTES:

1. In the *Fisheries Jurisdiction Case* ICJ Rep 1973 3, a Joint Opinion by five Judges held that 'State practice must be common, consistent and concordant' (at p. 50). However, it is implicit in the extracts cited above that the degree of consistency, generality and uniformity of State practice necessary for the formation of customary law may vary from case to case. The practice of States specially affected by a rule is of particular importance – see *North Sea Continental Shelf Case*, para. 74 – as is the requirement of *opinio juris*, for this is what distinguishes 'law' from 'habit'. In the *North Sea Continental Shelf Case*, the members of the Court adopted different approaches to finding *opinio juris*, although it seems that a rather more relaxed view of the necessary proof of *opinio juris* was favoured by the majority in *Nicaragua* v *USA*. In the *Danube Dams Case* the Court adopted the International Law Commission's (ILC) formulation concerning the scope of the customary law on the 'defence' of necessity with no analysis of State practice and no attempt to identify sufficient *opinio juris*.

2. Likewise, in the *Maritime Delimitation and Territorial Questions Between Qatar and Bahrain Case* (*Qatar* v *Bahrain*) ICJ Rep 2001, Qatar and Bahrain accepted that the relevant Articles of the Law of the Sea Convention 1982 represented customary law and thus should form the basis of the Court's judgment even though that treaty was not in force between them. The point is not that the 1982 Convention might be said to represent customary law (many commentators and States would not disagree), but rather that the Court was prepared to accept the parties' agreement that the treaty did indeed represent customary law without any substantial analysis of the point. In other words, the Court seems prepared to allow the parties to choose *in effect* to be governed by a treaty (even if neither or only one is a party to it) by the simple device of accepting the parties' agreement that it represents customary law. Once again, the context in which it is necessary to determine the validity of a particular 'source' of a rule of international law affects how the issue is dealt with.

3. It is obvious that many types of acts and omissions may amount to 'State practice' for the formation of customary law. There has been considerable comment on this point, with various academics arguing in favour of, or against, the inclusion in 'State practice' of such matters as verbal statements, discussions in international fora, votes in international organs, government position papers and diplomatic exchanges. Once again, Charney reminds us that any attempt to define the nature of customary law should take account of the realities of the way international affairs are conducted and Charlesworth and Chinkin (above) remind us that there is move to 'international' practice rather than 'State' practice.

B: Local custom

Asylum Case (*Colombia* v *Peru*)
ICJ Rep 1950 266, International Court of Justice

Following an unsuccessful coup in Peru in 1948, the leader of the rebel movement sought refuge and 'diplomatic asylum' in the Colombian Embassy in Lima, the Peruvian capital. The Peruvian government subsequently refused safe conduct for the rebel leader and the dispute was referred by agreement to the ICJ. One issue was whether a 'local custom' existed in Latin-America permitting one State to grant political asylum and thereby offer consequential protection to the asylum seeker.

The Colombian Government has . . . has relied on an alleged regional or local custom peculiar to Latin-American States.

The Party which relies on a custom of this kind must prove that this custom is established in such a manner that it has become binding on the other Party. The Colombian Government must prove that the rule invoked by it is in accordance with a constant and uniform usage practised by the States in question, and that this usage is the expression of a right appertaining to the State granting asylum and a duty incumbent on the territorial State. This follows from Article 38 of the Statute of the Court, which refers to international custom 'as evidence of a general practice accepted as law'. In support of its contention concerning the existence of such a custom, the Colombian Government has referred to a large number of . . . treaties . . .

Finally, the Colombian Government has referred to a large number of particular cases in which diplomatic asylum was in fact granted and respected. But it has not shown that the alleged rule . . . was invoked or – if in some cases it was in fact invoked – that it was, apart from conventional stipulations, exercised by the States as a duty incumbent on them and not merely for reasons of political expediency. The facts brought to the knowledge of the Court disclose so much uncertainty and contradiction, so much fluctuation and discrepancy in the exercise of diplomatic asylum and in the official views expressed on various occasions, there has been so much inconsistency in the rapid succession of conventions on asylum, ratified by some States and rejected by others, and the practice has been so much influenced by considerations of political expediency in the various cases, that it is not possible to discern in all this any constant and uniform usage, accepted as law, with regard to the alleged rule of unilateral and definitive qualification of the offence.

The Court cannot therefore find that the Colombian Government has proved the existence of such a custom. But even if it could be supposed that such a custom existed between certain Latin-American States only, it could not be invoked against Peru which, far from having by its attitude adhered to it, has, on the contrary, repudiated it by refraining from ratifying the Montevideo Conventions of 1933 and 1939, which were the first to include a rule concerning the qualification of the offence in matters of diplomatic asylum.

NOTE:

In the *Asylum Case*, the Court found against the existence of local custom because of lack of evidence. However, the possibility that local custom could exist in an appropriate case was confirmed in the *Rights of Passage over Indian Territory Case*, ICJ Rep 1960 6, where the Court observed that:

> [w]ith regard to Portugal's claim of a right of passage as formulated by it on the basis of local custom, it is objected on behalf of India that no local custom could be established between only two states. It is difficult to see why the number of states between which a local custom may be established on the basis of long practice must necessarily be larger than two. The Court sees no reason why long continued practice between two States accepted by them as regulating their relations should not form the basis of mutual rights and obligations between the two states.

C: Persistent objector

J. Charney, 'The Persistent Objector Rule and the Development of Customary International Law'

(1985) 56 BYBIL 1

The role of the dissenting State in the development of customary international law is difficult to identify. The positivists clearly held that no rule of international law could be binding on a State without its consent. Most modern theories of international law do not require that express consent be found before a rule of customary international law can be held to be binding on a State. Many authorities argue that a State can be bound by a rule of customary international law even though the State neither expressly nor tacitly consented to the rule. . . . No authority would permit a State unilaterally to opt out of an existing rule of customary international law, and few would permit new States to choose to exempt themselves from such rules.

Even though most authorities recognize that a State is not required to have expressly consented to be bound by a rule of customary international law, virtually all authorities maintain that a State which objects to an *evolving* rule of general customary international law can be exempted from its obligations. . . . The International Court decision that writers primarily rely upon to support this rule is the *Anglo-Norwegian Fisheries* case. In that judgment the International Court of Justice made an alternative finding that a coastline delimitation rule put forward by the United Kingdom 'would appear to be inapplicable as against Norway, in as much as she has always opposed any attempt to apply it to the Norwegian coast'.

When the question of consent is directly addressed, most writers argue that States do not have the free will to decide whether or not to be bound by rules of international law. The obligation to conform to rules of international law is not derived from the voluntary decision of a State to accept or reject the binding force of a rule of law. Rather, it is the societal context which motivates States to have an international law and obligates them to conform to its norms. . . .

If it is the societal context that is the source of the obligation to conform to specific rules of international law, then consent, either express or tacit, is irrelevant to the obligation. It may also appear to follow that if the societal context is the source, then an objection at any time, persistent or not, is irrelevant to the binding effect of a rule of law. If this is true, there is no place in international law for the persistent objector rule. A similar conclusion that the rule has no place in international law is reached if one maintains that consent is the basis of obligation. In that case, a particular persistent objector rule is redundant.

Only if one actually believes in the reality of the tacit consent theory of international legal obligation might there be any room for the persistent objector rule. In that case, it is difficult to limit its application only to overt dissent commenced at the formative stages of law development. . . .

At this point it might be wise to conclude that regardless of one's theory of international law, the persistent objector rule has no legitimate basis in the international legal system. Not only is the rule hard to reconcile with the current theories of international law, but the evidence which might be produced to support the rule is weak indeed. This conclusion does not explain why so many reputable international law authorities explicitly report the existence of the rule. Perhaps its *raison d'être* can be found in the dynamics of international law development.

. . . Customary international law is not static. It changes as the patterns of State behaviour change and *opinio juris* evolves to reflect current realities of obligation. Extant rules of law are subjected to change. Nations forge new law by breaking existing law, thereby leading the way for other nations to follow. Ultimately, new patterns of behaviour and obligation develop.

In the early stages a number of States may object to the new behaviour, but over time social pressures and modern realities will cause those reluctant States to conform to the new norm. On the other hand, some will seek to retain the traditional rule. The persistent objector rule becomes directly relevant when those resisting States continue to dissent from the new norm after it has replaced the old norm. At this stage the persistent objector rule promotes disharmony and discord in international relations. The international community will exert pressure to force the objector to conform to the new normative standard. . . . In fact, the two International Court of Justice cases which appear to support the persistent objector rule both arose in circumstances in which the new rule itself was in substantial doubt. Thus, it was significantly easier for the objector to maintain its status. No case is cited for a circumstance in which the objector effectively maintained its status after the rule became well accepted in international law. In fact, it is unlikely that such a status could be maintained in light of the realities of the international legal system. This is certainly the plight that befell the US, the UK and Japan in the law of the sea. Their objections to expanded coastal State jurisdiction were ultimately to no avail, and they have been forced to accede to 12-mile territorial seas and 200-mile exclusive economic zones.

It appears, therefore, that the persistent objector rule, if it really exists, focuses more on the process of law development than on the status of a State under stable international law. Its utility, if any, is to provide the State which objects to the evolution of a new rule of law with a tool it may use over the short term in its direct and indirect negotiations with the proponents of a new rule. The objecting State is armed with the theoretical right to opt out of the new rule. The proponents of the new rule are, as a consequence, encouraged to accommodate the objecting State or to utilize greater power to turn the objecting State to their will. At the same time, the persistent objector rule serves to soften the threat that the force of 'law' will impose a new and objectionable rule on the State that is content with the status quo. The persistent objector rule permits the objecting State to feel secure that it is not directly threatened, in an overt legal way, by changes in the law which it opposes. The legal system thereby appears to be fair and to permit an accommodation of views in the evolution of rules of law. It will be the political and social realities of the new status quo that will force the objecting State to conform to the new rule of law or the rest of the international community to accept on the basis of prescription the dissenter's unique status. It will not be a formal rule of uniform obligation that will procure conformity.

Viewed in this light, the persistent objector rule may be seen to be closely linked to the doctrine that in order to determine whether a rule of international law exists, one must examine the views and practices of the States whose interests are particularly affected. If the particularly affected States have not behaved in ways that conform to the purported rule of law, the International Court of Justice will be reluctant to hold in favour of that rule.

If any State will be the persistent objector, it will be the particularly affected State. Such a State will have interests directly at stake in the matter that is the subject of the rule of law under study. If it finds that the new rule is contrary to its interests, it will oppose the rule and will work for its rejection. As a particularly affected State, it will have leverage in determining the evolution of the applicable rule of law and will have the theoretical option of invoking the persistent objector rule. Thus both of these rules have one purpose, to force an accommodation of interests in the international community with respect to the evolution of new rules of law. . . .

In conclusion, it appears that the persistent objector rule is, at best, only of temporary or strategic value in the evolution of rules of international law. It cannot serve a permanent role, unless, of course, one really does believe that States have the independence freely to grant or withhold their consent to rules of customary international law.

O. Schachter, 'New Custom: Power, *Opinio Juris* and Contrary Practice' in J. Makarczyk (ed), *Theory of International Law at the Threshold of the 21st Century*
(1996), pp. 538–539

It will be recalled that in the *Nicaragua* Case the International Court pointed out that the 'instances of conduct' inconsistent with the *opinion juris* prohibiting force and intervention were generally treated as breaches of the rules and consequently did not override the finding of general practice confirming the *opinio juris*.

The problem of inconsistent practice (i.e. violations) comes up sharply in respect of declared norms of international human rights. . . . In the face of these facts, it is hard to conclude that the declared norms are confirmed by general and consistent practice. A similar problem arises in regard to other declared rules that prohibit State conduct in violation of basic human rights including, not least, the humanitarian law of armed conflict.

Most international lawyers seek to minimize the violations by emphasizing strong verbal condemnations and denials. The fact that *opinio juris* is manifested in international forums (usually in general terms) is regarded by some as sufficient to sustain the customary law status of the prohibition. However this conclusion requires some discrimination with respect to kinds of customary law involved. The notion that contrary practice should yield to *opinio juris* challenges the basic premise of customary law. It would not be acceptable in respect of the great body of customary rules – as for example, the law on jurisdiction, immunities, State responsibility, diplomatic privileges. In these areas, pertinent changes in State conduct usually create expectations of future behavior that modify the *opinio juris* on applicable law.

The legal perception is quite different in regard to prohibitions of State conduct that are strongly supported and important to international order and human values. Examples are the prohibitions of aggression, genocide, slavery, torture and systematic racial discrimination. . . .

It is worth noting that a characteristic of this category of legal norms is that they are brittle in the sense that violations are likely. For that very reason, the norm has to be maintained despite violations. The difference between international *opinio juris* in these cases and that in the other areas of customary law is empirically evident. It is a fact of international life evidenced by formal pronouncements of a general character and also by statements condemning conduct in particular cases.

NOTES:

1. In the *Anglo-Norwegian Fisheries Case*, ICJ Rep 1951 116, referred to by Charney, the United Kingdom objected to the delimitation of the territorial sea carried out by Norway by two Royal Decrees of 1935 and 1937. Part of the UK's objection rested on the fact that there was a customary rule of international law that 'closing lines' along the mouths of bays could be no longer than 10 nautical miles. As well as deciding that such a rule did not exist in general customary law, due to inconsistent State practice, the Court also observed that '[i]n any event the ten mile rule would appear to be inapplicable as against Norway as she has always opposed any attempt to apply it to the Norwegian coast'.

2. The theory of the persistent objector clearly has a role within the international legal system: the difficulty is to identify its true effect. In reality it is difficult for an objector to remain outside the rule indefinitely. Likewise, some types of contrary conduct are not regarded as 'objections' at all, but 'violations' to be condemned. As the above extracts suggest, perhaps it is a mistake to suppose that persistent objection/violation has the same effect irrespective of the content of the customary rule. The *Namibia Opinion* ICJ Rep 1971, 16 indicates that it would be impossible to be a persistent objector to a rule of *jus cogens* (see Chapter 3).

D: The relationship of custom and treaty law

Generally a treaty only binds the parties to it, whilst a rule of customary international law binds all States unless there is some local custom or persistent and effective objection. The two sources will interact and will occasionally come into conflict.

R. Baxter, 'Multilateral Treaties as Evidence of Customary International Law' (1965) 41 BYBIL 275, pp. 298–300

1. If reliance is to be placed on a multilateral treaty as evidence of customary international law, it is first necessary to establish whether the treaty was intended to be declaratory of existing customary international law or constitutive of new law. The silence of the treaty, which may necessitate resort to the *travaux préparatoires*, can make this a task of great difficulty.

2. If the treaty on its face purports to be declaratory of customary international law or if it can be established that such was the intent of its draftsmen, the treaty may be accepted as valid evidence of the state of customary international law. The weight it will carry varies in proportion to the number of parties and is also affected by the amount of consistent or inconsistent evidence of the state of

customary international law available from other sources, such as judicial decisions or diplomatic correspondence.

If it can be established that a treaty that purports to be declaratory of international law actually lays down new law – a burden which must be sustained by the opponent of the proffered evidence – the impact of the treaty may be weakened. It nevertheless remains that if a State declares that what is apparently new law is actually part of existing law, that very assertion counts in favour of the rule's incorporation into customary international law.

The clear formulation of rules in a codification treaty and the assent of a substantial number of States may have the effect of arresting change and flux in the state of customary international law. Although the treaty 'photographs' the state of the law as at the time of its entry into force as to individual States, it continues, so long as States remain parties to it, to speak in terms of the present. . . .

3. Early in the life of a treaty that is declaratory of customary law but has not yet entered into force, it carries weight as evidence of the state of the law. With the passage of time, its evidentiary force weakens. There still often remains a certain ambiguity about whether the lack of ratifications or accessions comes as the consequence of the fact that States disagree with the treaty or because the treaty has been so warmly received into customary international law that ratification of the treaty or accession to it would be supererogatory.

4. If a treaty was at the time of its adoption constitutive of new law, then the person or entity relying on the treaty as evidence of customary law has the burden of establishing that the treaty has subsequently been accepted into custom, either by express reference to this process by States and other authorities or by proof that the rule of the treaty is identical with customary law in the absence of the treaty. . . . Humanitarian treaties may, by reason of their special character, be an exception to this general rule. The adhesion of the great majority of the important States of the world to such an agreement may act in such a way as to impose the standards of the treaty on non-parties. But that view . . . requires acceptance of the notion that there is such a thing as true international legislation, by which the majority binds the dissenting or passive minority.

5. The advantage of the employment of a treaty as evidence of customary international law, as it was at the time of the adoption of the treaty or as it has come to be, is that it provides a clear and uniform statement of the rule to which a number of States subscribe. There is no problem of reconciling ambiguous and inconsistent State practice of varying antiquity and varying authority. The treaty speaks with one voice as of one time.

6. The convenience of reliance on the multilateral treaty is such that it may have a certain centripetal force, whether the agreement was initially declaratory or constitutive of the law. Inertia may lead advocates or decision-makers to drop other evidence of the law and to defer to the treaty because it speaks loudly and clearly. Thus the four elements of statehood listed in the Montevideo Convention on the Rights and Duties of States have become a standard expression of the definition of a State.

7. The passage of the rule of a treaty into customary international law may have certain consequences for the parties as well as non-parties. For example, if the treaty is accepted as a sound statement of customary international law, denunciation of the treaty by a party cannot absolve that State from its obligation to observe the rules of customary international law, proof of the existence of which is to be found in the treaty. . . .

8. Reliance on a multilateral treaty as evidence of customary international law is not conditional on any demonstration that the signatory States have actually observed the norms of the treaty for any length of time. The process of establishing the state of customary international law is one of demonstrating what States consider to be the measure of their obligations. The actual conduct of States in their relations with other nations is only a subsidiary means whereby the rules which guide

the conduct of States are ascertained. The firm statement by the State of what it considers to be the rule is far better evidence of its position than what can be pieced together from the actions of that country at different times and in a variety of contexts.

North Sea Continental Shelf Cases (Federal Republic of Germany v Denmark; FRG v The Netherlands)
ICJ Rep 1969 3, International Court of Justice

70. The Court must now proceed to the last stage in the argument put forward on behalf of Denmark and the Netherlands. This is to the effect that even if there was at the date of the Geneva Convention [on the Continental Shelf 1958] no rule of customary international law in favour of the equidistance principle, and no such rule was crystallized in Article 6 of the Convention, nevertheless such a rule has come into being since the Convention, partly because of its own impact, partly on the basis of subsequent State practice, – and that this rule, being now a rule of customary international law binding on all States, including therefore the Federal Republic, should be declared applicable to the delimitation of the boundaries between the Parties' respective continental shelf areas in the North Sea.

71. In so far as this contention is based on the view that Article 6 of the Convention has had the influence, and has produced the effect, described, it clearly involves treating that Article as a norm-creating provision which has constituted the foundation of, or has generated a rule which, while only conventional or contractual in its origin, has since passed into the general *corpus* of international law, and is now accepted as such by the *opinio juris*, so as to have become binding even for countries which have never, and do not, become parties to the Convention. There is no doubt that this process is a perfectly possible one and does from time to time occur: it constitutes indeed one of the recognized methods by which new rules of customary international law may be formed. At the same time this result is not lightly to be regarded as having been attained.

72. It would in the first place be necessary that the provision concerned should, at all events potentially, be of a fundamentally norm-creating character such as could be regarded as forming the basis of a general rule of law. . . .

73. With respect to the other elements usually regarded as necessary before a conventional rule can be considered to have become a general rule of international law, it might be that, even without the passage of any considerable period of time, a very widespread and representative participation in the convention might suffice of itself, provided it included that of States whose interests were specially affected. . . .

74. As regards the time element, the Court notes that it is over ten years since the Convention was signed, but that it is even now less than five since it came into force in June 1964, and that when the present proceedings were brought it was less than three years, while less than one had elapsed at the time when the respective negotiations between the Federal Republic and the other two Parties for a complete delimitation broke down on the question of the application of the equidistance principle. Although the passage of only a short period of time is not necessarily, or of itself, a bar to the formation of a new rule of customary international law on the basis of what was originally a purely conventional rule, an indispensable requirement would be that within the period in question, short though it might be, State practice, including that of States whose interests are specially affected, should have been both extensive and virtually uniform in the sense of the provision invoked; – and should moreover have occurred in such a way as to show a general recognition that a rule of law or legal obligation is involved.

Military and Paramilitary Activities in and against Nicaragua (Nicaragua v USA) (Merits)

ICJ Rep 1986 14, International Court of Justice

174. The Court would observe that, according to the United States argument, it should refrain from applying the rules of customary international law because they have been 'subsumed' and 'supervened' by those of international treaty law, and especially those of the United Nations Charter. Thus the United States apparently takes the view that the existence of principles in the United Nations Charter precludes the possibility that similar rules might exist independently in customary international law, either because existing customary rules had been incorporated into the Charter, or because the Charter influenced the later adoption of customary rules with a corresponding content.

175. The Court does not consider that, in the areas of law relevant to the present dispute, it can be claimed that all the customary rules which may be invoked have a content exactly identical to that of the rules contained in the treaties which cannot be applied by virtue of the United States reservation. . . .

177. But . . . even if the customary norm and the treaty norm were to have exactly the same content, this would not be a reason for the Court to hold that the incorporation of the customary norm into treaty-law must deprive the customary norm of its applicability as distinct from that of the treaty norm. The existence of identical rules in international treaty law and customary law has been clearly recognized by the Court in the *North Sea Continental Shelf cases*. To a large extent, those cases turned on the question whether a rule enshrined in a treaty also existed as a customary rule, either because the treaty had merely codified the custom, or caused it to 'crystallize', or because it had influenced its subsequent adoption. The Court found that this identity of content in treaty law and in customary international law did not exist in the case of the rule invoked, which appeared in one article of the treaty, but did not suggest that such identity was debarred as a matter of principle: on the contrary, it considered it to be clear that certain other articles of the treaty in question 'were . . . regarded as reflecting, or as crystallizing, received or at least emergent rules of customary international law' (*ICF Rep 1969*, p. 39, para. 63). More generally, there are no grounds for holding that when customary international law is comprised of rules identical to those of treaty law, the latter 'supervenes' the former, so that the customary international law has no further existence of its own.

178. There are a number of reasons for considering that, even if two norms belonging to two sources of international law appear identical in content, and even if the States in question are bound by these rules both on the level of treaty-law and on that of customary international law, these norms retain a separate existence. This is so from the standpoint of their applicability. In a legal dispute affecting two States, one of them may argue that the applicability of a treaty rule to its own conduct depends on the other State's conduct in respect of the application of other rules, on other subjects, also included in the same treaty. . . . But if the two rules in question also exist as rules of customary international law, the failure of the one State to apply the one rule does not justify the other State in declining to apply the other rule. Rules which are identical in treaty law and in customary international law are also distinguishable by reference to the methods of interpretation and application. A State may accept a rule contained in a treaty not simply because it favours the application of the rule itself, but also because the treaty establishes what that State regards as desirable institutions or mechanisms to ensure implementation of the rule. Thus, if that rule parallels a rule of customary international law, two rules of the same content are subject to separate treat-ment as regards the organs competent to verify their implementation, depending on whether they are customary rules or treaty rules. . . .

179. It will therefore be clear that customary international law continues to exist and to apply, separately from international treaty law, even where the two categories of law have an identical content. Consequently, in ascertaining the content of the customary international law applicable to

the present dispute, the Court must satisfy itself that the Parties are bound by the customary rules in question; but the Court is in no way bound to uphold these rules only in so far as they differ from the treaty rules which it is prevented by the United States reservation from applying in the present dispute.

JUDGE JENNINGS (Dissenting Opinion): Let us look first, therefore, at the relationship between customary international law, and Article 2, paragraph 4, and Article 51 of the United Nations Charter. The proposition, however, that, after the Charter, there exists alongside those Charter provisions on force and self-defence, an independent customary law that can be applied as an alternative to Articles 2, paragraph 4, and 51 of the Charter, raises questions about how and when this correspondence came about, and about what the differences, if any, between customary law and the Charter provisions, may be.

A multilateral treaty may certainly be declaratory of customary international law . . . It could hardly be contended that these provisions of the Charter were merely a codification of the existing customary law. The literature is replete with statements that Article 2, paragraph 4, – for example in speaking of 'force' rather than war, and providing that even a 'threat of force' may be unlawful – represented an important innovation in the law. . . . Even Article 51, though referring to an 'inherent' and therefore supposedly pre-existing, right of self-defence, introduced a novel concept in speaking of 'collective self-defence'. . . .

If, then, the Charter was not a codification of existing custom about force and self-defence, the question must then be asked whether a general customary law, replicating the Charter provisions, has developed as a result of the influence of the Charter provisions, coupled presumably with subsequent and consonant States' practice . . . But there are obvious difficulties about extracting even a scintilla of relevant 'practice' on these matters from the behaviour of those few States which are not parties to the Charter; and the behaviour of all the rest, and the *opinio juris* which it might otherwise evidence, is surely explained by their being bound by the Charter itself.

There is, however, a further problem: the widely recognized special status of the Charter itself. This is evident from paragraph 6 of Article 2, that:

> The Organization shall ensure that States which are not Members of the United Nations act in accordance with these Principles so far as may be necessary for the maintenance of international peace and security.

This contemplates obligations for non-members arising immediately upon the coming into operation of the Charter, which obligations could at that time only be derived, like those for Members, directly from the Charter itself. Even 'instant' custom, if there be such a thing, can hardly be simultaneous with the instrument from which it develops. There is, therefore, no room and no need for the very artificial postulate of a customary law paralleling these Charter provisions. . . .

That the Court has not wholly succeeded in escaping from the Charter and other multilateral treaties, is evident from even a casual perusal of the Judgment; the Court has in the event found it impossible to avoid what is in effect a consideration of treaty provisions as such. As the Court puts it, the Court 'can and must take them [the multilateral treaties] into account in determining the content of the customary law which the United States is also alleged to have infringed' (para. 183).

This use of treaty provisions as 'evidence' of custom, takes the form of an interpretation of the treaty text. Yet the Court itself acknowledges that treaty-law and customary law can be distinguished precisely because the canons of interpretation are different (para. 178). To indulge the treaty interpretation process, in order to determine the content of a posited customary rule, must raise a suspicion that it is in reality the treaty itself that is being applied under another name. Of course this way of going about things may be justified where the treaty text was from the beginning designed to be a codification of custom; or where the treaty is itself the origin of a customary law rule. But, as we have already seen, this could certainly not be said of Article 2, paragraph 4, or even Article 51, of the United Nations Charter; nor indeed of most of the other relevant multilateral treaty provisions.

The reader cannot but put to himself the question whether the Judgment would, in its main substance, have been noticeably different in its content and argument, had the application of the multilateral treaty reservation been rejected.

Vienna Convention on the Law of Treaties 1969

Article 38
Nothing . . . precludes a rule set forth in a treaty from becoming binding upon a third State as a customary rule of international law, recognised as such.

Article 53
A treaty is void if, at the time of its conclusion, it conflicts with a peremptory norm of general international law. For the purposes of the present Convention, a peremptory norm of general international law is a norm accepted and recognized by the international community of States as a whole as a norm from which no derogation is permitted and which can be modified only by a subsequent norm of general international law having the same character.

Article 64
If a new peremptory norm of international law emerges, any existing treaty which is in conflict with that norm becomes void and terminates.

NOTES:
1. The relationship between conventional (i.e. treaty law) and customary law is dealt with at length in the above extracts, and in this regard the majority opinion in *Nicaragua* v *USA* offers important guidance. It must be remembered, however, as Judge Jennings points out in that case, that 'particular' rules between two or more States will take precedence over general obligations, save where the latter constitute rules of *jus cogens*.
2. Although few would now doubt that rules of *jus cogens* do exist and that they take precedence over all treaties, there is no general agreement as to what rules have attained this status. The *Nicaragua Case* suggests the prohibition of the use of force as one example, and many would argue that the prohibition of crimes against humanity, the right of self-determination, the prohibitions of genocide and slavery and the freedom of the high seas should also be included. Such a belief is behind arguments denying that immunity can be enjoyed by States or individuals in respect of grave violation of human rights law (see Chapter 9). In *Committee of United States Citizens Living in Nicaragua* v *Reagan* 859 F 2d 929, a US Court of Appeal decided that a State's obligation to comply with a binding decision of the ICJ was not itself a *jus cogens* obligation, perhaps indicating that rules of *jus cogens* are concerned with substantive and not procedural obligations. However others argue that the principle *pacta sunt servanda* (treaties are binding in law) is a fundamental rule of international law.

SECTION 5: **General principles of law**

There are many different interpretations of Article 38(1)(c) of the ICJ Statute, and some international lawyers argue that its inclusion adds nothing to the totality of rights and duties already existing in international law. Certainly, however, 'general principles' have been referred to by the ICJ on a number of occasions, both as a source of substantive rules and as the reason why considerations of 'equity' may be used in the determination of disputes involving questions of international law.

G. von Glahn, *Law Among Nations*
(6th edn, 1986), pp. 22–24

General principles of law form the third source of international law. The meaning of 'general prin-ciples of law recognized by civilized nations' has been the subject of extensive discussion. Two major opinions prevail: one holds that the phrase embraces such general principles as pervade domestic jurisprudence and can be applied to international legal questions. Such principles might include the concept that both sides in a dispute should have a fair hearing, that no one should sit in judgment on his own case, and so on. The other view asserts that the phrase refers to general principles of law linked to natural law as interpreted during recent centuries in the Western world, that is, the trans-formation of broad universal principles of a law applicable to all of mankind into specific rules of international law. It must be assumed, however, that from a legal point of view, the law of nature represents at best a vague and ill-defined source of international law. Most modern writers appear to regard general principles of law as a secondary source of international law, infrequently used in practice but possibly helpful on occasion.

The former view concerning general principles of law is the one prevailing today. When this source of the law was written into the Statute of the Permanent Court of International Justice, the 1920 Committee of Jurists offered several interpretations of the source's meaning. It may well have been their purpose to avoid having an international court not hand down a decision because no 'positive applicable rule' existed. The phrase 'general principles' does enable a court, however, to go outside the generally accepted rules of international law and resort to principles common to various domestic legal systems. In fact, a number of court decisions and several law-making treaties refer to the general principles concept . . .

From a theoretical point of view, the acceptance of using general principles in fleshing out the body of international law means repudiating the extreme positivist doctrine that only rules created by means of the formal treaty process or a reliance on general custom are valid.

Thus it appears that, as yet, many international lawyers and diplomats doubt the validity of the claim that 'general principles' represent a truly usable source of international law.

International Status of South-West Africa Case, Advisory Opinion
ICJ Rep 1950 128, International Court of Justice

In 1950, the General Assembly requested the ICJ to give an Advisory Opinion on the status of South-West Africa (now Namibia) and its relationship with the Man-date power (South Africa), following the dissolution of the League of Nations in April 1946.

JUDGE McNAIR: What is the duty of an international tribunal when confronted with a new legal institution the object and terminology of which are reminiscent of the rules and institutions of private law? To what extent is it useful or necessary to examine what may at first sight appear to be relevant analogies in private law systems and draw help and inspiration from them? International law has recruited and continues to recruit many of its rules and institutions from private systems of law. Article 38(1)(c) of the Statute of the Court bears witness that this process is still active, and it will be noted that this article authorizes the Court to 'apply . . . (c) the general principles of law recognized by civilized nations'. The way in which international law borrows from this source is not by means of importing·private law institutions 'lock, stock and barrel', ready-made and fully equipped with a set of rules. It would be difficult to reconcile such a process with the application of 'the general principles of law'. In my opinion, the true view of the duty of international tribunals in this matter is to regard any features or terminology which are reminiscent of the rules and institutions of private law as an indication of policy and principles rather than as directly importing these rules and institutions.

River Meuse Case (*Netherlands* v *Belgium*)
PCIJ Ser A/B, (1937) No 70, pp. 76–77, Permanent Court of International Justice

JUDGE HUDSON (Individual Opinion): What are widely known as principles of equity have long been considered to constitute a part of international law, and as such they have often been applied by international tribunals. . . . A sharp division between law and equity, such as prevails in the administration of justice in some States, should find no place in international jurisprudence; even in some national legal systems, there has been a strong tendency towards the fusion of law and equity. Some international tribunals are expressly directed by the *compromis* which control them to apply 'law and equity'. . . . Of such a provision, a special tribunal of the Permanent Court of Arbitration said in 1922 that 'the majority of international lawyers seem to agree that these words are to be understood to mean general principles of justice as distinguished from any particular systems of jurisprudence'. . . . Numerous arbitration treaties have been concluded in recent years which apply to differences 'which are justifiable in their nature by reason of being susceptible of decision by the application of the principles of law or equity'. Whether the reference in an arbitration treaty is to the application of 'law and equity' or to justiciability dependent on the possibility of applying 'law or equity', it would seem to envisage equity as a part of law.

The Court has not been expressly authorized by its Statute to apply equity as distinguished from law. Nor, indeed, does the Statute expressly direct its application of international law, though as has been said on several occasions the Court is 'a tribunal of international law'. . . . Article 38 of the Statute expressly directs the application of 'general principles of law recognized by civilized nations', and in more than one nation principles of equity have an established place in the legal system. The Court's recognition of equity as a part of international law is in no way restricted by the special power conferred upon it 'to decide a case *ex aequo et bono*, if the parties agree thereto'. . . . It must be concluded, therefore, that under Article 38 of the Statute, if not independently of that Article, the Court has some freedom to consider principles of equity as part of the international law which it must apply.

M. Akehurst, 'Equity and General Principles of Law'
25 ICLQ (1976) 801

The three functions of equity
Despite occasional statements to the contrary, the absence of an express authorisation to apply equity does not necessarily mean that an international tribunal is forbidden to apply equity. . . .

Equity can perform three functions – it can be used to adapt the law to the facts of individual cases (equity *infra legem*); it can be used to fill gaps in the law (equity *praeter legem*); and it can be used as a reason for refusing to apply unjust laws (equity *contra legem*). These functions merge into one another to some extent; in particular, equity *infra legem* can be used in a wide number of situations, ranging from cases which differ only slightly from a strict application of the letter of the law, through cases where the spirit of the law is made to prevail over its letter, to cases where equitable exceptions are inferred into a rule of law. Consequently, a judge who wishes not to apply a rule of law can say that application of the letter of the law would be contrary to its spirit or that the legislator must have intended that there should be exceptions to the letter of the law (equity *infra legem*), or that the law does not apply to the case and that the judge can fill the resulting gap by recourse to equity (equity *praeter legem*) or that the law is unjust and should not be applied (equity *contra legem*). Not surprisingly, therefore, some (but not all) of the decisions of international tribunals are hard to fit into any one of the three classifications.

Is equity a source of international law?

The fact that tribunals often invoke equity does not necessarily mean that equity is a formal source of law. Counsel and judges in national courts frequently appeal to considerations of equity and justice when the law is uncertain, but this does not lead to equity being regarded as a source of national law. When deciding a doubtful case, a judge may point out that the rule he is laying down is just; he may also point out that it is a workable rule, which will be easy to apply and will yield predictable results in future cases. In both national and international law, similar appeals are often made to other extra-legal factors – religion, morality, good manners, neighbourliness, logic, reason, reasonableness, common sense, convenience, and political, economic, socio-logical, geographical and scientific factors. These factors are material sources of law; they are not formal sources. The same may well be true of equity. . . .

However, it would be unwise to make too much of this argument. The fact that international law is less developed institutionally than municipal law means that the difference between formal sources and material sources is less clear in international law than in municipal law. To a large extent the question whether equity is a formal source of international law is a purely verbal question; whichever way the question is answered, it is an undeniable fact that international tribunals often apply equity.

Dangers of applying equity

The fact that international tribunals often apply equity does not necessarily mean that it is desirable that they should apply equity.

One of the dangers of applying equity arises from the fact that equity provides exceptions to general rules. . . .

Normally States are deterred from breaking international law by fear of creating a precedent which can be used against them in subsequent cases. This fear is removed if one can invent an equitable exception to a rule; in such cases a State can continue to pay lip-service to the rule, while disregarding it and hoping that the precedent will not be copied by other States in other contexts. Such a state of affairs might not matter if compulsory judicial settlement existed in international law, but at present judicial settlement is optional and seldom used. In these circumstances there is a great danger that States will invoke equitable considerations as an exception to rules of law whenever obedience to the rules of law would be irksome . . .; the concept of equity could be used to give an aura of respectability to such exceptions, even though the States invoking them will probably refuse to allow the validity of the exceptions to be tested by an international tribunal. What makes this process particularly dangerous is that ideas of equity often vary according to the interests and culture of the State concerned.

The result is not only that respect for international law is weakened, but also that the rules of international law themselves become uncertain. Although it is desirable that rules of law should be just, it is perhaps even more desirable that they should be certain, clear and predictable.

The other main danger of applying equity lies in the fact that equity is subjective. . . .

Even in a national society, equity can sometimes 'vary with the length of the Chancellor's foot.' The problem is far more acute in the international society, where political, ethical and cultural values are far more heterogeneous than in a national society . . . One of the problems about equity is that it can often be defined only by reference to a particular ethical system. Consequently, although references to equity are meaningful in a national society which can be presumed to hold common ethical values, the position is entirely different in the international arena, where the most mutually antagonist philosophies meet in head-on conflict. Moreover, many of the issues which come before international tribunals are so complex and raise such finely-balanced points of conflicting interests that an equitable solution does not exactly leap to the eye, to put it mildly.

It is sometimes said to be a general principle of law that a judge can apply equity. Even if such a general principle exists, it cannot be transplanted into international law, because the homogeneity of values, which is the condition precedent for such a principle in municipal law, simply does not exist in international law.

In a legal system where there is no compulsory judicial settlement, the subjectiveness of equity is very dangerous. States will base claims on considerations which seem equitable to them but which do not seem equitable to their opponents; disputes will become not only more frequent, but harder to settle.

It is also dangerous for an international tribunal to base its decisions on equity. A judgment which seems equitable to the winning party may not seem equitable to the losing party, who will be tempted to accuse the tribunal of being biased and acting *ultra vires* and to refuse to execute the judgment. Moreover, if . . . the unpredictability of judicial decisions is a major reason for the reluctance of States to accept the jurisdiction of international tribunals, it is likely that the number of cases submitted to international tribunals will vary in inverse proportion to the reliance on equity by judges and arbitrators.

This may explain why international tribunals often couple references to equity with a simultaneous invocation of general principles of law, customary law, treaties . . . or previous arbitral decisions.

Frontier Dispute Case (*Burkina Faso* v *Mali*)
ICJ Rep 1985 6, International Court of Justice

In 1983, Burkina Faso and Mali agreed to submit their frontier dispute to a Chamber of the ICJ. In the light of submissions by both states, the Chamber considered the application of 'principles of equity' and its relationship to the ability of the Court to decide a case *ex aequo et bono* under Art. 38(2) of the Statute.

27. In their pleadings and oral arguments, the two Parties have advanced conflicting views on the question whether equity can be invoked in the present case. They both agree that no use should be made of the Chamber's power, under Article 38 of the Statute, to decide the case *ex aequo et bono* if they had agreed to this. However, Mali urges that account should be taken of 'that form of equity which is inseparable from the application of international law', which it sees as equivalent to equity *infra legem*. Although it did not object to this concept being resorted to, Burkina Faso considered that it was far from clear what the practical implications would be in this case. It emphasized that in the field of territorial boundary delimitation there is no equivalent to the concept of 'equitable principles' so frequently referred to by the law applicable in the delimitation of maritime areas. Mali did not question this statement; it explained that what it had in mind was simply the equity which is a normal part of the due application of law.

28. It is clear that the Chamber cannot decide *ex aequo et bono* in this case. Since the Parties have not entrusted it with the task of carrying out an adjustment of their respective interests, it must also dismiss any possibility of resorting to equity *contra legem*. Nor will the Chamber apply equity *praeter legem*. On the other hand, it will have regard to equity *infra legem*, that is, that form of equity which constitutes a method of interpretation of the law in force, and is one of its attributes. As the Court has observed: 'It is not a matter of finding simply an equitable solution, but an equitable

solution derived from the applicable law.' (*Fisheries Jurisdiction* . . .) How in practice the Chamber will approach recourse to this kind of equity in the present case will emerge from its application throughout this Judgment of the principles and rules which it finds to be applicable.

NOTES:
1. The use of concepts found in most legal systems would seem to be within the spirit of 'general principles'. In the *Factory Chorzow at Case* PCIJ Rep Ser A (1928) No. 17 the Court observed 'that it is a principle of international law, and even a general conception of law, that any breach of an engagement involves an obligation to make reparation'. If this view of Art. 38(1)(c) is correct, it is not clear whether general principles of national law can be regarded as 'formal' or 'material' sources of international law. However, in practice, they are designed to give efficacy and substance to international law and perhaps that is enough to warrant their inclusion in Art. 38.
2. The use of equity and its relationship to the *ex aequo et bono* power of Article 38 was also discussed in the *Rann of Kutch Arbitration* 50 ILR (1968) 2 where the Tribunal confirmed that 'equity forms part of International Law; therefore the Parties are free to present and develop their cases with reliance on principles of equity', but that an 'International Tribunal will have the wider power to adjudicate a case *ex aequo et bono*, and thus go outside the bounds of law, only if such power has been conferred on it by mutual agreement between the Parties'. A similar view was put forward by the arbitrators in *AMCO v Indonesia* 89 ILR 365.

SECTION 6: Judicial decisions and the writings of publicists

Simply because international law is a system of law considerable importance must attach to judicial decisions that purport to apply that law. This is so even though decisions of the ICJ are formally binding only between the parties to a dispute and are not to be taken as creating a system of precedent (Article 59, Statute of the ICJ below). Whether a system of precedent does exist in fact is a matter of some debate, as the Court's decisions can have a considerable impact on the international community (see Chapter 15). In addition, although there is a tendency to focus on the ICJ, in practice arbitration awards and decisions of other courts (including national courts) may be crucial in determining rights and duties under international law.

Statute of the International Court of Justice 1945

Article 59
The decision of the Court has no binding force except between the parties and in respect of that particular case.

The Paquete Habana
175 US SC Rep (1900) 677, United States Supreme Court

In 1898, two fishing vessels, *The Lola* and *The Paquete Habana* were seized by the United States Navy as Spanish prize during the Spanish-American War. One of the issues before the US Supreme Court was whether international law permitted the seizure of *bona fide* fishing vessels as prize. The case is an example of how decisions of national courts can be relevant in determining rules of international law; in this case the customary law of prize.

JUSTICE GRAY: International law is part of our law, and must be ascertained and administered by the courts of justice of appropriate jurisdiction as often as questions of right depending upon it are duly presented for their determination. For this purpose, where there is no treaty and no controlling executive or legislative act or judicial decision, resort must be had to the customs and usages of civilized nations, and, as evidence of these, to the works of jurists and commentators who by years of labor, research, and experience have made themselves peculiarly well acquainted with the subjects of which they treat. Such works are resorted to by judicial tribunals, not for the speculations of their authors concerning what the law ought to be, but for trustworthy evidence of what the law really is. . . .

Wheaton places among the principal sources of international law 'text-writers of authority, showing what is the approved usage of nations, or the general opinion respecting their mutual conduct, with the definitions and modifications introduced by general consent.' As to these he forcibly observes:

> Without wishing to exaggerate the importance of these writers, or to substitute, in any case, their authority for the principles of reason, it may be affirmed that they are generally impartial in their judgment. They are witnesses of the sentiments and usages of civilized nations, and the weight of their testimony increases every time that their authority is invoked by statesmen, and every year that passes without the rules laid down in their works being impugned by the avowal of contrary principles. Wheaton, *International Law* (8th ed.), para. 15.

NOTES:

1. Article 38 describes judicial decisions as 'a subsidiary means' for the determination of rules of law and Article 59 attempts to deny a system of precedent. However, the Court itself frequently uses its previous decisions as authority in later cases (e.g. as in the *Danube Dam Case* (see Chapter 3) para. 46, citing both contentious *and* advisory opinions), and cases such as the *North Sea Continental Shelf Cases* show how the Court can contribute significantly to the development of customary law.

2. The impact of decisions of national courts on the content and role of international law should not be underestimated. The series of *Pinochet* cases in the United Kingdom continue to exert considerable influence over the way in which human rights obligations and principles of sovereign immunity interact (see further, Chapter 9). Even if the *Pinochet* cases do not establish *as a matter of international law* the primacy of human rights law over principles of sovereign immunity, there is no doubt that the judgments will be used as a source of principles for the determination of this pressing and difficult issue in similar cases.

3. The impact of writers on the *corpus* of international law is, of course, never capable of scientific analysis. For example, the degree to which judges of the ICJ rely on published works (other than their own!) is rarely made clear, although greater reference is made in national courts when considering international law, as in *Paquete Habana* above.

SECTION 7: **Resolutions of international organisations**

United Nations Charter 1945

Article 10

The General Assembly may discuss any questions or any matters within the scope of the present Charter or relating to the powers and functions of any organs provided for in the present Charter, and, expect as provided for in Article 12, may make recommendations to the Members of the United Nations or to the Security Council or to both on any such questions or matters.

Article 18

1. Each Member of the General Assembly shall have one vote.

2. Decisions of the General Assembly on important questions shall be made by two-thirds majority of the Members present and voting. These questions shall include: recommendations with respect to the maintenance of international peace and security, the election of the non-permanent members of the Security Council, the election of the members of the Economic and Social Council, the election of the members of the Trusteeship Council . . ., the admission of new members to the United Nations, the suspension of the rights and privileges of membership, the expulsion of Members, questions relating to the operation of the trusteeship system, and budgetary questions.

3. Decisions on other questions, including the determination of additional categories of questions to be decided by a two-thirds majority, shall be made by a majority of the Members present and voting.

Article 25

The Members of the United Nations agree to accept and carry out the decisions of the Security Council in accordance with the present Charter.

B. Sloan, 'General Assembly Resolutions Revisited'

(1987) 58 BYBIL 93

Decisions

By virtue of powers expressly or impliedly authorized by the Charter, inherent in its nature or acquired through practice, the General Assembly may take decisions having binding force or operative effect. While these decisions concern mainly budgetary and internal organizational matters, some have direct and many have indirect external effects affecting obligations of States. . . .

Some decisions (budgetary resolutions under Article 17) are directly binding on members, while decisions having operative effect are 'action' to which, under Article 2(5), is appended a duty to give 'every assistance'. Determinations and interpretations involved in decisions are binding for the particular case and create precedents for the future.

The binding force and operative effect of decisions applies to all such resolutions validly adopted by the majorities specified in Article 18 of the Charter. The size of the vote is legally irrelevant, although a decision taken against strong opposition may result in a refusal of some States to co-operate. Thus from a practical point of view agreement or acceptance may be material even with respect to legally binding decisions.

Recommendations

Those resolutions of the General Assembly which are recommendations *stricto sensu*, granted that normally they are non-binding, nevertheless carry with them obligations of co-operation and good faith. . . . Whether recommendations are 'action' within the meaning of Article 2(5) may be debatable, but those resolutions which recommend action should entail the duty of assistance provided for in that article or at the very least an obligation not to interfere with action being taken by other States in accordance with the recommendation.

The foregoing obligations of co-operation, good faith and assistance apply to all validly adopted recommendations, without special regard to the size of the vote. The hortatory effect of recommendations will be strengthened by unanimity or near unanimity. Recommendations will also have value as precedents and may gain binding force through acceptance or estoppel.

Declarations

Declarations are a species of General Assembly resolutions based on established practice outside the express provisions of Chapter IV of the Charter. The practice of adopting declarations is consistent, universally accepted and 'immemorial' in the sense that it goes back to the very beginning of the UN. While the effect of declarations remains controversial, they are not recommendations and are not to be evaluated as such. . . . Where, however, there is an intent to declare law, whether customary, general principles or instant, spontaneous or new law, and the resolution is adopted by a unanimous or nearly unanimous vote or by genuine consensus, there is a presumption that the rules and principles embodied in the declaration are law. This presumption could only be overcome by evidence of substantial conflicting practice supported by an *opinio juris* contrary to that stated or implied in the resolution. If the declaration is adopted by a majority vote its evidentiary value is to be weighed in the light of all relevant factors. It would in any event be part of the material sources of customary law and would constitute an expression of *opinio juris*, or a lack of *opinio juris* for conflicting norms, of those States voting for the resolution.

Determinations, interpretations and agreement

As noted previously determinations, interpretations and agreement may be involved in any of the preceding categories of resolutions.

Determinations include findings of fact and characterizations. Such determinations will normally enjoy the weight of the resolution in which they are found. If embodied in a decision they will be binding for the purpose of that decision and will have precedential value in other situations. Determinations contained in a recommendatory resolution are entitled as a minimum to the same respect as the recommendation, but as findings and characterizations they may have greater or at least a different effect. They may justify States in accepting and acting on the determinations in situations not covered by the recommendation and in expecting other States to respect their action. Determinations in declarations confirming rules and principles as existing law will carry special evidentiary weight. Moreover, determinations, whether in decisions, recommendations or declarations, will have precedential value as a part of State practice.

Interpretations of the Charter, and sometimes of other treaties and of general international law, will also be found in all three categories of resolution. Interpretations involved in decisions are binding for that case. The binding force of interpretations for other situations, whether they are found in decisions, recommendations or declarations, depends on their general acceptability. . . .

Agreement in one form or another may also be involved in all three categories of resolution. Acceptance of a recommendation may convert a resolution into a binding agreement, or the status of a declaration may be confirmed by agreement. Even with respect to operative decisions, agreement may be necessary concerning certain aspects. For example, a resolution will through its own force establish a subsidiary organ, but the operation of that organ within the territory of a State may still depend on that State's acceptance or agreement.

Jus cogens and general principles

Special note should be taken of the role which General Assembly resolutions have played as a vehicle for expressing acceptance and recognition by the international community of States as a whole of norms of *jus cogens* and the similar role which they might play in recognizing other general principles of law in the sense of Article 38(1)(c) of the Statute of the International Court of Justice.

NOTES:

1. Resolutions of international organisations, of which the United Nations is the most significant, must be considered in two respects. First, there is the question whether such resolutions are binding in law on the members of the organisations, and there is agreement that the great majority are not. However, resolutions of the General Assembly regulating the internal affairs

of the UN Organisation (which includes all the 'important questions' in Article 18 except recommendations with respect to international peace and security) will in fact create situations that members of the Organisation cannot disregard, as with the election to various committees and matters of finance. Likewise, 'decisions' of the Security Council are formally binding, although the Council instead often uses its general power to make recommendations.

2. Second, there is the separate issue as to whether such resolutions, whether they are internally binding or not, have given rise to international law in another way, such as through the development of customary law or the elucidation of general principles. As well as the extracts immediately above, reference should also be made to the ICJ's reliance on Assembly resolutions as establishing *opinio juris* in *Nicaragua* v *USA*.

SECTION 8: **Soft law**

P. Weil, 'Towards Relative Normativity in International Law'
77 AJIL 413 (1983)

The structural weaknesses

3. As everyone knows, the international normative system, given the specific structure of the society it is called on to govern, is less elaborate and more rudimentary than domestic legal orders – which, or course, does not mean that it is their inferior or less 'legal' than they: it is just different.

Some of its structural weaknesses are too familiar to require lengthy treatment here: not only the inadequacy of its sanction mechanisms, but also the mediocrity of many of its norms. In regard to certain points, international law knows no norm at all, but a lacuna. As for others, the substance of the rule is still too controversial for it effectively to govern the conduct of states. On yet other points, the norm has remained at the stage of abstract general standards on which only the – necessarily slow – development of international law can confer concrete substance and precise meaning.

For some time, however, writers have been apt to point out a further weakness: alongside 'hard law,' made up of the norms creating precise legal rights and obligations, the normative system of international law comprises, they note, more and more norms whose substance is so vague, so uncompelling, that A's obligation and B's right all but elude the mind. One does not have to look far for examples of this 'fragile,' 'weak,' or 'soft law,' as it is dubbed at times: the 1963 Moscow Treaty banning certain nuclear weapon tests, Article I of which provides, *inter alia*, that 'each Party shall in exercising its national sovereignty have the right to withdraw from the Treaty if it decides that extraordinary events, related to the subject matter of this Treaty, have jeopardized the supreme interests of its country'; the numerous treaty provisions whereby the parties undertake merely to consult together, to open negotiations, to settle certain problems by subsequent agreement; and the purely hortatory or exhortatory provisions whereby they undertake to 'seek to,' 'make efforts to,' 'promote,' 'avoid,' 'examine with understanding,' 'act as swiftly as possible,' 'take all due steps with a view to,' etc. While particularly common in economic matters, there 'precarious' norms are similarly encountered in the political field, as witness, apart from the above-quoted Moscow Treaty provision, a recent Advisory Opinion of the International Court of Justice including obligations 'to co-operate in good faith' and 'to consult together' among the 'legal principles and rules' governing the relations between an international organization and a host country. Whether a rule is 'hard' or 'soft' does not, of course, affect its normative character. A rule of treaty or customary law may be vague, 'soft'; but, as the above examples show, it does not thereby cease to be a legal norm. In contrast, however definite the substance of a non-normative provision – certain clauses of the Helsinki Final Act, say, or of the Charter of Economic Rights and Duties of States – that will not turn it into a legal norm. Yet the fact remains that the proliferation of 'soft' norms, of what some also call 'hortatory' or 'programmatory' law, does not help strengthen the international normative system.

The conceptual weaknesses

4. Alongside those structural weaknesses – which a jurist may observe but is powerless to modify – the international normative system also suffers from failings that must rather be ascribed to a certain slackness in intellectual grasp. This time, it is not a question of inherent flaws but of conceptual weaknesses that jurists can strive to remove. One is already familiar and need not be dwelt upon, namely, the lack of rigor too often shown nowadays in handling the distinction between the non-normative and the normative. The other is more recent, and to it we shall devote our attention: it is the conception of variable normativity for which certain theories now in process of elaboration are paving the way.

The blurring of the normativity threshold

5. The acts accomplished by subjects of international law are so diverse in character that it is no simple matter for a jurist to determine what may be called the normativity threshold: *i.e.*, the line of transition between the nonlegal and the legal, between what does not constitute a norm and what does. At what point does a 'nonbinding agreement' turn into an international agreement, a promise into a unilateral act, fact into custom? Of course, this problem of the transition from nonlaw to law occurs in all legal systems, in particular under the guise of the distinction between moral and legal obligation. But the multiplicity of the forms of action secreted by the needs of international intercourse has rendered it more acute in that field than in any other, since in the international order neither prenormative nor normative acts are as clearly differentiated in their effects as in municipal systems. While prenormative acts do not create rights or obligations on which reliance may be placed before an international court of justice or of arbitration, and failure to live up to them does not give rise to international responsibility, they do create expectations and exert on the conduct of states an influence that in certain cases may be greater than that of rules of treaty or customary law. Conversely, the sanction visited upon the breach of a legal obligation is sometimes less real than that imposed for failure to honor a purely moral or political obligation.

If there is one field pervaded by this problem, it is surely that of the resolutions of international organizations. Today, the distinction between decisions, as creative of legal rights and obligations, and recommendations, as not creative of any 'legal obligation to comply with them,' has been rejected by some in favor of a more flexible conception: without crossing the normativity threshold, certain resolutions, it is said, nevertheless possess a 'certain legal value' that may vary not only from one resolution to another but, within the same resolution, from clause to clause. Henceforth, 'there are no tangible, clear, juridical criteria that demarcate with precision the zones of binding force'; there are only 'hazy, intermediate, transitional, embryonic, inchoate situations.' Even if resolutions do not attain full normative stature, they nevertheless constitute 'embryonic norms' of 'nascent legal force,' or 'quasi-legal rules.' In other words, there is no longer any straightforward either/or answer to the problem of the normative force of the acts of international organizations; it is all a matter of degree.

NOTE:

As the article by Wiel makes clear, the international legal system is imperfect and immature, at least by the standards of the national legal system. So-called 'soft law' is said to be a by-product of these deficiencies. However, even by the standards of the international legal system, this soft 'law' might not be law at all. Rather, it encompasses those principles, policies and expressions of intent that may well govern the conduct of States in certain situations, albeit that no legal obligation exists. These concepts are 'soft' because they lack the imperative quality of law, although they may acquire that status in due course through their transformation by the formal sources of law.

SECTION 9:   **Codification and development of international law**

The International Law Commission (ILC) was established by the General Assembly in 1947 to promote the codification and progressive development of international law. It consists of 34 members ('eminent jurists') sitting in an individual capacity and not as representatives of States. It holds a regular session each year and routinely has a number of projects in hand. Its proposals may well go on to form the basis of an international treaty. A good example is the Statute of the International Criminal Court (see Chapter 5). In addition, the Commission may produce a set of Draft Articles, hopefully to form the basis of a treaty, such as the ILC Draft Articles on State Responsibility. These Draft Articles might codify customary international law or aid in its development. It is often difficult to determine which parts of a set of Draft Articles represent the (customary) law as it now is as opposed to the law as the Commission would like it to be.

UK Statement to the Sixth Committee of the General Assembly, 12 November 1996
(1996) 67 BYBIL 703

I conclude this section of my statement with just one comment, which goes to the Commission's intriguing analysis of the relationship between codification and progressive development. The Commission take the view that the distinction between the two 'is difficult if not impossible to draw in practice, especially when one descends to the detail . . . necessary . . . to give more precise effect to a principle.' It is hard to cavil at that. There remains, however, a difference in kind, reflected in turn in the elusive but tantalising words of article 15 of the Commission's Statute. It would be worth an attempt to explore more deeply what it was that the General Assembly seemed to have in mind in 1947. However that may be, the distinction exists and the blurring of the dividing line which has characterised most of the Commission's work over the years may also have led to the blurring of another factor which to my mind remains very important. . . .

'Codification' is a process designed to pin down the unique 'right solution' which represents what the law is at the given moment. 'Progressive development', on the other hand, necessarily entails an element of choice as to how the law *should* develop; various solutions are possible, none uniquely right, even if one seems (to the Commission) better than others. It is quite possible that over the years the Commission, in eliding the distinction, has been guilty of disguising this element of choice. Policy choices have been presented in the language of codification, as if they were uniquely right solutions, or at least uniquely preferable solutions. It would seem far better for the Commission to acknowledge the element of choice, indeed to go out of its way to identify the choices and explain the criteria. To provide guidance in this way would not only make the entire process of choice and recommendation more transparent, it would also be of positive benefit to Governments in their responses if the Commission guided them on their way, possibly by pointing out the consequences foreseen from making one choice rather than another. This would not prevent, or even inhibit, the Commission from stating what its own preference would be.

H. Charlesworth and C. Chinkin, *The Boundaries of International Law: A Feminist Perspective*
(2000), p. 89

NGOs

There has been a dramatic proliferation in the numbers and activities of NGOs in the past years. This has been recognised by governments and NGO contributions are sought in various arenas. NGOs are increasingly achieving access to national policy-making bodies and offering advice to senior government officials. In turn this has had an impact upon regional and international decision-making. . . .

Similarly international NGOs have become increasingly visible and active in the negotiations before and during global summit meetings.

Despite their high profile, such NGO activities do not challenge the primacy of states in law-making. However influential their input, the final documents, whether in treaty or soft law form, are agreed on by states. More radical are proposals that have been made for the acceptance of the activities of NGOs as constitutive of practice for determining rules of customary international law. This, it is argued, would reflect the contemporary dynamics of the formation of international law. While this suggestion would import the different perspectives and priorities of NGOs into inter-national law-making, it raises some significant questions. One issue would be deciding which of the thousands of NGOs in existence would have this status. Another would be determining which of their activities could constitute 'practice'. A possible limitation on NGO participation in international law-making would be to focus on international NGOs that have observer status with the UN's ECOSOC This would ensure at least that the relevant NGOs had a formal commitment to the purposes and principles of the UN Charter. However, state hostility towards the mandates of particular NGOs can prevent ECOSOC recognition. It is also important to note that the agendas of NGOs are not necessarily produced with greater democracy or transparency than the agendas of individuals or states.

International civil society

The role of 'international civil society' has been presented as a counter-balance to the domination of states although the phenomenon of transnational citizen movements pre-dates the emergence of the state system of international organisation. The category of 'international civil society' is broader than that of NGOs and covers a range of both organised and unorganised, alternative and complementary groupings. In different contexts international civil society can embrace officials of international organisations, voluntary organisations, grassroots organisations and transnational social organisations. The concept also can encompass religious movements, professional groups such as lawyers, physicians, scientists or media personnel, business, trade and commerce repre-sentatives, trade unions, and indeed any body of persons that seeks to influence governments, to develop new modes of governance, to change international imperatives and to occupy political space. . . .

Richard Falk has argued that the role of 'international civil society' challenges state-centred inter-national law. He has postulated that states are no longer the sole legitimate source of law-making and that ideas from other bodies should not be ignored when determining the international norma-tive order. He has pointed to 'societal or populist' initiatives that respond to the failure of consti-tutional governments and international institutions to respond to particular events. International civil society thus acts without 'any authorization, directly or indirectly from government or the State'. It is promoted as an expression of democracy where popular will is expressed by concerned citizens, and constituting a truly 'universal law'.

NOTE:
The role of the ILC is one example of the way in which non-State entities can influence the development of international law. Non-governmental organisations, transnational corporations and individuals all contribute, in various ways to the sources of international law. The extract from Charlesworth and Chinkin continues this theme.

3

The Law of Treaties

Introductory note

Treaties are evidence of the express consent of States to regulate their interests according to international law. They are an important source of international law, as seen in Chapter 2, and are used with increasing frequency to codify, to crystallise and to develop international law, as they quickly reflect the changes in international society. The majority of international legal relationships between States are now governed by treaties.

The law of treaties is often equated with the law of contracts, but most analogies with contract law are misleading, particularly when dealing with multilateral treaties, being treaties between more than two parties. In multilateral treaties, the rights and obligations of each party in respect of each of the other parties may vary significantly, especially due to reservations to the terms of the treaty given by each party. Treaties can also be seen to have a legislative role in that, like some General Assembly resolutions, treaties impose binding rules on States that create rights and obligations.

As the number of treaties increases, it is necessary for rules to be developed which govern the obligations of States once they enter a treaty. These rules can be rules of general application to all treaties, whether they are bilateral or multilateral treaties, and whether their subject matter is commerce or human rights. The law of treaties concerns these rules, and includes such matters as the initial process of the formation of treaties and their entry into force, as well as the limitations (e.g. reservations) which States may place on their consent to be bound by a treaty. Principles of treaty interpretation and the procedures for invalidating and terminating treaties are also included, as is the substantive law in regard to these aspects.

SECTION 1: **Definition of a treaty**

The primary reason for determining whether certain agreements, statements or other action constitute a treaty, is that rights and obligations may then arise for which the law of treaties is applicable. Most treaties are concluded once the express consent of all the parties has been reached. However, occasionally, unilateral statements by a representative of a State have been construed as being binding on that State in its dealings with another State or States.

A: General definition of a treaty

Vienna Convention on the Law of Treaties 1969
1158 UNTS 331

Article 2 Use of Terms
1. For the purposes of the present Convention:
    (a) 'treaty' means an international agreement concluded between States in written form and governed by international law, whether embodied in a single instrument or in two or more related instruments and whatever its particular designation;

Case concerning Maritime Delimitation and Territorial Questions between Qatar and Bahrain **(Qatar v Bahrain) (Jurisdiction – First Phase)**
ICJ Rep 1994 112, International Court of Justice

This dispute related to competing claims of sovereignty over islands, shoals and maritime areas between these two Gulf States. The first aspect of the dispute to be considered by the Court was whether it had jurisdiction to decide the case. The basis of jurisdiction revolved around whether exchanges of letters between the heads of each State – by which it was agreed to submit the dispute to the Court – were treaties and so binding in international law. The court held that it had jurisdiction.

22. The Parties agree that the exchanges of letters of December 1987 constitute an international agreement with binding force in their mutual relations. Bahrain however maintains that the Minutes of 25 December 1990 were no more than a simple record of negotiations, similar in nature to the Minutes of the Tripartite Committee; that accordingly they did not rank as an international agreement and could not, therefore, serve as a basis for the jurisdiction of the Court.

23. The Court would observe, in the first place, that international agreements may take a number of forms and be given a diversity of names [see] Article 2, paragraph (1)(a), of the Vienna Convention on the Law of Treaties of 23 May 1969 . . .

Furthermore, as the Court said, in a case concerning a joint communiqué, 'it knows of no rule of international law which might preclude a joint communiqué from constituting an international agreement to submit a dispute to arbitration or judicial settlement' (*Aegean Sea Continental Shelf, Judgment, ICJ Reports 1978*, p. 39, para. 96). In order to ascertain whether an agreement of that kind has been concluded, 'the Court must have regard above all to its actual terms and to the particular circumstances in which it was drawn up' *(ibid.)*.

25. Thus the 1990 Minutes include a reaffirmation of obligations previously entered into; they entrust King Fahd with the task of attempting to find a solution to the dispute during a period of six months; and lastly, they address the circumstances under which the Court could be seised after May 1991.

Accordingly, and contrary to the contentions of Bahrain, the Minutes are not a simple record of a meeting, similar to those drawn up within the framework of the Tripartite Committee; they do not merely give an account of discussions and summarize points of agreement and disagreement. They enumerate the commitments to which the Parties have consented. They thus create rights and obligations in international law for the Parties. They constitute an international agreement.

27. The Court does not find it necessary to consider what might have been the intentions of the Foreign Minister of Bahrain or, for that matter, those of the Foreign Minister of Qatar. The two Ministers signed a text recording commitments accepted by their Governments, some of which were to be given immediate application. Having signed such a text, the Foreign Minister of Bahrain is not in a position subsequently to say that he intended to subscribe only to a 'statement recording a political understanding', and not to an international agreement.

29. The Court would observe that an international agreement of treaty that has not been registered with the Secretariat of the United Nations may not, according to the provisions of Article 102 of the Charter, be invoked by the parties before any organ on the United Nations. Non-registration or late registration, on the other hand, does not have any consequence for the actual validity of the agreement, which remains no less binding upon the parties.

30. The Court concludes that the Minutes of 25 December 1990, like the exchanges of letters of December 1987, constitute an international agreement creating rights and obligations for the Parties.

NOTES:
1. There are many designations used other than 'treaty' to refer to an international agreement, for example, 'convention', 'protocol', 'declaration', 'charter', 'covenant', 'agreement', 'concordat', although 'treaty' is the accepted generic term.
2. Article 2(1)(a) of the Vienna Convention on the Law of Treaties 1969 (above) confirms that it is the effect of an agreement, rather than the nomenclature attributed to it, that is relevant. In *Qatar v Bahrain* (above), the International Court of Justice indicated that an exchange of letters can constitute an international agreement binding on those States, while in *Legal Status of Eastern Greenland (Denmark v Norway)* PCIJ Rep 8, Ser A/B, (1933) No. 53, a declaration by the Norwegian Foreign Minister was found to be binding on Norway, although not as a treaty *per se*. See further discussion on unilateral declarations (below).
3. Article 80 of the Vienna Convention on the Law of Treaties provides that after a treaty enters into force, the treaty must be registered with the Secretariat of the United Nations. While an unregistered treaty remains legally binding between the parties, by virtue of Article 102 of the United Nations Charter, an unregistered treaty may not be invoked before the International Court of Justice or any other United Nations organ.
4. The Vienna Convention on the Law of Treaties applies only to treaties between States (Article 1); however, this does not affect the legality of agreements between States and other subjects of international law (Article 3). It is possible to have treaties between a State and international organisations and between international organisations, to which the law of treaties applies – see the Vienna Convention on the Law of Treaties Between States and International Organisations 1986, 25 ILM 543 (1986), Article 1. However, the capacity of international organisations to conclude treaties is governed by the constituent instrument or rules of that organisation (Article 6).
5. There are an increasing number of agreements between States and private entities, mainly dealing with commercial matters. The International Court of Justice has decided that the law of treaties does not apply to these agreements, because these agreements do 'not regulate in any way the relations between . . . Governments' (*Anglo-Iranian Oil Case (United Kingdom v Iran) (Preliminary Objection)* ICJ Rep 1952 93, at p. 112). However, in *Texaco Overseas Petroleum*

Company v *The Libyan Arab Republic* 53 ILR (1977) 389, the view was taken that private entities may be able to take advantage of general rules of international law in areas such as nationalisation/expropriation in order to invoke rights which result from the agreement with the State (see the extract from this case in Chapter 5). There are also some treaties (between States) which govern aspects of these agreements between States and private entities, for example, the Convention on the Settlement of Investment Disputes Between States and Nationals of Other States 1966 (see Chapter 15).

6. Some international agreements are intended not to be legally binding, and not to be 'governed by international law' as Article 2 of the Vienna Convention provides. A prominent example is the Final Act of the Helsinki Conference on Security and Co-operation in Europe 1975 (15 ILM 1292, (1975)), although the terms of this agreement might be used as evidence of State practice.

7. Sometimes a State can be legally bound even though it has acted unilaterally through its representatives. This position is explored in the extracts below.

B: Unilateral statements

Nuclear Test Cases (*Australia* v *France* and *New Zealand* v *France*) (*Merits*)

ICJ Rep 1974 253, International Court of Justice

Australia and New Zealand brought proceedings against France arising from nuclear tests conducted by France in the South Pacific. Before the Court had an opportunity to hear in full the merits of the case, statements were made by French authorities indicating that France would no longer conduct atmospheric nuclear tests. The court held by nine votes to six that, due to these statements by France, the claim of Australia and New Zealand no longer had any object and so the Court did not have to decide the issues in the case.

43. It is well recognized that declarations made by way of unilateral acts, concerning legal or factual situations, may have the effect of creating legal obligations. Declarations of this kind may be, and often are, very specific. When it is the intention of the State making the declaration that it should become bound according to its terms, that intention confers on the declaration the character of a legal undertaking, the State being thenceforth legally required to follow a course of conduct consistent with the declaration. An undertaking of this kind, if given publicly, and with an intent to be bound, even though not made within the context of international negotiations, is binding. In these circumstances, nothing in the nature of a *quid pro quo* nor any subsequent acceptance of the declaration, nor even any reply or reaction from other States, is required for the declaration to take effect, since such a requirement would be inconsistent with the strictly unilateral nature of the juridical act by which the pronouncement by the State was made. . . .

45. With regard to the question of form, it should be observed that this is not a domain in which international law imposes any special or strict requirements. Whether a statement is made orally or in writing makes no essential difference, for such statements made in particular circumstances may create commitments in international law, which does not require that they should be couched in written form. Thus the question of form is not decisive. . . .

46. One of the basic principles governing the creation and performance of legal obligations, whatever their source, is the principle of good faith. Trust and confidence are inherent in international co-operation, in particular in an age when this co-operation in many fields is becoming increasingly essential. Just as the very rule of *pacta sunt servanda* in the law of treaties is based on

good faith, so also is the binding character of an international obligation assumed by unilateral declaration. Thus interested States may take cognizance of unilateral declarations and place confidence in them, and are entitled to require that the obligation thus created be respected. . . . The Court must however form its own view of the meaning and scope intended by the author of a unilateral declaration which may create a legal obligation, and cannot in this respect be bound by the view expressed by another State which is in no way a party to the text.

49. Of the statements by the French Government now before the Court, the most essential are clearly those made by the President of the Republic. There can be no doubt, in view of his functions, that his public communications or statements, oral or written, as Head of State, are in international relations acts of the French State. His statements, and those of members of the French Government acting under his authority, up to the last statement made by the Minister of Defence (of 11 October 1974), constitute a whole. Thus, in whatever form these statements were expressed, they must be held to constitute an engagement of the State, having regard to their intention and to the circumstances in which they were made.

50. The unilateral statements of the French authorities were made outside the Court, publicly and *erga omnes*, even though the first of them was communicated to the Government of Australia. As was observed above, to have legal effect, there was no need for these statements to be addressed to a particular State, nor was acceptance by any other State required. The general nature and characteristics of these statements are decisive for the evaluation of the legal implications, and it is to the interpretation of the statements that the Court must now proceed. The Court is entitled to presume, at the outset, that these statements were not made *in vacuo*, but in relation to the tests which constitute the very object of the present proceedings, although France has not appeared in the case.

51. In announcing that the 1974 series of atmospheric tests would be the last, the French Government conveyed to the world at large, including the Applicant, its intention effectively to terminate these tests. It was bound to assume that other States might take note of these statements and rely on their being effective. The validity of these statements and their legal consequences must be considered within the general framework of the security of international intercourse, and the confidence and trust which are so essential in the relations among States. It is from the actual substance of these statements, and from the circumstances attending their making, that the legal implications of the unilateral act must be deduced. The objects of these statements are clear and they were addressed to the international community as a whole, and the Court holds that they constitute an undertaking possessing legal effect. The Court considers that the President of the Republic, in deciding upon the effective cessation of atmospheric tests, gave an undertaking to the international community to which his words were addressed. It is true that the French Government has consistently maintained, for example in a Note dated 7 February 1973 from the French Ambassador in Canberra to the Prime Minister and Minister for Foreign Affairs of Australia, that it "has the conviction that its nuclear experiments have not violated any rule of international law", nor did France recognize that it was bound by any rule of international law to terminate its tests, but this does not affect the legal consequences of the statements examined above. The Court finds that the unilateral undertaking resulting from these statements cannot be interpreted as having been made in implicit reliance on an arbitrary power of reconsideration. The Court finds further that the French Government has undertaken an obligation the precise nature and limits of which must be understood in accordance with the actual terms in which they have been publicly expressed.

NOTES:

1. It is very rare that a Court will find that a unilateral statement will bind a State. In *Frontier Dispute Case (Burkina Faso v Mali)* 1986 ICJ Rep 554, a Chamber of the International Court of Justice held that a statement made by the President of Mali at a press conference did not create legal obligations on Mali, especially as 'The Chamber considers that it has a duty to

show even greater caution when it is a question of a unilateral declaration not directed to any particular recipient.' (para 39).

2. In September 1995, New Zealand did not succeed in its attempt (in relation to non-atmospheric nuclear tests) to reopen the *Nuclear Test Cases* before the Court (see Chapter 12).

C: Nature of a treaty

M. Craven, 'Legal Differentiation and the Concept of the Human Rights Treaty in International Law'

11 *European Journal of International Law* (2000) 489, pp. 500–504

In their simplest form, treaties are conceived primarily in terms of an analogy with contracts in municipal law – that is, as consensual arrangements instituting, through the medium of legal rights and duties, a reciprocal exchange of goods or benefits. If that is the case the claim to non-reciprocity on the part of certain human rights treaties suggests that they are either an entirely novel form of treaty, or perhaps not treaties at all. Such a conclusion, however, is dependent upon the extent to which reciprocity is understood as a critical element of treaty law, and upon how that reciprocity is conceptualized. . . . [T]here seems no doubt that, according to the [Vienna] Convention [on the Law of Treaties], the 'agreement' is constituted in a mutual expression of consent. . . . In this context, the principle *pacta sunt servanda* [see below] must mean not just that 'promises shall be kept', as is so often assumed, but more specifically and literally, that 'agreements shall be followed'. It is, in other words, the multi-party, or relational, dimension of *pactum* that is central to the assumption of obligations in treaty law.

If treaties can only really be understood as 'agreements' between mutually consenting parties, it does not necessarily follow that they are to be regarded as 'reciprocal'. Indeed, it is apparent that as explanatory mediums the concepts of reciprocity and consent do not necessarily pull in the same direction. . . . Whilst theoretically distinct, each account of obligation exposes the incompleteness of the other: an emphasis on consent will potentially lead to one being bound by terms that are unfair; and an emphasis on reciprocity will potentially lead one to being bound in ways that one did not choose. . . . Consent and reciprocity are not, in that sense, mutually reinforcing, and indeed may supplant one another for the purposes of determining the presence of obligation in particular circumstances. . . .

Indeed, it is clear that the [Vienna] Convention does not invoke any concept of 'consideration' or 'cause' for the purpose of determining the obligatory effect of treaties. Such an understanding is reflected in general doctrine: it is possible after all, to conceive of treaties in which one state simply agrees to do something with no substantive or formal *quid pro quo*. The unconditional cession of territory from one state to another by means of a treaty might be a good example, as indeed may be the conclusion of a treaty of peace. . . .

Whilst it may be concluded, therefore, that treaties are not necessarily marked by any form of 'reciprocal exchange' of goods or benefits, the importance placed upon the 'mutuality' of consent suggest that some form of reciprocity might nevertheless be relevant. . . . Reciprocity [can be considered to be material exchange and psychological agreement as well as being] expressive of a mutual, but conditional, exchange of legal obligations in which the possession of rights and obliga-tions of one party are linked to (and perhaps dependent upon) those of the other party. . . . The logic of reciprocity, however, derives not so much from the nature of treaty relations, *per se*, but from the apparent imperatives of the decentralized international system. . . . It is only by reason of reciprocity, therefore, that states will be able to participate in international relations without expos-ing themselves unduly to the risks involved with non-compliance on the part of other states: it provides the means, in other words, by which states may effectively 'police' those obligations by means of self-help.

N. White, 'The United Nations System: Conference, Contract or Constitutional Order?'

4 *Singapore Journal of International and Comparative Law* (2000) 281, pp. 290–291

Attempts have been made, mainly since the adoption of the League of Nations Covenant in 1919 to suggest that there is a considerable distinction to be drawn between ordinary 'contractual' bilateral or multilateral treaties and 'constitutional' multilateral treaties. Such a suggestion was quite a radical departure from the view that international law was in essence private law between consenting states acting as equals, rather than any form of public law. . . . If we move from the post-1919 world order to the post-1945 order, the picture . . . is one of societal values shaping, informing and regulating the operation of a complex set of institutions, within a system framed by legal instruments of foundational significance. It is clear that the UN system is not governed by a series of treaties, but is governed by a complex constitution, with the UN Charter at its heart. . . . It is arguable that in 1945 the UN Charter was constructed as a constitutional document and not simply as an international treaty, a fact indicated by the opening words of the UN Charter – 'We the Peoples of the United Nations'. What is clear is that the Charter has become a constitution, indeed is the foundational constitutional document in the UN system.

NOTES:

1. Treaties may be categorised and compared in a number of ways: participation (bilateral/ multilateral, regional/global); subject matter (environment, sea, trade, human rights); structure (combinations of treaties/single treaty); and function. A treaty is both a procedural act and an obligation, with most of the law of treaties dealing with the former (eg formation, entry into force and termination).

2. As was noted in the introduction to this Chapter, treaties are sometimes considered to be contracts, sometimes legislation and sometimes constitutions. As is seen in the two extracts above, the nature of a treaty will often depend on the subject matter, the parties to the treaty and the effect of the treaty. Therefore it is arguable that, at least in relation to some treaties, the requirement of consent to treaties has not been 'frontally assaulted but cunningly outflanked' (P. Weil, 77 *American Journal of International Law* 413, 438).

3. Craven (above) notes that two of the key elements of a treaty are consent and reciprocity but these do not always operate coherently. He concludes that because human rights treaties 'not only serve to place certain limits upon the nature and scope of governmental authority but also contribute to the development of a justifiable basis for that authority (albeit in no unproblematic manner), they cannot therefore simply be regarded as the accidental data of an otherwise disinterested legal system' and so are not 'only treaties' (p. 519). See further in Chapter 6.

SECTION 2: Vienna Convention on the Law of Treaties 1969

The Vienna Convention on the Law of Treaties 1969 ('the Vienna Convention') is the principal instrument which governs the law of treaties. It entered into force on 27 January 1980, upon the deposit of the 35th instrument of ratification (pursuant to Article 84). As of 1 July 2002 there were 94 parties to the Vienna Convention. As its Preamble states, it was intended to codify and to develop the law of treaties.

A: General principles

I. Sinclair, *The Vienna Convention on the Law of Treaties*
(2nd edn, 1984), p. 1

Having regard to the significance of treaties as a primary source of international law, and having regard equally to the range and complexity of the law of treaties, it may be permissible to express satisfaction that this major enterprise in the field of codification and progressive development of international law – an enterprise which was embarked upon by the International Law Commission as early as 1949 – has achieved finality, and has achieved it in the form of a Convention which has, albeit after more than ten years, attracted sufficient support from States to bring it into force. But satisfaction must be tempered with realism. The Convention is the product of many conflicting interests and viewpoints and has the customary vices of compromise. Among these is a tendency to overcome points of difficulty by expressing rules at a level of generality and abstraction sufficient to hide the underlying divergencies.

B: Customary international law

Danube Dam Case (Gabcikovo-Nagymaros Project) (Hungary v Slovakia)
ICJ Rep 1997 7, International Court of Justice

46. The Court . . . has several times had occasion to hold that some of the rules laid down in [the Vienna Convention on the Law of Treaties] might be considered as a codification of existing contemporary law   . . .

99. The Court referred earlier to the question of the applicability to the present case of the Vienna Convention of 1969 on the Law of Treaties. The Vienna Convention is not directly applicable to the 1977 Treaty inasmuch as both States ratified that Convention only after the Treaty's conclusion. Consequently only those rules that are declaratory of customary international law are applicable . . . [T]his is the case . . . with Articles 60 to 62 of the Vienna Convention, relating to termination or suspension of the operation of a treaty.

Golder v United Kingdom
ECHR Ser A (1975) No 18, European Court of Human Rights

The Court had to determine if Art. 6(1) of the European Convention on Human Rights secured the right of access to the courts for every person seeking to commence proceedings to have her/his rights determined.

29. The submissions made to the Court were in the first place directed to the manner in which the Convention, and particularly Article 6 §1, should be interpreted. The Court is prepared to consider, as do the Government and the Commission, that it should be guided by Articles 31 to 33 of the Vienna Convention of 23 May 1969 on the Law of Treaties. That Convention has not yet entered into force and it specifies, at Article 4, that it will not be retroactive, but its Articles 31 to 33 enunciate in essence generally accepted principles of international law to which the Court has already referred on occasion. In this respect, for the interpretation of the European Convention account is to be taken of those Articles subject, where appropriate, to "any relevant rules of the organization" – the Council of Europe – within which it has been adopted (Article 5 of the Vienna Convention).

A. Aust, *Modern Treaty Law and Practice*
(2000), pp. 10–11

When questions of treaty law arise during negotiations, whether for a new treaty or about one concluded before the entry into force of the [Vienna] Convention, the rules set forth in the Convention are invariably relied upon even when the states are not parties to it. The writer [who was for many years a senior legal adviser in the British Foreign and Commonwealth Office] can recall at least three bilateral treaty negotiations when he had to respond to arguments of the other side which relied heavily on specific articles of the Convention, even though the other side had not ratified it. . . .

Whether a particular rule in the Convention represents customary international law is only likely to be an issue if the matter is litigated, and even then the Court or tribunal will take the Convention as its starting – and normally also its finishing – point. This is certainly the approach taken by the International Court of Justice, as well as other courts and tribunals, international and national. . . . There has as yet been no case where the Court has found that the Convention does not reflect customary law. But this is not so surprising. Despite what some critics of the Convention may say, as with any codification of the law the Convention inevitably reduces the scope for judicial law-making. For most practical purposes treaty questions are resolved by applying the rules of the Convention. To attempt to determine whether a particular provision of the Convention represents customary international law is now usually a rather futile task. . . . [T]he modern law of treaties is now authoritatively set out in the Convention.

NOTES:
1. The application of the Vienna Convention itself is limited both by parties and by timing. The Convention is binding only on its parties, and as such is unlikely to apply directly to multilateral agreements. However, as a codification of customary international law (as seen in the extracts above) the application of the Convention can be extended to all other treaties, including treaties between non-parties to the Convention and to treaties made prior to the Convention entering into force. Indeed, those provisions of the Vienna Convention which are not declaratory of customary international law may constitute presumptive evidence of emerging rules of international law.
2. Articles 31 and 32 of the Vienna Convention on the Law of Treaties have been referred to in other international judicial and arbitral decisions as being the customary international law method for interpreting treaty provisions, for example, in the *Territorial Dispute Case* (*Libya* v *Chad*) (below), para. 41.

SECTION 3:   **Formation and application of treaties**

A: Formation

Vienna Convention on the Law of Treaties 1969

Article 6 Capacity of States to conclude treaties
Every State possesses capacity to conclude treaties.

Article 7 Full powers
  1. A person is considered as representing a State for the purpose of adopting or authenticat-

ing the text of a treaty or for the purpose of expressing the consent of the State to be bound by a treaty if:

- (a) he produces appropriate full powers [these are defined in Article 2(1) (c)]; or
- (b) it appears from the practice of the States concerned or from other circumstances that their intention was to consider that person as representing the State for such purposes and to dispense with full powers.

Article 8 Subsequent confirmation of an act performed without authorisation

An act relating to the conclusion of a treaty performed by a person who cannot be considered under article 7 as authorised to represent a State for that purpose is without legal effect unless afterwards confirmed by that State.

Article 11 Means of expressing consent to be bound by a treaty

The consent of a State to be bound by a treaty may be expressed by signature, exchange of instruments constituting a treaty, ratification, acceptance, approval or accession, or by any other means if so agreed.

Article 12 Consent to be bound by a treaty expressed by signature

1. The consent of a State to be bound by a treaty is expressed by the signature of its representative when:
- (a) the treaty provides that signature shall have that effect;
- (b) it is otherwise established that the negotiating States were agreed that signature should have that effect; or
- (c) the intention of the State to give that effect to the signature appears from the full powers of its representative or was expressed during the negotiation.

Article 14 Consent to be bound by a treaty expressed by ratification, acceptance or approval

1. The consent of a State to be bound by a treaty is expressed by ratification when:
- (a) the treaty provides for such consent to be expressed by means of ratification;
- (b) it is otherwise established that the negotiating States were agreed that ratification should be required;
- (c) the representative of the State has signed the treaty subject to ratification; or
- (d) the intention of the State to sign the treaty subject to ratification appears from the full powers of its representative or was expressed during the negotiation.

2. The consent of a State to be bound by a treaty is expressed by acceptance or approval under conditions similar to those which apply to ratification.

Article 15 Consent to be bound by a treaty expressed by accession

The consent of a State to be bound by a treaty is expressed by accession when:
- (a) the treaty provides that such consent may be expressed by that State by means of accession;
- (b) it is otherwise established that the negotiating States were agreed that such consent may be expressed by that State by means of accession; or
- (c) all the parties have subsequently agreed that such consent may be expressed by that State by means of accession.

NOTES:

1. Care must be taken to distinguish between signatory and ratifying States. Most international treaties are made at international conferences where the text is adopted and often signed, but

legally binding consent to the treaty is conditional upon subsequent ratification or accession (Articles 14, 15) (though see Art. 18 below).

2. Generally a State will be legally bound by a treaty only once it has ratified the treaty or has otherwise signified its consent to be bound. This usually occurs after the State's internal political (and sometimes legal) processes to approve the terms of the treaty have been completed. States which were not signatories to the treaty indicate their consent to be legally bound by 'accession' not 'ratification' (Article 15).

3. A State may be legally bound by a treaty upon the signature of the treaty by the State (by its representative), but only if the treaty so provides, or if it is the intention of the State or of the parties to the treaty that signature would bind States (Article 11).

B: Entry into force

Vienna Convention on the Law of Treaties 1969

Article 18 Obligation not to defeat the object and purpose of a treaty prior to its entry into force
A State is obliged to refrain from acts which would defeat the object and purpose of a treaty when:
>   (a) it has signed the treaty or has exchanged instruments constituting the treaty subject to ratification, acceptance or approval, until it shall have made its intention clear not to become a party to the treaty; or
>   (b) it has expressed its consent to be bound by the treaty, pending the entry into force of the treaty and provided that such entry into force is not unduly delayed.

Article 24 Entry into force
1. A treaty enters into force in such manner and upon such date as it may provide or as the negotiating States may agree.

2. Failing any such provision or agreement, a treaty enters into force as soon as consent to be bound by the treaty has been established for all the negotiating States.

3. When the consent of a State to be bound by a treaty is established on a date after the treaty has come into force, the treaty enters into force for that State on that date, unless the treaty otherwise provides.

4. The provisions of a treaty regulating the authentication of its text, the establishment of the consent of States to be bound by the treaty, the manner or date of its entry into force, reservations, the functions of the depositary and other matters arising necessarily before the entry into force of the treaty apply from the time of the adoption of its text.

Article 28 Non-retroactivity of treaties
Unless a different intention appears from the treaty or is otherwise established, its provisions do not bind a party in relation to any act or fact which took place or any situation which ceased to exist before the date of the entry into force of the treaty with respect to that party.

Letter to the UN Secretary General from the Under Secretary of State for Arms Control and International Security of the United States of America, 6 May 2002
Dear Mr. Secretary-General:

This is to inform you, in connection with the Rome Statute of the International Criminal Court adopted on July 17, 1998, that the United States does not intend to become a party to the treaty. Accordingly, the United States has no legal obligations arising from its signature on December 31, 2000. The United States requests that its intention not to become a party, as expressed in this letter, be reflected in the depositary's status lists relating to this treaty.

Sincerely,

John R. Bolton

NOTES:

1. Many multilateral treaties provide that a certain number of States must have ratified (or acceded to) the treaty before the treaty enters into force. For example, the International Covenant on Civil and Political Rights provides in Article 49 that it will 'enter into force three months after the date of deposit with the Secretary-General of the United Nations of the thirty-fifth instrument of ratification or instrument of accession'.

2. As many multilateral treaties take many years to enter into force, Article 18 of the Vienna Convention is an important provision as it obliges States not to defeat the object and purpose of the treaty between their consent to be bound and the entry into force of the treaty. Even if a treaty is not in force, the fact that many States are bound by its terms may be evidence of State practice (see Chapter 2).

3. The United States of America's action in announcing that its signature was to have no legal effect is consistent with Art 18(a) of the Vienna Convention in that a State does not have the obligation not to defeat the object and purpose of a treaty if it has 'made its intention clear not to become a party to the treaty'. This action was expressly said not to be an 'unsigning' or 'de-signing' of a treaty (if such can occur).

4. A treaty can be amended by agreement between the parties, though a separate treaty (often known as a 'protocol') is the usual method for changing the provisions of a treaty. The rules governing amendments, are set out in Articles 39–41.

C: *Pacta sunt servanda*

Vienna Convention on the Law of Treaties 1969

Article 26 *Pacta sunt servanda*

Every treaty in force is binding on the parties to it and must be performed by them in good faith.

Report of the International Law Commission to the General Assembly

Yearbook of the International Law Commission (1966) vol II, 172, p. 211

(1) *Pacta sunt servanda* – the rule that treaties are binding on the parties and must be performed in good faith – is the fundamental principle of the law of treaties. Its importance is underlined by the fact that it is enshrined in the Preamble to the Charter of the United Nations. As to the Charter itself, paragraph 2 of Article 2 expressly provides that Members are to "fulfil in good faith the obligations assumed by them in accordance with the present Charter".

(2) There is much authority in the jurisprudence of international tribunals for the proposition that in the present context the principle of good faith is a legal principle which forms an integral part of the rule *pacta sunt servanda*. Thus, speaking of certain valuations to be made under articles 95 and 96 of the Act of Algeciras, the Court said in the *Case concerning Rights of Nationals of the United States of America in Morocco* (Judgment of 27 August 1954): "The power of making the valuation rests with the Customs authorities, but it is a power which must be exercised reasonably and in good faith". Similarly, the Permanent Court of International Justice, in applying treaty clauses prohibiting discrimination against minorities, insisted in a number of cases, that the clauses must be so applied

as to ensure the absence of discrimination in fact as well as in law; in other words, the obligation must not be evaded by a merely literal application of the clauses. Numerous precedents could also be found in the jurisprudence of arbitral tribunals. To give only one example, in the *North Atlantic Coast Fisheries* arbitration the Tribunal dealing with Great Britain's right to regulate fisheries in Canadian waters in which she had granted certain fishing rights to United States nationals by the Treaty of Ghent, said; ". . . from the Treaty results an obligatory relation whereby the right of Great Britain to exercise its right of sovereignty by making regulations is limited to such regulations as are made in good faith, and are not in violation of the Treaty."

NOTES:

1. The principle of *pacta sunt servanda* is considered to be the primary reason why there is compliance with treaty obligations. It derives from the consent of States and is a principle of customary international law (see Chapter 2). For there to be any significant legal regulation of the international community, the principle of *pacta sunt servanda* is required. If each State can rely on the other parties to a treaty to comply with the terms of that treaty (or at least not frustrate them – see Article 18 of the Vienna Convention on the Law of Treaties, above), then that State will also constantly seek to comply with its treaty obligations.

2. The International Law Commission (ILC) was established by General Assembly Resolution 174 (II) in 1947 to promote the progressive development of international law and its codification. Each session the ILC, made up of respected international lawyers (and hence a source of international law under para. 38(1)(d) of the Statute of the ICJ – see Chapter 2), submits to the General Assembly a report on its work. The Reports of the ILC are of some influence on the law of treaties as the Vienna Convention arose largely from the drafts of the ILC.

D: Impact on third states

Vienna Convention on the Law of Treaties 1969

Article 34 General rule regarding third States
A treaty does not create either obligations or rights for a third State without its consent.

Article 35 Treaties providing for obligations for third States
An obligation arises for a third State from a provision of a treaty if the parties to the treaty intend the provision to be the means of establishing the obligation and the third State expressly accepts that obligation in writing.

Article 36 Treaties providing for rights for third States
1. A right arises for a third State from a provision of a treaty if the parties to the treaty intend the provision to accord that right either to the third State, or to a group of States to which it belongs, or to all States, and the third State assents thereto. Its assent shall be presumed so long as the contrary is not indicated, unless the treaty otherwise provides.

2. A State exercising a right in accordance with paragraph 1 shall comply with the conditions for its exercise provided for in the treaty or established in conformity with the treaty.

Article 37 Revocation or modification of obligations or rights of third States
1. When an obligation has arisen for a third State in conformity with article 35, the obligation may be revoked or modified only with the consent of the parties to the treaty and of the third State, unless it is established that they had otherwise agreed.

2. When a right has arisen for a third State in conformity with article 36, the right may not be revoked or modified by the parties if it is established that the right was intended not to be revocable or subject to modification without the consent of the third State.

Article 38 Rules in a treaty becoming binding on third States through international custom
Nothing in articles 34 to 37 precludes a rule set forth in a treaty from becoming binding upon a third State as a customary rule of international law, recognized as such.

Vienna Convention on Succession of States in Respect of Treaties 1978
Reprinted in 72 AJIL 971 (1978)

This Convention entered into force on 6 November 1996 and, as at 1 July 2002, 17 States had ratified it.

Article 2 Use of terms
(b) "succession of States" means the replacement of one State by another in the responsibility for the international relations of territory; . . .

(f) "newly independent State" means a successor State the territory of which immediately before the date of the succession of States was a dependent territory for the international relations of which the predecessor State was responsible;

Article 5 Obligations imposed by international law independently of a treaty
The fact that a treaty is not considered to be in force in respect of a State by virtue of the application of the present Convention shall not in any way impair the duty of that State to fulfil any obligation embodied in the treaty to which it is subject under international law independently of the treaty.

Article 6 Cases of succession of States covered by the present Convention
The present Convention applies only to the effects of a succession of States occurring in conformity with international law and, in particular, the principles of international law embodied in the Charter of the United Nations.

Article 8 Agreements for the devolution of treaty obligations or rights from a predecessor State to a successor State
1. The obligations or rights of a predecessor State under treaties in force in respect of a territory at the date of a succession of States do not become the obligations or rights of the successor State towards other States parties to those treaties by reason only of the fact that the predecessor State and the successor State have concluded an agreement providing that such obligations or rights shall devolve upon the successor State.

2. Notwithstanding the conclusion of such an agreement, the effects of a succession of States on treaties which, at the date of that succession of States, were in force in respect of the territory in question are governed by the present Convention.

Article 9 Unilateral declaration by a successor State regarding treaties of the predecessor State
1. Obligations or rights under treaties in force in respect of a territory at the date of a

succession of States do not become the obligations or rights of the successor State or of other States parties to those treaties by reason only of the fact that the successor State has made a unilateral declaration providing for the continuance in force of the treaties in respect of its territory.

2. In such a case, the effects of the succession of States on treaties which, at the date of that succession of States, were in force in respect of the territory in question are governed by the present Convention.

Article 10 Treaties providing for the participation of a successor State

1. When a treaty provides that, on the occurrence of a succession of States, a successor State shall have the option to consider itself a party to the treaty, it may notify its succession in respect of the treaty in conformity with the provisions of the treaty or, failing any such provisions, in conformity with the provisions of the present Convention.

2. If a treaty provides that, on the occurrence of a succession of States, a successor State shall be considered as a party to the treaty, that provision takes effect as such only if the successor State expressly accepts in writing to be so considered.

3. In cases falling under paragraph 1 or 2, a successor State which establishes its consent to be a party to the treaty is considered as a party from the date of the succession of States unless the treaty otherwise provides or it is otherwise agreed.

Article 11 Boundary régimes

A succession of States does not as such affect:

  (a) a boundary established by a treaty; or
  (b) obligations and rights established by a treaty and relating to the régime of a boundary.

Article 12 Other territorial régimes

1. A succession of States does not as such affect:

  (a) obligations relating to the use of any territory, or to restrictions upon its use, established by a treaty for the benefit of any territory of a foreign State and considered as attaching to the territories in question;
  (b) rights established by a treaty for the benefit of any territory and relating to the use, or to restrictions upon the use, of any territory of a foreign State and considered as attaching to the territories in question.

2. A succession of States does not as such affect:

  (a) obligations relating to the use of any territory, or to restrictions upon its use, established by a treaty for the benefit of a group of States or of all States and considered as attaching to that territory;
  (b) rights established by a treaty for the benefit of a group of States or of all States and relating to the use of any territory, or to restrictions upon its use, and considered as attaching to that territory.

3. The provisions of the present article do not apply to treaty obligations of the predecessor State providing for the establishment of foreign military bases on the territory to which the succession of States relates.

Article 13 The present Convention and permanent sovereignty over natural wealth and resources

Nothing in the present Convention shall affect the principles of international law affirming the permanent sovereignty of every people and every State over its natural wealth and resources.

Article 15 Succession in respect of part of territory

When part of the territory of a State, or when any territory for the international relations of which a State is responsible, not being part of the territory of that State, becomes part of the territory of another State:

    (a) treaties of the predecessor State cease to be in force in respect of the territory to which the succession of States relates from the date of the succession of States; and

    (b) treaties of the successor State are in force in respect of the territory to which the succession of States relates from the date of the succession of States, unless it appears from the treaty or is otherwise established that the application of the treaty to that territory would be incompatible with the object and purpose of the treaty or would radically change the conditions for its operation.

Article 16 Position in respect of the treaties of the predecessor State

A newly independent State is not bound to maintain in force, or to become a party to, any treaty by reason only of the fact that at the date of the succession of States the treaty was in force in respect of the territory to which the succession of States relates.

Case Concerning the Arbitral Award of 31 July 1989 (Guinea-Bissau v Senegal)

83 ILR (1992) 1, Special Arbitration Tribunal

By a treaty in 1985, Guinea-Bissau and Senegal agreed to submit to arbitration a dispute over their maritime boundaries. At the core of the dispute was whether an agreement in 1960 between Portugal and France (the former colonial powers over the relevant territories) was binding on Guinea-Bissau and Senegal. The majority of the Tribunal held the 1960 agreement to be valid and binding.

33. A successor State can invoke before a tribunal all grounds of claim or objection which could have been invoked by the State to which it has succeeded. Consequently, Guinea-Bissau, as a successor State, is entitled to invoke before the Tribunal all the grounds of nullity which could have been raised by Portugal regarding the 1960 Agreement. Guinea-Bissau can also submit to the Tribunal any reasons for non-opposability to it of the Agreement, which in its view exclude succession to that Agreement. Similarly, Senegal can likewise invoke before the Tribunal all the grounds which, in its view, support the existence and validity of the Agreement and its effect in the present case.

Application of the Genocide Convention (Bosnia and Herzegovina v Yugoslavia (Serbia and Montenegro)) (Indication of Provisional Measures)

ICJ Rep 1993 325, International Court of Justice

The facts are set out in Chapter 15. One of the key issues was whether each new State that arose from the Former Yugoslavia could succeed to the Genocide Convention, which the Former Yugoslavia had ratified. The Court did not have to make a final decision on this matter at the provisional measures stage but Judge Weeramantry gave a Separate Opinion that dealt with the matter of succession to human rights treaties.

JUDGE WEERAMANTRY (Separate Opinion): The principle that a new State ought not in general to be fettered with treaty obligations which it has not expressly agreed to assume after it has attained statehood (the clean slate principle) is of considerable historical and theoretical importance. New States ought not, in principle, to be burdened with treaty-based responsibilities without their express consent. With the sudden advent into the international community of nearly eighty newly independent States in the late fifties and early sixties, there was a realization among them, in the words of Julius Stone, that: "their authority or their territory or both are burdened with debts, concessions, commercial engagements of various kinds or other obligations continuing on from the earlier colonial regime . . ." [Julius Stone, 'A common law for mankind?' (1960), 1 *International Studies*, pp. 430–432]. . . .

Theoretically, the clean slate principle can be justified on several powerful bases: the principle of individual State autonomy, the principle of self-determination, the principle of *res inter alios acta*, and the principle that there can be no limitations on a State's rights, except with its consent. Newly independent States should not have to accept as a *fait accompli* the contracts of predecessor States, for it is self-evident that the new State must be free to make its own decisions on such matters. The clean slate principle could also be described as an important corollary to the principle of self determination, which is of cardinal importance in modern international law. The principle of self determination could be emptied of an important part of its content if prior treaties automatically bind the new State. . . . Basic concepts of State sovereignty also require that any curtailment of the sovereign authority of a State requires the express consent of the State. If there is to be, in a given case, a deviation from the clean slate principle, sufficiently cogent reasons should exist to demonstrate that the new State's sovereignty is not being thereby impaired. The question needs therefore to be examined as to whether there is any impairment of State sovereignty implicit in the application of the principle of automatic succession to any given treaty.

Human rights and humanitarian treaties involve no loss of sovereignty or autonomy of the new State, but are merely in line with general principles of protection that flow from the inherent dignity of every human being which is the very foundation of the United Nations Charter. At the same time, it is important that the circle of exceptions should not be too widely drawn. Conceivably some human rights treaties may involve economic burdens, such as treaties at the economic end of the spectrum of human rights. It is beyond the scope of this Opinion to examine whether all human rights and humanitarian treaties should be exempted from the clean slate principle. It is sufficient for the purposes of this Opinion to note a variety of reasons why it has been contended that human rights and humanitarian treaties in general attract the principle of automatic succession. These reasons apply with special force to treaties such as the Genocide Convention or the Convention against Torture, leaving no room for doubt regarding automatic succession to such treaties. The international community has a special interest in the continuity of such treaties. . . . [He then sets out ten reasons why human rights and humanitarian treaties are exceptions to the general clean slate principle]

If the principle of continuity in relation to succession of States, adopted in Article 34(1) in the 1978 Vienna Convention on Succession of States in Respect of Treaties, is to apply to any treaties at all, the Genocide Convention must surely be among such treaties. . . . All of the foregoing reasons combine to create what seems to me to be a principle of contemporary international law that there is automatic State succession to so vital a human rights convention as the Genocide Convention. Nowhere is the protection of the quintessential human right – the right to life – more heavily concentrated than in that Convention. Without automatic succession to such a Convention, we would have a situation where the worldwide system of human rights protections continually generates gaps in the most vital part of its framework, which open up and close, depending on the break up of the old political authorities and the emergence of the new. The international legal system cannot condone a principle by which the subjects of these States live in a state of continuing uncertainty regarding the most fundamental of their human rights protections. Such a view would grievously tear the seamless fabric of international human rights protections, endanger peace, and lead the law astray from the Purposes and Principles of the United Nations, which all nations, new and old, are committed to pursue.

NOTES:
1. While the Vienna Convention principles with regard to third States' rights and obligations apply only to parties to that Convention, this rule is considered to represent customary

international law – see *Free Zones of Upper Savoy and the District of Gex Case (France v Switzerland)*, PCIJ Rep, Ser A/B (1932), No. 46. Article 12 of the Vienna Convention on Succession of States in Respect of Treaties (above) is also considered a rule of customary international law – see the *Danube Dam Case* (below). Where the treaty codifies customary international law then the third State would be bound by that law.

2. The Vienna Convention on Succession of States in Respect of Treaties 1978, reinforces the principle that a new State enters the international community with a 'clean slate'. This principle has some significant limitations – for example, a boundary treaty must be accepted – which are necessary for international peace and security (see Chapter 7). Judge Weeramantry (above) raises the possibility of other limitations to this principle, such as human rights and humanitarian law treaties. Generally, a new State will quickly become a party to many treaties, such as those concerning diplomatic relations, in order to participate effectively in the international community.

3. The issue of succession of States to treaties was important during the decolonisation era. It has become an immediate issue again with the break-up of the Soviet Union and Yugoslavia, for example, see Agreement on Succession Issues between the five successor States of the Former Yugoslavia (41 ILM 1 (2002)).

4. The special nature of the United Nations Charter (which is a treaty) may create obligations for non-parties to that treaty. Article 2(6) of the Charter provides: 'The [United Nations] Organization shall ensure that States which are not Members of the United Nations act in accordance with [its] Principles so far as may be necessary for the maintenance of international peace and security'. In practice non-parties do act in accordance with these principles. For example, Switzerland, which was not then a party to the Charter, acted consistently with the Security Council resolutions imposing economic sanctions against Iraq during the Gulf War (see Chapter 14). See also the *Reparations of Injuries Case* (Chapter 5), which dealt with the personality of the UN for non-parties.

SECTION 4: **Reservations to treaties**

Reservations are the means whereby states accept as many of the rights and obligations under a treaty as possible, while expressly stating that there are some provisions of the treaty which they cannot accept. Reservations can have the effect of excluding altogether the legal effect of a particular provision, or modifying or qualifying the extent of a provision.

A: General principles

Reservations to the Convention on the Prevention and Punishment of the Crime of Genocide
ICJ Rep 1951 15, International Court of Justice

The General Assembly sought an advisory opinion from the Court on the following questions:

In so far as concerns the Convention on the Prevention and Punishment of the Crime of Genocide in the event of a State ratifying or acceding to the Convention subject to a reservation made either on ratification or on accession, or on signature followed by ratification:

I. Can the reserving State be regarded as being a party to the Convention while still maintaining its reservation if the reservation is objected to by one or more of the parties to the Convention but not by others?

II. If the answer to Question I is in the affirmative, what is the effect of the reservation as between the reserving State and:

(a) The parties which object to the reservation?

(b) Those which accept it?

III. What would be the legal effect as regards the answer to Question I if an objection to a reservation is made:

(a) By a signatory which has not yet ratified?

(b) By a State entitled to sign or accede but which has not yet done so?

[As regards Question I]: It is well established that in its treaty relations a State cannot be bound without its consent, and that consequently no reservation can be effective against any State without its agreement thereto. It is also a generally recognized principle that a multilateral convention is the result of an agreement freely concluded upon its clauses and that consequently none of the contracting parties is entitled to frustrate or impair, by means of unilateral decisions or particular agreements, the purpose and *raison d'être* of the convention. To this principle was linked the notion of the integrity of the convention as adopted, a notion which in its traditional concept involved the proposition that no reservation was valid unless it was accepted by all the contracting parties without exception, as would have been the case if it had been stated during the negotiations. . . .

It must also be pointed out that although the Genocide Convention was finally approved unanimously, it is nevertheless the result of a series of majority votes. The majority principle, while facilitating the conclusion of multilateral conventions, may also make it necessary for certain States to make reservations. This observation is confirmed by the great number of reservations which have been made of recent years to multilateral conventions.

In this state of international practice, it could certainly not be inferred from the absence of an article providing for reservations in a multilateral convention that the contracting States are prohibited from making certain reservations. Account should also be taken of the fact that the absence of such an article or even the decision not to insert such an article can be explained by the desire not to invite a multiplicity of reservations. The character of a multilateral convention, its purpose, provisions, mode of preparation and adoption, are factors which must be considered in determining, in the absence of any express provision on the subject, the possibility of making reservations, as well as their validity and effect. . . .

The object and purpose of the Genocide Convention imply that it was the intention of the General Assembly and of the States which adopted it that as many States as possible should participate. The complete exclusion from the Convention of one or more States would not only restrict the scope of its application, but would detract from the authority of the moral and humanitarian principles which are its basis. It is inconceivable that the contracting parties readily contemplated that an objection to a minor reservation should produce such a result. But even less could the contracting parties have intended to sacrifice the very object of the Convention in favour of a vain desire to secure as many participants as possible. The object and purpose of the Convention thus limit both the freedom of making reservations and that of objecting to them. It follows that it is the compatibility of a reservation with the object and purpose of the Convention that must furnish the criterion for the attitude of a State in making the reservation on accession as well as for the appraisal by a State in objecting to the reservation. Such is the rule of conduct which must guide every State in the appraisal which it must make, individually and from its own standpoint, of the admissibility of any reservation. . . .

It results from the foregoing considerations that Question I, on account of its abstract character, cannot be given an absolute answer. The appraisal of a reservation and the effect of objections that might be made to it depend upon the particular circumstances of each individual case.

[As regards Question II]: The considerations which form the basis of the Court's reply to Question I are to a large extent equally applicable here. As has been pointed out above, each State which is a party to the Convention is entitled to appraise the validity of the reservation, and it exercises this right individually and from its own standpoint. As no State can be bound by a reservation to which it has not consented, it necessarily follows that each State objecting to it will or will not, on the basis of its individual appraisal within the limits of the criterion of the object and purpose stated above, consider the reserving State to be a party to the Convention.

Vienna Convention on the Law of Treaties 1969

Article 2 Use of terms

(d) For the purposes of the present Convention . . . 'reservation' means a unilateral statement, however phrased or named, made by a State, when signing, ratifying, accepting, approving or acceding to a treaty, whereby it purports to exclude or to modify the legal effect of certain provisions of the treaty in their application to that State.

Article 19 Formulation of reservations

A State may, when signing, ratifying, accepting, approving or acceding to a treaty, formulate a reservation unless:

(a) the reservation is prohibited by the treaty;
(b) the treaty provides that only specified reservations, which do not include the reservation in question, may be made; or
(c) in cases not falling under sub-paragraphs (a) and (b), the reservation is incompatible with the object and purpose of the treaty.

Article 23 Procedure regarding reservations

1. A reservation, an express acceptance of a reservation and an objection to a reservation must be formulated in writing and communicated to the contracting States and other States entitled to become parties to the treaty.

2. If formulated when signing the treaty subject to ratification, acceptance or approval, a reservation must be formally confirmed by the reserving State when expressing its consent to be bound by the treaty. In such a case the reservation shall be considered as having been made on the date of its confirmation.

3. An express acceptance of, or an objection to, a reservation made previously to confirmation of the reservation does not itself require confirmation.

4. The withdrawal of a reservation or of an objection to a reservation must be formulated in writing.

Belilos v *Switzerland*

ECHR Ser A (1988) Vol 132, European Court of Human Rights

Belilos claimed that she had not been given a fair trial in Switzerland in contravention of Article 6 of the European Convention on Human Rights. Switzerland objected to the case proceeding on the basis that, when it ratified the Convention, it had made an 'interpretative declaration' concerning Article 6, which had the effect of being a valid reservation under Article 64 of the Convention (which set out the requirements for a valid reservation). The Swiss 'interpretative declaration' was:

The Swiss Federal Council considers that the guarantee of fair trial in Article 6, paragraph 1 of the Convention . . . is intended solely to ensure ultimate control by the judiciary over the acts or decisions of the public authorities relating to such rights or obligations or the determination of such a charge.

The Court held that the Swiss 'interpretative declaration' was in reality a reservation. However, it was not a valid reservation (as being too broad in scope) within the requirements of Article 64. The Court then upheld the applicant's claim against Switzerland. The reasoning of the Court was as follows:

47. The [Swiss] Government derived an additional argument from the fact that there had been no reaction from the Secretary General of the Council of Europe or from the States Parties to the Convention. . . . The Swiss Government inferred that it could in good faith take the declaration as having been tacitly accepted for the purposes of Article 64. The Court does not agree with that analysis. The silence of the depository and the Contracting States does not deprive the Convention institutions of the power to make their own assessment. . . .

48. . . . Like the Commission and the Government, the Court recognises that it is necessary to ascertain the original intention of those who drafted the declaration. In its view, the documents show that Switzerland originally contemplated making a formal reservation but subsequently opted for the term 'declaration'. . . .

49. The question whether a declaration described as 'interpretative' must be regarded as a 'reservation' is a difficult one, particularly – in the instant case – because the Swiss Government has made both 'reservations' and 'interpretative declarations' in the same instrument of ratification. More generally, the Court recognises the great importance, rightly emphasised by the Government, of the legal rules applicable to reservations and interpretative declarations made by States Parties to the Convention. Only reservations are mentioned in the Convention, but several States have also (or only) made interpretative declarations, without always making a clear distinction between the two.

In order to establish the legal character of such a declaration, one must look behind the title given to it and seek to determine the substantive content. In the present case, it appears that Switzerland meant to remove certain categories of proceedings from the ambit of Article 6(1) and to secure itself against an interpretation of that Article which it considered to be too broad. However, the Court must see to it that the obligations arising under the Convention are not subject to restrictions which would not satisfy the requirements of Article 64 as regard reservations. Accordingly, it will examine the validity of the interpretative declaration in question, as in the case of a reservation, in the context of this provision. . . .

60. In short, the declaration does not satisfy two of the requirements of Article 64 of the Convention, with the result that it must be held to be invalid. At the same time, it is beyond doubt that Switzerland is, and regards itself as, bound by the Convention irrespective of the Validity of the declaration. Moreover, the Swiss Government recognised the Court's competence to determine the latter issue.

NOTES:

1. The *Belilos* case offers a useful discussion of the distinction between interpretative declarations and reservations. The status of the 'declaration' depends on an assessment of what it seeks to achieve, which is made by interpreting the text of the declaration and its legal effect (see below). If its effect is to make the State's consent to the treaty conditional upon the acceptance of the content of the declaration, rather than merely offering an interpretation of the treaty, the declaration will be treated as a reservation.

2. The rules in the Vienna Convention on reservations are based on the fundamental rule that

all States that are parties to a treaty should be subject to the same rights and obligations under it. This must always be the case with bilateral treaties, in which instance a reservation is better considered as a counter-offer which the other party can accept or refuse, resulting in either the conclusion or rejection of the treaty as drafted. However, where a multilateral treaty is concerned, a State may decide, for a variety of political, social and legal reasons, to restrict the extent to which it is bound by all of the treaty's obligations. This is usually done by making a written reservation to the treaty when signing, ratifying, accepting, approving or acceding to the treaty. Reservations can be withdrawn at any time. Most treaties today have some provision regarding reservations, in which case the provision on reservation in each treaty will apply instead of the Vienna Convention rules.

3. The extent to which reservations to treaties should be allowed in international law raises the conflict between the need to preserve the 'integrity' of a treaty (so that all parties are equally bound), against the desirability of securing wider participation in treaties. The latter is particularly the case where a treaty may be considered to be 'standard-setting', such as many human rights treaties (see Chapter 6) and the Law of the Sea Convention 1982 (see Chapter 10). However, in many cases the international tribunal considering a reservation will strive to interpret a reservation so that the object and propose of a treaty is upheld without compromising a State's limitation on its consent to be bound by that treaty.

4. The Articles in the Vienna Convention concerning reservations are generally in line with the conclusions reached by the International Court of Justice in the *Genocide case*. Thus this part of the Vienna Convention is considered to reflect customary international law.

5. A reservation may be made unless the treaty prohibits it, the reservation is not among an exhaustive list of specified permissible reservations or it is incompatible with the object and purpose of the treaty: see Article 19 of the Vienna Convention.

B: The legal effect of reservations

Vienna Convention on the Law of Treaties 1969

Article 20 Acceptance of and objection to reservations

1. A reservation expressly authorized by a treaty does not require any subsequent acceptance by the other contracting States unless the treaty so provides.

2. When it appears from the limited number of negotiating States and the object and purpose of a treaty that the application of the treaty in its entirety between all the parties is an essential condition of the consent of each one to be bound by the treaty, a reservation requires acceptance by all the parties.

3. When a treaty is a constituent instrument of an international organization and unless it otherwise provides, a reservation requires the acceptance of the competent organ of that organization.

4. In cases not falling under the preceding paragraphs and unless the treaty otherwise provides:

　　(a) acceptance by another contracting State of a reservation constitutes the reserving State a party to the treaty in relation to that other State if or when the treaty is in force for those States;

　　(b) an objection by another contracting State to a reservation does not preclude the entry into force of the treaty as between the objecting and reserving States unless a contrary intention is definitely expressed by the objecting State;

　　(c) an act expressing a State's consent to be bound by the treaty and containing a reservation is effective as soon as at least one other contracting State has accepted the reservation.

5. For the purposes of paragraphs 2 and 4 and unless the treaty otherwise provides, a reservation is considered to have been accepted by a State if it shall have raised no objection to the reservation by the end of a period of twelve months after it was notified of the reservation or by the date on which it expressed its consent to be bound by the treaty, whichever is later.

Article 21   Legal effects of reservations and of objections to reservations

1. A reservation established with regard to another party in accordance with articles 19, 20 and 23:

   (a) modifies for the reserving State in its relations with that other party the provisions of the treaty to which the reservation relates to the extent of the reservation; and

   (b) modifies those provisions to the same extent for that other party in its relations with the reserving State.

2. The reservation does not modify the provisions of the treaty for the other parties to the treaty *inter se*.

3. When a State objecting to a reservation has not opposed the entry into force of the treaty between itself and the reserving State, the provisions to which the reservation relates do not apply as between the two States to the extent of the reservation.

Article 22   Withdrawal of reservations and of objections to reservations

1. Unless the treaty otherwise provides, a reservation may be withdrawn at any time and the consent of a State which has accepted the reservation is not required for its withdrawal.

2. Unless the treaty otherwise provides, an objection to a reservation may be withdrawn at any time.

3. Unless the treaty otherwise provides, or it is otherwise agreed:

   (a) the withdrawal of a reservation becomes operative in relation to another contracting State only when notice of it has been received by that State;

   (b) the withdrawal of an objection to a reservation becomes operative only when notice of it has been received by the State which formulated the reservation.

English Channel Arbitration (*United Kingdom* v *France*)
54 ILR (1977) 6, Special Court of Arbitration

The case concerned the continental shelf boundary in the English Channel. Both States were parties to the Geneva Convention on the Continental Shelf 1958. However, France had entered reservations to Article 6 (regarding the equidistance principle) which were objected to by the United Kingdom and so the Court of Arbitration had to first determine the law applicable to the arbitration.

59. The Court considers that the answer to the question of the legal effect of the French reservations lies partly in the contentions of the French Republic and partly in those of the United Kingdom. Clearly, the French Republic is correct in stating that the establishment of treaty relations between itself and the United Kingdom under the Convention depended on the consent of each State to be mutually bound by its provisions; and that when it formulated its reservations to Article 6 it made its consent to be bound by the provisions of that Article subject to the conditions embodied in the reservations. There is, on the other hand, much force in the United Kingdom's observation that its rejection was directed to the reservations alone and not to Article 6 as a whole. In short, the disagreement between the two countries was not one regarding the recognition of Article 6 as applicable in their mutual relations but one regarding the matters reserved by the French Republic

from the application of Article 6. The effect of the United Kingdom's rejection of the reservations is thus limited to the reservations themselves. . . .

61. In a more limited sense, however, the effect of the rejection may properly, in the view of the Court, be said to render the reservations non-opposable to the United Kingdom. Just as the effect of the French reservations is to prevent the United Kingdom from invoking the provisions of Article 6 except on the basis of the conditions stated in the reservations, so the effect of their rejection is to prevent the French Republic from imposing the reservations on the United Kingdom for the purpose of invoking against it as binding a delimitation made on the basis of the conditions contained in the reservations. Thus, the combined effect of the French reservations and their rejection by the United Kingdom is neither to render Article 6 inapplicable *in toto*, as the French Republic contends, nor to render it applicable *in toto*, as the United Kingdom primarily contends. It is to render the Article inapplicable as between the two countries to the extent, but only to the extent, of the reservations; and this is precisely the effect envisaged in such cases by Article 21, paragraph 3 of the Vienna Convention on the Law of Treaties and the effect indicated by the principle of mutuality of consent.

62. The fact that Article 6 is not applicable as between the Parties to the extent that it is excluded by the French reservations does not mean that there are no legal rules to govern the delimitation of the boundary in areas where the reservation operates. On the contrary, as the International Court of Justice observed in the *North Sea Continental Shelf* cases, 'there are still rules and principles of law to be applied' (ICJ Rep 1969, paragraph 83); and these are the rules and principles governing delimitation of the continental shelf in general international law.

Memorandum by the United Kingdom's Department of Trade, March 1978
(1978) 49 BYBIL pp. 378–380

2. The basic effect of the Convention regime on reservations to multilateral conventions is as follows:

(a) States are entitled to formulate a reservation on signature, or ratification of, or accession to a treaty unless the treaty prohibits reservations or provides that only specified reservations, which do not include the reservation in question, may be made.

(b) Where the treaty is silent on reservations, States are entitled to formulate a reservation unless the reservation is incompatible with the object and purpose of the treaty. (This is the test laid down by the International Court of Justice in its Advisory Opinion on *Reservations to the Convention on Genocide*: ICJ Rep 1951, page 15.)

(c) Reservations to a restricted multilateral treaty require acceptance by all the parties, and reservations to a constituent instrument of an international organisation require the acceptance of the competent organ of that organisation, unless the treaty otherwise provides.

(d) In other cases, and unless the particular treaty otherwise provides:

(i) The express or tacit acceptance of a reservation by another contracting State constitutes the reserving State a party to the treaty in relation to that other State, tacit acceptance being assumed if no objection is raised within a specified period.

(ii) An objection to a reservation by another contracting State does not preclude the entry into force of the treaty as between the objecting and reserving States unless a contrary intention is definitely expressed by the objecting State.

(iii) An act expressing a State's consent to be bound by a treaty which contains a reservation is effective as soon as at least one other contracting State has accepted the reservation.

3. The basic principle in the case of a treaty which is silent on reservations therefore is that States are entitled to *formulate* a reservation unless the reservation is incompatible with the object and purpose of the treaty. The question whether a reservation is or is not incompatible with the object

and purpose of the treaty is, however, one on which there may be differing views. The State wishing to make the reservation will no doubt be of the view that the reservation is compatible with the object and purpose of the treaty. The other States may take the opposite view. If so, they are certainly entitled to object to the reservation; and they have a discretion to declare that the effect of their objection is to preclude the entry into force of the treaty as a whole as between the objecting and reserving States. It is not, however, only on this basis that other States may object to a reservation. State practice shows clearly that it is also permissible for a State to object to a reservation made by another State if the objecting State does not assert that the reservation is incompatible with the object and purpose of the treaty. . . .

In view of the very large role which tacit consent plays in the acceptance of reservations, it is in fact quite possible to envisage a situation in which even a reservation which was objectively incompatible with the object and purpose of the convention would be tacitly accepted by the majority (or, indeed, all) of the other contracting States. Because of the part played by tacit consent, it may well be preferable for a party which wishes to make a reservation not to seek the acceptance of the reservation by the other contracting States before ratifying or acceding to the convention in question.

D. Bowett, 'Reservations to Non-Restricted Multi-Lateral Treaties'
(1976) 48 BYBIL 67, pp. 88–90

An examination of recent State practice on reservations suggests that there is considerable uncertainty over the operation of the rules now embodied in the Vienna Convention. . . .

6. The question of 'permissibility' is always a question to be resolved as a matter of construction of the treaty and does *not* depend on the reactions of the Parties. Therefore, though each Party may have to determine whether it regards a reservation as permissible, in the absence of any 'collegiate' system it must do so on the basis of whether the treaty permits such a reservation. The issue of 'permissibility' is thus entirely separate from the issue of 'opposability', that is to say whether a Party accepts or does not accept a reservation which is permissible.

7. Parties may not accept an impermissible reservation.

8. As to permissible reservations, with non-restricted multilateral treaties, a reservation which is expressly authorized . . . above requires no acceptance and takes effect with the reserving State's acceptance of the treaty. That apart, permissible reservations may meet with the following three reactions from other Parties:

(i)   acceptance of the reservation: the effect is that the treaty is in force and the reservation takes full effect between the reserving and accepting States, on a reciprocal basis;

(ii)   objection to the reservation: the effect is that the treaty is in force, but *minus* the provision affected by the reservation *to the extent of the reservation*. The reservation is not 'opposable' to the objecting State;

(iii)   objection to the reservation and an express objection to the treaty's entering into force: the effect is that the reserving and objecting States are not in any treaty relationship. Neither the treaty nor the reservation is 'opposable' to the objecting State.

9. The objecting State, exercising either of the last two options set out in conclusion 8 above, is free to object on any ground: that is to say, its objection is not confined to the ground of 'incompatibility' with the object and purpose of the treaty.

NOTES:

1. While there is no need for a State to object to an impermissible reservation, the extract from Bowett sets out the three options available to a State when considering how to react to a permissible reservation. Note, however, that some reservations require the approval of all

State parties. If a State makes no express response to a reservation then it may be bound by virtue of Article 20(5) of the Vienna Convention (though this subsection does not represent customary international law). The extract from the Department of Trade memorandum shows that this tacit consent is not uncommon.

2. A valid reservation accepted by a party to the treaty modifies the treaty between it and the reserving State, but does not affect the treaty relations between the party and non-reserving States. Where a party has objected to a reservation (but not to the entry into force of the treaty between it and the reserving State) then the treaty is inapplicable between the party and the reserving State to the extent of the reservation. The *English Channel Arbitration* extract notes that the consequence of this position is that there is no express agreement between the two States concerning the issues covered by the reservation, but that other rules of international law may still apply.

3. The practical effect of these rules regarding reservations to multilateral treaties is that they become, in effect, a series of bilateral treaties with legal relations between States depending on how each State has reacted to other States' reservations.

C: Reservations to human rights treaties

General Comment on Issues Relating to Reservations
UN Human Rights Committee, General Comment No 24(52)
2 International Human Rights Reports 10 (1995)

This General Comment was made in response to concerns that the large number and broad range of reservations to the International Covenant on Civil and Political Rights (ICCPR: 'the Covenant') might undermine the effectiveness of the Covenant, as well as concerns about the effects of the application of the Vienna Convention to reservations to human rights treaties.

4. The possibility of entering reservations may encourage States which consider that they have difficulties in guaranteeing all the rights in the Covenant nonetheless to accept the generality of obligations in that instrument. Reservations may serve a useful function to enable States to adapt specific elements in their laws to the inherent rights of each person as articulated in the Covenant. However, it is desirable in principle that States accept the full range of obligations, because the human rights norms are the legal expression of the essential rights that every person is entitled to as a human being. . . .

8. Reservations that offend peremptory norms would not be compatible with the object and purpose of the Covenant. Although treaties that are mere exchanges of obligations between States allow them to reserve *inter se* application of rules of general international law, it is otherwise in human rights treaties, which are for the benefit of persons within their jurisdiction. Accordingly, provisions in the Covenant that represent customary international law (and *a fortiori* when they have the character of peremptory norms) may not be the subject of reservations. . . .

11. The Covenant consists not just of the specified rights, but of important supportive guarantees. These guarantees provide the necessary framework for securing the rights in the Covenant and are thus essential to its object and purpose. Some operate at the national level and some at the international level. Reservations designed to remove these guarantees are thus not acceptable. . . .

13. . . . A reservation cannot be made to the Covenant through the vehicle of the Optional Protocol but such a reservation would operate to ensure that the State's compliance with that obligation may not be tested by the Committee under the first Optional Protocol. . . .

17. [I]t is the Vienna Convention on the Law of Treaties that provides the definition of reservations

and also the application of the object and purpose test in the absence of other specific provisions. But the Committee believes that its provisions on the role of State objections in relation to reservations are inappropriate to address the problem of reservations to human rights treaties. Such treaties, and the Covenant specifically, are not a web of inter-State exchanges of mutual obligations. They concern the endowment of individuals with rights. The principle of inter-State reciprocity has no place, save perhaps in the limited context of reservations to declarations on the Committee's competence under article 41. And because the operation of the classic rules on reservations is so inadequate for the Covenant, States have often not seen any legal interest in or need to object to reservations. The absence of protest by States cannot imply that a reservation is either compatible or incompatible with the object and purpose of the Covenant.

18. It necessarily falls to the Committee to determine whether a specific reservation is compatible with the object and purpose of the Covenant. This is in part because, as indicated above, it is an inappropriate task for States parties in relation to human rights treaties, and in part because it is the task that the Committee cannot avoid in the performance of its functions. . . . Because of the special character of a human rights treaty, the compatibility of a reservation with the object and purpose of the Covenant must be established objectively, by reference to legal principles, and the Committee is particularly well placed to perform this task. The normal consequence of an unacceptable reservation is not that the Covenant will not be in effect at all for a reserving party. Rather, such a reservation will generally be severable, in the sense that the Covenant will be operative for the reserving party without benefit of the reservation.

Rawle Kennedy v *Trinidad and Tobago*

UN Human Rights Committee, 7 International Human Rights Reports 315 (2000)

Trinidad and Tobago had initially ratified the Optional Protocol to the Convention (which allows individuals to bring complaints ('communications') to the UN Human Rights Committee) and then denounced it (ie withdrew from the treaty) after a series of cases against it, especially in relation to Trinidad and Tobago's application of the death penalty. Trinidad and Tobago immediately reacceded to the Protocol but this time included a reservation. The reservation stated:

[T]he Human Rights Committee shall not be competent to receive and consider communications relating to any prisoner who is under sentence of death in respect of any matter relating to his prosecution, his detention, his trial, his conviction, his sentence or the carrying out of the death sentence on him and any matter connected therewith.

In this case the Committee had to consider the effect of this reservation in relation to a complaint about the death penalty against Trinidad and Tobago. It decided that the complaint was admissible despite the reservation.

6.7. The present reservation, which was entered after the publication of General Comment No. 24, does not purport to exclude the competence of the Committee under the Optional Protocol with regard to any specific provision of the Covenant, but rather to the entire Covenant for one particular group of complainants, namely prisoners under sentence of death. This does not, however, make it compatible with the object and purpose of the Optional Protocol. On the contrary, the Committee cannot accept a reservation which singles out a certain group of individuals for lesser procedural protection than that which is enjoyed by the rest of the population. In the view of the Committee, this constitutes a discrimination which runs counter to some of the basic principles embodied in the

Covenant and its Protocols, and for this reason the reservation cannot be deemed compatible with the object and purpose of the Optional Protocol. The consequence is that the Committee is not precluded from considering the present communication under the Optional Protocol.

NOTES:
1. The desirability to have as many States as possible acknowledging obligations to respect, protect and fulfil human rights obligations within their jurisdiction has meant that there are many States which ratify human rights treaties but, for political, social, economic or cultural reasons, make reservations. As a consequence, the Human Rights Committee (HRC) has tended to interpret such reservations very narrowly. Indeed, the its General Comment 24 (above) affirms the European Court of Human Rights decision in *Belilos* v *Switzerland* (above) that a reservation was invalid despite the lack of objections by any other States that were parties to that treaty.

2. Following the HRC's General Comment 24, many States, while recognising the different obligations imposed by various types of treaties, have expressed a preference for the maintenance of a universal reservations regime rather than the creation of a dual regime. The Vienna Convention, by striking a balance between the interests of States and individuals, is argued to provide a flexible system promoting universality of participation rather than hindering ratification: see, for example, 'Sixth Committee Concludes Consideration of Report of International Law Commission', *Press Release* GA/L/3058, 7 November 1997. The Comment has also been criticised for the role it envisages for the HRC in the determination of the permissibility of reservations (para. 18 above). States including the United Kingdom, the United States, France and Libya have argued that monitoring bodies to treaties such as the HRC should not be able to decide if a reservation is permissible, and that their role should be confined to making recommendations to States. However, a similar criticism has not been made of the European or Inter-American Courts of Human Rights decisions.

3. The HRC applied its General Comment 24 in the *Rawle Kennedy Case* (above). As a consequence, Trinidad and Tobago denounced the Optional Protocol again and did not reaccede. There is now no opportunity for any person in Trinidad and Tobago to bring a complaint to the HRC. While this is an undesirable consequence, the HRC would consider that it has now made clear that a State that makes a reservation that is incompatible with the object and purpose of a human rights treaty is actually undertaking no legal obligations and so its reservation should not be allowed to remain.

4. The reason why the HRC has taken this stance is because human rights treaties are not of the same nature as other treaties as there are usually no reciprocal obligations between States in such treaties. Accordingly, there is no self-interest for any State to enforce the obligations of other States under these types of treaties and also no incentive to object to any reservations, whether those reservations are permissible or not (see para 17 of the General Comment). It must be the case that the body given the responsibility to ensure compliance with a human rights treaty should determine the status of reservations to that treaty. It must also have the responsibility to determine the effect of reservations, even if the consequence is that a State party – because its reservation is deemed to be impermissible and severable – has greater obligations under the treaty than that State originally intended. While this position may be contrary to a concept of international law as based on States' consent, it is consistent with a broader view of the nature of both international law generally and international human rights law in particular.

SECTION 5: **Interpretation of treaties**

The manner in which the terms of a treaty are interpreted by an international tribunal can determine the extent of the rights and obligations of the parties to that treaty.

G. Fitzmaurice, 'The Law and Procedure of the International Court of Justice: Treaty Interpretation and Certain other Treaty Points'
(1951) 28 BYBIL 1

There are today three main schools of thought on the subject, which could conveniently be called the 'intentions of the parties' or 'founding fathers' school; the 'textual' or 'ordinary meaning of the words' school; and the 'teleological' or 'aims and objects' school. The ideas of these three schools are not necessarily exclusive of one another, and theories of treaty interpretation can be constructed (and are indeed normally held) compounded of all three. However, each tends to confer the primacy on one particular aspect of treaty interpretation, if not to the exclusion, certainly to the subordination of the others. Each, in any case, employs a different approach. For the 'intentions' school, the prime, indeed the only legitimate, object in to ascertain and give effect to the intentions, or presumed intentions, of the parties: the approach is therefore to discover what these were, or must be taken to have been. For the 'meaning of the text' school, the prime object is to establish what the text means according to the ordinary or apparent signification of its terms: the approach is therefore through the study and analysis of the text. For the 'aims and objects' school, it is the general purpose of the treaty itself that counts, considered to some extent as having, or as having come to have, an existence of its own, independent of the original intentions of the framers. The main object is to establish this general purpose, and construe the particular clauses in the light of it: hence it is such matters as the general tenor and atmosphere of the treaty, the circumstances in which it was made, the place it has come to have in international life, which for this school indicate the approach to interpretation. It should be added that this last, the teleological, approach has its sphere of operation almost entirely in the field of general multilateral conventions, particularly those of the social, humanitarian, and law-making type. All three approaches are capable, in a given case, of producing the same result in practice; but equally (even though the differences may, on analysis, prove to be more of emphasis and methodology than principle) they are capable of leading to radically divergent results.

Vienna Convention on the Law of Treaties 1969

Article 31 General rule of interpretation

1. A treaty shall be interpreted in good faith in accordance with the ordinary meaning to be given to the terms of the treaty in their context and in the light of its object and purpose.

2. The context for the purpose of the interpretation of a treaty shall comprise, in addition to the text, including its preamble and annexes:

> (a) any agreement relating to the treaty which was made between all the parties in connexion with the conclusion of the treaty;
> (b) any instrument which was made by one or more parties in connexion with the conclusion of the treaty and accepted by the other parties as an instrument related to the treaty.

3. There shall be taken into account, together with the context:

(a) any subsequent agreement between the parties regarding the interpretation of the treaty or the application of its provisions;

(b) any subsequent practice in the application of the treaty which establishes the agreement of the parties regarding its interpretation;

(c) any relevant rules of international law applicable in the relations between the parties.

4. A special meaning shall be given to a term if it is established that the parties so intended.

Article 32 Supplementary means of interpretation

Recourse may be had to supplementary means of interpretation, including the preparatory work of the treaty and the circumstances of its conclusion, in order to confirm the meaning resulting from the application of article 31, or to determine the meaning when the interpretation according to article 31:

(a) leaves the meaning ambiguous or obscure; or

(b) leads to a result which is manifestly absurd or unreasonable.

Article 33 Interpretation of treaties authenticated in two or more languages

1. When a treaty has been authenticated in two or more languages, the text is equally authoritative in each language, unless the treaty provides or the parties agree that, in case of divergence, a particular text shall prevail.

2. A version of the treaty in a language other than one of those in which the text was authenticated shall be considered an authentic text only if the treaty so provides or the parties so agree.

3. The terms of the treaty are presumed to have the same meaning in each authentic text.

4. Except where a particular text prevails in accordance with paragraph 1, when a comparison of the authentic texts discloses a difference of meaning which the application of articles 31 and 32 does not remove, the meaning which best reconciles the texts, having regard to the object and purpose of the treaty, shall be adopted.

Golder v *United Kingdom*

ECHR Ser A (1975) No 18, 14, European Court of Human Rights

In the way in which it is presented in the 'general rule' in Article 31 of the Vienna Convention, the process of interpretation of a treaty is a unity, a single combined operation; this rule, closely integrated, places on the same footing the various elements enumerated in the four paragraphs of the Article.

M. Koskenniemi, *From Apology to Utopia: The Structure of International Legal Argument*

(1989), pp. 291–294, 298–299

According to a subjective approach treaties bind because they express consent. An objective approach assumes that they bind because considerations of teleology, utility, reciprocity, good faith or justice require this. The history of the doctrine of treaty interpretation is the history of the contrast between these two approaches.

Doctrinal expositions and case-law on treaty interpretation usually start out by emphasizing that a text must first be so construed as to give effect to its 'normal', 'natural', 'ordinary' or 'usual' meaning. This seems supported both by the subjective as well as the objective understanding. 'Natural' meaning seems relevant as the most reliable guide to what the parties had consented to as well as what justice requires. But this position is not really a rule of interpretation at all. It assumes what was to be proved; that the expression has a certain meaning instead of another one. The doctrine of 'normal' meaning singularly fails to deal with the fact that already the ascertainment of the 'normal' requires interpretation and that the very emergence of the dispute conclusively proves this. . . .

It is often held that the principal goal of interpretation is to give effect to (subjective) party intentions. But it is virtually impossible to ascertain real, subjective party intent. In particular, doctrine lacks means to oppose its conception of party intent on a deviating conception proposed by the party itself. Besides, sometimes intent may seem like a relatively minor matter – peace treaties or human rights instruments being the obvious examples. The important point is, however, that if intent is to be the *goal* of interpretation, it cannot be used as a *means* for attaining it. . . .

But moving into the objective approach provides no solution. How can we know which interpretation (which behaviour, which teleology) manifests consent? The problem-solver should be capable of justifying his view about what it is that the text (party behaviour, contractual equilibrium) requires. Inasmuch he cannot justify it by referring to intent (because the argument started from the assumption that intent was not known) he must refer to some non-subjective criterion. The irony is, of course, that the system simultaneously denies there to be such a thing as an "objective normality" or any other non-subjective criterion by which the contractual relationship could be evaluated. It tells us only that we cannot proceed beyond our subjective views about such matters and that nobody has any duty to defer to another's subjective views. By this simple assumption – the rejection of natural law and intelligible essences – the liberal system of treaty interpretation deconstructs itself. . . .

The fusion of the subjective and objective understandings in this way resembles the tacit consent strategy. The subjective theory seems necessary to preserve the treaty's legitimacy. The objective view is needed to preserve the treaty's binding force. Neither can be maintained alone. Intent can be known only in its manifestations – which manifestations (text, behaviour, teleology etc.) count depends on whether they express intent. The subjective argument can be supported only by moving into an objective position. The objective argument can be held only on subjective premises. The argument is hopelessly circular. . . .

The problems of treaty interpretation lie deeper than the unclear character of treaty language. They lie in the contradiction between the legal principles available to arrive at an interpretation.

Applicant A v *Minister for Immigration and Ethnic Affairs*
(1997) 190 CLR 225, High Court of Australia

BRENNAN CJ: If a statute transposes the text of a treaty or a provision of a treaty into the statute so as to enact it as part of domestic law, the *prima facie* legislative intention is that the transposed text should bear the same meaning in the domestic statute as it bears in the treaty. To give it that meaning, the rules applicable to the interpretation of treaties must be applied to the transpose text and the rules generally applicable to the interpretation of domestic statutes give way.

Territorial Dispute Case (*Libyan Arab Jamahiriya* v *Chad*)
ICJ Rep 1994 6, International Court of Justice

The dispute revolved around whether a boundary between Libya and Chad had been established by a treaty in 1995 between Libya and France (the colonial power over Chad territory). The Court held, by 16 votes to 1, that the 1955 treaty did define the boundary. In reaching this conclusion it noted at paragraph 41 that Article 31 of the Vienna Convention reflected customary international law.

51. The parties could have indicated the frontiers by specifying in words the course of the boundary, or by indicating it on a map, by way of illustration or otherwise; or they could have done both. They chose to proceed in a different manner and to establish, by agreement, the list of international instruments from which the frontiers resulted, but the course for which they elected presents no difficulties of interpretation. That being so, the Court's task is clear:

> Having before it a clause which leaves little to be desired in the nature of clearness, it is bound to apply this clause as it stands, without considering whether other provisions

might with advantage have been added to or substituted for it. (*Acquisition of Polish Nationality*, Advisory Opinion, 1923, PCIJ, Series E. No. 7, p. 20.)

The text of Article 3 [of the 1955 treaty] clearly conveys the intention of the parties to reach a definitive settlement of the question of their common frontiers. Article 3 and Annex I are intended to define frontiers by reference to legal instruments which would yield the course of such frontiers. Any other construction would be contrary to one of the fundamental principles of interpretation of treaties, consistently upheld by international jurisprudence, namely that of effectiveness.

NOTES:

1. The main principle of interpretation of treaties is *pacta sunt servanda*, i.e. treaties are binding on the parties and must be performed in good faith (see above).

2. Article 31 combines all the major schools of treaty interpretation (identified in the extract by Fitzmaurice) into one rule, to be used in a 'single combined operation' (see *Golder v United Kingdom* above). In relation to the 'intentions of the parties' approach, it is the common intention of both parties that is relevant not the unshared intentions of each party. An approach limited to the intentions of the negotiators of the treaty may be appropriate with a bilateral treaty concerning trade and commerce. However, an objective approach, where current international law concepts are considered, is generally used where multilateral treaties dealing with human rights or maritime territory are in issue, being areas where international law has developed rapidly. Koskenniemi points out (above), that it is necessary to combine the subjective and objective approaches to treaty interpretation, as each by itself cannot provide a legally coherent solution. Indeed, one of the approaches that is being used more frequently is that of 'effectiveness' (see the *Territorial Dispute Case* above).

3. Judge Alvarez in the *Conditions on Admission to Membership of the UN (Second) Opinion* ICJ Rep 1950 10, considered that 'a treaty . . . acquires a life of its own. Consequently in interpreting it we must have regard to the exigencies of contemporary life, rather than the intentions of those who framed it.' His comment is persuasive and shows the important role of international bodies on the interpretation on treaties. This is was also seen in the section on reservations above. In the *Case concerning the Arbitral Award of 31 July 1989* (above), the Tribunal noted that a treaty 'must be interpreted in the light of the law in force at the date of its conclusion' (para. 85), i.e. using the doctrine of inter-temporal law (see Chapter 7).

4. Article 32 allows recourse to the *travaux préparatoires* of a treaty to resolve ambiguities and absurdities, although what constitutes preparatory work is not defined in the Vienna Convention. However, the extract from *Applicant A v Minister for Immigration and Ethnic Affairs* shows that national rules for the interpretation of legislation may be inappropriate for the interpretation of treaties under international law (see Chapter 4).

5. Many treaties are drawn up in more than one language as international participation increases. Where two versions of a treaty possess equal authority, but one version appears to have a wider meaning than the other, a court must adopt the more limited interpretation that can be made in conformity with both versions and which accords with the intention of the parties – see the *Mavrommatis Palestine Concessions Case* PCIJ Rep, Ser A, (1926) No. 2.

6. The more parties to a treaty, the greater the difficulty there may be in applying the principles set out in Articles 31 and 32 of the Vienna Convention. This will be because consistent subsequent practice may be hard to find; the initial object and purpose may be unclear; the original intentions of the parties may now be irrelevant; and the *travaux préparatoires* are unlikely to be binding on subsequent parties to the treaty. Accordingly, some flexibility in the approach by an international tribunal interpreting a treaty is usually necessary. However, on many occasions the tribunals have not indicated their approach to interpreting the treaty in issue.

SECTION 6: **Invalidity of treaties**

A treaty that complies with all the formal procedural aspects discussed above, may still be unenforceable if it is invalid. Due to the primacy of the consent of States, another party to a treaty can still agree to allow the treaty to remain in force despite there being a ground for invalidity (Article 45). The only grounds of invalidity where there has been much contention to date have been error (Article 48) and *jus cogens* (Articles 53 and 64).

A: General principles

Vienna Convention on the Law of Treaties 1969

Article 42 Validity and continuance in force of treaties

1. The validity of a treaty or of the consent of a State to be bound by a treaty may be impeached only through the application of the present Convention.

2. The termination of a treaty, its denunciation or the withdrawal of a party, may take place only as a result of the application of the provisions of the treaty or of the present Convention. The same rule applies to suspension of the operation of a treaty.

Article 43 Obligations imposed by international law independently of a treaty

The invalidity, termination or denunciation of a treaty, the withdrawal of a party from it, or the suspension of its operation, as a result of the application of the present Convention or of the provisions of the treaty shall not in any way impair the duty of any State to fulfil any obligation embodied in the treaty to which it would be subject under international law independently of the treaty.

Article 44 Separability of treaty provisions

1. A right of a party, provided for in a treaty or arising under article 56, to denounce, withdraw from or suspend the operation of the treaty may be exercised only with respect to the whole treaty unless the treaty otherwise provides or the parties otherwise agree.

2. A ground for invalidating, terminating, withdrawing from or suspending the operation of a treaty recognized in the present Convention may be invoked only with respect to the whole treaty except as provided in the following paragraphs or in article 60.

3. If the ground relates solely to particular clauses, it may be invoked only with respect to those clauses where:

(a) the said clauses are separable from the remainder of the treaty with regard to their application;

(b) it appears from the treaty or is otherwise established that acceptance of those clauses was not an essential basis of the consent of the other party or parties to be bound by the treaty as a whole; and

(c) continued performance of the remainder of the treaty would not be unjust.

4. In cases falling under articles 49 and 50 the State entitled to invoke the fraud or corruption may do so with respect either to the whole treaty or, subject to paragraph 3, to the particular clauses alone.

5. In cases falling under articles 51, 52 and 53, no separation of the provisions of the treaty is permitted.

Article 45 Loss of a right to invoke a ground for invalidating, terminating, withdrawing from or suspending the operation of a treaty

A State may no longer invoke a ground for invalidating, terminating, withdrawing from or suspending the operation of a treaty under articles 46 to 50 or articles 60 and 62 if, after becoming aware of the facts:

> (a) it shall have expressly agreed that the treaty is valid or remains in force or continues in operation, as the case may be; or
> (b) it must by reason of its conduct be considered as having acquiesced in the validity of the treaty or in its maintenance in force or in operation, as the case may be.

Article 46 Provisions of internal law regarding competence to conclude treaties

1. A State may not invoke the fact that its consent to be bound by a treaty has been expressed in violation of a provision of its internal law regarding competence to conclude treaties as invalidating its consent unless that violation was manifest and concerned a rule of its internal law of fundamental importance.

2. A violation is manifest if it would be objectively evident to any State conducting itself in the matter in accordance with normal practice and in good faith.

Article 47 Authority of representative to conclude treaties

If the authority of a representative to express the consent of a State to be bound by a particular treaty has been made subject to a specific restriction, his omission to observe that restriction may not be invoked as invalidating the consent expressed by him unless the restriction was notified to the other negotiating States prior to his expressing such consent.

Article 48 Error

1. A State may invoke an error in a treaty as invalidating its consent to be bound by the treaty if the error relates to a fact or situation which was assumed by that State to exist at the time when the treaty was concluded and formed an essential basis of its consent to be bound by the treaty.

2. Paragraph 1 shall not apply if the State in question contributed by its own conduct to the error or if the circumstances were such as to put that State on notice of a possible error.

3. An error relating only to the wording of the text of a treaty does not affect its validity; article 79 then applies.

Article 49 Fraud

If a State has been induced to conclude a treaty by the fraudulent conduct of another negotiating State, the State may invoke the fraud as invalidating its consent to be bound by the treaty.

Article 50 Corruption of a representative of a State

If the expression of a State's consent to be bound by a treaty has been procured through the corruption of its representative directly or indirectly by another negotiating State, the State may invoke such corruption as invalidating its consent to be bound by the treaty.

Article 51 Coercion of a representative of a State

The expression of a State's consent to be bound by a treaty which has been procured by the coercion of its representative through acts of threats directed against him shall be without any legal effect.

Article 52   Coercion of a State by the threat or use of force

A treaty is void if its conclusion has been procured by the threat or use of force in violation of the principles of international law embodied in the Charter of the United Nations.

Article 53   Treaties conflicting with a peremptory norm of general international law (*jus cogens*)

A treaty is void if, at the time of its conclusion, it conflicts with a peremptory norm of general international law. For the purposes of the present Convention, a peremptory norm of general international law is a norm accepted and recognized by the international community of States as a whole as a norm from which no derogation is permitted and which can be modified only by a subsequent norm of general international law having the same character.

Article 64   Emergence of a new peremptory norm of general international law (*jus congens*)

If a new peremptory norm of general international law emerges, any existing treaty which is in conflict with that norm becomes void and terminates.

NOTES:

1. The main grounds for impugning the validity of a treaty are those that affect the capacity of a party to consent (Articles 46 and 47); those that affect the reality of consent itself (Articles 48–52); and those that affect the lawfulness of the treaty (Articles 53 and 64).
2. It is uncertain whether the grounds set out in the Vienna Convention are the only grounds of invalidity. However, due to the fact that a treaty is usually negotiated by two or more States at arm's length, it could be argued that all grounds for invalidity must be interpreted narrowly. See, however, the discussion below concerning unequal treaties.
3. Article 103 of the United Nations Charter may also place a limitation on a State complying with its obligation under a treaty. It provides that 'in the event of a conflict between the obligations of the Members of the United Nations under the present Charter and their obligations under any other international agreement, their obligations under the present Charter shall prevail.'
4. A later treaty on the same subject-matter overrides an earlier treaty between the same States parties (Article 30, Vienna Convention). However there is uncertainty in regard to inconsistencies between a later treaty on a different subject-matter but which in effect overlaps with an earlier treaty. An example of this would be the World Trade Organization Agreements compared with multilateral environmental agreements such as the Convention on International Trade in Endangered Species 1973 (see Chapters 12 and 13).

B: Error

Temple of Preah Vihear Case (*Cambodia* v *Thailand*) (*Merits*)
ICJ Rep 1962 6, pp. 26–27, International Court of Justice

A map was prepared by the Mixed Franco-Siamese Commission pursuant to its delimitation of the boundary between Cambodia (then a French protective) and Thailand in 1904. This map placed the Temple in Cambodia.

[I]t is contended on behalf of Thailand, so far as the disputed area of Preah Vihear is concerned, that an error was committed, an error of which the Siamese authorities were unaware at the time when they accepted the map.

It is an established rule of law that the plea of error cannot be allowed as an element vitiating consent if the party advancing it contributed by its own conduct to the error, or could have avoided it, or if the circumstances were such as to put that party on notice of a possible error. The Court considers that the character and qualifications of the persons who saw the Annex I map on the Siamese side would alone make it difficult for Thailand to plead error in law. These persons included the members of the very Commission of Delimitation within whose competence this sector of the frontier had lain. But even apart from this, the Court thinks that there were other circumstances relating to the Annex I map which make the plea of error difficult to receive.

An inspection indicates that the map itself drew such pointed attention to the Preah Vihear region that no interested person, nor anyone charged with the duty of scrutinizing it, could have failed to see what the map was purporting to do in respect of that region. . . . The Siamese authorities knew it was the work of French topographical officers to whom they had themselves entrusted the work of producing the maps. They accepted it without any independent investigation, and cannot therefore now plead any error vitiating the reality of their consent. The Court concludes therefore that the plea of error has not been made out.

C: *Jus cogens*

Report of the International Law Commission to the General Assembly
Yearbook of the International Law Commission (1966) vol II, 172, pp. 247–248

(1) The view that in the last analysis there is no rule of international law from which States cannot at their own free will contract out has become increasingly difficult to sustain, although some jurists deny the existence of any rules of *jus cogens* in international law, since in their view even the most general rules still fall short of being universal. The Commission pointed out that the law of the Charter concerning the prohibition of the use of force in itself constitutes a conspicuous example of a rule in international law having the character of *jus cogens*. Moreover, if some Governments in their comments have expressed doubts as to the advisability of this article unless it is accompanied by provision for independent adjudication, only one questioned the existence of rules of *jus cogens* in the international law of today. Accordingly, the Commission concluded that in codifying the law of treaties it must start from the basis that today there are certain rules from which States are not competent to derogate at all by a treaty arrangement, and which may be changed only by another rule of the same character.

(2) The formulation of the article is not free from difficulty, since there is no simple criterion by which to identify a general rule of international law as having the character of *jus cogens*. Moreover, the majority of the general rules of international law do not have that character, and States may contract out of them by treaty. It would therefore be going much too far to state that a treaty is void if its provisions conflict with a rule of general international law. Nor would it be correct to say that a provision in a treaty possesses the character of *jus cogens* merely because the parties have stipulated that no derogation from that provision is to be permitted, so that another treaty which conflicted with that provision would be void. Such a stipulation may be inserted in any treaty with respect to any subject-matter for any reasons which may seem good to the parties. The conclusion by a party of a later treaty derogating from such a stipulation may, of course, engage its responsibility for a breach of the earlier treaty. But the breach of the stipulation does not, simply as such, render the treaty void . . . It is not the form of a general rule of international law but the particular nature of the subject-matter with which it deals that may, in the opinion of the Commission, give it the character of *jus cogens*.

(3) The emergence of rules having the character of *jus cogens* is comparatively recent, while international law is in process of rapid development. The Commission considered the right course to be to provide in general terms that a treaty is void if it conflicts with a rule of *jus cogens* and to leave the full content of this rule to be worked out in State practice and in the jurisprudence of

international tribunals. Some members of the Commission felt that there might be advantage in specifying, by way of illustration, some of the most obvious and best settled rules of *jus cogens* in order to indicate by these examples the general nature and scope of the rule contained in the article. Examples suggested included (a) a treaty contemplating an unlawful use of force contrary to the principles of the Charter, (b) a treaty contemplating the performance of any other act criminal under international law, and (c) a treaty contemplating or conniving at the commission of acts, such as trade in slaves, piracy or genocide, in the suppression of which every State is called upon to co-operate. Other members expressed the view that, if examples were given, it would be undesirable to appear to limit the scope of the article to cases involving acts which constitute crimes under international law; treaties violating human rights, the equality of States or the principle of self-determination were mentioned as other possible examples. The Commission decided against including any examples of rules of *jus cogens* in the article for two reasons. First, the mention of some cases of treaties void for conflict with a rule of *jus cogens* might, even with the most careful drafting, lead to misunderstanding as to the position concerning other cases not mentioned in the article. Secondly, if the Commission were to attempt to draw up, even on a selective basis, a list of the rules of international law which are to be regarded as having the character of *jus cogens*, it might find itself engaged in a prolonged study of matters which fall outside the scope of the present articles.

I. Sinclair, *The Vienna Convention on the Law of Treaties*
(1984), pp. 220–222

What conclusions can we draw so far from this analysis of the controversy surrounding the admissibility and application of the concept of *jus cogens* in international law? Perhaps one should stress at the outset that the 'great debate' on this issue involves taking a view on some of the fundamental and basic underpinnings of international law in general. It is no accident that some of the more vigorous Western proponents of *jus cogens* base their case largely upon private law analogies and upon concepts deriving from natural law. It is, equally, no accident that those who deny the existence of *jus cogens* found their denial in part upon considerations relating to State sovereignty and independence, and in part upon an analysis of the evidence of State practice; these are, of course, some of the hallmarks of the positivist approach. As de Visscher rightly points out the controversy surrounding *jus cogens* constitutes a renewal, in different terms, of the ancient doctrinal dispute between naturalists and positivists.

But there is a paradox here, particularly if one notes the enthusiasm of Soviet and other Eastern European publicists and official representatives for an extended application of the concept of *jus cogens* in international law. For those attached to Marxist-Leninist teachings there can be no place for any seed-bed of natural law in which *jus cogens* might take root. Equally, it might be thought unnatural that Soviet representatives, traditionally supporting some of the more exaggerated notions of State sovereignty, should come down in favour of a concept which postulates the existence of a superior international legal order. . . .

Whatever their doctrinal point of departure, the majority of jurists would no doubt willingly concede to the sceptics that there is little or no evidence in positive international law for the concept that nullity attaches to a treaty concluded in violation of *jus cogens*. But they would be constrained to admit that the validity of a treaty between two States to wage a war of aggression against a third State or to engage in acts of physical or armed force against a third State could not be upheld; and, having made this admission, they may be taken to have accepted the principle that there may exist norms of international law so fundamental to the maintenance of an international legal order that a treaty concluded in violation of them is a nullity.

Some (among whom may be counted the present author) would be prepared to go this far, but would immediately wish to qualify this acceptance of the principle involved by sketching out the limits within which it may be operative in present-day international law. In the first place, they would insist that, in the present state of international society, the concept of an 'international legal order' of hierarchically superior norms binding all States is only just beginning to emerge. Ideological differences and disparities of wealth between the individual nation States which make up the international community, combined with the contrasts between the objectives sought by them, hinder the development of an overarching community consensus upon the content of *jus cogens*. Indeed, it is the existence of these very differences and disparities which constitute the principal danger implicit in an unqualified recognition of *jus cogens*, for it would be only too easy to postulate as a norm of *jus cogens* a principle which happened neatly to serve a particular ideological or economic goal. In the second place, they would test any assertion that a particular rule constitutes a norm of jus cogens by reference to the evidence for its acceptance as such by the international community as a whole, and they would require that the burden of proof should be discharged by those who allege the *jus cogens* character of the rule.

Barcelona Traction, Light and Power Company Limited Case (*Belgium* v *Spain*) (*Second Phase*)
ICJ Rep 1970 3, International Court of Justice

33. [An] essential distinction should be drawn between the obligations of a State towards the international community as a whole, and those arising *vis-à-vis* another State in the field of diplomatic protection. By their very nature the former are the concern of all States. In view of the importance of the rights involved, all States can be held to have a legal interest in their protection; they are obligations *erga omnes*.

34. Such obligations derive, for example, in contemporary international law, from the outlawing of acts of aggression, and of genocide, as also from the principles and rules concerning the basic rights of the human person, including protection from slavery and racial discrimination. Some of the corresponding rights of protection have entered into the body of general international law (*Reservations to the Convention on the Prevention and Punishment of the Crime of Genocide, Advisory Opinion, ICJ Rep 1951*, p. 23); others are conferred by international instruments of a universal or quasiuniversal character.

NOTES:
1. There is much dispute concerning the concept of *jus cogens*. Many of the parties to the Vienna Convention have expressed some hesitation in accepting the principle. As the effect of *jus cogens* is to make a treaty contrary to *jus cogens* void, its operation could infringe dramatically a State's express consent to treaties, and could also be a limitation on a State's sovereignty to undertake international obligations. Nevertheless, there seems to be widespread acceptance of the concept of *jus cogens*, perhaps as part of the beneficial development of an international public order. If it is accepted that there can be rules of international law which have the character of *jus cogens*, then it must logically follow that treaties which conflict with those rules are void. The concept of *jus cogens* has also been applied outside the treaty context to State responsibility more generally (see Chapter 11).
2. Despite this, there is no general consensus as to what are the rules of international public order which comprise *jus cogens*. Some of the suggested rules are given in the above extracts, with the assumption being that an *erga omnes* obligation (being an obligation that enables every State to bring a claim based on that obligation) reflects a rule of *jus cogens*. Other rules of *jus cogens* often suggested include the right of self-determination, at least for colonial territories, and the requirement to settle disputes peacefully (see Chapters 6 and 15). There are few examples of a treaty being declared, or even claimed, to be void on the ground of it being inconsistent with *jus cogens*, though this claim was made in the *East Timor Case (Portugal v Australia)* (see Chapter 6) and it is likely that most States would refrain from making such treaties.

3. State practice could not be inconsistent with *jus cogens*, as then the peremptory norm would not be accepted and recognised by the international community. Thus, a customary international law rule must exist before a rule of *jus cogens* arises. It seems that one State may not be able to prevent a rule of *jus cogens* forming and being applied against it, as the International Court of Justice in the *Namibia Opinion* ICJ Rep 1971 16 (see below) seemed to imply that there was a *jus cogens* rule prohibiting racial discrimination that could be applied against the racially discriminatory apartheid government of South Africa.

D: Unequal treaties

P. Wesley-Smith, *Unequal Treaty 1898–1997: China, Great Britain and Hong Kong's New Territories*
(1980), pp. 184–185

There is no doubt that the Convention of Peking 1898 [concerning the New Territories of Hong Kong] is an unequal treaty and is so considered by the Peoples' Republic of China: the circumstances in which it was negotiated were inconsistent with the sovereignty and equality of both contracting parties and its burdens and advantages are non-reciprocal. This does not necessarily mean, however, that it is invalid according to modern international law. Although duress has been recognized, both in the 1969 Vienna Convention on the Law of Treaties and by the International Court of Justice, as a factor which might vitiate a treaty, it is a concept which must be very restrictively interpreted, and it is doubtful that the Convention of Peking 1898, which arguably was not brought about by force or even the explicit threat of force, can be considered invalid on this ground. The doctrine of changed circumstances (*rebus sic stantibus*) was frequently relied upon by nationalistic Chinese polemicists in the first decades of this century, and the Chinese delegation to Paris in 1919 specifically referred to the complete change in the balance of power since 1898 to justify 'retrocession' of leased territories. But this too has been approached cautiously by the international community and is of dubious application to the New Territories convention.

The notion is gradually developing, however, that inequality may itself be a sufficient ground for disputing the validity of a treaty. First, an unequal treaty could be void from the beginning (*ab initio*), without any effect in international law at any time; such a treaty would be incapable of abrogation or repudiation, for it has never subsisted as an agreement between the parties. Secondly, an unequal treaty could be not void but voidable, able to be annulled because of its inherent defects yet effective until annulment. In this second case it must further be determined who may abrogate the voidable unequal treaty, in what circumstances, and how.

NOTE:
There is no international consensus that inequality is a ground of invalidity of a treaty. The time of testing whether a treaty is invalid was given by the International Court of Justice in the *Namibia Opinion*, ICJ Rep 1971 16, at p. 31, where it was stated that 'an international instrument has to be interpreted and applied within the framework of the entire legal system prevailing at the time of the interpretation'.

E: Procedure for invoking the invalidity of a treaty

Vienna Convention on the Law of Treaties 1969

Article 65 Procedure to be followed with respect to invalidity, termination, withdrawal from or suspension of the operation of a treaty

1. A party which, under the provisions of the present Convention, invokes either a defect in its consent to be bound by a treaty or a ground for impeaching the validity of a treaty, terminating it, withdrawing from it or suspending its operation, must notify the other parties of its claim. The notification shall indicate the measure proposed to be taken with respect to the treaty and the reasons therefor.

2. If, after the expiry of a period which, except in cases of special urgency, shall not be less than three months after the receipt of the notification, no party has raised any objection, the party making the notification may carry out in the manner provided in article 67 the measure which it has proposed.

3. If, however, objection has been raised by any other party, the parties shall seek a solution through the means indicated in Article 33 of the Charter of the United Nations. . . .

5. Without prejudice to article 45, the fact that a State has not previously made the notification prescribed in paragraph 1 shall not prevent it from making such notification in answer to another party claiming performance of the treaty or alleging its violation.

Article 69 Consequences of the invalidity of a treaty

1. A treaty the invalidity of which is established under the present Convention is void. The provisions of a void treaty have no legal force.

2. If acts have nevertheless been performed in reliance on such a treaty:
    (a) each party may require any other party to establish as far as possible in their mutual relations the position that would have existed if the acts had not been performed;
    (b) acts performed in good faith before the invalidity was invoked are not rendered unlawful by reason only of the invalidity of the treaty.

3. In cases falling under articles 49, 50, 51 or 52, paragraph 2 does not apply with respect to the party to which the fraud, the act of corruption or the coercion is imputable.

4. In the case of the invalidity of a particular State's consent to be bound by a multilateral treaty, the foregoing rules apply in the relations between that State and the parties to the treaty.

Article 71 Consequences of the invalidity of a treaty which conflicts with a peremptory norm of general international law

1. In the case of a treaty which is void under article 53 the parties shall:
    (a) eliminate as far as possible the consequences of any act performed in reliance on any provision which conflicts with the peremptory norm of general international law; and
    (b) bring their mutual relations into conformity with the peremptory norm of general international law.

2. In the case of a treaty which becomes void and terminates under article 64, the termination of the treaty:
    (a) releases the parties from any obligation further to perform the treaty;
    (b) does not affect any right, obligation or legal situation of the parties created through the execution of the treaty prior to its termination; provided that those rights, obligations or situations may thereafter be maintained only to the extent that their maintenance is not in itself in conflict with the new peremptory norm of general international law.

SECTION 7: **Termination of treaties**

It is a consequence of a breach of some treaty obligations that an entitlement to terminate the treaty arises in the party or parties affected by the breach. There are certain grounds set out in the Vienna Convention that enable a party to proceed to terminate a treaty, though these can be waived (Article 45).

A: Grounds for termination

Vienna Convention on the Law of Treaties 1969

Article 45 Loss of a right to invoke a ground for invalidating, terminating, withdrawing from or suspending the operation of a treaty
A State may no longer invoke a ground for invalidating, terminating, withdrawing from or suspending the operation of a treaty under Articles 46 to 50 or Articles 60 and 62 if, after becoming aware of the facts:
> (a) it shall have expressly agreed that the treaty is valid or remains in force or continues in operation, as the case may be; or
> (b) it must by reason of its conduct be considered as having acquiesced in the validity of the treaty or in its maintenance in force or in operation, as the case may be.

Article 54 Termination of or withdrawal from a treaty under its provisions or by consent of the parties
The termination of a treaty or the withdrawal of a party may take place:
> (a) in conformity with the provisions of the treaty; or
> (b) at any time by consent of all the parties after consultation with the other contracting States.

Article 56 Denunciation of or withdrawal from a treaty containing no provision regarding termination, denunciation or withdrawal
1. A treaty which contains no provision regarding its termination and which does not provide for denunciation or withdrawal is not subject to denunciation or withdrawal unless:
> (a) it is established that the parties intended to admit the possibility of denunciation or withdrawal; or
> (b) a right of denunciation or withdrawal may be implied by the nature of the treaty.
2. A party shall give not less than twelve months' notice of its intention to denounce or withdraw from a treaty under paragraph 1.

Article 57 Suspension of the operation of a treaty under its provisions or by consent of the parties
The operation of a treaty in regard to all the parties or to a particular party may be suspended:
> (a) in conformity with the provisions of the treaty; or
> (b) at any time by consent of all the parties after consultation with the other contracting States.

Article 59 Termination or suspension of the operation of a treaty implied by conclusion of a later treaty

1. A treaty shall be considered as terminated if all the parties to it conclude a later treaty relating to the same subject-matter and:

(a) it appears from the later treaty or is otherwise established that the parties intended that the matter should be governed by that treaty; or

(b) the provisions of the later treaty are so far incompatible with those of the earlier one that the two treaties are not capable of being applied at the same time.

2. The earlier treaty shall be considered as only suspended in operation if it appears from the later treaty or is otherwise established that such was the intention of the parties.

Article 60 Termination or suspension of the operation of a treaty as a consequence of its breach

1. A material breach of a bilateral treaty by one of the parties entitles the other to invoke the breach as a ground for terminating the treaty or suspending its operation in whole or in part.

2. A material breach of a multilateral treaty by one of the parties entitles:

(a) the other parties by unanimous agreement to suspend the operation of the treaty in whole or in part or to terminate it either:

(i) in the relations between themselves and the defaulting State, or

(ii) as between all the parties;

(b) a party specially affected by the breach to invoke it as a ground for suspending the operation of the treaty in whole or in part in the relations between itself and the defaulting State;

(c) any party other than the defaulting State to invoke the breach as a ground for suspending the operation of the treaty in whole or in part with respect to itself if the treaty is of such a character that a material breach of its provisions by one party radically changes the position of every party with respect to the further performance of its obligations under the treaty.

3. A material breach of a treaty, for the purpose of this article, consists in:

(a) a repudiation of the treaty not sanctioned by the present Convention; or

(b) the violation of a provision essential to the accomplishment of the object or purpose of the treaty.

4. The foregoing paragraphs are without prejudice to any provision in the treaty applicable in the event of a breach.

5. Paragraphs 1 to 3 do not apply to provisions relating to the protection of the human person contained in treaties of a humanitarian character, in particular to provisions prohibiting any form of reprisals against persons protected by such treaties.

Article 61 Supervening impossibility of performance

1. A party may invoke the impossibility of performing a treaty as a ground for terminating or withdrawing from it if the impossibility results from the permanent disappearance or destruction of an object indispensable for the execution of the treaty. If the impossibility is temporary, it may be invoked only as a ground for suspending the operation of the treaty.

2. Impossibility of performance may not be invoked by a party as a ground for terminating, withdrawing from or suspending the operation of a treaty if the impossibility is the result of a breach by that party either of an obligation under the treaty or of any other international obligation owed to any other party to the treaty.

Article 62 Fundamental changes of circumstances

1. A fundamental change of circumstances which has occurred with regard to those existing

at the time of the conclusion of a treaty, and which was not foreseen by the parties, may not be invoked as a ground for terminating or withdrawing from the treaty unless:

    (a) the existence of those circumstances constituted an essential basis of the consent of the parties to be bound by the treaty; and

    (b) the effect of the change is radically to transform the extent of obligations still to be performed under the treaty.

2. A fundamental change of circumstances may not be invoked as a ground for terminating or withdrawing from a treaty:

    (a) if the treaty establishes a boundary; or

    (b) if the fundamental change is the result of a breach by the party invoking it either of an obligation under the treaty or of any other international obligation owed to any other party to the treaty.

3. If, under the foregoing paragraphs, a party may invoke a fundamental change of circumstances as a ground for terminating or withdrawing from a treaty it may also invoke the change as a ground for suspending the operation of the treaty.

Article 70 Consequences of the termination of a treaty

1. Unless the treaty otherwise provides or the parties otherwise agree, the termination of a treaty under its provisions or in accordance with the present Convention:

    (a)   releases the parties from any obligation further to perform the treaty;

    (b)   does not affect any right, obligation or legal situation of the parties created through the execution of the treaty prior to its termination.

2. If a State denounces or withdraws from a multilateral treaty, paragraph 1 applies in the relations between that State and each of the other parties to the treaty from the date when such denunciation or withdrawal takes effect.

Article 72 Consequences of the suspension of the operation of a treaty

1. Unless the treaty otherwise provides or the parties otherwise agree, the suspension of the operation of a treaty under its provisions or in accordance with the present Convention:

    (a) releases the parties between which the operation of the treaty is suspended from the obligation to perform the treaty in their mutual relations during the period of the suspension;

    (b) does not otherwise affect the legal relations between the parties established by the treaty.

2. During the period of the suspension the parties shall refrain from acts tending to obstruct the resumption of the operation of the treaty.

Report of the International Law Commission to the General Assembly
Yearbook of the International Law Commission (1966) vol II, 172, pp. 253–254, 257

(1) The great majority of jurists recognize that a violation of a treaty by one party may give rise to a right in the other party to abrogate the treaty or to suspend the performance of its own obligations under the treaty. A violation of a treaty obligation, as of any other obligation, may give rise to a right in the other party to take non-forcible reprisals, and these reprisals may properly relate to the defaulting party's rights under the treaty. Opinion differs, however, as to the extent of the right to abrogate the treaty and the conditions under which it may be exercised. Some jurists, in the absence of effective international machinery for securing the observance of treaties, are more impressed with the innocent party's need to have this right as a sanction for the violation of the treaty. They tend to formulate the right in unqualified terms, giving the innocent party a general right to abrogate the treaty in the event of a breach. Other jurists are more impressed with the risk that a State may allege a trivial or even fictitious breach simply to furnish a pretext for denouncing a treaty which it now finds

embarrassing. These jurists tend to restrict the right of denunciation to 'material' or 'fundamental' breaches and also to subject the exercise of the right to procedural conditions.

(2) State practice does not give great assistance in determining the true extent of this right or the proper conditions for its exercise. In many cases, the denouncing State has decided for quite other reasons to put an end to the treaty and, having alleged the violation primarily to provide a pretext for its action, has not been prepared to enter into a serious discussion of the legal principles involved. The other party has usually contested the denunciation primarily on the basis of the facts; and, if it has sometimes used language appearing to deny that *unilateral* denunciation is ever justified, this has usually appeared rather to be a protest against the one-sided and arbitrary pronouncements of the denouncing State than a rejection of the right to denounce when serious violations are established.

Fisheries Jurisdiction Case (*United Kingdom* v *Iceland*) (*Jurisdiction*)
ICJ Rep 1973 3, International Court of Justice

The United Kingdom, as part of what was known as 'the Cod War', applied to the Court claiming that the proposed extension of Iceland's exclusive fisheries jurisdiction from 12 miles to 50 miles was a breach of an agreement between the two States, evidenced by an Exchange of Notes in 1961. Iceland contended that the Court had no jurisdiction to hear the case and it also submitted that any agreement that it had with the United Kingdom not to extend its fisheries jurisdiction, was no longer binding due to a fundamental change of circumstances since that agreement.

The Court decided that it did have jurisdiction. It also considered that Art. 62 of the Vienna Convention on the Law of Treaties represented customary international law.

37. One of the basic requirements embodied in [Article 62] is that the change of circumstances must have been a fundamental one. In this respect the Government of Iceland has, with regard to developments in fishing techniques, referred ... to the increased exploitation of the fishery resources in the seas surrounding Iceland and to the danger of still further exploitation because of an increase in the catching capacity of fishing fleets. The Icelandic statements recall the exceptional dependence of that country on its fishing for its existence and economic development. . . .

38. The invocation by Iceland of its 'vital interests', which were not made the subject of an express reservation to the acceptance of the jurisdictional obligation under the 1961 Exchange of Notes, must be interpreted, in the context of the assertion of changed circumstances, as an indication by Iceland of the reason why it regards as fundamental the changes which in its view have taken place in previously existing fishing techniques. This interpretation would correspond to the traditional view that the changes of circumstances which must be regarded as fundamental or vital are those which imperil the existence or vital development of one of the parties.

43. Moreover, in order that a change of circumstances may give rise to a ground for invoking the termination of a treaty it is also necessary that it should have resulted in a radical transformation of the extent of the obligations still to be performed. The change must have increased the burden of the obligations to be executed to the extent of rendering the performance something essentially different from that originally undertaken. In respect of the obligation with which the Court is here concerned, this condition is wholly unsatisfied; the change of circumstances alleged by Iceland cannot be said to have transformed radically the extent of the jurisdictional obligation which is imposed in the 1961 Exchange of Notes. The compromissory clause enabled either of the parties to

submit to the Court any dispute between them relating to an extension of Icelandic fisheries jurisdiction in the waters above its continental shelf beyond the 12-mile limit. The present dispute is exactly of the character anticipated in the compromissory clause of the Exchange of Notes. Not only has the jurisdictional obligation not been radically transformed in its extent; it has remained precisely what it was in 1961.

Namibia Opinion
ICJ Rep 1971 16, International Court of Justice

The Security Council had resolved that South Africa's Mandate over South-West Africa (Namibia) was terminated, but this had been ignored by South Africa. The Security Council then resolved, by Resolution 276 (1970), that the continued presence of South Africa in Namibia was illegal, as had General Assembly Resolution 2145 (XXI). It sought an advisory opinion from the Court, asking what were the legal consequences for States of the continued presence of South Africa in Namibia notwithstanding Resolution 276 (1970). The Court held that South Africa was under an obligation to withdraw its administration in Namibia. It also held that other States were under an obligation not to recognise any acts by South Africa's administration in Namibia (see Chapter 6).

94. In examining this action of the General Assembly [under Resolution 2145 (XXI)] it is appropriate to have regard to the general principles of international law regulating termination of a treaty relationship on account of breach. For even if the mandate is viewed as having the character of an institution, as is maintained, it depends on those international agreements which created the system and regulated its application. As the Court indicated in 1962 "this Mandate, like practically all other similar Mandates" was "a special type of instrument composite in nature and instituting a novel international régime. It incorporates a definite agreement . . ." (ICJ Rep 1962, p. 331). The Court stated conclusively in that Judgment that the Mandate ". . . in fact and in law, is an international agreement having the character of a treaty or convention" (ICJ Rep 1962, p. 330). The rules laid down by the Vienna Convention on the Law of Treaties concerning termination of a treaty relationship on account of breach (adopted without a dissenting vote) may in many respects be considered as a codification of existing customary law on the subject. In the light of these rules, only a material breach of a treaty justifies termination, such breach being defined as:

(a) a repudiation of the treaty not sanctioned by the present Convention; or
(b) the violation of a provision essential to the accomplishment of the object or purpose of the treaty" (Art. 60, para. 3).

95. General Assembly resolution 2145 (XXI) determines that both forms of material breach had occurred in this case. By stressing that South Africa "has, in fact, disavowed the Mandate", the General Assembly declared in fact that it had repudiated it. The resolution in question is therefore to be viewed as the exercise of the right to terminate a relationship in case of a deliberate and persistent violation of obligations which destroys the very object and purpose of that relationship.

96. It has been contended that the Covenant of the League of Nations did not confer on the Council of the League power to terminate a mandate for misconduct of the mandatory and that no such power could therefore be exercised by the United Nations, since it could not derive from the League greater powers than the latter itself had. For this objection to prevail it would be necessary to show that the mandates system, as established under the League, excluded the application of the general principle of law that a right of termination on account of breach must be presumed to exist in respect of all treaties, except as regards provisions relating to the protection of the human person contained in treaties of a humanitarian character (as indicated in Art. 60, para. 5, of the Vienna

Convention). The silence of a treaty as to the existence of such a right cannot be interpreted as implying the exclusion of a right which has its source outside the treaty, in general international law, and is dependent on the occurrence of circumstances which are not normally envisaged when a treaty is concluded. . . .

101. It has been suggested that, even if the Council of the League had possessed the power of revocation of the Mandate in an extreme case, it could not have been exercised unilaterally but only in co-operation with the mandatory Power. However, revocation could only result from a situation in which the Mandatory had committed a serious breach of the obligations it had undertaken. To contend, on the basis of the principle of unanimity which applied in the League of Nations, that in this case revocation could only take place with the concurrence of the Mandatory, would not only run contrary to the general principle of law governing termination on account of breach, but also postulate an impossibility. For obvious reasons, the consent of the wrongdoer to such a from of termination cannot be required.

Danube Dam Case (Hungary v Slovakia)
7 ICJ Rep 1997 7, International Court of Justice

In 1977, Hungary and Czechoslovakia concluded a treaty to facilitate the construction of dams on the Danube River. Hungary later suspended works due to environmental concerns in response to which Czechoslovakia carried out unilateral measures. Slovakia became a party to the 1977 Treaty as successor to Czechoslovakia (see above on succession). Hungary then claimed the right to terminate the treaty, at which point the dispute was submitted to the International Court of Justice. Hungary also submitted that it was entitled to terminate the Treaty on the ground that Czechoslovakia/Slovakia had violated Articles of the Treaty by undertaking unilateral measures, culminating in the diversion of the Danube. The Court rejected Hungary's claim to terminate the treaty.

100. The 1977 Treaty does not contain any provision regarding its termination . . .

101. The Court will now turn to the first ground advanced by Hungary, that of the state of necessity. In this respect, the Court will merely observe that, even if a state of necessity is found to exist, it is not a ground for the termination of a treaty. It may only be invoked to exonerate from its responsibility a State which has failed to implement a treaty . . .

102. Hungary also relied on the principle of the impossibility of performance as reflected in Article 61 . . . [I]f the joint exploitation of the investment was no longer possible, this was originally because Hungary did not carry out most of the works for which it was responsible . . .; Article 61, paragraph 2, of the Vienna Convention expressly provides that impossibility of performance may not be invoked for the termination of a treaty by a party to that treaty when it results from that party's own breach of an obligation flowing from that treaty. . . .

104. Hungary further argued that it was entitled to invoke a number of events which, cumulatively, would have constituted a fundamental change of circumstances [changes of a political nature, the reduced economic viability of the Project, and the progress of environmental knowledge and international environmental law] . . . The changed circumstances advanced by Hungary are, in the Court's view, not of such a nature . . . that their effect would radically transform the extent of the obligations still to be performed in order to accomplish the Project. A fundamental change of circumstances must have been unforeseen; the existence of the circumstances must have constituted an essential basis of the consent of the parties to be bound by the treaty . . .

106. . . . [I]t is only a material breach of the treaty itself, by a State party to that treaty, which

entitles the other party to rely on it as a ground for terminating the treaty. The violation of other treaty rules or of rules of general international law may justify the taking of certain measures, including countermeasures, by the injured State, but it does not constitute a ground for termination under the law of treaties. . . .

108. . . . Czechoslovakia violated the Treaty only when it diverted the waters of the Danube into the bypass canal in October 1992. In constructing the works which would lead to the putting into operation of [the unilateral measure], Czechoslovakia did not act unlawfully.

In the Court's view, therefore, the notification of termination by Hungary on 19 May 1992 was premature.

NOTES:

1. A treaty can be terminated by the consent of the parties (Article 54). The main grounds in the Vienna Convention of contested termination are material breach (Article 60) and fundamental change of circumstances (Article 62). In both cases the Vienna Convention represents customary international law (see 2(ii) above). However, as can be seen in the above extracts from the *Fisheries Jurisdiction Case*, the *Namibia Opinion* and the *Danube Dam Case*, it can be difficult for a State to show evidence sufficient to prove that there has been a breach of a treaty that entitles a State to terminate the treaty.

2. A State cannot invoke its internal law as a justification for a failure to comply with a treaty unless it was objectively manifestly obvious to any State that the first State's consent to be bound by a treaty was contrary to an internal law of fundamental importance to that first State (Articles 27 and 46, Vienna Convention).

3. It is possible to suspend the operation of a treaty for a period of time, as an alternative to complete termination (Article 57). In certain instances, a treaty provision may be separated from the rest of the treaty (Article 44). There is no right of unilateral denunciation of a treaty, due to the principle of State's consent. The procedures for termination are set out in Articles 65 to 68, which provide procedural safeguards to afford the opportunity to a State which has breached a treaty to rectify its breach.

B: Other aspects of termination

Rainbow Warrior Arbitration (New Zealand v France)
82 ILR (1990) 499, Special Arbitration Tribunal

In 1985, French agents sank the Greenpeace ship, 'Rainbow Warrior', while it was in New Zealand waters. The dispute was referred to the Secretary-General of the United Nations, whose decision was accepted by the two States and formalised in a 1986 treaty. This treaty provided, *inter alia*, that the French agents would be transferred to a French military facility on the island of Hao for a period of not less than three years, except with the mutual consent of both States. Before the three-year period had elapsed, both agents had left the island without the consent of New Zealand. France was not a party to the Vienna Convention.

The Tribunal decided that France had breached its treaty obligations. It then examined the issue of whether this breach could be justified. The Tribunal decided that France had committed a violation of its international obligations. They held that the only damage was of a moral, political and legal nature so the remedy given was a declaration that France had breached international law.

75. . . . [F]or the decision of the present case, both the customary Law of Treaties and the

customary Law of State Responsibility are relevant and applicable. The customary Law of Treaties, as codified in the Vienna Convention, proclaimed in Article 26, under the title 'Pacta sunt servanda' that 'Every treaty in force is binding upon the parties to it and must be performed by them in good faith.' This fundamental provision is applicable to the determination whether there have been violations of that principle, and in particular, whether material breaches of treaty obligations have been committed.

Moreover, certain specific provisions of customary law in the Vienna Convention are relevant in this case, such as Article 60, which gives a precise definition of the concept of a material breach of a treaty, and Article 70, which deals with the legal consequences of the expiry of a treaty.

On the other hand, the legal consequences of a breach of a treaty, including the determination of the circumstances that may exclude wrongfulness (and render the breach only apparent) and the appropriate remedies for breach, are subjects that belong to the customary Law of State Responsibility.

The reason is that the general principles of International Law concerning State responsibility are equally applicable in the case of breach of treaty obligation, since in the international law field there is no distinction between contractual and tortious responsibility, so that any violation by a State of any obligation, of whatever origin, gives rise to State responsibility and consequently, to the duty of reparation. The particular treaty itself might of course limit or extend the general Law of State Responsibility, for instance by establishing a system of remedies for it.

The Permanent Court proclaimed this fundamental principle in the *Chorzow Factory (Jurisdiction)* case, stating:

> It is a principle of international law that the breach of an engagement involves an obligation to make reparation in an adequate form. Reparation, therefore, is the indispensable complement of a failure to apply a convention. (PCIJ, Series A, Nos. 9, 21 (1927)).

And the present Court has said:

> It is clear that refusal to fulfil a treaty obligation involves international responsibility. (*Peace Treaties* (second phase) 1950, ICJ Reports 221, 228).

The conclusion to be reached on this issue is that, without prejudice to the terms of the [1986 treaty] which the Parties signed and the applicability of certain important provisions of the Vienna Convention on the Law of Treaties, the existence in this case of circumstances excluding wrongfulness as well as the questions of appropriate remedies, should be answered in the context and in the light of the customary Law of State Responsibility.

NOTES:
1. A treaty can expressly provide for grounds of termination and processes for termination. In the absence of any express provision, the Vienna Convention should apply (see *Danube Dam Case*, above).
2. The law on State Responsibility (see Chapter 11) could give rise to other grounds relevant to termination. The Tribunal in the *Rainbow Warrior Case* (as confirmed in the *Danube Dam Case*) allowed a State to seek to justify its breach of a treaty obligation by relying on the exceptions within the law of State responsibility (for example, *force majeure* and distress). A similar decision was made by an Arbitration Tribunal in the *Air Services Agreement Case (France v United States)* 18 RIAA (1978) 416 where, in an action by a State to terminate a treaty in accordance with the procedures of the Vienna Convention, the issue of counter-measures was considered relevant.

4

International Law and National Law

Introductory note

The interaction between international law and national (or 'municipal' or 'domestic') law demonstrates the struggle between State sovereignty and the international legal order. While the international legal order seeks to organise international society in accordance with the general interests of the international community, State sovereignty can be used to protect a State against the intervention of international law into its national legal system. However, as international law expands into areas such as human rights and the environment (see Chapters 6 and 12), there has been a reduction in the areas of law which can be considered to be governed solely by the national law of a State.

While the tension between these two systems is often explained by reference to monistic or dualistic theories (see below), the resolution of this struggle is usually determined by the constitution of each State – the constitution having been created by political acts – and by the interpretation of the constitution and national laws by the national courts of each State. As a consequence, the application of international law within a national legal system will vary from State to State. Further, the lack of significant enforcement measures in international law has meant that it is often through national courts that international law is enforced, and therefore national law can often determine the effectiveness of international legal decisions and the lawfulness of international actions.

SECTION 1: **Theories**

H. Lauterpacht, *Oppenheim's International Law*
vol 1 (8th edn, 1955), pp. 37–39

According to what may be called the dualistic view, the Law of Nations and the Municipal Law of the several States are essentially different from each other. They differ, first, as regards their sources. The sources of Municipal Law are custom grown up within the boundaries of the State concerned and statutes enacted by the law-giving authority. The sources of International Law are custom grown up among States and law-making treaties concluded by them.

The Law of Nations and Municipal Law differ, secondly, regarding the relations they regulate.

Municipal Law regulates relations between the individuals under the sway of a State and the relations between the State and the individual. International Law, on the other hand, regulates relations between States.

The Law of Nations and Municipal Law differ, thirdly, with regard to the substance of their law: whereas Municipal Law is a law of a sovereign over individuals subjected to his sway, the Law of Nations is a law not above, but between, sovereign States, and is therefore a weaker law.

If the Law of Nations and Municipal Law differ as demonstrated, the Law of Nations can neither as a body nor in parts be *per se* a part of Municipal Law. Just as Municipal Law lacks the power of altering or creating rules of International Law, so the latter lacks absolutely the power of altering or creating rules of Municipal Law. If, according to the Municipal Law of an individual State, the Law of Nations as a body or in parts is considered to be part of the law of the land, this can only be so either by municipal custom or by statute, and then the respective rules of the Law of Nations have by adoption become at the same time rules of Municipal Law. Wherever and whenever such total or partial adoption has not taken place, municipal courts cannot be considered to be bound by International Law, because it has, *per se*, no power over municipal courts. And if it happens that a rule of Municipal Law is in indubitable conflict with a rule of the Law of Nations, municipal courts must apply the former. . . .

The above dualistic view is opposed by what may conveniently be called the monistic doctrine. The latter rejects all three premises of the dualists. It denies, in the first instance, that the subjects of the two systems of law are essentially different and maintains that in both it is ultimately the conduct of the individuals which is regulated by law, the only difference being that in the international sphere the consequences of such conduct are attributed to the State. Secondly, it asserts that in both spheres law is essentially a command binding upon the subjects of the law independently of their will. Thirdly, it maintains that International Law and Municipal Law, far from being essentially different, must be regarded as manifestations of a single conception of law. This is so not only for the terminological reason that it would be improper to give the same designation of law to two fundamentally different sets of rules governing the same conduct. The main reason for the essential identity of the two spheres of law is, it is maintained, that some of the fundamental notions of International Law cannot be comprehended without the assumption of a superior legal order from which the various systems of Municipal Law are, in a sense, derived by way of delegation. It is International Law which determines the jurisdictional limits of the personal and territorial competence of States. Similarly, it is only by reference to a higher legal rule in relation to which they are all equal, that the equality and independence of a number of sovereign States can be conceived. Failing that superior legal order, the science of law would be confronted with the spectacle of some sixty sovereign States [as at 1955] each claiming to be the absolutely highest and underived authority. It is admitted that municipal courts may be bound by the law of their States to enforce statutes which are contrary to International Law. But this, it may be said, merely shows that, in view of the weakness of International Law and organisation, States admit and tolerate what is actually a conflict of duties within the same legal system – a phenomenon not altogether unknown in other spheres of Municipal Law. In any case, from the point of view of International Law the validity of a pronouncement of a municipal court is in such case purely provisional. It still leaves intact the international responsibility of the State. It is a well recognised rule that a State is internationally responsible for the decisions of its courts, even if given in conformity with the law of the State concerned, whenever that law happens to be contrary to International Law.

G. Fitzmaurice, 'The General Principles of International Law Considered from the Standpoint of the Rule of Law'

(1957-II) 92 RC 5, pp. 70–71, 79–80

First of all . . ., a radical view of the whole subject may be propounded to the effect that the entire monist-dualist controversy is unreal, artificial and strictly beside the point, because it assumes something that has to exist for there to be any controversy at all – and which in fact does not exist – namely a *common field* in which the two legal orders under discussion both simultaneously have their spheres of activity. It is proposed here to state the case for this view. In order that there can be controversy about whether the relations between two orders are relations of *co-ordination* between self-existent independent orders, or relations of *subordination* of the one to the other, or of the other to the one – or again whether they are part of the same order, but both subordinate to a superior order – it is necessary that they should both be purporting to be, and in fact be, applicable in the same field – that is, to the same set of relations and transactions. . . .

International and domestic law having no common field, there is no need, nor would there be any point in discussing whether their relationship is one of co-ordination, or of subordination one to another, or of mutual subordination to a common superior order. There is no more point in discussing the abstract question of supremacy in regard to these two legal orders than, as has been seen, there would be in discussing whether abstract supremacy lay with English or French law. Such a question is necessarily meaningless. Each is supreme in its own field, and all that matters for this purpose is that international law is supreme in the international field. The very question of supremacy as between the two orders, national and international, is irrelevant, as is also that of the existence of some superior norm or order conferring supremacy. National law is not and cannot be a rival to international law in the international field, or it would cease to be national and become international, which, *ex hypothesi*, it is not. National law, *by definition*, cannot govern the action of, or relations with, other States. It may govern or fetter the action of its own State in such a way that the latter cannot fulfil its international obligations, but again, by definition only at the national level and without legal effect or operation beyond it. Formally, therefore, international and domestic law as *systems* can never come into conflict. What may occur is something strictly different, namely a conflict of *obligations*, or an inability for the State *on the domestic plane* to act in the manner required by international law. The supremacy of inter-national law in the international field does not in these circumstances entail that the judge in the municipal courts of the State must override local law and apply international law. Whether he does or can do this depends on the local law itself, and on what legislative or administrative steps can be or are taken to deal with the matter. The supremacy of international law in the international field simply means that if nothing can be or is done, the State will, on the international plane, have committed a breach of its international law obligations, for which it will be internationally respon-sible, and in respect of which it cannot plead the condition of its domestic law by way of absolu-tion. International law does not therefore in any way purport to govern the content of national law in the national field – nor does it need to. It simply says – and this is all it needs to say – that certain things are not valid according to international law, and that if a State in the application of its domestic law acts contrary to international law in these respects, it will commit a breach of its international obligations.

NOTES:
1. Lauterpacht indicates the two main theories dealing with the interaction between inter-national law and national law: dualism and monism. Fitzmaurice tries to take a median line by declaring that the systems of international law and national law have no common field, but his position is essentially dualist and is only descriptive not interpretative. Also, contrary to Fitzmaurice's view, the two systems do interact, for example, in human rights law and in economic law (Chapters 6 and 13).
2. While these theories are helpful in attempting to explain why international law and national law interact, rarely do courts or other judicial bodies reach conclusions on the issues before them by applying monism, dualism or any other theory (although see the reference to the 'dualistic' UK in *In Re Pinochet* [1999] 2 All ER 97). Instead, usually courts decide cases in the context of the particular constitutional rules and principles of the relevant State and in

accordance with that State's laws. As seen below, when courts do make use of theoretical approaches the terminology they use is often different from the international law terminology.

SECTION 2: National law on the international plane

As was shown in Chapter 2, national law can be of value when determining the sources of international law, particularly as it can be evidence of State practice as part of customary international law.

Brazilian Loans Case (France v Brazil)
PCIJ Ser A (1929) No 21, p. 124, Permanent Court of International Justice

In the context of a case concerning loans made by the Brazilian government, the Court had to consider the meaning and effect of French national law in a dispute between the two States.

Though bound to apply municipal law when circumstances so require, the Court, which is a tribunal of international law, and which, in this capacity, is deemed itself to know what this law is, is not obliged also to know the municipal law of the various countries. All that can be said in this respect is that the Court may possibly be obliged to obtain knowledge regarding the municipal law which has to be applied. And this it must do, either by means of evidence furnished it by the Parties or by means of any researches which the Court may think fit to undertake or to cause to be undertaken.

Once the Court has arrived at the conclusion that it is necessary to apply the municipal law of a particular country, there seems no doubt that it must seek to apply it as it would be applied in that country. It would not be applying the municipal law of a country if it were to apply it in a manner different from that in which that law would be applied in the country in which it is in force.

It follows that the Court must pay the utmost regard to the decisions of the municipal courts of a country, for it is with the aid of their jurisprudence that it will be enabled to decide what are the rules which, in actual fact, are applied in the country the law of which is recognized as applicable in a given case. If the Court were obliged to disregard the decisions of municipal courts, the result would be that it might in certain circumstances apply rules other than those actually applied; this would seem to be contrary to the whole theory on which the application of municipal law is based.

Of course the Court will endeavour to make a just appreciation of the jurisprudence of municipal courts. If this is uncertain or divided, it will rest with the Court to select the interpretation which it considers most in conformity with the law. But to compel the Court to disregard that jurisprudence would not be in conformity with its function when applying municipal law.

Barcelona Traction, Light and Power Company Limited Case (Belgium v Spain) (Second Phase)
ICJ Rep 1970 3, International Court of Justice

The issue arose in this case as to whether the national law concept of 'the company' was applicable in international law. As to the law regarding the nationality of the companies see the extract in Chapter 11.

37. In seeking to determine the law applicable to this case, the Court has to bear in mind the continuous evolution of international law. . . . These . . . changes have given birth to municipal

institutions, which have transcended frontiers and have begun to exercise considerable influence on international relations. One of these phenomena which has a particular bearing on the present case is the corporate entity.

38. In this field international law is called upon to recognize institutions of municipal law that have an important and extensive role in the international field. This does not necessarily imply drawing any analogy between its own institutions and those of municipal law, nor does it amount to making rules of international law dependent upon categories of municipal law. All it means is that international law has had to recognize the corporate entity as an institution created by States in a domain essentially within their domestic jurisdiction. This in turn requires that, whenever legal issues arise concerning the rights of States with regard to the treatment of companies and shareholders, as to which rights international law has not established its own rules, it has to refer to the relevant rules of municipal law. Consequently, in view of the relevance to the present case of the rights of the corporate entity and its shareholders under municipal law, the Court must devote attention to the nature and interrelation of those rights. . . .

50. In turning now to the international legal aspects of the case, the Court must, as already indicated, start from the fact that the present case essentially involves factors derived from municipal law – the distinction and the community between the company and the shareholder – which the Parties, however widely their interpretations may differ, each take as the point of departure of their reasoning. If the Court were to decide the case in disregard of the relevant institutions of municipal law it would, without justification, invite serious legal difficulties. It would lose touch with reality, for there are no corresponding institutions of international law to which the Court could resort. Thus the Court has, as indicated, not only to take cognizance of municipal law but also to refer to it. It is to rules generally accepted by municipal legal systems which recognize the limited company whose capital is represented by shares, and not to the municipal law of a particular State, that international law refers. In referring to such rules, the Court cannot modify, still less deform them.

Vienna Convention on the Law of Treaties 1969
1155 UNTS 331

Article 27   Internal law and observance of treaties
A party may not invoke the provisions of its internal law as justification for its failure to perform a treaty. This rule is without prejudice to Article 46.

Article 46   Provisions of internal law regarding competence to conclude treaties
1. A State may not invoke the fact that its consent to be bound by a treaty has been expressed in violation of a provision of its internal law regarding competence to conclude treaties as invalidating its consent unless that violation was manifest and concerned a rule of its internal law of fundamental importance.

2. A violation is manifest if it would be objectively evident to any State conducting itself in the matter in accordance with normal practice and in good faith.

NOTES:
1. As national courts are a part of the State – the State often being defined as comprising the executive, the legislature and the judiciary – the decisions of those courts, as well as the national law itself, can help to clarify the content of international law. As such, national law forms a part of the sources of international law (see Chapter 2).
2. Articles 27 and 46 of the Vienna Convention reflect customary international law in providing

that a State cannot rely on its national law as a justification for a breach of its international obligations (see *Polish Nationals in Danzig Case*, PCIJ Ser A/B (1932) No 44, 24). If a change in national law is required in order to enable a State to fulfil its international obligations, then the State must make that change or else mitigate its international responsibility by taking action under international law. International tribunals do award damages for injury arising out of decisions of national courts which have breached international law.

SECTION 3: **International law on the national plane**

A. Cassese, *International Law*
(2001), pp. 168–171, 180

Generally speaking, in the second half of the twentieth century, domestic systems gradually opened the door to international values and States became increasingly willing to bow to international law. Although each State is free to choose its own mechanism for implementing international rules, even a cursory survey of national legal systems shows that two basic modalities prevail.

The first is *automatic standing incorporation* of international rules. Such incorporation occurs whenever the national constitution, or a law (or, in the case of judge-made law, judicial decisions) enjoin that all State officials as well as all nationals and other individuals living on the territory of the State are bound to apply certain present or future rules of international law. In other words, an internal rule provides in a permanent way for the automatic incorporation into national law of any relevant rule of international (customary or treaty) law, without there being any need for the passing of an ad hoc national statute (subject to the exception of non-self-executing international rules). . . .

The second mechanism is *legislative ad hoc incorporation* of international rules. Under this system international rules become applicable within the State legal system only if and when the relevant parliamentary authorities pass *specific* implementing legislation. This legislation may take one of two principal forms. First, it may consist of an act of parliament translating the various treaty provisions into national legislation, setting out in detail the various obligations, powers, and rights stemming from those international provisions (*statutory ad hoc incorporation of international rules*). Second, the act of parliament may confine itself to enjoining the automatic applicability of the international rule within the national legal system, without reformulating that rule ad hoc (*automatic ad hoc incorporation of international law*). Thus, *in substance*, this mechanism works in a similar way to the one that we have termed above automatic standing incorporation (the only difference being that now the incorporation is effected on a case by case basis). In this case as well, State officials, and all the individuals concerned, become duty bound to abide by the international provisions to which the act of parliament makes reference. . . .

A survey of national legislation and case law shows that some States tend to put the international rules incorporated into the national legal system (whether automatically or through ad hoc legislative enactment) on the same footing as national legislation of domestic origin. As a consequence, the general principles governing relationships between rules having the same rank apply: *lex posterior derogat priori* (a subsequent law repeals or modifies or at any rate supersedes a previous law), *lex specialis derogat generali* (a special law prevails over a general law), *lex posterior generalis non derogat priori speciali* (a subsequent general law does not derogate from a prior special law). It follows that the national legislature may at any time pass a law amending or repealing a rule of international origin. True, in this case the State, if it applies the national law in lieu of the international rule, incurs international responsibility for a breach of international law. The fact remains, however, that the international rule is set aside by a simple act of parliament.

In contrast, other States tend to accord international rules a status and rank higher than that of national legislation. Such an approach is normally linked to the nature of their national constitution. Where the constitution is flexible (that is, it can be amended by simple Act of Parliament, or in any case the principle of legislative supremacy obtains), the only way of giving international rules overriding importance would be to entrench them, so that it is not possible for legislation passed by simple majority to modify them. Such a course of action, however, does not seem to have occurred so far in those States which have a flexible constitution.

Things are different where the constitution is rigid, in particular where it is 'functionally rigid' (that is, the constitution lays down special requirements for constitutional amendments and in addition sets up a court authorized to undertake judicial review of legislation so as to establish whether the legislature exceeds its powers and infringes the constitution). In these constitutional systems, if the constitution provides for the incorporation of international rules, normally those rules enjoy constitutional or quasi-constitutional status and therefore rank higher than normal law. It follows that the legislature is precluded from passing a law contrary to an international rule, unless of course this law is enacted through the special procedure required for constitutional legislation. The logic behind this approach is that international legal standards should always be regarded as having overriding importance. Therefore, in addition to binding the executive branch and all citizens, they cannot be set aside by simple parliamentary majority. Only under special circumstances, when compelling national interests prevail and a special majority (say, a two-thirds majority) is mustered in parliament, may those rules be overridden.

States tend to regulate national incorporation of international rules on the basis of two different requirements. First, they may have to choose between a statist (or nationalist) and an internationalist approach. Second, they may have to take into account the question of the relationship between the executive and legislative branch of government, and shape the mechanism for implementing international law accordingly. States choosing a statist or nationalist approach incline (i) to adopt legislative ad hoc incorporation and (ii) to put international rules on the same footing as national legislation of domestic origin. In contrast, States taking an international outlook tend (i) to opt for the automatic incorporation (whether standing or ad hoc) of international rules and (ii) to accord international rules a status and rank higher than that of national legislation. . . .

In sum, most States do not accord primacy to international rules in their national legal systems. Thus, it may be concluded that most members of the world community tend to play down the possible role of international legal standards in their domestic legal setting. This does not mean that they normally and systematically disregard international norms. The contrary is rather the rule. The failure of States to accord to international law pride of place in their legal systems only means that they do not intend to tie their hands formally, at the constitutional or legislative level. In other words, subject to the few exceptions already referred to [e.g. Greece, The Netherlands and Spain], States ultimately prefer not to enshrine in their constitutions or in their laws a firm and irrevocable commitment to unqualified observance of all international rules. To limit, at least in part, the markedly statist outlook taken by many States, courts may play a crucial role by stepping in to ensure compliance at the national level with international legal standards. Whenever their national legislation does not provide them with the legal means for making international values prevail, they have at least two interpretative principles available: that concerning the presumption in favour of international treaties, and the principle of speciality. . . . By judiciously resorting to either of these principles courts may make international law advance in a significant way.

Basic Law (*Grundgesetz*) of Germany

Article 25

The general rules of international law shall form part of federal law. They shall take precedence over the laws and create rights and duties directly for the inhabitants of the federal territory.

M. Kirby, 'Domestic Implementation of of International Human Rights Norms'

5 *Australian Journal of Human Rights* (1999) 109, 124–125

The age of reconciliation of international and national law has dawned. . . . It is a development as natural to the age as jumbo jets, international informatics, pandemics, global warming and the international economy. In this little planet, we are all ultimately bound together. Diminution in the human rights of others endangers peace and security elsewhere and offends the sensibilities of people everywhere, who are increasingly well informed on such matters. . . . [This] clearly involves the evolution of a new relationship between international and national law. The new relationship is coming, as [seen by] the many cases which require the application of international law, . . . by the use of international human rights jurisprudence filling the gaps of the [national] law and . . . it is coming as an interpretative principle to assist in the ascertainment of the meaning of national constitutions where they provide guarantees of fundamental rights and freedoms. It is an exciting and construct- ive time of legal creativity. But the ultimate question is whether judges and other lawyers, trained until now to think strictly in jurisdictional terms, can adapt their minds to a new way of thinking that is harmonious to the realities of the world about them.

NOTES:

1. Cassese notes the variety of methods that national law takes in relation to international law. He shows that the particular constitutional rules and principles of the relevant State, and its overall response to international law, determine how national law interacts with inter- national law. He and Kirby also indicate how the growing interdependence of States, global- isation and the increasing amount of international law all have an impact on national law.

2. Even where the Constitution appears to provide clear direct application of international law, in many cases, as in Germany and the United States (discussed below), this is still subject to interpretation by a Constitutional Court to ensure that the resulting national law (created by international law) is consistent with the constitution. Constitutional provisions incorporat- ing treaties and international customary law are often restrictively applied by national courts, and can be overridden by contrary national legislation and by inconsistent provisions of the constitution. In addition, evidence of customary law must be proved to the satisfaction of the national court and it is often the case that if a treaty is to be fully effective in national law then it will have to be incorporated in legislation generally.

3. While, as shown below, the United Kingdom applies a different approach to the incorpor- ation of international treaties than to the incorporation of international customary law, this distinction is not made in many other European States. While most Commonwealth States inherited versions of the common law developed in the United Kingdom, they usually also have a single document constitution. However, the majority have no constitutional provi- sion dealing with the impact of international law on national legal systems. As a result, national courts in Commonwealth States have generally adopted a similar approach to that employed in the United Kingdom.

4. There appears to be a definite development by national courts in all States to apply inter- national law into national law with increasing frequency. In most cases, the national courts use international law (including treaties and decisions by international bodies), sometimes through comparative law from other States, to assist in the interpretation of national law and to buttress the court's decisions. This is particularly the situation where the relevant inter- national law concerns human rights or otherwise grants rights to individuals.

5. Most States amend their national laws and practices to comply with international legally binding decisions of international bodies, such as the United Nations Security Council. This will include decisions about non-recognition of States, economic sanctions and the estab- lishment of international bodies, such as the International Criminal Tribunal for the Former

Yugoslavia, and (see Chapters 5, 14 and 15). Many States will also change their laws, including through decisions by national courts, as a result of international non-legally binding decisions by international bodies, such as human rights supervisory bodies (see Chapter 6).

SECTION 4: Examples of international law on the national plane

The following examples of national law applications of international law are chosen as they demonstrate the diversity of the mechanisms for implementing international law described by Cassese above.

A: United Kingdom

The United Kingdom does not have a single document constitution. Instead its constitution is ascertained by an examination of such material as legislation, judicial decisions and political or Parliamentary conventions and practices. One of the fundamental principles of its unwritten constitution is that of 'Parliamentary Sovereignty'. This has been defined as meaning that Parliament 'has, under the English constitution, the right to make or unmake any law whatever; and, further, that no person or body is recognised by the law of England as having a right to override or set aside the legislation of Parliament' (A. Dicey, *Introduction to the Study of the Law of the Constitution*, 5th edn, 1897, p. 38). The relationship between the law of the United Kingdom and international law is said to vary as between customary international law and treaty obligations.

(a) Treaties

International Tin Council Case (J. H. Rayner (Mincing Lane) Ltd v Department of Trade and Industry)
[1990] 2 AC 418, House of Lords

> This case was one of a number of actions brought by creditors against the International Tin Council ('ITC') after it was unable to meet its debts. The ITC was founded by a treaty (the Sixth International Tin Agreement or ITA 6) which operated in the United Kingdom pursuant to a Headquarters Agreement (another treaty), although neither treaty was incorporated in the national law of the United Kingdom. The claimants argued that the treaty provided them with a right of action against the States parties directly, rather than against the ITC. The House of Lords unanimously rejected the claimants' arguments.

LORD OLIVER: It is axiomatic that municipal courts have not and cannot have the competence to adjudicate upon or to enforce the rights arising out of transactions entered into by independent sovereign states between themselves on the plane of international law. . . . That is the first of the underlying principles. The second is that, as a matter of the constitutional law of the United Kingdom, the Royal Prerogative, whilst it embraces the making of treaties, does not extend to altering the law or conferring rights upon individuals or depriving individuals of rights which they enjoy in domestic law without the intervention of Parliament. Treaties, as it is sometimes expressed, are not self-executing. Quite simply, a treaty is not part of English law unless and until it has been incorporated into the law by legislation. so far as individuals are concerned, it is *res inter alios acta* from which they cannot derive rights and by which they cannot be deprived of rights or subjected to obligations; and it is outside the purview of the court not only because it is made in the conduct of foreign relations, which are a prerogative of the Crown, but also because, as a source of rights and obligations, it is irrelevant.

These propositions do not, however, involve as a corollary that the court must never look at or construe a treaty. Where, for instance, a treaty is directly incorporated into English law by Act of the legislature, its terms become subject to the interpretative jurisdiction of the court in the same way as any other Act of the legislature. *Fothergill* v *Monarch Airlines Ltd* [1981] AC 251 is a recent example. Again, it is well established that where a statute is enacted in order to give effect to the United Kingdom's obligations under a treaty, the terms of the treaty may have to be considered and, if necessary, construed in order to resolve any ambiguity or obscurity as to the meaning or scope of the statute. Clearly, also, where parties have entered into a domestic contract in which they have chosen to incorporate the terms of the treaty, the court may be called upon to interpret the treaty for the purposes of ascertaining the rights and obligations of the parties under their contract: see, for instance, *Philippson* v *Imperial Airways Ltd* [1939] AC 332.

Further cases in which the court may not only be empowered but required to adjudicate upon the meaning or scope of the terms of an international treaty arise where domestic legislation, although not incorporating the treaty, nevertheless requires, either expressly or by necessary implication, resort to be had to its terms for the purpose of construing the legislation (as in *Zoernsch* v *Waldock* [1964] 1 WLR 675) or the very rare case in which the exercise of the Royal Prerogative directly effects an extension or contraction of the jurisdiction without the constitutional need for internal legislation, as in *Post Office* v *Estuary Radio Ltd* [1968] 2 QB 740.

It must be borne in mind, furthermore, that the conclusion of an international treaty and its terms are as much matters of fact as any other fact. That a treaty may be referred to where it is necessary to do so as part of the factual background against which a particular issue arises may seem a statement of the obvious. But it is, I think, necessary to stress that the purpose for which such reference can legitimately be made is purely an evidential one. Which states have become parties to a treaty and when and what the terms of the treaty are are questions of fact. The legal results which flow from it in international law, whether between the parties inter so or between the parties or any of them and outsiders are not and they are not justiciable by municipal courts. . . .

The creation and regulation by a number of sovereign states of an international organisation for their common political and economic purposes was an act *jure imperii* and an adjudication of the rights and obligations between themselves and that organisation or, inter se, can be undertaken only on the plane of international law. The transactions here concerned – the participation and concurrence in the proceedings of the council authorising or countenancing the acts of the buffer stock manager – were transactions of sovereign states with and within the international organisation which they have created and are not to be subjected to the processes of our courts in order to determine what liabilities arising out of them attached to the members in favour of the ITC.

NOTES:
1. The power to conclude treaties in the United Kingdom is an exercise of the Royal Prerogative (as Lord Oliver notes in the *International Tin Council case*), being part of the monarch's powers exercised by the executive. As Parliament is the only national institution of the United Kingdom which can make law, the courts have required treaties to be incorporated, or implemented, by legislation into United Kingdom law before they will give full effect to the treaties (see e.g., the Torture Convention in *Ex parte Pinochet* [1999] 2 All ER 97).
2. The courts do refer to unincorporated treaties to resolve ambiguities in legislation (e.g.

Salomon v *Commissioners of Customs and Excise* [1967] 2 QB 116), or even in common law (e.g. *Derbyshire County Council* v *Times Newspapers* [1992] QB 770), in order to interpret national law in conformity with international law, so far as is possible. In undertaking this task of interpretation, the national courts interpret the treaty in accordance with the rules of international law, for example, by referring to the *travaux préparatoires* of the treaty (see *Fothergill* v *Monarch Airlines* [1981] AC 251). This has had some effect on the United Kingdom courts' interpretation of purely national law for example, where Parliamentary statements may now sometimes be taken into account (see *Pepper* v *Hart* [1993] AC 593).

3. The consequence of the general rule that unincorporated treaties cannot give rights or obligations in the United Kingdom is that claims based on an unincorporated treaty are non-justiciable by the courts, i.e. outside their jurisdiction. In *Arab Monetary Fund* v *Hashim (No 3)* [1991] 1 All ER 871 (the *AMF* case), the House of Lords avoided this consequence by finding that the relevant international organisation, which was created by a treaty, had been incorporated in the national law of at least one State (in that case the United Arab Emirates) and those laws gave the AMF a legal identity. Because the United Kingdom recognised that State, its national laws, and the effect of its national laws (as it does with nearly all States – see Chapter 5), the United Kingdom courts would recognise the legal identity of the AMF. In *Westland Helicopters Ltd* v *Arab Organisation for Industrialisation* [1995] 2 All ER 387, the Queen's Bench Division held that the law which the United Kingdom courts would apply in regard to the existence, constitution and representation of the international organisation was international law and not the national law of the State where the organisation was incorporated. It is at least arguable that this circumvents the non-justiciable rule.

(b) Customary international law

The United Kingdom has adopted the principle of 'incorporation' in regard to customary international law, by which that law automatically becomes part of the national law without need for legislative or judicial pronouncement.

Triquet v *Bath*
(1746) 3 Burr 1478; 97 ER 936, Court of King's Bench

LORD MANSFIELD: Lord Talbot [in *Buvot* v *Barbuit*] declared a clear opinion – 'That the law of nations, in its full extent was part of the law of England.' – 'That the Act of Parliament was declaratory; and occasioned by a particular incident.' – 'That the law of nations was to be collected from the practice of different nations, and the authority of writers.'

West Rand Central Gold Mining Co. v *The King*
[1905] 2 KB 391, Kings Bench Division

LORD ALVERSTONE CJ: [The proposition] that international law forms part of the law of England, requires a word of explanation and comment. It is quite true that whatever has received the common consent of civilized nations must have received the assent of our country, and that to which we have assented along with other nations in general may properly be called international law, and as such will be acknowledged and applied by our municipal tribunals when legitimate occasion arises for those tribunals to decide questions to which doctrines of international law may be relevant. But any doctrine so invoked must be one really accepted as binding between nations, and the international law sought to be applied must, like anything else, be proved by satisfactory evidence, which must shew either that the particular proposition put forward has been recognised and acted upon by our own country, or that it is of such a nature, and has been so widely and generally accepted, that it can hardly be supposed that any civilized State would repudiate it. The mere opinions of jurists, however eminent or learned, that it ought to be so recognised, are not in themselves sufficient. They must have received the express sanction of international agreement, or gradually have grown to be part of international law by their frequent practical recognition in dealings between various nations.

Trendtex Trading Corporation v *Central Bank of Nigeria*
[1977] QB 529, Court of Appeal

The issue arose in this case as to whether the common law principle of precedent applied to the integration of customary international law into the common law of the United Kingdom in circumstances where the rule of customary international law has been changed or superseded. A majority (Lord Denning MR, Shaw LJ, Stephenson LJ dissenting) concluded that changes to customary international law can effect changes to the common law.

LORD DENNING MR: . . . It is certain that international law does change. I would use of international law the words which Galileo used of the earth: "But it does move." International law does change: and the courts have applied the changes without the aid of any Act of Parliament. Thus, when the rules of international law were changed (by the force of public opinion) so as to condemn slavery, the English courts were justified in applying the modern rules of international law . . .

Seeing that the rules of international law have changed – and do change – and that the courts have given effect to the changes without any Act of Parliament, it follows to my mind inexorably that the rules of international law, as existing from time to time, do form part of our English law. It follows, too, that a decision of this court – as to what was the ruling of international law 50 or 60 years ago – is not binding on this court today. International law knows no rule of *stare decisis*. If this court today is satisfied that the rule of international law on a subject has changed from what it was 50 or 60 years ago, it can give effect to that change – and apply the change in our English law – without waiting for the House of Lords to do it.

SHAW LJ: May it not be that the true principle as to the application of international law is that the English courts must at any given time discover what the prevailing international rule is and apply that rule? . . .

What *is* immutable is the principle of English law that the law of nations (not what *was* the law of nations) must be applied in the courts of England. The rule of *stare decisis* operates to preclude a court from overriding a decision which binds it in regard to a particular rule of (international) law; it does not prevent a court from applying a rule which did not exist when the earlier decision was made if the new rule has bad the effect in international law of extinguishing the old rule.

NOTES:
1. Customary international law is applied by the United Kingdom courts as part of the common law. These courts may, however, feel unable to apply customary international law in the case before them because they have been unable to discover the relevant customary international law with sufficient certainty. As shown in the extract from the *West Rand*, the courts require clear evidence that a rule of customary international law exists before they will apply it. In seeking this evidence, the courts adopt the international law rules on the ascertainment of customary international law, i.e. evidence of general State practice and *opinio juris* (see Chapter 2).
2. As customary international law is part of the common law it can be overridden by unambiguous legislation. As seen in the *Trendtex* case, however, customary international law is not subject to the principle of *stare decisis*.
3. As with treaties, some matters of customary international law are non-justiciable by national courts (see *Buttes Gas & Oil Co* v *Hammer (Nos 2 and 3)* [1982] AC 88). Other matters are

affected by decisions of the executive – usually indicated by an executive certificate – and this certificate is often used in relation to the recognition of States (Chapter 5) and immunity from jurisdiction (Chapter 9).

4. It is difficult to justify the different rules for the application of treaties and of customary international law in the United Kingdom. The distinction is based on the principle of Parliamentary sovereignty, as only Parliament can change the laws of the United Kingdom. Thus, it is argued, because the conclusion of treaties is an act of the executive, treaties cannot be applied directly into United Kingdom law, while customary international law is common law and can be overridden by legislation and so does not infringe Parliamentary sovereignty. However, the signing of treaties is a public act of the executive for which questions can be raised in Parliament and, in any event, all treaties are laid before Parliament for at least 21 days before they are ratified (the 'Ponsonby rule') and so are subject to Parliamentary debate and possible review by a Parliamentary Committee. In contrast, customary international law is created by the practices of many States, including their treaty practice, for which actions by Parliament are rarely relevant. Therefore, Parliament has less influence on customary international law than on treaties. In addition, both types of international law can be overridden by contrary, unambiguous national legislation. As such, both treaties and customary international law should be treated in the same way by the United Kingdom courts and applied directly into national law unless national law is expressly contrary.

(c) *The impact of Europe on the United Kingdom*

The United Kingdom has ratified two treaties that have had significant effect on its national law. By the Treaty of Accession of the United Kingdom to the European Communities 1972, the United Kingdom became a party to the treaties, in particular to the Treaty of Rome 1957, which established the European Communities. Second, the European Convention on Human Rights and Fundamental Freedoms 1950, was ratified by the United Kingdom in 1951 (see further Chapter 6). Both treaties confer rights and obligations on the United Kingdom under international law, but the impact of each on the national law of the United Kingdom has been different.

By the European Communities Act 1972, the United Kingdom has incorporated the European Communities (now the European Union) treaties into its national law. More recently, the European Convention on Human Rights and Fundamental Freedoms was largely incorporated by the Human Rights Act 1998 that came into effect on 2 October 2000. By these actions it seems that considerable limitations on the United Kingdom's sovereignty have been created.

European Communities Act 1972 (United Kingdom)

2—(1) All such rights, powers, liabilities, obligations and restrictions from time to time created or arising by or under the Treaties, and all such remedies and procedures from time to time provided for by or under the Treaties, as in accordance with the Treaties are without further enactment to be given legal effect or used in the United Kingdom shall be recognised and available in law, and be enforced, allowed and followed accordingly; and the expression "enforceable Community right" and similar expressions shall be read as referring to one to which this subsection applies.

(2) Subject to Schedule 2 to this Act, at any time after its passing Her Majesty may by Order in Council, and any designated Minister or department may by regulations, make provision—

(a) for the purpose of implementing any Community obligation of the United Kingdom, or enabling any such obligation to be implemented, or of enabling any rights enjoyed or to be enjoyed by the United Kingdom under or by virtue of the Treaties to be exercised; or

(b) for the purpose of dealing with matters arising out of or related to any such obligation or rights or the coming into force, or the operation from time to time, of subsection (1) above;

and in the exercise of any statutory power or duty, including any power to give directions or to legislate by means of orders, rules, regulations or other subordinate instrument, the person entrusted with the power or duty may have regard to the objects of the Communities and to any such obligations or rights as aforesaid. . . .

(4) The provision that may be made under subsection (2) above includes, subject to Schedule 2 to this Act, any such provision (of any such extent) as might be made by Act of Parliament, and any enactment passed or to be passed, other than one contained in this Part of this Act, shall be construed and have effect subject to the foregoing provisions of this section; but, except as may be provided by any Act passed after this Act, Schedule 2 shall have effect in connection with the powers conferred by this and the following sections of this Act to make Orders in Council and regulations.

3—(1) For the purposes of all legal proceedings any question as to the meaning or effect of any of the Treaties, or as to the validity, meaning or effect of any community instrument, shall be treated as a question of law (and, if not referred to the European court, be for determination as such in accordance with the principles laid down by and any relevant decision of the European court).

(2) Judicial notice shall be taken of the Treaties, of the Official Journal of the Communities and of any decision of, or expression of opinion by, the European court on any such question as aforesaid.

Factortame Ltd v *Secretary of State for Transport (No 2)*
[1991] 1 AC 603, House of Lords

By the United Kingdom's Merchant Fishing Act 1988, 95 deep sea fishing vessels could not be registered as British fishing vessels as they were substantially managed and controlled by Spanish nationals and not by British nationals as required by the Act. The Act, and regulations under it, were challenged as infringing basic European Community rights, such as non-discrimination against a national of a member state of the European Communities. These latter rights became enforceable as British law in 1972 by virtue of the European Communities Act (see above). The Divisional Court sought a ruling from the Court of Justice of the European Communities (European Court of Justice). Due to the likely delay before that court had time to consider the matter in its entirety, the applicants sought an order from the House of Lords that the Merchant Fishing Act 1988 be not applied until a final ruling was given by the European Court of Justice.

LORD BRIDGE: My Lords, when this appeal first came before the House last year [[1990] 2 AC 85] your Lordships held that, as a matter of English law, the courts had no jurisdiction to grant interim relief in terms which would involve either overturning an English statute in advance of any decision by the European Court of Justice that the statute infringed Community law or granting an injunction against the Crown. It then became necessary to seek a preliminary ruling from the European Court of Justice as to whether Community law itself invested us with such jurisdiction. In the speech I delivered on that occasion, with which your Lordships agreed, I explained the reasons which led us to those conclusions. It will be remembered that, on that occasion, the House never directed its attention to the question how, if there were jurisdiction to grant the relief sought, discretion ought to be exercised in deciding whether or not relief should be granted.

In June of this year we received the judgment of the European Court of Justice (Case C213/89) ante, p. 852B *et seq.*, replying to the questions we had posed and affirming that we had jurisdiction, in the circumstances postulated, to grant interim relief for the protection of directly enforceable rights under Community law and that no limitation on our jurisdiction imposed by any rule of national law could stand as the sole obstacle to preclude the grant of such relief. In the light of this judgment we were able to conclude the hearing of the appeal in July and unanimously decided that relief should be granted in terms of the orders which the House then made, indicating that we would give our reasons for the decision later. . . .

Some public comments on the decision of the European Court of Justice, affirming the jurisdiction of the courts of member states to override national legislation if necessary to enable interim relief to be granted in protection of rights under Community law, have suggested that this was a novel and dangerous invasion by a Community institution of the sovereignty of the United Kingdom Parliament. But such comments are based on a misconception. If the supremacy within the European Community of Community law over the national law of member states was not always inherent in the EEC Treaty (Cmnd. 5179–II) it was certainly well established in the jurisprudence of the European Court of Justice long before the United Kingdom joined the Community. Thus, whatever limitation of its sovereignty Parliament accepted when it enacted the European Communities Act 1972 was entirely voluntary. Under the terms of the Act of 1972 it has always been clear that it was the duty of a United Kingdom court, when delivering final judgment, to override any rule of national law found to be in conflict with any directly enforceable rule of Community law. Similarly, when decisions of the European Court of Justice have exposed areas of United Kingdom statute law which failed to implement Council directives, Parliament has always loyally accepted the obligation to make appropriate and prompt amendments. Thus there is nothing in any way novel in according supremacy to rules of Community law in those areas to which they apply and to insist that, in the protection of rights under Community law, national courts must not be inhibited by rules of national law from granting interim relief in appropriate cases is no more than a logical recognition of that supremacy.

Although affirming our jurisdiction, the judgment of the European Court of Justice does not fetter our discretion to determine whether an appropriate case for the grant of interim relief has been made out. . . . Unlike the ordinary case in which the court must decide whether or not to grant interlocutory relief at a time when disputed issues of fact remain unresolved, here the relevant facts are all ascertained and the only unresolved issues are issues of law, albeit of Community law. Now, although the final decision of such issues is the exclusive prerogative of the European Court of Justice, that does not mean that an English court may not reach an informed opinion as to how such issues are likely to be resolved.

Human Rights Act 1998

The Human Rights Act came into force on 2 October 2000.

1. The Convention Rights

(1) In this Act "the Convention rights" means the rights and fundamental freedoms set out in—

    (a) Articles 2 to 12 and 14 of the Convention,

    (b) Articles 1 to 3 of the First Protocol, and

    (c) Articles 1 and 2 of the Sixth Protocol,

as read with Articles 16 to 18 of the Convention.

(2) Those Articles are to have effect for the purposes of this Act subject to any designated derogation or reservation (as to which see sections 14 and 15).

(3) The Articles are set out in Schedule 1.

(4) The Secretary of State may by order make such amendments to this Act as he considers appropriate to reflect the effect, in relation to the United Kingdom, of a protocol.

(5) In subsection (4) "protocol" means a protocol to the Convention—

(a) which the United Kingdom has ratified; or

(b) which the United Kingdom has signed with a view to ratification.

(6) No amendment may be made by an order under subsection (4) so as to come into force before the protocol concerned is in force in relation to the United Kingdom.

2. Interpretation of Convention rights

(1) A court or tribunal determining a question which has arisen in connection with a Convention right must take into account any—

(a) judgment, decision, declaration or advisory opinion of the European Court of Human Rights,

(b) opinion of the Commission given in a report adopted under Article 31 of the Convention,

(c) decision of the Commission in connection with Article 26 or 27(2) of the Convention, or

(d) decision of the Committee of Ministers taken under Article 46 of the Convention,

whenever made or given, so far as, in the opinion of the court or tribunal, it is relevant to the proceedings in which that question has arisen.

(2) Evidence of any judgment, decision, declaration or opinion of which account may have to be taken under this section is to be given in proceedings before any court or tribunal in such manner as may be provided by rules. . . .

3. Interpretation of legislation

(1) So far as it is possible to do so, primary legislation and subordinate legislation must be read and given effect in such a way which is compatible with Convention rights.

(2) This section—

(a) applies to primary legislation and subordinate legislation whenever enacted;

(b) does not affect the validity, continuing operation or enforcement of any incompatible primary legislation; and

(c) does not affect the validity, continuing operation or enforcement of any incompatible subordinate legislation if (disregarding any possibility of revocation) primary legislation prevents removal of the incompatibility. . . .

4. Declaration of incompatibility

(1) Subsection (2) applies in any proceedings in which a court determines whether a provision of primary legislation is compatible with a Convention right.

(2) If the court is satisfied that the provision is incompatible with a Convention right, it may make a declaration of that incompatibility.

(3) Subsection (4) applies in any proceedings in which a court determines whether a provision of subordinate legislation, made in the exercise of a power conferred under primary legislation, is compatible with a Convention right.

(4) If the court is satisfied—

(a) that the provision is incompatible with a Convention right, and

(b) that (disregarding any possibility of revocation) the primary legislation prevents removal of the incompatibility,

it may make a declaration on that incompatibility.

(5) In this section 'court' means—

(a) the House of Lords;

(b) the Judicial Council of the Privy Council;

(c) the Courts-Martial Appeal Court;

(d) in Scotland, the High Court of Justiciary sitting otherwise than as a trial court or the Court of Session;

(e) in England and Wales or Northern Ireland, the High Court or the Court of Appeal.

(6) A declaration under this section ('a declaration of incompatibility')—

(a) does not affect the validity, continuing operation or enforcement of the provision in respect of which it is given; and

(b) is not binding on the parties to the proceedings in which it is made. . . .

6. Acts of public authorities

(1) It is unlawful for a public authority to act in a way which is incompatible with a Convention right.

(2) Subsection (1) does not apply to an act if—

(a) as the result of one or more provisions of primary legislation, the authority could not have acted differently; or

(b) in the case of one or more provisions of, or made under, primary legislation which cannot be read or given effect in a way which is compatible with the Convention rights, the authority was acting so as to give effect to or enforce those provisions.

(3) In this section 'public authority' includes—

(a) a court or tribunal, and

(b) any person certain of whose functions are functions of a public nature, but does not include either House of Parliament or a person exercising functions in connection with proceedings in Parliament.

(4) In subsection (3) 'Parliament' does not include the House of Lords in its judicial capacity.

(5) In relation to a particular act, a person is not a public authority by virtue only of subsection (3)(b) if the nature of the act is private.

(6) 'An act' includes a failure to act but does not include a failure to—

(a) introduce in, or lay before, Parliament a proposal for legislation; or

(b) make any primary legislation or remedial order. . . .

19. Statements of compatibility

(1) A Minister of the Crown in charge of a Bill in either House of Parliament must, before Second reading of the Bill—

(a) make a statement to the effect that in his view the provisions of the Bill are compatible with the Convention rights ('a statement of compatibility'); or

(b) make a statement to the effect that although he is unable to make a statement of compatibility the government nonetheless wishes the House to proceed with the Bill.

(2) The statement must be in writing and be published in such manner as the Minister making it considers appropriate.

D. Feldman, 'Monism, Dualism and Constitutional Legitimacy'

20 *Australian Yearbook of International Law* (1999) 105, 114–115, 118–119

The new scheme introduced by the *Human Rights Act* 1998 . . . makes 'Convention rights' part of municipal law in the United Kingdom. 'Convention rights' are those rights arising under the European Convention on Human Rights that are identified in section 1 of the Act and set out in Schedule I, subject to various other provisions. Under section 2, the rights are to be interpreted taking into account the case-law of the Convention organs. By section 3, all legislation is to be interpreted so far as possible in a way that is compatible with Convention rights. Under section 6, a public authority (which includes courts and tribunals but excludes Parliament) acts unlawfully to the extent that it does anything which is incompatible with a Convention right, unless its action is required by primary legislation which cannot be interpreted so as to be compatible with Convention rights. Where primary legislation is incompatible with a Convention right, it is not thereby made invalid, but a superior court may make a declaration of incompatibility, which should lead to an amendment of the law. To assist parliamentary scrutiny, section 19 requires a Minister introducing a government Bill to Parliament to make a statement in writing (which is printed on the front cover of the Bill) that in his or her opinion the Bill either does or does not comply with Convention rights. Parliament is to establish a Joint Select Committee of its two Houses to monitor and report on matters relating to human rights in the United Kingdom and report to each House.

This structure preserves the doctrine of parliamentary sovereignty while providing a system for remedying violations of Convention rights in municipal courts and tribunals, whereas previously it would have been necessary for victims of violations to go to Strasbourg [where the European Court of Human Rights is based] for a remedy (after exhausting any domestic remedy which might have been available in municipal law). The 1998 Act, not the Convention, is the source of the authority for municipal tribunals to apply the rights. Even the meaning of the rights in municipal law is not necessarily the same as in international law, as the interpretation of the European Court of Human Rights provisions by Strasbourg organs is persuasive but not binding on municipal tribunals.

However, in practice the separation between municipal and international law is weakened. The Act recognises that the meaning of the Convention rights is dynamic rather than fixed, and acknowledges that the Strasbourg organs have a part to play in driving forward the interpretation of the rights. The Act also makes the Strasbourg case law dispositive of some questions of municipal law, particularly standing to assert Convention rights in proceedings under the Act. Furthermore, the obligation on courts and tribunals under section 2 of the Act to have regard to relevant case-law of the Strasbourg organs will inevitably bring other treaties into play, since the European Court of Human Rights regularly refers to instruments such as the International Covenant on Civil and Political Rights and the Convention on the Rights of the Child, as well as some 'soft law', norms or standards which are intended to guide decisions or actions but which are not intended to be legally enforceable, when interpreting provisions in the European Court of Human Rights.

These steps towards a more outward-looking approach to the development of municipal law in the United Kingdom, tentative though they may seem, represent a fundamental shift. Having been taken by Act of Parliament, the steps are procedurally legitimate, and the objective of protecting human rights should ensure that they are also morally legitimate. On the other hand, the change was not necessitated by any major constitutional upheaval. Nor was it the result of widespread public demands for improved protection for human rights. The *Human Rights Act* 1998 came about through long-term pressure from an influential minority of lawyers, parliamentarians, political scientists and journalists, building on concern about the United Kingdom's reputation abroad in the light of repeatedly having been held in violation of the European [Convention] of Human Rights in cases reaching the European Court of Human Rights. Had there been a sense that a Bill of Rights was historically, socially or constitutionally necessary (rather than just desirable), it would probably have been a more far-reaching instrument than the 1998 Act, giving greater weight to the international instruments and imposing stronger checks on parliamentary sovereignty. There would also probably have been a more intensive and far-reaching campaign of public consultation to ensure that the rights and methods of enforcement commanded maximum support among the population. Public support is important to make constitutional change in a democracy politically legitimate, and would help to maintain its legitimacy in the face of the possible unpopularity of some consequences of applying the rights and of some of the causes espoused by those who may assert them. Instead, the debate was mainly conducted by an informed élite within a charmed circle. . . .

One effect of these constitutional arrangements is to blur the distinction between international and municipal law. As in the United Kingdom under the *Human Rights Act* 1998, it is impossible to say what municipal law is in relation to human rights issues without reference to international law, and, in the case of South African courts, the case law of other jurisdictions, even where international law does not form part of municipal law. This presents a difficulty for dualist positivists. It is hard to accept that municipal law can be a closed system of rules when the system itself makes norms from other systems, over which it exercises no control, decisive of, or persuasive in, the determination of issues. Although these outside influences are likely to be limited in their application by the Constitution, they are not controlled by it. A mixed system like that now operating in the United Kingdom, and *a fortiori* that which has been adopted in South Africa, draws its operating rules from a range of sources, not all of which can be said to be legally validated by reference to criteria contained in the national constitution. This closely resembles Kelsen's model of a monist system in which the application of international law is subject to constitutional constraints.

NOTES:
1. Some jurists consider that European Union law is not international law but is a form of 'supra-national' law. They note the degree of integration of political, economic and social matters that has occurred between the member States of the European Union. As at 1 July 2002 there are 15 member States: Austria, Belgium, Denmark, Finland, France, Germany, Greece, Ireland, Italy, Luxembourg, The Netherlands, Portugal, Spain, Sweden, and the United Kingdom. There is a European Parliament (of limited power), a European exchange rate mechanism, and also European Union regulations which are binding on the member States. Yet, despite the unusual character of the European Union, it is clear that the determination of European Union laws, and their binding nature, is able to be made by the member States because of the treaties which they have ratified and the rights and obligations contained in those treaties. In the same way as other European treaties, such as the European Convention on Human Rights, are regional international law, European Union law is a part of international law and can be treated as such.
2. The European Communities Act 1972 is amended, if necessary, subsequent to the signature of each new European Union treaty.
3. The Court of Justice of the European Communities (the European Court of Justice) is the final interpreter of European Union law (by the power given in Article 177 of the Treaty of Rome 1957). This is confirmed by s 3(1) of the European Communities Act. However, the national implementation of European Union law and determination of any inconsistency between national law and European Union law are matters for the national legislatures and courts of the member States. Section 2(1) and (4) of the European Communities Act 1972 provide that all European law created and to be created has direct effect in the United Kingdom as if it were United Kingdom law. However, this position applies only to European regulations and some directives and not to all European law.
4. The Court of Justice of the European Communities has used the European Convention on Human Rights as an aid to interpretation. The EU has also now introduced an EU Charter of Fundamental Rights 2000 (40 ILM 266 (2001)) but it is not, as yet, legally enforceable.
5. Prior to the incorporation of the European Convention on Human Rights by the Human Rights Act, any cases involving human rights issues could only be brought before the European Commission and the Court of Human Rights. This resulted in a dismal record for the United Kingdom before these bodies. As Feldman shows, the condemnation of United Kingdom law, through findings of breaches of the Convention, and of the inability of United Kingdom courts to protect human rights, contributed to the use by the courts of the Convention as a constant source of reference and to the pressure by many judges and others to incorporate the Convention.

6. In the language of the Government, the purpose of the Human Rights Act was to see 'rights brought home'. The Act also establishes a parliamentary procedure to ensure the conformity of legislation with the Convention. As at July 2002 there have only been a few cases where the courts have held that legislation is incompatible with the Human Rights Act (e.g. *Wilson* v *First County Trust Ltd* [2001] 3 WLR 42). Not surprisingly, the courts have so far been rather tentative in their approach and it will require a few years' experience before it is clear what the general approach of the courts will be to the Human Rights Act. However, as Feldman shows, the existence of the Human Rights Act has already changed the interaction between the UK and international law.

B: Australia

Mabo v *Queensland (No 2)*
(1992) 175 CLR 1, High Court of Australia

BRENNAN J: If the international law notion that inhabited land may be classified as terra nullius no longer commands general support [see *Western Sahara Opinion*], the doctrines of the common law which depend on the notion that native peoples may be 'so low in the scale of social organization' that it is 'idle to impute to such people some shadow of the rights known to our law' (*In re Southern Rhodesia* (1919) AC, at pp 233–234) can hardly be retained. If it were permissible in past centuries to keep the common law in step with international law, it is imperative in today's world that the common law should neither be nor be seen to be frozen in an age of racial discrimination.

 Whatever the justification advanced in earlier days for refusing to recognize the rights and interests in land of the indigenous inhabitants of settled colonies, an unjust and discriminatory doctrine of that kind can no longer be accepted. The expectations of the international community accord in this respect with the contemporary values of the Australian people. The opening up of international remedies to individuals pursuant to Australia's accession to the Optional Protocol to the International Covenant on Civil and Political Rights . . . brings to bear on the common law the powerful influence of the Covenant and the international standards it imports. The common law does not necessarily conform with international law, but international law is a legitimate and important influence on the development of the common law, especially when international law declares the existence of universal human rights. A common law doctrine founded on unjust discrimination in the enjoyment of civil and political rights demands reconsideration. It is contrary both to international standards and to the fundamental values of our common law to entrench a discriminatory rule which, because of the supposed position on the scale of social organization of the indigenous inhabitants of a settled colony, denies them a right to occupy their traditional lands.

Minister of State for Immigration and Ethnic Affairs v *Teoh*
(1995) 183 CLR 273, High Court of Australia

MASON CJ and DEANE J: It is well established that the provisions of an international treaty to which Australia is a party do not form part of Australian law unless those provisions have been validly incorporated into our municipal law by statute. This principle has its foundation in the proposition that in our constitutional system the making and ratification of treaties fall within the province of the Executive in the exercise of its prerogative power whereas the making and the alteration of the law fall within the province of Parliament, not the Executive. So, a treaty which has not been incorporated into our municipal law cannot operate as a direct source of individual rights and obligations under that law. In this case, it is common ground that the provisions of the Convention have not been incorporated in this way. It is not suggested that the declaration made pursuant to s 47(1) of the Human Rights and Equal Opportunity Commission Act has this effect.

But the fact that the Convention has not been incorporated into Australian law does not mean that its ratification holds no significance for Australian law. Where a statute or subordinate legislation is ambiguous, the courts should favour that construction which accords with Australia's obligations under a treaty or international convention to which Australia is a party, at least in those cases in which the legislation is enacted after, or in contemplation of, entry into, or ratification of, the relevant international instrument. That is because Parliament, prima facie, intends to give effect to Australia's obligations under international law.

Apart from influencing the construction of a statute or subordinate legislation, an international convention may play a part in the development by the courts of the common law. The provisions of an international convention to which Australia is a party, especially one which declares universal fundamental rights, may be used by the courts as a legitimate guide in developing the common law. But the courts should act in this fashion with due circumspection when the Parliament itself has not seen fit to incorporate the provisions of a convention into our domestic law. Judicial development of the common law must not be seen as a backdoor means of importing an unincorporated convention into Australian law. A cautious approach to the development of the common law by reference to international conventions would be consistent with the approach which the courts have hitherto adopted to the development of the common law by reference to statutory policy and statutory materials. Much will depend upon the nature of the relevant provision, the extent to which it has been accepted by the international community, the purpose which it is intended to serve and its relationship to the existing principles of our domestic law.

In the present case, however, we are not concerned with the resolution of an ambiguity in a statue. Nor are we concerned with the development of some existing principle of the common law. The critical questions to be resolved are whether the provisions of the Convention are relevant to the exercise of the statutory discretion and, if so, whether Australia's ratification of the Convention can give rise to a legitimate expectation that the decision-maker will exercise that discretion in conformity with the terms of the Convention. The foregoing discussion of the stautus of the Convention in Australian law reveals no intrinsic reason for excluding its provisions from consideration by the decision-maker simply because it has not been incorporated into our municipal law.

[R]atification of a convention is a positive statement by the executive government of this country to the world and to the Australian people that the executive government and its agencies will act in accordance with the Convention. That positive statement is an adequate foundation for a legitimate expectation, absent statutory or executive indications to the contrary, that administrative decision-makers will act in conformity with the Convention . . . It is not necessary that a person seeking to set up such a legitimate expectation should be aware of the Convention or should personally entertain the expectation; it is enough that the expectation is reasonable in the sense that there are adequate materials to support it.

Nulyarimma v *Thompson*

(1999) 165 ALR 621, Federal Court of Australia

This case concerned the issue as to whether certain members of the Australian government had committed acts of genocide against the indigneous peoples of Australia. There was no relevant Australian legislation incorporating the Geno-cide Convention (see Chapter 3) and so the issue turned on whether genocide was a crime under customary international law and so was automatically part of Australian common law. While all judges accepted that the crime of genocide was a matter of customary international law, they differed as to the effect of creating such a common law crime had on Australian law. The Court unanimously held, on the basis of the particular facts of the case, that the claim was not successful.

WILCOX J: 18. I accept that the prohibition of genocide is a peremptory norm of customary international law, giving rise to a non-derogatable obligation by each nation State to the entire international community. This is an obligation independent of the Convention on the Prevention and Punishment of the Crime of Genocide. It existed before the commencement of that Convention in January 1951, probably at least from the time of the United Nations General Assembly resolution in December 1946. I accept, also, that the obligation imposed by customary law on each nation State is to extradite or prosecute any person, found within its territory, who appears to have committed any of the acts cited in the definition of genocide set out in the Convention. It is generally accepted this definition reflects the concept of genocide, as understood in customary international law.

19. It follows from the obligation to prosecute or extradite, imposed by international customary law on Australia as a nation State, that it would be constitutionally permissible for the Commonwealth Parliament to enact legislation providing for the trial within Australia of persons accused of genocide, wherever occurring. . . .

20. However, it is one thing to say Australia has an international legal obligation to prosecute or extradite a genocide suspect found within its territory, and that the Commonwealth Parliament may legislate to ensure that obligation is fulfilled; it is another thing to say that, without legislation to that effect, such a person may be put on trial for genocide before an Australian court. If this were the position, it would lead to the curious result that an international obligation incurred pursuant to customary law has greater domestic consequences than an obligation incurred, expressly and voluntarily, by Australia signing and ratifying an international convention. Ratification of a convention does not directly affect Australian domestic law unless and until implementing legislation is enacted. This seems to be the position even where the ratification has received Parliamentary approval, as in the case of the Genocide Convention. . . .

25. I think this passage brings home the point that it is difficult to make a general statement covering all the diverse rules of international customary law. It is one thing, it seems to me, for courts of a particular country to be prepared to treat a civil law rule like the doctrine of foreign sovereign immunity as part of its domestic law, whether because it is accepted by those courts as being "incorporated" in that law or because it has been "transformed" by judicial act. It is another thing to say that a norm of international law criminalising conduct that is not made punishable by the domestic law entitles a domestic court to try and punish an offender against that law.

26. Perhaps this is only another way of saying that domestic courts face a policy issue in deciding whether to recognise and enforce a rule of international law. If there is a policy issue, I have no doubt it should be resolved in a criminal case by declining, in the absence of legislation, to enforce the international norm. As Shearer pointed out, in the realm of criminal law "the strong presumption *nullum crimen sine lege* (there is no crime unless expressly created by law) applies". In the case of serious criminal conduct, ground rules are needed. Which courts are to have jurisdiction to try the accused person? What procedures will govern the trial? What punishment may be imposed? These matters need to be resolved before a person is put on trial for an offence as horrendous as genocide.

MERKEL J: 131. It is plain from a survey of the case law in England, Canada, New Zealand and Australia that the courts have had considerable difficulty in formulating the principles to be applied in determining when a court is to give its imprimatur to the "jural quality" of a rule of international law or put another way, whether a rule of customary international law has become part of domestic law. However, it appears that in Australia at least, Dixon J's "source" view [in *Chow Hung Ching* v *The King* (1949) 77 CLR 449] which equates generally with what I have loosely described as the common law adoption approach, holds sway over the incorporation or legislative adoption approaches.

132. The more difficult task is to define with some precision what is meant by the "source" view or the common law adoption approach. In my view, the approach can be formulated as follows:

1. A recognised prerequisite of the adoption in municipal law of customary international law is that the doctrine of public international law has attained the position of general acceptance by or assent of the community of nations "as a rule of international conduct, evidenced by international treaties and conventions, authoritative textbooks, practice and judicial decisions": see *Compania Naviera Vascongado* v *SS Cristina* [1938] AC 485 at 497 per Lord Macmillan. . . .

2. The rule must not only be established to be one which has general acceptance but the court must also consider whether the rule is to be treated as having been adopted or "received into, and so become a source of English law": see Holdsworth at 268 and *Chow Hung Ching* at 477 per Dixon J.

3. A rule will be adopted or received into, and so a source of, domestic law if it is "not inconsistent with rules enacted by statutes or finally declared by [the courts]": *Chung Chi Cheung* (at 168) per Lord Atkin. Plainly, international law cannot be received if it is inconsistent with a rule enacted by statute. However, the position is less clear with a rule that might be inconsistent with the common law. To the extent that international law is to be received into domestic law, it will have necessarily altered or modified the common law and, to that extent, might be said to be inconsistent with it. Thus, in my view a strict test of inconsistency could not have been intended.

4. A rule of customary international law is to be adopted and received unless it is determined to be inconsistent with, and therefore "conflicts" with, domestic law in the sense explained above. In such circumstances no effect can be given to it without legislation to change the law by the enactment of the rule of customary international law as law. . . . This approach subordinates rules of customary international law to domestic law thereby avoiding a fundamental difficulty of the incorporation approach which, by requiring the common law to invariably change to accord with rules of international law, subordinates the common law to customary international law.

5. The rules of customary international law, once adopted or received into domestic law have the "force of law" in the sense of being treated as having modified or altered the common law. The decision of the court to adopt and receive a rule of customary international law is declaratory as to what the common law is. . . .

6. As *Trendtex Trading* demonstrates international law evolves and changes from time to time. However, unlike the common law, the evolution of, and change, in international law is established by evidence and other appropriate material. Thus, it may be that in certain instances the adoption will only be as from the date the particular rule of customary law has been established. . . .

157. The above analysis . . . does not support the view that customary international law, whether civil or in respect of universal crimes, can only be incorporated into municipal law in common law states, like Australia, by legislation. A different situation arises in respect of international criminal law in respect of non-universal international crimes where extra-territoriality and the status of jus cogens, is absent. . . .

185. In the present case I have no difficulty in determining that the "end" or "goal" which the law serves will be better served by treating universal crimes against humanity as part of the common law in Australia. Further, a decision to incorporate crimes against humanity, including genocide, as part of Australia's municipal law at the end of the 20th century satisfies the criteria of experience, common sense, legal principle and public policy.

NOTES:
1. While treaties are not directly incorporated into the national law of Australia, the *Mabo* and *Teoh* cases both recognise the important influence of international law on the development of common law principles, and its role in the interpretation of ambiguous legislation that seeks to implement international obligations. The decision in *Teoh* takes this point a step further by examining the effect of international law on administrative decision-making. In *Newcrest Mining v Commonwealth* (1997) 147 ALR 42 before the High Court of Australia, Kirby J held (at p 148) that 'To the full extent that its text permits, Australia's Constitution, as the fundamental law of government in this country, accommodates itself to international law, including insofar as that law expresses basic rights'. See also Kirby's extra-judicial comments above.

2. The Australian government acted swiftly to reduce the effect of the *Teoh* decision. Arguing that the decision would create uncertainty as to the decision-making process of government officials, the Minister for Foreign Affairs and the Attorney-General stated that the mere fact that the government entered into an international treaty 'is not reason for raising any expectation that government decision-makers will act in accordance with the treaty if the relevant provisions of that treaty have not been enacted into domestic Australian law' (Joint Statement, *International Treaties and the High Court Decision in Teoh*, 10 May 1995). Successive governments have sought to restrict the application of the decicion in *Teoh* by passing legis-lation contrary to the decision. However, none of this legislation has yet been passed by Parliament.

3. The Court in *Nulyarimma v Thompson* clearly had difficulty in trying to determine if a matter was customary international law and, if so, what was its effect. All the Court found that the prohibition on genocide was customary international law (and *jus cogens*). The public policy grounds on which Wilcox (and the majority of the Court) held that a crime should not be unknown and, therefore, that common law crimes should not be developed is unconvincing where genocide is concerned. By the end of the twentieth century all Australians could be expected to believe that genocide was a crime.

C: South Africa

Constitution of the Republic of South Africa 1996

International agreements

231. (1) The negotiating and signing of all international agreements is the responsibility of the national executive.

(2) An international agreement binds the Republic only after it has been approved by reso-lution in both the National Assembly and the National Council of Provinces, unless it is an agreement referred to in subsection (3).

(3) An international agreement of a technical, administrative or executive nature, or an agreement which does not require either ratification or accession, entered into by the national executive, binds the Republic without approval by the National Assembly and the National Council of Provinces, but must be tabled in the Assembly and the Council within a reasonable time.

(4) Any international agreement becomes law in the Republic when it is enacted into law by national legislation; but a self-executing provision of an agreement that has been approved by Parliament is law in the Republic unless it is inconsistent with the Constitution or an Act of Parliament.

(5) The Republic is bound by international agreements which were binding on the Republic when this Constitution took effect.

Customary international law
232. Customary international law is law in the Republic unless it is inconsistent with the Constitution or an Act of Parliament.

Application of international law
233. When interpreting any legislation, every court must prefer any reasonable interpretation of the legislation that is consistent with international law over any alternative interpretation that is inconsistent with international law.

S v *Makwanyane & Mchunu*
1995 (3) SA (CC), Constitutional Court of South Africa

The key issue in this case was whether the death penalty was lawful under the South African Constitution. The Constitution was silent on this point. The Court considered the transitional Constitution (1993) but its terms, for these purposes, were similar to those of the 1996 Constitution. The Court held that the death penalty was unlawful.

CHASKALSON P: 34. . . . In interpreting the provisions of this [Constitution] a court of law shall promote the values which underlie an open and democratic society based on freedom and equality and shall, where applicable, have regard to public international law applicable to the protection of the rights entrenched in this [Constitution], and may have regard to comparable foreign case law.

35. Customary international law and the ratification and accession to international agreements is dealt with in *section* 231 [and 232–233] of the Constitution which sets the requirements for such law to be binding within South Africa. . . . [P]ublic international law would include non-binding as well as binding law. They may both be used . . . as tools of interpretation. International agreements and customary international law accordingly provide a framework within which the [Constitution] can be evaluated and understood, and for that purpose, decisions of tribunals dealing with comparable instruments, such as the United Nations Committee on Human Rights, the Inter-American Commission on Human Rights, the Inter-American Court of Human Rights, the European Commission on Human Rights, and the European Court of Human Rights, and in appropriate cases, reports of specialised agencies such as the International Labour Organisation may provide guidance as to the correct interpretation of [the Constitution].

NOTES:
1. The South African Constitution was adopted after the end of the apartheid era and after large number of other constitutions and treaties, particualrly human rights treaties, were reviewed. A great deal of national consultation and international input occurred before its adoption (see Feldman (above) in relation to the legitimacy this brings to the Constitution). The Constitution recognises the importance of international law on national law.
2. The Constitutional Court of South Africa has had to consider a significant number of key issues that have international law aspects. These have included cases concerning the right of access to health care and the right to housing (*Soobramoney* v *Minister of Health* 1998 (1) SA 765 and *Grootboom* v *Government of the Republic of South Africa* 2000 10 BHRC 84) – see also Chapter 6.

D: United States

The Constitution of the United States 1787
Article VI, section 2

This Constitution, and the Laws of the United States which shall be made in Pursuance thereof; and all Treaties made, or which shall be made, under the Authority of the United States, shall be the supreme Law of the Land; and the Judges in every State shall be bound thereby, any Thing in the Constitution or Laws of any State to the Contrary notwithstanding.

Sei Fujii v *State of California*
19 ILR (1952) 312, Supreme Court of California

A Japanese man who was ineligible for American citizenship, claimed that a Californian law which prevented him owning land was unenforceable as contrary to the United States Constitution and the United Nations Charter.

It is not disputed that the charter is a treaty, and our federal Constitution provides that treaties made under the authority of the United States are part of the supreme law of the land and that the judges in every state are bound thereby. USConst, Article VI. A treaty, however, does not automatically supersede local laws which are inconsistent with it unless the treaty provisions are self-excuting. In the words of Chief Justice Marshall: A treaty is:

> to be regarded in courts of justice as equivalent to an act of the Legislature, whenever it operates of itself, without the aid of any legislative provision. But when the terms of the stipulation import a contract – when either of the parties engages to perform a particular act, the treaty addresses itself to the political, not the judicial department; and the Legislature must execute the contract before it can become a rule for the court.
> *Foster* v *Neilson*, 1829, 2 Pet 253, 324, 7 LEd 415

In determining whether a treaty is self-executing courts look to the intent of the signatory parties as manifested by the language of the instrument, and, if the instrument is uncertain, recourse may be had to the circumstances surrounding its execution. . . . In order for a treaty provision to be operative without the aid of implementing legislation and to have the force and effect of a stature, it must appear that the framers of the treaty intended to prescribe a rule that, standing alone, would be enforceable in the courts. . . .

It is clear that the provisions of the preamble and of Article I of the charter which are claimed to be in conflict with the alien land law are not self-executing. They state general purposes and objectives of the United Nations Organization and do not purport to impose legal obligations on the individual member nations or to create rights in private persons. It is equally clear that none of the other provisions relied on by plaintiff is self-executing. Article 55 declares that the United Nations 'shall promote: . . . universal respect for, and observance of, human rights and fundamental freedoms for all without distinction as to race, sex, language, or religion,' and in Article 56, the member nations 'pledge themselves to take joint and separate action in co-operation with the Organization for the achievement of the purposes set forth in Article 55.' Although the member nations have obligated themselves to co-operate with the international organization in promoting respect for, and observance of, human rights, it is plain that it was contemplated that future legislative action by the several nations would be required to accomplish the declared objectives, and there is nothing to indicate that these provisions were intended to become rules of law for the courts of this country upon the ratification of the charter. . . .

The humane and enlightened objectives of the United Nations Charter are, of course, entitled to respectful consideration by the courts and Legislatures of every member nation, since that document expresses the universal desire of thinking men for peace and for equality of rights and opportunities. The charter represents a moral commitment of foremost importance, and we must not permit the spirit of our pledge to be compromised or disparaged in either our domestic or foreign affairs. We are satisfied, however, that the charter provisions relied on by plaintiff were not intended to supersede existing domestic legislation, and we cannot hold that they operate to invalidate the alien land law.

NOTES:

1. The United States Supreme Court has not been active in applying international law. It has required treaties to be 'self-executing' (see *Fujii*), or incorporated by national law, before they will be applied, despite the words of Article VI(2) of the Constitution (though see *The Paquete Habana* in Chapter 2). It has also ignored international law to protect its government's self-interest, as seen in *United States* v *Alvarez-Machain* 31 ILM (1992) 902, where the forcible abduction of a Mexican national from Mexico by United States government agents was allowed, in apparent contravention of a bilateral treaty and of the customary international law of human rights (see further in Chapter 8).

2. It is apparent from a number of cases that United States courts (like most national courts) require proof of the existence of customary international law before they will apply it – as common law – in the United States. See *Filartiga* v *Pena-Irala* 630 F 2nd 876 (1980) (Court of Appeals, Second Circuit), *Tel-Oren* v *Libyan Arab Republic* 726 F 2nd 774 (1984) (Court of Appeal, District of Columbia Circuit) and *Trajano* v *Marcos* 978 F 2nd 493 (1992) (Court of Appeal, Ninth Circuit).

5

Personality and Recognition

Introductory note

International law is unlike the law of national legal systems in that the persons or entities to which it applies are not always immediately apparent. National law applies, most obviously (though not exclusively), to natural or legal persons within the territorial borders and to 'nationals' of the home State. In a general way, the 'subjects' of national law, being the persons to whom the legal system is addressed, are reasonably well defined geographically and legally. International law has no territorial boundaries in the same sense and no comparable concept of 'nationals'. Consequently, its 'subjects' are harder to define and even to identify. Of course, the question of 'who' may be subject to international rights and duties is of considerable importance. If a 'State', group of persons, territorial entity (e.g. Northern Ireland, Quebec) or multinational corporation can be said to be a 'subject' of international law and have 'international personality' then it can be subject to the rights and duties of the international legal system. This will include procedural rights and obligations, such as the ability to make international claims before judicial tribunals and arbitration panels and the obligation to defend such claims.

The manner in which this valuable international personality is achieved is the subject of much debate. Does it depend on the application of objective rules of international law backed by factual criteria, on the attitude and actions of existing members of the international community, on a combination of these, or is it rather a purely political concept? To what extent does 'recognition' of the international personality of an entity actually confer that personality or, at the least, resolve doubts about disputed personality? Furthermore, in addition to having consequences on the international plane (such as the ability to make treaties, bring claims, participate in multinational events, be held accountable, etc.), international personality (or the absence thereof) may have consequences within the national legal systems of States. These consequences may indeed differ from to State to State. Thus 'recognition' of the statehood of an entity by the United Kingdom may be critical in determining the rights and duties of that State in the national law of the UK. Consequently, in this chapter materials are presented relating to the very concept of international personality, types of legal person under international law, recognition issues in international law and finally the consequences of recognition (or non-recognition) in national law.

SECTION 1: International legal personality

It is clear that there are many different types of international legal person. It is also clear that 'international personality' is not an absolute concept. It is relative in the sense that different types of international legal person may have different types or layers of international personality. Generally (and not exhaustively), international personality entails the ability to bring claims before international tribunals exercising an international legal jurisdiction, to enjoy rights and be subject to international legal obligations, to participate in international law creation, to enjoy the immunities attaching to international legal persons within national legal systems, to participate in international organisations and to conclude treaties. However, not all international persons have the full measure of personality for all purposes and it is a matter of debate whether it is true to say that an entity has 'international personality' if it exercises, say, only one of these attributes. The more that the emphasis is placed on 'States' as the foundation of international law and the international legal system, the less inclined one might be to accept the 'personality' of such diverse groups as Non-Governmental Organisations (e.g. Greenpeace), corporations (e.g. Microsoft) and non-independent territorial entities (e.g. Quebec, Palestine). To this extent we must recognise that both politics and legal theory play a part in helping to understand the concept of international personality.

A: Statehood

States are the most important subjects of international law. By definition, if an entity amounts to a 'State' it has the potential or 'capacity' to avail itself of all of the rights and to be subject to all of the duties known to the international system. Of course, individual States may have deliberately limited their capacity in respect of particular rights or duties, often by treaty (e.g. by accepting the Vienna Convention on Diplomatic Relations 1961 States limit their jurisdictional rights), but this does not detract from their paramount claim to those rights and duties. In effect, the rights and duties of States set the bench-mark for the other 'subjects' of international law.

Montevideo Convention on the Rights and Duties of States 1933
135 LNTS (1936) 19

Article 1
The State as a person of international law should possess the following qualifications: (a) a permanent population; (b) a defined territory; (c) government; and (d) capacity to enter into relations with other states.

Customs Regime between Germany and Austria Case
PCIJ Ser A/B (1931) No. 41, Permanent Court of International Justice

In a Protocol (i.e. treaty) signed at Geneva in October 1922, Austria undertook not to give up its independence in economic matters contrary to Article 88 of the Treaty of St-Germain. In a Protocol signed at Vienna in March 1931, Austria agreed to negotiate a customs union with Germany. The Council of the League of Nations requested an Advisory Opinion on whether this proposed union would violate the terms of the 1922 Protocol and Article 88 of the Treaty of St-Germain. A majority of the Court held that it would, and in his Separate Opinion, Judge Anzilotti discussed the nature of 'independence' in international law.

JUDGE ANZILOTTI: . . . With regard to the former, [the meaning of 'independence'] I think the foregoing observations show that the independence of Austria within the meaning of Article 88 is nothing else but the existence of Austria, within the frontiers laid down by the Treaty of Saint-Germain, as a separate State and not subject to the authority of any other State or group of States. Independence as thus understood is really no more than the normal condition of States according to international law; it may also be described as *sovereignty (suprema potestas)*, or *external sovereignty*, by which is meant that the State has over it no other authority than that of international law.

The conception of independence, regarded as the normal characteristic of States as subjects of international law, cannot be better defined than by comparing it with the exceptional and, to some extent, abnormal class of States known as 'dependent States.' These are States subject to the authority of one or more other States. The idea of dependence therefore necessarily implies a relation between a superior State (suzerain, protector, etc.) and an inferior or subject State (vassal, *protégé*, etc.); the relation between the State which can legally impose its will and the State which is legally compelled to submit to that will. Where there is no such relation of superiority and subordination, it is impossible to speak of dependence within the meaning of international law.

It follows that the legal conception of independence has nothing to do with a State's subordination to international law or with the numerous and constantly increasing states of *de facto* dependence which characterize the relation of one country to other countries.

It also follows that the restrictions upon a State's liberty, whether arising out of ordinary international law or contractual engagements, do not as such in the least affect its independence. As long as these restrictions do not place the State under the legal authority of another State, the former remains an independent State however extensive and burdensome those obligations may be.

United Nations Charter 1945

Article 2
1. . . . The Organization is based on the principle of the sovereign equality of all its Members. . . .

Article 4

1. Membership in the United Nations is open to all other peace-loving States which accept the obligations contained in the present Charter and, in the judgment of the Organization, are able and willing to carry out these obligations.

2. The admission of any such State to membership in the United Nations will be effected by a decision of the General Assembly upon the recommendation of the Security Council.

J. Crawford, 'The Criteria for Statehood in International Law'
(1976–77) 48 BYBIL 93

If the effect of positivist doctrine in international law was to place the emphasis, in matters of statehood, on the question of recognition, then the effect of modern doctrine and practice has been to return the attention to issues of statehood and status, independent of recognition. But there is nevertheless no generally accepted and satisfactory contemporary legal definition of statehood. This may well be because the question normally arises only in the borderline cases, where a new entity has emerged bearing some but not all of the characteristics of undoubted States. International lawyers are thus confronted with difficult problems of characterization; and, as has been suggested, such problems do not occur, and cannot be solved, except in relation to the particular issues and circumstances. But, it may be asked, are there any legal consequences which attach to statehood as such, but which are not legal incidents of other forms of international personality? To put it another way, is there a legal concept of statehood, or does the meaning of the term vary infinitely depending on the context? . . . [S]tatehood does appear to be a term of art in international law; though of course, like all legal, and especially international legal, concepts it is one of open texture. The following exclusive and general legal characteristics of States may be instanced.

1. In principle States have plenary competence to perform acts, make treaties and so on, in the international sphere: this is one meaning of the term 'sovereign' as applied to States.

2. In principle States are exclusively competent with respect to their internal affairs, a principle reflected by Article 2, paragraph 7 of the United Nations Charter. This does not of course mean that they are omnicompetent, in international law, with respect to those affairs: it does mean that their jurisdiction is prima facie both plenary and not subject to the control of other States.

3. In principle States are not subject to compulsory international process, jurisdiction or settlement, unless they consent, either in specific cases or generally, to such exercise.

4. States are regarded in international law as 'equal', a principle also recognized by the Charter (Article 2(1)). This is in part a restatement of the foregoing principles, but it may have certain other corollaries. It is a formal, not a moral or political, principle. It does not mean, for example, that all States are entitled to an equal vote in international organizations, merely that, in any international organization not based on equality, the consent of all the Members to the derogation from equality is required.

5. Finally, any derogations from these principles must be clearly established: in case of doubt an international court or tribunal will decide in favour of the freedom of action of States, whether with respect to external or internal affairs, or as not having consented to a specific exercise of international jurisdiction, or to a particular derogation from equality. This presumption – which is of course rebuttable in any given case – provides a useful indication as to the status of the entity in whose favour it is invoked. It will be referred to throughout this study as the *Lotus* presumption – its classic formulation being the judgment of the Permanent Court in *The Lotus*. . . .

If there is then a legal concept of statehood, it follows that the law must find some means of determining which entities are 'States', with the above attributes; in other words, of determining the criteria for statehood. It is with this that we are here concerned.

Two preliminary points should, however, be made. First, upon examination the exclusive attributes of States listed above are found not to prescribe specific rights, powers or liberties which all States must, to be States, possess: rather they are presumptions as to the existence of such rights, powers or liberties, rules that these exist unless otherwise provided for. This must be so, since the actual powers, rights and liberties of particular States vary considerably. The legal consequences of statehood are thus seen to be – paradoxically – matters of evidence, or rather of presumption. Predicated on a basic or 'structural' independence, statehood does not involve any necessary substantive rights. Equally the law recognizes no general duty on a State to maintain that independence: independence is protected while it exists, but there is no prohibition on its partial or permanent alienation. The legal concept of statehood provides a measure for determining whether in a given case rights have been acquired or lost.

Secondly, the criteria for statehood are rather special rules, in that their application conditions the application of most other international law rules. As a result, existing States have sometimes tended to assert more or less complete freedom of action with regard to new States. This may explain the reluctance of the International Law Commission to frame comprehensive definitions of statehood when engaged on other work – albeit work which assumed that the category 'States' is certain or ascertainable. It follows that, at the empirical level, the question must again be asked: whether, given the existence of international law rules determining what are 'States', those rules are sufficiently certain to be applied in specific cases, or else have been kept so uncertain or open to interpretation as not to constitute rules at all. And this question is independent of the point – which is accepted – that States may on occasions treat as a State an entity which does not come within the accepted definition of the term. The question is rather: can States legitimately refuse, under cover of the 'open texture' of rules, to treat entities as States which do in fact qualify? Preventing that is the point of having – if in fact we do have – 'objective' criteria for statehood.

H. Charlesworth and C. Chinkin, *The Boundaries of International Law*
(2000), pp. 124–134

Statehood confers the capacity to claim rights and duties under international law. Other entities, such as individuals and international inter-governmental and NGOs, can assert some degree of international personhood for particular purposes, but the state is considered the most complete expression of international legal personality. The state is of course an artificial entity, a means of allocating political control over territory. Its decisions, policies and strategies are those of the individuals and groups comprising its decision-making elites. International law regards states as independent and autonomous members of the international community. It tends to obliterate the differences between states by considering all states as formally equal, whatever their size, population, geography or wealth. In practice, however, disparities in size, population and wealth create great differences in power between states which are sometimes acknowledged in weighted voting systems in international organisations or differential treaty obligations. The fiction of equality is preserved through such arrangements being presented as dependent on the consent of all states parties.

The monolithic view of statehood upon which traditional international law doctrine depends significantly limits the scope of international law. One consequence is that it establishes a model for full international personality that other claimants for international status cannot replicate. Moreover, the idea of statehood constructed by international law creates a barrier between the entity of the state and those within it. This is exemplified externally by the principles of non-intervention and non-interference in the domestic affairs of states and internally by doctrines of immunity and non-justifiability. International legal theory has little to say about national decision-making processes, providing limited constraints on national action mainly through human rights principles. It is therefore not surprising that there has been little investigation by international lawyers of statehood's differential significance for women and men.

International legal doctrine on the state focuses on the criteria for, and the incidents of, statehood. . . .

A permanent population

International legal doctrine does not require a minimum number of inhabitants for an entity to qualify as a state. Indeed, the Montevideo definition gives no content to the notion of population, apart from the need for it to be permanent. The constitution of a population appears in many respects as a broad prerogative of statehood. The fact that the Vatican City is recognised as a state in international law suggests that there is no problem if an entity restricts its population almost entirely to adult men and that the population is reproduced asexually, through recruitment.

The concept of permanent population as a criterion of statehood assumes that populations are static. This is inaccurate in a number of ways. In the 1990s there were significant movements of peoples within and between states. For example, the UNHCR estimated that in 1997 there were 50 million forcibly displaced people around the world. . . .

Certain restraints on population have, however, been accepted as undermining a claim to statehood. For example, the 'homelands' or 'Bantustans' created by South Africa were never accepted as states by the international community. The UN General Assembly strongly condemned their establishment 'as designed to consolidate the inhuman policies of apartheid, to destroy the territorial integrity of the country, to perpetuate white minority domination and to dispossess the African people of South Africa of their inalienable rights'. . . . International practice, therefore, suggests that a certain form of racial policy may be significant but that other forms of population change are insignificant in the assessment of whether a particular group of people constitutes a permanent population. . . .

Defined territory

The territory of a state can vary greatly in size. The fact that the borders, or indeed existence, of a territorial entity are contested is considered no barrier to statehood. What is considered critical is that there be 'a certain coherent territory effectively governed'. A related international legal principle is the right of states to 'territorial integrity'. Article 2(4) of the UN Charter commits all member states to 'refrain in their international relations from the threat or use of force against the territorial integrity or political independence of any state'.

This concern with the coherence and integrity of territory presents the state as a bounded, unified entity. The notions of boundaries, borders, circumferences and peripheries have considerable power in legal rhetoric. Thus minority peoples do not qualify as full subjects of international law.

In the twentieth century territorial claims have expanded to include maritime areas and air space. Delimitation of such areas creates new problems to which traditional international law rules of acquisition of territory are inapplicable. New prescriptive regimes have been developed for these areas which emphasise the durability of the concern with boundary drawing. Innovative schemes for equitable sharing of resources in the post-colonial era such as the concept of 'the common heritage of mankind' have been controversial and resisted by a number of developed countries. In the context of the deep seabed and subsoil, the area beyond national jurisdiction and hence within the common heritage area, was greatly reduced by the extensive definition of the continental shelf. The envisaged operation of mining that area for the common benefit has been subsequently modified because of pressure from developed states, notably the United States and some member states of the EU in ways that effectively undermine the spirit of common heritage in favour of 'market-oriented approaches'.

Government

International law requires that an entity have an organised and effective government before it can be considered a state. Traditionally, there has been little concern with the *form* of the government, only its effectiveness. State practice indicates some outer limits on methods of achieving governmental stability, particularly at the time of the formation of a new entity. For example, the UN's refusal to recognise the declaration of independence of Ian Smith's government in Southern Rhodesia in 1965 was based on its purpose of enabling continued minority white rule, as well as its unilateral assertion. The notion of governmental power assumed in the definition of statehood, however, does not question women's exclusion from systems of power worldwide; indeed it can be seen to depend for its smooth functioning on particular versions of masculinity and femininity, which, like the Athenian *polis*, connect men with public political life and women with the private, domestic infrastructure that is necessary to sustain public life.

The criterion of an organised and effective government, like all the traditional international legal criteria of statehood, depends on a notion of state autonomy built on isolation and separation. It enables the state to be seen as a complete, coherent, bounded entity that speaks with one voice, obliterating the diversity of voices within the state. In this way, government can be seen as the head of the body of the state, which is made up of its population and territory. . . .

Capacity to enter into relations with other states

This criterion of statehood is generally understood to signify independence from the authority of other states, so that agreements with other states can be freely entered into. Independence, or its synonym in international law, sovereignty, is considered the principal criterion of statehood. . . . Sovereignty means both full competence to act in the international arena, for example by entering into treaties or by acting to preserve state security, and exclusive jurisdiction over internal matters, for example exercise of legislative, executive and judicial competence. Thus sovereignty is a doubled-sided principle: externally, it signifies equality of power, and internally, it signifies pre-eminence of power. The standard view of international law as an essentially consensual regime is a concomitant of sovereignty – a fully sovereign entity can only voluntarily accept restraints on its activities. This capacity distinguishes states from other non-state entities such as indigenous peoples. Consent to the regime of international law thus becomes the vehicle by which the sovereign independence of states is reconciled with the practical imperatives of co-existence with other states.

There are strong connections between the requirement of a defined territory, and the notions of independence and sovereignty. One aspect of the definition of territory and the creation of boundaries is precisely to foster independence and autonomy from other entities. . . .

That capacity to enter into international relations depends upon the willingness of other states to allow particular interests an international voice is illustrated by the somewhat anomalous position of the Holy See. The territorial state of the Vatican City is governed by the Holy See, which is a non-member state maintaining a permanent observer mission to the UN. The Holy See is regarded as the 'juridical personification' of the Roman Catholic Church. It is a full member of some UN specialised agencies and some European intergovernmental organisations. The Holy See receives and sends diplomatic representatives to other states. It can enter into treaties, address the UN General Assembly and participate as an associate member of the UN on the same basis as state delegations in UN conferences and meetings. It has exercised considerable influence within both the specialised agencies and at global conferences.

NOTES:
1. It is clear that the criteria of the Montevideo Convention have been accepted as the indicia of Statehood and have now passed into customary international law. However, the question remains whether these criteria are sufficient for Statehood, as well as being necessary. In his article, Crawford goes on to consider other possible conditions such as 'permanence', 'willingness and ability to observe international law', 'a certain degree of civilisation', 'recognition', the existence of a 'legal order' within the State, and 'legality'. This indicates that 'Statehood' is a rather more complex legal relationship than the Montevideo Convention suggests. Likewise, the European Community and Member State's Guidelines on Recognition of New States in Eastern Europe and the Soviet Union, and their Declaration on Yugoslavia (see below) appear to lay down additional criteria for Statehood, or at least for recognition of Statehood. However, as illustrated in the extract from Murphy (below) it is unwise to trumpet 'Western' notions of Statehood (e.g., democracy) as if they were accepted universally.

2. Another problem is who is competent to decide whether an entity has achieved the conditions laid down in the Montevideo Convention and any additional Statehood criteria. In this regard, membership of an international organisation may be strong evidence. Yet, the Saharan Arab Republic (Western Sahara) is a member of the OAU, although not the United Nations. As at January 2003 there are 191 members of the United Nations (see Appendix) but this excludes Taiwan, the Palestinian Autonomous Area, East Timor and Northern Cyprus. Membership of the United Nations is a prize for aspirant States, a good example being the admittance of Eritrea on its secession from Ethiopia.

B: Other territorial entities

Clearly there exist many other territorial creations that are not States as such but which also cannot accurately be described as 'merely' part of the metropolis of a an existing State. Taiwan provides a good example, being neither desirous itself of the status of 'statehood' (because it formally still adheres to a 'one China' policy) but in essence operating as an independent entity. Other, more difficult examples exist, such as the Palestinian Autonomous Area (the Gaza Strip and West Bank), Saharan Arab Republic and Chechnya. Then there are autonomous components of existing states such as Quebec (Canada), Northern Ireland (UK) and Montenegro (Yugoslavia). To what extent do these territorial entities have international personality? Does it matter that there *is* a link to a territorial space (like a State) and might many existing states once have been described in these terms (e.g. Namibia, Eritrea, and Bangladesh). So, are such entities really pre-States whose personality is diminished accordingly (but still exists) that may, or may not, acquire statehood depending on future developments?

Rights of Nationals of the United States in Morocco Case (France v United States)
ICJ Rep 1952 176, International Court of Justice

France instituted proceedings against the United States in October 1950 because of a dispute over the economic activities of US nationals in Morocco. These had been restricted by a Decree of 1948 issued by the French Resident General, much to the advantage of French nationals. This was alleged to be contrary to the General Act of Algeciras 1906, a multiparty treaty that guaranteed economic equality for aliens in Morocco. At the relevant time, Morocco was a French Protectorate. One question for the Court was to determine the status of Morocco in international law, for this could affect the rights of France to regulate the economic activities of foreign nationals.

It is common ground between the Parties that the characteristic of the status of Morocco, as resulting from the General Act of Algeciras of April 7th, 1906, is respect for the three principles stated in the Preamble of the Act, namely: 'the sovereignty and independence of His Majesty the Sultan, the integrity of his domains, and economic liberty without any inequality'. . . .

It is not disputed by the French Government that Morocco, even under the Protectorate, has retained its personality as a State in international law. The rights of France in Morocco are defined by the Protectorate Treaty of 1912. In economic matters France is accorded no privileged position in

Morocco. Such a privileged position would not be compatible with the principle of economic liberty without any inequality, on which the Act of Algeciras is based.

Reference Re Secession of Quebec
37 ILM 1340 (1998), Canadian Supreme Court

126. The recognized sources of international law establish that the right to self-determination of a people is normally fulfilled through *internal* self-determination – a people's pursuit of its political, economic, social and cultural development within the framework of an existing state. A right to *external* self-determination (which in this case potentially takes the form of the assertion of a right to unilateral secession) arises in only the most extreme of cases and, even then, under carefully defined circumstances. *External* self-determination can be defined as in the following statement from the *Declaration on Friendly Relations* . . . as

> The establishment of a sovereign and independent State, the free association or integration with an independent State or the emergence into any other political status freely determined by a *people* constitute modes of implementing the right of self-determination by *that people*. [Emphasis added.]

127. The international law principle of self-determination has evolved within a framework of respect for the territorial integrity of existing states. The various international documents that support the existence of a people's right to self-determination also contain parallel statements supportive of the conclusion that the exercise of such a right must be sufficiently limited to prevent threats to an existing state's territorial integrity or the stability of relations between sovereign states.

NOTES:

1. A similar opinion to that offered in the *US Nationals Case* had been given earlier in the *Nationality Decrees in Tunis and Morocco Case*, PCIJ Ser B, (1923) No 4, where the Court also noted that the 'extent of the powers of a protecting State in the territory of a protected State depends, first upon the Treaties between the protecting State and the protected State establishing the Protectorate, and, secondly, upon the conditions under which the Protectorate has been recognised by third Powers as against whom there is an intention to rely on the provisions of these Treaties'.

2. A clear example of entities tied to a territory and being classified as subjects of international law without being States *per se* were the peoples of the UN Trust Territories. Similar to League of Nation's Mandates, such territories were placed under the Trusteeship of a protecting State whose paramount duty was to promote the peoples' right of self-determination, On 1 October 1994, the last remaining Trusteeship territory (Palau) exercised its right of self-determination by becoming an independent state. The Republic of Palau, the Federated States of Micronesia and the Republic of the Marshall Islands were formerly part of the Pacific Trust Territory and all have become independent sovereign States. All three have entered into Compacts with the United States which, while not compromising their sovereignty, is a loose form of protectorate or free association. The Commonwealth of the Northern Mariana Islands, also part of the former Pacific Trust Territory, has exercised its right of self-determination by becoming a self-governing Commonwealth under the sovereignty of the United States. However, neither an exercise of the right of self-determination nor a successful secession need necessarily lead to Statehood, as seen in the *Quebec Secession Case* above (and see Chapter 7).

C: International organisations

International organisations are one of the growth areas of international law. When discussing international personality, it is tempting to think only of the major international multilateral organisations such as the United Nations, Organisation of African Unity (OAU), Organisation of American States (OAS) and the League of Arab States. There are also general organisations (such as the UN), organisations within organisations (e.g. UNESCO within the UN), regional organisations (e.g. the EU and OAS), single issue organisations (e.g. International Maritime Organisation), economic organisations (e.g. World Trade Organisation), military organisations (e.g. NATO), and even two-party organisations (e.g. UK-Ireland Decommissioning Body). All of these may well have international personality to some degree or another, and much will depend on the manner of their creation and the role they are designed to fulfil within the international legal order.

United Nations Charter

Article 104
The Organization shall enjoy in the territory of each of its Members such legal capacity as may be necessary for the exercise of its functions and the fulfilment of its purposes.

Article 105
1. The Organization shall enjoy in the territory of each of its Members such privileges and immunities as are necessary for the fulfilment of its purposes.
2. Representatives of the Members of the United Nations and officials of the Organization shall similarly enjoy such privileges and immunities as are necessary for the independent exercise of their functions in connection with the Organization. . . .

Reparations for Injuries Suffered in the Service of the United Nations Opinion
ICJ Rep 1949 174, International Court of Justice

> Following the assassination of Count Bernadotte, a UN official, in Jerusalem in 1948, the General Assembly requested the ICJ to give an Advisory Opinion on whether the United Nations had 'as an Organisation, the capacity to bring an international claim against the responsible *de jure* or *de facto* government with a view to obtaining the reparation due in respect of the damage caused (a) to the United Nations, (b) to the victim or the persons entitled through him?'. The Court held unanimously, in respect of (a) that the UN had such capacity *vis à vis* Members of the Organisation and non-members; and similarly by 11 votes to 4 in respect of question (b).

Competence to bring an international claim is, for those possessing it, the capacity to resort to the customary methods recognized by international law for the establishment, the presentation and the settlement of claims. Among these methods may be mentioned protest, request for an enquiry, negotiation, and request for submission to an arbitral tribunal or to the Court in so far as this may be authorized by the Statute.

This capacity certainly belongs to the State; a State can bring an international claim against another State. Such a claim takes the form of a claim between two political entities, equal in law, similar in form, and both the direct subjects of international law. It is dealt with by means of negotiation, and cannot, in the present state of the law as to international jurisdiction, be submitted to a tribunal, except with the consent of the States concerned.

When the Organization brings a claim against one of its Members, this claim will be presented in the same manner, and regulated by the same procedure. It may, when necessary, be supported by the political means at the disposal of the Organization. In these ways the Organization would find a method for securing the observance of its rights by the Member against which it has a claim.

But, in the international sphere, has the Organization such a nature as involves the capacity to bring an international claim? In order to answer this question, the Court must first enquire whether the Charter has given the Organization such a position that it possesses, in regard to its Members, rights which it is entitled to ask them to respect. In other words, does the Organization possess international personality? This is no doubt a doctrinal expression, which has sometimes given rise to controversy. But it will be used here to mean that if the Organization is recognized as having that personality, it is an entity capable of availing itself of obligations incumbent upon its Members. . . .

To answer this question, which is not settled by the actual terms of the Charter, we must consider what characteristics it was intended thereby to give to the Organization.

The subjects of law in any legal system are not necessarily identical in their nature or in the extent of their rights, and their nature depends upon the needs of the community. Throughout its history, the development of international law has been influenced by the requirements of international life, and the progressive increase in the collective activities of States has already given rise to instances of action upon the international plane by certain entities which are not States. This development culminated in the establishment in June 1945 of an international organization whose purposes and principles are specified in the Charter of the United Nations. But to achieve these ends the attribution of international personality is indispensable. . . .

The Charter has not been content to make the Organization created by it merely a centre 'for harmonizing the actions of nations in the attainment of these common ends' (Article 1, para. 4). It has equipped that centre with organs, and has given it special tasks. It has defined the position of the Members in relation to the Organization by requiring them to give it every assistance in any action undertaken by it (Article 2, para. 5), and to accept and carry out the decisions of the Security Council; by authorizing the General Assembly to make recommendations to the Members; by giving the Organization legal capacity and privileges and immunities in the territory of each of its Members; and by providing for the conclusion of agreements between the Organization and its Members. Practice – in particular the conclusion of conventions to which the Organization is a party – has confirmed this character of the Organization, which occupies a position in certain respects in detachment from its Members, and which is under a duty to remind them, if need be, of certain obligations. It must be added that the Organization is a political body, charged with political tasks of an important character, and covering a wide field namely, the maintenance of international peace and security, the development of friendly relations among nations, and the achievement of international co-operation in the solution of problems of an economic, social, cultural or humanitarian character (Article 1); and in dealing with its Members it employs political means. The 'Convention on the Privileges and Immunities of the United Nations' of 1946 creates rights and duties between each of the signatories and the Organization. . . . It is difficult to see how such a convention could operate except upon the international plane and as between parties possessing international personality.

In the opinion of the Court, the Organization was intended to exercise and enjoy, and is in fact exercising and enjoying, functions and rights which can only be explained on the basis of the possession of a large measure of international personality and the capacity to operate upon an international plane. It is at present the supreme type of international organization, and it could not carry out the intentions of its founders if it was devoid of international personality. It must be acknowledged that its Members, by entrusting certain functions to it, with the attendant duties and responsibilities, have clothed it with the competence required to enable those functions to be effectively discharged.

Accordingly, the Court has come to the conclusion that the Organization is an international person. That is not the same thing as saying that it is a State, which it certainly is not, or that its legal personality and rights and duties are the same as those of a State. Still less is it the same thing as saying that it is 'a super-State', whatever that expression may mean. It does not even imply that all its rights and duties must be upon the international plane, any more than all the rights and duties of a State must be upon that plane. What it does mean is that it is a subject of international law and capable of possessing international rights and duties, and that it has capacity to maintain its rights by bringing international claims. . . .

The next question is whether the sum of the international rights of the Organization comprises the right to bring the kind of international claim described in the Request for this Opinion. That is a claim against a State to obtain reparation in respect of the damage caused by the injury of an agent of the Organization in the course of the performance of his duties. Whereas a State possesses the totality of international rights and duties recognized by international law, the rights and duties of an entity such as the Organization must depend upon its purposes and functions as specified or implied in its constituent documents and developed in practice. The functions of the Organization are of such a character that they could not be effectively discharged if they involved the concurrent action, on the international plane, of fifty-eight or more Foreign Offices, and the Court concludes that the Members have endowed the Organization with capacity to bring international claims when necessitated by the discharge of its functions. . . .

[On Question 1 (a)] the question is concerned solely with the reparation of damage caused to the Organization when one of its agents suffers injury at the same time. It cannot be doubted that the Organization has the capacity to bring an international claim against one of its Members which has caused injury to it by a breach of its international obligations towards it. The damage specified in Question 1 (a) means exclusively damage caused to the interests of the Organization itself, to its administrative machine, to its property and assets, and to the interests of which it is the guardian. It is clear that the Organization has the capacity to bring a claim for this damage. As the claim is based on the breach of an international obligation on the part of the Member held responsible by the Organization, the Member cannot contend that this obligation is governed by municipal law, and the Organization is justified in giving its claim the character of an international claim.

When the Organization has sustained damage resulting from a breach by a Member of its international obligations, it is impossible to see how it can obtain reparation unless it possesses capacity to bring an international claim. It cannot be supposed that in such an event all the Members of the Organization save the defendant State must combine to bring a claim against the defendant for the damage suffered by the Organization. . . .

The question remains whether the Organization has 'the capacity to bring an international claim against the responsible *de jure* or *de facto* government with a view to obtaining the reparation due in respect of the damage caused (a) to the United Nations, (b) to the victim or to persons entitled through him' when the defendant State is not a member of the Organization.

In considering this aspect of Question 1 (a) and (b), it is necessary to keep in mind the reasons which have led the Court to given an affirmative answer to it when the defendant State is a Member of the Organization. It has now been established that the Organization has capacity to bring claims on the international plane, and that it possesses a right of functional protection in respect of its agents. Here again the Court is authorized to assume that the damage suffered involves the responsibility of a State, and it is not called upon to express an opinion upon the various ways in which that responsibility might be engaged. Accordingly the question is whether the Organization has capacity to bring a claim against the defendant State to recover reparation in respect of that damage or whether, on the contrary, the defendant State, not being a member, is justified in raising the objection that the Organization lacks the capacity to bring an international claim. On this point, the Court's opinion is that fifty States, representing the vast majority of the members of the international community, had the power, in conformity with international law, to bring into being an entity possessing objective international personality, and not merely personality recognized by them alone, together with capacity to bring international claims.

Accordingly, the Court arrives at the conclusion that an affirmative answer should be given to Question 1 (a) and (b) whether or not the defendant State is a Member of the United Nations.

United Nations General Assembly: Report of the Secretary-General, Administrative and Budgetary Aspects of the Financing of United Nations Peacekeeping Operations
37 ILM 700 (1998)

6. The international responsibility of the United Nations for the activities of United Nations forces is an attribute of its international legal personality and its capacity to bear international rights and obligations. It is also a reflection of the principle of State responsibility – widely accepted to be applicable to international organizations – that damage caused in breach of an international obligation and which is attributable to the State (or to the Organization), entails the international responsibility of the State (or of the Organization) and its liability in compensation.

7. In recognition of its international responsibility for the activities of its forces, the United Nations has since the inception of peacekeeping operations assumed its liability for damage caused by members of its' forces in the performance of their duties. In conformity with section 29 of the Convention on the Privileges and Immunities of the United Nations, it has undertaken in paragraph 51 of the model status-of-forces agreement (see A/451594) to settle by means of a standing claims commission claims resulting from damage caused by members of the force in the performance of their of official duties and which for reasons of immunity of the Organization and its Members could not have been submitted to local courts.

8. The undertaking to settle disputes of a private law nature submitted against it and the practice of actual settlement of such third-party claims – although not necessarily according to the procedure provided for under the status-of-forces agreement – evidence the recognition on the part of the United Nations that liability for damage caused by members of United Nations forces is attributable to the Organization.

Legality of the Threat or Use of Nuclear Weapons Opinion (WHO Advisory Opinion)
ICJ Rep 1996 66, International Court of Justice

The World Health Organisation (WHO) requested an advisory opinion on whether 'the use of nuclear weapons by a State in war or other armed conflict [would] be a breach of its obligations under international law including the WHO Convention'. At the same time, the General Assembly requested an advisory opinion in relation to the threat or use of nuclear weapons (see Chapter 14). In deciding that the Court did not have jurisdiction to decide on this request by WHO, the Court considered the personality of international organisations.

25. The Court need hardly point out that international organizations are subjects of international law which do not, unlike States, possess a general competence. International organizations are governed by the 'principle of speciality', that is to say, they are invested by the States which create them with powers, the limits of which are a function of the common interests whose promotion

those States entrusts to them. The Permanent Court of International Justice referred to this basic principle in the following terms:

> As the European Commission is not a State, but an international institution with a special purpose, it only has the functions bestowed upon it by the Definitive Statute with a view to the fulfilment of that purpose, but it has power to exercise those functions to their full extent, in so far as the Statute does not impose restrictions on it. (*Jurisdiction of the European Commission of the Danube*, Advisory Opinion, PCIJ, Series B, No. 14, p. 64.)

The powers conferred on international organizations are normally the subject of an express statement in their constituent instruments. Nevertheless, the necessities of international life may point to the need for organizations, in order to achieve their objectives, to possess subsidiary powers which are not expressly provided for in the basic instruments which govern their activities. It is generally accepted that international organizations can exercise such powers, known as 'implied' powers. . . .

In the opinion of the Court, to ascribe to the WHO the competence to address the legality of the use of nuclear weapons – even in view of their health and environmental effects – would be tantamount to disregarding the principle of speciality; for such competence could not be deemed a necessary implication of the Constitution of the Organization in the light of the purposes assigned to it by its member States.

International Tin Council Case (*Maclaine Watson* v *Department of Trade and Industry*)
[1989] Ch 72, Court of Appeal

The facts of this case are noted in Chapter 4. One aspect of the litigation was the claim made by the EEC in the Court of Appeal that it was entitled to sovereign immunity in the United Kingdom in respect of its dealings with the International Tin Council. In dealing with this submission, which was ultimately unsuccessful, Kerr LJ commented upon the place of the European Community/Union in the international legal order.

KERR LJ: There can be no doubt that the EEC has legal personality in international law. This is provided in the EEC Treaty to which I come shortly, and is therefore part of the law of the member states. In the case of the United Kingdom the relevant article is incorporated into our law by section 2 of the European Communities Act 1972. No doubt the EEC would also be recognised as a legal entity under the laws of non-member states, but we are not concerned with this question and I only mention it for the sake of completeness.

Next, there is equally no doubt that the EEC (European Union) exercises powers and functions which are analogous to those of sovereign states. In particular it has the *jus missionis* in the sense that it has permanent delegations in many non-member states and receives permanent representatives from many countries, and that all these missions have diplomatic status. Furthermore, apart from the right of legation, the EEC also has the *jus tractatus* as instanced by ITA 6 itself, i.e. the power to conclude or participate in treaties with sovereign states and international organisations. This power has also been widely used. Finally, the EEC enjoys certain sovereign powers to the extent to which these have been ceded to it by its members under the various EEC treaties, and from this cession it has derived its own legislative, executive and judicial organs whose acts and decisions take effect within the member states. On the other hand, the EEC differs from sovereign states in that it has no sovereignty over territory as such and no nationals or citizens.

NOTES:

1. The legal personality of the United Nations in international law and the national law of UN

members is also guaranteed by Article 1 of the Convention on the Privileges and Immunities of the United Nations 1946. State parties to this Convention commonly give effect to the legal personality of the UN in their national legal systems through legislation. See, for example, in the UK the International Organisations Acts 1968 and 1981, and (for example) in the Syria Legislative Decree No. 12 of 3 August 1953. In the *Reparations Opinion* (above). The Opinion indicates that the United Nations has 'objective' legal personality. It is not clear, however, whether this personality is opposable to (that is, enforceable against) non-members through recognition, or generally whether any State or group of States has the power to create an entity endowed with international personality where such personality *must* then be recognised by the international community at large.

2. In terms of functions, the United Nations can behave very much like a state. In the past it has had legal (if not factual) control over territory (for example, over Namibia pre-independence after terminating the Mandate of South Africa, and in East Timor prior to the latter's independence). Moreover, as the above extracts make clear, the UN has the ability both to bring claims and to be subject to liabilities under international law.

3. The *WHO Advisory Opinion* makes it clear that ultimately the full reach of an organisation's personality will depend on its constituent treaty, although note also how the Court in the *Reparations Opinion* was prepared to imply powers for the UN if these were necessary for the fulfilment of the general functions of the organisation. Ultimately, of course, an organisation's personality can be destroyed by its dissolution in accordance with international law. This was indeed the fate of the League of Nations.

4. The Vienna Convention on the Law of Treaties between International Organisations, or between States and International Organisations 1986, is significant not only because it establishes a comprehensive code of treaty law for international organisations, but also because its existence testifies to the importance of organisations as international legal persons. The fact that the rules of this Convention follow broadly the rules of the Vienna Convention on Treaties between States 1969 (see Chapter 3) is further evidence of this trend. Whether the generous legal personality enjoyed by international organisations can continue as their number proliferates remains to be seen. It may well be – and this is at present only a hypothesis – that the concept of international personality as it applies to international organisations becomes more sophisticated and layered as their numbers swell and their sphere of operations widens.

5. The European Union was one of the original signatories to the Agreement Relating to the Implementation of Part XI of the 1982 Convention on the Law of the Sea 1994 (see Chapter 10). In *French Republic* v *Commission of the European Communities*, C-327/91, 9 August 1994, the Court of Justice of the European Communities found that the European Commission had acted *ultra vires* in concluding a treaty with the United States on antitrust matters (on which see Chapter 8). The judgment is interesting in many respects for the constitutional law of the European Communities, but the important point for present purposes is that the Court did not doubt that the Communities (now the European Union) had personality in international law and with it the capacity to conclude treaties. Rather, the Court determined that the wrong organ of the Communities had concluded the treaty in question. Of course, this does not invalidate the agreement at international law because of the principle that non-compliance with internal rules concerning treaty-making capacity will not invalidate an otherwise valid international act save in the most exceptional circumstances (see Chapter 3).

6. It is possible for two States to create an entity enjoying international personality for limited purposes. In 1997 the UK and the Republic of Ireland established the Independent International Commission on Decommissioning in relation to Northern Ireland and this enjoys

certain international privileges and immunities, made operative in the United Kingdom under the International Organisations Act 1968.

D: Individuals

The place of individuals within the system of international law has been a cause of controversy for some considerable time. Originally, international law was a system of rules governing the relations between sovereign States, and many of the rules of the system still reflect this. Moreover, it remains true that many States are slow to allow individuals to have any rights and duties outside their own national legal systems. However, in recent years, the emergence of a substantial body of human rights law (see Chapter 6) and the development of personal criminal responsibility (see Chapter 7) have gone a considerable way to extend the scope of international law beyond its traditional areas. The personal criminal responsibility of individuals has been given new life by the establishment of an International Criminal Court (ICC) which formally came into existence on 1 July 2002. For some states (e.g. the USA) this is a controversial development for it institutionalises a jurisdiction that is neither State nor territorially based. It seems to cut at the root of State sovereignty by establishing a process by which nationals may be made subject to the jurisdiction of a non-State entity. Actually, this exercise of jurisdiction by non-State entity is not a new development, but it is both the extensive reach and the intended permanence of the ICC that marks it as one of the most profound developments in the international legal order since the UN Charter of 1945.

European Convention for the Protection of Human Rights and Fundamental Freedoms 1950
UKTS (1950) 70

Article 25

1. The Commission may receive petitions addressed to the Secretary General of the Council from any person, non-governmental organisation or group of individuals claiming to be the victim of a violation by one of the High Contracting Parties of the rights set forth in this Convention, provided that the High Contracting Party against which the complaint has been lodged has declared that it recognises the competence of the Commission to receive such petitions. Those of the High Contracting Parties who have made such a declaration undertake not to hinder in any way the effective exercise of this right.

Protocol 9 to the European Convention for the Protection of Human Rights and Fundamental Freedoms Broadening the Access to the Court for Individuals
30 ILM 693 (1991)

This Protocol modifies substantially the provisions of the ECHR. See further Chapter 6.

Optional Protocol to the International Covenant on Civil and Political Rights 1966
Annex to General Assembly Resolution 2200 A, (1966) 21 UNGAOR Supp (No 16) 59

Under the International Covenant on Civil and Political Rights 1966, States undertake to guarantee a number of rights to all persons within their territory and subject to their jurisdiction. This is fortified by a reporting system and an optional system of inter-State complaints to a Human Rights Committee (see further in Chapter 6). The Optional Protocol to this Convention allows for individual complaints to be brought against the State.

Article 1
A State Party to the Covenant that becomes a party to the present Protocol recognises the competence of the Committee to receive and consider communications from individuals subject to its jurisdiction who claim to be the victims of a violation by that State Party of any of the rights set forth in the Covenant. No communication shall be received by the Committee if it concerns a State Party to the Covenant which is not a party to the present Protocol.

Article 2
Subject to the provisions of Article 1, individuals who claim that any of their rights enumerated in the covenant have been violated and who have exhausted all available domestic remedies may submit a written communication to the Committee for consideration.

Attorney-General of the Government of Israel v *Eichmann*
36 ILR (1961) 5, District Court of Jerusalem

Eichmann, former head of the Jewish Office in Germany during the Second World War, was abducted by Israeli agents from Argentina in 1960 and brought to Israel to face charges of war crimes, crimes against humanity and crimes against the Jewish people. In Israel, he was prosecuted under the Nazi and Nazi Collaborators (Punishment) Law 1951. Defence counsel submitted, *inter alia*, that since Eichmann was a German national, he could not be subject to Israeli criminal jurisdiction.

The abhorrent crimes defined in the Law are not crimes under Israel law alone. These crimes, which struck at the whole of mankind and shocked the conscience of nations, are grave offences against the law of nations itself (*delicta juris gentium*). Therefore, so far from international law negating or limiting the jurisdiction of countries with respect to such crimes, international law is, in the absence of an International Criminal Court, in need of the judicial and legislative organs of every country to give effect to its criminal interdictions and to bring the criminals to trial. The jurisdiction to try crimes under international law is universal.

In re Piracy Jure Gentium
[1934] AC 586, Privy Council

Following the arrest of Chinese nationals on the high seas, the Judicial

Committee of the Privy Council was asked to consider whether actual robbery was an element of the offence of piracy *jure gentium*.

With regard to crimes as defined by international law, that law has no means of trying or punishing them. The recognition of them as constituting crimes, and the trial and punishment of the criminals, are left to the municipal law of each country. But whereas according to international law the criminal jurisdiction of municipal law is ordinarily restricted to crimes committed on its *terra firma* or territorial waters or its own ships, and to crimes by its own nationals wherever committed, it is also recognized as extending to piracy committed on the high seas by any national on any ship, because a person guilty of such piracy has placed himself beyond the protection of any State. He is no longer a national, but 'hostis humani generis' and as such he is justiciable by any State anywhere.

R v Bow Street Metropolitan Stipendiary Magistrate and others, ex parte Pinochet Ugarte (No 3)
[2000] 1 AC 147, House of Lords, pp. 106–108

Senator Pinochet, the ex-Head of State of Chile, was accused of various violations of the human rights of both Chilean and foreign nationals. A Spanish court had issued an arrest warrant in respect of alleged acts against Spanish nationals. While visiting London, Senator Pinochet was arrested on an extradition warrant pending extradition to Spain. One crucial issue was whether Senator Pinochet, as an ex-Head of State, enjoyed immunity from UK courts in respect of acts done while in office (see Chapter 9). If he was immune, he could not be extradited. One alleged offence was the crime of torture which, it was accepted by the Court, was a crime involving personal criminal responsibility and one triggering universal jurisdiction. As a result, Senator Pinochet was held not to have immunity in respect of some of the charges against him. However, although the courts decided that he was amenable to extradition, he was not eventually extradited to Spain due to his poor health.

LORD BROWNE-WILKINSON: Apart from the law of piracy, the concept of personal liability under international law for international crimes is of comparatively modern growth. The traditional subjects of international law are states not human beings. But consequent upon the war crime trials after the 1939–45 War, the international community came to recognise that there could be criminal liability under international law for a class of crimes such as war crimes and crimes against humanity. Although there may be legitimate doubts as to the legality of the Charter of the International Military Tribunal appended to the Agreement for the Prosecution and Punishment of the Major War Criminals of the European Axis (the Nuremberg Charter) (London, 8 August 1945; TS 27 (1946); Cmd 6903), in my judgment those doubts were stilled by the Affirmation of the Principles of International Law recognised by the Charter of Nuremberg Tribunal adopted by the United Nations General Assembly on 11 December 1946 (see UN GA Resolution 95(I) (1946)). That affirmation affirmed the principles of international law recognised by the Nuremberg Charter and the judgment of the tribunal and directed the committee on the codification of international law to treat as a matter of primary importance plans for the formulation of the principles recognised in the Nuremberg Charter. At least from that date onwards the concept of personal liability for a crime in international law must have been part of international law. In the early years State torture was one of the elements of a war crime. In consequence torture, and various other crimes against humanity, were linked to war or at least to hostilities of some kind. But in the course of time this linkage with war fell away and torture, divorced from war or hostilities, became an international crime on its own: see *Oppenheim's International Law* (9th edn, 1992) Vol 1, p 996; note 6 to Art. 18 of the ILC Draft Code of Crimes against the Peace and Security of Mankind; *Prosecutor v Anto Furundzija* (10 December 1998, unreported). Ever since 1945, torture on a large scale has featured as one of the crimes against humanity: see, for example, UN General Assembly Resolutions 3059 (1973), 3452 and 3453 (1975); Statutes of the International Criminal Tribunals for the Former Yugoslavia (Art. 5) (see the Statute of the International Tribunal for the Prosecution of Persons Responsible for Serious Violations of International Humanitarian Law Committed in the Territory of the Former Yugoslavia since 1991 (the Statute of the Tribunal for the Former Yugoslavia) (UN Security Council Resolution 827 (1993)) and Rwanda (Art. 3) (see the Statute of the International Tribunal for the Prosecution of Persons Responsible for Genocide and Other Serious Violations of International Humanitarian Law Committed in the Territory of Rwanda and Rwandan Citizens Responsible for Genocide and other such Violations committed in the territory of neighbouring states between 1 January 1994 and 31 December 1994 (the Statute of the Tribunal for Rwanda) (UN SC Resolution 955 (1994)).

Moreover, the Republic of Chile accepted before your Lordships that the international law prohibiting torture has the character of *jus cogens* or a peremptory norm, i.e. one of those rules of international law which have a particular status. In *Furundzija*'s case at para 153, the tribunal said:

> Because of the importance of the values it protects, [the prohibition of torture] has evolved into a peremptory norm or *jus cogens*, that is, a norm that enjoys a higher rank in the international hierarchy than treaty law and even 'ordinary' customary rules. The most conspicuous consequence of this higher rank is that the principle at issue cannot be derogated from by states through international treaties or local or special customs or even general customary rules not endowed with the same normative force . . . Clearly, the *jus cogens* nature of the prohibition against torture articulates the notion that the prohibition has now become one of the most fundamental standards of the international community. Furthermore, this prohibition is designed to produce a deterrent effect, in that it signals to all members of the international community and the individuals over whom they wield authority that· the prohibition of torture is an absolute value from which nobody must deviate. . . .

The *jus cogens* nature of the international crime of torture justifies states in taking universal jurisdiction over torture wherever committed. International law provides that offences *jus cogens* may be punished by any state because the offenders are 'common enemies of all mankind and all nations have an equal interest in their apprehension and prosecution': *Demjanjuk v Petrovsky* (1985) 603 F Supp 1468, 776 F 2d 571.

It was suggested by Miss Montgomery QC, for Senator Pinochet that although torture was contrary to international law it was not strictly an international crime in the highest sense. In the light of the authorities to which I have referred (and there are many others) I have no doubt that long before the Torture Convention, State torture was an international crime in the highest sense.

But there was no tribunal or court to punish international crimes of torture. Local courts could take jurisdiction: see *Demjanjuk*'s case and *A–G of Israel v Eichmann* (1961) 36 ILR 5. But the objective was to ensure a general jurisdiction so that the torturer was not safe wherever he went. For example, in this case it is alleged that during the Pinochet regime torture was an official, although unacknowledged, weapon of government and that, when the regime was about to end, it passed legislation designed to afford an amnesty to those who had engaged in institutionalised torture. If these allegations are true, the fact that the local court had jurisdiction to deal with the international crime of torture was nothing to the point so long as the totalitarian regime remained in power: a totalitarian regime will not permit adjudication by its own courts on its own shortcomings. Hence the demand for some international machinery to repress state torture which is not dependent upon the local courts where the torture was committed. In the event, over 110 states (including Chile, Spain and the United Kingdom) became state parties to the Torture Convention. But it is far from clear that none of them practised state torture. What was needed therefore was an international system which could punish those who were guilty of torture and which did not permit the evasion of punishment by the torturer moving from one state to another. The Torture Convention was agreed not in order to create an international crime which had not previously existed but to provide an international system under which the international criminal – the torturer – could find no safe haven. Burgers and Danelius (respectively the chairman of the United Nations Working Group on the Torture Convention and the draftsmen of its first draft) say in their *Handbook on the Convention against Torture and Other Cruel, Inhuman or Degrading Treatment or Punishment* (1984) p 131 that it was 'an essential purpose [of the Convention] to ensure that a torturer does not escape the consequences of his acts by going to another country'.

Rome Statute of the International Criminal Court 1998

As part of its work on the Draft Code of Crimes Against the Peace and Security of Mankind, the International Law Commission established a Working Group to examine the establishment of an International Criminal Court, being a court similar in operation to the ICJ but having jurisdiction over individuals charged with crimes against international law. A Statute (being a treaty) was adopted on 17 July 1998 by a conference of States in Rome. The ICC came into existence on 1 July 2002 in accordance with the terms of its Statute. As at August 2002 there are 77 parties, including the United Kingdom. A total of 139 states have signed the Statute, but this does not mean that they will all become parties in due course (see Chapter 3). For some of those States domestic legislation will be necessary to ensure compatibility between the State's international obligations and its national law. In this regard, the UK has enacted the International Criminal Court Act 2001.

PART I. ESTABLISHMENT OF THE COURT

Article 1
The Court

An International Criminal Court ('the Court') is hereby established. It shall be a permanent institution and shall have the power to exercise its jurisdiction over persons for the most serious crimes of international concern, as referred to in this Statute, and shall be complementary to national criminal jurisdictions.

Article 4
Legal status and powers of the Court

1. The Court shall have international legal personality. It shall also have such legal capacity as may be necessary for the exercise of its functions and the fulfilment of its purposes.
2. The Court may exercise its functions and powers, as provided in this Statute, on the territory of any State Party and, by special agreement, on the territory of any other State.

NOTES:

1. The first extract above concerns the ability of individuals to enforce directly such rights as they are given by international law. It is important to realise that in such cases individuals are in fact being accorded two distinct capacities as international legal persons. First, they are being accorded substantive rights in international law; secondly, they may also be accorded the procedural capacity to begin proceedings to enforce those rights without having to rely on States to do it for them. An example of the latter is the jurisdiction of the American Court of Human Rights under which States wishing to join the system must accept the possibility of complaints by individuals but have the option of whether to accept the Court's jurisdiction in cases of complaint by other States. By virtue of Protocol 11 to the European Convention for the Protection of Human Rights and Fundamental Freedoms (ECHR), all European States party to the ECHR must now allow any individual in their jurisdiction the right to bring a claim against a State to the European Court of Human Rights (see Article 34 of the Convention).

2. It is sometimes said that when individuals are granted rights by treaty (or indeed where they are under direct criminal obligations – see below), such persons are merely 'objects' of the law, not its subjects, because it is States that have both created this personality and who will vindicate it by either acting to enforce human rights obligations, or acting to enforce personal criminal responsibility. However, if international personality means having rights, duties or capacities in international law, this is not a valid distinction.

3. Individuals employed by the United Nations and Specialised Agencies usually have both substantive and procedural rights in relation to the terms and conditions of their employment. The substantive rights and enforcement provisions are not governed by the national law of any one State, but rather by an amorphous set of principles loosely referred to as the law of the international civil service. Employees with claims may well have recourse to judicial procedures governed by this species of international law and, in exceptional cases, matters may even find their way to the ICJ.

4. The personal criminal responsibility of individuals for certain crimes (e.g., piracy, war crimes, crimes against humanity, crimes against the peace) is now firmly established in international law. Until recently, however, the means of exercising this jurisdiction lay with national courts of States. Such courts usually were disposed to exercise this jurisdiction on behalf of the international community only when some additional motive or interest of their own existed, as with the *Eichmann* case in Israel and *US* v *Yunis* (1988) 681 F Supp 896 in the United States (hijacking of a US airline said to be air piracy and a crime of universal jurisdiction). The *Pinochet* case is not exactly of this type as it was an extradition hearing not a trial of the merits. Nevertheless, it indicates how national courts can be used to supplement the international judicial system.

5. In its attempt to establish an enforcement process that is independent of States, the Statute of the International Criminal Court indicates the way forward. Currently, there are two *ad hoc* tribunals (established by the Security Council) trying individuals accused of crimes against international law. The International Tribunal for the Prosecution of Persons Responsible for Serious Violations of International Humanitarian Law Committed in the Territory of the Former Yugoslavia since 1990, was established by Security Council Resolution 827 (1993), and the International Tribunal for Rwanda by Security Council Resolution 955 (1994) (see Chapters 6 and 15). These mark a sea change in the attitude of the international community to the personality of individuals and have resulted in a number of convictions: see, e.g., Yugoslav Tribunals – *Cases of Delalic, Mucic, Delic and Landzo*, 38 ILM 57 (1999) and *Prosecutor* v *Furundžija* 38 ILM 317 (1999). Individuals may be extradicted by national courts to stand trial: e.g., *Re Elizaphan Ntakirutimana* 37 ILM 398 (1997), extradited from the US for the Rwandan tribunal. In one sense, such personal responsibility is a counterpart to the increased

protection that individuals now enjoy under human rights law. A third tribunal that will deal with events arising out of the collapse of order in Sierra Leone is soon to be instituted. Note also that individuals within a State may be now be surrendered to the International Criminal Court and in the UK, the International Criminal Court Act 2001 makes provision for this eventuality.

E: Other international persons

There are a number of miscellaneous groups or bodies that have some measure of international personality. The precise ambit of this personality will usually depend on the acquiescence of, or recognition by, States.

Scarfo v *Sovereign Order of Malta*
24 ILR 1 (1957), Tribunal of Rome, Italy

> The plaintiff sued the Order for breach of his contract of employment as a doctor. The Order contended that the Italian courts had no jurisdiction, because it had acted in a sovereign capacity when making this contract, having regard to the fact that one of its duties as a sovereign Order was to care for the sick and wounded.

There can be no doubt that the Order of Malta is a sovereign entity and a subject of international law. . . .

The limitations on the sovereignty of the Order of Malta which undoubtedly exist result mainly from the absence of State territory and citizens, and also from the fact that it is a religious Order recognized by the Holy See and what may be termed a '*persona moralis in Ecclesia*' (which, by reason of its military, noble and knightly origin, occupies a special position). These limitations, however, are not such as to be able to negative its sovereignty. Its sovereignty exists in law and is determined by its own legal order which is entirely independent of that of other subjects of international law. The Order has its own administration and courts, and the right of active and passive legation (Article 2 of the Constitution) which has been recognized by the Holy See. The latter has approved a diplomatic representation of the Order (Article 4 of the new Constitution), and the right of legation is also recognized by the Italian State, which has a legation accredited to the Order of Malta. Thus the status of the Order as a subject of international law, at any rate *vis-à-vis* the Italian State, cannot be doubted because the Italian State, by establishing a legation, has recognized the sovereignty of the Order within its own territory.

Texaco Overseas Petroleum Company v *The Libyan Arab Republic*
53 ILR (1977) 389, Dupuy, Sole Arbitrator

> This dispute arose out of the nationalisation by Libya of foreign-owned oil interests in 1973–74. One question was whether the contract between the company and the State gave the company any rights enforceable at international law. After finding that the contract was an 'internationalised contract' (on which, see Chapter 11), Professor Dupuy, the arbitrator, commented on the status of Texaco.

DUPUY: The Tribunal must specify the meaning and the exact scope of internationalization of a contractual relationship so as to avoid any misunderstanding: indeed to say that international law governs contractual relations between a State and a foreign private party neither means that the latter is assimilated to a State nor that the contract entered into with it is assimilated to a treaty.

This distinction is worth making, because the situation of individuals, and more generally private persons, in respect of international law, has recently been the subject matter of important doctrinal debates on the occasion of which excessive positions sometimes may have been stated. . . .

This Tribunal will abstain from going that far: it shall only consider as established today the concept that legal international capacity is not solely attributable to a State and that international law encompasses subjects of a diversified nature. If States, the original subjects of the international legal order, enjoy all the capacities offered by the latter, other subjects enjoy only limited capacities which are assigned to specific purposes. The proposition which has just been stated is in conformity with the statement by the International Court of Justice in its *Advisory Opinion on Reparations of 11 April 1949* under which 'the subjects of law, in any legal system, are not necessarily identical in their nature or in the extent of their rights and their nature depends on the needs of the community' ([1949] ICJ 174, at 178). In other words, stating that a contract between a State and a private person falls within the international legal order means that for the purposes of interpretation and performance of the contract, it should be recognized that a private contracting party has specific international capacities. But, unlike a State, the private person has only a limited capacity and his quality as a subject of international law does enable him only to invoke, in the field of international law, the rights which he derives from the contract. . . .

Thus, the internationalization of certain contracts entered into between a State and a private person does not tend to confer upon a private person competences comparable to those of a State but only certain capacities which enable him to act internationally in order to invoke the rights which result to him from an internationalized contract.

NOTES:

1. The question whether any other entity may have international personality, even for a single purpose may depend on whether a State has granted or recognised that personality. In *Scarfo v Sovereign Order of Malta*, the Tribunal seems to indicate that the sovereignty of the Order is opposable to Italy because of the latter's recognition of the fact. This may mean that other States would not be bound to accept or give effect to that sovereignty without such recognition. The UK/Ireland Independent International Commission on Decommissioning may fall into this category.

2. Disputes between companies and States on the international plane depend very much on the specific agreement between the parties, as in *Texaco v Libya* and *BP v Libya*, 53 ILR (1974) 329. In many instances, a company has more economic power than the State and so can force a State to accept the international personality of companies. A number of formal systems for the settlement of certain disputes between States and foreign companies, which necessarily involve some measure of personality for the latter, have been established, e.g., by the Convention on the Settlement of Investment Disputes between States and Nationals of Other States 1966 and the Iran/US Claims Tribunal (see further in Chapters 11 and 15).

3. Likewise, Non-Governmental Organisations (NGOs) now play an increasing role in the international legal order, especially in areas such as environmental protection and human rights where States (and organisations created and controlled by States) cannot be relied upon to promote universally beneficial policies.

SECTION 2:   **Recognition in international law**

The role of 'recognition' in both international and national legal systems has traditionally aroused considerable debate. As a matter of international law, recognition is often described as 'declaratory' (being 'merely' a political act recognising a pre-existing state of affairs) or 'constitutive' (being a necessary act before the recognised entity can enjoy international personality). In national law, the 'home' State may choose variously to 'recognise' a foreign State and/or its Government, and such recognition may be '*de jure*' (accepting that the entity exists as of right) or simply '*de facto*' (recognising the existence of the entity but with concerns about its legitimacy). In any of these senses, the act of recognition may then have consequences within the national legal system.

A: General considerations

I. Brownlie, 'Recognition in Theory and Practice'
(1982) 53 BYBIL 197

With rare exceptions the theories on recognition have not only failed to improve the quality of thought but have deflected lawyers from the application of ordinary methods of legal analysis. The confusion which reigns is such that contemporary thinking does not even provide elementary methods of defining what the issues are in a given episode, much less the basis for solutions of the problems presented.

III 'Recognition': a Term of Art?

The standard works fail to warn the student of international law of the important fact that 'recognition' is not a term of art. Indeed, by implication, by dint of repetition and the constant introduction of the word into headings, the standard treatments give the firm impression that 'recognition' and its congener, 'non-recognition', are terms of art with a consistent content and legal significance. Nothing could be further from the truth.

The following proposition may be put by way of example:

> The Government of State A does not recognize [the Government of] State B (*or* the 'entity' calling itself [the Government of] State B).

This statement represents fairly normal usage (although there is no standard form applicable in these matters). In fact and as a matter of necessary interpretation, the proposition could bear two radically different meanings. It could mean that, in the opinion of State A, State B did not exist as such, that is to say that the entity or political organization concerned did not *qualify* in legal terms to be recognized because it did not satisfy the criteria of statehood. Examples of this type of non-recognition are rare. In the alternative, the proposition could signify that although State B was regarded as a State in law, and thus qualifying for recognition, State A was not willing to accord such recognition on political grounds. In this context 'non-recognition' is simply a code for a policy of hostility short of armed conflict and usually accompanied by a range of political and economic sanctions (the last word is not intended to indicate the legality of such measures). . . .

No assumption is made concerning the legal significance of the State A-State B (above) proposition in either of its possible meanings: the object is, first of all, to discover *what* State A purports to be doing or intends. The *legal appreciation* of what State A says or does is a further question, but it cannot be pursued unless the first enquiry is competently made.

The ultimate question at the first stage is, what is the intention of the government concerned? This may be derived from all the available evidence: diplomatic correspondence, statements in inter-national organizations, official views expressed in national assemblies and so forth. Charges of breaches of international law carry the very strong implication that the entity concerned is a State capable of bearing State responsibility. The terminology used is by no means a dominant feature. Moreover, the word 'recognition' need not be employed, provided the intention of the government concerned is clear. Thus the most common form of the recognition of new States involves the sending of a letter or telegram of felicitations by a Head of State to the Head of State or other appropriate organ of the new State: no formal words are called for and the intention of the recogniz-ing State is unambiguous.

The strange aspect of all this is that the correct approach – seeking the intention of the govern-ment concerned on the basis of the documents and other evidence – involves nothing more than ordinary legal technique: what did the government intend on the given occasion? No theory is called for to assist in this process. . . .

The writer's conviction that in the field of 'recognition' the role of theory has not been a happy one has already been made patent. In the literature the theories have tended to stand in front of the issues and to have assumed a 'theological' role as a body of thought with its own validity which tends to distract the student, and to play the role of master rather than servant. In spite of this it is useful (if not at all necessary) to confront the leading theories on their own terms.

By way of preface the complaint is to be made that the very approach in terms of the selection of *the* correct or preferred theory of recognition involves an immediate encouragement to the simpli-fied approach and a diversion from the deployment of ordinary legal analysis.

The most fashionable theory in twentieth-century doctrine has been the 'declaratory' theory. Briefly has expressed its essence in the following passage:

> The better view is that the granting of recognition to a new state is not a 'constitutive' but a 'declaratory' act; it does not bring into legal existence a state which did not exist before. A state may exist without being recognized, and if it does exist in fact, then, whether or not it has been formally recognized by other states, it has a right to be treated by them *as* a state. The primary function of recognition is to acknowledge as a fact something which has hitherto been uncertain, namely the independence of the body claiming to be a state, and to declare the recognizing state's readiness to accept the normal consequences of that fact, namely the usual courtesies of international intercourse.

The 'declaratory' view has much to commend it as a *general* approach, since it militates in favour of a legal and objective method of analysing situations. None the less the idea that an issue of statehood or of government (the criterion of effectiveness) involves the mere acknowledgement of a fact is really too simple. Certainly, questions of fact are foremost: but the legal criteria have to be *applied* and this may call for some rather nice assessments. . . . Such an assessment involves elem-ents of appreciation and the choice of a point in a crescent process: in other words the choice is, to a degree and unavoidably, arbitrary.

In general the 'declaratory' theory does not prepare the student of the problems of 'recogni-tion' for the task of evaluating the declarations of governments and the conduct of States in general. As in the *Tinoco* arbitration, a political non-recognition may be compatible with the view – perhaps expressed by the conduct of the same State – that a State (or government) objectively qualifies in law for recognition. Finally, the theory does not help in the case where the facts are clear but there is some feature of illegality, as in the case of Manchukuo (1932–45) or Rhodesia (1965–80).

In opposition to the 'declaratory' theory is the 'constitutive' theory, according to which the polit-ical act of recognition on the part of other States is a precondition of the existence of legal rights. In the more extreme version this amounts to saying that the very existence of a State may depend on the political decision of other States. In fact constitutivist doctrine takes various forms and in many cases its partisans give a mitigated version which allows that certain fundamental rights and duties arise prior to recognition. Such essays in coping with the position of the 'unrecognized State' involve an advance toward the 'declaratory' position.

In any event the core of the constitutivist theory is unacceptable. States cannot, by the device of withholding recognition, determine – and in effect thus repudiate – the content of their legal obligations toward other States. Indeed, in practice such conduct is difficult to find, since on examination policies of non-recognition turn out to be examples of political non-recognition of the kind Arbitrator Taft had to deal with in the *Tinoco Concessions* case.

All this having been said, it is necessary to recognize certain elements of truth in the constitutivist approach. As it has been suggested already, in many situations the facts which have to be subjected to legal evaluation involve a process and the court or foreign ministry official or other decision maker has to make a more or less arbitrary appreciation of the question of statehood or effective government. To this extent recognition involves an element of authoritative choice or 'certification'. There is a second element of truth which appears in those cases in which the entity concerned does not prima facie fit into the orthodox categories. Thus it can be argued that polities such as Andorra or the Holy See, which may not clearly qualify as States, but which none the less are generally accepted as having legal personality in international relations, may depend on the role of recognition in overcoming the apparent anomaly of status.

S. Murphy, 'Democratic Legitimacy and the Recognition of States and Governments'
(1999) 48 ICLQ 545

The traditional criteria for recognising States and governments have often been mixed with other factors. One of those factors is that democratic States, driven by deep-seated beliefs within their populace, tend to want to promote democracy in other States. With the considerable increase in the number of democratic States worldwide, there is little doubt that the trend is toward greater use of democratic legitimacy as a factor in recognition practice, and leads to certain tentative conclusions:

(1) There is no international norm obligating States not to recognise an emerging State simply because its political community is not democratic in nature. Were there such a norm, it might be accompanied by a norm permitting intervention so as to establish a democratic government.

(2) When a political community seeks recognition as a State, the existence of a democratic referendum whereby the people of the community proclaim themselves in favour of independence will be one important, but not decisive, element in the international community's decision to recognise it as a State. However, other elements will be equally important, including the international community's adherence to the modern version of the principle of *uti possidetis* and other means for maintaining peace and stability.

(3) When a non-democratic regime usurps a democratically elected government, the international community may react by refusing to recognise the new *de facto* government and imposing comprehensive economic sanctions, in an effort to cajole the new government into a transition back to democratic rule.

(4) However, while the international community is increasingly interested in democratic legitimacy as a factor in its recognition practice, there is an enduring desire to promote economic development, international peace and stability as well. These values – legitimacy, development and stability – do not always go hand in hand. Depending on the situation, one or the other value may dominate the decision within the international community regarding whether to recognise the State or government.

Regarding the role of democratic legitimacy as just another policy element in the practice of recognising States and governments may be regarded as an unattractive conclusion. Rather than resorting to a ready-made legal framework on recognition, policy-makers are left weighing various amorphous policy elements that provide little concrete guidance. Yet, finding the right solutions through the application of differing policies to different cases is what diplomacy is all about. Democratic legitimacy is an important concept and tool, but it should not serve as a straitjacket for governments and others as they seek to find solutions, on a case-by-case basis, that promote the welfare of peoples worldwide. Whether nurturing new democracies, restoring overthrown democracies, promoting the gradual transition from non-democracy to democracy, or pursuing values that do not necessarily entail 'democratic' means (such as promoting regional stability, economic development), the international community has an array of diplomatic and economic tools at its disposal, of which recognition practice is merely one.

Tinoco Arbitration (*United Kingdom* v *Costa Rica*)
1 RIAA (1923) 369, Taft, Sole Arbitrator

In January 1917, Frederico Tinoco came to power in Costa Rica after a *coup d'état*. His government concluded certain contracts with British corporations. After Tinoco's retirement in 1919, the old constitution was restored, and a Law of Nullities was passed annulling the contracts and other matters concluded during the Tinoco regime. The UK made claims in respect of the injuries to its nationals caused by these annulments. Two preliminary issues were the status of the Tinoco regime in international law, and whether the UK was estopped from pursuing the claim because of lack of recognition, either *de jure* or *de facto*, of the Tinoco government.

TAFT: But it is urged that many leading Powers refused to recognize the Tinoco government, and that recognition by other nations is the chief and best evidence of the birth, existence and continuity of succession of a government. Undoubtedly recognition by other Powers is an important evidential factor in establishing proof of the existence of a government in the society of nations. . . .

Probably because of the leadership of the United States in respect to a matter of this kind, her then Allies in the war, Great Britain, France and Italy, declined to recognize the Tinoco government. Costa Rica was, therefore, not permitted to sign the Treaty of Peace at Versailles, although the Tinoco government had declared war against Germany. . . .

The non-recognition by other nations of a government claiming to be a national personality, is usually appropriate evidence that it has not attained the independence and control entitling it by international law to be classed as such. But when recognition *vel non* of a government is by such nations determined by inquiry, not into its *de facto* sovereignty and complete governmental control, but into its illegitimacy or irregularity of origin, their non-recognition loses something of evidential weight on the issue with which those applying the rules of international law are alone concerned. What is true of the non-recognition of the United States in its bearing upon the existence of a *de facto* government under Tinoco for thirty months is probably in a measure true of the non-recognition by her Allies in the European War. Such non-recognition for any reason, however, cannot outweigh the evidence disclosed by this record before me as to the *de facto* character of Tinoco's government, according to the standard set by international law.

Second. It is ably and earnestly argued on behalf of Costa Rica that the Tinoco government cannot be considered a *de facto* government, because it was not established and maintained in accord with the constitution of Costa Rica of 1871. To hold that a government which establishes itself and maintains a peaceful administration, with the acquiescence of the people for a substantial period of time, does not become a *de facto* government unless it conforms to a previous constitution would be to hold that within the rules of international law a revolution contrary to the fundamental law of the existing government cannot establish a new government. This cannot be, and is not, true. The change by revolution upsets the rule of the authorities in power under the then existing fundamental law, and sets aside the fundamental law in so far as the change of rule makes it necessary. To speak of a revolution creating a *de facto* government, which conforms to the limitations of the old constitution is to use a contradiction in terms. The same government continues internationally, but not the internal law of its being. The issue is not whether the new government assumes power or conducts its administration under constitutional limitations established by the people during the incumbency of the government it has overthrown. The question is, has it really established itself in such a way that all within its influence recognize its control, and that there is no opposing force assuming to be a government in its place? Is it discharging its functions as a government usually does, respected within its own jurisdiction? . . .

It is further objected by Costa Rica that Great Britain by her failure to recognize the Tinoco government is estopped now to urge claims of her subjects dependent upon the acts and contracts of the Tinoco government. The evidential weight of such non-recognition against the claim of its *de facto* character I have already considered and admitted. The contention here goes further and precludes a government which did not recognize a *de facto* government from appearing in an international tribunal in behalf of its nationals to claim any rights based on the acts of such government.

To sustain this view a great number of decisions in English and American courts are cited to the point that a municipal court cannot, in litigation before it, recognize or assume the *de facto* character of a foreign government which the executive department of foreign affairs of the government of which the court is a branch has not recognized. This is clearly true. It is for the executive to decide questions of foreign policy and not courts. It would be most unseemly to have a conflict of opinion in respect to foreign relations of a nation between its department charged with the conduct of its foreign affairs and its judicial branch. But such cases have no bearing on the point before us. Here the executive of Great Britain takes the position that the Tinoco government which it did not recognize, was nevertheless a *de facto* government that could create rights in British subjects which it now seeks to protect. Of course, as already emphasized, its failure to recognize the *de facto* government can be used against it as evidence to disprove the character it now attributes to that government, but this does not bar it from changing its position.

EC Declaration on the Guidelines on Recognition of New States in Eastern Europe and the Soviet Union, December 1991
4 *European Journal of International Law* (1993) 72

In compliance with the European Council's request, Ministers have assessed developments in Eastern Europe and in the Soviet Union with a view to elaborating an approach regarding relations with new states.

In this connection they have adopted the following guidelines on the formal recognition of new states in Eastern Europe and in the Soviet Union:

The Community and its Member States confirm their attachment to the principles of the Helsinki Final Act and the Charter of Paris, in particular the principle of self-determination. They affirm their readiness to recognise, subject to the normal standards of international practice and the political realities in each case, those new states which, following the historic changes in the region, have constituted themselves on a democratic basis, have accepted the appropriate international obligations and have committed themselves in good faith to a peaceful process and to negotiations.

Therefore, they adopt a common position on the process of recognition of these new states, which requires:

— respect for the provisions of the Charter of the United Nations and the commitments subscribed to in the Final Act of Helsinki and in the Charter of Paris, especially with regard to the rule of law, democracy and human rights;

— guarantees for the rights of ethnic and national groups and minorities in accordance with the commitments subscribed to in the framework of the CSCE;

— respect for the inviolability of all frontiers which can only be changed by peaceful means and by common agreement'

— acceptance of all relevant commitments with regard to disarmament and nuclear non-proliferation as well as to security and regional stability;

— commitment to settle by agreement, including where appropriate by recourse to arbitration, all questions concerning state succession and regional disputes.

The Community and its Member States will not recognise entities which are the result of aggression. They would take account of the effects of recognition on neighbouring states.

The commitments to these principles opens the way to recognition by the Community and its Member States and to the establishment of diplomatic relations. It could be laid down in agreements.

EC Declaration on Yugoslavia, 16 December 1991
4 *European Journal of International Law* (1993) 72

In addition to the above Declaration, the EC also adopted a specific Declaration on Yugoslavia, inviting the former Republics to apply for recognition by 23 December 1991. Such recognition was to be conditional on fulfilment of the above Guidelines and also:

The Community and its member States also require a Yugoslav Republic to commit itself, prior to recognition, to adopt constitutional and political guarantees ensuring that it has no territorial claims towards a neighbouring Community State and that it will conduct no hostile propaganda activities versus a neighbouring Community State, including the use of a denomination which implies territorial claims.

NOTES:

1. The debate between proponents of the so-called 'declaratory' and 'constitutive' theories of recognition (see Brownlie above) should be read in conjunction with the materials on Statehood discussed earlier. Many international lawyers believe that the argument is fruitless because it does not assist in the resolution of 'real life' problems. Moreover, it may well be that the declaratory and constitutive theories are not dealing with the same question. There may be a difference between the circumstances in which a body may acquire the abstract right to exercise the capacities of Statehood on the international plane (declaratory) and the actual exercise of those capacities in a concrete case (constitutive).

2. The European Communities' guidelines were issued in response to the break up of the former federal States of Eastern Europe. Crucially, these guidelines go beyond simply requiring the attainment of the traditional criteria of Statehood found in Article 33 of the Montevideo Convention). They *appear* to require 'candidates' for recognition to meet conditions of a subjective and peculiarly Euro-centric nature including issues of governance (as described by Murphy). This has led some commentators to argue that the constitutive theory of recognition is gaining ground. However, an alternative view is that these guidelines represent the EC's minimum standards for the opening of inter-State relations, and that they are not intended to qualify the right of these entities to Statehood. Again, this may illustrate the difference between the achievement of international personality (e.g. Statehood) and its

effective exercise in the international community. Note that some non-European States have adopted these guidelines in determining recognition of the former Yugoslavia States – see (1993) 14 *Australian Year Book of International Law* 413.

3. The European Communities' Conference on Yugoslavia also established an Arbitration Commission (the Badinter Commission) to resolve certain questions of law submitted to it arising out of the dissolution of the former federal State of Yugoslavia (see Chapter 6). Among the issues referred to this Commission were the questions whether Bosnia-Hercegovina (Opinion No 4), Croatia (Opinion No 5), Macedonia (Opinion No 6), and Slovenia (Opinion No 7) had fulfilled the criteria for recognition laid down in the guidelines and the EC Declaration on Yugoslavia. Eventually, and in apparent disregard of the Commission's various findings, all four former members of the federation were recognised as States by the EC. These cases are fine examples of how recognition can be a powerful political tool, even though the recognition issue may be dressed up as purely a matter of law. The UK's failure to recognise a new Yugoslavia (that is, Serbia and Montenegro) until 1996 was overtly political.

4. The absence of international recognition of Statehood does not leave an entity powerless or unprotected in international law. As has been shown, international personality is relative. So, recognition by the international community of the *personality* (but not Statehood) of Kosovo and East Timor in 1999 is a necessary consequence of the community's intervention in those territories (see Chapter 14). Timor is now a State and the newest member of the United Nations.

B: Mandatory non-recognition in international law

Following the Unilateral Declaration of Independence by the Smith apartheid regime in Southern Rhodesia (now Zimbabwe) in 1965, the Security Council passed numerous resolutions condemning the action and eventually imposed economic sanctions. The resolution below clearly imposed a legal duty on States not to recognise the 'illegal regime'. It had been preceded by other resolutions (notably SC Res 216 (1965), 12 November 1965), which had called for non-recognition and thereby set the standard for future action.

Security Council Resolution 277 (1965) March 1970

The Security Council. . . .
Acting under Chapter VII of the Charter
    1. Condemns the illegal proclamation of republican status of the Territory by the illegal regime in Southern Rhodesia;
    2. Decides that Member States shall refrain from recognising this illegal regime or from rendering any assistance to it;
    3. Calls upon Member States to take appropriate measures, at the national level, to ensure that any act performed by officials and institutions of the illegal regime in Southern Rhodesia shall not be accorded any recognition, official or otherwise, including judicial notice, by the competent organs of their State;. . . .
    9. Decides, in accordance with Article 41 of the Charter and in furthering the objective of ending the rebellion, that Member States shall:
        (a) Immediately sever all diplomatic, consular, trade, military and other relations that they may have with the illegal regime in Southern Rhodesia, and terminate any representation that they may maintain in the territory;

   (b) Immediately interrupt any existing means of transportation to and from Southern
       Rhodesia.

NOTES:
1. Reference should be made to the ICJ's decision in the *Namibia Case*, ICJ Rep 1971 16, on
    the consequences of South Africa's continued illegal occupation of the territory after the
    termination of the Mandate (see Chapter 7). Essentially, the ICJ imposed a duty not to
    recognise the continuation of the Mandate. Likewise, in SC Res 541 of 18 November 1983,
    the Security Council called on all States not to recognise the Turkish Republic of Northern
    Cyprus as it had been created by the unlawful use of force by Turkey against Cyprus
    proper.
2. In reference to the prolonged litigation between the Kuwait Airways Corporation and the
    Iraqi Airways Company in UK courts arising out of the seizure of the former's aircraft follow-
    ing the Iraqi invasion in 1992, the UK has maintained strict non recognition – both *de facto*
    and *de jure* – of Iraq's alleged assumption of sovereign power over Kuwait (see (1997) 68 BYBIL
    519).

SECTION 3: **Recognition in national law**

A: Recognition in UK law:

(a) States

It is not only on the international plane that the question of international personality is important. On the national level also, it may well be crucial to know
whether an entity has international personality as a sovereign 'State' or 'government'. In the law of the United Kingdom, for example, the status of a foreign entity
can determine whether it has immunity from suit (see Chapter 9), whether it may
bring proceedings, and whether the laws emanating from that entity may be recognised in national courts. Whether an entity has this sovereign status (or any
existence in international law) may well depend on whether it has been 'recognised' by the authorities of the State in which it is acting, although, as is made clear
below, this is not the only way by which an entity may acquire the privileges
associated with such status.

Luther v *Sagor*
[1921] 1 KB 456, King's Bench Division

   The defendants imported wood into the UK that had been confiscated by the
   Soviet Government in 1919 and sold to them in 1920. The plaintiffs claimed to
   be owners of the wood. The issue was whether the UK recognised the Soviet
   Government. If so, a UK Court would accept the validity of the confiscation.

ROCHE J: Whether the decree in question is a valid legislative act which can be recognized as
such by the Courts of this country must, in my judgment, depend upon whether the power from
which it purports to emanate is what it apparently claims to be, a sovereign power, in this case the

sovereign power of the Russian Federative Republic. The proper source of information as to a foreign power, its status and sovereignty, is the Sovereign of this country through the Government . . . At all events, even if I were entitled to look elsewhere for information I am certainly not bound to do so, and in this case I know of no other sources of information available to which I can safely or properly resort.

I therefore propose to deal with the case upon the information furnished by His Majesty's Secretary of State for Foreign Affairs. The attitude proper to be adopted by a Court of this country with regard to foreign governments or powers I understand to be as follows: (1) If a foreign government is recognized by the Government of this country the Courts of this country may and must recognize the sovereignty of that foreign government and the validity of its acts . . . (2) If a foreign government, or its sovereignty, is not recognized by the Government of this country the Courts of this country either cannot, or at least need not, or ought not, to take notice of, or recognize such foreign government or its sovereignty. . . .

On these materials I am not satisfied that His Majesty's Government has recognized the Soviet Government as the Government of a Russian Federative Republic or of any sovereign state or power. I therefore am unable to recognize it, or to hold it has sovereignty, or is able by decree to deprive the plaintiff company of its property.

Carl Zeiss Stiftung v *Rayner & Keeler*

[1967] 1 AC 853, House of Lords

The defendants were trading under the name Carl Zeiss Stiftung and the plaintiffs were solicitors acting on behalf of an East German corporation of the same name, seeking an injunction against the defendants. The defendants contended that since the East German corporation was incorporated and administered under the laws of East Germany, the Court could not act to protect it, because the Courts of the UK would not give effect to the laws of a foreign 'State' or 'government' that had not been recognised formally by the UK.

LORD WILBERFORCE: It is as well, before considering the legal consequences of non-recognition, to appreciate what the respondents' contention involves. The Stiftung is a corporate body established for industrial and trading purposes under the law of Germany; one of whose constitutional organs – the special board – is an administrative authority exercising power at the place of the body's operations. As a fact, there is not doubt that at the relevant date this authority was there, that it was exercising its functions, that it was operating as the special board, that (this is proved by the evidence) it would be recognised by the local courts as so doing. Yet, so it is said, because the law and the order which set it up are derived from a body not recognised as a lawful government, this authority, *qua* organ of the Stiftung, has no legal existence; all its transactions in private law are void, as are presumably all other transactions carried out under its authority or by persons who derive their authority from it. By logical extension it seems to follow, and counsel for the respondents accepted, that there is, for many years has been and, until the attitude of Her Majesty's Government changes, will be, in East Germany a legal vacuum; subject only, it may be, to the qualification that pre-existing German law, so far as it can continue to be operated or have effect, may continue in force. Whether in fact it can continue to be operated to any great extent if its operation depends upon administrative or judicial authorities set up by the non-existent 'government' must be doubtful. But the respondents, so far from shrinking from these consequences, insist up on them as the necessary and, as they say, intended consequences of non-recognition. And correspondingly, they argue that if recognition were to be given by the courts to legislative acts of the non-recognised 'government' that would be tantamount to recognition of that government, and so in conflict with the policy of the executive.

My Lords, if the consequences of non-recognition of the East German 'government' were to bring in question the validity of its legislative acts, I should wish seriously to consider whether the invalidity so brought about is total, or whether some mitigation of the severity of this result can be found. As Locke said: 'A government without laws is, I suppose, a mystery in politics, inconceivable to human capacity and inconsistent with human society,' and this must be true of a society – at least a civilised and organised society – such as we know to exist in East Germany. In the United States some glimmerings can be found of the idea that non-recognition cannot be pressed to its ultimate logical limit, and that where private rights, or acts of everyday occurrence, or perfunctory acts of administration are concerned (the scope of these exceptions has never been precisely defined) the courts may, in the interests of justice and common sense, where no consideration of public policy to the contrary has to prevail, give recognition to the actual facts or realities found to exist in the territory in question. . . . No trace of any such doctrine is yet to be found in English law, but equally, in my opinion, there is nothing in those English decisions, in which recognition has been refused to particular acts of non-recognised governments, which would prevent its acceptance or which pre- scribes the absolute and total invalidity of all laws and acts flowing from unrecognised governments. In view of the conclusion I have reached on the effect to be attributed to non-recognition in this case, it is not necessary here to resort to this doctrine but, for my part, I should wish to regard it as an open question, in English law, in any future case whether and to what extent it can be invoked. . . .

Her Majesty's Government have not granted any recognition *de jure* or *de facto* to the 'German Democratic Republic' or its 'Government' – the inverted commas are as in the certificate itself. . . . There are only two questions which might arise in relation to the Eastern Zone. The first is whether it is admissible in the courts of this country to take account of the fact (if such be the case, as to which I shall make some observation later) that the USSR itself considers that there is in existence in the Eastern Zone a government independent of the USSR, *viz.*, the 'government' of the 'German Demo- cratic Republic.' In my opinion, the answer to this must be negative: to make any such assertion would be in direct contradiction to the certificate which states without qualification that the USSR and its Government is entitled *de jure* to exercise governing authority there and that nobody else is, either *de jure* or *de facto*. What view another state may take as to the legal or factual situation in any territory is irrelevant to the recognising (or non-recognising) state and, after the latter has defined its own attitude, is inadmissible in its courts. . . . The second question is whether consistently with the certificate it is possible to assert that the USSR is not *de facto* exercising governing authority or control in the Eastern Zone.

In stating that the USSR is exercising *de jure* governing authority and that no other body is exercising *de facto* authority, the two certificates to my mind say all that need or can be said. *De jure* recognition in all cases but one is the fullest recognition which can be given: the one exception is the case where there is concurrently some other body *de facto* exercising a rival authority to that of the '*de jure*' sovereign. . . . But any such possibility as this is . . . excluded by the terms of the certificates. . . . The certificates therefore in my opinion establish the USSR as *de jure* entitled to exercise governing authority and in full control of the area of the Eastern Zone.

NOTES:

1. The materials on recognition should be read with the change in UK practice clearly in mind, (see immediately below) remembering that the UK has not changed its position in respect of the recognition of *States*, where UK Foreign Office certificate will still be issued. For example, in *R v Commissioners for the Inland Revenue ex parte Resat Caglar* (1994), the UK Foreign Office certified that the UK did not recognise the so-called 'Turkish Republic of Northern Cyprus' as a State. As the affidavit said in that case, 'Her Majesty's Government views with concern the suggestion that the "TRNC" should be held to be a "Foreign state" [for the purposes of s. 321 of the Income and Corporation Taxes Act 1988] notwithstanding that it is not recognised as such by Her Majesty's Government'. A certificate confirming the recognition of the statehood

of the United Arab Emirates was issued in *BCCI (Overseas) Ltd* v *Price Waterhouse* [1997] 4 All ER 108, where it was also confirmed that the UK does not accord recognition to constituent territories of federal entities. (See also (1996) 67 BYIL, pp. 710–12.)

2. Under the State Immunity Act 1978, States are granted certain immunities from the jurisdiction of UK courts (see Chapter 9). Whether a body is a 'State' for these purposes is to be determined in accordance with s. 21, which specifies that a certificate issued by the Secretary of State for Foreign and Commonwealth Affairs shall be conclusive for the purposes of the Act, as in *BCCI* v *Price Waterhouse*. The fact that an unrecognised State may have no privileges or immunities in the UK has often been said to support the constitutive theory of recognition. If, however, the effects of non-recognition of a 'State' in the UK are dictated by a rule of UK national law, the status of such bodies in the UK says nothing of their status in international law.

3. When *Luther* v *Sagor* came to the Court of Appeal ([1921] 3 KB 532), the UK Foreign Office by then had indicated that the UK did indeed recognise the Soviet Government as the *de facto* government of Russia. This recognition was held to date from before the confiscation. Thus the appeal was allowed, as the defendant's title to the wood was confirmed, being bestowed by a sovereign act of a sovereign State.

4. The live issue at the heart of the *Carl Zeiss* case is now irrelevant – Germany is a united and sovereign State. However, the case illustrates both the power of the non-recognition doctrine and the extent to which UK courts would go to side-step it.

(b) Governments

UK Practice Statement on the Recognition of Governments, House of Lords

H.L. Deb. Vol. 48, cols 1121–22, April 1980

Previously, the United Kingdom had recognised foreign governments formally, either *de jure* or *de facto*. Although this was said to be based on the effectiveness of that government within a particular territory, it was often taken to be a sign of approval.

LORD CARRINGTON (Foreign Secretary): [W]e have conducted a re-examination of British policy and practice concerning the recognition of Governments. This has included a comparison with the practice of our partners and allies. On the basis of this review we have decided that we shall no longer accord recognition to Governments. The British Government recognises States in accordance with common international doctrine.

Where an unconstitutional change of régime takes place in a recognised State, Governments of other States must necessarily consider what dealings, if any, they should have with the new régime, and whether and to what extent it qualifies to be treated as the Government of the State concerned. Many of our partners and allies take the position that they do not recognise Governments and that therefore no question of recognition arises in such cases. By contrast, the policy of successive British Governments has been that we should make and announce a decision formally 'recognising' the new Government.

This practice has sometimes been misunderstood, and, despite explanations to the contrary, our 'recognition' interpreted as implying approval. For example, in circumstances where there might be legitimate public concern about the violation of human rights by the new régime, or the manner in which it achieved power, it has not sufficed to say that an announcement of 'recognition' is simply a neutral formality.

We have therefore concluded that there are practical advantages in following the policy of many other countries in not according recognition to Governments. Like them, we shall continue to decide the nature of our dealings with régimes which come to power unconstitutionally in the light of our assessment of whether they are able of themselves to exercise effective control of the territory of the State concerned, and seem likely to continue to do so.

House of Commons
H.C. Deb. Vol. 985, Written Answers, col. 385, 23 May 1980

This was the government's reply to a written question asking how UK Courts were now to assess a foreign entity claiming to be a sovereign government.

In future cases where a new régime comes to power unconstitutionally our attitude on the question whether it qualifies to be treated as a Government, will be left to be inferred from the nature of the dealings, if any, which we may have with it, and in particular on whether we are dealing with it on a normal Government to Government basis.

Somalia (A Republic) v Woodhouse Drake & Carey (Suisse) SA
[1993] 1 All ER 371, High Court

Somalia was suffering a civil war and it appeared that no faction was in effective control of the State. The plaintiffs claimed to be the 'Government of Somalia' and sought control over certain funds belonging to the Republic of Somalia. The issue was whether the plaintiffs were the 'Government of Somalia' and hence entitled to the funds. Following the UK practice (set out above), there was no Foreign Office certificate concerning the status of the plaintiffs.

HOBHOUSE J: The policy of the United Kingdom is now not to confer recognition upon governments as opposed to upon states. The new policy of Her Majesty's government was stated in two parliamentary answers in April and May 1980. . . . The position in English law before 1980 is conveniently set out in 18 *Halsbury's Laws* (4th edn) para 1431:

> A foreign government which has not been recognised by the United Kingdom government as either de jure or de facto government has no locus standi in the English courts. Thus it cannot institute an action in the courts . . . The English courts will not give effect to the acts of an unrecognised government. . . .

Thus, recognition by Her Majesty's government was the decisive matter and the courts had no role save to inquire of the executive whether or not it had recognised the government in question.

Some writers appear still to feel that the criterion remains one of recognition by the government of this country, the difference being that, whereas before 1980 the government would say expressly whether it recognised the foreign government, now it is to be left to be ascertained as a matter of inference: . . . The impracticality of the 'inferred recognition' theory as a legal concept for forensic use is obvious and it cannot be though that that was the intention of Her Majesty's government in giving the Parliamentary answers. The use of the phrase 'left to be inferred' is designed to fulfil a need for information in an international or political, not a judicial, context.

If recognition by Her Majesty's government is no longer the criterion of the locus standi of a foreign 'government' in the English courts and the possession of a legal persona in English law, what criteria is the court to apply? The answers do confirm one applicable criterion, namely whether the relevant regime is able of itself to 'exercise effective control of the territory of the State concerned' and is 'likely to continue to do so'; and the statement as to what is to be the evidence of the attitude of Her Majesty's government provides another – to be inferred from the nature of the dealings, if any, that Her Majesty's government has with it and whether they are on a normal government to government basis. The non-existence of such dealings cannot however be conclusive because their absence may be explained by some extraneous consideration – for example lack of occasion, the attitude of the regime to human rights, its relationship to another state. As the answers themselves acknowledge, the conduct of governments' in their relations with each other may be affected by considerations of policy as well as by considerations of legal characterisation. The courts of this country are now only concerned with the latter consideration. How much weight in this connection the courts should give to the attitude of Her Majesty's government was one of the issues before me. . .

It is clear from this letter [received by the plaintiffs' solicitors from the Foreign Office] that Her Majesty's government does not consider that there is at present any effective government in Somalia. It refers to 'factions' and treats the interim, government as merely one among a number of factions.

Accordingly, if the question before the court is to be decided upon the basis of the attitude adopted by Her Majesty's government, an order cannot be made in favour of the interim government or Crossman Block. The basis for its attitude is clearly not any disapproval of an established regime but rather that there is no regime which has control, let alone any administrative control which has the requisite element of stable continuity.

Mr Richards submitted that particular weight should be given to these communications. I have difficulty in accepting that submission without some qualification. Once the question for the court becomes one of making its own assessment of the evidence, making findings of fact on all the relevant evidence placed before it and drawing the appropriate legal conclusion, and is no longer a question of simply reflecting government policy, letters from the Foreign and Commonwealth Office become merely part of the evidence in the case. In the present case no problem of admissibility of evidence arises. In so far as the letters make statements about what is happening in the territory of some foreign state, such letters may not be the best evidence; but as regards the question whether Her Majesty's government has dealings with the foreign government it will almost certainly be the best and only conclusive evidence of that fact. Where Her Majesty's government is dealing with the foreign government on a normal government to government basis as the government of the relevant foreign state, it is unlikely in the extreme that the inference that the foreign government is the government of that state will be capable of being rebutted and questions of public policy and considerations of the interrelationship of the judicial and executive arms of Government may be paramount. . . . But now that the question has ceased to be one of recognition, the theoretical possibility of rebuttal must exist.

There is no decided English authority upon the effect of the 1980 answers. *GUR Corp* v *Trust Bank of Africa Ltd* was concerned with a question of the recognition of a state and the competence of a subordinate body within the recognised territory of that state under the laws of that state. The 1980 answers were referred to but were not the basis of the decision. Here no question of the recognition of a state is involved. Nor does this case involve any accredited representative of a foreign state in this country. Different considerations would arise if it did, since it would be contrary to public policy for the court not to recognise as a qualified representative of the head of state of the foreign state the diplomatic representative recognised by Her Majesty's government. There is no recognised diplomatic representative of the Republic of Somalia to the United Kingdom.

The statements of fact in the letters from the Foreign and Commonwealth Office are confirmed by the other evidence that is before the court concerning the actual situation in Somalia. The interim government is not governing that country and does not exercise administrative or any control over its territory and population. . . . The criteria of effective control referred to in the Parliamentary answers are clearly not satisfied. . . . The interim government clearly does not satisfy these criteria; the republic currently has no government.

However there are two other aspects upon which counsel for the interim government has relied. These are the recognition of the interim government by some other states and international bodies, and the fact that the interim government was set up by the Djibouti Agreement, which resulted from an international conference attended by many international states and bodies.

In evaluating these arguments it is relevant to distinguish between regimes that have been the constitutional and established government of a state and a regime which is seeking to achieve that position either displacing a former government or to fill a vacuum. Since the question is now whether a government *exists*, there is no room for more than one government at a time nor for separate de jure and de facto governments in respect of the same state. But a loss of control by a constitutional government may not immediately deprive it of its status, whereas an insurgent regime will require to establish control before it can exist as a government.

The argument based on the Djibouti Agreement does not assist the interim government. The Djibouti Agreement was not constitutional. It did not create a de jure status for the interim government in Somalia. The interim government was not and did not become the constitutional successor of the government of President Siad Barre. Accordingly, if the interim government is to be treated as the government of Somalia, it must be able to show that it is exercising administrative control over the territory of the republic. That it is not able to do. Accordingly that argument must fail.

As regards the argument of international recognition and recognition by the United Nations, although this does not as such involve control of territory or a population, it does correspond to one aspect of statehood. A classic definition of a state is that contained in art 1 of the Inter-American Convention on the Rights and Duties of States (Montevideo, 26 December 1933; 137 BFSP 282) as having − '(a) a permanent population; (b) a defined territory; (c) Government; and (d) capacity to enter into relations with other States.' Whilst illustrating that it is difficult to separate the recognition of a state from the recognition of a government of that state, this definition also shows that part of the function of a government of a state is to have relations with other states. This is also implicit in the reference in the 1980 parliamentary answers to dealings on a government to government basis.

Accordingly I consider that the degree of international recognition of an alleged government is a relevant factor in assessing whether it exists as the government of a state. But where, as here, the regime exercises virtually no administrative control at all in the territory of the state, international recognition of an unconstitutional regime should not suffice and would, indeed, have to be accounted for by policy considerations rather than legal characterisation; and it is, of course, possible for states to have relations with bodies which are not states or governments of states.

There is evidence from which it appears that the United Nations Organisation considers that there are persons whom it may treat as the representatives of the Republic of Somalia. Resolution 733 started with the words: 'Considering the request by Somilia for the Security Council to consider the situation in Somalia'. . . . This evidence is not wholly satisfactory. The attitude of the United Nations to interim government could be established in a more direct fashion and more authoritatively. . . . In any event, membership of an international organisation does not amount to recognition nor does a vote on credentials and representation issues: see Warbrick 'The new British policy on recognition of governments' (1981) 30 ICLQ 568 at 583, citing the Secretary General's memorandum 1950 UN Doc S/1466. But any apparent acceptance of the interim government by the United Nations and other international organisations and states does not suffice in the present case to demonstrate that the interim government is the government of the Republic of Somalia. The evidence the other way is too strong.

Accordingly, the factors to be taken into account in deciding whether a government exists as the government of a state are: (a) whether it is the constitutional government of the state; (b) the degree, nature and stability of administrative control, if any, that it of itself exercises over the territory of the state; (c) whether Her Majesty's government has any dealings with it and if so what is the nature of those dealings; and (d) in marginal cases, the extent of international recognition that it has the government of the state.

On the evidence before the court the interim government certainly does not qualify having regard to any of the three important factors.

NOTES:

1. The change in the UK practice concerning recognition (or rather non-recognition) of governments would seem to require a shift in the relationship between the UK government and UK courts. The burden of assessing the status of an entity claiming to be a foreign sovereign government has passed from the former to the latter. Indeed, although the cases decided soon after the change in practice (e.g. *Gur Corporation* v *Trust Bank of Africa* [1986] 3 WLR 583) suggest a deference to the Executive despite the change in practice, the *Somalia* case has made it clear that the role of the courts is now central. In this respect, the *Somalia* case is a decision of considerable importance. It is the clearest indication yet that the change in UK practice concerning recognition of governments has brought about a substantive change in the law of recognition. This has been confirmed by the decision in *Sierra Leone Telecommunications* v *Barclays Bank plc* [1998] 2 All ER 821.

2. The change in practice could simply have meant that UK courts would ask 'what course of dealings' does the UK have with the disputed entity, and then determine the status of that entity in line with the Foreign Office answer to this question. This would be a doctrine of recognition in all but name. In *Somalia* and *Sierra Leone*, it is made clear that the court may determine the status of an alleged foreign sovereign government by reference to its own criteria, only part of which is the 'course of dealings' that the UK has with the entity. Furthermore, the case opens up the possibility that a UK court will accept the sovereignty of a foreign government even if the UK government would, as a matter of policy, be opposed to such a move. In an action in the High Court of Hong Kong in 1991 (that is, while Hong Kong was under UK sovereignty), a Foreign Office reply indicated that the UK does not recognise Taiwan as a State and has no *official* dealings with any authority there ((1996) 67 BYIL, pp. 716–17). However, given that the reply makes it clear that the UK has *unofficial* dealings with the authorities in Taiwan, it would be possible for a UK court to conclude that Taiwan had a 'government' for the purposes of UK law.

(c) Foreign companies

One of the consequences of the non-recognition of a foreign State was that all companies incorporated under its (unrecognised) laws had no legal personality within the UK. Consequently, they could not sue or be sued. This was unfortunate for persons having commercial dealings with these companies which, for all intents and purposes, did exist and did engage in trade and commerce. This was substantially the issue in *Carl Zeiss* and *Gur* and, although the House of Lords sidestepped the issue by relying on the device of 'delegated sovereignty' (see above) the position was unsatisfactory. The issue has now been placed on a firmer legal footing by the enactment of the Foreign Corporations Act 1991.

Foreign Corporations Act 1991

1.—(1) If at any time—

    (a) any question arises whether a body which purports to have or, as the case may be, which appears to have lost corporate status under the laws of a territory which is not at that time a recognised State should or should not be regarded as having legal personality as a body corporate under the law of any part of the United Kingdom, and

    (b) it appears that the laws of that territory are at that time applied by a settled court system in that territory, that question and any other material question relating to the body shall be determined (and account shall be taken of those laws) as if that territory were a recognised State.

(2) For the purposes of subsection (1) above—

    (a) 'a recognised State' is a territory which is recognised by Her Majesty's Government in the United Kingdom as a State;

    (b) the laws of a territory which is so recognised shall be taken to include the laws of any part of the territory which are acknowledged by the federal or other central government of the territory as a whole; and

    (c) a material question is a question (whether as to capacity, constitution or otherwise) which, in the case of a body corporate, falls to be determined by reference to the laws of the territory under which the body is incorporated.

R v *Minister of Agriculture Fisheries & Food, ex parte S.P. Anastasiou (Pissouri) and Others*

noted at 54 CLJ 4 (1995)

The Turkish Republic of Northern Cyprus (TRNC) is not recognised as a State by the UK. Cypfruvex, a company incorporated in the TRNC was 81 per cent owned by the TRNC Government. The UK, despite not recognising the TRNC, accepted customs certificates from that entity and this enabled Cypfruvex to import citrus fruit into the UK. Fruit growers from the Republic of Cyprus (which was recognised by the UK) sought judicial review of the decision to accept these certificates. Cypfruvex sought leave of the court to intervene in these proceedings, and this was the issue before the Court. The Cypriot fruit growers argued that Cypfruvex could not intervene either because (i) in reality it represented the government of the TRNC, an unrecognised State, or (ii) it was a company incorporated in an unrecognised State. Popplewell J rejected the first contention, accepting that Cypfruvex was a legal person in its own right, irrespective of the identity of its shareholders. The second issue turned on the Foreign Corporations Act 1991.

POPPLEWELL J: The question of the status of Cypfruvex has involved consideration of the Foreign Corporations Act 1991.

There is no dispute but that the TRNC is not a recognised state. The territory to which it lays claim is legally the territory of the Republic of Cyprus. Cypfruvex has been set up by a state which is not recognised and which is treated as illegal.

On the face of the Act itself, it appears to me that the Court has to consider three questions:

Firstly, is there territory which is identifiable but which is not a recognised state? The answer to that is yes.

Secondly, is there a settled court system in that territory so that the laws of that territory are thereby applied? I am satisfied on the material in the papers that that is so.

Thirdly, in the instant case does the body (that is Cypfruvex) have corporate status under the court system operating in that territory? To that the answer is yes. . . .

Mr Vaughan submits that the territory occupied by the TRNC is in fact territory belonging to the Republic of Cyprus. It is occupied by a rebel government; accordingly, in the light of that passage, the matter has to be construed not in relation to the Foreign Corporations Act 1991 but with principles which prevailed before the passing of the Act. . . .

I confess that when I first read the Foreign Corporations Act 1991 it seemed to me abundantly clear what it meant . . . There may be a situation where a revolution is taking place where a relevant legal system has not yet been established; alternatively, whether it has been established in a piece of territory may be in doubt because the territory in question may not have been established. If a relevant legal system is in doubt, the question of its identification may need to be determined in accordance with previous principles. . . .

[I]f the matter were in doubt or appeared to result in an absurdity, the Court was entitled to look at the debates in Hansard in accordance with *Pepper v Hart*. Again, from an abundance of caution, I did. It is clear from what was said by the Lord Advocate in moving the second reading in the House of Lords and by the Solicitor General (as he then was) on the second reading in the Commons that the interpretation which the Court has put on this is the one that Parliament intended.

NOTES:

1. The above case was the first case where the Foreign Corporations Act 1991 was applied. Popplewell J interpreted and applied it consistently with its purpose: *viz* to give legal recognition to a company from an unrecognised State. Hence Cypfruvex could intervene. However, the question whether the UK could accept customs certificates from the TRNC had been referred to the European Court of Justice to see if such certificates complied with Community law. Subsequent to Popplewell's decision, the ECJ ruled that the UK could not accept such certificates because they were not issued by the legitimate authority in Cyprus. While the decision of Popplewell J was perfectly consistent with (and probably required by) the Foreign Corporations Act 1991, the ECJ decision was less than pragmatic and places a premium on policy. It is a retrograde step, at least considering the changes in recognition law and practice made in recent years in the UK. After the decision of the ECJ there is the further danger that the Foreign Corporations Act 1991 will be redundant in many areas of its operation, i.e. where there is an EC law element.

2. It is also important that Popplewell J refused to interpret the Foreign Corporations Act 1991 restrictively. He did not agree that whether a 'settled court system' existed was to be determined by reference to an affidavit of the Foreign Office. Clearly this is correct.

(d) International organisations

Arab Monetary Fund v *Hashim* (*No 3*)
[1990] 2 All ER 769, Court of Appeal

The Arab Monetary Fund (AMF) was an international organisation created by treaty. The UK was not a party to this treaty, and the AMF had not been given the status of a company in English law. The AMF sued Hashim for misappropriated funds. The defendant contended that the AMF had no status in English law and, therefore, could not maintain an action. It was not disputed that the AMF was a 'person' in international law. The question was, therefore, whether English law would 'recognise' the status of an international legal person, although that body had no separate English personality. The judgment of the Court of Appeal is noted below. On appeal to the House of Lords ([1991] 1 All ER 871), their lordships allowed the AMF to sue, but only because it had been incorporated in Abu Dhabi law and could be regarded as an Abu Dhabian corporation to be recognised under the 'conflict of laws' rules.

LORD DONALDSON MR: The decision of the House of Lords in the *International Tin Council* case [see above] . . . confirms that our courts have no competence to adjudicate on or to enforce rights arising out of transactions entered into by independent sovereign states between themselves on the plane of international law. It also confirms that treaties to which the United Kingdom government is a party, and a *fortiori* those to which it is not, are not self-executing. They do not therefore create rights and obligations. . . . Hence the need for the International Organisations Act 1968, which enables Her Majesty by Order in Council to 'confer on the organisation the legal capacities of a body corporate' if it is an organisation of which the United Kingdom government is a member or if it maintains or proposes to maintain an establishment in the United Kingdom and, in the former case, may also provide that it shall enjoy certain privileges and immunities (see ss 1(2) and 4(a)). The fund is not, of course, such an organisation, since the United Kingdom government is not a member and it does not propose to maintain an establishment in this country. The *International Tin Council* case itself was concerned with the extent to which such an Order in Council invested the organisation with a separate personality distinct from its constituent members and, if so, to what extent (if at all) liability, whether primary or secondary, for its obligations attached to its constituent members. The House of Lords answered the first question 'Yes' and the second question 'Not at all'. Neither question arises directly on this appeal, but the discussion of the nature of an international organisa-tion on which the legal capacities of a body corporate have been conferred casts some light on how English law would or should regard an international organisation on which an Abu Dhabi or United Arab Emirates decree has conferred similar capacities. . . .

As I see it, absent an Order in Council, an international organisation is something which, in the eyes of English law, is as much a fact as a tree, a road or a hill. But it is not a person and the law can only deal in the rights and liabilities of persons. Once it is touched by the magic wand of the Order in Council it becomes a person, but one which is quite unlike other persons. Self-evidently it is not a natural person. But equally it is not a United Kingdom juridical person; nor is it a foreign juridical person. It is a person *sui generis*, which has all the capacities of a United Kingdom juridical person, but is not subject to the controls to which such a person is subject under United Kingdom law. It is not a native, but nor is it a visitor from abroad. It comes from the invisible depths of outer space.

Westland Helicopters Ltd v *Arab Organisation for Industrialisation*
[1995] 2 All ER 387, Queen's Bench Division

> The AOI was an international organisation incorporated as a legal person in the national law of many States, but not the UK. In consequence, one question was whether the Bank had legal personality in the UK.

An international organisation would be recognised by English law as having legal personality if it had been accorded the legal capacity of a corporation under the law of one of its member states or the state where it had its seat (if that state was not a member state) and the fact that it had been accorded such capacity by more than one state did not mean that there was more than one international organisation for the English courts to recognise, but merely that there was more than one factual basis on which recognition could be accorded to the same organisation. Once it was accepted that an international organisation had been recognised by the English courts, questions as to the meaning, effect and operation of its constitution in so far as they arose between parties to the founding treaty were matters which could only be determined by reference to the treaty and to the principles of public international law, indeed, it would be contrary to the comity of nations for the English courts to impose the domestic law of one of the member states of the international organisa-tion as its governing law, particularly where the terms of the treaty included a provision expressly insulating the international organisation from the domestic law of any participating state. It followed that the proper law governing the existence, constitution and representation of the AOI was public international law and not Egyptian domestic law.

NOTE:

If an international organisation is 'personalised' in UK law then its status as a UK legal person is beyond doubt. This may arise through incorporation in the UK, or by statutory instrument under the International Organisations Acts. According to *Hashim*, an international organisation incorporated in the law of a State recognised by the UK has the personality of that State and so also has legal status in the UK. In the *Westland* case, a further step is taken by noting that, provided the organisation is incorporated in a recognised State, its 'true' legal attributes are to be determined by the treaty which established it – even if this treaty is unenacted in the UK. This case suggests that all international organisations now have personality in the UK – as defined by their constituent treaty. This is a long way from the non-recognition theory of the *International Tin Council* cases.

B: Recognition practice of other States

The recognition practice of other common law States is very similar to that of the UK.

Australia's New Recognition Policy
Department of Foreign Affairs and Trade: Backgrounder No 611, 16 March 1988

Previously Australia recognised (or did not recognise) both States and governments in existing States. We now recognise States only [as of 19 January 1988]. Recognition of a State essentially means acceptance of it as a fully independent and sovereign member of the community of nations. . . .

Under our old policy the recognition of a new [government] which had come to power in an existing State as the government of that State was technically a formal acknowledgment that the government was in effective control of that State and in a position to represent that State internationally. However, recognition of a new government inevitably led to public assumptions of approval or disapproval of the government concerned, and could thereby create domestic or other problems for the recognising government. On the other hand 'non-recognition' limited the non-recognising government's capacity to deal with the new regime.

Considerations such as these have led a number of western governments to change to a policy of recognising States only. Australia now follows this policy . . . In future, Australia will no longer announce that it recognises, or does not recognise, a new regime in an existing State. Australia's attitude to a new regime will be ascertained by the nature of our policies towards and relations with the new regime. Important indicators of Australia's attitude to a new regime will be: public statements; establishment of and/or the conduct of diplomatic relations with it; ministerial contact; and other contacts, such as entering into aid, economic or defence arrangements, technical and cultural exchanges.

Abandoning the device of recognition of governments will enable us to react more flexibly and quickly to developments and to avoid giving rise to speculation about recognition and, consequently, assumptions of approval.

First National City Bank v Banco Para El Comercio Exterior De Cuba
462 US 611 (1983), United States Court of Appeals

The Cuban Government established the Banco Para El Comercio Exterior De Cuba (Bancec) to serve as an official autonomous credit institution for foreign trade with full legal capacity. After a dispute over a contract with the applicant bank, the Cuban government seized the First National City Bank's assets in Cuba.

The issue was whether the Bancec's separate juridical status shielded it from liability for the acts of the Cuban Government.

Increasingly during this century, governments throughout the world have established separately constituted legal entities to perform a variety of tasks. . . . Freely ignoring the separate status of government instrumentalities would result in substantial uncertainty over whether an instrumentality's assets would be diverted to satisfy a claim against the sovereign, and might thereby cause third parties to hesitate before extending credit to a government instrumentality without the government's guarantee. As a result, the efforts of sovereign nations to structure their governmental activities in a manner deemed necessary to promote economic development and efficient administration would surely be frustrated. Due respect for the actions taken by foreign sovereigns and for principles of comity between nations, see *Hilton* v *Guyot*, 159 U.S. 113, 163–164 (1895), leads us to conclude – as the courts of Great Britain have concluded in other circumstances [*I Congreso del Partido*] that government instrumentalities established as juridical entities distinct and independent from their sovereign should normally be treated as such.

We find support for this conclusion in the legislative history of the Foreign Sovereign Immunities Act [US] (FSIA). During its deliberations, Congress clearly expressed its intention that duly created instrumentalities of a foreign State are to be accorded a presumption of independent status. . . . In discussing the legal status of private corporations, courts in the United States and abroad, have recognized that an incorporated entity – described by Chief Justice Marshall as 'an artificial being, invisible intangible, and existing only in contemplation of law' [*Trustees of Dartmouth College* v *Woodward*, 4 Wheat 518, 636 (1819)] – is not to be regarded as legally separate from its owners in all circumstances. Thus, where a corporate entity is so extensively controlled by its owner that a relationship of principal and agent is created, we have held that one may be held liable for the actions of the other. In addition, our cases have long recognized 'the broader equitable principle that the doctrine of corporate entity, recognized generally and for most purposes, will not be regarded when to do so would work fraud or injustice.' *Taylor* v *Standard Gas Co.*, 306 U.S. 307, 322 (1939). In particular, the Court has consistently refused to give effect to the corporate form where it is interposed to defeat legislative policies . . .

Giving effect to Bancec's separate juridical status in these circumstances, even though it has long been dissolved, would permit the real beneficiary of such an action, the Government of the Republic of Cuba, to obtain relief in our courts that it could not obtain in its own right without waiving its sovereign immunity and answering for the seizure of Citibank's assets – a seizure previously held by the Court of of Appeals to have violated international law. We decline to adhere blindly to the corporate form where doing so would cause such an injustice . . . Having dissolved Bancec and transferred its assets to entities that may be held liable on Citibank's counterclaim, Cuba cannot escape liability for acts in violation of international law simply by retransferring the assets to separate juridical entities. To hold otherwise would permit governments to avoid the requirements of international law simply by creating juridical entities whenever the need arises . . . Our decision today announces no mechanical formula for determining the circumstances under which the normally separate juridical status of a government instrumentality is to be disregarded. Instead, it is the product of the application of internationally recognized equitable principles to avoid the injustice that would result from permitting a foreign state to reap the benefits of our courts while avoiding the obligations of international law.

NOTES:

1. Most States have now adopted a policy of not formally recognising governments. Part of the reason for this is, as the above extract on Australia's policy shows, due to the assumptions of approval or non-approval that it can create.

2. The courts of all States tend to seek to minimise the effect of non-recognition on the ordinary activities of individuals and groups (and corporations) as well as to avoid fraud and injustice

(see *First National City Bank* above). However, the courts differ in the extent to which they will go beyond official government statements and executive certificates in order to acknowledge the realities of the situation – see *Attorney-General for Fiji* v *Robert Jones House* (New Zealand High Court) 80 ILR (1988) 1.

6

International Human Rights Law

Introductory note

The United Nations Charter begins with these words: 'We the Peoples of the United Nations determined . . . to reaffirm faith in fundamental human rights, in the dignity and worth of the human person, in the equal rights of men and women . . .'. This acknowledgement of the importance of human rights by all States which ratify the United Nations Charter has done much to stimulate the large amount of international law protecting human rights now in place. While there was considerable academic acceptance of international human rights law from an early date, and some national constitutions specifically provided for the protection of the human rights of their citizens, development of the protection of human rights in international law has generally been subsequent to the United Nations Charter.

The impact of international human rights on the international community is profound. For example, it has developed the role of the individual as a subject of international law, as discussed in Chapter 5; claims of title to territory cannot be made without some consideration of the rights of the inhabitants of that territory (see Chapter 7); and it has meant that a State's sovereignty has been limited, as the treatement of an individual by a State is a matter of international concern and not a matter purely for national jurisdiction (see Chapter 11). It has also changed many perceptions of the nature of international law, as seen in Chapter 1.

Human rights are a matter of international law, as the rights of humans do not depend on an individual's nationality and so the protection of these rights cannot be limited to the jurisdiction of any one State. Of course, national protection of human rights is vital, and many States do specifically provide for such protection. Also, both the protection and the enforcement of international human rights, as with all international law, can depend on national courts (as seen in Chapter 4). However, as most breaches of human rights are caused by a State acting against its own citizens or against those persons in its jurisdiction, much of international human rights law operates beyond the national legal system in order to afford redress to those whose human rights are infringed and to provide an international standard by which States can be judged. This chapter aims to introduce the principal ideas, issues and framework of international human rights law.

Ultimately, if human rights mean anything in international law, then the traditional international law of State-based jurisdictional exclusivity must give way to a realisation that the rights of humans matter more than the interests of States.

SECTION 1:   Human rights theories

The crux of international human rights law is to afford legal protection of human rights. To do this it is first necessary to decide what are human rights. Virtually all major legal theorists have considered the nature of human rights.

R. Wasserstrom, 'Rights, Human Rights and Racial Discrimination' in J. Rachels (ed), *Moral Problems*
(3rd edn, 1979), p. 12

First, [a human right] must be possessed by all human beings, as well as only by human beings. Second, because it is the same right that all human beings possess, it must be possessed equally by all human beings. Third, because human rights are possessed by all human beings, we can rule out as possible candidates any of those rights which one might have in virtue of occupying any particular status or relationship, such as that of parent, president or promisee. And fourth, if there are human rights, they have the additional characteristic of being assertable, in a manner of speaking, 'against the whole world'.

J. Shestack, 'The Jurisprudence of Human Rights' in T. Meron (ed), *Human Rights in International Law: Legal and Policy Issues*
(1984), pp. 70–71, 73–74, 77–82, 90–91, 96–99

One of the initial questions is what is meant by human rights. . . . How we understand the meaning of human rights will influence our judgments on such issues as which rights are regarded as absolute, which are universal, which should be given priority, which can be overruled by other interests, which call for international pressures, which can demand programs for implementation, and which will be fought for.

The definitional process is not easy. Consider first the term 'rights', a chameleonhued word as Professor Hohefeld ['Fundamental Legal Conceptions as Applied in Judicial Reasoning' (1913) 23 Yale LJ 16] has taught us. Certainly, as we examine the various rights dealt with in this volume, we will observe that 'rights' is an ambiguous term used to describe a variety of legal relationships. According to Hohefeldian analysis, 'right' sometimes is used in its strict sense of the right-holder being *entitled* to something with a correlative duty in another. Sometimes, 'right' is used to indicate an *immunity* from having a legal status altered. Sometimes it indicates a *privilege* to do something. Sometimes it refers to a *power* to create a legal relationship. . . .

Some scholars classify civil and political rights as types of immunities since they protect against encroachments of government. They are restraints on government in the nature of a command: 'Thou shalt not.' Generally, such negative restraints can be secured by fairly simple legislation. Economic, social, and cultural rights, on the other hand, are 'rights' in which affirmative action by the government is necessary. Therefore, they are viewed as claims upon the governments which may or may not be realized depending on such matters as availability of resources and other conditions.

If it were that simple, the logical conclusion would seem to be that civil and political rights (in the nature of immunities) deserve a hierarchical preference over contingent claims or expectations. But . . . Communist states and some Third World states often assert the reverse: that economic or social claims have a priority among the classes of rights. Indeed, it is frequently argued that achievement of economic and social rights is a pre-condition for other rights, that is, until the economic and social rights are realized a state is not in a condition to provide civil and political rights. . . . The authority for and the priorities to be assigned these two sets of rights involve issues of *real-politik* which have often sharply divided East and West, North and South. . . .

Finally, in the case of international human rights one is always faced with the question of what are rights worth where the type of enforcement procedures we find in a domestic system do not exist. It has often been said that there cannot be a right without a remedy. But is that so where there are various alternative forms of redress achieved through non-legal processes such as quiet diplomacy, threats of linkage, public opinion pressures, and other measures? . . .

Natural law: the autonomous individual
Natural law theory has underpinnings in Sophocles and Aristotle, but it was first elaborated by the stoics of the Hellenistic period and later of the Roman period. Natural law, they believed, embodied those elementary principles of justice which were right reason, i.e., in accordance with nature, unalterable and eternal. . . .

Natural law theory led to natural rights theory – the theory most closely associated with modern human rights. The chief exponent of this theory was John Locke, who developed his philosophy within the framework of seventeenth-century humanism and political activity. Locke imagined the existence of human beings in a state of nature. In that state men and women were in a state of freedom, able to determine their actions, and also in a state of equality in the sense that no one was subjected to the will or authority of another. To end the certain hazards and inconveniences of the state of nature, men and women entered into a contract by which they mutually agreed to form a community and set up a body politic. However, in setting up that political authority they retained the natural rights of life, liberty, and property which were their own. Government was obliged to protect the natural rights of its subjects and if government neglected this obligation it would forfeit its validity and office. . . .

Positivism: the authority of the state
Another approach to human rights study is that of legal positivism. . . . Under [classical] positivist theory, the source of human rights is to be found only in the enactments of a system of law with sanctions attached to it. Views on what the law *ought* to be have no place in law and are cognitively worthless. The need to distinguish with maximum clarity law as it *is* from what it *ought to be* is the theme that haunts positivist philosophers, and they condemned natural law thinkers because they had blurred this vital distinction. . . .

An influential moral philosopher, Professor H.L.A. Hart, [*The Concept of Law* (1961)] . . . finds the authority for the rules of law in the background of legal standards against which the government acts, standards that have been recognized and accepted by the community for that government. This legitimizes the decisions of the government and gives them the warp and woof of obligation that the naked commands of classical positivism lacked. . . . In short, he continues to argue for a concept of law which allows the invalidity of law to be distinguished from its morality. And this remains a basic difference between natural rights philosophy and positivist philosophy. . . .

Marxism: man as a specie being
[Marx] regarded the notion of individual rights as a bourgeois illusion. Concepts such as law, justice, morality, democracy, freedom, etc., are considered historical categories, whose content is determined by the material conditions of the life of a people and by their social circumstances. As the conditions of life change, so the content of notions and ideas may change. . . .

Marxist recognition of rights stems from its view of persons as indivisible from the social whole; only by meeting the will of the whole can the higher freedom of individuals be achieved. Under this view, even satisfaction of basic needs can become contingent on realization of societal goals such as industrialization or the building of communism. . . .

Theories based on justice

The monumental thesis of modern moral philosophy is John Rawls' *A Theory of Justice* [1971]. 'Justice is the first virtue of social institutions', says Rawls. Human rights, of course, are an end of justice; consequently, the role of justice is crucial to understanding human rights. No theory of human rights can be advanced today without considering Rawls' thesis.

Principles of justice, according to Rawls, provide a way of assigning rights and duties in the basic institutions of society. Those principles define the appropriate distribution of the benefits and burdens of social cooperation . . . The First Principle is that each person is to have an equal right to the most extensive total system of equal basic liberties compatible with a similar system of liberty for others. The Second Principle is that social and economic inequalities are to be arranged so they are both (a) to the greatest benefit of the least advantaged, and (b) attached to positions and offices open to all (equal opportunity).

The general conception of justice behind these principles is one of fairness and provides that all social primary goods – liberty and opportunity, income and wealth, and the bases of self-respect – are to be distributed equally unless an unequal distribution of any or all of these goods is to the advantage of the least favored. (This latter aspect is important in Rawls' theory and is known as the Difference Principle.) . . .

Theories based on dignity

McDougal, Lasswell, and Chen [*Human Rights and World Public Order: The Basic Policies of an International Law of Human Dignity* (1980)] follow what they call a value-policy oriented approach based on the protection of human dignity proceed on the premise that demands for human rights are demands for wide sharing in all the values upon which human rights depend and for effective participation in all community value processes. The interdependent values they specify are the demands relating to (1) respect, (2) power, (3) enlightenment, (4) well-being, (5) health, (6) skill, (7) affection, and (8) rectitude. They assemble a huge catalogue of the demands which satisfy those eight values, as well as all of the ways in which they are denigrated. . . .

The ultimate goal, as they see it, is a world community in which a democratic distribution of values is encouraged and promoted; all available resources are utilized to the maximum; and the protection of human dignity is regarded as a paramount objective of social policy. . . .

Theory based on equality of respect and concern

Dworkin [*Taking Rights Seriously* (1977)] proceeds from the postulate of political morality, i.e., that governments must treat all their citizens with equal concern and respect. . . . Dworkin next endorses the egalitarian character of the utilitarian principle that 'everybody can count for one, nobody for more than one'. . . . Under this principle he believes that the state may exercise wide interventionist functions in order to advance social welfare.

Dworkin believes that a right to liberty in general is too vague to be meaningful. However, certain specific liberties, such as freedom of speech, freedom of worship, rights of association and personal and sexual relations, do require special protection against government interference. This is so not because these preferred liberties have some special substantive or inherent value . . . but because of a kind of procedural impediment that these preferred liberties might face. The impediment is that if those liberties were left to a utilitarian calculation, that is, an unrestricted calculation of the general interest, the balance would be tipped in favor of restrictions. . . .

H. Lauterpacht, *International Law and Human Rights*

(1950), pp. 68–72

For human dignity and considerations of utility alike rebel against the idea of the State as the sole guardian of the interests of man. The purpose of the State is to safeguard the interests of the individual human being and to render possible the fulfilment, through freedom, of his wider duty to man and society. Some of these interests can be effectively safeguarded by the State in the international sphere. But it is inadmissible that the State should claim, in the conditions of the modern world, that it is the best instrument for protecting all these interests and that it is entitled to exclude from this legal sphere individuals and non-government bodies which may be created for that purpose. As within the State, so also in the international sphere the paramount danger arises when, in the words of John Stuart Mill in an eloquent concluding passage of his essay on Liberty, the State 'instead of calling forth the activity and the powers of individuals and bodies, . . . substitutes its own activities for theirs'. . . . The claim of the State to unqualified exclusiveness in the field of international relations was tolerable at a time when the actuality and the interdependence of the interests of the individual cutting across national frontiers were less obvious than they are today. It is this latter fact which explains why the constant expansion of the periphery of individual rights – an enduring feature of legal development – cannot stop short of the limits of the State. What is much more important, the recognition of the individual, by dint of the acknowledgment of his fundamental rights and freedoms, as the ultimate subject of international law, is a challenge to the doctrine which in reserving that quality exclusively to the State tends to a personification of the State as a being distinct from the individuals who compose it, with all that such personification implies. That recognition brings to mind the fact that, in the international as in the municipal sphere, the collective good is conditioned by the good of the individual human beings who comprise the collectivity. It denies, by cogent implication, that the corporate entity of the State is of a higher order than its component parts. It challenges the absolute moral superiority of groups, and in particular of the collective agency of the State which when thus artificially personified is prone to and certainly capable of disregard of all moral restraints.

. . . International law, which has excelled in punctillious insistence on the respect owed by one sovereign State to another, henceforth acknowledges the sovereignty of man. For fundamental human rights are rights superior to the law of the sovereign State. The hope, expressed by Emerson, that 'man shall treat with man as a sovereign state with a sovereign state' may be brought nearer to fruition by sovereign States recognising the duty to treat man with the respect which traditional law exacted from them in relation to other States. To that vital extent the recognition of inalienable human rights and the recognition of the individual as a subject of international law are synonymous. To that vital extent they both signify the recognition of a higher, fundamental law not only on the part of States but also, through international law, on the part of the organised international community itself. That fundamental law, as expressed in the acknowledgment of the ultimate reality and the independent status of the individual, constitutes both the moral limit and the justification of the international legal order. Through them, it implies the promise that the organised international society will not, in turn, degenerate into a tyrannical accumulation of power. It is that danger which has been for many the reason of the determined opposition to the idea of an organised commonwealth of nations embracing all humanity. In that perspective the acknowledgment of human rights and fundamental freedom on the part of the Members of the United Nations assumes an added significance of its own. The consequent recognition of the individual human being as a subject of international law lends to the law obtaining between sovereign States the beneficent complexion of a law of nations conceived as the universal law of mankind.

P. Gabel and D. Kennedy, 'Roll Over Beethoven'
36 Stanford LR 1 (1984), pp. 26, 33–34

This is the essence of the problem with rights discourse. People don't realise that what they are doing is recasting the real existential feelings that led them to become political people into an ideological framework that coopts them into adopting the very consciousness they want to transform. Without even knowing it, they start talking as if 'we' were rights-bearing citizens who are 'allowed' to do this or that by something called 'the state,' which is a passivising illusion – actually an hallucination which establishes the presumptive political legitimacy of the status quo. . . .

Exactly what people don't need is their *rights*. What they need are the actual forms of social life that have to be created through the building of movements that can overcome illusions about the nature of what is political, like the illusion that there is an entity called the state, that people possess rights. It may be necessary to use the rights argument in the course of political struggle, in order to make gains. But the thing to be understood is the extent to which it is enervating to use it. It's a diversion from true political language, political modes of communication about the nature of reality and what it is that people are trying to achieve. . . . [it is] an hallucination that as long as people believe in it, they will disempower themselves. . . . [A right] can be, in some circumstances, a marginal gain in power. It can force officials to obey their own rules. There are things about it that can lead to protective spaces that there's no reason for us to criticise. But it is critical for people not to 'return' this power to the state, to remember that the state is an illusion and that there are no rights.

H. Charlesworth, 'What are "Women's International Human Rights"?' in R. Cook (ed), *Human Rights of Women: National and International Perspectives* (1994), pp. 60, 68, 76

[T]he development of international human rights law generally has been partial and androcentric, privileging a masculine worldview. Non-governmental organizations have recently begun to document abuse of women that falls within the traditional scope of human rights law. But the very structure of this law has been built on silence of women. The fundamental problem women face worldwide is not discriminatory treatment compared with men, although this is a manifestation of the larger problem. Women are in an inferior position because they have no real power in either the public or the private worlds, and international human rights law, like most economic, social, cultural and legal constructs, reinforces this powerlessness. Noreen Burrows writes ['International Law and Human Rights: The Case of Women's Rights' in T. Campbell et al. (eds) *Human Rights: From Rhetoric to Reality*]: 'For most women, what it is to be human is to work long hours in agriculture or the home, to receive little or no renumeration, and to be faced with political and legal processes which ignore their contribution to society and accord no recognition of their particular needs.' A more fundamental treatment of the skewed nature of the international human rights system would redefine the boundaries of the traditional human rights canon, rather than tinkering with the limited existing model of non discrimination. . . .

It is worth noting . . . that, with the exception of the Convention on the Rights of the Child, all 'general' human rights instruments refer only to men. The importance of language in constructing and reinforcing the subordination of women has been much analyzed by feminist scholars, and the consistently masculine vocabulary of human rights law operates at both a direct and subtle level to exclude women. More basically, all international human rights law rests on and reinforces a distinction between public and private worlds, and this distinction operates to muffle, and often completely silence, the voices of women. . . .

How can international human rights law tackle the oppressed position of women worldwide? Women's international human rights must be developed on a number of fronts. Certainly the relevance of the traditional canon of human rights to women is important to document. The instruments and institutions of the 'first wave' of international law with respect to women must also be supported and strengthened. The potential of an individual complaints procedure under the Women's Convention, for example, should be seriously explored. At the same time, rights that focus on harms sustained by women in particular need to be identified and developed, challenging the public/private distinction by bringing rights discourse into the private sphere. But, most fundamental and important, we must work to ensure that women's voices find a public audience, to reorient the boundaries of mainstream human rights law so that it incorporates an understanding of the world from the perspective of the socially subjugated. One way forward in international human rights law is to challenge the gendered dichotomy of public and private worlds.

P. Williams, *The Alchemy of Race and Rights*

(1991), p. 164

[F]or the historically disempowered, the conferring of rights is symbolic of all the denied aspects of their humanity: rights imply a respect that places one in referential range of self and others, that elevates one's status from human body to social being. . . . 'Rights' feels new in the mouths of most black people. It is still deliciously empowering to say. It is the magic wand of inclusion and exclusion, of power and no power. The concept of rights, both positive and negative, is the maker of citizenship, our relation to others.

NOTES:

1. Understanding the different theories of human rights provides an insight into the content and interpretation of rights throughout this Chapter. For example, decisions as to whether any limitations can be allowed to be placed on human rights, questions of the allocation of priorities between human rights, the extent to which human rights are universal and concerns over the recognition of 'new' human rights, among many other issues, require some consideration of the concept of what is a human right. Wasserstrom's definition (above) is one of many definitions of human rights, with other theorists placing emphasis on human dignity, others on their role in developing every person's capacities and others on capabilities.

2. The theories summarised in the extracts above are only a selection of the major theories and are, necessarily, briefly described. Gabel and Kennedy are part of the Critical Legal Studies school of legal thought, and Charlesworth offers an example of the feminist perspective on human rights. In addition, the extract from wa Matua (4 below) examines the duties aspect of human rights. A number of the theories were formed within the context of national constitutional law, so there is some limitation on their relevance to international human rights law. However, they are important in that they illustrate some of the developments in the theoretical debates about human rights.

3. The first part of the extract from Shestack shows, by reference to Hohfeld's categories, that the use of the term 'rights' does not imply that if they are infringed then an individual is necessarily able to bring a claim against a State before a judicial body and directly enforce any decision made. However, by describing them as 'rights', it elevates these concepts from what could be considered to be purely moral standards to those having legal characteristics, as well as giving them moral and social power (as shown in Williams' extract). International human rights law constructs human rights as being only activated in relation to a State, however, the concept of human rights is not restricted to relationships only with a State (see D. Otto, 18 *Australian Year Book of International Law* (1997).

4. Shestack refers to the different types of rights, being civil and political rights (e.g., freedom from torture, right to a fair trial); economic, social and cultural rights (e.g., right to education, right to access to health care); and group or 'people' rights (e.g., freedom from genocide, right of self-determination). These rights are interdependent and of equal status. There is no hierarchy of rights because, as has often been said, 'rights begin with breakfast'. Therefore to categorise rights in terms of 'generations' is a mistake as it implies that some rights can only be respected, protected and fulfilled after other rights. In addition, as Shestack demonstrates, no one type of right requires one type of action or inaction by a State. For example, to ensure the right to a fair trial a State must finance a legal system with courts, judges, etc. Also, as is seen below in decisions by international tribunals, all rights are to some extent justiciable.

SECTION 2: **Human rights and the international community**

A: Universal obligations

The first major statement after the United Nations Charter on the international legal protection of human rights was the Universal Declaration of Human Rights. It is considered to set out some of the customary international law obligations on States with respect to the protection of human rights (see further below).

Universal Declaration of Human Rights 1948
General Assembly Resolution 217A (III)

The Universal Declaration of Human Rights was adopted by the General Assembly on 10 November 1948 by a vote of 48 in favour, none against and 8 abstentions, being Byelorussian SSR, Czechoslovakia, Poland, Saudi Arabia, South Africa, Ukrainian SSR, USSR, and Yugoslavia.

Preamble

Whereas recognition of the inherent dignity and of the equal and inalienable rights of all members of the human family is the foundation of freedom, justice and peace in the world,

Whereas disregard and contempt for human rights have resulted in barbarous acts which have outraged the conscience of mankind, and the advent of a world in which human beings shall enjoy freedom of speech and belief and freedom from fear and want has been proclaimed as the highest aspiration of the common people,

Whereas it is essential, if man is not to be compelled to have recourse, as a last resort, to rebellion against tyranny and oppression, that human rights should be protected by the rule of law,

Whereas it is essential to promote the development of friendly relations between nations,

Whereas the peoples of the United Nations have in the Charter reaffirmed their faith in fundamental human rights, in the dignity and worth of the human person and in the equal rights of men and women and have determined to promote social progress and better standards of life in larger freedom,

Whereas Member States have pledged themselves to achieve, in cooperation with the United Nations, the promotion of universal respect for and observance of human rights and fundamental freedoms,

Whereas a common understanding of these rights and freedoms is of the greatest importance for the full realization of this pledge.

Vienna Declaration and Programme of Action 1993
32 ILM 1661 (1993)

In June 1993, a World Conference on Human Rights was organised by the United Nations. All States participated and there was input from many non-governmental organisations and individuals. At the end of the conference, the Vienna Declaration was agreed by consensus.

Preamble

Recognising and affirming that all human rights derive from the dignity and worth inherent in the human person, and that the human person is the central subject of human rights and fundamental freedoms, and consequently should be the principal beneficiary and should participate actively in the realization of these rights and freedoms, . . .

Emphasising that the Universal Declaration of Human Rights, which constitutes a common standard of achievement for all peoples and all nations, is the source of inspiration and has been the basis for the United Nations in making advances in standard setting as contained in the existing international human rights instruments, in particular the International Convenant on Civil and Political Rights and the International Convenant on Economic, Social and Cultural Rights, . . .

1. The World Conference on Human Rights reaffirms the solemn commitment of all States to fulfil their obligations to promote universal respect for, and observance and protection of, all human rights and fundamental freedoms for all in accordance with the Charter of the United Nations, other instruments relating to human rights, and international law. The universal nature of these rights and freedoms is beyond question.

In this framework, enhancement of international cooperation in the field of human rights is essential for the full achievement of the purposes of the United Nations.

Human rights and fundamental freedoms are the birthright of all human beings; their protection and promotion is the first responsibility of Governments. . . .

4. The promotion and protection of all human rights and fundamental freedoms must be considered as a priority objective of the United Nations in accordance with its purposes and principles, in particular the purpose of international cooperation. In the framework of these purposes and principles, the promotion and protection of all human rights is a legitimate concern of the international community. The organs and specialized agencies related to human rights should therefore further enhance the coordination of their activities based on the consistent and objective application of international human rights instruments.

5. All human rights are universal, indivisible and interdependent and interrelated. The international community must treat human rights globally in a fair and equal manner, on the same footing, and with the same emphasis. While the significance of national and regional particularities and various historical, cultural and religious background must be borne in mind, it is the duty of States, regardless of their political, economic and cultural systems, to promote and protect all human rights and fundamental freedoms.

6. The efforts of the United Nations system towards the universal respect for, and observance of, human rights and fundamental freedoms for all, contribute to the stability and well-being necessary for peaceful and friendly relations among nations, and to improved conditions for peace and security as well as economic and social development, in conformity with the Charter of the United Nations. . . .

8. Democracy, development and respect for human rights and fundamental freedoms are interdependent and mutually reinforcing. Democracy is based on the freely expressed will of the people to determine their own political, economic, social and cultural systems and their full participation in all aspects of their lives. . . .

10. The World Conference on Human Rights reaffirms the right to development, as established in the Declaration on the Right to Development, as a universal and inalienable right and an integral part of fundamental human rights.

Prosecutor v *Tadić (Jurisdictional Phase)*

35 ILM 35 (1996), International Criminal Tribunal for the Former Yugoslavia

97. The impetuous development and propagation in the international community of human rights doctrines . . . has brought about significant changes in international law, notably in the approach to

problems besetting the world community, . . . [Thus a] state-sovereignty-oriented approach has been gradually supplanted by a human-being-oriented approach. Gradually the maxim of Roman law *hominum causa omne jus constitutum est* (all law is created for the benefit of human beings) has gained a firm foothold in the international community as well.

NOTES:

1. As seen in the Preambles to both the Universal Declaration of Human Rights and the Vienna Declaration, most human rights treaties explicitly assume that the rights enumerated in them pre-exist their legal formulation. Thus they adopt the theory that human rights derive from the inherent dignity of the human person.

2. Every State in the world has ratified at least one treaty that protects human rights. This extraordinary fact indicates the extent to which international human rights law is now a part of the international legal system. Of course, the ratification by States of a human rights treaty does not necessarily mean that they comply with their obligations under it, or that they accept all the terms of the treaty (see reservations below).

3. Human rights has made a significant impact on international law. It has particularly affected the sovereignty of States and the assumption that international law is solely a State-based system (as seen in the *Tadic* comment above). There is now general agreement that human rights are a matter of legitimate international concern and they are appropriately a part of the international legal system (see para. 4 of the Vienna Declaration above). The vast amount of international and regional instruments concerning both human rights in general and specific human rights – being evidence of State practice – testify to this. Therefore, a State can no longer claim that human rights is a matter within its exclusive 'domestic jurisdiction' within Article 2(7) of the United Nations Charter and so claim that the international community is not able to be concerned about human rights within that State. Instead, how a State treats all persons on its territory is not a matter for the State alone but is a matter of international law. International human rights law provides a standard whereby the conduct of each State in regard to human rights can be judged.

4. While there are many breaches of human rights by States, very rarely will a State claim that it is allowed to breach a human right. It will either deny the facts concerning the breach, or will try and justify its action by reference to some exception to, derogation on, or limitation of, those rights. In so doing, the State affirms the obligation to protect human rights, as was acknowledged by the International Court of Justice in *Military and Paramilitary Activities in and against Nicaragua* ICJ Rep 1986 14 (para. 185), when it held that if a State 'defends its conduct by appealing to exceptions or justifications contained within the [recognised international law] rule itself, then whether or not the State's conduct is in fact justifiable on that basis, the significance of that attitude is to confirm rather than to weaken the rule'.

B: Cultural relativism

If human rights are universal then they apply to all persons no matter where, or within which cultures, they live. However, if human rights are relative to each society or culture (hence the term 'cultural relativism') then any international system of protecting human rights could be seen as inappropriate.

F. Tesón, 'International Human Rights and Cultural Relativism'

25 *Virginia Journal of Human Rights* 869 (1985), 895

[The attitude of some cultural relativists implies that] countries that do not spring from a Western tradition may somehow be excused from complying with the international law of human rights. This elitist theory of human rights holds that human rights are good for the West but not for much of the non-Western world. Surprisingly, the elitist theory of human rights is very popular in the democratic West, not only in conservative circles but also, and even more often, among liberal and radical groups. The right-wing version of elitism embodies the position closely associated with colonialism, that backward peoples cannot govern themselves and that democracy only works for superior cultures. The left-wing version, often articulated by liberals who stand for civil rights in Western countries but support leftist dictatorships abroad, reflects a belief that we should be tolerant of and respect the cultural identity and political self-determination of Third World countries (although, of course, it is seldom the people who choose to have dictators; more often the dictators decide for them).

The position of relativist scholars who are human rights advocates illustrates an eloquent example of concealed elitism. Such persons find themselves in an impossible dilemma. On the one hand they are anxious to articulate an international human rights standard, while on the other they wish to respect the autonomy of individual cultures. The result is a vague warning against 'ethnocentrism,' and well-intentioned proposals that are deferential to tyrannical governments and insufficiently concerned with human suffering. Because the consequence of either version of elitism is that certain national or ethnic groups are somehow less entitled than others to the enjoyment of human rights, the theory is fundamentally immoral and replete with racist overtones.

I. Shivji, *The Concept of Human Rights in Africa*
(1989), pp. vii, 70–71

Human rights talk constitutes one of the main elements in the ideological armoury of imperialism. Yet from the point of view of the African people, human rights struggles constitute the stuff of their daily lives. . . . [T]he first important building-block of the new perspective on human rights in African [is that it] must be thoroughly anti-imperialist, thoroughly democratic and unreservedly in the interest of the 'people'.

Secondly, human rights, as we have seen, is an ideology. It ideologises certain social interests in the course of class struggles. And it plays either a legitimising role or a mobilising one. For the new perspective, the human rights ideology has to be appropriated in the interest of the people to play a mobilising role in their struggle against imperialism and compradorial classes and their state. Therefore the new perspective must distance itself openly from imperialist ideology of human rights at the international level and cultural-chauvinist/developmentalist ideology of the compradorial classes, at the national level. This is the second . . . building block. . . .

Thirdly, . . . the new conceptualisation must clearly break from both the metaphysics of natural law as well as the logical formalism and legalism of positive law. It must be rooted in the perspective of class struggle. This means, first, that counter-posed to the individualist/liberal paradigm must be the collectivist/revolutionary conception. The right-holder, if you like, is not exclusively an autonomous individual but a collective: a people, a nation, a nationality, a national group, an interest/social group, a cultural/oppressed minority, etc. But this notion of 'collective' must be clearly distinguished from a fascist concept where the 'collective' is expressed in the oppressor state or a revisionist-'marxist' concept where both the 'collective' and the state cease to bear any class character. Secondly, here right is not theorised simply as a legal right, which implies both a static and an absolutist paradigm, in the sense of an entitlement or a claim, but a means of struggle. In that sense it is akin to righteousness rather than right. Seen as a means of struggle, 'right' is therefore not a standard granted as charity from above but a standard-bearer around which people rally for struggle from below. By the same token, the correlate of 'right' is not duty (in the Hohfeldian sense) where duty-holders are identified and held legally or morally responsible but rather the correlate is power/privilege where those who enjoy such power/privilege are the subject of being exposed and struggled against. . . .

Therefore, the human rights vocabulary too undergoes transformation. In the new perspective one does not simply sympathise with the 'victims' of human rights violations and beg the 'violators' to mend their ways in numerous catalogued episodes of violations; rather one joins the oppressed/exploited/dominated or ruled against the oppressors/exploiters/dominant and ruling to expose and resist, with a view ultimately to overcome, the situation which generates human rights violations.

Finally, the new perspective lends a totally different meaning to the prioritization debate as well as a new content and form to human rights activity and community.

A. Farrag, 'Human Rights and Liberties in Islam' in J. Berting et al. (eds), *Human Rights in a Pluralist World: Individuals and Collectivities* (1990), pp. 133–134, 143

Islamic thought is distinctive for the connection it establishes between rights, duties and the imposition of the Divine Law. Obligation is the way to what is right; work is the road to acquistion and ownership, and political rights are rights and duties simultaneously. Education and instruction are also considered to be rights and, in the Islamic context, attain the level of a religious obligation. . . . Islamic jurisprudence, in general, speaks of the ramification of rights into financial, literary, moral and social rights. We may say in summary that a right is an interest which the revealed law does not preclude. It therefore constitutes a material or intangible benefit either for an individual or for a collectivity, which pertains to either of them, bringing advantage or precluding disadvantage. . . .

[Islam] does not constitute a mere collection of moral counsels, for Islam has laid down a body of individual and collective rights, which it guarantees, defends and protects without making any distinction between human beings for any reason, through the provisions of the Sharia, the very foundations of which are the realising of the best and unshakeable interests of man.

These rights in their sacred nature have been derived from God Himself: Muslims recognise the right of God in every individual and collective right. . . . Islam, which has laid down these rights, contains legal and legislative principles and rulings which serve to furnish the necessary guarantee for their execution and for the adherence of nations and governments to them. These principles are manifested in the [duty of 'enjoining good and forbidding evil' and the judiciary]. In this way, these rights which Islam has established are not simply noble and beautiful dreams, but have been a genuine fact of life for everyone.

Y. Ghai, 'Human Rights and Governance: The Asia Debate'
15 *Australian Yearbook of International Law* (1994) 1, pp. 5–18

It is easy to believe that there is a distinct Asian approach to human rights because some government leaders speak as if they represent the whole continent when they make their pronouncements on human rights. This view is reinforced because they claim that their views are based on perspectives which emerge from the Asian culture or religion or Asian realities. The gist of their position is that human rights as propounded in the West are founded on individualism and therefore have no relevance to Asia which is based on the primacy of the community. It is also sometimes argued that economic underdevelopment renders most of the political and civil rights (emphasised in the West) irrelevant in Asia. Indeed, it is sometimes alleged that such rights are dangerous in view of fragmented nationalism and fragile Statehood.

It would be surprising if there were indeed one Asian perspective, since neither Asian culture nor Asian realities are homogenous throughout the continent. All the world's major religions are represented in Asia, and are in one place or another State religions (or enjoy a comparable status: Christianity in the Philippines, Islam in Malaysia, Hinduism in Nepal and Buddhism in Sri Lanka and Thailand). To this list we may add political ideologies like socialism, democracy or feudalism which animate peoples and governments of the region. Even apart from religious differences, there are other factors which have produced a rich diversity of cultures. A culture, moreover, is not static and many accounts given of Asian culture are probably true of an age long ago. Nor are the economic circumstances of all the Asian countries similar. Japan, Singapore and Hong Kong are among the world's most prosperous countries, while there is grinding poverty in Bangladesh, India and the Philippines. The economic and political systems in Asia likewise show a remarkable diversity, ranging from semi-feudal kingdoms in Kuwait and Saudi Arabia, through military dictatorships in Burma and formerly Cambodia, effectively one party regimes in Singapore and Indonesia, communist regimes in China and Vietnam, ambiguous democracies in Malaysia and Sri Lanka, to well established democracies like India. There are similarly differences in their economic systems, ranging from tribal subsistence economies in parts of Indonesia through highly developed market economies of Singapore, Hong Kong and Taiwan and the mixed economy model of India to the planned economies of China and Vietnam. Perceptions of human rights are undoubtedly reflective of these conditions, and suggest that they would vary from country to country.

Perceptions of human rights are reflective of social and class positions in society. What conveys an apparent picture of a uniform Asian perspective on human rights is that it is the perspective of a particular group, that of the ruling elites, which gets international attention. What unites these elites is their notion of governance and the expediency of their rule. For the most part, the political systems they represent are not open or democratic, and their publicly expressed views on human rights are an emanation of these systems, of the need to justify authoritarianism and occasional repression. It is their views which are given wide publicity domestically and internationally. . . .

[S]ome Asian governments claim that their societies place a higher value on the community than in the West, that individuals find fulfilment in their participation in communal life and community tasks, and that this factor constitutes a primary distinction in the approach to human rights. . . . This argument is advanced as an instance of the general proposition that rights are culture specific.

The 'communitarian' argument is Janus-faced. It is used against the claim of universal human rights to distinguish the allegedly Western, individual-oriented approaches to rights from the community centred values of the East. Yet it is also used to deny the claims and assertions of communities in the name of national unity and stability. It suffers from at least two further weaknesses. First, it overstates the 'individualism' of Western society and traditions of thought. . . .

Secondly, Asian governments . . . fall into the easy but wrong assumption that they or the State are the 'community'. . . . Nothing can be more destructive of the community than this conflation. The community and State are different institutions and to some extent in a contrary juxtaposition. The community, for the most part, depends on popular norms developed through forms of consensus and enforced through mediation and persuasion. The State is an imposition on society, and unless humanised and democratised (as it has not been in most of Asia), it relies on edicts, the military, coercion and sanctions. It is the tension between them which has elsewhere underpinned human rights. In the name of the community, most Asian governments have stifled social and political initiatives of private groups. . . . Governments have destroyed many communities in the name of development or State stability. . . .

Another attack on the community comes from the economic, market oriented policies of the governments. Although Asian capitalism appears to rely on the family and clan associations, there is little doubt that it weakens the community and its cohesion. The organising matrix of the market is not the same as that of the community. Nor are its values or methods particularly 'communitarian'. The moving frontier of the market, seeking new resources, has been particularly disruptive of communities which have managed to preserve intact a great deal of their culture and organisation during the colonial and post-colonial periods. The emphasis on the market, and with it individual rights of property are also at odds with communal organisation and enjoyment of property. . . .

A final point is the contradiction between claims of a consensus and harmonious society, and the extensive arming of the State apparatus. The pervasive use of draconian legislation like administrative detention, disestablishment of societies, press censorship, and sedition, belies claims to respect alternative views, promote a dialogue, and seek consensus. The contemporary State intolerance of opposition is inconsistent with traditional communal values and processes.

NOTES:

1. It is clear that developed (Western) States promoted the international legal protection of human rights. It is also clear that some developed States press for the protection of certain rights (civil and political rights, such as freedom of expression) to the apparent exclusion of other rights. This does not mean that the concepts of human rights are solely Western concepts or that the rhetoric by some States equates to the legal position. Indeed, many of the rights protected by international law were promoted by developing States and theorists from those States. These include some of the economic, social and cultural rights as well as group rights, such as the right of self-determination. It should be recalled that all human rights are 'universal, indivisible and interdependent and interrelated' (see para. 5 of the Vienna Declaration, above).

2. While many societies, religions and cultures have not used the terminology of 'human rights', contemporary scholars have discerned the existence of concepts of human rights across the world, as is evident in the extracts from Shivji and Farrag above. This is consistent with the position that all humans have rights, as otherwise – as Teson shows – human rights would be elitist and discriminatory. The universal acceptance of the concepts of human rights can also be seen in the fact that all States have ratified at least one treaty protecting human rights.

3. Nevertheless, there is a need to recognise that, while the concepts of human rights are universal, the application of these rights within each society and culture will vary. This position was acknowledged in para. 5 of the Vienna Declaration (above) where the significance of different cultural backgrounds is to be 'borne in mind'. Those backgrounds are borne in mind by the international human rights supervisory bodies when they apply the relevant treaty (see the 'margin of appreciation' below). At the same time, as Ghai indicates, caution is needed so that too much weight is not given to the arguments of States seeking to assert their own authoritarian rule and to avoid their obligations to protect human rights. The voices of those whose rights are being violated must also be listened to.

SECTION 3: **International protection of human rights**

A: International instruments

The detailed provisions of most of the major international instruments protecting human rights can be found in books of documents on international law and on international human rights (e.g., M. Evans, *Blackstone's International Law Documents* and P. Ghandi, *Blackstone's Human Rights Documents*).

United Nations Charter

Article 1

The Purposes of the United Nations are: ...

3. To achieve international co-operation in solving international problems of an economic, social, cultural, or humanitarian character, and in promoting and encouraging respect for human rights and for fundamental freedoms for all without distinction as to race, sex, language, or religion.

Article 55

With a view to the reaction of conditions of stability and well-being which are necessary for peaceful and friendly relations among nations based on respect for the principle of equal rights and self-determination of peoples, the United Nations shall promote:

(a) higher standards of living, full employment, and conditions of economic and social progress and development;

(b) solutions of international economic, social, health, and related problems; and international cultural and educational co-operation; and

(c) universal respect for, and observance of, human rights and fundamental freedoms for all without distinction as to race, sex, language, or religion.

Article 56

All Members pledge themselves to take joint and separate action in co-operation with the Organization for the achievement of the purposes set forth in Article 55.

Article 68

The Economic and Social Council shall set up commissions in economic and social fields and for the promotion of human rights, and such other commissions as may be required for the performance of its functions.

Article 76

The basic objectives of the trusteeship system, in accordance with the Purposes of the United Nations laid down in Article I of the present Charter, shall be: . . .

(c) to encourage respect for human rights and for fundamental freedoms for all without distinction as to race, sex, language, or religion, and to encourage recognition of the interdependence of the peoples of the world.

International Covenant on Civil and Political Rights 1966
999 UNTS 171

This treaty entered into force on 23 March 1976. As at 1 July 2002, 148 States have ratified this Covenant.

Article 1

Article 1 concerns the right of self-determination (see 6(i) below) and Articles 6 to 27 set out the civil and political rights protected by the Covenant. These are: the right to life (Article 6); freedom from torture (Article 7); freedom from slavery (Article 8); right to liberty (Articles 9 and 10); freedom from imprisonment for failure to fulfil a contractual obligation (Article 11); freedom of movement (Article 12); freedom from expulsion of an alien (Article 13); right to a fair trial (Article 14); freedom from retroactive criminal laws (Article 15); right to recognition as a person (Article 16); right to privacy (Article 17); freedom of thought, conscience and religion (Article 18); freedom of expression (Article 19); prohibition against war propaganda and national, racial or religious hatred (Article 20); freedom of assembly (Article 21); freedom of association (Article 22); right to marry and found a family (Article 23); rights of a child (Article 24); right to vote and right of participation in political and public life (Article 25); freedom from discrimination (Article 26); rights of ethnic, religious and linguistic minorities (Article 27). A few of these articles are extracted here.

The (First) Optional Protocol to the Covenant deals with individual communications to the Human Rights Committee and is dealt with below. The Second Optional Protocol to the Covenant aims for the abolition of the death penalty.

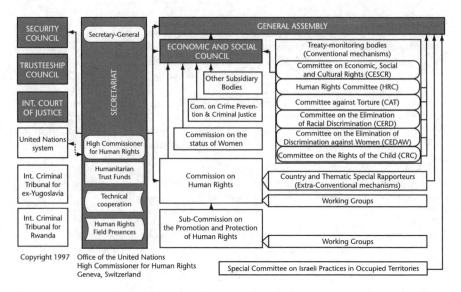

Figure 1 UN Human Rights Organizational Structure: Office of UN High Commissioner for Human Rights, **www.unhchr.ch**

Article 2

1. Each State Party to the present Covenant undertakes to respect and to ensure to all individuals within its territory and subject to its jurisdiction the rights recognized in the present Covenant, without distinction of any kind, such as race, colour, sex, language, religion, political or other opinion, national or social origin, property, birth or other status.

2. Where not already provided for by existing legislative or other measures, each State Party to the present Covenant undertakes to take the necessary steps, in accordance with its constitutional processes and with the provisions of the present Convenant, to adopt such legislative or other measures as may be necessary to give effect to the rights recognized in the present Covenant.

3. Each State Party to the present Covenant undertakes:

    (a) To ensure that any person whose rights or freedoms as herein recognized are violated shall have an effective remedy, notwithstanding that the violation has been committed by persons acting in an official capacity;

    (b) To ensure that any person claiming such a remedy shall have his right thereto determined by competent judicial, administrative or legislative authorities, or by any other competent authority provided for by the legal system of the State, and to develop the possibilities of judicial remedy;

    (c) To ensure that the competent authorities shall enforce such remedies when granted.

Article 3

The States Parties to the present Covenant undertake to ensure the equal right of men and women to the enjoyment of all civil and political rights set forth in the present Covenant.

Article 4

1. In time of public emergency which threatens the life of the nation and the existence of which is officially proclaimed, the State Parties to the present Covenant may take measure derogating from their obligations under the present Covenant to the extent strictly required by the exigencies of the situation, provided that such measures are not inconsistent with their other obligations under international law and do not involve discrimination solely on the ground of race, colour sex, language, religion or social origin.

2. No derogation from Articles 6, 7, 8 (paragraphs 1 and 2), 11, 15, 16 and 18 may be made under this provision.

3. Any State Party to the present Covenant availing itself of the right of derogation shall immediately inform the other States Parties to the present Covenant, through the intermediary of the Secretary-General of the United Nations of the provisions from which it has derogated and of the reasons by which it was actuated. A further communication shall be made, through the same intermediary on the date on which it terminates such derogation.

Article 5

1. Nothing in the present Covenant may be interpreted as implying for any State, group or person any right to engage in any activity or perform any act aimed at the destruction of any of the rights and freedoms recognized herein or at their limitation to a greater extent than is provided for in the present Covenant.

2. There shall be no restriction upon or derogation from any of the fundamental human rights recognized or existing in any State Party to the present Covenant pursuant to law, conventions, regulations or custom on the pretext that the present Covenant does not recognize such rights or that it recognizes them to a lesser extent.

Article 6

1. Every human being has the inherent right to life. This right shall be protected by law. No one shall be arbitrarily deprived of his life.

2. In countries which have not abolished the death penalty, sentence of death may be imposed only for the most serious crimes in accordance with the law in force at the time of the commission of the crime and not contrary to the provisions of the present Covenant and to the Convention on the Prevention and Punishment of the Crime of Genocide. This penalty can only be carried out pursuant to a final judgement rendered by a competent court. . . .

Article 7

No one shall be subjected to torture or to cruel, inhuman or degrading treatment or punishment. In particular, no one shall be subjected without his free consent to medical or scientific experimentation. . . .

Article 19

1. Everyone shall have the right to hold opinions without interference,

2. Everyone shall have the right to freedom of expression; this right shall include freedom to seek, receive and impart information and ideas of all kinds, regardless of frontiers, either orally, in writing or in print, in the form of art, or through any other media of his choice.

3. The exercise of the rights provided for in paragraph 2 of this article carries with it special duties and responsibilities. It may therefore be subject to certain restrictions, but these shall only be such as are provided by law and are necessary:

    (a) For respect of the rights or reputations of others;

    (b) For the protection of national security or of public order (*ordre public*), or of public health or morals. . . .

Article 26

All persons are equal before the law and are entitled without any discrimination to the equal protection of the law. In this respect, the law shall prohibit any discrimination and guarantee to all persons equal and effective protection against discrimination on any ground such as race, colour, sex, language, religion, political or other opinion, national or social origin, property, birth or other status.

Article 27

In those States in which ethnic, religious or linguistic minorities exist, persons belonging to such minorities shall not be denied the right, in community with the other members of their group, to enjoy their own culture, to profess and practice their own religion, or to use their own language.

International Covenant on Economic, Social and Cultural Rights 1966
993 UNTS 3

This treaty entered into force on 3 January, 1976. As at 1 July 2002, 145 States have ratified the Covenant.

Article 1 (right of self-determination) of this Covenant is in identical terms (see 6(i), and Article 5 (no destruction of rights) of this Covenant is in essentially the same terms (see above), as Articles 1 and 5 (respectively) of the International Covenant on Civil and Political Rights. Articles 6 to 15 of this Covenant set out the economic, social and cultural rights protected by the Covenant. These are: the right to work (Article 6); right to just and favourable conditions of work (Article 7); right to form and join trade unions (Article 8); right to social security (Article 9); protection of the family (Article 10); right to adequate standard of living (Article 11); right to highest attainable standard of physical and mental health (Article 12); right to education (Article 13); adoption of compulsory, free, primary education (Article 14); right to take part in cultural life, benefit from scientific progress and protection of copyright (Article 15). A few of these articles are extracted here.

Article 2

1. Each State Party to the present Covenant undertakes to take steps, individually and through international assistance and cooperation, especially economic and technical, to the maximum of its available resources, with a view to achieving progressively the full realization of the rights recognized in the present Covenant by all appropriate means, including particularly the adoption of legislative measures.

2. The States Parties to the present Covenant undertake to guarantee that the rights enunciated in the present Covenant will be exercised without discrimination of any kind as to race, colour, sex, language, religion, political or other opinion, national or social origin, property, birth or other status.

3. Developing countries, with due regard to human rights and their national economy, may determine to what extent they would guarantee the economic rights recognized in the present Covenant to non-nationals.

Article 3

The States Parties to the present Covenant undertake to ensure the equal right of men and women to the enjoyment of all economic, social and cultural rights set forth in the present Covenant.

Article 4
The States Parties to the present Covenant recognize that, in the enjoyment of those rights provided by the State in conformity with the present Covenant, the State may subject such rights only to such limitations as are determined by law only in so far as this may be compatible with the nature of these rights and solely for the purpose of promoting the general welfare in a democratic society. . . .

Article 7
The States Parties to the present Covenant recognize the right of everyone to the enjoyment of just and favourable conditions of work which ensure, in particular:
  (a) Remuneration which provides all workers, as a minimum, with:
    (i) Fair wages and equal remuneration for work of equal value without distinction of any kind, in particular women being guaranteed conditions of work not inferior to those enjoyed by men, with equal pay for equal work;
    (ii) A decent living for themselves and their families in accordance with the provisions of the present Covenant;
  (b) Safe and healthy working conditions;
  (c) Equal opportunity for everyone to be promoted in his employment to an appropriate higher level, subject to no considerations other than those of seniority and competence;
  (d) Rest, leisure and reasonable limitation of working hours and periodic holidays with pay, as well as remuneration for public holidays. . . .

Article 13
1. The States Parties to the present Covenant recognize the right of everyone to education. They agree that education shall be directed to the full development of the human personality and the sense of its dignity, and shall strengthen the respect for human rights and fundamental freedoms. They further agree that education shall enable all persons to participate effectively in a free society, promote understanding, tolerance and friendship among all nations and all racial, ethnic or religious groups, and further the activities of the United Nations for the maintenance of peace.

2. The States Parties to the present Covenant recognize that, with a view to achieving the full realization of this right:
  (a) Primary education shall be compulsory and available free to all;
  (b) Secondary education in its different forms, including technical and vocational secondary education, shall be made generally available and accessible to all by every appropriate means, and in particular by the progressive introduction of free education;
  (c) Higher education shall be made equally accessible to all, on the basis of capacity, by every appropriate means, and in particular by the progressive introduction of free education;
  (d) Fundamental education shall be encouraged or intensified as far as possible for those persons who have not received or completed the whole period of their primary education;
  (e) The development of a system of schools at all levels shall be actively pursued, an adequate fellowship system shall be established, and the material conditions of teaching staff shall be continuously improved.

3. The States Parties to the present Covenant undertake to have respect for the liberty of parents and, when applicable, legal guardians to choose for their children schools, other than those established by the public authorities, which conform to such minimum educational

standards as may be laid down or approved by the State and to ensure the religious and moral education of their children in conformity with their own convictions. . . .

NOTES:

1. When the Universal Declaration of Human Rights was agreed to in 1948, it was intended that a single treaty protecting all human rights would be drafted soon after, based on the Universal Declaration. It took nearly 20 years for the drafting to be completed and, due primarily to Cold War political pressure, instead of a single treaty, two treaties (called 'Covenants') were created dealing with different rights.

2. There are a vast array of international human rights treaties and other instruments sponsored by the United Nations which protect a specific right, or which protect a series of rights relating to a specific matter. For example, the International Convention on the Elimination of All Forms of Racial Discrimination 1966, the Convention on the Elimination of All Forms of Discrimination against Women 1979, the Convention on the Rights of the Child 1989 and the Declaration on the Right to Development 1986. A Declaration on the Rights of Indigenous People 1994 has been drafted (see Chapter 7) but it is still being considered by States, many of whom seem unwilling to see it progress into a Declaration approved by the General Assembly.

3. The proliferation of international instruments protecting specific human rights can be seen as an indication of the growing awareness that broad instruments protecting a wide variety of rights may not be sufficient to protect some rights which do not easily fit within that scheme. Many treaties enable States, and others, to focus on the need to protect a specific right or rights. This proliferation is also an example of the constant evolution of international society as its members begin to understand about those who are oppressed within the society and who require the protection of human rights instruments. At the same time, there is the criticism that the increasing volume of rights protected can dilute the power and coherence of international human rights law.

B: Procedure for protecting human rights

The United Nations has created a number of procedures for protecting and promoting human rights and ascertaining where human rights violations occur. Primarily these procedures are through independent bodies established by either general or specific human rights treaties, as well as some inter-governmental bodies operating directly within the United Nations system.

L. Henkin, 'International Law: Politics, Values and Functions'
13 (IV) *Recueil des Cours* 216 (1989)

Special [international] enforcement machinery has followed two principal tracks. Some has been established by particular human rights agreements, such as the Human Rights Committee under the [International] Covenant on Civil and Political Rights and the commissions and courts under the European and American conventions. A second track of enforcement consists of United Nations bodies – the General Assembly, the Economic and Social Council (ECOSOC), and especially the Human Rights Commission and its subsidiary units. Their activities are sometimes seen as politics, not law, but these bodies invoke norms and are properly seen as part of the enforcement system.

It is difficult to assess which of these 'tracks' has been more successful; surely they have both contributed to compliance. But they work differently. A monitoring body created by a human rights covenant or convention addresses only compliance by States parties to that agreement and only with the norms established by the agreement. The mandate, authority and procedures of the monitoring body are defined by the agreement. United Nations bodies, on the other hand, often address human rights issues as part of their general mandate as defined by the United Nations Charter and by General Assembly resolutions. They are not themselves monitoring bodies, but have sometimes created *ad hoc* monitors and have sometimes condemned violations. In principle, they might address human rights violations by virtually any State, since nearly all States are parties to the United Nations Charter; in fact, political bodies are likely to address only selected, dramatic human rights violations by selected countries. . . .

International human rights law benefits significantly from enforcement . . . by political bodies [that are within the UN system, as well as by bodies created by the human rights treaties]. In general, international political bodies have attended only to the enforcement of norms of extraordinary political significance such as the law of the Charter on the use of force, but political bodies have devoted extraordinary efforts to promoting law on human rights and for that and other reasons they have not avoided the demands of enforcement of – inducing compliance with – that law.

If law is politics, enforcement of law in the inter-State system is also heavily political. Political influence brought to bear in the organs and suborgans of the United Nations determined the enforcement machinery that found its way into covenants and conventions. . . . But United Nations bodies themselves have also been an arena for charges of human rights violations, sometimes evoking resolutions of condemnation.

One cannot appraise these activities with precision or with confidence, but clearly they have served as some inducement to terminate or mitigate violations, perhaps even as some deterrent. Political bodies, however, are subject to their own political laws. The larger bodies – notably the United Nations General Assembly – are more visible, more newsworthy, therefore more 'politicized', therefore less likely to apply human rights norms judicially, impartially. In such bodies, human rights are more susceptible to being subordinated to non-human rights considerations. There, voting, including 'bloc-voting', has led to 'selective targeting' of some States, sometimes exaggerating their violations, and overlooking those of other States, including some that are guilty of gross violations. Smaller political bodies, such as the Human Rights Commission, are also inhabited by government representatives concerned for State values and friendly relations, but increasingly they are able to be somewhat less 'political', more evenhanded, as well as more activist in the cause of human rights.

In monitoring human rights as in other matters, the influence of the United Nations bodies has reflected the transformation of the United Nations by the influx of new Members and the dominance of the Organization by the Third World. In general, Third World States have been committed to non-alignment and were therefore reluctant to support an active United Nations role in human rights monitoring, which, in the past at least, Communist States (and others particularly committed to State values) resisted. . . . On the other hand, African States provided a particular impetus to human rights activism when they led the United Nations to take a strong stance against apartheid, make it a perennial issue, adopt perennial resolutions of condemnation and exhortations to sanctions.

P. Alston 'Critical Appraisal of the UN Human Rights Regime', in P. Alston (ed), *The United Nations and Human Rights: A Critical Appraisal*
(1992), pp. 10–11

Since the Committee on the Elimination of Racial Discrimination (CERD) first met in January 1970, the [United Nations] treaty-based system has expanded at a rate which is without precedent in the field of international organization. By September 1991, when the Committee on the Rights of the Child (CRC) began its first session, there were eight treaty bodies already operating and another one foreshadowed once the International Convention on the Protection of the Rights of All Migrant Workers and Members of Their Families enters into force. Of these eight, five are almost identical in form and basic mandate. They are, in addition to the two already mentioned, the Human Rights Committee (HRC) (which first met in 1976), the Committee on the Elimination of Discrimination against Women (CEDAW) (1982), and the Committee against Torture (CAT) (1988).

Of the other three, two relate to apartheid issues. . . . The final treaty body, the Committee on Economic, Social and Cultural Rights (CESCR), is a curious hybrid in that it has been established by a Charter-based organ (the ECOSOC), ostensibly to advise it on the implementation of the relevant treaty (the Covenant on Economic, Social and Cultural Rights), but in reality to perform virtually all the Council's relevant treaty-based functions on its behalf. While the Committee can thus be abolished at any moment by the Council, it has been given a quasi-independent existence by being authorized by the latter to imitate in every significant way the role and working methods of the five other bodies that operate pursuant to specific treaty provisions.

In brief, each of the treaty bodies performs the task of monitoring States Paries' compliance with their obligations under the relevant treaty. Each of the five analysed in this [book] (HRC, CERD, CEDAW, CAT and CESCR) does so through a dialogue with the representatives of each of the States Parties on the basis of a detailed report (an 'initial' report, followed by 'periodic' reports at approximately four- to five-year intervals). The principal outcome of this process is the record of the resulting dialogue and the Committee's own summary of the key points, which provide an opportunity for individual members, or the Committee as a whole, to indicate the extent to which the State Party appears to be in compliance, or otherwise. Each of the Committees also adopts carefully drafted statements in the form of General Comments (or some comparable terminology), which purport to be based directly on the Committees' work in examining reports, and which seek to elaborate upon the normative content of specific rights or to address specific issues that have arisen. [Some] of the five Committees also deal with complaints from individuals alleging violations of their rights under the treaty concerned. . . . Finally, there is an interstate complaints mechanism which can be invoked before three of the treaty bodies (HRC, CERD and CAT). The latter mechanism has attracted no attention from States and seems unlikely to generate any 'business' in the foreseeable future, although the rekindling of long-dormant ethnic disputes ammong the States of Central and Eastern Europe might well provide an occasion for rewriting this record.

There is no formal hierarchy among the treaty bodies, although the Human Rights Committee tends to have the potentially most comprehensive mandate and to have been endowed with the greatest resources in terms of meeting time and Secretariat assistance. The relationship between the treaty bodies and the need for measures to promote better co-ordination, to reduce overlapping, and to rationalize the burden imposed on States that are parties to many of the treaties, have only recently begun to be addressed by UN organs.

Human Rights Committee, General Comments
36 UN GAOR, Supp 40 (A/36/40), annex VII and 37 UN GAOR,
Supp 40 (A/37/40), annex V; 1 IHRR (1994), pp. 2–5

Article 40(4) of the International Covenant on Civil and Political Rights (ICCPR) allows the Human Rights Committee to issue 'general comments' to States concerning compliance with the ICCPR. These general comments clarify the obligations of States under the ICCPR. An example is set out below.

General Comment 3
1. The Committee notes that article 2 of the Covenant generally leaves it to the States parties concerned to choose their method of implementation in their territories within the framework set

out in that article. It recognizes, in particular, that the implementation does not depend solely on constitutional or legislative enactments, which in themselves are often not per se sufficient. The Committee considers it necessary to draw the attention of States parties to the fact that the obligation under the Covenant is not confined to the respect of human rights, but that States parties have also undertaken to ensure the enjoyment of these rights to all individuals under their jurisdiction. This aspect calls for specific activities by the States parties to enable individuals to enjoy their rights. . . .

4. In this connection, it is very important that individuals should know what their rights under the Covenant (and the Optional Protocol, as the case may be) are and also that all administrative and judicial authorities should be aware of the obligations which the States party has assumed under the Covenant. To this end the Covenant should be publicized in all official languages of the State and steps should be taken to familiarize the authorities concerned with its contents as part of their training. It is desirable also to give publicity to the States party's cooperation with the Committee.

Bleir v *Uruguay*
1 Selected Decisions HRC (1982) 109, Human Rights Committee

The HRC can consider complaints from individuals under the (First) Optional Protocol to the ICCPR. As at 1 July 2002, there were 102 State parties to this treaty. In one of its 'views', the HRC considered a complaint against Uruguay.

Uruguay denied that it held a 'disappeared' person. Other evidence contradicted this denial. The HRC considered the issue of the burden of proof in human rights matters.

13.3 With regard to the burden of proof, this cannot rest alone on the author of the communication, especially considering that the author and the State party do not always have equal access to the evidence and that frequently the State party alone has access to relevant information. It is implicit in Article 4(2) of the Optional Protocol that the State party has the duty to investigate in good faith all allegations of violation of the Covenant made against it and its authorities, especially when such allegations are corroborated by evidence submitted by the author of the communication, and to furnish to the Committee the information available to it. In cases where the author has submitted to the Committee allegations supported by substantial witness testimony, as in this case, and where further clarification of the case depends on information exclusively in the hands of the State Party, the Committee may consider such allegations as substantial in the absence of satisfactory evidence and explanations to the contrary submitted by the State party.

Committee on Economic, Social and Cultural Rights, General Comments
UN Doc E/1991/23, 1 IHRR (1994) 6

No supervisory body was provided for in the International Covenant on Economic, Social and Cultural Rights (ICESCR) to consider compliance by State parties with that Covenant. Only in 1986 was the Committee on Economic, Social and Cultural Rights (CESCR) set up as a supervisory body to review the annual reports of States on compliance with the ICESCR. It is comprised of 18 independent experts. While this Committee does not have the power to deal with individual complaints, it has issued some General Comments similar to those issued by the Human Rights Committee. One example is set out below.

General Comment 3
The nature of States parties obligations

1. Article 2 is of particular importance to a full understanding of the Covenant and must be seen as having a dynamic relationship with all the other provisions of the Covenant. It describes the nature

of the general legal obligations undertaken by States parties to the Covenant. These obligations include both what may be termed (following the work of the International Law Commission) obligations of conduct and obligations of result. While great emphasis has sometimes been placed on the difference between the formulations used in this provision and that contained in the equivalent article 2 of the [ICCPR], it is not always recognized that there are also significant similarities. In particular, while the Covenant provides for progressive realization and acknowledges the constraints due to the limits of available resources, it also imposes various obligations which are of immediate effect. . . .

2. . . . Thus while the full realization of the relevant rights may be achieved progressively, steps towards that goal must be taken within a reasonably short time after the Covenant's entry into force for the States concerned. Such steps should be deliberate, concrete and targeted as clearly as possible to meeting the obligations recognized in the Covenant.

3. . . . In fields such as health, the protection of children and mothers, and education, as well as in respect of the matters dealt with in articles 6 to 9, legislation may also be an indispensable element for many purposes.

4. . . . However, the ultimate determination as to whether all appropriate measures have been taken [by a State] remains one for the Committee to take.

5. Among the measures which might be considered appropriate, in addition to legislation, is the provision of judicial remedies with respect to rights which may, in accordance with the national legal system, be considered justiciable. The Committee notes, for example that the enjoyment of the rights recognized, without discrimination, will often be appropriately promoted, in part, through the provision of judicial or other effective remedies. Indeed, those States parties which are also parties to the [ICCPR] are already obligated (by virtue of arts. 2 (paras. 1 and 3), 3 and 26) of that Covenant to ensure that any person whose rights or freedoms (including the right to equality and non-discrimination) recognized in that Covenant are violated, 'shall have an effective remedy' (art. 2(3)(a)). In addition, there are a number of other provisions in the [ICESCR], including articles 3, 7(a)(i), 8, 10(3), 13(2)(a), (3) and (4) and 15(3) which would seem to be capable of immediate application by judicial and other organs in many national legal systems. Any suggestion that the provisions indicated are inherently non-self-executing would seem to be difficult to sustain. . . .

8. The Committee notes that the undertaking 'to take steps . . . by all appropriate means including particularly the adoption of legislative measures' neither requires nor precludes any particular form of government or economic system being used as the vehicle for the steps in question, provided only that it is democratic and that all human rights are thereby respected. Thus, in terms of political and economic systems the Covenant is neutral. . . .

9. . . . The concept of progressive realization constitutes a recognition of the fact that full realization of all economic, social and cultural rights will generally not be able to be achieved in a short period of time. In this sense the obligation differs significantly from that contained in article 2 of the [ICCPR] which embodies an immediate obligation to respect and ensure all of the relevant rights. Nevertheless, the fact that realization over time, or in other words progressively, is foreseen under the Covenant should not be misinterpreted as depriving the obligation of all meaningful content. It is on the one hand a necessary flexibility device, reflecting the realities of the real world and the difficulties involved for any country in ensuring full realization of economic, social and cultural rights. On the other hand, the phrase must be read in the light of the overall objective, indeed the *raison d'être*, of the Covenant which is to establish clear obligations for States parties in respect of the full realization of the rights in question. It thus imposes an obligation to move as expeditiously and effectively as possible towards that goal. Moreover, any deliberately retrogressive measures in that regard would require the most careful consideration and would need to be fully justified by reference

to the totality of the rights provided for in the Covenant and in the context of the full use of the maximum available resources.

10. On the basis of the extensive experience gained by the Committee, as well as the body that preceded it, over a period of more than a decade of examining States parties' reports, the Committee is of the view that a minimum core obligation to ensure the satisfaction of, at the very least, minimum essential levels of each of the rights in incumbent upon every State party. Thus, for example, a State party in which any significant number of individuals is deprived of essential food-stuffs, of essential primary health care, of basic shelter and housing, or of the most basic forms of education is, prima facie, failing to discharge its obligations under the Covenant. If the Covenant were to be read in such a way as not to establish such a minimum core obligation, it would be largely deprived of its *raison d'être*. By the same token, it must be noted that any assessment as to whether a State has discharged its minimum core obligation must also take account of resource constraints applying within the country concerned. . . . In order for a State party to be able to attribute its failure to meet at least its minimum core obligations to a lack of available resources it must demonstrate that every effort has been made to use all resources that are at its disposition in an effort to satisfy, as a matter of priority, those minimum obligations.

11. The Committee wishes to emphasize, however, that even where the available resources are demonstrably inadequate, the obligation remains for a State party to strive to ensure the widest possible enjoyment of the relevant rights under the prevailing circumstances. Moreover, the obligations to monitor the extent of the realization, or more especially of the non-realization, of economic, social and cultural rights, and to devise strategies and programmes for their promotion, are not in any way eliminated as a result of resource constraints. . . .

12. Similarly, the Committee underlines the fact that even in times of severe resources constraints, whether caused by a process of adjustment, of economic recession, or by other factors, the vulnerable members of society can and indeed must be protected by the adoption of relatively low-cost targeted programmes.

NOTES:

1. The Economic and Social Council (ECOSOC) was set up in the United Nations Charter and it has a particular responsibility for human rights by Article 55 of the Charter (set out above). It has created a number of bodies to deal with human rights matters, including the Commission on Human Rights. This Commission is comprised of 54 State representatives. It has a group of independent legal experts to assist it – the Sub-Commission on Prevention of Discrimination and Protection of Minorities.

   The Commission can now consider, by virtue of ECOSOC Resolutions 1235 (XLII) and 1503 (XLVII), human rights abuses by enabling it to have an annual public debate on human rights and to consider privately individual States where a 'consistent pattern of gross and reliably attested violations of human rights' exists. While Special Rapporteurs and Working Parties have been set up to consider situations in particular States or about certain human rights in general (e.g., torture), the Commission's record of protecting human rights is poor, mainly due to the political pressures which can be directly placed on it by the States concerned. But the public political pressure it can place on States has assisted the legitimacy of international criticisms of governments that violate human rights.

2. As shown in the extract from Alston, each treaty body has slightly different powers and functions from each other body, though there are many similarities between them. The relationship is unclear between the various United Nations bodies which supervise and monitor compliance by States with their obligations under human rights treaties, and this can give rise to problems. There is some overlapping of functions, e.g., in areas of non-discrimination; some differences in protections provided which can cause concerns about

compatibility; little coordination between the bodies; and substantial material and logistical difficulties for States, particularly developing States, to provide numerous detailed reports. The appointment of a United Nations High Commissioner for Human Rights in 1993 has begun to lead to greater coordination between these bodies and Mary Robinson, who was the High Commissioner for Human Rights from 1997 to 2002, was an impressive international advocate for human rights.

3. The effectiveness of these bodies in leading to increased protection of human rights is open to debate. It is uncertain that a report-based system leads to any real changes, especially where the State is not subject to internal scrutiny by its population, before or after a report is presented, because of deliberate State restrictions on information. It is difficult to determine the extent to which States comply with recommendations by these bodies, even after a determination on an individual complaint, as any recommendation or determination by these bodies is not legally binding on the State concerned. However, many States do comply with the recommendations, e.g., changes to legislation by the United Kingdom and its introduction of a Bill of Rights in Hong Kong after pressure from the HRC, though often this compliance is not acknowledged. The public nature of the monitoring by these bodies and the potential for embarrassment of States when they are condemned for violations of human rights, can have some effect on States' behaviour, even if their response is more dictated by fear of losing investment or diplomatic clout. In this regard, non-governmental organisations can be vital (see below).

4. These international human rights bodies have clarified the legal obligations undertaken by States when they ratify human rights treaties. The obligations of States under human rights treaties are not reciprocal between States, rather the State has obligations and individuals or groups have rights, and so the State's obligations are unlikely to be closely monitored by States themselves (see paragraph 29 of the *Effect of Reservations case* below). Therefore, where human rights treaties are in issue there is a requirement for the supervisory body itself to ensure that States comply with their obligations. Generally these bodies have interpreted. State's obligations under human rights treaties broadly, as is seen above in the CESCR General Comment 3 (especially paragraphs 9 and 10), the HRC's General Comment 3 and its decision in such cases as *Bleir v Uruguay*. On the effect of individual complaints see Chapter 5.

5. As well as clarifying the general legal obligations of States under human rights treaties, the supervisory bodies can elaborate on the substantive rights themselves. For example, in the extracts above, it can be seen that the HRC's General Comment 6(5) suggests that violation of the right to life includes indirect deprivation of life by State inaction to prevent, for example, malnutrition.

6. The Security Council can make a decision on a matter which concerns human rights, if it considers that a threat to international peace and security is involved. Those decisions are binding on all member States of the United Nations, as provided by Article 25 of the United Nations Charter. Thus the Security Council has made decisions in regard to South Africa's apartheid system and its presence in Namibia and in respect of Iraq's actions during the 1990–91 Gulf War, particularly concerning the Kurds. The Security Council can also create new institutions to deal with violations of human rights such as the War Crimes Tribunal considering matters in Yugoslavia and Rwanda and the establishment of an International Criminal Court (see further Chapters 8 and 15).

7. Many United Nations organisations have some responsibility for issues that concern the protection of specific human rights, such as the United Nations Educational, Scientific and Cultural Organisation (UNESCO), the World Health Organisation (WHO), and even the World Bank, which should consider human rights breaches and environmental matters when deciding on funding (see Chapter 13). The International Labour Organisation (ILO) is particularly active in regard to labour rights, with ILO representatives (who are not limited to

States) being able to complain about abuses of these rights, and each State is required to produce an annual report.

C: Customary international law

Even if a State has not ratified a human rights treaty, it could be bound by customary international law to protect some human rights.

Namibia Opinion
ICJ Rep 1971 16, International Court of Justice

The facts of this case are set out in Chapter 3.

131. Under the Charter of the United Nations, the former Mandatory had pledged itself to observe and respect, in a territory having an international status, human rights and fundamental freedoms for all without distinction as to race. To establish instead, and to enforce, distinctions, exclusions, restrictions and limitations exclusively based on grounds of race, colour, descent or national or ethnic origin which constitute a denial of fundamental human rights is a flagrant violation of the purposes and principles of the Charter.

JUDGE AMMOUN (Separate Opinion): [The provisions of the Universal Declaration of Human Rights] are not binding *qua* international convention within the meaning of Article 38, paragraph 1(a), of the Statute of the Court, they can bind States on the basis of custom within the meaning of paragraph 1(b) of the same Article, whether because they constituted a codification of customary law as was said in respect of Article 6 of the Vienna Convention on the Law of Treaties, or because they have acquired the force of custom through a general practice accepted as law, in the words of Article 38, paragraph 1(b), of the Statute. One right which must certainly be considered a pre-existing binding customary norm which the Universal Declaration of Human Rights codified is the right to equality, which by common consent has ever since the remotest times been deemed inherent in human nature.

The equality demanded by the Namibians and by other peoples of every colour, the right to which is the outcome of prolonged struggles to make it a reality, is something of vital interest to us here, on the one hand because it is the foundation of other human rights which are no more than its corollaries and, on the other, because it naturally rules out racial discrimination and *apartheid*, which are the gravest of the facts with which South Africa, as also other States, stands charged. The attention I am devoting to it in these observations can therefore by no means be regarded as exaggerated or out of proportion.

Filartiga v Pena-Irala
630 F. 2nd 876 (1980), United States Court of Appeals, Second Circuit

This case raised the issue of whether torture was in breach of customary international law. Here the Court was considering the general impact of international human rights instruments.

The United Nations Charter (a treaty of the United States, see 59 Stat. 1033 (1945)) makes it clear that in this modern age a state's treatment of its own citizens is a matter of international concern. . . . For although there is no universal agreement as to the precise extent of the 'human rights and fundamental freedoms' guaranteed to all by the Charter, there is at present no dissent from the view that the guaranties include, at a bare minimum, the right to be free from torture. This prohibition has become part of customary international law, as evidenced and defined by the Universal

Declaration of Human Rights, General Assembly Resolution 217 (III)(A) (Dec. 10, 1948) which states, in the plainest of terms 'no one shall be subjected to torture.' The General Assembly has declared that the Charter precepts embodied in this Universal Declaration 'constitute basic principles of international law.' G.A.Res. 2625 (XXV) (Oct. 24, 1970). . . .

These UN declarations are significant because they specify with great precision the obligations of member nations under the Charter. Since their adoption, '[m]embers can no longer contend that they do not know what human rights they promised in the Charter to promote.' Sohn, 'A Short History of United Nations Documents on Human Rights,' in *The United Nations and Human Rights, 18th Report of the Commission* (Commission to Study the Organization of Peace ed. 1968). Moreover, a UN Declaration is, according to one authoritative definition, 'a formal and solemn instrument, suitable for rare occasions when principles of great and lasting importance are being enunciated.' 34 U.N. ESCOR, Supp. (No. 8) 15, U.N. Doc. E/cn.4/1/610 (1962) (memorandum of Office of Legal Affairs, UN Secretariat). Accordingly, it has been observed that the Universal Declaration of Human Rights 'no longer fits into the dichotomy of "binding treaty" against "non-binding pronouncement," but is rather an authoritative statement of the international community.' E. Schwelb, *Human Rights and the International Community* 70 (1964). Thus, a Declaration creates an expectation of adherence, and 'insofar as the expectation is gradually justified by State practice, a declaration may by custom become recognized as laying down rules binding upon the States.' 34 UN ESCOR, *supra*. Indeed, several commentators have concluded that the Universal Declaration has become *in toto*, a part of binding, customary international law. . . .

The treaties and accords cited above, as well as the express foreign policy of our own government, all make it clear that international law confers fundamental rights upon all people vis-à-vis their own governments. While the ultimate scope of those rights will be a subject for continuing refinement and elaboration, we hold that the right to be free from torture is now among them. . . .

NOTES:

1. It has been argued that the entire Universal Declaration of Human Rights embodies customary international law. While it does not bind States as a treaty obligation, it certainly may reflect ideals held by the international community. Any consideration of it as customary international law can only be made after an article by article examination, as was done in *Filartiga* v *Pena-Irala* in regard to the prohibition on torture. Nevertheless, the Universal Declaration has significantly influenced other international, regional and national human rights agreements. For example, it is referred to in the Preambles of the two International Human Rights Covenants set out above, and in each of the American and the European Conventions on Human Rights and the African Charter of Human and Peoples' Rights, as well as in the Helsinki Final Act. The latter is of particular importance, as it was signed by Czechoslovakia, Poland, the USSR, and Yugoslavia, each of which had abstained from the vote on the Universal Declaration in 1948, as well as by the United States, which has ratified few human rights treaties.

2. Many human rights – for example, right to life, freedom from torture, freedom from racial discrimination, prohibition on genocide, right to education, right of self-determination – can be considered to be customary international law and so binding on States which have not ratified treaties to protect those rights. Indeed, some of these rights may be *jus cogens*, as was accepted by the International Court of Justice in the *Barcelona Traction case* (see Chapter 3).

SECTION 4: **Regional human rights protection**

There are three regions where broad-based, binding human rights treaties have been ratified: Europe, the Americas and Africa. The principal treaties are not extracted here, nor are any detailed materials, as these are readily available elsewhere.

Commission to Study the Organization of Peace, *Regional Promotion and Protection of Human Rights*
(1980), 15

[There are] four grounds [for favouring regional human rights systems]: (1) the existence of geographic, historical, and cultural bonds among States of a particular region; (2) the fact that recommendations of a regional organization may meet with less resistance than those of a global body; (3) the likelihood that publicity about human rights will be wider and more effective; and (4) the fact that there is less possibility of 'general, compromise formulae,' which in global bodies are more likely to be based on 'considerations of a political nature'. . . .

Opposition to the establishment of regional human rights commissions has been expressed on numerous occasions by the Eastern European States and other Members of the United Nations, on several grounds. First, they argue that human rights, being global in nature and belonging to everyone, should be defined in global instruments and implemented by global bodies. 'The African and the Asian should have the same human rights as the European or the American.' Second, regional bodies in the human rights field would, at best, duplicate the work of United Nations bodies and, at worst, develop contradictory policies and procedures. . . . Third, the Eastern European States in particular object that any cooperation between regional commissions and the United Nations would add to the financial burdens of the latter. Fourth, several Western European States contend that preoccupation with regional arrangements might deflect official and public attention from the two International Covenants and delay their ratification.

It may be argued that the global approach and the regional approach to promotion and protection of human rights are not necessarily incompatible; on the contrary, they are both useful and complementary. The two approaches can be reconciled on a functional basis: the normative content of all international instruments, both global and regional, should be similar in principle, reflecting the Universal Declaration of Human Rights, which was proclaimed 'as a common standard of achievement for all peoples and all nations.' The global instrument would contain the minimum normative standard, whereas the regional instrument might go further, add further rights, refine some rights, and take into account special differences within the region and between one region and another.

Thus what at first glance might seem to be a serious dichotomy – the global approach and the regional approach to human rights – has been resolved satisfactorily on a functional basis. . . .

The further question arises whether if human rights commissions were established in certain regions, they might interpret international standards too narrowly and thus adversely affect the work of global bodies in this field. It might be necessary in such a case to establish the right of global institutions to consider a particular matter *de novo*.

Effect of Reservations on Entry into Force of the American Convention (Articles 74 and 75)
67 ILR (1982) 559, Inter-American Court of Human Rights

The Inter-American Court was asked to advise on the question: 'From what moment is a State deemed to have become a party to the American Convention on Human Rights when it ratifies or adheres to the Convention with one or more reservations: from the date of the deposit of the instrument of ratification or adherence or upon the termination of the period specified in Article 20 of the Vienna Convention on the Law of Treaties?' (See also Chapter 3, concerning the effects of reservations.)

29. The Court must emphasize, however, that modern human rights treaties in general, and the American Convention in particular, are not multilateral treaties of the traditional type concluded to accomplish the reciprocal exchange of rights for the mutual benefit of the contracting States. Their object and purpose is the protection of the basic rights of individual human beings, irrespective of their nationality, both against the State of their nationality and all other contracting States. In concluding these human rights treaties, the States can be deemed to submit themselves to a legal order within which they, for the common good, assume various obligations, not in relation to other States, but towards all individuals within their jurisdiction. . . .

32. It must be emphasized also that the Convention, unlike other international human rights treaties, including the European Convention, confers on private parties the right to file a petition with the Commission against any State as soon as it has ratified the Convention (Convention, Art. 44). By contrast, before one State may institute proceedings against another State, each of them must have accepted the Commission's jurisdiction to deal with inter-State communications. (Convention, Art. 45). This structure indicates the overriding importance the Convention attaches to the commitments of the States Parties *vis-à-vis* individuals, which can be readily implemented without the intervention of any other State.

33. Viewed in this light and considering that the Convention was designed to protect the basic rights of individual human beings irrespective of their nationality, against States of their own nationality or any other State Party, the Convention must be seen for what in reality it is: a multilateral legal instrument or framework enabling States to make binding unilateral commitments not to violate the human rights of individuals within their jurisdiction. . . .

THE COURT IS OF THE OPINION

By unanimous vote, that the Convention enters into force for a State which ratifies or adheres to it with or without a reservation on the date of the deposit of its instrument of ratification or adherence.

M. wa Matua, 'The Banjul Charter and the African Cultural Fingerprint: An Evaluation of the Language of Duties'

35 *Virginia Journal of International Law* 339 (1995), 368–373, 377–8

The African Charter on Human and Peoples' Rights (the African [or Banjul] Charter), the basis of Africa's continental human rights system, entered into force on October 21, 1986, upon ratification by a simple majority of member states of the Organization of African Unity (OAU). The African Charter has attracted criticism because it departs from the narrow formulations of other regional and international human rights instruments. In particular, it codifies the three generations of rights, including the controversial concept of peoples' rights, and imposes duties on individual members of African societies. While a number of scholars have focused attention on apparent tensions between human and peoples' rights, there has been little discussion of the notion of individual duties in the context of the African Charter. Yet a thorough understanding of the meaning of human rights, and the complicated processes through which they are protected and realized, would seem to link inextricably the concepts of human rights, peoples' rights, and duties of individuals. . . .

The duty/rights conception of the African Charter could provide a new basis for individual identification with compatriots, the community, and the state. It could forge and instill a national consciousness and act as the glue to reunite individuals and different nations within the modern state, and at the same time set the proper limits of conduct by state officials. The motivation and purpose behind the concept of duty in pre-colonial societies was to strengthen community ties and social cohesiveness, creating a shared fate and common destiny. This is the consciousness that the impersonal modern state has been unable to foster. It has failed to shift loyalties from the lineage and the community to the modern state, with its mixture of different nations.

The series of explicit duties spelled out in articles 27 through 29 of the African Charter could be read as intended to recreate the bonds of the pre-colonial era among individuals and between individuals and the State. They represent a rejection of the individual 'who is utterly free and utterly irresponsible and opposed to society' [Organisation of African Unity Draft Charter]. In a proper reflection of the nuanced nature of societal obligations in the pre-colonial era, the African Charter explicitly provides for two types of duties: direct and indirect. A direct duty is contained, for example, in Article 29(4) of the Charter which requires the individual to 'preserve and strengthen social and national solidarity, particularly when the latter is threatened.' There is nothing inherently sinister about this provision; it merely repeats a duty formerly imposed on members of pre-colonial communities. The African Charter provides an example of an indirect duty in Article 27(2), which states that '[t]he rights and freedoms of each individual shall be exercised with due regard to the rights of others, collective security, morality and common interest.' This duty is in fact a limitation on the enjoyment of certain individual rights. It merely recognizes the practical reality that in African societies, as elsewhere in the world, individual rights are not absolute. Individuals are asked to reflect on how the exercise of their rights in certain circumstances might adversely affect other individuals or the community. The duty is based on the presumption that the full development of the individual is only possible where individuals care about how their actions would impact on others. By rejecting the egotistical individual whose only concern is fulfilling self, Article 27(2) raises the level of care owed to neighbors and the community. Duties are also grouped according to whether they are owed to individuals or to larger units such as the family, society, or the state. Parents, for example, are owed a duty of respect and maintenance by their children. . . .

[I]n the pre-colonial era, and in the African Charter, duties are primarily owed to the family – nuclear and extended – and to the community, not to the State. In effect, the primacy attached to the family in the Charter places the family above the State, which is not the case under Communism. In pre-colonial Africa, unlike the former Soviet Union or Eastern Europe, duties owed to the family or community were rarely misused or manipulated to derogate from human rights obligations. The most damaging criticism of the language of duties in Africa sees them as 'little more than the formulation, entrenchment, and legitimation of state rights and privileges against individuals and peoples' [Okoth-Ogeno in R. Cohen (ed) Human Rights and Governance in Africa (1993)]. However, critics who question the value of including duties in the Charter point only to the theoretical danger that states might capitalize on the duty concept to violate other guaranteed rights. The fear is frequently expressed that emphasis on duties may lead to the 'trumping' of individual rights if the two are in opposition. It is argued that: If the state has a collective right and obligation to develop the society, economy, and polity (Article 29), then as an instrument it can be used to defend coercive state actions against both individuals and constituent groups to achieve state policies rationalized as social and economic improvement. . . .

The African Charter distinguishes human rights from peoples' or collective rights, but sees them in cooperation, not competition or conflict. The Charter's preambular paragraph notes this relationship and recognizes 'on the one hand, that fundamental human rights stem from the attributes of human beings, which justifies their national and international protection and on the other hand, that the reality and respect for peoples rights should necessarily guarantee human rights.' This unambiguous statement, notes van Boven [7 *Human Rights Law Journal* 1986], is conclusive proof of the Charter's view: human rights are inalienable and intrinsic to man individuals and are not in conflict with peoples' rights, which they complement. The exercise of sovereignty rights by a 'people' or 'peoples' as contemplated by the Charter is a necessary precondition for the enjoyment of individual rights. This dialectic between individual and peoples' rights is one of the bases for the Charter's imposition of duties on individuals. Solidarity between the individual and the greater society safeguards collective rights, without which individual rights would be unattainable.

NOTES:

1. One of the arguments in favour of regional human rights treaties is that they are seen as reflecting the cultures and societies of those within a State better than an international human rights treaty. Hence there should be an increased likelihood of States ratifying at least their region's human rights treaty. Each of the principal regional human rights treaties – the European Convention on Human Rights 1950 (ECHR), the American Convention on Human Rights 1978 (ACHR) and the African Charter of Human and Peoples' Rights 1981 (ACHPR) – has been ratified by nearly all States in their region (with the major exception of the United States of America in regard to the ACHR). Of course, there are a number of regions where there is no human rights treaty, such as Asia and the Pacific, despite some noble attempts.

2. Each of the principal regional human rights treaties protect primarily civil and political rights, though not in identical terms. The ACHPR also protects some economic, social and cultural rights, and these rights are protected (in slightly different terms) by separate regional treaties in Europe and the Americas (eg the European Social Charter 1961 (revised in 1998) and the Protocol on Economic Social and Cultural Rights 1988, respectively). The ACHPR also protects some group rights, such as the right of self-determination (see below), as well as including some provisions about individual's duties (as discussed by wa Matua above). Within Europe, the Organisation on Security and Cooperation in Europe (OSCE) has developed institutional structures for the protection of human rights, including an Office for Democratic Institutions and Human Rights and a High Commissioner on National Minorities.

3. The supervisory mechanisms for each of the principal regional human rights treaties are different. With the changes to the ECHR brought about by Protocol 11, there is now an entirely judicial system of supervision and a full-time Court under the ECHR, with a right of individual complaint directly to that Court from each of its State parties. The ACHR has a two-tier system of a Commission, which checks for admissibility and tries to reach a friendly settlement, and a Court (the Inter-American Court of Human Rights); while the ACHPR has a Commission, which can investigate and report on human rights complaints, though a Court has been agreed upon but is not yet in operation. In each case, though, the final supervision of compliance with a decision or report of the Court or Commission lies with an intergovernmental body of State representatives from that region. Each of the rights protected and the supervisory mechanisms adopted are justified on the basis of being reflective of the particular cultures of the region.

4. The ECHR system, being in active use for the longest period, is the most developed in international human rights law, at least in terms of its use by individuals, its respected supervisory bodies and compliance by States with the decisions made by those bodies. The Inter-American system is now active in both advisory opinions and consideration of individual complaints, and the African system is beginning to make progress. The combined impact of these regional systems has been to contribute significantly to the development of international law generally, such as in the increasing role of the individual in international law (see Chapter 5), and to the impact of (regional) international law in the national laws of many States (see Chapter 4).

SECTION 5: **Limitations on the human rights treaty obligations of states**

Human rights treaties, both international and regional, place legal obligations on States. However, as States themselves draft these treaties, there are limitations placed on the obligations of States under human rights treaties.

A: General limitations

Nearly all human rights have exceptions to, and/or limitations on, them. These limitations are to protect the rights of others and to protect the general interests of society, as human rights do not exist in a vacuum.

Handyside v *United Kingdom*
24 ECHR Ser A (1976), European Court of Human Rights

Handyside intended to publish *The Little Red Schoolbook* in the United Kingdom, and it had been available in other European States. It was seized under the United Kingdom Obscene Publications Act 1959, and he was convicted and fined. The Court held that there was no breach of Art. 10 (freedom of expression) as the restriction could be justified within Art. 10(2) on the ground of 'protection of morals'.

48. The Court points out that the machinery of protection established by the Convention is subsidiary to the national systems safeguarding human rights (judgment of 23 July 1968 on the merits of the *'Belgian Linguistic'* case, Series A no. 6, p. 35, § 10 *in fine*). The Convention leaves to each Contracting State, in the first place, the task of securing the rights and freedoms it enshrines. The institutions created by it make their own contribution to this task but they become involved only through contentious proceedings and once all domestic remedies have been exhausted (Article 26).

These observations apply, notably, to Article 10 § 2. In particular, it is not possible to find in the domestic law of the various Contracting States a uniform European conception of morals. The view taken by their respective laws of the requirements of morals varies from time to time and from place to place, especially in our era which is characterised by a rapid and far-reaching evolution of opinions on the subject. By reason of their direct and continuous contact with the vital forces of their countries, State authorities are in principle in a better position than the international judge to give an opinion on the exact content of these requirements as well as on the 'necessity' of a 'restriction' or 'penalty' intended to meet them. . . . Nevertheless, it is for the national authorities to make the initial assessment of the reality of the pressing social need implied by the notion of 'necessity' in this context.

Consequently, Article 10 § 2 leaves to the Contracting States a margin of appreciation. This margin is given both to the domestic legislator ('prescribed by law') and to the bodies, judicial amongst others, that are called upon to interpret and apply the laws in force. . . .

49. Nevertheless, Article 10 § 2 does not give the Contracting States an unlimited power of appreciation. The Court, which, with the Commission, is responsible for ensuring the observance of those States' engagements (Article 19), is empowered to give the final ruling on whether a 'restriction' or 'penalty' is reconcilable with freedom of expression as protected by Article 10. The domestic

margin of appreciation thus goes hand in hand with a European supervision. Such supervision concerns both the aim of the measure challenged and its 'necessity'; it covers not only the basic legislation but also the decision applying it, even one given by an independent court. In this respect, the Court refers to Article 50 of the Convention ('decision or . . . measure taken by a legal authority or any other authority') as well as to its own case-law (Engel and others judgment of 8 June 1976, Series A no. 22, pp. 41–42, § 100).

The Court's supervisory functions oblige it to pay the utmost attention to the principles character-ising a 'democratic society'. Freedom of expression constitutes one of the essential foundations of such a society, one of the basic conditions for its progress and for the development of every man. Subject to paragraph 2 of Article 10, it is applicable not only to 'information' or 'ideas' that are favourably received or regarded as inoffensive or as a matter of indifference, but also to those that offend, shock or disturb the State or any sector of the population. Such are the demands of that pluralism, tolerance and broadmindedness without which there is no 'democratic society'. This means, amongst other things, that every 'formality', 'condition', 'restriction' or 'penalty' imposed in this sphere must be proportionate to the legitimate aim pursued.

From another standpoint, whoever exercises his freedom of expression undertakes 'duties and responsibilities' the scope of which depends on his situation and the technical means he uses. The Court cannot overlook such a person's 'duties' and 'responsibilities' when it enquires, as in this case, whether 'restrictions' or 'penalties' were conducive to the 'protection of morals' which made them 'necessary' in a 'democratic society'.

50. It follows from this that it is in no way the Court's task to take the place of the competent national courts but rather to review under Article 10 the decisions they delivered in the exercise of their power of appreciation.

However, the Court's supervision would generally prove illusory if it did no more than examine these decisions in isolation; it must view them in the light of the case as a whole, including the publication in question and the arguments and evidence adduced by the applicant in the domestic legal system and then at the international level. The Court must decide, on the basis of the different data available to it, whether the reasons given by the national authorities to justify the actual measures of 'interference' they take are relevant and sufficient under Article 10 § 2. . . .

In these circumstances, despite the variety and the constant evolution in the United Kingdom of views on ethics and education, the competent English judges were entitled, in the exercise of their discretion, to think at the relevant time that the Schoolbook would have pernicious effects on the morals of many of the children and adolescents who would read it.

Toonen v *Australia*

1 *International Human Rights Reports* (1994) 97, United Nations Human Rights Committee

Toonen claimed that provisions of the Criminal Code of the Australian state of Tasmania (for which the State of Australia is responsible in international law) breached the rights contained in the ICCPR, including Article 17 (right to priv-acy), as they made criminal 'various forms of sexual conduct between men, including all forms of sexual contact between consenting adult homosexual men in private.' Tasmania was the only Australian state to have such laws, although they were rarely enforced. The HRC found that the existence of these laws breached Article 17. Subsequently, the Australian government complied with the HRC's views and, eventually, the Tasmanian provisions were repealed.

8.2 Inasmuch as article 17 is concerned, it is undisputed that adult consensual sexual activity in private is covered by the concept of 'privacy', and that Mr Toonen is actually and currently affected by the continued existence of the Tasmanian laws. The Committee considers that Sections 122(a), (c) and 123 of the Tasmanian Criminal Code 'interfere' with the author's privacy, even if these provisions have not been enforced for a decade. . . .

8.3 The prohibition against private homosexual behaviour is provided for by law, namely, Sections 122 and 123 of the Tasmanian Criminal Code. As to whether it may be deemed arbitrary, the Committee recalls that pursuant to its General Comment 16 (32) on article 17, the 'introduction of the concept of arbitrariness is intended to guarantee that even interference provided for by the law should be in accordance with the provisions, aims and objectives of the Covenant and should be, in any event, reasonable in the circumstances'. The Committee interprets the requirement of reasonableness to imply that any interference with privacy must be proportional to the end sought and be necessary in the circumstances of any given case.

8.5 As far as the public health argument of the Tasmanian authorities is concerned, the Committee notes that the criminalization of homosexual practices cannot be considered a reasonable means or proportionate measure to achieve the aim of preventing the spread of AIDS/HIV. . . .

8.6 The Committee cannot accept either that for the purposes of article 17 of the Covenant, moral issues are exclusively a matter of domestic concern, as this would open the door to withdrawing from the Committee's scrutiny a potentially large number of statutes interfering with privacy. It further notes that with the exception of Tasmania, all laws criminalizing homosexuality have been repealed throughout Australia and that, even in Tasmania, it is apparent that there is no consensus as to whether Sections 122 and 123 should not also be repealed. Considering further that these provisions are not currently enforced, which implies that they are not deemed essential to the protection of morals in Tasmania, the Committee concludes that the provisions do not meet the 'reasonableness' test in the circumstances of the case, and that they arbitrarily interfere with Mr Toonen's right under article 17, paragraph 1.

8.7 The State party has sought the Committee's guidance as to whether sexual orientation may be considered an 'other status' for the purposes of article 26. The same issue could arise under article 2, paragraph 1, of the Covenant. The Committee confines itself to noting, however, that in its view the reference to 'sex' in articles 2, paragraph 1, and 26 is to be taken as including sexual orientation.

10. Under article 2(3)(a) of the Covenant, the author, victim of a violation of article 17, paragraph 1, *juncto* 2, paragraph 1, of the Covenant, is entitled to a remedy. In the opinion of the Committee, an effective remedy would be the repeal of Sections 122(a), (c) and 123 of the Tasmanian Criminal Code.

NOTES:

1. Human rights do not exist in a vacuum and so many human rights have limitations in order to protect the rights of others or the general interests of society. For example, in the extracts from the ICCPR and ICESCR above, it can be seen that Article 19(3) of the ICCPR has general limitations on freedom of expression and Article 13(3) and (4) of the ICESCR has limitations on State actions to allow for parental choice of education. Sometimes rights have exceptions to protect perceived individual or State interests, such as the exception in regard to seniority and competence under Article 7(c) of the ICESCR and the exception for the death penalty in Article 6(2) of the ICCPR, though this is now prohibited by the Second Optional Protocol to that treaty. Article 7 of the ICCPR is an example of an absolute right.
2. The international and regional human rights supervisory bodies correctly see their role as being subsidiary to national protections of human rights, although with the authority to review compliance by the State with its human rights treaty obligations. However, as the decisions in *Handyside* v *UK* and *Toonen* v *Australia* make clear, the body will review the extent to which the limitations placed on the human right by the State is proportional to a

legitimate (and not arbitrary) aim pursued by the State to address a pressing social need in the State. Thus, when reviewing compliance with a treaty, these bodies may allow a degree of flexibility to a State, particularly in matters of moral views. This can be seen to be an application of appropriate cultural relativism (see above).

3. There are many other limitations on individuals or others being able to bring a claim successfully against a State under a human rights treaty. Of course, that State must be a party to the relevant treaty, but also the person complaining must have standing to bring the claim and must first have exhausted all effective national remedies. The view of the HRC in *Toonen* v *Australia* is unusual in that it was the mere existence of the law that gave rise to the violation of human rights. In addition, generally, the person making the complaint does not need to be a national of the State against which a complaint has been made, as it is territorial jurisdiction, not nationality, that is crucial.

B: Reservations

Many States place reservations on specific articles of human rights treaties. The law applicable to these reservations is slightly different to general treaty law due to the fact that human rights treaties do not primarily entail reciprocal rights and obligations between States – see Chapter 3.

C: Derogations

Most human rights treaties allow States to limit their obligations to protect certain human rights when a 'state of emergency' exists. The conditions necessary for lawful derogations are set out in the treaties.

Brannigan and McBride v *United Kingdom*
ECHR Ser A (1993) No 258–B, European Court of Human Rights

The two applicants had been detained for over four days by the police in Northern Ireland under the provisions of the United Kingdom Prevention of Terrorism (Temporary Provisions) Act 1984. The United Kingdom government conceded that it had breached Articles 5(3) and (5) of the ECHR as the applicants were not brought promptly before a judge after their detention. The issue was whether the derogation to the ECHR by the United Kingdom (explained in the extract below) exonerated it of any breach.

31. On 23 December 1988 the United Kingdom informed the Secretary General of the Council of Europe that the Government had availed itself of the right of derogation conferred by Article 15(1) [to the ECHR] to the extent that the exercise of powers under section 12 of the 1984 Act might be inconsistent with the obligations imposed by Article 5(3) of the Convention. . . .

43. The Court recalls that it falls to each Contracting State, with its responsibility for 'the life of [its] nation', to determine whether that life is threatened by a 'public emergency' and, if so, how far it is necessary to go in attempting to overcome the emergency. By reason of their direct and continuous contact with the pressing needs of the moment, the national authorities are in principle in a better position than the international judge to decide both on the presence of such an emergency and on the nature and scope of derogations necessary to avert it. Accordingly, in this matter a wide margin

of appreciation should be left to the national authorities (see the *Ireland* v *the United Kingdom* judgment of 18 January 1978, Series A No. 25, pp. 78–79, para. 207).

Nevertheless, Contracting Parties do not enjoy an unlimited power of appreciation. It is for the Court to rule on whether *inter alia* the States have gone beyond the 'extent strictly required by the exigencies' of the crisis. The domestic margin of appreciation is thus accompanied by a European supervision (ibid.). At the same time, in exercising its supervision the Court must give appropriate weight to such relevant factors as the nature of the rights affected by the derogation, the circumstances leading to, and the duration of, the emergency situation. . . .

47. Recalling its case-law in *Lawless* v *Ireland* (judgement of 1 July 1961, Series A No. 3, p. 56, para. 28) and *Ireland* v *The United Kingdom* (*loc. cit.*, Series A No. 25, p. 78, para. 205) and making its own assessment, in the light of all the material before it as to the extent and impact of terrorist violence in Northern Ireland and elsewhere in the United Kingdom (see paragraph 12 above) the Court considers there can be no doubt that such a public emergency existed at the relevant time.

It does not judge it necessary to compare the situation which obtained in 1989 with that which prevailed in December 1988 since a decision to withdraw a derogation is, in principle, a matter within the discretion of the State and since it is clear that the Government believed that the legislation in question was in fact compatible with the Convention (see paragraphs 49–51 below). . . .

[The Court then considered whether the measures taken were strictly required by the exigencies of the situation. In doing so, it considered four main questions:

    (i)   Was the derogation a genuine response to an emergency situation?
    (ii) Was the derogation premature?
    (iii) Was the absence of judicial control of extended detention justified?
    (iv) Were there safeguards against abuse of the detention power?]

59. It is not the Court's role to substitute its view as to what measures were most appropriate or expedient at the relevant time in dealing with an emergency situation for that of the Government which have direct responsibility for establishing the balance between the taking of effective measures to combat terrorism on the one hand, and respecting individual rights on the other (see the above-mentioned *Ireland* v *The United Kingdom* judgment, Series A No. 25, p. 82, para. 214 and the *Klass and Others* v *Germany* judgment of 6 September 1978, Series A No. 28, p. 23, para. 49). In the context of Northern Ireland where the judiciary is small and vulnerable to terrorist attacks, public confidence in the independence of the judiciary is understandably a matter to which the Government attach great importance. . . .

66. Having regard to the nature of the terrorist threat in Northern Ireland, the limited scope of the derogation and the reasons advanced in support of it, as well as the existence of basic safeguards against abuse, the Court takes the view that the Government have not exceeded their margin of appreciation in considering that the derogation was strictly required by the exigences of the situation. . . .

69. For the Government, it was open to question whether an official proclamation was necessary for purposes of Article 4 of the Covenant, since the emergency existed prior to the ratification of the Covenant by the United Kingdom and has continued to the present day. In any event, the existence of the emergency and the fact of derogation were publicly and formally announced by the Secretary of State for the Home Department to the House of Commons on 22 December 1988. Moreover there had been no suggestion by the United Nations Human Rights Committee that the derogation did not satisfy the formal requirements of Article 4. . . .

73. . . . In the Court's view, the [22 December 1988] statement, which was formal in character and made public the Government's intentions as regards derogation, was well in keeping with the notion of an official proclamation. It therefore considers that there is no basis for the applicant's arguments in this regard.

74. In the light of the above examination, the Court concludes that the derogation lodged by the United Kingdom satisfies the requirements of Article 15 and that therefore the applicants cannot validly complain of a violation under Article 5(3). It follows that there was no obligation under Article 5(5) to provide the applicants with an enforceable right to compensation.

S. Marks, 'Civil Liberties at the Margin: the UK Derogation and the European Court of Human Rights'
15 Oxford JLS (1995) 69, pp. 94–95

There can be no doubt that departure from normal human rights standards is unavoidable in some circumstances. What is in question is the purpose served by derogations provisions such as Article 15. Will they limit governmental freedom of action or will they preserve or even enhance it? Will they provide a ground for critical scrutiny of government policy or only a ground for defending governmental policy? Will they stand firm against repression or will they lend force to the criticism that human rights are useless, even counter-productive, in resisting repression? The Court's decision in *Brannigan & McBride* suggests that Article 15 may be substantially a helpmate for governments: a means of preserving governmental freedom of action; a ground primarily for defending government policy; a tame and yielding guard against repression. To this extent, the prospects for human rights protection under the Convention in a situation designated an 'emergency' appear less than encouraging. Derogation will be precluded in only the crassest of cases. And if this is so, then the prospects for human rights protection under the Convention generally are less than encouraging, for if derogations are to be widely permitted, then the opportunities for condoned non-compliance with certain rights and freedoms – including, so it seems, rights and freedoms potentially impinging on non-suspendable rights and freedoms – are correspondingly widened. And insofar as that occurs, do not all the Court's efforts to define and elaborate and strengthen those rights and freedoms begin to seem like mere tinkering? To take up a point made by Judge Makarczyk (dissenting) in *Brannigan & McBride*, the issue of the UK derogation is an issue of 'the integrity of the Convention system of protection as a whole'.

NOTES:
1. There is always the difficulty in determining whether any derogations from the application of human rights treaties should be allowed. If derogations are allowed, as is generally the case, then they could be used whenever a State simply considers it is expedient. This possibility is increased by the decision of the Court in *Brannigan and McBride* v *United Kingdom*, as is explained by Marks (above).
2. Different rights are considered non-derogable in different treaties though some rights, such as freedom from torture, are both universally non-derogable and have no legal limitations otherwise on their protection.

SECTION 6:   **The right of self-determination**

This right requires separate consideration because of its impact on different aspects of international law. In particular it has a direct effect on issues of sovereignty over territory (see Chapter 7).

A: International instruments

United Nations Charter

Article 1
The Purposes of the United Nations are: . . .

2. To develop friendly relations among nations based on respect for the principle of equal rights and self-determination of peoples, and to take other appropriate measures to strengthen universal peace.

Article 73
Members of the United Nations which have or assume responsibilities for the administration of territories whose peoples have not yet attained a full measure of self-government recognize the principle that the interests of the inhabitants of these territories are paramount, and accept as a sacred trust the obligation to promote to the utmost, within the system of international peace and security established by the present Charter, the well-being of the inhabitants of these territories, and to this end:

    (a) to ensure, with due respect for the culture of the peoples concerned, their political, economic, social and educational advancement, their just treatment, and their protection against abuses;

    (b) to develop self-government, to take due account of the political aspirations of the peoples, and to assist them in the progressive development of their free political institutions, according to the particular circumstances of each territory and its peoples and their varying stages of advancement;

    (c) to further international peace and security;

    (d) to promote constructive measures of development, to encourage research, and to co-operate with one another and, when and where appropriate, with specialized international bodies with a view to the practical achievement of the social, economic, and scientific purposes set forth in this Article; and

    (e) to transmit regularly to the Secretary-General for information purposes, subject to such limitation as security and constitutional considerations may require, statistical and other information of a technical nature relating to economic, social, and educational conditions in the territories for which they are respectively responsible other than those territories to which Chapters XII and XIII apply.

Declaration on the Granting of Independence to Colonial Territories and Peoples General Assembly Resolution 1514 (XV)
14 December 1960, UN Doc A/4684 (1960), GAOR 15th Session, Supp 16, p. 66

The General Assembly:

Convinced that all peoples have an inalienable right to complete freedom, the exercise of their sovereignty and the integrity of their national territory,

Solemnly proclaims the necessity of bringing to a speedy and unconditional end colonialism in all its forms and manifestations;

And to this end

Declares that:

1. The subjection of peoples to alien subjugation, domination and exploitation constitutes a denial of fundamental human rights, is contrary to the Charter of the United Nations and is an impediment to the promotion of world peace and co-operation.

2. All peoples have the right to self determination; by virtue of that right they freely determine their political status and freely pursue their economic, social and cultural development.

3. Inadequacy of political, economic, social or educational preparedness should never serve as a pretext for delaying independence.

4. All armed action or repressive measures of all kinds directed against dependent peoples shall cease in order to enable them to exercise peacefully and freely their right to complete independence, and the integrity of their national territory shall be respected.

5. Immediate steps shall be taken, in Trust and Non-Self-Governing Territories or all other territories which have not yet attained independence, to transfer all powers to the peoples of those territories, without any conditions or reservations, in accordance with their freely expressed will and desire, without any distinction as to race, creed or colour, in order to enable them to enjoy complete independence and freedom.

6. Any attempt aimed at the partial or total disruption of the national unity and the territorial integrity of a country is incompatible with the purposes and principles of the Charter of the United Nations.

7. All States shall observe faithfully and strictly the provisions of the Charter of the United Nations, the Universal Declaration of Human Rights and the present Declaration on the basis of equality, non-interference in the internal affairs of all States, and respect for the sovereign rights of all peoples and their territorial integrity.

General Assembly Resolution 1541 (XV) 15 December 1960, Principles VI–IX
UN Doc A/4684 (1960), GAOR 15th Session, Supp 16, p. 29

Principles which should guide Members in determining whether or not an obligation exists to transmit the information called for in Article 73 of the Charter of the United Nations.

Principle VI
A Non-Self-Governing Territory can be said to have reached a full measure of self-government by:

(a) Emergence as a sovereign independent State;
(b) Free association with an independent State; or
(c) Integration with an independent State.

International Covenant on Economic, Social and Cultural Rights 1966 and the International Covenant on Civil and Political Rights 1966, Common Article 1

Article 1
1. All peoples have the right of self-determination. By virtue of that right they freely determine their political status and freely pursue their economic, social and cultural development.

2. All peoples may, for their own ends, freely dispose of their natural wealth and resources without prejudice to any obligations arising out of international economic co-operation, based upon the principle of mutual benefit, and international law. In no case may a people be deprived of its own means of subsistence.

3. The States Parties to the present Covenant, including those having responsibility for the administration of Non-Self-Governing and Trust Territories, shall promote the realization of the right of self-determination, and shall respect that right, in conformity with the provisions of the Charter of the United Nations.

Declaration on Principles of International Law concerning Friendly Relations and Cooperation among States in Accordance with the Charter of the United Nations General Assembly Resolution 2625 (XXV) 24 October, 1970
UN Doc A/8028 (1970), 25 UN GAOR Supp (No 28) 121

The principle of equal rights and self-determination of peoples

By virtue of the principle of equal rights and self-determination of peoples enshrined in the Charter, all peoples have the right freely to determine, without external interference, their political status and to pursue their economic, social and cultural developement, and every State has the duty to respect this right in accordance with the provisions of the Charter.

Every State has the duty to promote, through joint and separate action, the realisation of the principle of equal rights and self-determination of peoples, in accordance with the provisions of the Charter, and to render assistance to the United Nations in carrying out the responsibilities entrusted to it by the Charter regarding the implementation of the principle in order:

(a) To promote friendly relations and co-operation among States; and
(b) To bring a speedy end to colonialism, having regard to the freely expressed will of the peoples concerned;

and bearing in mind that subjection of peoples to alien subjugation, domination and exploitation constitutes a violation of the principle, as well as a denial of fundamental human rights, and is contrary to the Charter of the United Nations.

Every State has the duty to promote through joint and separate action universal respect for the observance of human rights and fundamental freedoms in accordance with the Charter.

The establishment of a sovereign and independent State, the free association or integration with an independent State or the emergence into any other political status freely determined by a people constitute modes of implementing the right of self-determination by that people.

Every State has the duty to refrain from any forcible action which deprives peoples referred to above in the elaboration of the present principle of their right to self-determination and freedom and independence. In their actions against and resistance to such forcible action in pursuit of the exercise of their right to self-determination, such peoples are entitled to seek and to receive support in accordance with the purposes and principles of the Charter of the United Nations.

The territory of a colony or other non-governing territory has, under the charter of the United Nations, a status separate and distinct from the territory of the State administering it; and such separate and distinct status under the Charter shall exist until the people of the colony or non-self-governing territory have exercised their right of self-determination in accordance with the Charter and particularly its purposes and principles.

Nothing in the foregoing paragraph shall be construed as authorizing or encouraging any action which would dismember or impair, totally or in part, the territorial integrity or political unity of sovereign and independent States conducting themselves in compliance with the principle of equal rights and self-determination of peoples as described above and thus possessed of a government representing the whole people belonging to the territory without distinction as to race, creed or colour.

Every State shall refrain from any action aimed at the partial or total disruption of the national unity and territorial integrity of any other State or country.

NOTES:

1. The idea of self-determination has been part of the debate in the international community for nearly a century. In 1918, United States President Wilson warned that 'peoples may now be dominated and governed only by their own consent. 'Self-determination' is not a mere phrase. It is an imperative principle of action, which statesmen will henceforth ignore at their peril' (W. Wilson, *War Aims of Germany and Austria* (1918)). A few plebiscites to

discern the wishes of the peoples occurred between the two World Wars and the idea continued into the United Nations Charter. The right of self-determination was then applied to colonial territories, as seen above in the General Assembly Resolutions of 14 and 15 December 1960. The link between a colonial State's obligations under Article 73 of the United Nations Charter and its obligations to protect the right of self-determination became inseparable.

2. The right of self-determination was most clearly defined in common Article 1 of the two International Human Rights Covenants (above) and its limits were clarified by the Declaration on Principles of International Law (above). The right has also been declared in other international and regional instruments, such as Part VIII of the Helsinki Final Act 1975 (part of the OCSE process) and Article 20 of the ACHPR.

B: Clarification of the right of self-determination

Human Rights Committee, General Comment 12
39 UN GAOR, Supp 40 (A/39/40), pp. 142–3; 1 IHRR (1994), pp. 10–11

1. . . . The right of self-determination is of particular importance because its realization is an essential condition for the effective guarantee and observance of individual human rights and for the promotion and strengthening of those rights. It is for that reason that States set forth the right of self-determination in a provision of positive law in both Covenants and placed this provision as article 1 apart from and before all of the other rights in the two Covenants.

6. Paragraph 3 [of Article 1], in the Committee's opinion, is particularly important in that it imposes specific obligations on States parties, not only in relation to their own peoples but *vis-à-vis* all peoples which have not been able to exercise or have been deprived of the possibility of exercising their right to self-determination. . . . The obligations exist irrespective of whether a people entitled to self-determination depends on a State party to the Covenant or not. It follows that all States parties to the Covenant should take positive action to facilitate realization of and respect for the right of peoples to self-determination.

Namibia Opinion
ICJ Rep 1971 16, International Court of Justice

As part of its Advisory Opinion in this case (see Chapter 3), the Court dealt with the responsibility of a State for a colonial (or colonial-type) territory, and so considered the issues of both self-determination and the 'sacred trust' of a League of Nations Mandate over a territory, this 'sacred trust' now continuing under Article 73 of the United Nations Charter.

[T]he subsequent development of international law in regard to non-self-governing territories, as enshrined in the Charter of the United Nations, made the principle of self-determination applicable to all of them. . . . the ultimate objective of the sacred trust was the self-determination and independence of the peoples concerned. . . . As to the general consequences resulting from the illegal presence of South Africa in Namibia, all States should bear in mind that the injured entity is a people which must look to the international community for assistance in its progress towards the goals for which the sacred trust was instituted.

JUDGE AMMOUN (Separate Opinion): . . . Indeed one is bound to recognize that the right of peoples to self-determination, before being written into charters that were not granted but won in bitter struggle, had first been written painfully, with the blood of the peoples, in the finally awakened conscience of humanity. . . . If any doubts had remained on this matter [of the right of self-determination] in the mind of the States Members of the United Nations, they would not have resolved to proclaim the legitimacy of the struggle of peoples – and more specifically the Namibian people – to make good their right of self-determination. If this right is still not recognized as a juridical norm in the practice of a few rare States or the writings of certain even rarer theoreticians, the attitude of the former is explained by their concern for their traditional interests, and that of the latter by a kind of extreme respect for certain long-entrenched postulates of classic international law. Law is a living deed, not a brilliant honours-list of past writers whose work of course compels respect but who cannot, except for a few great minds, be thought to have had such a vision of the future that they could always see beyond their own times.

Final Report and Recommendations of an International Meeting of Experts on the Further Study of the Concept of the Right of People for UNESCO
22 February, 1990, SNS–89/CONF. 602/7

A people for the [purposes of the] rights of people in international law, including the right to self-determination, has the following characteristics:

(a) A group of individual human beings who enjoy some or all of the following common features:
    (i) A common historical tradition;
    (ii) Racial or ethnic identity;
    (iii) Cultural homogeneity;
    (iv) Linguistic unity;
    (v) Religious or ideological affinity;
    (vi) Territorial connection;
    (vii) Common economic life.
(b) The group must be of a certain number who need not be large (e.g. the people of micro States) but must be more than a mere association of individuals within a State.
(c) The group as a whole must have the will to be identified as a people or the consciousness of being a people – allowing that groups or some members of such groups, though sharing the foregoing characteristics, may not have the will or consciousness.
(d) Possibly the group must have institutions or other means of expressing its common characteristics and will for identity.

NOTES:
1. As was made clear in the *Namibia Opinion*, the right of self-determination is now a rule of customary international law, at least in its application to colonial territories. Indeed, the Special Rapporteur of the Sub-Commission on Prevention of Discrimination and Protection of Minorities, (H. Gros Espiell, *The Right to Self-Determination: Implementation of United Nations Resolutions*, 1980, pp. 11–13) considered that 'the exceptional importance of the principle of the self-determination of peoples in the modern world is such that . . . it is one of the cases of *jus cogens*'. This view has the support of many jurists and in the statements by a number of State authorities (see Chapter 3 on the concept of *jus cogens*). The application of the right to self-determination beyond colonial situations is examined in the next section.
2. There is a close connection between the protection of the right of self-determination and the protection of other human rights, as is indicated by the Human Rights Committee's General Comment above. There is even a connection with humanitarian law (see below), in that the Geneva Protocol I 1977 on the law relating to the protection of victims of armed conflict expressly includes situations where peoples are exercising their right of self-determination as being within its scope (Article 1(4)).
3. One of the principal difficulties in clarifying the right of self-determination is to decide the 'self' or 'peoples' who have this right. Many definitions have been considered, both objective

and subjective, and the UNESCO Report (above) brings most of these proposed definitions together. While it is certainly to the advantage of the 'people' concerned that they are recognised by States as a peoples having the right of self-determination, recognition is ultimately a political decision by States (see Chapter 5) which may not accord with the legal position. Above all, those entitled to the benefit of the protection of a human right should not be dependent on the whims of States.

C: Application of the right of self-determination

Western Sahara Opinion
ICJ Rep 1975 12, International Court of Justice

The facts are set out in Chapter 7.

THE COURT: [Affirmes] the decision in the [*Namibia Opinion*] and emphasises that the application of the right of self-determination requires a free and genuine expression of the will of the peoples concerned. . . . The validity of the principle of self-determination, defined as the need to pay regard to the freely expressed will of peoples, is not affected by the fact that in certain cases the General Assembly has dispensed with the requirement of consulting the inhabitants of a given territory. Those instances were based either on the consideration that a certain population did not constitute a "people" entitled to self-determination or on the conviction that a consultation was totally unnecessary, in view of special circumstances. . . .

The Court has already concluded that the two questions [for which an Advisory Opinion is sought] must be considered in the whole context of the decolonization process. The right of self-determination leaves the General Assembly a measure of discretion with respect to the forms and procedures by which that right is to be realized.

JUDGE DILLARD (Separate Opinion): . . . The pronouncements of the Court thus indicate, in my view, that a norm of international law has emerged applicable to the decolonization of those non-self-governing territories which are under the aegis of the United Nations. . . .

It seemed hardly necessary to make more explicit the cardinal restraint which the legal right of self-determination imposes. That restraint may be captured in a single sentence. It is for the people to determine the destiny of the territory and not the territory the destiny of the people. Viewed in this perspective it becomes almost self-evident that the existence of ancient "legal ties" of the kind described in the Opinion, while they may influence some of the projected procedures for decolonization, can have only a tangential effect in the ultimate choices available to the people. . . .

[I]t may be suggested that self-determination is satisfied by a free choice not by a particular consequence of that choice or a particular method of exercising it.

Frontier Dispute Case (Burkina Faso v Republic of Mali)
ICJ Rep 1986 554, Chamber of the International Court of Justice

Both States were formerly French colonies, being Upper Volta and French Sudan respectively. They failed to reach agreement concerning 300 kilometres of their common frontier, which was thought to be rich in mineral resources, and so submitted the dispute to a Chamber of the Court.

20. Since the two Parties have, as noted above, expressly requested the Chamber to resolve their dispute on the basis, in particular, of the 'principle of the intangibility of frontiers inherited from colonization', the Chamber cannot disregard the principle of *uti possidetis juris*, the application of which gives rise to this respect for intangibility of frontiers. Although there is no need, for the

purposes of the present case, to show that this is a firmly established principle of international law where decolonization is concerned, the Chamber nonetheless wishes to emphasize its general scope, in view of its exceptional importance for the African continent and for the two Parties. In this connection it should be noted that the principle of *uti possidetis* seems to have been first invoked and applied in Spanish America, inasmuch as this was the continent which first witnessed the phenomenon of decolonization involving the formation of a number of sovereign States on territory formerly belonging to a single metropolitan State. Nevertheless the principle is not a special rule which pertains solely to one specific system of international law. It is a general principle, which is logically connected with the phenomenon of the obtaining of independence, wherever it occurs. Its obvious purpose is to prevent the independence and stability of new States being endangered by fratricidal struggles provoked by the challenging of frontiers following the withdrawal of the administering power. . . .

Uti possidetis, as a principle which upgraded former administrative delimitations, established during the colonial period, to international frontiers, is therefore a principle of a general kind which is logically connected with this form of decolonization wherever it occurs. . . .

25. However, it may be wondered how the time-hallowed principle has been able to withstand the new approaches to international law as expressed in Africa, where the successive attainment of independence and the emergence of new States have been accompanied by a certain questioning of traditional international law. At first sight this principle conflicts outright with another one; the right of peoples to self-determination. In fact, however, the maintenance of the territorial status quo in Africa is often seen as the wisest course, to preserve what has been achieved by peoples who have struggled for their independence, and to avoid a disruption which would deprive the continent of the gains achieved by much sacrifice. The essential requirement of stability in order to survive, to develop and gradually to consolidate their independence in all fields, has induced African States judiciously to consent to the respecting of colonial frontiers, and to take account of it in the interpretation of the principle of self-determination of peoples.

26. Thus the principle of *uti possidetis* has kept its place among the most important legal principles, despite the apparent contradiction which explained its coexistence alongside the new norms. Indeed it was by deliberate choice that African States selected, among all the classic principles, that of *uti possidetis*. This remains an undeniable fact. In the light of the foregoing remarks, it is clear that the applicability of *uti possidetis* in the present case cannot be challenged merely because in 1960, the year when Mali and Burkina Faso achieved independence, the Organization of African Unity which was to proclaim this principle did not yet exist, and the above-mentioned resolution calling for respect for the pre-existing frontiers dates only from 1964.

Letter from United Kingdom's representative to the United Nations to the President of the Security Council, 28 April 1982

Security Council Official Record 37 Session Supp for April, May, June, pp. 47–49

The Falkland/Malvinas Islands were the subject of a long-running dispute between the United Kingdom and Argentina. Armed conflict occurred in April 1982. Argentina's claim is based primarily on a succession to the rights of Spain and France; continental integrity/contiguity; and a continual protest against the United Kingdom's claim as being contrary to international law as it is an exercise of sovereignty by it as a colonial power. The United Kingdom claim could have been based on discovery and perhaps conquest, but its principal claim is now centred on self-determination.

The Falkland Islanders are a people. The United Kingdom ratified both the Human Rights Covenants on their behalf. They are a permanent population. Over half of the people can trace back their roots on the Island to 1850. They have no other home. They have as is well known expressed their wishes regarding their political status in free and fair elections, the last having been held as recently as October 1981. The consistent practice of the United Nations shows that there is no minimum figure for a population to qualify for the right to self-determination: it suffices to cite the case of St. Helena, another South Atlantic island with about 4000 people whose right to self-determination has been consistently upheld. The United Kingdom cannot accept that the right of self-determination as enshrined in the Charter and the Human Rights Covenants is subject to a special exception in the case of the Falkland Islands. This conclusion is confirmed by the Declaration on Principles of International Law concerning Friendly Relations and Co-operation among States in accordance with the Charter of the United Nations, adopted by consensus in October 1970 [*see General Assembly resolution 2625 (XXV)*]. . . .

In particular, the present population of the Falkland Islands has been there, generation after generation, for the last 149 years, maintaining a viable pastoral economy and distinctive way of life. And whereas the French, the Spanish and the Buenos Aires colonies were very small (under 100 people), the only significant permanent population has been that from the mid-19th century to the present day, averaging just under 2000 persons.

Whilst no doubt much time and energy could be spent in reviewing the history of the Falkland Islands between the first settlement in 1764 and 1833, and whilst the United Kingdom is confident about the strength of its legal case over that period, these factors cannot be allowed to override the right of self-determination. In 1833, the age of the railway was just opening in Europe and it hardly seems appropriate to decide issues involving the welfare of people alive in the latter part of the 20th century on the basis of (disputed) events in the early part of the 19th century or even the 18th century. If the international community were to discount 149 years of history, there would hardly be an international boundary which did not immediately become subject to dispute.

Arbitration Committee of the International Conference on Yugoslavia, Opinion No 2

3 *European Journal of International Law* (1992), 183–4

This Committee (known as the Badinter Committee after its Chairperson) was established by the European Union States when they convened an International Conference on Yugoslavia in August 1991. The Committee's mandate seems to be to decide on legal matters brought to it by those concerned with seeking peace in Yugoslavia, but the binding quality of its decisions is unclear. Its opinions on recognition are considered in Chapter 5.

On 20 November 1991 the Chairman of the Arbitration Committee received a letter from Lord Carrington, Chairman of the Conference on Yugoslavia, requesting the Committee's opinion on the following question put by the Republic of Serbia:

> Does the Serbian population in Croatia and Bosnia-Herzegovina, as one of the constituent peoples of Yugoslavia, have the right to self-determination?

The Committee took note of the *aide-mémoires*, observations and other materials submitted by the Republics of Bosnia-Herzegovina, Croatia, Macedonia, Montenegro, Slovenia and Serbia, by the Presidency of the Socialist Federal Republic of Yugoslavia (SFRY) and by the 'Assembly of the Serbian People of Bosnia-Herzegovina'.

1. The Committee considers that, whatever the circumstances, the right to self-determination must not involve changes to existing frontiers at the time of independence (*uti possidetis juris*) except where the states concerned agree otherwise.

2. Where there are one or more groups within a state constituting one or more ethnic, religious or language communities, they have the right to recognition of their identity under international law. As the Committee emphasised in its Opinion No. 1 of 29 November 1991, published on 7 December, the

– now peremptory – norms of international law requires states to ensure respect for the rights of minorities. This requirement applies to all the Republics *vis-à-vis* the minorities on their territory.

The Serbian population in Bosnia-Herzegovina and Croatia must therefore be afforded every right accorded to minorities under international convention as well as national and international guarantees consistent with the principles of international law and the provisions of Chapter II of the draft Convention of 4 November 1991, which has been accepted by these Republics.

3. Article 1 of the two 1966 International Covenants on human rights establishes that the principle of the right to self-determination serves to safeguard human rights. By virtue of that right every individual may choose to belong to whatever ethnic, religious or language community he or she wishes.

In the Committee's view one possible consequence of this principle might be for the members of the Serbian population in Bosnia-Herzegovina and Croatia to be recognized under agreements between the Republics as having the nationality of their choice, with all the rights and obligations which that entails with respect to the states concerned.

4. The Arbitration Committee is therefore of the opinion:

(i) that the Serbian population in Bosnia-Herzegovina and Croatia is entitled to all the rights concerned to minorities and ethnic groups under international law and under the provisions of the draft Convention of the Conference on Yugoslavia of 4 November 1991, to which the Republics of Bosnia-Herzegovina and Croatia have undertaken to give effect; and

(ii) that the Republics must afford the members of those minorities and ethnic groups all the human rights and fundamental freedoms recognized in international law, including, where appropriate, the right to choose their nationality.

Case Concerning East Timor (*Portugal* v *Australia*)
ICJ Rep 1995 90, International Court of Justice

Portugal commenced these proceeding after the conclusion of a treaty between Australia and Indonesia concerning the delimitation of the continental shelf between Australia and East Timor. Portugal was then the administering authority over East Timor (being a non-self-governing territory). In 1975 Indonesian forces occupied East Timor and committed human rights violations. Portugal objected to Australia entering the treaty with Indonesia, *inter alia*, because it infringed the right of self-determination of the East Timorese people, which Portugal was meant to protect. Because Indonesia did not accept the jurisdiction of the ICJ, no case could be brought against Indonesia. The Court held (by 14 votes to 2) that it could not decide this case in the absence of Indonesia, as Indonesia's rights and obligations would have been affected by any judgment of the Court. Nevertheless, the Court made a few comments about the right of self-determination.

29. In the Court's view, Portugal's assertion that the right of peoples to self-determination, as it evolved from the Charter and from United Nations practice, has an *erga omnes* character, is irreproachable. The principle of self-determination of peoples has been recognized by the United Nations Charter and in the jurisprudence of the Court (see *Legal Consequences for States of the continued presence of South Africa in Namibia (South West Africa) notwithstanding Security Council Resolution 276 (1970), ICJ Reports 1971*, pp. 31–32, paras 52–53; *Western Sahara, ICJ Reports 1975*, pp. 31–33, paras 54–59); it is one of the essential principles of contemporary international law. . . .

31. The Court notes that the argument of Portugal under consideration rests on the premise that the United Nations resolutions, and in particular those of the Security Council, can be read as

imposing an obligation on States not to recognize any authority on the part of Indonesia over the territory and, where the latter is concerned, to deal only with Portugal. The Court is not persuaded, however, that the relevant resolutions went so far.

For the two Parties, the territory of East Timor remains a non-self-governing territory and its people has the right to self-determination. Moreover, the General Assembly, which reserves to itself the right to determine the territories which have to be regarded as non-self-governing for the purposes of the application of Chapter XI of the Charter, has treated East Timor as such a territory. The competent subsidiary organs of the General Assembly have continued to treat East Timor as such to this day. Furthermore, the Security Council, in its resolutions 384 (1975) and 389 (1976) has expressly called for respect for 'the territorial integrity of East Timor as well as the inalienable right of its people to self-determination in accordance with General Assembly resolution 1514 (XV).

Nor is it at issue between the Parties that the General Assembly has expressly referred to Portugal as the 'administering Power' of East Timor in a number of the resolutions it adopted on the subject of East Timor between 1975 and 1982, and that the Security Council has done so in its resolution 384 (1975). The Parties do not agree, however, on the legal implications that flow from the reference to Portugal as the administering Power in those texts.

32. The Court finds that it cannot be inferred from the sole fact that the above-mentioned resolutions of the General Assembly and the Security Council refer to Portugal as the administering Power of East Timor that they intended to establish an obligation on third States to treat exclusively with Portugal as regards the continental shelf of East Timor. The Court notes, furthermore, that several States have concluded with Indonesia treaties capable of application to East Timor but which do not include any reservation in regard to that Territory. . . .

37. The Court recalls in any event that it has taken note in the present judgment (paragraph 31) that, for the two Parties, the territory of East Timor remains a non-self-governing territory and its people has the right to self-determination.

H. Hannum, 'Minorities, Indigenous Peoples, and Self-Determination' in L. Henkin and J. Hargrove (eds), *Human Rights: An Agenda for the Next Century* (1994), pp. 7, 9–11

The growing recognition that the mere protection of individual human rights may not always be sufficient to guarantee legitimate values of group identity or demands for more effective participation in the larger society led to adoption of a plethora of new international instruments in the late 1980s and 1990s. Whether phrased in the technical terms of individual rights ('persons belonging to' minorities) or more broadly, these instruments constitute an explicit recognition of the fact that true democracy may require more than one-person, one-vote, and that the self-determination of states may not be sufficient to respond to demands by peoples for self-government. . . .

Like other 'peoples,' indigenous peoples claim the right to *self-determination*, although governments have been understandably reluctant to concede this point if 'self-determination' includes a right of secession. Certainly indigenous peoples should have a right to self-determination equal to that of other peoples, although this does not resolve the issue of the content of that right in the post-colonial era. These development offer ample evidence that the international community has begun to recognise that certain groups – whether peoples, nations, populations, communities, or minorities – deserve special protection, just as international law has recognized the special needs of other vulnerable groups, such as women, children, refugees, migrant workers, and detainees. However, it is also evident that no realistic assessment of the policy options available to either the United States or the international community can be based purely on definitional distinctions among ethnic groups, minorities, and peoples. Support for assertions of rights should be based on criteria applicable to all groups and designed to promote universally shared human values independent of the status of a group as a nation, people, or minority.

R. McCorquodale, 'Self-Determination: A Human Rights Approach'
(1994) 43 ICLQ 857, pp. 857, 883–5

Resolution of the extent of the exercise of the right of self-determination has been a vexed issue in the international community. Too frequently there has been resort to armed conflict as the means to resolve claims arising from the right. Despite the political, social and moral aspects of any resolution, international law needs to devise a coherent legal framework so that a structure for peaceful settlement is created which can apply to all the potentially competing claims and interests concerning the right of self-determination.

The right of self-determination applies to all situations where peoples are subject to oppression by subjugation, domination and exploitation by others. It is applicable to all territories, colonial or not, and to all peoples. The legal approaches to the right of self-determination which have been used so far have focussed on the 'peoples' and on the 'territory' involved. These have been shown to be too rigid to be able to be used in the present variety of applications and exercises of the right, especially to internal self-determination.

The human rights approach to the right of self-determination recognises that the right is a human right but is not an absolute human right. This approach relies on the general legal rules developed within the international human rights law framework to enable the limitations on the right to be discerned and elaborated. By interpreting the right in the context of current State practice and current international standards, full account can be given to the development of the right over time and to its broad range of possible exercises, in contrast to the restrictive 'territorial' approach which limit its exercise to secession or independence. Use can also be made of the broad and flexible rules concerning who is a 'victim' able to bring a claim for violation of a human right to give a flexible definition of 'peoples', which avoids the barrenness and rigidity of the 'peoples' approach.

The approach provides a coherent and consistent body of general legal rules by relying on the framework of international human rights law. By using this framework, the limitations on the right are discerned and considered. The right of self-determination does have limitations, both to protect the rights of others and to protect the general interests of society, especially the need to maintain international peace and security. But those limitations are applicable only in certain circumstances, such as where internal self-determination has already occurred, and where there is a pressing need for the limitations in the society concerned.

This approach is able to deal with the changing of values in international society away from the State-based international law towards a more flexible system. Indeed, many of the claims for self-determination arose because the unjust, State-based, international legal order failed to respond to legitimate aspirations of peoples. The limitations on the right of territorial integrity and *uti possidetis* are both attempts to reassert the exclusivity of the State in international law at the expense of the people of a territory. By reasserting the primacy of the State over the rights of people, these limitations are at odds with the development of international human rights law and so, under the human rights approach, are given priority over the right of self-determination only in restricted circumstances.

While the human rights approach does not make it possible to say in the abstract which peoples have the right of self-determination and the extent of any exercise of this right, it does provide a framework to enable every situation to be considered and all the relevant rights and interests to be taken into account, balanced and analysed. This balance means that the geo-political context of the right being claimed – the particular historical circumstances – and the present constitutional order of the State and of international society, is acknowledged and addressed. Thus a claim for the exercise of the right of self-determination by secession may be considered contrary to the pressing social need in the particular society for territorial integrity, or it may be able to be exercised by different means, such as by internal self-determination. The decision by the State as to the balance between its interests and the rights that need to be protected within its territory against the right of self-determination claimed by peoples within its territory is very important but it is not conclusive, as the

State, and the international community, must still comply with obligations under international human rights law. The increasing acceptance by States of these obligations could assist to foster international adjudication on claims concerning the infringement of the right of self-determination.

Thus the human rights approach to the right of self-determination creates a framework to balance competing rights and interests and seeks to provide legal rules to deal with disputes. Once this legal process has been completed then the relevant political and moral forces will be able to act on a clear and coherent legal position.

Reference Re Secession of Quebec
[1998] 2 SCR 217, 37 ILM 1342 (1998), Canadian Supreme Court

> The Canadian Supreme Court was asked several questions about whether Quebec could secede from Canada, including the following question: "Is there a right of self-determination under international law that would give the National Assembly, legislature or government of Quebec the right to effect the secession of Quebec from Canada unilaterally?"

111. It is clear that international law does not specifically grant component parts of sovereign states the legal right to secede unilaterally from their 'parent' state. . . . [P]roponents . . . are therefore left to attempt to found their argument . . . on the implied duty of states to recognize the legitimacy of secession brought about by the exercise of the well-established international law right of a 'people' to self-determination. . . .

114. The existence of the right of a people to self-determination is now so widely recognized in international conventions that the principle has acquired a status beyond 'convention' and is considered a general principle of international law. . . .

124. It is clear that 'a people' may include only a portion of the population of an existing state. The right to self-determination has developed largely as a human right, and is generally used in documents that simultaneously contain references to 'nation' and 'state'. The juxtaposition of these terms is indicative that the reference to 'people' does not necessarily mean the entirety of a state's population. . . .

125. While much of the Quebec population certainly shares many of the characteristics (such as a common language and culture) that would be considered in determining whether a specific group is a 'people', as do other groups within Quebec and/or Canada, it is not necessary to explore this legal characterization to resolve Question 2 appropriately. Similarly, it is not necessary for the Court to determine whether, should a Quebec people exist within the definition of public international law, such a people encompasses the entirety of the provincial population or just a portion thereof. Nor is it necessary to examine the position of the aboriginal population within Quebec. . . .

126. The recognized sources of international law establish that the right to self-determination of a people is normally fulfilled through internal self-determination a people's pursuit of its political, economic, social and cultural development within the framework of an existing state. A right to external self-determination (which in this case potentially takes the form of the assertion of a right to unilateral secession) arises in only the most extreme of cases and, even then, under carefully defined circumstances. . . .

130. . . . There is no necessary incompatibility between the maintenance of the territorial integrity of existing states, including Canada, and the right of a 'people' to achieve a full measure of self-determination. A state whose government represents the whole of the people or peoples resident within its territory, on a basis of equality and without discrimination, and respects the principles of self-determination in its own internal arrangements, is entitled to the protection under international law of its territorial integrity. . . .

133. The other clear case [in addition to colonial domination] where a right to external self-determination accrues is where a people is subject to alien subjugation, domination or exploitation outside a colonial context. This recognition finds its roots in the Declaration on Friendly Relations . . .

134. A number of commentators have further asserted that the right to self-determination may ground a right to unilateral secession in a third circumstance . . . when a people is blocked from the meaningful exercise of its right to self-determination internally, it is entitled, as a last resort, to exercise it by secession. The Vienna Declaration requirement that governments represent 'the whole people belonging to the territory without distinction of any kind' adds credence to the assertion that such a complete blockage may potentially give rise to a right of secession.

135. . . . Even assuming that the third circumstance is sufficient to create a right to unilateral secession under international law, the current Quebec context cannot be said to approach such a threshold. . . .

136. The population of Quebec cannot plausibly be said to be denied access to government. Quebecers occupy prominent positions within the government of Canada. Residents of the province freely make political choices and pursue economic, social and cultural development within Quebec, across Canada, and throughout the world. The population of Quebec is equitably represented in legislative, executive and judicial institutions. In short, to reflect the phraseology of the international documents that address the right to self-determination of peoples, Canada is a 'sovereign and independent state conducting itself in compliance with the principle of equal rights and self-determination of peoples and thus possessed of a government representing the whole people belonging to the territory without distinction'. . . .

139. We would not wish to leave this aspect of our answer to Question 2 without acknowledging the importance of the submissions made to us respecting the rights and concerns of aboriginal peoples in the event of a unilateral secession, as well as the appropriate means of defining the boundaries of a seceding Quebec with particular regard to the northern lands occupied largely by aboriginal peoples. However, the concern of aboriginal peoples is precipitated by the asserted right of Quebec to unilateral secession. In light of our finding that there is no such right applicable to the population of Quebec, either under the Constitution of Canada or at international law, but that on the contrary a clear democratic expression of support for secession would lead under the Constitution to negotiations in which aboriginal interests would be taken into account, it becomes unnecessary to explore further the concerns of the aboriginal peoples in this Reference.

140. As stated, an argument advanced by the *amicus curiae* on this branch of the Reference was that, while international law may not ground a positive right to unilateral secession in the context of Quebec, international law equally does not prohibit secession and, in fact, international recognition would be conferred on such a political reality if it emerged, for example, via effective control of the territory of what is now the province of Quebec.

141. It is true that international law may well, depending on the circumstances, adapt to recognize a political and/or factual reality, regardless of the legality of the steps leading to its creation. However, as mentioned at the outset, effectivity, as such, does not have any real applicability to Question 2, which asks whether a right to unilateral secession exists.

142. No one doubts that legal consequences may flow from political facts, and that 'sovereignty is a political fact for which no purely legal authority can be constituted.' . . . Secession of a province from Canada, if successful in the streets, might well lead to the creation of a new state. Although recognition by other states is not, at least as a matter of theory, necessary to achieve statehood, the viability of a would-be State in the international community depends, as a practical matter, upon recognition by other States. That process of recognition is guided by legal norms. However, international recognition is not alone constitutive of statehood and, critically, does not relate back to the date of secession to serve retroactively as a source of a 'legal' right to secede in the first place.

Recognition occurs only after a territorial unit has been successful, as a political fact, in achieving secession.

143. . . . [A]n emergent State that has disregarded legitimate obligations arising out of its previous situation can potentially expect to be hindered by that disregard in achieving international recognition, at least with respect to the timing of that recognition. On the other hand, compliance by the seceding province with such legitimate obligations would weigh in favour of international recognition.

NOTES:

1. The extent of the application of the right of self-determination is still subject to debate. The right has an economic, social and cultural dimension as well as a political dimension. While it is clear that the right of self-determination applies to all colonial situations, there has been increasing acceptance of the right in non-colonial situations. Namibia, East Timor and Palestine are examples of non-colonial territories where a right of self-determination has been internationally acknowledged, with the former two entities now being States. In addition, the Preamble to the Treaty on the Final Settlement With Respect to Germany 1990 (see Chapter 7) stated that the 'German people, freely exercising their right of self-determination, have expressed their will to bring about the unity of Germany as a State'. There have also been statements on the applications of the right to the break-ups of the former Soviet Union and Yugoslavia by the Badinter Committee (above) (and see Chapter 5).

2. The right of self-determination can be exercised in a variety of ways, with there being a strong presumption against secession or independence in non-colonial situations. Even in colonial situations other options to independence were available, as set out in General Assembly Resolution 1541 (above). At the same time, the right of self-determination has an 'internal' aspect, which enables a peoples within a State to exercise their right of self-determination by choosing their political status, the extent of their political participation and the form of their government. This aspect was proclaimed in the Declaration on Friendly Relations (above), as it provided that only 'a government representing the whole people belonging to the territory without distinction as to race, creed or colour' can be considered as complying with the right. This was relevant for the decision in *Reference Re Secession of Quebec* (above).

3. In any exercise of the right of self-determination, the rights of others must be taken into account, so that the human rights of all are protected. There are also State limitations on the right of self-determination, including the territorial integrity of a State and the principle of *uti possidetis*, being the respect for the established colonial boundaries. The purpose of the latter is to protect the territorial integrity and stability of newly independent States, as is stated in the *Case Concerning the Frontier Dispute*, above. This was reiterated by a Chamber of the International Court of Justice in the *Land, Island and Maritime Dispute Case* (*El Salvador* v *Honduras*) (*Merits*) ICJ Rep 1992 92, though it also noted (at p. 388) that '*uti possidetis juris* is essentially a retrospective principle, investing as international boundaries administrative limits intended originally for quite other purposes' (see further in Chapter 7). Thus, as McCorquodale makes clear in the extract above, care must be taken so that these limitations are applied only in appropriate situations and that they do not become another method by which States, and elites in non-States, assert their power in international law at the expense of the people of a territory and so violate the right of self-determination.

4. The impact on international law of the right of self-determination is potentially very broad, with its important impact on sovereignty over territory considered in Chapter 7, as it has an *erga omnes* character (see *East Timor* case). As Hannum points out, the right has potential relevance to minorities and indigenous peoples, as well as to women. It is also part of the movement away from an exclusively State-based system of international law.

SECTION 7: **International criminal law**

The framework of international human rights law is primarily based on States being legally obliged to protect human rights within their territory. If a violation of human rights occurs then the State is responsible. However, in some instances, individuals are directly responsible for violations of human rights. This occurs in the area of international criminal law, for which there is usually universal jurisdiction (see Chapter 8).

Judgment of the Nuremberg International Military Tribunal
41 AJIL 172 (1947)

That international law imposes duties and liabilities upon individuals as well as upon States has long been recognized . . . individuals can be punished for violations of international law. Crimes against international law are committed by men, not by abstract entities, and only by punishing individuals who commit such crimes can the provisions of international law be enforced.

Prosecutor v *Tadić (Jurisdictional Phase)*
35 ILM 35 (1996), International Criminal Tribunal for the Former Yugoslavia

134. [C]ustomary international law imposes [individual] criminal liability for serious violations of common Article 3 [of the Geneva Conventions for the Protection of Victims of War], as supplemented by other general principles and rules on the protection of victims of internal armed conflict, and for breaching certain fundamental principles and rules regarding means and methods of combat in civil strife. . . .

141. It is by now a settled rule of customary international law that crimes against humanity do not require a connection to international armed conflict . . . Indeed, . . . customary international law may not require a connection between crimes against humanity and any conflict at all [for an individual to be responsible at international law].

Prosecutor v *Furundžija*
38 ILM 317 (1999), International Criminal Tribunal for the Former Yugoslavia

143. The prohibition of torture laid down in international humanitarian law with regard to situations of armed conflict is reinforced by the body of international treaty rules on human rights: these rules ban torture both in armed conflict and in time of peace. In addition, treaties as well as resolutions of international organisations set up mechanisms designed to ensure that the prohibition is implemented and to prevent resort to torture as much as possible.

144. It should be noted that the prohibition of torture laid down in human rights treaties enshrines an absolute right, which can never be derogated from, not even in time of emergency (on this ground the prohibition also applies to situations of armed conflicts). This is linked to the fact . . . that the prohibition on torture is a peremptory norm or *jus cogens*. This prohibition is so extensive that States are even barred by international law from expelling, returning or extraditing a person to another State where there are substantial grounds for believing that the person would be in danger of being subjected to torture.

145. These treaty provisions impose upon States the obligation to prohibit and punish torture, as well as to refrain from engaging in torture through their officials. In international human rights law, which deals with State responsibility rather than individual criminal responsibility, torture is prohibited as a criminal offence to be punished under national law; in addition, all States parties to the

relevant treaties have been granted, and are obliged to exercise, jurisdiction to investigate, prosecute and punish offenders. Thus, in human rights law too, the prohibition of torture extends to and has a direct bearing on the criminal liability of individuals.

146. The existence of this corpus of general and treaty rules proscribing torture shows that the international community, aware of the importance of outlawing this heinous phenomenon, has decided to suppress any manifestation of torture by operating both at the interstate level and at the level of individuals. No legal loopholes have been left.

W. Schabas, *An Introduction to the International Criminal Court*
(2001), pp. 21–23

The International Criminal Court has jurisdiction over four categories of crimes: genocide, crimes against humanity, war crimes and aggression. In both the preamble to the Statute and in Article 5, these are variously described as 'the most serious crimes of concern to the international community as a whole'. Elsewhere, the Statute describes them as 'unimaginable atrocities that deeply shock the conscience of humanity' (preamble), 'international crimes' (preamble), and 'the most serious crimes of international concern' (Article 1).

The concept of 'international crimes' has been around for centuries. They were generally considered to be offences whose repression compelled some international dimension. Piracy, for example, was committed on the high seas. This feature of the crime necessitated special jurisdictional rules as well as cooperation between States. Similar requirements obtained with respect to the slave trade, trafficking in women and children, traffic in narcotic drugs, hijacking, terrorism and money laundering. It was indeed this sort of crime that inspired Trinidad and Tobago, in 1989, to reactivate the issue of an international criminal court within the General Assembly of the United Nations. Crimes of this type are already addressed in a rather sophisticated scheme of international treaties, and for this reason the drafters of the Rome Statute referred to them as 'treaty crimes'.

The crimes over which the International Criminal Court has jurisdiction are 'international' not so much because international cooperation is needed for their repression, although this is also true, but because their heinous nature elevates them to a level where they are of 'concern' to the international community. These crimes are somewhat more recent in origin than many of the so-called 'treaty crimes', in that their recognition and subsequent development is closely associated with the human rights movement that arose subsequent to World War II. They dictate prosecution because humanity as a whole is the victim. Moreover, humanity as a whole is entitled, indeed required, to prosecute them for essentially the same reasons as we now say that humanity as a whole is concerned by violations of human rights that were once considered to lie within the exclusive prerogatives of State sovereignty.

All four crimes within the jurisdiction of the Court were prosecuted, at least in an earlier and somewhat embryonic form, by the Nuremberg Tribunal and the other post-war courts. At Nuremberg, they were called crimes against peace, war crimes and crimes against humanity. The term 'crimes against peace' is now replaced by 'aggression'; while probably not identical, the two terms largely overlap. Although the term 'genocide' already existed at the time of the Nuremberg trial, and it was used by the prosecutors, the indictments against Nazi criminals for the genocide of European Jews were based on the charge of 'crimes against humanity'. But, in contemporary usage, the crime of 'genocide' is now subsumed within the broader concept of 'crimes against humanity'.

The definitions of crimes within the Nuremberg Charter are relatively laconic, and the scope of the four categories of crimes as they are now conceived has evolved considerably since that time. Since Nuremberg, the concepts of crimes against humanity and war crimes have also undergone considerable development and enlargement. For example, crimes against humanity can now take place in peacetime as well as during armed combat, and war crimes exist in non-international as well as in international armed conflict. The evolution in the definitions is somewhat reflected in the length of the definitions in the Rome Statute. . . . At Rome, States argued that the "principle of legality" dictated detailed and precise provisions setting out the punishable crimes.

The definition of the crimes in the Rome Statute is in some cases the result of recent treaties, such as the 1984 Convention Against Torture or the earlier Apartheid Convention. But much of the development in the definition of these crimes is attributed to the evolution of customary law, whose content is not always as easy to identify with clarity. The definitions of crimes set out in Articles 6 to 8 [genocide, crimes against humanity and war crimes], as completed by the Elements of Crimes, correspond in a general sense to the state of customary international law. The three categories of crimes are drawn from existing definitions and use familiar terminology. . . . Nevertheless, while the correspondence with customary international law is close, it is far from perfect. To answer concerns that the Statute's definitions of crimes be taken as a codification of custom, Article 10 of the Statute declares: 'Nothing in this Part shall be interpreted as limiting or prejudicing in any way existing or developing rules of international law for purposes other than this Statute'. . . . It will become more and more important in the future, because customary law should evolve and the Statute may not be able to keep pace with it. For example, it is foreseeable that international law may raise the age of prohibited military recruitment from fifteen, or consider certain weapons to be prohibited. As a result of Article 10, the Statute cannot provide comfort to those who argue against this evolution of customary law. But, of course, the logic of Article 10 cuts both ways. To those who claim that the Statute sets a new minimum standard, for example in the field of gender crimes, conservative jurists will plead Article 10 and stress the differences between the texts in the Statute and their less prolix ancestors in the Geneva Conventions and related instruments.

NOTES:

1. International criminal law is one area where international human rights law intersects with international humanitarian law, which is the law that protects persons during armed conflicts. Although the two legal systems have different theoretical and practical origins, they both aim to protect the rights of the oppressed and can complement each other. For example, in a state of emergency where a State has derogated from protecting human rights (see derogations above), international humanitarian law would usually still apply. See Chapter 14 for the international law of armed conflict.

2. The international crimes for which individuals are directly responsible include war crimes, crimes against humanity, genocide, torture, hostage taking and rape in armed conflict (see Schabas above and the crimes within the jurisdiction of the International Criminal Court extracted in Chapter 8). In these areas, the individual person, who is normally hidden behind the 'abstract entity' – as the Nuremberg Military Tribunal called it – of the legal personality of the State, becomes clearly the subject of international law. During the 1990s the international community has been developing institutional structures to deal with these crimes. The Security Council established two international tribunals for the former Yugoslavia and Rwanda and a permanent International Criminal Court came into existence on 1 July 2002, with jurisdiction over international crimes.

3. As seen in the extracts above from the decisions of the International Criminal Tribunal for the Former Yugoslavia, many of these international crimes are now customary international law. International bodies and national courts have been active in clarifying the parameters of these crimes, with the UK House of Lords in the *Pinochet Case* (*R v Bow Street Metropolitan Stipendiary Magistrate, ex parte Pinochet* – see Chapter 9) applying the Torture Convention to a former Head of State and the United Nations Committee Against Torture extending the definition of persons responsible for torture to include persons who are not State officials (see

Elmi v *Australia*, Communication No. 120/1998, 20 May 1999). These decisions reflect an understanding that international law is no longer solely a State-based system. Rather, international law is a system in which the human rights of all and the responsibilities of both States and individuals are a vital part of that system.

SECTION 8: Other issues

A: Non-governmental organisations

Non-governmental organisations (NGOs), being those voluntary organisations not comprised of State representatives, have a vital function in the protection of human rights.

J. Shestack, 'Sisyphus Endures: The International Human Rights NGO'
24 *New York Law School Law Review* 89 (1978), pp. 95–6, 103, 108, 114

An NGO, despite the drama of the acronym, is simply a voluntary organization. It cannot act with the power of law or the force available to governments. As a voluntary organization, the principal value objectives of the human rights NGO fall into the following categories: (1) consultation; (2) education; (3) mediation; (4) participation in government action; (5) catalyst to government action; and (6) restraining government action. These categories, of course, overlap and suffer from imprecision, but . . . they are useful in distinguishing among the alternative courses of action open to human rights NGOs, particularly within the UN framework. . . .

The fifth function is that of catalyst, acting as an initiator for social change. The reference here is not to the pressure role, which in a sense is also a catalytic role, but the broader, more intellectual sense of initiating creative concepts, ideas and directions. . . . A large share of the important human rights concepts have stemmed from ideas of voluntary organizations or individuals. . . . The Universal Declaration itself, the concept of a Human Rights Commission, the idea of a High Commissioner for Human Rights, the Convention on Religious Discrimination, are all ideas which sprung from NGOs. . . .

How, then, can international human rights NGOs restrain governments? The realistic answer for the time being lies outside of the UN structure. For international human rights NGOs the productive course appears to be increased concentration on creating competing spheres of influence, which will induce restraints on abuses. Two competing centers of influence, which may be powerful enough to affect repressive governments, are world opinion and the internal populace. . . .

[T]he evidence shows that human rights activity does produce beneficial results. Repressive governments do not issue press releases crediting human rights NGOs for inducing their action. Still, amnesties do get declared, prisoners are released, sentences are eased, and abuses are lessened. . . . The International Red Cross Committee is recognized as having a great influence on ameliorating prison conditions. Amnesty [International] has undoubtedly contributed to the release of thousands of prisoners. No one can assess precisely the affectiveness of human rights NGOs. But each NGO can point to case after case where the end result of its intercession was relief for a victim of a human rights violation. They add up to an impressive argument for the value of the human rights non-governmental organization.

NOTES:
1. It is impossible to determine the exact correlation between the efforts of NGOs and the protection of human rights, as Shestack notes above, but clearly their influence on States in

promoting and protecting human rights – and, it is hoped, preventing violations of human rights – through fact-finding, finding, publicity and action has had some impact. As well, information provided by NGOs is often used by human rights bodies to clarify a particular situation and to counter-balance a State's assertions of facts, as can be seen in the reference to them in the *Brannigan and McBride* v *United Kingdom* decision above. A few NGOs have some standing in United Nations organisations, which can enable them to comment on issues before those organisations.

2. There is some criticism that most international NGOs are based in, or funded by those living in, developed States and that they tend to be concerned primarily with civil and political rights. While there is substance to this criticism, there are NGOs which have broader concerns, including religious institutions and trade unions, and there has been some desire to establish local and national NGOs, which can link with international NGOs and so be more effective within each State to promote and protect human rights and prevent their abuse. There are, however, problems faced by NGOs, not least of which is physical and financial survival – particularly in States where freedom of association and freedom of expression are regularly violated – as States often act to discredit NGOs' legitimacy and the factual accuracy of their reports, despite the difficulties in obtaining accurate information on the protection of human rights in most States.

3. Education about human rights – to both individuals and governments – is a major way to prevent abuses of human rights. This was indicated in the Preamble to the Universal Declaration on Human Rights (see 2 above), which proclaimed that 'every individual every organ of society . . . shall strive by reaching and education to promote respect for these rights and freedoms and by progressive measures, national and international, to secure their universal and effective recognition and observance.'

B: Impact of globalisation

The process of globalisation has an impact on all areas of international law, through its reduction of the importance of territorial boundaries. One area on which it has had a particular impact is on international human rights law.

R. McCorquodale with R. Fairbrother, 'Globalization and Human Rights'
21 *Human Rights Quarterly* (1999) 735, 763–6

Economic globalization does have an impact on the protection of human rights. It simultaneously creates opportunities and presents challenges for the international legal protection of human rights. While there are understandable concerns about both economic globalization and the international legal protection of human rights in terms of their philosophical bases, both are part of the process of globalization in which political, economic, social, civil, and cultural relationships are not restricted to territorial boundaries and are not solely within the control of any one state. As a result, globalization and the international legal order are opportunities to end the absolute sovereignty of the state and, hence, to further the realization that how a state deals with those within its territory is no longer a matter exclusively within the domestic jurisdiction of a state. It is now a matter of legitimate international concern . . .

Nevertheless, international human rights law, caught within its framework of state responsibility for human rights violations, is unable to deal fully with the changes to state sovereignty accelerated by the process of globalization. Where the violator of human rights law is not a state or its agent but is, for example, a globalized economic institution [such as the World Bank or the IMF] or a transnational corporation, international human rights law finds it difficult to provide any redress to the victim. In such cases, international human rights law focuses on the responsibility of a state to adopt constitutional, legislative, judicial, administrative, and other measures to ensure that human rights within its territory are protected, no matter who the perpetrator may be. However, this approach tends to be ineffective where a state is unwilling or unable to take these measures due to the possible effect on investment by globalized economic institutions. Therefore, international human rights law needs to take the opportunities presented by globalization to develop a more flexible frame work within which responsibility for human rights violations is not state-based; states must provide appropriate mechanisms for all individuals, groups, and others to have standing to bring claims for any violation of human rights . . .

However, pressure still needs to be exerted to ensure that the globalized economic institutions do take international human rights law explicitly into account in all stages of their decision-making. Decision-making is still primarily driven by economic factors. As has been shown, there are some grounds for arguing that economic factors can improve human rights protection. However, because economic globalization is generated by a philosophy in which markets must be allowed to flourish while states are relegated to the role of assisting this flourishing, any benefits for human rights protection tend to be incidental and fragmentary. The globalized communications industry constantly restates these philosophies. Accordingly, as has been indicated, the dangers of economic globalization for human rights can outweigh these incidental benefits.

Furthermore, there is the possibility of the fragmentation of states. This fragmentation is fostered by shifting the decision-making processes away from governments and people to globalized economic institutions and transnational corporations which have a limited interest in the social and cultural welfare or the human rights of people in developing states.

A danger of economic globalization is its impact on the concepts and application of human rights. An example of this was seen in the right to development where only certain types of development, such as the construction of transportation infrastructures, have been included within the concept of this right. Another example is the dominance of globalization's focus on certain rights (civil and political) to the virtual exclusion of other rights. But the greater danger is that the values of the international community, embodied in the international legal order and created to protect human rights, are being challenged by the values of the global economic free market.

NOTES:

1. Globalisation is primarily an economic process, although it is also a political, social and cultural process. It is a process where developments in technology and communications, the creation of intricate international economic and trade arrangements, increasing activity by international organisations and transnational corporations are moving at a rapid pace and beyond the control of any one State. By diminishing the relevance of territorial boundaries, globalisation highlights the extent of interdependence of the international community. As such, the process of globalisation affects all aspects of international law, including territorial sovereignty and jurisdiction (see Chapters 7 and 8). At the same time it requires a reconsideration of the nature of international law so that it can deal effectively with intra-State and inter-State activities by non-State actors.

2. The focus on obligations in international human rights has tended to be on the responsibility of the State for the actions of the State and of public bodies. Yet often human rights are violated by private actors (see A. Clapham, *Human Rights in the Private Sphere* (1993)) such as transnational corporations, or by actions in the supposedly private sphere for which a State is traditionally not held to be responsible, such as domestic violence. Feminist legal theory has challenged this division into public/private spheres in the determination of when a State is responsible (see Charlesworth above). It is hoped that international human rights law will develop to protect the victim of a violation of human rights, no matter who is the violater, what is the cause or the place of the violation.

3. Only some aspects of international human rights law have been dealt with in this chapter. Other human rights issues will be referred to in later chapters, for example, human rights and

the environment (Chapter 12) and violations of rights in extradition/abduction cases (Chapter 8), or were raised in previous chapters, as with the role of the individual in international law considered in Chapter 5. Indeed, as noted at the beginning of this chapter, international human rights law continues to have a significant effect on most areas of international law.

7

Sovereignty over Territory

Introductory note

Sovereignty is one of the fundamental concepts in international law. It is an integral part of the principles of equality of States and of territorial integrity and political independence that are referred to in Art. 2 of the United Nations Charter. Sovereignty is crucial to the exercise of powers by a State over both its territory and the people living in that territory. Accordingly, Chapters 7, 8 and 10 are concerned primarily with issues of sovereignty. Further, as a corollary to a State's own sovereignty, it has responsibilities to respect the sovereignty of other States (see Chapter 9) and, perhaps, not to abuse its sovereignty, for example, by causing environmental damage (see Chapter 12).

SECTION 1: **Sovereignty and territory**

H. Hinsley, *Sovereignty*
(2nd edn, 1986), pp. 222, 225

The concept of sovereignty originated in the closer association of the developing state and the developing community which became inevitable when it was discovered that power had to be shared between them. The function of the concept was to provide the only formula which could ensure the effective exercise of power once this division of power or collaboration of forces had become inescapable. It was on this account that, to begin with, it placed the sovereignty in the rulership. As the community became still more complex the thesis of the sovereignty of the ruler was challenged by the thesis of the sovereignty of the people, and even by the thesis that the state and the notion of sovereignty were dispensable; but these arguments could not meet the primary need to ensure the effective exercise of power, the more so as the growing complexity of the community was serving to emphasize the importance of the state. . . . Since for practical purposes it has to be pre-supposed that each independent state in the international system is sovereign within its own territory, it has to be accepted of some states that they are sovereign in theory when in reality the historical development and the present condition of the territory in which they rule are not such as to have permitted the concept of sovereignty to emerge as the relevant or even as a possible basis for authority. Of some states, indeed, it has now to be accepted that they are sovereign even though they do not in fact rule effectively.

R. Jennings and A. Watts, *Oppenheim's International Law*
(9th edn, 1992), pp. 661–662

Boundaries of State territory are the imaginary lines on the surface of the earth which separate the territory of one State from that of another, or from unappropriated territory, or from the Open Sea. . . . [T]he distinction sometimes made between artificial and natural boundaries is geographic rather than legal, for so-called natural boundaries, making use of natural features such as rivers or mountains, usually need further definition in order to produce a precise boundary line.

Island of Palmas Case (*The Netherlands* v *United States*)
2 RIAA (1928) 829, Huber, Sole Arbitrator

The facts of this case are set out below.

Sovereignty in the relations between States signifies independence. Independence in regard to a portion of the globe is the right to exercise therein, to the exclusion of any other State, the functions of a State. The development of the national organisation of States during the last few centuries and, as a corollary, the development of international law, have established this principle of the exclusive competence of the State in regard to its own territory in such a way as to make it the point of departure in settling most questions that concern international relations. The special cases of the composite State, of collective sovereignty, etc., do not fall to be considered here and do not, for that matter, throw any doubt upon the principle which has just been enunciated. Under this reservation it may be stated that territorial sovereignty belongs always to one, or in exceptional circumstances to several States, to the exclusion of all others. The fact that the functions of a State can be performed by any State within a given zone is, on the other hand, precisely the characteristic feature of the legal situation pertaining in those parts of the globe which, like the high seas or lands without a master, cannot or do not yet form the territory of a State. . . .

Territorial sovereignty, as has already been said, involves the exclusive right to display the activities of a State. This right has as corollary a duty: the obligation to protect within the territory the rights of other States, in particular their right to integrity and inviolability in peace and in war, together with the rights which each State may claim for its nationals in foreign territory. Without manifesting its territorial sovereignty in a manner corresponding to circumstances, the State cannot fulfil this duty. Territorial sovereignty cannot limit itself to its negative side, i.e. to excluding the activities of other States; for it serves to divide between nations the space upon which human activities are employed, in order to assure them at all points the minimum of protection of which international law is the guardian.

Although municipal law, thanks to its complete judicial system, is able to recognize abstract rights of property as existing apart from any material display of them, it has none the less limited their effect by the principles of prescription and the protection of possession. International law, the structure of which is not based on any super-State organisation, cannot be presumed to reduce a right such as territorial sovereignty, with which almost all international relations are bound up, to the category of an abstract right, without concrete manifestations.

NOTES:
1. In the *North Atlantic Coast Fisheries Case* (*United Kingdom* v *United States*) 11 RIAA (1910) 167, the Permanent Court of Arbitration stated (at p. 180) that 'one of the essential elements of sovereignty is that it is to be exercised within territorial limits, and that, failing proof to the contrary, the territory is co-terminous with Sovereignty'. Territory is also one criterion for Statehood (see Chapter 5) and hence is essential for an entity to become a State.
2. Title to territory is not merely concerned with changes in the occupation of that territory but with changes in the right to territorial sovereignty (see R. Jennings, *The Acquisition of Territory in International Law*, (1963), p. 14). Despite the 'imaginary' nature of territorial boundaries (as

stated by Oppenheim) and the legal position that successor States are bound by boundary treaties, many disputes occur between States over territory. Many of these disputes occur due to hopes about potential natural resources. The International Court of Justice, and other international tribunals, have been generally effective in resolving those territorial boundary disputes which the parties have trusted to them (see Chapter 15).

3. Perspectives on the nature of sovereignty and its relationship to territory are changing. These are considered in Section 7, below.

SECTION 2: **Traditional means of acquisition of territory**

Traditionally there have been five means of acquisition of territory. These are occupation, prescription, cession, accretion (being the geographical addition of new territory – not discussed here), and conquest. They are of current value only as a means of exposition.

A: Occupation and prescription

Occupation is the exercise of sovereignty (often initially by discovery) over previously unclaimed territory (*terra nullius*). Prescription is the peaceful exercise of sovereignty for a reasonable period without objection by another State.

Clipperton Island Arbitration (France v Mexico)
2 RIAA (1932) 1105; transl. in 26 AJIL 390, Victor Emmanuel III, Sole Arbitrator

> Clipperton Island is situated in the Pacific Ocean, about 1,200 kilometres south west of Mexico. On 17 November 1858, a French lieutenant on board a commercial vessel cruising past the Island, declared the Island (which was uninhabited) to be French territory. The lieutenant notified the French consulate in Honolulu, which informed the Government of Hawaii and published the declaration of French sovereignty in a local Hawaiian journal. Very little was then done in relation to the Island by the French authorities. In 1897 a Mexican gun-boat landed and forced the three inhabitants to raise the Mexican flag, claiming that the Island had been discovered by Spain, to which Mexico was the successor State from 1836. The Arbitrator held that this discovery by Spain had not been proved, and that France had not abandoned her claim and so had title to the Island.

[T]he proof of an historic right of Mexico's is not supported by any manifestation of her sovereignty over the island, a sovereignty never exercised until the expedition of 1897; and the mere conviction that this was territory belonging to Mexico, although general and of long standing, cannot be retained.

Consequently, there is ground to admit that, when in November, 1858, France proclaimed her sovereignty over Clipperton, that island was in the legal situation of *territorium nullius*, and, therefore, susceptible of occupation.

The question remains whether France proceeded to an effective occupation, satisfying the conditions required by international law for the validity of this kind of territorial acquistion. In effect,

Mexico maintains, secondarily to her principal contention which has just been examined, that the French occupation was not valid, and consequently her own right to occupy the island which must still be considered as *nullius* in 1897.

In whatever concerns this question, there is, first of all, ground to hold as incontestable, the regularity of the act by which France in 1858 made known in a clear and precise manner, her intention to consider the island as her territory.

On the other hand, it is disputed that France took effective possession of the island, and it is maintained that without such a taking of possession of an effective character, the occupation must be considered as null and void.

It is beyond doubt that by immemorial usage having the force of law, besides the *animus occupandi*, the actual, and not the nominal, taking of possession is a necessary condition of occupation. This taking of possession consists in the act, or series of acts, by which the occupying state reduces to its possession the territory in question and takes steps to exercise exclusive authority there. Strictly speaking, and in ordinary cases, that only takes place when the state establishes in the territory itself an organization capable of making its laws respected. But this step is, properly speaking, but a means of procedure to the taking of possession, and, therefore, is not identical with the latter. There may also be cases where it is unnecessary to have recourse to this method. Thus, if a territory, by virtue of the fact that it was completely uninhabited, is, form the first moment when the occupying state makes its appearance there, at the absolute and undisputed disposition of that state, from that moment the taking of possession must be considered as accomplished, and the occupation is thereby completed. . . .

It follows from these premises that Clipperton Island was legitimately acquired by France on November 17, 1858. There is no reason to suppose that France has subsequently lost her right by *derelictio*, since she never had the *animus* of abandoning the island, and the fact that she has not exercised her authority there in a positive manner does not imply the forfeiture of an acquisition already definitively perfected.

Chamizal Arbitration (*Mexico* v *United States*)

11 RIAA (1911) 309, International Boundary Commission

The Rio Grande was established, by treaties dated 1848 and 1853, as being the boundary between Mexico and the United States. The river-bed moved over time. The Chamizal Tract lies between the old bed of the Rio Grande and the present bed of that river.

In the argument it is contended that the Republic of Mexico is estopped from asserting the national title over the territory known as "El Chamizal" by reason of the undisturbed, uninterrupted, and unchallenged possession of said territory by the United States of America since the treaty of Guadalupe Hidalgo.

Without thinking it necessary to discuss the very controversial question as to whether the right of prescription invoked by the United States is an accepted principle of the law of nations, in the absence of any convention establishing a term of prescription, the commissioners are unanimous in coming to the conclusion that the possession of the United States in the present case was not of such a character as to found a prescriptive title. Upon the evidence adduced it is impossible to hold that the possession of El Chamizal by the United States was undisturbed, uninterrupted, and unchallenged from the date of the treaty [to] the creation of a competent tribunal to decide the question. . . . On the contrary, it may be said that the physical possession taken by citizens of the United States and the political control exercised by the local and Federal Governments, have been constantly challenged and questioned by the Republic of Mexico, through its accredited diplomatic agents. . . .

The very existence of that convention precludes the United States from acquiring by prescription against the terms of their title, and, as has been pointed out above, the two Republics have ever since the signing of that convention treated it as a source of all their rights in respect of accretion to the territory on one side or the other of the river. Another characteristic of possession serving as a foundation for prescription is that it should be peaceable. . . .

Under these circumstances the commissioners have no difficulty in coming to the conclusion that the plea of prescription should be dismissed.

Western Sahara Opinion
ICJ Rep 1975 12, International Court of Justice

After much dispute over sovereignty to Western Sahara, the General Assembly, by Resolution 3292 (XXIX) adopted on 13 December 1974, sought an advisory opinion from the International Court of Justice on a number of questions, including the following:

I.   Was Western Sahara (Rio de Oro and Sakiet El Hamra) at the time of colonisation by Spain a territory belonging to no one (*terra nullius*)?

If the answer to the first question is in the negative,

II. What were the legal ties between this territory and the Kingdom of Morocco and the Mauritian entity?

The Court answered the first question in the negative but found legal ties between the territory and each of the two states.

79. Turning to Question I, the Court observes that the request specifically locates the question in the context of 'the time of colonization by Spain', and it therefore seems clear that the words 'Was Western Sahara ... a territory belonging to no one (*terra nullius*)?' have to be interpreted by reference to the law in force at that period. The expression '*terra nullius*' was a legal term of art employed in connection with 'occupation' as one of the accepted legal methods of acquiring sovereignty over territory. 'Occupation' being legally an original means of peaceably acquiring sovereignty over territory otherwise than by cession or succession, it was a cardinal condition of a valid 'occupation' that the territory should be *terra nullius* – a territory belonging to no-one – at the time of the act alleged to constitute the 'occupation' (cf. *Legal Status of Eastern Greenland*, PCIJ, Series A/B, No. 53, pp. 44 f. and 63 f.). In the view of the Court, therefore, a determination that Western Sahara was a '*terra nullius*' at the time of colonization by Spain would be possible only if it were established that at that time the territory belonged to no-one in the sense that it was then open to acquisition through the legal process of 'occupation'.

80. Whatever differences of opinion there may have been among jurists, the State practice of the relevant period indicates that territories inhabited by tribes or peoples having a social and political organization were not regarded as *terrae nullius*. It shows that in the case of such territories the acquisition of sovereignty was not generally considered as effected unilaterally through 'occupation' of *terra nullius* by original title but through agreements concluded with local rulers. On occasion, it is true, the word 'occupation' was used in a non-technical sense denoting simply acquisition of sovereignty; but that did not signify that the acquisition of sovereignty through such agreements with authorities of the country was regarded as an 'occupation' of a '*terra nullius*' in the proper sense of these terms. On the contrary, such agreements with local rulers, whether or not considered as an actual 'cession' of the territory, were regarded as derivative roots of title, and not original titles obtained by occupation of *terrae nullius*.

81. In the present instance, the information furnished to the Court shows that at the time of colonization Western Sahara was inhabited by peoples which, if nomadic, were socially and politically organized in tribes and under chiefs competent to represent them. It also shows that, in colonizing Western Sahara, Spain did not proceed on the basis that it was establishing its sovereignty over *terrae nullius*. In its Royal Order of 26 December 1884, far from treating the case as one of occupation of *terra nullius*, Spain proclaimed that the King was taking the Rio de Oro under his protection on the basis of agreements which had been entered into with the chiefs of the local tribes . . .

[Question II] . . . As the Permanent Court stated in the case concerning the *Legal Status of Eastern Greenland*, a claim to sovereignty based upon continued display of authority involves 'two elements each of which must be shown to exist: the intention and will to act as sovereign, and some actual exercise or display of such authority' (*ibid.*, pp. 45 f). True, the Permanent Court recognized that in the case of claims to sovereignty over areas in thinly populated or unsettled countries, 'very little in the way of actual exercise of sovereign rights' (*ibid.*, p. 46) might be sufficient in the absence of a competing claim. But, in the present instance, Western Sahara, if somewhat sparsely populated, was a territory across which socially and politically organized tribes were in constant movement and where armed incidents between these tribes were frequent. In the particular circumstances outlined in paragraphs 87 and 88 above, the paucity of evidence of actual display of authority unambiguously relating to Western Sahara renders it difficult to consider the Moroccan claim as on all fours with that of Denmark in the *Eastern Greenland* case. Nor is the difficulty cured by introducing the argument of geographical unity or contiguity. In fact, the information before the Court shows that the geographical unity of Western Sahara with Morocco is somewhat debatable, which also militates against giving effect to the concept of contiguity. Even if the geographical contiguity of Western Sahara with Morocco could be taken into account in the present connection, it would only make the paucity of evidence of unambiguous display of authority with respect to Western Sahara more difficult to reconcile with Morocco's claim to immemorial possession. . . .

93. In the view of the Court, however, what must be of decisive importance in determining its answer to Question II is not indirect inferences drawn from events in past history but evidence directly relating to effective display of authority in Western Sahara at the time of its colonization by Spain and in the period immediately preceding that time (cf. *Minquiers and Ecrehos, Judgment*, ICJ Reports 1953, p. 57). . . .

161. As already indicated in paragraph 70 of this Opinion, the General Assembly has made it clear, in resolution 3292 (XXIX), that the right of the population of Western Sahara to self-determination is not prejudiced or affected by the present request for an advisory opinion, nor by any other provision contained in that resolution. It is also clear that, when the General Assembly asks in Question II what were the legal ties between the territory of Western Sahara and the Kingdom of Morocco and the Mauritanian entity, it is addressing an enquiry to the Court as to the nature of these legal ties. This question, as stated in paragraph 85 above, must be understood as referring to such legal ties as may affect the policy to be followed in the decolonization of Western Sahara. In framing its answer, the Court cannot be unmindful of the purpose for which its opinion is sought. Its answer is requested in order to assist the General Assembly to determine its future decolonization policy and in particular to pronounce on the claims of Morocco and Mauritania to have had legal ties with Western Sahara involving the territorial integrity of their respective countries.

162. The materials and information presented to the Court show the existence, at the time of Spanish colonization, of legal ties of allegiance between the Sultan of Morocco and some of the tribes living in the territory of Western Sahara. They equally show the existence of rights, including some rights relating to the land, which constituted legal ties between the Mauritanian entity, as understood by the Court, and the territory of Western Sahara. On the other hand, the Court's conclusion is that the materials and information presented to it do not establish any tie of territorial sovereignty between the territory of Western Sahara and the Kingdom of Morocco or the Mauritanian

entity. Thus the Court has not found legal ties of such a nature as might affect the application of resolution 1514 (XV) in the decolonization of Western Sahara and, in particular, of the principle of self-determination through the free and genuine expression of the will of the peoples of the Territory (cf. paragraphs 54–59 above).

NOTES:

1. The concept of occupation was based on a notion of European hegemony over the 'uncivilised world'. Even if there were some inhabitants of a territory, it was still assumed that the territory was *terra nullius* if the inhabitants did not have obvious European forms of social or political institutions and so could be occupied. This concept of *terra nullius* was discredited in the *Western Sahara Opinion* (and see *Mabo* v *Queensland (No 2)* below).

2. With prescription, it is important that the sovereign actions be public and open, so that all interested States are aware of the actions and so, if appropriate, can protest. Though, as seen in the *Clipperton Island Case*, the amount of publicity given to the sovereign actions can be very limited.

B: Cession

Cession is the transfer of territory from one sovereign to another, usually by means of a treaty.

M. Davis, *Constitutional Confrontation in Hong Kong*
(1989), pp. 1, 136–137

In September of 1982 the British Prime Minister, Margaret Thatcher, reached agreement with Chinese leaders to 'enter into talks through diplomatic channels with the common aim of maintaining the stability and prosperity of Hong Kong'. While parts of the colony of Hong Kong had in the middle of the last century been ceded to Britain in perpetuity the largest section of the colony, the so called New Territories, was held under a lease that was due to expire in 1997. Protracted negotiations followed the 1982 announcement and resulted in the signing of the Sino-British Joint Declaration in 1984. Under the terms of the Joint Declaration China will resume sovereignty over the entire territory of Hong Kong on 1 July 1997. As suggested by the original 1982 announcement, the Joint Declaration seeks to maintain Hong Kong's stability and prosperity under a capitalist common law system and afford a high degree of autonomy. The Joint Declaration calls for the drafting by China of a Basic Law for Hong Kong to provide a framework or constitution for the future Hong Kong Special Administrative Region of the People's Republic of China [SAR], thus implementing China's announced policy of 'one country, two systems'. The final draft of the Basic Law has now been prepared and thus substantial movement towards Hong Kong's promised future has been made. . . .

The basis for this arrangement is thus a binding international agreement that provides for a level of self-government, constitutional democracy and foreign relations competence sufficient to ensure the successful operation of a capitalist region, even in the national context of a dramatically opposed Marxist-Leninist Chinese economic and political system. This is no small task and may demand more from autonomy than has ever been achieved before. Even the main cases for associated state status have not been marked by such contrast. It is in this context that the powers expressly afforded that bear on external support may exceed those often evident even with regard to associated states. It is difficult to imagine how anything less will achieve the policy objective.

In orchestrating the Joint Declaration's formula for Hong Kong, the Chinese government has in practice indicated a willingness to set aside many of the labels to which it is so strongly committed in rhetoric. In light of evolving notions of statehood and autonomy, they have taken the leading edge and contrived a formula designed to maintain adequate central control over foreign political and defence affairs, while otherwise permitting Hong Kong to conduct its own affairs. This formula aims to maintain the SAR in China's national orbit, and demonstrate the little which is demanded of the modern conception of sovereignty, while otherwise permitting Hong Kong to continue doing what it does well. . . .

On the positive side, the PRC is generally considered to have a good record for conformity to its treaty obligations unlike its purely domestic commitments. Nevertheless the rather liberal and inventive autonomy model evident in the Joint Declaration is generally inconsistent with Chinese policy and practice. Historically, the Chinese have rejected the internationalism implied by the Hong Kong formula in the Joint Declaration, a formula which preserves many aspects of Hong Kong's status as an international actor. Even committing this formula to an international treaty seems inconsistent with past practices. Historically, the Chinese have insisted on the inviolability and inalienability of national sovereignty. China has supported a positivist conception of sovereignty as the core of all fundamental principles of international law and as the foundation on which other international institutions and norms are based. Under this view, China would not invite international scrutiny of the Hong Kong formula or any other regional or human rights problem, such as that evident in Tibet. Such would be viewed as meddling in China's internal affairs.

In spite of this, the Joint Declaration at its heart seems to invite such scrutiny of the Hong Kong formula. Dr Roda Mushkat ['*Transition*', 14 Denver Jnl of International Law and Policy, p. 178] suggests that historically the Chinese have tacitly accepted a form of divided sovereignty over Hong Kong. Britain has 'effective sovereignty' while China has 'titular' or 'residual' sovereignty. The Joint Declaration and the draft Basic Law, therefore speak of 'resuming the exercise' of sovereignty. Nevertheless in its overall policy and practical content the Joint Declaration seems tacitly to continue this ambiguity. This creative ambiguity reflects a practical side of Chinese policy content.

Treaty on the Final Settlement With Respect to Germany
29 ILM 1186 (1990)

This treaty was entered into by France, the USSR, the United Kingdom and the United States, being the Four Powers which had rights and responsibilities over Berlin and Germany consequent upon the end of the Second World War, and also by the Federal Republic of Germany and the German Democratic Republic.

Article 1

1. The united Germany shall comprise the territory of the Federal Republic of Germany, the German Democratic Republic and the whole of Berlin. Its external borders shall be the borders of the Federal Republic of Germany and the German Democratic Republic and shall be definitive from the date on which the present Treaty comes into force. The confirmation of the definitive nature of the borders of the united Germany is an essential element of the peaceful order in Europe.

2. The united Germany and the Republic of Poland shall confirm the existing border between them in a treaty that is binding under international law.

3. The united Germany has no territorial claims whatsoever against other states and shall not assert any in the future.

4. The Governments of the Federal Republic of Germany and the German Democratic Republic shall ensure that the constitution of the united Germany does not contain any provision incompatible with these principles. This applies accordingly to the provisions laid down in the preamble, the second sentence of Article 23, and Article 146 of the Basic Law for the Federal Republic of Germany.

5. The Governments of the French Republic, the Union of Soviet Socialist Republics, the United Kingdom of Great Britain and Northern Ireland and the United States of America take formal note of the corresponding commitments and declarations by the Governments of the Federal Republic of Germany and the German Democratic Republic and declare that their implementation will confirm the definitive nature of the united Germany's borders.

Article 7

1. The French Republic, the Union of Soviet Socialist Republics, the United Kingdom of Great Britain and Northern Ireland and the United States of America hereby terminate their rights and responsibilities relating to Berlin and to Germany as a whole. As a result, the corresponding, related quadriparite agreements, decisions and practices are terminated and all related Four Power institutions are dissolved.

2. The united Germany shall have accordingly full sovereignty over its internal and external affairs.

NOTES:

1. Cession transfers all rights of sovereignty from one State to another. Yet the State transferring sovereignty cannot transfer more rights than it possesses. Due to the right of self-determination (see below and Chapter 6), now there is a requirement to consult the inhabitants of a territory before cession occurs.
2. The question of whether the 1898 treaties with China concerning Hong Kong are valid is considered in the section on Unequal Treaties in Chapter 3.
3. New states can acquire territory by succession, such as when the former Yugoslavia divided into separate States. This is discussed in Chapter 3.

C: Conquest

Conquest is the acquisition of territory by the use of force.

United Nations Charter
Declaration on Principles of International Law concerning Friendly Relations and Cooperation among States in Accordance with the Charter of the United Nations, General Assembly, Annex to Resolution 2625 (XXV), 24 October 1970

Article 2

4. All Members shall refrain in their international relations from the threat or use of force against the territorial integrity or political independence of any State, or in any other manner inconsistent with the Purposes of the United Nations.

Every State has the duty to refrain in its international relations from the threat or use of force against the territorial integrity or political independence of any State, or in any other manner inconsistent with the purposes of the United Nations. Such a threat or use of force constitutes a violation of international law and the Charter of the United Nations and shall never be employed as a means of settling international issues. . . .

The territory of a State shall not be the object of military occupation resulting from the use of force in contravention of the provisions of the Charter. The territory of a State shall not be the object of acquisition by another State resulting from the threat or use of force. No territorial acquisition resulting from the threat or use of force shall be recognized as legal. Nothing in the foregoing shall be construed as affecting:

(a) Provisions of the Charter or any international agreement prior to the Charter régime and valid under international law; or

(b) The powers of the Security Council under the Charter.

Security Council Resolution 662 (1990) adopted on 9 August 1990

The Security Council,

Recalling its resolutions 660 (1990) and 661 (1990),

Gravely alarmed by the declaration by Iraq of a 'comprehensive and eternal merger' with Kuwait,

Demanding, once again, that Iraq withdraw immediately and unconditionally all its forces to the positions in which they were located on 1 August 1990,

Determined to bring the occupation of Kuwait by Iraq to an end and to restore the sovereignty, independence and territorial integrity of Kuwait,

Determined also to restore the authority of the legitimate Government of Kuwait,

1. *Decides* that annexation of Kuwait by Iraq under any form and whatever pretext has no legal validity, and is considered null and void;

2. *Calls upon* all States, international organizations and specialized agencies not to recognize that annexation, and to refrain from any action or dealing that might be interpreted as an indirect recognition of the annexation;

3. *Further demands* that Iraq rescind its actions purporting to annex Kuwait;

4. *Decides* to keep this item on its agenda and to continue its efforts to put an early end to the occupation.

NOTES:

1. At least since the signing of the United Nations Charter, the use of force has been illegal in international law (see Chapter 13). Acquisitions of territory by force since that date are illegal and usually are condemned by the international community. Acquisitions of territory prior to that date are affected by 'intertemporal law'.

2. The doctrine of intertemporal law requires that sovereignty be considered in the light of the rules of international law that prevailed at the time at which the claim of sovereignty is based and not the rules of international law prevailing at the time the dispute is being adjudicated. While the creation of the entitlement to a territory is dependent on the rules of international law at the earlier time, it seems that the continued existence of that entitlement is dependent on the current rules of international law. This was made clear in the *Island of Palmas Case* (see below) where it was stated that 'a juridical fact must be appreciated in the light of the law contemporary with it, and not of the law in force at the time when a dispute in regard to it arises or falls to be settled. . . . [However] a distinction must be made between the creation of rights and the existence of rights. The same principle which subjects the act creative of a right to the law in force at the time the right arises, demands that the existence of [a] right, in other words, its continued manifestation, shall follow the conditions required by the evolution of law.'

SECTION 3: **Effective occupation**

Contemporary approaches to international law consider three primary matters with respect to sovereignty over territory: effective occupation, consent and the right of self-determination (see Chapter 6 for the latter). The main basis for establishing sovereignty over territory today is by effective occupation, being the continuous and peaceful display of sovereignty.

Island of Palmas Case (*The Netherlands* v *United States*)
2 RIAA (1928) 829, Huber, Sole Arbitrator

This dispute related to sovereignty over the Island of Palmas (or Miangas), just south of the Island of Mindanao in (present day) The Philippines. The United States' claim to the island was derived from Spain by way of cession under the Treaty of Paris 1898, and they relied, as successor to Spain, on acts of discovery, recognition by treaty and on contiguity. The Netherlands challenged this by relying on the historical connection between it and neighbouring States, of which the Island was a part, since about 1700, and on acts of sovereignty by The Netherlands since that date. The Arbitrator upheld the Netherlands' title to the Island.

Territorial sovereignty is, in general, a situation recognized and delimited in space, either by so-called natural frontiers as recognised by international law or by outward signs of delimitation that are undisputed, or else by legal engagements entered into between interested neighbours, such as frontier conventions, or by acts of recognition of States within fixed boundaries. If a dispute arises as to the sovereignty over a portion of territory, it is customary to examine which of the States claiming sovereignty possesses a title – cession, conquest, occupation, etc. – superior to that which the other State might possibly bring forward against it. However, if the contestation is based on the fact that the other Party has actually displayed sovereignty, it cannot be sufficient to establish the title by which territorial sovereignty was validly acquired at a certain moment; it must also be shown that the territorial sovereignty has continued to exist and did exist at the moment which for the decision of the dispute must be considered as critical. This demonstration consists in the actual display of State activities, such as belongs only to the territorial sovereign. . . .

Titles of acquisition of territorial sovereignty in present-day international law are either based on an act of effective apprehension, such as occupation or conquest, or, like cession, presuppose that the ceding and the cessionary Powers or at least one of them, have the faculty of effectively disposing of the ceded territory. In the same way natural accretion can only be conceived of as an accertion to a portion of territory where there exists an actual sovereignty capable of extending to a spot which falls within its sphere of activity. It seems therefore natural that an element which is essential for the constitution of sovereignty should not be lacking in its continuation. So true is this, that practice, as well as doctrine, recognizes – though under different legal formulae and with certain differences as to the conditions required – that the continuous and peaceful display of territorial sovereignty (peaceful in relation to other States) is as good as a title. The growing insistence with which international law, ever since the middle of the 18th century, has demanded that the occupation shall be effective would be inconceivable, if effectiveness were required only for the act of acquisition and not equally for the maintenance of the right. If the effectiveness has above all been insisted on in regard to occupation, this is because the question rarely arises in connection with territories in which there is already an established order of things. Just as before the rise of international law, boundaries of lands were necessarily determined by the fact that the power of a State was exercised within them, so too, under the reign of international law, the fact of peaceful and continuous display is still one of the most important considerations in establishing boundaries between States. . . .

[O]n the other hand the view is adopted that discovery does not create a definitive title of sovereignty, but only an "inchoate" title, such a title exists, it is true, without external manifestation. However, according to the view that has prevailed at any rate since the 19th century, an inchoate title of discovery must be completed within a reasonable period by the effective occupation of the region claimed to be discovered. This principle must be applied in the present case, for the reasons given above in regard to the rules determining which of successive legal systems is to be applied (the so-called intertemporal law). Now, no act of occupation nor, except as to a recent period, any exercise of sovereignty at Palmas by Spain has been alleged. But even admitting that the Spanish title still existed as inchoate in 1898 and must be considered as included in the cession under Article III of the Treaty of Paris, an inchoate title could not prevail over the continuous and peaceful display of authority by another State; for such display may prevail even over a prior, definitive title put forward by another State. . . .

Manifestations of territorial sovereignty assume, it is true, different forms, according to conditions of time and place. Although continuous in principle, sovereignty cannot be exercised in fact at every moment on every point of a territory. The intermittence and discontinuity compatible with the maintenance of the right necessarily differ according as inhabited or uninhabited regions are involved, or regions enclosed within territories in which sovereignty is incontestably displayed or again regions accessible from, for instance, the high seas. It is true that neighbouring States may by convention fix limits to their own sovereignty, even in regions such as the interior of scarcely explored continents where such sovereignty is scarcely manifested, and in this way each may prevent the other from any penetration of its territory. The delimitation of Hinterland may also be mentioned in this connection.

The United States base their claim on the titles of discovery, of recognition by treaty and of contiguity, i.e. titles relating to acts or circumstances leading to the acquisition of sovereignty; they have however not established the fact that sovereignty so acquired was effectively displayed at any time. The Netherlands on the contrary found their claim to sovereignty essentially on the title of peaceful and continuous display of State authority over the island. Since this title would in international law prevail over a title of acquistion of sovereignty not followed by actual display of State authority, it is necessary to ascertain in the first place, whether the contention of the Netherlands is sufficiently established by evidence, and, if so, for what period of time. . . .

The acts of the *East India Company* (Generale Geoctroyeerde Nederlandsch Oost-Indische Compagnie), in view of occupying or colonizing the regions at issue in the present affair must, in international law, be entirely assimilated to acts of the Netherlands State itself. From the end of the 16th till the 19th century, companies formed by individuals and engaged in economic pursuits (Chartered Companies), were invested by the State to whom they were subject with public powers for the acquisition and administration of colonies. The Dutch East India Company is one of the best known. . . .

As regards *contracts between a State* or a Company such as the Dutch East India Company and *native princes or chiefs of peoples* not recognized as members of the community of nations, they are not, in the international law sense, treaties or conventions capable of creating rights and obligations such as may, in international law, arise out of treaties. But, on the other hand, contracts of this nature are not wholly void of indirect effects on situations governed by international law; if they do not constitute titles in international law, they are none the less facts of which that law must in certain circumstances take account.

The title of discovery, if it had not been already disposed of by the Treaties of Münster and Utrecht would, under the most favourable and most extensive interpretation, exist only as an inchoate title, as a claim to establish sovereignty by effective occupation. An inchoate title however cannot prevail over a definite title founded on continuous and peaceful display of sovereignty. The title of contiguity, understood as a basis of territorial sovereignty, has no foundation in international law.

The title of recognition by treaty does not apply, because even if the Sangi States, with the dependency of Miangas, are to be considered as "held and possessed" by Spain in 1648, the rights of Spain to be derived from the Treaty of Münster would have been superseded by those which were acquired by the Treaty of Utrecht. Now if there is evidence of a state of possession in 1714 concerning the island of Palmas (or Miangas), such evidence is exclusively in favour of the Nether-lands. But even if the Treaty of Utrecht could not be taken into consideration, the acquiescence of Spain in the situation created after 1677 would deprive her and her successors of the possibility of still invoking conventional rights at the present time.

The Netherlands title of sovereignty, acquired by continous and peaceful display of State authority during a long period of time going probably back beyond the year 1700, therefore holds good.

Legal Status of Eastern Greenland Case (Norway v Denmark)

PCIJ Rep Ser A/B (1933) No 53, Permanent Court of International Justice

Norway occupied Eastern Greenland in July 1931, claiming that it was *terra nul-lius*, while Denmark insisted that Danish sovereignty existed over all Greenland from about 1721, at the time when Denmark and Norway were one State. The Court determined that Denmark had a valid title to Eastern Greenland.

Before proceeding to consider in detail the evidence submitted to the Court, it may be well to state that a claim to sovereignty based not upon some particular act or title such as a treaty of cession but merely upon continued display of authority, involves two elements each of which must be shown to exist: the intention and will to act as sovereign, and some actual exercise or display of such authority.

Another circumstance which must be taken into account by any tribunal which has to adjudicate upon a claim to sovereignty over a particular territory, is the extent to which the sovereignty is also claimed by some other Power. In most of the cases involving claims to territorial sovereignty which have come before an international tribunal, there have been two competing claims to the sover-eignty, and the tribunal has had to decide which of the two is the stronger. One of the peculiar features of the present case is that up to 1931 there was no claim by any Power other than Denmark to the sovereignty over Greenland. Indeed, up till 1921, no Power disputed the Danish claim to sovereignty.

It is impossible to read the records of the decisions in cases as to territorial sovereignty without observing that in many cases the tribunal has been satisfied with very little in the way of the actual exercise of sovereign rights, provided that the other State could not make out a superior claim. This is particularly true in the case of claims to sovereignty over areas in thinly populated or unsettled countries. . . . Legislation is one of the most obvious forms of the exercise of sovereign power. . . .

The conclusion to which the Court is led is that, bearing in mind the absence of any claim to sovereignty by another Power, and the Arctic and inaccessible character of the uncolonized parts of the country, the King of Denmark and Norway displayed during the period from the founding of the colonies by Hans Egede in 1721 up to 1814 his authority to an extent sufficient to give his country a valid claim to sovereignty, and that his rights over Greenland were not limited to the colonized area. . . . The result of all the documents connected with the grant of the [trading, hunting and mining] concession is to show that, on the one side, it was granted upon the footing that the King of Denmark was in a position to grant a valid monopoly on the East coast and that his sovereign rights entitled him to do so, and, on the other, that the concessionnaires in England regarded the grant of a monopoly as essential to the success of their projects and had no doubt as to the validity of the rights conferred. . . .

The concessions granted for the erection of telegraph lines and the legislation fixing the limits of territorial waters in 1905 are also manifestations of the exercise of sovereign authority.

In view of the above facts, when taken in conjunction with the legislation she had enacted applicable to Greenland generally, the numerous treaties in which Denmark, with the concurrence of the other contracting Party, provided for the non-application of the treaty to Greenland in general, and the absence of all claim to sovereignty over Greenland by any other Power, Denmark must be regarded as having displayed during this period of 1814 to 1915 her authority over the uncolonized part of the country to a degree sufficient to confer a valid title to the sovereignty.

NOTES:
1. It is clear that effective occupation or 'the continuous and peaceful display of territorial sovereignty . . . is a good as title' (see *Island of Palmas*, above). However, what number of sovereign acts are needed will depend on the nature of the territory, with thinly populated, inhospitable or uninhabited territory, such as in the *Eastern Greenland Case*, requiring very few acts.
2. The amount of evidence of effective occupation that is necessary for a State to show also depends, like all claims to territory, on the existence and nature of rival claims. Title to territory is, after all, relative not absolute.
3. The evidence of sovereign acts to show effective occupation must be acts by States or attributable to States. This would usually include acts by a State's military forces, legislation, administrative actions, treaties and the conduct of legal proceedings. Occasionally acts by private individuals or corporations can be attributable to a State, as happened in the *Island of Palmas Case*. The key issue is whether their actions are attributable to a State and there is an intention to act as a sovereign over that territory: see *Ethiopia/Eritrea* Boundary Commission decision 13 April 2002.
4. The effect of the doctrine of intertemporal law (see 2.(iii) above) was seen in the outcome of the *Island of Palmas Case*. The United States' main claim was based on discovery (by Spain, from which the United States had title by cession), a valid basis for title to territory (or at least an 'inchoate' title) in earlier centuries. However, the evidence showed that it was The Netherlands, by its sovereign acts, which had shown that it was in effective occupation during the relevant period. These acts, as being consistent with the current rules of international law, were held to prevail over even a prior definitive title, and so The Netherlands' claim succeeded.

SECTION 4: **Consent by other States**

As sovereignty over territory is determined on the basis of relative title, the acts of the other party, as well as the acts of the international community, in respect of the disputed territory, must be relevant.

A: Consent by the other party to the dispute

Temple of Preah Vihear Case (*Cambodia* v *Thailand*) (*Merits*)
ICJ Rep 1962 6, International Court of Justice

Cambodia claimed, as successor to France, sovereignty over an area of land which included the Temple of Preah Vihear. One of the key pieces of evidence upon which Cambodia relied was a map made in 1907 that showed the temple to be in French territory, and that map was sent to the authorities of Siam (now Thailand) (see also Chapter 3). The Court found that the Temple was situated in Cambodian territory.

It has been contended on behalf of Thailand that this communication of the maps by the French authorities was, so to speak, *ex parte*, and that no formal acknowledgment of it was either requested of, or given by, Thailand. In fact, as will be seen presently, an acknowledgment by conduct was undoubtedly made in a very definite way; but even if it were otherwise, it is clear that the circumstances were such as called for some reaction, within a reasonable period, on the part of the

Siamese authorities, if they wished to disagree with the map or had any serious question to raise in regard to it. They did not do so, either then or for many years, and thereby must be held to have acquiesced. . . .

The Court moreover considers that there is no legal foundation for the consequence it is attempted to deduce from the fact that no one in Thailand at that time may have known of the importance of the Temple or have been troubling about it. Frontier rectifications cannot in law be claimed on the ground that a frontier area has turned out to have an importance not known or suspected when the frontier was established.

It follows from the preceding findings that the Siamese authorities in due course received the Annex I map and that they accepted it. Now, however, it is contended on behalf of Thailand, so far as the disputed area of Preah Vihear is concerned, that an error was committed, an error of which the Siamese authorities were unaware at the time when they accepted the map.

It is an established rule of law that the plea of error cannot be allowed as an element vitiating consent if the party advancing it contributed by its own conduct to the error, or could have avoided it, or if the circumstances were such as to put that party on notice of a possible error. The Court considers that the character and qualifications of the persons who saw the Annex I map on the Siamese side would alone make it difficult for Thailand to plead error in law. These persons included the members of the very Commission of Delimitation within whose competence this sector of the frontier had lain. But even apart from this, the Court thinks that there were other circumstances relating to the Annex I map which make the plea of error difficult to receive.

An inspection indicates that the map itself drew such pointed attention to the Preah Vihear region that no interested person, nor anyone charged with the duty of scrutinizing it, could have failed to see what the map was purporting to do in respect of that region. . . . much the most significant episode consisted of the visit paid to the Temple in 1930 by Prince Damrong, formerly Minister of the Interior, and at this time President of the Royal Institute of Siam, charged with duties in connection with the National Library and with archaeological monuments. The visit was part of an archaelogical tour made by the Prince with the permission of the King of Siam, and it clearly had a quasi-official character. When the Prince arrived at Preah Vihear, he was officially received there by the French Resident for the adjoining Cambodian province, on behalf of the Resident Superior, with the French flag flying. The Prince could not possibly have failed to see the implications of a reception of this character. A clearer affirmation of title on the French Indo-Chinese side can scarcely be imagined. It demanded a reaction. Thailand did nothing. Furthermore, when Prince Damrong on his return to Bangkok sent the French Resident some photographs of the occasion, he used language which seems to admit that France, through her Resident, had acted as the host country.

The explanations regarding Prince Damrong's visit given on behalf of Thailand have not been found convincing by the Court. Looking at the incident as a whole, it appears to have amounted to a tacit recognition by Siam of the sovereignty of Cambodia (under French Protectorate) over Preah Vihear, through a failure to react in any way, on an occasion that called for a reaction in order to affirm or preserve title in the face of an obvious rival claim. What seems clear is that either Siam did not in fact believe she had any title – and this would be wholly consistent with her attitude all along, and thereafter, to the Annex I map and line – or else she decided not to assert it, which again means that she accepted the French claim, or accepted the frontier at Preah Vihear as it was drawn on the map.

B: Consent by other States

Legal Status of Eastern Greenland Case (*Norway* v *Denmark*)
PCIJ Rep Ser A/B (1933) No 53, Permanent Court of International Justice

The facts are set out above.

In order to establish the Danish contention that Denmark has exercised in fact sovereignty over all Greenland for a long time, Counsel for Denmark have laid stress on the long series of conventions – mostly commercial in character – which have been concluded by Denmark and in which, with the concurrence of the other contracting Party, a stipulation has been inserted to the effect that the convention shall not apply to Greenland. In the case of multilateral treaties, the stipulation usually takes the form of a Danish reserve at the time of signature. In date, these conventions cover the period from 1782 onwards. As pointed out in the earlier part of the judgment, the exclusion of Greenland is, with one exception, made without qualification. In that case alone it is 'the Danish colonies in Greenland' to which the treaty is not to apply. In many of these cases, the wording is quite specific; for instance, Article 6 of the Treaty of 1826 with the United States of America: 'The present Convention shall not apply to the Northern possessions of His Majesty the King of Denmark, that is to say Iceland, the Faerö Islands and Greenland. . . .'

The importance of these treaties is that they show a willingness on the part of the States with which Denmark has contracted to admit her right to exclude Greenland. To some of these treaties, Norway has herself been a Party, and these must be dealt with later because they are relied on by Denmark as constituting binding admissions by Norway that Greenland is subject to Danish sovereignty. For the purpose of the present argument, the importance of these conventions, with whatever States they have been concluded, is due to the support which they lend to the Danish argument that Denmark possesses sovereignty over Greenland as a whole. . . .

If the Parties were agreed that the treaty was not to apply in a particular area and the area is only designated by name, the natural conclusion is that no difference existed between them as to the extent of the area which that name covered. . . .

To the extent that these treaties constitute evidence of recognition of her sovereignty over Greenland in general, Denmark is entitled to rely upon them. These treaties may also be regarded as demonstrating sufficiently Denmark's will and intention to exercise sovereignty over Greenland.

C: Consent by the international community

Q. Wright, 'The Goa Incident'
56 AJIL 617 (1962)

This incident concerned the actions by India in December 1961 in occupying the Portuguese colonies of Goa, Damao and Diu on the western coast of the Indian sub-continent. A Security Resolution condemning India's use of force was vetoed by the USSR, with three other members of the Security Council voting against it.

The significant feature, however, of the Goa situation was that many of the new states, and also the Soviet Union, felt that colonialism was such an evil that the use of force to eliminate it should be tolerated. The argument was, in fact, political and moral rather than legal. . . .

Throughout Asia and Africa it is argued that ex-colonial peoples cannot be expected to accept the validity of the claims of colonial Powers to overseas territories acquired and maintained by force, on the theory, prevalent in the age of discoveries, that territories not in the possession of a Christian prince were "*territorium nullius*" subject to acquisition by Papal grant or by discovery and occupation without regard to the wishes of the native inhabitants. These peoples, it is argued, submitted because of military weakness, but never accepted the justifying theories of European jurists. . . .

The argument is, therefore, supported by the principle that positive international law rests on the express or tacit consent of the states bound by it. While European Powers may have recognized a customary rule permitting the acquisition of non-Christian territory by discovery and occupation, the rulers and peoples of such territories never recognized such a rule. . . . The conclusion seems to be that no action is likely to be taken by the United Nations, in which case the states of the world will, doubtless, recognize or acquiesce in the Indian annexation of Goa.

It should be noted that while individual recognition of the fruits of aggression is forbidden by Charter principles, as it was by the Stimson Doctrine of 1932, the United Nations itself may recognize a situation which it regards as, on the whole, beneficial, even if this situation originated in illegality.

NOTES:
1. Other States can consent to sovereignty by a claimant State either by positive actions, such as by recognition or by ratification of a treaty (as in the *Eastern Greenland Case*), or by acquiescence, where there is a failure to protest in a situation where some kind of reaction signifying objection is called for (as in the *Temple Case*). In the situation of Goa, the international community acknowledged Indian sovereignty, even though illegally obtained, over time, with Portugal itself recognising Indian sovereignty in 1974.
2. Consent by other States affects a State's claim to title to a territory in two main ways: it can mean that the other claimant State is precluded from denying the opposing State's title; or it can provide strong external evidence to support a State's claim. The role of consent by State is also important in understanding the nature of international law (see Chapter 1).

SECTION 5: **Limitations on sovereignty over territory**

A: The right of self-determination

The right of self-determination has a major impact on sovereignty over territory. The extent and application of the right are explained in Chapter 6 and *must* be considered in any issue of sovereignty over territory.

B: *Uti possidetis juris*

Uti possidetis juris, being the principle that colonial boundaries are maintained on independence, was also explained in Chapter 6 in the context of the right of self-determination (see especially the *Frontier Dispute Case* ICJ Rep 1986 554). This principle has an impact on the determination of territorial disputes.

Case Concerning the Land, Island and Maritime Frontier Dispute
(El Salvador v Honduras; Nicaragua intervening)
ICJ Rep 1992 355, Chamber of the International Court of Justice

The dispute between El Salvador and Honduras (for which Nicaragua was allowed to intervene – see Chapter 14) concerned the Gulf of Fonseca: the land around it;

the islands in it; and the waters of and beyond it. The aspect which is extracted here concerns the general issues of the land boundary dispute.

42. Thus the principle of *uti possidetis juris* is concerned as much with title to territory as with the location of boundaries; certainly a key aspect of the principle is the denial of the possibility of *terra nullius*.

43. To apply this principle is not so easy when, as in Spanish Central America, there were administrative boundaries of different kinds or degrees. . . . Besides, in addition to the various civil territorial jurisdictions, general or special, there were the ecclesiastical jurisdictions, which were supposed to be followed in principle, pursuant to general legislation, by the territorial jurisdiction of the main civil administrative units in Spanish America; such adjustment often needed, however, a certain span of time within which to materialize. . . . Moreover it has to be remembered that no question of international boundaries could ever have occurred to the minds of those servants of the Spanish Crown who established administrative boundaries; *uti possidetis juris* is essentially a retrospective principle, investing as international boundaries administrative limits intended originally for quite other purposes. . . .

57. As already mentioned above, El Salvador contends that the *uti possidetis juris* principle is the primary but not the only, legal element to be taken into consideration for the determination of the land boundary. It has put forward in addition in that respect a body of arguments referred to either as 'arguments of a human nature' or as arguments based on '*effectivités*'.

58. The factual considerations which El Salvador has brought to the attention of the Chamber fall into two categories. On the one hand, there are arguments and material relating to demographic pressures in El Salvador creating a need for territory, as compared with the relatively sparsely populated Honduras; and on the other the superior natural resources (e.g., water for agriculture and hydroelectric power) said to be enjoyed by Honduras. On the first point, El Salvador apparently does not claim that a frontier deriving from the principle of the *uti possidetis juris* could be adjusted subsequently (except by agreement) on the grounds of unequal population density, and this is clearly right. It will be recalled that the Chamber in the *Frontier Dispute* case emphasized that even equity *infra legem*, a recogised concept of international law, could not be resorted to in order to modify an established frontier inherited from colonization, whatever its deficiencies (see *ICJ Reports 1986*, p. 633, para. 149). El Salvador claims that such an inequality existed even before independence, and that its ancient possession of the territories in dispute, 'based on historic titles, is also based on reasons of crucial human necessity'. The Chamber will not lose sight of this dimension of the matter; but it is one without direct legal incidence. For the *uti possidetis juris*, the question is not whether the colonial province needed wide boundaries to accommodate its population, but where those boundaries actually were; and post-independence *effectivités*, where relevant, have to be assessed in terms of actual events, not their social origins. As to the argument of inequality of natural resources, the Court, in the case concerning the *Continental Shelf* (*Tunisia/Libyan Arab Jamahiriya*), took the view that economic considerations of this kind could not be taken into account for the delimitation of the continental shelf areas appertaining to two States (*ICJ Reports 1982*, p. 77, para. 107); still less can they be relevant for the determination of a land frontier which came into existence on independence. . . .

61. Both parties have invoked, in relation to this claim of El Salvador, the analysis in the Judgment of the Chamber of the Court in the *Frontier Dispute* case of the relationship between 'titles' and '*effectivités*' (*I.C.J. Reports 1986*, pp. 586–587, para. 63). The passage in question reads as follows:

> The role played in this case by such *effectivités* is complex, and the Chamber will have to weigh carefully the legal force of these in each particular instance. It must however state forthwith, in general terms, what legal relationship exists between such acts and the titles on which the implementation of the principle of *uti possidetis* is grounded. For this

purpose, a distinction must be drawn among several eventualities. Where the act corresponds exactly to law, where effective administration is additional to the *uti possidetis juris*, the only role of *effectivité* is to confirm the exercise of the right derived from a legal title. Where the act does not correspond to the law, where the territory which is the subject of the dispute is effectively administered by a State other than the one possessing the legal title, preference should be given to the holder of the title. In the event that the *effectivité* does not co-exist with any legal title, it must invariably be taken into consideration. Finally, there are cases where the legal title is not capable of showing exactly the territorial expanse to which it relates. The *effectivités* can then play an essential role in showing how the title is interpreted in practice. (*ICJ Reports 1986*, pp. 586–587, para. 63.)

62. With regard to the interrelation of title and *effectivité*, it should however be borne in mind that the *titulos* submitted to the Chamber by both Parties, including the 'formal title-deeds to commons' are not what are here referred to as 'the titles on which the implementation of the principle of *uti possidetis* is grounded'; as already explained, they can be compared to 'colonial *effectivités*', to the extent that they are acts of effective administration by the colonial authorities, not acts of private individuals. What the Chamber has to do in respect of the land frontier is to arrive at a conclusion as to the position of the 1821 *uti possidetis juris* boundary; to this end it cannot but take into account, for reasons already explained, the colonial *effectivités* as reflected in the documentary evidence of the colonial period submitted by the Parties. The Chamber may have regard also, in certain instances, to documentary evidence of post-independence *effectivités* when it considers that they afford indications in respect of the 1821 *uti possidetis juris* boundary, providing a relationship exists between the *effectivités* concerned and the determination of that boundary. . . .

67. . . . [T]he *uti possidetis juris* position can be qualified in other ways, for example, by acquiescence or recognition. There seems to be no reason in principle why these factors should not operate, where there is sufficient evidence to show that the parties have in effect clearly accepted a variation, or at least an interpretation, of the *uti possidetis juris* position.

M. Shaw, 'Case Concerning the Land, Island and Maritime Frontier Dispute . . .',
(1993) 42 ICLQ 929, pp. 931–933

The Chamber proceeded to examine in great detail each of the six disputed sectors of the land boundary. Several significant points arise as a result of this careful analysis that are worthy of brief mention.

First, the Chamber does appear to have established a clear threshold for the relevance or sufficiency of *effectivités*. On several occasions the Chamber dismissed varieties of practice as insufficient to be capable of affecting the decision. Without analysing in detail all such situations, it is not possible to determine whether the Chamber has been unduly restrictive in practice here, but there is no doubt that the test for sufficiency of *effectivités* remains to be elucidated.

Second, the Chamber seems to have paid particular attention to the role of *effectivités* in the context of establishing the acquiescence of one of the parties to the assertion of control by the other. It was emphasised that the Chamber did not consider that the effect of the application of the principle of *uti possidetis juris* was to freeze for all time the provincial boundaries which at the moment of independence became international boundaries. The States themselves could by agreement vary such boundaries. Additionally, 'some forms of activity, or inactivity, might amount to acquiescence in a boundary other than that of 1821' [at p. 408]. The Chamber found in one particular section that the conduct of Honduras from 1881 to 1972 (when a claim to the area appears first to have been made) amounted to such acquiescence.

In addition, in the context of a discussion of the legal situation of the islands, the Chamber noted in an important statement [at p. 565].

Where the relevant administrative boundary was ill-defined or its position disputed . . . the behaviour of the two newly independent states in the years following independence may well serve as a guide to where the boundary was, either in their shared view, or in the view acted on by one and acquiesced in by the other.

Third, the Chamber returned to the sensitive issue of the role of equity in boundary and territorial disputes – and not for the last time, it is suggested. It noted that where the line of the *uti possidetis juris* boundary could not be determined in a particular area, it was considered right to fall back upon equity *infra legem* and this in the specific context of an unratified delimitation arrived at in 1869, which could, therefore, be taken into account here. However, the Chamber wisely emphasised that grounds of unequal population density, for example, could not amount to a basis for changing an established frontier inherited from colonisation, whatever its deficiencies.

Fourth, it is interesting to note the comments by the Chamber with regard to the relevance of geographical features. The Chamber noted that where no conclusion unambiguously pointing to another boundary emerges from the documentary material, 'the suitability of topographical features to provide a readily identifiable and convenient boundary is a material aspect' [at p. 422] While this approach is relatively uncontentious as such, one must be extremely careful in not extending this hopefully modest expression. We are very far from the days of claimed natural frontiers, which always appeared to be on the far side of the border, and the dangers of permitting a form of geographical irredentism are too obvious to ignore.

NOTES:

1. The Chamber of the International Court of Justice in the *Land, Island and Maritime Dispute Case* was aware of the problem in using the principle of *uti possidetis* to form international boundaries from divisions of territory based on administrative convenience. But this principle, combined with issues of a general historical nature, can place limitations on determinations of sovereignty over territory.

2. Shaw comments on the interaction between the principles of *uti possidetis* and of *effectivités* and clarified the many issues of evidence which a court is required to weigh up in any territory boundary dispute.

3. In the *Case Concerning the Territorial Dispute* (*Libya* v *Chad*) ICJ Rep 1994 6 the Court stressed that there was a 'fundamental principle of the stability of boundaries' (para 72) and, accordingly, the terms of a treaty agreeing a boundary will be upheld as far as possible.

C: Indigenous people

The International Court of Justice in the *Western Sahara Opinion* (above) noted (at para. 80) that 'territories inhabited by tribes or peoples having a social and political organisation were not regarded as *terra nullius*'. This decision, and other matters, have had an impact on the claims of many indigenous peoples, particularly those where no treaty (or similar agreement) was entered into by a colonial power.

Mabo v *Queensland* (*No 2*)
(1992) 175 CLR 1, High Court of Australia

This case raised many issues of the continuing existence of native title and associated rights to land in Australia. No acts of cession or conquest had occurred on the particular islands in dispute (being the Murray Islands in the Torres Strait between Australia and Papua New Guinea) as they had been annexed by the application of common law and statute by the State of Queensland in the federation of Australia. The High Court decided, by 6:1, that native title did continue to exist in these circumstances.

BRENNAN J [with whom Mason CJ and McHugh J agreed]: Although the question whether a territory has been acquired by the Crown is not justiciable before municipal courts, those courts have jurisdiction to determine the consequences of an acquisition under municipal law. Accordingly, the municipal courts must determine the body of law which is in force in the new territory. By the common law, the law in force in a newly-acquired territory depends on the manner of its acquisition by the Crown. Although the manner in which a sovereign state might acquire new territory is a matter for international law, the common law has had to march in step with international law in order to provide the body of law to apply in a territory newly acquired by the Crown.

International law recognized conquest, cession, and occupation of territory that was terra nullius as three of the effective ways of acquiring sovereignty. No other way is presently relevant. The great voyages of European discovery opened to European nations the prospect of occupying new and valuable territories that were already inhabited. As among themselves, the European nations parcelled out the territories newly discovered to the sovereigns of the respective discoverers, provided the discovery was confirmed by occupation and provided the indigenous inhabitants were not organized in a society that was united permanently for political action. To these territories the European colonial nations applied the doctrines relating to acquisition of territory that was terra nullius. They recognized the sovereignty of the respective European nations over the territory of 'backward peoples' and, by State practice, permitted the acquisition of sovereignty of such territory by occupation rather than by conquest. . . . The enlarging of the concept of terra nullius by international law to justify the acquisition of inhabited territory by occupation on behalf of the acquiring sovereign raised some difficulties in the expounding of the common law doctrines as to the law to be applied when inhabited territories were acquired by occupation (or 'settlement', to use the term of the common law). . . .

It is one thing for our contemporary law to accept that the laws of England, so far as applicable, became the laws of New South Wales and of the other Australian colonies. It is another thing for our contemporary law to accept that, when the common law of England became the common law of the several colonies, the theory which was advanced to support the introduction of the common law of England accords with our present knowledge and appreciation of the facts. When it was sought to apply Lord Watson's assumption in *Cooper* v *Stuart* that the colony of New South Wales was 'without settled inhabitants or settled law' to Aboriginal society in the Northern Territory, the assumption proved false. In *Milirrpum* v *Nabalco Pty Ltd* Blackburn J said ((1971) 17 FLR 141 at 267)

> The evidence shows a subtle and elaborate system highly adapted to the country in which the people led their lives, which provided a stable order of society and was remarkably free from the vagaries of personal whim or influence. If ever a system could be called 'a government of laws, and not of men' it is that shown in the evidence before me. . . .

The theory of terra nullius has been critically examined in recent times by the International Court of Justice in its *Advisory Opinion on Western Sahara* . . . If the international law notion that inhabited land may be classified as terra nullius no longer commands general support, the doctrines of the common law which depend on the notion that native peoples may be 'so low in the scale of social organization' that it is 'idle to impute to such people some shadow of the rights known to our law' [In *re Southern Rhodesia* [1919] AC 211 at pp. 233–234] can hardly be retained. If it were permissible in past centuries to keep the common law in step with international law, it is imperative in today's world that the common law should neither be nor be seen to be frozen in an age of racial discrimination.

The fiction by which the rights and interests of indigenous inhabitants in land were treated as non-existent was justified by a policy which has no place in the contemporary law of this country. . . . Whatever the justification advanced in earlier days for refusing to recognize the rights and interests in land of the indigenous inhabitants of settled colonies, and unjust and discriminatory doctrine of that kind can no longer be accepted. The expectations of the international community accord in this respect with the contemporary values of the Australian people. The opening up of international remedies to individuals pursuant to Australia's accession to the Optional Protocol to the International Covenant on Civil and Political Rights brings to bear on the common law the powerful influence of the Covenant and the international standards it imports. The common law does not necessarily conform with international law, but international law is a legitimate and important influence on the development of the common law, especially when international law declares the existence of universal human rights. A common law doctrine founded on unjust discrimination in the enjoyment of civil and political rights demands reconsideration. It is contrary both to international standards and to the fundamental values of our common law to entrench a discriminatory rule which, because of the supposed position on the scale of social organization of the indigenous inhabitants of a settled colony, denies them a right to occupy their traditional lands.

Draft Declaration on the Rights of Indigenous People 1994
34 ILM 541 (1995)

This Declaration was drafted under the auspices of the United Nations Commission on Human Rights by representatives of both indigenous peoples and States. It has not yet been accepted by the State members of the General Assembly but a number of its provisions reflect possible ways forward in international law's response to indigenous peoples.

Article 31
Indigenous peoples, as a specific form of exercising their right to self-determination, have the right to autonomy or self-government in matters relating to their internal and local affairs, including culture, religion, education, information, media, health, housing, employment, social welfare, economic activities, land and resources management, environment and entry by non-members, as well as ways and means for financing these autonomous functions.

D: International territorial administration

States are not the only entities that can control territory. Territory can be controlled by non-State actors, such as armed opposition groups and national liberation movements (see Chapter 5), as well as by international organisations, the latter of which has a form of sovereignty over the territory.

R. Wilde, 'From Danzig to East Timor and Beyond: The Role of International Territorial Administration'
95 AJIL 583 (2001), pp. 584–587

To understand the official purposes of granting administrative control over territory to international organizations, one must appreciate how such control operates. In certain circumstances, states hand over responsibility for running camps, housing refugees and/ or internally displaced persons (refugee camps) to UNHCR [United Nations High Commissioner for Refugees]. . . . These camps resemble small cities where education, medical services, and basic infrastructure are provided by a network of international agencies under the control of UNHCR. More generally, UN agencies, notably the World Food Programme, implement programs of material assistance in a variety of places. . . . In Bosnia and Herzegovina, the OHR [Office of the High Representative of the International Community], created by the 1995 Dayton Agreement [Agreement on Peace in Bosnia and Herzegovina], has interpreted its vague powers in that Agreement to encompass various governmental acts, including the passing of laws and the dismissal of elected officials. . . . In June 1999, the United Nations Mission in Kosovo (UNMIK) was created to provide an 'interim administration' in that territory. In the same year, the United Nations Mission in East Timor (UNAMET) conducted a popular consultation on East Timor's future status, and the United Nations Transitional Authority in East Timor (UNTAET) was later created to administer the territory until independence.

Each project involves a claim made by an international organization relating to territorial administration. Here, 'territorial administration' refers to a formally constituted, locally based management structure operating with respect to a particular territorial unit; it can be limited (e.g., a territorial program concerned with certain matters) or plenary (e.g., a territorial government) in scope. The international organization asserts the right either to supervise and control the operation of this structure by local actors, or to operate the structure directly. The right is exercised from within the territory, and can pertain to the structure as a whole, or certain parts of it (e.g., the legislature). This activity should be contrasted with merely monitoring and/or assisting local actors in operating such a structure, although the distinction is sometimes difficult to make in practice, particularly in the case of conduct and assistance. The spatial identity of the international organization and its officials – as 'international' – is distinct from and opposed to the 'local' identity of the territorial unit and population affected, even if the organization's activities are limited to that territory and some of the 'internationals' are actually local nationals. This divergence between the two spatial identities marks the projects off from the European Communities [EC]. There, the EC institutions share the same spatial identity as the legal order in respect of which they perform administrative functions (even if this legal order cuts across the distinct legal orders of member states). Similarly, although the enjoyment of privileges and immunities in state territory gives international organizations near-exclusive administrative competence by default, such competence usually covers only the property and personnel of the organization (the provision of consular protection is similarly limited). . . .

International organizations first exercised territorial administration in the Free City of Danzig, where the League of Nations enjoyed certain governmental prerogatives from 1920 to 1939. In addition, the League administered the German Saar Basin (the Saar) between 1920 and 1935, and the Colombian town and district of Leticia (Leticia) from 1933 to 1934. It also appointed the president of the Upper Silesia Mixed Commission in 1922 and the chair of the Memel Harbor board in Lithuania in 1924. Immediately after the Second World War, Germany and Austria were administered by the Allies. With the creation of the United Nations, the new international organization was authorized in 1947 to exercise certain governmental powers in what would have become the Free Territory of Trieste, but the free territory plan was never realized.

The United Nations first exercised territorial administration in the 1960s, asserting various administrative prerogatives in the Congo between 1960 and 1964, and administering West Irian for seven months between 1962 and 1963. In 1967, the UN Council for what was then South West Africa (later Namibia) was established to administer the territory, but South Africa prevented the Council from taking up this role. Over twenty years later, in 1991 the United Nations was authorized to perform administrative functions in Western Sahara and Cambodia; although these functions were exercised in Cambodia from 1991 to 1992, they are yet to be fully performed in Western Sahara. From 1994 to 1996, a different institution – the EUAM – administered the city of Mostar in Bosnia and Herzegovina. Then, as part of the Dayton process, the territory of Eastern Slavonia, Baranja, and Western Sirmium (Eastern Slavonia) in Croatia was placed under UN administration from 1996 to 1998. In some of the aforementioned missions, and in others as well, the mandates of international organizations have called for the performance of two particular administrative functions: controlling or conducting some form of territory-wide popular consultation and/or 'community building' through the creation of local institutions.

ITA [International Territorial Administration] . . . is seen as a substitute for territorial administration as it is 'normally' practiced: by actors whose spatial identity, as local, corresponds to that of the territorial unit and its population. ITA has been and is being used as a device to replace local actors in the activity of administration either partially or fully, because of two perceived problems with the 'normal' model. In the first place, ITA is used to respond to a perceived sovereignty problem with the presence of local actors exercising control over the territory. In the second place, ITA is used to respond to a perceived governance problem with the conduct of governance by local actors. The first problem concerns the identity of the local actors being excluded from administration; the second problem concerns the quality of governance being exercised in the territory.

NOTES:

1. International law, like most law, responds to changes in society – political, ideological and moral – as seen in the way conquest has become an illegal mode of acquisition (see inter-temporal law, above). By denigrating the indigenous peoples' way of life, colonial powers (and even independent States) could claim that certain territory was *terra nullius* and so able to be occupied with minimal acts of sovereignty being necessary. As understanding and concern for indigenous peoples has increased, so have the challenges to the laws imposed on those peoples by the colonial powers. This challenge has been primarily before national courts.

2. The decision in *Mabo* v *Queensland (No 2)* (above) led to significant changes in the Australian legislation dealing with land (and other) rights of indigenous peoples. Similar case law – and resulting changes to legislation – has occurred elsewhere, particularly in New Zealand, Canada and the United States. In each State, the national courts have referred to international law developments in the protection of indigenous peoples. Some of these developments are discussed in Chapter 6.

3. Some protection for the inhabitants of a territory was intended by the League of Nations Mandate system, which was carried forward by the Trusteeship system of the United Nations. The main provisions of the United Nations system (Article 73 of the United Nations Charter) are set out in Chapter 6. The International Court of Justice had to consider the Trusteeship system in the *Case Concerning Certain Phosphate Lands in Nauru (Australia* v *Nauru)* ICJ Rep 1992 240. It is clear (from para 30 of the preliminary objections judgment) that the termination of a Trust by the General Assembly does not necessarily discharge all responsibilities of the State administering the Trust towards the inhabitants of the Trust territory. The Draft Declaration is another step in this (slow) process.

4. Control of territory by international organisations, particularly the United Nations, is a form of sovereignty over the territory. In relation to the United Nations operations in Kosovo and East Timor, a UN report said:

    These operations face challenges and responsibilities that are unique among United Nations field operations. No other operation must set and enforce the law, establish customs services and regulations, set and collect business and personal taxes, attract foreign investment, adjudicate property disputes and liabilities for war damage, reconstruct and operate all public utilities, creat a banking system, run schools and pay teachers, and collect the garbage (Brahimi Report on UN Peace Operations (UN Doc A/55/305-S/2000/809, para 77, 21 August 2000)).

    International administration of territory has a number of purposes (as Wilde indicates above), however it is unclear to what extent this type of administration has international legal responsibility for its actions compared to State responsibility (see Chapter 11).

SECTION 6: **Other territory**

A: Antarctica

'Map of National Claims in Antarctica' in G. Triggs, *The Antarctic Treaty Regime: Law, Environment and Resources*
(1987)

(see page 259)

The Antarctic Treaty 1959
UNTS 402 (1961) 71

The original parties to this Treaty were Argentina, Australia, Chile, France, New Zealand, Norway and the United Kingdom, each of whom asserted a claim of sovereignty to part or parts (including some overlapping claims) of Antarctica, together with Belgium, Japan, South Africa, the USSR and the United States. As at 1 July 2002 there are 45 State parties to this Treaty, with some having only 'observer' status. Regular meetings occur between the parties to the Treaty.

Article I
    1. Antarctica shall be used for peaceful purposes only. There shall be prohibited, *inter alia*, any measures of a military nature, such as the establishment of military bases and fortifications, the carrying out of military manoeuvres as well as the testing of any type of weapons.
    2. The present Treaty shall not prevent the use of military personnel or equipment for scientific research or for any other peaceful purpose.

Article IV
    1. Nothing contained in the present Treaty shall be interpreted as:
    (a) a renunciation by any Contracting Party of previously asserted rights of or claims to territorial sovereignty in Antarctica;
    (b) a renunication or diminution by any Contracting Party of any basis of claim to territorial sovereignty in Antarctica which it may have whether as a result of its activities or those of its nationals in Antarctica, or otherwise;
    (c) prejudicing the position of any Contracting party as regards its recognition or non-recognition of any other State's right of or claim or basis of claim to territorial sovereignty in Antarctica.
    2. No acts or activities taking place while the present Treaty is in force shall constitute a basis for asserting, supporting or denying a claim to territorial sovereignty in Antarctica or create any rights of sovereignty in Antarctica. No new claim, or enlargement of an existing claim, to territorial sovereignty in Antarctica shall be asserted while the present Treaty is in force.

Article XII
    1. (a) The present Treaty may be modified or amended at any time by unanimous agreement of the Contracting Parties . . .
    2. (a) If after the expiration of thirty years from the date of entry into force of the present Treaty, any of the Contracting Parties whose representatives are entitled to participate in the meetings provided for under Article IX so request by a communication addressed to the depositary Government, a Conference of all the Contracting Parties shall be held as soon as practicable to review the operation of the Treaty.

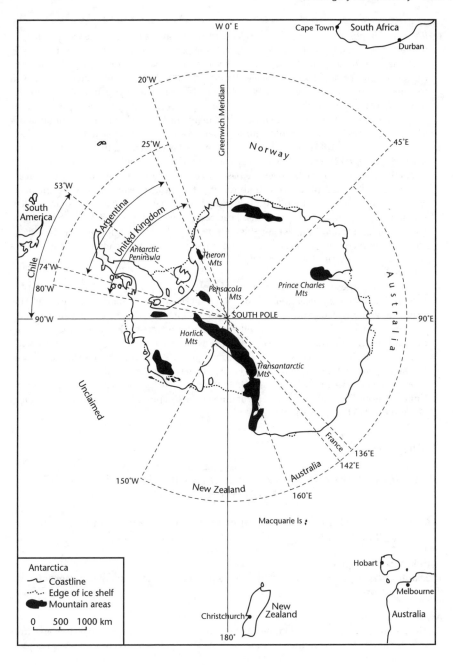

NOTES:
1. It seems that most of the original seven claimant States have relied upon the sector principle, whereby their claims extend by longitudinal lines to the South Pole. However, in 1977, Australia said (8 *Aust Yearbook IL* 307) that it did not make a sectoral claim 'because the concept of a sector carries with it the idea that it is a theoretical claim unrelated to activity in the area. In truth our claim . . . is based upon discovery and occupation. The degree of occupation of course is slight, but is adequate in regard to the circumstances prevailing in the area. . . . The lines of longitude are used on the mainland as a convenient description of our lateral boundaries'. This may represent the present position of the other States.
2. In the debate in the UK House of Commons in July 1989 concerning the Antarctic Minerals Act (see Chapter 12), the following was said by the relevant government minister: 'The Antarctic treaty has succeeded over the past 30 years because every member of that treaty system has exercised forbearance and no member has pushed its interest beyond the point where it can be tolerated by others. The treaty system has also depended on an implicit assumption that, once an agreement has been reached by consensus, all parties to that consensus will confirm and implement the agreement.' While this comment may be true in terms of the parties to the Antarctic Treaty, non-parties can be adversely affected by this consensus, which can freeze out any alternative approaches to sovereignty over the Antarctic.
3. In 1991, the parties to the Antarctic Treaty adopted a Protocol to the Treaty (30 ILM 1455 (1991)). This Protocol concerns environmental protection of the Antarctic and designates it a natural reserve devoted to peace and science (see Chapter 12). Despite this apparent change in the territorial status of the Antarctic, the legal position remains the same as in the Antarctic Treaty above. This was made clear by the words of the Final Act of the Eleventh Antarctic Treaty Special Consultative Meeting (which adopted to Protocol), which state that: 'The Meeting agreed that the contents of this Final Act are without prejudice to the legal position of any Party under Article IV of the Antarctic Treaty.' There is also the possible impact of the United Nations Convention on the Law of the Sea (see Chapter 10), particularly in relation to pollution and to the continental shelf.

B: Airspace

Chicage Convention on International Civil Aviation 1944
15 UNTS (1944) 295

As at 1 July 2002 there are 188 parties to this treaty, which came into force in January 1945.

Article 1 Sovereignty
The contracting States recognize that every State has complete and exclusive sovereignty over the airspace above its territory.

Article 2 Territory
For the purposes of this Convention the territory of a State shall be deemed to be the land areas and territorial waters adjacent thereto under the sovereignty, suzerainty, protection or mandate of such State.

Article 3 Civil and state aircraft
(a) This Convention shall be applicable only to civil aircraft, and shall not be applicable to state aircraft.

(b) Aircraft used in military, customs and police services shall be deemed to be state aircraft.

(c) No state aircraft of a contracting State shall fly over the territory of another State or land thereon without authorization by special agreement or otherwise, and in accordance with the terms thereof.

(d) The contracting States undertake, when issuing regulations for their state aircraft, that they will have due regard for the safety of navigation of civil aircraft.

Article 5 Right of non-scheduled flight

Each contracting State agrees that all aircraft of the other contraction States, being aircraft not engaged in scheduled international air services shall have the right, subject to the observance of the terms of this Convention, to make flights into or in transit non-stop across its territory and to make stops for non-traffic purposes without the necessity of obtaining prior permission and subject to the right of the State flown over to require landing. Each contracting State nevertheless reserves the right, for reasons of safety of flight, to require aircraft desiring to proceed over regions which are inaccessible or without adequate air navigation facilities to follow prescribed routes, or to obtain special permission for such flights.

Such aircraft, if engaged in the carriage of passengers, cargo, or mail for remuneration or hire on other than scheduled international air services, shall also, subject to the provisions of Article 7, have the privilege of taking on or discharging passengers, cargo, mail, subject to the right of any State where such embarkation or discharge takes place to impose such regulations, conditions or limitations as it may consider desirable.

Article 6 Scheduled air services

No scheduled international air service may be operated over or into the territory of a contracting State, except with the special permission or other authorization of that State, and in accordance with the terms of such permission or authorization.

Article 17 Nationality of aircraft

Aircraft have the nationality of the State in which they are registered.

Article 89 War and emergency conditions

In case of war, the provisions of this Convention shall not affect the freedom of action of any of the contracting States affected, whether as belligerents or as neutrals. The same principle shall apply in the case of any contracting State which declares a state of national emergency and notifies the fact to the Council.

Military and Paramilitary Activities in and against Nicaragua Case (*Nicaragua* v *United States*) (*Merits*)

ICJ Rep 1986 14, 111, International Court of Justice

The basic legal concept of State sovereignty in customary international law, expressed in, *inter alia*, Article 2, paragraph 1, of the United Nations Charter, extends to the internal waters and territorial sea of every State and to the air space above its territory. As to superjacent air space, the 1994 Chicago convention on Civil Aviation (Art. 1) reproduces the established principle of the complete and exclusive sovereignty of a State over the air space above its territory. That convention, in conjunction with the 1958 Geneva Convention on the Territorial Sea, further specifies that the sovereignty of the coastal State extends to the territorial sea and to the air space above it, as does the United Nations Convention on the Law of the Sea adopted on 10 December 1982. The Court has no doubt that these prescriptions of treaty-law merely respond to firmly established and longstanding tenets of customary international law.

S. Murphy, 'Aerial Incident off the Coast of China
95 AJIL 630 (2001), pp. 630–633

On April 1, 2001, a US EP-3E Aries II airplane on a routine surveillance mission near the Chinese coast was intercepted by two Chinese-built F-8 fighter jets and then collided with one of the jets, which was closely tailing it. The damaged US airplane – with its twenty-four crew members – issued a Mayday alarm and made an emergency landing on China's Hainan Island at Lingshui. The damaged Chinese fighter jet crashed into the water, and it was later determined that the pilot, Wang Wei, had died.

China immediately charged the United States with responsibility for the incident, stating that the US airplane had turned suddenly into the Chinese jet and then landed at Lingshui without permission. In addition to demanding an apology, China called upon the United States to end its frequent reconnaissance flights along the Chinese coast. The United States responded that the airplane had been operating outside Chinese territorial waters, that the EP-3E Aries II was a large, slow-moving airplane relative to the Chinese F-8, that Chinese jets had become increasingly aggressive in approaching and tailing US reconnaissance airplanes, and that the airplane had landed in distress. Consequently, no apology was appropriate, and China should allow the immediate return of the crew and the airplane to the United States. Chinese officials argued, in turn, that China had the right to exclude airplanes from flying over its exclusive economic zone, that the airplane should have received permission before landing in China, and that, in any event, China had the right to conduct an investigation into the incident. US officials took the position, however, that such flights outside a state's territory were permissible under international law and that an emergency landing in China was necessary through no fault of the United States.

The standoff between the two governments lasted eleven days. On April 11, the US ambassador to China, Joseph W. Prueher, sent a letter to the Chinese minister of foreign affairs, Tang Jiaxum, reflecting discussions between the two governments. The letter stated, in part:

> Both President Bush and Secretary of State Powell have expressed their sincere regret over your missing pilot and aircraft. Please convey to the Chinese people and to the family of pilot Wang Wei that we are very sorry for their loss. Although the full picture of what transpired is still unclear, according to our information, our severely crippled aircraft made an emergency landing after following international emergency procedures. We are very sorry the entering of China's airspace and the landing did not have verbal clearance, but very pleased the crew landed safely. We appreciate China's efforts to see to the well-being of our crew. In view of the tragic incident and based on my discussions with your representative, we have agreement to the following actions: Both sides agree to hold a meeting to discuss the incident. My government understands and expects that our aircrew will be permitted to depart China as soon as possible. . . .

On April 12, China allowed the twenty-four crew members to leave China. The next day, US Secretary of Defense Donald H. Rumsfeld stated that he had spoken with the pilot of the US airplane to ascertain the circumstances of the collision, and that he wished to make certain points about the incident and the practice of states regarding such matters.

> It is well-understood in international agreements that if an aircraft is in distress that it broadcast that on the accepted international channels. The pilot made a decision to head towards Hainan Island. I am told that . . . the crew made some 25 to 30 attempts to broadcast Mayday and distress signals, and to alert the world, as well as Hainan Island, that they were going to be forced to land there. . . . [T]hey really could not be aware as to whether or not their distress signals had been acknowledged. . . . We had every right to be flying where we were flying. They have every right to come up and observe our flight. . . .

> [Examples of] instances where one nation's aircraft landed at another nation's airport, but without permission and because of some sort of emergency. On February 27, 1974, a Soviet AN-24 reconnaissance aircraft was low on fuel and made an emergency landing at

Gambell Airfield in Alaska. The crew remained on the aircraft overnight. They were provided space heaters and food. They were refueled the next day and they departed. The crew was not detained and the aircraft was not detained. On April 6, 1993, a Chinese civilian airliner declared an in-flight emergency and landed in Shemya, Alaska, in the United States. It was apparently a problem of turbulence; very, very severe turbulence to the point that two people died, dozens were seriously injured, and the plane made an emergency landing on the US airfield. The aircraft was repaired and refueled without charge, and it departed. On 26 March, 1994, Russian military surveillance aircraft, monitoring a NATO anti-submarine warfare exercise, was low on fuel and made an emergency landing at Thule Air Base in Greenland. It was on the ground about six hours, the crew was fed, the aircraft was refueled and it departed.

Now, I mention these to point out that reconnaissance flights have been going on for decades. They are not unusual. They are well-understood by all nations that are involved in these types of matters. And in similar situations, nations have not detained crews and they have not kept aircraft.

The United States wished to repair the airplane and fly it out of China. After extensive US – China negotiations, however, the airplane was dismantled and then returned to the United States on July 3. Thereafter, the United States offered to pay $34,567 in compensation for costs relating to the emergency landing, but China rejected the offer as falling far short of the $1,000,000 it had requested.

NOTE:

The Chicago Convention attempts to provide international agreement as to the regulation and protection of civilian aircraft. Further, as a consequence of the destruction by Soviet military planes of Korean Airlines Flight 007 in September 1983, the United States said in the Security Council (22 ILM 1121 (1983)) that 'sovereignty neither requires nor permits the shooting down of airlines in peacetime'. However, the USSR replied that there was a 'sovereign right of every State to protect its borders including its airspace'. The issue remains contentious even for surveillance (spy) aircraft as seen in the extract above.

C: Outer space

Treaty on Principles Governing the Activities of States in the Exploration and Use of Outer Space, including the Moon and other Celestial Bodies 1967
610 UNTS (1967) 205

As at 1 July 2001, 96 States have ratified this Treaty, which entered into force in October 1967.

Article I

The exploration and use of outer space, including the moon and other celestial bodies, shall be carried out for the benefit and in the interests of all countries, irrespective of their degree of economic or scientific development, and shall be the province of all mankind.

Outer space, including the moon and other celestial bodies, shall be free for exploration and use by all States without discrimination of any kind, on a basis of equality and in accordance with international law, and there shall be free access to all areas of celestial bodies.

There shall be freedom of scientific investigation in outer space, including the moon and other celestial bodies, and States shall facilitate and encourage international co-operation in such investigation.

Article II

Outer space, including the moon and other celestial bodies, is not subject to national appropriation by claim of sovereignty, by means of use or occupation, or by any other means.

Article IV

States Parties to the treaty undertake not to place in orbit around the earth any objects carrying nuclear weapons or any other kinds of weapons of mass destruction, install such weapons on celestial bodies, or station such weapons in outer space in any other manner.

The moon and other celestial bodies shall be used by all States Parties to the Treaty exclusively for peaceful purposes. The establishment of military bases, installations and fortifications, the testing of any type of weapons and the conduct of military manoeuvres on celestial bodies shall be forbidden. the use of military personnel for scientific research or for any other peaceful purposes shall not be prohibited. The use of any equipment or facility necessary for peaceful exploration of the moon and other celestial bodies shall also not be prohibited.

Article VIII

A State Party to the Treaty on whose registry an object launched into outer space is carried shall retain jurisdiction and control over such object, and over any personnel thereof, while in outer space or on a celestial body. Ownership of objects launched into outer space, including objects landed or constructed on a celestial body, and of their component parts, is not affected by their presence in outer space or on a celestial body or by their return to the Earth. Such objects or component parts found beyond the limits of the state Party to the treaty on whose registry they are carried shall be returned to that State Party, which shall, upon request, furnish identifying data prior to their return.

Cosmos 954 Claim (Canada v USSR)
18 ILM 899 (1979), Claim Nos 15, 20–23

In January 1978, a Soviet satellite, which had a nuclear reactor, disintegrated through Canadian airspace on to Canadian territory. Canada issued a Statement of Claim to the USSR seeking compensation of six million dollars for cleaning up the affected area. The matter was settled by a payment of three million dollars without admission of liability. This is an extract from Canada's claim.

On behalf of CANADA: . . .

(a) *International agreements*

15. Under Article II of the Convention on International Liability for Damage caused by Space Objects, hereinafter also referred to as the Convention, 'A launching State shall be absolutely liable to pay compensation for damage caused by its space object on the surface of the earth. . . .' The Union of Soviet Socialist Republics, as the launching State of the cosmos 954 satellite, has an absolute liability to pay compensation to Canada for the damage caused by this satellite. The deposit of hazardous radioactive debris from the satellite throughout a large area of Canadian territory, and the presence of that debris in the environment rendering part of Canada's territory unfit for use, constituted 'damage to property' within the meaning of the Convention. . . .

20. The liability of the Union of Soviet Socialist Republics for damage caused by the satellite is also founded in Article VII of the Treaty on Principles Government the Activities of States in the Exploration and Use of Outer Space, including the Moon and Other Celestial Bodies, done in 1967, and to which both Canada and the Union of Soviet Socialist Republics are parties. This liability places an obligation on the Union of Soviet Socialist Republics to compensate Canada in accordance with

international law for the consequences of the intrusion of the satellite into Canadian air space and the deposit on Canadian territory of hazardous radioactive debris from the satellite.

(b) *General principles of international law*

21. The intrusion of the Cosmos 954 satellite into Canada's air space and the deposit on Canadian territory of hazardous radioactive debris from the satellite constitutes a violation of Canada's sovereignty. This violation is established by the mere face of the trespass of the satellite, the harmful consequences of this intrusion, being the damage caused to Canada by the presence of hazardous radioactive debris and the interference with the sovereign right of Canada to determine the acts that will be performed on its territory. International precedents recognize that a violation of sovereignty gives rise to an obligation to pay compensation.

22. The standard of absolute liability for space activities, in particular activities involving the use of nuclear energy, is considered to have become a general principle of international law. A large number of states, including Canada and the Union of Soviet Socialist Republics, have adhered to this principle as contained in the 1972 Convention on International Liability for Damage caused by Space Objects. The principle of absolute liability applies to fields of activities having in common a high degree of risk. It is repeated in numerous international agreements and is one of 'the general principles of law recognized by civilized nations' (Article 38 of the Statute of The International Court of Justice). Accordingly this principle has been accepted as a general principles of international law.

23. In calculating the compensation claimed, Canada has applied the relevant criteria established by general principles of international law according to which fair compensation is to be paid, by including in its claim only those costs that are reasonable, proximately caused by the intrusion of the satellite and deposit of debris and capable of being calculated with a reasonable degree of certainty.

NOTE:

In 1979 there was an Agreement Governing the Activities of States on the Moon and other Celestial Bodies. Although there are only 10 State parties to it (and none of the Permanent Members of the Security Council), it seeks to make the Moon and its resources part of the 'common heritage of mankind'. This is part of an attempt to make areas of the Earth and its surrounds beyond the sovereignty of any one State (see Chapter 12). This concept is also seen in developments in the law of the sea over the high seas (see Chapter 10) and over the environment (see Chapter 12), as well as placing pressure on the parties to the Antarctic treaty to make the Antarctic part of the common heritage of mankind.

SECTION 7: **Changing perceptions of sovereignty**

Case Concerning East Timor (*Portugal* v *Australia*)
ICJ Rep 1995 90, International Court of Justice

The facts of this case are set out in Chapter 6.

32. The Court finds that it cannot be inferred from the sole fact that the . . . resolution of the General Assembly and the Security Council refer to Portugal as the administering Power of East Timor that they intended to establish an obligation on third States to treat exclusively with Portugal as regards the continental shelf of East Timor. The Court notes, furthermore, that several States have concluded with Indonesia treaties capable of application to East Timor but which do not include any reservation in regard to that Territory.

JUDGE VERESHCHETIN (Separate Opinion): Besides Indonesia, . . . there is another 'third party' in this case, whose consent [was not sought]. . . . The 'third party' at issue is the people of East Timor. Since the [majority] Judgment is silent on this matter, one might wrongly conclude that the people, whose right of self-determination lies at the core of the whole case, have no role to play in the proceedings. This is not to suggest that the Court should have placed the States Parties to the case and the people of East Timor on the same level procedurally. . . . This is merely to say that the right of a people to self-determination, by definition, requires that the wishes of the people be at least ascertained and taken into account by the Court. . . . [There is a] necessity for the Court at least to ascertain the views of the East Timorese representatives of various trends of opinion on the subject matter of the Portuguese Application. . . . I believe that nowadays the mere denomination of a State as administering Power may not be interpreted as automatically conferring upon that State a general power to take action on behalf of the people concerned, irrespective of any concrete circumstances.

JUDGE SKUBISZEWSKI (Dissenting Opinion): East Timor has not been well served by the traditional interests and sovereignties of the strong. . . . [While] both Parties invoked the interests of the East Timorese people . . . they presented us with little or no evidence of what the actual wishes of that people were.

P. Allott, *Eunomia: New Order for a New World*
(1990), pp. 329–330

International society is recognizing itself as a society in which the state-societies are agents and instruments of the survival and prospering of human race. . . .

Sovereignty over territory will disappear as a category from the theory of international society and from its international law. . . . With the exclusion of the concept of sovereignty over territory, international society will find itself liberated at last to contemplate the possibility of delegating powers of government not solely by reference to an area of the earth's surface. Such a liberation will enable international society to do two things, in particular, which will open up rich new possibilities for its self-ordering (1) International society will be able to see international organizations at last as true international societies in their own right, not merely as co-operative ventures of the state-societies. (2) It will be possible for two or more state-societies to share in organizing the public realm of one and the same territory or of one and the same nation. . . . In this way, international society will be able to remove the greatest cause of war and of interminable self-destructive social struggle. Endless international and internal conflicts, costing the lives of countless human beings, have centred on the desire of this or that state-society to control this or that area of the earth's surface to the exclusion of this or that other state-society, the desire of this or that nation to be or not to be part of the structure-system of this or that state-society. International law has contributed next to nothing to the avoidance and the resolution of such conflicts. On the contrary, it has fueled them with the perverted passions generated by its primitive categories of *sovereignty* and *sovereignty over territory*.

R. McCorquodale, 'International Law, Boundaries and Imagination' in D. Miller and S. Hashmi (eds), *Boundaries and Justice*
(2001), pp. 136, 155–156

Boundaries are integral to international law. They are a cause of conflict and a reason for peace. They establish order and lead to disorder. They provide a protection and a weapon. They include and exclude. They define and divide. They are real and imagined. . . .

The prevailing concept of the international legal system is that territorial boundaries establish statehood and that territorial boundaries are the basis for state sovereignty (ownership). Accordingly, the distribution of natural resources, concepts of diversity, and the mobility of people are considered within this state-based framework, and the political autonomy of the state and territorial boundaries are completely entwined. The current international legal system recreates and affirms the dispositions by colonial powers, it privileges certain voices and silences others, and it restricts the identities of individuals to those defined by state boundaries. The effect of this is to reinforce the state-based framework of the international legal system and to limit the influence of other factors. This is because this system, as traditionally conceived 'naturalises and legitimises the subjugating and disciplinary effects of European, masculinist, heterosexual and capitalist regimes of power.' [D. Otto, 18 *Australian Yearbook of International Law* (1998)]

While territorial boundaries are artificially created by the international legal system, they tend to arise only from the imagination of these regimes of power. There is little room for the imagination of the developing states, of non-state actors, of women or of alternative concepts of the international legal system. Occasionally, these different imaginations do have some expression, such as in the development of internal self-determination and of the common heritage of mankind, but they are quickly limited by the prevailing international legal system. Law, in determining rules (and hence legal boundaries), is self-limiting because 'law purports to preserve institutional stability and continuity [and] reform must build from existing legal precedents and doctrines,' [K. Bartlett and R. Kennedy (eds) *Feminist Legal Theory* (1991)] and so law allows change incrementally from the status quo position. However, as the 'intrusive, intersubjective, and symbolic qualities of modern law continually interact with social practices and relationships, making legal change is an integral, necessary component of social change.' [K. Powers, *Wisconsin Law Review* (1979)]. It does leave open the possibilities for new imaginations of international law to emerge.

There are new ways to imagine the international legal role of territorial boundaries. Some of these ways are institutional, as seen in the multilevel sovereignties in Europe, and some are structural, such as the diminished importance of territorial boundaries due to the process of globalization. Above all, the new imaginations are conceptual. They have to be able 'to convert those borders from their prevailing postures as ramparts into a new veritable function as bridges' [A. Asiwaju in C. Schofield (ed) *Global Boundaries* (1994)], and to focus on relationships and not on imaginary constructs. This language of international law in relation to territorial boundaries must be in terms of an international society that is inclusive of all, allows all to find and use their voices, is creative of identity opportunities, and recognizes diversity within the universality of international society.

NOTES:

1. In the *East Timor Case*, the ICJ took the view that sovereignty over a territory does not necessarily reside in one State. In that case, the colonial (administering) State had some sovereign power but it was not an exclusive power. The State which occupied the territory had some sovereign power over the territory, at least in the day-to-day administration of the affairs of the territory, and this power may, perhaps, include the ability to enter treaties concerning the territory. In addition, the people of the territory have some sovereignty over the territory, as they have the right of self-determination, which can be exercised as they freely decide without external interference (see above). This is a significant power as it limits to some extent the power of all other possible sovereigns. The *East Timor Case* has affirmed the development of international law in restricting the absolute sovereignty of States, at least in respect of the right of self-determination. Subsequent to this decision, East Timor was administered by the United Nations until East Timor became a State in May 2002 (see above) and so there were further muliple sovereignties over the same territory.

2. Allott's view is that it is possible to reconceive international law so that State sovereignty over territory will disappear. Already such sovereignty is diminishing in importance as alternative sovereignties develop. These alternative sovereignties reflect the changes to the nature of international law (as reflected in the extract from McCorquodale) where States are no longer the only participants in the development of international law.

8

Jurisdictional Sovereignty

Introductory note

As noted in Chapter 7, 'sovereignty' is one of the most fundamental concepts known to international law. However, the 'sovereignty' of a State is a nebulous concept, comprising many facets, and its implications may be felt both in the national and international spheres. A State's administrative, judicial, executive and legislative activity is part of the exercise of its sovereignty, sometimes known as its jurisdictional sovereignty. The principal concern of this chapter is to examine the objects of a State's jurisdictional sovereignty (both natural and legal persons) and the circumstances in which it may be exercised.

The exercise of jurisdiction over persons and property by a State necessarily comprises action in the national sphere through its legislature, police force and courts. This action may also have international consequences, as where jurisdiction is exercised over a foreign national, or the assets of a foreign State or in respect of acts occurring outside the State's territory. In simple terms, jurisdiction is either 'prescriptive' or 'enforcement' in nature. Prescriptive jurisdiction describes a State's ability to define its own laws in respect of any matters it chooses. Enforcement jurisdiction describes a State's ability to enforce those laws and is necessarily dependent on the existence of prescriptive jurisdiction. As a general rule, a State's prescriptive jurisdiction is unlimited and a State may legislate for any matter irrespective of where the event occurs (even if in the territory of another State) or the nationality of the persons involved. However, the sovereign equality of states means that one State may not exercise its enforcement jurisdiction in a concrete sense (i.e. by arresting suspects, establishing courts) in another State's territory irrespective of the reach of its prescriptive jurisdiction, at least not without the latter State's consent. As a corollary to these principles, a State's enforcement jurisdiction within its own territory is presumptively absolute over all matters and persons situated therein. There are exceptions to this absolute territorial jurisdiction, as where persons are immune from the jurisdiction of local courts (see Chapter 9), but this occurs only by reason of a specific rule of international or national law to that effect.

The principles of jurisdiction are rules of international law that represent an attempt to regulate the extent to which one State's enforcement jurisdiction impinges or conflicts with another's. To put it another way, they attempt to resolve disputed questions of jurisdiction by determining which of two or more States competing to exercise an enforcement jurisdiction may properly do so.

In addition to *State* jurisdiction (i.e. jurisdictional sovereignty of States), it is now clear that there is an emerging body of international law that does not rely on States for the imposition of obligations on individuals. These rules foresee *international courts* trying persons according to *international law* for violations of obligations owed at international law, irrespective of the position in the local legal system of the individual concerned. This international jurisdiction is, of course, very different from national courts trying persons within its enforcement jurisdiction for matters which are contrary to national law, even if those matters be also contrary to international law and there is no doubt that it represents a threat to traditional notions of State sovereignty which see 'the State' as having exclusive power over its own nationals. This branch of international law – which is linked to principles of *universal jurisdiction* discussed below, is sometimes referred to as international criminal law because it imposes obligations on individuals that resemble crimes in national laws. Whether this is an accurate description of the emerging law is debatable, for there is no reason why these rules need be limited to events which resemble the familiar crimes of national law. Indeed, the essence of this 'international criminal law' is that it imposes obligations on individuals directly, which are directly enforceable before international tribunals regardless of the nationality of the perpetrator or any victim. One of these tribunals is the new International Criminal Court, possibly the most important institutional development in international law since the birth of the United Nations. Moreover, once the possibility of individual criminal responsibility at international law has been established – as now is certain – it is perfectly feasible that the system will develop to encompass international civil obligations.

SECTION 1: **General principles of jurisdiction**

United Nations Charter 1945

Article 2
The Organization and its Members, in pursuit of the Purposes stated in Article 1, shall act in accordance with the following Principles:

7. Nothing contained in the present Charter shall authorize the United Nations to intervene in matters which are essentially within the domestic jurisdiction of any State or shall require the Members to submit such matters to settlement under the present Charter; but this principle shall not prejudice the application of enforcement measures under Chapter VII.

SS Lotus Case (*France* v *Turkey*)

PCIJ Ser A (1927) No 9, Permanent Court of International Justice

A collision occurred on the high seas in the Mediterranean between a French steamer, the *Lotus*, and a Turkish steamer, *Boz-Kourt*, in which the latter was sunk with the loss of eight Turkish sailors. Upon the arrival of the *Lotus* at a Turkish port, its French officer on watch, Lieutenant Demons, was arrested on the criminal charge of involuntary manslaughter. By special agreement, the parties brought the matter before the Court, asking whether Turkey, by exercising its criminal jurisdiction in prosecuting the French citizen, was acting contrary to international law, in particular Article 15 of the Convention of Lausanne 1923. Held, by the casting vote of the President, that Turkey had not acted contrary to international law.

International law governs relations between independent States. The rules of law binding upon States therefore emanate from their own free will as expressed in conventions or by usages generally accepted as expressing principles of law and established in order to regulate the relations between these co-existing independent communities or with a view to the achievement of common aims. Restrictions upon the independence of States cannot therefore be presumed.

Now the first and foremost restriction imposed by international law upon a State is that – failing the existence of a permissive rule to the contrary – it may not exercise its power in any form in the territory of another State. In this sense jurisdiction is certainly territorial; it cannot be exercised by a State outside its territory except by virtue of a permissive rule derived from international custom or from a convention.

It does not, however, follow that international law prohibits a State from exercising jurisdiction in its own territory, in respect of any case which relates to acts which have taken place abroad, and in which it cannot rely on some permissive rule of international law. Such a view would only be tenable if international law contained a general prohibition to States to extend the application of their laws and the jurisdiction of their courts to persons, property and acts outside their territory, and if, as an exception to this general prohibition, it allowed States to do so in certain specific cases. But this is certainly not the case under international law as it stands at present. Far from laying down a general prohibition to the effect that States may not extend the application of their laws and the jurisdiction of their courts to persons, property and acts outside their territory, it leaves them in this respect a wide measure of discretion which is only limited in certain cases by prohibitive rules; as regards other cases, every State remains free to adopt the principles which it regards as best and most suitable . . .

In these circumstances, all that can be required of a State is that it should not overstep the limits which international law places upon its jurisdiction; within these limits, its title to exercise jurisdiction rests in its sovereignty.

Though it is true that in all systems of law the principle of the territorial character of criminal law is fundamental, it is equally true that all or nearly all these systems of law extend their action to offences committed outside the territory of the State which adopts them, and they do so in ways which vary from State to State. The territoriality of criminal law, therefore, is not an absolute principle of international law and by no means coincides with territorial sovereignty . . .

Consequently, once it is admitted that the effects of the offence were produced on the Turkish vessel, it becomes impossible to hold that there is a rule of international law which prohibits Turkey from prosecuting Lieutenant Demons because of the fact that the author of the offence was on board the French ship. . . . [T]here is no reason preventing the Court from confining itself to observing that, in this case, a prosecution may also be justified from the point of view of the so-called territorial principle . . .

It is certainly true that – apart from certain special cases which are defined by international law – vessels on the high seas are subject to no authority except that of the State whose flag they fly. In virtue of the principle of the freedom of the seas, that is to say, the absence of any territorial sovereignty upon the high seas, no State may exercise any kind of jurisdiction over foreign vessels upon them . . .

This conclusion could only be overcome if it were shown that there was a rule of customary international law which, going further than the principle stated above, established the exclusive jurisdiction of the State whose flag was flown. . . . In the Court's opinion, the existence of such a rule has not been conclusively proved . . .

The conclusion at which the Court has therefore arrived is that there is no rule of international law in regard to collision cases to the effect that criminal proceedings are exclusively within the jurisdiction of the State whose flag is flown. This conclusion moreover is easily explained if the manner in which the collision brings the jurisdiction of two different countries into play be considered. . . .

Neither the exclusive jurisdiction of either State, nor the limitations of the jurisdiction of each to the occurrences which took place on the respective ships would appear calculated to satisfy the requirements of justice and effectively to protect the interests of the two States. It is only natural that each should be able to exercise jurisdiction and to do so in respect of the incident as a whole. It is therefore a case of concurrent jurisdiction.

American Law Institute, *Restatement (Third) Foreign Relations Law of the United States*
(1987) pp. 232, 235–238

The rules given in this Restatement are said to reflect the law as given effect by Courts in the United States. In general, those Courts construe US national law so as not to conflict with international law (although see the case of *United States* v *Alvarez-Machain*, below). Moreover, the so-called 'principles of jurisdiction to prescribe' – being the applicable rules when two or more States are claiming jurisdiction over the same events – are not accepted by all scholars as reflecting customary international law.

§401. Categories of Jurisdiction
Under international law, a state is subject to limitations on

(a) jurisdiction to prescribe, i.e., to make its law applicable to the activities, relations, or status of persons, or the interests of persons in things, whether by legislation, by executive act or order, by administrative rule or regulation, or by determination of a court;

(b) jurisdiction to adjudicate, i.e., to subject persons or things to the process of its courts or administrative tribunals, whether in civil or in criminal proceedings, whether or not the state is a party to the proceedings;

(c) jurisdiction to enforce, i.e., to induce or compel compliance or to punish noncompliance with its laws or regulations, whether through the courts or by use of executive, administrative, police, or other nonjudicial action.

International law has long recognized limitations on the authority of states to exercise jurisdiction to prescribe in circumstances affecting the interests of other states. In the past, the jurisdiction of a state to make its law applicable in a translational context was determined by formal criteria supposedly derived from concepts of state sovereignty and power. In principle, it was accepted that a state had jurisdiction to exercise its authority within its territory and with respect to its nationals abroad. Ambiguous cases were seen as raising issues in the definition and application of those principles. . . . If the regulation of two (or more) states conflicted, that was unfortunate for the actor caught between two masters, but international law, it was thought, offered neither resolution nor remedy.

Increasingly, the practice of states has reflected conceptions better adapted to the complexities of contemporary international intercourse. State sovereignty was to be controlled by law, and its power tempered by reason and reasonableness. States have not in fact regulated all the foreign activities of their nationals (or affiliates of their nationals), nor every activity that could be said to have some effect in their territory. Attempts by some states – notably the United States – to apply their law on the basis of very broad conceptions of territoriality or nationality bred resentment and brought forth conflicting assertions of the rules of international law. Relations with Canada, and also with several states in Western Europe, have at times been strained by efforts of the United States to implement economic sanctions – against China, the Soviet Union, Cuba, and other states – through restraints on foreign subsidiaries of corporations based in the United States. . . . The application of antitrust and securities laws, on both governmental and private initiative, has reached beyond the territorial frontiers of the United States, and from time to time has been perceived by other states as intrusion into their rightful domain. . . . Partly in response to the reactions of other states, the United States has modified its assertions of jurisdiction in some areas . . .

Territoriality and nationality remain the principal bases of jurisdiction to prescribe, but in determining their meaning rigid concepts have been replaced by broader criteria embracing principles of reasonableness and fairness to accommodate overlapping or conflicting interests of states, and affected private interests. Courts and other decision makers, learning from the approach to comparable problems in private international law, are increasingly inclined to consider various interests, examine contacts and links, give effect to justified expectations, search for the 'center of gravity' of a given situation, and develop priorities. This Restatement follows this approach in adopting the principle of reasonableness.

§402. Bases of Jurisdiction to Prescribe
Subject to § 403, a state has jurisdiction to prescribe law with respect to

(1) (a) conduct that, wholly or in substantial part, takes place within its territory;

(b) the status of persons, or interests in things, present within its territory;

(c) conduct outside its territory that has or is intended to have substantial effect within its territory;

(2) the activities, interests, status, or relations of its nationals outside as well as within its territory; and

(3) certain conduct outside its territory by persons not its nationals that is directed against the security of the state or against a limited class of other state interests.

NOTES:
1. The limits of the 'domestic' or 'national' jurisdiction of a State have been altered over time by the development of international law. For example, national jurisdiction has generally been expanded by the changes in the extent of a State's maritime jurisdiction under the Law of the Sea (see Chapter 10), and it has been limited by international human rights law (see Chapter 6).
2. The Court in the *Lotus Case* (above) adopted a positivist view that prevents any limitations being placed on the sovereignty of States unless there is a clear rule to the contrary. This decision does not reflect contemporary customary international law, as now a State asserting jurisdiction over any given issue must show a positive basis of jurisdiction if challenged by a State having or alleging a greater jurisdictional right. Thus national courts must now seek a ground for the assertion of their jurisdiction, i.e. a reason why the local adjudication and enforcement process should proceed, at least in cases where another State may also have a claim to exercise enforcement jurisdiction.

SECTION 2: **Grounds for the assertion of jurisdiction by national courts**

The following section discusses the principles that national courts have used to explain why they should, or should not, exercise enforcement jurisdiction in any given case. The issue usually arises in cases where another State is claiming jurisdiction (perhaps through an application to extradite an offender), or where the defendant herself denies the national court's jurisdiction. In many cases, the subject matter of the case involves non-nationals or events wholly or partly performed abroad and often concerns criminal law. The principal grounds for the assertion of jurisdiction are where there is either a territorial or nationality link between the case and the court, as where the events take place in the State or are committed by a national of that State. An extension of these is the 'protective' and 'passive personality' principles, both of which are now being invoked more frequently. The 'effects doctrine' is a contentious ground for invoking national jurisdiction as it often has an extraterritorial reach and affects non-nationals. Its principal proponent is the United States. Lastly, 'universal' jurisdiction is a widely acknowledged ground for the assertion of jurisdiction by national courts over acts that are crimes under international law, or over acts that are so disruptive of the international legal order that any State may take enforcement measures without violating another State's jurisdictional rights and irrespective of where or by whom they were committed.

Speaking during the debate on the second reading in the House of Commons of the Jurisdiction (Conspiracy and Incitement) Bill, the Parliamentary Under-Secretary of State, Home Office, Mr Timothy Kirkhope, stated ((1997) 68 BYIL 575):

When introducing legislation aimed at combating international crime, we should be careful to ensure that the UK does not simply export its laws to other countries. Foreign Governments are responsible for determining what actions should be prohibited within their territories and how such behaviour should be dealt with under their laws. It is important to strike the right balance between dealing effectively with cross-border crime and avoiding impinging on other countries' laws . . .

The UK should deal with those who commit offences within our territory. That is the principle on which the jurisdiction of our courts is based. The interdepartmental review of extra-territorial jurisdiction, which reported last July . . . confirmed that that approach continues to be right for the United Kingdom . . .

It is worth saying a few words about the background that gave rise to the review of extra-territorial jurisdiction. Generally, criminal jurisdiction in the UK is territorially based. That means that conduct that would constitute an offence must have some connection with United Kingdom territory. Offences committed abroad by British nationals, unless they fall within a particular statutory provision, cannot normally be prosecuted in the UK.

The reasons for the primacy of the territorial principle are clear and twofold. In the first place, the criminal law of this country sets out what we as a nation believe about the sort of society in which we want to live. The law defines the conduct that is or is not acceptable: it defines the parameters and establishes the standard. We, and we alone, can say what actions should be proscribed by the criminal law. No one can do that for us and nor, in the generality of cases, should we attempt to do it for anyone else.

The second reason is equally strong. Under our system of justice, criminal trials depend to a major degree on the ability of the court to hear and assess evidence and to test out the truth of allegations by the cross-examination of witnesses. The best place for that to happen is clearly in the country where the crime occurred. The territorial basis of the criminal law has been, and in our view always should be, paramount.

Nevertheless, that principle has had to be modified in recent years. The report of the review of extra-territorial jurisdiction contains an important and fascinating account of the many and diverse ways in which, for very good reasons, the territoriality principle has been modified in recent times to co-operate further with other countries in the continuing battle with frontierless crime.

There are many such crimes, and as society and technology develop, the development of inter-national crime keeps pace. I can mention, for example, terrorism, hijacking, financial fraud, drug trafficking, fraud and forgery, art theft – indeed, there is a very long list . . .

In Europe, many countries already take extensive extra-territorial jurisdiction. That gives them some measure of control over the activities abroad of their countrymen but, unlike the United Kingdom, many are not prepared to extradite their own citizens. The reason is frequently found to be in their constitutions.

In contrast, we are prepared to extradite our citizens, subject of course to the normal safeguards. We have extradition arrangements with more than 100 countries. Even so, we have found that the absence of jurisdiction over the commission abroad of serious offences by British citizens can and does give rise to difficulties in circumstances in which we have not been able to extradite the individual.

As a result of those differences and of the difficulties that have arisen from time to time, there has been pressure to take wider jurisdiction, usually in areas where there is public and political concern.

NOTES:

1. The above statement concerning UK practice encapsulates the traditional approach to the exercise of an enforcement jurisdiction: that it is essentially territorial and nationality based. However, even in the UK this has given way to a more flexible approach, depending on the type of alleged criminal activity. In *R* v *Manning* [1999] 2 WLR 430, the traditional view was roundly criticised by the court, although the defects in that case are now abrogated by the entry into force of Part I of the Criminal Justice Act 1993. Note, however, that in addition to the above principles, a State may exercise an enforcement jurisdiction in respect of crimes against international law irrespective of the nationality of the perpetrator or locality of the offence. This 'universal' jurisdiction is considered below.

2. In *R* v *Cook* 38 ILM 271 (1999), the Canadian Supreme Court had to decide whether the Canadian Charter of Rights and Freedoms had extraterritorial effect, i.e. gave rights to a Canadian citizen arrested in the US in respect of acts committed in Canada. After noting that '[j]urisdictional competence on the basis of territoriality and nationality is an incident of sovereign equality and independence' and that there is a 'general prohibition in inter-national law against the extra-territorial application of domestic laws', the Court held that the granting of fundamental rights by the Charter was so important that it was not restricted to actions within Canada. This is a good example of the beneficial effect of extra-territoriality. However, as will be seen below, extraterritorial laws are usually both punitive to the individual and resented by other States.

A: Territorial

Compania Naviera Vascongado v Steamship 'Cristina'
[1938] AC 485, House of Lords

LORD MACMILLAN: It is an essential attribute of the sovereignty of this realm, as of all sovereign independent States, that it should possess jurisdiction over all persons and things within its territorial limits and all causes civil and criminal arising within these limits. This jurisdiction is exercised through the instrumentality of the duly constituted tribunals of the land.

R v Governor of Belmarsh Prison, ex parte Martin
[1995] 2 All ER 548, Court of Appeal

The United States sought the extradition of Martin to stand trial on terrorist charges. Their main evidence arose from telephone conversations between accomplices in the US and Martin in Ireland that had been intercepted in the US. Martin claimed that such evidence was inadmissible in an extradition hearing in England because the interception of telephone calls was an offence under the Interception of Communications Act 1985 unless proper procedure were followed. The US Agents making the telephone intercepts in the US would commit an offence under English law only if the Act had extraterritorial effect.

McCOWAN LJ: [A]s a matter of principle of English law, English criminal courts have no jurisdiction over persons resident abroad and committing offences abroad. In support of this proposition he relied on *MacLeod v A-G for New South Wales*. In giving the judgment of their Lordships, Lord Halsbury LC said ([1891]) AC 455 at 458–459):

> All crime is local. The jurisdiction over the crime belongs to the country where the crime is committed, and, except over her own subjects, Her Majesty and the Imperial Legislature have no power whatever. It appears to their Lordships that the effect of giving the wider interpretation to this statute necessary to sustain this indictment would be to comprehend a great deal more than Her Majesty's subjects; more than any persons who may be within the jurisdiction of the Colony by any means whatsoever; and that, therefore, if that construction were given to the statute, it would follow as a necessary result that the statute was ultrà vires of the Colonial Legislature to pass. Their Lordships are far from suggesting that the Legislature of the Colony did mean to give to themselves so wide a jurisdiction. The more reasonable theory to adopt is that the language was used, subject to the well-known and well-considered limitation, that they were only legislating for those who were actually within their jurisdiction, and within the limits of the Colony.

[O]nly the clearest possible language in any statute can create jurisdiction for English courts to deal with an alleged offence committed by a non-resident abroad . . .

In our judgment, the language of the statute is incapable of being construed as creating an offence triable in the United Kingdom, although committed by a non-resident by an act outside the United Kingdom.

NOTES:
1. A State's 'territory' for jurisdictional purposes extends to its land and dependent territories, airspace, aircraft, ships, territorial sea and, for limited purposes, to its contiguous zone, continental shelf and EEZ (see Chapter 10).

2. As is evident from the above two cases and the *Lotus Case* discussed in the preceding section, the principle of territorial jurisdiction is the preeminent ground for the assertion of jurisdiction. It ensures that all persons within a State's territory are subject to national law, save only for those granted immunity under international law. However, as the *Belmarsh* case illustrates, the principle of territoriality is also a limiting factor and national courts are slow to construe legislation as having an extraterritorial effect unless this is the clear intention of the legislature.

3. Most States assert jurisdiction over persons or events where any element of an event takes place within their territory: see Lord Diplock in *Treacy v Director of Public Prosecutions* [1971] AC 537. The 'objective' territorial principle permits a State to exercise its jurisdiction over all activities that are completed within its territory, even though some element constituting the crime or civil wrong took place elsewhere: see, e.g., the *Lotus Case, R v Sansom* [1991] 2 All ER 145 and *Liangsiriprasert v US Government* [1990] 2 All ER 866. The 'subjective' territorial principle permits a State to assert jurisdiction over matters commencing in its territory, even though the final element may have occurred abroad. In the UK, the Criminal Justice Act 1993, ss. 1–3 provide for the exercise of jurisdiction over certain offences where only an element of the offence occurs within the territory. See also the Civil Aviation (Amendment) Act 1996, which gives UK courts jurisdiction over persons (including non-nationals) committing offences on foreign aircraft while in flight to the UK. This Act is a hybrid between territorial and protective jurisdiction. In cases where two or more States may claim jurisdiction based on the territorial principle, the issue is often settled by negotiation, extradition to the most affected State or simply by an exercise of jurisdiction by the State having custody of the individual.

B: Nationality

Hague Convention on Certain Questions Relating to the Conflict of Nationality Laws, Articles 1–4
(1930) 179 *League of Nations Treaty Series* 89

Article 1
It is for each State to determine under its own law who are its nationals. This law shall be recognised by other States in so far as it is consistent with international conventions, international custom, and the principles of law generally recognised with regard to nationality.

Article 2
Any question as to whether a person possesses the nationality of a particular State shall be determined in accordance with the law of that State.

Article 3
Subject to the provisions of the present Convention, a person having two or more nationalities may be regarded as its national by each of the States whose nationality he possesses.

Nottebohm Case (Liechtenstein v Guatemala) (Second Phase)
ICJ Rep 1955 4, International Court of Justice

The facts are set out in Chapter 11.

It is . . . for every sovereign State, to settle by its own legislation the rules relating to the acquisition of its nationality, and to confer that nationality by naturalization granted by its own organs in accordance with that legislation. It is not necessary to determine whether international law imposes any limitations on its freedom of decision in this domain. Furthermore, nationality has its most immediate, its most far-reaching and, for most people, its only effects within the legal system of the State conferring it. Nationality serves above all to determine that the person upon whom it is conferred enjoys the rights and is bound by the obligations which the law of the State in question grants to or imposes on its nationals. This is implied in the wider concept that nationality is within the domestic jurisdiction of the State.

NOTES:

1. States have an inherent right to exercise jurisdiction over their own nationals irrespective of the place where the relevant acts occurred, even if all elements of the offence took place abroad. In fact, States tend to exercise this jurisdiction extraterritorially (i.e. in respect of acts committed abroad) only where the offence or civil wrong is particularly serious. The extent to which a national court will go to establish jurisdiction based on nationality in serious cases is illustrated by *Joyce* v *Director of Public Prosecutions*, where the defendant was said to owe allegiance to the English Crown even though his UK passport had been obtained unlawfully and had been surrendered in 1940. Common Law countries generally do not exercise jurisdiction based on nationality alone (that is, where there is no territorial connection at ᵃll) unless the offence is particularly serious (e.g., murder, certain sexual offences), the jurisdiction is required because of international agreements and/or the offence is also a crime under international law (e.g., War Crimes Act 1991 (UK)). For example, Australia relies on the nationality principle for its Crimes (Child Sex Tourism) Act 1994. As a counterpart, non-nationals found in the jurisdiction who are alleged to have committed on offence elsewhere may be extradited to the territory where the offence was actually committed: see, e.g., *R v Bow Street Metropolitan Stipendiary Magistrate, ex parte Pinochet (No 3)* [1999] 2 All ER 97 (see Chapter 9). This is without prejudice to the right of a State to take action against persons found on its territory who are non-nationals and where the offence occurred abroad if the alleged office is a crime under international law triggering universal jurisdiction.

2. The issue of how the nationality of an individual is to be determined is discussed in the *Nottebohm Case*, above. In principle, that case supposed that it was for each State to determine the criteria for awarding nationality, although the Court did suggest that in cases where two States were alleging that an individual was their national (as in that case), a 'genuine link' with a State had to be established before that nationality could be recognised. In this regard, the identification of the nationality of a company has given rise to much debate. See *Barcelona Traction Case*, ICJ Rep 1970 3 (see Chapter 11).

C: Protective principle

Harvard Research Convention on Jurisdiction with respect to Crime
29 AJIL Special Supplement (1935), 435

A State has jurisdiction with respect to any crime committed outside its territory by an alien against the security, territorial integrity or political independence of that State, provided that the act or omission which constitutes the crime was not committed in exercise of a liberty guaranteed the alien by the law of the place where it was committed.

Joyce v *Director of Public Prosecutions*
[1946] AC 347, House of Lords

Joyce was an American citizen who, as 'Lord Haw Haw', broadcast messages from Germany during the Second World War seeking to persuade the Allies to surrender. He had held a British passport for six years until 1940. He was convicted in the UK of high treason.

LORD JOWITT LC: The statute in question deals with the crime of treason committed within or, as was held in *R* v *Casement*, without the realm: it is general in its terms and I see no reason for limiting its scope except in the way that I indicated earlier in this opinion, viz.: that, since it is declaratory of the crime of treason, it can apply only to those who are capable of committing that crime. No principle of comity demands that a state should ignore the crime of treason committed against it outside its territory. On the contrary a proper regard for its own security requires that all those who commit that crime, whether they commit it within or without the realm should be amenable to its laws.

Attorney-General of the Government of Israel v *Eichmann*
36 ILR (1961) 5, District Court of Jerusalem

The facts of this case are set out in Chapter 5. The jurisdiction of the Israeli Court was unsuccessfully challenged and the Israeli Supreme Court upheld the decision of the District Court.

30. We have discussed at length the international character of the crimes in question because this offers the broadest possible, though not the only, basis for Israel's jurisdiction according to the law of nations. No less important from the point of view of international law is the special connection which the State of Israel has with such crimes, since the people of Israel (*Am Israel*), the Jewish people (*Ha'Am Ha'Yehudi*, to use the term in the Israel legislation), constituted the target and the victim of most of the said crimes. The State of Israel's 'right to punish' the accused derives, in our view, from two cumulative sources: a universal source (pertaining to the whole of mankind), which vests the right to prosecute and punish crimes of this order in every State within the family of nations; and a specific or national source, which gives the victim nation the right to try any who assault its existence.

This second foundation of criminal jurisdiction conforms, according to accepted terminology, to the protective principle (*compétence réelle*) . . .

Learned counsel for the defence has summed up his argument against the jurisdiction of the Israel legislator by stressing . . . that under international law there must be a connection between the State and the person who committed the crime and that in the absence of a 'recognized linking point' the State has no authority to inflict punishment for foreign offences.

33. When the question is presented in its widest form, as above, it seems to us that the answer cannot be in doubt. The 'linking point' between Israel and the accused (and for that matter any person accused of a crime against the Jewish people under this Law) is striking in the case of 'crime against the Jewish people', a crime that postulates an intention to exterminate the Jewish people in whole or in part . . .

34. The connection between the State of Israel and the Jewish people needs no explanation. The State of Israel was established and recognized as the State of the Jews . . .: this is the sovereign State of the Jewish people . . .

Indeed, this crime very deeply concerns the 'vital interests' of the State of Israel, and under the 'protective principle' this State has the right to punish the criminals. In terms of Dahm's thesis, the acts referred to in this Law of the State of Israel 'concern it more than they concern other States', and therefore according also to this author there exists a 'linking point'. The punishment of Nazi criminals does not derive from the arbitrariness of a country 'abusing' its sovereignty but is a legitimate and reasonable exercise of a right of penal jurisdiction.

36. Defence counsel contended that the protective principle cannot apply to this Law because that principle is designed to protect only an existing State, its security and its interests, whereas the State of Israel did not exist at the time of the commission of the said crimes . . . The right of the injured group to punish offenders derives directly, as Grotius explained . . . from the crime committed against them by the offender, and it is only want of sovereignty that denies it the power to try and punish the offender. If the injured group or people thereafter achieves political sovereignty in any territory, it may exercise such sovereignty for the enforcement of its natural right to punish the offender who injured it.

All this applies to the crime of genocide (including the 'crime against the Jewish people') which, although committed by the killing of individuals, was intended to exterminate the nation as a group.

Liangsiriprasert v *United States Government*
[1990] 2 All ER 866, Privy Council

A US agent persuaded a Thai drug smuggler to attend a meeting in Hong Kong (then a colony of the UK). Upon arrival, the Thai was arrested, and the Hong Kong Government acceded to the US's request for extradition. The appellant contended, *inter alia*, that the detention in Hong Kong was unlawful as the conspiracy to traffic in drugs was entered into outside Hong Kong and no overt act occurred in Hong Kong, so there was no offence in Hong Kong that gave Hong Kong jurisdiction to detain and then extradite the Thai.

[T]he inchoate crimes of conspiracy, attempt and incitement developed with the principal object of frustrating the commission of a contemplated crime by arresting and punishing the offenders before they committed the crime. If the inchoate crime is aimed at England with the consequent injury to English society, why should the English courts not accept jurisdiction to try it if the authorities can lay hands on the offenders, either because they come within the jurisdiction or through extradition procedures? If evidence is obtained that a terrorist cell operating abroad is planning a bombing campaign in London what sense can there be in the authorities holding their hand and not acting until the cell comes to England to plant the bombs, with the risk that the terrorists may slip through the net? Extradition should be sought before they have a chance to put their plan into action and they should be tried for the conspiracy or the attempt as the case may be. Furthermore, if one of the conspirators should chance to come to England, for whatever purpose, he should be liable to arrest and trial for the criminal agreement he has entered into abroad.

The Law Commission in *Territorial and Extra-Territorial Extent of the Criminal Law* (Working Paper No 29 (1970)) para 96 said:

As to conspiracies abroad to commit offences in England, we take the view that such conspiracies should not constitute offences in English Law unless overt acts pursuant thereto take place in England.

But why should an overt act be necessary to found jurisdiction? In the case of conspiracy in England the crime is complete once the agreement is made and no further overt act need to be proved as an ingredient of the crime. The only purpose of looking for an overt act in England in the case of a conspiracy entered into abroad can be to establish the link between the conspiracy and England or possibly to show the conspiracy is continuing. But if this can be established by other evidence, for example the taping of conversations between the conspirators showing a firm agreement to commit the crime at some future date, it defeats the preventative purpose of the crime of conspiracy to have to wait until some overt act is performed in pursuance of the conspiracy.

Unfortunately in this century crime has ceased to be largely local in origin and effect. Crime is now established on an international scale and the common law must face this new reality. Their Lordships can find nothing in precedent, comity or good sense that should inhibit the common law from regarding as justiciable in England inchoate crimes committed abroad which are intended to result in the commission of criminal offences in England. Accordingly, a conspiracy entered into in Thailand with the intention of committing the criminal offence of trafficking in drugs in Hong Kong is justiciable in Hong Kong even if no overt act pursuant to the conspiracy has yet occurred in Hong Kong.

NOTE:

The protective principle tends to be relied upon by a State only when its national security, or a matter of public interest, is in issue. This should be contrasted with the 'effects' doctrine considered below. *Liangsiriprasert* also raises the possibility of jurisdiction under the 'objective' territorial principle.

D: Passive personality

SS Lotus Case (*France* v *Turkey*)

PCIJ Ser A (1927) No 9, Permanent Court of International Justice

MOORE J (Dissenting Opinion): The substance of the jurisdictional claim is that Turkey has a right to try and punish foreigners for acts committed in foreign countries not only against Turkey herself, but also against Turks, should such foreigners afterwards be found in Turkish territory . . . I cannot escape the conclusion that it is contrary to well-settled principles of international law. . . .

This claim is defended by its advocates, and has accordingly been defended before the Court, on what is called the 'protective' principle [now known as the 'passive personality principle']; and the countries by which the claim has been espoused are said to have adopted the 'system of protection'.

What, we may ask, is this system? In substance, it means that the citizen of one country, when he visits another country, takes with him for his 'protection' the law of his own country and subjects those with whom he comes into contact to the operation of that law. In this way an inhabitant of a great commercial city, in which foreigners congregate, may in the course of an hour unconsciously fall under the operation of a number of foreign criminal codes. This is by no means a fanciful supposition; it is merely an illustration of what is daily occurring, if the 'protective' principle is admissible. It is evident that this claim is at variance not only with the principle of the exclusive jurisdiction of a State over its own territory, but also with the equally well-settled principle that a person visiting a foreign country, far from radiating for his protection the jurisdiction of his own country, falls under the dominion of the local law and, except so far as his government may diplomatically intervene in case of a denial of justice, must look to that law for his protection.

United States v *Yunis*

681 F. Supp 896 (1988), United States District Court, District of Columbia

Yunis, a Lebanese citizen, was lured by a US agent from Cyprus into a fishing boat that was in international waters. He was then arrested and transported to the US, where he was charged with hostage taking and piracy in connection with the hijacking in 1985 of an aircraft belonging to Royal Jordanian Airlines. No part of the offences occurred in the US, although two of the passengers were US citizens. The Court considered that it had jurisdiction over the prosecution of Yunis on the basis of both the passive personality and the universality principles (see below). The Court of Appeal, District of Columbia upheld the decision (30 ILM 463 (1991)).

This [passive personality] principle authorizes states to assert jurisdiction over offenses committed against their citizens abroad. It recognizes that each state has a legitimate interest in protecting the safety of its citizens when they journey outside national boundaries. Because American nationals were on board the Jordanian aircraft, the government contends that the Court may exercise jurisdiction over Yunis under this principle. Defendant argues that this theory of jurisdiction is neither recognized by the international community nor the United States and is an insufficient basis for sustaining jurisdiction over Yunis.

Although many international legal scholars agree that the principle is the most controversial of the five sources of jurisdiction, they also agree that the international community recognizes its legitimacy. Most accept that 'the extraterritorial reach of a law premised upon the . . . principle would not be in doubt as a matter of international law.' Paust, *Jurisdiction and Nonimmunity*, 23 Va.J. of Int'l Law, 191, 203 (1983). More importantly, the international community explicitly approved of the principle as a basis for asserting jurisdiction over hostage takers. As noted above, . . . the Hostage Taking Convention set forth certain mandatory sources of jurisdiction. But it also gave each signatory country discretion to exercise extraterritorial jurisdiction when the offense was committed 'with respect to a hostage who is a national of that state if that state considers it appropriate.' Art. 5(a)(d). Therefore, even if there are doubts regarding the international community's acceptance, there can be no doubt concerning the application of this principle to the offense of hostage taking, an offense for which Yunis is charged . . .

Defendant's counsel correctly notes that the Passive Personality principle traditionally has been an anathema to United States lawmakers. But his reliance on the Restatement (Revised) of Foreign Relations Laws for the claim that the United States can never invoke the principle is misplaced. In the past, the United States has protested any assertion of such jurisdiction for fear that it could lead to indefinite criminal liability for its own citizens. This objection was based on the belief that foreigners visiting the United States should comply with our laws and should not be permitted to carry their laws with them. Otherwise Americans would face criminal prosecutions for actions unknown to them as illegal. However, in the most recent draft of the Restatement, the authors noted that the theory 'has been increasingly accepted when applied to terrorist and other organized attacks on a state's nationals by reason of their nationality, or to assassinations of a state's ambassadors, or government officials.' Restatement (Revised) § 402, comment g . . . The authors retreated from their wholesale rejection of the principle, recognizing that perpetrators of crimes unanimously condemned by members of the international community, should be aware of the illegality of their actions. Therefore, qualified application of the doctrine to serious and universally condemned crimes will not raise the specter of unlimited and unexpected criminal liability.

NOTES:

1. The passive personality principle extends the nationality principle to apply to any crime

committed against a national of a State, wherever that national may be. The practice of States suggests that this ground for the assertion of jurisdiction is rarely advanced.

2. The US has altered its practice in recent years. Previously it had always protested to any State that sought to exercise passive personality jurisdiction over a national of the US while at the same time asserting the jurisdiction itself.

E: The 'effects' doctrine

Hartford Fire Insurance Co. v *California US Supreme Court*
113 S. Ct 2891 (1993), Noted by A. Lowenfeld, 89 AJIL 42 (1995)

The case arose out of an insurance crisis in the US. The plaintiffs alleged that London insurance companies, acting in the UK, had collaborated in refusing to grant reinsurance to certain US businesses except on terms agreed amongst themselves. This was said to violate the Sherman Act (a US Act prohibiting collusion). The UK defendants argued that their actions were legal in the place where they occurred, and further that they had acted in compliance with the UK law of regulation on where the insurance market. The Supreme Court, by a majority (5:4) held that the US court did have jurisdiction.

The English defendants did not deny that their actions had effects in the United States – indeed, direct and substantial effects. They argued, however, that their conduct was legal in the state where it took place; that they had operated in full compliance with a regime of regulation and self-regulation as prescribed by the British Parliament; and that under principles of international law and comity, as spelled out particularly in two major decisions of US courts of appeals – *Timberlane Lumber Co.* v *Bank of America* and *Mannington Mills Inc.* v *Congoleum Corp.* – as well as two generations of the *Restatement of the Foreign Relations Law of the United States*, jurisdiction to apply US law should not be exercised in this case.

In the much-discussed *Timberlane* case, it will be recalled, Judge Choy had written that the 'effects doctrine' as formulated by Judge Learned Hand in *Alcoa* is incomplete, because it fails to consider the interests of other nations in the application or nonapplication of United States law. Judge Choy had proposed a three-part test: first, to see if the challenged conduct had had *some* effect on the commerce of the United States – the minimum contact to support application of US law; second, to see if a greater showing could be made that the conduct in question imposed a burden or restraint on US commerce – i.e., whether the complaint stated a claim under the antitrust laws; and third, to consider 'the additional question which is unique to the international setting of whether the interests of, and links to, the United States . . . are sufficiently strong, vis-à-vis those of other nations, to justify an assertion of extraterritorial authority.'

Judge Choy then proceeded to set out seven factors by which to judge the third or 'ought to' question, based on a list of factors proposed some years earlier by Professor Kingman Brewster. Other courts and the *Restatement* (*Third*) modified the criteria somewhat, but for the most part adopted the approach of the *Timberlane* case . . .

Justice David Souter, for the majority of five, wrote: 'The only substantial question in this case is whether there is in fact a true conflict between domestic and foreign law.'

Justice Souter went on to acknowledge the argument of the London reinsurers, supported by the British Government, that applying the Sherman Act to their conduct would conflict significantly with British law. But British law did not *require* the agreements that were the basis of the challenge under the Sherman Act. All that British law did was to establish a regulatory – and largely self-regulatory – regime with which the challenged conduct was consistent. '[T]his,' said Justice Souter, citing the *Restatement*, 'is not to state a conflict. . . . No conflict exists, for these purposes, "where a person subject to regulation by two states can comply with the laws of both."' . . .

For the moment, I want to point out only that Justice Souter's opinion seems to equate 'conflict' with 'foreign compulsion.' For conflict, that is for inconsistent interests of states, *Timberlane* taught that one should evaluate or balance; for foreign compulsion, in contrast, we had understood since the *Nylon* and *Light Bulb* cartel cases of the early 1950s that no person would be required to do an act in another state that is prohibited by the law of that state or would be prohibited from doing an act in another state that is required by the law of that state; in other words, that the territorial preference would make balancing unnecessary. But Justice Souter said nothing about the controversial subject of balancing – either for or against – and barely mentioned *Timberlane*. 'We have no need in this case,' he concluded, 'to address other considerations that might inform a decision to refrain from the exercise of jurisdiction on grounds of international comity.'

To Justice Scalia and the four-person minority, the case looked entirely different. Justice Scalia started with two presumptions: first, that legislation of Congress, unless a contrary intent appears, 'is meant to apply only within the territorial jurisdiction of the United States'; and second, that 'an act of congress ought never to be construed to violate the law of nations if any other possible construction remains.' a quotation going back to Chief Justice Marshall, and that customary international law includes limitations on a nation's exercise of its jurisdiction to prescribe. The first point, of course, begs the question about whether one looks at conduct – here in London – or effect – here in the United States. If one looks at effect, then application of the Sherman Act would not be extraterritorial. In any event, Justice Scalia conceded that there were numerous precedents for application of the Sherman Act to conduct outside the United States. The second point, about customary international law, led Justice Scalia right to the series of court of appeals decisions from *Alcoa* to *Timberlane* and *Mannington Mills*, plus decisions by the U.S. Supreme Court in a series of seamen's cases cited to the Court by the English defendants, as well as the *Restatement*. 'Whether the Restatement precisely reflects international law in every detail matters little here,' he wrote, 'as I believe this case would be resolved the same way under virtually any conceivable test that takes account of foreign regulatory interests.' Justice Scalia went through the approach of the *Restatement*, including the factors set out in section 403(2). 'Rarely,' he concluded, perhaps exaggerating in order to emphasize his difference from the majority, 'would these factors point more clearly against application of United States law.'

Further, on the conclusion by the majority that a true conflict would exist only if compliance with US law would constitute violation of the other state's law, Justice Scalia wrote: 'That breathtakingly broad proposition, which contradicts the many cases discussed earlier, will bring the Sherman Act and other laws into sharp and unnecessary conflict with the legitimate interests of other countries – particularly our closest trading partners.'

'Statement of Principles by the United Kingdom Government concerning Jurisdiction in Anti-Trust Matters' in A. V. Lowe, *Extraterritorial Jurisdiction: An Annotated Collection of Legal Materials*
(1983), pp. 145–147

The basis on which personal jurisdiction may be exercised over foreign corporations

(1) Personal jurisdiction should be assumed only if the foreign company 'carries on business' or 'resides' within the territorial jurisdiction. . . .

(5) The normal rules governing the exercise of personal jurisdiction should not be extended in such a manner as to extend beyond proper limits the exercise of substantive jurisdiction in respect of the activities of foreigners abroad. Nor can the assertion of extended personal jurisdiction be justified on the basis that it is necessary for the enforcement of legislation which in itself exceeds the proper limits of substantive jurisdiction . . .

The basis on which substantive jurisdiction may be exercised in anti-trust matters

(1) On general principles, substantive jurisdiction in anti-trust matters should only be taken on the basis of either

(a) the territorial principle, or
(b) the nationality principle.

There is nothing in the nature of anti-trust proceedings which justifies a wider application of these principles than is generally accepted in other matters; on the contrary there is much which calls for a narrower application.

(2) The territorial principle justifies proceedings against foreigners and foreign companies only in respect of conduct which consists in whole or in part of some activity by them in the territory of the State claiming jurisdiction. A State should not exercise jurisdiction against a foreigner who or a foreign company which has committed no act within its territory. In the case of conspiracies the assumption of jurisdiction is justified:

(a) if the entire conspiracy takes place within the territory of the State claiming jurisdiction; or
(b) if the formation of the conspiracy takes place within the territory of the State claiming jurisdiction even if things are done in pursuance of it outside its territory; or
(c) if the formation of the conspiracy takes place outside the territory of the State claiming jurisdiction, but the person against whom the proceedings are brought has done things within its territory in pursuance of the conspiracy.

(3) The nationality principle justifies proceedings against nationals of the State claiming jurisdiction in respect of their activities abroad only provided that this does not involve interference with the legitimate affairs of other States or cause such nationals to act in a manner which is contrary to the laws of the State in which the activities in question are conducted.

Protection of Trading Interests Act 1980 (UK)

1. Overseas measures affecting United Kingdom trading interests

(1) If it appears to the Secretary of State—

(a) that measures have been or are proposed to be taken by or under the law of any overseas country for regulating or controlling international trade; and
(b) that those measures, in so far as they apply or would apply to things done or to be done outside the territorial jurisdiction of that country by persons carrying on business in the United Kingdom, are damaging or threaten to damage the trading interests of the United Kingdom,

the Secretary of State may by order direct that this section shall apply to those measures either generally or in their application to such cases as may be specified in the order.

(2) The Secretary of State may by order make provision for requiring, or enabling the Secretary of State to require, a person in the United Kingdom who carries on business there to give notice to the Secretary of State of any requirement or prohibition imposed or threatened to be imposed on that person pursuant to any measures in so far as this section applies to them by virtue of an order under subsection (1) above.

(3) The Secretary of State may give to any person in the United Kingdom who carries on business there such directions for prohibiting compliance with any such requirement or prohibition as aforesaid as he considers appropriate for avoiding damage to the trading interests of the United Kingdom.

2. Documents and information required by overseas courts and authorities

(1) If it appears to the Secretary of State—

    (a) that a requirement has been or may be imposed on a person or persons in the United Kingdom to produce to any court, tribunal or authority of an overseas country any commercial document which is not within the territorial jurisdiction of that country or to furnish any commercial information to any such court, tribunal or authority; or

    (b) that any such authority has imposed or may impose a requirement on a person or persons in the United Kingdom to publish any such document or information,

the Secretary of State may, if it appears to him that the requirement is inadmissible by virtue of subsection (2) or (3) below, give directions for prohibiting compliance with the requirement.

(2) A requirement such as is mentioned in subsection (1)(a) or (b) above is inadmissible—

    (a) if it infringes the jurisdiction of the United Kingdom or is otherwise prejudicial to the sovereignty of the United Kingdom; or

    (b) if compliance with the requirement would be prejudicial to the security of the United Kingdom or to the relations of the government of the United Kingdom with the government of any other country.

A. V. Lowe, 'US Extra-territorial Jurisdiction'

(1997) 46 ICLQ 378

This article discusses United States' Iran and Libya Sanctions Act 1996 (the D'Amato Act) and the Cuban Liberty and Democratic Solidarity (LIBERTAD) Act 1996 (the Helms–Burton Act). Both extend the jurisdiction of the United States to the activities of non-nationals occurring outside of the United States, even in cases where there is little demonstrable 'effect' within US territory.

Helms–Burton Title III creates a right for US nationals to bring actions in US courts to recover compensation from persons that 'traffic' in property in which the plaintiff has an interest and which was confiscated from anyone (regardless, it seems, of their nationality) by the Castro government at any time since 1959. That provision is objectionable in several respects.

First, there are established means for the settlement of claims arising from unlawful expropriations, by negotiations between the government of the national State of the victims and the government which did the expropriating. They have been used, successfully, by many States. . . .

Second, the process ignores established principles governing international claims. For instance, it permits recovery even where the property in question was not owned by a US citizen when it was taken – it may even have been owned by a Cuban national, in which case there could have been no violation of *international* law. It is enough, for the purposes of a Title III claim, that a US citizen has subsequently acquired an interest in it. In such cases Cuba did no wrong to any US citizen; and under international law it is for the national State of the person from whom the property was originally taken, and not for the United States, to take action to obtain redress.

Third, the non-US company now holding the property may have acquired it, for value, and used it, in a manner entirely lawful under the law of the place where the property is located, and under the national law of the company, and even under US law as it stood at the time of the acquisition. The property is theirs, according to the normal rules. Title III is tantamount to the ascription of a right to US nationals to expropriate this property owned by foreign businesses.

Fourth, in certain cases Title III imposes a penalty – the treble-damages provisions plainly have nothing to do with compensation – on non-US companies for transactions outside the United States, where the only link with the United States is the interest a US national had or has acquired in the property being handled. This is, in essence. a claim to jurisdiction on the basis of the 'passive personality' principle that the United States has itself vigorously opposed as contrary to international law.

Fifth, the provisions are an undesirable precedent. It is, for instance, difficult to see the United States welcoming the enactment of similar legislation by Arab States, permitting the recovery of compensation for property taken by Israel in East Jerusalem and other parts of the occupied territories.

The D'Amato provisions for the imposition of sanctions upon foreign businesses investing in Iran or Libya are in some ways even more extraordinary than the provisions of Helms–Burton. There seems to be no attempt whatever to tie the power to impose penalties upon violators of the law to any link between the United States and the alleged offender; no attempt to show even the semblance of respect for the principles of international law concerning the allocation of jurisdiction between States. It does not matter that the investment was made, or the goods supplied, by a non-US business operating outside the United States and having no links whatever with the United States. Under the D'Amato, Act the President is not instructed to act so as to keep US businesses in line with US foreign policy: he is instructed to act as a world policeman, imposing US law upon every person and every place on the planet. It does little to reassure those who think that many members of the US Congress do not understand international law at all, but see the world as one great federal State with the United States filling the role of the federal government.

However, the sanctions that are applicable under D'Amato – denial of export licences, of export assistance, of the right to import, and so on – do not appear to he extraterritorial. Like Title IV of Helms–Burton, they are 'frontier' measures, imposed (in the sense of the exercise of enforcement jurisdiction) at or within the frontiers of US territory. The objection is not that they exceed the limits, *ratione loci*, of US jurisdiction but, rather, that US jurisdiction is here used for inappropriate purposes.

There are, then, two kinds of objection. First, there are 'legal' objections: objections to the disregard of established legal principles and of US treaty obligations, and to the assertion of jurisdictional powers that the United States does not have; and, second, objections to what are seen as inappropriate uses by the United States of powers that it does have.

NOTES:

1. The 'effects' doctrine could be seen as an extension of the territorial principle where some part of an act might be said to occur on a State's territory, even if the only 'effect' is economic harm indirectly caused by that act. It can also be considered as an extension of the protective principle to situations other than national security, where issues considered of importance to a State are affected. As it mixes both these grounds of jurisdiction and has been so controversial, it is considered separately in this chapter.

2. The core element of the 'effects' doctrine is that it is an extraterritorial application of national laws where an action by a person with no territorial or national connection with a State has an effect on that State. It is the exercise of jurisdiction over non-nationals in respect of acts that occur abroad. Consequently, it may cause great offence to the State of nationality of the defendant or the State where the actions did occur. This is compounded if the act is actually legal in the place where it was performed. The result has been blocking legislation by other States, such as the Protection of Trading Interests Act (above) and the Canadian Foreign Extra-territorial Measures Act 1996 (36 ILM 111 (1997), EU Regulation No. 2271/96 Protecting

Against the Effects of the Extra-Territorial Application of Legislation Adopted by a Third Country (36 ILM 125 (1997)) and the Mexican Act to Protect Trade and Investment from Foreign Norms that Contravene International Law (36 ILM 133 (1997)). This type of legislation seeks to protect the activities of persons or companies behaving lawfully in the State where they are situated, even if the acts are unlawful under the 'effects' jurisdiction of another State.

3. The 'effects' doctrine is essentially an American one and originally applied in 'anti-trust' situations, i.e. where there are restrictive trade or anti-competitive agreements between corporations, even where there was no intent to cause any harm in the US. The doctrine has not been generally accepted, even by many other developed States. As noted above, many States have introduced legislation to limit the impact of the doctrine, or their courts have been alert to means to avoid applying it. In *Mannington Mills Inc* v *Congoleum Corporation* (1979) 595 F 2d 1287 the US Court of Appeals, Third Circuit, said 'When foreign nations are involved, however, it is unwise to ignore the fact that foreign policy, reciprocity, comity, and limitations of judicial power are considerations that should have a bearing on the decision to exercise or decline jurisdiction.' The most recent statement of the US authorities, *Restatement (Third) Foreign Relations Law of the United States* (1987), para 415, seems to be equivocal in its stance, asserting jurisdiction only where the principal purpose of the anti-trust agreement is to interfere in the commerce of the US and some effect on that commerce actually occurs. Otherwise it 'takes no position on the question whether intended or threatened effect (without actual effect) on the commerce of the United States satisfies the requirement of [the 'effects' doctrine]'. The *Hartford Fire Insurance* decision shows how easily the balance can come down in favour of exercising an extraterritorial jurisdiction.

4. The impact of US extraterritorial anti-trust laws on the trading interests of the European Union caused considerable friction between these two powerful trading blocs. At one point it seemed that a jurisdictional conflict was about to occur between US courts and the courts of the member States of the EU. The balancing approach of recent US decisions has mitigated this to some extent but a more reliable solution was needed. The result was the 1991 European Communities–US Agreement on the Application of Their Competition Laws, 30 ILM 1487 (1991), which instituted a system of cooperation in the enforcement of anti-trust legislation. Unfortunately, in *French Republic* v *Commission of the European Communities* [1994] ECR I-3641 the Court of Justice of the Communities declared that the European Commission had no power under Community law to enter into this Agreement. These deficiencies have now been rectified and the Agreement is in force – see Decision of 10 April 1995 [1995] OJ L 95/45.

5. The Court of Justice of the European Communities itself is not averse to utilising an 'effects' jurisdiction to protect its interests. In *Re Wood Pulp Cartel: Ahlström Osakeyhtio* v *EC Commission* [1988] 4 CMLR 901, the European Commission had determined that 41 woodpulp producers and two trade associations, all having registered offices outside the EC, had engaged in restrictive trade practices contrary to European Community law (primarily Art. 85 of the Treaty of Rome). The Court upheld the Commission's decision, by deciding that:

> the conclusion of an agreement which has had the effect of restricting competition in the Common Market, consists of conduct made up of two elements, the formation of the agreement . . . and the implementation thereof. . . . The decisive factor is . . . the place where it is implemented. The producers in this case implemented their pricing agreement within the Common Market. It is immaterial in that respect whether or not they had recourse to subsidiaries, agents, sub-agents or branches within the Community. . . . Accordingly, the Community's jurisdiction to apply its competition rules to such conduct is covered by the territorial principle as universally recognised in public international law.

6. In *Soering* v *UK* (1989) 11 ECHR 439 the European Court of Human Rights, in deciding that Soering's extradition to the US would be a breach by the UK of the European Convention on Human Rights because of the effect of the death penalty laws in the US, effectively extended the jurisdiction of this Convention to actions of States not parties to it. This could be considered consistent with the development of the international protection of human rights (see Chapter 6), but runs the risk of being an application in other States of European concepts of human rights.

F: Universality

American Law Institute, *Restatement (Third) Foreign Relations Law of the United States*
(1987), pp. 254–256

§404. Universal Jurisdiction to Define and Punish Certain Offenses
A state has jurisdiction to define and prescribe punishment for certain offenses recognized by the community of nations as of universal concern, such as piracy, slave trade, attacks on or hijacking of aircraft, genocide, war crimes, and perhaps certain acts of terrorism, even where none of the bases of jurisdiction indicated in §402 is present.

Comment
Universal jurisdiction over the specified offenses is a result of universal condemnation of those activities and general interest in cooperating to suppress them, as reflected in widely-accepted international agreements and resolutions of international organizations. These offenses are subject to universal jurisdiction as a matter of customary law. Universal jurisdiction for additional offenses is provided by international agreements, but it remains to be determined whether universal jurisdiction over a particular offense has become customary law for states not party to such an agreement. . . . A universal offense is generally not subject to limitations of time.

There has been wide condemnation of terrorism but international agreements to punish it have not, as of 1987, been widely adhered to, principally because of inability to agree on a definition of the offense. . . . Universal jurisdiction is increasingly accepted for certain acts of terrorism, such as assaults on the life or physical integrity of diplomatic personnel, kidnapping, and indiscriminate violent assaults on people at large.

United States v *Yunis*
681 F. Supp 896 (1988), United States District Court, District of Columbia

The facts are set out above.

PARKER J: The Universal principle recognizes that certain offenses are so heinous and so widely condemned that 'any state if it captures the offender may prosecute and punish that person on behalf of the world community regardless of the nationality of the offender or victim or where the crime was committed.' M. Bassiouini, II International Criminal Law, Ch. 6 at 298 (ed. 1986). The crucial question for purposes of defendant's motion is how crimes are classified as 'heinous' and whether aircraft piracy and hostage taking fit into this category.

Those crimes that are condemned by the world community and subject to prosecution under the Universal principle are often a matter of international conventions or treaties. *See Demjanjuk* v *Petrovsky*, 776 F.2d 571, 582 (6th Cir. 1985) (Treaty against genocide signed by a significant number of states made that crime heinous; therefore, Israel had proper jurisdiction over nazi war criminal under the Universal principle).

Both offenses [hijacking and hostage taking] are the subject of international agreements. A majority of states in the world community including Lebanon, have signed three treaties condemning aircraft piracy . . . These . . . demonstrate the international community's strong commitment to punish aircraft hijackers irrespective of where the hijacking occurred.

The global community has also joined together and adopted the International Convention for the Taking of Hostages an agreement which condemns and criminalizes the offense of hostage taking. Like the conventions denouncing aircraft piracy, this treaty requires signatory states to prosecute any alleged offenders 'present in its territory.'

In light of the global efforts to punish aircraft piracy and hostage taking, international legal scholars unanimously agree that these crimes fit within the category of heinous crimes for purposes of asserting universal jurisdiction. . . . In The Restatement (Revised) of Foreign Relations Law of the United States, a source heavily relied upon by the defendant, aircraft hijacking is specifically identified as a universal crime over which all states should exercise jurisdiction.

Our Circuit has cited the Restatement with approval and determined that the Universal principle, standing alone, provides sufficient basis for asserting jurisdiction over an alleged offender. See *Tel-Oren* v *Libyan Arab Republic*, 726 F.2d at 781, n. 7, Therefore, under recognized principles of international law, and the law of this Circuit, there is clear authority to assert jurisdiction over Yunis for the offenses of aircraft piracy and hostage taking. . . .

NOTES:

1. Universal jurisdiction is available irrespective of who committed the act and where it occurred. It depends solely on the nature of the offence committed, and principally is exercised by the State which has apprehended the alleged offender. The exercise of this jurisdiction can be supported as being a means of upholding the international legal order by enabling any State to exercise jurisdiction in respect of offences that are destructive of that order.

2. Other than piracy, the offences that are included within this ground of jurisdiction are not uniformly acknowledged and a number derive from treaty provisions e.g., International Convention Against the Taking of Hostages 1979. Genocide, piracy and, perhaps, slave trading may now be subject to a sufficient degree of consensus as may war crimes and crimes against humanity (Chapter 6) and, less certainly, drug trafficking. In the *Pinochet Case* (see Chapter 9) the House of Lords seemed to consider that torture was a crime that gave universal jurisdiction.

3. By way of contrast, in the *Case Concerning the Arrest Warrant of April 11 2000* (*Congo* v *Belgium*), ICJ Rep 14 February 2002, President Guillaume delivered a Separate Opinion that challenged the view that universal jurisdiction existed for a wide range of international crimes. In his view, 'in all systems of law, the principle of the territorial character of criminal law is fundamental' and any exceptions to this (e.g. by way of universal jurisdiction) needed clear evidence to be established. He conceded that customary international law did 'recognise one case of universal jurisdiction, that of piracy'. However, in his view, any other alleged matters of universal jurisdiction were actually examples of jurisdiction conceded by treaty and he agreed with Lord Slynn in the first (disapplied) House of Lords hearing in the *Pinochet Case* that there was no State practice or general consensus that all crimes against international law should be justicible in national courts on the basis of universality of jurisdiction. Its view draws a distinction between crimes against international law (i.e. matters for which individuals can be personally responsible) and universal jurisdiction (national courts having the power to try persons for such crimes). The existence of the former (which President Guillaume readily acknowledges) does not imply the latter. Of course, this is very

much a State-centred view, for it seeks to re-assert the pre-eminent rights of the territorial State or the State of nationality over an offence. It does not seem to be consistent with the views expressed, *inter alia*, in the *Eichmann Case* and by the majority in the second hearing of *Pinochet* in the House of Lords.

4. The Court in *US* v *Yunis* (above), noted that Lebanon, the State where the offences occurred and of which Yunis was a national, was unwilling or incapable of taking jurisdiction, and said that 'when another government harbors international terrorists or is unable to enforce international law, it is left to the world community to respond and prosecute the alleged terrorists. As long as governments which step into this enforcement role act within the constraints imposed by international and domestic law, their efforts to combat terrorism should be praised.' This may not be a view shared by non-western States, or by those States which have expressed some support for certain 'terrorist' organisations. In this regard, the UN Security Council imposed sanctions (now discharged) under Chapter VII of the United Nations Charter against Libya for its refusal to hand over persons allegedly involved in the Lockerbie bombing 748 (1992) (see Chapter 3) and the Council has acted in respect of the atrocities of September 11 2001 (see Chapter 14).

5. The question over which State may exercise jurisdiction over alleged terrorists is now very contemporary following the September 11 attacks. The US will not be deterred from exercising jurisdiction over any persons connected with these events. This has led to very serious concerns about US intentions with regard to persons detained as a result of the military intervention in Afghanistan. The basis of jurisdiction to try such persons – and before US military courts – solely because they have been captured in the course of military operations against the Taliban is uncertain and has aroused much criticism: see generally AJIL 2002, '*Agora, Military Commissions*'. For all intents and purposes these detainees are prisoners of war protected by international treaty and customary law. In contrast, territorial jurisdiction exists in respect of persons directly connected to the terrorist hijackings as this crime clearly unfolded on the territory of the US. More difficulties will be raised, however, by the potential application in the US of the death penalty to any person found guilty, especially if they are a national of a State where capital punishment is viewed as a grave violation of human rights (e.g. as in the European human rights system). The *Case LaGrand* (see Chapter 15) has already demonstrated the potential for international tension in such circumstances.

SECTION 3: **State jurisdiction and persons apprehended in violation of international law**

Unless a State is prepared to try a person in their absence from that territory, the exercise of enforcement jurisdiction over individuals depends on their physical presence in the territory of the acting State. There have been several cases where an individual has been removed forcibly from the territory of one State to be tried in another, either without the former State's consent or in violation of the procedures laid down in an extradition treaty between the former State and the State seeking to exercise jurisdiction. In such cases, the question arises whether the courts of the State seeking to exercise jurisdiction will object to the violation of the territorial sovereignty of the other State or will take cognisance of the fact that a treaty of extradition has not been complied with.

State v Ebrahim

31 ILM 888 (1991), Supreme Court of South Africa (Appellate Division)

The appellant, a South African citizen, was charged with treason. He had been abducted from Swaziland and transported to South Africa, most likely by agents of the South African Government. This was a violation of international law, being a violation of the territorial sovereignty of Swaziland, although Swaziland had not made an official protest. The appellant appealed against his conviction on the ground that the South African courts lacked jurisdiction because his appearance before them was brought about by a violation of international law. The appeal was allowed and the conviction set aside.

The first question to be decided in the present case is not what the relevant rules of international law are, but what those of our own law are. To answer this question it is necessary to examine our common law on this subject. . . .

Several fundamental legal principles are contained in these rules, namely the protection and promotion of human rights, good inter-state relations and a healthy administration of justice. The individual must be protected against illegal detention and abduction, the bounds of jurisdiction must not be exceeded, sovereignty must be respected, the legal process must be fair to those affected and abuse of law must be avoided in order to protect and promote the integrity of the administration of justice. This applies equally to the state. When the state is a party to a dispute, as for example in criminal cases, it must come to court with 'clean hands'. When the state itself is involved in an abduction across international borders, as in the present case, its hands are not clean.

Principles of this kind tesify to a healthy legal system of high standard. Signs of this development appear increasingly in the municipal law of other countries. . . .

It follows that, according to our common law, the trial court had no jurisdiction to hear the case against the appellant. Consequently his conviction and sentence cannot stand.

United States v Alvarez-Machain

31 ILM 902 (1992), United States Supreme Court

The appellant was a Mexican citizen. He was abducted from Mexico and transported to the US where he was charged with the kidnapping and murder of a US Drug Enforcement Agency agent. The case was dismissed in the lower courts on the ground that the abduction violated the US-Mexican extradition treaty. The Supreme Court held that the abduction did not violate the treaty and, further, that although the abduction may have been a violation of international law (the territorial integrity of Mexico), a US court could still exercise jurisdiction. In the Court's view, alleged violations of international law by the US were for the Executive alone. Dr Alvarez-Machain was eventually acquitted by a US Court and returned to Mexico.

[T]he language of the [US–Mexican extradition] Treaty, in the context of its history, does not support the proposition that the Treaty prohibits abductions outside of its terms. The remaining question, therefore, is whether the Treaty should be interpreted so as to include an implied term prohibiting prosecution where the defendant's presence is obtained by means other than those established by the Treaty. . . .

Respondent contends that the Treaty must be interpreted against the backdrop of customary international law, and that international abductions are 'so clearly prohibited in international law' that there was no reason to include such a clause in the Treaty itself. . . . The international censure of international adbuctions is further evidence, according to respondent, by the United Nations Charter and the Charter of the Organization of American States. . . .

More fundamentally, the difficulty with the support respondent garners from international law is that none of it relates to the practice of nations in relation to extradition treaties. In *Rauscher*, we implied a term in the Webster-Ashburton Treaty because of the practice of nations with regard to extradition treaties. In the instant case, respondent would imply terms in the extradition treaty from the practice of nations with regard to international law more generally. Respondent would have us find that the Treaty acts as a prohibition against a violation of the general principle of international law that one government may not 'exercise its police power in the territory of another state'. . . . There are many actions which could be taken by a nation that would violate this principle, including waging war, but it cannot seriously be contended an invasion of the United States by Mexico would violate the terms of the extradition treaty between the two nations.

In sum, to infer from this Treaty and its terms that it prohibits all means of gaining the presence of an individual outside of its terms goes beyond established precedent and practice. . . . The general principles cited by respondent simply fail to persuade us that we should imply in the United States-Mexico Extradition Treaty a term prohibiting international abductions.

Respondent and his *amici* may be correct that respondent's abduction was 'shocking', . . . and that it may be a violation of general international law principles. Mexico has protested the abduction of respondent through diplomatic notes . . . and the decision of whether respondent should be returned to Mexico, as a matter outside of the Treaty, is a matter for the Executive Branch. We conclude, however, that respondent's abduction was not in violation of the Extradition Treaty between the United States and Mexico . . . The fact of respondent's forcible abduction does not therefore prohibit his trial in a court in the United States for violations of the criminal laws of the United States.

R v *Horseferry Road Magistrates' Court, ex parte Bennett*
[1993] 3 All ER 138, House of Lords

Bennett, a New Zealand citizen, was wanted in the UK in respect of allegations of fraud. Bennett was located in South Africa and the UK police asked the South African police to send him forcibly to the UK. This was done. There was no extradition treaty between the UK and South Africa, although special extradition arrangements could have been made under the UK Extradition Act 1989. The House of Lords held that, if Bennett could prove his allegations, there would have been an abuse of the process because the manner by which he came before UK courts would have been a violation of international law and the rule of law.

LORD GRIFFITHS: The respondents have relied upon the United States authorities in which the Supreme Court has consistently refused to regard forcible abduction from a foreign country as a violation of the right by due process of law guaranteed by the Fourteenth Amendment to the Constitution: see in particular the majority opinion in *US* v *Alvarez-Machain* (1992) 112 S Ct 2188 reasserting the *Ker-Frisbie* rule (see *Ker* v *Illinois* (1886) 119 US 436 and *Frisbie* v *Collins* (1952) 342 US 519). I do not, however, find these decisions particularly helpful because they deal with the issue of whether or not an accused acquires a constitutional defence to the *jurisdiction* of the United States courts and not to the question whether, assuming the court has jurisdiction, it has a discretion to refuse to try the accused. . . .

Your Lordships are now invited to extend the concept of abuse of process a stage further. In the present case there is no suggestion that the appellant cannot have a fair trial, nor could it be suggested that it would have been unfair to try him if he had been returned to this country through extradition procedures. If the court is to have the power to interfere with the prosecution in the present circumstances it must be because the judiciary accept a responsibility for the maintenance of the rule of law that embraces a willingness to oversee executive action and to refuse to countenance behaviour that threatens either basic human rights or the rule of law.

My Lords, I have no doubt that the judiciary should accept this responsibility in the field of criminal law. The great growth of administrative law during the latter half of this century has occurred because of the recognition by the judiciary and Parliament alike that it is the function of the High Court to ensure that executive action is exercised responsibly and as Parliament intended. So also should it be in the field of criminal law and if it comes to the attention of the court that there has been a serious abuse of power it should, in my view, express its disapproval by refusing to act upon it.

Let us consider the position in the context of extradition. Extradition procedures are designed not only to ensure that criminals are returned from one country to another but also to protect the rights of those who are accused of crimes by the requesting country. Thus sufficient evidence has to be produced to show a prima facie case against the accused and the rule of speciality protects the accused from being tried for any crime other than that for which he was extradited. If a practice developed in which the police or prosecuting authorities of this country ignored extradition procedures and secured the return of an accused by a mere request to police colleagues in another country they would be flouting the extradition procedures and depriving the accused of the safeguards built into the extradition process for his benefit. It is to my mind unthinkable that in such circumstances the court should declare itself to be powerless and stand idly by; I echo the words of Lord Devlin in *Connelly* v *DPP* [1964] 2 All ER 401 at 442, [1964] AC 1254 at 1354:

> The courts cannot contemplate for a moment the transference to the executive of the responsibility for seeing that the process of law is not abused.

The courts, of course, have no power to apply direct discipline to the police or the prosecuting authorities, but they can refuse to allow them to take advantage of abuse of power by regarding their behaviour as an abuse of process and thus preventing a prosecution.

In my view your Lordships should now declare that where process of law is available to return an accused to this country through extradition procedures our courts will refuse to try him if he has been forcibly brought within our jurisdiction in disregard of those procedures by a process to which our own police, prosecuting or other executive authorities have been a knowing party.

LORD BRIDGE: Whatever differences there may be between the legal systems of South Africa, the United States, New Zealand and this country, many of the basic principles to which they seek to give effect stem from common roots. There is, I think, no principle more basic to any proper system of law than the maintenance of the rule of law itself. When it is shown that the law enforcement agency responsible for bringing a prosecution has only been enabled to do so by participating in violations of international law and of the laws of another state in order to secure the presence of the accused within the territorial jurisdiction of the court, I think that respect for the rule of law demands that the court take cognisance of that circumstance. To hold that the court may turn a blind eye to executive lawlessness beyond the frontiers of its own jurisdiction is, to my mind, an insular and unacceptable view. Having then taken cognisance of the lawlessness it would again appear to me to be a wholly inadequate response for the court to hold that the only remedy lies in civil proceedings at the suit of the defendant or in disciplinary or criminal proceedings against the individual officers of the law enforcement agency who were concerned in the illegal action taken. Since the prosecution could never have been brought if the defendant had not been illegally abducted, the whole proceeding is tainted. If a resident in another country is properly extradited here, the time when the prosecution commences is the time when the authorities here set the extradition process in motion. By parity of reasoning, if the authorities, instead of proceeding by way of extradition, have resorted to abduction, that is the effective commencement of the prosecution process and is the illegal foundation on which it rests. It is apt, in my view, to describe these circumstances, in the language used by Woodhouse J in *Moevao* v *Dept of Labour* [1980] 1 NZLR 464 at 476, as an 'abuse of the criminal jurisdiction in general' or indeed, in the language of Mansfield J in *US* v *Toscanino* (1974) 500 F 2d 267 at 276, as a 'degradation' of the court's criminal process. To hold that in these circumstances the court may decline to exercise its jurisdiction on the ground that its process has been abused may be an extension of the doctrine of abuse of process but is, in my view, a wholly proper and necessary one.

NOTES:
1. The South African and UK cases illustrate that there are circumstances in which national courts will refuse to exercise a jurisdiction that they undoubtedly possess because of the circumstances in which an exercise of that jurisdiction has become possible. A violation of international law in securing the defendant prevents the exercise of jurisdiction. In *Ebrahim*, the court refused to exercise jurisdiction even though the defendant was a national of the State and irrespective of whether the offended State had actually protested. Note, however, that the UK decision in *R* v *Staines Magistrates' Court, ex parte Westfallen* [1998] 4 All ER 210, appears to limit the *Bennett* principle. According to the Divisional Court, the national court should decline jurisdiction where the defendant was procured in violation of international law *only* if the UK had themselves acted illegally or procured or connived in the illegality of others. So, an unlawful deportation from another country would not prevent an exercise of jurisdiction by a UK court if the UK authorities simply stood by and let it occur rather than taking part in it. This is a fine line indeed, and does not support the principle behind declining jurisdiction as put forward in *Ebrahim*. In contrast, the decision in *Alvarez-Machain* seems arrogant and unprincipled and says more about the US attitude to the sovereign equality of States and the rule of international law than a thousand pronouncements by US ambassadors in the General Assembly.
2. This issue was also raised in *Attorney-General of the Government of Israel* v *Eichmann* (above), where Eichmann was abducted from Argentina by the Israeli Secret Service. Argentina protested, Israel expressed its regret, but the national court exercised jurisdiction. This case may perhaps be distinguished from the three extracted above because the crimes with which Eichmann was charged were crimes giving rise to universal jurisdiction, as opposed to crimes under the national laws of the abducting States.

SECTION 4: **Exercise of jurisdiction over persons by international tribunals and international criminal law**

A: International tribunals

As international law is a system of law that is concerned primarily with the relations of States, there have been few examples of international courts exercising jurisdiction over individuals. Some aspects of this issue are discussed in Chapters 5, 6 and 14. After the Second World War, two International Tribunals were established at Nuremberg and Tokyo to try individuals accused of war crimes, crimes of aggression and crimes against humanity. As well as being crimes giving rise to universal jurisdiction for the national courts of all States, these offences were said to be crimes under international law for which an international tribunal could properly exercise jurisdiction. Many defendants were found guilty and executed. For nearly 40 years after the Nuremberg and Tokyo trials, there were few developments in this field. However, in recent years, the international community has considered afresh the possibility of establishing an International Criminal Court to try individuals accused of certain offences, and concrete steps have been taken in respect of two recent outbreaks of international violence.

Rome Statute for an International Criminal Court 1998

The Statute of the International Criminal Court entered into force on 1 July 2002 and from that date the International Criminal Court (ICC) was in existence. At that date, there were 78 State parties, with many more anticipated once they had brought their national legislation into line with the requirements of the Statute. The UK became a party on 4 October 2001 and has enacted the International Criminal Court Act 2001. The Advance Team for the ICC is now preparing the ground for the full operation of the Court and the First Session of the Assembly of State Parties will take place in September 2002. The Court will be based in The Hague, The Netherlands along with the ICJ. The US will not become a party, being fundamentally opposed to the exercise of jurisdiction over its nationals by an international court (see Chapter 3).

Article 5 Crimes within the jurisdiction of the Court
1. The jurisdiction of the Court shall be limited to the most serious crimes of concern to the international community as a whole. The Court has jurisdiction in accordance with this Statute with respect to the following crimes:
(a) The crime of genocide;
(b) Crimes against humanity;
(c) War crimes;
(d) The crime of aggression.
2. The Court shall exercise jurisdiction over the crime of aggression once a provision is adopted in accordance with articles 121 and 123 defining the crime and setting out the conditions under which the Court shall exercise jurisdiction with respect to this crime. Such a provision shall be consistent with the relevant provisions of the Charter of the United Nations.

Article 11 Jurisdiction ratione temporis
1. The Court has jurisdiction only with respect to crimes committed after the entry into force of this Statute.
2. If a State becomes a Party to this Statute after its entry into force, the Court may exercise its jurisdiction only with respect to crimes committed after the entry into force of this Statute for that State, unless that State has made a declaration under article 12, paragraph 3.

Article 12 Preconditions to the exercise of jurisdiction
1. A State which becomes a Party to this Statute thereby accepts the jurisdiction of the Court with respect to the crimes referred to in article 5.

2. In the case of article 13, paragraph (a) or (c). the Court may exercise its jurisdiction if one or more of the following States are Parties to this Statute or have accepted the jurisdiction of the Court in accordance with paragraph 3:

(a) The State on the territory of which the conduct in question occurred or, if the crime was committed on board a vessel or aircraft, the State of registration of that vessel or aircraft;

(b) The State of which the person accused of the crime is a national.

3. If the acceptance of a State which is not a Party to this Statute is required under paragraph 2, that State may, by declaration lodged with the Registrar, accept the exercise of jurisdiction by the Court with respect to the crime in question. The accepting State shall cooperate with the Court without any delay or exception in accordance with Part 9.

Article 13 Exercise of jurisdiction

The Court may exercise its jurisdiction with respect to a crime referred to in article 5 in accordance with the provisions of this Statute if:

(a) A situation in which one or more of such crimes appears to have been committed is referred to the Prosecutor by a State Party in accordance with article 14;

(b) A situation in which one or more of such crimes appears to have been committed is referred to the Prosecutor by the Security Council acting under Chapter VII of the Charter of the United Nations; or

(c) The Prosecutor has initiated an investigation in respect of such a crime in accordance with article 15.

Article 16 Deferral of investigation or prosecution

No investigation or prosecution may be commenced or proceeded with under this Statute for a period of 12 months after the Security Council, in a resolution adopted under Chapter VII of the Charter of the United Nations, has requested the Court to that effect; that request may be renewed by the Council under the same conditions.

Article 17 Issues of admissibility

1. Having regard to paragraph 10 of the Preamble and article 1, the Court shall determine that a case is inadmissible where:

(a) The case is being investigated or prosecuted by a State which has jurisdiction over it, unless the State is unwilling or unable genuinely to carry out the investigation or prosecution;

(b) The case has been investigated by a State which has jurisdiction over it and the State has decided not to prosecute the person concerned, unless the decision resulted from the unwillingness or inability of the State genuinely to prosecute;

(c) The person concerned has already been tried for conduct which is the subject of the complaint, and a trial by the Court is not permitted under article 20, paragraph 3;

(d) The case is not of sufficient gravity to justify further action by the Court.

2. In order to determine unwillingness in a particular case, the Court shall consider, having regard to the principles of due process recognized by international law, whether one or more of the following exist, as applicable:

(a) The proceedings were or are being undertaken or the national decision was made for the purpose of shielding the person concerned from criminal responsibility for crimes within the jurisdiction of the Court referred to in article 5:

(b) There has been an unjustified delay in the proceedings which in the circumstances is inconsistent with an intent to bring the person concerned to justice;

(c) The proceedings were not or are not being conducted independently or impartially, and they were or are being conducted in a manner which, in the circumstances, is inconsistent with an intent to bring the person concerned to justice.

3. In order to determine inability in a particular case, the Court shall consider whether, due to a total or substantial collapse or unavailability of its national judicial system, the State is unable to obtain the accused or the necessary evidence and testimony or otherwise unable to carry out its proceedings.

Article 21 Applicable law

1. The Court shall apply:
   (a) In the first place, this Statute, Elements of Crimes and its Rules of Procedure and Evidence;
   (b) In the second place, where appropriate, applicable treaties and the principles and rules of international law, including the established principles of the international law of armed conflict.
   (c) Failing that, general principles of law derived by the Court from national laws of legal systems of the world including, as appropriate, the national laws of States that would normally exercise jurisdiction over the crime, provided that those principles are not inconsistent with this Statute and with international law and internationally recognized norms and standards.

2. The Court may apply principles and rules of law as interpreted in its previous decisions.

3. The application and interpretation of law pursuant to this article must be consistent with internationally recognized human rights, and be without any adverse distinction founded on grounds such as gender as defined in article 7, paragraph 3, age, race, colour, language, religion or belief, political or other opinion, national, ethnic or social origin, wealth, birth or other status.

International Tribunal for the Prosecution of Persons Responsible for Serious Violations of International Humanitarian Law Committed in the Territory of the Former Yugoslavia
SC Res 827 (1993)

The creation of this tribunal by the Security Council is part of the international community's response to the conflict that has engulfed the former State of Yugoslavia. Its purpose is simply to try individuals accused of violations of the laws of war and other atrocities. The first defendants have been indicted and tried, and there have been both convictions and acquittals.

Article 1 Competence of the International Tribunal
The International Tribunal shall have the power to prosecute persons responsible for serious violations of international humanitarian law committed in the territory of the former Yugoslavia since 1991 in accordance with the provisions of the present Statute.

Article 2 Grave breaches of the Geneva Conventions of 1949
The International Tribunal shall have the power to prosecute persons committing or ordering to be committed grave breaches of the Geneva Conventions of 12 August 1949 . . .

Article 3 Violations of the laws or customs of war
The International Tribunal shall have the power to prosecute persons violating the laws or customs of war . . .

Article 4 Genocide
1. The International Tribunal shall have the power to prosecute persons committing genocide . . .

Article 5 Crime against humanity
The International Tribunal shall have the power to prosecute persons responsible for the following crimes when committed in armed conflict, whether international or internal in character, and directed against any civilian population:

    (a) murder;

    (b) extermination;

    (c) enslavement;

    (d) deportation;

    (e) imprisonment;

    (f) torture;

    (g) rape;

    (h) persecutions on political, racial and religious grounds;

    (i) other inhuman acts.

Article 7 Individual criminal responsibility
1. A person who planned, instigated, ordered, committed or otherwise aided and abetted in the planning, preparation or execution of a crime referred to in articles 2 to 5 of the present Statute, shall be individually responsible for the crime.

2. The official position of any accused person, whether as Head of State or Government or as a responsible Government official, shall not relieve such person of criminal responsibility nor mitigate punishment.

3. The fact that any of the acts referred to in articles 2 to 5 of the present Statute was committed by a subordinate does not relieve his superior of criminal responsibility if he knew or had rason to know that the subordinate was about to commit such acts or had done so and the superior failed to take the necessary and reasonable measures to prevent such acts or to punish the perpetrators thereof.

4. The fact that an accused person acted pursuant to an order of a Government or of a superior shall not relieve him of criminal responsibility, but may be considered in mitigation if the International Tribunal determines that justice so requires.

Article 9 Concurrent jurisdiction
1. The International Tribunal and national courts shall have concurrent jurisdiction to prosecute persons for serious violations of international humanitarian law committed in the territory of the former Yugoslavia since 1 January 1991.

2. The International Tribunal shall have primacy over national courts. At any stage of the procedure, the International Tribunal may formally request national courts to defer to the competence of the International Tribunal in accordance with the present Statute and the Rules of Procedure and Evidence of the International Tribunal.

NOTES:

1. The Security Council has established a similar tribunal to deal with personal criminal responsibility arising out of the Rwandan civil war: see International Tribunal for Rwanda

established by SC Res. 955 (1994) and it now seems certain that a tribunal will be created to deal with events in Sierra Leone.

2. The trial of the Lockerbie bombing suspects (see Chapter 15) by a Scottish court in The Netherlands is an unusual example of cooperation in the field of enforcement jurisdiction, having both a national and an international flavour. The trial of the suspects was a pre-condition of the lifting of UN sanctions against Libya (now done), but the UK maintained throughout that the exercise of jurisdiction should fall to the State territorially affected (Scotland) and be according to its normal criminal laws. The establishment of a Scottish court, in The Netherlands, under the watching brief of the UN, met Libyan fears about partiality: see the Agreement between the [Government of The Netherlands] and the [UK Government] concerning a Scottish Trial in The Netherlands 38 ILM 926 (1999).

B: International criminal law

International criminal law is not a term of art. It is a loose description of a set of rules that deal with cross-border criminal matters. Some issues are not 'international' in the sense in which that term has been used throughout this collection of materials. Thus, the European Convention on Extradition 1957 and its Additional Protocol 1975 impose and regulate an obligation to extradite among State parties. However, the extradition crimes are not 'international' in the sense of being crimes against international law. These are crimes under the national laws of participating States for which there is international co-operation in enforcement and related matters. Of course there is overlap between matters relating to *international co-operation* in the field of criminal matters and *international crimes* properly so-called, as with the European Convention on the Suppression of Terrorism 1977.

It is not the purpose of this collection to deal extensively with international criminal law. Certain aspects of this emerging and developing field have been dealt with already. The concept of international crimes (piracy, slavery, genocide, torture, war of aggression, crimes against humanity, war crimes and possibly others) and their relationship with the principle of universal jurisdiction has been discussed above. The emergence of international tribunals, having an international competence in respect of international crimes, is now gathering pace. As we have seen, the International Criminal Court is established and no doubt will exercise its *international* jurisdiction in due course. This is already an achievement of the highest order and marks a sea-change in the way international law works. It can no longer be said that international law is only concerned with the enforcement of the rights and duties of States. Likewise, the Rwanda and Yugoslavia Tribunals are busy and the new Sierra Leone Tribunal is likely to be established in the very near future. Other matters relevant to 'international criminal law' in the sense of involving international legal rights and duties include the systems for the protection and promotion of human rights, both regional and general; the relationship between crimes of terror and the use of force by States; the law of State responsibility and jurisdictional questions; the law of humanitarian warfare; and the ever growing international personality of individuals and multinational corporations.

In terms of the law relating to international co-operation in criminal matters, there is a burgeoning list of international treaties, soft law, agreed protocols and informal cross-border working practices. The subject matter covers mutual assistance in criminal matters (e.g. European Convention on Mutual Assistance in Criminal Matters 1959), extradition arrangements, cross-border crimes such as money laundering, drug trafficking and people smuggling, internet crime, co-ordination of policing arrangements and arrest warrants (e.g. Interpol) and cross-border abduction (e.g. parental child abduction). In other words, a vast array of legal and practical measures designed to prevent, deter, detect and punish national crimes which have an international dimension.

9

Immunities from National Jurisdiction

Introductory note

In Chapter 5 on personality and recognition, it was suggested that a subject of international law enjoys certain privileges or rights, both in international and national law. One of the most important of these is the immunity from legal process enjoyed by States and international organisations and their representative in the courts of other States. This immunity can be split conveniently into State (or sovereign) immunity and diplomatic and consular immunities. The first concerns foreign States *per se*, (including the Head of State) while the second concerns the personal immunities enjoyed by representatives of those States. These immunities may be either because the particular individual or entity enjoys a certain status under their own law (sometimes called immunity *ratione personae*) and sometimes because of the substance of the matter in which the individual has become involved (sometimes called immunity *ratione materiae*). Generally speaking, immunity *ratione personae* – that is, simply because the entity or individual has a certain status (e.g. a Head of State or Ambassador) irrespective of the nature of the matter in which they have become involved – is more limited in scope and endures only while the status endures. Immunity *ratione materiae*, on the other hand, attaches because of the inherently sovereign nature of the incident in which the entity or individual has become embroiled and in consequence finds more favour with local courts and commentators. However, we should remember that these are descriptive labels, rather than analytical categories and that each claim of immunity must be judged within the factual matrix it occurs, including the relevant international rules (often found in treaty) and the particular approach of the relevant local court. By way of contrast, the immunities enjoyed by international organisations and their staff are purely functional in that they exist only to ensure that the organisation may operate effectively within States. Such immunities are granted by treaty and there are no difficult issues about 'dignity', 'international comity' and 'equality of nations' as there is with States.

In this Chapter, both the sections on State and diplomatic immunity deal with the position in international law generally and then the position in national law in particular. As far as most national legal systems are concerned, it should also be noted that a State (and hence its representatives) will not be able to benefit from immunity unless that State has been recognised as a 'Sovereign State' in accordance with the criteria discussed in Chapter 5.

The principle of internationally protected immunity for States and their representatives is a principle of international law. This has the immediate consequence that should a State fail to apply the principle of immunity in an appropriate case, it will be responsible under international law as in the *Arrest Warrant of 11 April 2000 Case (Democratic Republic of Congo v Belgium)*, ICJ Rep 14 February 2002, where Belgium international responsibility was engaged for issuing an arrest warrant against the Congolese Minister of Foreign Affairs in violation of the latter's immunity. However, the actual circumstances in which immunity is to be granted are usually settled by the national law of each State in an attempt to comply with that State's international obligations. For this reason the UK position is dealt with at some length. Reference will also be made to the law of other countries by way of comparison.

SECTION 1: State immunity in international law

A: General principles

In the recent past there has been considerable debate over whether a State's immunity before the courts of another State was 'absolute' or 'restrictive.' If absolute, a State was immune for all purposes and in all proceedings. If restrictive, a State was immune only in respect of its 'sovereign' acts, otherwise known as acts *juri imperii*, and not immune in respect of its private law or commercial acts, otherwise known as acts *jure gestionis*. It is now settled that States may grant only restrictive immunity to other States without incurring responsibility under international law. Necessarily, however, this means that national courts must be able to draw the distinction between acts *juri imperii* and *jure gestionis*. The extracts below consider these matters as well as the distinction between the principles of State immunity and other similar doctrines such as 'act of State' and non-justiciability.

I. Sinclair, 'The Law of Sovereign Immunity; Recent Developments'
(1980) 167 RC 113

The notion of immunity must also be distinguished from the notion of non-justiciability. Immunity, expressed in the maxim *par in parem non habet imperium*, is in principle concerned with the status of sovereign equality enjoyed by all independent States. . . . Non-justiciability, or lack of jurisdiction in the local courts by reason of the subject-matter, is a concept which, although it may be related, is distinct. Thus, a court may refuse to pronounce upon the validity of a law of a foreign State applying to matters within its own territory, on the ground that to do so would amount to an assertion of jurisdiction over the internal affairs of that State. . . .

If then immunity can be defined jurisprudentially as the correlative of a duty imposed upon the territorial State to refrain from exercising its jurisdiction over a foreign State, and if it must be distinguished from lack of jurisdiction in the territorial State by reason of the subject-matter, does it apply *ratione personae* or *ratione materiae*? The answer is probably both. Immunity applies *ratione personae* to identify the categories of persons, whether individuals, corporate bodies or unincorporated entities, by whom it may *prima facie* be claimable: and *ratione materiae* to identify whether substantively it may properly be claimed. . . .

6. *Acts jure imperii and jure gestionis*

Although it may appear that the distinction between acts *jure imperii* and acts *jure gestionis* is more objective than the distinction between the differing personalities or capacities of the State (because one is looking at the *nature* of the act rather than the capacity in which the State performs it), abundant difficulties remain. . . .

This is not to say that the distinction between acts *jure imperii* and acts *jure gestionis* is impractical and unworkable. It does at any rate furnish a general guideline sufficient to indicate that immunity must continue to be accorded in proceedings which put in issue the sovereign acts of foreign States. Given the multifarious and constantly expanding range of activities in which the modern State engages, any attempt to give an exhaustive definition or even enumeration of State activities which can be classified as activities *jure gestionis* is probably doomed to failure. . . .

It must however be admitted that there has been a tendency, in those civil law jurisdictions which have developed the restrictive immunity theory, to base it, at least in part, on the distinction between the State operating in the sphere of public law and the State operating in the sphere of private law. This has been a source of some confusion since, even in those States which apply the public law/private law dichotomy, there is no clear dividing line between what pertains to the sphere of public law and what pertains to the sphere of private law. . . . In any event, there is, as has already been noted, a very high degree of artificiality in the concept of the State acting as a private person. . . .

It is all very well to say that an individual can make a contract, but cannot expel an alien or legislate in such a way as to nationalise property. If one takes this simple dichotomy, it is no doubt easy to reach the conclusion that immunity should not be claimable by a State in respect of any contract which it has entered into, but may be claimed if what is in issue is the validity of legislative or administrative acts which it may have taken in exercise of its political (in the widest sense) functions. Here again, however, one confronts a dilemma of the kind presented in the English case of *Congreso del Partido*, for a State may enter into what is *prima facie* a pure commercial transaction, but may, for high policy reasons, decide subsequently to renege on the transaction. Does one look to the nature of the *original* transaction (purely commercial in nature) or to the nature of the subsequent breach?

7. Immunity and Act of State

This brings us neatly to the borderland between sovereign immunity and the act of State doctrine. . . .

Jurisprudentially, of course, the two doctrines are quite distinct. The residual rule of immunity in respect of acts *jure imperii* precludes the courts of the State of the forum from assuming jurisdiction in a case where a foreign State is directly or indirectly impleaded and where the validity of acts which it has performed in its sovereign capacity may be in issue. In other words, it operates as a bar *in limine* to the continuance of the proceedings. The 'act of State' doctrine on the other hand is not in any sense a bar to the assumption of jurisdiction, and it may be pleaded even in cases where the foreign State is neither directly nor indirectly impleaded. It may nonetheless be a defence . . . to proceedings in which the validity of foreign executive or legislative acts may be in issue. . . .

[T]here is little doubt that the preponderant practice of States now favours the concept that the jurisdictional immunities of States and their property should be limited by some kind of functional test. This suggests that one should go back to first principles and seek to discern the true foundation of the concept of sovereign immunity.

If one looks again at the classic judgment of Chief Justice Marshall in *Schooner Exchange* v *McFaddon*, one sees that it is based fundamentally on the principle that 'the jurisdiction of the nation within it is own territory is necessarily exclusive and absolute'. . . . He then goes on to propound the thesis that 'this full and absolute territorial jurisdiction being like the attribute of every sovereign, and being incapable of conferring extra-territorial power, would not seem to contemplate foreign sovereigns nor their sovereign rights as its objects'. . . . He then develops the theory of the express or implied licence whereunder the sovereign enters a foreign territory on the understanding that the territorial authorities will waive in his favour the exercise of part of their complete exclusive territorial jurisdiction.

If one takes this as the starting point, it will be seen that the whole topic of sovereign immunity appears in a new light. It operates by way of exception to the dominating principle of territorial jurisdiction. In other words, one does not start from an assumption that immunity is the norm, and that exceptions to the rule of immunity have to be justified. One starts from an assumption of non-immunity, qualified by reference to the functional need (operating by way of express or implied licence) to protect the sovereign rights of foreign States operating or present in the territory. . . .

This approach is not all that far removed from that suggested by Lauterpacht some 30 years ago. Lauterpacht indeed proposed the partial abolition of the rule of immunity of foreign States, subject to the following safeguards:

(1) Immunity must remain the rule with respect to the legislative acts of a foreign State and of measures taken in pursuance thereof (e.g., nationalization laws or decrees).

(2) Immunity must remain the rule in respect of the executive and administrative acts of the foreign State within its territory, such as alleged unjustified expulsion or exaction of dues or denial of justice.

(3) Immunity must remain with respect to contracts made with or by the foreign State which, by virtue of the rules of private international law applied by the courts of the State of the forum, lie outside their jurisdiction.

(4) No action should lie or execution be levied against a foreign State contrary to the accepted principles of international law in the matter of diplomatic immunities.

The one element in these . . . proposals which may warrant hesitation is the implied suggestion that there should be some real connection between the subject-matter of the dispute and the territorial jurisdiction of the courts of the State of the forum. . . .

To sum up, the continuing trend of comparative case-law on State immunity is in the direction of recognising and applying the restrictive theory. Various justifications have been advanced for the restrictive theory, none of which is wholly satisfactory. The reason is perhaps that the courts have sought to elaborate reasons for cutting down what they regarded as a pre-existing rule of immunity. This has led them on occasion to try to enumerate or define what is the content of those acts in respect of which immunity is *not* claimable. The equation may become easier to solve if one starts from the opposite assumption and seeks to elaborate or define more closely the class of cases in which, even on the restrictive theory, immunity may still have to be accorded. This in turn suggests that, for the purposes of the searching study upon which the International Law Commission have now embarked, attention could perhaps be focussed, not so much on the theoretical underpinnings of the distinction between acts *jure gestionis* and acts *jure imperii* or of the distinction between the differing capacities or personalities of the State, but rather on the functional need to maintain a measure of jurisdictional immunity for foreign States in order to ensure that the local courts do not call into question the validity of acts which they have performed in their own territory in exercise of their sovereign authority.

International Law Commission, Draft Articles on Jurisdictional Immunities of States and their Property

In 1978, the International Law Commission began the task of codifying the international legal principles on State immunity. It has now completed its task and the Draft Articles have been under consideration by the 6th (Legal) Committee of the UN General Assembly, although they have not been well received and their future is uncertain.

Article 1 Scope of the present articles
The present articles apply to the immunity of a State and its property from the jurisdiction of the courts of another State.

Article 2 Use of terms
1. For the purposes of the present articles:
    (a) 'court' means any organ of a State, however, named, entitled to exercise judicial functions;
    (b) 'State' means:
        (i)   the State and its various organs of government;
        (ii) constituent units of a federal State;
        (iii) political subdivisions of the State which are entitled to perform acts in the exercise of the sovereign authority of the State;
        (iv) agencies or instrumentalities of the State and other entities, to the extent that the are entitled to perform acts in the exercise of the sovereign authority of the State;
        (v)   representatives of the State acting in that capacity;
    (c) 'commercial transaction' means:
        (i)   any commercial contract or transaction for the sale of goods or supply of services.
        (ii) any contract for a loan or other transaction of a financial nature, including any obligation of guarantee or of indemnity in respect of any such loan or transaction;
        (iii) any other contract or transaction of a commercial, industrial, trading or professional nature, but not including a contract of employment of persons.

2. In determining whether a contract or transaction is a 'commercial transaction' under paragraph 1(c), reference should be made primarily to the nature of the contract or transaction, but its purpose should also be taken into account if, in the practice of the State which is a party to it, that purpose is relevant to determining the non-commercial character of the contract or transaction.

3. The provisions of paragraphs 1 and 2 regarding the use of terms in the present articles are without prejudice to the use of those terms or to the meanings which may be given to them in other international instruments or in the internal law of any State.

Article 5 State immunity
A state enjoys immunity, in respect of itself and its property, from the jurisdiction of the courts of another State subject to the provisions of the present articles.

Article 10 Commercial transactions
1. If a State engages in a commercial transaction with a foreign natural or juridical person and, by virtue of the applicable rules of private international law, differences relating to the commercial transaction fall within the jurisdiction of a court of another State, the State cannot invoke immunity from that jurisdiction in a proceeding arising out of that commercial transaction.

2. Paragraph 1 does not apply:
(a) in the case of a commercial transaction between States; or
(b) if the parties to the commercial transaction have expressly agreed otherwise.

3. The immunity from jurisdiction enjoyed by a State shall not be affected with regard to a proceeding which relates to a commercial transaction engaged in by a State enterprise or other entity established by the State which has an independent legal personality and is capable of:
(a) suing or being sued; and
(b) acquiring, owning or possessing and disposing of property, including property which the State has authorized it to operate or manage.

European Convention on State Immunity 1972
11 ILM 470 (1972)

The 41 Articles of the European Convention cover all aspects of State immunity, and the optional Additional Protocol of 14 Articles establishes a European Tribunal to settle disputes arising out of the Convention that cannot be settled by a State's national law. At August 2002, the Convention was in force with 8 parties and the Additional Protocol with 6 parties. Apart from its general provisions, the main impact of this Convention was to introduce a mechanism for the enforcement of judgments against States. Previously, many States still allowed absolute immunity against enforcement, even though there was only restrictive immunity for adjudication of the dispute.

Article 20

1. A Contracting State shall give effect to a judgment given against it by a court of another Contracting State:
(a) if, in accordance with the provisions of Articles 1 to 13, the State could not claim immunity from jurisdiction; and
(b) if the judgment cannot or can no longer be set aside if obtained by default, or if it is not or is no longer subject to appeal or any other form of ordinary review or to annulment.

2. Nevertheless, a Contracting State is not obliged to give effect to such a judgment in any case:
(a) where it would be manifestly contrary to public policy in that State to do so, or where, in the circumstances, either party had no adequate opportunity fairly to present his case;
(b) where proceedings between the same parties, based on the same facts and having the same purpose:
   (i) are pending before a court of that State and were the first to be instituted;
   (ii) are pending before a court of another Contracting State, were the first to be instituted and may result in a judgment to which the State party to the proceedings must give effect under the terms of this Convention;
(c) where the result of the judgment is inconsistent with the result of another judgment given between the same parties:
   (i) by a court of the Contracting State, if the proceedings before that court were the first to be instituted or if the other judgment has been given before the judgment satisfied the conditions specified in paragraph 1 (b); or
   (ii) by a court of another Contracting State where the other judgment is the first to satisfy the requirements laid down in the present Convention;
(d) where the provisions of Article 16 have not been observed and the State has not entered an appearance or has not appealed against a judgment by default.

3. In addition, in the cases provided for in Article 10, a Contracting State is not obliged to give effect to the judgment:

  (a) if the courts of the State of the forum would not have been entitled to assume jurisdiction had they applied, *mutatis mutandis*, the rules of jurisdiction (other than those mentioned in the Annex to the present Convention) which operate in the State against which judgment is given; or

  (b) if the court, by applying a law other than that which would have been applied in accordance with the rules of private international law of that State, has reached a result different from that which would have been reached by applying the law determined by those rules.

However, a Contracting State may not rely upon the grounds of refusal specified in sub-paragraphs (a) and (b) above if it is bound by an agreement with the State of the forum on the recognition and enforcement of judgments and the judgment fulfils the requirement of that agreement as regards jurisdiction and, where appropriate, the law applied.

Article 23
No measures of execution or preventive measures against the property of a Contracting State may be taken in the territory of another Contracting State except where and to the extent that the State has expressly consented thereto in writing in any particular case.

Holland v *Lampen-Wolfe*
[2001] 1 WLR 1573, House of Lords

The claimant was employed at a US military base in the UK in an educational capacity. The defendant, also an employee of the US made disparaging remarks about the claimant's teaching. The claimant sued for libel and the US raised the defence of state immunity. The House of Lords held that the matter fell outside the UK State Immunity Act 1978 (on which see below) because it was related to a function of the armed forces of a State (see s 16, State Immunity Act 1978) and so was to be treated under the common law. Their Lordships thus had cause to consider the nature of State immunity.

LORD MILLET: It is an established rule of customary international law that one state cannot be sued in the courts of another for acts performed *jure imperii*. The immunity does not derive from the authority or dignity of sovereign States or the need to protect the integrity of their governmental functions. It derives from the sovereign nature of the exercise of the State's adjudicative powers and the basic principle of international law that all States are equal. The rule is *'par in parem non habet imperium'*: see *I Congreso del Partido* [1983] 1 AC 244, 262, per Lord Wilberforce. As I explained in *Reg* v *Bow Street Metropolitan Stipendiary Magistrate, ex parte Pinochet Ugarte (No 3)* [2000] 1 AC 147, 269, it is a subject-matter immunity. It operates to prevent the official and governmental acts of one state from being called into question in proceedings before the courts of another. The existence of the doctrine is confirmed by the European Convention on State Immunity (1972) (Cmnd 5081), the relevant provisions of which are generally regarded as reflecting customary international law. In according immunity from suit before the English courts to foreign States the State Immunity Act 1978 and the common law give effect to the international obligations of the United Kingdom.

Where the immunity applies, it covers an official of the state in respect of acts performed by him in an official capacity. In the present case, it is common ground that at all material times the defendant acted in his capacity as an official of the United States Department of Defense, being the department responsible for the armed forces of the United States present in the United Kingdom. The United States has asserted immunity on behalf of the defendant. Dr. Holland has not challenged the proposition that, if the United States is entitled to the immunity it claims, that immunity bars the present proceedings.

NOTES:

1. In *Kuwait Airways Corporation v Iraqi Airways Co (Nos 4 and 5)* [2002] 2 WLR 1353, the House of Lords returned to the legal issues arising out of Iraq's invasion of Kuwait in 1990 and the subsequent seizure and use by Iraq and an Iraqi company of aircraft owned by the Kuwait Airways Corporation. Questions of State immunity had been litigated before the House in *Kuwait Airways Corporation v Iraqi Airways Co* [1995] 1 WLR 1147 (see below). The present case concerned liability and damages in tort. One issue was whether the UK court must recognise the Iraqi law that had confiscated the aircraft and that gave title to the Iraqi company. If this Iraqi law was valid in a UK court, the chances of liability for wrongful use were much diminished as the Iraqi company could show good title to the aircraft. Normally, a UK court would be obliged to give effect to a law of a foreign sovereign State and the principle of non-justicibility would mean that the UK court could not pronounce on the validity of that law: it had to accept it. However, the House of Lords noted that the invasion of Kuwait was a violation of a rule of *jus cogens* (the prohibition of the use of force) and that clear rules of international law existed nullifying all the effects of the invasion. In such circumstances, the House of Lords concluded that there was an exception to the principle of non-justicibility so that a UK court could pronounce on the validity of a foreign State's laws where the relevant rules of international law were clear and manageable. Consequently, the UK court did not have to accept the validity of the Iraqi law because it was perpetuated in consequence of, and in pursuance of, a course of action declared illegal under international law. Clearly, this is a significant development, not only in terms of the relationship between UK law and international law (in that it seems to afford a primacy to international law over normal rules of UK law), but also because it may precipitate many more challenges to the laws of foreign States that might be thought to be contrary to principles of international law.

2. As a matter of legal theory, the Draft Articles propose a principle of absolute immunity (Article 5) and then detract from that in Part III, Articles 10 to 17. The result is a set of Articles establishing restrictive immunity turning on the distinction between acts *juri imperii* and acts *jure gestionis*. Certain activities are presumptively not immune: employment contracts (Article 11), acts causing personal injury or damage to property (Article 12), acts relating to immoveable property (Article 13), to intellectual property (Article 14), to State ships (Article 16), matters concerning companies (Article 15), and certain arbitration proceedings (Article 17). Importantly, Article 10 attempts a definition of a 'commercial transaction' in which the purpose of the disputed activity may be relevant in making the decision.

B: Theories

The Schooner Exchange v *McFaddon*
7 Cranch 116 (1812), US Supreme Court

MARSHALL CJ: The jurisdiction of the nation within its own territory is necessarily exclusive and absolute. It is susceptible of no limitation not imposed by itself. Any restriction upon it, deriving validity from an external source, would imply a diminution of its sovereignty to the extent of the restriction, and an investment of that sovereignty to the same extent in that power which could impose such restriction.

All exceptions, therefore, to the full and complete power of a nation within its own territories, must be traced up to the consent of the nation itself. They can flow from no other legitimate source. This consent may be either express or implied. . . .

This full and absolute territorial jurisdiction being alike the attribute of every sovereign, and being incapable of conferring extraterritorial power, would not seem to contemplate foreign sovereigns nor their sovereign rights as its objects. One sovereign being in no respect amenable to another; and being bound by obligations of the highest character not to degrade the dignity of his nation, by placing himself or its sovereign rights within the jurisdiction of another, can be supposed to enter a foreign territory only under an express license, or in the confidence that the immunities belonging to his independent sovereign station, though not expressly stipulated, are reserved by implication, and will be extended to him.

This perfect equality and absolute independence of sovereigns, and this common interest impelling them to mutual intercourse, and an interchange of good offices with each other, have given rise to a class of cases in which every sovereign is understood to waive the exercise of a part of that complete exclusive territorial jurisdiction, which has been stated to be the attribute of every nation.

1st. One of these is admitted to be the exemption of the person of the sovereign from arrest or detention within a foreign territory.

If he enters that territory with the knowledge and license of its sovereign, that license, although containing no stipulation exempting his person from arrest, is universally understood to imply such stipulation.

2d. A second case, standing on the same principles with the first, is the immunity which all civilized nations allow to foreign ministers.

3d. A third case in which a sovereign is understood to cede a portion of his territorial jurisdiction is, where he allows the troops of a foreign prince to pass through his dominions. . . .

The preceding reasoning has maintained the propositions that all exemptions from territorial jurisdiction must be derived from the consent of the sovereign of the territory; that this consent may be implied or expressed; and that when implied, its extent must be regulated by the nature of the case, and the views under which the parties requiring and conceding it must be supposed to act.

Victory Transport Inc v *Comisaria General de Abastecimientos y Transpertos*
35 ILR (1964) 110, United States Second Circuit Court of Appeals

The defendants (an organ of the Spanish Government), entered into a charter agreement with the plaintiffs. An arbitration clause provided for arbitration in New York in the event of a dispute. The defendants claimed State immunity.

SMITH J: The conceptual difficulties involved in formulating a satisfactory method of differentiating between acts *jure imperii* and acts *jure gestionis* have led many commentators to declare that the distinction is unworkable. However, the Supreme Court has made it plain that when the State Department has been silent on the question of immunity in a particular case, it is the court's duty to determine for itself whether the foreign sovereign is entitled to immunity 'in conformity to the principles accepted by the department of the Government charged with the conduct of foreign relations'. . . . And since the State Department has publicly pronounced its adherence to the distinction, we must apply it to the facts of this case.

The purpose of the restrictive theory of sovereign immunity is to try to accommodate the interest of individuals doing business with foreign Governments in having their legal rights determined by the courts, with the interest of foreign Governments in being free to perform certain political acts without undergoing the embarrassment or hindrance of defending the propriety of such acts before foreign courts. Sovereign immunity is a derogation from the normal exercise of jurisdiction by the courts and should be accorded only in clear cases. Since the State Department's failure or refusal to suggest immunity is significant, we are disposed to deny a claim of sovereign immunity that has not been 'recognized and allowed' by the State Department unless it is plain that the activity in question falls within one of the categories of strictly political or public acts about which sovereigns have traditionally been quite sensitive. Such acts are generally limited to the following categories:

(1) internal administrative acts, such as expulsion of an alien;

(2) legislative acts, such as nationalization;

(3) acts concerning the armed forces;

(4) acts concerning diplomatic activity;

(5) public loans.

We do not think that the restrictive theory adopted by the State Department requires sacrificing the interests of private litigants to international comity in other than these limited categories. Should diplomacy require enlargement of these categories, the State Department can file a suggestion of immunity with the court. Should diplomacy require contraction of these categories, the State Department can issue a new or clarifying policy pronouncement.

NOTES:

1. There are various theories put forward to explain the basis of State immunity, although the view put forward by Marshall CJ in *The Schooner Exchange*, above, is generally regarded as the most apposite. It is echoed in the speech of Lord Millet in *Lampen-Wolfe* extracted above. Note, however, that as we come to consider the immunity of individuals derived from their status (e.g. immunity *ratione personae* such as with Heads of State, Ambassadors etc.), it seems that its justification is purely functional, in that it ensures that the individual may carry out their functions as an officer of the State. As noted in the *Arrest Warrant Case*, ICJ Rep February 2002, para. 53, 'the immunities accorded to Ministers of Foreign Affairs are not granted for their personal benefit, but to ensure the effective performance of their functions on behalf of their respective states.'

2. In reality, of course, it is not generally the theory behind immunity that is important. The important issue is whether the local court adopts absolute or restrictive immunity in its approach to states and how that distinction is to be drawn. The European Convention clearly favours a restrictive approach and this is the *effect* of the ILC's Draft Articles, even if they are less explicit.

3. The *Victory Transport Case* gives some indication of the way in which the principle of restrictive immunity can be applied in practice. However, *Trendtex Trading Corp v Central Bank of Nigeria* [1977] 2 WLR 356, *I Congreso del Partido* [1981] 3 WLR 328 *United States v The Public Service Alliance of Canada* 32 ILM 1 (1993) and *Holland v Lampen-Wolfe* (below) suggest other methods for deciding whether an act was *jure imperii* or *jure gestionis*.

SECTION 2: **The relationship between immunity and acts contrary to international law**

By its very nature, a successful plea of immunity removes either a State or an individual from the jurisdiction of a local court. While this may generate outrage in the local state, it is a generally accepted consequence of the need to preserve the sovereign equality of States on a practical as well as a theoretical level. However, what is the position where the State or individual claiming immunity is alleged to have committed an act which is itself contrary to international law, such as a gross violation of human rights. In such cases, there is a tension between those rules of international law requiring immunity to be given and those rules of international law generally regarded as of central importance to the international legal order and for violation of which an individual may be held personally responsible in addition to engaging the responsibility of the State. For example, can a Head of State or an Ambassador claim immunity from the jurisdiction of local courts in respect of alleged war crimes, or torture, or crimes against humanity or genocide. Is immunity or human rights to prevail?

The matter has now been considered in a number of cases before both international and local courts. Factors that have been considered relevant are: whether sovereign equality of States should be surrendered in the face of human rights violations; whether the individual was acting in an official capacity; whether the individual had caused a breach of a rule of *jus cogens*; whether the individual could be held personally responsible under international law for the alleged acts; and whether the individual was at the time of trial in the local court still holding the official position that appears to attract the immunity.

R v Bow Street Metropolitan Stipendiary Magistrate and others, ex parte Pinochet Ugarte (Amnesty International and others intervening) (No 3)
[1999] 2 All ER 97, House of Lords

Senator Pinochet, the ex-Head of State of Chile, had been detained in London pending an extradition request from Spain. It was alleged that he had authorised acts of torture while in office against, *inter alia*, Spanish nationals. Senator Pinochet claimed immunity as an ex-Head of State. One issue was whether he could be immune in respect of acts that might be regarded as crimes of universal jurisdiction under customary international law and that, in any event, attracted universal jurisdiction under the Torture Convention. The House of Lords held (Lord Goff dissenting) that there could be no immunity.

State immunity
LORD BROWNE-WILKINSON: This is the point around which most of the argument turned. It is of considerable general importance internationally since, if Senator Pinochet is not entitled to immunity in relation to the acts of torture alleged to have occurred after 29 September 1988 it will be the first time, so far as counsel have discovered, when a local domestic court has refused to afford immunity to a Head of State or former Head of State on the grounds that there can be no immunity against prosecution for certain international crimes.

Given the importance of the point, it is surprising how narrow is the area of dispute. There is general agreement between the parties as to the rules of statutory immunity and the rationale which underlies them. The issue is whether international law grants State immunity in relation to the international crime of torture and, if so, whether the Republic of Chile is entitled to claim such immunity even though Chile, Spain and the United Kingdom are all parties to the Torture Convention and therefore 'contractually' bound to give effect to its provisions from 8 December 1988 at the latest.

It is a basic principle of international law that one sovereign State (the forum state) does not adjudicate on the conduct of a foreign State. The foreign state is entitled to procedural immunity from the processes of the forum State. This immunity extends to both criminal and civil liability. State immunity probably grew from the historical immunity of the person of the monarch. In any event, such personal immunity of the Head of State persists to the present day: the Head of State is entitled to the same immunity as the State itself. The diplomatic representative of the foreign State in the forum State is also afforded the same immunity in recognition of the dignity of the State which he represents. This immunity enjoyed by a Head of State in power and an ambassador in post is a complete immunity attaching to the person of the Head of State or ambassador and rendering him immune from all actions or prosecutions whether or not they relate to matters done for the benefit of the State. Such immunity is said to be granted *ratione personae*.

What then when the ambassador leaves his post or the Head of State is deposed? . . . The continuing partial immunity of the ambassador after leaving post is of a different kind from that enjoyed *ratione personae* while he was in post. Since he is no longer the representative of the foreign State he merits no particular privileges or immunities as a person. However in order to preserve the integrity of the activities of the foreign State during the period when he was ambassador, it is necessary to provide that immunity is afforded to his *official* acts during his tenure in post. If this were not done the sovereign immunity of the state could be evaded by calling in question acts done during the previous ambassador's time. Accordingly under Art. 39(2) the ambassador, like any other official of the state, enjoys immunity in relation to his official acts done while he was an official. This limited immunity, *ratione materiae*, is to be contrasted with the former immunity *ratione personae* which gave complete immunity to all activities whether public or private.

In my judgment at common law a former Head of State enjoys similar immunities, *ratione materiae*, once he ceases to be Head of State. He too loses immunity *ratione personae* on ceasing to be Head of State . . . As ex-Head of State he cannot be sued in respect of acts performed whilst Head of State in his public capacity: *Hatch v Baez* (1876) 7 Hun 596. Thus, at common law, the position of the former ambassador and the former Head of State appears to be much the same: both enjoy immunity for acts done in performance of their respective functions whilst in office.

The question then which has to be answered is whether the alleged organisation of State torture by Senator Pinochet (if proved) would constitute an act committed by Senator Pinochet as part of his official functions as Head of State. It is not enough to say that it cannot be part of the functions of the head of state to commit a crime. Actions which are criminal under the local law can still have been done officially and therefore give rise to immunity *ratione materiae*. The case needs to be analysed more closely.

Can it be said that the commission of a crime which is an international crime against humanity and *jus cogens* is an act done in an official capacity on behalf of the State? I believe there to be strong ground for saying that the implementation of torture as defined by the Torture Convention cannot be a State function. . . .

I have doubts whether, before the coming into force of the Torture Convention, the existence of the international crime of torture as *jus cogens* was enough to justify the conclusion that the organisation of state torture could not rank for immunity purposes as performance of an official function. At that stage there was no international tribunal to punish torture and no general jurisdiction to permit or require its punishment in domestic courts. Not until there was some form of universal jurisdiction for the punishment of the crime of torture could it really be talked about as a fully constituted international crime. But in my judgment the Torture Convention did provide what was missing: a worldwide universal jurisdiction. Further, it required all member states to ban and outlaw torture: Art 2. How can it be for international law purposes an official function to do something which international law itself prohibits and criminalises? Thirdly, an essential feature of the international crime of torture is that it must be committed 'by or with the acquiesence of a public official or other person acting in an official capacity.' As a result all defendants in torture cases will be state officials. Yet, if the former Head of State has immunity, the man most responsible will escape liability while his inferiors (the chiefs of police, junior army officers) who carried out his orders will be liable. I find it impossible to accept that this was the intention.

Finally, and to my mind decisively, if the implementation of a torture regime is a public function giving rise to immunity *ratione materiae*, this produces bizarre results. Immunity *ratione materiae* applies not only to ex-Heads of State and ex-ambassadors but to all State officials who have been involved in carrying out the functions of the State. Such immunity is necessary in order to prevent State immunity being circumvented by prosecuting or suing the official who, for example, actually carried out the torture when a claim against the Head of State would be precluded by the doctrine of immunity. If that applied to the present case, and if the implementation of the torture regime is to be treated as official business sufficient to found an immunity for the former Head of State, it must also be official business sufficient to justify immunity for his inferiors who actually did the torturing. Under the Convention the international crime of torture can only be committed by an official or someone in an official capacity. They would all be entitled to immunity. It would follow that there can be no case outside Chile in which a successful prosecution for torture can be brought unless the state of Chile is prepared to waive its right to its officials' immunity. Therefore the whole elaborate structure of universal jurisdiction over torture committed by officials is rendered abortive and one of the main objectives of the Torture Convention – to provide a system under which there is no safe haven for torturers – will have been frustrated. In my judgment all these factors together demonstrate that the notion of continued immunity for ex-Heads of State is inconsistent with the provisions of the Torture Convention.

For these reasons in my judgment if, as alleged, Senator Pinochet organised and authorised torture after 8 December 1988 he was not acting in any capacity which gives rise to immunity *ratione materiae* because such actions were contrary to international law, Chile had agreed to outlaw such conduct and Chile had agreed with the other parties to the Torture Convention that all signatory states should have jurisdiction to try official torture (as defined in the Convention) even if such torture were committed in Chile.

LORD MILLET: Two overlapping immunities are recognised by international law: immunity *ratione personae* and immunity *ratione materiae*. They are quite different and have different rationales.

Immunity *ratione personae* is a status immunity. An individual who enjoys its protection does so because of his official status. It ensures for his benefit only so long as he holds office. While he does so he enjoys absolute immunity from the civil and criminal jurisdiction of the national courts of foreign states. But it is only narrowly available. It is confined to serving Heads of State and heads of diplomatic missions, their families and servants. It is not available to serving heads of government who are not also Heads of State, military commanders and those in charge of the security forces, or their subordinates. It would have been available to Hitler but not to Mussolini or Tojo.

The immunity of a serving Head of State is enjoyed by reason of his special status as the holder of his State's highest office. He is regarded as the personal embodiment of the State itself. It would be an affront to the dignity and sovereignty of the State which he personifies and a denial of the equality of sovereign States to subject him to the jurisdiction of the municipal courts of another State, whether in respect of his public acts or private affairs. His person is inviolable; he is not liable to be arrested or detained on any ground whatever. The head of a diplomatic mission represents his Head of State and thus embodies the sending state in the territory of the receiving state. While he remains in office he is entitled to the same absolute immunity as his Head of State, in relation both to his public and private acts.

This immunity is not in issue in the present case. Senator Pinochet is not a serving Head of State. If he were, he could not be extradited. It would be an intolerable affront to the Republic of Chile to arrest him or detain him.

Immunity *ratione materiae* is very different. This is a subject matter immunity. It operates to prevent the official and governmental acts of one state from being called into question in proceedings before the courts of another, and only incidentally confers immunity on the individual. It is therefore a narrower immunity but it is more widely available. It is available to former Heads of State and heads of diplomatic missions, and any one whose conduct in the exercise of the authority of the State is afterwards called into question, whether he acted as head of government, government minister, military commander or chief of police, or subordinate public official. The immunity is the same whatever the rank of the office holder. This too is common ground. It is an immunity from the civil and criminal jurisdiction of foreign national courts, but only in respect of governmental or official acts. The exercise of authority by the military and security forces of the State is the paradigm example of such conduct. The immunity finds its rationale in the equality of sovereign States and the doctrine of non-interference in the internal affairs of other States . . . The immunity is sometimes also justified by the need to prevent the serving Head of State, or diplomat, from being inhibited in the performance of his official duties by fear of the consequences after he has ceased to hold office. This last basis can hardly be prayed in aid to support the availability of the immunity in respect of criminal activities prohibited by international law.

Case Concerning the Arrest Warrant of 11 April 2000 (Democratic Republic of the Congo v Belgium)
ICJ Rep 14 February 2002, International Court of Justice

A Belgian investigating judge had issued an international arrest warrant against the serving Congolese Minister of Foreign Affairs. The warrant was in respect of alleged serious violations of international humanitarian law, including crimes against humanity. Congo claimed that this constituted a violation of the sovereignty of the Congo and a contravention of the sovereign equality of States. An essential issue was whether the Minister was entitled to immunity from the Belgian criminal process while a serving Minister, even though the alleged crimes would, if proven, amount to serious breaches of international law. The Court found in favour of the Congo.

53. In customary international law, the immunities accorded to Ministers for Foreign Affairs are not granted for their personal benefit, but to ensure the effective performance of their functions on behalf of their respective States. In order to determine the extent of these immunities, the Court must therefore first consider the nature of the functions exercised by a Minister for Foreign Affairs. The Court further observes that a Minister for Foreign Affairs, responsible for the conduct of his or her State's relations with all other States, occupies a position such that, like the Head of State or the Head of Government, he or she is recognized under international law as representative of the State solely by virtue of his or her office. . . .

54. The Court accordingly concludes that the functions of a Minister for Foreign Affairs are such that, throughout the duration of his or her office, he or she when abroad enjoys full immunity from criminal jurisdiction and inviolability. That immunity and that inviolability protect the individual concerned against any act of authority of another State which would hinder him or her in the performance of his or her duties.

55. In this respect, no distinction can be drawn between acts performed by a Minister for Foreign Affairs in an 'official' capacity, and those claimed to have been performed in a 'private capacity', or, for that matter, between acts performed before the person concerned assumed office as Minister for Foreign Affairs and acts committed during the period of office. Thus, if a Minister for Foreign Affairs is arrested in another State on a criminal charge, he or she is clearly thereby prevented from exercising the functions of his or her office. The consequences of such impediment to the exercise of those official functions are equally serious, regardless of whether the Minister for Foreign Affairs was, at the time of arrest, present in the territory of the arresting State on an 'official' visit or a 'private' visit,

regardless of whether the arrest relates to acts allegedly performed before the person became the Minister for Foreign Affairs or to acts performed while in office, and regardless of whether the arrest relates to alleged acts performed in an 'official' capacity or a 'private' capacity. Furthermore, even the mere risk that, by travelling to or transiting another State a Minister for Foreign Affairs might be exposing himself or herself to legal proceedings could deter the Minister from travelling internationally when required to do so for the purposes of the performance of his or her official functions.

56. The Court will now address Belgium's argument that immunities accorded to incumbent Ministers for Foreign Affairs can in no case protect them where they are suspected of having committed war crimes or crimes against humanity. . . .

Belgium begins by pointing out that certain provisions of the instruments creating international criminal tribunals state expressly that the official capacity of a person shall not be a bar to the exercise by such tribunals of their jurisdiction.

Belgium also places emphasis on certain decisions of national courts, and in particular on the judgments rendered on 24 March 1999 by the House of Lords in the United Kingdom and on 13 March 2001 by the Court of Cassation in France in the *Pinochet* and *Qaddafi* cases respectively, in which it contends that an exception to the immunity rule was accepted in the case of serious crimes under international law. Thus, according to Belgium, the *Pinochet* decision recognizes an exception to the immunity rule when Lord Millett stated that '[i]nternational law cannot be supposed to have established a crime having the character of a *jus cogens* and at the same time to have provided an immunity which is co-extensive with the obligation it seeks to impose', or when Lord Phillips of Worth Matravers said that 'no established rule of international law requires state immunity *rationae materiae* to be accorded in respect of prosecution for an international crime'. As to the French Court of Cassation, Belgium contends that, in holding that, 'under international law as it currently stands, the crime alleged [acts of terrorism], irrespective of its gravity, does not come within the exceptions to the principle of immunity from jurisdiction for incumbent foreign Heads of State', the Court explicitly recognized the existence of such exceptions.

57. The Congo, for its part, states that, under international law as it currently stands, there is no basis for asserting that there is any exception to the principle of absolute immunity from criminal process of an incumbent Minister for Foreign Affairs where he or she is accused of having committed crimes under international law.

In support of this contention, the Congo refers to State practice, giving particular consideration in this regard to the *Pinochet* and *Qaddafi* cases, and concluding that such practice does not correspond to that which Belgium claims but, on the contrary, confirms the absolute nature of the immunity from criminal process of Heads of State and Ministers for Foreign Affairs. Thus, in the *Pinochet* case, the Congo cites Lord Browne-Wilkinson's statement that '[t]his immunity enjoyed by a head of state in power and an ambassador in post is a complete immunity attached to the person of the head of state or ambassador and rendering him immune from all actions or prosecutions . . .'. According to the Congo, the French Court of Cassation adopted the same position in its *Qaddafi* judgment, in affirming that 'international custom bars the prosecution of incumbent Heads of State, in the absence of any contrary international provision binding on the parties concerned, before the criminal courts of a foreign State'.

58. The Court has carefully examined State practice, including national legislation and those few decisions of national higher courts, such as the House of Lords or the French Court of Cassation. It has been unable to deduce from this practice that there exists under customary international law any form of exception to the rule according immunity from criminal jurisdiction and inviolability to incumbent Ministers for Foreign Affairs, where they are suspected of having committed war crimes or crimes against humanity.

The Court has also examined the rules concerning the immunity or criminal responsibility of persons having an official capacity contained in the legal instruments creating international criminal tribunals. It finds that these rules likewise do not enable it to conclude that any such an exception exists in customary international law in regard to national courts.

In view of the foregoing, the Court accordingly cannot accept Belgium's argument in this regard.

59. It should further be noted that the rules governing the jurisdiction of national courts must be carefully distinguished from those governing jurisdictional immunities: jurisdiction does not imply absence of immunity, while absence of immunity does not imply jurisdiction. Thus, although various international conventions on the prevention and punishment of certain serious crimes impose on States obligations of prosecution or extradition, thereby requiring them to extend their criminal jurisdiction, such extension of jurisdiction in no way affects immunities under customary international law, including those of Ministers for Foreign Affairs. These remain opposable before the courts of a foreign State, even where those courts exercise such a jurisdiction under these conventions.

60. The Court emphasizes, however, that the *immunity* from jurisdiction enjoyed by incumbent Ministers for Foreign Affairs does not mean that they enjoy *impunity* in respect of any crimes they might have committed, irrespective of their gravity. Immunity from criminal jurisdiction and individual criminal responsibility are quite separate concepts. While jurisdictional immunity is procedural in nature, criminal responsibility is a question of substantive law. Jurisdictional immunity may well bar prosecution for a certain period or for certain offences; it cannot exonerate the person to whom it applies from all criminal responsibility.

61. Accordingly, the immunities enjoyed under international law by an incumbent or former Minister for Foreign Affairs do not represent a bar to criminal prosecution in certain circumstances.

First, such persons enjoy no criminal immunity under international law in their own countries, and may thus be tried by those countries' courts in accordance with the relevant rules of domestic law.

Secondly, they will cease to enjoy immunity from foreign jurisdiction if the State which they represent or have represented decides to waive that immunity.

Thirdly, after a person ceases to hold the office of Minister for Foreign Affairs, he or she will no longer enjoy all of the immunities accorded by international law in other States. Provided that it has jurisdiction under international law, a court of one State may try a former Minister for Foreign Affairs of another State in respect of acts committed prior or subsequent to his or her period of office, as well as in respect of acts committed during that period of office in a private capacity.

Fourthly, an incumbent or former Minister for Foreign Affairs may be subject to criminal proceedings before certain international criminal courts, where they have jurisdiction.

Al-Adsani v *UK*
34 EHRR (2002) 273, European Court of Human Rights

The claimant alleged that he had been tortured in Kuwait by a relative of the Head of State of Kuwait. He further alleged that Kuwait itself should be held responsible and issued civil proceedings in the UK. While denying that it was in any way responsible, Kuwait claimed State immunity. The UK court upheld immunity on the ground that the alleged acts of personal injury were done outside the UK by a foreign sovereign and were immune under the UK State Immunity Act 1978. In consequence, the claimant pursued the UK under the European Convention on Human Rights alleging a violation of Art. 3 (prohibition of torture) and a violation of Art. 6 (right to a fair and public hearing). The European

Court decided unanimously that the UK had not violated Art. 3, not least because all relevant acts were done outside UK jurisdiction by a person for whom the UK was not responsible. The claim under Art. 6 raised more difficult issues. Its essence was that a plea of sovereign immunity necessarily barred a fair trial and that in the context of an alleged claim of torture, the grant of sovereign immunity was not a legitimate aim of the UK and, even if it was, that it was disproportionate. By a vote of nine to eight, the Court held that there was no violation of Art. 6.

53. The right of access to court is not, however, absolute, but may be subject to limitations; these are permitted by implication since the right of access by its very nature calls for regulation by the State. In this respect, the Contracting States enjoy a certain margin of appreciation, although the final decision as to the observance of the Convention's requirements rests with the Court. It must be satisfied that the limitations applied do not restrict or reduce the access left to the individual in such a way or to such an extent that the very essence of the right is impaired. Furthermore, a limitation will not be compatible with Article 6 § 1 if it does not pursue a legitimate aim and if there is no reasonable relationship of proportionality between the means employed and the aim sought to be achieved.

54. The Court must first examine whether the limitation pursued a legitimate aim. It notes in this connection that sovereign immunity is a concept of international law, developed out of the principle *par in parem non habet imperium*, by virtue of which one State shall not be subject to the jurisdiction of another State. The Court considers that the grant of sovereign immunity to a State in civil proceedings pursues the legitimate aim of complying with international law to promote comity and good relations between States through the respect of another State's sovereignty.

55. The Court must next assess whether the restriction was proportionate to the aim pursued. It recalls that the Convention has to be interpreted in the light of the rules set out in the Vienna Convention of 23 May 1969 on the Law of Treaties, and that Article 31 § 3 (c) of that treaty indicates that account is to be taken of 'any relevant rules of international law applicable in the relations between the parties'. The Convention, including Article 6, cannot be interpreted in a vacuum. The Court must be mindful of the Convention's special character as a human rights treaty, and it must also take the relevant rules of international law into account (see, *mutatis mutandis*, the *Loizidou* v *Turkey* judgment of 18 December 1996, *Reports* 1996–VI, § 43). The Convention should so far as possible be interpreted in harmony with other rules of international law of which it forms part, including those relating to the grant of State immunity.

56. It follows that measures taken by a High Contracting Party which reflect generally recognised rules of public international law on State immunity cannot in principle be regarded as imposing a disproportionate restriction on the right of access to court as embodied in Article 6 § 1. Just as the right of access to court is an inherent part of the fair trial guarantee in that Article, so some restrictions on access must likewise be regarded as inherent, an example being those limitations generally accepted by the community of nations as part of the doctrine of State immunity.

61. While the Court accepts, on the basis of these authorities, that the prohibition of torture has achieved the status of a peremptory norm in international law, it observes that the present case concerns not, as in the *Furundzija* and *Pinochet* decisions, the criminal liability of an individual for alleged acts of torture, but the immunity of a State in a civil suit for damages in respect of acts of torture within the territory of that State. Notwithstanding the special character of the prohibition of torture in international law, the Court is unable to discern in the international instruments, judicial authorities or other materials before it any firm basis for concluding that, as a matter of international

law, a State no longer enjoys immunity from civil suit in the courts of another State where acts of torture are alleged.

64. As to the amendment to the FSIA, the very fact that the amendment was needed would seem to confirm that the general rule of international law remained that immunity attached even in respect of claims of acts of official torture. Moreover, the amendment is circumscribed in its scope: the offending State must be designated as a State sponsor of acts of terrorism, and the claimant must be a national of the United States. The effect of the FSIA is further limited in that after judgment has been obtained, the property of a foreign State is immune from attachment or execution unless one of the statutory exceptions applies (see para. 24 above).

65. As to the *ex parte Pinochet (No 3)* judgment, the Court notes that the majority of the House of Lords held that, after the Torture Convention and even before, the international prohibition against official torture had the character of *jus cogens* or a peremptory norm and that no immunity was enjoyed by a torturer from one Torture Convention State from the criminal jurisdiction of another. But, as the Working Group of the ILC itself acknowledged, that case concerned the immunity *ratione materiae* from criminal jurisdiction of a former head of State, who was at the material time physically within the United Kingdom. As the judgments in the case made clear, the conclusion of the House of Lords did not in any way affect the immunity *ratione personae* of foreign sovereign States from the civil jurisdiction in respect of such acts (see in particular, the judgment of Lord Millett, mentioned in paragraph 34 above). In so holding, the House of Lords cited with approval the judgments of the Court of Appeal in the *Al-Adsani* case itself.

66. The Court, while noting the growing recognition of the overriding importance of the prohibition of torture, does not accordingly find it established that there is yet acceptance in international law of the proposition that States are not entitled to immunity in respect of civil claims for damages for alleged torture committed outside the forum State. The 1978 Act, which grants immunity to States in respect of personal injury claims unless the damage was caused within the United Kingdom, is not inconsistent with those limitations generally accepted by the community of nations as part of the doctrine of State immunity.

67. In these circumstances, the application by the English courts of the provisions of the 1978 Act to uphold Kuwait's claim to immunity cannot be said to have amounted to an unjustified restriction on the applicant's access to court.

It follows that there has been no violation of Article 6 § 1 in this case.

NOTES:

1. It appears from the judgments in *Pinochet*, that there were two connected grounds for denying immunity. Either, an ex-Head of State only enjoyed immunity in respect of acts done while he was a Head of State if these were in exercise of his official functions and torture could not be an official function. This is the essence of Lord Browne-Wilkinson's analysis. Alternatively, immunity could not attach to acts that were themselves in violation of fundamental rules of international law and the prevention of torture was such a rule of *jus cogens*. This is the essence of Lord Millet's analysis and he linked denial of immunity with international crimes attracting universal jurisdiction. Lord Millet's view has a certain logic about it: as immunity is available in respect of violation of national laws, but can never be available in respect of violations of international law. However, this has not been followed in subsequent cases. For his part, Lord Goff (dissenting) could find nothing in customary law or the Torture Convention suggesting that immunity *ratio materiae* was removed for an ex-Head of State.

2. The issue in the *Arrest Warrant* Case concerned a current serving State representative and it is no surprise that the ICJ (following a classical State-based approach to international law) determined that such a person's immunity covered all matters, including alleged violations

of international human rights law. It was immunity *ratione personae*. Indeed, the ICJ was clear that such immunity extended even to non-official acts while the individual was still serving. Given that the *Pinochet Case* concerned an ex-State representative, the cases are not inconsistent, for it seems that if the national court has an ex-representative before it, it need accord immunity only to official acts done while in office (i.e. a limited immunity *ratione materiae*). The ICJ was quick to point out that immunity from jurisdiction does not imply immunity from responsibility. Hence, the ICJ identifies ways (e.g. in para. 61) in which a person who is immune from one type of jurisdiction may nevertheless be made to bear their criminal responsibility.

3. The European Court of Human Rights in the *Al-Adsani* case (above) did not merely consider the relation between the procedural right to a fair hearing (Art. 6) and State immunity. It also considered the underlying right (to freedom from torture) that was sought to be vindicated by that hearing. This approach has been followed by the Court in two cases against the UK: personal injury (*McElhinney*) and sex discrimination (*Fogarty*). Thus it seems that these issues are not sufficient to defeat a claim of immunity, at least not when the issue was a civil suit against a foreign State. Taken together, they amount to a controversial defence of the principle of State immunity in those cases where the alleged violation for which immunity is claimed is a violation of human rights' obligations. The cases are different from *Pinochet* in that a *State* not an *individual* was involved and they also concerned civil not criminal proceedings. Nevertheless, the House of Lords robust assertion in *Pinochet* that crimes of torture cannot attract immunity must now be read with some caution.

4. In general terms, while it seems that the immunity of individuals will be denied in the face of grave violations of international law when that individual no longer represents the State and his actions were not 'official', the immunity of the State itself has not yet been overcome by the application of human rights law. Of course, as the Court makes clear in the *Al-Adsani* decision, it will be a new question in each case whether the grant of immunity was legitimate and proportionate. Consequently, the grant of immunity to a foreign State might still constitute a violation of the Convention by the 'home' State in particular circumstances. The Court has sought to weld together human rights law and sovereign immunity principles and this is to be welcomed given that they all spring from 'international law'. Yet, it remains to be seen whether the balance is well struck or sustainable in the face of the criticism these three decisions attracted (see e.g. [2002] CLJ 246).

SECTION 3: **State immunity in the United Kingdom**

The law in the UK is governed substantially by the State Immunity Act 1978. For matters falling outside this statute or issues arising before its enactment, the common law prevails. The *I Congreso* case is the leading common law authority now supplemented by *Holland* v *Lompen-Wolfe*. Cases that mark the progression from absolute to restrictive immunity in the UK have been omitted as they are now of largely historical interest only, though some of them are discussed in *I Congreso*.

A: General principles

I Congreso del Partido

[1981] 3 WLR 328, House of Lords

In 1973, two ships, *The Marble Islands* and *The Playa Larga* were carrying sugar to Chile on behalf of Cubazucar, a Cuban State enterprise. After a coup in Chile, *The Playa Larga* (essentially owned by Cuba) was ordered to return to Cuba with most of her sugar unloaded, and *The Marble Islands* (essentially chartered to Cuba) was ordered to Vietnam where the sugar was sold. The plaintiffs, who were owners of the sugar, brought an action *in rem* (i.e. to hold the ship) against *I Congreso*, a ship also owned by Cuba. Cuba claimed State immunity. The case was decided at common law, the issue arising before the 1978 Act. The House of Lords rejected the plea of immunity in respect of both ships: in regard to *The Playa Larga* because at all times the actions of Cuba were as owners and not by virtue of sovereign authority, and in regard to *The Marble Islands* (Lords Wilberforce and Edmund Davies dissenting) because the sale of the sugar to Vietnam was made under Cuban law, being analogous to conversion in the law of torts, and not by virtue of the sovereign authority of Cuba.

LORD WILBERFORCE: Until 1975 it would have been true to say that England, almost alone of influential trading nations (the United States of America having changed its position under the Tate letter in 1952) continued to adhere to a pure, absolute, doctrine of state immunity in all cases. . . . In 1977 there were reported two landmark cases – *The Philippine Admiral* [1977] AC 373 and *Trendtex Trading Corporation Ltd* v *Central Bank of Nigeria* [1977] QB 529. In *The Philippine Admiral* the Judicial Committee of the Privy Council, in an appeal from Hong Kong, declined to follow *The Porto Alexandre* [1920] P 30 and decided to apply the 'restrictive' doctrine to an action *in rem* against a state-owned trading vessel. In the comprehensive judgment which was delivered on behalf of the Board, it was said that to do so was more consonant with justice. It was further commented that it was open to the House of Lords to move away from the absolute rule of immunity in actions *in personam*. Sitting in this House I would unhesitantly affirm as part of English law the advance made by *The Philippine Admiral* [1977] AC 373 with the reservation that the decision was perhaps unnecessarily restrictive in, apparently, confining the departure made to actions *in rem*. . . . In fact there is no anomaly and no distinction. The effect of *The Philippine Admiral* [1977] AC 373 if accepted, as I would accept it, is that as regards state-owned trading vessels, actions, whether commenced *in rem* or not, are to be decided according to the 'restrictive' theory.

The other landmark authority (*Trendtex* [1977] QB 529), a decision of the Court of Appeal, establishes that, as a matter of contemporary international law, the 'restrictive' theory should be generally applied. In that case what was involved was not a claim relating to a trading ship, but one based on a commercial letter of credit arising out of a purchase of cement. The case was not appealed to this House, and since there may be appeals in analogous cases it is perhaps right to avoid commitment to more of the admired judgment of Lord Denning MR than is necessary. Its value in the present case lies in the reasoning that if the act in question is of a commercial nature, the fact that it was done for governmental or political reasons does not attract sovereign immunity.

On the basis of these cases I have no doubt that the 'restrictive' doctrine should be applied to the present case, though the relevant events chronologically preceded both *The Philippine Admiral* [1977] AC 373 and *Trendtex* [1977] QB 529. Indeed this was not disputed by either side in these appeals. The issue is as to the limits of the doctrine: merely to state that the 'restrictive' doctrine applies is to say little more than that a state has no absolute immunity as regards commercial or trading transactions, but where immunity begins and ends has yet to be determined.

It is necessary to start from first principle. The basis upon which one state is considered to be immune from the territorial jurisdiction of the courts of another state is that of 'par in parem' which effectively means that the sovereign or governmental acts of one state are not matters upon which the courts of other states will adjudicate.

The relevant exception, or limitation, which has been engrafted upon the principle of immunity of states, under the so called 'restrictive theory,' arises from the willingness of states to enter into commercial, or other private law, transactions with individuals. It appears to have two main foundations: (a) It is necessary in the interest of justice to individuals having such transactions with states to allow them to bring such transactions before the courts. (b) To require a state to answer a claim based upon such transactions does not involve a challenge to or inquiry into any act of sovereignty or governmental act of that state. It is, in accepted phrases, neither a threat to the dignity of that state, nor any interference with its sovereign functions.

When therefore a claim is brought against a state . . . and state immunity is claimed, it is necessary to consider what is the relevant act which forms the basis of the claim: is this, under the old terminology, an act 'jure gestions' or is it an act 'jure imperii': is it . . . a 'private act' or is it a 'sovereign or public act,' a private act meaning in this context an act of a private law character such as a private citizen might have entered into. It is upon this point that the arguments in these appeals is focussed. . . .

The activities of states cannot always be compartmentalised into trading or governmental activities; and what is one to make of a case where a state has, and in the relevant circumstances, clearly displayed, both a commercial interest and a sovereign or governmental interest? To which is the critical action to be attributed? Such questions are the more difficult since they arise at an initial stage in the proceedings and, in all probability, upon affidavit evidence. This difficulty is inherent in the nature of the 'restrictive' doctrine, introducing as it does an exception, based upon a certain state of facts, to a plain rule. But as was said in the *Empire of Iran* case . . .

> The fact that it is difficult to draw the line between sovereign and non-sovereign state activities is no reason for abandoning the distinction. International law knows of other similar difficulties . . . The distinction between sovereign and non-sovereign state activities cannot be drawn according to the purpose of the state transaction and whether it stands in a recognizable relation to the sovereign duties of the state. For, ultimately, activities of state, if not wholly then to the widest degree, serve sovereign purposes and duties, and stand in a still recognizable relationship to them. Neither should the distinction depend on whether the state has acted commercially. Commercial activities of states are not different in their nature from other non-sovereign state activities. . . .

Under the 'restrictive' theory the court has first to characterise the activity into which the defendant state has entered. Having done this, and (assumedly) found it to be of a commercial, or private law, character, it may take the view that contractual breaches, or torts, prima facie fall within the same sphere of activity. It should then be for the defendant state to make a case . . . that the act complained of is outside that sphere, and within that of sovereign action. . . .

The conclusion which emerges is that in considering, under the 'restrictive' theory whether state immunity should be granted or not, the court must consider the whole context in which the claim against the state is made, with a view to deciding whether the relevant act(s) upon which the claim is based, should, in that context, be considered as fairly within an area of activity, trading or commercial, or otherwise of a private law character, in which the state has chosen to engage, or whether the relevant act(s) should be considered as having been done outside that area, and within the sphere of governmental or sovereign activity.

Holland v Lampen-Wolfe

[2000] 1 WLR 1573, House of Lords

The primary facts are stated above. Under s 16(2) State Immunity Act 1978 (see below) the Act 'does not apply to proceedings relating to anything done by or in relation to the armed forces of a State while present in the United Kingdom'. The House of Lords decided that this section should be given a wide meaning and thus the employment of a person in an educational capacity on a US military base was 'in relation to' the armed forces of a State and so was not covered by the Act. The matter thus fell to be considered under the common law.

LORD MILLET: Accordingly the question is whether, in accordance with the law laid down in *I Congreso del Partido* [1983] 1 AC 244, 262, the act complained of was *jure imperii* or *jure gestionis*. This must be judged against the background of the whole context in which the claim is made. The question is not an altogether easy one, but I have come to the conclusion that the Court of Appeal was correct to designate the act complained of as being *jure imperii*.

In *Littrell v United States of America (No 2)* [1995] 1 WLR 82 the plaintiff claimed damages for personal injuries arising from medical treatment which he had received at a United States military hospital in the United Kingdom while a serving member of the United States Air Force. It was conceded that section 16(2) applied, so that the case fell to be decided at common law. The Court of Appeal held that the proceedings were barred by state immunity. Hoffmann LJ said, at pp. 94–95:

> The context in which the act took place was the maintenance by the United States of a unit of the United States Air Force in the United Kingdom. This looks about as imperial an activity as could be imagined. But it would be facile to regard this context as determinative of the question. Acts done within that context could range from arrangements concerning the flights of the bombers–plainly *jure imperii* – to ordering milk for the base from a local dairy or careless driving by off-duty airmen on the roads of Suffolk. Both of the latter would seem to me to be *jure gestionis*, fairly within an area of private law activity. I do not think that there is a single test or "bright line" by which cases on either side can be distinguished. Rather, there are a number of factors which may characterise the act as nearer to or further from the central military activity . . . Some acts are wholly military in character, some almost entirely private or commercial and some in between. . . .

The Court of Appeal could find no material distinction between the medical treatment provided in that case and the educational services provided in the present one. I agree with them that the provision of education for members of the armed forces and their families is, in modern conditions, as much a normal and necessary part of the overall activity of maintaining those forces as is the provision of medical treatment.

It is, of course, true that the action is an action for defamation, not for the negligent provision of professional services. The *Littrell* case is clearly distinguishable on this ground. But I do not regard the distinction as material. The defendant was responsible for supervising the provision of educational services to members of the United States armed forces in the United Kingdom and their families. He published the material alleged to be defamatory in the course of his duties. If the provision of the services in question was an official or governmental act of the United States, then so was its supervision by the defendant. I would hold that he was acting as an official of the United States in the course of the performance of its sovereign function of maintaining its armed forces in this country.

State Immunity Act 1978

This Act was designed primarily to meet the UK's obligations under the European Convention (above) and the earlier Brussels Convention for the Unification of Certain Rules relating to the Immunity of State Owned Vessels 1920.

1. General immunity from jurisdiction

(1) A State is immune from the jurisdiction of the courts of the United Kingdom except as provided in the following provisions of this Part of this Act.

(2) A court shall give effect to the immunity conferred by this section even though the State does not appear in the proceedings in question.

2. Submission to jurisdiction

(1) A State is not immune as respects proceedings in respect of which it has submitted to the jurisdiction of the courts of the United Kingdom.

(2) A State may submit after the dispute giving rise to the proceedings has arisen or by a prior written agreement; but a provision in any agreement that it is to governed by the law of the United Kingdom is not to be regarded as a submission.

(3) A State is deemed to have submitted –

(a) if it has instituted the proceedings; or

(b) subject to subsections (4) and (5) below, if it has intervened or taken any step in the proceedings.

(4) Subsection (3)(b) above does not apply to intervention or any step taken for the purpose only of –

(a) claiming immunity; or

(b) asserting an interest in property in circumstances such that the State would have been entitled to immunity if the proceedings had been brought against it.

3. Commercial transactions and contracts to be performed in United Kingdom

(1) A State is not immune as respects proceedings relating to –

(a) a commercial transaction, entered into by the State; or

(b) an obligation of the State which by virtue of a contract (whether a commercial transaction or not) falls to be performed wholly or partly in the United Kingdom.

(2) This section does not apply if the parties to the dispute are States or have otherwise agreed in writing; and subsection (1)(b) above does not apply if the contract (not being a commercial transaction) was made in the territory of the State concerned and the obligation in question is governed by its administrative law.

(3) In this section 'commercial transaction' means –

(a) any contract for the supply of goods or services;

(b) any loan or other transaction· for the provision of finance and any guarantee or indemnity in respect of any such transaction or of any other financial obligation; and

(c) any other transaction or activity (whether of a commercial, industrial, financial, professional or other similar character) into which a State enters or in which it engages otherwise than in the exercise of sovereign authority;

but neither paragraph of subsection (1) above applies to a contract of employment between a State and an individual.

4. Contracts of employment

(1) A State is not immune as respects proceedings relating to a contract of employment between the State and an individual where the contract was made in the United Kingdom or the work is to be wholly or partly performed there.

(2) Subject to subsections (3) and (4) below, this section does not apply if –

(a) at the time when the proceedings are brought the individual is a national of the State concerned; or

(b) at the time when the contract was made the individual was neither a national of the United Kingdom nor habitually resident there; or

(c) the parties to the contract have otherwise agreed in writing. . . .

5. Personal injuries and damage to property

A State is not immune as respects proceedings in respect of –

(a) death or personal injury; or

(b) damage or loss of tangible property,

caused by an act or omission in the United Kingdom.

6. Ownership, possession and use of property

(1) A State is not immune as respects proceedings relating to –

(a) any interest of the State in, or its possession or use of, immovable property in the United Kingdom; or

(b) any obligation of the State arising out of its interest in, or its possession or use of, any such property.

(2) A State is not immune as respects proceedings relating to any interest of the State in movable or immovable property, being an interest arising by way of succession, gift or *bona vacantia*.

(3) The fact that a State has or claims an interest in any property shall not preclude any court from exercising in respect of it any jurisdiction relating to the estates of deceased persons or persons of unsound mind or to insolvency, the winding up of companies or the administration of trusts.

(4) A court may entertain proceedings against a person other than a State notwithstanding that the proceedings relate to property –

(a) which is in the possession or control of a State; or

(b) in which a State claims an interest,

if the State would not have been immune had the proceedings been brought against it or, in a case within paragraph (b) above, if the claim is neither admitted nor supported by prima facie evidence.

10. Ships used for commercial purposes

(1) This section applies to –

(a) Admiralty proceedings; and

(b) proceedings on any claim which could be made the subject of Admiralty proceedings.

(2) A State is not immune as respects –

(a) an action *in rem* against a ship belonging to that State; or

(b) an action *in personam* for enforcing a claim in connection with such a ship,

if, at the time when the cause of action arose, the ship was in use or intended for use for commercial purposes.

(3) Where an action *in rem* is brought against a ship belonging to a State for enforcing a claim in connection with another ship belonging to that State, subsection (2)(a) above does not apply as respects the first-mentioned ship unless, at the time when the cause of action relating to the other ship arose, both ships were in use or intended for use for commercial purposes.

(4) A State is not immune as respects –

(a) an action *in rem* against a cargo belonging to that State if both the cargo and the ship carrying it were, at the time when the cause of action arose, in use or intended for use for commercial purposes; or

(b) an action *in personam* for enforcing a claim in connection with such a cargo if the ship carrying it was in use or intended for use as aforesaid.

(6) Sections 3 to 5 above do not apply to proceedings of the kind described in subsection (1) above if the State in question is a party to the Brussels Convention and the claim relates to the operation of a ship owned or operated by that State, the carriage of cargo or passengers on any such ship or the carriage of cargo owned by that State on any other ship.

11. Value added tax, customs duties etc

A State is not immune as respects proceedings relating to its liability for—
> (a) value added tax, and duty of customs or excise or any agricultural levy; or
> (b) rates in respect of premises occupied by it for commercial purposes.

13. Other procedural privileges

(1) No penalty by way of committal or fine shall be imposed in respect of any failure or refusal by or on behalf of a State to disclose or produce any document or other information for the purposes of proceedings to which it is a party.

(2) Subject to subsection (3) and (4) below –
> (a) relief shall not be given against a State by way of injunction or order for specific performance or for the recovery of land or other property; and
> (b) the property of a State shall not be subject to any process for the enforcement of a judgment or arbitration award or, in an action *in rem*, for its arrest, detention or sale.

(3) Subsection (2) above does not prevent the giving of any relief or the issue of any process with the written consent of the State concerned; and any such consent (which may be contained in a prior agreement) may be expressed so as to apply to a limited extent or generally; but a provision merely submitting to the jurisdiction of the courts is not to be regarded as a consent for the purposes of this subsection.

(4) Subsection (2)(b) above does not prevent the issue of any process in respect of property which is for the time being in use or intended for use for commercial purposes; but, in a case not falling within section 10 above, this subsection applies to property of a State party to the European Convention on State Immunity only if –
> (a) the process is for enforcing a judgment which is final within the meaning of section 18(1)(b) below and the State has made a declaration under Article 24 of the Convention; or
> (b) the process is for enforcing an arbitration award.

(5) The head of a State's diplomatic mission in the United Kingdom, or the person for the time being performing his functions, shall be deemed to have authority to give on behalf of the State any such consent as is mentioned in subsection (3) above and, for the purposes of subsection (4) above, his certificate to the effect that any property is not in use or intended for use by or on behalf of the State for commercial purposes shall be accepted as sufficient evidence of that fact unless the contrary is proved.

14. States entitled to immunities and privileges

(1) The immunities and privileges conferred by this Part of this Act apply to any foreign or commonwealth State other than the United Kingdom; and references to a State include reference to –
> (a) the sovereign or other head of that State in his public capacity;
> (b) the government of that State; and
> (c) any department of that government,

but not to any entity (hereafter referred to as a 'separate entity') which is distinct from the executive organs of the government of the State and capable of suing or being sued.

(2) A separate entity is immune from the jurisdiction of the courts of the United Kingdom if, and only if –

    (a) the proceedings relate to anything done by it in the exercise of sovereign authority; and

    (b) the circumstances are such that a State (or, in the case of proceedings to which section 10 above applies, a State which is not a party to the Brussels Convention) would have been so immune.

    (3) If a separate entity (not being a State's central bank or other monetary authority) submits to the jurisdiction in respect of proceedings in the case of which it is entitled to immunity by virtue of subsection (2) above, subsections (1) to (4) of section 13 above shall apply to it in respect of those proceedings as if references to a State were references to that entity.

    (4) Property of a State's central bank or other monetary authority shall not be regarded for the purposes of subsection (4) of section 13 above as in use or intended for use for commercial purposes; and where any such bank or authority is a separate entity subsections (1) to (3) of that section shall apply to it as if references to a State were references to the bank or authority.

    (5) Section 12 above applies to proceedings against the constituent territories of a federal State; and Her Majesty may by Order in Council provide for the other provisions of this Part of this Act to apply to any such constituent territory specified in the Order as they apply to a State.

    (6) Where the provisions of this Part of this Act do not apply to a constituent territory by virtue of any such Order subsections (2) and (3) above shall apply to it as if it were a separate entity.

16. Excluded matters

    (1) This Part of this Act does not affect any immunity or privilege conferred by the Diplomatic Privileges Act 1964 or the Consular Relations Act 1968; and –

    (a) section 4 above does not apply to proceedings concerning the employment of the members of a mission within the meaning of the Convention scheduled to the said Act of 1964 or of the members of a consular post within the meaning of the Convention scheduled to the said Act of 1968;

    (b) section 6(1) above does not apply to proceedings concerning a State's title to or its possession of property used for the purposes of a diplomatic mission.

    (2) This Part of this Act does not apply to proceedings relating to anything done by or in relation to the armed forces of a State while present in the United Kingdom and, in particular, has effect subject to the Visiting Forces Act 1952.

    (3) This Part of this Act does not apply to proceedings to which section 17(6) of the Nuclear Installations Act 1965 applies.

    (4) This Part of this Act does not apply to criminal proceedings.

    (5) This Part of this Act does not apply to any proceedings relating to taxation other than those mentioned in section 11 above.

20. Heads of State

    (1) Subject to the provisions of this section and to any necessary modifications, the Diplomatic Privileges Act 1964 shall apply to –

    (a) a sovereign or other head of State;

    (b) members of his family forming part of his household; and

    (c) his private servants,

as it applies to the head of a diplomatic mission, to members of his family forming part of his household and to his private servants.

    (2) The immunities and privileges conferred by virtue of subsection (1)(a) and (b) above shall not be subject to the restrictions by reference to nationality or residence mentioned in Article 37(1) or 38 in Schedule 1 to the said Act of 1964.

    (3) Subject to any direction to the contrary by the Secretary of State, a person on whom

immunities and privileges are conferred by virtue of subsection (1) above shall be entitled to the exemption conferred by section 8(3) of the Immigration Act 1971.

(4) Except as respects value added tax and duties of customs or excise, this section does not affect any question whether a person is exempt from, or immune as respects proceedings relating to, taxation.

(5) This section applies to the sovereign or other head of any State on which immunities and privileges are conferred by Part I of this Act and is without prejudice to the application of that Part to any such sovereign or head of State in his public capacity.

NOTES:
1. In *Littrell* v *United States of America (No 2)* [1994] 4 All ER 203, where the Court of Appeal held that the alleged negligent medical treatment of a US serviceman by US medical personnel, on a US military base in the UK, was an act *jure imperii* because of the whole context in which it occurred. Normally, medical treatment would be regarded as an act *jure gestionis* and this case demonstrates why neither a 'purpose' nor 'nature' test can be applied without reference to the background context. In *Kuwait Airways Corp.* v *Iraqi Airways* (below), the House of Lords adopted Lord Wilberforce's test in *I Congreso* without dissent and so the 'nature in context' approach is likely to be applied in all cases where the common law governs the issue and, probably, where the UK State Immunity Act 1978 refers to 'sovereign authority'.
2. As well as regulating the circumstances in which immunity may be claimed, the State Immunity Act also identifies those persons or entities who may claim such immunity as being 'the State'. Section 14 (above) is most relevant for legal entities claiming to be part of the government apparatus of an existing State, and under section 21 the Secretary of State for Foreign Affairs may stipulate conclusively whether the claimant is indeed a 'State' for the purposes of this Act. Note the interesting Swiss case of *Swissair* v *X and Another* 82 ILR (1985) 36, where a Swiss court held that a national of the local state could not claim the immunity belonging to a foreign State even if it (the national) had acted on behalf of the foreign State.
3. It is not altogether clear whether the UK legislation is on all fours with the ILC Draft Articles as they stand at present. In particular, the State Immunity Act 1978 allows little room for the 'purpose' of the transaction to be considered when deciding upon immunity, whereas this is an important element in the ILC Draft.

B: Who may claim immunity: States and separate entities

Trendtex Trading Corp v *Central Bank of Nigeria*
[1977] 2 WLR 356, Court of Appeal

The Central Bank of Nigeria was modelled on the Bank of England. It had issued a letter of credit in favour of the plaintiff, to pay for cement that was to be used to build army barracks in Nigeria. The Central Bank refused to pay for the cement or for charges incurred by delay at the port of delivery (demurrage). The Bank claimed state immunity. As well as accepting unequivocally that immunity was restrictive, Lord Denning considered whether the Bank was an organ of the State of Nigeria so as to be entitled to immunity at all.

LORD DENNING: . . . If we are still bound to apply the doctrine of absolute immunity, there is, even so, an important question arising upon it. The doctrine grants immunity to a foreign government or its department of state, or any body which can be regarded as an 'alter ego or organ' of the government. But how are we to discover whether a body is an 'alter ego or organ' of the government?

The cases on this subject are difficult to follow, even in this country: let alone those in other countries. And yet, we have to find what is the rule of international law for all of them. It is particularly difficult because different countries have different ways of arranging internal affairs. In some countries the government departments conduct all their business through their own offices – even ordinary commercial dealings – without setting up separate corporations or legal entities. In other countries they set up separate corporations or legal entities which are under the complete control of the department, but which enter into commercial transactions, buying and selling goods, owning and chartering ships, just like any ordinary trading concern. This difference in internal arrangements ought not to affect the availability of immunity in international law. A foreign department of state ought not to lose its immunity simply because it conducts some of its activities by means of a separate legal entity. . . .

Another problem arises because of the internal laws of many countries which grant immunities and privileges to its own organisations. Some organisations can sue, or be sued, in their courts. Others can not. In England we have had for centuries special immunities and privileges for 'the Crown' – a phrase which has been held to cover many governmental departments and many emanations of government departments – but not nationalised commercial undertakings. . . . It includes even the Forestry Commission. . . . It cannot be right that international law should grant or refuse absolute immunity according to the immunities granted internally. I would put on one side, therefore, our cases about the privileges, prerogatives and exceptions of the 'Crown'.

It is often said that a certificate by the ambassador, saying whether or not an organisation is a department of state, is of much weight, though not decisive: see *Krajina* v *Tass Agency* [1949] 2 All ER 274. But even this is not to my mind satisfactory. . . .

I confess that I can think of no satisfactory test except that of looking to the functions and control of the organisation. I do not think that it should depend on the foreign law alone. I would look to all the evidence to see whether the organisation was under government control and exercised governmental functions.

Kuwait Airways Corporation v *Iraqi Airways Co.*
[1995] 1 WLR 1147, House of Lords

Following the invasion of Kuwait by Iraq in August 1990, the Iraqi Government ordered the defendants to transport the plaintiff's aircraft to Iraq. Subsequently, the ownership of the aircraft was purportedly transferred to the defendants. A key issue was whether the defendants were entitled to immunity under s. 14(2) of the State Immunity Act 1978 as a 'separate entity' exercising sovereign authority in circumstances where the State itself would have been immune. A majority of the Court (3:2) held that the defendants were not immune in respect of all actions occurring after the purported transfer of ownership as such actions were not done in the exercise of sovereign authority but as 'owner'.

LORD GOFF: I turn next to the question whether I.A.C. [Iraqi Airways Co.] is entitled to claim immunity from jurisdiction on the principles embodied in section 14(2) of the State Immunity Act 1978, as a separate entity distinct from the organs of government of the State of Iraq and capable of suing and being sued. . . .

It follows that both conditions have to be satisfied if I.A.C. is to be entitled to immunity. However, as I see it, the central question in the present case is whether the acts performed by I.A.C. to which the proceedings relate were performed in the exercise of sovereign authority, which here means acta jure imperii (in the sense in which that expression has been adopted by English law from public international law).

Section 14 of the Act, however so far as it relates to separate entities, plainly has its origin in article 27 of the [European] Convention [on State Immunity], which provides:

1. For the purposes of the present Convention, the expression 'Contracting State' shall not include any legal entity of a Contracting State which is distinct therefrom and is capable of suing or being sued, even if that entity has been entrusted with public functions.

2. Proceedings may be instituted against any entity referred to in paragraph 1 before the courts of another Contracting State in the same manner as against a private person; however, the courts may not entertain proceedings in respect of acts performed by the entity in the exercise of sovereign authority (*acta jure imperii*).

3. Proceedings may in any event be instituted against any such entity before those courts if, in corresponding circumstances, the courts would have had jurisdiction if the proceedings had been instituted against a Contracting State.

I interpolate that it seems probable that the expressions 'any entity' and 'separate entity' in section 14 of the Act are intended to refer to an entity or separate entity of a state, a construction which is reinforced by the description in section 14(1) of such an entity as being 'distinct from the executive organs of the government of the State,' and by the fact that section 14(1) finds it necessary to provide expressly that references to a state do not include references to such an entity. However, although the point was touched upon in argument, it does not arise directly for decision in the present case, there being no doubt that I.A.C. is a separate entity of the State of Iraq. . . .

The two conditions imposed by section 14(2) (viz. that the proceedings must relate to something done by the separate entity in the exercise of sovereign authority, and that the circumstances must be such that a state would have been so immune) derive from paragraphs 2 and 3 of article 27 of the Convention. The question however arises whether immunity is excluded in the case of acta jure gestionis under the first or the second of these conditions. The puzzle arises from the fact that commercial transactions within section 3 appear to be excluded both as something not done in the exercise of sovereign authority under the first condition (i.e. not acta jure imperii as stated in article 27(2) of the Convention), and as a case in which (by virtue of section 3) a state would not be immune under the second condition. This tautology appears to be the effect of the introduction into section 3 of the Act of an exception relating to commercial transactions, while at the same time enacting section 14(2) in a form reflecting article 27 of a Convention which did not recognise any such exception. The logical answer would appear to be first to apply the condition in section 14(2)(*a*), which would have the effect of excluding acta jure gestionis, with the practical effect that questions relating to commercial transactions should not arise under section 14(2)(*b*). The latter subsection would of course still apply in other cases in which a state would not have been immune, as for example where there had been a submission to the jurisdiction within section 2. At all events, in considering whether acts done by a separate entity are or are not acts done by it in the exercise of sovereign authority under section 14(2)(*a*), it would, in my opinion, be appropriate to have regard to the English authorities relating to the distinction between acta jure imperii and acta jure gestionis as adopted from public international law, including the statement of principle by Lord Wilberforce in the *I Congreso del Partido* [1983] 1 AC 244, to which I have already referred. Such an approach is consistent with the opinion expressed by Lord Diplock in *Alcom Ltd v Republic of Columbia* [1984] AC 580, 600, that section 14(2) comes close to adopting the straightforward dichotomy between acta jure imperii and acta jure gestionis which had become familiar doctrine in public international law.

I wish to add in parenthesis that there appear at first sight to be differences between the exception relating to commercial transactions introduced in section 3 of the Act, and the distinction between acta jure imperii and acta jure gestionis as drawn by Lord Wilberforce in the *I Congreso del Partido*. In the first place, Lord Wilberforce recognised, at p. 263D, that, even where a state engages in trade, it remains a state and is capable at any time of sovereign or governmental action.

Accordingly, the inquiry still had to be made whether the relevant acts were within or outside the trading commercial activity. I suppose that it is possible (though I express no opinion on the point) that the same inquiry may have to be made under section 3 of the Act, when considering whether the proceedings relate to a commercial transaction. Second, Lord Wilberforce, at p. 267C, considered acta jure gestionis to be acts 'within an area of activity, trading or commercial, or otherwise of a private law character. . . .' However, having regard to the very broad definition of 'commercial transactions' in section 3(3) of the Act, it is probable that most, if not all, of the actions of a private law character in which a separate entity of a state is likely to engage will fall within that definition. At all events I do not consider that these differences (such as they are) should require us to construe the words 'in the exercise of sovereign authority' in section 14(2)(a) otherwise than in accordance with the accepted meaning of acta jure imperii, especially as that is plainly in accordance with article 27(2) of the Convention, which is reflected in section 14(2) of the Act.

It is apparent from Lord Wilberforce's statement of principle that the ultimate test of what constitutes an act jure imperii is whether the act in question is of its own character a governmental act, as opposed to an act which any private citizen can perform. It follows that, in the case of acts done by a separate entity, it is not enough that the entity should have acted on the directions of the state, because such an act need not possess the character of a governmental act. To attract immunity under section 14(2), therefore, what is done by the separate entity must be something which possesses that character. . . .

But where an act done by a separate entity of the state on the directions of the state does not possess the character of a governmental act, the entity will not be entitled to state immunity, though it may be able to invoke a substantive defence such as force majeure despite the fact that it is an entity of the state: see, e.g., *C. Czarnikow Ltd v Centrela Handlu Zagranicznego Rolimpex* [1979] AC 351. Likewise, in the absence of such character, the mere fact that the purpose or motive of the act was to serve the purposes of the state will not be sufficient to enable the separate entity to claim immunity under section 14(2) of the Act.

LORD MUSTILL (Dissenting): . . . My Lords, I think it clear that sections 3 and 14(2) [of the State Immunity Act 1978], read together, call for an inquiry in three stages, which in the context of the present facts may be stated as follows. First, what 'thing' or things alleged to have been done by I.A.C. are the subject of the proceedings against which I.A.C. claims to be immune? Secondly, did these things amount to a 'commercial transaction' within the extended definition in section 3(3)(c)? Finally, were these things done by I.A.C. in the exercise of sovereign authority?

As to the first question, although it may in some cases be difficult to be sure precisely what things alleged to have been done by the defendant are the subject of the proceedings, particularly if the issue of immunity is raised before the plaintiffs' claim is pleaded, there is no such problem here. The statement of claim is perfectly clear, and is of central importance in identifying and limiting the matters constituting the cause of action in respect of which the plaintiffs sought a money judgment. . . . The plaintiffs allege a proprietary tort which I.A.C. committed by wrongfully remaining in possession of the aircraft and refusing to give them back, thus causing the plaintiffs to lose their entire value. . . .

Accordingly, at the second state of the inquiry it must be asked whether, if the relevant defendant had been the Republic of Iraq, it would have been entitled to immunity against a claim based on an allegation that the Republic had wrongfully retained the aircraft and refused to hand them back. Since Iraq is a sovereign and therefore entitled to a prima facie general immunity under section 1 of the Act, the answer would be affirmative unless the claim fell within one of the exceptions in Part I which in the present instance means section 3. Thus the immunity of Iraq against the hypothetical claim contemplated by section 14(2)(b) would depend on whether the retention and non-return of the aircraft was a 'commercial transaction.' I venture to think that without the expanded definition in section 3(3)(c) it could not plausibly be suggested that the retention of the aircraft was a 'transaction' and still less that it was 'commercial.' It was quite simply a wrongful detention, with no commercial attributes. The rationale of the common law doctrine of the restricted immunity, of which section 3 is the counterpart, is that where the sovereign chooses to doff his robes and descend into the market place he must take the rough with the smooth, and having condescended to engage in mundane commercial activities he must also condescend to submit himself to an adjudication in a foreign court on whether he has in the course of those activities undertaken obligations which he has failed to fulfil. A claim of the present kind falls entirely outside this reasoning. Equally, although the meaning of 'commercial transactions' is broadened by section 3(3)(c) to embrace an 'activity' as well as a 'transaction,' the word is qualified by the parenthesis '(whether of a commercial, industrial, financial, professional or other similar character),' which conforms with the general policy which I have suggested. In my opinion the plaintiffs' claim for wrongful misappropriation is within neither the letter nor the spirit of the commercial exception to the general immunity of the state.

There remains the third stage of the inquiry, which is whether the retention of the aircraft was 'done by [I.A.C.] in the exercise of sovereign authority.' This is much more difficult, since a separate entity is not sovereign and has no authority. For my part, I do not think that section 14(2)(a) can simply be an echo of section 3, or Part I of the Act as a whole, for otherwise it would duplicate section 14(2)(b): and section 14 as a whole assumes that the state may be immune in circumstances where an entity is not. The immunities of the sovereign and of the entity are of an entirely different character. The former is a matter of status, inherent in the nature of the person or body claiming it, and all-embracing except where specifically excluded by the Act. By contrast the separate entity has no status entitling it to a general immunity, and is endowed by section 14 only with a case-by-case immunity in the situations there described. Moreover, the immunities differ in extent as well as kind, for there must be many activities of separate entities which could not on any view be described as done under sovereign authority for the purposes of section 14(2)(a), but which if done by the sovereign would lie outside the 'commercial transaction' exception, and all the other exceptions in Part I of the Act, and hence would attract the general immunity under section 1.

Assuming, therefore, that section 14(2)(a) is intended to create an additional requirement for immunity, one must ask again what is meant by the reference to things done by the entity in the exercise of a sovereign authority which the entity does not possess. The best I can do, to convey what I believe to be the flavour of section 14(2)(a), is to assert that the entity is immune only if in some sense the act, although not done by the sovereign, is a manifestation of the sovereign's authority, Looking at the matter in this way, it is not enough to show that a sovereign act was an essential preliminary to the conduct by the entity of which the plaintiff complains, for the sovereign quality of the train of events may have died away by the time that the entity comes to play its part; so it is not in my opinion sufficient for I.A.C. to claim immunity in respect of items c. and d. of the particulars just because the conduct of Iraq in the early stages, which put I.A.C. in a position where the acts in question could be done, may, for the sake of argument be assumed to have had a sovereign character. But in the present case I cannot detect any change in the character of the successive events. Put at its bluntest and most colourful, the plaintiffs' complaint is that the Republic of Iraq stole the aircraft and that I.A.C. is unlawfully in possession of them. It is not an accident that when this complaint was clothed in the language of a civil pleading the same cause of action founded on the same allegations of fact, and leading to the same monetary claim, was asserted against both defendants alike: and it appears to me that in this respect the pleader's instinct was right. In my opinion I.A.C. was not acting autonomously, but in harness with the Republic of Iraq, and under the shadow of the sovereign authority by which the latter itself was acting, so that its acts were a manifestation of that authority.

For these reasons I would for my part hold that all three conditions, for the immunity of I.A.C. are satisfied in relation, to the whole of the claim advanced in the writ. I would therefore propose that the writ and all subsequent proceedings, including the judgment and the various steps taken by way of execution should be set aside.

NOTE:

As well as difficult questions about exactly what organ is 'the State' for the purposes of claiming immunity, the above cases demonstrate that even 'separate entities' may be entitled to immunity if (a) they exercise sovereign authority and (b) the State would have been immune in the circumstances of the case. Technically, the question of whether the entity claiming immunity is 'separate' is logically prior to whether it was exercising sovereign authority: that is, the exercise or non-exercise of sovereign authority should not determine whether it is 'separate' or not. In this sense, 'sovereign authority' appears to be used to describe the purpose/nature of the particular action undertaken by an entity that the court has already decided is 'separate'. However, as the *Kuwait* case shows, it is easy to conflate the issues. The judges in the minority took the view that the whole episode – the transfer and subsequent use of the aircraft – was done in the exercise of sovereign authority (in circumstances where the State itself would have been immune) and so attracted immunity.

C: Heads of State

A Head of State either amounts to 'the State' itself for the purpose of attracting immunity when he or she is acting in a public capacity (s. 14(1)(a), State Immunity Act 1978) or enjoys immunity equivalent to a Head of Diplomatic Mission (s. 20(1), State Immunity Act 1978). Necessarily, there is some overlap.

Bank of Credit and Commerce International (Overseas) Ltd v *Price Waterhouse*
[1997] 4 All ER 108

> The liquidators of the plaintiff bank commenced certain actions against the defendants, who were the bank's former auditors. The defendants sought to bring into those proceedings Abu Dhabi, which was a constituent territory of the United Arab Emirates (a recognised State), and issued a third party notice against Sheikh Zayed, the Ruler of Abu Dhabi and President of the United Arab Emirates. Sheikh Zayed applied to set aside the notice on the ground that he was immune from suit as a diplomatic agent under Article 31 of the Vienna Convention on Diplomatic Relations, as set out in Sch. 1 to the Diplomatic Privileges Act 1964, by virtue of s. 20(1)(a) of the State Immunity Act 1978. The defendants contended that they were bringing proceedings against Sheikh Zayed in his public capacity as the Ruler and the embodiment of Abu Dhabi, and that since the territory was not immune from suit as a separate entity under s. 14(2) of the 1978 Act, as it had not acted in the exercise of the sovereign authority of the United Arab Emirates, neither was he.
>
> The Court held that Sheikh Zayed was immune from suit under s. 20(i) as being equivalent to a Head of Mission. The 'public capacity' of the Sheikh did not arise as no recognised State was involved.

LADDIE J: The 1978 Act includes two significant provisions relating to the sovereign or head of state, that is to say a sovereign or head of state of a state recognised by virtue of the issue of a suitable certificate . . . [Under s. 20(i)(a)] the head of state has all the immunities bestowed on diplomatic personnel such as ambassadors. Secondly, in some cases, it is possible to bring proceedings against the head of state as representing the state itself. Because that is so, s. 14(1)(a) of the 1978 Act provides:

The immunities and privileges conferred by this Part of this Act apply to any foreign or commonwealth State other than the United Kingdom; and references to a State include references to – (a) the sovereign or other head of that State in his public capacity. . . .

This means that when a head of a recognised state is acting in his private capacity, he has the same immunities as say, the ambassador of that state under the 1964 Act. On the other hand, when acting in his public capacity, effectively as the embodiment of the state, he has all the immunities the state has under the 1978 Act, it would appear at first blush that the immunities are cumulative, thus the fact that he has immunities when acting in a public capacity, does not detract from the immunities derived from the 1964 Act by virtue of s. 20(1) of the 1978 Act. (See in this regard s. 16 of the 1978 Act.)

This construction appears to me to be consistent with the underlying purpose of this legislation. In so far as the sovereign or head of state is acting in a public capacity on behalf of that state, he is clothed with the immunity that the state has. When acting in this capacity, the head of state and the state are, to some extent, indistinguishable. On the other hand, when acting in any other capacity, it is sensible that he should have immunity equivalent to that enjoyed by the state's diplomatic staff.

NOTES:

1. The *Pinochet Case* (above) held that the immunity of a former Head of State exists in respect of acts done while he or she was in office if those acts were 'official', a view endorsed in a similar context in the *Arrest Warrant Case* (*Congo* v *Belgium*) above. Lord Goff dissented on the ground that there is no rule of international law denying immunity in cases of torture. However, what is unclear is whether immunity is denied because 'torture' can *never* be an official act under international law *or* because the crime of torture is an international crime and immunity does not apply for crimes against international law. The second view – that there is no immunity for crimes against international law – has a coherency about it that avoids national courts having to decide what an 'official' act is. It also firmly establishes immunity as being immunity from the national laws of a State, not from international law itself (see further section 2 above).

2. A serving Head of State has, virtually, absolute immunity while in office: either because he or she is 'the State' within the 1978 Act, or because of the personal immunities enjoyed as if he or she was Head of Mission. However, if there is no immunity for crimes against international law (which is unclear: see *Al-Adsani* v *UK* above) it then should not matter whether the Head of State is currently in office or not. In fact, as the *Arrest Warrant Case* makes clear, there is no exception to the rule of virtual absolute immunity for a serving senior State representative. Immunity *ratione personae* is not lost even if massive human rights violations are alleged.

D: Interpreting the State Immunity Act

Alcom Ltd v *Republic of Colombia*
[1984] AC 580, House of Lords

The plaintiffs had secured judgment in default against Colombia, and now sought to enforce that judgment against monies held in the Colombian Embassy's London bank account. The Colombian Ambassador had certified that the monies in the account were used for the running of the Embassy. The issue was whether the monies were 'property' used for 'commercial purposes' within s. 13 of the State Immunity Act 1978.

LORD DIPLOCK: The crucial question of construction for your Lordships is whether a debt . . . falls within the description contained in section 13(4) of 'property which is for the time being in use or intended for use for commercial purposes.' ... . What is clear beyond all question is that if the expression 'commercial purposes' in section 13(4) bore what would be its ordinary and natural meaning in the context in which it there appears, a debt representing the balance standing to the credit of a diplomatic mission in a current bank account used for meeting the day-to-day expenses of running the mission would fall outside the subsection.

'Commercial purposes,' however, is given by section 17(1) the extended meaning which takes one back to the comprehensive definition of 'commercial transaction' in section 3(3). Paragraph (a) of this tripartite definition refers to *any* contract for the supply of goods or services, without making any exception for contracts in either of these two classes that are entered into for purposes of enabling a foreign state to do things in the exercise of its sovereign authority either in the United Kingdom or elsewhere. This is to be contrasted with the other paragraph of the definition that is relevant to the instant case, paragraph (c), which on the face of it would be comprehensive enough to include all transactions into which a state might enter, were it not that it does specifically preserve immunity from adjudicative jurisdiction for transactions or activities into which a state enters or in which it engages in the exercise of sovereign authority, other than those transactions that are specifically referred to either in paragraph (a) or in paragraph (b), with the latter of which the instant appeal is not concerned. ... .

My Lords, the decisive question for your Lordships is whether in the context of the other provisions of the Act to which I have referred, and against the background of its subject matter, public international law, the words 'property which is for the time being in use or intended for use for commercial purposes,' appearing as an exception to a general immunity to the enforcement jurisdiction of United Kingdom courts accorded by section 13(2) to the property of a foreign state, are apt to describe the debt represented by the balance standing to the credit of a current account kept with a commercial banker for the purpose of meeting the expenditure incurred in the day-to-day running of the diplomatic mission of a foreign state.

Such expenditure will, no doubt, include *some* moneys due under contracts for the supply of goods or services to the mission, to meet which the mission will draw upon its current bank account; but the account will also be drawn upon to meet many other items of expenditure which fall outside even the extended definition of 'commercial purposes' for which section 17(1) and section 3(3) provide. The debt owed by the bank to the foreign sovereign state and represented by the credit balance in the current account kept by the diplomatic mission of that state as a possible subject matter of the enforcement jurisdiction of the court is however one and indivisible; it is not susceptible of anticipatory dissection into the various uses to which moneys drawn upon it might have been put in the future if it had not been subjected to attachment by garnishee proceedings. Unless it can be shown by the judgment creditor who is seeking to attach the credit balance by garnishee proceedings that the bank account was earmarked by the foreign state solely (save for *de minimis* exceptions) for being drawn upon to settle liabilities incurred in commercial transactions, as for example by issuing documentary credits in payment of the price of goods sold to the state, it cannot, in my view, be sensibly brought within the crucial words of the exception for which section 13(4) provides.

NOTE:

A State or other entity entitled to immunity may submit to the jurisdiction by waiver. However, in UK law at least, that waiver must be express, by words or conduct intended to operate as a waiver. So, in *London Branch of the Nigerian Universities Commission v Bastians* [1995] ICR 358, an uncompleted form returned to an Industrial Tribunal (via the UK Foreign Office) by the Commission was not a waiver, and in *Malaysian Industrial Development Authority v Jeyasingham* [1998] ICR 307, the employer's notice of appearance was not a waiver and, in any event, it had not been offered by the High Commissioner, the only person who could waive Malaysian immunity according to s. 2(7) of the State Immunity Act 1978.

SECTION 4: **State immunity in other States**

The following cases illustrate how the restrictive approach to State immunity is applied in other States. They also illustrate just how difficult it can be to make a distinction between sovereign and commercial acts.

United States v *The Public Service Alliance of Canada*
32 ILM 1 (1993), Canadian Supreme Court

Canadian workers were in dispute with the United States Government regarding their employment on a US military base in Canada. The US Government claimed immunity. The matter was decided by the Canadian Supreme Court on the basis of the Canadian State Immunity Act 1982. The Court decided that contracts of employment at a military base were, in their context, a sovereign activity even though their nature was essentially commercial.

LA FOREST J: The crux of this appeal is the proper interpretation of s. 5 of the *State Immunity Act*. It reads:

5. A foreign state is not immune from the jurisdiction of a court in any proceedings that relate to any commercial activity of the foreign state. . . .

Certain aspects of employment at the base are commercial, but in other respects the employment relationship is infused with sovereign attributes. . . . In the courts below and on the hearing of this appeal, considerable importance was attached to the distinction between the nature of the employment relationship (a valid consideration under the statute) and the purpose of that relationship (purportedly an invalid consideration). I find it difficult if not impossible to distinguish in a principled manner between the nature and purpose of employment relationships, and I would thus decline to follow this approach. Nature and purpose are interrelated, and it is impossible to determine the former without considering the latter. I do not accept that the definition of 'commercial activity' in the Act precludes consideration of its purpose. . . . However, if consideration of purpose is helpful in determining the nature of an activity, then such considerations should be and are allowed under the Act. . . .

Before delving into the specific questions posed by this case, it is useful to consider first the common law antecedents of the *State Immunity Act* and then to compare Canada's codification of the common law with the statutory model in the United States. As will become apparent, the law in this area reveals a consistent pattern of development that has arrived at a point where state activity can be characterized only after appreciating its entire context. Rigid dichotomies between the 'nature' and 'purpose' of state activity are not helpful in this analysis.

This passage [cited from the judgment of Lord Wilberforce in *I Congreso*] underscores the point that the state activity in question will often possess a hybrid nature – one public, the other private. In light of this reality, Lord Wilberforce did not attempt to surmount the conceptual difficulties inherent in formulating a precise method of differentiating between acts *jure imperii* and acts *jure gestionis*. Instead, he opted for a contextual approach. . . . The entire context includes both the nature and purpose of the act. Lord Wilberforce noted, at p. 272, that, 'I agree that the purpose . . . is not decisive but it may throw some light upon the nature of what was done.'

It seems to me that a contextual approach is the only reasonable basis of applying the doctrine of restrictive immunity. The alternative is to attempt the impossible – an antiseptic distillation of a 'once-and-for-all' characterisation of the activity in question, entirely divorced from its purpose. It is true that purpose should not predominate, as this approach would convert virtually every act by commercial agents of the state into an act *jure imperii*. However, the converse is also true. Rigid adherence to the 'nature' of an act to the exclusion of purpose would render innumerable government activities *jure gestionis*. Neither of these extremes offers an appropriate resolution of the problem.

Société Iranienne Du Gaz v *Société Pipeline Service*
noted in 85 AJIL 696 (1991), French Court of Cassation

Société Pipeline Service sued the National Iranian Gas Company for monies owed over the construction of a pipeline. The National Gas Company (NIGC) raised a plea of immunity, which was accepted by the Court because of the function and purpose that NIGC was fulfilling when it entered into the contract.

From the decision of the Court of Cassation . . . it appears that NIGC based its plea of immunity on the consideration that it was intimately linked to the Iranian Government and that its activities relating to gas transmission throughout Iran were intended to meet the needs of a 'public service' (*service public*). The court of appeal had considered this line of argument irrelevant because the decisive factor in determining the issue of immunity was the nature of the transaction. In its view, under the French *lex fori*, the transaction fell within the category of a 'public work subcontract,' which should be characterized as a purely commercial transaction. The Court of Cassation disagreed with that characterization, stating: 'Foreign states and instrumentalities acting under the direction or on behalf of states are entitled to immunity from suit not only in regard to governmental acts but also in respect of acts performed in furtherance of a public service.'

This decision is surprising. It is contrary to a consistent line of cases in which the Court of Cassation had held that, for the implementation of immunity rules, the relevant factor is the nature of the transaction from which the dispute arises, rather than its purpose. The nature of the transaction has been considered decisive in cases involving both immunity from suit and immunity from execution. . . .

Under the circumstances, the rationale of the *NIGC* decision is not readily apparent. It may be that the Court of Cassation was influenced by domestic administrative law concepts regarding the respective jurisdictions of the administrative and judicial courts. If that were the case, the *NIGC* decision would be a matter of concern because these concepts are not as clear as would be desirable. To project them into the international arena would inject unwarranted uncertainties into the implementation of immunity rules. Another possibility is that the Court may have been influenced by nonlegal considerations due to the improvement in the political climate between France and Iran.

Controller and Auditor-General v *Sir Ronald Davidson*
[1996] 2 NZLR 84, New Zealand Court of Appeal

A Commission of Inquiry (the Davidson Inquiry) was established in New Zealand to investigate certain tax matters. An element in the impugned transactions was tax credits issued by the Government of the Cook Islands. For the purposes of the action, the Cook Islands was treated as a fully sovereign independent State. The issue was whether the issue of tax credits by the Cook Islands Government was a sovereign act attracting immunity. New Zealand had no immunity legislation.

COOKE P: Sovereign immunity is of course accepted by the New Zealand Courts. . . . The two leading expositions of the doctrine and the commercial exception to it evolved in recent times are the speech of Lord Wilberforce in *I Congreso del Partido* [see above] and the speech of Lord Goff of Chieveley in *Kuwait Airways Corp.* v *Iraqi Airways Co.* [see above].

Seen in isolation, the issuing of a tax credit is an act which could only be performed by a state. At least on the surface, it would by itself attract sovereign immunity. But the affidavit of the Commissioner of Inquiry and the evidence already before him show prima facie that the Cook Islands Government Property Corporation, in the buying and selling of promissory notes was integrally involved in the tax credit transactions. Dealing in promissory notes is an activity which any private citizen can perform. As a whole the transactions may be called the sale of tax credits, but, if that description is too loose, it is at least cleat that there is apparently strong evidence of ostensibly commercial sale-and-purchase contracts as a key component of the arrangements. *I Congreso and Kuwait Airways* and the other authorities cited to us do not deal with mixed-up transactions of this kind. . . . Clearly they fall within the commission's terms of reference. Their commercial aspects is so significant that one can have no doubt that the doctrine of sovereign immunity must be excluded in relation to the whole inquiry. A government which descends to this extent into the market place cannot fairly expect total immunity. Its auditors and financial advisers can be in no better position. . . .

In the present era of civilisation and international law I should think that a Court would be going too far if it were to allow a general exception of iniquity to the doctrine of sovereign immunity. The invasion of Kuwait was treated as iniquitous by the United Nations and no doubt was so regarded by many countries, yet in the *Kuwait Airways* case the House of Lords held unanimously that the seizure of Kuwait civil aircraft was protected by sovereign immunity. On the other band, as noted in the American Law Institute's *Restatement of The Law The foreign Relations Law of the United States* (1987), vol. 1, s. 461c. 'In principle, a foreign state is responsible for violations of domestic law by terrorist acts committed by its agents'. The assassination case of *Letelier* v *Republic of Chile* 488 F Supp 665 (DDC, 1980) is one of the supporting authorities cited.

One can speculate that the law may gradually but steadily develop, perhaps first excepting from sovereign immunity atrocities or the use of weapons of mass destruction, perhaps ultimately going on to except acts of war not authorised by the United Nations. But this is [to] peer optimistically into the future far beyond the bounds of anything falling to be decided in the present judicial review proceedings.

NOTE:

The denial of immunity in the above case follows from the characterisation of the tax scheme as a commercial transaction. The contextual approach (see *I Congreso* and *Holland* v *Lampen-Wolfe*) is used this time to deny immunity, even though the giving of a tax credit is itself a governmental act. Cooke P also touches on the issue of denying immunity in cases that strike at the heart of the international order, irrespective of whether they can be truly regarded as 'commercial' or not.

SECTION 5: **The immunities of international organisations and their staff**

As was seen in Chapter 5, international organisations may well have international legal personality. Furthermore, the functions of some international organisations may be so important that they and their staff are granted privileges and immunities in order both to protect them from the vagaries of each State's domestic legal system and in order to facilitate their functions. The most obvious candidate for such immunities is the United Nations and its subsidiary and related organisations. The Convention on the Privileges and Immunities of the United Nations 1946 (which has 146 parties) and the Convention on the Privileges of the Specialised Agencies 1947 (which has 108 parties) establish and codify the immunities that the UN and its staff enjoy. These are quite extensive, ranging from the immunity from legal process (as with State immunity) to the immunity of UN staff members from income tax, and civil and criminal procedures in similar fashion to diplomats. Such privileges and immunities will be effective against all States which have signed the Conventions and have given effect to their provisions in their national law. They are protected vigorously: see ICJ Advisory Opinion on the *Difference Relating to Immunity from Legal Process of a Special Rapporteur of the Commission on Human Rights*, 38 ILM 873 (1999). There is no reason why other international organisations should not have certain privileges and immunities, although this will stem from specific treaties establishing those agreements and specific provisions of national law. In the *International Tin Council Case* [1988] 3 All ER 257, it was held that the EEC (now European Union) has no such immunity.

In the UK, whether an international organisation (and its staff) has immunity from legal process and other obligations depends on (i) whether it has legal capacity in the UK (see Chapter 5) and (ii) whether such immunity is enshrined in UK law. For example, the United Nations has such capacity and immunity under the International Organisations Acts 1968 and 1981.

In *Arab Monetary Fund* v *Hashim (No 4)* [1996] 1 Lloyd's Rep 589, the defendant contended that he was immune from the process of recovery (of an alleged bribe) because he was an employee of an international organisation. The Court of Appeal dismissed the submission on the grounds that such immunity existed for official acts only. In fact, the scope of staff immunities may not be so limited, especially if domestic legislation equates such staff to diplomatic status. In *Atkinson* v *Inter-American Development Bank*, 38 ILM 91 (1999), the US Court of Appeals for Columbia District held the Bank absolutely immune, as an international organisation, irrespective of whether it was engaged in a commercial activity. Of course, such immunity is for the organisation and its staff and not for private contractors to the Bank: *International Bank for Reconstruction and Development* v *District of Columbia* 38 ILM 818 (1999).

SECTION 6: **Diplomatic and consular immunities**

A: In international law

The law of diplomatic privileges and immunities is as old as the system of international law itself. They exist in the main because of the identity of a particular person, being the diplomat or consular representative of a foreign sovereign State and as such essentially immunities *ratione personae*. It is clear that these immunities from the jurisdiction of the 'host' State, being the State where the representatives are stationed, exist in order that the representative may carry out his functions effectively and without interference. Thus, although diplomatic privileges and immunities may seem to benefit an individual personally, that is not their *raison d'être*. As a matter of international law, the relevant principles are to be found in the multilateral treaty extracted below, supplemented by customary international law.

Vienna Convention on Diplomatic Relations 1961
UNTS 500 (1965) 95

The Convention was adopted by a UN Conference on Diplomatic Intercourse and Immunities in April 1961, and entered force in April 1964. At August 2002, there were parties to the Convention. As well as being one of the most widely ratified multilateral treaties, much of the Convention also reflects existing customary international law.

Article 9

1. The receiving state may at any time and without having to explain its decision, notify the sending state that the head of the mission or any member of the diplomatic staff of the mission is *persona non grata* or that any other member of the staff of the mission is not acceptable. In any such case, the sending state shall, as appropriate, either recall the person concerned or terminate his functions with the mission. A person may be declared *non grata* or not acceptable before arriving in the territory of the receiving state.

2. If the sending state refuses or fails within a reasonable period to carry out its obligations under paragraph 1 of this article, the receiving state may refuse to recognize the person concerned as a member of the mission.

Article 22

1. The premises of the mission shall be inviolable. The agents of the receiving state may not enter them, except with the consent of the head of the mission.

2. The receiving state is under a special duty to take all appropriate steps to protect the premises of the mission against any intrusion or damage and to prevent any disturbance of the peace of the mission or impairment of its dignity.

3. The premises of the mission, their furnishings and other property thereon and the means of transport of the mission shall be immune from search, requisition, attachment or execution.

Article 24

The archives and documents of the mission shall be inviolable at any time and wherever they may be.

Article 27

1. The receiving state shall permit and protect free communication of the part of the mission for all official purposes. In communicating with the government and the other missions and consulates of the sending state, wherever situated, the mission may employ all appropriate

means, including diplomatic couriers and messages in code or cipher. However, the mission may install and use a wireless transmitter only with the consent of the receiving state.

2. The official correspondence of the mission shall be inviolable. Official correspondence means all correspondence relating to the mission and its functions.

3. The diplomatic bag shall not be opened or detained.

4. The packages constituting the diplomatic bag must bear visible external marks of their character and may contain only diplomatic documents or articles intended for official use.

5. The diplomatic courier, who shall be provided with an official document indicating his status and the number of packages constituting the diplomatic bag, shall be protected by the receiving state in the performance of his functions. He shall enjoy personal inviolability and shall not be liable to any form of arrest or detention.

Article 29

The person of a diplomatic agent shall be inviolable. He shall not be liable to any form of arrest or detention. The receiving state shall treat him with due respect and shall take all appropriate steps to prevent any attack on his person, freedom or dignity.

Article 30

1. The private residence of a diplomatic agent shall enjoy the same inviolability and protection as the premises of the mission.

2. His papers, correspondence and, except as provided in paragraph 3 of Article 31, his property, shall likewise enjoy inviolability.

Article 31

1. A diplomatic agent shall enjoy immunity from the criminal jurisdiction of the receiving state. He shall also enjoy immunity from its civil and administrative jurisdiction, except in the case of:

    (a) a real action relating to private immovable property situated in the territory of the receiving state, unless he holds it on behalf of the sending state for the purposes of the mission;

    (b) an action relating to succession in which the diplomatic agent is involved as executor, administrator, heir or legatee as a private person and not on behalf of the sending state;

    (c) an action relating to any professional or commercial activity exercised by the diplomatic agent in the receiving state outside his official functions.

2. A diplomatic agent is not obliged to give evidence as a witness.

3. No measures of execution may be taken in respect of a diplomatic agent except in the cases coming under sub-paragraphs (a), (b) and (c) of paragraph 1 of this article, and provided that the measures concerned can be taken without infringing the inviolability of his person or of his residence.

4. The immunity of a diplomatic agent from the jurisdiction of the receiving state does not exempt him from the jurisdiction of the sending state.

Article 32

1. The immunity from jurisdiction of diplomatic agents and of persons enjoying immunity under Article 37 may be waived by the sending state.

2. Waiver must always be express.

3. The initiation of proceedings by a diplomatic agent or by a person enjoying immunity from jurisdiction under Article 37 shall preclude him from invoking immunity from jurisdiction in respect of any counter-claim directly connected with the principal claim.

4. Waiver of immunity from jurisdiction in respect of civil or administrative proceedings shall not be held to imply waiver of immunity in respect of the execution of the judgment, for which a separate waiver shall be necessary.

Article 39

1. Every person entitled to privileges and immunities shall enjoy them from the moment he enters the territory of the receiving state on proceeding to take up his post or, if already in its territory, from the moment when his appointment is notified to the Ministry for Foreign Affairs or such other ministry as may be agreed.

Article 41

1. Without prejudice to their privileges and immunities, it is the duty of all person enjoying such privileges and immunities to respect the laws and regulations of the receiving state. They also have a duty not to interfere in the internal affairs of that state.

2. All official business with the receiving state entrusted to the mission by the sending state shall be conducted with or through the Ministry for Foreign Affairs of the receiving state or such other ministry as may be agreed.

3. The premises of the mission must not be used in any manner incompatible with the functions of the mission as laid down in the present Convention or by other rules of general international law or by any special agreements in force between the sending and the receiving state.

Article 42

A diplomatic agent shall not in the receiving state practise for personal profit any professional or commercial activity.

US Diplomatic and Consular Staff in Iran Case (*United States* v *Tehran*)

ICJ Rep 1980 3, International Court of Justice

On 4 November 1979, Iranian students seized the US Embassy in Tehran and a number of consulates in outlying cities. The Iranian authorities failed to protect the Embassy and later appeared to adopt the students' actions (see Chapter 11). Over 50 US nationals (mostly diplomatic and consular staff) were held for 444 days. The US sought a declaration, *inter alia*, that Iran had violated the two Vienna Conventions, and calling for the release of the hostages and the vacation of the Embassy and consulates. The Court considered whether the initial attack by the students could be attributed to the Iranian Government, the conduct of Iran at that time and subsequently, and whether Iran was therefore in violation of its international obligations.

68. The Court is therefore led inevitably to conclude, in regard to the first phase of the events which has so far been considered, that on 4 November 1979 the Iranian authorities:

(a) were fully aware of their obligations under the conventions in force to take appropriate steps to protect the premises of the United States Embassy and its diplomatic and consular staff from any attack and from any infringement of their inviolability, and to ensure the security of such other persons as might be present on the said premises;

(b) were fully aware, as a result of the appeals for help made by the United States Embassy, of the urgent need for action on their part;

(c) had the means at their disposal to perform their obligations;

(d) completely failed to comply with these obligations.

Similarly, the Court is led to conclude that the Iranian authorities were equally aware of their obligations to protect the United States Consulates at Tabriz and Shiraz, and of the need for action on their part, and similarly failed to use the means which were at their disposal to comply with their obligations.

69. The second phase of the events which are the subject of the United States' claims comprises the whole series of facts which occurred following the completion of the occupation of the United States Embassy by the militants, and the seizure of the Consulates at Tabriz and Shiraz. The occupation having taken place and the diplomatic and consular personnel of the United States' mission having been taken hostage, the action required of the Iranian Government by the Vienna Conventions and by general international law was manifest. Its plain duty was at once to make every effort, and to take every appropriate step, to bring these flagrant infringements of the inviolability of the premises, archives and diplomatic and consular staff of the United States Embassy to a speedy end, to restore the Consulates at Tabriz and Shiraz to United States control, and in general to re-establish the status quo and to offer reparation for the damage.

76. The Iranian authorities' decision to continue the subjection of the premises of the United States Embassy to occupation by militants and of the Embassy staff to detention as hostages, clearly gave rise to repeated and multiple breaches of the applicable provisions of the Vienna Conventions even more serious than those which arose from their failure to take any steps to prevent the attacks on the inviolability of these premises and staff.

84. The Vienna Conventions of 1961 and 1963 contain express provisions to meet the case when members of an embassy staff, under the cover of diplomatic privileges and immunities, engage in such abuses of their functions as espionage or interference in the internal affairs of the receiving State. It is precisely with the possibility of such abuses in contemplation that Article 41, paragraph 1, of the Vienna Convention on Diplomatic Relations, and Article 55, paragraph 1, of the Vienna Convention on Consular Relations, provide

> Without prejudice to their privileges and immunities, it is the duty of all persons enjoying such privileges and immunities to respect the laws and regulations of the receiving State. They also have a duty not to interfere in the internal affairs of that State.

Paragraph 3 of Article 41 of the 1961 Convention further states: 'The premises of the mission must not be used in any manner incompatible with the functions of the missions . . .': an analogous provision, with respect to consular premises is to be found in Article 55, paragraph 2, of the 1963 Convention.

85. Thus, it is for the very purpose of providing a remedy for such possible abuses of diplomatic functions that Article 9 of the 1961 Convention on Diplomatic Relations stipulates:

> 1. The receiving State may at any time and without having to explain its decision, notify the sending State that the head of the mission or any member of the diplomatic staff of the mission is *persona non grata* or that any other member of the staff of the mission is not acceptable. . . .

Beyond that remedy for dealing with abuses of the diplomatic function by individual members of a mission, a receiving State has in its hands a more radical remedy if abuses of their functions by members of a mission reach serious proportions. This is the power which every receiving State has, at its own discretion, to break off diplomatic relations with a sending State and to call for the immediate closure of the offending mission.

86. The rules of diplomatic law, in short, constitute a self-contained regime which, on the one hand, lays down the receiving State's obligations regarding the facilities, privileges and immunities to be accorded to diplomatic missions and, on the other, foresees their possible abuse by members of

the mission and specifies the means at the disposal of the receiving State to counter any such abuse. These means are, by their nature, entirely efficacious, for unless the sending State recalls the member of the mission objected to forthwith, the prospect of the almost immediate loss of his privileges and immunities, because of the withdrawal by the receiving State of his recognition as a member of the mission, will in practice compel that person, in his own interest, to depart at once. But the principle of the inviolability of the persons of diplomatic agents and the premises of diplomatic missions is one of the very foundations of this long-established regime, to the evolution of which the traditions of Islam made a substantial contribution. . . . Even in the case of armed conflict or in the case of a breach in diplomatic relations those provisions require that both the inviolability of the members of a diplomatic mission and of the premises, property and archives of the mission must be respected by the receiving State. Naturally, the observance of this principle does not mean – and this the Applicant Government expressly acknowledges – that a diplomatic agent caught in the act of committing an assault or other offence may not, on occasion, be briefly arrested by the police of the receiving State in order to prevent the commission of the particular crime. But such eventualities bear no relation at all to what occurred in the present case.

92. It is a matter of deep regret that the situation which occasioned those observations has not been rectified since they were made. Having regard to their importance the Court considers it essential to reiterate them in the present Judgment. The frequency with which at the present time the principles of international law governing diplomatic and consular relations are set at naught by individuals or groups of individuals is already deplorable. But this case is unique and of very particular gravity because here it is not only private individuals or groups of individuals that have disregarded and set at naught the inviolability of a foreign embassy, but the government of the receiving State itself. Therefore in recalling yet again the extreme importance of the principles of law which it is called upon to apply in the present case, the Court considers it to be its duty to draw the attention of the entire international community, of which Iran itself has been a member since time immemorial, to the irreparable harm that may be caused by events of the kind now before the Court. Such events cannot fail to undermine the edifice of law carefully constructed by mankind over a period of centuries, the maintenance of which is vital for the security and well-being of the complex international community of the present day, to which it is more essential than ever that the rules developed to ensure the ordered progress of relations between its members should be constantly and scrupulously respected.

Radwan v Radwan

[1972] 3 All ER 967, Family Division

The essential issue in this case was whether the Consulate-General of the (then) United Arab Republic (Egypt-Syria) in London was part of the territory of that State, so as to enable a divorce obtained on those premises to be recognised under the Divorces and Legal Separations Act 1971 as a divorce obtained outside the British Isles. The judge considered both the nature of an Embassy and the general nature of diplomatic and consular immunities.

CUMMING-BRUCE J: Three principles have been invoked to explain the admitted principle that diplomatic premises and property are inviolable by the agents of the receiving state: (a) The strict extra-territorial fiction. The premises are regarded by a legal fiction as outside the territory of the receiving state and as part of the territory of the sending state. (b) The representative theory. The premises are immune from entry without consent of the head of the mission, as the mission represents or personifies the sovereignty of the sending state. (c) The theory of functional necessity. The immunity is granted by the receiving state because it is necessary to enable the mission to carry out its functions.

Counsel for the Queen's Proctor submits, and I agree, that (a) should be discarded as obsolete in the sense that international lawyers have long regarded it as unsound, and it is inconsistent with modern foreign decisions and international convention. He asks me to prefer (c) to (b), although both avoid the practical dangers which (a) is liable to produce.

This view is rested on the foundation of the consensus of authors learned in international law, the approach of courts of law abroad in such cases in modern times as have involved consideration of the immunity of diplomatic land and buildings, and inferences from the international conventions by which civilised states in modern times have sought to define the immunities which they will accord to diplomatic missions. I develop these three heads separately. . . .

I quote and adopt the observations of Mr J E S Fawcett:

> But there are two popular myths about diplomats and their immunities which we must clear away: one is that an embassy is foreign territory, and the other is that a diplomat can incur no legal liabilities in the country in which he is serving. The first is a confusion between territory or property and jurisdiction over it, and it is important to clarify it for it has sometimes arisen over ships and aircraft. The building occupied by a foreign embassy and the land on which it stands are part of the territory of what we call the receiving state: it is therefore under the jurisdiction of that state. But the members of the mission and their activities in the embassy are primarily under the control and jurisdiction of the sending state. International law avoids conflict between these jurisdictions by laying down rules to cover the whole field of diplomatic relations. These rules have been embodied in the Vienna Convention 1961, which may be taken as reflecting existing law and practice. This Convention, and that on Consular Relations drawn up in 1963, are among the first steps – we shall meet others on the law of the sea – in the successful codification of international law. The premises of a mission are inviolable, and the local authorities may enter them only with the consent of the head of the mission. But this does not make the premises foreign territory or take them out of the reach of the local law for many purposes: for example, a commercial transaction in an embassy may be governed by the local law, particularly tax law; marriages may be celebrated there only if conditions laid down by the local law are met; and a child born in it will, unless his father has diplomatic status, acquire the local nationality.

This so exactly represents the conclusion to which I have come, after looking at the textbooks to which I have referred, that I think it unnecessary in this judgment to quote other passages of eminent authorities.

R. Higgins, 'UK Foreign Affairs Committee Report on the Abuse of Diplomatic Immunities and Privileges: Government Response and Report'
80 AJIL 135 (1986)

After the killing of a British policewoman in April 1984 by shots fired from the Libyan Peoples Bureau, the Foreign Secretary instituted a review of the Vienna Conventions from the UK perspective. This resulted in a report by the Foreign Affairs Committee (*The Abuse of Diplomatic Immunities and Privileges* 1985) and a Government White Paper in response.

The White Paper contains much that is of interest to the student of diplomatic privileges and immunities. The view is taken that the Vienna Convention has become, even for nonparties, the modern customary law on the matter, so that even if termination of acceptance were legally possible, a state would be left in substantially the same position. . . .

The White Paper points out that the Vienna Convention contains no objective definition of staff categories, and that checks after notification thus usually have to relate to such questions as nationality, residence and family status: '[I]t is virtually impossible in most cases for the FCO to tell whether a person should more properly be described as a diplomat or as a member of the administrative and technical staff or indeed as a member of the mission at all.' The answer has to lie in information coming from other sources (including exchanges of information within the European Community) and in the willingness to use the persona non grata sanction where appropriate.

As the Government explains, the Vienna Conference sought, but failed, to provide a definition of 'members of the family forming part of the household'. On the vexed question of adult children, the United Kingdom practice is to accept children aged 18 or over, provided they are clearly resident with the members of the mission and are not engaged in employment on a permanent basis. In an interesting comment, the White Paper notes, 'Our acceptance or rejection of a notification is not in itself conclusive of status. In doubtful cases it is for a court to rule on the status of a dependant should he for instance be accused of a criminal offence.'

NOTE:
The above extracts deal with the substantive principles of international law that require a State to grant diplomatic privileges and immunities. Parties to the Vienna Convention must ensure that their national courts meet the standards of those treaties, while non-parties will be governed by a similar standard in customary international law. Failure to meet the obligation the US involves international responsibility (see *LaGrand Case* (Chapter 15)).

B: In the United Kingdom

The UK is a party to the Vienna Convention above. In order to ensure compliance with its international obligations, it was necessary to pass national legislation that gave diplomats immunity from that process in UK courts.

Diplomatic Privileges Act 1964

2. Application of Vienna Convention
(1) Subject to section 3 of this Act, the Articles set out in Schedule 1 to this Act (being Articles of the Vienna Convention on Diplomatic Relations signed in 1961) shall have the force of law in the United Kingdom and shall for that purpose be construed in accordance with the following provisions of this section.

3. Restriction of privileges and immunities
(1) If it appears to Her Majesty that the privileges and immunities accorded to a mission of Her Majesty in the territory of any State, or to persons connected with that mission, are less than those conferred by this Act on the mission of that State or on persons connected with that mission, Her Majesty may be an Order in Council withdraw such of the privileges and immunities so conferred from the mission of that State or from such persons connected with it as appears to Her Majesty to be proper.

4. Evidence
If in any proceedings any question arises whether or not any person is entitled to any privilege or immunity under this Act a certificate issued by or under the authority of the Secretary of State stating any fact relating to that question shall be conclusive evidence of that fact.

7. Saving for certain bilateral arrangements

(1) Where any special agreement or arrangement between the Government of any State and the Government of the United Kingdom in force at the commencement of this Act provides for extending—

(a) such immunity from jurisdiction and from arrest or detention, and such inviolability of residence, as are conferred by this Act on a diplomatic agent; or

(b) such exemption from duties (whether of customs or excise) chargeable on imported goods, taxes and related charges as is conferred by this Act in respect of articles for the personal use of a diplomatic agent;

to any class of person, or to articles for the personal use of any class of person, connected with the mission of that State, that immunity and inviolability or exemption shall so extend, so long as that agreement or arrangement continues in force.

Empsom v *Smith*

[1966] 1 QB 426, Court of Appeal

> The defendant was an administrative officer with the Canadian High Commission. The plaintiff sued for breach of a tenancy agreement and the defendant claimed diplomatic immunity. The dispute arose before the passing of the 1964 Act, but the defendant did not apply for the writ to be set aside until November 1964, by which time the 1964 Act had come into force. The plaintiff appealed to the Court of Appeal, which allowed her appeal.

DIPLOCK LJ: If the defendant had applied before the passing of the Diplomatic Privileges Act, 1964, to have the plaintiff's action dismissed there would have been no answer to his application. But he delayed until November, 1964. By that date his right to immunity from civil suit had been curtailed by that Act which applies to the United Kingdom the provisions of the Vienna Convention on Diplomatic Relations, 1961, contained in the schedule to the Act. By the combined effect of articles 31 and 37 of the Convention as a member of the administrative and technical staff of the mission his immunity from the civil jurisdiction of the courts of the United Kingdom does not extend to acts performed outside the course of his duties. Whether he is entitled to immunity in any particular suit no longer depends solely upon his status but also upon the subject-matter of the suit.

It is elementary law that diplomatic immunity is not immunity from legal liability but immunity from suit. . . . Statutes relating to diplomatic immunity from civil suit are procedural statutes. The Diplomatic Privileges Act, 1964, is in my view clearly applicable to suits brought after the date on which that statute came into force in respect of acts done before that date. If, therefore, the plaintiff had issued her plaint after October 1, 1964, instead of before, the action could not have been dismissed upon the ground of diplomatic privilege unless and until the court had determined the issue: whether or not the defendant's acts alleged by the plaintiff to constitute her cause of action against him were acts performed outside the course of his duties. It is, to say the least, arguable that acts done by the defendant in relation to his tenancy of his private residence in London were performed by him outside the course of his duties. But this issue is one which can be decided only upon evidence.

It follows therefore that until steps were taken to set it aside or to dismiss the action the plaintiff's plaint was no nullity: it was a valid plaint. If the defendant had, with the permission of his High Commissioner, appeared to it before October 1, 1964, the procedural bar to the hearing would have been removed. So, too, if the defendant had ceased to be en poste while the plaint was still outstanding the action could then have proceeded against him. I can see no reason in logic or the law of nations why the position should be any different when the procedural bar has been removed by Act of Parliament – particularly when that Act of Parliament gives statutory effect to an international convention, by which sovereign states have mutually waived in part immunities for members of the staff of their foreign missions to which they were formerly entitled by the law of nations.

R v *Secretary of State for the Home Department, ex parte Bagga*
[1991] 1 All ER 777, Court of Appeal

The applicant had arrived in the UK on 13 November 1981, and his appointment was notified to the Foreign Office on 25 November. He was employed by the Indian High Commission on a diplomatic passport. He left the UK when his employment ended, and on his return, entry was refused. The question for the Court of Appeal was whether exemption from immigration controls depended either on notification of diplomatic status to the Foreign Office or entry in the UK (or taking up of employment if already here). In passing, the Court also considered whether immunities under the 1964 Act depended on arrival, employment or notification.

PARKER J: It is abundantly clear from art. 39 of the [Vienna Convention on Diplomatic Relations] that the immunities will be enjoyed on entry to take up a post and that it is only when a person already in the country is appointed that the immunities depend on notification. . . .

We are however, not concerned with enjoyment of diplomatic immunities but with exemption from immigration control. This is dependent and dependent only on whether the person concerned 'is a member of a mission within the meaning of the 1964 Act or is a member of the family and forms part of the household of such a member or is a person otherwise entitled to the like immunity from jurisdiction as is conferred by that Act on a diplomatic agent.'

Approaching the matter *de novo* I would have no hesitation in concluding that, as a matter of construction, someone arriving to take up a post or, if already in this country, on becoming employed as a member of the mission is exempt from immigration control from the moment of entry or commencement of employment whether or not there had been any notification to the Foreign Office.

NOTES:
1. The Convention on Consular Relations is enacted in the Consular Relations Act 1968. The Articles of the Vienna Convention on Diplomatic Relations referred to in s. 2 of the Diplomatic Privileges Act are Articles 1, 22–24, 27–40. Article 45 was incorporated into UK law by the Diplomatic and Consular Premises Act 1987.
2. As the ICJ observed in the *US Diplomatic and Consular Staff in Iran Case*, the law of diplomatic immunities is one of the most important areas of international law. The immunities contained in these Conventions are far-reaching, and many commentators have questioned whether they go too far. Indeed, they appear to offer protection to the diplomat, but seem to deny the host State the opportunity of defending itself from hostile actions by that diplomat, especially if diplomatic agents are seen (or believed) to be engaged in criminal activities. See the decision of the Australian High Court in *Minister for Foreign Affairs and Trade* v *Magno* (1992) 112 ALR 529.

10

Law of the Sea

Introductory note

The law of the sea is of great importance to the world community. This is reflected in the wealth of treaty law, customary law and judicial decisions concerning this subject. The most important of all is the United Nations Law of the Sea Convention 1982, which entered into force on 16 November 1994. This is a multilateral treaty of considerable significance, and the conclusion in July 1994 of an Agreement Relating to the Implementation of Part XI of the Convention in regard to deep sea mining means that many States once reluctant to ratify the Convention have become parties, including the United Kingdom and other members of the European Union. Moreover, even if there are some States that choose not to ratify the 1982 Convention and 1994 Agreement (such as the United States), many of the Convention's principles have now passed into the corpus of customary international law and are used as the basis for the settlement of disputes between States not bound by the Convention in their relations with each other: see, for example, *Case Concerning Maritime Delimitation and Territorial Questions between Qatar and Bahrain (Qatar v Bahrain)* 16 March 2001. In addition, there are four other Conventions concerning the law of the sea stemming from the First UN Conference on the Law of the Sea in 1958. Although still in force to some extent for the parties to them, these 1958 Conventions are gradually being superseded by the 1982 Convention and customary law. At August 2002, there were 141 parties to the Law of the Sea Convention 1982 (and 112 parties to the 1994 Agreement), 62 parties to the Convention on the High Seas 1958, 37 parties to the Convention on Fishing and Conservation of the Living Resources of the High Seas 1958 and 57 parties to the Convention on the Continental Shelf 1958.

SECTION 1: Law of the Sea Convention 1982

The 1982 Convention was the result of nine years' work by the Third United Nations Conference on the Law of the Sea. It is a comprehensive multilateral treaty covering all aspects of the use of the sea and sea bed. The Convention should be viewed as an integrated whole, for the development of the text was the result of compromise and bargain between the various fluctuating interest groups. Nevertheless, it soon became clear that States of the developed world were not prepared to accept Part XI of the Convention as it was originally drafted. This led to concern for the overall efficacy of the Convention, a matter now resolved by the 1994 Agreement. Consequently an overall view of the Convention requires an understanding of the changes made by the 1994 Agreement. This is addressed more fully below.

D. Anderson, 'Legal Implications of the Entry into Force of the UN Convention on the Law of the Sea'
(1995) 44 ICLQ 313

On 16 November 1993, Guyana became the 60th State to ratify the 1982 Convention. Consequently, in accordance with Article 308, the Convention came into force, as modified provisionally by the 1994 Agreement relating to Part XI (Deep Sea Bed), on 16 November 1994. The Agreement came into force – thus modifying the Convention permanently – on 28 July 1996.

To sum up the status of the Convention: it has entered into force for the States parties and they are implementing it. In addition, various international organisations such as the United Nations, the International Maritime Organisation and the new International Seabed Authority are implementing different parts of it. However, Part XI has been qualified by the new Agreement, which is being applied provisionally, pending its entry into force, resulting in an interim or transitional regime. Moreover, the first election of the Tribunal has been postponed to allow more time for States to ratify or accede. The Convention is not in force as a treaty for non-States parties; but many of them are observing it in practice, both directly and as members of the organisations. Some non-parties are also joining in the provisional application of the new Agreement. . . .

III. Legal implications of entry into force of the Convention and the provisional application of the Agreement

A. For States Parties
The entry into force of the Convention carries with it the normal implications under the Vienna Convention of the Law of Treaties. That is to say, as between the States parties to the Convention, the basic rule of *pacta sunt servanda* applies. Their relations in many maritime matters are governed by the Convention. More widely, the relevant practice of the States parties must be based on the Convention. States are repealing legislation based on the terms of the Geneva Conventions and enacting new laws in line with the Convention. Entry into force will result in an addition to State practice by States which are parties. . . .

Article 311(1) provides that the Convention is to prevail, as between the States parties, over the Geneva Conventions on the Law of the Sea of 1958. As the number of parties grows, the Convention will prevail to an increasing extent. This provision signals rather clearly a formal stage in the process of evolution in the law of the sea. The law as it stood in the 1960s, following the First and Second UN Conferences on the Law of the Sea, is giving way more and more. The process of evolution began many years ago, at least by the 1970s when the 200-mile limit was accepted; but it has accelerated since 1982. Entry into force marks and formalises the change.

The Convention of 1982 breaks much new ground: new concepts abound. Entry into force of all Parts of the Convention (subject to the qualifications mentioned above) means that States parties can take advantage of possibilities set out in the different Parts and Annexes. Equally, each State party has to accept claims by other States parties based on the Convention. A party to the Convention must therefore accept new concepts articulated in its terms, for example the archipelagic State under Part IV, the fishing rights of landlocked States under Article 69 and extended pollution jurisdiction under Part XII.

. . . It is very likely that the provisions of the Convention of 1982 will be the primary influence on State practice worldwide. Entry into force will lead to legitimisation *ex post facto* of some past practice, e.g. archipelagic claims.

B. For Non-Parties

As regards States which have not yet become parties to the Convention, as a matter of strict law its provisions are not binding upon them: Vienna Convention, Article 34. However, many of these States have already been applying much of the Convention, day by day, since 1982, or even earlier in some respects. Many provisions are expressive of rules of customary law. States have been following the Convention in matters such as the 12-mile territorial sea and the 200-mile economic zone, as well as rights of passage. They have ceased to protest about a wide range of claims by other States in line with, or explicitly based on, the Convention. Many of these non-parties are industrialised States with major maritime interests: in many cases they are applying provisionally the Agreement adopted on 28 July 1994 and enjoying membership on a provisional basis of the Authority. They are also helping to pay for the Authority from the UN budget, on a temporary basis. They are preparing to ratify or accede in many cases. . . .

IV. The nature of the Convention

Apart from Part XI, there is little room in the Convention for our old friends the 'persistent dissenters' or 'objectors': they were all represented at the Conference and afforded ample opportunity to argue their cases. Some unique problems faced by single States met with sympathetic responses: for example, Bangladesh and Norway both benefited from special provisions. But the Conference did not accept all such special pleas: the element of a negotiation, leading to the adoption of an overall negotiated text, has now to be taken into account in assessing the strength of what may have become lost causes. . . .

The Convention balances the differing interests of States. The typical balance is between the rights and interests of the coastal State and those of the distant water State or flag State. But there are other balances: between States interested in mining manganese nodules and the generality of States (a balance which has been adjusted by the Agreement of 28 July 1994); between the land-locked State and the transit State; and between the broad-margin State and the international community as a whole. The Convention has been described as a 'package deal' by some commentators; but the expression is not entirely apt in that it has too strong a contractual flavour. The process of balancing was done on individual issues, as well as on clusters of issues (e.g. 12-mile limit/straits passage/200-mile limit), in the Second Committee. In many instances the process was one of finding middle ground or the equitable solution more than of contractual dealing.

The text which emerged at the end of the Conference was a negotiated text. It is a text of high intrinsic quality. It is coherent, internally balanced and forward-looking (especially on environmental issues). At the same time, it takes into account the historical development of the law of the sea through customary law, decisions by international tribunals and the Geneva Conventions, much of which it incorporates or 're-enacts' (often with updating). The Convention represents codification, consolidation, progressive development and the conscious revision or reform of the law of the sea. . . .

VI. Settlement of disputes

The Convention is remarkable in providing for compulsory settlement of disputes by recourse to the International Court of Justice, or the International Tribunal for the Law of the Sea, or to conciliation, arbitration or special arbitration. One or other of these mechanisms is applicable to almost all disputes. This is the first time that a major convention in the field of international law has provided not for an optional system for the settlement of disputes (as in 1958, 1961 and 1963) but, rather, for compulsory dispute settlement, albeit subject to some exceptions or possibilities to opt out in Article 298. . . .

The International Tribunal for the Law of the Sea is to have jurisdiction over deep seabed mining disputes, including disputes between the States parties and the International Seabed Authority (Article 187). Consortia, i.e. private parties, may appear before its Seabed Disputes Chamber. The International Court's jurisdiction is confined to States. . . .

The creation of this new standing Tribunal could turn out to have wide-spread implications. States parties may refer to the Tribunal disputes not simply to do with the international seabed area and the mining of metallic nodules. The Tribunal may also be called upon to decide disputes in areas such as navigation, fishing, access to the sea or maritime boundaries. . . .

D. Anderson, 'British Accession to the UN Convention on the Law of the Sea' (1997) 46 ICLQ 761

On 21 July 1997 the Foreign and Commonwealth Secretary announced the United Kingdom's decision to accede to the United Nations Convention on the Law of the Sea ('the Convention'), a decision which was acted upon four days later in New York. The United Kingdom thus became the 119th State to establish its consent to be bound by the Convention and the 82nd party to the Agreement of July 1994 on the Implementation of its Part XI ('the Implementation Agreement').

II. The terms of accession to the Convention

At the time of accession, the British government made five declarations. As well as specifying the dependencies to which the Convention was to apply and making a notification concerning membership of the European Community made by other EC States for the purposes of Annex IX, the declarations were notable in expressly rejecting all declarations made by other States which were inconsistent with the terms of the Convention. In addition, two declarations, one by Spain about Gibraltar and the other by Argentina about the Falkland Islands and South Georgia and the South Sandwich Islands, were both expressly rejected. . . .

(a) General

The United Kingdom cannot accept any declaration or statement made or to be made in the future which is not in conformity with articles 309 and 310 of the Convention.

Article 309 of the Convention prohibits reservations and exceptions (except those expressly permitted by other articles of the Convention). Under article 310 declarations and statements made by a State cannot exclude or modify the legal effect of the provisions of the Convention in their application to the State concerned.

III. The implementation of the convention in UK law and practice

Methods of implementing the Convention around the world have varied considerably. The Convention, in other words, does not prescribe any particular methods by which States parties give effect to its terms at the national level. Some States parties have given the Convention the direct force of law under their constitutions or have enacted extensive new laws (e.g. Germany, whilst others have amended their existing legislation in a single Act (e.g. Australia). Several Commonwealth countries have comprehensive Acts which follow the Convention, topic by topic, making appropriate provisions for the different maritime zones. The choice of method depends to a large extent upon the constitutional arrangements in each State party and . . . the United Kingdom adopted its own methods.

Most Parts of the Convention were found on examination to give rise to a need for legislation in order to implement them. In some instances the legislation was new, for example where fresh or further provision was found to be required. Recent legislation in the fields of shipping, navigation and the control of marine pollution has been expressly framed to give effect to the Convention. In many other cases, however, existing legislation has been relied upon: this existing legislation includes Acts passed during the late 1980s and the early 1990s in anticipation of possible future accession, as well as earlier legislation passed in order to give effect to the Geneva Conventions on the Law of the Sea of 1958, notably the Continental Shelf Act 1964. . . .

IV. Concluding remarks

The legislation implementing the Convention in the United Kingdom is extensive, although a completely piecemeal approach was adopted to its enactment. Legislation is spread over many different volumes of *Halsbury's Statutes*. The practitioner cannot reach for a single text such as the German *Gesetz* of 1995. Much of the United Kingdom's legislation is of very recent date, particularly as a result of the consolidation of the merchant shipping legislation in 1995, and it is supplemented by EC regulations and directives in several fields, notably fisheries, shipping and environmental protection. In most instances, the role of the legislation in question in giving effect to the Convention is not made explicit: only in a minority of cases does the legislation refer to the Convention. Powers are in place to enable the government to fulfil the vast majority of the obligations arising from accession. A very few matters, such as aspects of deep seabed mining, have been left until there is a need to take fresh powers when the circumstances of the day will no doubt be taken into account.

The United Kingdom became the fourth Permanent Member of the Security Council and the eleventh member of the European Community to establish its consent to be bound by the Convention. Almost all Commonwealth countries, many of them having played key roles in the Conference, have become parties. . . . Only one or two States appear to be actively opposed to important provisions in the Convention, primarily as a result of conflicting jurisdictional claims and outstanding maritime boundaries with neighbours.

The States parties today come from all regions of the world and represent all the many different types of interests in the seas and oceans, including maritime and coastal States, flag and port States, developing and developed States, landlocked and transit States, as well as island, archipelagic and straits States. The Convention, together with the Implementation Agreement, is well on its way to achieving the goal of universal participation. The three institutions constituted by the Convention, namely the International Seabed Authority, the International Tribunal for the Law of the Sea and the Commission on the Limits of the Continental Shelf, have all been established and have started work. The United Kingdom's accession has strengthened further the regime of the Convention, including its institutions.

NOTES:
1. The above extract indicates the position now that the 1982 Convention and 1994 Agreement have entered into force.
2. The impact of the Convention on customary law was considerable even before it entered into force. The decisions of the ICJ given before 16 November 1994 confirm this. Many of its provisions have passed into customary law, although for its parties the Convention will prevail in the event of any inconsistencies. The 1982 Convention will also prevail for State parties over any inconsistent obligations they may have *inter se* under the 1958 Geneva Conventions on the Law of the Sea (see Convention Art. 311).
3. In the *Case Concerning Maritime Delimitation and Territorial Questions Between Qatar and Bahrain* (*Qatar* v *Bahrain*), Merits, ICJ Reports, 16 March 2001, the 1982 Convention was not in force between the two States because it had been ratified only by Bahrain. However, both parties agreed that the provisions of the Convention which would have been applicable did indeed represent customary international law and this was adopted readily by the ICJ. In the main, these were uncontroversial matters dealing with applicable rules of maritime

delimitation (e.g. the 'equidistance/special circumstance' rule). One contested issue was the status of 'low-tide elevations' in customary law, being small areas of land mass that were visible only at low tide. A majority of the Court take the view that the LOS 1982 provision (Art. 13) reflected customary international law, especially in relation to its implication that sovereignty could exist over these areas and that in principle they could be used for various purposes in delimiting (i.e. extending) a coastal State's powers over the maritime area. (This was not the result in this dispute because of 'special circumstances'). Judge Oda, in his Separate Opinion, dissented from this view because he could discern no State practice sufficient to support the majority's contention. In particular, he was concerned that the Court's jurisprudence might well encourage the use of these low tide elevations for construction of installations for economic or recreational purposes and that this would have a profound impact on the future development of the law of the sea. Judge Oda has sounded notes of caution before about the way the ICJ interprets and applies the 1982 Convention and this recent criticism is in the same vein. As ever, his criticism is well-founded and has a strong practical base. It is likely to be ignored.

4. In the *Eritrea/Yemen Arbitration, Second Stage, Maritime Delimitation*, December 1999 (see http://www.pca-cpa.org), the parties had submitted a dispute to the Permanent Court of Arbitration under an Arbitration Agreement. The Award in the Second Stage notes at para. 130 that 'the requirement to take into account the United Nations Convention on the Law of the Sea of 1982 is important because Eritrea has not become a party to that Convention but has in the Arbitration Agreement thus accepted the application of provisions of the Convention that are found to be relevant to the present stage. There is no reference in the Arbitration Agreement to the customary law of the sea, but many of the relevant elements of customary law are incorporated in the provisions of the Convention'.

SECTION 2: The territorial sea and the contiguous zone

A: Territorial sea

The territorial sea is a belt of water immediately lying off the coast. It is an area over which the coastal State has full sovereignty and in this sense it is legally equivalent to land territory. All coastal States may enjoy a territorial sea for this is inherent in sovereignty. Historically, the seaward limit of the territorial sea extended so far as the coastal State could effectively exercise sovereignty from the coast: usually a limit of three miles, being the range of a canon-ball! This hardened in to a rule that three miles was the acceptable seaward extent of territorial sea. In the late twentieth century, it became clear that many states favoured an extension of the limit of the territorial sea, not least to preserve coastal states rights and security. The LOS 1982 now provides for a limit of 12 miles (Art. 3) and this is generally accepted to reflect customary international law. According to the most recent published survey of the UK Hydrographic Office (Jan 2001), only 11 states claimed a territorial sea greater than 12 miles.

Necessarily, it becomes important to know from which point the territorial sea can be measured. Twelve nautical miles from where? Various methods exist, but it must be remembered that the location of delimitation points can seriously affect the amount of sea brought within the coastal state's territorial sphere. This is particularly acute where the 'base point' is an island or low tide elevation located some way off the coast. Such areas may have a significant impact on the reach of coastal state sovereignty and sometimes a disproportionate affect – as in the *Qatar* v *Bahrain* Case (above) where the existence of low-tide elevations was discounted in delimiting the territorial sea precisely because of their disproportionate effect on the maritime boundary between the two States.

Anglo-Norwegian Fisheries Case (UK v Norway)
ICJ Rep 1951 116, International Court of Justice

The UK objected to the method of delimitation employed by Norway to define its territorial sea. Essentially, the Norwegian method was to draw straight lines (baselines) from selected points on the coast from which the breadth of the territorial sea could be measured. Norway alleged that this was necessary because of the fragmented nature of her coastline (the *skjaergaard*), and it meant that the baselines assumed a geometrical and regular pattern. One consequence was that a greater proportion of water on the landward side of the baseline became 'internal waters'. The ICJ confirmed the legality of the straight baseline system, and its judgment was incorporated substantially in the 1958, and subsequently, the 1982 Conventions.

The Court has no difficulty in finding that, for the purpose of measuring the breadth of the territorial sea, it is the low-water mark as opposed to the high-water mark, or the mean between the two tides, which has generally been adopted in the practice of States. This criterion is the most favourable to the coastal State and clearly shows the character of territorial waters as appurtenant to the land territory. The Court notes that the Parties agree as to this criterion, but that they differ as to its application. . . .

Three methods have been contemplated to effect the application of the low-water mark rule. The simplest would appear to be the method of the *tracé parallèle*, which consists of drawing the outer limit of the belt of territorial waters by following the coast in all its sinuosities. This method may be applied without difficulty to an ordinary coast, which is not too broken. Where a coast is deeply indented and cut into, as is that of Eastern Finnmark, or where it is bordered by an archipelago such as the 'skjægaard' along the western sector of the coast here in question, the base-line becomes independent of the low-water mark, and can only be determined by means of a geometric construction. In such circumstances the line of the low-water mark can no longer be put forward as a rule requiring the coast line to be followed in all its sinuosities; nor can one speak of exceptions when contemplating so rugged a coast in detail. Such a coast, viewed as a whole, calls for the application of a different method. Nor can one characterize as exceptions to the rule the very many derogations which would be necessitated by such a rugged coast. The rule would disappear under the exceptions.

The arcs of circles method, which is constantly used for determining the position of a point or object at sea, is a new technique in so far as it is a method for delimiting the territorial sea. . . . Its purpose is to secure the application of the principle that the belt of territorial waters must follow the line of the coast. It is not obligatory by law, as was admitted by Counsel for the United Kingdom Government in his oral reply. . . .

The principle that the belt of territorial waters must follow the general direction of the coast makes it possible to fix certain criteria valid for any delimitation of the territorial sea; these criteria will be elucidated later. The Court will confine itself at this stage to noting that, in order to apply this principle, several States have deemed it necessary to follow the straight base-lines method and that they have not encountered objections of principle by other States. This method consists of selecting appropriate points on the low-water mark and drawing straight lines between them. This has been done, not only in the case of well-defined bays, but also in cases of minor curvatures of the coast line where it was solely a question of giving a simpler form to the belt of territorial waters. . . .

[On the validity of the specific straight baseline system preferred by Norway, the Court noted that] It does not at all follow that, in the absence of rules having the technically precise character alleged by the United Kingdom Government, the delimitation undertaken by the Norwegian Government in 1935 is not subject to certain principles which make it possible to judge as to its validity under international law. The delimitation of sea areas has always an international aspect; it cannot be dependent merely upon the will of the coastal State as expressed in its municipal law. Although it is true that the act of delimitation is necessarily a unilateral act, because only the coastal State is competent to undertake it, the validity of the delimitation with regard to other States depends upon international law.

In this connection, certain basic considerations inherent in the nature of the territorial sea, bring to light certain criteria which, though not entirely precise, can provide courts with an adequate basis for their decisions, which can be adapted to the diverse facts in question.

Among these considerations, some reference must be made to the close dependence of the territorial sea upon the land domain. It is the land which confers upon the coastal State a right to the waters off its coasts. It follows that while such a State must be allowed the latitude necessary in order to be able to adapt its delimitation to practical needs and local requirements, the drawing of base-lines must not depart to any appreciable extent from the general direction of the coast.

Another fundamental consideration, of particular importance in this case, is the more or less close relationship existing between certain sea areas and the land formations which divide or surround them. The real question raised in the choice of base-lines is in effect whether certain sea areas lying within these lines are sufficiently closely linked to the land domain to be subject to the regime of internal waters. This idea, which is at the basis of the determination of the rules relating to bays, should be liberally applied in the case of a coast, the geographical configuration of which is as unusual as that of Norway.

Finally, there is one consideration not to be overlooked, the scope of which extends beyond purely geographical factors: that of certain economic interests peculiar to a region, the reality and import-ance of which are clearly evidenced by a long usage.

Law of the Sea Convention 1982

The 1982 Convention repeats with only minor modifications the Articles of the 1958 Geneva Convention on the Territorial Sea and the Contiguous Zone.

Article 2 Legal status of the territorial sea, of the air space over the territorial sea and of its bed and subsoil

1. The sovereignty of a coastal State extends beyond its land territory and internal waters and, in the case of an archipelagic State, its archipelagic waters, to an adjacent belt of sea, described as the territorial sea.

2. This sovereignty extends to the air space over the territorial sea as well as to its bed and subsoil.

3. The sovereignty over the territorial sea is exercised subject to this Convention and to other rules of international law.

Article 3 Breadth of the territorial sea
Every State has the right to establish the breadth of its territorial sea up to a limit not exceeding 12 nautical miles, measured from baselines determined in accordance with this Convention.

Article 4 Outer limit of the territorial sea
The outer limit of the territorial sea is the line every point of which is at a distance from the nearest point of the baseline equal to the breadth of the territorial sea.

Article 5 Normal baseline
Except where otherwise provided in this Convention, the normal baseline for measuring the breadth of the territorial sea is the low-water line along the coast as marked on large-scale charts officially recognized by the coastal State.

Article 7 Straight baselines
1. In localities where the coastline is deeply indented and cut into, or if there is a fringe of islands along the coast in its immediate vicinity, the method of straight baselines joining appropriate points may be employed in drawing the baseline from which the breadth of the territorial sea is measured.

2. Where because of the presence of a delta and other natural conditions the coastline is highly unstable, the appropriate points may be selected along the furthest seaward extent of the low-water line and, notwithstanding subsequent regression of the low-water line, the straight baselines shall remain effective until changed by the coastal State in accordance with this Convention.

3. The drawing of straight baselines must not depart to any appreciable extent from the general direction of the coast, and the sea areas lying within the lines must be sufficiently closely linked to the land domain to be subject to the régime of internal waters.

4. Straight baselines shall not be drawn to and from low-tide elevations, unless lighthouses or similar installations which are permanently above sea level have been built on them or except in instances where the drawing of baselines to and from such elevations has received general international recognition.

5. Where the method of straight baselines is applicable under paragraph 1, account may be taken, in determining particular baselines, of economic interests peculiar to the region concerned, the reality and the importance of which are clearly evidenced by long usage.

6. The system of straight baselines may not be applied by a State in such a manner as to cut off the territorial sea of another State from the high seas or an exclusive economic zone.

Article 8 Internal waters
1. Except as provided in Part IV, waters on the landward side of the baseline of the territorial sea form part of the internal waters of the state.

2. Where the establishment of a straight baseline in accordance with the method set forth in article 7 has the effect of enclosing as internal waters areas which had not previously been considered as such, a right of innocent passage as provided in this Convention shall exist in those waters.

Article 17 Right of innocent passage
Subject to this Convention, ships of all States, whether coastal or land-locked, enjoy the right of innocent passage through the territorial sea.

Article 19 Meaning of innocent passage
1. Passage is innocent so long as it is not prejudicial to the peace, good order or security of

the coastal State. Such passage shall take place in conformity with this Convention and with other rules of international law.

2. Passage of a foreign ship shall be considered to be prejudicial to the peace, good order or security of the coastal State if in the territorial sea it engages in any of the following activities:

(a) any threat or use of force against the sovereignty, territorial integrity or political independence of the coastal State, or in any other manner in violation of the principles of international law embodied in the Charter of the United Nations;

(b) any exercise or practice with weapons of any kind;

(c) any act aimed at collecting information to the prejudice of the defence or security of the coastal State;

(d) any act of propaganda aimed at affecting the defence or security of the coastal State;

(e) the launching, landing or taking on board of any aircraft;

(f) the launching, landing or taking on board of any military device;

(g) the loading or unloading of any commodity, currency or person contrary to the customs, fiscal, immigration or sanitary laws and regulations of the coastal State;

(h) any act of wilful and serious pollution contrary to this Convention;

(i) any fishing activities;

(j) the carrying out of research or survey activities;

(k) any act aimed at interfering with any system of communication or any other facilities or installations of the coastal State;

(l) any other activity not having a direct bearing on passage.

Corfu Channel Case (UK v Albania) (Merits)
ICJ Rep 1949 4, International Court of Justice

In October 1946, British warships sought to pass through the North Corfu Strait. Two were badly damaged by mines, allegedly laid by Albania. After deciding that this strait was a strait used for international navigation, one issue was whether the passage of British warships was 'innocent', so as to be permissible under customary international law.

It is, in the opinion of the Court, generally recognized and in accordance with international custom that States in time of peace have a right to send their warships through straits used for international navigation between two parts of the high seas without the previous authorization of a coastal State, provided that the passage is *innocent*. Unless otherwise prescribed in an international convention, there is no right for a coastal State to prohibit such passage through straits in time of peace. . . .

The Albanian Government has further contended that the sovereignty of Albania was violated because the passage of the British warships on October 22nd, 1946, was not an *innocent passage*. The reasons advanced in support of this contention may be summed up as follows: The passage was not an ordinary passage, but a political mission; the ships were manœuvring and sailing in diamond combat formation with soldiers on board; the position of the guns was not consistent with innocent passage; the vessels passed with crews at action stations; the number of the ships and their armament surpassed what was necessary in order to attain their object, and showed an intention to intimidate and not merely to pass; the ships had received orders to observe and report upon the coastal defences and this order was carried out.

It is shown by the Admiralty telegram of September 21st, cited above, and admitted by the United Kingdom Agent, that the object of sending the warships through the Strait was not only to carry out a passage for purposes of navigation, but also to test Albania's attitude. . . . The legality of this measure taken by the Government of the United Kingdom cannot be disputed, provided that it was carried out in a manner consistent with the requirements of international law. The 'mission' was designed to affirm a right which had been unjustly denied. The Government of the United Kingdom was not bound to abstain from exercising its right of passage which the Albanian Government had illegally denied.

It remains, therefore, to consider whether the *manner* in which the passage was carried out was consistent with the principle of innocent passage, and to examine the various contentions of the Albanian Government in so far as they appear to be relevant. . . .

It is shown by the evidence that the ships were not proceeding in combat formation, but in line, one after the other, and that they were not manœuvring until after the first explosion. . . . It is known . . . that ships, when using the North Corfu Strait, must pass with armament in fore and aft position. That this order was carried out during the passage on October 22nd is stated by the Commander-in-Chief, Mediterranean, in a telegram of October 26th to the Admiralty. . . . In the light of this evidence, the Court cannot accept the Albanian contention that the position of the guns was inconsistent with the rules of innocent passage.

In the above-mentioned telegram of October 26th, the Commander-in-Chief reported that the passage 'was made with ships at action stations in order that they might be able to retaliate quickly if fired upon again'. In view of the firing from the Albanian battery on May 15th, this measure of precaution cannot, in itself, be regarded as unreasonable. But four warships – two cruisers and two destroyers – passed in this manner, with crews at action stations, ready to retaliate quickly if fired upon. They passed one after another through this narrow channel, close to the Albanian coast, at a time of political tension in this region. The intention must have been, not only to test Albania's attitude, but at the same time to demonstrate such force that she would abstain from firing again on passing ships. Having regard, however, to all the circumstances of the case, as described above, the Court is unable to characterize these measures taken by the United Kingdom authorities as a violation of Albania's sovereignty.

USA/USSR Joint Statement on Uniform Interpretation of Rules of International Law Governing Innocent Passage
23 September 1989
28 ILM 1444 (1989)

For maritime States, the right of innocent passage is of special importance. This joint statement is significant for it confirms (at least for these two States) that the Articles in the 1982 Convention reflect customary international law.

1. The relevant rules of international law governing innocent passage of ships in the territorial sea are stated in the 1982 United Nations Convention on the Law of the Sea (Convention of 1982), particularly in Part II, Section 3.

2. All ships, including warships, regardless of cargo, armament or means of propulsion, enjoy the right of innocent passage through the territorial sea in accordance with international law, for which neither prior notification nor authorization is required.

3. Article 19 of the Convention of 1982 sets out in paragraph 2 an exhaustive list of activities that would render passage not innocent. A ship passing through the territorial sea that does not engage in any of those activities is in innocent passage. . . .

5. Ships exercising the right of innocent passage shall comply with all laws and regulations of the coastal State adopted in conformity with relevant rules of international law as reflected in Articles 21, 22, 23 and 25 of the Convention of 1982. . . .

7. If a warship engages in conduct which violates such laws or regulations or renders its passage

not innocent and does not take corrective action upon request, the coastal State may require it to leave the territorial sea, as set forth in Article 30 of the Convention of 1982. In such case the warship shall do so immediately.

NOTES:
1. While there was early agreement over the nature of the territorial sea as a belt of water adjacent to the coast over which the coastal State exercised sovereignty, there was considerable disagreement over the permissible breadth of the territorial sea. The 1958 Convention on the Territorial Sea and Contiguous Zone contains no relevant provision, and a Second United Conference on the Law of the Sea in 1962 failed by one vote to adopt a compromise solution. The provision adopted in the 1982 Convention reflects customary law and is in any event binding on the parties. To some extent, however, the issue has become less pressing given the extension of State jurisdiction seawards under the Continental Shelf and Exclusive Economic Zone regimes (see below).
2. A problem related to that of the width of the territorial sea has been the method of its delimitation. The matter was brought to a head by the *Anglo–Norwegian Fisheries Case*, above, where the Court accepted the use of the 'straight baseline' system by Norway, at least in its dealings with the United Kingdom. The straight baseline system now seems to be valid *erga omnes*, irrespective of the opposition or agreement of other States, provided that the shape of the coastline merits its application. However, there are very many examples of the use of straight, geometric baselines in circumstances not falling within Art. 7 of the 1982 Convention. It could be that customary international law is outstripping the Convention so as to permit straight baselines in all cases. The UK has made it clear that it opposes such baselines where they are not justified by the terms of Art. 7 of the 1982 Convention.
3. The Territorial Sea Act 1987 was passed in the UK in response to developments in State practice since 1958 and is in accordance with Art. 3 of the 1982 Convention.

B: The contiguous zone

Law of the Sea Convention 1982

Article 33
1. In a zone contiguous to its territorial sea, described as the contiguous zone, the coastal State may exercise the control necessary to:
   (a) prevent infringement of its customs, fiscal, immigration or sanitary laws and regulations within its territory or territorial sea;
   (b) punish infringement of the above laws and regulations committed within its territory or territorial sea.
2. The contiguous zone may not extend beyond 24 nautical miles from the baselines from which the breadth of the territorial sea is measured.

Sorensen and Jensen, Case No. 3134
89 ILR (1991) 78, Supreme Court of Chile

The two defendants were foreign nationals charged with various crimes arising out of a collision 41 miles off the Chilean coast. They submitted that the Chilean courts lacked territorial jurisdiction. Chile had a 12-mile territorial sea, 12-mile contiguous zone, and a 200-mile Exclusive Economic Zone (EEZ).

3. Article 593 of the Chilean Civil Code provides that the maritime area contiguous to the territorial sea covers a further twelve miles beyond the territorial sea, which itself extends for twelve miles from the coast. Chile is therefore entitled to exercise jurisdiction over an area of twenty-four miles from the coast, with regard to the prevention and punishment of offences against the Chilean laws and regulations concerning customs, fiscal, immigration and sanitary matters. Article 596 of the Civil Code establishes that Chile enjoys exclusive sovereignty over the area beyond twenty-four miles and up to two hundred miles from its coast, with respect solely to economic matters.

4. In the light of the above considerations . . . it must be concluded that, since the events at issue occurred forty-one miles from the coast, they took place outside national territory, so that the Chilean courts are unable to exercise jurisdiction . . . Chilean criminal jurisdiction is limited to facts occurring within the national territory.

SECTION 3: **The continental shelf**

A: General principles

The continental shelf is rich in natural resources and highly prized by coastal States fortunate enough to possess a continental margin. It is not surprising, therefore, that this is one area of the law of the sea where reasonably detailed rules have emerged governing the rights to explore and exploit the resources of this region. These customary rules are mirrored and developed in the 1982 Convention. Many of the principles of continental shelf delimitation have developed through the jurisprudence of the ICJ and this is certainly one area where it can claim to have had significant success. Problems do remain however, such as the differences between the provisions of the 1958 and 1982 Conventions on the seaward limit of the continental shelf. The 1958 Convention adopts a criterion of exploitability, while the 1982 Convention favours an automatic right to a shelf within 200 miles, with an extension if geomorphology permits. Clearly, for State parties to the 1982 Convention the matter is now settled. For other States, it may be that customary international law has developed to such an extent that the 1958 Convention is redundant.

Geneva Convention on the Continental Shelf 1958
499 UNTS 311

Article 1
For the purpose of these articles, the term 'continental shelf' is used as referring (a) to the seabed and subsoil of the submarine areas adjacent to the coast but outside the area of the territorial sea, to a depth of 200 metres or, beyond that limit, to where the depth of the superjacent waters admits of the exploitation of the natural resources of the said areas; (b) to the seabed and subsoil of similar submarine areas adjacent to the coasts of islands.

Article 6
1. Where the same continental shelf is adjacent to the territories of two or more states

whose coasts are opposite each other, the boundary of the continental shelf appertaining to such states shall be determined by agreement between them. In the absence of agreement, and unless another boundary line is justified by special circumstances, the boundary is the median line, every point of which is equidistant from the nearest points of the baselines from which the breadth of the territorial sea of each state is measured.

2. Where the same continental shelf is adjacent to the territories of two adjacent states, the boundary of the continental shelf shall be determined by agreement between them. In the absence of agreement, and unless another boundary line is justified by special circumstances, the boundary shall be determined by application of the principle of equidistance from the nearest points of the baselines from which the breadth of the territorial sea of each state is measured.

3. In delimiting the boundaries of the continental shelf, any lines which are drawn in accordance with the principles set out in paragraphs 1 and 2 of this article should be defined with reference to charts and geographical features as they exist at a particular date, and reference should be made to fixed permanent identifiable points on the land.

Law of the Sea Convention 1982

Article 76 Definition of the continental shelf

1. The continental shelf of a coastal State comprises the sea-bed and subsoil of the submarine areas that extend beyond its territorial sea throughout the natural prolongation of its land territory to the outer edge of the continental margin, or to a distance of 200 nautical miles from the baselines from which the breadth of the territorial sea is measured where the outer edge of the continental margin does not extend up to that distance.

2. The continental shelf of a coastal State shall not extend beyond the limits provided for in paragraphs 4 to 6.

3. The continental margin comprises the submerged prolongation of the land mass of the coastal State, and consists of the sea-bed and subsoil of the shelf, the slope and the rise. It does not include the deep ocean floor with its oceanic ridges or the subsoil thereof.

4. (a) For the purposes of this Convention, the coastal State shall establish the outer edge of the continental margin wherever the margin extends beyond 200 nautical miles from the baselines from which the breadth of the territorial sea is measured, by either:

    (i) a line delineated in accordance with paragraph 7 by reference to the outermost fixed points at each of which the thickness of sedimentary rocks is at least 1 per cent of the shortest distance from such point to the foot of the continental slope; or

    (ii) a line delineated in accordance with paragraph 7 by reference to fixed points not more than 60 nautical miles from the foot of the continental slope.

  (b) In the absence of evidence to the contrary, the foot of the continental slope shall be determined as the point of maximum change in the gradient at its base.

5. The fixed points comprising the line of the outer limits of the continental shelf on the sea-bed, drawn in accordance with paragraph 4(a) (i) and (ii), either shall not exceed 350 nautical miles from the baselines from which the breadth of the territorial sea is measured or shall not exceed 100 nautical miles from the 2,500 metre isobath, which is a line connecting the depth of 2,500 metres.

6. Notwithstanding the provisions of paragraph 5, on submarine ridges, the outer limit of the continental shelf shall not exceed 350 nautical miles from the baselines from which the breadth of the territorial sea is measured. This paragraph does not apply to submarine elevations

that are natural components of the continental margin, such as its plateaux, rises, caps, banks and spurs.

7. The coastal State shall delineate the outer limits of its continental shelf, where that shelf extends beyond 200 nautical miles from the baselines from which the breadth of the territorial sea is measured, by straight lines not exceeding 60 nautical miles in length, connecting fixed points, defined by co-ordinates of latitude and longitude.

10. The provisions of this article are without prejudice to the question of delimitation of the continental shelf between States with opposite or adjacent coasts.

Article 77 Rights of the coastal State over the continental shelf

1. The coastal State exercises over the continental shelf sovereign rights for the purpose of exploring it and exploiting its natural resources.

2. The rights referred to in paragraph 1 are exclusive in the sense that if the coastal State does not explore the continental shelf or exploits its natural resources, no one may undertake these activities without the express consent of the coastal State.

3. The rights of the coastal State over the continental shelf do not depend on occupation, effective or notional, or on any express proclamation.

4. The natural resources referred to in this Part consist of the mineral and other non-living resources of the sea-bed and subsoil together with living organisms belonging to sedentary species, that is to say, organisms which, at the harvestable stage, either are immobile on or under the sea-bed or are unable to move except in constant physical contact with the sea-bed or the subsoil.

Article 78 Legal status of the superjacent waters and air space and the rights and freedoms of other states

1. The rights of the coastal State over the continental shelf do not affect the legal status of the superjacent waters or of the air space above those waters.

2. The exercise of the rights of the coastal State over the continental shelf must not infringe or result in any unjustifiable interference with navigation and other rights and freedoms of other States as provided for in this Convention.

Article 79 Submarine cables and pipelines on the continental shelf

1. All States are entitled to lay submarine cables and pipelines on the continental shelf, in accordance with the provisions of this article.

2. Subject to its right to take reasonable measures for the exploration of the continental shelf, the exploitation of its natural resources and the prevention, reduction and control of pollution from pipelines, the coastal State may not impede the laying or maintenance of such cables or pipelines.

3. The delineation of the course for the laying of such pipelines on the continental shelf is subject to the consent of the coastal State.

Article 82 Payments and contributions with respect to the exploitation of the continental shelf beyond 200 nautical miles

1. The coastal State shall make payments or contributions in kind in respect of the exploitation of the non-living resources of the continental shelf beyond 200 nautical miles from the baselines from which the breadth of the territorial sea is measured.

3. A developing State which is a net importer of a mineral resource produced from its continental shelf is exempt from making such payments or contributions in respect of that mineral resource.

4. The payments or contributions shall be made through the Authority, which shall

distribute them to States Parties to this Convention, on the basis of equitable sharing criteria, taking into account the interests and needs of developing States, particularly the least developed and the land-locked among them.

Article 83 Delimitation of the continental shelf between states with opposite or adjacent coasts

1. The delimitation of the continental shelf between States with opposite or adjacent coasts shall be effected by agreement on the basis of international law, as referred to in Article 38 of the Statute of the International Court of Justice, in order to achieve an equitable solution.

2. If no agreement can be reached within a reasonable period of time, the States concerned shall resort to the procedures provided for in Part XV.

3. Pending agreement as provided for in paragraph 1, the States concerned, in a spirit of understanding and co-operation, shall make every effort to enter into provisional arrangements of a practical nature and, during this transitional period, not to jeopardize or hamper the reaching of the final agreement. Such arrangements shall be without prejudice to the final delimitation.

4. Where there is an agreement in force between the States concerned, questions relating to the delimitation of the continental shelf shall be determined in accordance with the provisions of that agreement.

NOTE:

As Art. 76 makes clear, the outer edge of the *legal* institution of the shelf may extend beyond 200 miles if the physical feature continues. In order to establish with clarity where such shelf rights end, there is a Commission on the Limits of the Continental Shelf whose purpose it is to consider data etc., submitted by coastal States concerning the outer edge of the shelf beyond 200 miles, to provide technical and scientific advice, and to make recommendations.

B: Delimitation of the shelf

Delimitation of a shared continental shelf between opposite or adjacent States has provided the ICJ with considerable work. The relevant legal provisions are found in Art. 6 of the 1958 Convention, Art. 83 of the 1982 Convention and customary international law. As is evident from the extracts below there is little agreement as to how these legal principles can be given practical effect in concrete cases. In addition, reference must also be made to the principles applicable to delimitation of the EEZ and so-called single maritime boundaries: that is, a delimitation of the continental shelf, EEZ, territorial sea and contiguous zone (or any combination thereof) between opposite or adjacent States by means of a single boundary rather than a boundary for each jurisdictional zone.

Gulf of Maine Case (Canada v USA)
ICJ Rep 1984 246, Chamber of the International Court of Justice

The facts of this case are given below. The following extract indicates the general approach of the ICJ to the question of shelf delimitation.

81. In a matter of this kind, international law – and in this respect the Chamber has logically to refer primarily to customary international law – can of its nature only provide a few basic legal principles, which lay down guidelines to be followed with a view to an essential objective. It cannot

also be expected to specify the equitable criteria to be applied or the practical, often technical, methods to be used for attaining that objective – which remain simply criteria and methods even where they are also, in a different sense, called 'principles'. Although the practice is still rather sparse, owing to the relative newness of the question, it too is there to demonstrate that each specific case is, in the final analysis, different from all the others, that it is monotypic and that, more often than not, the most appropriate criteria, and the method or combination of methods most likely to yield a result consonant with what the law indicates, can only be determined in relation to each particular case and its specific characteristics. . . .

82. The same may not, however, be true of international treaty law. There is, for instance, nothing to prevent the parties to a convention – whether bilateral or multilateral – from extending the rules contained in that convention to aspects which it is less likely that customary international law might govern.

111. A body of detailed rules is not to be looked for in customary international law which in fact comprises a limited set of norms for ensuring the co-existence and vital co-operation of the members of the international community, together with a set of customary rules whose presence in the *opinion juris* of States can be tested by induction based on the analysis of a sufficiently extensive and convincing practice, and not by deduction from preconceived ideas. It is therefore unrewarding, especially in a new and still unconsolidated field like that involving the quite recent extension of the claims of States to areas which were until yesterday zones of the high seas, to look to general international law to provide a ready-made set of rules that can be used for solving any delimitation problems that arise. A more useful course is to seek a better formulation of the fundamental norm, on which the Parties were fortunate enough to be agreed, and whose existence in the legal convictions not only of the Parties to the present dispute, but of all States, is apparent from an examination of the realities of international legal relations.

112. What general international law prescribes in every maritime delimitation between neighbouring States could therefore be defined as follows:
(1) No maritime delimitation between States with opposite or adjacent coasts may be effected unilaterally by one of those States. Such delimitation must be sought and effected by means of an agreement, following negotiations conducted in good faith and with the genuine intention of achieving a positive result. Where, however, such agreement cannot be achieved, delimitation should be effected by recourse to a third party possessing the necessary competence.
(2) In either case, delimitation is to be effected by the application of equitable criteria and by the use of practical methods capable of ensuring, with regard to the geographic configuration of the area and other relevant circumstances, an equitable result.

North Sea Continental Shelf Cases (*Federal Republic of Germany* v *Denmark; FRG* v *The Netherlands*)
ICJ Rep 1969 3, International Court of Justice

The FRG and Denmark and, the FRG and The Netherlands had failed to agree on the division of their common continental shelf. The FRG was not a party to the 1958 Convention and thus Art. 6 was not binding on it as a matter of treaty law. Denmark and The Netherlands argued that the 'equidistance-special circumstance' rule in that Article was now part of customary international law. The FRG objected, especially since the equidistance principle would operate unjustly where there was a concave coast such as here. The Court decided that Art. 6 did not reflect customary international law (see Chapter 2), and thus went on to discuss what principles of customary law were applicable to continental shelf delimitation.

83. The legal situation therefore is that the Parties are under no obligation to apply either the 1958 Convention, which is not opposable to the Federal Republic, or the equidistance method as a mandatory rule of customary law, which it is not. But as between States faced with an issue concerning the lateral delimitation of adjacent continental shelves, there are still rules and principles of law to be applied. . . .

85. It emerges from the history of the development of the legal régime of the continental shelf, which has been reviewed earlier, that the essential reason why the equidistance method is not to be regarded as a rule of law is that, if it were to be compulsorily applied in all situations, this would not be consonant with certain basic legal notions which . . . have from the beginning reflected the *opinio juris* in the matter of delimitation; those principles being that delimitation must be the object of agreement between the States concerned, and that such agreement must be arrived at in accordance with equitable principles. On a foundation of very general precepts of justice and good faith, actual rules of law are here involved which govern the delimitation of adjacent continental shelves – that is to say, rules binding upon States for all delimitations; – in short, it is not a question of applying equity simply as a matter of abstract justice, but of applying a rule of law which itself requires the application of equitable principles, in accordance with the ideas which have always underlain the development of the legal régime of the continental shelf in this field, namely:

(a) the parties are under an obligation to enter into negotiations with a view to arriving at an agreement, and not merely to go through a formal process of negotiation as a sort of prior condition for the automatic application of a certain method of delimitation in the absence of agreement; they are under an obligation so to conduct themselves that the negotiations are meaningful, which will not be the case when either of them insists upon its own position without contemplating any modification of it;

(b) the parties are under an obligation to act in such a way that, in the particular case, and taking all the circumstances into account, equitable principles are applied, – for this purpose the equidistance method can be used, but other methods exist and may be employed, alone or in combination, according to the areas involved;

(c) . . . the continental shelf of any State must be the natural prolongation of its land territory and must not encroach upon what is the natural prolongation of the territory of another State.

89. It must next be observed that, in certain geographical circumstances which are quite frequently met with, the equidistance method, despite its known advantages, leads unquestionably to inequity, in the following sense:

(a) The slightest irregularity in a coastline is automatically magnified by the equidistance line as regards the consequences for the delimitation of the continental shelf. Thus it has been seen in the case of concave or convex coastlines that if the equidistance method is employed, then the greater the irregularity and the further from the coastline the area to be delimited, the more unreasonable are the results produced. So great an exaggeration of the consequences of a natural geographical feature must be remedied or compensated for as far as possible, being of itself creative of inequity.

(b) In the case of the North Sea in particular, where there is no outer boundary to the continental shelf, it happens that the claims of several States converge, meet and intercross in localities where, despite their distance from the coast, the bed of the sea still unquestionably consists of continental shelf. A study of these convergences, as revealed by the maps, shows how inequitable would be the apparent simplification brought about by a delimitation which, ignoring such geographical circumstances, was based solely on the equidistance method.

91. Equity does not necessarily imply equality. There can never be any question of completely refashioning nature, and equity does not require that a State without access to the sea should be allotted an area of continental shelf, any more than there could be a question of rendering the situation of a State with an extensive coastline similar to that of a State with restricted coastline. Equality is to be reckoned within the same plane, and it is not such natural inequalities as these that equity could remedy. . . .

95. The institution of the continental shelf has arisen out of the recognition of a physical fact; and the link between this fact and the law, without which that institution would never have existed, remains an important element for the application of its legal régime. The continental shelf is, by definition, an area physically extending the territory of most coastal States into a species of platform which has attracted the attention first of geographers and hydrographers and then of jurists. . . . The appurtenance of the shelf to the countries in front of whose coastlines it lies, is therefore a fact, and it can be useful to consider the geology of that shelf in order to find out whether the direction taken by certain configurational features should influence delimitation because, in certain localities, they point-up the whole notion of the appurtenance of the continental shelf to the State whose territory it does in fact prolong.

96. . . . This is one of the reasons why the Court does not consider that markedly pronounced configurations can be ignored; for, since the land is the legal source of the power which a State may exercise over territorial extensions to seaward, it must first be clearly established what features do in fact constitute such extensions. Above all is this the case when what is involved is no longer areas of sea, such as the contiguous zone, but stretches of submerged land; for the legal régime of the continental shelf is that of a soil and a subsoil, two words evocative of the land and not of the sea.

97. Another factor to be taken into consideration in the delimitation of areas of continental shelf as between adjacent States is the unity of any deposits. The natural resources of the subsoil of the sea in those parts which consist of continental shelf are the very object of the legal régime established subsequent to the Truman Proclamation. . . .

98. A final factor to be taken account of is the element of a reasonable degree of proportionality which a delimitation effected according to equitable principles ought to bring about between the extent of the continental shelf appertaining to the States concerned and the lengths of their respective coastlines, – these being measured according to their general direction in order to establish the necessary balance between States with straight, and those with markedly concave or convex coasts, or to reduce very irregular coastlines to their truer proportions. . . .

English Channel Arbitration (UK v France)
54 ILR (1977) 6, Special Court of Arbitration

Having failed to negotiate a delimitation of their shared continental shelf, the UK and France submitted the dispute to an *ad hoc* Court of Arbitration. Both States were parties to the 1958 Continental Shelf Convention. The Court considered, therefore, the meaning of Art. 6 of that Convention and its relationship to customary law (see Chapter 3).

48. The Court accordingly finds that the Geneva Convention of 1958 on the Continental Shelf is a treaty in force, the provisions of which are applicable as between the Parties to the present proceedings under Article 2 of the Arbitration Agreement. This finding, the Court wishes at the same time to emphasise, does not mean that it regards itself as debarred from taking any account in these proceedings of recent developments in customary law. On the contrary, the Court has no doubt that

it should take due account of the evolution of the law of the sea in so far as this may be relevant in the context of the present case.

68. Article 6, as both the United Kingdom and the French Republic stress in the pleadings, does not formulate the equidistance principle and 'special circumstances' as two separate rules. The rule there stated in each of the two cases is a single one, a combined equidistance-special circumstances rule. This being so, it may be doubted whether, strictly speaking, there is any legal burden of proof in regard to the existence of special circumstances. The fact that the rule is a single rule means that the question whether 'another boundary is justified by special circumstances' is an integral part of the rule providing for application of the equidistance principle. . . .

69. . . . Clearly, this feature of Article 6 further underlines the full liberty of the Court in appreciating the geographical and other circumstances relevant to the determination of the continental shelf boundary, and at the same time reduces the possibility of any difference in the appreciation of these circumstances under Article 6 and customary law.

70. The Court does not overlook that under Article 6 the equidistance principle ultimately possesses an obligatory force which it does not have in the same measure under the rules of customary law; for Article 6 makes the application of the equidistance principle a matter of treaty obligation for Parties to the Convention. But the combined character of the equidistance-special circumstances rule means that the obligation to apply the equidistance principle is always one qualified by the condition 'unless another boundary line is justified by special circumstances'. . . . In short, the rôle of the 'special circumstances' condition in Article 6 is to ensure an equitable delimitation; and the combined 'equidistance-special circumstances rule', in effect, gives particular expression to a general norm that, failing agreement, the boundary between States abutting on the same continental shelf is to be determined on equitable principles. . . . In other words, even under Article 6 it is the geographical and other circumstances of any given case which indicate and justify the use of the equidistance method as the means of achieving an equitable solution rather than the inherent quality of the method as a legal norm of delimitation.

75. It follows from the foregoing paragraphs that . . . the Court considers that Article 6 is applicable, in principle, to the delimitation of the continental shelf as between the Parties under the Arbitration Agreement. This does not, however, mean that the Court considers the rules of customary law discussed in the judgment in the *North Sea Continental Shelf* cases to be inapplicable in the present case.

Continental Shelf Case (*Tunisia* v *Libya*)
ICJ Rep 1982 18, International Court of Justice

The parties requested the ICJ to indicate the principles and rules of international law that they should bear in mind when negotiating a treaty delimiting their continental shelf. The Court was directed specifically to take account of equitable principles and any 'new trends' accepted at the Third UN Conference on the Law of the Sea. Neither State was a party to the 1958 Convention and both pleaded that the equidistance principle was inappropriate.

44. Both Parties to the present case have in effect based their argument upon the idea that because a delimitation should, in accordance with the Judgment in the *North Sea Continental Shelf* cases, leave to each Party 'all those parts of the continental shelf that constitute a natural prolongation of its land territory into and under the sea' . . ., therefore the determination of what constitutes such natural prolongation will produce a correct delimitation. The Court in 1969 did not regard an equitable delimitation and a determination of the limits of 'natural prolongation' as synonymous, since in the operative clause of its Judgment, just quoted, it referred only to the delimitation being

effected in such a way as to leave 'as much as possible' to each Party the shelf areas constituting its natural prolongation. . . . The Court is therefore unable to accept the contention of Libya that 'once the natural prolongation of a State is determined, delimitation becomes a simple matter of complying with the dictates of nature'. It would be a mistake to suppose that it will in all cases, or even in the majority of them, be possible or appropriate to establish that the natural prolongation of one State extends, in relation to the natural prolongation of another State, just so far and no farther, so that the two prolongations meet along an easily defined line. Nor can the Court approve the argument of Tunisia that the satisfying of equitable principles in a particular geographical situation is just as much a part of the process of the identification of the natural prolongation as the identification of the natural prolongating is necessary to satisfy equitable principles. The satisfaction of equitable principles is, in the delimitation process, of cardinal importance, as the Court will show later in this Judgment, and identification of natural prolongation may, where the geographical circumstances are appropriate, have an important role to play in defining an equitable delimitation, in view of its significance as the justification of continental shelf rights in some cases; but the two considerations – the satisfying of equitable principles and the identification of the natural prolongation – are not to be placed on a plane of equality.

70. Since the Court considers that it is bound to decide the case on the basis of equitable principles, it must first examine what such principles entail, divorced from the concept of natural prolongation which has been found not to be applied for purposes of delimitation in this case. The result of the application of equitable principles must be equitable. . . .

71. Application of equitable principles is to be distinguished from a decision *ex aequo et bono*. The Court can take such a decision only on condition that the Parties agree (Art. 38, para. 2, of the Statute), and the Court is then freed from the strict application of legal rules in order to bring about an appropriate settlement. The task of the Court in the present case is quite different: it is bound to apply equitable principles as part of international law, and to balance up the various considerations which it regards as relevant in order to produce an equitable result. While it is clear that no rigid rules exist as to the exact weight to be attached to each element in the case, this is very far from being an exercise of discretion or conciliation; nor is it an operation of distributive justice.

73. It should first be recalled that exclusive rights over submarine areas belong to the coastal State. The geographic correlation between coast and submerged areas off the coast is the basis of the coastal State's legal title. . . . Adjacency of the sea-bed to the territory of the coastal State has been the paramount criterion for determining the legal status of the submerged areas, as distinct from their delimitation, without regard to the various elements which have become significant for the extension of these areas in the process of the legal evolution of the rules of international law. . . .

81. The 'relevant circumstances which characterize the area' are not limited to the facts of geography or geomorphology, either as a matter of interpretation of the Special Agreement or in application of the equitable principle requiring all relevant circumstances to be taken into account. Apart from the circumstance of the existence and interests of other States in the area, and the existing or potential delimitations between each of the Parties and such States, there is also the position of the land frontier, or more precisely the position of its intersection with the coastline, to be taken into account. In that connection, the Court must in the present case consider a number of alleged maritime limits resulting from the conduct of the States concerned. It has further to give due consideration to the historic rights claimed by Tunisia, and to a number of economic considerations which one or the other Party has urged as relevant.

JUDGE GROS (Dissenting Opinion): . . . I find myself in disagreement with the Judgment in respect of the way in which the Court set about the search for an equitable delimitation of the continental shelf areas as between the Parties, which I find contrary to the concept of the role of equity in the delimitation of a continental shelf adopted by the Court in its 1969 Judgment [in the *North Sea Continental Shelf Cases*]. . . .

11. Thus the Court contents itself . . . with some generalities on the equidistance method without giving the reasons why it has not been employed. Moreover, there is no prior examination to justify such a decision, when the Court, in acting in this way, contradicts the indications it gave on this point in 1969. The reasons referred to in the first lines of paragraph 89 of the 1969 Judgment for discarding equidistance, which 'in certain geographical conditions [could lead] unquestionably to inequity', were based on particular geographical configurations and on their unquestionably inequitable effect, two factors that require examination. Yet in the present case nothing was done to investigate the precise effect on an equidistance line of the relevant geographical features in the area of continental shelf under consideration, the 'unreasonable' (the word used in para. 89) results which the equidistance method might produce and any modifications to be therefore envisaged. If the Court stated in 1969 that the concurrent use of various methods could, in certain situations, enable the desired equitable solution to be achieved, there was, precisely, all the more necessity to try several methods, certainly including equidistance in the sector close to the coast and farther out, to compare their effects, to investigate whether disproportionate effects resulted from this, that or the other relevant geographical feature, to weigh the equities and only to decide in full possession of the facts. This was not done, and this lack of a systematic search for the equitable has produced a result the equity of which remains to be proved.

12. The Court's first task was thus to see what an equidistance line would produce in order to identify the 'extraordinary, unnatural or unreasonable' result to which, it is said, this method might lead. . . .

16. When the Court, in its 1969 Judgment, did not rest content with saying that a continental shelf delimitation should be carried out in accordance with equitable principles, but amassed safeguards by characterizing equity as the application of some lengthily expounded rules and principles of law, taking account of carefully specified factors, it was defining its conception of the role of equity in the delimitation of the continental shelf. While the Court is entitled to change its conception of equity in comparison with the 1969 Judgment, the use of a few quotations from that Judgment does not suffice to prove that no such change has taken place. What is in issue here is the substance of the law applicable to the delimitation of the continental shelf, not the old or novel formulae employed but the decisions taken and the reasons given in the present Judgment; and it is on those points that I differ entirely from the present views of the Court.

To simplify, I need only begin with a few general remarks. The question is: exactly what meaning should be ascribed to equity in the delimitation of continental shelf areas, leaving aside all discussion of equity in municipal law, equity in the philosophy of law and the diversity of possible equities? A court only decides the case before it without being able to deliver judgments of principle with a general scope. Here, equity is the goal, and the way to reach that goal is to apply to the relevant facts such legal methods and reasoning as are suited to the various factors that go to make up that unique phenomenon which is the case referred to the court.

18. There is a profound gulf between an equitable solution to a problem of continental shelf delimitation which is founded upon the rules of law applicable to relevant facts accurately and fully taken into account, and an equitable solution which is founded upon subjective and sometimes divided assessments of the facts, regardless of the law of delimitation, through an eclectic approach to a result unrelated to the extant factors and without any verification other than calculations prompted by chance of coincidence. That is a solution not through equity, but through a compromise sought at one and the same time between the claims of the Parties and the opinions held within the Court.

19. Much more is here involved than a difference of opinion as to how equity should be conceived: what is at issue is the decision dividing a continental shelf between two States which requested that it be delivered in accordance with the law. If a State claiming a right to an area of

continental shelf really possesses that right such as it describes it, it is not equity to deprive it of it but an error of law, and therein lies a far-reaching complaint since the judgments of the Court are irreversible as between the Parties. Equity is not a sort of independent and subjective vision that takes the place of law. The Judgment states that there can be no question in the instant case of applying *ex aequo et bono*. Statements are one thing, the effective pronouncements of the Judgment are another.

Continental Shelf Case (*Libya* v *Malta*)
ICJ Rep 1985 13, International Court of Justice

The parties by special agreement requested the Court to indicate the principles and rules applicable to the delimitation of their shared continental shelf, and also how such principles could be applied in practice. The two States were, 'opposite' rather than 'adjacent'. The 1958 Convention did not apply. The Court considered the 'distance' principle and the extent to which regard must be paid to the Exclusive Economic Zone when delimiting the shelf.

33. In the view of the Court, even though the present case relates only to the delimitation of the continental shelf and not to that of the exclusive economic zone, the principles and rules underlying the latter concept cannot be left out of consideration. As the 1982 Convention demonstrates, the two institutions – continental shelf and exclusive economic zone – are linked together in modern law. Since the rights enjoyed by a State over its continental shelf would also be possessed by it over the sea-bed and subsoil of any exclusive economic zone which it might proclaim, one of the relevant circumstances to be taken into account for the delimitation of the continental shelf of a State is the legally permissible extent of the exclusive economic zone appertaining to that same State. This does not mean that the concept of the continental shelf has been absorbed by that of the exclusive economic zone; it does however signify that greater importance must be attributed to elements, such as distance from the coast, which are common to both concepts.

34. For Malta, the reference to distance in Article 76 of the 1982 Convention represents a consecration of the 'distance principle'; for Libya, only the reference to natural prolongation corresponds to customary international law. It is in the Court's view incontestable that, apart from those provisions, the institution of the exclusive economic zone, with its rule on entitlement by reason of distance, is shown by the practice of States to have become a part of customary law. . . . Although the institutions of the continental shelf and the exclusive economic zone are different and distinct, the rights which the exclusive economic zone entails over the sea-bed of the zone are defined by reference to the régime laid down for the continental shelf. Although there can be a continental shelf where there is no exclusive economic zone, there cannot be an exclusive economic zone without a corresponding continental shelf. It follows that, for juridical and practical reasons, the distance criterion must now apply to the continental shelf as well as to the exclusive economic zone; and this quite apart from the provision as to distance in paragraph 1 of Article 76. This is not to suggest that the idea of natural prolongation is now superseded by that of distance. What it does mean is that where the continental margin does not extend as far as 200 miles from the shore, natural prolongation, which in spite of its physical origins has throughout its history become more and more a complex and juridical concept, is in part defined by distance from the shore, irrespective of the physical nature of the intervening sea-bed and subsoil. The concepts of natural prolongation and distance are therefore not opposed but complementary; and both remain essential elements in the juridical concept of the continental shelf. . . .

46. The normative character of equitable principles applied as a part of general international law is important because these principles govern not only delimitation by adjudication or arbitration, but

also, and indeed primarily, the duty of Parties to seek first a delimitation by agreement, which is also to seek an equitable result.

49. It was argued by Libya that the relevant geographical considerations include the landmass behind the coast, in the sense that that landmass provides in Libya's view the factual basis and legal justification for the State's entitlement to continental shelf rights, a State with a greater landmass having a more intense natural prolongation. The Court is unable to accept this as a relevant consideration. Landmass has never been regarded as a basis of entitlement to continental shelf rights, and such a proposition finds no support in the practice of States, in the jurisprudence, in doctrine, or indeed in the work of the Third United Nations Conference on the Law of the Sea. . . .

50. It was argued by Malta, on the other hand, that the considerations that may be taken account of include economic factors and security. . . . The Court does not however consider that a delimitation should be influenced by the relative economic position of the two States in question, in such a way that the area of continental shelf regarded as appertaining to the less rich of the two States would be somewhat increased in order to compensate for its inferiority in economic resources. Such considerations are totally unrelated to the underlying intention of the applicable rules of international law. . . .

51. Malta contends that the 'equitable consideration' of security and defence interests confirms the equidistance method of delimitation, which gives each party a comparable lateral control from its coasts. Security considerations are of course not unrelated to the concept of the continental shelf. They were referred to when this legal concept first emerged, particularly in the Truman Proclamation. However, in the present case neither Party has raised the question whether the law at present attributes to the coastal State particular competences in the military field over its continental shelf, including competence over the placing of military devices. In any event, the delimitation which will result from the application of the present Judgment is, as will be seen below, not so near to the coast of either Party as to make questions of security a particular consideration in the present case.

58. [T]o use the ratio of coastal lengths as of itself determinative of the seaward reach and area of continental shelf proper to each Party, is to go far beyond the use of proportionality as a test of equity, and as a corrective of the unjustifiable difference of treatment resulting from some method of drawing the boundary line. . . . Its weakness as a basis of argument, however, is that the use of proportionality as a method in its own right is wanting of support in the practice of States, in the public expression of their views at (in particular) the Third United Nations Conference on the Law of the Sea, or in the jurisprudence. . . . That does not however mean that the 'significant difference in lengths of the respective coastlines' is not an element which may be taken into account at a certain stage in the delimitation process; this aspect of the matter will be returned to at the appropriate stage in the further reasoning of the Court.

NOTE:
As regards delimitation of the shelf between opposite and adjacent States, the ICJ has attempted to develop a set of criteria to enable a delimitation to be made that is objectively valid and based on legal principle rather than abstract justice. The move from the formalistic approach of the *North Sea Cases* to the flexible result-orientated approach of *Tunisia* v *Libya*, *Libya* v *Malta* and *Denmark* v *Norway* (see below) has been welcomed by some and rejected by others. Essentially, customary international law, the 1958 Convention and the 1982 Convention are all said to require the same result: an equitable solution. However, it is questionable whether the principles and rules identified by the Court enable States to delimit their shelf themselves with any degree of certainty.

SECTION 4: **The Exclusive Economic Zone**

A: General principles

The Exclusive Economic Zone, or EEZ, is a post-1958 development, largely brought about because of the pressure to extend coastal States' rights beyond the territorial sea. The zone is particularly important for those States that have little or no geological continental shelf, such as many States in South America. Although the principle of the EEZ is firmly established in customary international law (see *Tunisia* v *Libya* above), it is important to consider the relationship between this maritime zone and that of the territorial sea and continental shelf. All three represent different aspects of the seaward extension of coastal State jurisdiction developed in the second half of the twentieth century. In this regard, the extracts considered above in relation to shelf delimitation provide considerable evidence as to how EEZ delimitation should be conducted. The entry into force of the 1982 Convention also brings with it detailed provisions regulating use of the EEZ that were absent from customary international law. The UK has not formally claimed an EEZ around its mainland although it claims specific rights (such as fishing and conservation) over a zone of similar extent. The UK has claimed on EEZ in respect of some of its dependent territories such as Bermuda and South Georgia.

Law of the Sea Convention 1982

Article 55 Specific legal régime of the exclusive economic zone
The exclusive economic zone is an area beyond and adjacent to the territorial sea, subject to the specific legal régime established in this Part, under which the rights and jurisdiction of the coastal State and the rights and freedoms of other States are governed by the relevant provisions of this Convention.

Article 56 Rights, jurisdiction and duties of the coastal state in the exclusive economic zone
    1. In the exclusive economic zone, the coastal State has:
        (a) sovereign rights for the purpose of exploring and exploiting, conserving and managing the natural resources, whether living or non-living, of the waters superjacent to the sea-bed and of the sea-bed and its subsoil, and with regard to other activities for the economic exploitation and exploration of the zone, such as the production of energy from the water, currents and winds;
        (b) jurisdiction as provided for in the relevant provisions of this Convention with regard to:
            (i)   the establishment and use of artificial islands, installations and structures;
            (ii) marine scientific research;
            (iii) the protection and preservation of the marine environment;
        (c) other rights and duties provided for in this Convention.
    2. In exercising its rights and performing its duties under this Convention in the exclusive economic zone, the coastal State shall have due regard to the rights and duties of other States and shall act in a manner compatible with the provisions of this Convention.

3. The rights set out in this article with respect to the sea-bed and subsoil shall be exercised in accordance with Part VI.

Article 57 Breadth of the exclusive economic zone

The exclusive economic zone shall not extend beyond 200 nautical miles from the baselines from which the breadth of the territorial sea is measured.

Article 58 Rights and duties of other states in the exclusive economic zone

1. In the exclusive economic zone, all States, whether coastal or land-locked, enjoy, subject to the relevant provisions of this Convention, the freedoms referred to in article 87 of navigation and overflight and of the laying of submarine cables and pipelines, and other internationally lawful uses of the sea related to these freedoms, such as those associated with the operation of ships, aircraft and submarine cables and pipelines, and compatible with the other provisions of this Convention.

2. Articles 88 to 115 and other pertinent rules of international law apply to the exclusive economic zone in so far as they are not incompatible with this Part.

3. In exercising their rights and performing their duties under this Convention in the exclusive economic zone, States shall have due regard to the rights and duties of the coastal State and shall comply with the laws and regulations, adopted by the coastal State in accordance with the provisions of this Convention and other rules of international law in so far as they are not incompatible with this Part.

Article 61 Conservation of the living resources

1. The coastal State shall determine the allowable catch of the living resources in its exclusive economic zone.

2. The coastal State, taking into account the best scientific evidence available to it, shall ensure through proper conservation and management measures that the maintenance of the living resources in the exclusive economic zone is not endangered by over-exploitation. As appropriate, the coastal State and competent international organizations, whether subregional, regional or global, shall co-operate to this end.

Article 70 Right of geographically disadvantaged states

1. Geographically disadvantaged States shall have the right to participate, on an equitable basis, in the exploitation of an appropriate part of the surplus of the living resources of the exclusive economic zones of coastal States of the same subregion or region, taking into account the relevant economic and geographical circumstances of all the States concerned and in conformity with the provisions of this article and of articles 61 and 62.

Article 74 Delimitation of the exclusive economic zone between states with opposite or adjacent coasts

1. The delimitation of the exclusive economic zone between States with opposite or adjacent coasts shall be effected by agreement on the basis of international law as referred to in Article 38 of the Statute of the International Court of Justice, in order to achieve an equitable solution.

2. If no agreement can be reached within a reasonable period of time, the States concerned shall resort to the procedures provided for in Part XV.

3. Pending agreement as provided for in paragraph 1, the States concerned, in a spirit of understanding and co-operation, shall make every effort to enter into provisional arrangements of a practical nature and, during this transitional period, not to jeopardize or hamper the

reaching of the final agreement. Such arrangements shall be without prejudice to the final delimitation.

    4. Where there is an agreement in force between the States concerned, questions relating to the delimitation of the exclusive economic zone shall be determined in accordance with the provisions of that agreement.

NOTES:
1. As with the continental shelf, the coastal State has 'sovereign rights' over the EEZ. However, the 1982 Convention also imposes obligations on coastal States as the counterpart of the benefits that coastal States gained from the EEZ.
2. The EEZ regime is legally distinct from that of the continental shelf, although they may well overlap physically. In this respect it is important to consider the differences between the two legal regimes as they are set out in the 1982 Convention. However, should a case arise where opposite or adjacent States request a delimitation of only their respective EEZs, Art. 74 of the 1982 Convention is so similar in content to Art. 83 on shelf delimitation that the same principles would be relevant (though possibly with different emphasis).
3. The extent to which the continental shelf and the EEZ should share the same delimitation solution between opposite or adjacent States has been the source of much academic and judicial comment. The *Gulf of Maine Case*, *Denmark v Norway (Jan Mayen)*, *Eritrea*, and *Qatar v Bahrain* have considered this matter at length (see below).

B: A common maritime boundary

The following cases concern the delimitation of more than one maritime zone between opposite or adjacent states. The principles are similar to those discussed in the section on shelf delimitation, although there is the logically prior question of whether it will always be 'equitable' for the continental shelf and the EEZ to share a common maritime boundary.

Gulf of Maine Case (Canada v USA)
ICJ Rep 1984 246, Chamber of the International Court of Justice

    The parties asked a five-judge Chamber of the ICJ to determine a single boundary dividing their fisheries zones and shared continental shelf in the Gulf of Maine area. The 1958 Convention was in force between the parties. Once again, Judge Gros is critical of the reasoning of the Chamber.

116. [T]he question therefore arises whether the fact (already noted by the Chamber) that the 1958 Convention on the Continental Shelf is in force between the Parties does or does not make it obligatory to use, for the delimitation requested in the present case, the method specified in Article 6 of that Convention and, by implication, the application of the criterion on which it is based. . . .

118. The Chamber therefore takes the view that if a question as to the delimitation of the continental shelf only had arisen between the two States, there would be no doubt as to the mandatory application of the method prescribed in Article 6 of the Convention, always subject, of course, to the condition that recourse is to be had to another method or combination of methods where special circumstances so require.

119. The purpose of the present proceedings is not, however, to obtain a delimitation of the continental shelf alone, as it might have been if they had taken place prior to the adoption by the two

Parties of an exclusive fishery zone and the consequent emergence of the idea of delimitation by a single line. Their purpose is – and both Parties have abundantly emphasized the fact – to draw a single delimitation line for both the continental shelf and the superjacent fishery zone. It is doubtful whether a treaty obligation which is in terms confined to the delimitation of the continental shelf can be extended, in a manner that would manifestly go beyond the limits imposed by the strict criteria governing the interpretation of treaty instruments, to a field which is evidently much greater, unquestionably heterogeneous, and accordingly fundamentally different. Apart from this formal, but important, considuration, there is the more substantive point that such an interpretation would, in the final analysis, make the maritime water mass overlying the continental shelf a mere accessory of that shelf. Such a result would be just as unacceptable as the converse result produced by simply extending to the continental shelf the application of a method of delimitation adopted for the 'water column' only and its fish resources.

125. The Chamber must therefore conclude in this respect that the provisions of Article 6 of the 1958 Convention on the Continental Shelf, although in force between the Parties, do not entail either for them or for the Chamber any legal obligation to apply them to the single maritime delimitation which is the subject of the present case.

JUDGE GROS (Dissenting Opinion): In redefining the law of maritime delimitation on the basis of Articles 74 and 83 of the 1982 Convention the Chamber has exposed the disservice rendered international law by the Third United Nations Conference; I have summed up this formulation in two words: agreement + equity. As the concept of agreement has nothing to do with the work of judges, only equity remains. But if there is any legal concept to which each attaches his own meaning, it is equity. . . . What is the equity referred to in any remnant of the law of maritime delimitation that may survive in 1984?

28. The Chamber's Judgment follows the line of thought of the Court's, thus confirming that there has been a break in the case-law in relation to the 1969 Judgment and the 1977 Decision. In a dissenting opinion appended to the Judgment of 1982 I have already expressed my reaction as to the nub of the problem raised by this new view of equity, and it seems to me useless to repeat it here. . . .

29. The decisive reason for my not having accepted the conception of today's Judgment, in which the Chamber enlarges upon that of the Court in 1982, continues to reside in the fact that equity does not consist in a successive search for equality, proportionality, result; each of these considerations is a way of applying equity, it is a choice made in the manner of applying the law and not an accumulation of equities which there is nothing to forbid supplementing with such others as one may glimpse in that frame of mind. One must not narrow down the law of delimitation to two words, agreement plus equity, only to equate that equity with judicial discretion.

46. The 1958 Convention on the Continental Shelf posits an equidistance special-circumstances rule, a single rule which is clear: if there are no special circumstances, equidistance must be applied. The 1969 Judgment and the 1977 Decision were based on that rule and interpreted it in the desire to seat international law firmly on a concept of rigour in the application of an equity dependent on that existing law. When the Judgment of 1982 decided, in paragraphs 109 and 110, to summarize the development of customary law on continental shelf delimitation, it took sides in the combat against the idea of equidistance by 'as a first step' depriving it of any 'preferential status' as a method, thus creating for negotiators and, subsequently, judges something like a thought prohibition. This ban is now renewed by the Judgment of 1984. The difference between the international law on the continental shelf of 1958 and the swerve to a new direction in 1982 is therefore fundamental. It would seem that the idea of conducting a preliminary examination in terms of the equidistance method is so feared that it has to be proscribed. It is difficult to grasp the necessity of such an *a priori* opposition to the very notion of equidistance having any useful role to play in searching for an equitable solution.

47. So far as its doctrine is concerned, the present Judgment can be summed up in four words: the result is equitable. This is tantamount to expecting States that come to the Court to accept this new basis of the function of the judge as one freed from the positive law he is charged to apply. The 1969 Judgment and the 1977 Decision had erected guardrails to the use of the concept of equity; these the 1982 Judgment and the present one have thrown down. . . . The course taken since February 1982 has been to indulge in an equity beyond the law, detached from any established rules, based solely on whatever each group of judges seised of a case declares itself able and free to appreciate in accordance with its political or economic views of the moment. This is to transform the International Court of Justice into a court of equity, as Judges Sir Arnold McNair and Sir Gerald Fitzmaurice had warned in their time. Since 1982 we have been witnessing not merely a new trend in jurisprudence but a different manner of settling inter-State disputes.

Maritime Delimitation in the Area Between Greenland and Jan Mayen (Denmark v Norway)

ICJ Rep 1993 38, International Court of Justice

Denmark made an application to the Court requesting delimitation of its maritime boundary with Norway in the area surrounding Jan Mayen island, a Norwegian island off the coast of Greenland, part of Denmark. Denmark claimed a single delimitation line corresponding to a 200-mile zone, while Norway relied on equidistance. This was the first case in which delimitation based on the compulsory jurisdiction of the Court and not by agreement of the parties. The consequences of this – particularly whether the Court could actually draw a boundary (which it did) and what law was applicable – are dealt with in the dissenting opinion of Vice-President Oda.

41. The Parties also differ on the question whether what is required is one delimitation line or two lines, Denmark asking for 'a single line of delimitation of the fishery zone and continental shelf area', and Norway contending that the median line constitutes the boundary for delimitation of the continental shelf, and constitutes also the boundary for the delimitation of the fishery zone, i.e., that the two lines would coincide, but the two boundaries would remain conceptually distinct. . . .

42. At first sight it might be thought that asking for the drawing of a single line and asking for the drawing of two coincident lines amounts in practical terms to the same thing. There is, however, in Norway's view, this important difference, that the two lines, even if coincident in location, stem from different strands of the applicable law, the location of the one being derived from the 1958 Convention, and the location of the other being derived from customary law. . . .

44. It is sufficient for it to note, as do the Parties, that the 1958 Convention is binding upon them, that it governs the continental shelf delimitation to be effected, and that it is certainly a source of applicable law, different from that governing the delimitation of fishery zones. The Court will therefore examine separately the two strands of the applicable law; the effect of Article 6 of the 1958 Convention applicable to the delimitation of the continental shelf boundary, and then the effect of the customary law which governs the fishery zone.

45. It may be observed that the Court has never had occasion to apply the 1958 Convention. . . . In the present case, both States are parties to the 1958 Convention and, there being no joint request for a single maritime boundary as in the *Gulf of Maine* case, the 1958 Convention is applicable to the delimitation of the continental shelf between Greenland and Jan Mayen.

47. Regarding the law applicable to the delimitation of the fishery zone, there appears to be no decision of an international tribunal that has been concerned only with a fishery zone; but there are

cases involving a single dual-purpose boundary asked for by the parties in a special agreement, for example the *Gulf of Maine* case, already referred to, which involved delimitation of 'the continental shelf and fishery zones' of the parties. The question was raised during the hearings of the relationship of such zones to the concept of the exclusive economic zone as proclaimed by many States and defined in Article 55 of the 1982 United Nations Convention on the Law of the Sea. Whatever that relationship may be, the Court takes note that the Parties adopt in this respect the same position, in that they see no objection, for the settlement of the present dispute, to the boundary of the fishery zones being determined by the law governing the boundary of the exclusive economic zones, which is customary law; however the Parties disagree as to the interpretation of the norms of such customary law. . . .

49. Turning first to the delimitation of the continental shelf, since it is governed by Article 6 of the 1958 Convention, and the delimitation is between coasts that are opposite, it is appropriate to begin by taking provisionally the median line between the territorial sea baselines, and then enquiring whether 'special circumstances' require 'another boundary line'. Such a procedure is consistent with the words in Article 6, 'In the absence of agreement, and unless another boundary line is justified by special circumstances, the boundary is the median line.'

Thus, in respect of the continental shelf boundary in the present case, even if it were appropriate to apply, not Article 6 of the 1958 Convention, but customary law concerning the continental shelf as developed in the decided cases, it is in accord with precedents to begin with the median line as a provisional line and then to ask whether 'special circumstances' require any adjustment or shifting of that line.

52. Turning now to the delimitation of the fishery zones, the Court must consider, on the basis of the sources listed in Article 38 of the Statute of the Court, the law applicable to the fishery zone, in the light also of what has been said above (paragraph 47) as to the exclusive economic zone. Of the international decisions concerned with dual-purpose boundaries, that in the *Gulf of Maine* case – in which the Chamber rejected the application of the 1958 Convention, and relied upon the customary law – is here material. After noting that a particular segment of the delimitation was one between opposite coasts, the Chamber went on to question the adoption of the median line 'as final without more ado', and drew attention to the 'difference in length between the respective coastlines of the two neighbouring States which border on the delimitation area' and on that basis affirmed 'the necessity of applying to the median line as initially drawn a correction which, though limited, will pay due heed to the actual situation' (*ICJ Reports 1984*, pp. 334–335, paras. 217, 218).

54. The Court is now called upon to examine every particular factor of the case which might suggest an adjustment or shifting of the median line provisionally drawn. The aim in each and every situation must be to achieve 'an equitable result'. From this standpoint, the 1958 Convention requires the investigation of any 'special circumstances'; the customary law based upon equitable principles on the other hand requires the investigation of 'relevant circumstances'. . . .

56. Although it is a matter of categories which are different in origin and in name, there is inevitably a tendency towards assimilation between the special circumstances of Article 6 of the 1958 Convention and the relevant circumstances under customary law, and this if only because they both are intended to enable the achievement of an equitable result. This must be especially true in the case of opposite coasts where, as has been seen, the tendency of customary law, like the terms of Article 6, has been to postulate the median line as leading prima facie to an equitable result. It cannot be surprising if an equidistance-special circumstances rule produces much the same result as an equitable principles-relevant circumstances rule in the case of opposite coasts, whether in the case of a delimitation of continental shelf, of fishery zone, or of an all-purpose delimitation of continental shelf, of fishery zone, or of an all-purpose single boundary. . . .

60. Both Parties have brought to the Court's attention various circumstances which they each

regard as appropriate to be taken into account for the purposes of the delimitation. Neither Party has however presented these specifically in the context of the possible adjustment or shifting of a median line provisionally drawn: Norway, because it argues that the median line itself is the correct and equitable solution, and Denmark, because it contends that the median line should not be used, even as a provisional solution. Denmark does however, assert that, on the basis of the 1958 Convention, it could contend,

> that the island of Jan Mayen, *par excellence*, falls within the concept of 'special circumstances' and should be given no effect on Greenland's 200-mile continental shelf area.

87. Having thus completed its examination of the geophysical and other circumstances brought to its attention as appropriate to be taken into account for the purposes of the delimitation of the continental shelf and the fishery zones, the Court has come to the conclusion that the median line adopted provisionally for both, as first stage in the delimitation, should be adjusted or shifted to become a line such as to attribute a larger area of maritime space to Denmark than would the median line. The line drawn by Denmark 200 nautical miles from the baselines of eastern Greenland would however be excessive as an adjustment, and would be inequitable in its effects. The delimitation line must therefore be drawn within the area of overlapping claims, between the lines proposed by each Party. . . .

VICE PRESIDENT ODA (Dissenting Opinion): 5. It appears to me that Denmark fails to appreciate certain concepts of the law of the sea. *In the first place*, it does not seem to grasp the proper concept of the exclusive economic zone, the concept adopted in the 1982 United Nations Convention on the Law of the Sea. . . . *Secondly*, Denmark seems to pay little heed to the regime of the continental shelf which is fated – at least under the contemporary law of the sea – to exist in parallel with the régime of the exclusive economic zone. . . . *Thirdly*, Denmark seems to confuse *title* to the continental shelf or the exclusive economic zone with the concept of *delimitation* of overlapping sea-areas. . . .

Problem 1: The Fishery Zone (However Called) Is Not Identical to the Exclusive Economic Zone

20. There is certainly no provision in the 1982 Convention that relates to a 200-mile 'fishery zone' as such. The 'fishing zone' (or 'fishery zone') which Denmark and Norway established respectively (and which Denmark mentions in its Application) is *not* the exclusive economic zone as defined in that Convention.

23. As the concept of the 'fishery zone' has no standing, at least in the 1982 Convention, and still remains a merely *political* concept, I would have liked the Court to have taken a clear stance with respect to the confusion . . . between the concepts of the 'exclusive economic zone' and the 'fishery zone'. Its failure to do so leads me to wonder what will become in future of the concept of the exclusive economic zone, as provided for in that Convention. I am afraid that the concept of the 'exclusive economic zone' will appear completely obsolete, even before the 1982 Convention has come into force.

Problem 2: The Régime of the Continental Shelf is Independent of the Concept of the Exclusive Economic Zone

25. How is it possible for Denmark to presuppose the identity of the boundary of the exclusive economic zone (for that is what it really alludes to) with that of the continental shelf, when both régimes originated against different backgrounds and exist in parallel? Is it the intention of Denmark to contend that the original, or proper, régime of the continental shelf has completely crumbled away, to be replaced by the new régime of the exclusive economic zone?. . . .

69. [I]n spite of the practical identity between Article 74 and Article 83, there is, of course, no guarantee that the delimitation of the exclusive economic zone and the delimitation of the

continental shelf will necessarily be identical. The 'equitable solution' to be reached by negotiation in the delimitation of the exclusive economic zones and that of the continental shelf areas can certainly be different, as the 'special' or 'relevant' circumstances to be taken into account when defining a delimitation line may well be different in each case.

(a) One or two delimitation lines?

70. Whether the boundary of the continental shelf areas and the boundary of the exclusive economic zone are or are not identical will depend quite simply on the result of each delimitation, which can well be different with respect to the two different areas. In the absence of an agreement between the States concerned, one cannot presuppose a single delimitation for two separate and independent regimes, the exclusive economic zone and the continental shelf, although the possibility of an eventual coincidence of the two lines may not be excluded.

71. I have however, some sympathy with the Danish attitude and with the Court's tendency to prefer a single maritime boundary, since, if the acceptance of wider claims to coastal jurisdiction over offshore fisheries had been seen as inevitable, those two régimes should have been amalgamated in the new law of the sea. What is deplorable about the new order in the oceans (which was being prepared in UNCLOS III) is the fact that an immature concept of the exclusive economic zone has been introduced to coexist with the previously accepted concept of the continental shelf which has been re-defined and thus transformed, and that the concept of the exclusive economic zone has in fact had the effect of ousting the latter concept. . . .

73. However, in spite of all I have said, the two regimes of the exclusive economic zone and the continental shelf exist separately and in parallel in the 1982 United Nations Convention, hence in existing international law, and the delimitation for each is different.

(b) Role of the third party in the delimitation of maritime boundaries

77. When a question is to be resolved by agreement, if that agreement cannot be achieved because of a divergence of views on various relevant elements governing the negotiation, that failure to reach agreement – assuming good faith – will not have been due to a difference in the interpretation of international law but to a difference in the concepts of equity upheld by each party.

78. The function of the third party in assisting the parties in dispute could be either to suggest concrete guidelines for the evaluation of each of the above-mentioned relevant elements in order to assign them a proper place in the negotiations or to proceed itself to choose a line by weighing up the relevant factors or elements from among an infinite variety of possibilities so that an equitable solution may be reached.

79. The most that can be done by this Court, *as a judicial tribunal applying international law*, is to declare that the lines of delimitation for the exclusive economic zone and the continental shelf, respectively, must be drawn by agreement between the Parties, as provided for in the 1982 United Nations Convention, from among the infinite possibilities lying *somewhere* between the line asked for by Denmark and the other line asked for by Norway. . . .

(e) Effecting a delimitation ex aequo et bono

88. Only in a case in which the parties in dispute have asked the Court by agreement to effect a maritime delimitation *ex aequo et bono* is it qualified to examine what factors or elements should be taken into account as relevant, and to what degree such factors or elements should be evaluated when it is determining the line to be drawn or indicating a concrete line based on its own evaluation of the relevant factors and elements.

89. I must add furthermore that, if a single maritime delimitation for the continental shelf and the exclusive economic zone is to be effected by the Court in response to a joint request by the parties in

dispute, then the parties have to agree which factors or elements relevant to either the exclusive economic zone or the continental shelf (or, in other words, relevant to either fishery resources or mineral resources), are to be given priority. The Court is not competent even as an arbitrator to decide the priority of either the exclusive economic zone or the continental shelf unless expressly requested to do so by the parties.

Case Concerning the Delimitation of Maritime Areas Between Canada and France (St Pierre and Miquelon)
31 ILM 1145 (1992), Court of Arbitration

The islands of St Pierre and Miquelon lie off the coast of Canada opposite Newfoundland. By a Special Agreement the two parties established a five-judge Court of Arbitration to determine a single delimitation line for the territorial sea, continental shelf and EEZ of the islands and Canada. Both parties had ratified the 1958 Convention on the Continental Shelf, but the court held, following *Gulf of Maine*, that this was applicable only to a case involving delimitation of the shelf alone. The Court considered various circumstances that may be relevant in achieving an equitable delimitation. Once again, there is a powerful dissent because of the apparent arbitrariness of the actual delimitation line – the so-called 'mushroom and stem'.

38. The Parties are in agreement with respect to the fundamental norm to be applied in this case, which requires the delimitation to be effected in accordance with equitable principles, or equitable criteria, taking account of all the relevant circumstances, in order to achieve an equitable result. The underlying premise of this fundamental norm is the emphasis on equity and the rejection of any obligatory method. However, the Parties disagree with respect to the principles or criteria that should govern the equitable decision of this dispute, placing their emphasis on different principles or criteria.

40. This Court will adhere to the established judicial opinion to the effect that in a single or all purpose delimitation operation, Article 6 of the Convention on the Continental Shelf has not 'mandatory force even between States which are parties to the Convention'. (*ICJ Reports 1984*, para. 124). . . .

41. Moreover, if the purpose of invoking Article 6 is to derive from it support for equidistance, it must be observed that Article 6 does not provide for equidistance 'tout court' but equidistance when there are no special circumstances. . . .

45. Undoubtedly, the difference in length of all the relevant coasts of the Parties is an important factor to take into account for an equitable delimitation, in order to avoid disproportionate results and, subsequently, to test the equitableness of the solution finally adopted. However, the Court cannot accept the contention that particular segments of coast may have an increased or diminished projection depending on their length. The extent of the seaward projections will depend, in every case, on the geographical circumstances; for example, a particular coast, however short, may have a seaward projection as far as 200 miles, if there are no competing coasts that could require a curtailed reach. . . .

49. In the view of this Court there are no grounds for contending that the extent of the maritime rights of an island depends on its political status.

63. This Court considers that the proper use of proportionality as a test of equity was well described by the International Court of Justice in its 1985 judgment in the *Libya/Malta* case. At paragraph 66 the Court defined its proper role:

It is however one thing to employ proportionality calculations to check a result; it is another thing to take note, in the course of the delimitation process, of the existence of a very marked difference in coastal lengths, and to attribute the appropriate significance to that coastal relationship, without seeking to define it in quantitative terms which are only suited to the ex-post assessment of relationships of coast to area.

65. This Court does not consider that either of the proposed solutions [by the parties] provides even a starting point for the delimitation. The Court's conclusion is similar to that drawn by the Chamber of the International Court of Justice in the *Gulf of Maine* case, namely 'that it must undertake this final stage of the task entrusted to it and formulate its own solution independently of the proposals made by the Parties'.

JUDGE WEIL (Dissenting Opinion): 1. The Agreement which set up this Court of Arbitration requested the Court to carry out the delimitation of the maritime areas appertaining to France and to Canada 'in accordance with the principles and rules of international law applicable in the matter'. I am at a loss to identify what principles and rules can have justified on a legal basis the delimitation which has been decided, and I fear that the Decision may in some respects jeopardise the development of the law of maritime delimitation which the *Libya/Malta* judgment had spectacularly impelled in the direction of a greater legal security. . . .

11. I must confess that I fail to understand how the majority of the Court can have endorsed that strange theory [of frontal projection: put forward by Canada]. It is true that '[w]here a constant distance is used to define the seaward extension of a coastal State . . . the maritime zone of a coastal State . . . is not to be thought of as a platform in front of its coast, but as a broad belt of sea surrounding its territory in every direction'. A maritime projection determined by a given distance from the coast cannot be measured only in a direction perpendicular to the general direction of the coastline and along the breadth of that coastline. It radiates in all directions, creating an oceanic envelope round the coastal facade. In one word, it is radial. This was already, with regard to the territorial sea, the significance of the cannon-shot rule: the cannon shoots in all directions, giving rise to that 'belt of territorial waters' to which the International Court of Justice has referred. The same rule applies today for the 200-mile zone.

12. The frontal projection theory has been rejected by the practice of States both for the determination of outside limits and for the delimitation of adjacent States. The outer limits of maritime jurisdictions are commonly determined today by reference to the so-called arcs of circles method which consists, as is well known, of drawing arcs of circles of a given radius (12 miles for the territorial sea, 200 miles for the exclusive economic zone or fisheries zone) from basepoints on the coast. By definition, these arcs of circles are drawn in all directions, with no particular preference for the frontal or perpendicular direction. . . .

16. The Decision invokes a second argument in support of its solution, namely the principle of non-encroachment. . . .

17. There can of course be no question of putting in doubt the principle of non-encroachment, which is one of the pillars of the law of maritime delimitation. Besides, as the Decision itself acknowledges (para. 67), any delimitation necessarily involves some mutual cut-off and encroachment, in this sense that each of the States concerned must renounce a part of the area to which it would be entitled if the other State did not exist. There is more than that, however: in order to arrive at an equitable result, the mutual cut-off and enchroachment from which the maritime frontier emerges must be shared in a balanced and reasonable manner between the two States and so that the sacrifice is not borne solely by one of them. The delimitation exercise and the assessment of the equitable result must not be approached solely from the point of view of one of the States, in such a way as to assume to be inequitable any line which does not essentially safeguard the integrity of the

projections of one of the States, thereby privileging the latter over the projections of the former. . . .

19. It was not the task of the Court to define the French area starting from the axiomatic presupposition that the whole of that region was Canadian in its essence or in its nature. The French area was not going to be determined by way of subtraction from the Canadian area. The Court was not called upon to reason as though its task were to define what was going to be granted to France. This is not what the Agreement requested it to do but rather to 'carry out the delimitation . . . of the maritime areas appertaining to France and the maritime areas appertaining to Canada'. For the Court, delimitation should have constituted a bipolar operation. . . .

20. Having thus rebutted the justifications invoked by the Decision, both for the corridor and for the asymmetric cap, I might be tempted to paraphrase what the International Court of Justice has said in the *Libya/Malta* case with regard to the Libyan claim: 'nothing else remains' in the solution adopted 'that can afford an independent principle and method for drawing the boundary, unless the reference to the lengths of coastlines is taken as such'. However, even though in some quarters there is an impression that this is how the majority of the Court approached the problem, the fact remains – and this alone matters from the legal standpoint – that the proportionality between the lengths of the coastlines and the corresponding maritime areas is not the only factor on which the Decision bases its solution.

23. One may however go even further and deplore that this Court should not have renounced the proportionality test in its quantified form, which nothing obliged it to adopt.

Case Concerning Maritime Delimitation and Territorial Questions between Qatar and Bahrain (Qatar v Bahrain) (Merits)
ICJ Reports 2001, International Court of Justice

The parties asked the ICJ to draw a single maritime boundary consequent upon the resolution of certain territorial questions relating to islands in the area.

167. The Parties are in agreement that the Court should render its decision on the maritime delimitation in accordance with international law. Neither Bahrain nor Qatar is party to the Geneva Conventions on the Law of the Sea of 29 April 1958; Bahrain has ratified the United Nations Convention on the Law of the Sea of 10 December 1982 but Qatar is only a signatory to it. Customary international law, therefore, is the applicable law. Both Parties, however, agree that most of the provisions of the 1982 Convention which are relevant for the present case reflect customary law. . . .

169. It should be kept in mind that the concept of 'single maritime boundary' may encompass a number of functions. In the present case the single maritime boundary will be the result of the delimitation of various jurisdictions. In the southern part of the delimitation area, which is situated where the coasts of the Parties are opposite to each other, the distance between these coasts is nowhere more than 24 nautical miles. The boundary the Court is expected to draw will, therefore, delimit exclusively their territorial seas and, consequently, an area over which they enjoy territorial sovereignty.

170. More to the north, however, where the coasts of the two States are no longer opposite to each other but are rather comparable to adjacent coasts, the delimitation to be carried out will be one between the continental shelf and exclusive economic zone belonging to each of the Parties, areas in which States have only sovereign rights and functional jurisdiction. Thus both Parties have differentiated between a southern and a northern sector. . . .

173. The Court observes that the concept of a single maritime boundary does not stem from multilateral treaty law but from State practice, and that it finds its explanation in the wish of States to establish one uninterrupted boundary line delimiting the various – partially coincident – zones of maritime jurisdiction appertaining to them. In the case of coincident jurisdictional zones, the determination of a single boundary for the different objects of delimitation:

can only be carried out by the application of a criterion, or combination of criteria, which does not give preferential treatment to one of these . . . objects to the detriment of the other, and at the same time is such as to be equally suitable to the division of either of them,

as was stated by the Chamber of the Court in the *Gulf of Maine* case (*ICJ Reports 1984*, p. 327, para. 194). In that case, the Chamber was asked to draw a single line which would delimit both the continental shelf and the superjacent water column.

174. Delimitation of territorial seas does not present comparable problems, since the rights of the coastal State in the area concerned are not functional but territorial, and entail sovereignty over the sea-bed and the superjacent waters and air column. Therefore, when carrying out that part of its task, the Court has to apply first and foremost the principles and rules of international customary law which refer to the delimitation of the territorial sea, while taking into account that its ultimate task is to draw a single maritime boundary that serves other purposes as well.

212. The Court observes that the method of straight baselines, which is an exception to the normal rules for the determination of baselines, may only be applied if a number of conditions are met. This method must be applied restrictively. Such conditions are primarily that either the coastline is deeply indented and cut into, or that there is a fringe of islands along the coast in its immediate vicinity.

213. The fact that a State considers itself a multiple-island State or a *de facto* archipelagic State does not allow it to deviate from the normal rules for the determination of baselines unless the relevant conditions are met. The coasts of Bahrain's main islands do not form a deeply indented coast, nor does Bahrain claim this. It contends, however, that the maritime features off the coast of the main islands may be assimilated to a fringe of islands which constitute a whole with the mainland.

214. The Court does not deny that the maritime features east of Bahrain's main islands are part of the overall geographical configuration; it would be going too far, however, to qualify them as a fringe of islands along the coast. The islands concerned are relatively small in number. Moreover, in the present case it is only possible to speak of a 'cluster of islands' or an 'island system' if Bahrain's main islands are included in that concept. In such a situation, the method of straight baselines is applicable only if the State has declared itself to be an archipelagic State under Part IV of the 1982 Convention on the Law of the Sea, which is not true of Bahrain in this case.

215. The Court, therefore, concludes that Bahrain is not entitled to apply the method of straight baselines. Thus each maritime feature has its own effect for the determination of the baselines, on the understanding that, on the grounds set out before, the low-tide elevations situated in the overlapping zone of territorial seas will be disregarded. It is on this basis that the equidistance line must be drawn.

JUDGE ODA: 13. With regard to the 'southern sector', the Court applies the principles and rules governing the boundary of the territorial sea and states:

In the southern part of the delimitation area, which is situated where the coasts of the Parties are opposite to each other, the distance between these coasts is nowhere more than 24 nautical miles. The boundary the Court is expected to draw will, therefore, delimit exclusively their territorial seas and, consequently, an area over which they enjoy territorial sovereignty. (Judgment, para. 169.)

I cannot agree with the Court in its view that the maritime boundary in the southern part of this region should be the line of delimitation of the *territorial sea*. I think that the Court's misunderstanding of this dispute stems from the Court's failure to take account of the background of the case. . . .

A review of the history of oil development in the Gulf and the successive bilateral agreements concluded among the Gulf States over the last several decades leads me to submit that Qatar and Bahrain were contemplating the delimitation between themselves of the sea areas for oil exploitation. It is patently clear that the two States *never* thought that they would be engaged in a dispute concerning the delimitation of their respective *territorial seas*. That is, I believe, the reason why the Parties employ the expression 'the maritime boundary' (Bahrain) or 'single maritime boundary' (Qatar), but never the boundary of the *territorial sea*, in their respective submissions. To repeat, both Qatar and Bahrain talk about the 'maritime boundary' or 'single maritime boundary' because their concern does not lie with the delimitation of the *territorial sea*. The Court is *not* correct in attempting to apply the rules and principles governing the boundary of the *territorial sea* in the southern part of the region at issue.

16. Even if, for the sake of argument, the 'southern sector' is to be delimited according to the rules and principles governing the boundary of the *territorial sea*, as the Court suggests, it appears to me that the Court is also mistaken in its interpretation of those rules and principles. The Court recommends that the boundary of the territorial sea (in the southern sector) should be drawn in accordance with Article 15 of the 1982 United Nations Convention on the Law of the Sea (which is quoted in full in the Judgment at paragraph 175 and is virtually identical to Article 12, paragraph 1, of the 1958 Convention on the Territorial Sea and the Contiguous Zone), which is 'to be regarded as having a customary character' (Judgment, para. 176).

17. The Court states that Article 15 of the 1982 United Nations Convention 'is often referred to as the "equidistance/special circumstances" rule' (Judgment, para. 176), and also that

> the equidistance/special circumstances rule, which is applicable in particular to the delimitation of the territorial sea, and the equitable principles/relevant circumstances rule, as it has been developed since 1958 in case-law and State practice with regard to the delimitation of the continental shelf and the exclusive economic zone, are closely interrelated.
> (Judgment, para. 231)

The fact of the matter is that the equidistance/special circumstances rule, so named by certain scholars after the 1958 Convention on the Continental Shelf, has been referred to mainly in connection with the delimitation of the continental shelf but, as far as I am aware, *not* in connection with the delimitation of the territorial sea. I wish to make this point because the Court, in this connection as well, appears to me to have confused the rules applicable to the boundary of the territorial sea with those applicable to the boundary of the continental shelf.

18. For the territorial sea, the *principle* is that the 'median line' is to be used, although there may be exceptions to this principle where necessary because of historic title *or* other special circumstances. This rule is manifestly *not* the same as the one applicable to the boundary of the continental shelf. . . .

20. The general rules established in the provisions in the 1958 Convention on 'limits of the territorial sea' (Part I, Sect. II) remain in the 1982 UN Convention (Part II, Sect II). I have in paragraph 6 of this opinion expressed my concern regarding islets and low-tide elevations in connection with the territorial issues but I must repeat those concerns here in connection with the maritime delimitation. This is necessary because in the present case the islets and low-tide elevations are really the most crucial points, leaving aside the matter of sovereignty over the Hawar Islands, in determining the maritime boundary.

The extension of the breadth of the territorial sea to 12 miles would have resulted in a radical change in the context of the concepts of low-tide elevation, island and islet, straight baselines, etc., which were introduced in 1958 to reflect customary international law at that time. It is extremely important to note that the provisions of the 1958 Convention relating to the territorial sea, its boundary and other elements which might affect the boundary were, as a whole, designed to meet the situation under the 3-mile rule and were adopted at a time when the 3-mile limit for the territorial sea prevailed. By the 1970s, only two decades after the 1958 Conference, there was no longer any doubt that a 12-mile limit for the territorial sea would eventually become the rule.

Although this change in the limit would have greatly affected the new régime of the territorial sea, the 1982 United Nations Convention was adopted at UNCLOS III without any careful consideration being given to this change of situation, namely from the generally accepted three-mile limit to the suggested 12-mile limit of the territorial sea. I greatly doubt whether certain provisions relating to 'limits of the territorial sea' adopted in 1958 and copied in 1982 (provisions on which the Court relies in the present Judgment) can today be considered to be customary international law when the overall conditions (those pertaining to the territorial sea in particular) have changed dramatically over the intervening decades.

21. I fear that the Court's statement in the present Judgment concerning the boundary of the territorial sea to be applied in the southern part of the sea areas in question (where there are a number of scattered low-tide elevations and islets in extremely shallow sea waters) will, in future, be taken as jurisprudence relating to maritime delimitation. I feel compelled to repeat and emphasize that the manner in which the Court has taken the rules and principles concerning the boundary of the territorial sea which might have been in effect when the three-mile limit prevailed and applied them to the boundary of the 12-mile sea-belt (territorial sea) in the southern part of the area in question is quite inappropriate.

Eritrea/Yemen Arbitration, Second Stage, Maritime Delimitation
Permanent Court of Arbitration December 1999, http://www.pca-cpa.org

The parties had requested the Permanent Court of Arbitration (PCA) to resolve a number of territorial and maritime issues. In the First Phase, the PCA had considered a number of territorial questions and had made an Award. The Second Stage dealt with the remaining maritime issues.

Award of the Arbitration Court
129. The task of the Tribunal in the present Stage of this Arbitration is defined by Article 2 of the Arbitration Agreement, and is to 'result in an award delimiting the maritime boundaries'. The term 'boundaries' is here used, it is reasonable to assume, in its normal and ordinary meaning of denoting an international maritime boundary between the two State Parties to the Arbitration; and not in the sense of what is usually called a maritime 'limit', such as the outer limit of a territorial sea or a contiguous zone; although there might be places where these limits happen to coincide with or be modified by the international boundary.

130. Article 2 also provides that, in determining the maritime boundaries, the Tribunal is to take 'into account the opinion it will have formed on questions of territorial sovereignty, the United Nations Convention on the Law of the Sea, and any other pertinent factor'. The reasons for taking account of the Award on Sovereignty are clear enough and both Parties have agreed in their pleadings that, in the Second Stage, there can be no question of attempting to reopen the decisions made in the First Award. The requirement to take into account the United Nations Convention on the Law of the Sea of 1982 is important because Eritrea has not become a party to that Convention but has in the Arbitration Agreement thus accepted the application of provisions of the Convention that are found to be relevant to the present stage. There is no reference in the Arbitration Agreement to the customary law of the sea, but many of the relevant elements of customary law are incorporated in the provisions of the Convention. 'Any other pertinent factors' is a broad concept, and doubtless includes various factors that are generally recognised as being relevant to the process of delimitation

such as proportionality, non-encroachment, the presence of islands, and any other factors that might affect the equities of the particular situation.

131. It is a generally accepted view, as is evidenced in both the writings of commentators and in the jurisprudence, that between coasts that are opposite to each other the median or equidistance line normally provides an equitable boundary in accordance with the requirements of the Convention, and in particular those of its Articles 74 and 83 which respectively provide for the equitable delimitation of the EEZ and of the continental shelf between States with opposite or adjacent coasts. Indeed both Parties to the present case have claimed a boundary constructed on the equidistance method, although based on different points of departure and resulting in very different lines.

132. The Tribunal has decided, after careful consideration of all the cogent and skilful arguments put before them by both Parties, that the international boundary shall be a single all-purpose boundary which is a median line and that it should, as far as practicable, be a median line between the opposite mainland coastlines. This solution is not only in accord with practice and precedent in the like situations but is also one that is already familiar to both Parties. . . . In the present stage the Tribunal has to determine a boundary not merely for the purposes of petroleum concessions and agreements, but a single international boundary for all purposes. For such a boundary the presence of islands requires careful consideration of their possible effect upon the boundary line; and this is done in the explanation which follows. Even so it will be found that the final solution is that the international maritime boundary line remains for the greater part a median line between the mainland coasts of the Parties.

134. First, it is necessary to deal with a complication that arises in the present case concerning this general rule of measuring from the low-water line. . . .

135. In this matter the Tribunal prefers the Eritrean argument that the use of the low-water line is laid down by a general international rule in the Convention's Article 5, and that both Parties have agreed that the Tribunal is to take into account the provisions of the Convention in deciding the present case. The median line boundary will, therefore, be measured from the low-water line, shown on the officially recognised charts for both Eritrea and Yemen, in accordance with the provision in Article 5 of the Convention. . . .

136. There is also a problem relating to both the northern and the southern extremities of the international boundary line. The Tribunal has the competence and the authority according to the Arbitration Agreement to decide the maritime boundary between the two Parties. But it has neither competence nor authority to decide on any of the boundaries between either of the two Parties and neighbouring States. It will therefore be necessary to terminate either end of the boundary line in such a way as to avoid trespassing upon an area where other claims might fall to be considered.

M. Evans, 'Delimitation and the Common Maritime Boundary'
(1994) 64 BYBIL 283

II. The EEZ and the continental shelf – one regime or two?

There are a variety of opinions as to the nature of the relationship between the zones. It is not the intention here to examine the cogency of the various options, or to decide between them. Rather, a number of them will simply be identified. Nor is this an exhaustive adumbration. As has already been intimated, there is a spectrum, and the positions that are outlined below seem to represent the chief points upon it. . . .

1. *Absorption*

The first possibility is that the acceptance of the EEZ into customary international law has had the effect of eclipsing the continental shelf to the extent that there is, in reality, only one zone, that being the EEZ. . . . The 1982 Convention includes in Article 56, which sets out the rights, jurisdiction and duties of the coastal State in the EEZ, the proviso that 'The rights set out in this article with respect to the sea-bed and subsoil shall be exercised in accordance with Part VI'. The better view is that this assures the primacy of the shelf regime over the EEZ as regards rights to the sea-bed and subsoil. No matter what its ambit, however, it is clear that it provides no support for the view that the continental shelf has been 'absorbed' by the EEZ, and such a view would now appear to be untenable.

There is little by way of State practice to support the 'absorption' theory. . . .

A more significant reason for not attributing much weight to these scraps of support is that it is unnecessary to declare a continental shelf in order to exercise sovereign rights over it. . . .

2. *Assimilation*

Assimilation is the process by which the two zones merge with each other so as to take on the character of an entirely novel zone which is capable of definition in terms of either component, and will often be expressed as being 'the EEZ' or 'the continental shelf' but which has, in fact, acquired its own *sui generis* nature. Such an outcome would, in some respects, mirror the actual development of the EEZ, which itself 'grew out of' the pre-existing zones (that is, the continental shelf and exclusive fishing zone) and took on a life of its own. In short, the two regimes would become one.

It must be said that there is, on the face of it, little evidence of such an assimilation. It is possible to argue that the practice of States in declaring 'maritime zones' without specifying whether these are the EEZ and/or the continental shelf (plus exclusive fishing zone, if jurisdiction over the water column is also included) could stand as evidence for such a trend. State practice of this nature is, however, meagre and difficult to evaluate. The chief problem, once again, is that since rights over the continental shelf exist *ipso facto* and *ab initio* it is unnecessary to make a specific claim to the continental shelf in order to exercise jurisdiction over it. The mere fact that a State chooses not to mention the continental shelf in legislation establishing a maritime zone provides no basis upon which to conclude that it is turning its back on the regime. . . .

3. *Parallelism*

The essence of parallelism is that although the continental shelf and the EEZ remain separate regimes, they should be construed as existing in harmony with each other. Moreover, when possible, they should be developed in a fashion that moves them closer together, in order to facilitate an ultimate unity between them. The name with which this theory is enextricably linked is that of Judge Shigeru Oda. He has expounded this theory in separate and dissenting opinions of the ICJ and in his writings, and it has been taken up by other academic writers.

Parallelism has two chief planks. First, that since the legal extent of the continental shelf, now enshrined in Article 76(1) the 1982 Convention, grew up alongside the development of the EEZ it must be interpreted in the light of it. This means that the distance principle has replaced natural prolongation as the dominant factor in title to areas of continental shelf situated within 200 miles of the coast. Judge Oda advanced this thesis in the *Tunisia/Libya* case, and it was ultimately accepted by the ICJ in the *Libya/Malta* case, although the Court allowed natural prolongation a residual role even within this distance. The second plank is that both regimes grant coastal States similar sovereign rights over the sea-bed and subsoil. This is a virtually unassailable proposition.

Having established this 'parallelism' within the common 200-mile area, a 'parallelism' is then identified between the sea-bed and subsoil jurisdiction within the 200-mile area and those areas that lie beyond it, but within the continental margin. . . .

4. *Separatism*

The final possible form of relationship is that of no formal relationship at all. That is to say, international law accepts that there are two separate regimes which can co-exist, and both can provide title to the same jurisdictional rights. States would be free to choose which regime to utilize. Whilst there is no inherent conflict between the regimes, there is neither reason for seeking, nor pressure towards, some form of doctrinal accommodation or amalgamation.

Separatism, however, can itself take on several forms. Most importantly, it can recognize that there is a possibility that the two regimes may come into conflict and provide for the inherent superiority of one of them should this occur. As has already been seen, this is the better view of the meaning of Article 56(3) of the 1982 Convention.

All of the State practice cited above in refutation of absorption stands evidence to the existence of separate regimes. Not all, however, can fairly be said to reflect the interpretation of the Convention that ascribes primacy to the shelf regime. Most is simply neutral on the question. The legislation of several States does, however, support the argument that the continental shelf takes priority over the EEZ by placing the sea-bed and subsoil areas that fall within the EEZ under the governance of pre-exiting continental shelf legislation. A clear example of this approach was afforded by the USSR when it expressly provided that

> The rights and jurisdictions set out in this article with respect to the sea-bed of the eco-nomic zone and its subsoil shall be exercised in accordance with the legislation of the USSR concerning the continental shelf of the USSR. . . .

There is little direct evidence to support the alternative proposition that the EEZ takes primacy over the continental shelf. The reason for this is that such a view is so close to 'absorption' as to be all but indistinguishable from it. Moreover, there is no practical purpose in holding such a view. The argument that the continental shelf regime takes precedence over that of the EEZ where the two come into conflict is based upon the juridicial differences between them – the *ipso facto* and *ab initio* nature of continental shelf rights, compared to the contingent, albeit exclusive, right to the EEZ. The arguments that would place the EEZ in a hierarchically superior position have no such underpinning and are based on the same views as support absorption, that is, a prudential assessment that it is the most appropriate arrangement to adopt. There would seem to be no reason for not going that one stage further and adopting the more extreme theory.

This conclusion effectively takes us full circle and concludes this presentation of alternative views.

NOTES:

1. The above cases, together with those in the section on the continental shelf, illustrate the debate between various scholars and judges as to the proper approach to maritime delimita-tion. There is an essential difference between those who favour relatively fixed criteria such as 'equidistance' or 'natural prolongation' and those who believe that relatively open-ended general equitable principles possibly combined with a presumptive distance criterion (i.e. 200 miles from the coast) are required to meet the unique nature of each maritime zone.

2. It is clear from the recent case law that there is a trend towards delimitation of single mari-time boundaries between opposite and adjacent states: one boundary for all the overlapping zones of influence. Whatever the legal difficulties with such an approach under the strict terms of the 1982 Convention, it is probable that most States would regard this as a pragmatic and workable solution. There are enough jurisdictional conflicts within the law of the sea without adding to them by preferring different boundary lines for different types of maritime zone. In time – or even possibly at this time – customary international law will change to reflect this realism.

3. The majority judgment in *Qatar* v *Bahrain* adopts as a rule of customary international law the equidistance/special circumstances rule. It also notes that 'low-tide elevations' may be used as a baseline for measuring the equidistance line and that this represents customary law. However, the majority then note that if the low tide elevations were used in this case to help draw the median line, they would produce a disproportionate (and hence inequitable) effect. So, the 'special circumstances' in this case that cause the 'normal' median line to be varied are the very low tide elevations that customary law (and the 1982 Convention) say may be used. In effect, the low tide elevations are ignored as a basis for drawing the median line. Judge Oda

takes exception to the underlying reasoning of the majority judgment. He disagrees that the southern sector should be delimited as if it were territorial sea because at the time the dispute was submitted to the ICJ the relevant area was outside either States' claims to territorial jurisdiction. He further challenges the Court's application of the rules on territorial sea delimitation, even assuming they are relevant.

4. In *Qatar v Bahrain*, the ICJ make no reference to the award in *Yemen v Eritrea*. In fact, with respect to maritime delimitation, both judgments generally apply a 'land dominates the sea' approach. However, there are real differences in each tribunals' application of the rules concerning acquisition of land territory, especially islands. These issues are explored in Chapter 7, but given that maritime delimitation was parasitic on the resolution of the land territorial questions, it is unfortunate that these two tribunals adopted such different approaches to the question of sovereignty over islands when the broad sweep of the issues were very similar.

SECTION 5: The high seas and related matters

The area of sea beyond national jurisdiction is known as the 'high seas'. For all practical purposes this means that the high seas commence from the outer edge of the territorial sea or the outer edge of the EEZ, should one exist. Waters that are not part of an EEZ but that are super-adjacent to a continental shelf that extends beyond 200 miles from the coast are also high seas, as are those beyond the territorial sea if no EEZ has been claimed. The 'freedom of the seas' has legal as well as political connotations, and it has been one of the cornerstones of maritime law ever since the rejection of the doctrine of 'closed seas' in the seventeenth century. Many jurists would argue that the freedom of the seas has attained the status of *jus cogens*.

Law of the Sea Convention 1982

Article 86 Application of the provisions of this part
The provisions of this Part apply to all parts of the sea that are not included in the exclusive economic zone, in the territorial sea or in the internal waters of a State, or in the archipelagic waters of an archipelagic State. This article does not entail any abridgement of the freedoms enjoyed by all States in the exclusive economic zone in accordance with article 58.

Article 87 Freedom of the high seas
1. The high seas are open to all States, whether coastal or land-locked. Freedom of the high seas is exercised under the conditions laid down by this Convention and by other rules of international law. It comprises, *inter alia*, both for coastal and land-locked States:

(a) freedom of navigation;
(b) freedom of overflight;
(c) freedom to lay submarine cables and pipelines, subject to Part VI;
(d) freedom to construct artificial islands and other installations permitted under international law, subject to Part VI;

(e) freedom of fishing, subject to the conditions laid down in section 2;

(f) freedom of scientific research, subject to Parts VI and XIII.

2. These freedoms shall be exercised by all States with due regard for the interests of other States in their exercise of the freedom of the high seas, and also with due regard for the rights under this Convention with respect to activities in the Area.

Article 88 Reservation of the high seas for peaceful purposes

The high seas shall be reserved for peaceful purposes.

Article 89 Invalidity of claims of sovereignty over the high seas

No State may validly purport to subject any part of the high seas to its sovereignty.

Article 90 Right of navigation

Every State, whether coastal or land-locked, has the right to sail ships flying its flag on the high seas.

Article 99 Prohibition of the transport of slaves

Every State shall take effective measures to prevent and punish the transport of slaves in ships authorized to fly its flag and to prevent the unlawful use of its flag for that purpose. Any slave taking refuge on board any ship, whatever its flag, shall *ipso facto* be free.

Article 100 Duty to co-operate in the repression of piracy

All States shall co-operate to the fullest possible extent in the repression of piracy on the high seas or in any other place outside the jurisdiction of any State.

Article 101 Definition of piracy

Piracy consists of any of the following acts:

(a) any illegal acts of violence or detention, or any act of depredation, committed for private ends by the crew or the passengers of a private ship or a private aircraft, and directed:

  (i) on the high seas, against another ship or aircraft, or against persons or property on board such ship or aircraft;

  (ii) against a ship, aircraft, persons or property in a place outside the jurisdiction of any State;

(b) any act of voluntary participation in the operation of a ship or of an aircraft with knowledge of facts making it a pirate ship or aircraft;

(c) any act of inciting or of intentionally facilitating an act described in subparagraph (a) or (b).

Article 108 Illicit traffic in narcotic drugs or psychotropic substances

1. All States shall co-operate in the suppression of illicit traffic in narcotic drugs and psychotropic substances engaged in by ships on the high seas contrary to international conventions.

Article 110 Right of visit

1. Except where acts of interference derive from powers conferred by treaty, a warship which encounters on the high seas a foreign ship, other than a ship entitled to complete immunity in accordance with articles 95 and 96, is not justified in boarding it unless there is reasonable ground for suspecting that:

(a) the ship is engaged in piracy;

(b) the ship is engaged in the slave trade;

(c) the ship is engaged in authorized broadcasting and the flag State of the warship has jurisdiction under article 109;

(d) the ship is without nationality; or

(e) though flying a foreign flag or refusing to show its flag, the ship is, in reality, of the same nationality as the warship.

Article 111 Right of hot pursuit

1. The hot pursuit of a foreign ship may be undertaken when the competent authorities of the coastal State have good reason to believe that the ship has violated the laws and regulations of that State. Such pursuit must be commenced when the foreign ship or one of its boats is within the internal waters, the archipelagic waters, the territorial sea or the contiguous zone of the pursuing State, and may only be continued outside the territorial sea or the contiguous zone if the pursuit has not been interrupted. It is not necessary that, at the time when the foreign ship within the territorial sea or the contiguous zone receives the order to stop, the ship giving the order should likewise be within the territorial sea or the contiguous zone. If the foreign ship is within a contiguous zone, as defined in article 33, the pursuit may only be undertaken if there has been a violation of the rights for the protection of which the zone was established.

2. The right of hot pursuit shall apply *mutatis mutandis* to violations in the exclusive economic zone or on the continental shelf, including safety zones around continental shelf installations, of the laws and regulations of the coastal State applicable in accordance with this Convention to the exclusive economic zone or the continental shelf, including such safety zones.

3. The right of hot pursuit ceases as soon as the ship pursued enters the territorial sea of its own State or of a third State.

4. Hot pursuit is not deemed to have begun unless the pursuing ship has satisfied itself by such practicable means as may be available that the ship pursued or one of its boats or other craft working as a team and using the ship pursued as a mother ship is within the limits of the territorial sea, or, as the case may be, within the contiguous zone or the exclusive economic zone or above the continental shelf. The pursuit may only be commenced after a visual or auditory signal to stop has been given at a distance which enables it to be seen or heard by the foreign ship.

5. The right of hot pursuit may be exercised only by warships or military aircraft, or other ships or aircraft clearly marked and identifiable as being on government service and authorized to that effect.

6. Where hot pursuit is effected by an aircraft:

(a) the provisions of paragraphs 1 to 4 shall apply *mutatis mutandis*;

(b) the aircraft giving the order to stop must itself actively pursue the ship until a ship or another aircraft of the coastal State, summoned by the aircraft, arrives to take over the pursuit, unless the aircraft is itself able to arrest the ship. It does not suffice to justify an arrest outside the territorial sea that the ship was merely sighted by the aircraft as an offender or suspected offender, if it was not both ordered to stop and pursued by the aircraft itself or other aircraft or ships which continue the pursuit without interruption.

Article 112 Right to lay submarine cables and pipelines

1. All States are entitled to lay submarine cables and pipelines on the bed of the high seas beyond the continental shelf.

Article 116 Right to fish on the high seas

All States have the right for their nationals to engage in fishing on the high seas subject to:

(a) their treaty obligations;

(b) the rights and duties as well as the interests of coastal States provided for, *inter alia*, in article 63, paragraph 2, and articles 64 to 67; and

(c) the provisions of this section.

Article 117 Duty of states to adopt with respect to their nationals measures for the conservation of the living resources of the high seas

All States have the duty to take, or to co-operate with other States in taking, such measures for their respective nationals as may be necessary for the conservation of the living resources of the high seas.

Article 121 Régime of Islands

1. An island is a naturally formed area of land, surrounded by water, which is above water at high tide.

2. Except as provided for in paragraph 3, the territorial sea, the contiguous zone, the exclusive economic zone and the continental shelf of an island are determined in accordance with the provisions of this Convention applicable to other land territory.

3. Rocks which cannot sustain human habitation or economic life of their own shall have no exclusive economic zone or continental shelf.

NOTES:

1. Although the 'high seas' are not open to acquisition by any State, the Geneva Convention on the High Seas 1958, the Geneva Convention on the Fishing and Conservation of Living Resources of the High Seas 1958, and the 1982 Convention contain fairly detailed rules about activities on, in or under the high seas. They also deal with matters such as the question of jurisdiction over vessels and structures (e.g., oil platforms), broadly speaking granting such jurisdiction to the 'flag State', except in cases of crimes against international law (such as piracy and slavery) where jurisdiction is universal. Had the Court been able to adjudicate on the merits in the *Fisheries Jurisdiction Case (Spain v Canada)* (below), States may well have been offered valuable guidance on the extent to which they may exercise limited jurisdiction over high seas areas for specific purposes, e.g., fisheries, either as a result of customary international law or of relevant treaty law. In regard to environmental impacts, see Chapter 12.

2. The development of maritime zones extending 200 miles seaward from the coast has necessarily led to a shrinking of waters legally classed as 'high seas'. The 1982 Convention contains certain compensatory provisions for maritime States, including the right of 'transit passage' through straits used for international navigation and the right of passage through archipelagic waters. The advent of mining in the deep sea bed (see below) and claims to a continental shelf beyond the 200-mile limit will not affect the legal status of the super-adjacent waters, although there will of necessity be some reduction in the scope of the freedoms of the seas contained in Art. 87 of the Convention.

3. In the *Fisheries Jurisdiction Case (Spain v Canada)* ICJ Rep 1998, Canada had seized a Spanish vessel fishing on the high seas some 245 miles from the Canadian coast, albeit within an area regulated by the Northwest Atlantic Fisheries Organization (NAFO). The ICJ decided that it lacked jurisdiction over the merits because a Canadian reservation excluded ICJ jurisdiction over 'disputes arising out of or concerning conservation and management measures taken by Canada with respect to vessels fishing in the NAFO Regulatory Area'. The issue was settled by Canada and Spain (and the EU) though with each side maintaining its view of the applicable law.

4. As seen in the *Qatar* and *Yemen* cases, the question of sovereignty over islands is intimately connected with the reach of a State's maritime jurisdiction. Not only can islands have their

own territorial sea, contiguous zone, shelf regime and EEZ, they are important in the delimitation of general maritime boundaries between opposite and adjacent States, especially
where islands lie close to the coast of more than one State. Qatar, Bahrain, Yemen and Eritrea
have settled just such a dispute, but for others States (e.g. Greece and Turkey in the Aegean
Sea), the unresolved status of islands is seriously hampering the full exploitation of the
resources of overlapping maritime zones.

5. In November 2001, the United Nations Educational, Scientific and Cultural Organisation
    (UNESCO) adopted a Convention on the Protection of Underwater Cultural Heritage (41
    ILM 40 (2002)). Although expressly preserving the rights and duties of States under the
    1982 Convention (and customary international law), the Convention proposes a substantial
    and comprehensive regime for the protection of underwater cultural heritage (so called
    'UCH') in all of the specific maritime zones: territorial sea, contiguous zone, continental
    shelf, EEZ and Deep Sea Area. The particular obligations with respect to UCH in these zones
    are not identical, as befitting the different rights and duties of States in each sphere.

SECTION 6: **The deep sea bed**

Part XI of the 1982 Convention proved to be the most controversial aspect of this
wide-ranging treaty. It soon became clear that a majority of developed States would
not ratify the Convention because they disagreed with the regime established to
regulate mining in the deep sea bed area. Although the non-participation of these
States would not prevent the Convention from entering into force, clearly the
Convention as a whole would have had a limited impact with so many maritime
(developed) States refusing to ratify it. Furthermore, the prospect of any deep sea
mining from which the international community would benefit, remained remote
while the only States financially and technologically able to undertake it were
preparing to act independently of the Convention. This led eventually to the
Agreement Relating to Part XI of the Convention 1994. This has been generally
accepted by the developed States and has now led to widespread ratification of the
Convention itself. In essence, this Agreement modifies the deep sea bed regime
found in Part XI and is to be regarded as an integral part of the Convention. No
State can become bound by the Agreement unless it first becomes bound by the
Convention.

There is no doubt that the deep sea bed area – the area 'beyond the limits of
national jurisdiction' – is not open to the sovereignty of any State. More importantly, the area is now accepted as 'the common heritage of mankind', meaning
that the benefits of any mining activity must be shared in some measure with all
members of the international community, not just among those willing and able
to undertake deep sea mining. The original Part XI of the Convention was an
attempt to give effect to the principle of common heritage. The dissenting
developed States did not object to the principle of common heritage, but rather to
the manner in which the unmodified Convention proposed to carry it out in
practice.

Law of the Sea Convention 1982

Article 1 Use of terms and scope

1. For the purposes of this Convention:
   (1) 'Area' means the sea-bed and ocean floor and subsoil thereof, beyond the limits of national jurisdiction;
   (2) 'Authority' means the International Sea-Bed Authority;
   (3) 'activities in the Area' means all activities of exploration for, and exploitation of, the resources of the Area. . . .

Part XI: Deep Sea Bed
Article 136 Common heritage of mankind

The Area and its resources are the common heritage of mankind.

Article 137 Legal status of the area and its resources

1. No State shall claim or exercise sovereignty or sovereign rights over any part of the Area or its resources, nor shall any State or natural or juridical person appropriate any part thereof. No such claim or exercise of sovereignty or sovereign rights, nor such appropriation shall be recognized.

2. All rights in the resources of the Area are vested in mankind as a whole, on whose behalf the Authority shall act. These resources are not subject to alienation. The minerals recovered from the Area, however, may only be alienated in accordance with this Part and the rules, regulations and procedures of the Authority.

3. No State or natural or juridical person shall claim, acquire or exercise rights with respect to the minerals recovered from the Area except in accordance with this Part. Otherwise, no such claim, acquisition or exercise of such rights shall be recognized.

Article 140 Benefit of mankind

1. Activities in the Area shall, as specifically provided for in this Part, be carried out for the benefit of mankind as a whole, irrespective of the geographical location of States, whether coastal or land-locked, and taking into particular consideration the interests and needs of developing States and of peoples who have not attained full independence or other self-governing status recognized by the United Nations in accordance with General Assembly resolution 1514 (XV) and other relevant General Assembly resolutions.

2. The Authority shall provide for the equitable sharing of financial and other economic benefits derived from activities in the Area through any appropriate mechanism, on a non-discriminatory basis, in accordance with article 160, paragraph 2(f)(i).

Article 141 Use of the area exclusively for peaceful purposes

The Area shall be open to use exclusively for peaceful purposes by all States, whether coastal or land-locked, without discrimination and without prejudice to the other provisions of this Part.

Article 144 Transfer of technology

1. The Authority shall take measures in accordance with this Convention:
   (a) to acquire technology and scientific knowledge relating to activities in the Area; and
   (b) to promote and encourage the transfer to developing States of such technology and scientific knowledge so that all States Parties benefit therefrom.

Ambassador Malone, Statement before the Subcommittee on Oceanography of the House of Representatives Committee on Merchant Marine and Fisheries, United States Congress, 28 April 1981
76 AJIL 9 (1981)

This extract summarises the objections to the *original* scheme of the Convention.

- The Draft Convention places under burdensome international regulation the development of all of the resources of the seabed and subsoil beyond the limits of national jurisdiction, representing approximately two-thirds of the earth's submerged lands. These resources include polymetallic nodules. They also include mineral deposits beneath the surface of the seabed about which nothing is known today, but which may be of very substantial economic importance in the future.
- The Draft Convention would establish a supranational mining company, called the Enterprise, which would benefit from significant discriminatory advantages relative to the companies of industrialized countries. Arguably, it could eventually monopolize production of seabed minerals. Moreover, the Draft Convention requires the US and other nations to fund the initial capitalization of the Enterprise, in proportion to their contributions to the UN.
- Through its transfer of technology provisions, the Draft Convention compels the sale of proprietary information and technology now largely in US hands. Under the Draft Convention, with certain restrictions, the Enterprise, through mandatory transfer, is guaranteed access on request to the seabed mining technology owned by private companies and also technology used by them but owned by others. The text further guarantees similar access to privately-owned technology by any developing country planning to go into seabed mining. We must also carefully consider how such provisions relate to security-related technology.
- The Draft Convention limits the annual production of manganese nodules from the deep seabed, as well as the amount which any one company can mine for the first twenty years of production. The stated purpose of these controls is to avoid damaging the economy of any country which produces the same commodities on land. In short, it attempts to insulate land-based producers from competition with seabed mining. In doing so, the draft treaty could discourage potential investors, thereby creating artificial scarcities. In allocating seabed production, the International Seabed Authority is granted substantial discretion to select among competing applicants. Such discretion could be used to deny contracts to qualified American companies.
- The Draft Convention creates a one-nation, one-vote international organization which is governed by an Assembly and a 36-member Executive Council. In the Council, the Soviet Union and its allies have three guaranteed seats, but the US must compete with its allies for any representation. The Assembly is characterized as the 'supreme' organ and the specific policy decisions of the Council must conform to the general policies of the Assembly.
- The Draft Convention provides that, after fifteen years of production, the provisions of the treaty will be reviewed to determine whether it has fulfilled overriding policy considerations, such as protection of land-based producers, promotion of Enterprise operations and equitable distribution of mining rights. If two-thirds of the States Parties to the treaty wish to amend provisions concerning the system of exploitation, they may do so after five years of negotiation and after ratification by two-thirds of the States Parties. If the US were to disagree with duly ratified changes, it would be bound by them nevertheless, unless it exercised its option to denounce the entire treaty.
- The Draft Convention imposes revenue-sharing obligations on seabed mining corporations which would significantly increase the costs of seabed mining.
- The Draft Convention imposes an international revenue-sharing obligation on the production of hydrocarbons from the continental shelf beyond the 200-mile limit. Developing countries that are net-importers of hydrocarbons are exempt from the obligation.

- The Draft Convention contains provisions concerning liberation movements, like the PLO, and their eligibility to obtain a share of the revenues of the Seabed Authority.

D. Anderson, 'Further Efforts to Ensure Universal Participation in the United Nations Convention on The Law of the Sea'
(1994) 43 ICLQ 886

At the outset of the consultations in July 1990 some nine specific topics (later reduced to eight, with the deferment of the environment) had been indentified as obstacles to ratification of the Convention by the industrialised States. They were: (1) costs to State parties; (2) the Enterprise; (3) decision-making; (4) the review conference; (5) transfer of technology; (6) production limitation; (7) compensation fund; (8) financial terms of contracts.

D. The terms for entry into force of the new agreement
In order to meet the concerns of States which had already ratified the Convention, the provisions in the proposed agreement about its entry into force provided a special option for such States. They could establish their consent to be bound by the agreement by means of a system of tacit consent. At a later stage in the consultations, the arrangement required a prior signature of the agreement in the case of States which had ratified the Convention. Signature was perceived to give added certainty to the process of establishing consent. These arrangements were set out in Article 5 of the agreement.

In order to meet the concerns of developing countries, both ratifiers and non-ratifiers alike, that their concessions might still fail to attract ratifications from major countries which had shown interest in deep seabed mining, a special requirement was included in Article 6 about entry into force. Entry into force of the agreement requires 40 ratifications, etc., of which at least seven must be States to which paragraph 1(a) of Resolution II of the Third UN Conference on the Law of the Sea applies (namely Belgium, Canada, France, Germany, Italy, Japan, the Netherlands, Russia, the United Kingdom and the United States, plus India and China: South Korea joined this group in August 1994). Five of the seven must be developed States. Such States would contribute a significant amount to the cost of the ISA, especially if they included the United States, Japan, Germany, France and the United Kingdom. . . .

F. Legal Status of the Agreement
The agreement provides that the annex thereto is an integral part of the agreement. The fundamental obligation on States parties is to implement Part XI in accordance with the terms of the agreement. In the event of any inconsistency between its terms and those of Part XI, the provisions of the agreement are to prevail and the two are to be interpreted and applied together as a single instrument. Provision is made for States to express their consent to be bound by the agreement by the ususal methods of signature not subject to ratification, or signature subject to ratification followed by ratification, or signature and recourse to the tacit procedure described above, as well as by means of accession. . . .

The agreement is clearly a treaty, governed by the Vienna Convention on the Law of Treaties. Although it does not expressly amend any provisions of Part XI, there is no doubt that the agreement will result in the terms of Part XI being implemented, interpreted and applied in a new way, as described in the annex. . . .

G. The Adoption of the Resolution and Signature of the Agreement
On July 27 [1994], the resumed 48th session of the General Assembly took up again Agenda item 36, Law of the Sea. . . . The Resolution [incorporating the Agreement] was adopted without change by a vote of 121 to 0, with 7 abstentions, on 28 July (G.A. Res. 48/263). On 29 July, the Agreement was opened for signature for one year at UN Headquarters in New York. The Agreement was signed by 41 States at a ceremony in the General Assembly Hall. In the following days 8 further signatures were affixed. . . .

H. Concluding Remarks

The origins of the Secretary-General's consultations can be traced back to the statement made by the Chairman of the Group of 77 at the end of the meeting of the Prepatatory Commission in the summer of 1989. This led directly to the opening of the consultations during 1990, amid some trepidation from all sides. The consultations started out with a specific agenda of eight problems perceived by developed countries and although other suggestions about the best approach were made from several sources, in the end it was this approach based on following the specific agenda and finding solutions to the eight problems which found expression in the draft agreement and its annex. Implicit in this approach was acceptance of both the principle of the common heritage of mankind, as it would be articulated, and a UN-administered system of mining. Gradually, the indus-trialised countries were able to demonstrate their wish to negotiate seriously, especially following the election of the Clinton administration. The member States of the European Union, together with the Union itself, were staunch supporters of the process. The deposit of the 60th ratification in November 1993 was greeted with different reactions from ratifiers and non-ratifiers, but in the event it turned out to be helpful in that it provided all concerned with a target date, November 1994, for finishing the consultations and drawing up the necessary new arrangements. Although hard bargain-ing continued until the very end of the consultations, they took place in a constructive, non-confrontational atmosphere between the different groups, notably between the Group of 77 and the industrialised countries. The new Agreement takes account of the political and economic changes, including a growing reliance on market principles and similar market-orientated approaches to economic issues, which have taken place since 1982. As a result, there now exist much improved prospects for universal participation in the UN Convention on the Law of the Sea, together with the Agreement on the Implementation of Part XI: 1994 could be a milestone towards the attainment of that goal.

Agreement Relating to the Implementation of Part XI of the United Nations Convention on the Law of the Sea General Assembly Resolution and Annex, 17 August 1994
33 ILM 1099 (1994)

Article 1 Implementation of Part XI
1. The States Parties to this Agreement undertake to implement Part XI in accordance with this Agreement.
2. The Annex forms an integral part of this Agreement.

Article 2 Relationship between this Agreement and Part XI
1. The provisions of this Agreement and Part XI shall be interpreted and applied together as a single instrument. In the event of any inconsistency between this Agreement and Part XI, the provisions of this Agreement shall prevail.
2. Articles 309 to 319 of the Convention shall apply to this Agreement as they apply to the Convention.

Article 4 Consent to be bound
1. After the adoption of this Agreement, any instrument of ratification or formal confirm-ation of or accession to the Convention shall also represent consent to be bound by this Agreement.
2. No state or entity may establish its consent to be bound by this Agreement unless it has previously established or establishes at the same time its consent to be bound by the Convention. . . .

Article 5   Simplified procedure

1. A state or entity which has deposited before the date of the adoption of this Agreement an instrument of ratification or formal confirmation of or accession to the Convention and which has signed this Agreement in accordance with article 4, paragraph 3(c), shall be considered to have established its consent to be bound by this Agreement 12 months after the date of its adoption, unless that State or entity notifies the depositary in writing before that date that it is not availing itself of the simplifed procedure set out in this article.

Annex

SECTION 1.   COSTS TO STATES PARTIES AND INSTITUTIONAL ARRANGEMENTS

1. The powers and functions of the Authority shall be those expressly conferred upon it by the Convention. The Authority shall have such incidental powers, consistent with the Convention, as are implicit in, and necessary for, the exercise of those powers and function with respect to activities in the Area.

SECTION 2.   THE ENTERPRISE

1. The Secretariat of the Authority shall perform the functions of the Enterprise until it begins to operate independently of the Secretariat. . . .

2. The Enterprise shall conduct its initial deep seabed mining operations through joint ventures. Upon the approval of a plan of work for exploitation for an entity other than the Enterprise, or upon receipt by the Council of an application for joint-venture operation with the Enterprise, the Council shall take up the issue of the functioning of the Enterprise independently of the Secretariat of the Authority. If joint-venture operations with the Enterprise accord with sound commercial principles, the Council shall issue a directive pursuant to article 170, paragraph 2, of the Convention providing for such independent functioning.

3. The obligation of States Parties to fund one mine site of the Enterprise as provided for in Annex IV, article 11, paragraph 3, of the Convention shall not apply and States Parties shall be under no obligation to finance any of the operations in any mine site of the Enterprise or under its joint-venture arrangements.

6. Article 170, paragraph 4, Annex IV and other provisions of the Convention relating to the Enterprise shall be interpreted and applied in accordance with this section.

SECTION 3.   DECISION-MAKING

1. The general policies of the Authority shall be established by the Assembly in collaboration with the Council.

2. As a general rule, decision-making in the organs of the Authority should be by consensus.

3. If all efforts to reach a decision by consensus have been exhausted, decision by voting in the Assembly on questions of procedure shall be taken by a majority of members present and voting, and decisions on questions of substance shall be taken by a two-thirds majority of members present and voting, as provided for in article 159, paragraph 8, of the Convention.

SECTION 5.   TRANSFER OF TECHNOLOGY

1. In addition to the provisions of article 144 of the Convention, transfer of technology for the purpose of Part XI shall be governed by the following principles:

    (a) The Enterprise, and developing States wishing to obtain deep seabed mining technology, shall seek to obtain such technology in fair and reasonable commercial terms and conditions on the open market, or through joint-venture arrangements;

    (b) If the Enterprise or developing States are unable to obtain deep seabed mining technology, the Authority may request all or any of the contractors and their respective sponsoring State or States to cooperate with it in facilitating the acquisition of deep seabed mining technology by the Enterprise or its joint venture, or by a developing State or States seeking to acquire such technology on fair and reasonable commercial terms and conditions, consistent with the effective protection of intellectual property rights. . . .

2. The provisions of Annex III, article 5, of the Convention shall not apply.

'Oceans Policy and the Law of the Sea Convention' Memorandum on US Policy, Transmitted with US Secretary of State Warren Christopher's Letter to Chairman of the Senate Committee on Foreign Relations Announcing US Signature of the 1982 Convention and 1994 Agreement
88 AJIL 733 (1994)

[The 1994 Agreement] sets forth economic and commercial principles that are consistent with our free market philosophy and which form the basis for developing rules and regulations establishing a management regime when interest in commercial mining emerges.

The Agreement retains the institutional outlines of Part XI but scales back the structure and links the activation and operation of institutions to the actual development of concrete interest in seabed mining. Of fundamental importance, it alters Part XI to provide the United States, and other states with major economic interests, a voice in decisionmaking commensurate with those interests. The United States, acting alone, can block decision[s] on issues of major financial or budgetary significance in a Finance Committee. Acting alone, the United States can block decisions to distribute revenues from mining (e.g., to liberation movements) in the executive Council. Other substantive decisions can be blocked in the Council by the United States and two of our allies acting in concert.

The mandatory technology transfer provisions are replaced by provisions for the promotion of technology transfer through cooperative arrangements (e.g., joint ventures) and through procurement on the open market. Importantly, such initiatives are to be based on 'fair and reasonable commercial terms and conditions, including effective protection of intellectual property rights.' Although the prospective operating arm (the Enterprise) is retained, the executive Council must decide whether and when it is to become operational. Moreover, the Agreement subjects the Enterprise to the same obligations as other miners and removes the obligation of developed [s]tates to finance it.

The Agreement limits assistance to land-based producers of minerals to adjustment assistance financed out of a portion of royalties from future seabed mining. It also replaces the production control regime of Part XI by the application of GATT principles on subsidization. The Agreement further replaces the detailed and burdensome financial obligations imposed on miners by a future system for recovering economic rents based on systems applicable to land-based mining and provides that it be designed to avoid competitive incentives or disincentives for seabed mining. The Agreement provides for grandfathering in the mining consortia licensed under US law on the basis of terms and conditions 'similar to and no less favourable than' those granted to French, Japanese, Russian, Indian and Chinese companies whose mine site claims have already been registered by the Law of the Sea Preparatory Committee. Finally, substantial financial obligations at the exploration stage are eliminated.

In short, the Agreement achieves a restructuring of Part XI of the Convention which is consistent with our economic principles as well as our need to ensure adequate United States influence over decisions made by the institutions of the regime. In doing so, it achieves the fundamental United States objective of guaranteed United States access to deep seabed resources on the basis of reasonable terms and conditions.

NOTES:

1. The Articles of the 1982 Convention extracted above give the general scheme of the deep sea bed regime. The detailed matters to which developed States objected are generally found in the original Annexes to the Convention and it is largely these that have been modified by the 1994 Agreement. The precise details of the modifications are quite complicated, although a general idea can be obtained from the above extracts. Particular attention should be paid to the writings of David Anderson, who was the chief UK representative throughout the process, who was a member of the 'boat group' whose work led directly to the 1994 Agreement, and is now a judge of the International Tribunal for the Law of the Sea. There is no doubt that the conclusion of the Agreement and the subsequent widespread participation in the Convention is a major achievement of the United Nations.

2. Although the United States signed the 1994 Agreement, it is still not a party to the 1982 Convention or the Agreement. It is thus not legally bound by either treaty and had to vacate its provisional membership of the Seabed Authority on 16 November 1998.

SECTION 7: Peaceful settlement of disputes

Part XV of the 1982 Convention requires States to settle compulsorily peacefully any disputes concerning the Convention. Failing a bilateral settlement, Art. 286 provides that any dispute be submitted for compulsory settlement to one of the tribunals having jurisdiction. These include the International Tribunal for the Law of the Sea (ITLOS), established by the Convention itself, the ICJ, and an arbitral or special arbitral tribunal constituted under the Convention. Peaceful settlement is thus compulsory.

UN Division for Ocean Affairs and the Law of the Sea
Briefing Note: 17 February 1999

International Tribunal for the Law of the Sea
The International Tribunal for the Law of the Sea is the central forum established by the *United Nations Convention on the Law of the Sea* for the peaceful settlement of disputes. Its seat is at the Free and Hanseatic City of Hamburg, Germany. The Tribunal may sit and exercise its functions elsewhere whenever it considers this desirable.

Jurisdiction
The jurisdiction of the Tribunal comprises all disputes and all applications submitted to it in accordance with the *United Nations Convention on the Law of the Sea* and all matters specifically provided for in any other agreement which confers jurisdiction on the Tribunal.

The Tribunal has exclusive jurisdiction, through its Seabed Disputes Chamber, with respect to disputes relating to activities in the international seabed Area. These matters include disputes between States Parties concerning the interpretation or application of the provisions of the Convention, along with those of the *Agreement relating to the Implementation of the Part XI of the Convention*, concerning the deep seabed Area; and disputes between States Parties or a contractor and the International Seabed Authority.

The Tribunal, through its Seabed Disputes Chamber, has jurisdiction to provide advisory opinions at the request of the Assembly or the Council of the International Seabed Authority on legal questions arising within the scope of their activities.

The Tribunal has special jurisdiction in matters calling for provisional measures. Failing agreement between parties to a dispute within two weeks of the request by either party for provisional measures, the Tribunal, or with respect to activities in the Area, the Seabed Disputes Chamber, may prescribe, modify or revoke provisional measures.

Where the authorities of a States Party have detained a vessel flying the flag of another State Party and it is alleged that the detaining State has not complied with the provisions of the Convention for the prompt release of the vessel or its crew upon the posting of a reasonable bond or other financial security, the question of release from detention may be submitted to the Tribunal, failing agreement between the Parties within ten days from the time of detention.

Composition

The Tribunal is composed of 21 independent members elected by States Parties to the Convention on the Law of the Sea from among persons with recognized competence in the field of the law of the sea and representing the principal legal systems of the world. The first election was held in August 1996. . . .

In hearing a dispute, all available members of the Tribunal may sit, although a quorum of 11 members is required to constitute the Tribunal. All disputes and applications submitted to the Tribunal shall be heard and determined by it, unless the dispute is to be submitted to the Seabed Disputes Chamber or the parties request that it be submitted to a special chamber.

The Seabed Disputes Chamber is to be composed of 11 members selected by a majority of the members of the Tribunal from among them. . . . A quorum of seven members is required to constitute the Chamber.

In addition to the Seabed Disputes Chamber, the Tribunal will form annually a chamber composed of five of its members which may hear and determine disputes by summary procedure. The Tribunal will also form special chambers for dealing with a particular dispute submitted to it if the parties so request. The composition of those chambers will be determined by the Tribunal with the approval of the parties. Finally, the Tribunal may form such other chambers, composed of three or more its members, as it considers necessary for dealing with particular categories of disputes. . . .

Applicable Law

The Tribunal will apply the provisions of the *United Nations Convention on the Law of the Sea* and other rules of international law not incompatible with the Convention in deciding disputes submitted to it. It does, however, have to the power to decide a case *ex aequo et bono*, if the parties so agree.

Procedure

Disputes are to be submitted to the Tribunal, depending on the case, either by notification of a special agreement, or by written application, addressed to the Registrar.

The Tribunal and its Seabed Disputes Chamber have the power to prescribe provisional measures. If the Tribunal is not in session or a sufficient number of its members is not available to constitute a quorum, the provisional measures can be prescribed by the chamber of summary procedure. Such measures are subject to review and revision by the Tribunal. . . .

States Parties not party to a dispute but which consider that they have an interest of a legal nature which may be affected by the decision in any dispute may submit a request to the Tribunal to be permitted to intervene. Whenever the interpretation or application of the Convention or any other agreement is in question, the Registrar will notify all States Parties to the Convention or to such agreements. Those parties have the right to intervene in the proceedings.

Decisions of the Tribunal are final and shall be complied with by all the parties to the dispute. However, decisions will not have a binding force except between the parties in respect of the particular dispute.

NOTE:

The International Tribunal for the Law of the Sea (ITLOS) heard its first case in 1997, being an application by St Vincent and the Grenadines for the 'prompt release' of a vessel seized by Guinea for alleged violations of Guinean customs law: see (1999) 49 ICLQ 187. ITLOS has to date dealt with 10 applications: five concerning prompt release of vessels seized by the coastal state; three concerning provisional measures pending determination of the substantive issue and two other matters. The most recent case (*The MOX Plant Case*) was brought by Ireland against the United Kingdom concerning the latter's operation of a nuclear re-processing plant and its effects on Ireland's rights as guaranteed by the 1982 Convention.

11

....

State Responsibility

Introductory note

The international legal system offers considerable benefits to a State, from conferring recognition of its sovereignty to protecting its territorial integrity. Accordingly, as part of a State's consent to the operation of that system, it must accept corresponding legal obligations. Primarily, it must accept responsibility for its actions that have an effect on other international legal persons and the international community. As stated by Judge Huber in the *Spanish Zone of Morocco Claims Case* (1925) 2 RIAA 615: 'responsibility is the necessary corollary of a right. All rights of an international character involve international responsibility.'

State responsibility arises from the violation by a State (or other competent international legal person) of an international obligation. That obligation can be one of customary international law or a treaty obligation. The violation must be due to conduct attributable to a State. The enforcement of this responsibility is generally undertaken by a State either on its own behalf or on behalf of its injured nationals. However, as each State (or other legal person) may decide for itself whether to enforce an apparent violation of an international obligation by another State, it is possible that no legal action will be taken against a State that has clearly violated international law. Additionally, as States themselves largely determine the scope of customary international law, they can allow certain exceptions to international obligations, and so determine for themselves when State responsibility exists.

The law of State responsibility can be divided conveniently into two parts, although it must be emphasised that this is for the purposes of exposition only. First, issues of general concern, comprising the nature of State responsibility, attribution (imputability) of internationally unlawful acts to the State, the mechanics of enforcement (including nationality of claims, exhaustion of local remedies), and defences to responsibility. Such matters are relevant irrespective of the type of international obligation said to have been violated and apply as much to an alleged violation of a treaty as to alleged mistreatment of a national abroad contrary to customary international law. Second, there is a subset of substantive rules concerning international responsibility for the mistreatment of aliens (i.e. non-nationals). These rules indicate both when a State will be responsible for such mistreatment and the consequences of such responsibility. In particular, international law is concerned with the expropriation of assets owned by foreign nationals and the issue of whether this is unlawful under international law.

SECTION 1: **The nature of State responsibility**

Factory at Chorzów (*Claim for Indemnity*) *Case* (*Germany* v *Poland*) (*Merits*)
PCIJ Ser A (1928) No 17, Permanent Court of International Justice

[T]he Court observes that it is a principle of international law, and even a general conception of law, that any breach of an engagement involves an obligation to make reparation . . . reparation is the indispensable complement of a failure to apply a convention, and there is no necessity for this to be stated in the convention itself.

International Law Commission, Articles on Responsibility of States for Internationally Wrongful Acts
August 2001, Special Rapporteur James Crawford

The International Law Commission (ILC) has been considering the general topic of state responsibility for a number of years. The ILC in August 2001 adopted a set of Articles and they stand as a code of the general principles of state responsibility. They have been commented on extensively by States and they command widespread, though not universal support. As ever, some parts of them remain controversial (e.g. Articles 40 and 41) and some aspects of the (huge) topic of responsibility are still to be completed (e.g. liability for injury to aliens). Nevertheless, the Articles may form the basis of an international treaty, although the content of some (but certainly not all) already reflects customary international law.

Article 1 Responsibility of a state for its internationally wrongful acts
Every internationally wrongful act of a State entails the international responsibility of that State.

Article 2 Elements of an internationally wrongful act of a State
There is an internationally wrongful act of a State when conduct consisting of an action or omission:
        (a) Is attributable to the State under international law; and
        (b) Constitutes a breach of an international obligation of the State.

Article 3 Characterization of an act of a State as internationally wrongful
The characterization of an act of a State as internationally wrongful is governed by international law. Such characterization is not affected by the characterization of the same act as lawful by internal law.

Article 12 Existence of a breach of an international obligation
There is a breach of an international obligation by a State when an act of that State is not in conformity with what is required of it by that obligation, regardless of its origin or character.

Article 28 Legal consequences of an internationally wrongful act

The international responsibility of a State which is entailed by an internationally wrongful act in accordance with the provisions of Part One involves legal consequences as set out in this Part.

Article 29 Continued duty of performance

The legal consequences of an internationally wrongful act under this Part do not affect the continued duty of the responsible State to perform the obligation breached.

Article 30 Cessation and non-repetition

The State responsible for the internationally wrongful act is under an obligation:
>   (a) To cease that act, if it is continuing;
>   (b) To offer appropriate assurances and guarantees of non-repetition, if circumstances so require.

Article 40 Application of this chapter

1. This chapter applies to the international responsibility which is entailed by a serious breach by a State of an obligation arising under a peremptory norm of general international law.

2. A breach of such an obligation is serious if it involves a gross or systematic failure by the responsible State to fulfil the obligation.

Article 41 Particular consequences of a serious breach of an obligation under this chapter

1. States shall cooperate to bring to an end through lawful means any serious breach within the meaning of article 40.

2. No State shall recognize as lawful a situation created by a serious breach within the meaning of article 40, nor render aid or assistance in maintaining that situation.

3. This article is without prejudice to the other consequences referred to in this Part and to such further consequences that a breach to which this chapter applies may entail under international law.

Article 48 Invocation of responsibility by a State other than an injured state

1. Any State other than an injured State is entitled to invoke the responsibility of another State in accordance with paragraph 2 if:
>   (a) The obligation breached is owed to a group of States including that State, and is established for the protection of a collective interest of the group; or
>   (b) The obligation breached is owed to the international community as a whole.

2. Any State entitled to invoke responsibility under paragraph 1 may claim from the responsible State:
>   (a) Cessation of the internationally wrongful act, and assurances and guarantees of non-repetition in accordance with article 30; and
>   (b) Performance of the obligation of reparation in accordance with the preceding articles, in the interest of the injured State or of the beneficiaries of the obligation breached.

3. The requirements for the invocation of responsibility by an injured State under articles 43, 44 and 45 apply to an invocation of responsibility by a State entitled to do so under paragraph 1.

Article 58: Individual responsibility

These articles are without prejudice to any question of the individual responsibility under international law of any person acting on behalf of a State.

406 State Responsibility

ILC Commentary on the Draft Articles
Official Records of the General Assembly, Fifty-sixth session, Supplement No 10
(A/56/10), chp.IV.E.2), Commentary on Draft Article 40

[T]he present Articles do not recognize the existence of any distinction between State crimes and delicts for the purposes of Part One. On the other hand, it is necessary for the Articles to reflect that there are certain *consequences* flowing from the basic concepts of peremptory norms of general international law and obligations to the international community as a whole within the field of State responsibility. Whether or not peremptory norms of general international law and obligations to the international community as a whole are aspects of a single basic idea, there is at the very least substantial overlap between them. The examples which the International Court has given of obligations towards the international community as a whole all concern obligations which, it is generally accepted, arise under peremptory norms of general international law. Likewise the examples of peremptory norms given by the Commission in its commentary to what became Article 53 of the Vienna Convention involve obligations to the international community as a whole. But there is at least a difference in emphasis. While peremptory norms of general international law focus on the scope and priority to be given to a certain number of fundamental obligations, the focus of obligations to the international community as a whole is essentially on the legal interest of all States in compliance – i.e., in terms of the present Articles, in being entitled to invoke the responsibility of any State in breach. Consistently with the difference in their focus, it is appropriate to reflect the consequences of the two concepts in two distinct ways. First, serious breaches of obligations arising under peremptory norms of general international law can attract additional consequences, not only for the responsible State but for all other States. Secondly, all States are entitled to invoke responsibility for breaches of obligations to the international community as a whole. The first of these propositions is the concern of the present chapter; the second is dealt with in Article 48.

(1) Article 40 serves to define the scope of the breaches covered by the chapter. It establishes two criteria in order to distinguish serious breaches of obligations under peremptory norms of general international law from other types of breaches. The first relates to the character of the obligation breached, which must derive from a peremptory norm of general international law. The second qualifies the intensity of the breach, which must have been serious in nature. Chapter III only applies to those violations of international law that fulfil both criteria.

(2) The first criterion relates to the character of the obligation breached. In order to give rise to the application of this chapter, a breach must concern an obligation arising under a peremptory norm of general international law. In accordance with Article 53 of the Vienna Convention on the Law of Treaties, a peremptory norm of general international law is one which is accepted and recognized by the international community of States as a whole as a norm from which no derogation is permitted and which can be modified only by a subsequent norm of general international law having the same character. The concept of peremptory norms of general international law is recognized in international practice, in the jurisprudence of international and national courts and tribunals and in legal doctrine.

(3) It is not appropriate to set out examples of the peremptory norms referred to in the text of Article 40 itself, any more than it was in the text of Article 53 of the Vienna Convention. The obligations referred to in Article 40 arise from those substantive rules of conduct that prohibit what has come to be seen as intolerable because of the threat it presents to the survival of States and their peoples and the most basic human values.

(4) Among these prohibitions, it is generally agreed that the prohibition of aggression is to be regarded as peremptory . . . There also seems to be widespread agreement with other examples listed in the Commission's commentary to Article 53: viz., the prohibitions against slavery and the slave trade, genocide, and racial discrimination and apartheid.

(5) Although not specifically listed in the Commission's commentary to Article 53 of the Vienna Convention, the peremptory character of certain other norms seems also to be generally accepted. This applies to the prohibition against torture as defined in article 1 of the Convention against Torture and Other Cruel, Inhuman or Degrading Treatment or Punishment of 10 December 1984. In the light of the International Court's description of the basic rules of international humanitarian law applicable in armed conflict as intransgressible in character, it would also seem justified to treat these as peremptory. Finally, the obligation to respect the right of self-determination deserves to be mentioned. As the International Court noted in the *East Timor* case, ... [t]he principle of self-determination ... is one of the essential principles of contemporary international law, which gives rise to an obligation to the international community as a whole to permit and respect its exercise. ...

(7) Apart from its limited scope in terms of the comparatively small number of norms which qualify as peremptory, Article 40 applies a further limitation for the purposes of the chapter, viz. that the breach should itself have been serious. A serious breach is defined in paragraph 2 as one which involves a gross or systematic failure by the responsible State to fulfil the obligation in question. The word serious signifies that a certain order of magnitude of violation is necessary in order not to trivialize the breach and it is not intended to suggest that any violation of these obligations is not serious or is somehow excusable.

(8) To be regarded as systematic, a violation would have to be carried out in an organized and deliberate way. In contrast, the term gross refers to the intensity of the violation or its effects; it denotes violations of a flagrant nature, amounting to a direct and outright assault on the values protected by the rule. The terms are not of course mutually exclusive; serious breaches will usually be both systematic and gross. Factors which may establish the seriousness of a.violation would include the intent to violate the norm; the scope and number of individual violations, and the gravity of their consequences for the victims. It must also be borne in mind that some of the peremptory norms in question, most notably the prohibitions of aggression and genocide, by their very nature require an intentional violation on a large scale.

P. Allott, 'State Responsibility and the Unmaking of International Law'
29 *Harvard International Law Journal* 1 (1988)

For almost four decades the International Law Commission has been working on the topic of state responsibility. The Commission's work raises fundamental questions not only about the state of contemporary international law but also about the existence and functioning of the Commission itself. There is reason to believe that the Commission's long and laborious work on state responsibility is doing serious long-term damage to international law and international society. ...

To international lawyers from the United States and other countries with similar interests and backgrounds, state responsibility was essentially a matter of codifying the obligations of states in the treatment of aliens. In the Harvard draft convention and at the 1930 Hague Conference, the topic was known as 'Responsibility of States for Damage Done in Their Territory to the Person or Property of Foreigners.'

In contrast, international lawyers from Latin America and other countries with similar interests viewed state responsibility as essentially a matter of confining the diplomatic protection of aliens within limits which respected the sovereignty of all states. The particular history and culture of Latin America had led writers from that region to take significantly different views not only of diplomatic protection and state responsibility but also of the fundamental nature and principles of international law . . .

It is possible to extract from the earlier codification efforts three different approaches to the technical problem of codifying the law of state responsibility. These might be called the 'delicts' approach (identifying the delictual acts which give rise to responsibility, such as denial of justice, expropriation, or government-sponsored personal injury), the 'obligations' approach (identifying the obligations, breach of which gives rise to responsibility, including obligations other than those regarding the treatment of individual aliens), and the 'principles' approach (determining the rules and principles of international law applying to all kinds of unlawful acts) . . .

The aspect of the draft articles on state responsibility that demands our particular attention is their fundamental structural feature – the postulation of a concept of 'responsibility-arising-from-wrongfulness' distinct from the wrongful act and from the consequences of a wrongful act. This middle category is a dangerous fiction, an unnecessary intrusion into the systematic structure of a legal system. But it is not merely analytically unnecessary. In the particular case of international law, it entails consequences of the most serious and undesirable kind.

The draft articles are based on the initial premise that state responsibility results from the 'internationally wrongful act of a State.' [The English text of the draft articles uses the unexpected word 'wrongful,' with its interesting moral overtone, rather than the word 'unlawful.' 'Wrongful' first appeared in the English version of Ago's original memorandum of 1962, . . . to render the French word '*illicite*.' A note in Ago's report, *Second Report on State Responsibility, by Mr. Roberto Ago, Special Rapporteur*, . . . says that the English-speaking members of the Commission preferred it to the word 'illicit.' The 1929 Harvard draft had used the word 'wrongful' in only one article, the provisions otherwise being phrased in terms of breach of obligation and responsibility. It should also be noted that the Commission long ago dispensed with the term 'state responsibility' and has adopted the term 'international responsibility,' except in the title of the topic on its agenda.] The internationally wrongful act of a state involves conduct 'attributable to the State under international law' that 'constitutes a breach of an international obligation of the State.' The act of a state is to be characterized as internationally wrongful only 'by international law.' Putting these ideas together, 'every internationally wrongful act of a State entails the international responsibility of that State.'

In short, the draft articles postulate that all the different kinds of obligation and different kinds of breach give rise to a single kind of consequence called 'responsibility.' Responsibility in this sense has two characteristics: (a) it has a particular substantive content of its own; and (b) it gives rise to certain further consequences in terms of liabilities, rights, and, eventually, remedies.

In the normal course of events, a wrongful act entails painful consequences: a judgment and possibly a penalty. The Benthamite price of lawbreaking is the risk of pain, not the possibility of an idea. The wages of sin are death, not responsibility for sin. In the terms of legal analysis, wrongdoing gives rise to a liability in the offender owed to others who have rights which may be enforced by legal processes. Liability is not a consequence of some intervening concept of responsibility. It is a direct consequence flowing from the nature of the wrong (the content of the rights of the offended party and the duties of the offender) and from the nature of the actual wrongful act in the given case (in particular, the content of the specific rights and duties which have been affected by the breach in question). The remedies available are a function of integrating the nature of the liability in the given case with the nature of the particular wrongful act . . .

Two especially vicious consequences result from using responsibility as a general and independent category in international law. First, it consecrates the idea that wrongdoing is the behavior of a general category known as 'states' and is not the behavior of morally responsible human beings. It therefore obscures the fact that breaches of international law are attributable formally to the legal persons known as states but morally to the human beings who determine the behaviour of states.

Second, if responsibility exists as a legal category, it must be given legal substance. In particular, general conditions of responsibility have to be created which are then applicable to all rights and duties. The net result is that the deterrent effect of the imposition of responsibility is seriously compromised, not only by notionalizing it (the first vicious consequence) but also by leaving room for argument in every conceivable case of potential responsibility (the second vicious consequence). When lawyers leave room for argument there is much room for injustice.

NOTES:
1. The International Law Commission was established in 1947 by the General Assembly for the purpose of codifying and progressively developing international law. Its 34 members are usually international lawyers, and a Special Rapporteur is appointed for each legal topic being considered and she/he prepares a report (or many reports) based on State practice, discussions, doctrine, etc. In some areas the draft conventions or 'articles' issued by the ILC are considered to be, at least in part, representative of customary international law, and may become the basis for a multilateral treaty.
2. The 2001 Articles are a mixture of progressive development of the law and codification of existing customary law. Necessarily, the Articles will help to promote the development of new customary law on similar lines to the content of the Articles. Indeed, the *Nicaragua Case* and the *Danube Dam Case* (see below) make it clear that earlier versions of the Articles have already had this effect.
3. There is still some concern over Articles 40 and 41 dealing with breaches of peremptory rules of international law (rules of *jus cogens*). For some States, including the UK, these Articles cannot represent customary law, although they are almost so vague as to have no real effect. They are, in effect, a compromise between those States wanting a full concept of international crimes (see the much criticised old Draft Art. 19 of the 1980 Draft Articles, not replicated in the 2001 Draft) and those States unconvinced that any special consequences should flow from certain 'important' or fundamental rules of international law. As the Special Rapporteur makes clear in his Fourth Report (UN Doc. A/CN 4/517, August 2000) the point is to identify rules of international law that create obligations towards the international community as a whole (the rules of *jus cogens*) rather than obligations owed only to particular States with whom the violator might be bound in law. The Rapporteur continues that these Articles are 'a framework for the progressive development, within a narrow compass, of a concept which is or ought to be broadly acceptable. On the one hand it does not call into question established understandings of the conditions for State responsibility. On the other hand, it recognises that there can be egregious breaches of obligations owed to the community as a whole, breaches which warrant some response by the community and by its members'.

SECTION 2: **Attribution**

A: Officials

International Law Commission, Articles on State Responsibility
August 2001, Special Rapporteur James Crawford

Article 4 Conduct of organs of a State
1. The conduct of any State organ shall be considered an act of that State under international law, whether the organ exercises legislative, executive, judicial or any other functions, whatever position it holds in the organization of the State, and whatever its character as an organ of the central government or of a territorial unit of the State.

2. An organ includes any person or entity which has that status in accordance with the internal law of the State.

Article 5 Conduct of persons or entities exercising elements of governmental authority
The conduct of a person or entity which is not an organ of the State under Article 4 but which is

empowered by the law of that State to exercise elements of the governmental authority shall be considered an act of the State under international law, provided the person or entity is acting in that capacity in the particular instance.

Article 6 Conduct of organs placed at the disposal of a State by another State
The conduct of an organ placed at the disposal of a State by another State shall be considered an act of the former State under international law if the organ is acting in the exercise of elements of the governmental authority of the State at whose disposal it is placed.

Article 7 Excess of authority or contravention of instructions
The conduct of an organ of a State or of a person or entity empowered to exercise elements of the governmental authority shall be considered an act of the State under international law if the organ, person or entity acts in that capacity, even if it exceeds its authority or contravenes instructions.

Article 8 Conduct directed or controlled by a State
The conduct of a person or group of persons shall be considered an act of a State under international law if the person or group of persons is in fact acting on the instructions of, or under the direction or control of, that State in carrying out the conduct.

Article 9 Conduct carried out in the absence or default of the official authorities
The conduct of a person or group of persons shall be considered an act of a State under international law if the person or group of persons is in fact exercising elements of the governmental authority in the absence or default of the official authorities and in circumstances such as to call for the exercise of those elements of authority.

Article 10 Conduct of an insurrectional or other movement
1. The conduct of an insurrectional movement which becomes the new government of a State shall be considered an act of that State under international law.

2. The conduct of a movement, insurrectional or other, which succeeds in establishing a new State in part of the territory of a pre-existing State or in a territory under its administration shall be considered an act of the new State under international law.

3. This article is without prejudice to the attribution to a State of any conduct, however related to that of the movement concerned, which is to be considered an act of that State by virtue of articles 4 to 9.

Article 11 Conduct acknowledged and adopted by a State as its own
Conduct which is not attributable to a State under the preceding articles shall nevertheless be considered an act of that State under international law if and to the extent that the State acknowledges and adopts the conduct in question as its own.

Caire Claim (France v Mexico)
5 RIAA (1929) 516 (transl. for the authors by Mr M. Nasta) French-Mexican Claims Commission

Caire, who was French, was killed in Mexico during a revolution by Mexican soldiers after refusing to give them money. The relevant question for the Commission was what was 'the responsibility of Mexico for actions of individual military personnel, acting without orders or against the wishes of their commanding officers and independently of the needs and aims of the revolution'.

PRESIDING COMMISSIONER VERZIJL: [The] solution [to the question asked] is to be found by having regard to the general principles governing the conditions of the international responsibility of States for acts committed by their public officials. However, this statement requires the following remarks:

(a) the special features distinguishing military from civil officials influence the conditions and the extent of the responsibility caused by their acts. . . .

(c) Mexico, having assumed the responsibility for damages caused by non-governmental, i.e. revolutionary, forces, is also responsible for their acts, as if they were committed by military forces under the control of the lawful government . . .

I should like to make clear first of all that I am interpreting the said principles in accordance with the doctrine of the 'objective responsibility' of the State, that is, the responsibility for the acts of the officials or organs of a State, . . . even in the absence of any 'fault' of its own. It is widely known that theoretical conceptions in this sphere have advanced a great deal in recent times . . . I can say that I regard them as perfectly correct in that they tend to impute to the State, on an international plane, the responsibility for all the acts committed by its officials or organs which constitute criminal acts from the point of view of the law of nations, no matter if the official or organ in question has acted within or exceeded the limits of his competence. 'It is generally agreed,' as M. Bourquin has rightly said, 'that acts committed by the officials and agents of a State entail the international responsibility of that State, even if the perpetrator did not have specific authorisation. This responsibility does not find its justification in general principles – I mean those principles regulating the judicial organisation of the State. The act of an official is only judicially established as an act of State if such an act lies within the official's sphere of competence. The act of an official operating beyond his competence is not an act of State. It should not in principle, therefore, affect the responsibility of the State. If it is accepted in international law that the position is different, it is for reasons peculiar to the mechanism of international life; it is because it is felt that international relations would become too difficult, too complicated and too insecure if foreign States were obliged to take into account the often complex judicial arrangements that regulate competence in the internal affairs of a State. From this it is immediately clear that in the hypothesis under consideration the international responsibility of the State is purely *objective* in character, and that it rests on an idea of *guarantee*, in which the subjective notion of fault plays no part.'

But in order to be able to admit this so-called objective responsibility of the State for acts committed by its officials or organs outside their competence, they must have acted at least to all appearances as competent officials or organs, or they must have used powers or methods appropriate to their official capacity. . . .

If the principles stated above are applied to the present case, and if it is taken into account that the perpetrators of the murder of M.J.-B. Caire were military personnel occupying the ranks of 'major' and 'capitan primero' aided by a few privates, it is found that the conditions of responsibility formulated above are completely fulfilled. . . . Under these circumstances, there remains no doubt that, even if they are to be regarded as having acted outside their competence, which is by no means certain, and even if their superior officers issued a counter-order, these two officers have involved the responsibility of the State, in view of the fact that they acted in their capacity of officers and used the means placed at their disposition by virtue of that capacity.

Corfu Channel Case (UK v *Albania*) (*Merits*)
ICJ Rep 1949 4, International Court of Justice

Two British warships were damaged by mines during transit of the Corfu Channel, which was within the Albanian territorial sea (see Chapter 10). One question submitted to the Court concerned whether Albania was responsible under international law for the damage to the warships and the loss of life of the British sailors.

It is clear that knowledge of the minelaying cannot be imputed to the Albanian Government by reason merely of the fact that a minefield discovered in Albanian territorial waters caused the explosions of which the British warships were the victims. It is true, as international practice shows, that a State on whose territory or in whose waters an act contrary to international law has occurred, may be called upon to give an explanation. It is also true that that State cannot evade such a request by limiting itself to a reply that it is ignorant of the circumstances of the act and of its authors. The State may, up to a certain point, be bound to supply particulars of the use made by it of the means of information and inquiry at its disposal. But it cannot be concluded from the mere fact of the control exercised by a State over its territory and waters that that State necessarily knew, or ought to have known, of any unlawful act perpetrated therein, nor yet that it necessarily knew, or should have known, the authors. This fact, by itself and apart from other circumstances, neither involves *prima facie* responsibility nor shifts the burden of proof.

On the other hand, the fact of this exclusive territorial control exercised by a State within its frontiers has a bearing upon the methods of proof available to establish the knowledge of that State as to such events. By reason of this exclusive control, the other State, the victim of a breach of international law, is often unable to furnish direct proof of facts giving rise to responsibility. Such a State should be allowed a more liberal recourse to inferences of fact and circumstantial evidence. This indirect evidence is admitted in all systems of law, and its use is recognized by international decisions. It must be regarded as of special weight when it is based on a series of facts linked together and leading logically to a single conclusion.

The Court must examine therefore whether it has been established by means of indirect evidence that Albania has knowledge of minelaying in her territorial waters independently of any connivance on her part in this operation. The proof may be drawn from inferences of fact, provided that they leave *no room* for reasonable doubt.

Southern Pacific Properties (Middle East) Ltd v Arab Republic of Egypt
32 ILM 933 (1993), International Centre for the Settlement of Investment Disputes

Southern Pacific entered into a contract with Egypt to develop land for tourism around the sites of the Pyramids at Giza. There was considerable opposition in Egypt, especially because of the possibility of disturbance of undiscovered antiquities. Egyptian authorities withdrew Southern Pacific's permission to develop the site. Southern Pacific claimed compensation and damages. The dispute to be decided fell according to international legal principles because the contract provided for arbitration by the International Centre for the Settlement of Investment Disputes. Egypt claimed, *inter alia*, that certain acts of Egyptian officials were null and void under Egyptian law and could not therefore be attributable to the State itself.

81. The Respondent has contended that certain acts of Egyptian officials upon which the Claimants rely are under Egyptian law, legally non-existent or absolutely null and void. . . . The Respondent argues further that certain decisions of high-ranking government officials are invalid because they were not taken pursuant to the procedures prescribed by Egyptian law.

82. It is possible that under Egyptian law certain acts of Egyptian officials, including even Presidential Decree No. 475, may be considered legally nonexistent or null and void or susceptible to invalidation. However, these acts were cloaked with the mantle of Governmental authority and communicated as such to foreign investors who relied on them in making their investments.

83. Whether legal under Egyptian law or not, the acts in question were the acts of Egyptian authorities, including the highest executive authority of the Government. These acts, which are now alleged to have been in violation of the Egyptian municipal legal system, created expectations protected by established principles of international law. A determination that these acts are null and void under municipal law would not resolve the ultimate question of liability for damages suffered by the victim who rallied on the acts. If the municipal law does not provide a remedy, the denial of of any remedy whatsoever cannot be the final answer. . . .

85. The principle of international law which the Tribunal is bound to apply is that which establishes the international responsibility of States when unauthorised or *ultra vires* acts of officials have been performed by State agents under cover of their official character. If such unauthorised or *ultra vires* acts could not be ascribed to the State, all State responsibility would be rendered illusory. For this reason.

> . . . the practice of states has conclusively established the international responsibility for unlawful acts of state organs, even if accomplished outside the limits of their competence and contrary to domestic law. (Sorensen (ed.), *Manual of Public International Law*, New York 1968, at p. 548.)

NOTE:

In *Paraguay* v *USA (Provisional Measures)* 1998 ILM 810, Paraguay requested the International Court to grant provisional measures staying the execution of a Paraguyan national who had been tried and convicted in the United States. The basis of the claim was not that an execution *per se* was internationally unlawful, but that the US courts had denied Paraguay its right of consular access to the accused. The attribution of the acts of US courts to the US was indisputable. However, while the ICJ granted the provisional measures (which the US ignored), some members of the Court were concerned lest the ICJ interfere with US' sovereignty in criminal matters in respect of acts done within its territory. There is but a fine line between attributable acts that violated Paraguay's rights and attributable acts that violated the rights of the accused. The former are certainly within the realm of international law and state responsibility, the latter might be 'only' a matter for national law. The matter was revisited in the *LaGrand Case (Germany* v *United States)* 27 June 2001 (see Chapter 15), where two German nationals were executed in the US following their convictions for serious offences. The US admitted that it had failed to advise the two accused of their right to see a German Consular official under international law (the Vienna Convention on Consular Relations 1963) but, more importantly, the US had failed to follow the ICJ's order of provisional measures' indicating that the US should take steps to attempt to prevent the execution of the German nationals pending the ICJ hearing. The German nationals were executed. For the first time, the ICJ decided that an order for provisional measures was binding in international law and, consequentially the US incurred responsibility for failing to abide by them.

B: Private persons

United States Diplomatic and Consular Staff in Tehran Case (United States v *Iran)*
ICJ Rep 1980 3, International Court of Justice

This case arose from the occupation by a group of Iranian citizens of the United States Embassy in Tehran and the taking of the Embassy staff as hostages (see further in Chapter 9).

56. The events which are the subject of the United States' claims fall into two phases which it will be convenient to examine separately.

57. The first of these phases covers the armed attack on the United States Embassy by militants on 4 November 1979, the overrunning of its premises, the seizure of its inmates as hostages, the appropriation of its property and archives and the conduct of the Iranian authorities in the face of those occurrences. The attack and the subsequent overrunning, bit by bit, of the whole Embassy premises, was an operation which continued over a period of some three hours without any body of police, any military unit or any Iranian official intervening to try to stop or impede it from being carried through to its completion. The result of the attack was considerable damage to the Embassy premises and property, the forcible opening and seizure of its archives, the confiscation of the archives and other documents found in the Embassy and, most grave of all, the seizure by force of its diplomatic and consular personnel as hostages, together with two United States nationals.

58. No suggestion has been made that the militants, when they executed their attack on the Embassy, had any form of official status as recognized 'agents' or organs of the Iranian State. Their conduct in mounting the attack, overruning the Embassy and seizing its inmates as hostages cannot, therefore, be regarded as imputable to that State on that basis. Their conduct might be considered as itself directly imputable to the Iranian State only if it were established that, in fact, on the occasion in question the militants acted on behalf of the State, having been charged by some competent organ of the Iranian State to carry out a specific operation. The information before the Court does not, however, suffice to establish with the requisite certainty the existence at that time of such a link between the militants and any competent organ of the State.

59. Previously, it is true, the religious leader of the country, the Ayatollah Khomeini, had made several public declarations inveighing against the United States as responsible for all his country's problems. In so doing, it would appear, the Ayatollah Khomeini was giving utterance to the general resentment felt by supporters of the revolution at the admission of the former Shah to the United States. The information before the Court also indicates that a spokesman for the militants, in explaining their action afterwards, did expressly refer to a message issued by the Ayatollah Khomeini, on 1 November 1979. . . . In the view of the Court, however, it would be going too far to interpret such general declarations of the Ayatollah Khomeini to the people or students of Iran as amounting to an authorization from the State to undertake the specific operation of invading and seizing the United States Embassy. . . .

69. The second phase of the events which are the subject of the United States' claims comprises the whole series of facts which occurred following the completion of the occupation of the United States Embassy by the militants, and the seizure of the Consulates at Tabriz and Shiraz. The occupation having taken place and the diplomatic and consular personnel of the United States' mission having been taken hostage, the action required of the Iranian Government by the Vienna Conventions and by general international law was manifest. Its plain duty was at once to make every effort, and to take every appropriate step, to bring these flagrant infringements of the inviolability of the premises, archives and diplomatic and consular staff of the United States Embassy to a speedy end, to restore the Consulates at Tabriz and Shiraz to United States control, and in general to re-establish the status quo and to offer reparation for the damage.

70. No such step was, however, taken by the Iranian authorities. . . .

71. In any event expressions of approval of the take-over of the Embassy, and indeed also of the Consulates at Tabriz and Shiraz, by militants came immediately from numerous Iranian authorities, including religious, judicial, executive, police and broadcasting authorities. Above all, the Ayatollah Khomeini himself made crystal clear the endorsement by the State . . . The result of that policy was fundamentally to transform the legal nature of the situation created by the occupation of the Embassy and the detention of its diplomatic and consular staff as hostages. The approval given to these facts by the Ayatollah Khomeini and other organs of the Iranian State, and the decision to

perpetuate them, translated continuing occupation of the Embassy and detention of the hostages into acts of that State. The militants, authors of the invasion and jailers of the hostages, had now become agents of the Iranian State for whose acts the State itself was internationally responsible.

Military and Paramilitary Activities in and against Nicaragua (*Nicaragua* v *US*) (*Merits*)
ICJ Rep 1986 14, International Court of Justice

The aspect of the dispute relevant here was whether the military activities of a significant insurrection movement, the *contras*, against the Nicaraguan government were imputable to the United States (see further Chapters 2 and 14).

114. The Court notes that according to Nicaragua, the *contras* are no more than bands of mercenaries which have been recruited, organized, paid and commanded by the Government of the United States. This would mean that they have no real autonomy in relation to that Government. Consequently, any offences which they have committed would be imputable to the Government of the United States, like those of any other forces placed under the latter's command. In the view of Nicaragua, '*stricto sensu*, the military and paramilitary attacks launched by the United States against Nicaragua do not constitute a case of civil strife. They are essentially the acts of the United States.' If such a finding of the imputability of the acts of the *contras* to the United States were to be made, no question would arise of mere complicity in those acts, or of incitement of the *contrast* to commit them.

115. The Court has taken the view . . . that United States participation, even if preponderant or decisive, in the financing, organizing, training, supplying and equipping of the *contras*, the selection of its military or paramilitary targets, and the planning of the whole of its operation, is still insufficient in itself, on the basis of the evidence in the possession of the Court, for the purpose of attributing to the United States the acts committed by the *contrast* in the course of their military or paramilitary operations in Nicaragua. All the forms of United States participation mentioned above, and even the general control by the respondent State over a force with a high degree of dependency on it, would not in themselves mean, without further evidence, that the United States directed or enforced the perpetration of the acts contrary to human rights and humanitarian law alleged by the applicant State. Such acts could well be committed by members of the *contras* without the control of the United States. For this conduct to give rise to legal responsibility of the United States, it would in principle have to be proved that that State had effective control of the military or paramilitary operations in the course of which the alleged violations were committed.

116. The Court does not consider that the assistance given by the United States to the *contras* warrants the conclusion that these forces are subject to the United States to such an extent that any acts they have committed are imputable to that State. It takes the view that the *contras* remain responsible for their acts, and that the United States is not responsible for the acts of the *contras*, but for its own conduct vis-à-vis Nicaragua, including conduct related to the acts of the *contras*. What the Court has to investigate is not the complaints relating to alleged violations of humanitarian law by the *contras*, regarded by Nicaragua is imputable to the United States, but rather unlawful acts for which the United States may be responsible directly in connection with the activities of the *contras*.

NOTE:
In the *Tadic Case* (1997 ILM 908), the International Criminal Tribunal for the Former Yugoslavia considered whether the acts of the individual could be attributable to the former Federal Republic of Yugoslavia (Serbia and Montenegro). There was no doubt that the accused was an agent of

the Bosnian Serb military, so the question became whether the acts of the Bosnia Serb authorities were attributable to the former Federal Republic. By a majority, the Tribunal found that the acts of the Bosnia Serb authorities could not be attributable to the former Federal Republic, for similar reasons to that relied on by the ICJ in the *Nicaragua Case* (above): lack of evidence of direct control of military operations as opposed to 'mere' shared aims. Despite the fact that the Tribunal accepted that the assistance of the former Federal Republic was 'crucial' to the ability of the Bosnian Serb military to take offensive action and that they (the Bosnian Serbs) were almost completely dependant on war material supplied by the former Federal Republic, this was insufficient for attribution. In his dissent, the President disagreed that 'effective control' was solely decisive in the question of attribution. He argued that the *Nicaragua Case* established two distinct tests for attribution: either agency in general (established by control on one side and dependency on the other), or where a specific act was delegated to the actor, wherein responsibility could exist for that act alone. He concluded that 'effective control' is vital for the acts of independent individuals (or groups), but that it is irrelevant where tasks are delegated because the fact of that delegation proves that the act is attributable. In short, where tasks are delegated, the individual or group is no longer 'independent' of the State at all. The matter is now covered by ILC Article 8.

C: Officials of successful revolutionary movements

International Law Commission, Articles on Responsibility of States for Internationally Wrongful Acts
August 2001, Special Rapporteur James Crawford

Article 10 Conduct of an insurrectional or other movement
　　1. The conduct of an insurrectional movement which becomes the new government of a State shall be considered an act of that State under international law.
　　2. The conduct of a movement, insurrectional or other, which succeeds in establishing a new State in part of the territory of a pre-existing State or in a territory under its administration shall be considered an act of the new State under international law.
　　3. This article is without prejudice to the attribution to a State of any conduct, however related to that of the movement concerned, which is to be considered an act of that State by virtue of articles 4 to 9.

ILC Commentary on the Draft Articles
Official Records of the General Assembly, Fifty-sixth session, Supplement No. 10
(A/56/10), chp.IV.E.2), Commentary on Draft Article 10

(1) Article 10 deals with the special case of attribution to a State of conduct of an insurrectional or other movement which subsequently becomes the new government of the State or succeeds in establishing a new State.

(2) At the outset, the conduct of the members of the movement presents itself purely as the conduct of private individuals. It can be placed on the same footing as that of persons or groups who participate in a riot or mass demonstration and it is likewise not attributable to the State. Once an organized movement comes into existence as a matter of fact, it will be even less possible to attribute its conduct to the State, which will not be in a position to exert effective control over its activities. The general principle in respect of the conduct of such movements, committed during the continuing struggle with the constituted authority, is that it is not attributable to the State under international law. In other words, the acts of unsuccessful insurrectional movements are not

attributable to the State, unless under some other article of chapter II, for example in the special circumstances envisaged by article 9 . . .

(4) The general principle that the conduct of an insurrectional or other movement is not attributable to the State is premised on the assumption that the structures and organization of the movement are and remain independent of those of the State. This will be the case where the State successfully puts down the revolt. In contrast, where the movement achieves its aims and either installs itself as the new government of the State or forms a new State in part of the territory of the pre-existing State or in a territory under its administration, it would be anomalous if the new regime or new State could avoid responsibility for conduct earlier committed by it. In these exceptional circumstances, article 10 provides for the attribution of the conduct of the successful insurrectional or other movement to the State. The basis for the attribution of conduct of a successful insurrectional or other movement to the State under international law lies in the continuity between the movement and the eventual government . . .

(15) Exceptional cases may occur where the State was in a position to adopt measures of vigilance, prevention or punishment in respect of the movement's conduct but improperly failed to do so. This possibility is preserved by paragraph 3 of article 10, which provides that the attribution rules of paragraphs 1 and 2 are without prejudice to the attribution to a State of any conduct, however related to that of the movement concerned, which is to be considered an act of that State by virtue of other provisions in Chapter II. The term however related to that of the movement concerned is intended to have a broad meaning. Thus the failure by a State to take available steps to protect the premises of diplomatic missions, threatened from attack by an insurrectional movement, is clearly conduct attributable to the State and is preserved by paragraph 3.

(16) A further possibility is that the insurrectional movement may itself be held responsible for its own conduct under international law, for example for a breach of international humanitarian law committed by its forces. The topic of the international responsibility of unsuccessful insurrectional or other movements, however, falls outside the scope of the present Articles, which are concerned only with the responsibility of States.

Short v *Iran*
(1987–III) 16 Iran-US CTR 76, Iran-United States Claims Tribunal

This claim was based on the loss of employment benefits and personal property caused by the alleged forceful expulsion of the claimant from Iran following the Islamic Revolution in Iran in 1978–79.

31. In examining whether the Claimant's departure from Iran was due to acts or circumstances attributable to the Respondent, the Tribunal has to take into account the existence of a revolutionary situation in Iran during the period under consideration. . . .

33. Where a revolution leads to the establishment of a new government the State is held responsible for the acts of the overthrown government insofar as the latter maintained control of the situation. The successor government is also held responsible for the acts imputable to the revolutionary movement which established it, even if those acts occurred prior to its establishment, as a consequence of the continuity existing between the new organization of the State and the organization of the revolutionary movement. *See* Draft Articles on State Responsibility, *supra*, Commentary on Article 15, paras. 3 and 4, 1975 Y.B. Int'l L. Comm'n, Vol. 2 at 100. These rules are of decisive importance in the present Case, since the Claimant departed from Iran on 8 February 1979, a few days before the proclamation on 11 February of the Islamic Revolutionary Government. At that time, the revolutionary movement had not yet been able to establish control over any part of Iranian territory, and the Government had demonstrated its loss of control.

34. The Claimant relies on acts committed by revolutionaries and seeks to attribute responsibility for their acts to the government that was established following the success of the Revolution. He is unable, however, to identify any agent of the revolutionary movement, the actions of which compelled him to leave Iran. The acts of supporters of a revolution cannot be attributed to the government following the success of the revolution just as the acts of supporters of an existing government are not attributable to the government. This was clearly recalled by the International Court of Justice in *United States Diplomatic and Consular Staff in Tehran (United States v Iran)*, 1980 ICJ 3, 29, para. 58 (Judgment of 24 May 1980). . . . In these circumstances, the Tribunal is of the view that the Claimant has failed to prove that his departure from Iran can be imputed to the wrongful conduct of Iran. The claim is therefore dismissed.

D: Acts of unsuccessful, or ongoing, revolutionary movements or secessionists

Asian Agricultural Products Ltd (AAPL) v *Republic of Sri Lanka*
30 ILM 577 (1991), International Centre for the Settlement of Investment Disputes

Sri Lankan security forces destroyed an installation belonging to a company partly owned by AAPL. The Sri Lankan security forces claimed that the installation was being used by the 'Tamil Tigers', a secessionist movement in Sri Lanka. The Tribunal concluded that although Sri Lanka was not responsible for the acts of the Tamil Tigers, it was responsible in its own right for failure to exercise due diligence in protecting AAPL's property.

72. It is generally accepted rule of International Law, clearly stated in international arbitral awards and in the writings of the doctrinal authorities, that:

(i)   A State on whose territory an insurrection occurs is not responsible for loss or damage sustained by foreign investors unless it can be shown that the Government of that state failed to provide the standard of protection required, either by treaty, or under general customary law, as the case may be; and

(ii) Failure to provide the standard of protection required entails the state's international responsibility for losses suffered, regardless of whether the damages occurred during an insurgents' offensive act [or] resulting from governmental counter-insurgency activities.

73. The long established arbitral case-law was adequately expressed by Max Huber, the *Rapporteur* in the *Spanish Zone of Morocco* claims (1923), in the following terms:

The principle of non-responsibility in no way excludes the duty to exercise a certain degree of vigilance. If a state is not responsible for the revolutionary events themselves, it may nevertheless be responsible, for what its authorities do or not do to ward the consequence, within the limits of possibility. . . .

76. In the light of all the above-mentioned arbitral precedents, it would be appropriate to consider that adequate protection afforded by the host State authorities constitutes a primary obligation, the failure to comply with which creates international responsibility. Furthermore, 'there is an extensive and consistent state practice supporting the duty to exercise due diligence' (BROWNLIE, *System of the Law of Nations, State Responsibility – Part 1*, Oxford, 1986, p. 162).

As a doctrinal authority, relied upon by both Parties during the various stages of their respective pleadings in the present case, Professor Brownlie stated categorically that:

There is general agreement among writers that the rule of non-responsibility cannot apply where the government concerned has failed to show due diligence (*Principles of Public International Law*, Third Edition, Oxford, 1979, p. 453).

After reviewing all categories of precedents, including more recent international judicial case-law, the learned Oxford University Professor arrived, not only to confirm that international responsibility arises from the mere 'failure to exercise due diligence' in providing the required protection, but also to note 'a sliding scale of liability related to the standard of due diligence' (*State Responsibility. op. cit.* p. 162 and p. 168).

NOTES:

1. In one sense, no real entity exists which is 'the State', it being a construct of international law. However, individuals act in the name of 'the State' and may use 'the State' as a shield against direct personal responsibility. Acts done in the name of 'the State' include the normal daily functions of the State's police force, judiciary, armed forces and government ministers. Note, however, Chapters 5 and 6 in regard to individual responsibility for international crimes which is not affected or dominated by State responsibility: see ILC Art. 58 and note also the Commentary to Draft Art. 10, above. It is also clear that when such individuals act for the State, there is no restriction on the types of obligation for which the State itself may be responsible should the official occasion a breach. So, in the *Case Concerning the Application of the Convention on the Prevention and Punishment of the Crime of Genocide (Bosnia & Herzegovina* v *Yugoslavia) (Preliminary Objections)* ICJ Rep. 1996 at p. 565, the Court accepted that a State could be held directly responsible for genocide even though the actual events were ordered or carried out by individuals and the individuals were also directly responsible under international law.

2. The two main theories on the responsibility of States are 'objective responsibility', where a State is strictly liable for all acts of its officials, and 'subjective responsibility', where it is necessary to show some fault or negligence by the State in its control of the official concerned. The former is preferred, and is the approach taken in ILC Art. 10 and, to a slightly lesser extent, in the *Caire Claim*. However, as both *Short* and the *AAPL* case illustrate, some element of fault, negligence or lack of due diligence may be required where the State is said to be 'responsible' for the acts of insurrectionists. Nevertheless, in the case of unsuccessful rebellions, the better view is that the existing government is responsible for failure to fulfill *its* own obligations (albeit only if acting negligently) rather than being responsible for the acts of persons dedicated to its overthrow.

3. International law attempts to regulate the conduct of States but rarely can it regulate directly the conduct of individuals. Therefore, it is necessary that a State be held responsible for all cases of acts or omissions by any person actually or apparently acting as an official of the State, except where it would not be reasonable for any injured non-national to have expected that the person was acting in the capacity of an official of the State. Otherwise the injured non-national has recourse only against the official personally and within the national law of the State of that official: see the *Southern Pacific Case* below.

SECTION 3: **Enforcement**

A: Ability to bring a claim

(a) *General interest in a matter*

South West Africa Cases **(*Ethiopia* v *South Africa; Liberia* v *South Africa*)**
(Preliminary Objections)
ICJ Rep 1962 319, International Court of Justice

An application was brought by Ethiopia and Liberia, as members of the United Nations, against South Africa, alleging that South Africa was not acting in accordance with the Mandate it had been given by the League of Nations (as later assumed by the United Nations). South Africa objected to the Court having jurisdiction to hear the case on the ground, *inter alia*, that Art. 7 of the Mandate did not give the applicants any standing to bring a claim. The majority of the Court rejected this objection.

JUDGE JESSUP (Separate Opinion): International law has long recognized that States may have legal interests in matters which do not affect their financial, economic, or other 'material', or, say, 'physical' or 'tangible' interests.

One type of illustration of this principle of international law is to be found in the right of a State to concern itself, on general humanitarian grounds, with atrocities affecting human beings in another country. In some instances States have asserted such legal interests on the basis of some treaty, as, for example, some of the representations made to the Belgian Government on the strength of the Berlin Act of 1885, concerning the atrocities in the Belgian Congo in 1906–1907. In other cases, the assertion of the legal interest has been based upon general principles of international law, as in remonstrances against Jewish pogroms in Russia around the turn of the century and the massacre of Armenians in Turkey. . . .

States have also asserted a legal interest in the general observance of the rules of international law. For example, in the cases of *Manouba* and *Carthage*, as submitted by France and Italy to the Permanent Court of Arbitration in 1913, in addition to claims for material damage, France claimed 100,000 francs for the 'moral and political injury resulting from the failure to observe international common law . . .'. Although the Permanent Court did not award damages on this ground, the Arbitral Tribunal in the case of the *I'm Alone* between the United States and Canada in 1935, awarded in addition to amounts for compensation for material damage, a sum of $25,000, 'as a material amend in respect of the wrong' . . .

It is impossible to escape the conclusion that paragraph 2 of Article 7 of the South West Africa Mandate was intended to recognize and to protect the general interests of Members of the international community in the Mandates System just as somewhat comparable clauses recognize this broad interest in the minority treaties, in the Constitution of the International Labour Organisation and, as more recently, in the Genocide Treaty and in some of the trusteeship agreements concluded under the United Nations. When the Mandate treaties were concluded, it was disputes over these broad interests which were contemplated.

South West Africa Cases (*Ethiopia* v *South Africa; Liberia* v *South Africa*)
(**Second Phase**)
ICJ Rep 1966 6, International Court of Justice

By the time the Court came to consider the merits of this case, the Court's composition had changed, and, by the casting vote of the President, the Court held that the specific applicants had no interest to bring the application.

44. [I]t may be said that a legal right or interest need not necessarily relate to anything material or 'tangible', and can be infringed even though no prejudice of a material kind has been suffered. In this connection, the provisions of certain treaties and other international instruments of a humanitarian character, and the terms of various arbitral and judicial decisions, are cited as indicating that, for instance, States may be entitled to uphold some general principle even though the particular contravention of it alleged has not affected their own material interests; – that again, States may have a legal interest in vindicating a principle of international law, even though they have, in the given case, suffered no material prejudice, or ask only for token damages. Without attempting to discuss how far, and in what particular circumstances, these things might be true, it suffices to point out that, in holding that the Applicants in the present case could only have had a legal right or interest in the 'special interests' provisions of the Mandate, the Court does not in any way do so merely because these relate to a material or tangible object. Nor, in holding that no legal right or interest exists for the Applicants, individually as States, in respect of the 'conduct' provisions, does the Court do so because any such right or interest would not have a material or tangible object. The Court simply holds that such rights or interests, in order to exist, must be clearly vested in those who claim them, by some text or instrument, or rule of law; – and that in the present case, none were ever vested in individual members of the League under any of the relevant instruments, or as a constituent part of the mandates system as a whole, or otherwise.

88. For these reasons the Court, bearing in mind that the rights of the Applicants must be determined by reference to the character of the system said to give rise to them, considers that the 'necessity' argument falls to the ground for lack of verisimilitude in the context of the economy and philosophy of that system. Looked at in another way moreover, the argument amounts to a plea that the Court should allow the equivalent of an '*actio popularis*', or right resident in any member of a community to take legal action in vindication of a public interest. But although a right of this kind may be known to certain municipal systems of law, it is not known to international law as it stands at present: nor is the Court able to regard it as imported by the 'general principles of law' referred to in Article 38, paragraph 1(c), of its Statute.

NOTE:
This decision in the 1966 *South West Africa Cases* ignores the interest that all States have in the maintenance of international law. The requirement of some 'special damage' to be shown by an applicant cannot be appropriate where a region, or the international community, is affected by breaches of international obligations but no one State is specially affected, for example, by pollution of the high seas. In this connection, the new ILC Articles 40 and 41 are relevant (see above).

(b) *Diplomatic protection: the nature of a State's claim*

Panevezys-Saldutiskis Railway Case (*Estonia* v *Lithuania*) (**Preliminary Objections**)
PCIJ Ser A/B (1939) No 76, Permanent Court of International Justice

In the opinion of the Court, the rule of international law on which the first Lithuanian objection is based is that in taking up the case of one of its nationals, by resorting to diplomatic action or international judicial proceedings on his behalf, a State is in reality asserting its own right, the right to ensure in the person of its nationals respect for the rules of international law. This right is necessarily limited to intervention on behalf of its own nationals because, in the absence of a special agreement, it is the bond of nationality between the State and the individual which alone confers upon the State the right of diplomatic protection, and it is as a part of the function of diplomatic protection that the right to take up a claim and to ensure respect for the rules of international law must be envisaged. Where the injury was done to the national of some other State, no claim to which such injury may give rise falls within the scope of the diplomatic protection which a State is entitled to afford nor can it give rise to a claim which that State is entitled to espouse.

NOTE:

As the State brings an international claim for its own injury, it is under no obligation to pay any reparation received by it to the national actually injured. For example, although in the UK the Government may in its discretion pass on to the injured national some or all of the compensation it receives, there is no right to such compensation: *Lonhro v ECGD* [1996] 4 All ER 673. The International Law Commission proposes to consider the topic of 'Diplomatic Protection' and have established a Working Group to begin the process. This Group has agreed that it will base its consideration on the rules of diplomatic protection as they exist in customary international law, that the exercise of diplomatic protection is the right of a State, that due regard must be had to the emerging ability of individuals to enforce their own rights directly under international law. It will focus on the procedural aspects of diplomatic protection (nationality of claims, admissibility, exhaustion of remedies, etc.) and it would not consider the substantive law (breach of which gives rise to a claim in the first place) unless this was necessary for the elucidation of the procedural rules. This will be a long and arduous task.

(c) Diplomatic protection of natural persons: nationality of claims

Nottebohm Case (*Liechtenstein* v *Guatemala*)
ICJ Rep 1955 4, International Court of Justice

Liechtenstein instituted proceedings against Guatemala, seeking a declaration by the Court that in 1943 Guatemala had unlawfully expelled, and seized the property of, Mr Nottebohm, who had been naturalised under the laws of Liechtenstein. Nottebohm was born in Germany in 1881 and had German nationality until his naturalisation by Liechtenstein. In 1905 he went to Guatemala, where he resided and conducted his business activities until 1943, although he occasionally went to Germany, and a few times to Liechtenstein, on holiday. He visited Liechtenstein in October 1939, one month after the outbreak of the Second World War, and applied there for naturalisation. Guatemala's main objection was that Liechtenstein's claim was inadmissible, as Liechtenstein could not extend diplomatic protection to Nottebohm in a claim against Guatemala. The Court upheld Guatemala's objection.

In order to decide upon the admissibility of the Application, the Court must ascertain whether the nationality conferred on Nottebohm by Liechtenstein by means of a naturalization which took place in the circumstances which have been described, can be validly invoked as against Guatemala, whether it bestows upon Liechtenstein a sufficient title to the exercise of protection in respect of Nottebohm as against Guatemala and therefore entitles it to seise the Court of a claim relating to him . . .

The naturalization of Nottebohm was an act performed by Liechtenstein in the exercise of its domestic jurisdiction. The question to be decided is whether that act has the international effect here under consideration. . . .

[A] State cannot claim that the rules it has thus laid down are entitled to recognition by another State unless it has acted in conformity with this general aim of making the legal bond of nationality accord with the individual's genuine connection with the State which assumes the defence of its citizens by means of protection as against other States.

According to the practice of States, to arbitral and judicial decisions and to the opinions of writers, nationality is a legal bond having as its basis a social fact of attachment, a genuine connection of existence, interests and sentiments, together with the existence of reciprocal rights and duties. It may be said to constitute the juridical expression of the fact that the individual upon whom it is conferred, either directly by the law or as the result of an act of the authorities, is in fact more closely connected with the population of the State conferring nationality than with that of any other State. Conferred by a State, it only entitles that State to exercise protection vis-à-vis another State, if it constitutes a translation into juridical terms of the individual's connection with the State which has made him its national.

These facts clearly establish, on the one hand, the absence of any bond of attachment between Nottebohm and Liechtenstein and, on the other hand, the existence of a long-standing and close connection between him and Guatemala, a link which his naturalization in no way weakened. That naturalization was not based on any real prior connection with Liechtenstein, nor did it in any way alter the manner of life of the person upon whom it was conferred in exceptional circumstances of speed and accommodation. In both respects, it was lacking in the genuineness requisite to an act of such importance, if it is to be entitled to be respected by a State in the position of Guatemala. It was granted without regard to the concept of nationality adopted in international relations.

Guatemala is under no obligation to recognize a nationality granted in such circumstances. Liechtenstein consequently is not entitled to extend its protection to Nottebohm vis-à-vis Guatemala and its claim must, for this reason, be held to be inadmissible.

Iran-United States Case No. A/18

(1984–1) 5 Iran-USCTR 251, Iran-United States Claims Tribunal

The issue was whether the Tribunal had jurisdiction over claims against Iran by persons who were, under US law, citizens of the US and who were, under Iranian law, citizens of the Islamic Republic of Iran.

On 12 April 1930, a Convention was concluded at The Hague 'Concerning Certain Questions relating to the Conflict of Nationality Laws' (the 'Hague Convention'). As Article 1 of that Convention makes plain, a determination by one State as to who are its nationals will be respected by another State 'in so far as it is consistent' with international law governing nationality. International law, then, does not determine who is a national, but rather sets forth the conditions under which that determination must be recognized by other States . . .

While *Nottebohm* itself did not involve a claim against a State of which Nottebohm was a national, it demonstrated the acceptance and approval by the International Court of Justice of the search for the real and effective nationality based on the facts of a case, instead of an approach relying on more formalistic criteria. The effects of the *Nottebohm* decision have radiated throughout the international law of nationality . . .

This trend toward modification of the Hague Convention rule of non-responsibility by search for the dominant and effective nationality is scarcely surprising as it is consistent with the contemporaneous development of international law to accord legal protections to individuals, even against the State of which they are nationals. Moreover . . ., many of the relevant decisions, even in the 19th century, reflected similar concerns by giving weight to domicile.

Thus, the relevant rule of international law which the Tribunal may take into account for purposes of interpretation, as directed by Article 31, paragraph 3(c), of the Vienna Convention, is the rule that flows from the *dictum* of *Nottebohm*, the rule of real and effective nationality, and the search for 'stronger factual ties between the person concerned and one of the States whose nationality is involved'. In view of the pervasive effect of this rule since the *Nottebohm* decision, the Tribunal concludes that the references to 'national' and 'nationals' in the Algiers Declarations must be understood as consistent with that rule unless an exception is clearly stated. As stated above, the Tribunal does not find that the text of the Algiers Declarations provides such a clear exception.

For the reasons stated above, the Tribunal holds that it has jurisdiction over claims against Iran by dual Iran-United States nationals when the dominant and effective nationality of the claimant during the relevant period from the date the claim arose until 19 January 1981 was that of the United States. [The question of interpretation posed in this case by the Government of Iran relates only to claims against Iran; however, it follows that the reasoning in this Decision is equally applicable to any claims against the United States.] In determining the dominant and effective nationality, the Tribunal will consider all relevant factors, including habitual residence, center of interests, family ties, participation in public life and other evidence of attachment.

To this conclusion the Tribunal adds an important caveat. In cases where the Tribunal finds jurisdiction based upon a dominant and effective nationality of the claimant, the other nationality may remain relevant to the merits of the claim. . . .

(d) *Diplomatic protection of legal persons: nationality of claims*

Barcelona Traction, Light and Power Company Limited Case (*Belgium* v *Spain*) (Second Phase)
ICJ Rep 1970 3, International Court of Justice

Belgium brought a claim on behalf of its nationals, who comprised the vast majority of shareholders in the Barcelona Traction, Light and Power Company Limited, a company incorporated in Canada. This company had been affected by acts of the Spanish authorities. The Court upheld the Spanish objections to Belgium's ability to bring the claim.

35. In the present case it is therefore essential to establish whether the losses allegedly suffered by Belgian shareholders in Barcelona Traction were the consequence of the violation of obligations of which they were the beneficiaries. In other words: has a right of Belgium been violated on account of its nationals' having suffered infringement of their rights as shareholders in a company not of Belgian nationality?

36. Thus it is the existence or absence of a right, belonging to Belgium and recognized as such by international law, which is decisive for the problem of Belgium's capacity. . . . It follows that the same question is determinant in respect of Spain's responsibility towards Belgium. Responsibility is the necessary corollary of a right. In the absence of any treaty on the subject between the Parties, this essential issue has to be decided in the light of the general rules of diplomatic protection.

37. In seeking to determine the law applicable to this case, the Court has to bear in mind the continuous evolution of international law. Diplomatic protection deals with a very sensitive area of international relations, since the interest of a foreign State in the protection of its nationals confronts the rights of the territorial sovereign, a fact of which the general law on the subject has had to take cognizance in order to prevent abuses and friction. From its origins closely linked with international commerce, diplomatic protection has sustained a particular impact from the growth of international economic relations, and at the same time from the profound transformations which have taken place in the economic life of nations. These latter changes have given birth to municipal institutions, which have transcended frontiers and have begun to exercise considerable influence on international relations. One of these phenomena which has a particular bearing on the present case is the corporate entity.

44. Notwithstanding the separate corporate personality, a wrong done to the company frequently causes prejudice to its shareholders. But the mere fact that damage is sustained by both company and shareholder does not imply that both are entitled to claim compensation. Thus no legal conclusion can be drawn from the fact that the same event caused damage simultaneously affecting several natural or juristic persons.

47. The situation is different if the act complained of is aimed at the direct rights of the shareholder as such. It is well known that there are rights which municipal law confers upon the latter distinct from those of the company, including the right to any declared dividend, the right to attend and vote at general meetings, the right to share in the residual assets of the company on liquidation. Whenever one of his direct rights is infringed, the shareholder has an independent right of action. On this there is no disagreement between the Parties. But a distinction must be drawn between a direct infringement of the shareholder's rights, and difficulties or financial losses to which he may be exposed as the result of the situation of the company. . . . Only in the event of the legal demise of the company are the shareholders deprived of the possibility of a remedy available through the company; it is only if they became deprived of all such possibility that an independent right of action for them and their government could arise.

67. In the present case, Barcelona Traction is in receivership in the country of incorporation. Far from implying the demise of the entity or of its rights, this much rather denotes that those rights are preserved for so long as no liquidation has ensued. Though in receivership, the company continues to exist. Moreover, it is a matter of public record that the company's shares were quoted on the stock-market at a recent date.

69. The Court will now turn to the second possibility, that of the lack of capacity of the company's national State to act on its behalf. The first question which must be asked here is whether Canada – the third apex of the triangular relationship – is, in law, the national State of Barcelona Traction.

70. In allocating corporate entities to States for purposes of diplomatic protection, international law is based, but only to a limited extent, on an analogy with the rules governing the nationality of individuals. The traditional rule attributes the right of diplomatic protection of a corporate entity to the State under the laws of which it is incorporated and in whose territory it has its registered office. These two criteria have been confirmed by long practice and by numerous international instruments. This notwithstanding, further or different links are at times said to be required in order that a right of diplomatic protection should exist. Indeed, it has been the practice of some States to give a company incorporated under their law diplomatic protection solely when it has its seat (*siège social*) or management or centre of control in their territory, or when a majority or a substantial proportion of the shares has been owned by nationals of the State concerned. Only then, it has been held, does there exist between the corporation and the State in question a genuine connection of the kind familiar from other branches of international law. However, in the particular field of the diplomatic protection of corporate entities, no absolute test of the 'genuine connection' has found general acceptance. Such tests as have been applied are of a relative nature, and sometimes links with one State have had to be weighed against those with another. In this connection reference has been made to the *Nottebohm* case. In fact the Parties made frequent reference to it in the course of the proceedings. However, given both the legal and factual aspects of protection in the present case the Court is of the opinion that there can be no analogy with the issues raised or the decision given in that case.

71. In the present case, it is not disputed that the company was incorporated in Canada and has its registered office in that country . . .

78. The Court would here observe that, within the limits prescribed by international law, a State may exercise diplomatic protection by whatever means and to whatever extent it thinks fit, for it is its own right that the State is asserting. Should the natural or legal persons on whose behalf it is acting

consider that their rights are not adequately protected, they have no remedy in international law. All they can do is to resort to municipal law, if means are available, with a view to furthering their cause or obtaining redress. The municipal legislator may lay upon the State an obligation to protect its citizens abroad, and may also confer upon the national a right to demand the performance of that obligation, and clothe the right with corresponding sanctions. However, all these questions remain within the province of municipal law and do not affect the position internationally.

79. The State must be viewed as the sole judge to decide whether its protection will be granted, to what extent it is granted, and when it will cease. It retains in this respect a discretionary power the exercise of which may be determined by considerations of a political or other nature, unrelated to the particular case. Since the claim of the State is not identical with that of the individual or corporate person whose cause is espoused, the State enjoys complete freedom of action. Whatever the reasons for any change of attitude, the fact cannot in itself constitute a justification for the exercise of diplomatic protection by another government, unless there is some independent and otherwise valid ground for that.

80. This cannot be regarded as amounting to a situation where a violation of law remains without remedy: in short, a legal vacuum. There is no obligation upon the possessors of rights to exercise them. Sometimes no remedy is sought, though rights are infringed. To equate this with the creation of a vacuum would be to equate a right with an obligation.

81. The cessation by the Canadian Government of the diplomatic protection of Barcelona Traction cannot, then, be interpreted to mean that there is no remedy against the Spanish Government for the damage done by the allegedly unlawful acts of the Spanish authorities. It is not a hypothetical right which was vested in Canada, for there is no legal impediment preventing the Canadian Government from protecting Barcelona Traction. Therefore there is no substance in the argument that for the Belgian Government to bring a claim before the Court represented the only possibility of obtaining redress for the damage suffered by Barcelona Traction and, through it, by its shareholders.

94. In view, however, of the discretionary nature of diplomatic protection, considerations of equity cannot require more than the possibility for some protector State to intervene, whether it be the national State of the company, by virtue of the general rule mentioned above, or, in a secondary capacity, the national State of the shareholders who claim protection. In this connection, account should also be taken of the practical effects of deducing from considerations of equity any broader right of protection for the national State of the shareholders. It must first of all be observed that it would be difficult on an equitable basis to make distinctions according to any quantitative test: it would seem that the owner of 1 per cent and the owner of 90 per cent of the share-capital should have the same possibility of enjoying the benefit of diplomatic protection. The protector State may, of course, be disinclined to take up the case of the single small shareholder, but it could scarcely be denied the right to do so in the name of equitable considerations. In that field, protection by the national State of the shareholders can hardly be graduated according to the absolute or relative size of the shareholding involved.

96. The Court considers that the adoption of the theory of diplomatic protection of shareholders as such, by opening the door to competing diplomatic claims, could create an atmosphere of confusion and insecurity in international economic relations. The danger would be all the greater inasmuch as the shares of companies whose activity is international are widely scattered and frequently change hands. It might perhaps be claimed that, if the right of protection belonging to the national States of the shareholders were considered as only secondary to that of the national State of the company, there would be less danger of difficulties of the kind contemplated. However, the Court must state that the essence of a secondary right is that it only comes into existence at the time when the original right ceases to exist. As the right of protection vested in the national State of the company cannot be regarded as extinguished because it is not exercised, it is not possible to accept

the proposition that in case of its non-exercise the national States of the shareholders have a right of protection secondary to that of the national State of the company. . . .

100. In the present case, it is clear from what has been said above that Barcelona Traction was never reduced to a position of impotence such that it could not have approached its national State, Canada, to ask for its diplomatic protection, and that, as far as appeared to the Court, there was nothing to prevent Canada from continuing to grant its diplomatic protection to Barcelona Traction if it had considered that it should do so.

101. For the above reasons, the Court is not of the opinion that, in the particular circumstances of the present case, *jus standi* is conferred on the Belgian Government by considerations of equity.

United Kingdom Rules regarding the Taking Up of International Claims by Her Majesty's Government, July 1983
(1983) 54 BYBIL 520

Rule I

HMG will not take up the claim unless the claimant is a United Kingdom national and was so at the date of the injury.

Rule II

Where the claimant has become or ceases to be a UK national after the date of the injury, HMG may in an appropriate case take up his claim in concert with the government of the country of his former or subsequent nationality.

Rule III

Where the claimant is a dual national, HMG may take up his claim, (although in certain circumstances it may be appropriate for HMG to do so jointly with the other government entitled to do so). HMG will not normally take up his claim as a UK national if the respondent State is the State of his second nationality, but may do so if the respondent State has, in the circumstances which gave rise to the injury, treated the claimant as a UK national.

Rule IV

HMG may take up the claim of a corporation or other juridical person which is created and regulated by the law of the United Kingdom or of any territory for which HMG are internationally responsible.

Rule V

Where a UK national has an interest, as a shareholder or otherwise, in a company incorporated in another State, and that company is injured by the acts of a third State, HMG may normally take up his claim only in concert with the government of the State in which the company is incorporated. Exceptionally, as where the company is defunct, there may be independent intervention.

Rule VI

Where a UK national has an interest, as a shareholder or otherwise, in a company incorporated in another State and of which it is therefore a national, and that State injures the company, HMG may intervene to protect the interests of that UK national.

Comment

In some cases the State of incorporation of a company does not possess the primary national interest in the company. A company may be created for reasons of legal or economic advantage under the law of one State though nearly all the capital is owned by nationals of another. In such circumstances, the State in which the company is incorporated may have little interest in protecting it, while the State to which the nationals who own the capital belong has considerable interest in so doing. In the Barcelona Traction Case, the International Court of Justice denied the existence under customary international law of an inherent right for the national State of shareholders in a foreign company to exercise diplomatic protection. However, the majority of the Court accepted the existence of a right to protect shareholders in the two cases described in Rules V and VI (when the company is defunct, and where the State in which the company is incorporated, although theoretically the legal protector of the company, itself causes injury to the company).

Where the capital in a foreign company is owned in various proportions by nationals of several States, including the United Kingdom, it is unusual for HMG to make representations unless the States whose nationals hold the bulk of the capital will support them in making representations.

NOTES:

1. The *Barcelona Traction Case* can be criticised for drawing an unnecessary distinction between when diplomatic protection can be exercised for natural and legal persons. The corporation may have little 'genuine link' with its State of incorporation, and that State may have little interest in that corporation or any connection with that corporation's activities, particularly where it is a 'tax haven' State. Also, by acknowledging that there could be an exception to the general principle where the State of incorporation is the State which has acted against the corporation, the Court in the *Barcelona Traction Case* and the provision of Rule VI above, give special international protection to those shareholders who, by good fortune, own shares in a corporation where the majority of shareholders do not reside in the State of incorporation.

2. To require a corporation to be defunct and so lacking any legal personality – and not merely to be without any assets – before the State of the shareholders can bring a claim, is to ignore the situation that shareholders are the 'economic reality' behind the 'corporate fiction' of a corporation. Consequently, some specialist settlement regimes – such as the US-Iran Claims Tribunal – define the nationality of a claim of a company by reference to the nationality of its shareholders.

3. Attempts have been made to limit the situations where a State can intervene, by diplomatic protection of its nationals, in a contractual dispute between a State and non-national. The 'Calvo clause' is the main example of this. It is a clause of a contract, usually in terms to the effect that 'under no conditions shall the intervention of foreign diplomatic agents be permitted, in any matter related to this contract'. In the *North American Dredging Company Claim* 4 RIAA (1926) 26, the Mexico-United States General Claims Commission said that the clause meant that the terms of the contract were binding on the non-national but did not prevent an application by him to his State for protection against violations of international law arising from his contract or otherwise. It also did not, and could not, prevent a State bringing diplomatic protection itself, as that was a right of a sovereign State. Some limitations also can be placed on the right of diplomatic protection by specific agreement between States, as seen in the Convention on the Settlement of Investment Disputes between States and Nationals of Other States 1966 (ICSID Convention) (see further below and in Chapter 15). Article 27(1) of that Convention provides that:

> no Contracting State shall give diplomatic protection, or bring an international claim, in respect of a dispute which one of its nationals and another Contracting State shall have consented to submit or shall have submitted to arbitration under this Convention, unless

such other Contracting State shall have failed to abide by and comply with the award rendered in such dispute.

B: Exhaustion of local remedies

Norwegian Loans Case (France v Norway)
ICJ Rep 1957 9, International Court of Justice

France brought a claim on behalf of its nationals who were holders of Norwegian bonds. Norway objected to the action on the ground, *inter alia*, that remedies in the Norwegian courts had not been exhausted.

JUDGE LAUTERPACHT (Separate Opinion): [T]he requirement of exhaustion of local remedies is not a purely technical or rigid rule. It is a rule which international tribunals have applied with a considerable degree of elasticity. In particular, they have refused to act upon it in cases in which there are, in fact, no effective remedies available owing to the law of the State concerned or the conditions prevailing in it. . . .

The Norwegian Government has contended that the burden of proving the inefficacy of local remedies rests upon France. There is, in general, a degree of unhelpfulness in the argument concerning the burden of proof. However, some *prima facie* distribution of the burden of proof there must be. This being so, the following seems to be the accurate principle on the subject: (1) As a rule, it is for the plaintiff State to prove that there are no effective remedies to which recourse can be had; (2) no such proof is required if there exists legislation which on the face of it deprives the private claimants of a remedy; (3) in that case it is for the defendant State to show that, notwithstanding the apparent absence of a remedy, its existence can nevertheless reasonably be assumed; (4) the degree of burden of proof thus to be adduced ought not to be so stringent as to render the proof unduly exacting.

Finnish Shipowners Arbitration (Finland v United Kingdom)
3 RIAA (1934) 1479, Bagge, Single Arbitrator

During the First World War, 13 ships belonging to Finnish shipowners were used by the UK Government, of which four were lost. After fruitless negotiation, the Finnish shipowners submitted the case to the Admiralty Transport Arbitration Board in the UK. This Board decided in January 1926, that the ships were not requisitioned by the UK but by Russia, and so no compensation was payable. No appeal was taken from this decision. The matter was later brought by Finland before an international arbitration tribunal. The UK objected on the ground that the Finnish shipowners had not exhausted local remedies in the UK. The Arbitrator rejected this objection.

The remedy of appeal relied on by the British Government may be said always to be open to a claimant in that sense that there is a right to file a notice of appeal and to have the contentions of the appellant as to his formal right of appeal dealt with by the Court of Appeal. It is, however, common ground that this is not sufficient to bring in the local remedies rule; the remedy must be effective and adequate.

A remedy of appeal is effective only if the Court of Appeal may enter into the merits of the case. But even this does not exhaust the condition of effectiveness under international law. . . . The rule as to local remedies is not a rule devised for the purpose of preventing international claims from being made because they are, or are thought to be ill founded, but it is based upon quite different conceptions: in cases of the present character the basis of the rule is that the foreign State should, first of all, be given the opportunity of redressing the wrong alleged. Whether a wrong has really been committed is a different question altogether, with which the international rule under discussion is not concerned; the only point under that rule is: Does the municipal means of redress exist? . . .

[T]he respondent State is entitled, first of all to discharge its responsibility by doing justice in its own way, but also to the investigation and adjudication of its own tribunals upon the questions of law and fact which the claim involves and then on the basis of this adjudication to appreciate its international responsibility and to meet or reject the claim accordingly.

According to the principles approved by the Arbitrator every relevant contention, whether it is well founded or not, brought forward by the claimant Government in the international procedure, must under the local remedies rule have been investigated and adjudicated upon by the highest competent municipal court.

The parties in the present case, however, agree – and rightly – that the local remedies rule does not apply where there is no effective remedy. And the British Government, as previously mentioned, submit that this is the case where a recourse is obviously futile. It is evident that the British Government there include not only cases where recourse is futile because on formal grounds there is no remedy or no further remedy, e.g. where there is no appealable point of law in the judgement, but also cases where on the merits of the claim recourse is obviously futile, e.g. where there may be appealable points of law but they are obviously insufficient to reverse the decision of the Court of first instance. The British Government, however, contend that in this latter case the merits must be considered upon the hypothesis that every allegation of fact in the claim is true and every legal proposition upon which it is based is correct.

The Arbitrator is of the same opinion, with the reservation only that, of course, where it is, as here, a question of remedy on appeal, and contentions of fact maintained by the claimant Government but rejected by the Arbitration Board, are not appealable, such contentions may not be taken as well founded. . . . [T]he Arbitrator comes to the conclusion that the appealable points of law, whether directly referring to British requisition or not, obviously would have been insufficient to reverse the decision of the Arbitration Board as to there not being a British requisition and that, in consequence, there was no effective remedy against this decision.

Elettronica Sicula SpA (ELSI) Case (United States v Italy)
ICJ Rep 1989 15, Chamber of the International Court of Justice

The dispute arose out of the requisition by Italy of the plant and other assets of ELSI, an Italian corporation wholly owned by two US corporations, Raytheon and Machlett. Prior to this requisition, due to financial difficulties, the US corporations had begun to plan for the liquidation of ELSI. The US claimed compensation for the two US corporate shareholders of ELSI pursuant to a treaty (the 'FCN Treaty') with Italy, as the planned liquidation was intended to pay the creditors in full, while the requisition meant that creditors received less than 1 per cent of their claims and the shareholders received nothing. Italy had objected to the admissibility of the claim on the ground that the US corporations had failed to exhaust the remedies available to them in Italy. This objection was unanimously rejected by the Chamber.

The Chamber has no doubt that the parties to a treaty can therein either agree that the local remedies rule shall not apply to claims based on alleged breaches of that treaty; or confirm that it shall apply. Yet the Chamber finds itself unable to accept that an important principle of customary international law should be held to have been tacitly dispensed with, in the absence of any words making clear an intention to do so. . . .

51. The United States further argued that the local remedies rule would not apply in any event to

the part of the United States claim which requested a declaratory judgment finding that the FCN Treaty had been violated. The argument of the United States is that such a judgment would declare that the United States own rights under the FCN Treaty had been infringed; and that to such a direct injury the local remedies rule, which is a rule of customary international law developed in the context of the espousal by a State of the claim of one of its nationals, would not apply. The Chamber, however, has not found it possible in the present case to find a dispute over alleged violation of the FCN Treaty resulting in direct injury to the United States, that is both distinct from, and independent of, the dispute over the alleged violation in respect of Raytheon and Machlett. . . .

52. Moreover, when the Court was, in the *Interhandel* case, faced with a not dissimilar argument by Switzerland that in that case its 'principal submission' was in respect of a 'direct breach of international law' and therefore not subject to the local remedies rule, the Court, having analysed that 'principal submission', found that it was bound up with the diplomatic protection claim, and that the Applicant's arguments 'do not deprive the dispute . . . of the character of a dispute in which the Swiss Government appears as having adopted the cause of its national . . .' (*Interhandel, Judgment, ICJ Reports 1959*, p. 28). In the present case, likewise, the Chamber has no doubt that the matter which colours and pervades the United States claim as a whole, is the alleged damage to Raytheon and Machlett, said to have resulted from the actions of the Respondent. Accordingly, the Chamber rejects the argument that in the present case there is a part of the Applicant's claim which can be severed so as to render the local remedies rule inapplicable to that part. . . .

[T]he local remedies rule does not, indeed cannot, require that a claim be presented to the municipal courts in a form, and with arguments, suited to an international tribunal, applying different law to different parties: for an international claim to be admissible, it is sufficient if the essence of the claim has been brought before the competent tribunals and pursued as far as permitted by local law and procedures, and without success. . . . It thus appears to the Chamber to be impossible to deduce, from the recent jurisprudence cited, what the attitude of the Italian courts would have been had Raytheon and Machlett brought an action, some 20 years ago, in reliance on Article 2043 of the Civil Code in conjunction with the provisions of the FCN Treaty and the Supplementary Agreement. Where the determination of a question of municipal law is essential to the Court's decision in a case, the Court will have to weight the jurisprudence of the municipal courts, and 'If this is uncertain or divided, it will rest with the Court to select the interpretation which it considers most in conformity with the law' (*Brazilian Loans, PCIJ, Series A, Nos. 20/21*, p. 124). In the present case, however, it was for Italy to show, as a matter of fact, the existence of a remedy which was open to the United States stockholders and which they failed to employ. The Chamber does not consider that Italy has discharged that burden.

63. It is never easy to decide, in a case where there has in fact been much resort to the municipal courts, whether local remedies have truly been 'exhausted'. But in this case Italy has not been able to satisfy the Chamber that there clearly remained some remedy which Raytheon and Machlett, independently of ELSI, and of ELSI's trustee in bankruptcy, ought to have pursued and exhausted. Accordingly, the Chamber will now proceed to consider the merits of the case.

NOTES:
1. The principle of the equality of States requires that the State responsible for an international wrong must first be given an opportunity to redress the wrong in its own legal system. However, the principle applies only where a diplomatic protection claim is made (i.e. a claim on 'behalf' of an injured national), and not where there is direct injury to a State, as then a submission to a national court would be inappropriate. A State can by specific agreement waive the local remedies rule, as was done by the US and Iran when establishing the Iran-United States Claims Tribunal (see below).
2. In the *Ambatielos Arbitration (Greece v United Kingdom)* 12 RIAA (1956) 83, the Commission of

Arbitration decided that if an appeal was futile because of the neglect of the national to call relevant evidence, then the rule of exhaustion of local remedies was not satisfied and so the international arbitration tribunal was prevented from deciding the claim. The various international and regional human rights tribunals have also upheld the principle of the exhaustion of local remedies (see Chapter 6).

C: Special enforcement regimes

It is in the nature of international relations that two or more States may be embroiled in an international controversy that affects the lives and well-being of many of their nationals. These events – such as the Islamic Revolution in Iran 1978/9 or the Iraq/Kuwait Gulf War 1990/91 – may give rise to international responsibility because of injury to the nationals of the disputants or because of injury directly to the States themselves. These claims could be settled on an *ad hoc* basis, with each individual claim being heard by a tribunal specially composed for the task or adjudicated by means of a generic claims procedure specifically established for that purpose. The latter will save time and money, will promote consistency of legal reasoning and allows the disputing States to choose the procedural and substantive legal rules they find most suitable. Good examples are provided by the US-Iran Claims Tribunal, established by the parties to deal with claims by nationals against either State after the Islamic Revolution, and the United Nations Compensation Commission established by the UN Security Council in 1991 (SC Res 687) to provide compensation to natural and legal persons suffering loss because of Iraq's unlawful invasion of Kuwait. The former Tribunal is essentially judicial, and many of its awards have contributed significantly to the development of the law of State responsibility. The UN Commission is rather more administrative in scope, although it decides which claimants may share in the compensation fund established from Iraq's oil revenues. Finally, States may sometimes enter into what are known as 'lump sum' settlements with other States that are alleged to be internationally responsible for some violation of international law. Under such settlements, the alleged delinquent State will pay a sum in full and final settlement of all claims. The final sum usually will *not* have been calculated by reference to the actual loss of the nationals of the claimant State. Examples include the US-Cambodia (1994) and US-Vietnam (1995) Claims Settlement Agreements, whereby both Cambodia and Vietnam agreed to pay a lump sum in full and final settlement of US claims and those of its nationals.

SECTION 4: Circumstances precluding wrongfulness (defences)

International Law Commission, Articles on Responsibility of States for Internationally Wrongful Acts

August 2001, Special Rapporteur James Crawford

Article 20 Consent

Valid consent by a State to the commission of a given act by another State precludes the wrongfulness of that act in relation to the former State to the extent that the act remains within the limits of that consent.

Article 21 Self-defence

The wrongfulness of an act of a State is precluded if the act constitutes a lawful measure of self-defence taken in conformity with the Charter of the United Nations.

Article 22 Countermeasures in respect of an internationally wrongful act

The wrongfulness of an act of a State not in conformity with an international obligation towards another State is precluded if and to the extent that the act constitutes a countermeasure taken against the latter State in accordance with Chapter II of Part Three.

Article 23 *Force majeure*

1. The wrongfulness of an act of a State not in conformity with an international obligation of that State is precluded if the act is due to *force majeure*, that is the occurrence of an irresistible force or of an unforeseen event, beyond the control of the State, making it materially impossible in the circumstances to perform the obligation.

2. Paragraph 1 does not apply if:
   (a) the situation of *force majeure* is due, either alone or in combination with other factors, to the conduct of the State invoking it; or
   (b) the State has assumed the risk of that situation occurring.

Article 24 Distress

1. The wrongfulness of an act of a State not in conformity with an international obligation of that State is precluded if the author of the act in question has no other reasonable way, in a situation of distress, of saving the author's life or the lives of other persons entrusted to the author's care.

2. Paragraph 1 does not apply if:
   (a) the situation of distress is due, either alone or in combination with other factors, to the conduct of the State invoking it; or
   (b) the act in question is likely to create a comparable or greater peril.

Article 25 Necessity

1. Necessity may not be invoked by a State as a ground for precluding the wrongfulness of an act not in conformity with an international obligation of that State unless the act:
   (a) is the only way for the State to safeguard an essential interest against a grave and imminent peril; and
   (b) does not seriously impair an essential interest of the State or States towards which the obligation exists, or of the international community as a whole.

2. In any case, necessity may not be invoked by a State as a ground for precluding wrongfulness if:
   (a) the international obligation in question excludes the possibility of invoking necessity; or
   (b) the State has contributed to the situation of necessity.

Article 26 Compliance with peremptory norms

Nothing in this chapter precludes the wrongfulness of any act of a State which is not in conformity with an obligation arising under a peremptory norm of general international law.

Article 27 Consequences of invoking a circumstance precluding wrongfulness

The invocation of a circumstance precluding wrongfulness in accordance with this chapter is without prejudice to:

(a) compliance with the obligation in question, if and to the extent that the circumstance precluding wrongfulness no longer exists;

(b) the question of compensation for any material loss caused by the act in question.

ILC Commentary on the Draft Articles

Official Records of the General Assembly, Fifty-sixth session, Supplement No 10
(A/56/10), Chp.IV.E.2), Commentary on Circumstances Precluding Wrongfulness

(1) Chapter V sets out six circumstances precluding the wrongfulness of conduct that would otherwise not be in conformity with the international obligations of the State concerned. The existence in a given case of a circumstance precluding wrongfulness in accordance with this chapter provides a shield against an otherwise well-founded claim for the breach of an international obligation. The six circumstances are: consent (article 20), self-defence (article 21), countermeasures (article 22), *force majeure* (article 23), distress (article 24) and necessity (article 25). Article 26 makes it clear that none of these circumstances can be relied on if to do so would conflict with a peremptory norm of general international law. Article 27 deals with certain consequences of the invocation of one of these circumstances.

(2) Consistently with the approach of the present articles, the circumstances precluding wrongfulness set out in Chapter V are of general application. Unless otherwise provided, they apply to any internationally wrongful act whether it involves the breach by a State of an obligation arising under a rule of general international law, a treaty, a unilateral act or from any other source. They do not annual or terminate the obligation; rather they provide a justification or excuse for non-performance while the circumstance in question subsists. This was emphasized by the International Court in the *Gabčíkovo-Nagymaros Project* case. . . . Thus a distinction must be drawn between the effect of circumstances precluding wrongfulness and the termination of the obligation itself. The circumstances in Chapter V operate as a shield rather than a sword. As Fitzmaurice noted, where one of the circumstances precluding wrongfulness applies, the non-performance is not only justified, but looks towards a resumption of performance as soon as the factors causing and justifying the non-performance are no longer present.

Rainbow Warrior Arbitration (*New Zealand* v *France*)

82 ILR (1990) 499, France-New Zealand Arbitration Tribunal

The facts are set out in Chapter 3. Among many submissions, France claimed that the health of its nationals gave rise to the defences of *force majeure* and distress and, further, that these were available defences to a claim of State responsibility based on breach of a treaty even though such defences were not regarded as reasons for non-performance of a treaty obligation in the law of treaties.

(1) According to Article 2 of the Supplementary Agreement, the Tribunal was required to reach its decision on the basis of

. . . the Agreements concluded between the Government of New Zealand and the Government of the French Republic by Exchange of Letters of 9 July 1986, this Agreement and the applicable rules and principles of customary international law.

Both the customary international law of treaties and the law of State responsibility were thus relevant. From the law of treaties, codified in the Vienna Convention on the Law of Treaties, 1969, the principle *pacta sunt servanda* and the provisions relating to the consequences of material breach and the expiry of agreements were particularly relevant. However, international law made no distinction between contractual and tortious liability. It followed that the violation by a State of a treaty obligation gave rise to State responsibility and had therefore to be evaluated in the light of the principles of the law of State responsibility, including the determination of the circumstances which might exclude wrongfulness. . . .

(2) Of the principles which the International Law Commission, in its Draft Articles on State Responsibility, had recognized as grounds for excluding wrongfulness. three – *force majeure* (Article 31), distress (Article 32) and necessity (Article 33) – might be relevant to the present case.

(a) *Force majeure* was cast in absolute terms and applied only where circumstances rendered compliance by a State with an international obligation impossible. It did not apply where, as here, circumstances merely made compliance more difficult or burdensome. . . .

(b) Distress had to be distinguished from the more controversial notion of necessity. What was involved in distress was a choice between departure from an international obligation and a serious threat to the life or physical integrity of a State organ or of persons entrusted to its care. Necessity, on the other hand, was concerned with departure from international obligations on the ground of vital interests of State. For distress to be applicable in the cases of Major Mafart and Captain Prieur, three conditions were requested:

(i) the existence of exceptional medical or other circumstances of an elementary nature of extreme urgency, provided that a prompt recognition of the existence of those circumstances was subsequently obtained from, or demonstrated by, the other Party;

(ii) the re-establishment of the original situation of compliance in Hao as soon as the circumstances of emergency had disappeared; and

(iii) a good faith attempt to obtain the consent of New Zealand under the terms of the First Agreement. . . .

Danube Dam Case
The Case Concerning the Gabcikovo-Nagymaros Project (Hungary/Slovakia)
ICJ Rep 1997 7, International Court of Justice

Czechoslovakia and Hungary agreed by Treaty in 1977 to construct a series of dams along the Danube. In 1989 Hungary abandoned work on its part of the project. In 1991, Czechoslovakia began work on a unilateral modification to the original scheme ('Variant C') and put this into effect in October 1992. In the intervening period (May 1992), Hungary purported to terminate the Treaty. Having failed to negotiate a solution, the parties (now Slovakia, following the division of the Czech-Slovak State) submitted various questions to the Court. One major issue concerned the parties' alleged responsibility for breach of treaty. The ICJ confirmed the *Rainbow Warrior* view that a State could rely on general 'circumstances precluding wrongfulness' when denying a breach of treaty and were not limited to 'treaty-specific' defences. The Court also confirmed that the then ILC Draft Article on 'necessity' (now Art. 25) represented customary international law.

47. Nor does the Court need to dwell upon the question of the relationship between the law of treaties and the law of State responsibility, to which the Parties devoted lengthy arguments, as those two branches of international law obviously have a scope that is distinct. A determination of whether a convention is or is not in force, and whether it has or has not been properly suspended or denounced, is to be made pursuant to the law of treaties. On the other hand, an evaluation of the

extent to which the suspension or denunciation of a convention, seen as incompatible with the law of treaties, involves the responsibility of the State which proceeded to it, is to be made under the law of State responsibility.

Thus the Vienna Convention of 1969 on the Law of Treaties confines itself to defining – in a limitative manner – the conditions in which a treaty may lawfully be denounced or suspended; while the effects of a denunciation or suspension seen as not meeting those conditions are, on the contrary, expressly excluded from the scope of the Convention by operation of Article 73. It is moreover well established that, when a State has committed an internationally wrongful act, its international responsibility is likely to be involved whatever the nature of the obligation it has failed to respect (cf. *Interpretation of Peace Treaties with Bulgaria, Hungary and Romania Second Phase, Advisory Opinion, ICJ Reports 1950*, p. 228, and see Article 17 of the Draft Articles on State Responsibility provisionally adopted by the International Law Commission on first reading, *Yearbook of the International Law Commission*, 1980, Vol. II, Part 2, p. 32).

NOTES:

1. The defences or, as the ILC Articles entitle them, 'circumstances precluding wrongfulness', indicate the extent to which States have control over their own responsibility through the development of exceptions to the imposition of liability. Moreover, as the *Rainbow Warrior* and *Danube Dam* cases illustrate, most defences to State responsibility are generally applicable and are not limited to breaches of certain kinds of obligations (see Commentary on the Draft Article). Thus, the Vienna Convention on the Law of Treaties is arguably not exhaustive as to the circumstances in which a State can be excused non-performance of a treaty obligation (see Chapter 3).

2. The *Rainbow Warrior* case also illustrates how the interpretation of the extent of an international legal obligation can be crucial to determining the existence of State responsibility or the appropriate remedy. France was under an obligation to detain the French agents in the Pacific 'for a period not less than three years'. At first sight, this might be thought to mean that the total period of detention should be three years, and this was the view of Sir Kenneth Keith, dissenting. The majority, however, determined that France's obligation was to detain the agents for an absolute period of three years from the date of their first incarceration. Consequently, once three years had passed in absolute terms, France was no longer under an obligation and the agents could not be returned to the island, irrespective of how long they had actually been there. France might be responsible for their unlawful removal within the three-year period but France's obligation ended once three years had passed.

3. In the extract from *Danube Dam* the Court touches on the relationship between the law of treaties and the law of State responsibility. Its conclusion – that there is almost a two-stage test, with treaty law determining validity and State responsibility determining liability – is superficially attractive. However, it might be thought artificial and unnecessarily complicated, especially as it is difficult to see how State relations can be forensically dissected in the way the Court suggests.

SECTION 5: **Treatment of aliens**

One important aspect of State responsibility concerns the obligations that a State owes to nationals of other States within its territory. Thus, mistreatment of these nationals by organs or officers of the State may give rise to responsibility on the international plane. This will not arise out of every incident in which a non-national is harmed (either physically or economically) but applies when the 'host' State has fallen below the standard of treatment that international law requires it to show to 'aliens'. Importantly, this responsibility can arise either directly through an act or omission attributable to the State that causes physical or economic harm to the non-national, or indirectly where the territorial sovereign is guilty of a 'denial of justice', being cases where the non-nationals are prejudiced in their attempts to obtain a national law remedy in a dispute against any other party (e.g., another private individual). If there is a failure to treat a non-national according to the standard required by international law, it is then the State of nationality of the non-national that may pursue, at its option, an action on the international plane against the territorial sovereign.

G. Hackworth, *Digest of International Law*
(1943), vol 5, pp. 471–472

The admission of aliens into a State immediately calls into existence certain correlative rights and duties. The alien has a right to the protection of the local law. He owes a duty to observe that law and assumes a relationship toward the State of his residence sometimes referred to as 'temporary allegiance.'

The State has the right to expect that the alien shall observe its laws and that his conduct shall not be incompatible with the good order of the State and of the community in which he resides or sojourns. It has the obligation to give him that degree of protection for his person and property which he and his State have the right to expect under local law, under international law, and under treaties and conventions between his State and the State of residence. Failure of the alien or of the State to observe these requirements may give rise to responsibility in varying degrees, the alien being amenable to the local law or subject to expulsion from the State, or both, and the State being responsible to the alien or to the State of which he is a national.

We are here concerned primarily with responsibility of the State. State responsibility may arise directly or indirectly. It does not arise merely because an alien has been injured or has suffered loss within the State's territory. If the alien has suffered an injury at the hands of a private person his remedy usually is against that person, and State responsibility does not arise in the absence of a dereliction of duty on the part of the State itself in connection with the injury, as for example by failure to afford a remedy, or to apply an existing remedy. When local remedies are available the alien is ordinarily not entitled to the interposition of his government until he has exhausted those remedies and has been denied justice. This presupposes the existence in the State of orderly judicial and administrative processes. In theory an unredressed injury to an alien constitutes an injury to his State, giving rise to international responsibility.

Neer Claim (United States v Mexico)
4 RIAA (1926) 60, Mexico-United States General Claims Commission

> Mr Neer, a national of the United States, was working in Mexico when he was stopped by armed men and shot. It was claimed that the Mexican authorities were not diligent in their investigations into the murder and that they should pay damages to Neer's family. This was rejected by the Commission.

Without attempting to announce a precise formula, it is in the opinion of the Commission possible . . . to hold (first) that the propriety of governmental acts should be put to the test of international standards, and (second) that the treatment of an alien, in order to constitute an international delinquency, should amount to an outrage, to bad faith, to wilful neglect of duty, or to an insufficiency of governmental action so far short of international standards that every reasonable and impartial man would readily recognize its insufficiency. Whether the insufficiency proceeds from deficient execution of an intelligent law or from the fact that the laws of the country do not empower the authorities to measure up to international standards is immaterial. . . . In the light of the entire record in this case the Commission is not prepared to hold that the Mexican authorities have shown such lack of diligence or such lack of intelligent investigation in apprehending and punishing the culprits as would render Mexico liable before this Commission.

Harvard Draft Convention on the Responsibility of States for Damage done in their Territory to the Person or Property of Foreigners
23 AJIL (1929), Special Supplement 133

Article 9
Denial of justice exists when there is a denial, unwarranted delay or obstruction of access to courts, gross deficiency in the administration of judicial or remedial process, failure to provide those guarantees which are generally considered indispensable to the proper administration of justice, or a manifestly unjust judgement. An error of a national court which does not produce manifest injustice is not a denial of justice.

NOTES:
1. Responsibility arising through a denial of justice may occur even though the initial act against the non-national (even if it was committed by the State) did not itself give rise to State responsibility, and even if the non-national is pursuing a perfectly ordinary action against another party in the national courts. Further, there may be a denial of justice giving rise to responsibility if the non-national is the object of local judicial action. For example, in the *Chattin Claim* 4 RIAA (1927) 282, Mexico was held internationally responsible for inadequacies and unfairness in the trial of Chattin on charges of embezzlement.
2. Many issues relating to the treatment of non-nationals (and nationals) are now within international human rights law (see Chapter 6).

SECTION 6: **Nationalisation/expropriation of non-nationals' property**

An area where the issues of State responsibility have raised significant opposing views, mainly due to the changes in the composition and number of States in the international community, is in regard to the nationalisation/expropriation of non-nationals' property by a State. The basic rule that a non-national takes the law of a

State as it finds it has now been modified by international law. The terms 'national-isation' and 'expropriation' are used interchangeably here.

A: Right to nationalise/expropriate

Texaco Overseas Petroleum Company v *Libyan Arab Republic*
53 ILR (1977) 389, Dupuy, Sole Arbitrator

Oil concessions were granted by the Libyan Government which gave exclusive rights to search for, extract and sell oil from Libyan territory. In order to ensure contractual stability, there were 'stabilisation' clauses in the concessions that sought to remove any impact on the concessions of changes in Libyan law. In particular, the clauses provided:

Clause 16
1. The Government of Libya will take all the steps necessary to ensure that the Company enjoys all the rights conferred by this Concession. The contractual rights expressly created by this concession shall not be altered except by mutual consent of the parties.

2. This Concession shall throughout the period of its validity be construed in accord-ance with the Petroleum Law and the Regulations in force on the date of execution of the agreement of amendment by which this paragraph 2 was incorporated into this concession agreement. Any amendment to or repeal of such Regulations shall not affect the contractual rights of the Company without its consent.

Clause 28
. . .
7. This Concession shall be governed by and interpreted in accordance with the prin-ciples of law of Libya common to the principles of international law and in the absence of such common principles then by and in accordance with the general principles of law, including such of those principles as may have been applied by international tribunals.

In 1971, the new Libyan Government nationalised Texaco's entire interest in the concession. The dispute was heard by an Arbitrator, in accordance with clause 28 of the contract.

[I]t is a well-known rule that nationalizations do not, in principle, produce any extra-territorial effect and that they cannot, in any case, impair or affect the existence of companies as legal entities which do not have the nationality of the nationalizing State.

59. This being so, the right of a State to nationalize is unquestionable today. It results from international customary law, established as the result of general practices considered by the inter-national community as being the law. The exercise of the national sovereignty to nationalize is regarded as the expression of the State's territorial sovereignty. Territorial sovereignty confers upon the State an exclusive competence to organize as it wishes the economic structures of its territory and to introduce therein any reforms which may seem to be desirable to it. It is an essential prerogative of sovereignty for the constitutionally authorized authorities of the State to choose and build freely an economic and social system. International law recognizes that a State has this prerogative just as it has the prerogative to determine freely its political regime and its constitutional institutions. The exclusive nature of such a right is in fact confirmed by the fact that in practice a

decision to nationalize very often is made by the organ which is regarded as the supreme level in the internal hierarchy of State institutions. . . .

60. [I]nternational practice as expressed within the framework of diplomatic protection for nationals abroad has hardly varied at all; it has not endeavored to limit as a matter of principle a power expressing the sovereignty of the State, but simply to claim reparation in one form or another, for the benefit of those who were injured by nationalization measures . . .

Thus, the recognition by international law of the right to nationalize is not sufficient ground to empower a State to disregard its commitments, because the same law also recognizes the power of a State to commit itself internationally, especially by accepting the inclusion of stabilization clauses in a contract entered into with a foreign private party.

73. Thus, in respect of the international law of contracts, a nationalization cannot prevail over an internationalized contract, containing stabilization clauses, entered into between a State and a foreign private company. The situation could be different only if one were to conclude that the exercise by a State of its right to nationalize places that State on a level outside of and superior to the contract and also to the international legal order itself, and constitutes an 'act of government' ('acte de gouvernement') which is beyond the scope of any judicial redress or any criticism. . . .

As regards the question of permanent sovereignty, a well-known distinction should be made as to enjoyment and exercise. The State granting the concession retains the permanent enjoyment of its sovereign rights; it cannot be deprived of the right in any way whatsoever; the contract which it entered into with a private company cannot be viewed as an alienation of such sovereignty but as a limitation, partial and limited in time, of the exercise of sovereignty. Accordingly, the State retains, within the areas which it has reserved, authority over the operations conducted by the concession holder, and the continuance of the exercise of its sovereignty is manifested, for example, by the various obligations imposed on its contracting party, which is in particular subjected to fiscal obligations that express unquestionably the sovereignty of the contracting State.

Starratt Housing Corporation v *Iran*
(1983-III) 4 Iran-USCTR 122, Iran-United States Claims Tribunal

The claimants argued that their property interests had been effectively nationalised due to actions of Iran, such as collapse of the banking system, freezing of assets of a subsidiary, harassment of personnel, appointment of a manager of the company by Iran, and reduction in the American workforce in Iran due to the Iranian Revolution.

It is undisputed in this case that the Government of Iran did not issue any law or decree according to which the Zomorod Project or Shah Goli expressly was nationalized or expropriated. However, it is recognized in international law that measures taken by a State can interfere with property rights to such an extent that these rights are rendered so useless that they must be deemed to have been expropriated, even though the State does not purport to have expropriated them and the legal title to the property formally remains with the original owner. . . . It has, however, to be borne in mind that assumption of control over property by a government does not automatically and immediately justify a conclusion that the property has been taken by the government, thus requiring compensation under international law. . . .

There is no reason to doubt that the events in Iran prior to January 1980 to which the Claimants refer, seriously hampered their possibilities to proceed with the construction work and eventually paralysed the Project. But investors in Iran, like investors in all other countries, have to assume a risk that the country might experience strikes, lock-outs, disturbances, changes of the economic and political system and even revolution. That any of these risks materialized does not necessarily mean that property rights affected by such events can be deemed to have been taken. A revolution as such does not entitle investors to compensation under international law. . . .

NOTES:
1. For the purpose of expropriation, the 'property' of non-nationals includes land, physical assets, shares, intellectual property rights, and contractual rights. A mere breach of contract by a State that has entered into a contract with a non-national is not an expropriation and will not give rise to State responsibility unless the contract has been internationalised: see *Texaco* above. However, the destruction of the non-national's ordinary contractual rights (i.e. in a contract not internationalised), in the sense that those contractual rights are appropriated by the State, can amount to an expropriation. In *Southern Pacific Properties* (below), the Tribunal rejected Egypt's argument that expropriation of contractual rights are not compensatable in international law.
2. In the *ELSI Case* (above), a Chamber of the International Court of Justice recognised that preventing a corporation's right to manage and control its own affairs could amount to a 'disguised expropriation'. In that case it concluded that no such 'disguised expropriation' had occurred. However, in *Shahin Shane Ebrahimi* v *Government of the Islamic Republic of Iran* (see below), the US-Iran Claims Tribunal concluded that the appointment of directors of the company by Iran amounted to an expropriation. The Tribunal said that 'a finding of expropriation is warranted whenever events demonstrate that the owner was deprived of fundamental rights of ownership and it appears that this deprivation is not merely ephemeral'.

B: Application of international law

Texaco Overseas Petroleum Company v *Libyan Arab Republic*
53 ILR (1977) 389, Dupuy, Sole Arbitrator

27. One cannot fail, in fact, on this point to recall the famous dictum stated by the Permanent Court of International Justice, in its judgments in the cases relating to the *Serbian and Brazilian Loans*:

> Any contract which is not a contract between States in their capacity as subjects of international law is based on the municipal law of some country. The question as to what this law is forms the subject of that branch of law which is at the present day usually described as private international law or the theory of conflict of laws. (*Case Concerning Various Serbian Loans Issued in France* [1929] PCIJ, Ser. A, No. 20, at 41.)

29. However, because it is a long time since the Permanent Court of International Justice delivered its judgments in the cases relating to the *Serbian and Brazilian Loans*, juridical analysis has been much refined in this field, in particular under the influence of contractual practice. This tends more and more to 'delocalize' the contract or, if one prefers, to sever its automatic connections to some municipal law: so much so that today when the municipal law of a given State, and particularly the municipal law of the contracting State, governs the contract, it is by virtue of the agreement between the parties and no longer by a privileged and so to speak mechanical application of the municipal law, as at a certain time was believed. Under the pressure of the needs of international trade, the principle of the autonomy of the will of the parties appears today to be much more significant than at the end of the 1920s.

42. International arbitration case law confirms that the reference to the general principles of law is always regarded to be a sufficient criterion for the internationalization of a contract. . . . The recourse to general principles is to be explained not only by the lack of adequate legislation in the

State considered (which might have been the case, at one time, in certain oil Emirates). It is also justified by the need for the private contracting party to be protected against unilateral and abrupt modifications of the legislation in the contracting State; it plays, therefore, an important role in the contractual equilibrium intended by the parties. . . .

Another process for the internationalization of a contract consists in inserting a clause providing that possible differences which may arise in respect of the interpretation and the performance of the contract shall be submitted to arbitration.

Such a clause has a twofold consequence:

— on the one hand, as this Tribunal has already noted . . ., the institution of arbitration shall be that established by international law.
— on the other hand, as regards the law applicable to the merits of the dispute itself, the inclusion of an arbitration clause leads to a reference to the rules of international law.

Even if one considers that the choice of international arbitration proceedings cannot by itself lead to the exclusive application of international law, it is one of the elements which makes it possible to detect a certain internationalization of the contract. . . . It is therefore unquestionable that the reference to international arbitration is sufficient to internationalize a contract, in other words, to situate it within a specific legal order – the order of the international law of contracts. . . .

A third element of the internationalization of the contracts in dispute results from the fact that it takes on a dimension of a new category of agreements between States and private persons: economic development agreements . . . Thus, the internationalization of certain contracts entered into between a State and a private person does not tend to confer upon a private person competences comparable to those of a State but only certain capacities which enable him to act internationally in order to invoke the rights which result to him from an internationalized contract. . . .

It follows that the reference made by the contracts under dispute to the principles of Libyan law does not nullify the effect of internationalization of the contracts which has already resulted from their nature as economic development agreements and recourse to international arbitration for the settlement of disputes. The application of the principles of Libyan law does not have the effect of ruling out the application of the principles of international law, but quite the contrary: it simply requires us to combine the two in verifying the conformity of the first with the second.

C: Unlawful nationalisation/expropriation

Libyan American Oil Company (LIAMCO) v *Libyan Arab Republic*
62 ILR (1977) 140, Mahmassani, Sole Arbitrator

The facts here were nearly identical to those of the *Texaco Case* above.

LIAMCO contends that such [expropriation] measures are wrongful, because they are politically motivated, discriminatory and confiscatory.

As to the contention that the said measures were politically motivated and not in pursuance of a legitimate public purpose, it is the general opinion in international theory that the public utility principle is not a necessary requisite for the legality of a nationalization. This principle was mentioned by Grotius and other later publicists, but now there is no international authority, from a judicial or any other source, to support its application to nationalization. Motives are indifferent to international law, each State being free:

to judge for itself what it considers useful or necessary for the public good . . . The object pursued by it is of no concern to third parties . . .

This assertion is easily comprehensible, because nationalization in itself usually presupposes a general policy or political plan in support of which it is executed.

However, political motivation may take the shape of discrimination as a result of political retaliation. That is what was sustained by LIAMCO in its contention of the discriminatory character of its nationalization measures.

It is clear and undisputed that non-discrimination is a requisite for the validity of a lawful nationalization. This is a rule well established in international legal theory and practice. . . . Therefore, a purely discriminatory nationalization is illegal and wrongful. . . .

From the . . . facts, it appears, that LIAMCO was not the first company to be nationalized, nor was it the only oil company nor the only American company to be nationalized by the first nationalization Act, nor was it nationalized alone on the date of the second nationalization Act. Other companies were nationalized before it, other American and Non-American companies were nationalized with it and after it, and other American companies are still operating in Libya.

Thus, it may be concluded from the above that the political motive was not the predominant motive for nationalization, and that such motive *per se* does not constitute a sufficient proof of a purely discriminatory measure. . . .

In its second method of estimating compensation, LIAMCO maintains that even lawful nationalization of a long term concession agreement entails adequate compensation which must include the profit lost, i.e. the current value of the economic benefits which the concessionnaire would have realized over the term of the contract.

This second method refers to lawful nationalization as distinguished from wrongful taking. Such distinction has already been clearly pointed out by the Permanent Court of International Justice in a dictum recorded in the *Chorzow Factory Case* in 1922. It clarified that, whereas in a wrongful taking the injured party must be restored to its original rights, – on the contrary in a lawful expropriation where the only wrongful act was the failure to pay the just price of what had been expropriated, the compensation due should be the value of the undertaking at the time of dispossession . . .

In conclusion, it may be safely laid down that it is lawful to nationalize concession rights before the expiry of the concession term, provided that the measure be not discriminatory nor in breach of treaty, and provided that compensation be duly paid.

Amoco International Finance v *Iran*
(1987–I) 15 Iran-USCTR 189, Iran-United States Claims Tribunal

This case concerned the nationalisation by Iran of the interest of a subsidiary of Amoco (Khemco), formed to construct and to operate a natural gas processing plant. The Tribunal considered the claim under a Treaty of Amity, Economic Relations and Consular Rights 1955 between the US and Iran and under the relevant rules of customary international law.

192. Undoubtedly, the first principle established by the Court [in the *Chorzów Factory Case*] is that a clear distinction must be made between lawful and unlawful expropriations, since the rules applicable to the compensation to be paid by the expropriating State differ according to the legal characterization of the taking. . . . Such a principle has been recently and expressly confirmed by the celebrated *AMINOIL* case, also invoked by both Parties. . . .

193. According to the Court in *Chorzów Factory*, an obligation of reparation of all the damages sustained by the owner of expropriated property arises from an unlawful expropriation. The rules of international law relating to international responsibility of States apply in such a case. They provide for *restitutio in integrum*: restitution in kind or, if impossible, its monetary equivalent. If need be, 'damages for loss sustained which would not be covered by restitution' should also be awarded. . . .

On the other hand, a lawful expropriation must give rise to 'the payment of fair compensation', . . . or of 'the just price of what was expropriated'. . . . Such an obligation is imposed by a specific rule of the international law of expropriation.

196. *Restitutio* is well defined by the Court. It means the restitution in kind or, if that is impossible, the payment of the monetary equivalent. In both cases the principle on which it lies is the same: 'that reparation must, as far as possible, wipe out all the consequences of the illegal act and reestablish the situation which would, in all probability, have existed if this act had not been committed'. . . . One essential consequence of this principle is that the compensation 'is not necessarily limited to the value of the undertaking at the moment of dispossession' (plus interest to the day of payment). According to the Court, 'this limitation would be admissible only if the Polish Government [the expropriating State] has had the right to expropriate, and if its wrongful act consisted merely in not having paid . . . the just price of what was expropriated'. This last statement is of paramount importance: It means that the compensation to be paid in case of a lawful expropriation (or of a taking which lacks only the payment of a fair compensation to be lawful) is limited to the value of the undertaking at the moment of the dispossession, i.e., 'the just price of what was expropriated'.

206. The case law developed since the judgment of the Court has generally followed the principles set forth in this judgment, at least on the distinction between lawful and unlawful expropriation. It is particularly remarkable that all the awards which adopted the standard of *restitutio* relate to expropriation found unlawful. . . .

209. 'Just compensation' has generally been understood as a compensation equal to the full value of the expropriated assets. This is confirmed in the wording of Article IV, paragraph 2, which refers to 'the full equivalent of the property taken'. The Tribunal does not see any material difference between this phrase and the usual term of 'just compensation'.

NOTES:

1. As indicated at the end of the extract from the *LIAMCO Case*, a breach of a treaty creates an unlawful nationalisation, as it is a breach of an international obligation. This was the situation in the *German Interests in Upper Silesia Case* (*Merits*) (*Germany v Poland*) PCIJ Ser A (1928), No. 7, and the *Factory at Chorzów (Claim for Indemnity) Case* (see below).
2. In *British Petroleum Exploration Company (Libya) Limited* v *Libyan Arab Republic* 53 ILR (1974) 329, the facts were that, in December 1971, the Libyan Revolutionary Command Council passed the BP Nationalisation Law, for the express purpose of retaliation for the UK's failure to prevent Iran occupying some islands in the Gulf, over which claims had been made by States which were under the protection of the UK. Lagergren, the Sole Arbitrator held that 'the taking by the Respondent of the property, rights and interests of the Claimant clearly violates public international law as it was made for purely extraneous political reasons and was arbitrary and discriminatory in character'. However, it would be rare that a State would express its reasons for nationalising property in such clear terms as these, or that an arbitrator would be prepared to criticise the public purpose motives of a State. Accordingly, the approach in the *LIAMCO Case* of considering the discriminatory nature of the particular nationalisation is preferable.
3. One basis for the distinction between lawful and unlawful expropriation is that in the latter case the corporation could not have taken account of that particular risk when it decided to invest in the host State. It is arguable that failure to pay any compensation at all may make the expropriation unlawful.

D: Compensation

(a) *Principles*

Factory at Chorzów (Claim for Indemnity) Case (Germany v *Poland) (Merits)*
PCIJ Ser A (1928) No 17, Permanent Court of International Justice

The case arose after the end of World War I, when Upper Silesia, which had previously been German territory, became part of Poland. A German corporation had established a nitrate factory at Chorzów in Upper Silesia pursuant to a contract with the German Government. However, the new Polish Government took possession of the factory. Germany sought reparation.

The Court . . . regarded reparation as the corollary of the violation of the obligations resulting from an engagement between States. . . .

It is a principle of international law that the reparation of a wrong may consist in an indemnity corresponding to the damage which the nationals of the injured State have suffered as a result of the act which is contrary to international law. . . . The reparation due by one State to another does not however change its character by reason of the fact that it takes the form of an indemnity for the calculation of which the damage suffered by a private person is taken as the measure. The rules of law governing the reparation are the rules of international law in force between the two States concerned, and not the law governing relations between the State which has committed a wrongful act and the individual who has suffered damage. . . .

On approaching this question, it should first be observed that, in estimating the damage caused by an unlawful act, only the value of property, rights and interests which have been affected and the owner of which is the person on whose behalf compensation is claimed, or the damage done to whom is to serve as a means of gauging the reparation claimed, must be taken into account. This principle, which is accepted in the jurisprudence of arbitral tribunals, has the effect, on the one hand, of excluding from the damage to be estimated, injury resulting for third parties from the unlawful act and, on the other hand, of not excluding from the damage the amount of debts and other obligations for which the injured party is responsible. . . .

The essential principle contained in the actual notion of an illegal act – a principle which seems to be established by international practice and in particular by the decisions of arbitral tribunals – is that reparation must, as far as possible, wipe out all the consequences of the illegal act and reestablish the situation which would, in all probability, have existed if that act had not been committed. Restitution in kind, or, if this is not possible, payment of a sum corresponding to the value which a restitution in kind would bear; the award, if need be, of damages for loss sustained which would not be covered by restitution in kind or payment in place of it – such are the principles which should serve to determine the amount of compensation due for an act contrary to international law.

Anglo-Iranian Oil Case (United Kingdom v *Iran)*
United Kingdom Memorial to the Court

The notion that compensation should be 'prompt, adequate and effective' is usually known as the 'Hull Formula', after an American Secretary of State.

30. [I]t is clear that the nationalization of the property of foreigners, even if not unlawful on any other ground, becomes an unlawful confiscation unless provision is made for compensation which is adequate, prompt and effective. By 'adequate' compensation is meant 'the value of the undertaking at the moment of dispossession, plus interest to the day of judgment' – per the Permanent Court of International Justice in the *Chorzów Factory (Claim for Indemnity) (Merits)* case, . . . The second

requirement, 'promptness', has already been referred to in the authorities quoted in the above paragraphs and has to some extent been defined by these authorities. It is, however, desirable to specify in greater detail what the Government of the United Kingdom understands by 'promptness'. There have, in fact, been pronouncements that prompt compensation means immediate payment in cash. . . . The Government of the United Kingdom is, however, prepared to admit that deferred payment may be interpreted as satisfying the requirement of payment in accordance with the rules of international law if

(a) the total amount to be paid is fixed promptly;

(b) allowance for interest for late payment is made;

(c) the guarantees that the future payments will in fact be made are satisfactory, so that the person to be compensated may, if he so desires, raise the full sum at once on the security of the future payments.

30A.   The third requirement is summed up in the word 'effective' and means that the recipient of the compensation must be able to make use of it. He must, for instance, be able, if he wishes, to use it to set up a new enterprise to replace the one that has been expropriated or to use it for such other purposes as he wishes. Monetary compensation which is in blocked currency is not effective because, where the person to be compensated is a foreigner, he is not in a position to use it or to obtain the benefit of it. The compensation therefore must be freely transferable from the country paying it and, so far as that country's restrictions are concerned, convertible into other currencies.

Resolution on Permanent Sovereignty over Natural Resources
GA Res. 1803 (XVII) 1962, paras 1–4, 8; 17 UN GAOR Supp (No 17), pp. 15–16

This Resolution was passed by a vote of 87 for, 2 against (France and South Africa), and 12 abstentions (being mainly socialist States).

1. The right of peoples and nations to permanent sovereignty over their natural wealth and resources must be exercised in the interest of their national development and of the well-being of the people of the State concerned.

3. In cases where authorization is granted, the capital imported and the earnings on that capital shall be governed by the terms thereof, by the national legislation in force, and by international law. The profits derived must be shared in the proportions freely agreed upon, in each case, between the investors and the recipient State, due care being taken to ensure that there is no impairment, for any reason, of that State's sovereignty over its natural wealth and resources.

4. Nationalization, expropriation or requisitioning shall be based on grounds or reasons of public utility, security or the national interest which are recognized as overriding purely individual or private interests, both domestic and foreign. In such cases the owner shall be paid appropriate compensation, in accordance with the rules in force in the State taking such measures in the exercise of its sovereignty and in accordance with international law. In any case where the question of compensation gives rise to a controversy, the national jurisdiction of the State taking such measures shall be exhausted. However, upon agreement by sovereign States and other parties concerned, settlement of the dispute should be made through arbitration or international adjudication.

8. Foreign investment agreements freely entered into by or between sovereign States shall be observed in good faith; States and international organizations shall strictly and conscientiously respect the sovereignty of peoples and nations over their natural wealth and resources in accordance with the Charter and the principles set forth in the present resolution.

Resolution on the Charter of Economic Rights and Duties of States, Articles 1, 2
GA Res 3281 (XXIX) 1974, 29 UN GAOR Supp (No 31), p. 52

This Resolution was adopted by 118 votes in favour, 6 against (Belgium, Denmark, Federal Republic of Germany, Luxembourg, UK and US), and 10 abstentions.

Article 1

Every State has the sovereign and inalienable right to choose its economic system as well as its political, social and cultural systems in accordance with the will of its people, without outside interference, coercion or threat in any form whatsoever.

Article 2

1. Every State has and shall freely exercise full permanent sovereignty, including possession, use and disposal, over all its wealth, natural resources and economic activities.
2. Each State has the right:
   (a) To regulate and exercise authority over foreign investment within its national jurisdiction in accordance with its laws and regulations and in conformity with its national objectives and priorities. No State shall be compelled to grant preferential treatment to foreign investment;
   (b) To regulate and supervise the activities of transnational corporations within its national jurisdiction and take measures to ensure that such activities comply with its laws, rules and regulations and conform with its economic and social policies. Transnational corporations shall not intervene in the internal affairs of a host State. Every State should, with full regard for its sovereign rights, co-operate with other States in the exercise of the right set forth in this subparagraph;
   (c) To nationalize, expropriate or transfer ownership of foreign property, in which case appropriate compensation should be paid by the State adopting such measures, taking into account its relevant laws and regulations and all circumstances that the State considers pertinent. In any case where the question of compensation gives rise to a controversy, it shall be settled under the domestic law of the nationalizing State and by its tribunals, unless it is freely and mutually agreed by all States concerned that other peaceful means be sought on the basis of the sovereign equality of States and in accordance with the principle of free choice of means.

Texaco Overseas Petroleum Company v *Libyan Arab Republic*
53 ILR (1977) 389, Dupuy, Sole Arbitrator

87. Substantial differences . . . exist between Resolution 1803 (XVII) and the subsequent Resolutions as regards the role of international law in the exercise of permanent sovereignty over natural resources. This aspect of the matter is directly related to the instant case under consideration; this Tribunal is obligated to consider the legal validity of the above-mentioned Resolutions and the possible existence of a custom resulting therefrom . . .

Refusal to recognize any legal validity of United Nations Resolutions must, however, be qualified according to the various texts enacted by the United Nations. These are very different and have varying legal value, but it is impossible to deny that the United Nations' activities have had a significant influence on the content of contemporary international law. In appraising the legal validity of the above-mentioned Resolutions, this Tribunal will take account of the criteria usually taken into consideration, i.e., the examination of voting conditions and the analysis of the provisions concerned . . .

On the basis of the circumstances of adoption mentioned above and by expressing an *opinio juris communis*, Resolution 1803 (XVII) seems to this Tribunal to reflect the state of customary law existing in this field. Indeed, on the occasion of the vote on a resolution finding the existence of a customary rule, the States concerned clearly express their views. The consensus by a majority of States belonging to the various representative groups indicates without the slightest doubt universal recognition of the rules therein incorporated, i.e., with respect to nationalization and compensation the use of the rules in force in the nationalizing State, but all this in conformity with international law.

88. While Resolution 1803 (XVII) appears to a large extent as the expression of a real general will, this is not at all the case with respect to the other Resolutions mentioned above, which has been demonstrated previously by analysis of the circumstances of adoption. In particular, as regards the Charter of Economic Rights and Duties of States, several factors contribute to denying legal value to those provisions of the document which are of interest in the instant case.

— In the first place, Article 2 of this Charter must be analyzed as a political rather than as a legal declaration concerned with the ideological strategy of development and, as such, supported only by non-industrialized States . . .

The absence of any connection between the procedure of compensation and international law and the subjection of this procedure solely to municipal law cannot be regarded by this Tribunal except as a *de lege ferenda* formulation, which even appears *contra legem* in the eyes of many developed countries. Similarly, several developing countries, although having voted favorably on the Charter of Economic Rights and Duties of States as a whole, in explaining their votes regretted the absence of any reference to international law.

89. Such an attitude is further reinforced by an examination of the general practice of relations between States with respect to investments. This practice is in conformity, not with the provisions of Article 2(c) of the above-mentioned Charter conferring exclusive jurisdiction on domestic legislation and courts, but with the exception stated at the end of this paragraph. Thus a great many investment agreements entered into between industrial States or their nationals, on the one hand, and developing countries, on the other, state, in an objective way, the standards of compensation and further provide, in case of dispute regarding the level of such compensation, the possibility of resorting to an international tribunal. In this respect, it is particularly significant in the eyes of this Tribunal that no fewer than 65 States, as of 31 October 1974, had ratified the Convention on the Settlement of Investment Disputes between States and Nationals of other States, dated March 18, 1966.

90. The argument of the Libyan Government, based on the relevant resolutions enacted by the General Assembly of the United Nations, that any dispute relating to nationalization or its consequences should be decided in conformity with the provisions of the municipal law of the nationalizing State and only in its courts, is also negated by a complete analysis of the whole text of the Charter of Economic Rights and Duties of States.

From this point of view, even though Article 2 of the Charter does not explicitly refer to international law, this Tribunal concludes that the provisions referred to in this Article do not escape all norms of international law.

Shahin Shane Ebrahimi v *Government of the Islamic Republic of Iran*
noted at 89 AJIL 385 (1995), US-Iran Claims Tribunal

The claimants alleged that the Government of Iran had expropriated their rights as shareholders in an Iranian construction firm. The Tribunal agreed but found it unnecessary to decide whether the compensation was lawful or unlawful. There was considerable discussion as to whether compensation should be 'prompt adequate and effective' or merely 'appropriate'. In addition, there was controversy over the method of calculating such compensation, especially whether the measure of compensation could be affected (i.e. lowered) by the damage done to the economic prospects of the business as a result of the expropriation. In principle, this should not be acceptable.

The claimants claimed 'prompt adequate and effective compensation' for the taking, relying on the Treaty of Amity between the United States and Iran, which provides for compensation equal to 'the full equivalent of the property taken.' They asserted that this amount must be equal to the fair market value of the Company as a going concern, including good will and likely future profitability. Claimants called upon the Tribunal to determine the amount that a willing buyer would have paid a willing seller 'without regard to "any diminution of value due to the nationali[z]ation itself or the anticipation thereof, and excluding consideration of events thereafter that might have increased or decreased the value of the shares."' Iran opposed this request, arguing that the Company was no longer a going concern at the time of the taking and that changes in government policy concerning construction works had diminished the value of the Company, as had mismanagement prior to the expropriation.

With respect to the proper standard of compensation, the Tribunal concluded that, 'while international law undoubtedly sets forth an obligation to provide compensation for property taken, international law theory and practice do not support the conclusion that the "prompt, adequate and effective" standard represents the prevailing standard of compensation. . . . Rather, customary international law favors an "appropriate" compensation standard.' While holding that this rule permits compensation to be determined' in a flexible manner, that is, taking into account the specific circumstances of each case,' the Tribunal stated that this rule 'must not be construed either to always require partial compensation or to always exclude full compensation.' It noted in this regard that the practice of the Tribunal has 'typically' been to award full compensation.

With respect to the implications of the legality *vel non* of the taking, the Tribunal pointed to its own decisions calling for full compensation both in the case of a large-scale nationalization where the taking was determined to be 'of a lawful character' and in the case of a discrete appropriation 'regardless of whether the expropriation was lawful.' It noted, however, that the distinction between a lawful and an unlawful taking was irrelevant in the present case, where claimants sought compensation for *damnum emergens* (including compensation for tangible and intangible assets and future prospects) but not for *lucrum cessans* (i.e., lost profits), because compensation for *damnum emergens* (but not for *lucrum cessans*) could be awarded regardless of the legality of the taking.

In establishing the Company's fair value, the Tribunal rejected Iran's contention that, 'because of the general climate of hostility against wealthy individuals during 1979,' the Company had no market value since no 'reasonable' private purchaser would have come forward. The Tribunal reasoned, first, that the fair market valuation, which 'carries with it an inherent degree of abstract analysis,' does not require the Tribunal to identify a 'concrete candidate buyer.' It reasoned further that Iran was precluded from arguing that the valuation must take account of the expropriation or the threat thereof. Nevertheless, the Tribunal refused to calculate its valuation of the Company's good will on the basis of the Company's past profitability, '[g]iven the changes that accompanied the Islamic Revolution.' Instead, concluding that 'the market value of the Company was less than the replacement cost of its tangible assets,' the Tribunal made a substantial deduction to the net asset value for 'negative goodwill.' The Tribunal concluded that the Company's fair market value was U.S. $5.2 million, together with interest and certain legal fees and costs.

While concurring in the result 'in order to form the requisite majority,' Judge Allison wrote separately to express his disagreement with the Tribunal's reliance on the 'amorphous,' 'ill-defined' and 'essentially meaningless' appropriate compensation standard. He specifically contested the Tribunal's decision to determine compensation 'taking into account the specific circumstances of each case,' which Allison contended was a mandate to consider 'the political and social conditions prevailing in the nationalizing State at the time of the taking.'

In support of his contention that the appropriate compensation rule is 'unjustifiable and out of step with the times,' he reviewed the history of the compensation doctrine, with particular emphasis on the confrontation between the Hull Doctrine of prompt, adequate and effective compensation and the rival doctrine of appropriate compensation (sometimes referred to ambiguously as the Calvo Doctrine).

Judge Allison contended that enactments like UN General Assembly Resolution 1803, far from being declarative of customary international law, represented the design of certain countries to use the forum of the General Assembly 'to alter − not reflect − the existing international regime' in an attempt to create a 'new' international economic order. However, he asserted that even during the 1970s, 'when the forces bent on undermining the traditional rule were at the peak of their influence,' 'it is clear that such a repudiation did not occur.' He characterized the *TOPCO*, *LIAMCO*, and *AMINOIL* decisions as vindicating the principle of *restitutio in integrum* while deliberately avoiding 'coming down decisively upon the side of either Secretary Hull or of Colonel Ghadaffi.'

He cited the various bilateral investment treaties, the World Bank's Guidelines on the Treatment of Foreign Direct Investment, and section 712 of the *Restatement (Third) of the Foreign Relations Law of the United States* (1987) as evidence that the Calvo Doctrine was a short-lived historical phenomenon that had 'languished and died' and that current practice is grounded in the Hull Doctrine. He found it particularly significant that in this decade the Soviet Union, Argentina and Mexico, all formerly staunch proponents of the Calvo Doctrine, have embraced the principle of full compensation.

Judge Allison also expressed disagreement with certain elements of the Tribunal's finding on valuation. He argued that the Tribunal's assignment of a negative value to the Company's good will in light of 'the supposed uncertainty of [the Company's] business prospects attributable to the Islamic revolution' violated the principle that the value of an expropriated asset is to be determined without reference to the effects of the act of expropriation. He also took issue with the Tribunal's interest award of 8.6 percent simple interest, both because the figure was below the 10 percent simple interest customarily awarded by Chamber Three and, more fundamentally, because the interest awarded was simple rather than compound.

Judge Arangio-Ruiz's opinion is troubling in three respects. First, the opinion takes no notice whatsoever of the existence of the Treaty of Amity between Iran and the United States, which the Tribunal heretofore has held in a number of cases to be the *lex specialis* of the case, prevailing over *lex generalis* or customary law. Second, the opinion opts for the appropriate compensation standard in preference to the Hull formula as the appropriate rule of customary international law without citing any international tribunal award that upholds a less-than-full-value standard. Finally, although the opinion announces that the appropriate compensation formula does not exclude an award of full compensation for the expropriated property and although it pays lip service to the principle that the effects of the expropriation are not to be considered in determining the value of the expropriated property, it nevertheless makes a deduction from net asset value for what it terms 'negative goodwill.' This deduction, which diminished the award by 13 percent, apparently represents an application of the appropriate compensation standard's mandate to 'tak[e] into account the specific circumstances of each case.' Hence, in spite of Judge Allison's effort to limit the reach of the opinion by asserting that 'despite its erroneous theoretical postulations [the award in the present case does] accept the full compensation standard.' it is more accurate to acknowledge that the opinion represents an application of the principle that 'once the full value of the property has been properly evaluated, the compensation to be awarded must be appropriate to reflect the pertinent facts and circumstances of each case.'

NOTES:

1. There are clearly competing views as to how to determine compensation. The resolutions of the General Assembly reflect the change in the international community's appreciation of the position of developing States. The approaches all recognise an obligation to pay compensation but they differ as to the means of determining that amount of compensation ('prompt, adequate and effective' or 'appropriate'), the method for deciding it (international law, national law or a combination), and who decides it (the State of the injured non-national, the State nationalising or an international arbitral tribunal). The Arbitration Tribunal in *Government of Kuwait* v *American Independent Oil Co. (Aminoil)* 66 ILR (1982) 518, at p. 602, noted that 'as regards States which welcome foreign investment, and which even engage in it themselves, it could be expected that their attitude towards compensation should not be such as to render foreign investment useless, economically'. The decision in *Shahin* adds a further complication as it appears to accept that the amount of compensation can be reduced because of the loss in value of the expropriated asset caused by the very act of expropriation.

2. It seems that the current practice of developed States in entering bilateral treaties dealing with foreign investment is to provide in the treaty that compensation in terms of the Hull Formula (above) will apply. In the most recent statement of the US position (American Law Institute, *Restatement (Third) Foreign Relations Law of the US* (1987) para. 712), the accepted principle is called 'just' compensation but it is essentially a reiteration of the Hull Formula. However, due to the need to reach a settlement of these disputes, on many occasions these States have accepted lump sums of less than the full value of the loss and payment has been made over a period of time.

(b) *Amount of compensation*

Amoco International Finance v *Iran*

(1987–I) 15 Iran-USCTR 189, Iran-United States Claims Tribunal

The facts are set out above. The Tribunal rejected the two methods of determining the 'appropriate' compensation proposed by the parties, being net book value and discounted cash flow. It requested them to calculate their loss according to the going concern method.

217. For the purpose of valuing the compensation due in case of the lawful expropriation of an asset, market value, apparently, is the most commendable standard, since it is also the most objective and the most easily ascertained when a market exists for identical or similar assets, i.e., when such assets are the object of a continuous flow of free transactions. The price at which these transactions take place is the reflection of the perceptions of value of a great number of willing buyers and sellers. . . .

219. Market value, on the other hand, is an ambiguous concept, to say the least (it might be more accurate to term it misleading), when an open market does not exist for the expropriated asset or for goods identical or comparable to it. . . .

220. The truth is that the absence of a market giving rise to the fixing of an objective market value compels recourse to alternative methods of valuation . . . A great number of such methods have been advocated by parties involved in cases of nationalization, such as net book value, replacement value, DCF calculation, etc. Their proponents inevitably contend that these methods permit a determination of 'full value', the just price, an adequate or equitable value, and so on. None of these values can, however, legitimately be labelled 'market value'. . . . Rather the Tribunal must determine,

ex post facto, the most equitable compensation required by the applicable law for a compulsory taking, excluding any speculative factor. Its first duty is to avoid any unjust enrichment or deprivation of either Party.

255. More generally, the theory that net book value is the appropriate standard of compensation in all cases of lawful expropriation overlooks the fact that a nationalized asset is not only a collection of discrete tangible goods (equipments, stocks and, possibly, grounds and buildings). It can include intangible items as well, such as contractual rights and other valuable assets, such as patents, know-how, goodwill and commercial prospects. To the extent that these various components exist and have an economic value, they normally must be compensated, just as tangible goods, even if they are not listed in the books. Furthermore, nationalization does not take place in order to disperse, by auction, the assets of the expropriated undertaking, or to use them for other purposes. On the contrary, the undertaking is nationalized as a going concern to be placed as such under State control, with a view to developing its activity and allowing the community to benefit fully from its returns. Therefore, the fact that the expropriated assets form a going concern can certainly not be disregarded at the time of the valuation of the compensation to be paid.

256. It should not be concluded from these remarks, however, that net book value is of no interest in the matter of compensation for expropriation . . . After its expropriation Khemco remained a going concern, even if it was at some time merged into NPC, and the plant from which it had drawn its revenues continued to be exploited as late as the subsequent events permitted. Going concern value, accordingly, is the measure of compensation in this case.

264. Going concern value encompasses not only the physical and financial assets of the undertaking, but also the intangible valuables which contribute to its earning power, such as contractual rights (supply and delivery contracts, patent licences and so on), as well as goodwill and commercial prospects. . . . In the present Case, the legitimate expectations [to use the term in Aminoil] of the Parties can only be deduced from the history of the concern and from its various components, as well as from the terms of the Khemco Agreement, taking into account the circumstances prevailing at the time of the taking. Finally, the liabilities of Khemco at the valuation date have to be deducted from the total value so determined.

Southern Pacific Properties (Middle East) Ltd v *Arab Republic of Egypt*
32 ILM 933 (1993), International Centre for the Settlement of Investment Disputes

The facts are set out above. The arbitrators found that the expropriation was lawful and that 'fair' compensation should be paid. They discussed various ways in which this could be achieved.

183. Thus, the Claimants are seeking 'compensation' for a lawful expropriation, and not 'reparation' for an injury caused by an illegal act such as a breach of contract. The cardinal point to be borne in mind, then, in determining the appropriate compensation is that, while the contracts could no longer be performed, the Claimants are entitled to receive fair compensation for what was expropriated rather than damages for breach of contract.

184. The Claimants contend that the measure of compensation for the taking of an ongoing enterprise should be equal to the value of the enterprise at the time of taking, and that such value depends on the revenues that the enterprise would have generated had the taking not occurred. In quantifying this value, the Claimants rely primarily on the so-called 'discounted cash flow' ('DCF') method. This method is intended to determine the present value of the future earnings expected to be generated by an investment. In applying the DCF method, the Claimants have first estimated the net revenues that would have been earned over the initial eighteen-year period of development, and then discounted that revenue flow to a present value, which, according to the Claimants,

represents the value of SPP(ME)'s rights as of May 28, 1978 – the date when the project was cancelled.

186. The Respondent contests the applicability of the DCF method on the grounds that it leads to speculative results and takes no account of the real value of the expropriated assets, in particular, the Respondent contends that in the present case the project was not sufficiently developed to yield the data necessary for a meaningful DCF analysis.

187. The Respondent has also submitted an expert opinion to the effect that the DCF method of valuation is unsuitable in this case because of the inherent uncertainties of the project and the fragility of a calculation which depends on forecasting cash flows almost twenty years into the future on the basis of revenues generated over a period of little more than a year. The Respondent has also cited the earlier ICC award in this case, where the tribunal refused to apply the DCF method on the ground that when the project was cancelled 'the great majority of the work had still to be done.' Finally, the Respondent argues that the DCF method would lead to unjust enrichment of the Claimants.

188. In the Tribunal's view, the DCF method is not appropriate for determining the fair compensation in this case because the project was not in existence for a sufficient period of time to generate the data necessary for a meaningful DCF calculation.

189. In these circumstances, the application of the DCF method would, in the Tribunal's view, result in awarding 'possible but contingent and undeterminate damage which, in accordance with the jurisprudence of arbitral tribunals, cannot be taken into account.' (*Chorrow Factory* case. *Series A. No. 17*, 1928, at p. 51).

198. The Tribunal will turn now to the Claimant's alternative claim for compensation [a fair measure of compensation], which is essentially a claim for 'out-of-pocket' expenses plus an amount to compensate the Claimants for what they have called 'the loss of the opportunity to make a commercial success of the project.'

NOTES:

1. In *Government of Kuwait* v *American Independent Oil Co. (Aminoil)* (see above), the Tribunal deducted the amount due to Kuwait in terms of taxation, royalties, etc., from the amount due to the corporation, calculated a 'reasonable', rate of interest (7.5 per cent), and took account of inflation. The amount of compensation awarded was to be determined by a balancing process to reach an equitable amount. An amount of nearly $US 180 million was awarded.

2. In each of the claims against Libya, the matters were eventually settled, although on different terms. In the *BP Case*, Libya agreed that BP was entitled to £62.4 million, but all except £17.4 million was set-off against Libyan claims for taxation and royalties. The *Texaco Case* was settled on the terms that Libya agreed to supply the corporations with crude oil for 15 months to the value of US$76 million. After LIAMCO had tried for four years to enforce in national courts its award, the matter was eventually settled for an undisclosed amount.

3. It seems probable that the amount of compensation for unlawful expropriation (i.e. expropriation that is unlawful, irrespective of whether any compensation is offered) will be greater than compensation payable for a lawful expropriation (i.e. an expropriation that will become unlawful only if no compensation is paid). This was discussed *obiter* in *Shahin Shane Ebrahimi* v *Government of the Islamic Republic of Iran*. Occasionally, compensation for unlawful expropriation is called 'damages' and may include an element for lost future profits. Actual loss suffered, however measured, is sometimes said to be the basis of compensation for lawful expropriation, although it must be relevant in cases of unlawful expropriation. In fact, awards have demonstrated a tendency to steer a middle course between competing claims, without explicitly relying on either the Hull formula or the 'appropriate' standard: see, e.g., *Southern Pacific Properties* and 'fair' compensation. This is preferable as it frees the issue of measuring compensation from fruitless theoretical arguments. It is unfortunate that *Shahin Shane* goes against this trend.

12

International Environmental Law

Introductory note

International environmental law challenges many fundamental concepts of traditional international law. It puts new limits on State sovereignty, it intrudes into the domestic jurisdiction and territorial integrity of States, it creates greater responsibilities for States, and it involves many non-State entities in the process of international law. The global nature of environmental issues means that national action by itself, while important, may be insufficient, and that significant international cooperation is required.

'The environment' is a description of physical matter that encompasses the air, the sea, the land, natural resources, flora and fauna, and cultural heritage (being items of archaelogical, historical, artistic and scientific interest). It can also be a description of a non-physical sense of surroundings and perceptions. Protection of the environment includes the control, reduction and elimination of existing causes of damage to the environment, the prevention and prohibition of additional kinds of damage, and the preservation and rational use of the environment. While the term 'the environment' has been criticised, and terms such as 'ecosystems' and 'biological diversity' have been proposed as alternatives, 'the environment' is a generally understood term and will be used here.

In the last few decades concern and awareness about the need for environmental protection has increased dramatically, both nationally and internationally. One way of putting this concern into action is the law, being a means to structure and regulate behaviour. International environmental law includes many treaties and declarations, a body of State practice, and some compliance mechanisms, as well as a development towards the introduction of flexible instruments to achieve compliance.

There are many competing interests to be taken into account when seeking to protect the environment, including population growth and poverty. In particular, the paramountcy of economic development, including the right of States to determine their own development goals and how they are to be achieved, has tended to force compromises in the law protecting the environment. Unlike international human rights law, it seems that there is no initial presumption in favour of protecting the environment. These tensions between economic development, environment and sovereignty necessarily challenge the ability of international law to protect the environment, so require recourse to non-legal processes. In addition, it is clear that international organisations, non-governmental organisations and individuals are having a greater input in this area than in almost any other area of international law.

SECTION 1: **The context**

A: Environmental context

The World Commission on Environment and Development, *Our Common Future*
(1987), pp. 22–23

> This Commission was established in response to a request from the General Assembly in Resolution 38/161 in December 1983. It was chaired by Gro Harlem Brundtland, former Prime Minister of Norway.

Over the course of this century, the relationship between the human world and the planet that sustains it has undergone a profound change. When the century began neither human numbers nor technology had the power radically to alter planetary system. As the century closes, not only do vastly increased human numbers and their activities have that power, but major, unintended changes are occurring in the atmosphere, in soils, in waters, among plants and animals, and in the relationships among all of these. The rate of change is outstripping the ability of scientific disciplines and our current capabilities to assess and advise. It is frustrating the attempts of political and economic institutions, which evolved in a different, more fragmented world, to adapt and cope. It deeply worries many people who are seeking ways to place those concerns on the political agendas.

The onus lies with no one group of nations. Developing countries face the obvious life-threatening challenges of desertification, deforestation, and pollution, and endure most of the poverty associated with environmental degradation. The entire human family of nations would suffer from the disappearance of rain forests in the tropics, the loss of plant and animal species, and changes in rainfall patterns. Industrial nations face the life-threatening challenges of toxic chemicals, toxic wastes, and acidification. All nations may suffer from the releases by industrialized countries of carbon dioxide and of gases that react with the ozone layer, and from any future war fought with the nuclear arsenals controlled by those nations. All nations will have a role to play in changing trends, and in righting an international economic system that increases rather than decreases inequality, that increases rather than decreases numbers of poor and hungry. . . .

The changes in human attitudes that we call for depend on a vast campaign of education, debate, and public participation. This campaign must start now if sustainable human progress is to be achieved. . . . We are unanimous in our conviction that the security, well-being, and very survival of the planet depend on such changes, now.

NOTE:
Concerns about the increasing degradation and destruction of the environment, as well as the awareness that environmental issues are not contained within State borders, have been major factors behind the development of international environmental law.

B: Legal context

Stockholm Declaration on the Human Environment 1972
Report of the UN Conference on the Human Environment
11 ILM 1416 (1972)

Principle 1

Man has the fundamental right to freedom, equality and adequate conditions of life, in an environment of a quality that permits a life of dignity and well-being, and he bears a solemn responsibility to protect and improve the environment for present and future generations. In this respect, policies promoting or perpetuating apartheid, racial segregation, discrimination, colonial and other forms of oppression and foreign domination stand condemned and must be eliminated.

Principle 2

The natural resources of the earth including the air, water, land, flora and fauna and especially representative samples of natural ecosystems must be safeguarded for the benefit of present and future generations through careful planning or management, as appropriate.

Principle 3

The capacity of the earth to produce vital renewable resources must be maintained and, wherever practicable, restored or improved.

Principle 4

Man has a special responsibility to safeguard and wisely manage the heritage of wildlife and its habitat which are now gravely imperilled by a combination of adverse factors. Nature conservation including wildlife must therefore receive importance in planning for economic development.

Principle 5

The non-renewable resources of the earth must be employed in such a way as to guard against the danger of their future exhaustion and to ensure that benefits from such employment are shared by all mankind.

Principle 6

The discharge of toxic substances or of other substances and the release of heat, in such quantities or concentrations as to exceed the capacity of the environment to render them harmless, must be halted in order to ensure that serious or irreversible damage is not inflicted upon ecosystems. The just struggle of the peoples of all countries against pollution should be supported.

Principle 7

States shall take all possible steps to prevent pollution of the seas by substances that are liable to create hazards to human health, to harm living resources and marine life, to damage amenities or to interfere with other legitimate uses of the sea.

Principle 8

Economic and social development is essential for ensuring a favourable living and working environment for man and for creating conditions on earth that are necessary for the improvement of the quality of life. . . .

Principle 21

States have, in accordance with the Charter of the United Nations and the principle of international law, the sovereign right to exploit their own resources pursuant to their own environmental policies, and the responsibility to ensure that activities within their jurisdiction or control do not cause damage to the environment of other States or of areas beyond the limits of national jurisdiction. . . .

Principle 23

Without prejudice to such criteria as may be agreed upon by the international community, or to standards which will have to be determined nationally, it will be essential in all cases to consider the systems of values prevailing in each country and the extent of the applicability of standards which are valid for the most advanced countries but which may be inappropriate and of unwarranted social cost for the developing countries.

Rio Declaration on Environment and Development, United Nations Conference on Environment and Development
31 ILM 876 (1992)

Principle 1

Human beings are at the centre of concerns for sustainable development. They are entitled to a healthy and productive life in harmony with nature.

Principle 2

States have, in accordance with the Charter of the United Nations and the principles of international law, the sovereign right to exploit their own resources pursuant to their own environmental and developmental policies, and the responsibility to ensure that activities within their jurisdiction or control do not cause damage to the environment of other States or of areas beyond the limits of national jurisdiction.

Principle 3

The right to development must be fulfilled so as to equitably meet developmental and environmental needs of present and future generations.

Principle 4

In order to achieve sustainable development, environmental protection shall constitute an integral part of the development process and cannot be considered in isolation from it.

Principle 5

All States and all people shall cooperate in the essential task of eradicating poverty as an indispensable requirement for sustainable development, in order to decrease the disparties in standards of living and better meet the needs of the majority of the people of the world.

Principle 6

The special situation and needs of developing countries, particularly the least developed and those most environmentally vulnerable, shall be given special priority. International actions in the field of environment and development should also address the interests and needs of all countries.

Principle 7

States shall cooperate in a spirit of global partnership to conserve, protect and restore the health and integrity of the Earth's ecosystem. In view of the different contributions to global environmental degradation, States have common but differentiated responsibilities. The developed countries acknowledge the responsibility that they bear in the international pursuit of sustainable development in view of the pressures their societies place on the global environment and of the technologies and financial resources they command.

Principle 8

To achieve sustainable development and a higher quality of life for all people, States should reduce and eliminate unsustainable patterns of production and consumption and promote appropriate demographic policies.

Principle 9
States should cooperate to strengthen endogenous capacity-building for sustainable development by improving scientific understanding through exchanges of scientific and technological knowledge, and by enhancing the development, adaptation, diffusion and transfer of technologies, including new and innovative technologies.

Principle 10
Environmental issues are best handled with the participation of all concerned citizens, at the relevant level. At the national level, each individual shall have appropriate access to information concerning the environment that is held by public authorities, including information on hazardous materials and activities in their communities, and the opportunity to participate in decision-making processes. States shall facilitate and encourage public awareness and participation by making information widely available. Effective access to judicial and administrative proceedings, including redress and remedy, shall be provided.

Principle 11
States shall enact effective environmental legislation. Environmental standards, management objectives and priorities should reflect the environmental and developmental context to which they apply. Standards applied by some countries may be inappropriate and of unwarranted economic and social cost to other countries, in particular developing countries.

Principle 12
States should cooperate to promote a supportive and open international economic system that would lead to economic growth and sustainable development in all countries, to better address the problems of environmental degradation. Trade policy measures for environmental purposes should not constitute a means of arbitrary or unjustifiable discrimination or a disguised restriction on international trade. Unilateral actions to deal with environmental challenges outside the jurisdiction of the importing country should be avoided. Environmental measures addressing transboundary or global environmental problems should, as far as possible, be based on an international consensus.

Principle 13
States shall develop national law regarding liability and compensation for the victims of pollution and other environmental damage. States shall also cooperate in an expeditious and more determined manner to develop further international law regarding liability and compensation for adverse effects of environmental damage caused by activities within their jurisdiction or control to areas beyond their jurisdiction.

Principle 14
States should effectively cooperate to discourage or prevent the relocation and transfer to other States of any activities and substances that cause severe environmental degradation or are found to be harmful to human health.

Principle 15
In order to protect the environment, the precautionary approach shall be widely applied by States according to their capabilities. Where there are threats of serious or irreversible damage, lack of full scientific certainty shall not be used as a reason for postponing cost-effective measures to prevent environmental degradation.

Principle 16
National authorities should endeavour to promote the internalization of environmental costs and the use of economic instruments, taking into account the approach that the polluter should, in principle, bear the cost of pollution, with due regard to the public interest and without distorting international trade and investment. . . .

Principle 22
Indigenous people and their communities, and other local communities, have a vital role in environmental management and development because of their knowledge and traditional practices. States should recognize and duly support their identity, culture and interests and enable their effective participation in the achievement of sustainable development.

Principle 23
In the environment and natural resources of people under oppression, domination and occupation shall be protected.

Principle 24
Warfare is inherently destructive of sustainable development. States shall therefore respect international law providing protection for the environment in times of armed conflict and cooperate in its further development, as necessary.

E. Brown-Weiss, 'Introductory Note on the United Nations Conference on Environment and Development'
31 ILM 814 (1992), pp. 814–15

[Agenda 21, which set out specific actions to be taken as a consequence of the Rio Declaration] includes a set of priority actions and a basket of means for accomplishing these priority actions. Priorities are grouped into the following categories:

— achieving sustainable growth, as through integrating environment and development in decision-making;
— fostering an equitable world, as by combating poverty and protecting human health;
— making the world habitable by addressing issues of urban water supply, solid waste management, and urban pollution;
— encouraging efficient resource use, a category which includes management of energy resources, care and use of fresh water, forest development, management or fragile eco systems, conservation of biological diversity, and management of land resources;
— protecting global and regional resources, including the atmosphere, oceans and seas, and living marine resources; and
— managing chemicals and hazardous and nuclear wastes.

Many of the action items in this agenda are very specific and advance significantly beyond the actions now in place in many countries.

The most controversial section of this part of Agenda 21 during the Rio Conference was the section on protecting the atmosphere. Saudi Arabia did not want this section to address renewable energy resources as environmentally sound energy resources. This is the only section in this part of Agenda 21 which was completely rewritten during the UNCED Conference.

The other part of Agenda 21 addresses the instruments for achieving environmentally sustainable development, which include legal instruments, international institutional arrangements, and finances, among others. In the section on international legal instruments, countries identify four priorities: review and assessment of relevant international law; further development of implementation mechanisms and compliance measures; effective participation by all countries in the international law-making process; and attention to the range and effectiveness of dispute resolution techniques.

Countries have agreed to establish a new Commission for Sustainable Development to monitor and review the implementation of Agenda 21. This will be an intergovernmental commission at the ministerial level which will report to the United Nations Economic and Social Council. . . . On the crucial issue of financing environmentally sustainable development, countries agreed that new and additional resources were needed, and that all available mechanisms of financing should be used.

This includes the Global Environmental Facility of the World Bank [30 ILM 1735 (1991)], but does not limit financing to it. The industrialized countries did not agree to commit 0.7% of their GNP to assist developing countries, as the Group of 77 had demanded.

NOTES:
1. The international obligations to protect the environment were largely initiated by the Stockholm Declaration. As a result of the Stockholm Declaration (made by 113 States) and Conference, the United Nations Environment Programme (UNEP) was established and is now based in Nairobi, Kenya. The World Charter for Nature 1982 (UN General Assembly Resolution 37/7, 28 October 1982) followed ten years after the Stockholm Declaration and other major conferences on the environment have included one in Rio in 1992 (above), where more than 170 states participated, and one held in Johannesburg in 2002.
2. The principles of the Rio Declaration and the provisions of Agenda 21, an 800 page document setting out actions which need to be taken, are generally considered be a turning point in increasing the commitment of States to take action to protect the environment. Undoubtedly one of the achievements of the Rio Conference was to place environmental issues high on the agenda of the international community. The Rio Conference was also a further step from the Stockholm Declaration towards more definite international legal obligations on States to protect the environment, with a number of key treaties agreed there: Conventions on Climate Change and on Biological Diversity (see below).
3. The importance of financial assistance in environmental protection is seen in the extract from Brown Weiss. In addition, World Bank funding of certain projects has had severe environmental impact, for example, the effect of economic developments in rainforests in the Amazon Basin and other fragile eco-systems. Therefore, the World Bank and some other development banks have now included environmental issues as a consideration in their financial assistance decision-making. Since the Rio Conference, agreement has been reached to make the Global Environment Facility into a permanent financial mechanism that will provide funds to developing States for activities that protect the environment (33 ILM 1273 (1994)).
4. All these documents reaffirm that protection of the environment requires international cooperation. They also show an awareness of the needs of developing States, so that 'environmental imperialism' by developed States does not occur; as well as the need to continue to undertake scientific, economic and social research into the environment.

SECTION 2: **Environmental theories**

The development of international environmental law has been influenced by different philosophical approaches to that law, particularly in regard to the rights and obligations conferred on States and individual actors.

C. Stone, 'Should Trees have Standing? – Toward Legal Rights for Natural Objects'
45 *Southern Californian Law Review* 450 (1972)

Now, to say that the natural environment should have rights is not to say anything as silly as that no one should be allowed to cut down a tree. We say human beings have rights, but – at least as of the time of this writing – they can be executed. Corporations have rights, but they cannot plead the fifth amendment . . . Thus, to say that the environment should have rights is not to say that it should have every right we can imagine, or even the same body of rights as human beings have. Nor is it to say that everything in the environment should have the same rights as every other thing in the environment.

What the granting of rights does involve has two sides to it. The first involves what might be called the legal-operational aspects; the second, the psychic and sociopsychic aspects. . . . First and most obviously, if the term ['legal rights'] is to have any content at all, an entity cannot be said to hold a legal right unless and until *some public authoritative body* is prepared to give *some amount of review* to actions that are colorably inconsistent with that 'right.' . . . But for a thing to be a *holder of legal rights*, something more is needed than that some authoritative body will review the actions and processes of those who threaten it. . . . They are, first, that the thing can institute legal actions *at its behest*; second, that in determining the granting of legal relief, the court must take *injury to it* into account; and, third, that relief must run to the *benefit of it*. . . .

It is not inevitable, nor is it wise, that natural objects should have no rights to seek redress on their own behalf. It is no answer to say that streams and forests cannot have standing because streams and forests cannot speak. Corporations cannot speak either; nor can states, estates, infants, incompetents, municipalities or universities. Lawyers speak for them, as they customarily do for the ordinary citizen with legal problems. One ought, I think, to handle the legal problems of natural objects as one does the problems of legal incompetents – human beings who have become vegetable. . . .

On a parity of reasoning, we should have a system in which, when a friend of a natural object perceives it to be endangered, he can apply to a court for the creation of a guardianship. Natural objects would have standing in their own right, through a guardian; damage to and through them would be ascertained and considered as an independent factor; and they would be the beneficiaries of legal awards. But these considerations only give us the skeleton of what a meaningful rights-holding would involve. To flesh out the 'rights' of the environment demands that we provide it with a significant body of rights for it to invoke when it gets to court. . . .

Witness the School Desegregation Cases [in the US] which, more importantly than to integrate the schools (assuming they did), awakened us to moral needs which, when made visible, could not be denied. And so here, too, in the case of the environment, the Supreme Court may find itself in a position to award 'rights' in a way that will contribute to a change in popular consciousness. It would be a modest move, to be sure, but one in furtherance of a large goal: the future of the planet as we know it.

A. Springer, *The International Law of Pollution – Protecting the Global Environment in a World of Sovereign States*
(1983), pp. 31–33

Scholars have questioned whether the present international legal system is sufficiently developed to resolve the disputes that arise over environmental issues and, more generally, to provide a constructive, forward-looking framework for environmental protection. Reflecting the decentralized nature of the international political context, international law accords to the state a degree of control over human activity within its boundaries that often appears incompatible with effective protection of the biosphere. . . . In critiques perhaps less sweeping, other scholars have attacked the limitations of both the existing norms of environmental protection and the mechanisms available to implement them.

On the normative level, international law traditionally relies on state practice and treaties for the creation of rules restricting state freedom. [Particularly in environmental matters], which have only recently become of significant international concern, rules often must be deduced from general state practice in the form of principles such as the 'reasonable use' of shared resources. What constitutes a 'reasonable use' as derived from past practice may be the very activity that has given rise to the present environmental threat, and even in a contemporary setting, military and other interests may have inherent priority in the minds of national leaders. When the immediate political fate of a nation is weighed against the future of the human species, uses concomitant with political survival, even though they threaten the long-term existence of mankind, may win acceptance as reasonable. . . .

A treaty approach, while offering the potential of greater specificity in normative standards, is also viewed as having significant limitations. Most basic is the necessity of arriving at a consensus among all states with a significant impact in an area of environmental concern. Differing state perceptions of their national self-interest and a general reluctance to commit themselves to overly restrictive rules can make this an extremely difficult and time-consuming process. Common environmental standards may be seen as imposing unfair economic burdens on developing countries, and the net result of negotiations may be weak obligations reflecting the lowest common denominator among participating states. Where prodded by major environmental accidents, such as the *Torrey Canyon* oil spill, what Goldie ['Development of International Environmental Law: An Appraisal' in Hargrove, *Law, Institutions and the Global Environment* (1976)] has termed a 'fire-brigade mentality' on the part of negotiators may produce reactive ad hoc agreements with limited general application. Furthermore, nonparticipation of states with a potential environmental impact can limit the effectiveness of whatever obligations are eventually agreed upon. In the case of the oceans, the use of 'flags of convenience could greatly stultify, if not render completely ineffective, an international regime for controlling pollution from tankers, pipelines, deep-sea mining and high seas mineral extraction from seawater.'

Finally, the consequence of violating the 'pollution limits' is often simply to impose legal liability and require payment of compensation, a penalty that may do little either to satisfy the injured party or to prevent future pollution. Thus, from a critical perspective, the standards of international environmental law are perceived as insufficiently restrictive and creating, at best, a patchwork system of normative restraints on environmental degradation. . . .

Under traditional international law, a state must meet relatively restrictive standards to attempt to invoke the responsibility of another state for polluting activity. Injury must be shown to an interest that the claimant state is legally entitled to protect. . . . Both state-to-state correspondence and third-party dispute-settlement mechanisms can be criticized: the former, for its tendency to produce 'compromise' solutions designed primarily to resolve divisive international disputes rather than to promote environmental protection; and the latter, for their limited jurisdiction and inaccessibility to nonstate claimants. . . . Politically, environmental issues may not be seen as sufficiently significant to risk jeopardizing the government's interest in promoting cooperative relations in other areas. From a legal perspective rules of reciprocity may discourage a state from criticizing a neighbor for transboundary pollution with moderate impact if it wishes to retain the right to 'protect' similar pollution that may be generated within its borders.

International organizations have also been the target of criticism for the limited role that states have been willing to give them in the creation and implementation of binding environmental standards. With power to do little more than recommend measures for national adoption, and lacking even the ability to receive and comment on complaints of member states, the United Nations Environment program (UNEP) has been cited as an example of the 'relative primitiveness of environmental protection.' The need for a UNEP is evidenced by the previously fragmented approach to international organization in environmental matters in which a plethora of specialized agencies carved out particular areas of competence, a development hardly conductive to the holistic perspective that many feel is so urgently needed. Where international organizations do offer the potential to perform at least a catalytic function, there is still the problem of creating within the organization a sufficiently unified and environmentally conscious consensus to permit effective policy action. The Intergovernmental Maritime Consulatative Organization (IMCO), for example, has been accused of being unduly influenced by the shipping interests its marine-pollution programs are designed to regulate, and the International Whaling Commission has had great difficulty in persuading its membership to adopt catch limits that recognize the endangered status of several important species.

E. Brown-Weiss, 'Our Rights and Obligations to Future Generations for the Environment'
84 AJIL 198 (1990) pp. 198–205

In Fairness to Future Generations [E. Brown-Weiss (1989)] argues that we, the human species, hold the natural environment of our planet in common with all members of our species: past generations, the present generation, and future generations. As members of the present generation, we hold the earth in trust for future generations. At the same time, we are beneficiaries entitled to use and benefit from it.

There are two relationships that must shape any theory of intergenerational equity in the context of our natural environment: our relationship to other generations of our own species and our relationship to the natural system of which we are a part. . . . The purpose of human society must be to realize and protect the welfare and well-being of every generation. This requires sustaining the life-support systems of the planet, the ecological processes and the environmental conditions necessary for a healthy and decent human environment. . . .

It is not enough, however, to apply a theory of intergenerational equity only among generations. It also carries an intragenerational dimension. When future generations become living generations, they have certain rights and obligations to use and care for the planet that they can enforce against one another. Were it otherwise, members of one generation could allocate the benefits of the world's resources to some communities and the burdens of caring for it to others and still potentially claim on balance to have satisfied principles of equity among generations. . . .

I have proposed three basic principles of intergenerational equity. First, each generation should be required to conserve the diversity of the natural and cultural resource base, so that it does not unduly restrict the options available to future generations in solving their problems and satisfying their own values, and should also be entitled to diversity comparable to that enjoyed by previous generations. This principle is called 'conservation of options.' Second, each generation should be required to maintain the quality of the planet so that it is passed on in no worse condition than that in which it was received, and should also be entitled to planetary quality comparable to that enjoyed by previous generations. This is the principle of 'conservation of quality.' Third, each generation should provide its members with equitable rights of access to the legacy of past generations and should conserve this access for future generations. This is the principle of 'conservation of access.'

These proposed principles constrain the actions of the present generation in developing and using the planet, but within these constraints do not dictate how each generation should manage its resources.

These principles of intergenerational equity form the basis of a set of intergenerational obligations and rights, or planetary rights and obligations, that are held by each generation. These rights and obligations derive from each generation's position as part of the intertemporal entity of human society. . . . The planetary, or intergenerational, rights proposed in *In Fairness to Future Generations* are not rights possessed by individuals. They are, instead, *generational* rights, which must be conceived of in the temporal context of generation. Generations hold these rights as groups in relation to other generations – past, present and future. . . .

Enforcement of these intergenerational rights is appropriately done by a guardian or representative of future generations as a *group*, not of future individuals, who are of necessity indeterminate. While the holder of the right may lack the capacity to bring grievances forward and hence depends upon the representative's decision to do so, this inability does not affect the existence of the right or the obligation associated with it.

M. Anderson, 'Human Rights Approaches to Environmental Protection' in A. Boyle and M. Anderson (eds), *Human Rights Approaches to Environmental Protection*
(1996), p. 1

What are the advantages and disadvantages of using a human rights approach rather than an approach based in regulation, criminal law, or the law of tort? Looking to the advantages, several are apparent. First, a human rights approach is a strong claim, a claim to an absolute entitlement theoretically immune to the lobbying and trade-offs which characterize bureaucratic decision-making. Its power lies in its ability to trump individual greed and short-term thinking. A second advantage is that the procedural dimensions of an environmental right can provide access to justice in a way that bureaucratic regulation, or tort law, simply cannot. A robust environmental right can mobilize redress where other remedies have failed. This is particularly important in cases like the Asian Rare Earth litigation in Malaysia, where proof of causation and other technical barriers make tort law ineffective. It was also important in the Indian context, where procedural simplicity has made environmental rights highly attractive to aggrieved parties. An environmental right may serve as the ultimate 'safety net' to catch legitimate claims which have fallen through the procedural cracks of public and private law. Thirdly, a human rights approach may stimulate concomitant political activism on environmental issues. Concerned citizens and NGOs are more likely to rally around a general statement of right than a highly technical, bureaucratic regulation expressed in legalese. Fourthly, a human rights approach can provide the conceptual link to bring local, national, and international issues within the same frame of legal judgment. At present, environmental damage is unequally distributed at both the national and international level; a non-discriminatory human rights standard could facilitate comparison, and foster political mobilization linking local concerns with more global issues. For example, . . . the operations of the World Bank could be made subject to a human rights standard which would apply equally to its international transactions, its national pro-grammes, and its local projects. Fifthly, a general expression of right can be interpreted creatively as issues and contexts change. This is evident in the Indian jurisprudence, where the right to a healthy environment held to be implicit in the right to life has been given more precise definition on a case-by-case basis as specific disputes have come before the courts. Thus, definitions and trade-offs evolve gradually in the light of experience rather than needing to be defined comprehensively and rigidly in a single piece of regulatory legislation.

A number of disadvantages are also apparent. . . . First of all, it is not clear to what extent a simple right may address the complex and often technical issues of environmental management. Environ-mental protection, in both decision-making and implementation, requires a legal language capable of incorporating highly technical specifications, distinguishing among industrial processes, evaluating elusive causal relationships, and protecting complicated biological and ecological systems. Not all issues can be resolved in the simple language of rights (although environmental rights may be supplemented with technical expertise and specific standards) . . . [and] disputes which essentially require the balancing of interests may be more difficult to resolve where two rights-holders are involved. . . . Secondly, a rights approach may not address the relationships of political economy which underlie much environmental damage. The causes of environmental damage – including technology choice, forms of production, and distribution of the social product – will not be addressed by a right directed merely to their symptoms. If environmental rights serve as nothing more than symbolic gestures, as in Hungary, or as mere palliatives which inculcate a sense of environmental responsibility while denigration of the environment continues largely unabated, then those rights may be positively counter-productive, drawing attention away from the structural causes of environmental change. Just as the prescription of anti-diarrhoea drugs in the poorer villages of Bangladesh can only be an expensive and ineffective short-term remedy for people without access to clean drinking water, likewise, the right to object to environmental damage will have little effect unless the social and economic forces causing the damage are confronted directly. Thirdly, rights, especially procedural rights, may be used by affluent groups or 'cosmetic environmentalists' to protect a privileged quality of life, which may impose further environmental costs upon the dispossessed or environmentally vulnerable communities, who are in turn denied access to justice by poverty or lack of institutional skills. Legal recognition of environmental rights will not necessarily change anything unless disadvantaged groups possess economic and political power to mobilize legal institutions. Fourthly, the expansion of rights-based litigation may well displace other forms of legal remedy, such as tort law or negotiated settlements, which are better suited to environmental issues. This danger is identified in the Indian context . . . [where] writ petitions under the Constitution are now displacing statutory regulation and civil suits as the main means of distributing environmental benefits and burdens. This raises the twin dangers of inconsistent standards and the transfer of essentially bureaucratic functions to the courts. Fifthly . . . the language of human rights may politicize and draw attention to environmental claims in a way that may attract more overt opposition from polluters, or even exacerbate government repression. Sometimes what may be easily achieved by quiet lobbying and technical regulation may not be possible through public campaigns and prominent litigation. And the explicit incorporation of environmental rights into the Malaysian legal system may invite a series of statutory restrictions and limitations which may leave environmentalists with fewer rights than they held at the outset.

On balance, our deliberations show that human rights approaches to environmental protection offer many attractions, and could play a key role in fostering equitable and sustainable human communities. If very real problems of theory and practice remain, they should stimulate careful analysis and jurisprudential innovation rather than intellectual surrender.

Danube Dam Case (Hungary v *Slovakia)*

ICJ Rep 1997 7, International Court of Justice

The facts of this case are set out in Chapter 3.

JUDGE WEERAMANTRY (Separate Opinion): The problem of steering a course between the needs of development and the necessity to protect the environment is a problem alike of the law of development and the law of the environment. Both these vital and developing areas of the law require, and indeed assume, the existence of a principle which harmonizes both needs. . . .

The people of both Hungary and Slovakia are entitled to development for the furtherance of their happiness and welfare. They are likewise entitled to the preservation of their human right to the protection of their environment . . .

The protection of the environment is . . . a vital part of contemporary human rights doctrine, for it is a *sine qua non* for numerous human rights such as the right to health and the right to life itself. It is scarcely necessary to elaborate on this, as damage to the environment can impair and undermine all the human rights spoken of in the Universal Declaration and other human rights instruments . . .

While, therefore, all peoples have the right to initiate development projects and enjoy their benefits, there is likewise a duty to ensure that those projects do not significantly damage the environment. . . . The concept of sustainable development is thus a principle accepted not merely by the developing countries, but one which rests on a basis of worldwide acceptance.

When we enter the arena of obligations which operate *erga omnes* rather than *inter partes*, rules based on individual fairness and procedural compliance may be inadequate . . . International environmental law will need to proceed beyond weighing the rights and obligations of parties within a closed compartment of individual State interest, unrelated to the global concept of humanity as a whole.

NOTES:

1. Theoretical approaches to international environmental law continue to expand (and see also the final section of this Chapter). In a significant development, the World Commission on

Environment and Development adopted the concept of 'sustainable development' to recognise the competing claims made by many States for the preservation of the environment and by developing States for the right to development. Principles of sustainable development encourage development in a manner and by methods which do not compromise the ability of future generations, and other States, to meet their own needs. The *Danube Dam* case shows that sustainable development has gained international approval. Another approach is to see an international public duty on states to act in the public interest, and that the public interest is to ensure that its citizens are not harmed by actions having effects on the environment.

2. Approaches to international environmental law are generally described in anthropocentric terms, with humans at the centre, with a responsibility to save, protect and preserve the environment. This leads, for example, to the acceptance of a human right to a clean environment (see Anderson above). However, the law could be conceived in terms of an environmentally-centred concern, so that the environment would be preserved for its own sake and not only to maintain human life and human interests. In *Sierra Club* v *Morton* 405 US 727 (1972), before the Supreme Court of the United States, Douglas J said eloquently:

> The voice of the inanimate object, therefore, should not be stilled. That does not mean that the judiciary takes over the managerial functions from the federal agency. It merely means that before these priceless bits of Americana (such as a valley, an alpine meadow, a river or a lake) are forever lost or are so transformed as to be reduced to the eventual rubble of our urban environment, the voice of the existing beneficiaries of these environmental wonders should be heard.

3. In *Minors Oposa* v *DENR* (below), the Supreme Court of the Philippines adopted Brown-Weiss's theory on intergenerational equity when deciding whether a group had standing to sue on environmental issues before a national court. Also, in *López Ostra* v *Spain* (below) environmental issues were considered in terms of human rights.

SECTION 3: **International obligations**

There are now a vast array of international instruments concerning environmental matters and nearly all States have agreed to some international instrument that contains provisions relating to the protection of the environment.

A: Obligation not to cause transboundary environmental damage

Trail Smelter Arbitration (*US* v *Canada*)
3 RIAA (1941) 1905, 1965–1966, Arbitral Tribunal

A smelter commenced production in 1896 near Trail, British Columbia, Canada. From 1925 to at least 1937, damage occurred in the State of Washington, United States, due to the sulphur dioxide emitted from the smelter. The two States agreed to submit the dispute to arbitration to determine the amount of compensation payable but, importantly, Canada did not dispute liability. The Tribunal decided that damage had occurred since 1 January 1932, and that the indemnity to be paid was $78,000.

The Tribunal . . . finds that . . . under the principles of international law, as well as of the law of the United States, no State has the right to use or permit the use of its territory in such a manner as to cause injury by fumes in or to the territory of another or the properties or persons therein, when the case is of serious consequence and the injury is established by clear and convincing evidence. . . .

Considering the circumstances of the case, the Tribunal holds that the Dominion of Canada is responsible in international law for the conduct of the Trail Smelter. . . . [I]t is, therefore, the duty of the Government of the Dominion of Canada to see to it that this conduct should be in conformity with the obligation of the Dominion under international law as herein determined. . . . So long as the present conditions in the Columbia River Valley prevail, the Trail Smelter shall be required to refrain from causing any damage through fumes in the State of Washington; the damaged herein referred to and its extent being such as would be recoverable under the decisions of the courts of the United States in suits between private individuals. The indemnity for such damage should be fixed in such manner as the Governments . . . should agree upon.

NOTES:

1. The *Trail Smelter* decision was that there is an obligation on States not to cause transboundary environmental damage. This obligation is often known as the 'preventative principle' or 'Principle 21/2' as it is based on the identical words of Principle 21 of the Stockholm Declaration (above) and Principle 2 of the Rio Declaration (above). These both provide that States have 'the responsibility to ensure that activities within their jurisdiction or control do not cause damage to the environment of other States or of areas beyond the limits of national jurisdiction.'

2. This obligation has been repeated in many international instruments and is customary international law. For example, in *Nuclear Test Case 1995* (*New Zealand* v *France*) ICJ Rep 1995 288, Judge Weeramantry held: '[There is] a fundamental principle of environmental law which must here be noted. It is well entrenched in international law and goes as far back as the *Trail Smelter* case . . . and perhaps beyond. This basic principle [is] that no nation is entitled by its own activities to cause damage to the environment of any other nation.'

3. State responsibility may be able to be invoked in the environmental area where there is an intentional abuse of rights over territory and where a right to compensation arises from an otherwise lawful exercise of sovereignty, as with nationalisation (see Chapter 11). It could also be extended to include an obligation to provide information on environmental damage and to cooperate in the mitigation and reduction of harm caused.

B: Obligation of cooperation

Resolution on the Charter of Economic Rights and Duties of States
GA Res 3281 (XXIX) 1974, 29 UN GAOR Supp (No 31), p. 55

Article 30
The protection, preservation and enhancement of the environment for the present and future generations is the responsibility of all States. All States shall endeavour to establish their own environmental and developmental policies in conformity with such responsibility. The environmental policies of all States should enhance and not adversely affect the present and future development potential of developing countries. All States have the responsibility to ensure that activities within their jurisdiction or control do not cause damage to the environment of other States or of areas beyond the limits of national jurisdiction. All States should co-operate in evolving international norms and regulations in the field of the environment.

Convention on Biological Diversity 1992
31 ILM 818 (1992)

This Convention is discussed below.

Article 16. Access to and Transfer of technology

1. Each Contracting Party, recognizing that technology includes biotechnology, and that both access to and transfer of technology among Contracting Parties are essential elements for the attainment of the objectives of this Convention, undertakes subject to the provisions of this Article to provide and/or facilitate access for and transfer to other Contracting Parties of technologies that are relevant to the conservation and sustainable use of biological diversity or make use of genetic resources and do not cause significant damage to the environment.

2. Access to and transfer of technology referred to in paragraph 1 above to developing countries shall be provided and/or facilitated under fair and most favourable terms, including on concessional and preferential terms where mutually agreed, and, where necessary, in accordance with the financial mechanism established by Articles 20 and 21. In the case of technology subject to patents and other intellectual property rights, such access and transfer shall be provided on terms which recognize and are consistent with the adequate and effective protection of intellectual property rights. The application of this paragraph shall be consistent with paragraphs 3, 4 and 5 below.

P-T. Stoll, 'The International Environmental Law of Cooperation' in Wolfrum (ed), *Enforcing Environmental Standards: Economic Mechanisms as Viable Means?*
(1996) pp. 39, 63–4, 87–8, 92

Cooperation, . . . by its very definition points to some interest that parties do have in common. Taken to the reverse, one may state, that cooperation is called for where States have agreed upon some common interest. . . . States seem to have accepted such common interest only in fairly limited number of cases. Common spaces and situations of massive pollution are examples. The recently discussed notion of international environmental security may become another one. In these cases States arguably have a [customary international law] duty to cooperate alongside other obligations, as for instance to comply to standards and obligations. . . . These findings . . . [that there is a customary international law duty to cooperate] apply to more specific obligations on cooperation, as for instance to information exchange, technological [transfer] and financial cooperation. Any such obligation is based on the same common interest, which has to be initially agreed upon by States. . . .

As regards compliance, cooperation may become relevant under four different aspects. *First*, cooperation plays an important role in gathering and disseminating information and thus may contribute to transparency. *Second*, the provision of additional resources by means of technical or financial cooperation may be considered to foster complaince in cases where it can be deemed that a particular State party is in need for such resources. On the contrary, it may be discussed, whether cooperation may be denied in order to redress or sanction an act of non-compliance. *Third*, it has to be discussed, if the provision of technical and financial cooperation may be claimed as a precondition of implementation and complaince. *Fourth*, cooperation may be called for in order to develop additional mechanisms of enforcement, for instance liability rules. . . . The existence of an international environmental law of cooperation can be argued on the basis of the structure of common interests involved and specific elements. As has been seen, it is to a great extent hard treaty law.

NOTES:

1. The Charter of Economic Rights and Duties of States, which was strongly supported by developing and socialist States, expresses both the obligation not to cause transboundary

environmental damage and to cooperate. The obligation to cooperate is found in most of the major environmental law instruments, such as in Article 9 of the Rio Declaration (above).

2. The obligation to cooperate has many elements, as Stoll makes clear. One of the major practical aspects of this obligation has been in relation to technology transfer, as seen in Article 16 of the Convention on Biological Diversity.

C: Precautionary principle

Framework Convention on Climate Change 1992
31 ILM 849 (1992)

This Convention is discussed below.

Article 3: Principles

3. The Parties should take precautionary measures to anticipate, prevent or minimize the causes of climate change and mitigate its adverse effects. Where there are threats of serious or irreversible damage, lack of full scientific certainty should not be used as a reason for postponing such measures, taking into account that policies and measures to deal with climate change should be cost-effective so as to ensure global benefits at the lowest possible cost. To achieve this, such policies and measures should take into account different socio-economic contexts, be comprehensive, cover all relevant sources, sinks and reservoirs of greenhouse gases and adaptation, and comprise all economic sectors. Efforts to address climate change may be carried out cooperatively by interested Parties.

B. Dickson, 'The Precautionary Principle in CITES: A Critical Assessment'
39 *Natural Resources Journal* 211 (1999), p. 211

Since 1987 the precautionary principle has become a popular principle in international environmental law. In 1990 the UN Secretary General remarked that the principle 'has been endorsed by all recent international forums' and in 1992 the principle was incorporated in the Rio Declaration on Environment and Development. But this surge in popularity was not accompanied by a consensus on the wording of the principle. Formulations vary from agreement to agreement. . . .

It is possible to make two helpful distinctions to guide one through the plethora of formulations of the precautionary principle that are found in international agreements. All versions of the principle offer guidance on how to respond when there is some evidence, but not proof, that a human practice is damaging the environment. The first distinction concerns the general nature of that guidance. One version of the principle calls for action to be taken against the practice that may be causing environmental damage. This type can be termed the 'action-guiding' version of the principle. This version is found most frequently in agreements dealing with marine pollution. For example, the formulation of the principle that is offered in the 1989 report of the Nordic Council's International Conference on the Pollution of the Seas is an instance of this version. The report speaks of: the need for an effective precautionary approach, with that important principle intended to safeguard the marine ecosystem by, amongst other things, eliminating and preventing pollution emissions where there is reason to believe that damage or harmful effects are likely to be caused, even where there is inadequate or inconclusive scientific evidence to prove a causal link between emissions and effects. The second version of the precautionary principle simply stipulates that the fact that it is uncertain whether a practice is causing environmental harm should not be used as a reason for not taking action against that practice. This version does not call directly for action. Rather, it restricts what can be considered as a reason for inaction. It will therefore be termed the 'deliberation-guiding' version. Instances of this version are found in many of the more general environmental agreements. It appears, for example, in Principle 15 of the Rio Declaration on Environment and Development. In order to protect the environment, the precautionary approach shall be widely applied by States according to their capabilities. Where there are threats of serious or irreversible damage, lack of full scientific certainty shall not be used as a reason for postponing cost-effective measures to prevent environmental degradation. This version of the precautionary principle is less stringent than the action-guiding version. For the action-guiding version requires that something be done in response to the threat, while the deliberation-guiding version does not. It might be objected that this distinction between the two versions cannot be maintained because deliberation is itself a type of action and therefore both versions of the principle are action-guiding. However, this objection misses the point in that the action referred to in the label 'action-guiding' is action against the practice that may be causing environmental damage. It is certainly the case that deliberation is itself a type of action. Indeed, the type of institutional deliberation about policy that is in question here will almost certainly involve actions, however narrow the meaning of 'action.' Nevertheless, the deliberation-guiding version, unlike the action-guiding version, does not call for action against the practice that may be causing damage. It simply places constraints on what can be considered in the course of deliberation about whether to undertake this sort of action. Thus, the terms 'action-guiding' and 'deliberation-guiding' remain rough but appropriate labels for the two versions of the precautionary principle.

The second distinction is one of degree. Formulations of the precautionary principle are more or less determinate. There are several aspects to the degree of specificity of the principle. A formulation of the principle may be concerned with a more or less specific part of the environment; it may be concerned with a more or less specifically defined type of threat; or it may be concerned with more or less specific types of action for responding to the threat. Judged against two of these three criteria, the formulation found in the Rio Declaration is clearly less determinate than the Nordic Council's formulation. The Rio formulation is concerned with all parts of the environment, it does not mention specific threats and it makes no assumptions about what type of response is appropriate (other than that it must be cost-effective). The Nordic Council's formulation, in contrast, is concerned specifically with marine ecosystems and the threat from pollution. It does not specify what action should be undertaken in response to the threat, although it does require that pollution emissions must be eliminated and prevented. . . .

Moreover, whenever environmental problems display the complexity illustrated by the conservation of terrestrial wildlife, any version of the principle that prevents the consideration of relevant factors will be open to criticism. This favors treating the precautionary principle either as a principle rather than as a rule, or as a deliberation-guiding and indeterminate rule. But, however understood, the principle should not be treated as a means for circumventing difficult, value-laden decisions.

NOTES:

1. The precautionary principle is found in most of the major environmental law instruments, at least since 1992, such as in Article 15 of the Rio Declaration (above) and Article 6 and Annex II of the Agreement for the Implementation of the Provisions of UNCLOS relating to the Conservation and Management of Highly Migratory Fish Stocks 1995 (34 ILM 1542 (1995)).

2. The precautionary principle is a vital part of the long-term protection of the environment, especially in the usual environmental situation where there is no scientific certainty. The existence of this uncertainty cannot be used, under this principle, as a justification of action or inaction due to the possibility of serious or irreversible damage by such action or inaction.

D: Intergenerational equity

Framework Convention on Climate Change 1992
31 ILM 849 (1992)

This Convention is discussed below.

Article 3 Principles

1. The Parties should protect the climate system for the benefit of present and future generations of humankind, on the basis of equity and in accordance with their common but differentiated responsibilities and respective capabilities. Accordingly, the developed country Parties should take the lead in combating climate change and the adverse effects thereof.

Minors Oposa v *Secretary of the Department of Environment and Natural Resources* (DENR)

33 ILM 173 (1994), Supreme Court of the Philippines

The plaintiffs sought an order against the Philippines government requiring it to discontinue existing and further timber and other licensing agreements on the basis that deforestation from the timber logging was causing environmental damage. The Court had to consider, *inter alia*, if the plaintiffs had standing to sue and a cause of action. It decided, unanimously, that they did have both standing to sue and a justiciable cause of action.

Petitioners minors assert that they represent their generation as well as generations yet unborn. We find no difficulty in ruling that they can, for themselves, for others of their generation and for the succeeding generations, file a class suit. Their personality to sue on behalf of the succeeding generations can only be based on the concept of intergenerational responsibility insofar as the right to a balanced and healthful ecology is concerned. Such a right, as hereinafter expounded, considers the 'rhythm and harmony of nature.' Nature means the created world in its entirety. Such rhythm and harmony indispensably include, *inter alia*, the judicious disposition, utilization, management, renewal and conservation of the country's forest, mineral, land, waters, fisheries, wildlife, off-shore areas and other natural resources to the end that their exploration, development and utilization be equitably accessible to the present as well as future generations. Needless to say, every generation has a responsibility to the next to preserve that rhythm and harmony for the full enjoyment of a balanced and healthful ecology. Put a little differently, the minors assertion of their right to a sound environment constitutes, at the same time, the performance of their obligation to ensure the protection of that right for the generations to come. . . .

The complaint focuses on one specific fundamental legal right – the right to a balanced and healthful ecology. . . . While the right to a balanced and healthful ecology is to be found under the Declaration of Principles and State Policies [of the 1987 Constitution of the Philippines] and not under the Bill of Rights, it does not follow that it is less important than any of the civil and political rights enumerated in the latter. Such a right belongs to a different category of rights altogether for it concerns nothing less than self-preservation and self-perpetuation – aptly and fittingly stressed by the petitioners – the advancement of which may even be said to predate all governments and constitutions. As a matter of fact, these basic rights need not even be written in the Constitution for they are assumed to exist from the inception of humankind. If they are now explicitly mentioned in the fundamental charter, it is because of the well-founded fear of its framers that unless the rights to a balanced and healthful ecology and to health are mandated as state policies by the Constitution itself, thereby highlighting their continuing importance and imposing upon the state a solemn obligation to preserve the first and protect and advance the second, the day would not be too far when all else would be lost not only for the present generation, but also for those to come – generations which stand to inherit nothing but parched earth incapable of sustaining life.

The right to a balanced and healthful ecology carries with it the correlative duty to refrain from impairing the environment. . . . The said right implies, among many other things, the judicious management and conservation of the country's forests. Without such forests, the ecological or environmental balance would be irreversibly disrupted. . . . Thus, the right of the petitioners (and all those they represent) to a balanced and healthful ecology is as clear as the DENR's duty – under its mandate and by virtue of its powers and functions under EO No 192 and the Administrative Code of 1987 – to protect and advance the said right. A denial or violation of that right by the other who has the correlative duty or obligation to respect or protect the same gives rise to a cause of action.

NOTES
1. The concept of intergenerational equity in relation to international environmental law was developed by Brown Weiss (see above), though the concept of custodianship on behalf of future generations is much older (e.g. *Pacific Fur Seals Arbitration* (1893) 1 Moore's Int Arb Awards 755). It is found in many of the major environmental law instruments, including the CITES Convention (see below) and in the Preamble to the International Whaling Convention 1946.
2. Intergenerational equity essentially comprises two elements: an inter/intra-generational element, where there is a relationship that is both spatial (between members of the present generation) and temporal (between members of future generations; and an equity, or fairness, element. The precautionary principle (above) could be considered to be part of inter-generational equity and technology transfer (being part of the obligation of cooperation) could be considered as part of intragenerational equity.

E: Other general State responsibilities towards the environment

Agreement between Australia and Nauru for the Settlement of the Case in the International Court of Justice Concerning Certain Phosphate Lands in Nauru
32 ILM 1474 (1993)

Nauru had brought a claim before the International Court of Justice against Australia, as one of the joint administering authorities (together with New Zealand and the United Kingdom) of Nauru when Nauru was a Trust territory. Nauru claimed reparation for the failure of Australia to remedy the environmental damage it caused to Nauru by mining for phosphates there. Australia's preliminary objections were rejected by the Court (ICJ Rep 1992 240), but the case was settled by the terms of this Agreement before the merits were considered.

Article 1
    (1) Australia agrees that, in an effort to assist the Republic of Nauru in its preparations for its post-phosphate future, it shall pay the Republic of Nauru a cash settlement of one hundred and seven million dollars ($A107 million) as follows:
        (a) The sum of ten million dollars ($A10 million) on or before 31 August 1993.
        (b) The sum of thirty million dollars ($A30 million) as soon as it may lawfully be paid and not later than 31 December 1993.
        (c) The sum of seventeen million dollars ($A17 million) on 31 August 1994.
        (d) An amount of fifty million dollars ($A50 million) to be paid at an annual rate of $2.5 million dollars, maintained in real terms by reference to the Australian Bureau of Statistics' non-farm GDP deflator, for twenty years commencing in the financial year 1993–94.
The above payments are made without prejudice to Australia's long-standing position that it bears no responsibility for the rehabilitation of the phosphate lands worked out before 1 July 1967.
    (2) At the end of the 20 year period referred to in paragraph (1)(d) the Republic of Nauru

shall continue to receive development co-operation assistance from Australia at a mutually agreed level.

NOTES:

1. The conditions determining the international responsibility of a State are set out in Chapter 11. It would seem from the above extracts that the principles concerning imputability of acts to a State extend to where a State corporation causes pollution, or even where a State refuses to take any legislative, judicial or administrative action against perpetrators of environmental damage (who are often non-State bodies, as seen in *López Ostra* (below)).

2. There may be a general interest of all States, being a right *erga omnes*, to seek to enforce environmental obligations, as suggested by Australia in its pleadings in the *Nuclear Tests Cases* (see Chapter 3 – pleadings are found at 178 Pleadings (1973) 333–336). To this end, the concept of State sovereignty will have to be limited so that a common interest of the entire international community can be upheld. The reluctance of States to use international law to define the legal responsibility of the USSR, in regard to the transboundary pollution caused by the Chernobyl nuclear power plant accident in April 1986, highlights the difficulty in relying on States alone to determine the extent of State responsibility.

3. The OECD has recommended the principle that the 'polluter pays' in relation to accidental pollution (28 ILM 1320 (1989)). This principle is gaining increasing recognition, such as in Article 16 of the Rio Declaration (above) and Article 174(2) of the Treaty on European Union (below). Before the principle can operate, there must first be a recognition by States of their responsibility to ensure that the environment is protected adequately.

4. There is a general principle of common but differentiated responsibility in international environmental law. This principle clarifies that, whilst all States have responsibilities for the environment, these responsibilities are not necessarily evenly divided amongst all States, with developing States and industrialised States, in particular, often having different responsibilities. This is seen, for example, in Principles 6 and 7 of the Rio Declaration (above).

5. Principle 24 of the Rio Declaration (above) indicates how armed conflicts can harm the environment. An example is the deliberate oil spill by Iraq during the Gulf War in February 1991. As yet there is no clear obligation on States to protect the environment during armed conflicts, though it is possible for the Security Council to decide that an action by a State which causes environmental damage could be a threat to international peace and security (see Chapter 14). Article 55 of Additional Protocol I provides: '1. Care shall be taken in warfare to protect the natural environment against widespread, long-term and severe damage. This protection includes a prohibition of the use and methods or means of warfare which are intended or may be expected to cause such damage to the natural environment and thereby to prejudice the health or survival of the population.'

SECTION 4:   **Selected environmental treaties**

There are hundreds of international environmental law treaties and other instruments. The following is a selection of some of the more interesting and broad-based ones.

A: Global treaties

(a) *Atmosphere*

Vienna Convention for the Protection of the Ozone Layer 1985
26 ILM 1516 (1987)

As at 1 July 2002, 184 States have ratified this Convention.

Article 1 Definitions
For the purposes of this Convention:

1. 'The ozone layer' means the layer of atmospheric ozone above the planetary boundary layer.

Article 2 General obligations
1. The Parties shall take appropriate measures in accordance with the provisions of this Convention and of those protocols in force to which they are party to protect human health and the environment against adverse effects resulting or likely to result from human activities which modify or are likely to modify the ozone layer.

2. To this end the Parties shall, in accordance with the means at their disposal and their capabilities:

   (a) Co-operate by means of systematic observation, research and information exchange in order to better understand and assess the effects of human activities on the ozone layer and the effects on human health and the environment from modification of the ozone layer;

   (b) Adopt appropriate legislative or administrative measures and co-operate in harmonising appropriate policies to control, limit, reduce or prevent human activities under their jurisdiction or control should it be found that these activities have or are likely to have adverse effects resulting from modification or likely modification of the ozone layer;

   (c) Co-operate in the formulation of agreed measures, procedures and standards for the implementation of this Convention, with a view to the adoption of protocols and annexes;

   (d) Co-operate with competent international bodies to implement effectively this Convention and protocols to which they are party.

3. The provisions of this Convention shall in no way affect the right of Parties to adopt, in accordance with international law, domestic measures additional to those referred to in paragraphs 1 and 2 above, nor shall they affect additional domestic measures already taken by a Party, provided that these measures are not incompatible with their obligations under this Convention.

4. The application of this article shall be based on relevant scientific and technical considerations.

Framework Convention on Climate Change 1992
31 ILM 849 (1992)

This treaty was signed during the Rio Conference and as at 1 July 2002, 111 States have ratified this Convention.

Article 2 Objective

The ultimate objective of this Convention and any related legal instruments that the Conference of the Parties may adopt is to achieve, in accordance with the relevant provisions of the Convention, stabilization of greenhouse gas concentrations in the atmosphere at a level that would prevent dangerous anthropogenic interference with the climate system. Such a level should be achieved within a time-frame sufficient to allow ecosystems to adapt naturally to climate change, to ensure that food production is not threatened and to enable economic development to proceed in a sustainable manner. . . .

Article 4 Commitments

1. All Parties, taking into account their common but differentiated responsibilities and their specific national and regional development priorities, objectives and circumstances, shall:

   (a) Develop, periodically update, publish and make available to the Conference of the Parties, in accordance with Article 12, national inventories of anthropogenic emissions by sources and removals by sinks of all greenhouse gases not controlled by the Montreal Protocol, using comparable methodologies to be agreed upon by the Conference of the Parties;

   (b) Formulate, implement, publish and regularly update national and, where appropriate, regional programmes containing measures to mitigate climate change by addressing anthropogenic emissions by sources and removals by sinks of all greenhouse gases not controlled by the Montreal Protocol, and measures to facilitate adequate adaptation to climate change; . . .

   (j) Communicate to the Conference of the Parties information related to implementation, in accordance with Article 12.

7. The extent to which developing country Parties will effectively implement their commitments under the Convention will depend on the effective implementation by developed country Parties of their commitments under the Convention related to financial resources and transfer of technology and will take fully into account that economic and social development and poverty eradication are the first and overriding priorities of the developing country Parties.

8. In the implementation of the commitments in this Article, the Parties shall give full consideration to what actions are necessary under the Convention, including actions related to funding, insurance and the transfer of technology, to meet the specific needs and concerns of developing country Parties arising from the adverse effects of climate change and/or the impact of the implementation of response measures, especially on:

   (a) Small island countries;

   (b) Countries with low-lying coastal areas;

   (c) Countries with arid and semi-arid areas, forested areas and areas liable to forest decay;

   (d) Countries with areas prone to natural disasters;

   (e) Countries with areas liable to drought and desertification;

   (f) Countries with areas of high urban atmospheric pollution;

   (g) Countries with areas with fragile ecosystems, including mountainous ecosystems;

   (h) Countries whose economic are highly dependent on income generated from the production, processing and export, and/or on consumption of fossil fuels and associated energy-intensive products; and

   (i) Land-locked and transit countries.

Further, the Conference of the Parties may take actions, as appropriate, with respect to this paragraph. . . .

Article 7 Conference of the parties

1. A Conference of the Parties is hereby established.

2. The Conference of the Parties, as the supreme body of this Convention, shall keep under regular review the implementation of the Convention and any related legal instruments that the Conference of the Parties may adopt, and shall make, within its mandate, the decisions necessary to promote the effective implementation of the Convention. To this end, it shall:

(a) Periodically examine the obligations of the Parties and the institutional arrangements under the Convention, in the light of the objective of the Convention, the experience gained in its implementation and the evolution of scientific and technological knowledge;

(b) Promote and facilitate the exchange of information on measures adopted by the Parties to address climate change and its effects, taking into account the differing circumstances, responsibilities and capabilities of the Parties and their respective commitments under the Convention;

Kyoto Protocol 1998
Conference of the Parties to the Framework Convention on Climate Change
37 ILM 22 (1998)

This Protocol has been ratified by 74 States as at 1 July 2002, and is the result of negotiations by the Conference of Parties established under Article 7 of the Framework Convention (above).

Article 3

1. The Parties included in Annex 1 shall, individually or jointly, ensure that their aggregate anthropogenic carbon dioxide equivalent emissions of the greenhouse gases listed in Appendix A do not exceed their assigned amounts . . . with a view to reducing their overall emissions of such gases by at least 5 per cent below 1990 levels in the commitment period 2008 to 2012.

2. Each party included in Annex 1 shall, by 2005, have made demonstrable progress in achieving its commitments under this Protocol. . . .

Article 6

1. For the purpose of meeting its requirements under Article 3, any party included in Annex 1 may transfer to, or acquire from, any other such Party emission reduction units resulting from projects aimed at reducing anthropogenic emissions by sources or enhancing anthropogenic removals by sinks of greenhouse gases in any sector of the economy, provided that:

(a) Any such project has the approval of the Parties involved . . .

(d) The acquisition of emission reduction units shall be supplemental to domestic actions for the purposes of meeting commitments under Article 3 . . .

3. A Party included in Annex 1 may authorize legal entities to participate, under its responsibility, in actions leading to the generation, transfer or acquisition under this Article of emission reduction units. . . .

Article 12

1. A clean development mechanism is hereby defined.

2. The purpose of the clean development mechanism shall be to assist the Parties not included in Annex 1 in achieving sustainable development and in contributing to the ultimate objective of the Convention, and to assist Parties included in Annex 1 in achieving compliance with their quantified emission limitation and reduction commitments under Article 3.

3. Under the clean development mechanism
   (a) Parties not included in Annex 1 will benefit from project activities resulting in certified emission reductions; and
   (b) Parties included in Annex 1 may use the certified emissions reductions accruing from such project activities to contribute to compliance with part of their quantified emission limitation and reduction commitments under Article 3. . . .

Article 16 bis

The Conference of Parties shall define the relevant principles, modalities, rules and guidelines, in particular for verification, reporting and accountability for emissions trading. The parties included in Annex B may participate in emissions trading for the purposes of fulfilling their commitments under Article 3 of this Protocol. Any such trading shall be supplemental to domestic actions for the purpose of meeting quantified emission limitation and reduction commitments under that Article.

NOTES:

1. One of the first environmental treaties involving both Western and Eastern European States was the Convention on Long-Range Transboundary Air Pollution (18 ILM 1442 (1979)). The Convention provides a system for the exchange of environmental information, a common method adopted both to advance general knowledge on the pollution of the air and sea and also as a (albeit weak) supervisory means to ensure compliance with the Convention.

2. The Framework Convention on Climate Change and subsequent Kyoto Protocol embody the approach that is being taken within many areas of environmental law, taking account of each State's level of development, particular geographical characteristics and access to resources. In late 2001 the parties to the Framework Convention continued this approach in the Marrakesh Accords. Similar bifurcated procedures are also emerging in international trade law (see Chapter 13).

3. Under the Kyoto Protocol the difference between Annex 1 (which is a list of developed or industrialised States) and non-Annex 1 Parties (developing States or States in transition to a market economy) is particularly apparent in the methods provided to States to reduce emissions through 'emission trading'. Emission trading, it is argued, allows polluters flexibility in choosing how to control and reduce air pollution, enabling reductions to be achieved in the most cost-efficient manner. Article 6 enables developed States to undertake 'joint implementation' projects whereby a State can earn emission 'credits' by investing in projects in other developed States. Article 16 *bis* also enables developed States to participate in emission trading to meet reduction targets (that are set out in Annex B to the Protocol) as long as the trading is supplemental to domestic reduction activities. Article 12, in contrast, enables developed States to initiate environmental projects designed to reduce emissions or create greenhouse 'sinks' (usually reforestation or afforestation projects) in non-Annex 1 Parties, and to use the 'emission reductions' to count towards their own reduction targets. The United States, which is a signatory to the Kyoto Protocol, indicated in 2001 that it would not ratify this Protocol.

4. The advance of scientific knowledge can outstrip the parties' mutual expectations. Within two years of the signing of the Vienna Convention, the signatories issued the Helsinki Declaration on the Protection of the Ozone Layer (28 ILM 1300 (1989)), agreeing to phase out CFC gases earlier than proposed by the Vienna Convention.

5. One long-running issue in international environmental law concerns the impact of nuclear testing on the atmosphere. Despite a variety of treaties, such as the Comprehensive Test Ban Treaty 1996 (35 ILM 1439 (1996)), and cases before the ICJ (see *Nuclear Tests Case* in Chapter 3 and *Legality of the Threat or Use of Nuclear Weapons Opinion* in Chapter 14), States continue to test nuclear weapons.

(b) *Marine environment*

Law of the Sea Convention 1982
21 ILM 1261 (1982)

This Convention is discussed extensively in Chapter 10.

Article 192 General obligation
States have the obligation to protect and preserve the marine environment.

Article 193 Sovereign right of States to exploit their natural resources
States have the sovereign right to exploit their natural resources pursuant to their environmental policies and in accordance with their duty to protect and preserve the marine environment.

Article 194 Measures to prevent, reduce and control pollution of the marine environment
1. States shall take, individually or jointly as appropriate, all measures consistent with this Convention that are necessary to prevent, reduce and control pollution of the marine environment from any source, using for this purpose the best practicable means at their disposal and in accordance with their capabilities, and they shall endeavour to harmonize their policies in this connection.

2. States shall take all measures necessary to ensure that activities under their jurisdiction or control are so conducted as not to cause damage by pollution to other States and their environment, and that pollution arising from incidents or activities under their jurisdiction or control does not spread beyond the areas where they exercise sovereign rights in accordance with this Convention.

3. The measures taken pursuant to this Part shall deal with all sources of pollution of the marine environment. These measures shall include, *inter alia*, those designed to minimize to the fullest possible extent:
  (a) the release of toxic, harmful or noxious substances, especially those which are persistent, from land-based sources, from or through the atmosphere or by dumping;
  (b) pollution from vessels, in particular measures for preventing accidents and dealing with emergencies, ensuring the safety of operations at sea, preventing intentional and unintentional discharges, and regulating the design, construction, equipment, operation and manning of vessels;
  (c) pollution from installations and devices used in exploration or exploitation of the natural resources of the sea-bed and subsoil, in particular measures for preventing accidents and dealing with emergencies, ensuring the safety of operations at sea, and regulating the design, construction, equipment, operation and manning of such installations or devices;
  (d) pollution from other installations and devices operating in the marine environment, in particular measures for preventing accidents and dealing with emergencies, ensuring the safety of operations at sea, and regulating the design, construction, equipment, operation and manning of such installations or devices.

4. In taking measures to prevent, reduce or control pollution of the marine environment, States shall refrain from unjustifiable interference with activities carried out by other States in the exercise of their rights and in pursuance of their duties in conformity with this Convention.

5. The measures taken in accordance with this Part shall include those necessary to protect and preserve rare or fragile ecosystems as well as the habitat of depleted, threatened or endangered species and other forms of marine life.

NOTES:
1. There are many other treaties concerning air and marine pollution, for example, the International Convention for the Prevention of Pollution from Ships (MARPOL) 1973 (12 ILM 1319 (1973)). There are also treaties about preservation of fish and other maritime resources, e.g. Agreement for the Implementation of the Provisions of UNCLOS relating to the Conservation and Management of Highly Migratory Fish Stocks 1995 (34 ILM 1542 (1995)) and Convention on the Protection and Use of Transboundary Watercourses and International Lakes 1992 (31 ILM 1312 (1992)).
2. The Basel Convention on the Control of Transboundary Movements of Hazardous Wastes and their Disposal 1989 (28 ILM 649 (1989)) seeks to establish the right to prohibit the import of hazardous wastes and limit their export. The Convention is designed to reduce hazardous waste generation by increasing the cost of its exportation, and to prevent what has been called the 'environmental racism' that results from the export of such wastes to developing States. The underlying objectives of the Convention have been affirmed in Principle 14 of the Rio Declaration (above).

(c) *Wildlife and biological diversity*

Convention on International Trade in Endangered Species of Wild Fauna and Flora 1973
12 ILM 1085 (1973)

As at 1 July 2002, 158 States have ratified this Convention.

Article II Fundamental principles

1. Appendix I shall include all species threatened with extinction which are or may be affected by trade. Trade in specimens of these species must be subject to particularly strict regulation in order not to endanger further their survival and must only be authorized in exceptional circumstances.

2. Appendix II shall include:
   (a) all species which although not necessarily now threatened with extinction may become so unless trade in specimens of such species is subject to strict regulation in order to avoid utilization incompatible with their survival; and
   (b) other species which must be subject to regulation in order that trade in specimens of certain species referred to in sub-paragraph (a) of this paragraph may be brought under effective control.

3. Appendix III shall include all species which any Party identifies as being subject to regulation within it jurisdiction for the purpose of preventing or restricting exploitation, and as needing the co-operation of other parties in the control of trade.

4. The Parties shall not allow trade in specimens of species included in Appendices I, II and III except in accordance with the provisions of the present Convention. . . .

Article VIII Measures to be Taken by the Parties

1. The Parties shall take appropriate measures to enforce the provisions of the present Convention and to prohibit trade in specimens in violation thereof. These shall include measures:
   (a) to penalize trade in, or possession of, such specimens, or both; and
   (b) to provide for the confiscation or return to the State of export of such specimens.

2. In addition to the measures taken under paragraph 1 of this Article, a Party may, when it deems it necessary, provide for any method of internal reimbursement for expenses incurred as a result of the confiscation of a specimen traded in violation of the measures taken in the application of the provisions of the present Convention.

Convention on Biological Diversity 1992
31 ILM 818 (1992)

This treaty was signed during the Rio Conference and as at 1 July 2002, 183 States have ratified this Convention.

Article 1 Objectives

The objectives of this Convention, to be pursued in accordance with its relevant provisions, are the conservation of biological diversity, the sustainable use of its components and the fair and equitable sharing of the benefits arising out of the utilization of genetic resources, including by appropriate access to genetic resources and by appropriate transfer of relevant technologies, taking into account all rights over those resources and to technologies, and by appropriate funding. . . .

Article 8 *In-situ* Conservation

Each Contracting Party shall, as far as possible and as appropriate:

(a) Establish a system of protected areas or areas where special measures need to be taken to conserve biological diversity;

(b) Develop, where necessary, guidelines for the selection, establishment and management of protected areas or areas where special measures need to be taken to conserve biological diversity;

(c) Regulate or manage biological resources important for the conservation of biological diversity whether within or outside protected areas, with a view to ensuring their conservation and sustainable use;

(d) Promote the protection of ecosystems, natural habitats and the maintenance of viable populations of species in natural surroundings;

(e) Promote environmentally sound and sustainable development in areas adjacent to protected areas with a view to furthering protection of these areas;

(f) Rehabilitate and restore degraded ecosystems and promote the recovery of threatened species, *inter alia*, through the development and implementation of plans or other management strategies;

(g) Establish or maintain means to regulate, manage or control the risks associated with the use and release of living modified organisms resulting from biotechnology which are likely to have adverse environmental impacts that could affect the conservation and sustainable use of biological diversity, taking also into account the risks to human health;

(h) Prevent the introduction of, control or eradicate those alien species which threaten ecosystems, habitats or species;

(i) Endeavour to provide the conditions needed for compatibility between present uses and the conservation of biological diversity and the sustainable use of its components;

(j) Subject to its national legislation, respect, preserve and maintain knowledge, innovations and practices of indigenous and local communities embodying traditional lifestyles relevant for the conservation and sustainable use of biological diversity and promote their wider application with the approval and involvement of the holders of such knowledge, innovations and practices and encourage the equitable sharing of the benefits arising from the utilization of such knowledge, innovations and practices;

(k) Develop or maintain necessary legislation and/or other regulatory provisions for the protection of threatened species and populations;

(l) Where a significant adverse effect on biological diversity has been determined pursuant to Article 7, regulate or manage the relevant processes and categories of activities; and

(m) Cooperate in providing financial and other support for *in-situ* conservation outlined in subparagraphs (a) to (l) above, particularly to developing countries.

Article 9 *Ex-situ* Conservation

Each Contracting Party shall, as far as possible and as appropriate, and predominantly for the purpose of complementing *in-situ* measures:

    (a) Adopt measures for the *ex-situ* conservation of components of biological diversity, preferably in the country of origin of such components; . . .

Article 23

    4. The Conference of the Parties shall keep under review the implementation of this Convention, and, for this purpose, shall:

    (a) Establish the form and the intervals for transmitting the information to be submitted in accordance with Article 26 and consider such information as well as reports submitted by any subsidiary body;

    (b) Review scientific, technical and technological advice on biological diversity provided in accordance with Article 25; . . .

Article 26 Reports

Each Contracting Party shall, at intervals to be determined by the Conference of the Parties, present to the Conference of the Parties, reports on measures which it has taken for the implementation of the provisions of this Convention and their effectiveness in meeting the objective of this Convention.

NOTES:

1. The mechanisms for supervising compliance with the Convention on Biological Diversity are similar to the Framework Convention on Climate Change (see above), with a body of State representative which reviews periodic reports. There is also some provision for financial assistance to developing States.
2. In 2000, the Cartagena Protocol on Biosafety 2000 was signed as Protocol to the Convention on Biological Diversity. As at 1 July 2002 there were 21 State parties to the Protocol. The Protocol 'seeks to protect biological diversity from the potential risks of modern biotechnology, particularly living modified organisms. It contains advance information procedures with a Biosafety Clearing-House to faciliate information exchange. The Protocol uses a precautionary approach as it reaffirms the precaution language in Principle 15 of the Rio Declaration (see above).
3. States also have an obligation to identify and to preserve the natural and cultural heritage where they have ratified the Convention for the Protection of the World Cultural and Natural Heritage 1972 (11 ILM 1358 (1972)). This heritage includes items of archaeological, historical, artistic and scientific interest, and geological formations. While there may be reasons for allowing the freedom of movement of cultural objects, these should not be placed above the original community's wishes. The Convention also establishes the World Heritage Committee, which can place certain property of 'outstanding and universal value' on the World Heritage List.

B: Regional obligations

Treaty of the European Union

As at 1 July 2002, there were 15 State parties to this treaty.

Article 174 (formerly Article 130R)
1. Community policy on the environment shall contribute to pursuit of the following objectives:
— preserving, protecting and improving the quality of the environment;
— protecting human health;
— prudent and rational utilization of natural resources;
— promoting measures at international level to deal with regional or worldwide environmental problems.

2. Community policy on the environment shall aim at a high level of protection taking into account the diversity of situations in the various regions of the Community. It shall be based on the precautionary principle and on the principles that preventive action should be taken, that environmental damage should as a priority be rectified at source, and that the polluter should pay.

In this context, harmonisation measures answering environmental protection requirements shall include, where appropriate, a safeguard clause allowing Member States to take provisional measures for non-economic environmental reasons, subject to a Community inspection procedure.

3. In preparing its policy on the environment, the Community shall take account of:
— available scientific and technical data;
— environmental conditions in the various regions of the Community;
— the potential benefits and costs of action or lack of action;
— the economic and social development of the Community as a whole and the balanced development of its regions.

4. Within their respective spheres of competence, the Community and the Member States shall cooperate with third countries and the competent international organisations. The arrangements for Community cooperation may be the subject of agreements between the Community and third parties concerned . . .

The previous subparagraph shall be without prejudice to Member States' competence to negotiate in international bodies and to conclude international agreements.

North American Agreement on Environmental Cooperation 1994
32 ILM 1480 (1994)

The United States, Canada and Mexico are parties to this treaty.

Article 2: General commitments
1. Each party shall, with respect to its own territory:
(a) periodically prepare and make publicly available reports on the state of the environment;
(b) develop and review environmental emergency preparedness measures;
(c) promote education in environmental matters, including environmental law;
(d) further scientific research and technology development in respect of environmental matters;
(e) assess, as appropriate, environmental impacts; and
(f) promote the use of economic instruments for the efficient achievement of environmental goals. . . .

Article 6: Private Access to Remedies
1. Each party shall ensure that interested person may request the Party's competent authorities to investigate alleged violations of its environmental laws and regulations and shall give such requests due consideration in accordance with law.

2. Each party shall ensure that persons with a legally recognized interest under its law in a particular matter have appropriate access to administrative, quasi-judicial or judicial proceedings for the enforcement of the Party's environmental laws and regulations . . .

NOTES:

1. The North American Agreement on Environmental Cooperation was negotiated as a side agreement to the North American Free Trade Agreement (NAFTA), one of the first times that trade and the environment have been on the same treaty agenda. This treaty is important because, unlike the majority of international environmental instruments, it provides a private right of action whereby individuals can sue another State party to enforce environmental laws.

2. There are now a considerable number of directives, and some regulations, issued by the European Union concerning the environment. These directives create obligations on the member States to implement them as appropriate, and the regulations are directly binding on the member States (see Chapter 4). Also, the Court of Justice of the European Communities has had a series of cases before it in which it has decided that there have been breaches of environmental obligations by member States.

C: Protection of particular territory

There have been a number of treaties that have dealt with environmental protection of particular territories that are outside the traditional sovereignty of any one State. This territory includes the moon and other celestial bodies, the deep sea bed and the Antarctic. There are also areas of environmental interest that cross State borders rather than being outside the sovereign territory of any one State, such as the Amazon. In contrast with regional treaties that are based on a pre-existing economic association, such territories have been the focus of specific declarations and treaties.

Protocol on Environmental Protection to the Antarctic Treaty 1991
30 ILM 1461 (1991)

This Protocol was adopted by the State parties to the Antarctic Treaty (see Chapter 7).

Article 2 Objective and designation
The Parties commit themselves to the comprehensive protection of the Antarctic environment and dependent and associated ecosystems and hereby designate Antarctica as a natural reserve, devoted to peace and science.

Article 3 Environmental principles
1. The protection of the Antarctic environment and dependent and associated ecosystems and the intrinsic value of Antarctica, including its wilderness and aesthetic values and its value as an area for the conduct of scientific research, in particular research essential to understanding the global environment, shall be fundamental considerations in the planning and conduct of all activities in the Antarctic Treaty area.
2. To this end:
   (a) activities in the Antarctic Treaty area shall be planned and conducted so as to limit adverse impacts on Antarctic environment and dependent and associated ecosystems; . . .

(d) regular and effective monitoring shall take place to allow assessment of the impacts of ongoing activities, including the verification of predicted impacts;

(e) regular and effective monitoring shall take place to facilitate early detection of the possible unforeseen effects of activities carried on both within and outside the Antarctic Treaty area on the Antarctic environment and dependent and associated ecosystems. . . .

Article 7 Prohibition of mineral resource activities
Any activity relating to mineral resources, other than scientific research, shall be prohibited.

Article 8 Environmental impact assessment
1. Proposed activities referred to in paragraph 2 below shall be subject to the procedures set out in Annex I for prior assessment of the impacts of those activities on the Antarctic environment or on dependent or associated ecosystems according to whether those activities are identified as having:

(a) less than a minor or transitory impact;

(b) a minor or transitory impact; or

(c) more than a minor or transitory impact.

2. Each Party shall ensure that the assessment procedures set out in Annex I are applied in the planning processes leading to decisions about any activities undertaken in the Antarctic Treaty area pursuant to scientific research programmes, tourism and all other governmental and non-governmental activities in the Antarctic Treaty area for which advance notice is required under Article VII (5) of the Antarctic Treaty, including associated logistic support activities. . . .

Article 12 Functions of the Committee
1. The functions of the Committee [for Environmental Protection] shall be to provide advice and formulate recommendations to the Parties in connection with the implementation of this Protocol, including the operation of its Annexes, for consideration at Antarctic Treaty Consultative Meetings, and to perform such other functions as may be referred to it by the Antarctic Treaty Consultative Meetings. . . .

Article 17 Annual report by parties
1. Each Party shall report annually on the steps taken to implement this Protocol. Such reports shall include notifications made in accordance with Article 13(3), contingency plans established in accordance with Article 15 and any other notifications and information called for pursuant to this Protocol for which there is no other provision concerning the circulation and exchange of information.

2. Reports made in accordance with paragraph 1 above shall be circulated to all Parties and to the Committee, considered at the next Antarctic Treaty Consultative Meeting, and made publicly available.

Amazon Declaration 1989
28 ILM 1303 (1989)

Bolivia, Brazil, Colombia, Ecuador, Guyana, Peru, Suriname and Venezuela are signatories to this Declaration and are the Parties to the Treaty for Amazonian Cooperation (17 ILM 1045 (1978)), which promotes the rational use of natural resources with the objective of maintaining a balance between economic growth and environmental cooperation.

2. Conscious of the importance of protecting the cultural, economic and ecological heritage of our Amazon regions and of the necessity of using this potential to promote the economic and social development of our peoples, we reiterate that our Amazon heritage must be preserved through the rational use of the resources of the region, so that present and future generations may benefit from this legacy of nature. . . .

4. We reaffirm the sovereign right of each country to manage freely its natural resources, bearing in mind the need for promoting the economic and social development of its people and the adequate conservation of the environment. In the exercise of our sovereign responsibility to define the best ways of using and conserving this wealth and in addition to our national efforts and to the co-operation among our countries, we express our willingness to accept co-operation from countries in other regions of the world, as well as from international organizations, which might contribute to the implementation of national and regional projects and programmes that we decide freely to adopt without external impositions, in accordance with the priorities of our Governments.

5. We recognize that the defence of our environment requires the study of measures, both bilateral and regional, to prevent contamination-causing accidents and to deal with their consequences once they have occurred.

6. We stress that the protection and conservation of the environment in the region, one of the essential objectives of the Treaty for Amazonian Co-operation to which each of our nations is firmly committed, cannot be achieved without improvement of the distressing social and economic conditions that oppress our peoples and that are aggravated by an increasingly adverse international context. . . .

8. We emphasize the need for the concerns expressed in the highly developed countries in relation to the conservation of the Amazon environment to be translated into measures of co-operation in the financial and technological fields. We call for the establishment of new resource flows in additional and concessional terms to projects oriented to environmental protection in our countries, including pure and applied scientific research, and we object to attempts to impose conditionalities in the allocation of international resources for development. We expect the establishment of conditions to allow free access to scientific knowledge, to clean technologies and to technologies to be used in environmental protection and we reject any attempts made to use legitimate ecological concerns to realize commercial profits. This approach is based above all on the fact that the principal causes for the deterioration of the environment on a world-wide scale are the patterns of industrialization and consumption as well as waste in the developed countries.

NOTES:
1. States have made territorial claims to the Antarctic, though these have been placed on hold under the Antarctic Treaty 1959 (see Chapter 7). The Final Act of the special consultative meeting that adopted the above Protocol made clear that the Protocol is agreed without prejudice to the legal position of any party to the Antarctic Treaty.
2. The moon has been declared to be part of the common heritage of mankind – see Agreement Governing the Activities of States on the Moon and other Celestial Bodies 1979 (Chapter 7) – as has the deep sea bed – see Art. 136 of the Law of the Sea Convention 1982 (Chapter 10). No territorial claim had been made to these areas by any State.
3. The Amazon Declaration recognises the difficulties in protecting the environment in those States with low levels of economic development. Some developing States have sought technology transfers from developed States to assist in sustainable development in order to prevent development in a manner that is as environmentally damaging as has been the development by the developed States.

SECTION 5: **Relationship of the environment with other international law issues**

A: Human rights and the environment

López Ostra v *Spain*
20 EHRR (1994) 277, European Court of Human Rights

> The applicants lived in a town where there were a large number of leather industries (tanneries). One tannery released gas fumes and other smells of such intensity that local residents were evacuated for three months in 1988. Some of these smells have not disappeared. The applicants brought a complaint to the European Court of Human Rights based, *inter alia*, on a violation of Article 8 (right to privacy) by the government in not acting to deal with the smells or the tannery.

51. Naturally, severe environmental pollution may affect individuals' well-being and prevent them from enjoying their homes in such a way as to affect their private and family life adversely, without, however, seriously endangering their health. Whether the question is analysed in terms of a positive duty on the State – to take reasonable and appropriate measures to secure the applicant's rights under paragraph 1 of Article 8 – as the applicant wishes in her case, or in terms of an 'interference by a public authority' to be justified in accordance with paragraph 2, the applicable principles are broadly similar. In both contexts regard must be had to the fair balance that has to be struck between the competing interests of the individual and of the community as a whole, and in any case the State enjoys a certain margin of appreciation. Furthermore, even in relation to the positive obligations flowing from the first paragraph of Article 8, in striking the required balance the aims mentioned in the second paragraph may be of a certain relevance (see, in particular, the *Rees* v *The United Kingdom* judgment of 17 October 1986, Series A no. 106, p. 15, § 37, and the *Powell and Rayner* v *The United Kingdom* judgment of 21 February 1990, Series A no. 172, p. 18, § 41). . . .

55. . . . At all events, the Court considers that in the present case, even supposing that the municipality did fulfil the functions assigned to it by domestic law (see paragraphs 27 and 28 above), it need only establish whether the national authorities took the measures necessary for protecting the applicant's right to respect for her home and for her private and family life under Article 8 (see, among other authorities and *mutatis mutandis*, the *X and Y* v *The Netherlands* judgment of 26 March 1985, series A no. 91, p. 11, § 23). . . .

57. The Government drew attention to the fact that the town had borne the expense of renting a flat in the centre of Lorca, in which the applicant and her family lived from 1 February 1992 to February 1993. . . . The Court notes, however, that the family had to bear the nuisance caused by the plant for over three years before moving house with all the attendant inconveniences. They moved only when it became apparent that the situation could continue indefinitely and when Mrs López Ostra's daughter's paediatrician recommended that they do so. . . . Under these circumstances, the municipality's offer could not afford complete redress for the nuisance and inconvenience to which they had been subjected.

58. Having regard to the foregoing, and despite the margin of appreciation left to the respondent State, the Court considers that the State did not succeed in striking a fair balance between the interest of the town's economic well-being – that of having a waste-treatment plant – and the applicant's effective enjoyment of her right to respect for her home and her private and family life. There has accordingly been a violation of Article 8.

NOTES:
1. Human rights and the environment have been linked by theorists (see above) as well as in case law. For a discussion of human rights generally see Chapter 6.
2. National legislation to protect the environment is continually growing. However, the *Minors Oposa* (above) and *Tasmanian Dams Case* ((1983) 158 CLR 1, before the High Court of Australia) highlight the difficulty of attempts to enforce international environment standards in national courts, particularly because procedural issues, such as standing to bring a claim. The 1974 Nordic Convention on the Protection of the Environment (13 ILM 591 (1974)) is an unusual treaty, in that it gives some rights to individuals affected by environmentally harmful activities in another contracting State to bring a claim in their own State. A private right of action is also provided by the North American Agreement on Environmental Cooperation (below).

B: Trade and the environment

P. Galizzi, 'Economic Instruments as Tools for the Protection of the International Environment'
(1997) *European Environmental Law Review* 155, 155–157

The use of economic instruments [such as charges and taxes, tradeable permits, deposit-refund systems, subsidies and enforcement incentives] as a means for the protection of the environment was developed within the OECD for application at the national level in Member States but its application at an international level is now also being considered. The idea underlying the use of these instruments, also known as market-based mechanisms, is the belief that through their use it is possible to provide incentives to guide human behaviour. In other words, economic instruments will use market forces to influence behaviour in a way which is favourable to the environment, through the detrimental consequences which would follow non-environmentally-friendly behaviour or the forfeiture of benefits by potential polluters. Economic instruments have several advantages: for example, they result in a more cost-effective allocation of pollution costs; they offer greater flexibility of methods to achieve certain environmental goals; there is no burden on the public purse, etc. But there are also some problems, related to the operation of the market and its regulation. There is always the need to set initial goals and standards; this requires interaction between command and control systems and market-based mechanisms.

As stated above, support for the application of economic instruments for international environmental protection is a recent phenomenon. . . . Several references can be found in Agenda 21 adopted at the United Nations Conference on the Environment and Development. Principle 16 of the Rio Declaration also suggests the use of these instruments at the national level. More importantly, some relevant treaties, like the Montreal Protocol on Substances that Deplete the Ozone Layer and the Climate Change Convention, seem to envisage the use of these instruments to reach their environmental objectives. . . .

These economic instruments, however, should be adapted to the structure of the existing international community. Developmental differences between the various countries should be taken into consideration specifically, and balances should be found to avoid increasing these differences. In particular, the provision of financial assistance and aid to developing countries, the promotion of the integration of economic and environmental objectives in the work of the more important international economic agencies, as well as national aid, should play fundamental roles. The example set by the Montreal Protocol Fund is a very encouraging experience in this direction and the same can be said for the development of the policy of the World Bank. Last, but not least, it remains to be seen what effect the Global Environmental Facility will have, but the first phase of its operation gives rise to a certain optimism.

According to one author, the integration of international environmental law within international economic law will result in the 'subordination of environmental policies to economic imperatives' [Pallemaerts in Sands (ed)]. This view cannot be shared; in my opinion, environmental concerns are part of the problems the international community faces and they must be seen in relation to all the other problems facing the world. Furthermore, it seems that the integration of environmental law within economic law has so far been beneficial for what is the final goal of this subject – the protection of the environment. Experience in human rights law, which has always been isolated by the work of international economic institutions, should be a reminder of how this separation could be detrimental.

NOTES:
1. The issues arising from the interaction of international economic law, particularly trade, and the environment are significant. The linking of environment and trade through the World Trade Organisation (WTO) and the General Agreement on Tariffs and Trade (GATT) framework has been a significant development for environmental protection.
2. While multilateral environmental treaties have in many instances used bans on imports and exports of species, goods or technologies to protect the environment, the WTO/GATT system has introduced rules on the use of such trade measures. This system establishes a general prohibition on import and export bans with only limited environmental exceptions that continue to be narrowly read by WTO dispute resolution panels (see Chapter 13). The result has been that environmental purposes have generally been trumped by economic considerations.
3. After much pressure, the World Bank has begun to take environmental matters into account, for example, an Inspection Panel has been created that allows individuals who believe that they will be affected detrimentally by a project in a State that is to be funded by the World Bank to ask the Panel to investigate their claim (Resolution No. 93–6, 1993). The Bank can do this even if the State is opposed to such investigation. A similar system operates in the Asian Development Bank and the Inter-American Development Bank. These issues are considered further in Chapter 13.
4. Galizzi shows how there are already economic aspects of international environmental law. He demontrates how these, combined with effective environmental policies of the international economic bodies, can contribute positively to the protection of the environment.

SECTION 6: **The future**

P. Sands, 'The Environment, Community and International Law'
30 *Harvard International Law Journal* 393 (1989)

The unwillingness of states to act as guardians of the environment does not mean, however, that there has been a complete lack of action on the basis of existing rules of international environmental law or that international law has been irrelevant. Additionally, non-governmental organizations (NGOs) such as Greenpeace International, Friends of the Earth, and World Wide Fund for Nature have been active for many years in identifying threats to the environment, in attempting to force governments to take measures to protect the environment, and in signalling breaches of existing international environmental regulations. In many respects, such NGOs have come to be the primary source of expression for the international desire to protect the environment, and number among its most effective guardians.

The increasing urgency of environmental problems requires pragmatic and practical approaches.

This Article suggests one course of action that could be followed if the law is to have a role in the protection of the international environment. This course includes three steps, each of which entails a considerable change in the way have traditionally understood international society in legal terms. First, the political reality that non-governmental organizations are important participants in international society ought to be given legal expression. Second, the notion of environmental rights ought to be established on the international plane. And third, international law should recognize a role for NGOs as legal guardians of those rights. Specifically, NGOs should be granted standing to enforce these rights in the international arena by negotiating with states and appearing before international institutions and tribunals. . . .

In excluding these non-governmental organizations from fuller participation in the affairs of international society, the international legal system establishes a notion of community and participant which fails to reflect an important reality and which lacks effectiveness. One consequence of this flawed structure is the inability of traditional international law to give effect to a large number of peoples' expressed desire for environmental protection.

D. Bodansky, 'The Legitimacy of International Governance: A Coming Challenge for International Environmental Law'
93 AJIL 596 (1999), pp. 596, 603–4, 623–4

Until now, international lawyers have tended to focus on what environmental standards are needed and how those standards can be made effective. But as decision-making authority gravitates from the national to the international level, the question of legitimacy will likely emerge from the shadows and become a central issue in international environmental law. . . . Legitimacy concerns the justification of authority; it provides grounds for deferring to another's decision, even in the absence of coercion or rational persuasion. Thus far, international environmental law has developed on a different basis, through a consensual rather than an authoritative process. States have negotiated and adopted international rules that they believe are in their self-interest, rather than recognize the rulemaking authority of international institutions. They realize that they cannot solve some transnational or global environmental problem through individual action, so they agree to collective action by means of reciprocol exchange of promises – they agree, for example, to limit their use of ozone-depleting substances or to impose restrictions on the import and export of endangered species. . . .

The process of globalization has put mounting strains on the State system. Environmental problems are increasingly escaping the control of individual States and international institutions have often been too weak to step into the breach. The result has been a 'decision-making deficit', an erosion in the ability of government to address environmental problems effectively. In the long run, overcoming this deficit will require stronger international institutions and decision-making mechanisms. But, as the case of the European Union illustrates, the stronger the institution, the greater the concern about its legitimacy. Unless the issue of legitimacy is addressed, it is likely to act as a drag on the development and effectiveness of international environmental regimes. . . .

Unless some other basis of legitimacy can be found, the continuing centrality of State consent (which remains, by default, the principle source of legitimacy for international environmental law) is likely to limit the possibilities of international governance. When States have common interests, and the issues involved are relatively technical, States might agree to establish institutions with flexible, non-consensus decision-making procedures, as they have done in the ozone regime. In such cases, general consent confers legitimacy initially, and technical expertise helps maintain this legitimacy on a continuing basis. But this approach is unlikely to work for problems such as climate change, where states have a much wider range of interests, and the issues involved are highly political. This is a sobering conclusion, but one that clarifies the challenges that lie ahead for international environmental law.

P. Birnie and A. Boyle, *International Law and the Environment*
(2nd edn, 2002), pp. 751–755

A sceptic assessing the present state of international environmental law might make three main criticisms: that it remains preponderantly 'soft' in character, unsystematic and insufficiently comprehensive in scope, and weak in matters of compliance and enforcement. As we have seen, there are some grounds for such criticisms but, for the most part, they overlook the significance of the broad framework for further development of the law to protect the environment that has now been established, and in certain respects fail to take account of what has been achieved since 1972. . . .

How one responds to these criticisms is largely a function of one's views on the nature of international law and the way in which the international legal system functions. . . . Certainly, there is no doubt that the content of customary international environmental law today is much less modest than was true in 1972. Even if in practice customary environmental law has not been the subject of much judicial elaboration or of widely accepted codification, is has exercised an influence, both in structuring the resolution of environmental disputes, such as those involving water-courses or fisheries conservation, and as a basis for negotiation of treaty regimes. . . . [I]t must be accepted that the main part of international environmental law comprises the treaty regimes. . . . The impact of these, both on customary law and in themselves, should not, however, be under-estimated. . . . [M]ost of the major global agreements, including the Rio treaties and the 1982 UNCLOS, enjoy wide participation, are in force, and have begun to exert significant influence on national environmental law and practice. Contrary to a frequently asserted claim, there is no evidence of widespread non-compliance with such treaties. . . . [A] more pertinent critique is that international regulatory regimes are sometimes ineffective, constrained by the competing demands of economic development and the difficulty of securing consensus on detailed regulations and standards. . . . This should not be surprising. The effectiveness of environmental regulation cannot be separated from value judgments about economic, social, and cultural priorities. . . .

However, what these [international] treaties have done . . . is to change the basis and perspective of international environmental law. Having started as a system of rules limited largely to liability for transboundary damage, resource allocation, and the resolution of conflicting uses of common spaces, international law now accommodates a preventive, and in this sense precautionary, approach to the protection of the environment on a global level. This is a necessary and inevitable development if international environmental law is to address major global and regional environmental issues; it involves much greater emphasis on environmental regulation, and gives less prominence to liability for damage as the law's main response to environmentally harmful activities. To this extent, the development of contemporary international law reflects a comparable transformation during this century in national environmental law throughout much of the developed, industrialized world. As a consequence, the most convincing characterization of international environmental law is no longer that of neighbourly relations, but of environmental trusteeship, with certain institutional similarities to the protection of social and economic human rights, and a comparable concern for community interests at a global level, and not merely those of states *inter se*. These considerations help explain the increasing use of institutional supervision as the primary form of environmental dispute resolution, regulation, and supervision, and the relatively limited resort to judicial bodies. Thus any examination of the functioning of the international legal system as regards protection of the environment must start with the realization that the role of courts is inevitably secondary in this context, limited to the settling of bilateral problems, or to providing judicial review of the operation of treaty regimes and international institutions. . . . Thus the primary concern of future development should properly be to address deficiencies of existing institutions, not to introduce radical innovations in the judicial machinery and process.

From this perspective, the problems of environmental law-making, implementation, and compliance are essentially political and institutional in character. They are best seen as a reflection of the difficulties of securing international cooperation on global environmental management within a complex and diffuse structure of political authority and of the deeply conflicting priorities among developed and developing states. . . . Yet the major virtue of the present international political system is precisely that in matters of global interdependence, such as protection of the environment, it compels negotiation of a balance of interests and requires consensus if a framework of rules is to attain global acceptance. No group of states, including developing nations, are deprived of influence in this system, as they might well be under a majoritarian model of decision-making; competing priorities, including those of economic development, must also be fully accommodated. . . .

If states have generally preferred to avoid resort to supranational law-making institutions, or supranational enforcement, it does not follow that their sovereignty has remained unaffected by the growth of international environmental law and the emergence of the environment as an issue of global concern. What is clear is not only that states are now subject to obligations of restraint and control in the use of their territory and natural resources, as well as the exploitation of common spaces, but, more significantly, notions of common heritage, common interest, common concern and inter-generational equity have extended the scope of international law, and the legitimate interest of other states, into the management of every state's domestic environment, at least in respect of certain issues such as global climate change and conservation of biodiversity. Moreover, the characterization of environmental quality as a human rights issue, potentially affording individuals a claim to protection in national and international law against their own government and those of other states, is likely to effect another radical transformation in the nature of sovereignty or sovereign rights over natural resources and the environment in general. These developments indicate that while sovereignty may remain a focus of conflict and resistance to further encroachments on national autonomy, it is no longer a decisive objection.

The development of modern international environmental law, starting essentially in the 1960s, has been one of the most remarkable exercises in international law-making, comparable only to the law of human rights and international trade law in the scale and form it has taken. The system which has emerged from this process is neither primitive nor without effect, though equally it has many weaknesses. . . . [I]t will be sufficient to observe the reality that international environmental law has provided the framework for much political and scientific co-operation, for measures of economic assistance and distributive equity, for the resolution of international disputes, for the promotion of greater transparency and public participation in national decision-making, and for the adoption and harmonization of a great deal of national environmental law. These developments have clearly not been without considerable significance, and have laid the foundations of a new system of global environmental order.

NOTES:

1. Many of the restrictions on international environmental protection are social, economic and political rather than legal. Instability and territorial disputes, desire for development and problems of poverty, overpopulation and lack of human rights and inequities in the international community, all hinder environmental protection. Also, an integrated interdisciplinary approach involving at least natural and social scientists is required to assist in the development of an international environmental policy. Only from the basis of such a policy can international environmental law develop further.

2. The fact that environmental issues interact with other international legal matters, such as human rights and trade, means that the future development of international environmental law must also deal with these issues.

13

International Economic Law

Introductory note

With a flurry of developments during the past decade, international economic law has become a distinct and distinctive part of the international legal system. While the regulation of inter-State trade has always been an aspect of international law, the creation of international institutions, definite rules governing a wide range of economic matters and the provision of dispute settlement methods has created a body of law described as international economic law. The focus of this chapter will be on international trade law aspects of international economic law.

International economic law influences developments in other areas of international law. For example, the involvement in international economic law of entities other than States, in particular transnational corporations, is part of the movement of international law away from being a State-only system. International economic law also challenges some concepts of State sovereignty and territorial integrity, as well as often being both part of the processes of globalisation and a potential regulator of those processes. Indeed, international economic law issues, as Jackson makes clear below, are now found on the front pages of daily newspapers.

SECTION 1: Defining international economic law

J. Jackson, 'International Economic Law: Reflections on the "Boilerroom" of International Relations' in C. Ku and P. Diehl (eds), *International Law: Classic and Contemporary Readings*
(1998), pp. 509–11

At the outset, it is appropriate to ask what we mean by 'international economic law.' This phrase can cover a very broad inventory of subjects: embracing the law of economic transactions; government regulation of economic matters; and related legal relations including litigation and international institutions for economic relations. Indeed, it is plausible to suggest that ninety per cent of international law work is in reality international economic law in some form or another. Much of this, of course, does not have the glamour or visibility of nation-state relations (use of force, human rights, intervention, etc.), but does indeed involve many questions of international law and particularly treaty law. Increasingly, today's international economic law issues are found on the front pages of the daily newspapers. . . .

In trying to describe international economic law, I would like to mention four characteristics about the subject:

(1) International Economic Law (IEL) can not be separated or compartmentalized from general or 'public' international law. The activities and cases relating to IEL contain much practice which is relevant to general principles of international law, especially concerning treaty law and practice. Conversely general international law has considerable relevance to economic relations and transactions . . .

(2) The relationship of international economic law to national or 'municipal' law is particularly important. It is an important part of understanding international law generally, but this 'link,' and the interconnections between IEL and municipal law are particularly significant to the operation and effectiveness of IEL rules. For example, an important question is the relationship of treaty norms to municipal law, expressed by such phrases as 'self executing' or 'direct application.'

(3) As the title phrase – international economic law – suggests, there is necessarily a strong component of multi-disciplinary research and thinking required for those who work on IEL projects. Of course, 'economics' is important and useful, especially for understanding the policy motivations of many of the international and national rules on the subject . . . In addition to economics, of course, other subjects are highly relevant. Political science (and its intersection with economics found generally in the 'public choice' literature) is very important, as are many other disciplines, such as cultural history and anthropology, geography, etc.

(4) As previously noted, work on IEL matters often seems to necessitate more empirical study than some other international law subjects. Empirical research, however, does not necessarily mean statistical research, in the sense used in many policy explorations. For some key issues of international law there are too few 'cases' on which to base statistical conclusions (such as correlations), so we are constrained to use a more 'anecdotal', or case study approach. This type of empiricism, however, is nevertheless very important, and a good check on theory or on sweeping generalizations of any kind.

NOTE:
As Jackson notes, international economic law is found within many areas of international law and a significant number of activities that lead to the development of international law are economically generated. Some of the extent of international economic law will be considered in this chapter, though only a representative sample will be given.

SECTION 2:   **Main international economic institutions**

Primarily, international economic law is founded on the desire of States and other entities to regulate international finance and trade. This was in part motivated by the belief that closer economic integration between States provided a means for ensuring enhanced global security. The institutions to enable this to happen and to supervise compliance have evolved since 1945.

M. Pryles, J. Waincymer and M. Davies, *International Trade Law: Cases and Materials*
(1996), pp. 92–93, 712–13

After the [Second World War], key political advisers in the United States and England believed that institutional mechanisms should be established to try to avoid a repetition of the protectionist trade policies of the 1930s. A meeting was held at Bretton Woods, which unveiled a comprehensive plan to set up mechanisms dealing with national trade, investment and foreign exchange. The three prongs of that system were to be the International Monetary Fund (IMF), the International Bank for Reconstruction and Development (the World Bank) and an International Trade Organisation (ITO).

The IMF was intended to provide short-term finance to countries in balance of payments difficulties. The World Bank was to provide long-term capital to support growth and development. The ITO was to promote a liberal trading system by proscribing certain protectionist trade rules. Of the three, the IMF and the World Bank were duly established. The ITO fell by the wayside, with its intended functions taken over by the General Agreement on Tariffs and Trade (the GATT). The GATT and its successor, the World Trade Organisation (WTO), are the most important trade-oriented institutions as they shape domestic import and export laws that directly affect all international sale of goods transactions and now cover trade in services as well. . . .

The GATT is an unusual institution primarily because it was only originally intended as an interim agreement until the International Trade Organisation was established, but through political circumstances, it has become the dominant organisation and body of rules dealing with intergovernmental trading relationships. The original agreement was signed on 30 October 1947. . . . Those signatories agreed to apply the GATT on a provisional basis under a Protocol of Provisional Application as from 1 January 1948.

Over time, GATT developed an institutional structure, a permanent home in Geneva and a secretariat. Modifications to the Agreement were made through negotiating Rounds, the last and most important of which was the Uruguay Round which was . . . completed [in 1994]. The final Agreement under that Round proposed establishment of a World Trade Organisation which would oversee the workings of the GATT and a new General Agreement on Trade in Services . . .

Because the GATT Agreement was only intended as an interim device until the ITO was created, it did not establish any institutional framework necessary for an ongoing international trade regulating organisation. When the ITO failed to eventuate, however, most key trading nations wanted to see GATT broaden its ambit to effectively act in a similar fashion. As a result, GATT slowly developed institutional and dispute settlement elements over the 40-odd years of its history, at the same time as its rules developed a central place in moulding and regulating world trade relationships.

The GATT worked on two levels. The first was the day-to-day level where the existing rules sought to circumscribe protectionist government activity, where disputes were sought to be resolved and where discussions could be held on general issues. The second level involved negotiating Rounds. These were lengthy multilateral trade negotiations aimed at improving liberalisation and the general structure of the Agreement. In the early years, the key focus of these Rounds was to promote further tariff reductions on a reciprocal negotiating basis. Later Rounds dealt with other trade rules and protectionist barriers besides tariffs. The Rounds were as follows: Geneva Round 1947, Annecy Round 1948, Torquay Round 1950, Geneva Round 1956, Dillon Round 1960–1961, Kennedy Round 1964–1967, Tokyo Round 1973–1979, Uruguay Round 1986–1994. The Uruguay Round has been the most significant of all the Rounds to date, not the least because it proposed the establishment of a new organisation, the World Trade Organisation (WTO) to subsume the GATT Agreement and the GATT organisational structure.

Agreement Establishing the World Trade Organization 1994, Article II

1. The WTO shall provide the common institutional framework for the conduct of trade relations among its Members in matters related to the agreements and associated legal instruments included in the Annexes to this Agreement.

2. The agreements and associated legal instruments included in Annexes 1, 2 and 3

(hereinafter referred to as 'Multilateral Trade Agreements') are integral parts of this Agreement, binding on all Members.

3. The agreements and associated legal instruments included in Annex 4 (hereinafter referred to as 'Plurilateral Trade Agreements') are also part of this Agreement for those Members that have accepted them, and are binding on those Members. The Plurilateral Trade Agreements do not create either obligations or rights for Members that have not accepted them.

D. Driscoll, 'The IMF and the World Bank: How do they Differ?' in *International Monetary Fund Publications*
http://www.imf.org

Known collectively as the Bretton Woods Institutions after the remote village in New Hampshire, USA, where they were founded by the delegates of 44 nations in July 1944, the [World] Bank and the [International Monetary Fund (IMF)] are twin intergovernmental pillars supporting the structure of the world's economic and financial order. That there are two pillars rather than one is no accident. The international community was consciously trying to establish a division of labor in setting up the two agencies. . . .

Both are in a sense owned and directed by the governments of member nations . . . [and] virtually every country on earth is a member of both institutions. Both institutions concern themselves with economic issues and concentrate their efforts on broadening and strengthening the economies of their member nations. . . . The fundamental difference is this: the Bank is primarily a development institution; the IMF is a cooperative institution that seeks to maintain an orderly system of payments and receipts between nations. Each has a different purpose, a distinct structure, receives its funding from different sources, assists different categories of members, and strives to achieve distinct goals through methods peculiar to itself.

At Bretton Woods the international community assigned to the World Bank the aims implied in its formal name, the International Bank for Reconstruction and Development (IBRD), giving it primary responsibility for financing economic development. The Bank's first loans were extended during the late 1940s to finance the reconstruction of the war-ravaged economies of Western Europe. When these nations recovered some measure of economic self-sufficiency, the Bank turned its attention to assisting the world's poorer nations, known as developing countries, to which it has since the 1940s loaned more than $US330 billion. The World Bank has one central purpose: to promote economic and social progress in developing countries by helping to raise productivity so that their people may live a better and fuller life.

The international community assigned to the IMF a different purpose. In establishing the IMF, the world community was reacting to the unresolved financial problems instrumental in initiating and protracting the Great Depression of the 1930s: sudden, unpredictable variations in the exchange values of national currencies and a wide-spread disinclination among governments to allow their national currency to be exchanged for foreign currency. Set up as a voluntary and cooperative institution, the IMF attracts to its membership nations that are prepared, in a spirit of enlightened self-interest, to relinquish some measure of national sovereignty by abjuring practices injurious to the economic well-being of their fellow member nations. The rules of the institution, contained in the IMFs Articles of Agreement signed by all members, constitute a code of conduct. The code is simple: it requires members to allow their currency to be exchanged for foreign currencies freely and without restriction, to keep the IMF informed of changes they contemplate in financial and monetary policies that will affect fellow Members' economies, and, to the extent possible, to modify these policies on the advice of the IMF to accommodate the needs of the entire membership. To help nations abide by the code of conduct, the IMF administers a pool of money from which members can borrow when they are in trouble. The IMF is not, however, primarily a lending institution as is the Bank. It is first and foremost an overseer of its Members' monetary and exchange rate policies and a guardian of the code of conduct. . . .

The World Bank is an investment bank, intermediating between investors and recipients, borrowing from the one and lending to the other. Its owners are the governments of its 180 member nations with equity shares in the Bank . . . the IMF is not a bank and does not intermediate between investors and recipients. . . . [Its] resources come from quota subscriptions, or membership fees, paid in by the IMF's . . . member countries [which are virtually all States]. Each member contributes to this pool of resources a certain amount of money proportionate to its economic size and strength (richer countries pay more, poorer less). While the Bank borrows and lends, the IMF is more like a credit union whose members have access to a common pool of resources (the sum total of their individual contributions) to assist them in times of need. . . .

The World Bank exists to encourage poor countries to develop by providing them with technical assistance and funding for projects and policies that will realize the countries' economic potential. The Bank views development as a long-term, integrated endeavor. . . .

[Today the IMF has three main functions]. First, the IMF continues to urge its members to allow their national currencies to be exchanged without restriction for the currencies of other member countries. . . . Second, in place of monitoring Members' compliance with their obligations in a fixed exchange system, the IMF supervises economic policies that influence their balance of payments in the presently legalized flexible exchange rate environment. . . . Third, the IMF continues to provide short- and medium-term financial assistance to member nations that run into temporary balance of payments difficulties. The financial assistance usually involves the provision by the IMF of convertible currencies to augment the afflicted member's dwindling foreign exchange reserves, but only in return for the government's promise to reform the economic policies that caused the balance of payments problem in the first place.

NOTES:

1. As at 1 July 2002, there are 144 State members of the WTO. There are also 32 States which have observer status, which enables them to attend WTO meetings but also requires them to begin accession negotiations within five years of becoming observers.

2. The WTO Agreement provides that all annexed agreements are integral parts of the Agreement (Article II: 2). The annexed agreements include the Multilateral Agreement on Trade in Goods, such as GATT 1994 (which incorporates GATT 1947 with a few minor amendments), the Agreement on Agriculture, the Agreement on the Application of Sanitary and Phytosanitary Measures (SPS Agreement), the Agreement on Textiles and Clothing, the Agreement on Technical Barriers to Trade, the Agreement on Trade-related Investment Measures, the Agreement on Implementation of Article VI of the GATT 1994, the Agreement on Subsidies and Countervailing Measures; the General Agreement on Trade in Services, the Agreement on Trade-related Aspects of Intellectual Property Rights (TRIPS), and the Understanding on Rules and Procedures Governing the Settlement of Disputes (DSU).

3. The WTO Agreement also provides for the creation of bodies responsible for overseeing the functioning of the WTO and the annexed ('covered') agreements set out above. The Ministerial Conference, composed of ministerial representatives of every member state, meets every two years and is the main body responsible for the functioning of the WTO. The General Council, also a representative body, is charged with overseeing the WTO between meetings of the Ministerial Conference. The General Council also convenes as the Dispute Settlement Body under the DSU (Article IV) and is responsible in this capacity for overseeing dispute settlement procedures within the WTO, such as monitoring compliance with decisions of dispute settlement bodies (see below). Separate councils also exist for Trade in Goods, Trade in Services and TRIPS to oversee the respective agreements. A number of committees have also been created to examine specific issues of relevance to the WTO such as the Committee on Trade and the Environment.

4. Article XVI:1 of the WTO Agreement declares that 'except as otherwise provided under this

Agreement or the Multilateral Trade Agreements, the WTO shall be guided by the decisions, procedures and customary practices followed by the Contracting Parties to GATT 1947 and the bodies established in the framework of GATT 1947'. This emphasises the continuing relevance of earlier GATT practice to current international economic law.

5. The World Bank consists of two separate institutions: the International Bank for Reconstruction and Development, and the International Development Association, which lends all its resources to States with the lowest *per capita* income. The World Bank umbrella also includes the Multilateral Investment Guarantee Agency, which acts as an insurance agency liaising on World Bank funding projects, and the International Centre for the Settlement of Investment Disputes, which provides a dispute settlement regime applying both to agreements between States and agreements between private investors and States (see Chapter 15).

6. While there is no formal relationship between the World Bank, the International Monetary Fund (IMF) and the GATT/WTO system, the organisations do operate with some collaboration. For example, Article III of the Agreement Establishing the World Trade Organisation provides that 'With a view to achieving greater coherence in global economic policy-making, the WTO shall cooperate, as appropriate, with the International Monetary Fund and with the International Bank for Reconstruction and Development and its affiliated agencies.'

SECTION 3: **Key principles of international trade law**

There are four key principles that underpin international trade law relating to trade in goods: binding of tariffs; most favoured nation treatment; national treatment obligation; and tariffication. The binding of tariffs and tariffication principles relate solely to trade in goods, however, the most favoured nation treatment and national treatment principles have been incorporated where relevant in other international trade agreements, such as the General Agreement on Trade in Services.

A: Binding of tariffs

Binding of tariffs is a principle by which individual States agree to tariff levels for particular products and 'bind' those tariff levels in schedules to the GATT. There is a schedule for each State, which can be renegotiated at the various negotiating Rounds (see above). States agree not to raise tariffs above those levels contained in the schedules and the GATT provides for compensatory adjustments and other remedies where a State does raise tariffs above its bound level (Article XXVIII).

B: Most favoured nation treatment

General Agreement on Tariffs and Trade 1947, Article I

1. With respect to customs duties and charges of any kind imposed on or in connection with importation or exportation or imposed on the international transfer of payments for imports or exports, and with respect to the method of levying such duties and charges, and with respect to all rules and formalities in connection with importation and exportation, and with respect to all matters referred to in paragraphs 2 and 4 of Article III, any

advantage, favour, privilege or immunity granted by any contracting party to any product originating in or destined for any other country shall be accorded immediately and unconditionally to the like product originating in or destined for the territories of all other contracting parties.

NOTES:

1. The most favoured nation (MFN) clause embodies the norm of non-discrimination, prohibiting discrimination between trading partners (States). The principle provides that any special treatment given to a product from one trading partner must be available to all like products originating in, or destined for, other Contracting Parties. As a result a Contracting Party cannot treat the trade of any trading partners more favourably than trade with a Contracting Party. The meaning of 'like product' is discussed further below.

2. In practice the MFN clause means that a tariff concession made by one State with another is in effect made with all other parties, without the conceding party being able to demand a *quid pro quo* as a condition for the extension of the concession. This obligation has been blamed for limiting the readiness of contracting parties to make offers and concessions in multilateral negotiations, particularly when larger economies appear unwilling to act reciprocally. However, arguably, unconditional most favoured nation treatment does help spread trade liberalisation more quickly by reducing the process of tariff negotiations.

3. The principle of most favoured nation treatment in GATT 1947 has been subject to much criticism because, despite the legal obligations found in Article I, there are both departures in trade practice and exceptions within the GATT itself. These exceptions generally relate to preferential trading arrangements, regional trading arrangements or in regard to developing States, as is discussed below.

C: National treatment obligation

Whereas the MFN principle is designed to prevent discrimination between foreign imports, the national treatment obligation is directed at the prevention of discrimination between domestic producers and foreign producers.

General Agreement on Tariffs and Trade 1947, Article III

1. The contracting parties recognize that internal taxes and other internal charges, and laws, regulations and requirements affecting the internal sale, offering for sale, purchase, transportation, distribution or use of products, and internal quantitative regulations requiring the mixture, processing or use of products in specified amounts or proportions, should not be applied to imported or domestic products so as to afford protection to domestic production.

2. The products of the territory of any contracting party imported into the territory of any other contracting party shall not be subject, directly or indirectly, to internal taxes or other internal charges of any kind in excess of those applied, directly or indirectly, to like domestic products. Moreover, no contracting party shall otherwise apply internal taxes or other internal charges to imported or domestic products in a manner contrary to the principles set forth in paragraph 1. . . .

4. The products of the territory of any contracting party imported into the territory of any other contracting party shall be accorded treatment no less favourable than that accorded to like products of national origin in respect of all laws, regulations and requirements affecting their internal sale, offering for sale, purchase, transportation, distribution or use.

Japan – Taxes on Alcoholic Beverages

WT/DS8/AB/R WT/DS10/AB/R WT/DS11/AB/R, Adopted 11 November 1996, pp. 17, 21–22, World Trade Organization, Report of the Appellate Body

The broad and fundamental purpose of Article III is to avoid protectionism in the application of internal tax and regulatory measures. More specifically, the purpose of Article III 'is to ensure that internal measures "not be applied to imported or domestic products so as to afford protection to domestic production"'. Toward this end, Article III obliges Members of the WTO to provide equality of competitive conditions for imported products in relation to domestic products. '[T]he intention of the drafters of the Agreement was clearly to treat the imported products in the same way as the like domestic products once they had been cleared through customs. Otherwise indirect protection could be given'. Moreover, it is irrelevant that 'the trade effects' of the tax differential between imported and domestic products, as reflected in the volumes of imports, are insignificant or even non-existent; Article III protects expectations not of any particular trade volume but rather of the equal competitive relationship between imported and domestic products. Members of the WTO are free to pursue their own domestic goals through internal taxation or regulation so long as they do not do so in a way that violates Article III or any of the other commitments they have made in the WTO Agreement.

NOTES:

1. The national treatment obligation explicitly recognises the tariff bindings to which States have committed themselves. Thus, once border duties have been paid in accordance with a State's tariff bindings, the principle of national treatment operates to prohibit any additional burdens being placed discriminately on the foreign producer or products.

2. The Appellate Body in both the *Japanese Beverages* case and *European Union – Measures Affecting Asbestos and Asbestos Containing Products* (the *Asbestos* case) (Report of the Appellate Body, WT/DS135/AB/R, 12 March 2001) differentiated between Article III:1, which they stated contains 'general principles', and Articles III:2 and III:4, which regulates specific obligations regarding internal taxes and charges, and internal laws and regulations respectively. The Appellate Body in the *Japanese Beverages* case declared (at p. 20) that 'Article III:1 articulates a general principle that internal measures should not be applied so as to afford protection to domestic production. This general principle informs the rest of Article III'.

3. Article III:2 comprises two distinct principles and Article III:1 informs each sentence in a different manner. The first sentence establishes that if imported products are taxed in excess of like domestic products, then that tax measure is inconsistent with Article III. The Appellate Body in the *Japanese Beverages* case determined (at p. 21) that it is not necessary to establish that the measure is in effect protectionist, but only that the tax measure is inconsistent with the general principle set out in the first sentence. With regard to the phrase 'in excess of', the Appellate Body in the *Japanese Beverages* case held (at p.27) that '[e]ven the smallest amount of "excess" is too much'.

4. The Appellate Body in the *Asbestos* case confirmed that the 'general principle' recognised in the *Japanese Beverages* case (above) also informs Article III:4 such that there must be 'consonance between the objective pursued by Article III, and enunciated in the "general principle" articulated in Article III:1, and the interpretation of the specific expression of this principle in the text of Article III:4' (at paragraph 98). Article III:4, therefore, is concerned to prevent the application of internal regulations 'in a manner which effects the competitive relationship, in the marketplace, between the domestic and imported products' (at paragraph 98).

5. The determination of whether imported and domestic products are 'like products' is determined on a case-by-case basis. The Appellate Body in the *Asbestos* case recognised (at paragraph 101) four categories of characteristics that like products might share: '(i) the physical

properties of the products: (ii) the extent to which the products are capable of serving the same or similar end-uses; (iii) the extent to which consumers perceive and treat the products as alternative means of performing particular functions in order to satisfy a particular want or demand; and (iv) the international classification of the products for tariff purposes'.

6. Article III:2 requires an analysis of whether the imported and domestic products are 'directly competitive or substitutable products', whether they are 'not similarly taxed', and whether the dissimilar taxation affords protection to domestic production. The Appellate Body in the *Japanese Beverages* case held (pp. 27–36) that 'directly competitive or substitutable products' is a broader category than 'like products'; that 'not similarly taxed' is something more than being a little more in excess; and that to determine whether the tax affords protection to domestic production the effect of the measure on each product must be analysed.

7. Article III:4 deals more specifically with discrimination against imported like products by internal laws, regulations and requirements. The Appellate Body in the *Asbestos* case held that 'the determination of likeness under Article III:4 is, fundamentally, a determination about the nature and extent of a competitive relationship between and among products.' (at paragraph 99). The Appellate Body further noted (at paragraph 99) that the scope of 'like' in Article III:4 is broader than the same term in Article III:2 but that the provision is not broader than 'the combined product scope of the two sentences of Article III:2'. The Appellate Body considered that a difference in the product scope of the two provisions would 'frustrate a consistent application of the "general principle" in Article III:1' as fiscal and non-fiscal measures covered by the provisions are often used to achieve the same ends (at paragraph 99). The two United States *Tuna-Dolphins* cases (30 ILM 1594 (1991) (see below) and 33 ILM 839 (1993)), highlight the difficulty in distinguishing between measures that are part of an internal regulatory system, such as border bans on non-dolphin-friendly tuna (which are permissible so long as they are consistent with the Article III national treatment obligations) and prohibitions or restrictions on imports under Article XI (see next subsection).

8. A general exception to the national treatment obligation is provided in Article III:8, which permits government agencies to favour domestic producers for the purposes of government procurement.

D: Tariffication

The principle of tariffication prohibits the use of quotas on imports or exports and the use of licences on the importation or exportation of goods in or out of a contracting party. The principle attempts to ensure that there are no non-tariff barriers to trade.

General Agreement on Tariffs and Trade 1947, Article XI

1. No prohibitions or restrictions other than duties, taxes or other charges, whether made effective through quotas, import or export licences or other measures, shall be instituted or maintained by any contracting party on the importation of any product of the territory of any other contracting party or on the exportation or sale for export of any product destined for the territory of any other contracting party.

NOTES:

1. The goal of Article XI is to promote the conversion of all non-tariff barriers into tariff barriers, which can then be reduced through multilateral negotiation. By reducing all barriers to trade into a common monetary form, the barriers are both easier to compare and to negotiate. Non-tariff barriers are generally considered to represent a greater impediment to liberalised

international trade as they are, *inter alia*, less transparent than tariffs and can therefore be open to corruption and subject to arbitrary decision-making by administering officials.

2. An exception to this principle of tariffication is provided in Article XIII of GATT, which permits developing States to impose quantitative restrictions on a temporary basis for balance of payments or infant industry reasons (see below). Other exceptions allow the use of export prohibitions or restrictions to meet internal shortages (Article XI:2) and allow a State to safeguard its external financial position and its balance of payments (Articles XII and XIII:B).

SECTION 4: **Exceptions to the key principles of international trade law**

Despite the commitment by the GATT Contracting Parties to the above principles, the GATT includes many exceptions to its key obligations. If it is determined that a State is in breach of its obligations under the GATT, it must then be asked whether the State's actions fall within an exception and therefore still comply with GATT rules.

A: General exceptions

General Agreement on Tariffs and Trade 1947, Article XX

General Exceptions

Subject to the requirement that such measures are not applied in a manner which would constitute a means of arbitrary or unjustifiable discrimination between countries where the same conditions prevail, or a disguised restriction on international trade, nothing in this Agreement shall be construed to prevent the adoption or enforcement by any contracting party of measures:

(a) necessary to protect public morals;

(b) necessary to protect human, animal or plant life or health;

(c) relating to the importations or exportations of gold or silver;

(d) necessary to secure compliance with laws or regulations which are not inconsistent with the provisions of this Agreement, including those relating to customs enforcement, the enforcement of monopolies operated under paragraph 4 of Article II and Article XVII, the protection of patents, trade marks and copyrights, and the prevention of deceptive practices;

(e) relating to the products of prison labour;

(f) imposed for the protection of national treasures of artistic, historic or archaeological value;

(g) relating to the conservation of exhaustible natural resources if such measures are made effective in conjunction with restrictions on domestic production or consumption.

United States – Restrictions in Imports of Tuna (Tuna-Dolphins 1)
30 ILM 1594 (1991), GATT Panel Report

6.2 The Panel wished to note the fact, made evident during its consideration of this case, that the provisions of the [GATT] impose few constraints on a contracting party's implementation of domestic environmental policies. The Panel recalled . . . that under these provisions, a contracting party is free to tax or regulate imported products and like domestic products as long as its taxes or regulations do not discriminate against imported products or afford protection to domestic producers, and a contracting party is also free to tax or regulate domestic production for environmental purposes. As a corollary to these rights, a contracting party may not restrict imports of a product merely because it originates in a country with environmental policies different from its own.

6.3 The Panel further recalled its finding that the import restrictions examined in this dispute, imposed to respond to differences in environmental regulation of producers, could not be justified under the exceptions in Articles XX(b) or XX(g). These exceptions did not specify criteria limiting the range of life or health protection policies, or resource conservation policies, for the sake of which they could be invoked. It seemed evident to the Panel that, if the Contracting Parties were to permit import restrictions in response to differences in environmental policies under the general agreement, they would need to impose limits on the range of policy differences justifying such responses and to develop criteria so as to prevent abuse. If the Contracting Parties were to decide to permit trade measures of this type in particular circumstances it would therefore be preferable for them to do so not by interpreting Article XX, but by amending or supplementing the provisions of the general agreement or waiving obligations thereunder. Such an approach would enable the Contracting Parties to impose such limits and develop such criteria.

United States – Standards for Reformulated and Conventional Gasoline
WT/DS2/AB/R, 29 April 1996, pp. 16–17, World Trade Organization, Report of Appellate Body

This case concerned a US measure designed to limit the pollution from the combustion of gasoline. Acceptable levels of pollution were calculated by reference to 1990 levels, referred to as baselines, which could be determined using two methods: one permitted refiners to establish individual baselines and the other was a statutory baseline based on average US levels. Foreign refiners, unlike US domestic refiners, were generally only able to use the statutory baseline which was claimed to be discriminatory in violation of the national treatment obligation.

In order that the justifying protection of Article XX may be extended to it, the measure at issue must not only come under one or another of the particular exceptions – paragraphs (a) to (j) – listed under Article XX; it must also satisfy the requirements imposed by the opening clauses of Article XX. The analysis is, in other words, two-tiered: first, provisional justification by reason of characterization of the measure under XX(g); second, further appraisal of the same measure under the introductory clauses of Article XX.

The chapeau [the introductory part of an Article] by its express terms addresses, not so much the questioned measure or its specific contents as such, but rather the manner in which that measure is applied. It is, accordingly, important to underscore that the purpose and object of the introductory clauses of Article XX is generally the prevention of "abuse of the exceptions of [what was later to become] Article [XX]." This insight drawn from the drafting history of Article XX is a valuable one. The chapeau is animated by the principle that while the exceptions of Article XX may be invoked as a matter of legal right, they should not be so applied as to frustrate or defeat the legal obligations of the holder of the right under the substantive rules of the [GATT]. If those exceptions are not to be abused or misused, in other words, the measures falling within the particular exceptions must be applied reasonably, with due regard both to the legal duties of the party claiming the exception and the legal rights of the other parties concerned. . . .

It is of some importance that the Appellate Body point out what this [decision] does *not* mean. It does not mean, or imply, that the ability of any WTO Member to take measures to control air pollution or, more generally, to protect the environment, is at issue. That would be to ignore the fact that Article XX of the [GATT] contains provisions designed to permit important state interests –

including the protection of human health, as well as the conservation of exhaustible natural resources – to find expression. The provisions of Article XX were not changed as a result of the Uruguay Round of Multilateral Trade Negotiations. Indeed, in the preamble to the WTO Agreement and in the Decision on Trade and Environment, there is specific acknowledgement to be found about the importance of coordinating policies on trade and the environment. WTO Members have a large measure of autonomy to determine their own policies on the environment (including its relationship with trade), their environmental objectives and the environmental legislation they enact and implement. So far as concerns the WTO, that autonomy is circumscribed only by the need to respect the requirements of the [GATT] and the other covered agreements.

United States – Import Prohibition of Certain Shrimp and Shrimp Products
WT/DS58/AB/R, 12 October 1998, paragraphs 156 – 57, 159, World Trade Organisation, Report of the Appellate Body

The US, in an attempt to reduce the death of sea turtles associated with shrimp harvesting, imposed an import ban on any shrimp harvested using fishing technology that could adversely affect certain species of sea turtle listed as endangered under US legislation. The Panel and the Appellate Body found that the US measure, despite falling within Article XX(g), constituted arbitrary and unjustifiable discrimination and did not therefore satisfy the chapeau of Article XX.

156. Turning then to the chapeau of Article XX, we consider that it embodies the recognition on the part of WTO Members of the need to maintain a balance of rights and obligations between the right of a Member to invoke one or another of the exceptions of Article XX, specified in paragraphs (a) to (j), on the one hand, and the substantive rights of the other Members under the GATT 1994, on the other hand. Exercise by one Member of its right to invoke an exception, such as Article XX(g), if abused or misused, will, to that extent, erode or render naught the substantive treaty rights in, for example, Article XI:1, of other Members. Similarly, because the GATT 1994 itself makes available the exceptions of Article XX, in recognition of the legitimate nature of the policies and interests there embodied, the right to invoke one of those exceptions is not to be rendered illusory. The same concept may be expressed from a slightly different angle of vision, thus, a balance must be struck between the *right* of a Member to invoke an exception under Article XX and the *duty* of that same Member to respect the treaty rights of the other Members. . . .

157. In our view, the language of the chapeau makes clear that each of the exceptions in paragraphs (a) to (j) of Article XX is a *limited and conditional* exception from the substantive obligations contained in the other provisions of the GATT 1994, that is to say, the ultimate availability of the exception is subject to the compliance by the invoking Member with the requirements of the chapeau. . . .

159. The task of interpreting and applying the chapeau is, hence, essentially the delicate one of locating and marking out a line of equilibrium between the right of a Member to invoke an exception under Article XX and the rights of the other Members under varying substantive provisions (e.g., Article XI) of the GATT 1994, so that neither of the competing rights will cancel out the other and thereby distort and nullify or impair the balance of rights and obligations constructed by the Members themselves in that Agreement. The location of the line of equilibrium, as expressed in the chapeau, is not fixed and unchanging; the line moves as the kind and the shape of the measures at stake vary and as the facts making up specific cases differ.

NOTES:
1. The method of interpretation adopted in the *Reformulated Gasoline* case requires the

provisional justification of a measure as a particular Article XX exception, and then further appraisal of the measure under the introduction (or 'chapeau') of the Article. The Appellate Body in the *Reformulated Gasoline* case determined that the Article XX exceptions concern the measures in question whereas the chapeau is concerned with the application of that measure.

2. The Panels in both *Tuna-Dolphins* cases considered that Article XX(b) and (g) could not be used to justify measures having extrajurisdictional application, such as an import ban aimed at forcing another State to change its environmental policy. The *Tuna-Dolphins 1* Panel (at paragraph 5.27) considered that this would permit States 'unilaterally [to] determine ... policies from which other parties could not deviate without jeopardising their rights under the General Agreement'. Although the Appellate Body in the *Shrimp Turtle* case did not consider that the extra-jurisdictional effect of a measure rendered it *prima facie* incapable of justification under the Article XX exceptions, its report indicates that unilateral measures will generally be inconsistent with the chapeau.

3. The narrow interpretation applied in a number of cases concerning environmental measures to the particular environmental exceptions in Article XX(b) and (g) has created the perception amongst environmental groups that the WTO places commercial concerns above environmental protection. Dispute settlement bodies have indicated that there is little possibility of a State justifying a trade related environmental measure under Article XX unless it relies on a multilateral environmental treaty that is in force between the parties (see Chapter 12) or has attempted to negotiate an agreement with the States concerned. By emphasising the object and purpose of the GATT 1994 and the WTO Agreement these decisions confirm that their central focus is the promotion of economic development through trade and a desire to deter States from resorting to environmental reasons for protectionist measures. This emphasis is seen, for example, in the last paragraph of the *Reformulated Gasoline* case (above).

B: Security exceptions

Article XXI of GATT provides for exceptions for security reasons.

General Agreement on Tariffs and Trade 1947, Article XXI

Nothing in this Agreement shall be construed

    (a) to require any contracting party to furnish any information the disclosure of which it considers contrary to its essential security interests; or

    (b) to prevent any contracting party from taking any action which it considers necessary for the protection of its essential security interests

        (i) relating to fissionable materials or the materials from which they are derived;

        (ii) relating to the traffic in arms, ammunition and implements of war and to such traffic in other goods and materials as is carried on directly or indirectly for the purpose of supplying a military establishment;

        (iii) taken in time of war or other emergency in international relations; or

    (c) to prevent any contracting party from taking any action in pursuance of its obligations under the United Nations Charter for the maintenance of international peace and security.

NOTES:

1. The basic justification for invoking the security exception is to provide for national defence and security by securing the production of goods essential for defence. These exceptions have been very broadly interpreted by Panels. However, where the exception has been invoked for

more overtly political reasons, Panels tend to be wary of allowing the exception. For example, one aspect of the intervention by the United States in the affairs of Nicaragua (see *Nicaragua* v *United States* ICJ Rep 1986 in Chapter 14) was that the US government modified Nicaragua's sugar quotas. A GATT Panel found the US actions were in breach of Article XIII:2 (requiring negotiation of any such alterations) but was not prepared to decide the US's claim that its actions were justified for security reasons under Article XXI (GATT, *GATT Activities 1986*, pp. 58–59).

2. Article XXI(c) provides an exception permitting trade sanctions imposed in the performance of State's obligations under the United Nations Charter (see Chapter 14). Under this exception, sanctions imposed against the Republic of South Africa during the apartheid era and against Iraq for the invasion of Kuwait, were permitted within the GATT framework.

C: Regional trading arrangements

The principles of most favoured nation and national treatment are potentially threatened by the development of preferential trading arrangements such as the European Union and the North American Free Trade Agreement.

General Agreement on Tariffs and Trade 1947, Article XXIV

Territorial Application – Frontier Traffic – Customs Unions and Free-trade Areas

4. The contracting parties recognize the desirability of increasing freedom of trade by the development, through voluntary agreements, of closer integration between the economies of the countries parties to such agreements. They also recognize that the purpose of a customs union or of a free-trade area should be to facilitate trade between the constituent territories and not to raise barriers to the trade of other contracting parties with such territories.

5. Accordingly, the provisions of this Agreement shall not prevent, as between the territories of contracting parties, the formation of a customs union or of a free-trade area or the adoption of an interim agreement necessary for the formation of a customs union or of a free-trade area; *Provided* that:

(a) with respect to a customs union, or an interim agreement leading to a formation of a customs union, the duties and other regulations of commerce imposed at the institution of any such union or interim agreement in respect of trade with contracting parties not parties to such union or agreement shall not on the whole be higher or more restrictive than the general incidence of the duties and regulations of commerce applicable in the constituent territories prior to the formation of such union or the adoption of such interim agreement, as the case may be;

(b) with respect to a free-trade area, or an interim agreement leading to the formation of a free-trade area, the duties and other regulations of commerce maintained in each of the constituent territories and applicable at the formation of such free-trade area or the adoption of such interim agreement to the trade of contracting parties not included in such area or not parties to such agreement shall not be higher or more restrictive than the corresponding duties and other regulations of commerce existing in the same constituent territories prior to the formation of the free-trade area, or interim agreement as the case may be; and

(c) any interim agreement referred to in sub-paragraphs (a) and (b) shall include a plan and schedule for the formation of such a customs union or of such a free-trade area within a reasonable length of time.

Turkey – Restrictions on Imports of Textile and Clothing Products
WT/DS34/AB/R, 22 October 1999, World Trade Organisation, Report of the Appellate Body

58. Accordingly, . . . we are of the view that Article XXIV may justify a measure which is inconsistent with certain other GATT provisions. However, in a case involving the formation of a customs union, this 'defence' is only available when two conditions are fulfilled. First, the party claiming the benefit of this defence must demonstrate that the measure at issue is introduced upon the formation of a customs union that fully meets the requirements of sub-paragraphs 8(a) and 5(a) of Article XXIV. And, second, that party must demonstrate that the formation of that customs union would be prevented if it were not allowed to introduce the measure at issue. Again, *both* these conditions must be met to have the benefit of the defence under Article XXIV.

NOTES:

1. The regional trade exception provides for the establishment of three types of regional trading arrangements that can operate as exceptions to the GATT framework: customs unions; free-trade areas; and interim arrangements that lead to the establishment of either a customs union or a free-trade area. Customs unions involve an abolition of import duties between members and the imposition of a common external tariff against all non-members of the customs union. To be permitted under GATT, the duties and restrictions on trade applying to non-members cannot be on the whole more restrictive than before the formation of the customs union (Article XXIV:5(a)). A free-trade area is less integrated than a customs union, with the abolition of import duties between members and the retention of independent tariffs against non-members. To be permitted under GATT, tariffs with non-members cannot be on the whole more restrictive than before the formation of the free-trade area (Article XXIV:5(b)).

2. While regional trading arrangements may appear to be a form of protectionism, it is possible that such an arrangement between similar States can provide faster and deeper economic integration that can lead to later multilateral trade liberalisation. This can occur outside the complex negotiating process of GATT.

D: Developing States

Developing States have 'special and differential status' under the GATT. However, some of these exceptions are illusory.

Note, 'Developing Countries and Multilateral Trade Agreements: Law and the Promise of Development'
108 *Harvard Law Review* 1715 (1994), pp. 1723–24

Together, the GATT and UNCTAD [the United Nations Conference on Trade and Development] arguably created substantial access for DCs [developing countries] to ICs' [industrialized countries] markets and therefore presumably helped increase DCs' exports. At the same time, however, these regimes often exacerbated or at least failed to improve DCs' trade imbalances. And although the prevailing multilateral trade regimes may not have caused DC's economic dependence, they have not lessened it. A cynical view might attribute these failures to trade rules that seemed – in their scope, the provisions for their enforcement, and their actual enforcement – not to reform, but only to reinforce the North-South economic hierarchy . . .

ICs have consistently created rules that affronted the principles upon which they had purported to establish the GATT. First, even amidst the GATT's original declarations of principle and accompanying rules, the ICs fashioned for themselves several exceptions to address domestic concerns. Most notable from the DCs' perspective, the United States prevented the GATT from addressing agriculture and textiles, so that it could maintain subsidies and other protectionist measures for US industry. Because DCs' comparative advantage lay overwhelmingly in these goods, their omission from the GATT severely attenuated the trade benefits the agreement could confer upon DCs. The GATT also included an escape clause that allowed governments to determine unilaterally when 'unforeseen developments . . . cause [d] or threaten [ed] serious injury to domestic producers' and to withdraw temporarily from their GATT obligations [Art. XIX]. Although the GATT's Article XVIII also incorporated DCs' request for an allowance to withdraw temporarily in order to promote domestic economic development, Article XVIII, unlike the escape clause, required the withdrawing country to gain explicit GATT approval through an elaborate procedure.

World Trade Organisation, Doha Declaration
WT/MIN(01)/DEC/1, 20 November 2001

2. International trade can play a major role in the promotion of economic development and the alleviation of poverty. We recognise the need for all our peoples to benefit from the increased opportunities and welfare gains that the multilateral trading system generates. The majority of WTO Members are developing countries. We seek to place their needs and interests at the heart of the Work Program adopted in this Declaration. Recalling the Preamble to the Marrakesh Agreement, we shall continue to make positive efforts designed to ensure that developing countries, especially least developing countries among them, secure a share in the growth of world trade commensurate with the needs of their economic development. In this context, enhanced market access, balanced rules, and well targeted, sustainably financed technical assistance and capacity building programs have important roles to play.

3. We recognise the particular vulnerability of the least-developed countries and the special structural difficulties they face in the global economy. We are committed to addressing the marginalisation of least-developed countries in international trade and to improving their effective participation in the multilateral trading system. . . .

42. . . . We recognise that the integration of the LDCs [Least-Developed Countries] into the multilateral trading system requires meaningful market access, support for the diversification of their production and export base, and trade-related technical assistance and capacity building. We agree that the meaningful integration of LDCs into the trading system and the global economy will involve efforts by all WTO Members. We commit ourselves to the objective of duty-free, quota-free market access for products originating from LDCs . . . We further commit ourselves to consider additional measures for progressive improvements in market access for LDCs.

NOTES:

1. A number of provisions of the GATT are intended to assist developing States. For example, under Article XVIII developing States are allowed to impose restrictions on imports, generally implemented as quantitative restrictions in the form of quotas or licences, either for balance of payments reasons or to foster infant industries. Further, Article XVI:8 states that other Contracting Parties do not expect reciprocity for commitments made by them to reduce trade barriers to trade from developing States, and Article XXXVII establishes the commitment of industrialised States to reduce barriers to the trade of developing States.

2. In the 1970s a Generalised System of Preferences (GSP) was introduced through the United Nations Conference on Trade and Development (UNCTAD). It was designed to update the system of colonial preferences arranged in 1947, by creating preferential trading arrangements between developed and developing States. These preferences could be granted by a

developed State as it chose, and were subject to a 'waiver', granted by the Contracting Parties, that permitted derogation from the MFN requirements of Article I.
3. The Doha Declaration came after at least two years of sustained concern by developing States and wide-spread public protests against the WTO. Much of this was based on increasing evidence that the free trade and globalization processes fostered by the WTO were having an unequal and heavy impact on developing States (see Chapter 6 in relation to globalisation and its impact on human rights). The impact on State sovereignty is discussed in 7. below.

SECTION 5: **Dispute resolution**

Under the original GATT procedures, Articles XXII and XXIII provided for bilateral consultations between disputing States. If this method failed to resolve the dispute, States had the option of using good offices, or entering into mediation and conciliation before a request for a GATT Panel was made. While there is no mention of a Panel in the GATT 1947, the practice developed that after the dispute was referred to the Council of Contracting Parties, a Panel of experts was established to hear the dispute. The Council would then adopt the Panel's report if any Contracting Party did not oppose it. However, these procedures were seen as being insufficiently rules-based and too dependent on consensus between the disputing States, compliance with Panels' decisions was variable, and it was incapable of taking account of broader issues such as environmental and labour standards. Thus the Uruguay Round established a new unified, streamlined and strengthened dispute resolution system.

Understanding on Rules and Procedures Governing the Settlement of Disputes 1994

Article 1
1. The rules and procedures of this Understanding shall apply to disputes brought pursuant to the consultation and dispute settlement provisions of the agreements listed in Appendix 1 to this Understanding (referred to in this Understanding as the 'covered agreements'). The rules and procedures of this Understanding shall also apply to consultations and the settlement of disputes between Members concerning their rights and obligations under the provisions of the Agreement Establishing the World Trade Organization (referred to in this Understanding as the 'WTO Agreement') and of this Understanding taken in isolation or in combination with any other covered agreement. . . .

Article 3
1. Members affirm their adherence to the principles for the management of disputes heretofore applied under Articles XXII and XXIII of GATT 1947, and the rules and procedures as further elaborated and modified herein.
2. The dispute settlement system of the WTO is a central element in providing security and predictability to the multilateral trading system. The Members recognize that it serves to preserve the rights and obligations of Members under the covered agreements, and to clarify the existing provisions of those agreements in accordance with customary rules of interpretation of public international law. Recommendations and rulings of the DSB cannot add to or diminish the rights and obligations provided in the covered agreements. . . .

7. Before bringing a case, a Member shall exercise its judgement as to whether action under these procedures would be fruitful. The aim of the dispute settlement mechanism is to secure a positive solution to a dispute. A solution mutually acceptable to the parties to a dispute and consistent with the covered agreements is clearly to be preferred. In the absence of a mutually agreed solution, the first objective of the dispute settlement mechanism is usually to secure the withdrawal of the measures concerned if these are found to be inconsistent with the provisions of any of the covered agreements. The provision of compensation should be resorted to only if the immediate withdrawal of the measure is impracticable and as a temporary measure pending the withdrawal of the measure which is inconsistent with a covered agreement. The last resort which this Understanding provides to the Member invoking the dispute settlement procedures is the possibility of suspending the application of concessions or other obligations under the covered agreements on a discriminatory basis *vis-à-vis* the other Member, subject to authorization by the DSB of such measures.

J. Trachtman, 'The Domain of WTO Dispute Resolution'
40 *Harvard International Law Journal* 333 (1999)

Many trade diplomats, environmentalists and scholars have expressed concern regarding the magnitude of decision-making power allocated to World Trade Organization (WTO) dispute resolution panels and the WTO Appellate Body. While trade diplomats and scholars have expressed pride at the Uruguay Round achievement of more binding and more 'law-oriented' dispute resolution, the same group and a variety of non-governmental organizations (NGOs) and other commentators question the jurisdictional scope of dispute resolution. After all, should these small tribunals, lacking direct democratic legitimacy, determine profound issues such as the relationship between trade and environmental values or trade and labor values? Many voices, including this author's, have called for greater international legislation in these important fields. . . .

[W]here decision-making authority is allocated to a dispute resolution body, less specific standards are consistent with a transfer of power to an international organization – the dispute resolution body itself – while more specific rules are more consistent with the reservation of continuing power by member states. From a more critical standpoint, it might be argued that allocation of authority to a transnational dispute resolution body by virtue of standards can be used as a method to integrate *sub rosa*, and outside the visibility of democratic controls.

It will be recalled that article 3(2) of the DSU provides that the vocation of dispute settlement is to preserve and to clarify rights and obligations under the covered agreements 'in accordance with customary rules of public international law.' This phrase has been interpreted by the Appellate Body to refer to the interpretative rules of the Vienna Convention [on Law of Treaties]. . . .

To understand the role of dispute resolution, one must recognize that dispute resolution is not simply a mechanism for neutral application of legislated rules but is itself a mechanism of legislation and of governance. We must also recognize that today dispute resolution often works in tandem with legislation in that dispute resolution tribunals function in part as agents of legislatures. Moreover, legislatures, intentionally or unintentionally but often efficiently, delegate wide authority to dispute resolution.

The WTO dispute resolution process begins with a requirement of consultations. If consultations are unsuccessful, the complaining state may request the establishment of a three-person panel to consider the matter. The panel issues a report which may be appealed to the Appellate Body. The panel report, as it may be modified by the Appellate Body, is subject to adoption by the Dispute Settlement Body (DSB) of the WTO. Adoption is automatic unless there is a consensus not to adopt the report. What is the vocation of WTO dispute resolution? There are several answers. Panels determine the facts. They determine those facts that are relevant under the applicable law, so that they must determine the applicable law and relevant facts concurrently and interactively. Interestingly, because of a design flaw in the DSU, the Appellate Body has no right of remand. Therefore, the

Appellate Body is constrained where it determines to apply law for which the panel has made no findings of fact. Within the determination of the applicable law are several subfunctions. First, panels (and here the Appellate Body acts as well) determine which law is applicable, by virtue of factors including, but not limited to, the activity, the location, the persons, and the timing. Second, where there is a dispute regarding the meaning of the law, the panel must definitively interpret the law. Third, where the law does not apply by its specific terms but was intended to address the issue, the panel may construe the law. Fourth, the law may have a lacuna and therefore not provide a response. Fifth, where two legal rules overlap, the panel must determine whether both were meant to apply or whether one takes precedence. Sixth, where two legal rules conflict, the panel must determine whether the laws are of unequal or equal stature. If they are of equal stature, the panel must determine how to accommodate both. As shall be discussed in more detail below, one persistent problem of the WTO legal system is the recognition and application of legal rules from outside the system. Penultimately, after the complete determination of the applicable law, the tribunal applies the law to the facts. Finally, the tribunal may fashion a remedy: it may recommend a resolution to be adopted by the DSB. . . .

The disparity between the positive law dispute resolution system of the WTO and the more political, natural law style of dispute resolution available in connection with most other forms of international law raises jurisprudential and practical concern. How can a WTO dispute resolution decision ignore other international law? On the other hand, how can the WTO dispute resolution process purport to interpret and apply non-WTO international law? While present WTO law seems clearly to exclude direct application of non-WTO international law, this position seems unsustainable as increasing conflicts between trade values and non-trade values arise. These conflicts may be addressed through standards such as the exceptional provisions of article XX, or by legislated rules regarding the more specific interaction between trade values and non-trade values.

NOTES:

1. The WTO Agreement established a Dispute Settlement Body (DSB), consisting of the General Council of the WTO (comprised of all State parties), which convenes to discharge the functions of the DSB under the Understanding on Rules and Procedures Governing the Settlement of Disputes 1994 (DSU).

2. Article 3 of the DSU embodies both the legal and the political aspects of dispute resolution. Article 3.2 emphasizes the rule-based nature of the system, providing that the DSB can interpret and apply the rights and obligations only under the covered agreements as they have been negotiated, with no capacity for law-making. This view of the system is augmented by the automatic right of a State to the establishment of a Panel; the adoption of a Panel report within 60 days unless there is an appeal or a consensus in the DSB to reject the report; and an appeals process with a report within 60 days. Article 3.7, however, entrenches the principle that a State must consider the probable success of an action, taking into account interests other than its own in service of the goal of maintaining an effective world trading system. This provision shows an emphasis on mutually satisfactory solutions with the DSB as a forum for the diplomatic discussion and resolution of trade disputes.

3. The DSU established a permanent Appellate Body for appeals from Panel decisions (Article 17). This Body is to be comprised of persons of recognised authority, with demonstrated expertise in law, international trade and the subject matter of the covered agreements generally, who are unaffiliated with any government. The Appellate Body was established to create legal certainty regarding the developing GATT/WTO jurisprudence, with its decisions now being the most authoritative statements of economic law in the GATT/WTO system. Decisions of the Panel and the Appellate Body since 1995 can found on the WTO website: http://www.wto.org/wto/dispute/dispute.htm.

4. The DSU is also designed to improve compliance by the introduction of surveillance

procedures with regard to the compliance with recommendations or rulings of the DSB (Article 21). In addition, the DSB has power to authorise compensation or the suspension of concessions if a State fails to comply with those recommendations or rulings, including same sector or cross-sector retaliation (Article 22).

5. Overall, the dispute settlement procedure is designed to reduce the use of unilateral action. However, while the DSU makes illegal any unilateral interpretations or determinations of violations of the GATT, in practice it may depend on whether an affected State is determined to pursue a matter to a DSB decision. There is also the issue, as Trachtman raises, of the compliance of the WTO DSB with general international law. On international dispute settlement generally, see Chapter 15.

SECTION 6: **The expanding scope of international economic law**

A significant feature of the Uruguay Round in 1994 was that it brought several new areas into the multilateral trade regime, including intellectual property, services, sanitary and phystosanitary measures and investment. It also strengthened the GATT rules on subsidies and countervailing duties and anti-dumping. A few of these areas will be briefly considered.

A: Intellectual property

In general, intellectual property rights give monopolistic rights to the holder of the patent, copyright, licence, etc., which seems in conflict with concepts of free trade. The merging of these concepts was effected in the Agreement on Trade-related Aspects of Intellectual Property Rights (TRIPS).

Agreement on Trade-related Aspects of Intellectual Property Rights 1994

Article 27 Patentable Subject Matter

1. [P]atents shall be available for any inventions, whether products or processes, in all fields of technology, provided that they are new, involve an inventive step and are capable of industrial application. Subject to paragraph 4 of Article 65, paragraph 8 of Article 70 and paragraph 3 of this Article, patents shall be available and patent rights enjoyable without discrimination as to the place of invention, the field of technology and whether products are imported or locally produced.

Article 65 Transitional Arrangements

1. Subject to the provisions of paragraphs, 2, 3 and 4, no Member shall be obliged to apply the provisions of this Agreement before the expiry of a general period of one year following the date of entry into force of the WTO Agreement.

4. To the extent that a developing country Member is obliged by this Agreement to extend product patent protection to areas of technology not so protectable in its territory on the general date of application of this Agreement for that Member, as defined in paragraph 2, it may delay

the application of the provisions on product patents of Section 5 of Part II to such areas of technology for an additional period of five years.

V. Shiva, 'Biotechnological Development and the Conservation of Biodiversity', in V. Shiva and I. Moser (eds), *Biopolitics: A Feminist and Ecological Reader on Biotechnology*

(1995), pp. 193–95, 208–11

In the dominant paradigm, technology is seen as being above society both in its structure and evolution, in its offering of technological fixes, and in its technological determinism. It is seen as a source of solutions to problems that lie in society, and is rarely perceived as a source of new social problems . . . The technocratic approach to biotechnology portrays the evolution of the technology as self-determined and views social sacrifice as a necessity. Human rights, including the right to a livelihood, must therefore be sacrificed for property rights that give protection to the innovation processes. Ironically, a process based on the sacrifice of human rights continues to be projected as automatically leading to human well-being.

The sacrifice of people's rights to create new property rights it not new. It has been part of the hidden history of the rise of capitalism and its technological structures. The laws of private property which arose during the fifteenth and sixteenth centuries simultaneously eroded people's common rights to the use of forests and pastures while creating the social conditions for capital accumulation through industrialization. The new laws of private property were aimed at protecting individual rights to property as a commodity, while destroying collective rights to commons as a basis of sustenance . . . The scene for such a shift is now being set to allow the emergence of a biotechnical era of corporate and industrial growth. . . .

Patents and intellectual property rights are at the centre of the protection of the right to profits. Human rights are at the centre of the protection of the right to life, which is threatened by the new biotechnologies as they expand the domain of capital accumulation while introducing new risks and hazards for citizens.

World Trade Organisation, Doha Declaration on the TRIPS Agreement and Public Health
WT/MIN(01)/DEC/2, 14 November 2001

3. We agree that the TRIPS Agreement does not and should not prevent Members from taking measures to protect public health. Accordingly, while reiterating our commitment to the TRIPS Agreement, we affirm that the Agreement can and should be interpreted and implemented in a manner supportive of WTO Members' right to protect public health and, in particular, to promote access to medicines for all. In this connection, we reaffirm the right of WTO Members to use, to the full, the provisions in the TRIPS Agreement, which provide flexibility for this purpose.

5. . . . Each Member has the right to grant compulsory licences and the freedom to determine the grounds upon which such licences are granted. Each Member has the right to determine what constitutes a national emergency or other circumstances of extreme urgency, it being understood that public health crises, including those relating to HIV/AIDS, tuberculosis, malaria and other epidemics, can represent a national emergency or other circumstances of extreme urgency.

6. We recognize that WTO Members with insufficient or no manufacturing capacities in the pharmaceutical sector could face difficulties in making effective use of compulsory licensing under the TRIPS Agreement. We instruct the Council for TRIPS to find an expeditious solution to this problem and to report to the General Council before the end of 2002.

NOTES:
1. The protection afforded to intellectual property rights under TRIPS is quite extensive and, as Drahos points out, has global consequences. However, these consequences may not always be positive. Shiva explains the potential cost in terms of human rights that could result (see also Chapter 6).
2. Shiva's fears were confirmed in the *Indian Patents Case* (WT/DS79/1), a decision by the WTO Appellate Body on 2 September 1998. The Appellate Body inquired into whether India's administrative system for filing of patents under its Patents Act 1970 provided sufficient protection of intellectual property rights. It concluded that India did not comply with its obligations under the TRIPS Agreement. In determining whether Indian legislation and practice complied with India's obligations under the TRIPS Agreement, the Appellate Body claimed that it was not delving inappropriately into Indian law, but only performing an assessment as to whether the Indian law was in conformity with TRIPS. This is an important issue of the extent to which an international tribunal can investigate internal State measures.
3. A similar case occurred in South Africa. The South African government introduced the Medicines and Related Substances Control Amendment Act 1997 to bring in three important measures designed to facilitate access to cheaper drugs: it enabled the parallel import of patented drugs; it required pharmacists to dispense cheaper generic versions of off-patent medicines if possible; and it established a pricing committee to facilitate the development of a transparent system for pricing medicines. The Act did not allow the import of generic versions of patented drugs. After initial political pressure, including the threat of WTO action by the United States government, to withdraw the Act ended, the large pharmaceutical corporations commenced a case before the South African courts seeking a declaration that the legislation was unconstitutional. The pharmaceutical corporations claimed that the Act abrogated a number of their rights under the South African Constitution, particularly freedom from arbitrary deprivation of property, and urged that the relevant rights be interpreted in accordance with TRIPS. Before the court could make its decision, the pharmaceutical corporations dropped their claim after wide-spread public protests and complaints by other developing States. One direct response to this case was the Doha Declaration on TRIPS and Public Health (above).

B: Sanitary and phytosanitary measures

The Sanitary and Phytosanitary Measures Agreement (SPS), like TRIPS, shifts the scope of international economic law.

Agreement on the Application of Sanitary and Phytosanitary Measures 1994

Article 2
1. Members have the right to take sanitary and phytosanitary measures necessary for the protection of human, animal or plant life or health, provided that such measures are not inconsistent with the provisions of this Agreement.
2. Members shall ensure that any sanitary or phytosanitary measure is applied only to the extent necessary to protect human, animal or plant life or health, is based on scientific principles and is not maintained without sufficient scientific evidence ...
3. Members shall ensure that their sanitary and phytosanitary measures do not arbitrarily or unjustifiably discriminate between Members where identical or similar conditions prevail ...

Sanitary and phytosanitary measures shall not be applied in a manner which would constitute a disguised restriction on international trade.

4. Sanitary or phytosanitary measures which conform to the relevant provisions of this Agreement shall be presumed to be in accordance with the obligations of the Members under the provisions of GATT 1994 which relate to the use of sanitary or phytosanitary measures, in particular the provisions of Article XX(b).

ANNEX A

Sanitary or phytosanitary measure – Any measure applied:

(a) to protect animal or plant life or health within the territory of the Member from risks arising from the entry, establishment or spread of pests, diseases, disease-carrying organisms or disease-causing organisms;

(b) to protect human or animal life or health within the territory of the Member from risks arising from additives, contaminants, toxins or disease-causing organisms in foods, beverages or foodstuffs;

(c) to protect human life or health within the territory of the Member from risks arising from diseases carried by animals, plants or products thereof, or from the entry, establishment or spread of pests; or

(d) to prevent or limit other damage within the territory of the Member from the entry, establishment or spread of pests.

Sanitary or phytosanitary measures include all relevant laws, decrees, regulations, requirements and procedures including, *inter alia*, end product criteria; processes and production methods; testing, inspection, certification and approval procedures; quarantine treatments including relevant requirements associated with the transport of animals or plants, or with the materials necessary for their survival during transport; provisions on relevant statistical methods, sampling procedures and methods of risk assessment; and packaging and labelling requirements directly related to food safety.

NOTES:

1. The SPS Agreement imposes obligations on States that have nothing to do with a discriminatory trading regime. The focus is moved away from whether a particular measure is discriminatory or amounts to a barrier to international trade, and towards the development of uniform standards.

2. Under Articles 2 and 3 of the SPS Agreement, a State can introduce or maintain an SPS measure that results in a higher standard of protection than that based on international standards only if there is scientific justification, or where a State has engaged in a process of risk assessment and risk management under Article 5, which is designed to minimise negative trade effects. In *Australia – Measures Affecting Importation of Salmon* (WT/DS18/AB/R, Report of the Appellate Body adopted 6 November 1998) – in a complaint brought by Canada – it was found that the risk assessment performed was insufficient, and that the measure in question amounted to an arbitrary or unjustifiable distinction, resulting in discrimination or a disguised restriction on international trade in breach of Article 5.

C: Subsidies and dumping

The main issue with subsidies and dumping is whether the original action (dumping or subsidisation) or the response (anti-dumping duty or counter-vailing duty) is the greater threat to international free trade.

General Agreement on Tariffs and Trade 1994, Articles VI and XVI

Article VI: Anti-dumping and Countervailing Duties

1. The contracting parties recognize that dumping, by which products of one country are introduced into the commerce of another country at less than the normal value of the products, is to be condemned if it causes or threatens material injury to an established industry in the territory of a contracting party or materially retards the establishment of a domestic industry. For the purposes of this Article, a product is to be considered as being introduced into the commerce of an importing country at less than its normal value, if the price of the product exported from one country to another:

    (a) is less than the comparable price, in the ordinary course of trade, for the like product when destined for consumption in the exporting country, or,

    (b) in the absence of such domestic price, is less than either

        (i) the highest comparable price for the like product for export to any third country in the ordinary course of trade, or

        (ii) the cost of production of the product in the country of origin plus a reasonable addition for selling cost and profit . . .

Article XVI: Subsidies

1. If any contracting party grants or maintains any subsidy, including any form of income or price support, which operates directly or indirectly to increase exports of any product from, or to reduce imports of any product into, its territory, it shall notify the Contracting Parties in writing of the extent and nature of the subsidization, of the estimated effect of the subsidization on the quantity of the affected product or products imported into or exported from its territory and of the circumstances making the subsidization necessary. In any case in which it is determined that serious prejudice to the interests of any other contracting party is caused or threatened by any such subsidization, the contracting party granting the subsidy shall, upon request, discuss with the other contracting party or parties concerned, or with the Contracting Parties, the possibility of limiting the subsidization.

NOTES:

1. In early GATT texts there was little regulation of subsidies, though, over time, this was changed. In the Uruguay Round, the Agreement on Subsidies and Countervailing Measures 1994 (SCM) introduced the first definition of subsidies, and placed limitations on the use of countervailing duties. To be able to respond to a subsidy with a countervailing duty, the subsidy must be specific to an enterprise or industry, rather than applying generally.

2. Article VI provides for the imposition of anti-dumping duties on dumped products up to the level of the margin of the dumping, that is, the difference between the export price of the good and its domestic price, provided that the imports are causing material injury to the importing State (Article VI:2). The provisions of GATT do not ban dumping, rather they provide a permitted response that would otherwise be in breach of GATT. In effect, therefore, while subsidies are strongly prohibited, dumping is only condemned.

3. The Uruguay Round saw the adoption of the Agreement on the Implementation of Article IV of GATT 1994. This agreement adopted a series of tests about how to determine whether a good has been dumped, and made it harder for a State to establish a material injury. The Agreement also established a process for the investigation of dumping charges and the imposition of anti-dumping duties.

SECTION 7: **International economic law and State sovereignty**

The sovereignty of States could be considered to be under threat by the integration and interdependence of the world economy, and the resulting inability of governments to give force to national policy objectives because of the ratification of international economic agreements.

A. Orford, 'Locating the International: Military and Monetary Interventions After the Cold War'
38 *Harvard International Law Journal* 443 (1997), pp. 464–67, 470

The IMF and the World Bank influence the policies of governments in two ways. First, they directly influence government policy through the imposition of conditions on access to credits and loans. Such conditions may even relate explicitly to issues of 'governance,' despite the explicit prohibition in the Articles of Agreement of the Bank against interference in the political affairs of any member state. The IMF and the World Bank are also able to influence the direction of government policies indirectly. First, due to the weight that private banks place on the IMF's approval, such approval determines a country's creditworthiness and thus its ability to access private capital markets. Second, the IMF exercises influence through its role in organising debt rescheduling. Since 1982, the IMF has played a central role in arranging for private banks to take part in concerted or coordinated lending packages. The involvement of the IMF is seen as desirable, not only because it provides extra liquidity, but more importantly because private banks assume that a lending package that includes the imposition of IMF conditionality will guarantee better and more stable economic policies in the debtor country . . .

Decision-making over ever larger areas of what was once considered to be central to popular sovereignty and substantive democracy is now treated as legitimately within the province of economists in institutions such as the IMF and the World Bank. The supposedly economic and technocratic changes required by those institutions shape the policy choices available to governments, alter existing constitutional and political arrangements, determine the extent to which people in many states can access health care, education, pensions, and social security, and shape labour markets – thus affecting functions that go to the heart of political and constitutional authority. The shifting of decision-making authority from governments to international economic institutions affects both popular sovereignty and substantive democracy. In some cases, IMF and World Bank conditions have also challenged existing constitutional and governmental arrangements.

Japan – Taxes on Alcoholic Beverages
WT/DS8/AB/R, WT/DS10/AB/R, WT/DS11/AB/R, Adopted 11 November 1996, p. 16,
World Trade Organisation, Report of the Appellate Body

The WTO Agreement is a treaty – the international equivalent of a contract. It is self-evident that in an exercise of their sovereignty, and in pursuit of their own respective national interests, the Members of the WTO have made a bargain. In exchange for the benefits they expect to derive as Members of the WTO, they have agreed to exercise their sovereignty according to the commitments they have made in the WTO Agreement.

S. Croley and J. Jackson, 'WTO Dispute Procedures, Standard of Review and Deference to National Governments'

90 *AJIL* 193 (1996), pp. 193–95, 211–12

Increasing international economic interdependence is obviously becoming a growing challenge to governments, which are frustrated by their limited capacities to regulate or control cross-border economic activities. Many subjects trigger this frustration, including interest rates, various fraudulent or criminal activities, product standards, consumer protection, environmental issues and prudential concerns for financial services. Although it has been said that 'all politics is local,' it has also been said, with considerable justification, that 'all economics is international'. . . .

Even if one recognizes that some concepts of 'sovereignty' are out of date or unrealistic in today's interdependent world, the word still raises important questions about the relationship of international rules and institutions to national governments, and about the appropriate roles of each in such matters as regulating economic behaviour that crosses national borders. The GATT dispute settlement procedures have increasingly confronted these questions, including the degree to which, in a GATT (and now WTO) dispute settlement procedure, an international body should 'second-guess' a decision of a national government agency concerning economic regulations that are allegedly inconsistent with an international rule. . . . This issue is not unique to GATT or the WTO, of course; nor even to 'economic affairs,' as literature in the human rights arena indicates. . . .

In many ways [concerns over the power of WTO institutions] go to a central problem for the future of the trading system – how to reconcile competing views about the allocation of power between national governments and international institutions on matters of vital concern to many governments, as well as the domestic constituencies of some of those governments. They also raise important 'constitutional' questions about international institutions and the potential need for 'checks and balances' against misuse or misallocation of power in and for those institutions.

On the one hand, effective international cooperation depends in part upon the willingness of sovereign states to constrain themselves by relinquishing to international tribunals at least minimum power to interpret treaties and articulate international obligations. Recognizing the necessity of such power does not lessen the importance at the national level of decision-making expertise, democratic accountability or institutional efficiency. On the other hand, nations and their citizens – and particularly those particular interests within nation-states that are reasonably successful at influencing their national political actors – will want to maintain control of the government decisions. . . . Admittedly, the word 'sovereignty' has been much abused and misused; nevertheless, if the term refers to policies and concepts that focus on an appropriate allocation of power between international and national governments, and if one is willing to recognize that nation-states ought still to retain powers for effective governing of national (or local) democratic constituencies in a variety of contexts and cultures – perhaps using theories of 'subsidiarity' – then a case can be made for at least some international deference to national decisions, even decisions regarding interpretations of international agreements . . . And there is no *a priori* reason why coordination values must, in every case across every context, trump sovereignty values. Some trade-off is necessary.

NOTES:

1. It is clear from Orford's and Croley and Jackson's analyses, that both the ratification of international economic agreements and the application of these agreements by the international economic institutions have placed significant limits on State sovereignty. While this is part of the increasing interdependence of States, it can have severe consequences on those who operate within the national systems. One consequence is seen in the impact on human rights (see Chapter 6). It is also evidence of the increasing power of corporations, particularly transnational corporations, over States as it is often these corporations which prompt the action taken by States and the corporations may effectively manage the litigation under the DSB.

2. An additional concern is that some aspects of international economic law are leading to the 'levelling down' of labour and environmental standards, creating a 'lowest common denominator' effect on national social policies. Indeed, one of the most significant impacts on international economic law in the past few years has been the combined effect of those who seek to include social and human values within this law and 'anti-globalisation' forces, first seen in a major way at a meeting of the WTO in Seattle in 1999. This is discussed below.

SECTION 8: **Future directions**

J. Bhagwati, 'The Agenda of the WTO', in P. Van Dijck and G. Faber (eds), *Challenges to the New World Trade Organization*
(1996), pp. 28–32, 38–39

[I]f you look back at the 1950s and 1960s, the contrast between the developing countries and the developed countries was striking and made the South strongly pessimistic about the effects of integration into the world economy while the North was instead firmly optimistic . . .

Today, however, the situation is almost reversed. The fears of integration into the world economy are being heard, but not from the developing countries which see great good from it as they have extensively undertaken what the GATT calls 'autonomous' reductions in their trade barriers, that is unilateral reductions outside the GATT context of reciprocal reductions. Of course, not all these reductions, and increased openness to inward DFI [direct foreign investment], have resulted from changed convictions in favour of the liberal international economic order and its benefits to oneself, though the failure of policies based on the old pro-inward-orientation views and the contrasting success of the Far Eastern countries following the pro-outward-orientation views have certainly played an important role, especially in Latin America and Asia. But some measure of the shift must also be ascribed to necessity resulting from the conditionality imposed by The World Bank and, at times, by the IMF, as several debt-crisis-afflicted countries flocked to these institutions for support in the 1980s, and equally from their own perceived need to restore their external viability by liberal domestic and international policies designed to reassure and attract DFI.

But if the South has moved to regard integration into the world economy as an opportunity rather than a peril, it is the North that is now fearful. In particular, the fear has grown, after the experience with the decline in the real wages of the unskilled in the USA and with the decline in their employ-ment in Europe in the 1970s and 1980s, that by trading with the South with its abundance of unskilled labour, the North will find its own unskilled labour at risk. The demand for protection that follows is not the old and defunct 'pauper-labour' argument which asserted falsely that trade between the South and the North could not be beneficial. Rather, it is the theoretically more defens-ible, income-distributional argument that trade with countries with paupers will produce paupers in our midst, that trade with the developing countries will produce more poor at home. . . .

But the key question is whether the cause of this phenomenon is trade with the South, as unions and many politicians feel, or rapid modern information-based technical change that is increasingly substituting unskilled labour with computers that need skilled rather than unskilled labour. As always, there is debate among economists about the evidence: but the preponderant view today among the trade experts is that the evidence for linking trade with the South to the observed distress among the unskilled to date is extremely thin, at best.

D. Leebron, 'Linkages'
96 *AJIL* 5 (2002), pp. 5–6, 26–27

Trade and the environment. Trade and workers' rights. Trade and competition policy. Trade and eighteen million tiny feet. It begins to resemble a question from an IQ test: which of the preceding pairs of issues does not fit? Increasingly, it seems there is no pairing with trade for which some argument cannot be made. The 'trade and . . .' industry is booming. The growth of the 'trade and . . .' business derives from two converging forces. First, more issues are now regarded as trade related in the narrow sense that the norms governing those issues affect trade, or conversely, that changes in trade flows affect the realization of those norms. Second, an increasing number of substantive areas are the subject of international coordinated action or multilateral agreements. Even if conduct in such areas does not directly affect trade flows, the creation of formalized regimes governing them raises the question how such regimes should be related to the trade regime and whether, for example, trade sanctions should be employed to enforce non-trade policies and agreements. In three important areas – human rights, workers' rights, and environmental protection – claims are based in part on concerns for the welfare of those in other nations. Domestic measures alone cannot address such concerns, and means (short of war) are therefore sought to influence governments abroad.

These issues came to the fore in both official negotiations and street protests at the Third Ministerial Conference of the World Trade Organization held in Seattle in 1999. Many developed nations sought to link issues of environmental protection and labor standards to the trade negotiations, an effort that most developing nations vehemently opposed. . . .

A claim that issues should be linked ultimately rests on the view that the resolution of one issue or group of related issues will or should affect, or be affected by, the resolution of the other issues or group of issues. Such interdependence might result solely from the actions of the claimant, meaning that the claimant's position on the resolution of one of the issues will potentially be affected by how the other issue is resolved. Alternatively, the claimant might not assert that its position on one issue is dependent on the other, but only suggest that for exogenous reasons the two issues ought to be resolved together. . . . [T]he linkage claim might in this sense be strategic or substantive or both. . . .

The general presumption in the multilateral context appears to be that strategic linkage across regimes or issue areas that are not substantively related . . . is unfair or counterproductive. This will not always be the case, but it leads most nations to resist it. Perhaps the fundamental problem boils down to the lack of consensus as to whether the linked issue ought to be the subject of an international agreement, or at least doubt as to whether a strong international regime is appropriate to the governance of that issue. That is, it seems inappropriate to use linkage to create pressure to reach an agreement on a subject on which few believe there should be a multilateral agreement at all. Where linkage is sought, it generally ought to be by weaker means that do not undermine the ability to reach agreements. Substantive linkage, on the other hand, provokes an array of responses for both substantive and strategic reasons. Where it is strongly supported (as for linking labor and environmental issues with trade), such linkage can probably not be resisted altogether. Rather, the goal must be to choose the means of linkage that most effectively advance the policies sought to be linked (e.g., environmental and labor), without undermining the ability to reach agreement and make progress in the other regime. Interpretive linkage holds promise in this respect, and the WTO now seems in effect to have endorsed this approach. With regard to the role of environmental agreements and norms in the interpretation of GATT obligations, for example, the WTO dispute panels have basically done an about-face. They have moved from a wooden, formalistic approach that largely ignored the evolution of international environmental law, to one that tries in a nuanced way to incorporate this evolution into a dynamic interpretation of the GATT rules [see *Shrimp Case* above].

Carefully tailoring the modality of linkage to the substantive (or on occasion strategic) claims advanced for linkage will enable us to see that these are not all-or-nothing claims but, rather, steps in the evolution of a complex multilateral regulatory framework across a variety of issue areas. Linkage so pursued should not obstruct agreement; on the contrary, it should further enhance the coherence of that multilateral world and the legitimacy of its institutions. In general, however, linkage ought not to substitute for attempts to formulate and improve the distinct international regimes that govern the linked areas. Regime borrowing and sanction linkage in particular tend to reflect frustration and disappointment with the borrowing regime (or non-regime) governing the issue area to be linked. In most such situations, linkage is a second-best solution. It would be preferable to develop the unsatisfactory regime independently.

NOTES:

1. Bhagwati shows how international economic law has developed over the past decades. This development will continue at an increasing pace and will raise more issues. The issues identified by Bhagwati and Leebron include the link between labour issues and trade, trade and the environment and the interaction between international organisations.

2. There are concerns as to whether international economic institutions are capable of dealing with social issues, such as labour, environmental and human rights matters. Yet these institutions must begin to take more account of these issues in their decision-making in order to ensure that they remain relevant and effective for the long-term benefit of all members of the international community.

3. The power of transnational corporations will affect the roles of international economic institutions and the development of international economic law. It is vital for the effectiveness of international law that these organisations come within the international legal framework.

14

The Use of Force, Collective Security and Peacekeeping

Introductory note

The fact that States frequently use armed force against each other is painfully obvious. This fact is not evidence of the 'failure' of international law. All societies, whether they be international or national, suffer from the use of violence by their members to resolve some of their disputes. One of the tasks of law when faced with this fact is to regulate the use of force by the members of the community. International law seeks to do this in two ways. First, by stipulating a paramount obligation not to use force to settle disputes with only limited exceptions. This prohibition of the use of force is a rule of *jus cogens*: *Military and Paramilitary Activities in and against Nicaragua* Case (see Chapter 2). Second, by having at its disposal a procedure whereby the international community itself may use force against a malefactor. These are known respectively as the rules on the 'unilateral use of force' and the rules of 'collective security'.

SECTION 1: **The unilateral use of force**

At one stage in the development of international law, States were entitled to resort to war, or to use force short of war, to achieve their aims. The United Nations Charter definitively changed this with its legal obligation not to use force (see Art. 2(4) of the Charter below), though does not mean that outbreaks of international violence will not occur. The use of force by a State is said to be 'unilateral' when it occurs without the authorisation of a competent international organisation, such as the Security Council of the United Nations. It is possible, therefore, for a use of force to be unilateral in this sense even though it involves more than one acting State. An example is the NATO military action against Yugoslavia (Serbia and Montenegro) during the Kosovo crisis of 1998/9, the legitimacy of which is discussed more fully below. In addition, a unilateral use of force may become superseded or suspended by, or even run concurrently with, a collective use of force under the mandate of collective security, as where unilateral acts become authorised by such a competent organisation. An example is the initially unilateral use of force by States in defence of Kuwait following Iraq's invasion in 1990, which subsequently became an exercise in collective security. Other examples of the unilateral use of force (lawful and unlawful) include the invasion of Cambodia by Vietnam in 1978/9, the invasion of Afghanistan by the USSR in 1980/5, the invasion of Panama by the United States in 1989 and the US-led intervention in Afghanistan in 2001/2002 following the September 2001 terrorist attacks.

The use of force is today governed by the rules found in the UN Charter, regional assistance treaties such as that governing the Organisation of American States (OAS) and customary international law. In addition, some jurists argue that certain customary rights to use force have survived the advent of the UN Charter and, further, that the right of self-defence under customary law is wider than that found in Art. 51 of the Charter. Others claim that the Charter represented a new beginning and that the content of the rules on use of force are to be found solely within it or in new rules of customary international law that have come to reflect its values.

A: The general scheme

United Nations Charter

Article 1
The Purposes of the United Nations are:
1. To maintain international peace and security, and to that end: to take effective collective measures for the prevention and removal of threats to the peace, and for the suppression of act of aggression or other breaches of the peace, and to bring about by peaceful means, and in conformity with the principles of justice and international law, adjustment or settlement of international disputes or situations which might lead to a breach of the peaces; ...

Article 2
3. All Members shall settle their international disputes by peaceful means in such a manner that international peace and security, and justice, are not endangered.
4. All Members shall refrain in their international relations from the threat or use of force against the territorial integrity or political independence of any State, or in any other manner inconsistent with the Purposes of the United Nations.

I. Brownlie and C. Apperley, 'Kosovo Crisis Inquiry: Memorandum on the International Law Aspects'
49 ICLQ 878 (2000), pp. 884–886

31. The scheme of the Charter consists of giving a monopoly of the use of force to the Security Council, but providing for specific exceptions in the case of the right of individual or collective self-defence, in accordance with the provisions of Article 51.

32. Article 2 of the Charter prescribes the principles which bind both the Organization and its Members. It is sometimes argued that the phrase 'against the territorial integrity or political independence' of any State in paragraph 4 of Article 2 can be given a restrictive meaning, which would permit forcible intervention provided this did not involve an annexation of territory.

33. The negotiating history is as follows. In Chapter II of the Dumbarton Oaks Proposals the fourth principle provided simply: 'All members of the Organization shall refrain in their international relations from the threat or use of force in any manner inconsistent with the purposes of the Organization'. At San Francisco an Australian amendment introduced phraseology substantially identical with the final text of paragraph 4. A Brazilian amendment would have provided:

> All members of the Organization shall refrain in their international relations from any intervention in the foreign or domestic affairs of any other member of the Organization, and from resorting to threats or use of force, if they are not in accord with the methods and decisions of the Organization. In the prohibition against intervention there shall be understood to be included any interference that threatens the national security of another member of the Organization, directly or indirectly threatens its territorial integrity, or involves the exercise of any excessively foreign influences on its destinies.

Ecuador wished to apply a paragraph to Chapter II in these terms:

> The declaration that an attempt by a State against the territorial integrity or inviolability, against the sovereignty or political independence of another State, shall be considered as an act of aggression against all the States which constitute the International Community.

34. In the first Committee of Commission I several delegates referred to the necessity of incorporating in Chapter II an express undertaking that the world Organization should insure the territorial integrity and political independence of Member States. The Committee rejected the Brazilian amendment but adopted the Australian amendment which had been accepted by the drafting subcommittee. In the discussion the Norwegian Delegate expressed an opinion that 'it should be made clear in the Report to the Commission that this paragraph 4 did not contemplate any use of force, outside of action by the Organization, going beyond individual or collective self-defence. He was himself in favour of omitting the specific phrase relating to "territorial integrity and political independence" since this was, on the one hand, a permanent obligation under international law and, on the other hand, could be said to be covered by the phrase "sovereign equality" as suggested in the commentary by the *Rapporteur*.' There is no indication in the records that the phrase was intended to have a restrictive effect.

35. In the Commission Belaunde of Peru pointed out that paragraph 1 of Chapter II lacked any reference to the idea of the personality of the State but that the elements of personality had been incidentally inserted in paragraph 4 and that this did not establish absolute respect for sovereignty and territorial integrity. The *Rapporteur* of Committee I explained that paragraphs 1 and 4 protected the personality of the State as well as its territorial integrity and political independence. The Commission adopted paragraph 4 in the form proposed by Committee I.

36. The conclusion warranted by the *travaux préparatoires* is that the phrase under discussion was not intended to be restrictive but, on the contrary, to give more specific guarantees to small States and that it cannot be interpreted as having a qualifying effect. If it is asserted that the phrase may have a qualifying effect then writers making this assertion face the difficulty that it involves an admission that there is an ambiguity, and in such a case recourse may be had to *travaux préparatoires*, which reveal a meaning contrary to that asserted.

37. In the Seventh Edition of *Oppenheim's International Law*, Volume II, published in 1952, the distinguished editor, Sir Hersch Lauterpacht, explains the position thus:

> Neither is the obligation not to resort to force or threats of force limited by the words 'against the territorial integrity or political independence of any State.' Territorial integrity, especially where coupled with 'political independence' is synonymous with territorial inviolability. Thus a State would be acting in breach of its obligations under the Charter if it were to invade or commit an act of force within the territory of another State, in anticipation of an alleged impending attack or in order to obtain redress, without the intention of

interfering permanently with the territorial integrity of that State. The prohibition of paragraph 4 is absolute except with regard to the use of force in fulfillment of the obligations to give effect to the Charter or in pursuance of action in self-defence consistently with the provisions of Article 51 of the Charter discussed in the following Section. (p.154).

38. The position was confirmed, 25 years later, in 1970, in the Declaration on Principles of International Law Concerning Friendly Relations and Co-operation. The Declaration provides evidence of the consensus among States on the meaning of the principles of the Charter.

M. McDougal and F. Feliciano, 'The Initiation of Coercion: A Multi-Temporal Analysis'
52 AJIL (1958) 241

The following extract is taken from the work of the proponents of a multi-dimensional approach to the use of force. Although the language is difficult, essentially the idea is that the use of force must be looked at in its complete context, and its usefulness (and hence legality) must be judged in terms of certain 'values' rather than according to 'dry' legal rules that may not reflect the realities of international life. The thesis is fully developed in the authors' major work, *Law and Minimum World Public Order*.

The first step, we submit, towards contact with reality is reference to, and careful orientation in, the factual process of coercion across national boundaries. In broad preliminary characterization, this process of coercion may be described in terms of various *participants* applying to each other coercion of alternately accelerating and decelerating degrees of intensity, for a wide range of *objectives*, utilizing *methods* which include the employment of all known distinctive strategies or instruments of policy, under the variable *conditions* of a world arena in continuous flux. It may be observed that, in the course of this process of coercion, the participants assert against each other many varying claims respecting the lawfulness and unlawfulness of the particular coercive practices being utilized by or against them, invoking both world prescriptions and world opinion to fortify their respective assertions.

The description we suggest of factual coercion in terms of 'process' is intended not merely to convey a sense of the variety in participant, purpose, modality and claim, but also to emphasize the facts of *continuity* – continuity in coercive action and reaction and in assertion and counter-assertion – and of *changing intensities in degree*, from the mildest to the most severe applications of coercion. Between the two extremes of 'pure' peace and 'total' war, the states of the world arena may in these terms be observed continuously to engage each other for power and other values, by all instruments of policy, in a *continuum* of degrees in coercive practices, ranging from the least intense to the most intense. . . . Rationality, in fine, in the determination of 'when war begins' requires not a marking of one or even a few dates in a calendar, nor a search for one decisive factor, for the applicability *in abstracto* of prescriptions, but rather the clarification of what world community policies are uniquely relevant to varying claims of authority at varying stages in coercion processes. A policy-oriented approach is not a single-factor but a multiple-factor approach; rational policy is not uni-temporal but multi-temporal.

. . . From such contextual orientation, an inquirer might, it is to be hoped, much more effectively seek to perform the various intellectual tasks deemed essential to policy-oriented study, including: the clarification of policies, the observation and comparison through time of past trends in decision, the identification in relative detail of the more significant conditioning elements, the projection of past trends into future probabilities, and the recommendation of preferred alternatives designed to secure the values of a free society.

T. Franck, 'Who Killed Article 2(4)?'

64 AJIL (1970) 809

[T]oday the high-minded resolve of Article 2(4) mocks us from its grave. That the rules against the use of force should have had so short a life appears due to various factors. The rules, admirable in themselves, were seemingly predicated on a false assumption: that the wartime partnership of the Big Five would continue, providing the means for policing the peace under the aegis of the United Nations. They appeared to address themselves to preventing conventional military aggression at the very moment in history when new forms of attack were making obsolete all prior notions of war and peace strategy. And the Charter itself provided enough exceptions and ambiguities to open the rules to deadly erosion . . .

Unfortunately these ambitious projects were founded on an invalid premise: that the Security Council would be able to discharge its responsibility as the United Nations' principal organ for world peacekeeping. . . . The Security Council . . ., in all but procedural matters, can only act with the assent of nine members, including the affirmative vote or at least the benevolent abstention of each of the Big Five. Almost from the moment the San Francisco Charter was signed, this essential prerequisite for UN collective enforcement action – the unanimity of the great Powers – was seen to be an illusion. . . . As Chapter VII was seen to rust, increasing use began to be made of Articles 51, 52, and 53, which set out the rights of states themselves, under certain exceptional circumstances, to resort to various kinds of force outside the United Nations frame-work, until today, through practice, the exceptions have overwhelmed the rule and transformed the system.

Article 51 of the UN Charter permits the use of armed force by a state responding in self-defense to an armed attack. This right to respond can either be exercised individually by the state attacked or collectively by a group of states going to its rescue. At first glance, such an exception would appear to be both inevitable and modest . . .

The simplicity of this is, however, misleading. In the first place, the failure of UN enforcement machinery has not been occasional but endemic, and so, concomitantly, has the resort to 'self-defense.' Equally important, since there is usually no way for the international system to establish conclusively which state is the aggressor and which the aggrieved, wars continue to occur, as they have since time immemorial, between parties both of which are using force allegedly in 'self-defense.'

The outright lie about who attacked first is not, however, the only or, probably, the principal problem. The most significant factor in complicating the 'simple' right of self-defense accorded by Article 51, rather, has been the changing nature of warfare itself. . . . Modern warfare . . . has inconveniently by-passed Queensberry-like practices. It tends, instead, to proceed along two radic-ally different lines, one too small and the other too large to be encompassed effectively by Article 51. These two categories are, first, wars of agitation, infiltration and subversion carried on by proxy through national liberation movements; and, second, nuclear wars involving the instantaneous use, in a first strike, of weapons of near-paralyzing destructiveness.

Ambiguities and complexities thus lurk behind the misleadingly simple rule in Article 2(4) prohibit-ing the use of force in international relations and in the carefully delimited exceptions to that rule. Changing circumstances of international relations, of the way nations perceive their self-interest, of strategy and tactics, have combined to take advantage of these latent ambiguities, enlarging the exceptions to the point of virtually repealing the rule itself.

A particularly significant part in this development has been played by regional organizations. Articles 52 and 53 of the Charter have been interpreted to legitimate the use of force by regional organizations in their collective self-interest, and, specifically, the rôle and primacy of regional organ-izations in settling disputes between their members. These exceptions to Article 2(4) and their application in practice have played an important, perhaps the most important, rôle in the growth of international violence over these past twenty-five years . . .

The prohibition against the use of force in relations between states has been eroded beyond recognition, principally by three factors: 1, the rise of wars of 'national liberation'; 2, the rising threat of wars of total destruction; 3, the increasing authoritarianism of regional systems dominated by a super-Power. These three factors may, however, be traced back to a single circumstance: the lack of congruence between the international legal norm of Article 2(4) and the perceived national interest of states, especially the super-Powers.

L. Henkin, 'The Reports of the Death of Article 2(4) are Greatly Exaggerated'
65 AJIL (1971) 544

It is difficult to quarrel with Dr Franck's diagnosis of the ills of the Charter. . . . Distracted and distraught by these ills, one can indeed fall into the conclusion that Article 2(4) is virtually dead, but that, I believe, would mistake the lives and the ways of the law.

My principal difference with Dr Franck's diagnosis is that it judges the vitality of the law by looking only at its failures. The purpose of Article 2(4) was to establish a norm of national behavior and to help deter violation of it. Despite common misimpressions, Article 2(4) has indeed been a norm of behavior and has deterred violations. In inter-state as in individual penology, deterrence often cannot be measured or even proved, but students of politics agree that traditional war between nations has become less frequent and less likely. The sense that war is not done has taken hold, and nations more readily find that their interests do not in fact require the use of force after all. . . . Even where force is used, the fact that it is unlawful cannot be left out of account and limits the scope, the weapons, the duration, the purposes for which force is used. . . .

Many will refuse credit to Article 2(4), attributing the lack of traditional war to other factors – to nuclear weapons and the changing character of war, to greater territorial stability, to other changes in national interests reducing national temptation to use force. If it were so, Article 2(4) would not be the less a norm: law often reflects dispositions to behavior as much as it shapes them. . . . The occasions and the causes of war remain. What has become obsolete is the notion that nations are as free to indulge it as ever, and the death of that notion is accepted in the Charter. . . .

The fissures of the Charter are worrisome but they, too, are not as wide in international life as they loom in academic imagination. Pre-emptive war as 'anticipatory self-defense' has been hypothesized by many professors but asserted by few governments: . . . A few nations have falsely claimed self-defense against actual attack, but there are effective limits to unwarranted claims, in what nations dare assert and what others will believe . . .

The regional loophole, too, is not as wide as might seem, dangerous but not fatal. There have been few instances of groups claiming the right to do together what the Charter forbids them singly, and little reason to expect that it will happen frequently in future . . .

Dr Franck's dramatic title makes its point, and his cry of alarm is warranted and necessary. But one must not allow it to be seized by the 'super-realists' to prove that the effort to control international violence by law has again failed and the Charter is now as irrelevant as the Kellogg-Briand Pact. For me, if Article 2(4) were indeed dead, I should have to conclude that it rules – not mocks – us from the grave. In fact, despite common misimpressions (from which it suffers in common with other international law) Article 2(4) lives and can live. No government, no responsible official of government, has been prepared or has wished to pronounce it dead. Article 2(4) was written by practical men who knew all about national interest. They believed the norms they legislated to be in their nations' interest, and nothing that has happened in the past twenty-five years suggests that it is not. There is reason to pray and strive for the change in individual and national perceptions which Dr Franck invokes, but the need is not to condemn Article 2(4) to death and pray for its resurrection in the end of days when men and nations will not learn war any more. The need is for citizens, policy-makers, national societies, transnational and international bodies to be reminded that this law is indeed in the national interest of all nations; that a decision to initiate force always involves a preference for one national interest over another; that in the cost-accounting of national interest a decision to go to war grossly depreciates the tangible cost to the citizen – in life, in welfare, in aspiration – and usually prefers the immediate and short-sighted to the longer, deeper national interest.

Military and Paramilitary Activities in and against Nicaragua Case
(*Nicaragua* v *USA*)
ICJ Rep 1986 14, International Court of Justice

Nicaragua alleged that the United States was responsible for certain military operations in Nicaraguan territory that were directed at the legitimate government. These included the mining of Nicaraguan ports and support for the *contra* rebels. These actions were said to violate Art. 2(4) of the Charter and customary international law. The Court determined that it lacked jurisdiction to try issues based on the Charter because the United States had legitimately refused consert to the Court having jurisdiction in cases concerning multilateral treaties. However, the Court did have jurisdiction over questions of customary law (see Chapter 2), and so it was crucial to determine whether the prohibition of Art. 2(4) had passed in to customary law.

188. The Court thus finds that both Parties take the view that the principles as to the use of force incorporated in the United Nations Charter correspond, in essentials, to those found in customary international law. The Parties thus both take the view that the fundamental principle in this area is expressed in the terms employed in Article 2, paragraph 4, of the United Nations Charter. . . . The Court has however to be satisfied that there exists in customary international law an *opinio juris* as to the binding character of such abstention. This *opinio juris* may, though with all due caution, be deduced from, *inter alia*, the attitude of the Parties and the attitude of States towards certain General Assembly resolutions, and particularly resolution 2625 (XXV) entitled 'Declaration on Principles of International Law concerning Friendly Relations and Co-operation among States in accordance with the Charter of the United Nations' . . .

190. A further confirmation of the validity as customary international law of the principle of the prohibition of the use of force expressed in Article 2, paragraph 4, of the Charter of the United Nations may be found in the fact that it is frequently referred to in statements by State representatives as being not only a principle of customary international law but also a fundamental or cardinal principle of such law . . .

JUDGE SETTE-CAMARA (Separate Opinion): I firmly believe that the non-use of force as well as non-intervention – the latter as a corollary of equality of States and self-determination – are not only cardinal principles of customary international law but could in addition be recognized as peremptory rules of customary international law which impose obligations on all States.

JUDGE JENNINGS (Dissenting Opinion): There is no doubt that there was, prior to the United Nations Charter, a customary law which restricted the lawful use of force, and which correspondingly provided also for a right to use force in self-defence; as indeed the use of the term 'inherent' in Article 51 of the United Nations Charter suggests. The proposition, however, that, after the Charter, there exists alongside those Charter provisions on force and self-defence, an independent customary law that can be applied as alternative to Articles 2, paragraph 4, and 51 of the Charter, raises questions about how and when this correspondence came about, and about what the differences, if any, between customary law and the Charter provisions, may be. . . .

It could hardly be contended that these provisions of the Charter were merely a codification of the existing customary law. The literature is replete with statements that Article 2, paragraph 4, – for example in speaking of 'force' rather than war, and providing that even a 'threat of force' may be unlawful – represented an important innovation in the law. . . . Even Article 51, though referring to an 'inherent' and therefore supposedly pre-existing, right of self-defence, introduced a novel concept in speaking of 'collective self-defence' . . .

If, then, the Charter was not a codification of existing custom about force and self-defence, the question must then be asked whether a general customary law, replicating the Charter provisions, has developed as a result of the influence of the Charter provisions, coupled presumably with subsequent and consonant States' practice . . . But there are obvious difficulties about extracting even a scintilla of relevant 'practice' on these matters from the behaviour of those few States which are not parties to the Charter; and the behaviour of all the rest, and the *opinio juris* which it might otherwise evidence, is surely explained by their being bound by the Charter itself . . .

That the Court has not wholly succeeded in escaping from the Charter and other multilateral treaties, is evident from even a casual perusal of the Judgment; the Court has in the event found it impossible to avoid what is in effect a consideration of treaty provisions as such. As the Court puts it, the Court 'can and must take them [the multilateral treaties] into account in determining the content of the customary law which the United States is also alleged to have infringed' (para. 183).

This use of treaty provisions as 'evidence' of custom, takes the form of an interpretation of the treaty text. Yet the Court itself acknowledges that treaty-law and customary law can be distinguished precisely because the canons of interpretation are different (para. 178). To indulge the treaty interpretation process, in order to determine the content of a posited customary rule, must raise a suspicion that it is in reality the treaty itself that is being applied under another name. Of course this way of going about things may be justified where the treaty text was, from the beginning, designed to be a codification of custom; or where the treaty is itself the origin of a customary law rule. But, as we have already seen, this could certainly not be said of Article 2, paragraph 4, or even Article 51, of the United Nations Charter; nor indeed of most of the other relevant multilateral treaty provisions.

The reader cannot but put to himself the question whether the Judgment would, in its main substance, have been noticeably different in its content and argument, had the application of the multilateral treaty reservation been rejected.

NOTES:

1. The paramount obligation not to resort to force, as found in Art. 2(4) and in customary international law, can now be regarded as a rule of *jus cogens*. Its importance is illustrated by the number of times it is recited in resolutions of the General Assembly and Security Council. It is clear also that the obligation not to resort to force is much more than a political slogan. It has real legal content. This means that States that resort to force face two barriers. First, they are faced with a legal presumption that their conduct is illegal, so is up to the State resorting to force to prove the legitimacy of its actions. Second, if a State's conduct can be described as 'unlawful' rather than merely immoral or 'dangerous', it may suffer action by the Security Council or, as is more likely, from the odium of other States. This can be a powerful sanction in the world of *real politik*, as with the isolation and subsequent subjugation of Iraq after its invasion of Kuwait and the international isolation of Yugoslavia (Serbia and Montenegro) following the Bosnia and Kosovo incidents. The general rejection of the use of force by the international community, even when that is not expressed by formal condemnation or sanctions, can have far reaching reciprocal consequences. So, while the US-led intervention

in Afghanistan in 2001/2002 cannot easily be justified under international law (although there may be a self-defence argument: see below), the fact that it was in response to a terrorist atrocity quelled even the fiercest critics of the United States. In fact, the criticism that has emerged is largely in respect of the US treatment of captives after the intervention, not of the intervention itself.

2. The 'restrictive' and 'permissive' schools of interpretation are discussed in some of the above extracts. The crucial question is the extent to which the 'permissive' school would allow the unilateral use of force to settle disputes without reliance on one of the recognised exceptions. This would accomodate the use of force in novel situations. Consequently, much turns on the interpretation of Art. 2(4).

3. The *Nicaragua Case* is perhaps the most important judicial pronouncement on the law relating to the unilateral use of force. The ICJ found itself in the position of having to decide the merits according to customary international law due to a limitation on its jurisdiction (see Chapter 2). Undoubtedly, this confirms the continuing validity of customary international law principles, although a majority of the Court did not agree that these principles granted wider freedom of action than the UN Charter. In fact, the majority decision is premised on the fact – some would say assumption – that the law of the Charter and customary international law have coincided in all material respects. The ICJ currently is seised of an application by Yugoslavia against certain members of NATO in respect of the latter States' military action against Yugoslavia during the Kosovo crisis. Whilst the Court has decided on some jurisdiction issues, it has not yet considered the merits: *Legality of the Use of Force Case*, available at www.icj-cij.org/.

B: Individual self-defence

The Caroline Case
29 Brit & For St Papers

The *Caroline* was an American ship that had been used by Canadian rebels to harass the authorities in Canada. While it was moored in an American port close to the border, it was attacked by the British and destroyed. The legality of the action was raised when Great Britain sought the release of one of the men involved in the attack. Webster's formulation in a letter is regarded as the *locus classicus* of customary self-defence.

Mr Webster to Mr Fox
Washington, April 24, 1841

The Undersigned has now to signify to Mr Fox that the Government of The United States has not changed the opinion which it has heretofore expressed to Her Majesty's Government of the character of the act of destroying the *Caroline*.

It does not think that that transaction can be justified by any reasonable application or construction of the right of self-defence, under the laws of nations. It is admitted that a just right of self-defence attaches always to nations as well as to individuals, and is equally necessary for the preservation of both. But the extent of this right is a question to be judged of by the circumstances of each particular case, and when its alleged exercise has led to the commission of hostile acts within the territory of a Power at peace, nothing less than a clear and absolute necessity can afford ground of justification . . .

Under these circumstances, and under those immediately connected with the transaction itself, it will be for Her Majesty's Government to show upon what state of facts, and what rules of national law, the destruction of the *Caroline* is to be defended. It will be for that Government to show a necessity of self-defence, instant, overwhelming, leaving no choice of means, and no moment for deliberation. It will be for it to show, also, that the local authorities of Canada, even supposing the necessity of the moment authorized them to enter the territories of The United States at all, did nothing unreasonable or excessive; since the act, justified by the necessity of self-defence, must be limited by that necessity, and kept clearly within it.

United Nations Charter

Article 51
Nothing in the present Charter shall impair the inherent right of individual or collective self-defence if an armed attack occurs against a Member of the United Nations, until the Security Council has taken measures necessary to maintain international peace and security. Measures taken by members in the exercise of this right of self-defence shall be immediately reported to the Security Council and shall not in any way affect the authority and responsibility of the Security Council under the present Charter to take at any time such action as it deems necessary in order to maintain or restore international peace and security.

J. de Arechega, 'General Course in Public International Law'
(1978) 159 *Recueil des Cours* 9

A strict interpretation of Article 51 of the Charter is attacked from two sides: by those who contend that underlying this provision there is a broad right of self-defence resulting from customary law which has not been limited by the Charter and, on the other side, by those who claim that whatever the terms of Article 51 may be, a legitimate exercise of self-defence arises in support of the right of self-determination.

The combined effect of Article 2(4) and Article 51 of the Charter is that the individual use of force by States is prohibited unless a State is exercising 'the inherent right of individual or collective self-defence if an armed attack occurs'. The Charter incorporates in Article 51, as an essential condition for the existence of the inherent right of self-defence, the precise and restrictive notion of 'armed attack', in French 'une agression armée'. The Charter does not refer to 'use or threat of force' as in Article 2(4) nor to 'a threat to the peace, breach of the peace or act of aggression' as in Article 39. The authorization to use force in self-defence is limited by an 'if' clause, by a condition of fact 'which is comparatively clear, objective, easy to prove, difficult to misinterpret or fabricate' . . .

It has been contended however that Article 51 does not 'cut down the customary right (of self-defence) and make it applicable only to the case of resistance to armed attack by another State'.

The arguments in support of this view are that the right of self-defence does not have its source in the Charter, but is an independent right rooted in general international law, and the purpose of Article 51 was simply to remove possible doubts as to the impact of the Security Council's powers upon the right of States individually and collectively to have recourse to force in self-defence. The *travaux préparatoires* show that Article 51 was introduced for the purpose of harmonising regional organizations for defence with the powers and responsibilities given to the Security Council.

These arguments do not seem convincing nor in accordance with the canons of treaty interpretation agreed at the Vienna Conference on the Law of Treaties. Whatever may have been the reasons which inspired the proposal to include Article 51 in the Charter, the fact remains that this provision was inserted and that the crucial reference to an 'armed attack' is contained in it. . . .

In support of the idea that the Charter preserved a supposed pre-existing customary law of self-defence, the argument is made that the qualification of self-defence as an inherent right . . . in

Article 51 cannot have any other meaning than referring back to general international law or to a general principle of law.

It does not appear possible, however, to attribute to this adjective the effect of annulling the substantive meaning of the whole text of Article 51.

The so-called customary law of self-defence supposedly pre-existing the Charter, and dependent on this single word, simply did not exist. Before 1945 self-defence was not a legal concept but merely a political excuse for the use of force. For the concept of legitimate defence to come into existence, it is necessary that a corresponding notion of illegitimate use of force already exists. . . .

It is only with the United Nations Charter that the prohibition of force and consequently the legitimacy of self-defence have become established as symmetrical legal concepts. It follows that to exercise self-defence legitimately, a State must comply with all the requirements established in Article 51 of the Charter and not with some loose conditions mentioned in a diplomatic incident between the United States and the United Kingdom some 140 years ago, as was the case of the *Caroline*. . . .

The only aspect of general international law which is relevant in the application of Article 51 is the general principle of law that the defensive action must be commensurate with and in proportion to the armed attack which gave rise to the exercise of the right of self-defence. The object of self-defence is precisely to put an end to the armed attack: it would not be permissible for a State, in the course of its defence, to seize and keep the resources and territory of the attacker.

The Charter requirement that a prior armed attack should occur before the right of self-defence arises does not mean that it is necessary to wait for the armed attack to strike in order lawfully to use force in self-defence. It is sufficient that the armed attack has been launched. . . .

Military and Paramilitary Activities in and against Nicaragua Case (*Nicaragua* v *USA*)
ICJ Rep 1986 14 International Court of Justice

193. The general rule prohibiting force allows for certain exceptions. In view of the arguments advanced by the United States to justify the acts of which it is accused by Nicaragua, the Court must express a view on the content of the right of self-defence, and more particularly the right of collective self-defence. First, with regard to the existence of this right, it notes that in the language of Article 51 of the United Nations Charter, the inherent right (or 'droit natural') which any State possesses in the event of an armed attack, covers both collective and individual self-defence. Thus, the Charter itself testifies to the existence of the right of collective self-defence in customary international law . . .

194. . . . In view of the circumstances in which the dispute has arisen, reliance is placed by the Parties only on the right of self-defence in the case of an armed attack which has already occurred, and the issue of the lawfulness of a response to the imminent threat of armed attack has not been raised. Accordingly the Court expresses no view on that issue. The Parties also agree in holding that whether the response to the attack is lawful depends on observance of the criteria of the necessity and the proportionality of the measures taken in self-defence. Since the existence of the right of collective self-defence is established in customary international law, the Court must define the specific conditions which may have to be met for its exercise, in addition to the conditions of necessity and proportionality to which the Parties have referred.

195. In the case of individual self-defence, the exercise of this right is subject to the State concerned having been the victim of an armed attack. Reliance on collective self-defence of course does not remove the need for this. There appears now to be general agreement on the nature of the acts which can be treated as constituting armed attacks. In particular, it may be considered to be agreed that an armed attack must be understood as including not merely action by regular armed forces across an international border, but also 'the sending by or on behalf of a State of armed bands,

groups, irregulars or mercenaries, which carry out acts of armed force against another State of such gravity as to amount to' (*inter alia*) an actual armed attack conducted by regular forces, 'or its substantial involvement therein'. This description, contained in Article 3, paragraph (g), of the Definition of Aggression annexed to General Assembly resolution 3314 (XXIX), may be taken to reflect customary international law. The Court sees no reason to deny that, in customary law, the prohibition of armed attacks may apply to the sending by a State of armed bands to the territory of another State, if such an operation, because of its scale and effects, would have been classified as an armed attack rather than as a mere frontier incident had it been carried out by regular armed forces. But the Court does not believe that the concept of 'armed attack' includes not only acts by armed bands where such acts occur on a significant scale but also assistance to rebels in the form of the provision of weapons or logistical or other support. Such assistance may be regarded as a threat or use of force, or amount to intervention in the internal or external affairs of other States.

JUDGE JENNINGS (Dissenting Opinion): The question of what constitutes 'armed attack' for the purposes of Article 51, and its relation to the definition of aggression, are large and controversial questions in which it would be inappropriate to become involved in this opinion. It is of course a fact that collective self-defence is a concept that lends itself to abuse. One must therefore sympathize with the anxiety of the Court to define it in terms of some strictness (though it is a little surprising that the Court does not at all consider the problems of the quite different French text: 'où un Membre . . . est l'objet d'une agression armée'). There is a question, however, whether the Court has perhaps gone too far in this direction.

The Court (para. 195) allows that, where a State is involved with the organization of 'armed bands' operating in the territory of another State, this, 'because of its scale and effects', could amount to 'armed attack' under Article 51; but that this does not extend to 'assistance to rebels in the form of the provision of weapons or logistical or other support' (*ibid.*). Such conduct, the Court goes on to say, may not amount to an armed attack; but 'may be regarded as a threat or use of force, or amount to intervention in the internal or external affairs of other States' (*ibid.*).

It may readily be agreed that the mere provision of arms cannot be said to amount to an armed attack. But the provision of arms may, nevertheless, be a very important element in what might be thought to amount to armed attack, where it is coupled with other kinds of involvement. Accordingly, it seems to me that to say that the provision of arms, coupled with 'logistical or other support' is not armed attack is going much too far. Logistical support may itself be crucial. . . . If there is added to all this 'other support', it becomes difficult to understand what it is, short of direct attack by a State's own forces, that may not be done apparently without a lawful response in the form of collective self-defence; nor indeed may be responded to at all by the use of force or threat of force, for, to cite the Court again, 'States do not have a right of "collective" armed response to acts which do not constitute an "armed attack"' . . .

This looks to me neither realistic nor just in the world where power struggles are in every continent carried on by destabilization, interference in civil strife, comfort, aid and encouragement to rebels, and the like. The original scheme of the United Nations Charter, whereby force would be deployed by the United Nations itself, in accordance with the provisions of Chapter VII of the Charter, has never come into effect. Therefore an essential element in the Charter design is totally missing. In this situation it seems dangerous to define unnecessarily strictly the conditions for lawful self-defence so as to leave a large area where both a forcible response to force is forbidden, and yet the United Nations employment of force, which was intended to fill that gap, is absent.

J. Hargrove, 'The Nicaragua Judgment and the Future of the Law of Force and Self-Defence'
81 AJIL 135 (1987)

The Court had put itself into a position that required it to apply exclusively customary international law, largely derivative from the United Nations Charter but nevertheless separate. Its most important conclusions of law relating to force and self-defense were the following:

(1) That the conduct of the United States in 'training, arming, equipping, financing and supplying the *contra* forces or otherwise encouraging, supporting and aiding military and paramilitary activities in and against Nicaragua,' where these activities involved the use of force, violated the customary law obligation of the United States not to use force against another state. The same was true of some seven specified 'attacks,' as well as the mining of Nicaraguan waters, which the Court found imputable to the United States.

(2) That since an 'armed attack' is necessary to justify resort to force in self-defense by the United States, the US claim of the right of self-defense failed because (a) the provision of arms or 'logistical or other support' to armed forces operating in the territory of another state does not amount to an 'armed attack' . . . and (b) certain 'military incursions' or 'military attacks' by the Nicaraguan Government into Honduran and Costa Rican territory, while found by the Court to be difficult to appraise legally, apparently did not amount to 'armed attacks.'

(3) That although the supply of arms to armed forces within another state's territory, as alleged against Nicaragua, could amount to an unlawful use of force, and might therefore justify 'proportionate countermeasures' even if not – as just indicated – the use of force in 'self-defense,' such countermeasures could only be taken by the victim state itself, and not by a third state such as the United States acting collectively with it. The Court strongly suggested, but so far as I can ascertain did not explicitly assert, that the victim state's 'proportionate countermeasures' might themselves include the use of force . . .

Thus, the Court appears to have asserted the following as to the rules of customary international law:

- The prohibition of 'force' does indeed prohibit all forms of physical violence, and all kinds of complicity in it, and not just conventional open hostilities by a state's own military forces.
- Only some of these acts of force, however, can be resisted by force in self-defense, no matter how reasonably necessary and proportionate the latter may be, because only some amount to an 'armed attack.' . . .
- Some of those unlawful acts of force that cannot be resisted by force in self-defense, however, may be resisted by 'proportionate countermeasures' by the victim. It remains an open question whether these countermeasures by the victim state might include acts of force, although the Court strongly suggests that they might . . . But in no such case may a third state participate in countermeasures involving force, and to do so is a violation of the prohibition on the use of force between states.

What are we to make of this? . . .

(1) Any suggestion that there are any acts of unlawful force between states that international law forbids a state from defending against by proportionate force, by the means and to the extent reasonably necessary to protect itself, degrades the concept of international law, and diminishes the inducement for a responsible political leader to take its constraints seriously into account in conflict situations in the actual planning and conduct of that state's affairs.

(2) The premise underlying the proposition that some acts of force cannot be resisted by force in self-defense is that, because the language of Article 51 is not identical to that of Article 2(4), some acts of unlawful force are not to be regarded as 'armed attacks.' That premise is otherwise

unsupported by the language of Article 51, which in no way limits itself to especially large, direct or important armed attacks . . .

(3) The Court was not free to treat the proposition that some acts of force cannot be resisted by force in self-defense as if writing on a tabula rasa. For it had been considered and specifically rejected by UN member states in the course of protracted negotiations in a sister principal organ of the United Nations [the General Assembly on the question of a Definition of Aggression] . . .

(4) The further details of the Court's pronouncement compound the injury. For as indicated earlier, either the Court was saying (a) that there are some acts of force that nobody, not even the victim, may resist by proportionate measures of force; or it was saying (b) that the victim may resist by force, provided it does so alone. There is little to be said in explanation of the latter position other than that it is simply a second arbitrary announcement of the Court, stacked on the first: one is at a loss to find any basis in the language of the Charter, or in the experience of states – weak or strong – for concluding that *legally* some acts of force must be fended off alone, while others can be resisted with the help of one's friends . . .

(5) The tentative invention of this new exception to Article 2(4) – 'forcible countermeasures' – is perhaps only the most obvious specific consequence of the Court's treatment of customary law as the law of the case. In general, the Court did not – as it could well have done – find customary law on matters of force and self-defense to be just a ghostly replica of the Charter, conveniently available to do the same jobs as the Charter when for technical reasons the Charter could not be employed. Instead, customary law was discovered to be a separate and different realm, waiting to be charted by the Court, resembling the Charter in important respects but containing other features that differ from the Charter and could not have been predicted from a reading of it.

(6) The cumulative effect of all the foregoing is that the law of force and self-defense as it emerges from the Court has become highly arbitrary, intricate and technical, but at the same time more uncertain.

Legality of the Threat or Use of Nuclear Weapons Opinion
ICJ Rep 1996, International Court of Justice

In 1994 the General Assembly resolved to request an Advisory Opinion on the question 'Is the threat or use of nuclear weapons in any circumstances permitted under international law?'. The Court agreed to give such an opinion.

38. The Charter contains several provisions relating to the threat and use of force. In Article 2, paragraph 4, the threat or use of force against the territorial integrity or political independence of another State or in any other manner inconsistent with the purposes of the United Nations is prohibited . . .

This prohibition of the use of force is to be considered in the light of other relevant provisions of the Charter. In Article 51, the Charter recognizes the inherent right of individual or collective self-defence if an armed attack occurs. A further lawful use of force is envisaged in Article 42, whereby the Security Council may take military enforcement measures in conformity with Chapter VII of the Charter.

39. These provisions do not refer to specific weapons. They apply to any use of force, regardless of the weapons employed. The Charter neither expressly prohibits, nor permits, the use of any specific weapon, including nuclear weapons. A weapon that is already unlawful *per se*, whether by treaty or custom, does not become lawful by reason of its being used for a legitimate purpose under the Charter.

40. The entitlement to resort to self-defence under Article 51 is subject to certain constraints. Some of these constraints are inherent in the very concept of self defence. Other requirements are specified in Article 51.

41. The submission of the exercise of the right of self-defence to the conditions of necessity and proportionality is a rule of customary international law. As the Court stated in the case concerning *Military and Paramilitary Activities in and against Nicaragua (Nicaragua v United States of America)* (ICJ Reports 1986, p. 94, para. 176): 'there is a specific rule whereby self-defence would warrant only measures which are proportional to the armed attack and necessary to respond to it, a rule well established in customary international law'. This dual condition applies equally to Article 51 of the Charter, whatever the means of force employed.

42. The proportionality principle may thus not in itself exclude the use of nuclear weapons in self-defence in all circumstances. But at the same time, a use of force that is proportionate under the law of self-defence, must, in order to be lawful, also meet the requirements of the law applicable in armed conflict which comprise in particular the principles and rules of humanitarian law.

44. Beyond the conditions of necessity and proportionality, Article 51 specifically requires that measures taken by States in the exercise of the right of self-defence shall be immediately reported to the Security Council, this article further provides that these measures shall not in any way affect the authority and responsibility of the Security Council under the Charter to take at any time such action as it deems necessary in order to maintain or restore international peace and security. These requirements of Article 51 apply whatever the means of force used in self defence.

46. Certain States asserted that the use of nuclear weapons in the conduct of reprisals would be lawful. The Court does not have to examine, in this context, the question of armed reprisals in time of peace, which are considered to be unlawful. Nor does it have to pronounce on the question of belligerent reprisals save to observe that in any case any right of recourse to such reprisals would, like self-defence, be governed *inter alia* by the principle of proportionality.

47. In order to lessen or eliminate the risk of unlawful attack, States sometimes signal that they possess certain weapons to use in self-defence against any State violating their territorial integrity or political independence. Whether a signalled intention to use force if certain events occur is or is not a 'threat' within Article 2, paragraph 4, of the Charter depends upon various factors. If the envisaged use of force is itself unlawful, the stated readiness to use it would be a threat prohibited under Article 2, paragraph 4. Thus it would be illegal for a State to threaten force to secure territory from another State, or to cause it to follow or not follow certain political or economic paths. The notions of 'threat' and 'use' of force under Article 2, paragraph 4, of the Charter stand together in the sense that if the use of force itself in a given case is illegal (for whatever reason) the threat to use such force will likewise be illegal. In short, if it is to be lawful, the declared readiness of a State to use force must be a use of force that is in conformity with the Charter. For the rest, no State (whether or not it defended the policy of deterrence) suggested to the Court that it would be lawful to threaten to use force if the use of force contemplated would be illegal.

48. Some States put forward the argument that possession of nuclear weapons is itself an unlawful threat to use force. Possession of nuclear weapons may indeed justify an inference of preparedness to use them. In order to be effective, the policy of deterrence, by which those States possessing or under the umbrella of nuclear weapons seek to discourage military aggression by demonstrating that it will serve no purpose, necessitates that the intention to use nuclear weapons be credible. Whether this is a 'threat' contrary to Article 2, paragraph 4, depends upon whether the particular use of force envisaged would be directed against the territorial integrity or political independence of a State, or against the Purposes of the United Nations or whether, in the event that it were intended as a means of defence, it would necessarily violate the principles of necessity and proportionality. In any of these circumstances the use of force, and the threat to use it, would be unlawful under the law of the Charter . . .

Replies in the following manner to the question put by the General Assembly:

A. Unanimously,
    There is in neither customary nor conventional international law any specific authorization of the threat or use of nuclear weapons;
B. By eleven votes to three,
    There is in neither customary nor conventional international law any comprehensive and universal prohibition of the threat or use of nuclear weapons as such;
C. Unanimously,
    A threat or use of force by means of nuclear weapons that is contrary to Article 2, paragraph 4, of the United Nations Charter and that fails to meet all the requirements of Article 51, is unlawful;
D. Unanimously,
    A threat or use of nuclear weapons should also be compatible with the requirements of the international law applicable in armed conflict, particularly those of the principles and rules of international humanitarian law, as well as with specific obligations under treaties and other undertakings which expressly deal with nuclear weapons;
E. By seven votes to seven, by the President's casting vote,
    It follows from the above-mentioned requirements that the threat or use of nuclear weapons would generally be contrary to the rules of international law applicable in armed conflict, and in particular the principles and rules of humanitarian law;
    However, in view of the current state of international law, and of the elements of fact at its disposal, the Court cannot conclude definitively whether the threat or use of nuclear weapons would be lawful or unlawful in an extreme circumstance of self-defence, in which the very survival of a State would be at stake;
F. Unanimously,
    There exists an obligation to pursue in good faith and bring to a conclusion negotiations leading to nuclear disarmament in all its aspects under strict and effective international control.

VICE-PRESIDENT SCHWEBEL (Dissenting Opinion): The . . . first paragraph of Paragraph 2E of the holdings [above] is followed by the Court's ultimate, paramount – and sharply controverted – conclusion in the case, narrowly adopted by the President's casting vote . . . This is an astounding conclusion to be reached by the International Court of Justice. Despite the fact that its Statute 'forms an integral part' of the United Nations Charter, and despite the comprehensive and categorical terms of Article 2, paragraph 4, and Article 51 of that Charter, the Court concludes on the supreme issue of the threat or use of force of our age that it has no opinion. In 'an extreme circumstance of self-defence, in which the very survival of a State would be at stake', the Court finds that international law and hence the Court have nothing to say. After many months of agonizing appraisal of the law, the Court discovers that there is none. When it comes to the supreme interests of State, the Court discards the legal progress of the Twentieth Century, puts aside the provisions of the Charter of the United Nations of which it is 'the principal judicial organ', and proclaims, in terms redolent of *Realpolitik*, its ambivalence about the most important provisions of modern international law. If this was to be its ultimate holding, the Court would have done better to have drawn on its undoubted discretion not to render an Opinion at all.

JUDGE WEERAMANTRY (Dissenting Opinion): . . . Self-defence raises probably the most serious problems in this case. The second sentence in paragraph 2(E) of the dispositif states that, in the current state of international law and of the elements of fact at its disposal, the Court cannot conclude definitively whether the threat or use of nuclear weapons would be lawful or unlawful in an extreme circumstance of self-defence, in which the very survival of a state would be at stake. I have voted against this clause as I am of the view that the threat or use of nuclear weapons would not be lawful in any circumstances whatsoever, as it offends the fundamental principles of the ius in bello. This conclusion is clear and follows inexorably from well-established principles of international law.

If a nation is attacked, it is clearly entitled under the United Nations Charter to the right of self-defence. Once a nation thus enters into the domain of the ius in bello, the principles of humanitarian law apply to the conduct of self-defence, just as they apply to the conduct of any other aspect of military operations. We must hence examine what principles of the ius in bello apply to the use of nuclear weapons in self-defence.

The first point to be noted is that the use of force in self-defence (which is an undoubted right) is one thing and the use of nuclear weapons in self-defence is another. The permission granted by international law for the first does not embrace the second, which is subject to other governing principles as well.

All of the seven principles of humanitarian law discussed in this Opinion apply to the use of nuclear weapons in self-defence, just as they apply to their use in any aspect of war. Principles relating to unnecessary suffering, proportionality, discrimination, non-belligerent states, genocide, environmental damage and human rights would all be violated, no less in self-defence than in an open act of aggression. The ius in bello covers all use of force, whatever the reasons for resort to force. There can be no exceptions, without violating the essence of its principles . . .

It is necessary to reiterate here the undoubted right of the state that is attacked to use all the weaponry available to it for the purpose of repulsing the aggressor. Yet this principle holds only so long as such weapons do not violate the fundamental rules of warfare embodied in those rules. Within these constraints, and for the purpose of repulsing the enemy, the full military power of the state that is attacked can be unleashed upon the aggressor. While this is incontrovertible, one has yet to hear an argument in any forum or a contention in any academic literature, that a nation attacked, for example, with chemical or biological weapons is entitled to use chemical or biological weapons in self-defence, or to annihilate the aggressor's population. It is strange that the most devastating of all the weapons of mass destruction can be conceived of as offering a singular exception to this most obvious conclusion following from the bedrock principles of humanitarian law . . .

H. Charlesworth and C. Chinkin, *The Boundaries of International Law: A Feminist Perspective*
(2000), p. 260 *et seq.*

The principles of international law relating to armed conflict can be seen as resting on a series of dichotomies: international/internal; independence/dependence; intervention/non-intervention; order/anarchy; integrity/disintegration; self-defence/illegal use of force. These binary oppositions are coded in a gendered way, with the first term connected with 'male' characteristics and the second, 'female'. The international legal regime upholds the first set of concepts: for example article 2(4) of the UN Charter prohibits the unilateral use of force in international relations against the territorial integrity or political independence of any state.

The only UN Charter exception to this prohibition is article 51 which reiterates the 'inherent' right of states to individual and collective self-defence. The enormous literature on the legal doctrine of self-defence assumes that the use of force by states is inevitable and that legal doctrines need to be interpreted accordingly. The concept of self-defence is not defined in article 51 and customary international law criteria remain applicable. These require the use of force to be necessary, proportionate and reasonable, that there be no alternative course of action, nor time for deliberation. The ICJ clarified some aspects of self-defence under customary international law in the *Nicaragua* case, setting out two preconditions to the legitimate use of force in collective self-defence. First, the target state must have declared that it had been subject to an armed attack and second, it must have requested assistance from the state purporting to act in collective self-defence. The ICJ also considered the related customary international norm of non-intervention, holding that illegal intervention not amounting to an armed attack does not legitimate the use of armed force either in self-defence or as a form of counter-intervention.

As we discussed in chapter 5, the notion of the state and its attributes that is assumed in international law is a limited one. The emphasis on the integrity of territory in the law on the use of force mimics the idea of the individual, detached and separate from society, entitled to resist any unsolicited contact. The image of the autonomous (male) individual, on which the idea of statehood and the concern with sovereignty within territorial boundaries rests, makes the interests of the international community and of individuals appear of secondary importance to those of a single, threatened state. It also reinforces images of women as unbounded and unequal to men within the state.

The inadequacy of the international legal regime on the use of force is illustrated by the reaction to the invasion of Kuwait by Iraq in 1990. The invasion was quickly condemned by the international community. Kuwait's right to individual and collective self-defence in response to an armed attack was asserted and economic sanctions imposed to facilitate the removal of Iraqi forces from Kuwait. Without any assessment of the effectiveness of economic sanctions, the use of 'all necessary means' was shortly afterwards mandated by the Security Council to achieve this objective. Allied forces under American command subsequently defeated the Iraqi forces. The surrender of Iraqi President Saddam Hussein in accordance with the stringent terms of Security Council Resolution 687 signified the triumphant completion of this operation. The expulsion of Iraq from Kuwait in 1991 is regularly presented as a paradigm of the successful military operation of international law.

Much attention was given to the actions of Saddam Hussein after the military surrender in 1991, but little was given to those of the returned Kuwaiti government. The 'liberation' of Kuwait was accompanied by significant violations of women's rights. First, no Kuwaiti woman could be said to be 'liberated' in the narrow sense of formal participation in democratic rights as Kuwait continued to deny suffrage to women. Second, women were not freed from the fear and actuality of violence that accompanied the occupation. A rape epidemic was reported in Kuwait after 'liberation' at levels worse than during the Iraqi occupation. Particular victims were women migrant workers from Sri Lanka, the Philippines, Palestine and India raped by armed men in Kuwaiti army or police uniform. The attitude of these men was reportedly that the women 'deserved' their treatment for 'supporting' the Iraqis, or that the attackers could be excused some excesses because of their recent difficult time. Although there was no evidence of deliberate government policy, Kuwaiti government responsibility could be based upon its failure to protect civilians by investigating allegations and prosecuting accused persons, especially where rapes were committed by men in uniform. Instead a climate of impunity prevailed. Third, a large number of women domestic workers were unable to leave Kuwait and sought refuge in various embassies in Kuwait City in early 1992. In many cases their employers had taken their passports and refused to pay their fares home, effectively trapping them in a modern form of slavery. Although these women were effectively hostages, international law offered them no protection.

NOTES:

1. The debate between the restrictive and permissive schools of thought on the law of the use of force (see above) is carried over to the dispute about the scope of the right of self-defence. If self-defence is the only exception to the general prohibition on the use of force apart from collective security, its precise ambit is crucial. The permissive doctrine does not consider that self-defence is available only where an 'armed attack' occurs – either because Art. 51 was not intended to replace the customary law (*The Caroline Case*), or because Art. 51 preserves by its terms ('inherent') that customary law. The restrictive school sees Art. 51 as the single and narrowly interpreted exception to a wide-ranging prohibition on the use of force.

2. The three major issues concerning self-defence are: first, whether lawful self-defence is limited in time to responses to ongoing attacks, as opposed to past or anticipated attacks; second, whether force in self-defence may be used to respond to a non-forceful threat, such as economic aggression; and third, whether self-defence is lawful only when an attack is made on State territory, as opposed to State interests. The *Nicaragua Case* considers the second of these questions, particularly what kind of action amounts to an 'armed attack' so as to justify self-defence.

C: Self-defence and terrorist attacks

The law on self-defence – whatever its precise content – is designed principally to deal with State-on-State attacks. This was the experience of States at the time the Charter was drafted. Today States are subject to attack by non-State entities that may, or may not, have roots or links with established States. Indeed, the *Nicaragua Case* touches on some of these issues when discussing the role of the *contra* rebels and their military opponents. Of course, where the 'terrorist group' (or 'freedom fighters') is so closely linked with a State that their actions can be regarded as those of the State itself (see Chapter 11), then the traditional rules on self-defence are more obviously relevant. However, many groups have no direct connection to any particular State (or perhaps they are linked with many) and then the traditional formulation is harder to apply. Necessarily, these groups must have a base or organisation somewhere, but should this 'host' State be held accountable and so susceptible to military action in self-defence? Is it relevant that the 'host' State might be unwilling or unable to deal with the group? Alternatively, is military action against the group permitted as an exception to Art. 2(4) of the Charter, provided that it does not compromise the 'political independence or territorial integrity' of the host State?

These issues were brought sharply into focus by the atrocities committed in the United States on 11 September 2001. One response was the invasion of Afghanistan, the State 'hosting' the terrorist movement. The result was the removal of its governing authority (the Taliban).

S. Murphy (ed), 'Contemporary Practice of the United States Relating to International Law'
96 AJIL 236 (2002)

The United States regarded the September 11 incidents as comparable to a military attack. In the week following the attacks, President Bush declared a national emergency and called to active duty the reserves of the US armed forces. He also signed into law a joint resolution of Congress that, after noting that 'the President has authority under the Constitution to take action to deter and prevent acts of international terrorism against the United States,' provided in Section 2:

(a) IN GENERAL. That the President is authorized to use all necessary and appropriate force against those nations, organizations, or persons he determines planned, authorized, committed, or aided the terrorist attacks that occurred on September 11, 2001, or harbored such organizations or persons, in order to prevent any future acts of international terrorism against the United States by such nations, organizations or persons.

Further, in a speech to the Congress on September 20, President Bush declared: 'On September 11th, enemies of freedom committed an act of war against our country.' The President created an Office of Homeland Security, as well as a Homeland Security Council, charged with developing and coordinating the implementation of a comprehensive national strategy to secure the United States from terrorist threats of attacks. The potential for further attacks was confirmed when, in late September, European law enforcement authorities uncovered a fully developed plan to blow up the U.S. Embassy in Paris. Intelligence reports of possible further attacks deemed credible by U.S. authorities led the Federal Bureau of Investigation (FBI) on October 11 and 29 to issue global alerts that more terrorist attacks might be carried out against U.S. targets in the United States or abroad . . .

The reaction of the global community was largely supportive. At the United Nations, the Security Council unanimously adopted on September 12 a resolution condemning 'the horrifying terrorist attacks,' which the Council regarded, 'like any act of international terrorism, as a threat to international peace and security.' Further, on September 28, the Security Council unanimously adopted, under Chapter VII of the UN Charter, a U.S.-sponsored resolution that obligates all member states to deny financing, support, and safe haven to terrorists, that calls for expanded information-sharing among member states, and that establishes a Security Council committee for monitoring implementation of these measures on a continuous basis. While the two resolutions did not expressly authorize the use of force by the United States, they both affirmed – in the context of such incidents – the inherent right of individual and collective self-defense, as well as the need 'to combat by all means' the 'threats to international peace and security caused by terrorist acts.' By contrast, the General Assembly condemned the 'heinous acts of terrorism' but did not characterize those acts as 'attacks' or recognize a right to respond in self-defense. Instead, that body called for 'international cooperation to bring to justice the perpetrators, organizers and sponsors' of the incidents. The form of cooperation was not specified, but a variety of conventions are already in place that address cooperation among states in dealing with violent or terrorist offenses.

The North Atlantic Council of the North Atlantic Treaty Organization (NATO) decided on September 12 that, if it was determined that the incidents were directed from abroad against the United States, 'it shall be regarded as an action covered by Article 5 of the Washington Treaty, which states that an armed attack against one or more of the Allies in Europe or North America shall be considered an attack against them all.' On October 2, after being briefed on the known facts by the United States, the council determined that the facts were 'clear and compelling' and that 'the attack against the United States on 11 September was directed from abroad and shall therefore be regarded as an action covered by Article 5 of the Washington Treaty.'

Similarly, the Organization of American States meeting of ministers of foreign affairs resolved:

> That these terrorist attacks against the United States of America are attacks against all American states and that in accordance with all the relevant provisions of the Inter-American Treaty of Reciprocal Assistance (Rio Treaty) and the principal of continental solidarity, all States Parties to the Rio Treaty shall provide effective reciprocal assistance to address such attacks and the threat of any similar attacks against any American state, and to maintain the peace and security of the continent.

On October 7, the United States informed the UN Security Council that it had been the victim of 'massive and brutal attacks' and that it was exercising its right of self-defense in taking actions in Afghanistan against Al Qaeda terrorist-training camps and Taliban military installations.

> In accordance with Article 51 of the Charter of the United Nations. I wish, on behalf of my Government, to report that the United States of America, together with other States, has initiated actions in the exercise of its inherent right of individual and collective self-defence following the armed attacks that were carried out against the United States on 11 September 2001.

The attacks on 11 September 2001 and the ongoing threat to the United States and its nationals posed by the Al-Qaeda organization have been made possible by the decision of the Taliban regime to allow the parts of Afghanistan that it controls to be used by this organization as a base of operation. Despite every effort by the United States and the international community, the Taliban regime has refused to change its policy. From the territory of Afghanistan, the Al-Qaeda organization continues to train and support agents of terror who attack innocent people throughout the world and target United States nationals and interests in the United States and abroad.

In response to these attacks, and in accordance with the inherent right of individual and collective self-defence, United States armed forces have initiated actions designed to prevent and deter further attacks on the United States. These actions include measures against Al-Qaeda terrorist training camps and military installations of the Taliban regime in Afghanistan. In carrying out these actions, the United States is committed to minimizing civilian casualties and damage to civilian property. In addition, the United States will continue its humanitarian efforts to alleviate the suffering of the people of Afghanistan. We are providing them with food, medicine and supplies.

After the Security Council met for two hours to hear the U.S. and UK justifications for acting in self-defense, the President of the Security Council (Ireland's UN ambassador, John Ryan) stated that the unanimity of support expressed in the Security Council's two prior resolutions 'is absolutely maintained.'

On the same day as the above proceedings in the Security Council, the United States and the United Kingdom launched attacks against Al Qaeda and Taliban targets in Afghanistan (twenty-six days after the September 11 incidents).

Security Council Resolution 1368 (2001)
12 September 2001

The Security Council,

Reaffirming the principles and purposes of the Charter of the United Nations,

Determined to combat by all means threats to international peace and security caused by terrorist acts,

Recognizing the inherent right of individual or collective self-defence in accordance with the Charter,

1. *Unequivocally condemns* in the strongest terms the horrifying terrorist attacks which took place on 11 September 2001 in New York, Washington, DC and Pennsylvania and *regards* such acts, like any act of international terrorism, as a threat to international peace and security;

2. *Expresses* its deepest sympathy and condolences to the victims and their families and to the people and Government of the United States of America;

3. *Calls* on all States to work together urgently to bring to justice the perpetrators, organizers and sponsors of these terrorist attacks and *stresses* that those responsible for aiding, supporting or harbouring the perpetrators, organizers and sponsors of these acts will be held accountable;

4. *Calls also* on the international community to redouble their efforts to prevent and suppress terrorist acts including by increased cooperation and full implementation of the relevant international anti-terrorist conventions and Security Council resolutions, in particular resolution 1269 (1999) of 19 October 1999;

5. *Expresses* its readiness to take all necessary steps to respond to the terrorist attacks of 11

September 2001, and to combat all forms of terrorism, in accordance with its responsibilities under the Charter of the United Nations;

    6. *Decides* to remain seized of the matter.

Security Council Resolution 1373 (2001)
28 September 2001

The Security Council,

    Reaffirming the inherent right of individual or collective self-defence as recognized by the Charter of the United Nations as reiterated in resolution 1368 (2001),

    Reaffirming the need to combat by all means, in accordance with the Charter of the United Nations, threats to international peace and security caused by terrorist acts,

    Recognizing the need for States to complement international cooperation by taking additional measures to prevent and suppress, in their territories through all lawful means, the financing and preparation of any acts of terrorism,

    Reaffirming the principle established by the General Assembly in its declaration of October 1970 (resolution 2625 (XXV)) and reiterated by the Security Council in its resolution 1189 (1998) of 13 August 1998, namely that every State has the duty to refrain from organizing, instigating, assisting or participating in terrorist acts in another State or acquiescing in organized activities within its territory directed towards the commission of such acts,

    Acting under Chapter VII of the Charter of the United Nations,

    1. *Decides* that all States shall:

        (a) Prevent and suppress the financing of terrorist acts;

        (b) Criminalize the wilful provision or collection, by any means, directly or indirectly, of funds by their nationals or in their territories with the intention that the funds should be used, or in the knowledge that they are to be used, in order to carry out terrorist acts;

        (c) Freeze without delay funds and other financial assets or economic resources of persons who commit, or attempt to commit, terrorist acts or participate in or facilitate the commission of terrorist acts; of entities owned or controlled directly or indirectly by such persons; and of persons and entities acting on behalf of, or at the direction of such persons and entities, including funds derived or generated from property owned or controlled directly or indirectly by such persons and associated persons and entities;

        (d) Prohibit their nationals or any persons and entities within their territories from making any funds, financial assets or economic resources or financial or other related services available, directly or indirectly, for the benefit of persons who commit or attempt to commit or facilitate or participate in the commission of terrorist acts, of entities owned or controlled, directly or indirectly, by such persons and of persons and entities acting on behalf of or at the direction of such persons;

    2. *Decides also* that all States shall:

        (a) Refrain from providing any form of support, active or passive, to entities or persons involved in terrorist acts, including by suppressing recruitment of members of terrorist groups and eliminating the supply of weapons to terrorists;

        (b) Take the necessary steps to prevent the commission of terrorist acts, including by provision of early warning to other States by exchange of information;

        (c) Deny safe haven to those who finance, plan, support, or commit terrorist acts, or provide safe havens;

        (d) Prevent those who finance, plan, facilitate or commit terrorist acts from using their respective territories for those purposes against other States or their citizens;

(e) Ensure that any person who participates in the financing, planning, preparation or perpetration of terrorist acts or in supporting terrorist acts is brought to justice and ensure that, in addition to any other measures against them, such terrorist acts are established as serious criminal offences in domestic laws and regulations and that the punishment duly reflects the seriousness of such terrorist acts;

(f) Afford one another the greatest measure of assistance in connection with criminal investigations or criminal proceedings relating to the financing or support of terrorist acts, including assistance in obtaining evidence in their possession necessary for the proceedings;

(g) Prevent the movement of terrorists or terrorist groups by effective border controls and controls on issuance of identity papers and travel documents, and through measures for preventing counterfeiting, forgery or fraudulent use of identity papers and travel documents;

3. *Calls* upon all States to:

(a) Find ways of intensifying and accelerating the exchange of operational information, especially regarding actions or movements of terrorist persons or networks; forged or falsified travel documents; traffic in arms, explosives or sensitive materials; use of communications technologies by terrorist groups; and the threat posed by the possession of weapons of mass destruction by terrorist groups;

(b) Exchange information in accordance with international and domestic law and cooperate on administrative and judicial matters to prevent the commission of terrorist acts;

(c) Cooperate, particularly through bilateral and multilateral arrangements and agreements, to prevent and suppress terrorist attacks and take action against perpetrators of such acts;

(d) Become parties as soon as possible to the relevant international conventions and protocols relating to terrorism, including the International Convention for the Suppression of the Financing of Terrorism of 9 December 1999;

(e) Increase cooperation and fully implement the relevant international conventions and protocols relating to terrorism and Security Council resolutions 1269 (1999) and 1368 (2001);

(f) Take appropriate measures in conformity with the relevant provisions of national and international law, including international standards of human rights, before granting refugee status, for the purpose of ensuring that the asylum-seeker has not planned, facilitated or participated in the commission of terrorist acts;

(g) Ensure, in conformity with international law, that refugee status is not abused by the perpetrators, organizers or facilitators of terrorist acts, and that claims of political motivation are not recognized as grounds for refusing requests for the extradition of alleged terrorists;

4. *Notes* with concern the close connection between international terrorism and transnational organized crime, illicit drugs, money-laundering, illegal arms-trafficking, and illegal movement of nuclear, chemical, biological and other potentially deadly materials, and in this regard *emphasizes* the need to enhance coordination of efforts on national, subregional, regional and international levels in order to strengthen a global response to this serious challenge and threat to international security;

5. *Declares* that acts, methods, and practices of terrorism are contrary to the purposes and principles of the United Nations and that knowingly financing, planning and inciting terrorist acts are also contrary to the purposes and principles of the United Nations;

6. *Decides* to establish, in accordance with rule 28 of its provisional rules of procedure, a Committee of the Security Council, consisting of all the members of the Council, to monitor

implementation of this resolution, with the assistance of appropriate expertise, and *calls upon* all States to report to the Committee, no later than 90 days from the date of adoption of this resolution and thereafter according to a timetable to be proposed by the Committee, on the steps they have taken to implement this resolution;

  7.   *Directs* the Committee to delineate its tasks, submit a work programme within 30 days of the adoption of this resolution, and to consider the support it requires, in consultation with the Secretary-General;

  8.   *Expresses* its determination to take all necessary steps in order to ensure the full implementation of this resolution, in accordance with its responsibilities under the Charter;

  9.   *Decides* to remain seized of this matter.

NOTES:
1. At no time has the Security Council authorised the use of force against Afghanistan. However, neither the Security Council nor the General Assembly has criticised or condemned the US and its allies for their military action. As the extract from *Contemporary Practice of the United States* makes clear, it is claimed as a legitimate act of self-defence. Few have publicly taken issue with this and it may be that the international community has accepted that *anticipatory* self-defence (i.e. fear or likelihood of future terrorist attacks) can be lawful. Alternatively, perhaps self-defence *after* an armed attack is permissible if it is both punitive in aim and deterrent in effect?
2. SC Resolution 1373 is a collective enforcement resolution under Chapter VII of the Charter (on which generally see below). It is noteworthy that it requires States to impose a number of sanctions against *terrorism* and terrorist *groups* without actually naming any State. This is the first time that a Chapter VII enforcement resolution has been expressed in such general terms without being directed at a specific State or localised situation.
3. In SC Resolution 1378 (2001) of 14 November 2001, the Council condemns the Taliban 'for allowing Afghanistan' to be used as a terrorist base and expressly welcomes the attempts by the Afghan people to establish a new administration. Does the resolution by overtly supporting the destruction of the government of a member State thereby tacitly endorse the US action in overthrowing that regime?
4. While there are few who cannot understand the motives for the US action, questions do remain about its legitimacy. Questions which may, of course, be answered by the employment of a wide concept of self-defence. The Security Council's apparent willingness to condone (without authorising) the action and its acceptance of the demise of the Taliban government of Afghanistan is unusual and may set an unfortunate precedent.

D: Collective self-defence

Military and Paramilitary Activities in and against Nicaragua Case (*Nicaragua* v *USA*)
ICJ Rep 1986 14, International Court of Justice

  196. The question remains whether the lawfulness of the use of collective self-defence by the third State for the benefit of the attacked State also depends on a request addressed by that State to the third State . . .

  199. At all events, the Court finds that in customary international law, whether of a general kind or that particular to the inter-American legal system, there is no rule permitting the exercise of collective self-defence in the absence of a request by the State which regards itself as the victim of an armed attack. The Court concludes that the requirement of a request by the State which is the victim of the alleged attack is additional to the requirement that such a State should have declared itself to have been attacked.

200. At this point, the Court may consider whether in customary international law there is any requirement corresponding to that found in the treaty law of the United Nations Charter, by which the State claiming to use the right of individual or collective self-defence must report to an international body, empowered to determine the conformity with international law of the measures which the State is seeking to justify on that basis. . . . As the Court has observed above (paragraphs 178 and 188), a principle enshrined in a treaty, if reflected in customary international law, may well be so unencumbered with the conditions and modalities surrounding it in the treaty. Whatever influence the Charter may have had on customary international law in these matters, it is clear that in customary international law it is not a condition of the lawfulness of the use of force in self-defence that a procedure so closely dependent on the content of a treaty commitment and of the institutions established by it, should have been followed. On the other hand, if self-defence is advanced as a justification for measures which would otherwise be in breach both of the principle of customary international law and of that contained in the Charter, it is to be expected that the conditions of the Charter should be respected. Thus for the purpose of enquiry into the customary law position, the absence of a report may be one of the factors indicating whether the State in question was itself convinced that it was acting in self-defence.

JUDGE JENNINGS (Dissenting Opinion): Another matter which seems to call for brief comment, is the treatment of collective self-defence by the Court. The passages beginning with paragraph 196 seem to take a somewhat formalistic view of the conditions for the exercise of collective self-defence. Obviously the notion of collective self-defence is open to abuse and it is necessary to ensure that it is not employable as a mere cover for aggression disguised as protection, and the Court is therefore right to define it somewhat strictly. Even so, it may be doubted whether it is helpful to suggest that the attacked State must in some more or less formal way have 'declared' itself the victim of an attack and then have, as an additional 'requirement', made a formal request to a particular third State for assistance. . . . It may readily be agreed that the victim State must both be in real need of assistance and must want it and that the fulfilment of both these conditions must be shown. But to ask that these requirements take the form of some sort of formal declaration and request might sometimes be unrealistic.

   But there is another objection to this way of looking at collective self-defence. It seems to be based almost upon an idea of vicarious defence by champions: that a third State may lawfully come to the aid of an authenticated victim of armed attack provided that the requirements of a declaration of attack and a request for assistance are complied with. But whatever collective self-defence means, it does not mean vicarious defence; for that way the notion is indeed open to abuse. The assisting State is not an authorized champion, permitted under certain conditions to go to the aid of a favoured State. The assisting State surely must, by going to the victim State's assistance, be also, and in *addition* to other requirements, in some measure defending itself. There should even in 'collective self-defence' be some real element of self involved with the notion of defence. . . . (It may be objected that the very term 'self-defence' is a common law notion, and that, for instance, the French equivalent of 'légitime défense' does not mention 'self'. Here, however, the French version is for once, merely unhelpful; it does no more than beg the question of what is 'légitime'.).

NOTE:

The issue here is whether collective self-defence is the joint exercise of individual rights (Jennings), or whether it is the exercise of a right by one or more States on behalf of the 'attacked' State (the Court). For example, after the invasion of Kuwait and the threat to Saudi Arabia, did the coalition deploy forces because it was also threatened in a way that gave *it* a right of self-defence, or did the coalition respond to assist Kuwait and Saudi Arabia in the exercise of their rights of self-defence?

E: The right to protect nationals

M. Akehurst, 'The Use of Force to Protect Nationals Abroad'
5 *Int Relations* 3 (1976/77)

[A] broad interpretation of Article 2(4) [i.e., that it prohibits all use of force] does not necessarily mean that the use of force to protect nationals abroad is illegal, because Article 51, one of the exceptions to the ban on the use of force laid down in Article 2(4), permits members of the United Nations to use force in self-defence, and it could be argued that the use of force to protect nationals abroad is a form of self-defence. . . . Even a narrow interpretation of Article 51, which would allow States to use force in self-defence only after an armed attack has occurred, would not necessarily be fatal to the view that it is lawful to use force to protect nationals abroad, because it could be argued that an armed attack on nationals abroad is equivalent to an armed attack on the State itself, since population is an essential ingredient of Statehood. However, most of the authors who adopt a narrow interpretation of Article 51 do not consider that it is lawful to use force to protect nationals abroad; they believe that force may be used in defence of a State's nationals only when they are present on the national State's territory . . .

It is further submitted that even the use of force for the protection of nationals abroad is contrary to the United Nations Charter. Virtually every example of the use of force for this purpose since 1945 has provoked protests from other States that such use of force is illegal. Admittedly some writers argue that the use of force for this purpose is permitted by Article 51 of the Charter, but that is not the only way in which Article 51 can be interpreted. Indeed, there are cogent reasons for interpreting Article 51 restrictively, so as to exclude the use of force in Article 51 is an exception to the prohibition of the use of force in Article 2(4), and it is a general principle of interpretation that exceptions to a general rule should be narrowly interpreted in order not to undermine the general rule. Moreover, to equate an attack on nationals abroad with an attack on the national State, as some writers do, is fallacious. Nationals cannot be identified with the national State for all purposes; for instance, a State possesses sovereign immunity in foreign courts, but its nationals do not.

NOTE:
The right to protect nationals can be justified on two grounds: either it is an aspect of self-defence, so that an attack on nationals intended to equate with an attack on the State itself, or it is a right exempt from Art. 2(4) because it is not (and does not compromise) 'territorial integrity or political independence'. An example of an allegedly lawful rescue of nationals was the Israeli operation at Entebbe airport, Uganda in 1976. The justification was advanced (though not widely accepted) by the United States in respect of its invasion of Panama in 1989: see 84 AJIL (1990) 494 for a critical appraisal.

F: Humanitarian intervention

Kosovo is part of the Republic of Serbia, itself part of the Federal Republic of Yugoslavia. From early 1998 onwards, Serbian forces were engaged in widespread and verifiable human rights abuses directed against the ethnic Kosovars. The Kosovo Liberation Army were engaged in an armed struggle against the Serbian forces. The result, in January–March 1999, was the displacement of over 300,000 people. Attempts at a diplomatic solution either failed or were not pursued fully. On 24 March 1999, NATO began military operations against Serbian forces, both in Kosovo and in greater Yugoslavia. These ceased formally on 20 June 1999.

Transcript of Press Conference by the UK Secretary of State for Defence, George Robertson, London, Thursday 25 March 1999

Last night the Air Forces of Belgium, Canada, Denmark, France, Germany, Italy, the Netherlands, Norway, Portugal, Spain, Turkey and the United Kingdom and the United States were all involved in the allied military action. We are in no doubt that NATO is acting within international law and our legal justification rests upon the accepted principle that force may be used in extreme circumstances to avert a humanitarian catastrophe. NATO's action has received support inside the UN Security Council from the United States, France, Argentina, Slovenia, Malaysia, Gambia, Bahrain, the Netherlands and Gabon. Outside of Russia and China, only Namibia disagreed with the military action in the Security Council, and in the wider United Nations we know of only opposition from India and understandably Belarus and the Former Republic of Yugoslavia itself.

We believe that military action is clearly justified in the circumstances of Kosovo given the undisputed humanitarian emergency and the rejection by Milosevic [President of Yugoslavia] of all diplomatic efforts.

I. Brownlie and C. Apperley, 'Kosovo Crisis Inquiry: Memorandum on the International Law Aspects'
49 ICLQ 878 (2000) pp. 886–894

(c) *The Legal Status of Humanitarian Intervention*

41. There is no sufficient evidence of the existence of a legal right of States, whether acting individually or jointly, to use force for humanitarian purposes. The alleged right is not compatible with the United Nations Charter. Thus it is not surprising that the sources of international law covering a period of 40 years fail to provide any substantial support for the legality of humanitarian intervention.

42. The relevant authorities will be reviewed in chronological order. Whilst the survey of opinion is not exhaustive, it is nonetheless fairly extensive and clearly represents the majority view.

43. Brownlie, *International Law and the Use of Force by States*, Oxford, 1963, pp. 338–342. The writer's conclusion is as follows:

> It must be admitted that humanitarian intervention has not been *expressly* condemned by either the League Covenant, the Kellogg-Briand Pact, or the United Nations Charter. Indeed, such intervention would not constitute resort to force as an instrument of national policy. It is necessary nevertheless to have regard to the general effect and the underlying assumptions of the juridical developments of the period since 1920. In particular it is extremely doubtful if this form of intervention has survived the express condemnations of intervention which have occurred in recent times or the general prohibition of resort to force to be found in the United Nations Charter.

44. Professor Schwebel, *Hague Academy Lectures* (1972).

In his substantial review of the subjects of aggression and intervention Professor Schwebel does not make a single reference to humanitarian intervention.

48. Jimenez de Arechaga, *Recueil des Cours*, Hague Academy, Vol. I (1978), pp. 86–116.

This detailed survey of the legal regime relating to the use of force by States clearly excludes the legality of humanitarian intervention. Professor Jimenez de Arechaga is a distinguished representative of Latin-American expertise and was President of the International Court of Justice, 1976–9, having served on the Court since 1970.

50. Professor Schachter, *Michigan Law Review*, Vol. 82 (1984), pp. 1620–1646 at p. 1629.

In 1984 Professor Oscar Schachter expressed the following opinion:

Nonetheless, governments by and large (and most jurists) would not assert a right to forcible intervention to protect the nationals of another country from the atrocities carried out in that country. An exception was the intervention of Indian troops to protect Bengalis in East Pakistan during the 1971 civil war in Pakistan. India's ethnic links and the refugee influx into its own territory, as well as hostility toward Pakistan, were factors influencing its military intervention. It is interesting that despite considerable sympathy for the oppressed Bengalis, a large number of the UN General Assembly called on India to withdraw its forces.

The reluctance of governments to legitimize foreign invasion in the interest of humanitarianism is understandable in the light of past abuses by powerful states. States strong enough to intervene and sufficiently interested in doing so tend to have political motives. They have a strong temptation to impose a political solution in their own national interest. Most governments are acutely sensitive to this danger and show no disposition to open article 2(4) up to a broad exception for humanitarian intervention by means of armed force.

52. British Foreign Office (Foreign Policy Document No.148): *British Year Book of Int.Law*, Vol. 57 (1986)

The key passage reads thus:

II.22. In fact, the best case that can be made in support of humanitarian intervention is that it cannot be said to be unambiguously illegal. To make that case, it is necessary to demonstrate, in particular by reference to Article 1(3) of the UN Charter, which includes the promotion and encouragement of respect for human rights as one of the Purposes of the United Nations, that paragraphs 7 and 4 of Article 2 do not apply in cases of flagrant violations of human rights. But the overwhelming majority of contemporary legal opinion comes down against the existence of a right of humanitarian intervention, for three main reasons: first, the UN Charter and the corpus of modern international law do not seem specifically to incorporate such a right; secondly, state practice in the past two centuries, and especially since 1945, at best provides only a handful of genuine cases of humanitarian intervention, and, on most assessments, none at all; and finally, on prudential grounds, that the scope of abusing such a right argues strongly against its creation. As Akehurst argues, 'claims by some states that they are entitled to use force to prevent violations of human rights may make other states reluctant to accept legal obligations concerning human rights'. In essence, therefore, the case against making humanitarian intervention an exception to the principle of non-intervention is that its doubtful benefits would be heavily outweighed by its costs in terms of respect for international law. (footnote omitted) (p. 614 at p. 619)

64. Professor Bruno Simma, writing in the *European Journal of International Law*, Vol.10 (1999), pp. 1–22, regards the use of force for humanitarian purposes as incompatible with the U.N. Charter in the absence of the authorisation of the Security Council. Professor Simma reaches the following conclusions:

This article has attempted to demonstrate that, while the threat of armed force employed by NATO against the FRY in the Kosovo crisis since the fall of 1998 is illegal due to the lack of a Security Council authorization, the Alliance made every effort to get as close to legality as possible by, first, following the thrust of, and linking its efforts to, the Council resolutions which did exist and second, characterizing its action as an urgent measure to avert even greater humanitarian catastrophes in Kosovo, taken in a state of humanitarian necessity.

The lesson which can be drawn from this is that unfortunately there do occur 'hard cases' in which terrible dilemm as must be faced and imperative political and moral considerations may appear to leave no choice but to act outside the law. The more isolated these instances remain, the smaller will be their potential to erode the precepts of international law, in our case the UN Charter. As mentioned earlier, a potential boomerang effect of such breaches can never be excluded, but this danger can at least be reduced by indicating the concrete circumstances that led to a decision *ad hoc* being destined to remain singular. In this regard, NATO has done a rather convincing job.

In the present author's view, only a thin red line separates NATO's action on Kosovo from international legality. But should the Alliance now set out to include breaches of the UN Charter as a regular part of its strategic programme for the future, this would have an immeasurably more destructive impact on the universal system of collective security embodied in the Charter. To resort to illegality as an explicit *ultima ratio* for reasons as convincing as those put forward in the Kosovo case is one thing. To turn such an exception into a general policy is quite another. If we agree that the NATO Treaty does have a hard legal core which even the most dynamic and innovative (re-) interpretation cannot erode, it is NATO's subordination to the principles of the United Nations Charter (at p. 22).

(d) *Conclusion on the Sources of International Law*

66. The works quoted above represent the considered opinion on the issue of 18 authorities. Only those writers with recognised professional standing have been included. They represent 12 nationalities. Three authors (Schwebel, Jimenez de Arechaga and Ruda) have been President of the International Court of Justice.

67. Only a minority among international lawyers have adopted the view that humanitarian intervention is lawful. The leading authorities may be cited as the more senior members of this minority. Professor Thomas Franck has expressed the following carefully conditional opinion on the subject:

Again, pragmatic escape from the conundrum posed in a 'hard case' requires application of a rule of reasonableness. The strict application of Article 51 is reasonable, in almost all cases. An exception may be made, however, where effective government has ceased to exist in the place where the danger to lives has arisen. In that event, however, other normative practice also becomes relevant. A modern customary law of humanitarian intervention is beginning to take form which may condone action to protect lives, providing it is short and results in fewer casualties than would have resulted from non-intervention. This practice does not distinguish between rescuing persons who are citizens of the intervening State, other aliens, or citizens of the State in which the intervention occurs. A State which purports to intervene to prevent danger to its own citizens but ignores the needs of others would be in violation of the new customary norm which it seeks to invoke. Moreover, as with 'anticipatory self-defence', the State which acts in violation of the general prohibition on intervention has the onus of demonstrating the existence of a genuine, immediate and dire emergency which could not be redressed by means less violative of the law. The emerging normative practice also requires an exhaustion of the multilateral remedies established by the Charter system.

68. Judge Rosalyn Higgins has produced an extended examination of the issues, which deserves to be quoted in full:

Under contemporary international law, may a State militarily intervene in another territory to rescue citizens under threat? Under customary international law, such activity was widely tolerated. But is it still allowed under the Charter? Let us examine the legal and policy issues.

Even minor military incursions are unlawful uses of force. It is quite clear, from the practice under the Charter and otherwise, that the Charter law does not simply prohibit major clashes between entire armies, while allowing smaller scale military interventions.

Attacks by single planes, for example, are as much a violation of Article 2(4) as would be an attack by a squadron. And it is not really feasible to engage in a rescue operation of threatened nationals without engaging in some use of force, which is prohibited by the terms of Article 2(4).

But does that dispose of the matter? There are several reasons for thinking that it does not. First, what Article 2(4) prohibits is the use of force against the territorial integrity or political independence of a State, or in any other manner inconsistent with the purposes of the United Nations. It can easily be seen that even a single plane attacking a country is a use of force against its territorial integrity. But is the answer so clear when the military intervention is not an attack on the State as such, but an operation simply designed to be able to rescue and remove one's threatened citizens? Is that really a use of force against the territorial integrity of a State or is it not rather a violation of sovereignty – in the same way as a civilian aircraft which enters airspace without permission will surely be violating sovereignty – but still not attacking the State or its territorial integrity? It would seem that hostile intent, coupled with military activity against the State (and beyond the minimum needed for the rescue), is what would distinguish a violation of sovereignty from an attack upon a State's territorial integrity.

If we can satisfy ourselves that humanitarian intervention does not violate the prohibition against the use of force against a State's territorial integrity, then we can feel fairly confident that no other prohibition in Article 2(4) is being violated. A military action to end a hijacking, for example, would not be force against a State's political independence (unless it was intended to overthrow the Government), and nor would it seem to be contrary to the purposes of the Charter, being directed towards the preservation of human life.

There is a different way of looking at the whole question – instead of looking to see whether a humanitarian intervention violates Article 2(4), looking instead at the permitted use of force under Article 51. That approach focuses rather on self-defence, and brings us back to the question of harm to one's nationals and self-defence. It is very similar to, but not quite the same as, the question we asked ourselves before. Instead of saying: 'Is an attack on a foreign citizen an attack on the State, which therefore entitles self-defence?' the question is the simpler one of whether a State can claim that military action to rescue one's citizens is an exercise of self-defence. Again, cautious support has sometimes been offered for this view. Professor Sir Humphrey Waldock (later Judge Waldock), giving his General Course in 1952, said that a State could use force to rescue nationals 'as an aspect of self-defence', if the threat of injury was imminent, if there was a failure or inability on the part of the territorial sovereign to protect them, and if the measures of protection were strictly confined to the object of protecting them. These criteria would all seem to have been met in the Entebbe situation. There an Israeli civilian airliner was hijacked to Entebbe; the then President, Adi Amin, far from endeavouring to negotiate the safe release of the passengers, provided further arms for the hijackers and ominously separated the Jewish from the non-Jewish passengers. The dangers seemed extremely imminent and the rescue operation was directed only to procuring the safety of the passengers.

The following may be noted: a claim of humanitarian intervention based on self-defence could only be advanced in respect of nationals, because it is predicated on the argument that the State is being harmed through injury to its nationals, and can therefore respond in self-defence. But a claim of humanitarian intervention based on the argument that no violation of Article 2(4) is entailed, would not logically be limited to the protection of one's own nationals. Either Article 2(4) is or is not violated by such activity – but nothing turns upon whether those being rescued are nationals or not.

The general question has yet to be judicially determined, though it did arise in an incidental way in the *Tehran Hostages* case before the International Court of Justice, 1980. The Court was seised of an application by the United States to deal with the merits of that issue – namely, whether the State of Iran was in violation of the Vienna Convention on Diplomatic Relations 1961 or international law more generally, by any attributability to it of the acts of those who had taken United States diplomats in Tehran hostage. The matter had already been, for several months, the subject of attempts at resolution elsewhere – there had been Security Council resolutions, a United Nations fact-finding commission set up, and an Order of the Court calling for the release of the hostages. No progress had been made. While the merits of the case were before the Court the United States engaged upon an ill-fated military attempt at rescuing the hostages. If one takes the Waldock tests, one question immediately presented itself; whether the hostages were in immediate danger of injury or harm (over and above the harm already occasioned by their very detention). The Court carefully did not pronounce upon the lawfulness or not of the United States action, but in some carefully chosen phrases indicated that it thought it inappropriate for the action to have been mounted while the matter was before the Court.

Many writers do argue against the lawfulness of humanitarian intervention today. They make much of the fact that in the past the right has been abused. It undoubtedly has. But then so have there been countless abusive claims of the right to self-defence. That does not lead us to say that there should be no right of self-defence today. We must face the reality that we live in a decentralized international legal order, where claims may be made either in good faith or abusively. We delude ourselves if we think that the role of norms is to remove the possibility of abusive claims ever being made. The role of norms is the achievement of values for the common good. Whether a claim invoking any given norm is made in good faith or abusively will always require contextual analysis by appropriate decision-makers – by the Security Council, by the International Court, by various international bodies. We can think of recent invocations of the right of humanitarian intervention – ranging from the Belgian and French interventions in Stanleyville in 1963, to the United States intervention in Grenada in 1987, to the Israeli intervention in Entebbe in 1976. We are all capable of deciding, on the facts at our disposal, in which of these foreigners were really at imminent risk, which interventions were bona fide for reasons of humanitarian necessity, and which were not. Nor am I persuaded by another, related argument sometimes advanced – that humanitarian intervention should be regarded as impermissible, because, in the international legal system, there is no compulsory reference to impartial decision-makers, and States finish up judges in their own cause. There are a variety of important decision-makers, other than courts, who can pronounce on the validity of claims advanced; and claims which may in very restricted exceptional circumstances be regarded as lawful should not *a priori* be disallowed because on occasion they may be unjustly invoked.

72. The proponents of humanitarian intervention are distinctly in a minority. More significant, however, is the position in customary international law, which depends upon the practice of States based upon *opinio juris*, that is to say, a belief that the action is in accordance with international law. There can be no doubt that the United Nations Charter can be modified by the congruent practice of the Member States crystallising as a new principle of customary law. But there is a burden of proof upon proponents of a change in the customary law. The central point is the absence of evidence of a change of view by a majority of States. The assertions of legality made by the British and other Governments in relation to the military operations against Yugoslavia were unaccompanied by any particulars of supporting State practice.

73. The experts who support the legality of humanitarian intervention do not provide even incipiently convincing evidence of State practice in support. Professor Franck refers to the customary law 'beginning to take form' (in 1993). Judge Higgins refers to three episodes. The first is the Belgian and French interventions in Stanleyville in 1963. The difficulty with this episode is that the Government in Zaire gave its consent. The second episode invoked is the United States' intervention in Grenada in 1983. This is an odd precedent. Various States, including Canada, had nationals on the island but they were not consulted. The reasons publicly advanced by the United Kingdom Government in relation to Grenada did not include a reference to humanitarian intervention. The Entebbe rescue operation of 1976 is rarely invoked as a precedent. Professor Dinstein places it within the category of self-defence. The attitude of States generally, as revealed in the Security Council debate at the time, either took the form of criticism on legal grounds or, in some cases, a waiver of the illegality.

74. In conclusion, there is very little evidence to support assertions that a new principle of customary law legitimating humanitarian intervention has crystallised.

C. Greenwood, 'International Law and the NATO Intervention in Kosovo Memorandum submitted to the Foreign Affairs Committee of the House of Commons'
49 ICLQ 926, pp. 929–934

To determine whether this case holds good in international law involves the consideration of two questions:

- (a) Does international law recognise a right of humanitarian intervention in cases of overwhelming humanitarian necessity? and
- (b) If so, were the circumstances in Kosovo as at 24 March 1999 such that this right became applicable?

In my opinion, the answer to both questions is 'yes'.

3 Does international law recognise a right of humanitarian intervention in cases of overwhelming humanitarian necessity?
It has been argued that, because the United Nations Charter contains a prohibition of the use of force and no express exception for humanitarian intervention, there can be no question of international law recognising a right of humanitarian intervention. That is, however, to take too rigid a view of international law.

This approach ignores the fact that international law in general and the United Nations Charter in particular do not rest exclusively on the principles of non-intervention and respect for the sovereignty of the State. The values on which the international legal system rests also include respect for human rights and 'the dignity and worth of the human person'. Upholding those rights is one of the purposes of the United Nations and of international law. While nobody would suggest that intervention is justified whenever a State violates human rights, international law does not require that respect for the sovereignty and integrity of a State must in all cases be given priority over the protection of human rights and human life, no matter how serious the violations of those rights perpetrated by that State.

Moreover, international law is not confined to treaty texts. It includes customary international law. That law is not static but develops through a process of State practice, of actions and the reaction to those actions. Since 1945, that process has seen a growing importance attached to the preservation of human rights. Where the threat to human rights has been of an extreme character, States have been prepared to assert a right of humanitarian intervention as a matter of last resort. Two instances are particularly important. First, in the summer of 1990 the Economic Community of West African States (ECOWAS) intervened in Liberia in an attempt to put a stop to appalling violations of human rights occurring in the civil war there. That action was not mandated by the Security Council but more than two years later the Council formally gave support to it. The ECOWAS action met with little or no international opposition.

Secondly, in April 1991, the United Kingdom, United States of America and a number of other States intervened in northern Iraq to create 'safe havens' to enable the large numbers of refugees and displaced persons to return home in safety. While the Security Council had earlier condemned the Iraqi repression of the civilian population as a threat to international peace and security in SCR 688 (1991), that resolution was not legally binding and did not authorise military action. In 1992 a no-fly zone was imposed in southern Iraq to protect the civilian population there. The United Kingdom Government defended these actions as the exercise of an exceptional right to intervene on humanitarian grounds. These actions received widespread international support. Moreover, with the exception of Iraq, very few States challenged the assertion of a right of humanitarian intervention in this case.

It has frequently been objected that there is no consensus about the existence of a right of humanitarian intervention or the conditions in which such a right exists. This objection has some force in that there is undoubtedly controversy about the existence of a right of humanitarian intervention, as reaction to NATO's action in Kosovo has demonstrated. Nevertheless, it is not a persuasive objection. International law does not require unanimity amongst States, let alone amongst writers, and there is controversy about many principles of international law. There has always been, for example, considerable debate over whether the right of self-defence extends to pre-emptive action in the face of an imminent armed attack or permits military action by a State only once it has actually been subjected to attack. Yet the practice of a majority of States (including the United Kingdom) and considerations of common sense strongly suggest that a limited right of anticipatory self-defence exists. In the case of humanitarian intervention, the logic of the principles on which international law is based and the preponderance of modern practice strongly favours the view that such a right is part of contemporary international law. It is noticeable that many of the expressions of opinion hostile to the existence of a right of humanitarian intervention pre-date the important practice of the 1990s, such as the Liberian and Iraqi interventions, or are based upon extreme interpretations of what might constitute humanitarian intervention. In practice, States have asserted a right of humanitarian intervention only in the extreme circumstances outlined in the previous paragraph.

A second objection often raised to humanitarian intervention is that it would be open to abuse. This is, of course, a policy objection, rather than a reason for asserting that there is no right of humanitarian intervention in existing law. Moreover, it is not persuasive. All rights are capable of being abused. The right of self-defence has undoubtedly been the subject of abuse but it is never seriously suggested that international law should not include the right of a State to defend itself. The fact that a State may make an unfounded claim to intervene in a bad case is not a sufficient reason for denying all States the right of intervention in cases where the objective conditions for intervention are met.

In my opinion modern customary international law does not exclude all possibility of military intervention on humanitarian grounds by States, or by an organisation like NATO. It does, however, treat the right of humanitarian intervention as a matter of last resort and confines it to extreme cases, where the following conditions are satisfied:

(a) that there exists – or there is an immediate threat of – the most serious humanitarian emergency involving large scale loss of life; and
(b) military intervention is necessary, in that it is the only practicable means by which that loss of life can be ended or prevented.

These are objective criteria and, in determining whether they are met in any individual case, the existence of authoritative and impartial acceptance of the existence of an emergency and the need for military action is obviously of great importance.

. . .

UK Parliamentary Select Committee on Foreign Affairs, Fourth Report, (2000)

Introduction

124. The Government has consistently asserted that the military action taken in the Kosovo campaign has been lawful, and that NATO would not have acted outside the principles of international law. Both Ministers told us that states had the right to use force in the case of 'overwhelming humanitarian necessity where, in the light of all the circumstances, a limited use of force is justifiable as the only way to avert a humanitarian catastrophe.' A number of difficult questions of law (as well as difficult questions of fact) arise.

125. These legal questions are not arcane. There is a need for a system of law governing the conduct of states, just as the internal affairs of states should be governed by the rule of law. An agreed system of law is particularly important where the use of force is concerned. It is in the national interest of the United Kingdom that an international order based on law should exist, and that individual states, or groups of states, should not be able to interpret the law perversely in their immediate interest. When the law is clear, there can be a consensus; when there is ambiguity, international stability and the mechanisms of collective security set up through the United Nations are threatened.

Was military intervention legal?

United Nations Approval

126. The Charter of the United Nations was described by Professor Simma as 'not just one multilateral treaty among others, but an instrument of singular legal weight, something akin to a "constitution" of the international community.' The Charter prohibits the threat or use of force except in self defence or when the Security Council determines that there is a threat to peace, breach of the peace or act of aggression, in which case the Security Council may determine (under Chapter VII) that force should be employed 'to maintain or restore international peace and security.' The NATO military intervention was patently not an act of self defence, nor was there any specific Security Council authorisation for the operation. As Dr Jones Parry told us, none of the three classic bases for intervention (a UN Security Council Resolution; an invitation to intervene; or self-defence) applied in the case of Kosovo.

Uniting for Peace

128. There is a procedure at the United Nations known as 'Uniting for Peace'. This can help a blockage in the Security Council to be bypassed by reference to the General Assembly. Uniting for Peace is relevant only when a peace-and-security issue is on the Security Council agenda and the Council is prevented from exercising its 'primary responsibility' to deal with it by veto of one of its permanent members. Though Article 12 of the UN Charter bars the General Assembly from making any recommendation in respect of any dispute or situation where the Security Council is exercising its functions, except at Security Council request, a procedural vote to refer a matter to the General Assembly requires the affirmative vote of nine members of the Security Council and is not subject to veto. The Uniting for Peace procedure was used against the United Kingdom and France over their intervention in Suez in 1956. In the case of Kosovo, the General Assembly could have been called into special session and could, by two-thirds majority, have supported military action. Professor Adam Roberts told us that he had suggested this procedure after Rambouillet failed, but had been rebuffed by the FCO, which was uncertain that the two thirds majority would have been achieved, and which regarded the General Assembly as in any case a cumbersome procedure to use since resolutions passed there could not easily be modified. Dr Jones Parry told us that the Government had considered a resort to the General Assembly, but had rejected the option. He pointed out that, though a resolution of the General Assembly would

have been particularly persuasive, the UN Charter still specified that military action required Security Council endorsement. Our conclusion is that *Operation Allied Force* was contrary to the specific terms of what might be termed the basic law of the international community – the UN Charter, although this might have been avoided if the Allies had attempted to use the Uniting for Peace procedures.

Customary International Law: Intervention for Humanitarian Purposes (Humanitarian Intervention)

129. International law is not, however, static. It develops both through the agreement of new treaties and other international instruments, and through the evolution of customary law. The Charter of the United Nations has been interpreted in different ways in the half century since it was written. As Professor Greenwood pointed out, some parts of the Charter have been conveniently ignored, while, since the end of the Cold War, the provisions of Article 2(7) which forbid intervention in internal affairs of states have been widened to allow such intervention on the grounds that what is happening internally in the state threatens international peace and security. Moreover, it is at least arguable that the preponderant will of the international community ought not to be held to ransom by the exercise of the veto (or threat of the exercise of the veto) by a minority, or indeed only one, of the permanent members of the Security Council. As Professor Greenwood put it, 'an interpretation of international law which would forbid intervention to prevent something as terrible as the Holocaust, unless a permanent member could be persuaded to lift its veto, would be contrary to the principles on which modern international law is based as well as flying in the face of the developments of the last fifty years.' We also note the fact that a veto by China on 25 February 1999 prevented the Security Council from authorising a six month extension of the term of the UN Preventive Deployment Force (UNPREDEP) in Macedonia. It was commonly believed that this veto was cast because of the establishment of diplomatic relations with Taiwan by Macedonia. One country's veto should not force the international community to sit on the sidelines and watch appalling human rights violations continue unchecked. We discuss the issue of the morality of the intervention, as distinct from its legality, below.

130. Supporters of NATO's position argue that a new right has developed in customary international law – the right of humanitarian intervention. The argument in favour of the existence of this right was set out by Professor Greenwood. Dame Pauline Neville-Jones was clear that NATO action had been lawful, and Professor Lowe told us that NATO action (if a breach of a fifty year old Charter) was 'consonant with the way international customary law is developing.' Professor Reisman put it thus: 'when human rights enforcement by military means is required, it should, indeed be the responsibility of the Security Council acting under the Charter. But when the Council cannot act, the legal requirement continues to be to save lives.'

131. Professor Greenwood conceded that the right of humanitarian intervention was based on state practice, but that this was state practice which had evolved in the past 10 years since the end of the Cold War. Although the interventions of India in East Pakistan (1971), Vietnam in Cambodia (1978), and Tanzania in Uganda (1979) had the effect of putting an end to massive human rights violations in each case, the intervening states relied ultimately on arguments of self-defence to justify their actions, even if reference was also made to the humanitarian situation. Only the interventions of ECOWAS in Liberia (1990) and the intervention by the USA, the United Kingdom and France in northern Iraq (1992) seem to have been unambiguously humanitarian in their stated aims. Professor Greenwood told us that the very short time scale over which the new practice had been apparent was unsurprising in international law, where a custom could develop much more quickly than in domestic law. Moreover, he argued that customary law formed a much more important part of international law than it did of domestic law.

132. An entirely contrary view is taken by Professor Brownlie, who provided the Committee with an exhaustive review of the authorities, including jurists of twelve nationalities, three of whom had been President of the International Court of Justice. He concluded that 'there is very little evidence to support assertions that a new principle of customary law legitimating humanitarian intervention has crystallised.' We are persuaded that Professor Greenwood was too ambitious in saying that a new customary right has developed. We conclude that, at the very least, the doctrine of humanitarian intervention has a tenuous basis in current international customary law, and that this renders NATO action legally questionable. . . .

NOTES:

1. As human rights becomes the watchword of the millenium, many international lawyers are arguing for a right to use force to intervene in the domestic affairs of other States to prevent and suppress large-scale violations of human rights. If the intervention is with the consent of the territorial sovereign, there are fewer problems. If, however, the intervention is 'non-permissive', it would appear to run counter to Art. 2(4) and various pronouncements of the General Assembly. There is particular concern that alleged humanitarian interventions usually result in the overthrow of the incumbent government – Vietnam in Cambodia, 1979; India in East Pakistan (Bangladesh), 1971; but, notably, not in Kosovo in 1998/9. Brownlie would not agree with Lillich's starting point that humanitarian intervention was established in customary international law, let alone the conclusion that it has survived the Charter.

2. The theoretical debate about the lawfulness of humanitarian intervention is not simply for academics. Our view of humanitarian intervention reveals much about the way we think of international law generally. The 'classicists' regard the formation of law as stemming from the practice of States and, *ipso facto*, the absence of instances of intervention for the protection of human rights, or the absence of acceptance of the legitimacy of such action in those cases where humanitarian concern has been part of the motive for acting, is all they need to 'prove' that such conduct is illegal. So called 'realists', on the other hand, see law as a tool for the achievement of community goals and argue that the right of humanitarian intervention need not be established by such strict criteria. It is enough if the right is necessary and is not specifically prohibited. While classicists appear to be willing to sacrifice human suffering in favour of upholding the formal legitimacy of the law-creating process (although they would disagree with this criticism), realists argue in favour of the use of force to achieve certain 'values' which, of course, may not be the values that promote a stable international community. Others may consider that the protection of human rights is more important in the international community than technical breaches of previous State practice.

3. The Kosovo action represents a turning point in (at least) the UK's attitude to the use of force for humanitarian intervention. There was a hint in respect of the UK's intervention to protect the Kurds and marsh-Arabs in Iraq in 1991 in that the intervention was said to be justified in order to prevent an humanitarian catastrophe, but the statements made at the time of Kosovo are the most explicit justification yet from the UK. However, even then, the UK government chose to stress the moral imperatives of its action (and see also the *4th Report* cited above): government statements directly addressing the legality of the action were few. Moreover, although there had been Security Council resolutions supporting NATO's attempts to resolve matters peacefully and to verify the attempted cease-fires (SC Res 1160, 1199 and 1203 of 1998), the Security Council had not given authority to use force, or even 'all necessary means'. The NATO action was thus without specific Security Council approval: it was not a UN enforcement action under Chapter VII of the Charter, nor a UN peacekeeping operation.

4. Note that Yugoslavia has instituted proceedings in the ICJ against NATO nations alleging an unlawful use of force.

5. On 10 June 1999, the Security Council adopted SC Res 1244 as NATO bombing had ceased and Serbian forces were withdrawing. This Resolution, adopted under Chapter VII of the Charter (and so binding), authorised the Secretary-General to establish in Kosovo an interim international civilian administration under which the people could move towards substantial autonomy within Serbia. Pending the assumption of full control by the United Nations Interim Administration Mission in Kosovo (UNMIK), a NATO-led military force (KFOR) was authorised to preserve the peace. The presence of these forces was agreed to by Yugoslavia. Thus, the unilateral action evolved into a multilateral/permissive action.

G: Intervention by invitation

L. Doswald-Beck, 'The Legal Validity of Military Intervention by Invitation of the Government'
(1985) 56 BYBIL 189

Since the Second World War, there have been numerous instances of troops being sent to another State allegedly upon invitation of its government. Many texts would support a principle unequivocally in favour of the legality of such intervention, and there is certainly no doubt that a State can legally send troops to another State upon invitation for certain limited operations. . . . However, certain recent texts express doubts as to the validity of intervention by invitation where foreign troops are to be used to quell an insurrection. The reasons given for such doubts are variously stated to be the inability of a shaky regime to represent the State as its government, a conflict with the principle of self-determination or a violation of the duty of non-intervention in the internal affairs of another State.

It is submitted that there is, at the least, a very serious doubt whether a State may validly aid another government to suppress a rebellion, particularly if the rebellion is widespread and seriously aimed at the overthrow of the incumbent regime . . .

With regard to the origin of the norm of non-intervention in internal affairs, this can best be seen, in this author's opinion, in the *travaux préparatoires* to Resolution 2131. The principle of non-intervention in internal affairs is, in effect, an attempt to limit outside neo-colonial attempts to influence events in other countries for the intèrests of the intervening country. The policy behind the norm is a recognition that countries intervene in practice for their own benefit and major powers have an interest in not allowing the influence of an adversary power to be strengthened in this way. The policy interest of weaker countries is self-evident as well as the general wish to avoid the escalation of violence. It is to be expected, however, that these norms will be broken when a State considers it imperative to do so in certain circumstances, or when it considers that it can be got away with, but this is quite normal with any legal system and does not in itself derogate from the norm when that norm is clearly expressed and not in doubt. It is submitted that this is the case with the law of non-intervention in internal affairs.

The effect of this new customary law is to revolutionize the traditional law, which held that a State can intervene to help a government suppress a rebellion unless belligerency is declared. . . . It is this that now regulates intervention in civil war and represents the modern law.

NOTE:
A legitimate government may invite the forces of another State on to its territory for any purpose lawful under international law, i.e. not for genocide, wars of aggression, or to prevent an exercise of self-determination. However, intervention by invitation usually occurs in the context of a civil war, where two competing governments claim to be the 'legitimate' government. In such

circumstances, to allow intervention by invitation serves only to encourage dictatorial interference by other States. There is also the problem of fabricated invitations, as with the alleged invitation made by the government of Afghanistan to the Soviet Union in 1979, and the allegedly valid invitation made by the Governor-General of Grenada to the United States in 1984.

H: Reprisals

D. Bowett, 'Reprisals Involving Recourse to Armed Force'
66 AJIL 1 (1972)

Few propositions about international law have enjoyed more support than the proposition that, under the Charter of the United Nations, the use of force by way of reprisals is illegal. Although, indeed, the words 'reprisals' and 'retaliation' are not to be found in the Charter, this proposition was generally regarded by writers and by the Security Council as the logical and necessary consequence of the prohibition of force in Article 2(4), the injunction to settle disputes peacefully in Article 2(3) and the limiting of permissible force by states to self-defense . . .

In recent years, and principally though not exclusively in the Middle East, this norm of international law has acquired its own 'credibility gap' by reason of the divergence between the norm and the actual practice of states . . .

Clearly, if self-defense is a permissible use of force and reprisals are not, the distinction between the two is vital . . .

Reprisals and self-defense are forms of the same generic remedy, self-help. They have, in common, the preconditions that:

(1) The target state must be guilty of a prior international delinquency against the claimant state.

(2) An attempt by the claimant state to obtain redress or protection by other means must be known to have been made, and failed, or to be inappropriate or impossible in the circumstances.

(3) The claimant's use of force must be limited to the necessities of the case and proportionate to the wrong done by the target state.

The difference between the two forms of self-help lies essentially in their aim or purpose. Self-defense is permissible for the purpose of protecting the security of the state and the essential rights – in particular the rights of territorial integrity and political independence – upon which that security depends. In contrast, reprisals are punitive in character: they seek to impose reparation for the harm done, or to compel a satisfactory settlement of the dispute created by the initial illegal act, or to compel the delinquent state to abide by the law in the future. . . .

This seemingly simple distinction abounds with difficulties. Not only is the motive or purpose of a state notoriously difficult to elucidate but, even more important, the dividing line between protection and retribution becomes more and more obscure as one moves away from the particular incident and examines the whole context in which the two or more acts of violence have occurred. Indeed, within the whole context of a continuing state of antagonism between states, with recurring acts of violence, an act of reprisal may be regarded as being at the same time both a form of punishment and the best form of protection for the future, since it may act as a deterrent against future acts of violence by the other party. . . .

In fact, the records of the Security Council are replete with cases where states have invoked self-defense in this broader sense but where the majority of the Council have rejected this classification and regarded their action as unlawful reprisals. These cases are worth the study, for they illustrate the importance of this question – Is the legality of the action to be determined solely by reference to the prior illegal act which brought it about or by reference to the whole context of the relationship between the two states?

Weighing the advantages against the disadvantages, however, it would seem that the approach of the Security Council in assessing whether a case for lawful self-defense has been made out has been somewhat unrealistic. To confine this assessment to the incident and its immediate 'cause,' without regard to the broader context of the past relations between the parties and events arising there-from, is to ignore the difficulties in which states may be placed, especially in relation to guerrilla activities. The result is not only that the Council finds itself being accused of being 'one-sided' but it may also be forced to characterize as reprisals (and therefore illegal) action which, on a broader view of self-defense, might be regarded as legitimate. Or, even worse, the Council characterizes such action as an unlawful reprisal but, realizing the difficulties faced by the 'defendant' state, does not make any formal condemnation and thus appears to be condoning action which it holds is illegal.

US State Department, 'Memorandum on US Practice with Respect to Reprisals'
73 AJIL 489 (1979)

In conclusion, it is clear that the United States has taken the categorical position that reprisals involving the use of force are illegal under international law; that it is generally not willing to con-demn reprisals without also condemning provocative terrorist acts; and that it recognizes the dif-ficulty of distinguishing between proportionate self-defense and reprisals but maintains the distinc-tion. Where the United States has itself possibly engaged in reprisal action involving the use of force, characterization of the action has been confused by equating it also with self-defense. These so-called reprisal incidents took place in the context of a war justified by the United States Government as collective self-defense, and on this basis, could be distinguished from the reprisal raids conducted by Israel. It is also clear that the United States has determined that patterns of attacks can constitute a level of 'armed attack' justifying the use of force in self-defense.

I: Self-determination

H. Wilson, *International Law and the Use of Force by National Liberation Movements*
(1989), pp. 130–136

One of the most common justifications of the use of force by national liberation movements is the plea of self-defence. . . .

First, in some cases liberation movements and States supporting them have justified their use of force based on a right of self-defence against the original colonial invasion. . . . This argument is not particularly persuasive because of the principle of intertemporal law, by which the acquisition of a territory by force at a time when the use of force to acquire territory was not illegal confers good title. . . .

The more common argument made to support the plea of self-defence is that colonialism, by its very nature, is permanent aggression and any other conception of colonialism misrepresents its true nature. Therefore colonial peoples have a right, consistent with the Charter's norms, to defend themselves. . . .

Such a liberal interpretation of self-defence was not in accord with the views of the Western Bloc nor with many of the Latin American States. In the first place, a number of countries were still of the opinion that Article 51 applied to the right of self-defence for States. . . .

Secondly, both the Western and Eastern Bloc States were sceptical about such a broad interpret-ation of Article 51 which, in their view, would undermine the prohibition of the use of force and return the idea of 'self-help' to international law. They supported the view that the important clause of Article 51 was that an *armed attack* must take place for there to be a right of self-defence. . . .

There is a third argument posed for the legitimization of the use of force based on a right of self-defence which is less vulnerable to the criticisms of the Western powers although it still has failed to convince that group. By the 1970 Declaration on Principles of International Law, member States of the United Nations agreed by consensus that a people who have a right to self-determination have a status in law separate and distinct from that of the State administering them, and that every State has the duty to refrain from the use of force to deprive such peoples of their right of self-determination. If the colonial power initiates the use of force, some argue that the people, represented by their liberation movement, have the authority to use force in self-defence. In other words, national liberation movements have the same authority as subjects of international law as sovereign States. They are still prohibited from resorting to the threat or use of force in their relations with the colonial power, but they may defend themselves against armed attack in accordance with Article 51 of the Charter.

The Third World States have not been eager to embrace this limited justification because it does not legitimize the eradication of colonialism by force of arms if necessary. . . .

The plea of self-defence was only one of the legal arguments proposed by the anti-colonial States. In a way, it was a justification within the bounds of the Charter of a more fundamental idea: that the denial of self-determination by colonial domination, alien occupation, or racism is so abhorrent that the use of force to eradicate these evils is justified irrespective of any prohibition of the use of force. In other words, wars of national liberation are an exception to the general prohibition of the use of force and anti-colonialism is part of a higher law.

Several Third World and Eastern Bloc States have argued that wars of national liberation are not prohibited by the Charter because Article 2(4) was referring to territorial aggrandizement. Wars of national liberation, in contrast, are fought to eradicate an agreed evil, and are therefore exempt from this prohibition.

Although the idea that wars of national liberation are exceptions to the general rule prohibiting the threat or use of force is widely accepted by Third World and Eastern Bloc States, it is not accepted by the Western States where sympathy for the ends of securing self-determination does not justify the use of force as a means. Many critics, quite rightly, have seen in this argument overtones of the medieval concept of a just war.

Finally, there is a third legal argument, less challenging of the traditional norms of international law than either the right of self-defence for peoples or the idea of a higher law. Quite simply, it is the explicit acceptance of a right of revolution by national liberation movements. . . . The law as it stands is still not agreed upon. However, some conclusions can be made about the current state of affairs.

1. National liberation movements have an international legal personality unlike that of other non-governmental organizations. This status is based on the right of the peoples which they represent to self-determination.

2. There is general agreement that wars of national liberation are not strictly internal armed conflicts.

3. The use of force to deny the free exercise of a people's right to self-determination is contrary to the principles of international law.

4. The right of a people to self-determination may legitimize the recognition of a government which would otherwise be premature.

5. The authority of national liberation movements to use force is not agreed upon as a matter of international law. Such authority is actively supported by the newly independent States and the Eastern Bloc States, but has never been accepted by an established government confronting a liberation movement, or by the Western States. Practice in the UN, particularly the Declaration on Principles of International Law and the Declaration on Aggression, both adopted without vote, does not resolve the fundamental differences of opinion over the status of national liberation movements and the extent of their authority as a matter of law. However, the trend over the last four decades

and since 1960 in particular has been toward the extension of the authority to use force to national liberation movements.

NOTE:
The alleged right of 'national liberation movements' to use force to achieve self-determination, and the alleged right of other States to assist them with force to achieve this objective, is controversial. If permitted, both rights would seriously erode the prohibition on the use of force. For this reason, it is strongly resisted by some States, though favoured by the developing States in the General Assembly. See the discussion of self-determination in Chapter 6.

SECTION 2: Collective security

In contrast to the unilateral use of force, a collective use of force occurs where the use of force (or other coercive measures) is used under the authority of a competent international organisation, usually in promotion of international community goals. Again, the actual force may be employed by one or many States, but whichever acts, they do so for the benefit of the international community at large and with its imprimatur. There was an attempt to establish a tentative system of collective security under the Covenant of the League of Nations but it was not until the United Nations Charter that a legally effective system came into being. Essentially, if the UN Security Council makes a determination that there has been a 'threat to the peace, breach of the peace or act of aggression' under Art. 39 of the Charter, it may go on to exercise its powers under Chapter VII. These are listed in Arts 40 to 42 and involve both military and non-military sanctions. Prior to the end of the Cold War, this power was used sparingly, partly because of institutional strictures (such as the power of veto enjoyed by the five Permanent Members of the Security Council) and partly because of a lack of political will both to initiate enforcement action and bear its consequences. The post-Cold War era of cooperation between the Permanent Members on the Council has resulted in a revival of the Council's enforcement role. Non-military sanctions have been imposed in recent years on Haiti, Libya, and parts of the former Yugoslavia (all now lifted), with military action authorised against or in Somalia, Yugoslavia, Iraq (being the most comprehensive and substantial instance of enforcement action to date) and East Timor. In 2000, the Council imposed certain limited embargoes on Eritrea and Ethiopia as a result of renewed conflict.

A: The Security Council

United Nations Charter
CHAPTER VII ACTION WITH RESPECT TO THREATS TO THE PEACE, BREACHES OF
THE PEACE, AND ACTS OF AGGRESSION

Article 39
The Security Council shall determine the existence of any threat to the peace, breach of the peace, or act of aggression and shall make recommendations, or decide what measures shall be taken in accordance with Articles 41 and 42, to maintain or restore international peace and security.

Article 40
In order to prevent an aggravation of the situation, the Security Council may, before making the recommendations or deciding upon the measures provided for in Article 39, call upon the parties concerned to comply with such provisional measures as it deems necessary or desirable. Such provisional measures shall be without prejudice to the rights, claims or position of the parties concerned. The Security Council shall duly take account of failure to comply with such provisional measures.

Article 41
The Security Council may decide what measures not involving the use of armed force are to be employed to give effect to its decisions, and it may call upon the Members of the United Nations to apply such measures. These may include complete or partial interruption of economic relations and of rail, sea, air, postal, telegraphic, radio, and other means of communication, and the severance of diplomatic relations.

Article 42
Should the Security Council consider that measures provided for in Article 41 would be inadequate or have proved to be inadequate, it may take such action by air, sea, or land forces as may be necessary to maintain or restore international peace and security. Such action may include demonstrations, blockade, and other operations by air, sea, or land forces of Members of the United Nations.

Article 43
1. All Members of the United Nations, in order to contribute to the maintenance of international peace and security, undertake to make available to the Security Council, on its call and in accordance with a special agreement or agreements, armed forces, assistance, and facilities, including rights of passage, necessary for the purpose of maintaining peace and security.

2. Such agreement or agreements shall govern the numbers and types of forces, their degree of readiness and general location, and the nature of the facilities and assistance to be provided.

3. The agreement or agreements shall be negotiated as soon as possible on the initiative of the Security Council. They shall be concluded between the Security Council and Members or between the Security Council and groups of Members and shall be subject to ratification by the signatory States in accordance with their respective constitutional processes.

H. Kelsen, 'Collective Security and Collective Self-Defence under the Charter of the United Nations'
42 AJIL 783 (1948)

Collective security is the main purpose of the United Nations, just as it was the main purpose of its predecessor, the League of Nations. What does collective security mean? . . . We speak of collective security when the protection of the rights of the states, the reaction against the violation of the law, assumes the character of a collective enforcement action. . . . The difference between such kind of collective security and the status of self-help is relatively small. . . . The difference between the most primitive type of collective security and the state of self-help consists only in that, in the case of collective security, states not directly violated in their rights are obliged to assist the violated state; whereas in the state of self-help under general international law, they are only allowed to do so.

A higher degree of collective security is reached if the collective enforcement actions provided for in the constitution of the international community are centralized, that is to say, if these actions are to be decided upon and directed by a central organ of the community. Such centralization of the use of force may be combined with the obligation imposed upon the individual members not to use force on their own initiative in their mutual relations, to abandon completely the principle of self-help – the use of force being reserved exclusively to the central organ of the community competent to take enforcement actions against members. In case of such centralization of the use of force, the force monopoly of the community is much more evident than in case of decentralization.

Collective security reaches the highest possible degree when the obligation of the members to refrain from the use of force is guaranteed by their disarmament, when the force monopoly of the community is constituted not only by the exclusive right of a central organ to take enforcement actions against members, but also by the fact that only a central organ of the international community has armed forces at its disposal to be employed against delinquent member states, whereas the single members of the community are allowed only to keep a police force for the maintenance of law and order among their subjects, that is to say, for enforcement actions against individuals. By such a high degree of centralization, the international community is about to be transformed into a national community, the union of states into a state.

However, the centralization of the use of force – be it in a state or in a true international organization – is possible only with an important limitation. This limitation refers to the case of self-defense. Self-defense is not identical with self-help; it is a special case of self-help. It is self-help against a specific violation of the law, against the illegal use of force, not against other violations of the law. Self-defense is the use of force by a person illegally attacked by another. The attack against which the use of force as an act of self-defense is permitted must have been made or must be intended to be made by force. Self-defense is that minimum of of self-help which, even within a system of collective security based on a centralized force monopoly of the community, must be permitted. As such it is recognized by national as well as by international law, within the state as well as within international organizations.

Examples of Security Council Resolutions
Security Council Resolution 678 (1990)

The Security Council . . .

Acting under Chapter VII of the Charter of the United Nations,

1. *Demands* that Iraq comply fully with resolution 660 (1990) and all subsequent relevant resolutions and decides, while maintaining all its decisions, to allow Iraq one final opportunity, as a pause of goodwill, to do so;

2. *Authorizes* Member States co-operating with the Government of Kuwait, unless Iraq on or before 15 January 1991 fully implements, as set forth in paragraph 1 above, the

foregoing resolutions, to use all necessary means to uphold and implement Security Council resolution 660 (1990) and all subsequent relevant resolutions and to restore international peace and security in the area.

Security Council Resolution 1264 (1999)

The Security Council . . .

Reiterating its welcome for the successful conduct of the popular consultation of the East Timorese people of 30 August 1999 and *taking note* of its outcome, which it regards as an accurate reflection of the views of the East Timorese people . . .

Deeply concerned also at the attacks on the staff and premises of the United Nations Mission in East Timor (UNAMET), on other officials and on international and national humanitarian personnel . . .

Appalled by the worsening humanitarian situation in East Timor, particularly as it affects women, children and other vulnerable groups . . .

Expressing its concern at reports indicating that systematic, widespread and flagrant violations of international humanitarian and human rights law have been committed in East Timor, and *stressing* that persons committing such violations bear individual responsibility,

Determining that the present situation in East Timor constitutes a threat to peace and security,

Acting under Chapter VII of the Charter of the United Nations,

1. *Condemns* all acts of violence in East Timor, *calls* for their immediate end and *demands* that those responsible for such acts be brought to justice;

3. *Authorizes* the establishment of a multinational force under a unified command structure, pursuant to the request of the Government of Indonesia conveyed to the Secretary-General on 12 September 1999, with the following tasks: to restore peace and security in East Timor, to protect and support UNAMET in carrying out its tasks and, within force capabilities, to facilitate humanitarian assistance operations, and *authorizes* the States participating in the multinational force to take all necessary measures to fulfil this mandate;

6. *Welcomes* the offers by Member States to organize, lead and contribute to the multi-national force in East Timor, *calls on* Member States to make further contributions of personnel, equipment and other resources and *invites* Member States in a position to contribute to inform the leadership of the multinational force and the Secretary-General; . . .

NOTES:
1. Resolution 1264 (1999) on East Timor is for all intents and purposes an 'enforcement action' within Chapter VII of the Charter and, although there is no explicit reference to Art. 39 of the Charter, there is a formal determination of a 'threat to the peace'. The Resolution notes that Indonesia has agreed to cooperate with the multilateral force but there is no suggestion of 'permission' here (as such would be legally unnecessary in the light of the resolution). As well as being in response to violations of human rights etc., this is the first clear example of Chapter VII UN action in support of the right of self-determination.
2. As with the Yugoslavia case, there is no requirement in Resolution 1264 that States *must* make military forces available for enforcement action: instead, there is the now standard (in such cases) authorisation for individual States or groups of States to take 'all necessary measures' to achieve UN goals. For the relevant Yugoslavian authorisation see S.C. Res. 1031 (1995).

3. In one sense, the original scheme of the Charter for collective security has failed. No agreements have been concluded under Art. 43 and there are no instances of the Security Council *requiring* States to use force against a malefactor, although it has 'decided' that States should impose non-military sanctions. However, the Council has assumed the power to authorise States to use force on behalf of the international community, and this was the approach adopted in the resolutions concerning Iraq, Somalia, Yugoslavia and East Timor. The Somalian situation is interesting as the Council exercised its enforcement powers in respect of a dispute that was essential domestic – that is, where the threat to 'international' peace and security emanated entirely from within Somalia. Likewise, the Council's economic and diplomatic sanctions against Libya was the first time that enforcement powers had been used to combat and punish an act of terrorism (the bombing of a Pan Am flight over Lockerbie), albeit one for which a State is held responsible. As noted above, this has now been extended to a general enforcement action (non-military sanction) against terrorism following September 11.
4. It is only the Security Council that can formally terminate an enforcement action, be it military or economic. Thus, the sanctions against Haiti are no longer in operation and the long-standing economic sanctions against South Africa were lifted in SC Res 919 (1994). Sanctions against Libya and Yugoslavia have been lifted following the resolution by agreement of the Lockerbie (see Chapter 5) and Bosnia cases respectively. For a full analysis of the Security Council's approach to authorisation powers see N. Blokker 'Is the Authorization Authorized?' Powers and Practice of the UN Security Council to Authorize the use of force by Coalition of the Able and Willing – 11 EJIL (2000), p. 541.

B: The General Assembly

The apparent failure of the Security Council to take effective enforcement action in the years 1945–1990 led some States to seek alternative methods of galvanising the international community into action against delinquent States. The General Assembly Resolution somewhat hopefully entitled 'Uniting for Peace' was the manifestation of these concerns. The resolution purported to confirm the Assembly's latent powers to recommend enforcement action in the event of deadlock in the Council. Not surprisingly, the constitutionality of this procedure generated considerable criticism, although the current vitality of the Council has made the issue moot.

Uniting for Peace Resolution
GA Res 377 (V) 1950

The General Assembly

1. Resolves that if the Security Council, because of lack of unanimity of the permanent members, fails to exercise its primary responsibility for the maintenance of international peace and security in any case where there appears to be a threat to the peace, breach of the peace, or act of aggression, the General Assembly shall consider the matter immediately with a view to making appropriate recommendations to Members for collective measures, including in the case of a breach of the peace or act of aggression the use of armed force when necessary, to maintain or restore international peace and security. If not in session at the time, the General Assembly may meet in emergency special session within twenty-four hours of the request therefore. . . .

7. Invites each Member of the United Nations to survey its resources in order to determine the

nature and scope of the assistance it may be in a position to render in support of any recommendations of the Security Council or of the General Assembly for the restoration of international peace and security.

8. Recommends to the State Members of the United Nations that each Member maintain within its national armed forces elements so trained, organized and equipped that they could promptly be made available, in accordance with its constitutional processes, for service as a United Nations unit or units, upon recommendation by the Security Council or the General Assembly, without prejudice to the use of such elements in exercise of the right of individual or collective self-defence recognized in Article 51 of the Charter.

Certain Expenses of the United Nations Opinion
ICJ Rep 1962 151, International Court of Justice

The General Assembly assesses members' financial contributions to the running of the Organisation under Art. 17 of the Charter. A number of States refused to pay their contributions in respect of two peacekeeping forces created under the direction of the Assembly. They argued that the Assembly was not competent to levy contributions in respect of such bodies, because the Charter assigned the maintenance of international peace and security to the Security Council. The ICJ was asked for an advisory opinion.

Article 24 of the Charter provides:

> In order to ensure prompt and effective action by the United Nations, its Members confer on the Security Council primary responsibility for the maintenance of international peace and security, . . .

The responsibility conferred is 'primary', not exclusive. This primary responsibility is conferred upon the Security Council, as stated in Article 24, 'in order to ensure prompt and effective action'. To this end, it is the Security Council which is given a power to impose an explicit obligation of compliance if for example it issues an order or command to an aggressor under Chapter VII. It is only the Security Council which can require enforcement by coercive action against an aggressor.

The Charter makes it abundantly clear, however, that the General Assembly is also to be concerned with international peace and security. Article 14 authorizes the General Assembly to 'recommend measures for the peaceful adjustment of any situation, regardless of origin, which it deems likely to impair the general welfare or friendly relations among nations, including situations resulting from a violation of the provisions of the present Charter setting forth the purposes and principles of the United Nations'. The word 'measures' implies some kind of action, and the only limitation which Article 14 imposes on the General Assembly is the restriction found in Article 12, namely, that the Assembly should not recommend measures while the Security Council is dealing with the same matter unless the Council requests it to do so. Thus while it is the Security Council which, exclusively, may order coercive action, the functions and powers conferred by the Charter on the General Assembly are not confined to discussion, consideration, the initiation of studies and the making of recommendations; they are not merely hortatory. Article 18 deals with '*decisions*' of the General Assembly 'on important questions'. These 'decisions' do indeed include certain recommendations, but others have dispositive force and effect . . . [In light of the fact that both forces were established only with the consent of the receiving state, and in view of the terms of the relevant Assembly and Council resolutions, the Court was of the opinion that neither action constituted 'enforcement' within Chapter VII of the Charter.]

C: Regional organisations

United Nations Charter

Article 52

1. Nothing in the present Charter precludes the existence of regional arrangements or agencies for dealing with such matters relating to the maintenance of international peace and security as are appropriate for regional action, provided that such arrangements or agencies and their activities are consistent with the Purposes and Principles of the United Nations.

2. The Members of the United Nations entering into such arrangements or constituting such agencies shall make every effort to achieve pacific settlement of local disputes through such regional arrangements or by such regional agencies before referring them to the Security Council.

3. The Security Council shall encourage the development of pacific settlement of local disputes through such regional arrangements or by such regional agencies either on the initiative of the States concerned or by reference to the Security Council.

4.The Article in no way impairs the application of Articles 34 and 35.

Article 53

1. The Security Council shall, where appropriate, utilize such regional arrangements or agencies for enforcement action under its authority. But no enforcement action shall be taken under regional arrangements or by regional agencies without the authorization of the Security Council, with the exception of measures against any enemy State, as defined in paragraph 2 of this Article provided for pursuant to Article 107 or in regional arrangements directed against renewal of aggressive policy on the part of any such State, until such time as the Organization may, on request of the Governments concerned, be charged with the responsibility for preventing further aggression by such a State.

2. The term 'enemy State' as used in paragraph 1 of this Article applies to any State which during the Second World War has been an enemy of any signatory of the present Charter.

Article 54

The Security Council shall at all times be kept fully informed of activities undertaken or in contemplation under regional arrangements or by regional agencies for the maintenance of international peace and security.

M. Akehurst, 'Enforcement Action by Regional Agencies with special reference to the Organisation of American States'

(1967) 42 BYBIL 175

Article 53 of the Charter states that no enforcement action may be taken by regional agencies or under regional arrangements without the authorization of the Security Council. What does 'enforcement action' mean? . . . Communist States argued that all sanctions imposed by a regional agency constituted 'enforcement action'; that sanctions might only be imposed in order to deal with a threat to the peace, a breach of the peace or an act of aggression (and not, for instance, in order to bring about the downfall of a Communist government in Cuba); and that they might not be imposed without the authorization of the Security Council.

The United States and its allies, on the other hand, maintained that 'enforcement action', necessitating Security Council authorization, referred only to military action, and that a regional agency could employ any non-military sanctions it liked, without Security Council authorization, against a member which presented a threat to the peace or which broke the rules of the organization. A number of arguments were put forward in support of this contention.

Firstly, it was said that enforcement naturally connoted force . . .

Secondly, it was urged that this interpretation reflected the basic principle of the Charter that military force was the monopoly of the Security Council and could not be used by States except in self-defence. It was only natural, then, that Security Council authorization was needed before regional agencies could use force, because otherwise it would be too easy to evade Article 2(4). But there was no corresponding reason why regional agencies should need Security Council authorization to do things which any State could lawfully do on its own.

This brings us to the third and principal argument used by the supporters of the OAS – that any State is at liberty to break off economic relations with another State at will and that groups of States are entitled to do the same on a concerted basis, whether the groups are regional or not . . .

There is one other possible argument in support of the OAS position . . . Under Article II(2) of the United Nations Charter, as interpreted in the *Expenses* case, the General Assembly cannot take enforcement action; the Security Council is the only United Nations organ which has that power. But the General Assembly has, from the beginning, claimed the right to recommend members to break off diplomatic or economic relations with particular States. If the General Assembly passes such a recommendation and members comply with it, no one would suggest that they are thereby infringing the Security Council's monopoly of enforcement action and acting illegally. Why, then, should States not be able to comply with a similar recommendation made by a regional agency of which they are members?

NOTE:

The right of the United Nations to utilise regional organisations for properly authorised enforcement action is not in doubt. The crucial question is the extent to which regional organisations can authorise the use of force against their own members when the Security Council has not authorised the action. Article 53 is quite clear that 'enforcement action' cannot be undertaken without Council approval and Article 103 establishes the primacy of the UN Charter over all other treaties. Hence NATO action in the Kosovo crisis does not become lawful simply because it was legitimate under NATO treaties. There was no UN authorisation in that case (see above). This limitation has led some members of regional organisations to claim that force can be authorised against a member provided it does not amount in a technical sense to 'enforcement action' e.g., in respect of the US-led invasion of Grenada in 1985, though this is of doubtful merit.

D: The overlap between self-defence and collective security

E. Rostow, 'Until What? Enforcement Action or Collective Self-Defense'
85 AJIL 506 (1991)

Should the Persian Gulf war of 1990–1991 be characterized as an 'international enforcement action' of the United Nations Security Council or as a campaign of collective self-defense approved, encouraged, and blessed by the Security Council?

This is not simply a nice and rather metaphysical legal issue, but an extremely practical one. The question it presents is whether the control and direction of hostilities in the gulf, their termination, and the substance of the settlement they produce were handled by the Council as the Korean War was handled, that is, as a campaign of collective self-defense, or as the United Nations' first 'international enforcement action.' According to some international lawyers, characterizing the gulf war as a Security Council 'enforcement action' under the untried procedures of Articles 42–50 of the Charter would in effect eviscerate Article 51, make the exercise of each state's 'inherent' right of self-defense subject to the permission of the Security Council, threaten the veto power of the permanent members of the Security Council, and thus lead to extremely grave and perhaps insoluble political difficulty. It could even destroy the United Nations.

1. Enforcement action or collective defense?

In Security Council Resolution 661 of August 2, 1990, the Council condemned the Iraqi invasion and annexation of Kuwait and affirmed 'the inherent right of individual or collective self-defence, in response to the armed attack by Iraq against Kuwait, in accordance with Article 51 of the Charter.' In the same resolution, it 'decided' that, 'notwithstanding paragraphs 4 through 8 above' – that is, the paragraphs decreeing sanctions – 'nothing in the present resolution shall prohibit assistance to the legitimate Government of Kuwait.'

In taking this step, was the Security Council seeking to preempt the field? Was it embarking on a two-track course that would combine the Security Council's 'decision'-making authority under the Charter with the sovereign right of states to defend themselves as they saw fit? Or was it simply calling on the member states to come to the defense of Kuwait, as it did in the Korean case forty years ago? What are the legal and practical differences between 'enforcement actions' conducted by the Security Council and exercises of the inherent 'right of individual or collective self-defence' carried out by individual countries with or without the blessing of the Security Council?

In the Persian Gulf crisis, Security Council Resolution 678 '[a]uthorizes Member States co-operating with the Government of Kuwait . . . to use all necessary means to uphold [the earlier resolutions] and to restore international peace and security in the area.' Except for the word 'authorizes,' the resolution is clearly one designed to encourage and support a campaign of collective self-defense, and therefore not a Security Council enforcement action. Instead of attempting to direct such an operation itself, the Council 'requests the States concerned' to keep it regularly informed about their progress. The Security Council held no meetings on the gulf crisis between November 29, 1990, when Resolution 678 was adopted, and February 14, 1991, when it met in secret session to discuss the political aspects of the end of the war. And the initial cease-fire in the gulf war was achieved as a practical matter not by an agreed Security Council resolution but by President Bush's ultimatum of February 28, 1991.

Thus, the practice followed in implementing Resolution 678 and in terminating hostilities has been that of an allied military campaign in defense of Kuwait directed by officers of the United States and the associated nations. Does the word 'authorized' in Resolution 678 mean that the member states which cooperated with Kuwait in driving Iraq out of that country could not have done so without the Council's 'authority'? As Professor Glennon points out, Resolution 678 is in fact permissive, like Resolution 83 of June 27, 1950, adopted by the Security Council during the Korean War. It imposes no legally binding obligation under Article 25 of the Charter. In Glennon's words, it 'merely exhorts, authorizes or recommends,' leaving to the member states the decision whether to cooperate in the effort of the allied coalition to liberate Kuwait. The word 'authorizes' in Resolution 678 should not therefore be considered to transform a military campaign of self-defense into an enforcement action . . .

The ultimate legal question presented by the Persian Gulf crisis of 1990–1991 is whether the Security Council can insist that no state exercise its rights of individual and collective self-defense without prior Security Council permission. Such permission could be blocked by the veto of one of the permanent members – or, indeed, by the inaction of a Council majority. In the gulf crisis, as Resolutions 660, 661, and 678 made explicit, the Council conceived of its actions as supplementing the programs of collective self-defense organized by the United States, not as supplanting them. It did not claim to be the exclusive agency for assuring compliance with Article 2(4) of the Charter but, on the contrary, affirmed the dual character of the United Nations as a political body: the Security Council may act, and so may the countries willing to exercise their rights of individual and collective self-defense. The United States and other countries carefully resisted any formal encroachment on the right of self-defense by the Security Council. On the other hand, the United States has also seemed to rely on the Council's 'approval' of its organized self-defense efforts as an 'authorization of the use of force.' Despite the strenuous efforts of the United States, the record shows some anomalies and ambiguities.

The practice of subordinating the right of self-defense to a requirement of prior Security Council permission would be fatal to the right of states to defend themselves. What the Charter prescribes is precisely the opposite rule: that the aggrieved state and its friends and allies may decide for themselves when to exercise their rights of individual and collective self-defense until peace is restored or the Security Council, by its own affirmative vote, decides that self-defense has gone too far and become a threat to the peace. However, under the rule urged by some in the gulf controversy, the right of self-defense would cease to be 'inherent' in sovereignty but would exist at the sufferance of the Security Council. In the light of its text, its history, and the nature of the state system, it is impossible to interpret Article 51 to permit such a result.

The right of individual and collective self-defense is the essence of sovereignty and the ultimate guaranty of the survival of states when all else fails. At the San Francisco Conference in 1945, which produced the United Nations Charter, France and some other states contended that Article 51 was not necessary, because no treaty could qualify the sovereign right of individual and collective self-defense. The article was adopted, however, in order to make the French point unmistakably clear. And its placement at the end of chapter VII defines the concurrent relationship between 'enforcement actions' of the Security Council and the use of force as an act of 'individual or collective self-defence.'

NOTE:
The Gulf War brought the relationship between collective self-defence and collective security into relief for the first time. Clearly, States could have come to the assistance of Kuwait – which had suffered an armed attack – and repelled Iraq solely in reliance on the right of (collective) self-defence. Political motives and the need to build an international coalition clothed with the authority of the United Nations played a large part in why they did not. However, Rostow's championing of the right of self-defence (which, he claims, can be terminated only by a positive resolution of the Council) does appear to inhibit the operation of the collective security provisions of the Charter.

SECTION 3: **Peacekeeping**

The United Nations has had a peacekeeping role since the earliest days of the organisation. The factual matrix of peacekeeping – as opposed to peace enforcing – is that a United Nations force is interposed in a conflict with the sole purpose of observing, fostering, or perhaps maintaining by its presence (though not by positive use of force) a ceasefire or disengagement. As a legal concept, the essence of peacekeeping is that the UN force enters and operates within a territory only with the consent of the government, group or groups exercising sovereignty within it. It is a consensual operation and can be terminated by the withdrawal of the consent of the territorial sovereign. Moreover, while the mandate of a peacekeeping force can be changed by the Security Council into one of peace enforcement action that does not require the consent of the territorial sovereign, this step will not be taken lightly. In this respect, a consensual peacekeeping operation can be instigated by action of the

General Assembly, Security Council, or even the UN Secretary-General, although it is most likely to be instigated by the Council.

Statement of C. Harper, Legal Adviser, US Department of State before the Legislation and National Security Subcommittee of the House of Representatives Government Operations Committee, US Congress
3 March 1994

To begin with, the United Nations Charter provides an extensive and flexible international legal framework for the conduct of peace operations. Chapter VI of the Charter authorizes the Security Council to investigate any situation that might endanger the maintenance of international peace and security and to make recommendations for the peaceful resolution of such disputes.

Chapter VII of the Charter authorizes the Security Council to determine the existence of a threat or breach of the peace or act of aggression and to make recommendations or decide on measures of a mandatory character to restore and maintain the peace. This may include economic and diplomatic sanctions or a broad range of military actions. The Council used Chapter VII, for example, for the imposition of mandatory sanctions on Iraq and Serbia and to authorize the use of force to enforce its decisions concerning those countries. UN Member States are required by the UN Charter to carry out decisions of the Council.

Typically, military operations aoproved by the Security Council are conducted by the forces of UN Member States, contributed and organized on an ad hoc basis for each operation. Operational control may be exercised by UN commanders as in the case of the UNOSOM operation in Somalia and the UNPROFOR operation in Bosnia), or may be exercised by one or more of the states involved (as was the case in the Gulf War and the initial US operations in Somalia). Article 43 of the Charter provides for the possibility of special agreements with UN Members to make units of the armed forces available on the call of the Council, but no such agreements have ever been concluded. . . .

First, you asked whether certain terms relating to peace operations needed to be defined or clarified as a matter of law. Our response is that this is not legally necessary. The mandate of the Security Council for each operation defines its scope and character, including the mission and command arrangements for the operation.

It is of course useful in general policy discussions to have a common understanding of the meaning of various terms used. In this area, we use the term 'peacekeeping' to refer to operations carried out with the consent of the states or other significant parties involved; these are traditionally non-combat operations (except for the purpose of self-defense) and are normally undertaken to monitor and facilitate implementation of an existing truce arrangement and in support of diplomatic efforts to achieve a political settlement of the dispute.

We use the term 'peace enforcement' to refer to operations involving the use of threat of force to preserve, maintain or restore international peace and security or to deal with breaches of the peace or acts of aggression; these operations are authorized by the Security Council under Chapter VII of the Charter and do not require the consent of the states or other parties involved. We use the term 'peace operations' to refer to the entire scope of peacekeeping and peace enforcement activities.

NOTE:

Typical examples of UN peacekeeping operations are the UN Observer Group in Central America (ONUCA: 1989–92; established by the UN Secretary-General and the Security Council), UN Operation in the Congo (ONUC; 1960–64; established by the Security Council and the General Assembly), UN Interim Force in Lebanon (UNIFIL: 1978–present; established by the Security Council and the UN Secretary-General) and UN Mission in Ethiopia and Eritrea (UNMEE): 2000 – present established by the Security Council).

15

Peaceful Settlement of International Disputes

Introductory note

An international legal order, as with any effective legal system, must have some rules in regard to the settlement of disputes. These rules are particularly necessary in an international community where States are not equal in terms of diplomatic power, access to weapons or access to resources, and where there is the potential for massive harm to people and to territory. That these disputes should be settled peacefully is a direct corollary of the prohibition of the use of force seen in the previous chapter.

The legal obligation to settle disputes peacefully may now have the character of *jus cogens*, at least if the non-use of force has that character (see Chapter 14). However, this obligation does not prescribe any specific method of peaceful settlement to be used, or that a dispute must be settled at all. Instead it provides that if an attempt is made to settle the dispute, it must be done peacefully.

The traditional assumption is that States must consent to the international legal order (see Chapter 2), so even if a State consents to a particular means or to a body to settle the dispute peacefully, generally that State cannot be compelled to comply with any decision which results. Nevertheless, in most instances States do comply with decisions of international judicial, quasi-judicial or other international supervisory bodies. This may be due to moral, economic, social or political pressure, or as part of an acknowledgement of an international legal order.

Relatively few international disputes are settled by the International Court of Justice. Nevertheless, its position as a permanent international court and the wide impact of its decisions in clarifying and developing international law, requires consideration of its structure and jurisdiction to a greater extent than its actual dispute-settling role would suggest.

SECTION 1: **General obligation on States**

United Nations Charter

Article 2
3. All Members shall settle their international disputes by peaceful means in such a manner that international peace and security, and justice, are not endangered.

Article 33
1. The parties to any dispute, the continuance of which is likely to endanger the mainten-ance of international peace and security, shall, first of all, seek a solution by negotiation, enquiry, mediation, conciliation, arbitration, judicial settlement, resort to regional agencies or arrangements, or other peaceful means of their own choice.

2. The Security Council shall, when it deems necessary, call upon the parties to settle their dispute by such means.

Status of Eastern Carelia Case
PCIJ Ser B (1923), No. 5, Permanent Court of International Justice

It is well established in international law that no State can, without its consent, be compelled to submit its disputes with other States either to mediation or to arbitration, or to any other kind of pacific settlement.

NOTE:
What constitutes an 'international dispute' was considered by the International Court of Justice in the Advisory Opinion of *Interpretation of Peace Treaties Case* ICJ Rep 1950 65. It held that:

> whether there exists an international dispute is a matter for objective determination. The mere denial of the existence of a dispute [by a State] does not prove its non-existence. . . . There has thus arisen a situation in which the two sides hold clearly opposite views concerning the ques-tion of the performance or non-performance of treaty obligations. Confronted with such a situation, the Court must conclude that international disputes have arisen.

SECTION 2: **Non-judicial settlement procedures**

A: General procedures

D. Bowett, 'Contemporary Developments in Legal Techniques in the Settlement of Disputes'
180 *Receuil des Cours* 169 (1983-II)

The principle of settlement of disputes by *peaceful* means is, of course, one of the principles basic to the whole structure of international society. Its juxtaposition in Article 2(3) of the United Nations Charter with Article 2(4) is no accident of drafting: for it is the corollary of the prohibition of the use or threat of force as a means of resolving international disputes. This emerges clearly from the Manila Declaration on the Peaceful Settlement of Disputes adopted by the General Assembly in 1982 at its thirty-seventh session: for there the constant reiteration of the obligation not to use force for the settlement of disputes emphasizes the fundamental link between these two Charter provisions.

Yet settlement of disputes by *peaceful* means is not the same as settlement by *legal* means. Realistically, we have to accept that the vast majority of disputes will be settled by political rather than by legal means. Settlement is normally achieved by negotiation, with or without the assistance of some third party. The third party may be a State or an organ of some organization such as the Security Council, or the Council of Ministers of the Organization for African Unity, or the Council, or the Arab League. And the third party involvement may be formalized good offices, or mediation, or conciliation; or it may be quite informal, and undertaken as a more or less routine part of the functioning of the many international organizations, or even the diplomatic function.

Yet, whatever its form, these techniques of settlement are rarely indifferent to the legal rights of the parties. Obviously, the relevance of the law will depend on how far the parties invoke legal arguments. In general, however, they will do so and the settlement process has to take account of them. The eventual settlement would, however, be normally expected to embody elements of a compromise: and, indeed, willingness to compromise is deemed something of a virtue.

Clearly, however, there are occasions when the parties prefer settlement by *legal* means, and by that I mean resort to either arbitration or judicial settlement. It is the characteristic of these techniques that they involve the application of law – to the exclusion of political discretion or, indeed, any other 'non-legal' factors – and result in a binding award or judgment. At least, that is the theory.

H. Wilson, *The Labour Government 1964–1970: A Personal Record*
(1971), pp. 112–113

The Rann of Kutch is an area north-west of Bombay on the Arabian Sea, and was the subject of a territorial dispute between India and Pakistan which resulted in the use of force in 1965. The boundary was eventually judicially settled by a judicial tribunal in 1968.

We [the United Kingdom Government] were able to make progress with the Rann of Kutch dispute, which had become more dangerous with the outbreak of fighting on the Kashmir border. Mr Shastri [Prime Minister of India] was at Chequers, President Ayub [of Pakistan] at Dorneywood. After dinner, when my guests went up to the Long Gallery for coffee and drinks and informal discussion, I [United Kingdom Prime Minister Harold Wilson] took the chance of sounding out the Indian Prime Minister about the dispute, and we were soon looking at maps. 'Was this track essential? Could Pakistan move along that one? Suppose it were only police and not troops involved in this area, and guns moved back in that one?' Gradually the sticking-points became clearer. Meanwhile, a similar process was going on at Dorneywood. Each tentative advance or embryo concession was passed through private secretaries from one house to the other and we began to make progress.

On the next evening the roles were reversed. I took Ayub aside after dinner, Arthur Bottomley engaged Shastri. . . . We . . . passed on to the Rann of Kutch problem, again exchanging messages point by point with Dorneywood. By midnight, putting together the moves in both houses, we were moving towards a possible settlement. Both our guests accepted my proposal that, with the Queen's permission, we might retire for a few minutes from the Royal dinner for the Commonwealth prime ministers to see if an agreement could be worked out. Detailed briefing was prepared in the Commonwealth Office, and on the night of Tuesday, 22nd June [1965], when we were all at Buckingham Palace, by prior arrangement with Her Majesty we went to a prepared room and quickly reached the basis of a settlement. The two British High Commissioners followed this up with their host Governments and, a cease-fire was signed on 30th June and announced by me in Parliament.

NOTES:
1. Article 33 of the United Nations Charter suggests a range of dispute settlement methods. Many of these methods are substantially non-judicial, for example, negotiation, enquiry,

mediation and conciliation. States can decide for themselves how to resolve their disputes peacefully – see *Status of Eastern Carelia Case* above.

2. The distinction between legal and non-legal means of settling disputes is given in the extract from Bowett. As seen from the memoirs of Harold Wilson, a non-legal method was applied in the Rann of Kutch settlement. The settlement reached was then put into a legally binding agreement, which included an agreement to arbitrate the dispute – *Rann of Kutch Arbitration* 7 ILM 633 (1968).

3. The introduction of a third party into a dispute is often used once the parties are unable to resolve the dispute by negotiation. The extent of the role of the third party varies from being merely a channel of communication between the parties to an active promoter of solutions after undertaking its own investigations. It can even be a national solution involving international actors, as in the Lockerbie case above. In that case, after one of the two men was found guilty, the Libyan government has reportedly offered compensation to the victims on condition that sanctions against it are lifted (see below).

B: United Nations procedures

United Nations Charter

Article 36

1. The Security Council may, at any stage of a dispute of the nature referred to in Article 33 or of a situation of like nature, recommend appropriate procedures or methods of adjustment.

2. The Security Council should take into consideration any procedures for the settlement of the dispute which have already been adopted by the parties.

3. In making recommendations under this Article the Security Council should also take into consideration that legal disputes should as a general rule be referred by the parties to the International Court of Justice in accordance with the provisions of the Statute of the Court.

Article 37

1. Should the parties to a dispute of the nature referred to in Article 33 fail to settle it by the means indicated in that Article, they shall refer it to the Security Council.

2. If the Security Council deems that the continuance of the dispute is in fact likely to endanger the maintenance of international peace and security, it shall decide whether to take action under Article 36 or to recommend such terms of settlement as it may consider appropriate.

Article 38

Without prejudice to the provisions of Articles 33 to 37, the Security Council may, if all the parties to any dispute so request, make recommendations to the parties with a view to a pacific settlement of the dispute.

K. Annan, *Prevention of Armed Conflict, Report of the Secretary-General of the United Nations, 2001*

United Nations Document A/55/985–S/2001/574

9. The Security Council has stressed the importance of responding to the root causes of conflict and the need to pursue long-term effective preventive strategies. The Council has further noted that a coherent peace-building strategy, encompassing political, developmental, humanitarian and human rights programmes, can play a key role in conflict prevention. In this regard, I would like to

draw a clear distinction between regular developmental and humanitarian assistance programmes, on the one hand, and those implemented as a preventive or peace-building response to problems that could lead to the outbreak or recurrence of violent conflict, on the other.

10. An investment in long-term structural prevention is ultimately an investment in sustainable development: first, because it is obvious that sustainable development cannot take place in the midst of actual or potential conflict, and second, because armed conflict destroys the achievements of national development. In some cases, as we have recently witnessed, protracted conflicts have undermined the very existence of such States as Somalia and Afghanistan. Effective conflict prevention is a prerequisite for achieving and maintaining sustainable peace, which in turn is a pre-requisite for sustainable development. When sustainable development addresses the root causes of conflict, it plays an important role in preventing conflict and promoting peace.

11. In the current era of diminishing international development assistance, the donor community is increasingly reluctant to provide development support to States that are on the brink of or in the midst of conflict. Investing in conflict prevention offers the potential for multiple returns for national development over the long term. More effective prevention strategies would save not only hundreds of thousands of lives but also billions of dollars. Funds currently spent on military action could instead be available for poverty reduction and equitable sustainable development, which would further reduce the risks of war and disaster. Conflict prevention and sustainable development are mutually reinforcing.

12. The role of the United Nations is principally to assist national Governments and their local counterparts in finding solutions to their problems by offering support for the development of national and regional capacities for early warning, conflict prevention and long-term peace-building. Such assistance is premised on the principle of consent of the affected Member States. In practice, international cooperation in this domain is often by invitation of the State or States concerned.

13. The development and humanitarian agencies of the United Nations system, together with the Bretton Woods institutions, have a vital role to play in creating a peaceful environment, as well as addressing the root causes of conflicts at the early stages of prevention.

NOTES:
1. Since the end of the Cold War the Security Council has been able to take action to settle disputes. Some of this action has been by force, as in the Gulf War, and some by peace-keeping operations, as in Namibia and Cambodia, as was seen in Chapter 14. In the extract above, Annan deals with the peace-building strategies of the United Nations, which can extend from seeking to resolve disputes between States to assisting in the process of demo-cratic elections.
2. The Secretary-General of the United Nations has used the 'good offices' function of the position to settle disputes, either personally or through an appointed representative. Regional organisations are also involved in settling disputes peacefully. He can be involved in many ways, as seen in the negotiations for solution to the Lockerbie case (see below), which led to a trial of two Libyan men before a Scottish court in The Netherlands (see above).
3. The interaction between the roles of the Security Council and the International Court of Justice in the peaceful settlement of disputes, as provided for in Article 36(3) of the United Nations Charter, is dealt with below.

SECTION 3: **Arbitration**

International Law Commission Draft Articles on Arbitral Procedure, *Report to the General Assembly*
ILC Ybk (1953), vol II, 202

According to established law and practice, international arbitration is a procedure for the settlement of disputes between States by a binding award on the basis of law and as the result of an undertaking voluntarily accepted. It is also of the essence of the traditional law of arbitral procedure . . . that the arbitrators chosen should be either freely selected by the parties or, at least, that the parties should have been given the opportunity of a free choice of arbitrators. The same principle of free determination by the parties applies to the competence of the arbitral tribunal, the law to be applied and the procedure to be followed by the tribunal.

O. Schachter, 'The Enforcement of International Judicial and Arbitral Decisions'
54 AJIL 1 (1960)

In legal doctrine, the principle that an arbitral award or a judicial decision is binding upon the parties and must be carried out in good faith has been accepted without dissent. The *compromis* almost invariably provides for the obligatory effect of the award; and even apart from this, there is a well-settled rule of customary law that such decisions are binding on the losing state. Thus, in connection with the Model Rules of Arbitral Procedure prepared by the International Law Commission, no government has suggested any reservation to the provision stating that the award is binding upon the parties when it is rendered and must be carried out in good faith. . . . Against the rule that decision is binding, the unsuccessful party will assert the doctrine of nullity or of impossibility of performance. Rarely, if ever, is the failure to comply unsupported by a legal claim; the decision, it will be argued, cannot be binding if it is invalid under law or unenforceable in practice. An abundant literature has grown up on the excuses for non-performance. The principles of nullity and impossibility are universally recognized, but there is a variety of views on the specific conditions of their application. Three conditions are most generally formulated in this literature as grounds of nullity: (1) excess of power, (2) corruption of a member of the tribunal, or (3) a serious departure from a fundamental rule of procedure. In practice, it is the first – excess of power – which is the most likely formula to be asserted for justifying non-performance. . . .

But even under present conditions enforcement measures may have a significance which should not be overlooked. The very fact that recourse to arbitration and judicial settlement is infrequent and uncertain increases the prejudicial effect that a single case of non-compliance will have on future submissions of disputes. If enforcement measures are not available or if they are inadequate, the sense of frustration is compounded, not only to the detriment of the rule of law but also quite possibly to an extent that may involve a direct threat to international peace.

A. Redfern and J. Hunter, *International Commercial Arbitration*
(3rd edn, 1999), pp. 1–27

International commercial arbitration is a way of resolving disputes which the parties choose for themselves. It is private, it is effective and, in most parts of the world, it is now the generally accepted method of resolving international business disputes. International commercial arbitrations take place daily, in different countries and against different legal and cultural backgrounds; because they take place by agreement between the parties, and are conducted in private, there is an informality about them which is striking. There are no national flags or other symbols of state authority. There are no ushers, wigs or gowns – simply a group of people seated around a row of tables, in a room hired for the occasion. To an outsider, it would look as if a conference or business meeting was in progress: it is not very like a legal proceeding at all.

Yet the appearance conceals the reality. It is true that the parties themselves choose to arbitrate, as an alternative to litigation or to other methods of dispute resolution. It is true too that, to a large extent, the arbitrators and the parties may choose for themselves the procedures to be followed. If they want a 'fast-track' arbitration they may have one. If they want to dispense with the disclosure of documents or the evidence of witnesses, they may do so. Indeed, they may dispense with the hearing itself if they wish. Nonetheless, the practice of resolving disputes by international commercial arbitration – a practice which increases in popularity each year – only works because it is held in place by a complex system of national laws and international treaties. Even a comparatively simple international commercial arbitration may require reference to as many as four different national systems or rules of law. First, there is the law that governs recognition and enforcement of the agreement to arbitrate. Then there is the law which governs (or regulates) the actual arbitration proceedings themselves. Next (and in most cases, most importantly) there is the law or the set of rules which the arbitral tribunal has to apply to the substantive matters in dispute before it. Finally, there is the law that governs recognition and enforcement of the award of the arbitral tribunal.

These laws may well be the same. The law that governs the arbitral proceedings (which will usually be the national law of the place of arbitration) may also be the applicable law – that is, the law which governs the substantive matters in issue. But this is not necessarily so. The applicable law (which is also known as the 'governing law' or 'the proper law of the contract', in Dicey's celebrated phrase) may be a different system of law. For example, an arbitral tribunal sitting in England, governed (or regulated) by English law as the law of the place of arbitration, may well be required to apply French law as the proper law of the contract. Moreover, the proper law of the contract may not necessarily be a given national system of law: it may be international law; or a blend of national law and international law; or even an assemblage of rules of law known as international trade law, transnational law, the 'modern law merchant' (the so-called *lex mercatoria*) or by some other appropriate title. Finally, because most international arbitrations take place in a country which is not that of the parties, the system of law which governs recognition and enforcement of the award of the arbitral tribunal will usually be different from that which governs the arbitral proceedings themselves. . . . [There are four] significant features of the process of international commercial arbitration . . .: the agreement to arbitrate; the choice of arbitrators; the decision of the arbitral tribunal; [and] the enforcement of the award. . . .

Two main criteria are used, either alone or in conjunction, to define the term 'international' in the context of an international commercial arbitration. The first involves analysing the *nature of the dispute*, so that an arbitration is treated as international if it 'involves the interests of international trade'. The second involves focusing attention on the *parties*: their nationality or habitual place of residence or, if (as is usually the case) the party is a corporate entity, the seat of its central control and management. On this criterion, to take a simple example, an arbitration between a British company and a French company would be an international arbitration, much as the annual rugby match between England and France is an international match. Some national systems of law have adopted the first approach; some have adopted the second; and others have followed the [UNCITRAL] Model Law in selecting a mixture of the two. . . .

The principal distinction that is commonly drawn is between *ad hoc* arbitration and institutional arbitration. Accordingly, it is appropriate to consider first the distinction between the two and then to look at some of the most important arbitral institutions operating in the field of international and commercial arbitration. An *ad hoc* arbitration is conducted under rules of procedure which are adopted for the purposes of the arbitration. These rules of procedure may have been drawn up by one of the non-commercial international organisations such as UNCITRAL; or they may be specifically drawn up by the parties, or by the arbitral tribunal, or by some combination of the above. Ad hoc arbitrations may take place under the provisions of a 'tailor-made' submission agreement, which itself establishes the arbitral tribunal and sets out the governing law, the place (or 'seat') of arbitration and the procedural rules upon which the parties have agreed. More usually however, an *ad hoc* arbitration arises under an arbitration clause in the contract between the parties.

An 'institutional' arbitration is one that is administered by one of the many specialist arbitral institutions under its own rules of arbitration. There are many such institutions. Amongst the better known are the American Arbitration Association, the Inter-American Commission of Commercial Arbitration, the International Centre for the Settlement of Investment Disputes, the International Chamber of Commerce, and the London Court of International Arbitration. There are also regional arbitral institutions, such as those of Zurich, Stockholm and Vienna. The rules of these arbitral institutions tend to follow a similar pattern, although they are expressly formulated for arbitrations that are to be administered by the institution concerned; and they generally arise under an institutional arbitration clause in the agreement between the parties. The clause recommended by the ICC, for instance, states: 'All disputes arising in connection with the present contract shall be finally settled under the Rules of Conciliation and Arbitration of the International Chamber of Commerce by one or more arbitrators appointed in accordance with the said Rules.' In common with other institutional clauses, this clause is a convenient short-form method of incorporating into the agreement between the parties a detailed book of rules that will govern any arbitration that may take place in the future. An obvious advantage of such a clause is that even if, at some future stage, one party proves reluctant to go ahead with arbitration proceedings, it will nevertheless be possible to arbitrate effectively, because a set of rules exists to regulate the way in which the arbitral tribunal is to be appointed and the arbitration is to be administered and conducted.

M. Sornarajah, 'Power and Justice in Foreign Investment Arbitration'
14 *Journal of International Arbitration* (1997) 103, 139–140

The vestiges of an old order based on power continues to dictate the course of developments in international foreign investment arbitration. It has been given additional impetus in recent times by the process of globalization and the seeming weakening of the resolve of developing States to press for the restructuring of the international economic order. Seizing upon this situation, new techniques of advancing the flow of foreign investment are being attempted. The old strategy of devising a system of foreign investment protection through the system of arbitration has been revived with new vigour in recent times. The tendency is most visible in the recent ICSID jurisprudence. The widening of jurisdiction by expanding notions of corporate nationality and the notion of arbitration without privity are clear examples of the tendency to assume jurisdiction over disputes in circumstances where consent is unclear. The creation of new substantive principles such as due process requirements before the termination of the foreign investment and the continuing emphasis on sanctity of contracts are spurious uses of the notion that general principles of law are a source of international law. These constitute instances of power being utilized in order to create 'law' to achieve the objective of investment protection without taking into account the context in which the foreign investment operated.

The system of international arbitration is intended to be a neutral system but it does not appear to have operated as such in the course of its development, at least as far as arbitration of foreign investment disputes are concerned. Arbitrators have shown a keenness to develop rules which favour foreign investment protection and have discarded rules which may permit a more balanced assessment of the issues presented in a dispute. Such trends are destructive of the objectives of international arbitration as a method of dispute settlement. The mechanism of arbitration still remains a viable method for the settlement of foreign investment disputes but there must be an evolution of more justice-oriented rules shaping its course.

Lockerbie Case: Scottish Trial in The Netherlands
Letter from UN Secretary-General to the Security Council, 5 April 1999
UN Doc. S/1999/378

The facts of the Lockerbie case are set out below. After a number of years of negotiations, it was agreed that a trial of the two main suspects (of Libyan nationality) would be held before a Scottish court (as the incident happened in Scottish (British) territory) but in a 'neutral' location, being The Netherlands. The eventual consequence was the finding by the Scottish court that one of the two men was guilty of murder (40 ILM 582 (2001)). This letter sets out the way by which this method of dispute settlement was agreed.

On 27 August 1998, the Security Council adopted resolution 1192 (1998), in which it welcomed the initiative for the trial of the two persons charged with the bombing of Pan Am flight 103 before a Scottish court sitting in the Netherlands, as contained in the letter dated 24 August 1998 from the Acting Permanent Representatives of the United Kingdom of Great Britain and Northern Ireland and of the United States of America and its attachments, and the willingness of the Government of the Netherlands to cooperate in the implementation of the initiative. In that resolution, the Security Council called upon the Government of the Netherlands and the Government of the United Kingdom to take such steps as were necessary, including the conclusion of arrangements with a view to enabling the court sitting in the Netherlands to exercise jurisdiction in respect of the trial of the two persons charged with the bombing of Pan Am flight 103. As has already been reported, that request has already been met. On 18 September 1998, the Government of the Netherlands and the Government of the United Kingdom signed an agreement concerning a trial in the Netherlands before a Scottish court, and subsequently they enacted the necessary legislation to give effect to the agreement [see 38 ILM 926 (1999)]. I should like to express my deep appreciation to both Governments for their willingness, in the interest of finding a constructive resolution to the matter at hand, to take this unprecedented step enabling a national court of one country to conduct a trial in another country.

By resolution 1192 (1998), the Council further requested the Secretary-General, after consultation with the Government of the Netherlands, to assist the Libyan Government with the physical arrangements for the safe transfer of the two accused from the Libyan Arab Jamahiriya direct to the Netherlands. I am pleased to inform the Security Council that, as requested in the resolution, all the necessary assistance has been provided to the Libyan Government and that today, 5 April 1999, the two accused have safely arrived in the Netherlands on board a United Nations aircraft. During the flight the two accused were accompanied by my representative, Mr Hans Corell, the Legal Counsel, who has been in charge of the operation. After the aircraft landed at 9.45 a.m., New York time, at Valkenburg airport in the Netherlands, the two accused were detained by the Dutch authorities, as provided for in paragraph 7 of Security Council resolution 1192 (1998), pending their transfer for the purpose of trial before the Scottish court sitting in the Netherlands. . . . Today's development would not have been possible without the demonstration of goodwill on the part of all the parties concerned and without their commitment to resolving all the issues related to the implementation of Security Council resolution 1192 (1998) in a satisfactory and mutually acceptable manner.

As has already been reported informally to the members of the Security Council, given the complex and sensitive nature of the arrangements foreseen in resolution 1192 (1998), issues of both a political and legal nature were raised by the Libyan Government regarding the implementation of the resolution. Those issues needed to be clarified to the satisfaction of all the parties concerned in order to achieve understanding on the implementation of the resolution.

Legal issues as well as practical arrangements related to the implementation of the resolution were discussed in October and November 1998 between the United Nations Legal Counsel, Mr Hans Corell, and a Libyan legal team, headed by Mr Kamel Hassan Maghur. They were resolved to the satisfaction of all those concerned . . . With a view to achieving progress in resolving some of the sensitive political issues of concern to the Libyan Government, on 5 December 1998, I travelled to the Libyan Arab Jamahiriya and had fruitful and constructive discussions with the Leader of the Revolution, Colonel Muammar Qaddafi, and senior Libyan officials. Following my visit, I sought the assistance of the Governments of South Africa and Saudi Arabia, with which I have been constantly in close touch to coordinate our joint efforts in search of a fair solution to the pending issues. I should like, therefore, to express my appreciation to the Government of the Libyan Arab Jamahiriya and all the other parties concerned for their willingness to demonstrate sufficient flexibility in arriving at a mutually acceptable solution. I should like, in particular, to express gratitude to the Governments of Saudi Arabia and South Africa for their efforts and assistance.

Paragraph 8 of Security Council resolution 1192 (1998) provides, *inter alia*, that if the Secretary-General reports to the Council that the two accused have arrived in the Netherlands for the purpose of trial before the Scottish court sitting in the Netherlands . . . the measures set forth in Security Council resolutions 748 (1992) and 883 (1993) shall be suspended immediately. As noted above, these requirements of the resolution have been met. . . . Therefore, following the suspension of the measures referred to above, I shall proceed as expeditiously as possible with the preparation of this report; The Libyan Arab Jamahiriya has already provided extensive information and the necessary assurances on this matter, including to the Security Council.

Finally, let me also express the hope that the spirit of cooperation now established, will be maintained in future and that the start of the trial will mark the beginning of a process leading to the normalization of relations among all parties concerned for the benefit of the international community as a whole. Accept, Sir, the assurances of my highest consideration.

(Signed) Kofi A. ANNAN

NOTES:

1. Arbitration is a device for leaving the settlement of disputes as much in the hands of the parties as is possible. It can be conducted confidentially and can be quicker and cheaper than ICJ proceedings. When the parties conclude an agreement, they generally settle the law to be applied to the agreement, and also the method of settlement of any disputes which may arise, including the place where the dispute is to be settled, by whom and in accordance with what procedures. They have much more freedom of choice than in court settlement, where there is a standing panel of judges with its own procedural rules.

2. States may choose arbitration as the method to settle a dispute between them, even if the dispute concerns territorial boundaries or treaty interpretation. Examples include the *English Channel Arbitration Case* 54 ILR (1977) 6 (see Chapter 3) and the *Air Services Agreement Case* 18 RIAA (1978) 416. In these situations, the States agree on the form of arbitration and the membership of the arbitration tribunal, usually with an arbitrator appointed by each State and the third arbitrator either appointed jointly by the States or by the already appointed arbitrators.

3. An international tribunal can be set up for a limited purpose in order to decide specific disputes between two States. An example is the Iran-United States Claims Tribunal, which was established in 1981 pursuant to the Declaration of Algiers (20 ILM 223 (1981)) after the taking of the United States Embassy and staff in Iran and the consequent freezing of Iranian assets in the United States (see *United States Diplomatic and Consular Staff in Tehran Case* in Chapter 11 and below). This Tribunal has jurisdiction over claims by nationals of the United States against Iran, claims by nationals of Iran against the United States, and claims between the two States.

4. In international commercial arbitrations between a State and an international corporation, there are a number of arbitration treaties which are supervised by international arbitration institutions, as is indicated by Redfern and Hunter. These treaties provide procedural rules which can be adopted by the parties if they consider them appropriate. This system, though,

has been criticised for favouring one group of interests over others, as seen in the extract from Sornarajah.

5. A major consideration in choosing arbitration as a means of settling a dispute between a State and an international corporation will be that the international corporation may not wish to be subjected to the courts of the State with which it has contracted (as seen in Chapter 11 in regard to expropriation/nationalisation). Agreements are made to limit a State's ability to interfere in, or to frustrate, an arbitration by, for example, claiming State immunity or giving diplomatic protection (e.g., Articles 26 and 27 of the ICSID Convention). Sometimes pressure from other States can compel arbitration, e.g. in *Santa Elena* v *Costa Rica*, (ICSID Final Award 17 February 2000) the ICSID Arbitral Tribunal noted that 'a $US175,000,000 loan Inter-American Development Bank to Costa Rica was delayed at the behest of the US until Costa Rica consented to refer the *Santa Elena* case to international arbitration' (para. 25).

6. In order to reduce the possibility of intervention by a State's courts in an international commercial arbitration occurring on its territory, the United Nations Commission on International Trade Law (UNCITRAL) proposed in 1985 a Model Law on International Commercial Arbitration (24 ILM 1302 (1985)). The purpose of this Model Law is to encourage each State to adopt it as part of its national legislation and so to standardise international treatment of these arbitrations. As Schachter indicates, there are certain circumstances where the decision of an arbitral tribunal may not be final. However, very often economic pressures, such as the desire for foreign investment – which usually demands a relatively stable legal system and confidence that law will be complied with – or pressures from other States (e.g. *Santa Elena* v *Costa Rica* above), facilitates a State's compliance with an arbitration decision.

SECTION 4: **Specific international tribunals**

There has been a vast growth in the number of international tribunals, both judicial and non-judicial, in the past few decades. Sands (below) puts these developments in context and the following notes offer some information on some of the major international tribunals.

P. Sands, 'Turtles and Torturers: the Transformation of International Law'
33 *New York University Journal of International Law and Politics* 527 (2001), 553–6

The international judiciary has evolved beyond recognition in the past two decades. In 1893, there were no standing international courts. In 1946, there was just one, the International Court of Justice in The Hague. Today, there are over twenty-five permanent international courts and tribunals, competent to hear cases brought by one State against another and, increasingly, providing for a forum within which non-State actors can litigate internationally. Some of these courts are familiar, particularly the European Court of Justice in Luxembourg and the European Court of Human Rights in Strasbourg. . . . [There is] the WTO's Appellate Body (arguably the single most powerful international court today) [,] the new International Tribunal for the Law of the Sea, [and] The World Bank's International Centre for the Settlement of Investment Disputes. . . . [There are also] the criminal tribunals for the former Yugoslavia and for Rwanda, which are rather better known, and the International Criminal Court (ICC), whose Statute was adopted in July 1998 in Rome. . . .

These and other regional and global judicial bodies have transformed the landscape of international law. States have created fertile conditions for international litigation and a powerful new international judiciary. This new judiciary has taken on a life of its own and has already, in many instances, shown itself unwilling to defer to traditional conceptions of sovereignty and state power.

The mere existence of these bodies is being felt around the world. I have little doubt that the *Pinochet* case would have taken a very different turn if there had not been the Nuremberg and Tokyo tribunals, the Yugoslavia and Rwanda tribunals, and the Statute of the ICC to rely upon, reflecting a desire to promote more effectively international criminal law and the protection of fundamental human rights. It is difficult to prove a causal relationship between various acts and developments at different levels of governance, but it seems clear that the creation of the ICC, the arrest of Senator Pinochet, and the indictment of President Milosovic by the International Criminal Tribunal for the Former Yugoslavia – all of which took place within a year of each other and each of which is without precedent – reflect a changing consciousness in which the international and the domestic intersect and are mutually reinforcing, and a set of 'international' values emerges, capable of being applied at the national level.

Beyond this background effect, the creation of these new international courts 'judicializes' international relations, increasingly subjecting international disputes to binding third-party adjudication and providing new avenues of appeal from the decisions of national courts. There is a double effect: (1) national courts begin, cautiously perhaps, to look over their shoulders to possible international appeal, and (2) the international decisions are themselves removed from the political control of states and put into the hands of what is, in effect, a new international player: the international judiciary. These developments transform the way we think about international law. States lose a degree of control in the 'making' of international law, since the line between interpretation and legislation can often be a hard one to draw, and a more level playing field is created. The decisions in the *Shrimp/Turtle* and *Pinochet* tribunals have, through the process of interpretation of a set of rules adopted by states, transformed their potential impact. In the *Shrimp/Turtle* case, we have seen how an issue which previously would have been decided by international negotiation and diplomatic action – on the basis of an assumed equality of states but where in reality great discrepancies in sovereign power tilt the balance in favor of the economically and politically powerful – is instead subject to binding judicial decision. We have also seen how these international judges can take the text of the GATT and give to it a meaning and effect which, in all probability, a majority of the state members of the WTO would not have intended. So, who are the seven members of the Appellate Body? How did they get elected, or appointed? From which source do they obtain their legitimacy? How far do they have to go before they cross the line of what states will consider to be acceptable? Who judges the judges? These are questions that have barely been addressed as international courts take on a life of their own and take international law beyond the preservation of peace and harmony amongst nations. An international judiciary has been created on the basis of no planning or long-term vision or strategy.

A: International criminal tribunals

As was seen in Chapters 6 and 8, there have been several international bodies established to deal with international crimes.

By Resolutions 827 (1993) and 955 (1994) the Security Council established the International Criminal Tribunal for the former Yugoslavia and the International Criminal Tribunal for Rwanda. These Tribunals share similar jurisdictional bases and structures (see Chapter 8) with regard to international crimes (see Chapter 6). They were established by means of Security Council resolutions, which are binding on all States, rather than being established by a treaty, due to a concern that the States which were most affected by the conflicts would not become parties to the relevant treaty. These Security Council resolutions were made under Chapter VII of the United Nations Charter, based on the potential threats to international peace and security that arose as a result of the conflicts (see Chapter 14).

One reason why these International Tribunals were established was because the Security Council took the view that in the absence of an international institution to bring war criminals to justice, there would be a continuing cycle of reprisals and conflict that would continue to threaten international peace and security. Prompted by this reasoning, the international community moved to establish by treaty a permanent criminal court. At a conference in Rome in 1998, 120 States voted in favour of the Rome Statute for the International Criminal Court, with 21 abstentions and 7 votes against (including the United States). This Statute (a treaty) entered into force on 1 July 2002, after receiving more than 60 ratifications. As discussed in Chapter 6, the establishment of an International Criminal Court is a major step forward in the enforcement of the law against international crimes.

B: Human rights supervisory bodies

International human rights law has a large number of bodies that supervise compliance with treaties protecting human rights. These are set out in Chapter 6, and include both human rights treaty-based Committees, that can consider both periodic State reports and individual complaints, and United Nations Commissions that can consider gross and systematic human rights violations. In addition, a number of these bodies, such as the Inter-American Commission on Human Rights, can seek to settle the matter prior to a final judicial or quasi-judicial decision. The impact of these international human rights supervisory bodies on the settlement of human rights disputes, including through national law and courts, is significant and is growing.

C: International economic law

As explained in Chapter 13, a detailed dispute settlement procedure was created by the World Trade Organization (WTO). The Understanding on Dispute Settlement (DSU) was incorporated into the Agreement establishing the WTO and is designed to provide a unitary system for dispute settlement that is applicable for all of the Uruguary Round Agreements regulating international trade. This system replaced the (temporary) procedures under the General Agreement on Tariffs and Trade (GATT).

D: Other specific international tribunals

Under the Law of the Sea Convention 1982, dispute settlement occurs by a variety of methods, including the International Tribunal for the Law of the Sea, though there are some issues that are expressly exempted from any form of compulsory dispute settlement (see Chapter 10). This Tribunal was formed in 1996, after the Convention came into force.

SECTION 5: **International Court of Justice**

The International Court of Justice (ICJ) was created in 1945. It is substantially a continuation of the Permanent Court of International Justice (PCIJ), which was created in 1921. Article 92 of the United Nations Charter describes the ICJ as 'the principal judicial organ of the United Nations', with the Statute of the ICJ being 'an integral part' of the Charter.

A: General

Statute of the International Court of Justice

Article 2
The Court shall be composed of a body of independent judges, elected regardless of their nationality from among persons of high moral character, who possess the qualifications required in their respective countries for appointment to the highest judicial offices, or are jurisconsults of recognized competence in international law.

Article 3
1. The Court shall consist of fifteen members, no two of whom may be nationals of the same State.

Article 26
1. The Court may from time to time form one or more chambers, composed of three or more judges as the Court may determine, for dealing with particular categories of cases; for example, labour cases and cases relating to transit and communications.
2. The Court may at any time form a chamber for dealing with a particular case. The number of judges to constitute such a chamber shall be determined by the Court with the approval of the parties.
3. Cases shall be heard and determined by the chambers provided for in this Article if the parties so request.

Article 27
A judgment given by any of the chambers provided for in Articles 26 and 29 shall be considered as rendered by the Court.

Article 31
1. Judges of the nationality of each of the parties shall retain their right to sit in the case before the Court.
2. If the Court includes upon the Bench a judge of the nationality of one of the parties any other party may choose a person to sit as judge. Such person shall be chosen preferably from among those persons who have been nominated as candidates as provided in Articles 4 and 5.
3. If the Court includes upon the Bench no judge of the nationality of the parties, each of these parties may proceed to choose a judge as provided in paragraph 2 of this Article.

Article 34

 1. Only States may be parties in cases before the Court.

NOTES:

1. By Article 93 of the United Nations Charter, all members of the United Nations are parties to the Statute of the ICJ. Other States can become parties to the Statute on conditions determined by the Security Council. In this way, five States have become parties to the Statute, often prior to their becoming members of the United Nations: for example, Switzerland (1946), Liechtenstein (1949), Japan (1953), San Mariono (1953), and Nauru (1988).
2. The judges of the ICJ tend to be appointed with the standard United Nations considerations of geographical distribution being taken into account, and with each of the five permanent members of the Security Council having a national as a judge on the ICJ.
3. The use of Chambers of the ICJ has not proved very successful, because there were some problems as to whether the parties should be able to choose the judges they wish for the Chamber, certain judges were regularly chosen and some were never chosen and there is much more weight given to a decision by the full Court.
4. There have been concerns about the apparent politicisation of the judges of the ICJ, with judges rarely voting against the claims of the State of which they are a national and decisions being seen as representing a particular political philosophy. The concern about politicisation is increased by the ability of each State that is a party in a contentious case before the ICJ to appoint judges *ad hoc* (under Article 31 of the Statute), usually being judges of that State's nationality, who are seen to represent the views of that State to the other judges of the ICJ. This may be the inevitable result of the nature of international law (or most law), as it cannot be removed from the political realities or from the various theoretical concepts underlying it (see Chapter 1). The Court has suggested that no person should be appointed a judge *ad hoc* who has acted as an agent, counsel or advocate before the Court within three years of his/her appointment (Practice Direction VII, 7 February 2002).

B: Jurisdiction in contentious cases

Statute of the International Court of Justice

Article 36

 1. The jurisdiction of the Court comprises all cases which the parties refer to it and all matters specially provided for in the Charter of the United Nations or in treaties or conventions in force.

 2. The States Parties to the present Statute may at any time declare that they recognize as compulsory *ipso facto* and without special agreement, in relation to any other State accepting the same obligation, the jurisdiction of the Court in all legal disputes concerning:

   (a) the interpretation of a treaty;
   (b) any question of international law;
   (c) the existence of any fact which, if established, would constitute a breach of an international obligation;
   (d) the nature or extent of the reparation to be made for the breach of an international obligation.

 3. The declarations referred to above may be made unconditionally or on condition of reciprocity on the part of several or certain States, or for a certain time.

 4. Such declarations shall be deposited with the Secretary-General of the United Nations, who shall transmit copies thereof to the parties to the Statute and to the Registrar of the Court.

5. Declarations made under Article 36 of the Statute of the Permanent Court of International Justice and which are still in force shall be deemed, as between the parties to the present Statute, to be acceptances of the compulsory jurisdiction of the International Court of Justice for the period which they still have to run and in accordance with their terms.

6. In the event of a dispute as to whether the Court has jurisdiction the matter shall be settled by the decision of the Court.

Declarations Accepting Compulsory Jurisdiction of the International Court of Justice

ICJ Ybk, (1988–89), 71, 73–74, 94–95; 24 ILM 1742 (1985)

As at 1 July 2002 there were 64 Declarations in force under Article 36(2). The following are examples:

Haiti

[Translation from the French]   4 X 21
On behalf of the Republic of Haiti, I recognize the jurisdiction of the Permanent Court of International Justice as compulsory.

(*Signed*) F. Addor, Consul.

India

18 IX 74.
I have the honour to declare, on behalf of the Government of the Republic of India, that they accept, in conformity with paragraph 2 of Article 36 of the Statute of the Court, until such time as notice may be given to terminate such acceptance, as compulsory *ipso facto* and without special agreement, and on the basis and condition of reciprocity, the jurisdiction of the International Court of Justice over all disputes other than:

(1) disputes in regard to which the parties to the dispute have agreed or shall agree to have recourse to some other method or methods of settlement;

(2) disputes with the government of any State which is or has been a Member of the Commonwealth of Nations;

(3) disputes in regard to matters which are essentially within the domestic jurisdiction of the Republic of India;

(4) disputes relating to or connected with facts or situations of hostilities, armed conflicts, individual or collective actions taken in self-defence, resistance to aggression, fulfilment of obligations imposed by international bodies, and other similar or related acts, measures or situations in which India is, has been or may in future be involved;

(5) disputes with regard to which any other party to a dispute has accepted the compulsory jurisdiction of the International Court of Justice exclusively for or in relation to the purposes of such dispute; or where the acceptance of the Court's compulsory jurisdiction on behalf of a party to the dispute was deposited or ratified less than 12 months prior to the filling of the application bringing the dispute before the Court;

(6) disputes where the jurisdiction of the Court is or may be founded on the basis of a treaty concluded under the auspices of the League of Nations, unless the Government of India specially agree to jurisdiction in each case;

(7) disputes concerning the interpretation or application of a multilateral treaty unless all the parties to the treaty are also parties to the case before the Court or Government of India specially agree to jurisdiction;

(8) disputes with the government of any State with which, on the date of an application to bring a dispute before the Court, the Government of India has no diplomatic relations or which has not been recognized by the Government of India;

(9) disputes with non-sovereign States or territories;

(10) disputes with India concerning or relating to:

(a) the status of its territory or the modification or delimitation of its frontiers or any other matter concerning boundaries;

(b) the territorial sea, the continental shelf and the margins, the exclusive fishery zone, the exclusive economic zone, and other zones of national maritime jurisdiction including for the regulation and control of marine pollution and the conduct of scientific research by foreign vessels;

(c) the condition and status of its island, bays and gulfs and that of the bays and gulfs that for historical reasons belong to it;

(d) the airspace superjacent to its land and maritime territory; and

(e) the determination and delimitation of its maritime boundaries.

(11) disputes prior to the date of this declaration, including any dispute the foundations, reasons, facts, causes, origins, definitions, allegations or bases of which existed prior to this date, even if they are submitted or brought to the knowledge of the Court hereafter.

2. This declaration revokes and replaces the previous declaration made by the Government of India on 14 September 1959.

New Delhi, 15 September 1974.

(*Signed*) Swaran Singh, Minister for External Affairs.

United Kingdom Of Great Britain And Northern Ireland

1 l 69.

I have the honour, by direction of Her Majesty's Principal Secretary of State for Foreign and Commonwealth Affairs, to declare on behalf of the Government of the United Kingdom of Great Britain and Northern Ireland that they accept as compulsory *ipso facto* and without special convention, on condition of reciprocity, the jurisdiction of the International Court of Justice, in conformity with paragraph 2 of Article 36 of the Statute of the Court, until such time as notice may be given to terminate the acceptance, over all disputes arising after 24 October 1945, with regard to situations or facts subsequent to the same date, other than:

(i) any dispute which the United Kingdom

(a) has agreed with the other Party or Parties thereto to settle by some other method of peaceful settlement; or

(b) has already submitted to arbitration by agreement with any State which had not at the time of submission accepted the compulsory jurisdiction of the International Court of Justice;

(ii) disputes with the government of any other country which is a Member of the Commonwealth with regard to situations or facts existing before 1 January 1969;

(iii) disputes in respect of which any other Party to the dispute has accepted the compulsory jurisdiction of the International Court of Justice only in relation to or for the purpose of the dispute; or where the acceptance of the Court's compulsory jurisdiction on behalf of any other Party to the dispute was deposited or ratified less than twelve months prior to the filing of the application bringing the dispute before the Court.

2. The Government of the United Kingdom also reserve the right at any time, by means of a notification addressed to the Secretary-General of the United Nations, and with effect as from the

moment of such notification, either to add to, amend or withdraw any of the foregoing reservations, or any that may hereafter be added.

New York, 1 January 1969.

(*Signed*) L. C. Glass.

United States of America

26 VIII 46.

I, Harry S. Truman, President of the United States of America, declare on behalf of the United of America, under Article 36, paragraph 2, of the Statute of the International Court of Justice, and in accordance with the Resolution of 2 August 1946 of the Senate of the United States of America (two-thirds of the Senators present concurring therein), that the United States of America recognizes as compulsory *ipso facto* and without special agreement, in relation to any other State accepting the same obligation, the jurisdiction of the International Court of Justice in all legal disputes hereafter arising concerning

(a) the interpretation of a treaty;
(b) any question of international law;
(c) the existence of any fact which, if established, would constitute a breach of an international obligation;
(d) the nature or extent of the reparation to be made for the breach of an international obligation;

Provided, that this declaration shall not apply to

(a) disputes the solution of which the parties shall entrust to other tribunals by virtue of agreements already in existence or which may be concluded in the future;
(b) disputes with regard to matters which are essentially within the domestic jurisdiction of the United States of America as determined by the United States of America; or
(c) disputes arising under a multilateral treaty, unless (1) all parties to the treaty affected by the decision are also parties to the case before the Court, or (2) the United States of America specially agrees to jurisdication; and

Provided further, that this declaration shall remain in force for a period of five years and thereafter until the expiration of six months after notice may be given to terminate this declaration.

Done at Washington this fourteenth day of August 1946.

(*Signed*) Harry S. Truman.

6 IV 84.

I have the honour on behalf of the Government of the United States of America to refer to the declaration of my Government of 26 August 1946 concerning the acceptance by the United States of America of the compulsory jursidiction of the International Court of Justice, and to state that the aforesaid declaration shall not apply to disputes with any Central American State or arising out of or related to events in Central America, any of which disputes shall be settled in such manner as the parties to them may agree.

Notwithstanding the terms of the aforesaid declaration, this proviso shall take effect immediately and shall remain in force for two years, so as to foster the continuing regional dispute settlement process which seeks a negotiated solution to the interrelated political, economic and security problems of Central America.

(*Signed*) George P. Shultz, Secretary of State of the United States of America.

October 7, 1985

Dear Mr Secretary General:

I have the honor on behalf of the Government of the United States of America to refer to the declaration of my Government of 26 August 1946, as modified by my note of 6 April 1984, concerning the acceptance by the United States of America of the compulsory jurisdiction of the

International Court of Justice, and to state that the aforesaid declaration is hereby terminated, with effect six months from the date hereof.
Sincerely yours,
George P. Shultz

Norwegian Loans Case (France v Norway)
ICJ Rep 1957 9, International Court of Justice

Both France and Norway had made declaration under Article 36(2) accepting the compulsory jurisdiction of the ICJ. Norway objected to France commencing the action, which concerned the rights of French holders of Norwegian bonds, as it claimed that the issue was essentially a matter within Norway's 'domestic jurisdiction'. Although Norway did not have such a reservation (often called an 'automatic' reservation) to its declaration, it submitted that it could rely on the fact that France did have such a reservation. The Court upheld Norway's submission. However, Judge Lauterpacht made a few comments about such 'automatic' reservations.

THE COURT: [I]n the present case the jurisdiction of the Court depends upon the Declarations made by the Parties in accordance with Article 36, paragraph 2, of the Statute on condition of reciprocity; and that, since two unilateral declarations are involved, such jurisdiction is conferred upon the Court only to the extent to which the Declarations coincide in conferring it. A comparison between the two Declarations shows that the French Declaration accepts the Court's jurisdiction within narrower limits than the Norwegian Declaration; consequently the common will of the parties, which is the basis of the Court's jurisdiction, exists within these narrower limits indicated by the French reservation. . . .

In accordance with the condition of reciprocity to which acceptance of the compulsory jurisdiction is made subject in both Declarations and which is provided for in Article 36, paragraph 3, of the Statute, Norway, equally with France, is entitled to except from the compulsory jurisdiction of the Court disputes understood by Norway to be essentially within its national jurisdiction.

JUDGE LAUTERPACHT (Separate Opinion): I consider that as the French Declaration of Acceptance excludes from the jurisdiction of the Court "matters which are essentially within the national jurisdiction as understood by the Government of the French Republic" – the emphasis being here on the words "as understood by the Government of the French Republic" – it is for the reason of that latter qualification an instrument incapable of producing legal effects before this Court and of establishing its jurisdiction. This is so for the double reason that: (a) it is contrary to the Statute of the Court; (b) the existence of the obligation being dependent upon the determination by the Government accepting the Optional Clause, the Acceptance does not constitute a legal obligation. That Declaration of Acceptance cannot, accordingly, provide a basis for the jurisdiction of the Court. Norway has not accepted the jurisdiction of the Court on any other basis. The Court therefore has no jurisdiction.

If that type of reservation is valid, then the Court is not in the position to exercise the power conferred upon it – in fact, the duty imposed upon it – under paragraph 6 of Article 36 of its Statute. . . . The French reservation is thus not only contrary to one of the most fundamental principles of international – and national – jurisprudence according to which it is within the inherent power of a tribunal to interpret the text establishing its jurisdiction. It is also contrary to a clear specific provision of the Statute of the Court as well as to the general Articles 1 and 92 of the Statute and of the Charter, respectively, which require the Court to function in accordance with its Statute. Now what is the result of the fact that a reservation or part of it are contrary to the provisions of the Statute of the Court? The result is that that reservation or that part of it is invalid.

Military and Paramilitary Activities in and against Nicaragua Case (*Nicaragua* v *USA*)

ICJ Rep 1984 392, International Court of Justice

The United States had made a Declaration in April 1984 (see above) limiting its Optional Clause Declaration. It did this after it became clear that the dispute with Nicaragua was to be placed before the Court. The Court considered that the limitation had no effect on the present case.

59. Declarations of acceptance of the compulsory jurisdiction of the Court are facultative, unilateral engagements, that States are absolutely free to make or not to make. In making the declaration a State is equally free either to do so unconditionally and without limit of time for its duration, or to qualify it with conditions or reservations. In particular, it may limit its effect to disputes arising after a certain date; or it may specify how long the declaration itself shall remain in force, or what notice (if any) will be required to terminate it. . . .

60. In fact, the declarations, even though they are unilateral acts, establish a series of bilateral engagements with other States accepting the same obligation of compulsory jurisdiction, in which the conditions, reservations and time-limit clauses are taken into consideration. . . .

64. The Court would also recall that in previous cases in which it has had to examine the reciprocal effect of declarations made under the Optional Clause, it has determined whether or not the 'same obligation' was in existence at the moment of seising of the Court, by comparing the effect of the provisions, in particular the reservations, of the two declarations at that moment. . . .

65. In sum, the six months' notice clause forms an important integral part of the United States Declaration and it is a condition that must be complied with in case of either termination or modification. Consequently, the 1984 notification, in the present case, cannot override the obligation of the United States to submit to the compulsory jurisdiction of the Court vis-à-vis Nicaragua, a State accepting the same obligation.

Legality of Use of Force Case (*Provisional Measures*) (*Federal Republic of Yugoslavia* v *Belgium, Canada, France, Germany, Italy, Netherlands, Portugal, Spain, United Kingdom and United States*)

38 ILM 950 (1999), International Court of Justice

The Federal Republic of Yugoslavia (FRY) brought this case against ten North Atlantic Treaty Organization (NATO) States in relation to events that were occurring during the armed conflict between NATO and the FRY in Kosovo (being a constituent part of the FRY). The ICJ declined to order provisional measures against any of the respondent States and made some comments about the Court's jurisdiction.

18. Whereas the Court is mindful of the purposes and principles of the United Nations Charter and of its own responsibilities in the maintenance of peace and security under the Charter and the Statute of the Court;

19. Whereas the Court deems it necessary to emphasize that all parties appearing before it must act in conformity with their obligations under the United Nations Charter and other rules of international law, including humanitarian law; . . .

47. Whereas there is a fundamental distinction between the question of the acceptance by a State of the Court's jurisdiction and the compatibility of particular acts with international law; the former requires consent; the latter question can only be reached when the Court deals with

the merits after having established its jurisdiction and having heard full legal arguments by both parties;

48. Whereas, whether or not States accept the jurisdiction of the Court, they remain in any event responsible for acts attributable to them that violate international law, including humanitarian law; whereas any disputes relating to the legality of such acts are required to be resolved by peaceful means, the choice of which, pursuant to Article 33 of the Charter, is left to the parties;

49. Whereas in this context the parties should take care not to aggravate or extend the dispute;

50. Whereas, when such a dispute gives rise to threat to the peace, breach of the peace or act of aggression, the Security Council has special responsibilities under Chapter VII of the Charter . . .

The Court Rejects the Request for Provisional Measures.

NOTES

1. The ICJ has jurisdiction to attempt to settle a dispute only if the parties to the dispute consent to the ICJ so doing. Partly for this reason, many international disputes never reach the ICJ. As is evident from the decision in the *Legality of Use of Force Case*, both the ICJ and States still have obligations under international law to settle disputes peacefully irrespective of whether the ICJ has jurisdiction in a particular instance. In *Armed Activities on the Territory of the Congo (Congo v Rwanda) (Provisional Measures)* ICJ Rep 2002, the ICJ reaffirmed that there is a 'fundamental distinction' between the Court having jurisdiction and whether an act is in violation of international law.

2. The main methods by which the ICJ has jurisdiction in contentious cases are where the parties specifically agree to submit a defined dispute to it (a *compromis*), as was the case in the various *Continental Shelf Cases* (see Chapter 10); by a compromissory clause in a multilateral or bilateral treaty, where the treaty provides for reference of certain disputes to the Court, as in the *United States Diplomatic and Consular Staff in Tehran Case*, ICJ Rep 1980 3 (below); or where the parties have made a declaration under Article 36(2), known as the 'Optional Clause', accepting the compulsory jurisdiction of the Court in all matters not specifically excluded by the State, as the parties had done (or appeared to have done) in the *Nicaragua Case*. A number of these declarations were made to the PCIJ's jurisdiction and remain current for the ICJ due to Articles 36(5) and 37 of the ICJ Statute.

3. It is argued that one difficulty of the Optional Clause method of accepting jurisdiction is that the State so declaring has perhaps little control over deciding whether the particular dispute is appropriate for settlement by the ICJ. There are few declarations which, like Haiti's, do not have any reservations. India's Commonwealth reservation (see above (2)) was declared to be a valid reservation in *Aerial Incident of 10 August 1999* (*Pakistan v India* ICJ Rep 2000, para 44). The vast majority of States either have not made any declaration under the Optional Clause, or have significant reservations in their declarations, such as India's. Of the five Permanent Members of the Security Council, only the United Kingdom has a current declaration under the Optional Clause, and that declaration includes reservations. This has the effect of reducing the ability of the ICJ to settle international disputes and decreasing the possibility of the ICJ clarifying and developing international law.

4. The concept of reciprocity allows a State to rely on a reservation by another State party to the ICJ even if that reservation has not been made by the first State, as seen in the *Norwegian Loans Case*, above.

5. In the *Qatar v Bahrain (Jurisdiction – Second Phase) Case* (see Chapter 3), the ICJ decided, as a matter of treaty interpretation, that the treaty in question gave each State the ability to bring a claim to the ICJ unilaterally.

6. In many of the cases brought to the ICJ, one party objects to the jurisdiction of the ICJ and the Court has to decide the question of whether it has jurisdiction before proceeding to decide the merits of the dispute. However, the Court can leave the issue of jurisdiction until

its considerations of the merits if the two are inextricably linked. Nevertheless, the Court has sometimes shown a marked reluctance to find that it does not have jurisdiction, although in the *Fisheries Jurisdiction Case (Spain* v *Canada)* (see Chapter 10) the Court applied a Canadian reservation and declined jurisdiction.

C: Absent third parties

On a number of occasions, two States have submitted disputes to the ICJ, even though other States, which may be affected by any resolution of the dispute, have not been parties to the case. This can cause considerable difficulties for the Court.

Case Concerning Certain Phosphate Lands in Nauru (*Nauru* v *Australia*) (*Jurisdiction*)
240 1992 ICJ Rep, International Court of Justice

Nauru brought a claim against Australia, which had been one of the administering authorities of Nauru when it had been a Trust territory, for reparations for environmental damage caused by phosphate mining on Nauru. One of Australia's objections to the Court having jurisdiction of the matter was that the other two administering authorities – New Zealand and the United Kingdom – were not parties before the Court (due to their reservations about the Court's jurisdiction). The Court decided that it did have jurisdiction. The case settled before the merits were considered (see Chapter 12).

In the present case, the interests of New Zealand and the United Kingdom do not constitute the very subject-matter of the judgment to be rendered on the merits of Nauru's Application . . . In the present case, the determination of the responsibility of New Zealand or the United Kingdom is not a prerequisite for the determination of the responsibility of Australia, the only object of Nauru's claim. . . . In the present case, a finding by the Court regarding the existence or the content of the responsibility attributed to Australia by Nauru might well have implications for the legal situation of the two other States concerned, but no finding in respect of that legal situation will be needed as a basis for the Court's decision on Nauru's claims against Australia. Accordingly, the Court cannot decline to exercise its jurisdiction.

Case Concerning East Timor (*Portugal* v *Australia*)
ICJ Rep 1995 90, International Court of Justice

The facts of this case are set out in Chapter 6. Because Indonesia did not accept the jurisdiction of the ICJ, no case could be brought against Indonesia. The Court held (by 14 votes to 2) that it could not decide this case in the absence of Indonesia, as Indonesia's rights and obligations would have been affected by any judgment of the Court.

26. The Court recalls in this respect that one of the fundamental principles of its Statue is that it cannot decide a dispute between States without the consent of those States to its jurisdiction. This principle was reaffirmed in the judgment given by the Court in the case of the *Monetary Gold Removed from Rome in 1943* and confirmed in several of its subsequent decisions. . . .

28. The Court has carefully considered the argument advanced by Portugal which seeks to separate Australia's behaviour from that of Indonesia. However, in the view of the Court, Australia's

behaviour cannot be assessed without first entering into the question why it is that Indonesia could not lawfully have concluded the 1989 Treaty, while Portugal allegedly could have done so; the very subject-matter of the Court's decision would necessarily be a determination whether, having regard to the circumstances in which Indonesia entered and remained in East Timor, it could or could not have acquired the power to enter into treaties on behalf of East Timor relating to the resources of its continental shelf. The Court could not make such a determination in the absence of the consent of Indonesia.

JUDGE VERESHCHETIN (Separate Opinion): Besides Indonesia, in the absence of whose consent the Court is prevented from exercising its jurisdiction over the Application, there is another 'third party' in this case, whose consent was sought neither by Portugal before filling the Application with the Court, nor by Australia before concluding the Timor Gap treaty. Nevertheless, the applicant State has acted in this Court in the name of this 'third party' and the Treaty has allegedly jeopardized its natural resources. The 'third party' at issue is the people of East Timor.

Since the judgment is silent on this matter, one might wrongly conclude that the people, whose right to self-determination lies at the core of the whole case, have no role to play in the proceedings. This is not to suggest that the Court could have placed the States Parties to the case and the people of East Timor on the same level procedurally. Clearly, only States may be parties in cases before the Court (Art. 34 of the Statute of the Court). This is merely to say that the right of a people to self-determination, by definition, requires that the wishes of the people concerned at least be ascertained and taken into account by the Court.

NOTES
1. In a number of decisions by the ICJ, particularly on continental shelf delimitation, the Court has been careful to avoid deciding on aspects of a case which could overlap with claims of third States, for example, in the *Continental Shelf Case (Libya* v *Malta)* ICJ Rep 1984 3 (see Chapter 10), the Court did not decide on part of the maritime boundary which could have affected Italy (see also notes on intervention below).
2. As Judge Vereshchetin pointed out in the *East Timor* case, there can be other interested parties (including non-States) which could be directly affected by a judgment of the ICJ but which do not, or cannot, appear before the Court.
3. There are also many instances of the absence of an actual party to the case, usually where that party objects to the Court taking jurisdiction of the matter. An example was the absence of the United States at the merits stage of the *Nicaragua* case. (see Chapter 2 and below).

D: Provisional measures

Statute of the International Court of Justice

Article 41

1. The Court shall have the power to indicate, if it considers that circumstances so require, any provisional measures which ought to be taken to preserve the respective rights of either party.

2. Pending the final decision, notice of the measure suggested shall forthwith be given to the parties and to the Security Council.

Military and Paramilitary Activities in and against Nicaragua Case
(*Nicaragua* v *USA*) (Request for the Indication of Provisional Measures)
ICJ Rep 1984 169, International Court of Justice

Nicaragua's main request was that the United States should cease and refrain from any action restricting, blocking or endangering access to or from Nicaraguan ports and, in particular, to cease the laying of mines. The Court indicated these provisional measures.

24. Whereas on a request for provisional measures the Court need not, before deciding whether or not to indicate them, finally satisfy itself that it has jurisdiction on the merits of the case, or, as the case may be, that an objection taken to jurisdiction is well-founded, yet it ought not to indicate such measures unless the provisions invoked by the Applicant appear, prima facie, to afford a basis on which the jurisdiction of the Court might be founded; . . .

26. Whereas the Court will not now make any final determination of the question of the present validity or invalidity of the declaration of 24 September 1929, and the question whether or not Nicaragua accordingly was or was not, for the purpose of Article 36, paragraph 2, of the Statute of the Court a 'State accepting the same obligation' as the United States of America at the date of filing of the Application, so as to be able to rely on the United States declaration of 26 August 1946, nor of the question whether, as a result of the declaration of 6 April 1984, the present Application is excluded from the scope of the acceptance by the United States of the compulsory jurisdiction of the Court; whereas however the Court finds that the two declarations do nevertheless appear to afford a basis on which the jurisdiction of the Court might be founded;

27. Whereas by the terms of Article 41 of the Statute the Court may indicate provisional measures only when it considers that circumstances so require to preserve the rights of either party; . . .

40. Whereas the decision given in the present proceedings in no way prejudges the question of the jurisdiction of the Court to deal with the merits of the case or any questions relating to the merits themselves, and leaves unaffected the right of the Governments of the United States of America and the Republic of Nicaragua to submit arguments in respect of such jurisdiction or such merits;

JUDGE SCHWEBEL (Dissenting Opinion): . . . It is beyond dispute that the Court may not indicate provisional measures under its Statute where it has no jurisdiction over the merits of the case. Equally, however, considerations of urgency do not or may not permit the Court to establish its jurisdiction definitively before it issues an order of interim protection. Thus the Court has built a body of precedent which affords it the authority to indicate provisional measures if the jurisdiction which has been pleaded appears, prima facie, to afford a basis on which the Court's jurisdiction might be founded. Whether 'might' means 'possibly might' or 'might well' or 'might probably' is a question of some controversy. The nub of the matter appears to be that, while in deciding whether it has jurisdiction on the merits, the Court gives the defendant the benefit of the doubt, in deciding whether it has jurisdiction to indicate provisional measures, the Court gives the applicant the benefit of the doubt. In the present case, the Court, in my view, has given the applicant the benefit of a great many doubts.

The result is that States which have, by one route or another, submitted to the Court's compulsory jurisdiction in advance of a particular dispute, run the risk of being the object of an order indicating provisional measures even though (as in the *Anglo-Iranian Oil Co.* case) the Court may eventually conclude that jurisdiction on the merits is lacking. Thus the tactical disadvantage which the minority of States which has adhered to the Optional Clause generally suffers, as compared with that majority which has not submitted declarations under the Optional Clause at all, may be markedly greater than was conceived at the time declarations were submitted or has been perceived since.

A ready solution to this problem which comports with the maintenance of the Court's jurisdiction is not obvious. But one step which the Court itself can take is to ensure that the parties, at the stage of argument on provisional measures, are afforded the time required to prepare to argue issues of jurisdiction in depth. A second step is to ensure that the Court itself is afforded the requisite time to deliberate issues of jurisdiction in depth and to formulate its order in accordance with its internal judicial practice.

J. Merrills, 'Interim Measures of Protection and the Substantive Jurisdiction of the International Court'
(1977) 36 *Cambridge Law Journal* 86

It is agreed that a decision by the Court to consider the merits of a request for interim measures in no way prejudices its later decision as to its substantive jurisdiction. The question is whether, and to what extent, it is necessary for the Court to investigate that substantive jurisdiction at the interim measures stage.

Five possible answers must be considered: that the Court's substantive jurisdiction must be clearly established before an award of interim measures can be contemplated; that substantive jurisdiction is irrelevant to a request for interim measures; that the Court must be satisfied that there is prima facie some possibility of jurisdiction on the merits; that the Court must find its substantive jurisdiction to be probable; and, finally, that jurisdiction is simply one of the 'circumstances' to be considered by the Court when it is asked to act under Article 41. . . .

The five approaches we have considered indicate that the extent of the Court's power to indicate interim measures depends on the relative importance assigned to two indisputable features of the Court's statute: the intention to make interim measures an effective, if temporary, remedy and the voluntary nature of international adjudication. . . .

The difference between the two most persuasive approaches is thus one of emphasis: state sovereignty versus the effectiveness of international legal remedies. . . .

Ultimately, the balancing of these considerations in order to decide how far the Court should go in investigating the question of its jurisdiction when deciding an application for interim measures of protection turns on the role of the International Court in one's model of the international system.

A state centred model places international adjudication at the periphery of affairs and treats the Court and its activities as nothing more than a reflection of the legal constraints which states are prepared to accept. On this view there is ample justification for the Court's refusing to indicate interim measures when its jurisdiction can be seriously challenged.

A law-centred or normative model of the world presents a different picture. The Court is seen as an institution designed to maintain and promote legal values in international affairs. On this view, while the voluntary nature of international adjudication is acknowledged, an assumption that interim measures may be indicated is favoured, not just because of the practical advantages, outlined earlier, but because in the last analysis if one believes that international law is more important than national sovereignty and that the Court's function is to ensure that interstate relations are governed by law, a temporary fetter on one party's actions seems a small price to pay for the prevention of irreparable invasion of another's rights.

LaGrand Case (*Germany* v *United States*)
ICJ Rep 2001, International Court of Justice

Germany sought provisional measures against the United States to halt the execution of two German nationals in Arizona. The jurisdiction of the Court was under the Vienna Convention on Consular Relations 1963. On 3 March 1999, the Court ordered provisional measures, which essentially sought the delay of the execution until the ICJ case was heard on the merits (ICJ Rep 1999 9). The

United States court nevertheless executed the two men. Germany sought an order that the United States had not complied with the ICJ provisional measures order and the Court (by 13 votes to 2) granted that order.

109. In short, it is clear that none of the sources of interpretation referred to in the relevant Articles of the Vienna Convention on the Law of Treaties, including the preparatory work, contradict the conclusions drawn from the terms of Article 41 read in their context and in the light of the object and purpose of the Statute. Thus, the Court has reached the conclusion that orders on provisional measures under Article 41 have binding effect.

110. The Court will now consider the Order of 3 March 1999. This Order was not a mere exhortation. It had been adopted pursuant to Article 41 of the Statute. This Order was consequently binding in character and created a legal obligation for the United States. . . .

115. The review of the above steps taken by the authorities of the United States with regard to the Order of the International Court of Justice of 3 March 1999 indicates that the various competent United States authorities failed to take all the steps they could have taken to give effect to the Court's Order. The Order did not require the United States to exercise powers it did not have; but it did impose the obligation to 'take all measures at its disposal to ensure that Walter LaGrand is not executed pending the final decision in these proceedings'. The Court finds that the United States did not discharge this obligation. Under these circumstances the Court concludes that the United States has not complied with the Order of 3 March 1999.

NOTES:
1. The decision on provisional (interim) measures requirements in the *Nicaragua Case* (above) has been repeated by the ICJ in a number of cases, including the *Arbitral Award of July 1989 Case* ICJ Rep 1990 64; *Passage Through the Great Belt Case* ICJ Rep 1991 12; the *Genocide Convention Case* ICJ Rep 1993 325; and the *Vienna Convention on Consular Relations Case (Paraguay v United States)* ICJ Rep 1998 248. The Court seems gradually to be liberalising its view as to what circumstances warrant the granting of interim measures.
2. The decision in *LaGrand* clarifies that an order of provisional measures by the ICJ is a binding order. Failure to comply with the order is grounds for a claim by the affected State.
3. Merrills points out the tension between State consent and making international adjudication effective. The Court's recent approach to provisional measures could be seen as limiting the role of State consent. This approach is understandable where the protection of natural resources, the environment or human rights are in issue. Judge Vereshchetin, in his dissenting opinion in the *Legality of Use of Force Case (Provisional Measures)* (see above), thought that the ICJ has power to make provisional orders beyond its powers under Article 41, as he said that 'the Court is inherently empowered, at the very least, immediately to call upon the Parties neither to aggravate nor to extend the conflict and to act in accordance with their obligations under the Charter of the United Nations. This power flows from its responsibility for the safeguarding of international law and from major considerations of public order.'

E: Intervention

Statute of the International Court of Justice

Article 62
1. Should a State consider that it has an interest of a legal nature which may be affected by the decision in the case, it may submit a request to the Court to be permitted to intervene.
2. It shall be for the Court to decide upon this request.

Article 63

1. Whenever the construction of a convention to which States other than those concerned in the case are parties is in question, the Registrar shall notify all such States forthwith.

2. Every State so notified has the right to intervene in the proceedings; but if it uses this right, the construction given by the judgment will be equally binding upon it.

Rules of the International Court of Justice

ICJ Acts and Documents Concerning the Organisation of the Court No 5 (1989)

Article 81

1. An application for permission to intervene under the terms of Article 62 of the Statute, signed in the manner provided for in Article 38, paragraph 3, of these Rules, shall be filed as soon as possible, and not later than the closure of the written proceedings. In exceptional circumstances, an application submitted at a later stage may however be admitted.

2. The application shall state the name of an agent. It shall specify the case to which it relates, and shall set out:

(a) the interest of a legal nature which the State applying to intervene considers may be affected by the decision in that case;

(b) the precise object of the intervention;

(c) any basis of jurisdiction which is claimed to exist as between the State applying to intervene and the parties to the case.

Article 82

1. A State which desires to avail itself of the right of intervention conferred upon it by Article 63 of the Statute shall file a declaration to that effect, signed in the manner provided for in Article 38, paragraph 3, of these Rules. Such a declaration shall be filed as soon as possible, and not later than the date fixed for the opening of the oral proceedings. In exceptional circumstances a declaration submitted at a later stage may however be admitted.

2. The declaration shall state the name of an agent. It shall specify the case and the convention to which it relates and shall contain:

(a) particulars of the basis on which the declarant State considers itself a party to the convention;

(b) identification of the particular provisions of the convention the construction of which it considers to be in question;

(c) a statement of the construction of those provisions for which it contends;

(d) a list of the documents in support, which documents shall be attached.

3. Such a declaration may be filed by a State that considers itself a party to the convention the construction of which is in question but has not received the notification referred to in Article 63 of the Statute.

Case Concerning Land, Island and Maritime Frontier Dispute Case (El Salvador v Honduras) (Nicaragua Intervention)

ICJ Rep 1992 92, Chamber of the International Court of Justice

The dispute between El Salvador and Honduras concerned the Gulf of Fonseca. This lies on the Pacific coast of three States, with the north-west coast being the territory of El Salvador, the south-east coast being the territory of Nicaragua, and Honduran territory lying on the coast between them. By Special Agreement between El Salvador and Honduras the dispute was brought before a Chamber of the Court. Nicaragua sought to intervene in regard to the delimitation of the waters of the Gulf, the legal situation of the islands in the Gulf, the legal situation of the maritime spaces outside the Gulf, and the legal régime of the waters of the Gulf itself. El Salvador objected to any intervention, but Honduras did not object to Nicaragua being permitted to intervene for the sole purpose of expressing its views on the legal status of the waters within the Gulf. The Chamber, unanimously, decided that Nicaragua could intervene only in regard to the legal régime of the waters of the Gulf.

58. If a State can satisfy the Court that it has an interest of a legal nature which may be affected by the decision in the case, it may be permitted to intervene in respect of that interest. But that does not mean that the intervening State is then also permitted to make excursions into other aspects of the case. This is recognized by Nicaragua . . . In the Chamber's opinion, however, it is clear, first, that it is for a State seeking to intervene to demonstrate convincingly what it asserts, and thus to bear the burden of proof; and, second, that it has only to show that its interest 'may' be affected, not that it will or must be affected. . . . Nevertheless, there needs finally to be clear identification of any legal interests that may be affected by the decision on the merits. A general apprehension is not enough. The Chamber needs to be told what interests of a legal nature might be affected by its eventual decision on the merits. . . .

90. So far as the object of Nicaragua's intervention is 'to inform the Court of the nature of the legal rights of Nicaragua which are in issue in the dispute', it cannot be said that this object is not a proper one: it seems indeed to accord with the function of intervention. . . . It seems to the Chamber however that it is perfectly proper, and indeed the purpose of intervention, for an intervener to inform the Chamber of what it regards as its rights or interests, in order to ensure that no legal interest may be 'affected' without the intervener being heard; and that the use in an application to intervene of a perhaps somewhat more forceful expression is immaterial, provided the object actually aimed at is a proper one. . . .

92. In the light of these statements, it appears to the Chamber that the object stated first in Nicaragua's Application, namely 'generally to protect the legal rights of the Republic of Nicaragua in the Gulf of Fonseca and the adjacent maritime areas by all legal means available', is not to be interpreted as involving the seeking of a judicial pronouncement on Nicaragua's own claims. The 'legal means available' must be those afforded by the institution of intervention for the protection of a third State's legal interests. So understood, that object cannot be regarded as improper. . . .

96. . . . The competence of the Court in this matter of intervention is not, like its competence to hear and determine the dispute referred to it, derived from the consent of the parties to the case, but from the consent given by them, in becoming parties to the Court's Statute, to the Court's exercise of its powers conferred by the Statute. There is no need to interpret the reference in Article 36, paragraph 1, of the Statute to 'treaties in force' to include the Statute itself; acceptance of the Statute entails acceptance of the competence conferred on the Court by Article 62. Thus the Court has the competence to permit an intervention even though it be opposed by one or both of the parties to the case; as the Court stated in 1984, 'the opposition [to an intervention] of the parties to a case is, though very important, no more than one element to be taken into account by the Court' (*ICJ Reports 1984*, p. 28, para. 46). The nature of the competence thus created by Article 62 of the Statute is definable by reference to the object and purpose of intervention, as this appears from Article 62 of the Statute. . . . It is therefore clear that a State which is allowed to intervene in a case, does not, by reason only of being an intervener, become also a party to the case. It is true, conversely, that, provided that there be the necessary consent by the parties to the case, the intervener is not prevented by reason of that status from itself becoming a party. . . .

100. It thus follows also from the juridical nature and from the purposes of intervention that the existence of a valid link of jurisdiction between the would-be intervener and the parties is not a

requirement for the success of the application. On the contrary, the procedure of intervention is to ensure that a State with possibly affected interests may be permitted to intervene even though there is no jurisdictional link and it therefore cannot become a party. . . .

101. The Chamber therefore concludes that the absence of a jurisdictional link between Nicaragua and the Parties to this case is no bar to permission being given for intervention.

C. Chinkin, 'Third Party Intervention before the ICJ'
80 AJIL 495 (1986)

One often repeated policy – reiterated by certain judges of the International Court – justifying a flexible attitude towards intervention is to promote economy of litigation for the efficient administration of justice. Certainly, the inclusion of the procedure in the Court's Statute stems from the recognition that international disputes rarely, if ever, fit neatly into a bilateral pattern. Rather, because of the interdependence of international relations, events that culminate in international adjudication will affect different actors in different ways and with varying intensity. Where this impact is upon the legal interests of other states, principles of economy and efficiency may require that pertinent submissions be presented along with the main proceedings.

In sum, by allowing third-party intervention, the Court could avoid the possible duplication of proceedings. It could also gain a wider perspective on the entire series of actions culminating in the litigation than that presented by the original parties and thus be better informed about all aspects of the dispute. Finally, easier access to the international judicial arena and the increased participation in international adjudication that could be expected to result would promote the peaceful settlement of disputes, recognized as one of the fundamental norms of international law. . . .

Where states have brought a dispute before the Court, especially through special agreement, which precludes a jurisdictional conflict, the Court may well determine that it can best serve the interests of the international community by adjudicating that dispute without allowing intervention, as that may lead the original parties to withdraw their acceptance of the Court's authority. Admittedly, this represents a limited view of the Court's role, but it may be a realistic one, allowing the Court to resolve specific disputes between states that will accept its ruling. If other interests are affected by its decision, they can be resolved at a subsequent time and, possibly, in another forum. The Court may not want to risk jeopardizing the successful resolution of the original dispute by widening its ambit through the overready acceptance of intervention.

This latter view of the Court's role is supported by the concept of party autonomy in international adjudication and necessarily entails restricting intervention. It recognizes that facilitating intervention could prove counter-productive by discouraging states from initiating a contentious suit for fear that they might be unable to control its course and eventual outcome if the dispute were widened beyond their direct concerns. It is also argued that third-party intervention runs counter to other fundamentals of international law such as the equality of states, consent and reciprocity in international adjudication.

NOTES:

1. Intervention pursuant to Article 63 was granted by the ICJ in the *Haya de la Torre Case*, ICJ Rep 1951 71, but the *Land, Island and Maritime Frontier Dispute Case* was the first case in the history of both the ICJ and the PCIJ in which a State has been accorded permission to intervene solely under Article 62, or its equivalent. However, Article 62 gives the Court a discretion not to allow an intervention, even if an interest of a legal nature, an appropriate object and a jurisdictional link are shown. In *Sovereignty over Pulau Ligitan and Pulau Sipadan (Indonesia v Malaysia) (The Philippines Intervention)* ICJ Rep 2001, the Court refused The Philippines application to intervene because it considered that no interest of a legal nature was demonstrated, as the claims by Indonesia and Malaysia did not relate to the issue on which The Philippines sought to intervene.

2. When the ICJ gave its final decision in the *Land Island and Maritime Frontier Dispute Case* (ICJ Rep 1992 92), it held that because Nicaragua was not formally a party to the case before the Court it was not bound by the Court's decision. This is consistent with the Court's view that no jurisdictional link is required for intervention, but, as Judge Oda pointed out in his Dissenting Opinion, this means that Nicaragua is not bound by the Court's lengthy determination of sovereignty over all the islands, maritime and other territory in dispute. This is not a good result if international legal order for settling disputes is desired.

3. In a number of the cases where intervention has been sought, the Court has taken into account the arguments of the intervening State in its ultimate decision on the case. It has done so by limiting its decision so as not to infringe the potential rights of the intervening State, as with Italy's application to intervene in the *Continental Shelf Case* (*Libya* v *Malta*) ICJ Rep 1984 3 (see Chapter 10).

4. While the consent of the parties to a case before the ICJ is important and must be considered by the Court, the ICJ is meant to be a body whose purpose is to settle international disputes between States. Its decisions do have an impact wider than simply on the parties to the case, and most cases brought to the Court by two parties are formulated in a bilateral manner, which may not reflect the multifaceted interests involved. If the Court's decisions on principles of international law are to be based on a full appreciation of the legal situation, then interventions (perhaps including those by non-States) may have to be allowed more frequently. In this way the Court can operate more effectively as a means to settle disputes peacefully, to promote international peace and justice, and to further the development of international law (see also the comments of the Court in the *Legality of Use of Force Case (Provisional Measures)* above).

F: Obligations to comply with decisions

Statute of the International Court of Justice

Article 59
The decision of the Court has no binding force except between the parties and in respect of that particular case.

United Nations Charter

Article 94
1. Each Member of the United Nations undertakes to comply with the decision of the International Court of Justice in any case to which it is a party.

2. If any party to a case fails to perform the obligations incumbent upon it under a judgment rendered by the Court, the other party may have recourse to the Security Council, which may, if it deems necessary, make recommendations or decide upon measures to be taken to give effect to the judgment.

NOTES:
1. In the *Territorial Dispute Case* (*Libya* v *Chad*) ICJ Rep 1994 6 (see Chapter 3), the parties enforced the decision rapidly, with a treaty to implement the decision being signed by the parties two months after the decision, and, within less than two more months, the parties had acted to remove troops from the disputed area. Such quick enforcement is, however, rare.

2. Some of the decisions of the ICJ have not been complied with by a party to the dispute. In some cases a party has even refused to appear before the ICJ when it is deciding the case, as did the United States in the decision on the merits of *Nicaragua* v *US*. The Security Council may later decide not to take any action itself, due to a veto being used. However, there is still a number of alternative methods of enforcing decisions available to a State, of which diplomatic and economic pressures are used the most often. In *LaGrand* (above) the Court clarified that a provisional measures order is binding and lack of compliance with it is a ground for action by the affected State.

3. As has been noted on a number of occasions, the lack of the ability to ensure enforcement of international law is one of the principal difficulties of the international legal system. If legal enforcement measures are not available or are inadequate, then lack of complete resolution of the dispute can threaten international peace and security and it can diminish the development of an international legal order. If the peaceful settlement of disputes is customary international law (let alone if it has the character of *jus cogens*), then it must include an obligation to comply with any decision which aims to settle an international dispute.

G: Advisory opinions

United Nations Charter

Article 96

1. The General Assembly or the Security Council may request the International Court of Justice to give an advisory opinion on any legal question.

2. Other organs of the United Nations and specialized agencies, which may at any time be so authorized by the General Assembly, may also request advisory opinions of the Court on legal questions arising within the scope of their activities.

Statute of the International Court of Justice

Article 65

1. The Court may give an advisory opinion on any legal question at the request of whatever body may be authorized by or in accordance with the Charter of the United Nations to make such a request.

2. Questions upon which the advisory opinion of the Court is asked shall be laid before the Court by means of a written request containing an exact statement of the question upon which an opinion is required, and accompanied by all documents likely to throw light upon the question.

Article 66

1. The Registrar shall forthwith give notice of the request for an advisory opinion to all States entitled to appear before the Court.

2. The Registrar shall also, by means of a special and direct communication, notify any State entitled to appear before the Court or international organization considered by the Court, or, should it not be sitting, by the President, as likely to be able to furnish information on the question, that the Court will be prepared to receive, within a time limit to be fixed by the President, written statements, or to hear, at a public sitting to be held for the purpose, oral statements relating to the question. . . .

Interpretation of Peace Treaties Opinion

ICJ Rep 1950 65, International Court of Justice

A number of States, which were parties to the post-Second World War peace treaties with Bulgaria, Hungary and Romania, had claimed that those latter States had violated the provisions of the treaties concerning their human rights obligations. The treaties provided for commissions to decide disputes between the parties, with each party to appoint one commissioner and a third member to be agreed or, failing agreement, to be appointed by the Secretary-General of the United Nations. Bulgaria, Hungary and Romania refused to appoint any commissioner. The Court was asked to advise the General Assembly as to whether the Secretary-General could nevertheless appoint the third member. The Court answered this question in the negative. Bulgaria, Hungary and Romania had objected to the Advisory Opinion as they had not consented to it.

The consent of States, parties to a dispute, is the basis of the Court's jurisdiction in contentious cases. The situation is different in regard to advisory proceedings even where the Request for an Opinion relates to a legal question actually pending between States. The Court's reply is only of an advisory character: as such, it has no binding force. It follows that no State, whether a Member of the United Nations or not, can prevent the giving of an Advisory Opinion which the United Nations considers to be desirable in order to obtain enlightenment as to the course of action it should take. The Court's Opinion is given not to the States, but to the organ which is entitled to request it; the reply of the Court, itself an 'organ of the United Nations', represents its participation in the activities of the Organization, and, in principle, should not be refused. . . .

Article 65 of the Statute is permissive. It gives the Court the power to examine whether the circumstances of the case are of such a character as should lead it to decline to answer the Request. In the opinion of the Court, the circumstances of the present case are profoundly different from those which were before the Permanent Court of International Justice in the *Eastern Carelia* case (Advisory Opinion No. 5), when that Court declined to give an Opinion because it found that the question put to it was directly related to the main point of a dispute actually pending between two States, so that answering the question would be substantially equivalent to deciding the dispute between the parties, and that at the same time it raised a question of fact which could not be elucidated without hearing both parties. . . . In the present case the Court is dealing with a Request for an Opinion, the sole object of which is to enlighten the General Assembly as to the opportunities which the procedure contained in the Peace Treaties may afford for putting an end to a situation which has been presented to it. That being the object of the Request, the Court finds in the opposition to it made by Bulgaria, Hungary and Romania no reason why it should abstain from replying to the Request.

Western Sahara Opinion

ICJ Rep 1975 12, International Court of Justice

The details of the questions put by the General Assembly for an advisory opinion by the ICJ are set out in Chapter 7.

17. It is true that, in order to reply to the questions [put by the General Assembly], the Court will have to determine certain facts, before being able to assess their legal significance. However, a mixed question of law and facts is none the less a legal question within the meaning of Article 96, paragraph 1, of the Charter and Article 65, paragraph 1 of the Statute [of the ICJ]. . . .

18. The view has been expressed that in order to be a 'legal question' . . . a question must not be of a historical character, but must concern or affect existing rights or obligations . . . the references to 'legal question' . . . are not to be interpreted restrictively.

19. . . . It has undoubtedly been the usual situation for an advisory opinion of the Court to pronounce on existing rights and obligations, or on their coming into existence, modification or

termination, or on the powers of international organs. However, the Court may also be requested to give its opinion on questions of law which do not call for any pronouncement of that kind, though they may have their place within a wider problem the solution of which could involve such matters. . . .

23. . . . In exercising this discretion [under Article 65], the International Court of Justice, like the Permanent Court of International Justice, has always been guided by the principle that as a judicial body, it is bound to remain faithful to the requirements of its judicial character even in giving advisory opinions. . . . It has also said that the reply of the Court, itself an organ of the United Nations, represents its participation in the activities of the Organisation and, in principle, should not be refused. By lending its assistance in the solution of a problem confronting the General Assembly, the Court would discharge its functions as the principal judicial organ of the United Nations. The Court has further said only 'compelling reasons' should lead it to refuse to give a requested advisory opinion. . . .

73. In any event, to what extent or degree its opinion will have an impact on the action of the General Assembly is not for the Court to decide. The function of the Court is to give an opinion based on law, once it has come to the conclusion that the questions put to it are relevant and have a practical and contemporary effect and, consequently, are not devoid of object or purpose.

74. In the light of [these] considerations . . . the Court finds no compelling reason, in the circumstances of the present case, to refuse to comply with a request by the General Assembly for an advisory opinion.

NOTE:
It is rare for the ICJ to decline give an advisory opinion to the reasons given in the two case extracts above. Similarly, in contentious cases, the ICJ seems inclined to accept that it has jurisdiction over a dispute, if at all possible.

SECTION 6:   International Court of Justice and the Security Council

As the ICJ indicated in the extract from the *Western Sahara Opinion*, above, the ICJ sees itself as an important organ of the United Nations and it has an obligation to offer its legal opinion when requested to do so. In para. 73 of that case, the ICJ said that it is not concerned about the impact its decision will have on the General Assembly. However, because the Security Council (as distinct from the General Assembly) can take decisions on legal matters that bind all States, there is an issue of the power of the ICJ in relation to the Security Council when the Security Council decides on matters of law.

United States Diplomatic and Consular Staff in Tehran Case (*United States* v *Iran*)
ICJ Rep 1980 3, International Court of Justice

This case arose from the occupation of the United States Embassy in Tehran (see further in Chapter 11), and was heard by the Court prior to the release of the Embassy staff. Iran, in a letter to the Court, had stated that the violations of diplomatic and consular law alleged by the United States could not be examined by the Court as they were part of a current political dispute, the dispute was before the Security Council, and the Secretary-General of the United Nations had established a Commission to settle the matter.

[L]egal disputes between sovereign States by their very nature are likely to occur in political contexts, and often form only one element in a wider and long-standing political dispute between the States concerned. Yet never has the view been put forward before that, because a legal dispute submitted to the Court is only one aspect of a political dispute, the Court should decline to resolve for the parties the legal questions at issue between them. Nor can any basis for such a view of the Court's functions or jurisdiction be found in the Charter or the Statute of the Court; if the Court were, contrary to its settled jurisprudence, to adopt such a view, it would impose a far-reaching and unwarranted restriction upon the role of the Court in the peaceful solution of international disputes . . .

Whereas Article 12 of the Charter expressly forbids the General Assembly to make any recommendation with regard to a dispute or situation while the Security Council is exercising its functions in respect of that dispute or situation, no such restriction is placed on the functioning of the Court by any provision of either the Charter or the Statute of the Court. The reasons are clear. It is for the Court, the principal judicial organ of the United Nations, to resolve any legal questions that may be in issue between parties to a dispute; and the resolution of such legal questions by the Court may be an important, and sometimes decisive, factor in promoting the peaceful settlement of the dispute . . . The establishment of the Commission by the Secretary-General with the agreement of the two States cannon, therefore, be considered in itself as in any way incompatible with the continuance of parallel proceedings before the Court. Negotiation, enquiry, mediation, conciliation, arbitration and judicial settlement are enumerated together in Article 33 of the Charter as means for the peaceful settlement of disputes. As was pointed out in the *Aegean Sea Continental Shelf* case, the jurisprudence of the Court provides various examples of cases in which negotiations and recourse to judicial settlement by the Court have been pursued *pari passu*. In that case, in which also the dispute had been referred to the Security Council, the Court held expressly that "the fact that negotiations are being actively pursued during the present proceedings is not, legally, any obstacle to the exercise by the Court of its judicial functions" (*ICJ Reports 1978*, p. 12, para. 29).

Lockerbie Case (Case Concerning Questions of Interpretation and Application of the 1971 Montreal Convention arising from the Aerial Incident at Lockerbie) *(Libya* v *United States; Libya* v *United Kingdom)* (Request for the Indication of Provisional Measures)

ICJ Rep 1992 3, p. 114, International Court of Justice

This case arose as a consequence of the explosion, caused by a bomb, of Pan Am Flight 103 on 21 December 1988, over Lockerbie in the United Kingdom, killing all passengers and crew and some residents of Lockerbie. Investigations by American and British authorities (and, later, French authorities) came to the conclusion that two Libyan nationals were responsible. Requests, and demands, that these men be handed to American and British authorities were refused by Libya. Libya maintained that it would cooperate with enquiries but that it could not extradite its nationals under its constitution (such a provision is found in many States' laws). Libya then requested, on 18 January 1992, an arbitration of the matter under Article 14(1) of the Montreal Convention for the Suppression of Unlawful Acts Against the Safety of Civil Aviation 1974, as Libya claimed the matter raised issues of interpretation and application of that Convention.

On 21 January, the Security Council, of which the United States, the United Kingdom and France are permanent members, passed a resolution (Resolution 731 (1992)) urging Libya to respond fully to the demands of those States to hand over the men. Before the expiry of the six-month period of notice of an arbitration request (as required by Article 14), Libya applied on 3 March 1992, to the ICJ for a declaration that Libya, in refusing immediately to hand over the men, had complied with the Montreal Convention. It also requested an order for provisional measure to protect its rights under international law. The ICJ heard the request for provisional measures from 26 to 28 March 1992, and began to prepare its judgment. However, on 31 March, at the instigation of the United States, the United Kingdom and France, the Security Council passed a resolution (Resolution 748 (1992)) imposing sanctions on Libya for non-compliance with its earlier resolution. The ICJ then gave its decision on 14 April 1992.

The ICJ decided, by 11 votes to 5, not to grant Libya's request for provisional measures. The decision given here is in the case *Libya* v *United States*, though the decision in *Libya* v *United Kingdom* was essentially identical.

42. Whereas both Libya and the United States, as Members of the United Nations, are obliged to accept and carry out the decisions of the Security Council in accordance with Article 25 of the Charter; whereas the Court, which is at the stage of proceedings on provisional measures, considers that prima facie this obligation extends to the decision contained in resolution 748 (1992); and whereas, in accordance with Article 103 of the Charter, the obligations of the Parties in that respect prevail over their obligations under any other international agreement, including the Montreal Convention;

43. Whereas the Court thus not at this stage called upon to determine definitively the legal effect of Security Council resolution 748 (1992), considers that, whatever the situation previous to the adoption of that resolution, the rights claimed by Libya under the Montreal Convention cannot now be regarded as appropriate for protection by the indication of provisional measures;

44. Whereas, furthermore, an indication of the measures requested by Libya would be likely to impair the rights which appear prima facie to be enjoyed by the United States by virtue of Security Council resolution 748 (1992);

JUDGE SHAHABUDDEEN (Separate Opinion): Whatever might have been the previous position, resolution 748 (1992) of the Security Council leaves the Court with no conclusion other than that to which it has come. This is the result not of imposition of superior authority – there is none – but of the fact that, in finding the applicable law, the Court must take account of the resolution in so far as it effects the enforceability of the rights for the protection of which Libya is seeking interim measures. The validity of the resolution, though contested by Libya, has, at this stage, to be presumed (see the general principle in *Legal Consequences for States of the Continued Presence of South Africa in Namibia (South West Africa) notwithstanding Security Council Resolution 276 (1970)*, ICJ Reports 1971, p. 22, para 20). Article 25 of the Charter of the United Nations obliges Libya to comply with the decision set out in the resolution (*ibid.*, pp. 52–53). By virtue of Article 103 of the Charter, that obligation prevails over any conflicting treaty obligation which Libya may have (*Military and Para-military Activities in and against Nicaragua (Nicaragua* v *United States of America)*, ICJ Reports 1984, p. 440 para. 107). Treaty obligations can be overridden by a decision of the Security Council imposing sanctions (Paul Reuter, *Introduction to the Law of Treaties*, 1981, p. 113. para 228, and Sir

Gerald Fitzmaurice, *The Law and Procedure of the International Court of Justice*, 1986, Vol. 2, p. 431). Hence, assuming that Libya has the rights which it claims, prima facie they could not be enforced during the life of the resolution.

Several cases demonstrate, in one way or another, that the Court is not precluded from acting by the mere circumstances that the matter in contest is also under consideration by another organ of the United Nations (see, *inter alia*, United States Diplomatic and Consular Staff in Tehran, ICJ Reports 1980, p. 22, para. 40; and *Military and Paramilitary Activities in and against Nicaragua (Nicaragua* v *United States of America) Provisional Measures*, ICJ Reports 1984, pp. 185–186, and, same case, *Jurisdiction and Admissibility*, ICJ Reports 1984, pp. 433–436). In this case, it happens that the decision which the Court is asked to give is one which would directly conflict with a decision of the Security Council. That is not an aspect which can be overlooked. Yet, it is not the juridical ground of today's Order. This results not from any collision between the competence of the security Council and that of the Court, but from a collision between the obligations of Libya under the decision of the Security Council and any obligations which it may have under the Montreal Convention. The Charter says that the former prevail . . .

JUDGE BEDJAOUI (Dissenting Opinion): 22. . . . if the simple but essential distinction . . . is borne in mind, between the quite specific juridical dispute submitted to the Court and the much wider political dispute brought before the Security Council, it becomes perfectly understandable that, given its functions, and powers, the Court has no alternative but to refrain from entertaining any aspect whatever of the political solutions arrived at by the Security Council. The Court's attitude in this respect continues to be defensible *so long as* no aspect of these political solutions adopted by the Council sets aside, rules out or renders impossible the juridicial solution expected of the Court. It is clear that, in this case, it is the judicial function itself which would be impaired. Indeed, this is what is happening here in the area where these two disputes overlap, where the solution arrived at by the Council to the question of the extradition of two individuals deprives a solution found by the Court of all meaning.

23. Such a situation, in which, on the basis of the case, the Court should have indicated provisional measures solely in order to protect a right that the Security Council annihilates by its resolution 748 (1992) when the case is *sub judice*, is not satisfactory for the judicial function. It is even less so when one of the two Respondents, the United States of America, asks the Court quite simply to refrain from exercising its judicial duty and to bow to the Security Council 'in order to avoid any conflict' with it. . . . In the past the Security Council awaited the Court's decision.

Case concerning Application of the Convention on the Prevention and Punishment of the Crime of Genocide (Bosnia and Herzegovina v Yugoslavia (Serbia and Montenegro)) (Indication of Provisional Measures)
ICJ Rep 1993 325, International Court of Justice

The Republic of Bosnia-Herzegovina instituted proceedings against the Federal Republic of Yugoslavia (Serbia and Montenegro) claiming that the latter were responsible for the commission of genocide in Bosnia-Herzegovina. The former Yugoslavia had previously ratified the Genocide Convention. Bosnia-Herzegovina also requested provisional measures to prevent on-going genocide. The Court made two decisions indicating provisional measures, in April and September 1993. Judge *ad hoc* Lauterpacht gave a Separate Opinion in the latter instance.

JUDGE LAUTERPACHT (Separate Opinion): 99. This is not to say that the Security Council can act free of all legal controls but only that the Court's power of judicial review is limited. That the Court has some power of this kind can hardly be doubted, though there can be no less doubt that it does not embrace any right of the Court to substitute its discretion for that of the Security Council in determining the existence of a threat to the peace, a breach of the peace or an act of aggression, or the political steps to be taken following such a determination. But the Court, as the principle judicial organ of the United Nations, is entitled, indeed bound, to ensure the rule of law within the United Nations system and, in cases properly brought before it, to assist on adherence by all United Nations organs to the rules governing their operations ...

100. The present case, however, cannot fall within the scope of the doctrine just enunciated. This is because the prohibition of genocide, unlike the matters covered by the Montreal Convention in the *Lockerbie* case to which the terms of Article 103 could be directly applied, has generally been accepted as having the status not of an ordinary rule of international law but of *jus cogens*. Indeed, the prohibition of genocide has long been regarded as one of the few undoubted examples of *jus cogens*. Even in 1951, in its Advisory Opinion on *Reservations to the Convention on the Prevention and Punishment of the Crime of Genocide*, the Court affirmed that genocide was 'contrary to moral law and to the spirit and aims of the United Nations' (a view repeated by the Court in paragraph 51 of today's Order) and that

> the principles underlying the Convention are provisions which are recognized by civilized nations as binding on States even without any conventional obligation (*ICJ Reports 1951*, p. 22).

An express reference to the special quality of the prohibition of genocide may also be seen in the work of the International Law Commission in the preparation of Article 50 of the draft articles on the Law of Treaties (*Year-book of the International Law Commission*, 1966, Vol, II, pp. 248–249) which eventually materialised in Article 53 of the Vienna Convention on the Law of Treaties and in the same Commission's commentary on Article 19 (international crimes and delicts) of the draft articles on State Responsibility (*Yearbook of the International Law Commission*, 1976, Vol, II, Pt. 2, p. 103). The concept of *jus cogens* operates as a concept superior to both customary international law and treaty. The relief which Article 103 of the Charter may give the Security Council in case of conflict between one of its decisions and an operative treaty obligation cannot – as a matter of simple hierarchy of norms – extend to a conflict between a Security Council resolution and *jus cogens*. Indeed, one only has to state the opposite proposition thus – that a Security Council resolution may even require participation in genocide – for its unacceptability to be apparent.

101. Nor should one overlook the significance of the provision in Article 24(2) of the Charter that, in discharging its duties to maintain international peace and security, the Security Council shall act in accordance with the Purposes and Principles of the United Nations. Amongst the Purposes set out in Article 1(3) of the Charter is that of achieving international co-operation 'in promoting and encouraging respect for human rights and for fundamental freedoms for all without distinction as to race, sex, language or religion'.

102. Now, it is not to be contemplated that the Security Council would ever deliberately adopt a resolution clearly and deliberately flouting a rule of *jus cogens* or requiring a violation of human rights. But the possibility that a Security Council resolution might inadvertently or in an unforeseen manner lead to such a situation cannot be excluded. And that, it appears, is what has happened here. On this basis, the inability of Bosnia-Herzegovina sufficiently strongly to fight back against the Serbs and effectively to prevent the implementation of the Serbian policy of ethnic cleansing is at least in part directly attributable to the fact that Bosnia-Herzegovina's access to weapons and equipment has been severely limited by the embargo. Viewed in this light, the Security Council resolution can be see as having in effect called on Members of the United Nations,

albeit unknowingly and assuredly unwillingly, to become in some degree supporters of the genocidal activity of the Serbs and in this manner and to that extent to act contrary to a rule of *jus cogens*.

103. What legal consequences may flow from this analysis? One possibility is that, in strict logic, when the operation of paragraph 6 of Security Council resolution 713 (1991) began to make Members of the United Nations accessories to genocide, it ceased to be valid and binding in its operation against Bosnia-Herzegovina; and that Members of the United Nations then became free to disregard it. Even so, it would be difficult to say that they then became positively obliged to provide the Applicant with weapons and military equipment.

104. There is, however, another possibility that is, perhaps, more in accord with the realities of the situation. It must be recognized that the chain of hypotheses in the analysis just made involves some debatable links – elements of fact, such as that the arms embargo has led to the imbalance in the possession of arms by the two sides and that that imbalance has contributed in greater or lesser degree to genocidal activity such as ethnic cleansing; and elements of law, such as that genocide is *jus cogens* and that a resolution which becomes violative of *jus cogens* must then become void and legally ineffective. It is not necessary for the Court to take a position in this regard at this time. Instead, it would seem sufficient that the relevance here of *jus cogens* should be drawn to the attention of the Security Council, as it will be by the required communication to it of the Court's Order, so that the Security Council may give due weight to it in future reconsideration of the embargo. . . .

106. While, of course, the principle thrust of a finding that paragraph 6 of Security Council resolution 713 (1991) may conflict with *jus cogens* must lie in the direction of third States which may be willing to supply arms to Bosnia-Herzegovina, that does not mean that such a conclusion could have no place in an order operative between Bosnia-Herzegovina and Yugoslavia in the present proceedings. There may well be advantage for Bosnia-Herzegovina (it is not for the Court to determine) in being able to say that the Court had identified a source of doubt regarding the validity of the embargo resolution which, though not directly operative by itself, requires that the Security Council give the matter further consideration.

NOTES:
1. The decision in the *Lockerbie Case* above was on whether provisional measures should be granted and not on the merits of the case. However, as Judge Shahabuddeen indicates, a number of important legal issues could be raised when the merits of the case are considered. The second Security Council resolution had a direct impact on the decision in the case, as seen in a joint Separate Opinion by Judges Evenson, Tarassov, Guillaume and Aguilar Mawdsley, where it is made clear that, prior to the second Security Council resolution, Libya was within its rights to refuse to extradite its nationals and the United States and the United Kingdom were entitled to take any action consistent with international law. Eventually, the matter was settled by a trial of two Libyan men before a Scottish Court in the The Netherlands (see above).
2. Most of the judges in the *Lockerbie Case*, as indicated in the decisions of Judge Shahabuddeen and Judge Bedjaoui, as well as Judge Lauterpacht in the *Genocide in Yugoslavia Case*, seem to take the view that the ICJ could undertake judicial review of a decision of the Security Council, even though this review could be exercised only in limited circumstances. This view raises the issue of the constitutional structure of the international community, particularly as between the Security Council and the ICJ. The power relationship between these two organs is not made explicit in the United Nations Charter, except that Art. 36(3) (above) provides that the Security Council should take into consideration that legal disputes should be referred to the ICJ. The difficulty is that a political decision by the Security Council can have legal impacts. Hence, Judge Bedjaoui's view that any conflict of powers between the two

organs would occur only where the Security Council has made a decision which renders judicial determination of a case futile.

3. In order to settle international disputes peacefully, it is necessary that a variety of measures, legal and non-legal, are available. However, if international law is to exist as a properly functioning legal system then its institutions must abide by the rule of law. Therefore, the Security Council must comply with law in making its decisions and it must allow the ICJ to review whether decisions of the Security Council are in accordance with international law.

APPENDIX

Member States of the United Nations

The 191 Member States of the UN (as at 1 October 2002) and the dates on which they joined are listed below. Details on any changes of status and/or of name are set out on the United Nations Internet site: http://www.un.org/.

Afghanistan (19 November 1946)
Albania (14 December 1955)
Algeria (8 October 1962)
Andorra (28 July 1993)
Angola (1 December 1976)
Antigua and Barbuda (11 November 1981)
Argentina (24 October 1945)
Armenia (2 March 1992)
Australia (1 November 1945)
Austria (14 December 1955)
Azerbaijan (9 March 1992)
Bahamas (18 September 1973)
Bahrain (21 September 1971)
Bangladesh (17 September 1974)
Barbados (9 December 1966)
Belarus (24 October 1945)
Belgium (27 December 1945)
Belize (25 September 1981)
Benin (20 September 1960)
Bhutan (21 September 1971)
Bolivia (14 November 1945)
Bosnia and Herzegovina (22 May 1992)
Botswana (17 October 1966)
Brazil (24 October 1945)
Brunei Darussalam (21 September 1984)
Bulgaria (14 December 1955)
Burkina Faso (20 September 1960)
Burundi (18 September 1962)
Cambodia (14 December 1955)
Cameroon (20 September 1960)
Canada (9 November 1945)
Cape Verde (16 September 1975)

Central African Republic (20 September 1960)
Chad (20 September 1960)
Chile (24 October 1945)
China (24 October 1945)
Colombia (5 November 1945)
Comoros (12 November 1975)
Congo (20 September 1960)
Congo (Democratic Republic of the) (20 September 1960)
Costa Rica (2 November 1945)
Côte d'Ivoire (20 September 1960)
Croatia (22 May 1992)
Cuba (24 October 1945)
Cyprus (20 September 1960)
Czech Republic (19 January 1993)
Denmark (24 October 1945)
Djibouti (20 September 1977)
Dominica (18 December 1978)
Dominican Republic (24 October 1945)
Ecuador (21 December 1945)
Egypt (24 October 1945)
El Salvador (24 October 1945)
Equatorial Guinea (12 November 1968)
Eritrea (28 May 1993)
Estonia (17 September 1991)
Ethiopia (13 November 1945)
Fiji (13 October 1970)
Finland (14 December 1955)
France (24 October 1945)
Gabon (20 September 1960)
Gambia (21 September 1965)
Georgia (31 July 1992)
Germany (18 September 1973)

Ghana (8 March 1957)
Greece (25 October 1945)
Grenada (17 September 1974)
Guatemala (21 November 1945)
Guinea (12 December 1958)
Guinea-Bissau (17 September 1974)
Guyana (20 September 1966)
Haiti (24 October 1945)
Honduras (17 December 1945)
Hungary (14 December 1955)
Iceland (19 November 1946)
India (30 October 1945)
Indonesia (28 September 1950)
Iran (Islamic Republic of) (24 October 1945)
Iraq (21 December 1945)
Ireland (14 December 1955)
Israel (11 May 1949)
Italy (14 December 1955)
Jamaica (18 September 1962)
Japan (18 December 1956)
Jordan (14 December 1955)
Kazakhstan (2 March 1992)
Kenya (16 December 1963)
Kiribati (14 September 1999)
Korea (Democratic People's Republic of) (17 September 1991)
Korea (Republic of) (17 September 1991)
Kuwait (14 May 1963)
Kyrgyzstan (2 March 1992)
Laos (People's Democratic Republic) (14 December 1955)
Latvia (17 September 1991)
Lebanon (24 October 1945)
Lesotho (17 October 1966)
Liberia (2 November 1945)
Libya (Libyan Arab Jamahiriya) (14 December 1955)
Liechtenstein (18 September 1990)
Lithuania (17 September 1991)
Luxembourg (24 October 1945)
Macedonia (The former Yugoslav Republic of) (8 April 1993)
Madagascar (20 September 1960)

Malawi (1 December 1964)
Malaysia (17 September 1957)
Maldives (21 September 1965)
Mali (28 September 1960)
Malta (1 December 1964)
Marshall Islands (17 September 1991)
Mauritania (7 October 1961)
Mauritius (24 April 1968)
Mexico (7 November 1945)
Micronesia (Federated States of) (17 September 1991)
Moldova (Republic of) (2 March 1992)
Monaco (28 May 1993)
Mongolia (27 October 1961)
Morocco (12 November 1956)
Mozambique (16 September 1975)
Myanmar (19 April 1948)
Namibia (23 April 1990)
Nauru (14 September 1999)
Nepal (14 December 1955)
Netherlands (10 December 1945)
New Zealand (24 October 1945)
Nicaragua (24 October 1945)
Niger (20 September 1960)
Nigeria (7 October 1960)
Norway (27 November 1945)
Oman (7 October 1971)
Pakistan (30 September 1947)
Palau (15 December 1994)
Panama (13 November 1945)
Papua New Guinea (10 October 1975)
Paraguay (24 October 1945)
Peru (31 October 1945)
Philippines (24 October 1945)
Poland (24 October 1945)
Portugal (14 December 1955)
Qatar (21 September 1971)
Romania (14 December 1955)
Russian Federation (24 October 1945)
Rwanda (18 September 1962)
Saint Kitts and Nevis (23 September 1983)
Saint Lucia (18 September 1979)

Saint Vincent and the Grenadines (16 September 1980)
Samoa (15 December 1976)
San Marino (2 March 1992)
Sao Tome and Principe (16 September 1975)
Saudi Arabia (24 October 1945)
Senegal (28 September 1960)
Seychelles (21 September 1976)
Sierra Leone (27 September 1961)
Singapore (21 September 1965)
Slovakia (19 January 1993)
Slovenia (22 May 1992)
Solomon Islands (19 September 1978)
Somalia (20 September 1960)
South Africa (7 November 1945)
Spain (14 December 1955)
Sri Lanka (14 December 1955)
Sudan (12 November 1956)
Suriname (4 December 1975)
Swaziland (24 September 1968)
Sweden (19 November 1946)
Switzerland (10 September 2002)
Syria (Syrian Arab Republic) (24 October 1945)
Tajikistan (2 March 1992)
Tanzania (United Republic of) (14 December 1961)
Thailand (16 December 1946)
Timor-Leste (East Timor) (27 September 2002)
Togo (20 September 1960)
Tonga (14 September 1999)
Trinidad and Tobago (18 September 1962)
Tunisia (12 November 1956)
Turkey (24 October 1945)
Turkmenistan (2 March 1992)
Tuvalu (5 September 2000)
Uganda (25 October 1962)
Ukraine (24 October 1945)
United Arab Emirates (9 December 1971)
United Kingdom of Great Britain and Northern Ireland (24 October 1945)
United States of America (24 October 1945)
Uruguay (18 December 1945)
Uzbekistan (2 March 1992)
Vanuatu (15 September 1981)
Venezuela (15 November 1945)
Vietnam (20 September 1977)
Yemen (30 September 1947)
Yugoslavia (Federal Republic of) (1 November 2000)
Zambia (1 December 1964)
Zimbabwe (25 August 1980)

INDEX